MALAY-ENGLISH ENGLISH-MALAY
Dictionary

Revised Edition

A.E. Coope

HIPPOCRENE BOOKS
New York

Introduction : Malay-English Section

This dictionary uses the new system of spelling introduced by the Malaysian (and Indonesian) Government in 1972. Students are advised to obtain the excellent little handbook on the subject compiled by the Dewan Bahasa dan Pustaka and published by the Ministry of Education. The dictionary is intended for non-Malays who wish to obtain a real mastery of Malay by speaking and by reading both some part of the old romances and semihistories and, at the other end of the scale, newspapers and modern writings generally.

I have not included all the many English words in common use, unless used in a restricted or expanded sense, e.g. (as Malayanised) *setail*, *gustang* and *joli*. Nor have I included many anglicisms and neologisms which crop up from time to time and may represent a temporary blossoming. For students should notice that Malays often avoid the introduction of new words by neatly adapting homely words of everyday speech to new usages while still retaining their basic original meaning.

Consider the use of the word *perentis* to mean "pioneer". It originally could only mean the man who cuts the *rentis* (trace) as the indispensable preliminary to the opening of a plantation or other enterprise. The modern meaning is new, but the basic meaning remains.

Consider also the word *sorok* meaning "to conceal by withdrawing" (e.g. claws). How beautifully it fits as describing the "stealthy withdrawing", i.e. hoarding, of some basic commodity: *penyorok beras*, rice-hoarder. To me the most pleasing of such adaptions is that of the word *rantau*. Its basic meaning is the reach of a river, i.e. the area between two bends, which to the traditional old-time riverine Malay represented his known world or "these parts". Now his world has extended far, but *rantau ini*, "these parts" is still used to cover it. Indeed, not long ago I read a speech by the Prime Minister on the subject of South-East Asia, a vast area; he still called it *rantau ini*.

A.E.C.

Publisher's Note

This Revised Edition includes a number of new headwords and commonly used phrases and idioms, as well as examples of simple sentences. Further improvement has been made on spelling, based on the latest 'Daftar Ejaan Rumi Bahasa Malaysia', published by the Dewan Bahasa dan Pustaka.

Numerals

It appears convenient to group numerals together in a brief statement instead of scattering them about the dictionary.

CARDINAL NUMBERS

one, se, suatu, satu.
two, dua.
three, tiga.
four, empat, pat.
five, lima.

six, enam, nam.
seven, tujuh.
eight, lapan, delapan.
nine, sembilan.
ten, sepuluh.

Se is not much used except in conjunction with another word, as in *sepuluh*, one ten. *Suatu* conveys rather the idea of 'a' than specifically 'one': one day, *suatu hari*. Eleven is *sebelas*; twelve, *dua-belas* and so on up to nineteen, *sembilan-belas*. Twenty is *dua-puluh*; thirty, *tiga-puluh* and so on up to ninety, *sembilan-puluh*. A hundred is *seratus*, a thousand, *seribu*; ten thousand is *selaksa* and a million, *sejuta*, though the English 'million' may be used.

In forming compound numbers no 'and' is used: thus, 2 436 is *dua ribu, empat ratus, tiga-puluh enam*.

ORDINAL NUMBERS

First is *yang pertama* or *yang kesatu*; second, *yang kedua*; third, *yang ketiga* and so on. But this usage tends to be clumsy and in speech the Anglicism *nombor* is often used: nineteenth, *nombor sembilan-belas*.

Cardinal numbers are used in dates: March 10th, *sepuluh hari bulan March*.

In speech, as a rule only the last two figures of the current century are given: 1960, *tahun enam puluh*. When all four figures are given they are likely to be expressed as *tahun seribu, sembilan ratus, enam-puluh*, not *tahun sembilan-belas enam-puluh*.

THE CALENDAR

As regards months, the 'English' calendar is used. The Arabic months are used for the calculation of the festivals, etc., of Islam; no one of these months coincides exactly with any one 'English' month.

The days of the week are as follows: Sunday, *hari Ahad, hari Minggu*; Monday, *hari Isnin*: Tuesday, *hari Selasa*; Wednesday, *hari Rabu*; Thursday, *hari Khamis*; Friday, *hari Jumaat*, Saturday, *hari Sabtu*.

Among foreigners the following may still be heard: Sunday, *hari Minggu*; Monday, *hari satu*; Tuesday, *hari dua*; Wednesday, *hari tiga*; Thursday, *hari empat*; Friday, *hari lima*; Saturday, *hari enam*. Bear in mind that to Malays night precedes day; so *malam Ahad* means Saturday night, not Sunday night.

Numeral Coefficients

In Malay (as in Chinese) a word called in English a numeral coefficient is placed between a number and most nouns; thus one says *seekor kucing* (one tail of cat) for 'one cat'. Nearly all nouns, except abstract nouns and nouns representing capacity, weight and distance, take numeral coefficients, of which there are a considerable number. Usage varies somewhat in different localities.

Words used as numeral coefficients nearly all have their own individual meaning and can be used separately in that meaning. In the following list the individual meaning of each numeral coefficient is given in brackets after it.

The commonest numeral coefficients are:

Orang (person) for human beings;

ékor (tail) for all members of the animal kingdom, whether tailed or not, except sometimes for molluscs;

buah (fruit) for large and, to some extent, shapeless objects, e.g. ships, countries, rocks, books and houses (but for houses in a row the word *pintu* (door) is generally used);

biji (seed) for smaller objects, e.g. eggs, fruit, cups, plates, stones and (often) molluscs.

The above four numeral coefficients are by far the most common.

Others in general use are:

butir (grain, particle) for nuts, gems, eggs, pebbles and other small objects; sometimes it is used for houses and in places on the East Coast it used to be quite commonly used for human beings;

pucuk (shoot) for letters, guns, cannon; in some parts for casting-nets (*jala*) and needles;

lai, helai for tenuous objects such as pieces of paper, leaves and cloth;

kutum, kuntum (bud, blossom) for flowers;

bilah (thin strip, bar) for metal-bladed objects such as knives and sometimes needles;

kaki (leg) for long-stemmed flowers and umbrellas;

laras (smooth cylinder, barrel) for guns;

batang (stem) for trees, poles, sticks, pencils, pens, cigarettes and umbrellas;

puntung (fag-end) for teeth;

rawan for nets;

bidang (expansive, expanse), for sails, nets, mats and large pieces of cloth;

urat (sinew) for string;

utas (coil, skein) for necklaces, cords, chains and sometimes nets;

patah (to break) for words (e.g. *dua tiga patah* — two or three words);

hentuk (curve) for curved objects such as rings and fish-hooks;

tangkai (stalk) for long-stemmed flowers;

lembar (thread) for strands or flat delicate objects, expecially sheets of paper;

keping (piece) for planks, slabs and flat objects generally.

It will be seen that in nearly all cases there is a sort of basic resemblance between the numeral coefficient and the object to which it is attached, except in the case of *lai* (and *helai*) and *rawan* whose use other than as coefficients doubtless has a meaning which seems to have been forgotten.

Index of Abbreviations

With regards to dialectical differences, it should be made plain that the allocation of a word to a particular locality is not intended to be exclusive. For example where a word is marked 'Kel' the implication is that the word is not used throughout the Malay Peninsula and has been observed in Kelantan; it may well be used in some parts outside Kelantan, especially those on the East coast.

A

aba [KN], father; (an informal address by a son to his father); *ayah*; *bapa*; ~ *di rumahkah?*, is your father at home?

abad [KN], Ar. 1. century; *sains dan teknologi dalam ~ keduapuluh satu*, science and technology in the 21st century; *ber~-~*, for centuries. 2. eternity, the endless future, in contradistinction to the endless past *(azal)*; also used for 'century'; cf. **kurun**.

abadi [KS], Ar. eternal; everlasting; *keamanan yang ~*, everlasting peace; *meng~kan*, to perpetuate, to immortalize; *ke~an*, perpetuity.

abadiat [KN], Ar. eternity.

abah [KN], 1. ~ = **aba**; 2. direction; *tak tentu ~nya*, a constant change of directions; *meng~kan*, to direct, to steer, show the way.

abah-abah [KN], tackle, gear, harness; ~ *kuda*, horse's gear (reins, saddle etc.).

abai [KS], *meng~kan* [KK], to neglect, to make light of, ignore; *dia meng~kan tugas dan tanggung-jawabnya*, he neglects his duty and responsibility; *peng~an*, careless, slovenly, indifference, negligence.

abaimana [KN], anus; the lower orifices of the body (with reference to ritual purification — *istinja)*.

abal-abal [KN], Kel, Treng. shelter, screen; *~daratan*, the shelter of the land; also *abar-abar*.

abang [KN], elder brother; a cousin or friend older than oneself; ~ *saya pegawai kanan di pejabat itu*, my elder brother is a senior officer in that department; used as a method of address, esp. by a woman to her husband or lover; *~ku* is sometimes used (to a younger person) for 'my husband'.

abakus [KN], abacus; cf. *dekak-dekak*.

abau [KN], a large swamp tortoise.

abdi [KN], Ar. slave, servant; *~-~ itu telah memperoleh kebebasan*, the slaves were emancipated; *meng~*, to be a slave or servant to; *peng~an*, slavery, enslavement.

Abdullah [KN], Ar. the name of the father of the Prophet; a common Malay name, often shortened to **Dollah**.

abjad [KN], Ar. the alphabet according to the numerical values of the letters as used in divination; *istilah-istilah sains itu disusun mengikut ~*, the scientific terms are arranged in alphabetical order.

abrak [KN], Ar. mica; a type of transparent mineral substance.

abstrak [KN], abstract; not real or solid; *perkataan lapar adalah sesuatu yang ~*, the word 'hunger' is an abstract noun.

abu [KN], Ar. 1. father of, e.g., in proper names such as Abu-Bakar. Abu-Bakar is a common Malay name (after Abu-Bakar, father-in-law of the Prophet and, after the Prophet's death, the first Caliph). 2. ashes, cinders, dust; *ular ~*, a name for the hamadryad; *meng~i mata*, to 'throw dust in the eyes', deceive; *menjadi ~ angin*, to become dust before the wind, be completely destroyed; also *abuk* and *habuk*; *seperti ~ di atas tunggul* (prov.), an insignificant husband.

abuk [KN], dust, powder, ash; ~ *gergaji*, saw-dust; *ber~*, fluently (as though dust flew); *peng~ mata*, dust in the eyes, 'eye-wash'; *warna ~ rokok*, charcoal-grey; *tempat ~ rokok*, ashtray.

abur [KS], Ind. *meng~* [KK], to lavish; *peng~* [KN], a lavish spender.

acah [KK], a variant of *acan*; *meng~-~*, to 'make passes', as in making a threatened or pretended attack; *petinju itu meng~-~ lawannya*, the boxer made a feint attack on his opponent.

acan [KK], Ked. to mimic; to feint, to make as if about to hit, to bait with pretended attacks; also *acah; di~,* tricked.

acap [KS], 1. ~ *kali,* often; *pada mulanya dia ~kali membuat kesalahan semasa menaip,* at the beginning she often made mistakes in her typing. 2. immersed, covered over, as by weeds or water; *kakinya ter~ ke lumpur,* his legs were caught in the mud.

acar [KN], 1. Hind. pickles; ~ *rampai,* mixed pickles. 2. Ked. a rubbish-hole.

acara [KN], Skr. a rule of conduct; a religious observance; programme, agenda; ~ *berikutnya ialah persembahan tarian singa;* next in the programme is the lion dance performance; *peng~,* Master of Ceremonies.

Acih [KN], Acheen.

aci [KN], 1. ~-~, the lever by which the boom of a Malay boat is turned round and round so as to fold up the sail; also *caci.* 2. done!, agreed; *sudah ~,* it is settled; *tak ~* it is off, 'it won't do!' as in the case of a foul. 3. axle.

acik [KN], aunty (actual or honorary).

acu [KK], to threaten; to attempt or appear to attempt without fully carrying out; *meng~-~kan,* to brandish, flourish; *~kan senapang pada,* to point a gun at; to test, to try; to try on; Kel. Treng. please!

acuan [KN], a mould, matrix, a model (e.g. of a proposed building); *bagaimana ~ begitulah kuihnya;* (prov.), like father like son.

acuh [KS], *~kan,* to value, deem important, to pay attention; ~ *tak ~,* half-heartedly, casually, off-handedly; *melihat ~ tak ~,* to watch without paying particular attention; *sikap ~ tak ~,* an attitude of indifference or apathy.

acum [KK], *meng~,* to incite to make trouble, to egg on, make mischief; *percubaan hendak meng~ kedua teman itu bermusuhan,* an attempt to provoke the two friends to quarrel; *acuman,*

incitement; *peng~,* a person who incites or provoke.

acung [KK], Ind. to raise one's hand; *sesiapa yang, ingin bertanya, sila meng~kan tangun,* those who would like to ask, please raise your hand. 2. kick.

ada [KK], to be; to be present, to exist; to be at home (to a visitor); to appertain to, to have; ~ *orang,* there are people (present); ~ *laut, ~lah perompak,* there are seas, there are pirates; *saya ~ duit* (colloquial), I have money; *meng~kan,* to create, call into existence, to appoint, to produce, to provide, to hold (an election), to give (a party); *ke~an,* state, existence, condition, position, circum-stances; *meng~-ng~,* to act in an affected manner, 'put on an act', give oneself airs; *meng~-ng~kan,* to concoct (as excuses), to 'work up' (a scheme, trick); ~ *nya,* existence, actual state; *demikianlah ~ nya,* such is the state of affairs (a phrase often found in writing, rounding off a passage: frequently shortened to ~ *nya* alone); *berada* is sometimes used as a more polite way of saying, 'to be present'; also *orang yang ber~,* people of standing; ~ *sahaja,* always there, inevitably present (e.g. as poverty, some diseases); ~-~ *sahaja,* id., *se~-~nya (sahaja),* what there is, such as happens to be available; *makanlah se~-~nya sahaja!* take pot-luck!; ~ *tak?* are there? (are there or aren't there?); ~ *tak ~,* whatever (of them) may be, if there are any; ~ *udang di balik batu* (prov.), to have an axe to grind.

adab [KN], Ar. respect, courtesy, manners (especially propriety in behaviour to one's elders or superiors), rules of politeness, etiquette, good manners; *setiap orang seharusnya memiliki ~ yang baik,* everyone is expected to be courteous; *dengan ~,* courteously; *bi~,* disrespectful; *ber~,* courteous; *per~an,* culture, civilization, advancement; also *adap.*

Adam [KN], Ar. a proper name, Adam; *nabi* ~, Adam, the common ancestor of all men; *anak* ~ or *bani* ~, humanity, mankind; *zaman Tok* ~, in Adam's time, i.e., in the dim and distant past.

adang, 1. obstruct; intercept; barring a passage; opposing a barrier to; *meng*~, to interpose between, to keep something off; *meng*~ *musuh*, to keep the foe at a distance. 2. ~~~, at times, sometimes; = *kadang-kadang*; *peng*~, obstruction, obstacles; *peng*~*an*, place where there is an obstruction.

adas [KN], ~ *manis*, aniseed; ~ *pedas*, fennel.

adat [KN], Ar, custom; customary law; customary behaviour; proper behaviour; courtesy; law; ~ *Minangkabau*, the (customary) law of Minangkabau or ~ *perpatih*, social and political customs still partly prevailing in Negri Sembilan; *seperti* ~ *nya*, as was his custom; *ber*~, in accordance with custom; proper, courteous; ~ *resam*, manners and customs; ~ *isti*~, customs and ceremonies, customary ceremonies; *membawa* ~ (polite), to menstruate; *ber*~, customary, conforming to custom; *ter*~, (usage, etc.) established as a custom; ~ *kebiasaan*, customs and usages.

adegan [KN], Jav. (etym.?) a scene, an incident (from a film); *dia berlakon sebagai kapten dalam* ~ *di atas kapal*, he played the role of a captain in a scene on board the ship.

adik [KN], younger brother or sister; cousin younger than oneself; a term of endearment to one slightly younger than oneself; ~ *ber*~, of brothers and sisters; *mengaku* ~ *ber*~, to accept as a brother or sister, i.e., to terminate a closer relation in a friendly manner, or to set a limit to possible relations; ~ *sepupu*, a (younger) first cousin; ~ *kakak*, brothers and sisters; ~~ *seperut*, born of the same mother; ~ *kandung(an)*, id.

memper~*kan*, look upon as a brother or sister.

adikara [KN], Skr. majestic; sometimes used in Ind. to mean dictator.

adil [KS], Ar. just, fair, honest — used of superiors being just to their subordinates or of a judge being impartial; *kami menghormati orang yang* ~, we respect impartial people; *peng*~, magistrate, referee; *peng*~ *keamanan*, Justice of the Peace; *menteri ke*~*an*, Minister of Justice; *hari peng*~*an*, day of judgement; *meng*~*kan*, examine, weigh up and decide a case fairly.

adinda [KN], younger brother or sister as used by royalty and in letters; a more courteous variant of *adik*; used esp. in poetry as a mode of address from a man to his loved one.

adiraja [KN], Skr. very royal; royal by descent; a component part of many Malay titles of distinction; also **diraja**.

adjektif [KK], adjective also **rupanama**.

adiwarna [KS], Skr. glowing with colour, resplendent.

adu [KK], 1. pitting; matching one against another; getting up a contest; *meng*~ *biri-biri*, pitting rams against one another; *meng*~ *untung*, *meng*~ *nasib*, id., to try one's luck; used also for to seek one's fortune; *meng*~ *kekuatan (terhadap)*, to have a trial of strength (with); *meng*~ *bertinju*, to match (persons) in boxing; *meng*~, *meng*~ *hal*, to lay a complaint; ~*an*, plaintiff, complainant; also *peng*~*an*, a complaint; *per*~*an*, contest or competition; *per*~*an cantik*, beauty contest; *kena* ~, to be sued; *yang kena* ~, defendant; *ber*~ *akal*, to match wits; *meng*~*dombakan*, Ind. to play off one against another; to set by the ears. 2. *ber*~, to sleep (of a prince); *per*~*n*, a couch; *bilik per*~*an*, a bedroom.

aduh [K Srn], alas!, oh!; ~, *lampu mati*, oh dear! The lights are out; *meng*~, to say alas! to utter an exclamation of pain; *orang yang luka itu meng*~

kesakitan; the injured man is moaning from pain.

aduhai [K Srn], alas!, oh!, = **aduh.**

aduk [KK], Ind. kneading or mixing; *campur* ~, a mixture; miscellaneous; *mencampur~kan,* to mix; *jangan mencampur~kan urusan peribadi dengan usahaniaga,* don't mix personal and business affairs.

adun [KS], 1. finery in dress; *~kan pengantin,* to deck out a bridegroom. 2. *~an,* dough; *meng~,* to knead; to mix, to combine ingredients; *meng~ tepung dan air,* to knead flour and water.

afdal [KS], Ind. meritorious, outstanding, of the first importance.

afiat [KS], Ar. health, good health; *sihat dan* ~, id.

Aflatun [KN], Ar. Plato.

afrit [KN], Ar. a malicious giant spirit.

aga [KK], *memper~kan,* to show off.

agah [KK], *meng~, ber~-~,* to crow, of a baby, to chuckle; *senyum meng~,* to smile and chuckle.

agak [KN], 1. conjecture, guessing; *~-~,* approximately, as far as one can guess; more or less; *~nya dia kurang senang dengan pekerjaannya,* it appears he isn't happy with his job; *~ gerangan,* if by chance; *ter~-~,* hesitatingly; to hesitate. 2. Ind. rather, somewhat.

agal [KN], the leathery turtle; also Treng., *agar.*

agam [KS], Pk. manly, big, stout, tall; *tubuhnya* ~, he is tall and burly.

agama [KN], Skr. religion; *~ Islam,* the Muslim religion; *ke~an,* religious bigotry, clericalism; *~ karut,* false doctrine, a heretical creed; *~ sesat,* id.; *keras ber~,* deeply and strictly religious; also **igama** and **ugama.**

agan [KK], *mati ber~,* to die without visible cause; to die from natural causes; to seem alive in death.

agar [KPhbg], 1. Ind. in order that, so that, = **supaya;** *belajarlah bersungguh-sungguh ~ lulus peperiksaan,* study seriously so that you could pass your exam. 2. *~-~,* a seaweed, *Gracilaria*

lichenoides, Eucheuma spinosum, used for making jelly; gelatine.

agas [KN], a sandfly.

agen [KN], dealer; *~ kereta,* car dealer.

agih [KK], a share agreed upon, the share to be allotted to anyone; *~kan,* to distribute; *meng~kan harta,* to divide property.

aguk [KN], a breast ornament worn by children, and at weddings by women.

agung [KS], large, great, main (in certain expressions only); *tiang* ~, the mainmast; *layar* ~, the mainsail; *~ alam,* a prince of the earth; royal or general; supreme (of Rulers); *konsul* ~, Consul-General; *pengakap* ~, Chief Scout; *meng~kan,* to extol; *meng~kan Tuhan,* to glorify God; to give preferential treatment to; *mesyuarat* ~, General Meeting; see **tuan.**

agus [KS], Jav. fair, handsome.

agut [KK], 1. nodding the head (from weakness); *orang tua ~-~,* doddering old man; 2. gasping for breath.

Ahad [KN], Ar. 1. one, first; *hari* ~, Sunday. 2. covenant; *ahli al-~,* people of the covenant, i.e., Christians and Jews.

ahli [KN], Ar. versed in, expert in; member (as of a Council or Club); *~-al-nujum,* an astrologer; *~ bersekutu,* associate member; *~-~ yang cendekia,* well-informed circles; *~ penimbang,* assessor; *~ penerbang,* airman; *~ biasa,* ordinary member; *~ kekal,* permanent member; *~ bahasa,* linguist; *~ agama,* theologian; *~ perniagaan,* businessman; *~ 'sains',* scientist; *~ sejarah,* historian; *~ dandan,* hair-stylist; *~ berenang,* swimming expert; *~ sukan,* athlete; *~ lumba,* runner; *~ ketimuran,* orientalist; *~ alkitab,* people of the Book, i.e., Arabs, Jews and Christians; *ke~an,* expertise, skill; *berlakon bukan ke~an saya,* acting is not my forte; *ke~an perang,* the art of war; ~ is also used politely for 'spouse'; also *ahlu.*

Ahmad [KN], Ar. Much Commended; an epithet of the Prophet, now used as a proper name.

Ahmadiah [KN], see **Kadiani**.

ahmak [KS], Ar. dense, stupid; *fikiran yang ~*, a foolish idea.

ahwal [KN], Ar. things, matters, events, occurences; *segala hal ~ perkara itu*, all the facts of the case.

aib [KS], Ar. a shame, a disgrace; *memberi ~*, to put to shame, to disgrace; *meng~kan; perbuatannya meng~kan*, his conduct was a disgrace; *ke'an*, dishonour, shame, disgrace.

ain [KN], 1. Ar. eyes; *nuru'l ~*, light of the eyes. 2. *~ -ul-banat*, the name of a cloth mentioned in romances. 3. an Arabic letter corresponding roughly to **a**.

air [KN], water, liquid, juice, sap; *~ bah*, a flood; *~ batu*, ice; *~ gula*, syrup; *~ keras*, spirits; *~ liur*, saliva; *menerbitkan ~ liur*, to make one's mouth water; *~ madu*, honey; *~ mata*, tears; *~ mawar*, rose-water; *~ minum*, drinking water; *~ muka*, expression of face; sometimes, complexion; *~ pasang*, the rising tide; *~ peluh*, perspiration; *~ surut*, the falling tide; *~ tawar*, fresh water; *~ teh*, tea; *~ terjun*, a waterfall; *buang ~ besar*, to defecate; *buang ~ kecil*, to urinate (polite); *mata ~*, a spring; *~ timpas*, low tide; *~ pasang penuh*, high tide; *tanah ~*, territories, used for 'fatherland'; *~ mata jatuh ke dalam*, weeping inwardly; *meng~kan*, to irrigate; *per~an*, waters (pertaining to a country); *ke~an*, waterlogged; *~ kencing*, urine; *~ kencing iblis*, (sl.) whisky; *~ wangi*, scent, perfume; *~ utama jiwa*, the Water of Life; *~ tolak bala*, holy water; *~ api*, corrosive acid, esp. vitriol, sometimes, caustic soda; *~ sembahyang*, water for ritual ablutions; *istiadat membatalkan ~ sembahyang*, the formal touching (e.g., by clasping hand) of bride by bridegroom at close of wedding ceremony; *menjatuhkan ~ muka*, to embarrass.

Aisah [KN], Ar. = **Esah**, q.v.

ajaib [KS], Ar. wonderful, miraculous, strange; *benda yang ~*, a curio; an extraordinary article; *ini ubat ~*, this drug works wonders; *ke~an*, wonder, strangeness, marvel; *meng~kan*, puzzling.

ajak [KK], *meng~*, to invite, to urge, persuade to action; *meng~ dia ke rumah*, invite him over; *~-~ ayam*, insincere invitation (because a hen cackles invitingly before eating something itself); *~ bertumbuk*, to challenge to fight (with fists).

ajal [KN], Ar. destiny; destined hour of death; allotted span of life; *tiada sampai ~nya*, his time (to die) has not yet come; *sebelum ~ berpantang mati* (prov.), a man can only die once.

ajar [KK], 1. teaching, instruction; to warn, advise; *~kan*, to teach; *bel~, mempel~i*, to learn; *saya harus mempel~i fakta-fakta ini*, I have to acquaint myself with these facts; *pel~an*, learning; the thing taught or learnt; *peng~an*, the art of teaching, the process of teaching; lectures; *peng~*, a teacher; *~an*, teaching, a lesson; (fig.) a lesson in the sense of a warning; *kurang ~*, badly brought-up, rude; *masuk ~*, well brought-up; *pel~an permulaan*, elementary education; *tak makan ~*, unruly, 'won't be told'; *melawat sambil bel~*, to go on a study tour; *pel~*, a student; *terpel~, berpel~an*, well-educated. 2. Skr. *~~* ascetics, disciples of an ascetic teacher.

aji [KN], Jav. royal; *rama ~*, or *bapa ~*, sovereign, father, sire; *kakang ~*, royal brother; *sang ~*, king, sacred majesty.

ajnabi [KN], Ar. those with whom marriage is not barred by reason of consanguinity; cf. **Muhrim**.

ajnas [KN], Ar. miscellanies, sorts; *tuhfatu'l-~*, 'a gift of various articles', a common expression in epistolary language to describe the letter itself.

aju [KK], *meng~kan*, offer, put forward; *meng~kan permintaan*, to make a request.

ajuk [KK], 1. to repeat, to mimic (not necessarily in ridicule); *cakap ~,* direct reported speech, as opposed to *cakap pindah.* 2. *meng~,* fathom; *meng~ dalamnya laut,* to fathom the sea; *~kan,* investigation, scrutiny.

ajun [KS], farthest from the mark; last in the competition; *meng~,* to make preparations.

akad [KN], Ar. contract, esp. marriage contract *(~ nikah); menjalankan ~ nikah, melangsungkan ~ nikah, melakukan ~ nikah,* to perform a marriage ceremony; *ber~ jual-beli,* to make a firm contract of sale; also **akat.**

akak = kakak.

akal [KN], Ar. primarily conveys the idea of reasoning power, understanding, human intelligence, the essential qualities distinguishing man from beast. But by extension it is used with many shades of meaning: the mind as the organ of thought, brains, tact, commonsense, gumption, 'nous': a proper mental attitude to problems of conduct; a plan, a scheme, a trick; *ber~,* intelligent; *panjang ~,* resourceful; *tajam ~,* quick witted; *~ baligh,* maturity, years of discretion; *mencari ~,* to devise a plan; *kehabisan ~,* at wits' end; *mati ~,* to give up hope, despair, *tidak diterima dek ~,* unworthy of acceptance, preposterous; *tidak termakan dalam ~,* seems incredible; *~kan,* (sl.) *meng~i,* to outwit, get the better of by cunning; *~ tak sekali tiba,* you can't make plans on the spur of the moment; *hilang ~,* to 'lose one's head', become flustered; *medan ~ kilat,* Brains' Trust.

akan [K Phbg], to, approach to; motion towards; intention to; *budak yang ~ mengaji,* a boy about to study; *~ daku,* to me; *~ dia,* to him; *~-~,* like, resembling, very similar to; *se~-~,* almost exactly like; *tak ~,* cannot be, not likely!

akar [KN], root, fibre; a climbing or creeping plant; *tak ada rotan ~ pun berguna,* if you cannot get a rattan (prov.), any fibre will be useful (half a loaf is better than no bread); *berakar,* to take root; *berakar-urat,* rooted, taken root; *berakar-tunjang,* deeply rooted; *ber~-umbi,* id.; *~ periuk,* medicinal herbs; *~ bahar,* a peculiar seaweed, wearing of which as a bracelet is believed to prevent rheumatis B; *akar kata,* root word; *~ kayu,* a liana; *~ serabut,* fibrous roots; *~ sokong,* laterals; *~ menyelar,* creeping roots above ground; *~ tunjang,* tap-root; *~ jangkar,* visible, stilt-like roots, as of the mangrove; *~ udara,* aerial roots.

akas [KS], 1. lively, nimble, deft. 2. returned, reverted; *~nya,* vice versa; *~kan,* to reverse (as gear).

akbar [KS], Ar. most great, almighty; *Allahu ~,* God is Almighty; *tahun Haji ~,* Great Pilgrimage year (i.e., a year in which the first day of the Haji ceremony, i.e., the 9th *Zulhijjah,* falls on a Friday).

akhbar [KN], Ar. news, a newspaper.

akhir [KN], Ar. last, the end; *~ nya,* in the end; *~-zaman,* for ever, to the end of time; *ber~* to end, to reach the end; *kali yang ter~ sekali saya —,* the last time I —; *perlawanan separuh ~,* semi-final; *yang ter~ tetapi tidak kurang pentingnya,* last but not least.

akhirat [KN], Ar. the life to come, the day of judgement; the World to Come.

akhlak [KN], Ar, morals, moral character; also *ikhlak; sudah rosak ~nya,* his character has been spoiled.

akhwan [KN], Ar. brothers; also **ikhwan.**

aki [KN], *to' ~,* grandfather.

akibah [KN], Ar. consequences, results; as a result of; also *akibat; dia menjadi lumpuh ~ kemalangan itu,* she's crippled as a result of the accident.

akidah [KN], belief, faith.

akik [KN] Ar, agate, cornelian, coral; covers almost any red semi-precious stone.

akikah [KN], Ar. the ritual shaving of a child's head for the first time; also **kekah.**

akil baligh [KS], grown up, maturity; *dia*

sudah ~ sekarang, he's grown-up now.

akrab [KS], near, close, intimate; *dia teman ~ saya,* he's a dear friend of mine.

aksi [KN], Ind. 1. action, movement esp. as opposed to speech. 2. smart, good-looking; also act, pretend; *tindakannya hanya ber~ sahaja,* she didn't really lose her temper, it was just a put-on.

aktif [KS], active, busy, industrious; *meng~kan,* activate, make active; *ke~an,* activity, effort, diligence.

aku [KN], 1. I, me, myself; *~ semua,* we; *~ sekalian,* id. 2. *meng~,* to admit, *meng~ kalah;* to throw in the towel, to accept (a fact), to confess; *peng~an,* recognition, declaration, admission; *~an,* id.; *meng~i,* to 'recognize' (e.g. a new Government).

akur [KK], Ind. consent, accord; to concur.

al, Ar. the, only used in Arabic expressions such as *~-marhum,* the late (Ruler), and *~-hamdulillah,* thanks be to God.

ala [KKtr], 1. on, upon, according to, in the fashion of -; *pakaian ~ Barat,* to dress like Westerners; *~ kadarnya,* to the extent of his ability; *~ kulihal juga,* just as well, might do. 2. = **hala.** 3. expression of surprise (= *Allah?).*

alabangka [KN], Port. a crowbar.

alah [KS], to be worsted, to lose (a contest); *~ kepada,* to be susceptible to (as a disease), allergic to; *~kan* and *meng~kan,* to vanquish; *ber~,* to give way, make a concession; *meng~,* to submit; to be meek, submissive; *bersifat meng~,* to be defeatist; *tak mahu meng~ dengan jiran,* to want to keep up with the Joneses (i.e., the neighbours); *~ membeli menang memakai* (prov.) cheapest is dearest.

alaihi, Ar. upon him, to him; *~ wassalam,* on Whom be peace, an exclamation often following the name of a saint or prophet, cf., **sallalahu;** *iblis ~ laanat,* the Devil, may he be accursed.

alaikum, Ar. upon you, to you; *salam ~!,* peace be unto you!, a common greeting between Muslims.

alak [KK], Kel. to urge on, encourage, to call upon to make an effort, to rally.

alam [KN], 1. Ar. the world, universe; nature, material phenomena; *~ ta-biat,* the world of nature; *~ tabii,* id.; sometimes shortened to *alam* simply; *tabiat ~,* natural trait; *~ lepas,* the outside world; *pertubuhan pencinta ~,* Nature Society; *pergi ke ~ yang baka,* to go to the World of Eternity, to die; *~ maya,* this transitory world; *empat penjuru ~,* the four corners of the world; *~ semula jadi,* nature untouched by man; *isi ~,* the world of nature; *~ kitaran (sekitaran), ~ keliling,* environment; *bencana ~,* natural disasters, 'acts of God'. 2. knowing best; *Allahu ~,* God knows best; *~i, meng~i,* to experience; *meng~i penderitaan,* to take the hard knocks; *peng~an,* experience.

alamak [KSrn], exclamation of surprise.

alamat [KN], Ar. sign, token; a portent, omen; *~ akan hujan,* signs that it's going to rain; *~ surat,* the address on an envelope; *dengan ~ (d.a.),* care of, c/o (in address).

alan-alan [KN], a jester; a buffoon; a clown.

alang [KN], 1. cross, across; *~ balai,* the cross-beams over an audience-hall; *~an,* the bar at an estuary; *meng~,* to obstruct (by putting something in the way), cause difficulties; *meng~kan leher suruh sembelih,* to stretch out one's neck and ask for one's throat to be cut, 'to stick one's neck out', suicidal act, foolish risks. 2. slight (in importance), of little account; *~ kepalang,* id.; *bukan ~~,* of no little importance, important, weighty; *~ ~an,* half-hearted, slight; *~ kah,* it is of no little importance that..., a semi-sarcastic interrogative enhancing the force of a statement; *~kah cantik rumahmu!* what a nice house you have!, *~~,* since you are going to, taking it

7

that. 3. **Alang,** a name often given to an 'intermediate' child, i.e., not the eldest nor expected to be the youngest of a family.

alap [KS], sedate, slow, quiet.

alar [KN], Pah. the child of a slave (of the class known as *hulur).*

alas [KN], 1. foundation, basis, framework, stand; ~ *kaki,* a footstool; ~ *perut,* a snack, a 'bite'; *peng~ tangan,* armrest, arm of chair; ~ *baju,* the lining of a coat; ~ *rumah,* the foundations of a house; so *~an,* pretext, excuse, grounds; *meng~,* to support, serve as a foundation for; *kedua belah tapak tangan meng~ tengkuk,* (lying) with both hands behind the neck; *meja ber~ kain putih,* a table covered with a white cloth. 2. Jav. *~an,* jungle.

alat [KN], Ar. equipment, appurtenances, appliances; ~ *jentera,* machinery generally; ~ *kerajaan,* regalia; ~ *pandang-dengar,* audiovisual aids; ~ *perang* and ~ *senjata,* military equipment; *~i* and *meng~kan,* to fit out; ~ *penangkap suara,* sound-recording machine; *kereta ber~,* armoured car; ~ *solek,* toilet articles; *per~an,* requisites; *per~ulis* (short for *per~an tulis),* stationery; ~ *perlengkapan,* kit, equipment; ~ *penyejuk,* cooling system; ~ *pemanas,* heating system; ~ *pencari,* detecting device, esp. for underwater objects, mines, etc.; ~ ~ *untuk bertukang sendiri,* 'to do it yourself kit'; *memper~kan,* to use as a tool, (fig.) to make use of someone for one's own purposes ('as a tool'); *dia tahu memper~ orang,* he knows how to manipulate people.

algoja-algojo [KN], Port. an excutioner.

alhamdullilah, Ar. thank God; ~ *segalanya berjalan dengan baik,* thank God! everything worked out fine.

Ali [KN], Ar. the son-in-law of the Prophet, husband of Fatimah; he was the fourth Caliph; a common Malay name; *perniagaan ~ Baba,* Ali Baba's trade,

sarcastic expression for trade carried on by foreigners, esp. Chinese, using licences specially issued to Malays and sold by them.

Alias [KN], Ar. Elias, a proper name, often shortened to Lias; *nabi ~,* the Prophet Elijah.

ali-ali [KN], a sling; *rajut ~-~,* the socket of a sling.

alif [KN], the name of the first letter of the alphabet, *~-ba-ta,* the Malay alphabet; *mengikut peraturan ~-ba-ta,* in alphabetical order.

alih [KK], moving, to shift; ~ *kata,* change a topic; to transplant (trees); *meng~kan pokok perbualan,* to change the subject; *ber~ hari,* after the turn of day, i.e., afternoon; *meng~ duduknya,* shifting his (sitting) position; *ber~ tadah,* to alter one's views; *per~an,* transition, transformation; *ber~ angin,* to have a change of air, go on a trip; *~-~,* then it happened that, suddenly, = *tiba-tiba;* also **kalih.**

alim [KS], Ar. learned, religious; *orang ~,* a savant, a theologian; *~-ulama,* religious dignitaries; *~-~ kucing,* sly humbug.

alin [KK], *mengalin,* to massage with magic art, so as to extract a toxic foreign body.

alir [KK], flowing; floating downstream; *meng~,* to flow; *meng~kan,* to set floating; *tali ~,* a floating line used for catching crocodiles; *~an,* flow of events, circumstances, system, creed, progress, course of action; *~an fikiran,* trend of opinion; *air yang meng~,* flowing, as opposed to static, water, *meng~kan,* to wash away, carry away in current.

alis [KN], Jav. the eyebrow.

alit [KN], colouring the edge of the eyelid (with kohl).

alkah [KN], Ar. foetus, embryo.

alkali [KN], [scientific term in chemistry]; *benda seperti soda yang bercampur dengan asid menjadi garam,* any of various substances that form chemical salts when combined with acids.

alku [KN], a go-between, a pimp.

Allah [KN], Ar. God, ~ *Taala,* God Most High; *Insha* ~, God willing; ~ *yarham;* often used respectfully to mean 'the late...', *kerana* ~, for God's sake; *hamba* ~, the servants of God, i.e., mankind, but esp. the poor; ~ *subhana-hu wa-taala* (s.w.t.), God ever to be praised, Most High; *la ilaha ila* ~, there is no God but God, the opening words of the Muslim creed; ~ *itu Pengampun lagi Penyayang,* God, the Merciful and Compassionate (from the Arabic *al-rahman al-rahim);* ~ *Yang Maha Mengetahui,* God the All-knowing.

allahumma, Ar. my God; O God!

almarhum, see **marhum.**

almari [KN], Port. a wardrobe, a cupboard, an almeirah; ~ *buku,* book-case.

almasih [KN], Jesus Christ.

alpa [KS], Skr. carelessness, negligence, to treat with carelessness; also *lepa;* ~ *akan kewajipannya,* to neglect one's duty.

alti [KS], Ar. clever, smart.

alu [KN], 1. a pestle, a pounder. 2. *meng~ng~kan,* to welcome a guest with assiduous attention. 3. *ikan* ~-~, a barracuda.

Al-Quran [KN], the Koran.

aluminium [KN], *kertas aluminium,* aluminum foil.

alumni [KN], derived from alumnus, *lulusan, bekas pelajar sesebuah sekolah, kolej atau universiti,* former students of a school, college or university.

alun [KN], 1. ground-swell; long rolling waves; *ber~* and *meng~,* to roll up, of the sea; *~an suara,* tone of voice; *suara ber~ kasar,* voice rising to an angry pitch; *meng~kan,* to cause to resound (a tune or song) by playing or singing. 2. Jav. ~-~, the esplanade in front of a Javanese Palace.

alur [KN], the channel of a river, the hollowed-out bed of a stream; *~an kapal,* the wake of a ship; *~an,* a groove; *ber~,* grooved; ~ *tenggala,* a furrow.

am [KS], general, common, as opposed to special *(khas); pengetahuan* ~, general knowledge.

ama [KN], 1. a gnat, an atom, a microbe, a mote, a minute insect parasite; also *hama.* 2. Ar. ~ *baada,* well then, and after that ... an opening to a Malay letter.

amah [KN], 1. a Chinese nurse; a maidservant. 2. Tam. mother.

amal [KN], Ar. good works in the eyes of God; *~kan,* to persist in doing (any thing); so *~an,* habit, practice; *ber~,* to do meritorious work; *meng~kan petua,* to put rules into practice; *pada ~annya,* in practice (as opposed to in theory); *membuat* ~ *ibadatnya,* to practice one's religion; ~ is used esp. of 'works' as opposed to faith *(iman),* esp. charitable works; *rumah* ~, a Home; *pertunjukan* ~, charity show.

aman [KN], Ar. peace, safety, security; *ke~an,* state of security, peacefulness; *meng~kan,* to pacify; *peng~an,* act of creating peace.

amanah [KN], Ar. charge, trust; *menaruh* ~, to leave a charge, of dying men; *meng~kan,* trust, confide, entrust; *pecah* ~, breach of trust; *orang* ~, a trustworthy person; *Jajahan Amanat,* Trust Territory; *pemegang* ~, a trustee; *lembaga* ~, board of trustees; *memberi* ~, to give a charge, a precept; also *amanat.*

amang [KN], 1. foreign elements or by-products in tin. 2. *meng~,* to threaten, to menace.

amar [KN], Ar. order, edict; the commands of the Deity; *~an,* a warning, caution.

amarah [KK] = **marah.**

amat [KKtr], very; *kau* ~ *baik hati,* you're terribly nice, (c) *ter~,* surpassingly; *yang ter~ mulia,* Most Illustrious, a title of honour given to the heir to a throne, the Ruler being *yang maha mulia* (His Highness) and lesser princes being ~ *mulia* (Very Illustrious); *amati,* ~-~i and *memper~-~i,* to look very closely at, to devote careful attention to.

ambai [KN], a purse-net fixed in estuaries.

ambal [KN], 1. ~an, a procession; ber~ a~an, in procession, trooping after. 2. a rug.

amban [KN], bamboos lashed to a boat's side to increase its buoyancy.

ambang [KN], the threshold of a door; meng~, e.g. bulan meng~; to seem just to rest on the horizon, of the sun or moon; to remain motionless in the air, of a bird, or in the water, of a fish; cinta ~~an, 'wishing' when the moon just appears over the horizon — a propitious time according to Malay belief.

ambar [KN], 1. Ar. ambergris. 2. tawar ~, also tawar-hambar; most insipid, tasteless; tertawa ~, to laugh feebly, snigger.

ambik = ambil.

ambil [KK], taking over, acquiring; taking and retaining (and not merely picking up); ~ pedoman, to set the course by the compass; meng~, to take; meng~ bahagian, to take part; meng~ akan menantu, to take as a son-in-law; to give one's daughter in marriage to; meng~ di-hati, to take to heart; to bear a grudge over; meng~ berat, to take seriously, take to heart; ~ muka, to try to ingratiate oneself; ~ tahu, to observe, take note of; to meddle, interfere; suka sangat ~ tahu hal orang, too fond of taking note of other people's affairs, inquisitive; ~ ada (sahaja), take what one can get without careful choice; ~ alih, to take over (adopt plan, take over business, administration, job, etc.).

ambin [KN], 1. a scarf to support a child borne on the back; a strap or band-support generally; mengambin, to carry in such a band. 2. Ind. dais, bench, sleeping-platform.

amboi [KSrn], hullo, oh!, an exclamation of astonishment.

ambul [KK], 1. meng~, to rebound (e.g., as a spear). 2. meng~, to fish with an un-weighted line, as for cuttle-fish.

ambulans [KN], ambulance.

Ambun [KN], negeri ~, Amboyna.

ambung [KN], 1. a back basket, knapsack. 2. [KK], meng~, to surge up, of waves, to bounce. 3. ~~, a sea-shore shrub (Scoevola Koenigii).

ambus [KK], meng~, to run away, 'beat it'; ber~!, beat it!, be off with you!

amil [KN], Ar. almsman, person entrusted with the collection of fitrah; sometimes in literature pegawai peng~ orang baharu (bagi tentera) is used for recruiting officer.

amin [KSrn], Ar. amen; be it so!; meng~kan, to keep repeating the word amen.

amir [KN], Ar. an emir, a chief; ~u'l-mukminin, Commander of the Faithful; ~u'l bahar, admiral.

ampai [KK], hanging and waving loosely; ~an kain, a clothes-line; ~~, a small stinging jelly-fish; ~~, sometimes used for tentacles; see **empai**; cf. **lampai**.

ampang [KN], dam; = **empang**.

ampat = **empat**.

ampu [KN], holding up by pressure from below; meng~, [KK], to hold up, to support (as corsets hold up the brests); (kain) peng~ susu, also **coli**, a brassiere; meng~ bodek, to 'suck-up', be a lickspittle; kaki ~, a sycophant; peng~, id.

ampuan [KN], tengku ~, a raja's principal wife.

amuk [KK], a furious attack; meng~, to run amok, to attack furiously; (fig.) to rampage, storm.

ampul [KK], meng~, to swell out, to be blown out.

ampun [KN], pardon, forgiveness; grant of privilege by Ruler; minta ~, to ask forgiveness; ~i, ~kan and meng~kan, to forgive; peng~an beramai-ramai, general amnesty.

ampung [KK], float, drifting, to drift; cf. **apung**, **lampung** etc.

amput [KK], (vulg.) to copulate.

amra [KN], Hind. the hog-plum; ~ *disangka kedondong,* (prov.) you never know till you have tried.

amris [KN], Ar. *urat* ~, the muscles and veins at the side of the throat; the throat; the jugular vein; *tulang* ~, the hyoid bone; also *meris.*

ana [KN], Ar. I, me.

anai-anai [KN], the white ant.

anak [KN], child, offspring, issue; the young of an animal; the native (of a place); the relationship of an accessory to a principal object or of a component part to a whole; ~-~, a puppet, a doll, an image; ~ *angkat,* a child by adoption; ~ *anjing,* a puppy; ~ *ayam,* a chick; ~ *air,* a rivulet; ~ *bini,* family, wife and family; ~ *buah* (1) descendants generally, (2) the people under the charge of a headman or chief; ~ *buangan,* a foundling; ~ *pungutan,* id.; ~ *cucu,* descendants; ~ *dagang,* a foreigner; ~ *dara,* a maiden; ~ *dayung,* an oarsman; ~ *gampang,* an illegitimate child of doubtful paternity; ~ *genta,* the clapper of a bell; ~ *gobek,* a betel-nut pounder; ~ *gundik,* a son by a secondary wife; ~ *haram,* an illegitimate child; ~ *jari,* a finger; ~ *kembar,* a twin; ~ *kunci,* a key; ~ *laki-laki,* a boy, a son; ~ *leher,* the front of the neck; ~ *lidah,* the uvula; ~ *emas,* born slave; but *meng~-emaskan,* to treat as superior, give preferential treatment to, as opposed to *meng~-tirikan,* treat as a step-child, i.e., neglect, slight, treat as inferior; ~ *marak,* baby fish, fry; ~ *murid,* a pupil; ~ *negeri,* a native of the country; ~ *orang,* other people's children (esp. their daughters); ~ *panah,* an arrow; ~ *perahu,* a boatman; ~ *perempuan,* a girl, a daughter; ~ *piatu,* an orphan; ~ *raja,* a prince; ~ *rambut,* the fringe of hair over the forehead; ~ *roda,* the spoke of a wheel; ~ *sulung,* the eldest-born; ~ *sumbang,* a child of incest; ~ *sungai,* a small tributary stream; ~ *tangga,* a step, a rung of a ladder; ~ *telinga,* the external gristly portion of the ear; ~ *teruna,* a bachelor, an unmarried youth; ~ *tiri,* a step-child; ~ *tunggal,* an only child; *ber~,* to be possessed of a child, to bear a child; to be born; *ber~(kan),* to bear a child; *ber~ kurang bulan,* a premature birth; ~ *di luar nikah,* born out of wedlock; ~ *kematian ibu,* motherless child; ~ *haram jadah,* bastard (= *haram zadah,* see **haram**); ~ *kemanakan,* nephew, niece; ~ *penakan,* id.; *ke~-~an,* childish; *bersikap ke~-~an,* behaving childishly; ~ *orang baik,* a good birth; ~ *tekak,* the uvula; *memperanakkan,* to beget; *penganak,* a sort of drum; *peranakan,* born in the country, natives, usually of persons of foreign race, esp. Tamil Muslims.

anakanda [KN], son — a courtly and literary form of **anak**.

analisa [KN], Ind. *meng~,* to analyse.

anang [KN], my son; a variant of **anak** occurring in Malayo-Javanese literature.

anasir [KN], Ar. elements, viz., air, fire, earth and water; so (fig.) the elements of, e.g., society; ~ *yang tidak diingini,* undersirable elements; ~ *subersib,* subversive elements.

anbia [KN], Ar. prophets; the plural of **nabi**.

ancai [KS], careless, = **cuai;** *meng~kan,* to neglect, be remiss about.

ancak [KN], platters for offerings of food placed in baskets for evil spirits; *buang* ~, to make such offerings.

ancam [KN], Jav. threat, menace; *perkerjaannya ter~,* his career is in jeopardy; *~an,* threat; *peng~,* person who threatens.

ancu [KN], 1. a large raft of the Sumatran type. 2. cross-beams under a *nibung* flooring.

ancuk [KK], *ber~,* to pair, to copulate (coarse).

ancung [KN], a glazed earthenware pot, esp. for ginger.

anda [KN], 1. Skr. the musk-glands in a civet; ~ *kesturi,* the name of a Malay sweetmeat. 2. Ar. you; also **anta.**

andai [KN], 1. the hook to which the sheet of a Malay sail is attached. 2. *~nya,* perhaps; *~nya rancangan ini gagal, saya akan bertanggungjawab sepenuhnya,* in the event this plan fails, I'll take full responsibility; *~-kata,* supposing; *se~nya,* on the understanding that, if it be; *peng~an,* assumption.

andak [KK], 1. to reef, (fig.) to decrease, e.g., expenditure; *meng~kan layar,* to reef a sail. 2. *Andak,* a Malay name for a fourth or fifth child, if female.

Andalas [KN], an ancient name of Sumatra.

andam [KN] Pers. the dressing of the hair above the forehead; the fringe of a bride; *meng~,* to trim, as fringe or moustache; *mabuk ~,* 'fringe-dizzy', of a girl excited at the prospect of her hoped-for wedding.

andang [KN], 1. a torch of dry leaves, etc. 2. *~~,* the yard on a ship or boat. 3. mole, birthmark.

andar [KK], Ar. *mati ~,* to perish for nothing (of deaths from inexplicable causes or murders in which the perpetrator is never traced).

andas [KN], a block with a flat surface; an anvil.

andeka [KN], 1. Jav. you — a pronoun of the second person used in addressing people of rank. 2. the vengeful sacrosanctity of a hereditary non-sovereign chief (= *daulat* of rulers); Pk. *adika.*

andil [KN], Ind. a portion, a share, esp. in a company.

Andoman [KN], Skr., Ked. Hanoman, q.v.; see **Doman.**

anduh [KK], support by means of a sling; *~an sekuci,* the slings under a boat at the davits; *tali ~,* the lashings of a gun-carriage; *kayu peng~,* splints, as for a broken limb.

andui [KN], a cradle, esp. one extempo-

rised from a bit of cloth; *peng~ tidur,* a lullaby.

andung [KN], the dracaena (botanical) (*Cordyline terminalis*).

andur [KN], a buffalo-sleigh; also *anur.*

aneh [KS], Ind. odd, unusual; *kelakuannya ~,* he acts strange; *ke~an,* wonder; *ini salah satu ke~ dunia,* this is one of the wonders of the world.

aneka [KS], Skr. all sorts of, various; *barang mainan yang ber~ warna,* multi-coloured toys; *serba ~,* of different kinds; also *neka; ~ warta,* news-items; *~ ragam,* variegated, varieties (of amusements), a variety show; *~ warna,* of many colours; *ber~,* diversified.

angan [KN], *~~,* thoughts, ideas, the mind; *siti juga di-~~~,* my lady is ever in my thoughts; *melayangkan ~~,* to be pensive, daydream; *ber~-~,* to day-dream; lost to reality; *~-~kan,* to imagine to oneself; *~~~,* visions of the future.

angga [KN], tine of the horn of a deer; *mer~ tanduk,* with branching horns.

anggai [KN], a sign (in very high-flown language), = **isyarat.**

anggal [KS], buoyant, lightly laden; *~kan,* to lighten (as ship, by removing cargo).

anggap [KK], 1. a challenging invitation at a game; *ber~-~an,* in turns, turn and turn about. 2. to take note of, consider, comment on; *meng~ sepi,* to scorn, think lightly of; *meng~ rendah,* to demean, to downgrade; *jangan meng~ rendah orang lain,* never downgrade others; *salah ~,* to take offence; *~an umum,* public opinion.

anggar [KK], reckoning, calculation; *~an pelayaran,* navigation (as a science); *membuat ~,* to take bearings; to make an estimate. 2. *ber~,* to halt for a moment, to pause; *~an burung,* a bird's habitual perching place.

anggara [KS], see **angkara.**

anggerik [KN], an orchid.

anggit [KK], fastening together; *rotan peng~ atap,* a rattan for fastening attaps; *rotan ~,* the rattan binding outside a drum.

anggota [KN], Skr. limbs; ~ *tiruan,* artificial limb; ~ is used (fig.) for members of an association; bodily member or organ; sometimes, a person.

angguk [KK], to nod the head; ~-*anggik,* bob up and down (as boats); *tali* ~, bobstay; *meng*~-~, to pitch, as a ship; *ter*~-~, pitching wildly (of a ship or (fig.) of a man's gait); ~-~ *balam,* a vague nod, indicating assent; *pak* ~, a 'nodder', a yes-man, one who agrees to everything.

anggul [KK], to lift at the bows, to pitch (of a boat).

anggun [KS], elegant; *dia kelihatan* ~ *dengan pakaian barunya,* she looked elegant in her new dress.

anggur [KN], 1. transplanting by budding. 2. Pers. the vine, grapes (by simile) grapeshot, shot; *air* ~, wine; *buah* ~, grapes; *taruk* ~, a vine-shoot; ~ *roda,* ball bearings. 3. better, rather, it were better that. 4. *meng*~, to be out of work; *peng*~*an,* unemployment.

angguri [KN], *kain angguri,* cloth used for a pilgrim's *jubah.*

angin [KN], a wind, a breeze, a current of air; ~ *barat,* a west wind; ~ *darat,* a land breeze; ~ *gila,* an uncertain wind; ~ *puting beliung,* a whirlwind; ~ *sakal,* a head-wind; ~ *turutan,* a following wind; ~ *haluan,* id.; ~ *paksa,* favourable wind; ~ *selembubu,* an eddying wind; ~ *haluan,* id.; *cakap* ~, empty talk; *di atas* ~, the windward and so — west, countries from which ships used to come in the southwest monsoon; *di bawah* ~, the leeward and so — Malaya, Burma, etc., countries to which people come from the west during the southwest monsoon; ~ *tetap,* trade wind (constant wind); ~ *berkala,* seasonal winds; *kematian* ~, dead calm; becalmed; *kepala* ~, flighty; *kincir* ~, windmill; *makan* ~, to set well in a breeze (of a sail); to take a holiday; *mata* ~, the direction from which the wind is blowing;

menjaring ~, to waste time; *percaya* ~, vain hopes or expectations; *penyakit* ~, a generic name for internal diseases which it is hard to diagnose; *sakit* ~ *tofan,* Pen. suffering from syphilis; *pokok* ~, a stormcloud; ~*kan,* to dry in a current of air, *per*~*an,* a clothes drier; *tempat per*~*an,* a holiday resort; *berlaga dengan* ~, to hit it off with, get on well with (generally with negative); *goda* ~, Treng. a whirlwind; *habuk* ~, dust before the wind, completely destroyed; *'brek'* ~, vacuum brake; *khabar* ~, rumour; ~-~, vague rumours, vague talk; *'tayar' tak ber*~, a flat tyre.

angka [KN], Skr. a numerical figure, a cypher; ~ *dua,* the figure two, the reduplication mark; ~ *bulat* = ~ *penuh;* whole number; ~ *ganjil,* odd number; ~ *genap,* even number; ~ *pecahan,* fractions, ~ *perpuluhan,* decimals; ~ *pokok,* cardinal numbers; ~ *berturut-turut,* ordinal numbers; *per*~*an,* statistics.

angkara [KS], Skr. gross brutality or disrespect, violence to a girl or woman, any gross and violent action; persecution; *hina* ~, a low brute; *setua* ~, a fabulous monster of great strength.

angkasa [KN], Skr. the regions of the air, the heavens; *dewa* ~, a celestial deity; *unggas* ~, a bird of the air; ~ is used to denote the region of the air immediately over a place: *di* ~ *Singapura,* over Singapore; ~ *luar,* the stratosphere; ~ *lepas,* outer space; *ruang* ~, the region of the upper heavens, space; ~*wan,* cosmonaut, astronaut.

angkat [KK], raising, lifting, bringing up; *anak* ~, an adopted child; ~-~, gait, bearing; *balai* ~-~, a temporary platform; ~*kan,* to raise, to lift; ~*an,* an expeditionary force, a corps, an organisation; a generation; ~*an* is also used to describe groups of persons sharing similar views or taste; ~*an muda,* the younger generation; *Angkatan 50,* the Fifty

Group, a body of writers, coming into prominence about 1945; *Angkatan Udara di Raja,* R.A.F.; *Angkatan Laut,* Navy; *Angkatan Bersenjata,* the Armed Forces; ~*an raja di raja,* the hearse at a sovereign's funeral; *ber~,* to go (of a prince); ~ *sumpah,* to take the oath; ~ *bungkus,* to clear out bag and baggage, move house; ~ *muka,* to assert oneself, stand up for oneself, ~ *mata,* to feel better, feel relieved; ~ *kaki,* to 'walk out' (e.g., from a meeting); ~ *punggung,* to 'buzz off' (coarse); ~ *senjata,* to take up arms; *bapa* ~, an adoptive father; *ber~,* to set out, start.

angkit [KK], raising (small light objects), to pick up; *belat* ~-~, chicks.

angklung [KN], Ind. a type of musical instrument.

angkuh [KS], proud, haughty, arrogant.

angkuk [KN], figure-head of local small boat.

angkup [KN], tweezers, forceps, pincers.

angkut [KK], lifting or carrying with an effort, 'hoicking'; ~-~, the mason-bee; *peng~an,* transport.

anglo [KN], Ch. a brazier.

anglung [KN], Ch. a pavilion, a summerhouse.

angsa [KN], Skr. a goose.

angsana [KN], the ansena-tree; also *sena.*

angsoka [KN], Skr. the name of a tree *(Pavetta Indica).*

angut [KS], day-dreaming, e.g., under the influence of opium.

ani [KN], 1. *meng~,* Hind., to arrange the pattern on a weaver's loom; *peng~,* a rack for the spools; a weaver; ~*an,* the warping machine in a loom (kek). 2. Ind. ~-~, a kind of reaping knife.

aniaya [KN], Skr. oppression, injustice; *berbuat* ~ *pada,* to oppress; *meng~i,* id.; *peng~,* tyrant, oppressor.

aning-aning [KN], a large blue wasp; also **naning**.

anja [KN], *ber~-~, ter~-~,* spoilt, see **manja**.

anjak [KK], to shift one's position slightly, edging away; *ber~,* to move slightly, to 'budge'; *meng~,* to move shift; to transplant.

anjal [KK], *meng~,* to rebound, spring back (as elastic).

anjang [KN], name of a fourth child in a family.

Anjiman [KN], Eng. *kapal* ~, an East Indiaman (ship).

anjing [KN], a dog; dog, as a term of abuse; ~-~, the muscle of the calf; ~ *hutan,* a wild dog; *anak* ~, a puppy; *gembala* ~, a dog-boy; *gigi* ~, the canine teeth; *meng~,* Kel. to be recalcitrant, 'answer back'; ~ *buruk kepala,* dog with rotten head, (met.) for a disgusting and contemptible person, 'a leper'; *penyakit* ~ *gila,* rabies; ~ *laut,* a seal.

anjung [KN], the projecting front room of a Malay house, a room over a porch; *meng~,* to project, hold up high, flatter.

anjur [KK], *meng~,* to project, to stretch out; *peng~,* front file of soldiers, leaders in a procession, leader, especially political leader; promoter, vanguard of a movement; *meng~* also used for, to proffer, bring forward, suggest; to initiate (a plan); ~*an,* a suggestion, a 'lead', an injunction.

ansur [KK], = **angsur**; *bertolak* ~, to compromise; *ber~,* gradually; *ber~ baik,* getting better; *ber~-~,* in instalments; ~*an,* an instalment.

anta [KN], 1. Ṣkr. existence, entity, nature; *ber~ indera,* divine; *ber~ loka,* earthly, mundane; ~ *kesuma,* flowery, the name given to a Malay dish (made of sweet potato). 2. Skr. *Naga Antaboga,* a great serpent.

anta [KN], Ar. you; also **anda**.

antah [KN], 1. the husk of grain. 2. ~-~, descendants in the fifth generation. 3. *negeri* ~-*ber~,* Never-never Land, Ruritania, Utopia (though not necessarily an ideal country); any imaginary and romatic country. (Probably ~ is a variant of *entah,* so that ~-*ber~* carries the idea of Dunno-where Land).

antan

antan [KN], a pestle.
antap [KS], heavy for its size, esp. of a child.
antar [KK] = hantar.
antar-antar [KN], a ramrod; a pounder.
antara [KPhbg, KKtr], Skr. space between; time between; *di ~*, during the interval between; in the space between; among; *ingat ~ belum kena*, think before you are involved in anything (look before you leap) (prov.); *per~an*, medium, means, commission; *~-bangsa*, international; *~ lain*, among others; *per~*, mediator.
antelas [KN], Ar. satin.
antero [KBil], Port. the whole; *~ Kelang*, the whole of Klang.
antih [KK], *meng~*, to spin (thread).
anting [KK], hanging down and swaying, pendulous; *untang-~* —id. of many objects swaying at a time; *~-~*, a earpendant; *burung ~-~*, racquettailed drongo *(Dissemuros platurus)*.
antuk [KS], 1. *meng~*, to be drowsy or sleepy; *orang meng~ disurungkan bantal*, the sleepy man gets a pillow pushed over to him, a saying expressing the idea of timely help. 2. [KK] colliding; *ber~*, to collide; *gigi ber~*, chattering teeth; *ter~*, in collision; *sudah ter~ baharu tengadah*, to look up after the collision (to shut the stable door after the steed has been stolen) (prov.).
antul [KK], *meng~*, to rebound.
antun [KS], 1. *ber~*, to be particular about one's dress. 2. Pk. slow, stately of speech or gait.
anu [KN], what's his name, what you may call it; *~ itu*, that thingumajig; of person or thing whose name one does not wish to mention; sometimes *~* is used as an exordium to a sentence, much like 'er, er'; in English; *si-~*, so-and-so; *di kampung ~*, at such-and-such a place.
anuan [KN], title, heading as of article.
anugerah [KN], Skr. favour, grace; the gift of a superior to an inferior; *~,*

apam

meng~i, to bestow, to confer a favour on.
anut [KK], to follow, adhere to (a creed); *meng~i Islam*, to follow the creed of Islam; *peng~*, follower.
anyam [KK], plaiting, basket and mat-work; *meng~*, to plait; *~an*, products of weaving or plating.
anyang [KN], 1. food such as clams, cockles which are not cooked but served with spices. 2. to root about in rubbish, as a pig grouting.
apa [KS], 1. what; *dia orang ~?* what is he?; *~-buat?* what are you doing?; *~-~*, whatever; *~ adanya; saya akan makan ~ adanya*, I'll eat what's here; *~ bila*, when, whenever, *~ fasal?* why?; *~-guna?*, what is the use?; *~ kala*, when, whenever; *~ lagi?* what then?, why, of course!; in some contexts *~ lagi?* means, how much more! or how much less!; *~lah*, and so on and so on; *~ macam?* how?, what kind of?, in what way?; *~ buat*, why?; *buat ~?*, why?; *~ sebab?*, why?; *~tah?*, what?; *barang ~*, whatever; *beberapa*, in some quantity; some, several; *berapa?*, in what quantity?, how many, how much?; *tak ber~*, not very; *bet~?*, how?, why?; *ken~* and *meng~?*, why?; *si~?*, who?; *ti~ meng~*, or (coll.) *tidak ~*, no matter, never mind; *tidak ~ ~*, saya tidak *~ ~*, I'm all right; *~tah lagi?*, still more or still less; *~kah?* how is it that? why?, what (on earth)?; *~ tidaknya?* why not?, what's wrong with the idea?; *~ boleh buat*, can't help it; *peng~kan*, (us. with a negative), to do something to a person, e.g. esp. inflict a punishment. Nowadays *~* when introducing a question does not necessarily mean 'what?': it does hardly more than mark the sentence as a question; *~ sahaja*, what have you. 2. *buluh ~*, a dwarf bamboo.
apabila [KKtr], when, whenever.
apak [KS] = hapak, stinking, as a sweaty person, frowsy.
apakala [KKtr], when, whenever.
apam [KN], Tam. a thin cake; *~ balik*, an

15

~ baked on both sides, turn-over.

apas [KS], striking, effective (of costume), smart appearance, elegant.

api [KN], fire, a light; *rumah* ~, a lighthouse; ~-~, a generic name for a number of trees of the mangrove class; a kind of fire-fly; *asap* ~, smoke; *bara* ~, live embers; *batu* ~, flint; (fig.) firebrand, mischief-maker; *bunga* ~, sparks, fireworks; *dimakan* ~, burnt; *gobek* ~, a fire syringe; *gunung ber*~, a volcano; *kapal* ~, a steamship; *kayu* ~, firewood; *kereta* ~, a railway; *laut* ~, the fiery sea (hell); *periuk* ~, mine, a bomb, a shell; *semut* ~, a long black stinging ant; *ber*~, flaming; *meng*~*kan*, to inflame, excite; *per*~*an*, brazier, stove; chafing-dish; ~ *diangan*, fire for warming; ~ *dalam sekam*, fire in chaff, met. for hidden dangers which may burst out or for smouldering (and dangerous) ill-feeling.

apih [KN], 1. a Chinese purse. 2. = **apik** IV.

apik [KS], 1. spruce, smart, neat, 2. *cakap upak-*~, tale-bearing, mischievous or inconsistent talk; also **rapik**. 3. N.S. ~*kan*, to take heed of, deem important. 4. Ch. daddy, gaffer.

apilan [KN], a gun-shield.

apit [KN], wedging between two surfaces (not connected by a hinge); a printing-press; *meng*~, to press, between two surfaces; so (fig.) to support (by standing beside); *peng*~, an assessor at a trial, the best man at a wedding; *ter*~, wedged in between; ~-~, a breakback trap (for rats or squirrels); ~ is used also for 'inside' at football; *bukit ber*~, twin hills joined by a col.

apiun [KN], Ar. opium.

apum [KN], a cake resembling (but not identical with) the *apam*.

apung [KK], drifting; flotsam; *laksana* ~ *ditengah laut*, like driftwood on the waves (helpless), (prov.), *ter*~-~, drifting about, floating about.

ara [KN], a generic name for trees of the fig type; *menanti* ~ *tak berge-*

tah, to wait for the fig to lose its sap (an endless wait), (prov.).

Arab [KN], Ar. Arabian, Arabic; *negeri* ~, Arabia; *bahasa* ~, Arabic.

Arabiah [KN], Arabia; ~ *Saudiah*, Saudi Arabia.

arah [KN], direction; ~ *ke laut*, towards the sea; *sekeliling* ~, on all sides, in all directions; *tak tentu* ~, in confusion; *tak tahu* ~, to get disoriented; *tak ada* ~, Kel. uncertain what to do, at wit's end; *meng*~*kan*, to direct (an enterprise); *Peng*~, a Director, Producer; ~*an*, a directive, an instruction for guidance; *mengalih* ~, to change course.

arai [KN], 1. ~ *jem*~, hanging loosely, as partly broken twigs, 2. the dried blossom stalk on a coconut tree.

arak [KN], 1. *ber*~, to march in procession; *per*~*an*, a procession; a processional car; *per*~*an tunjuk perasaan*, a procession by way of political demonstration; *meng*~, to march in procession; to conduct in procession, usher along; *meng*~ *panji-panji*, to troop the colour; *peng*~, a forerunner, a presage; *awan peng*~ *hujan*, clouds presaging rain. 2. Ar. arrack; rice spirit; spirits; liquor.

arakian [KKtr], furthermore.

aral [KN], Ar. an obstacle; a difficulty; hindrance; ~ *melintang*, an obstacle in one's path.

aram [KK], 1. grudge; ~-~, bearing a grudge. 2. ~-*tem*~, clouded over (as the moon). 3. ~-~, a scaffolding.

arang [KN], charcoal; *kayu* ~, ebony; ~ *batu*, coal; ~ *padu*, seam coal; ~ *di muka*, defilement; shame, disgrace; *sapu* ~ *di muka*, to insult publicly, disgrace; *hapuskan* ~ *di muka*, to avenge an insult or a disgrace; *berkerat rotan ber-patah* ~, (prov.), friendships irreparably broken by quarrels.

aras [KN], 1. rising to a level with; on a level with, a level; *meng*~ *awan*, to rise to the cloud line; ~ *laut*, sea-level. 2. 'opened' check (chess). 3. Ar. the throne of God.

arbaa [KN] = **rabu** II.

argus [KN], guinea-pig.

ari [KN], 1. *kulit* ~, the inner skin (under the cuticle). 2. ~-~ , the part of the body between the navel and the pubes; *bulu* ~- ~, pubic hair. 3. Ar. halter; *meng~ (kuda)*, to put a halter on (a horse). 4. ~, younger brother or sister.

aria [KN], 1. (nautical) lower away! 2. title of a prince; word used while coaxing.

arif [KS], Ar. one who knows, the wise; *seperti kata* ~, in the words of the wise; *Arif* is used as a proper name, *meng~*, understand, know, comprehend.

arifin [KN], Ar. wise men; the wise — plural of **arif**.

arih [KS], *meng~*, put out or stretch out the hands etc., to embrace; *dia meng~kan tangannya hendak memeluk saya*, he holds out his hands to embrace me.

arik, [KK], *meng~*, pull (oar), awake, sleepless.

aring [KS], 1. foul-smelling, as a urinal. 2. the small piece of worked steel below the guard of the blade of *keris*.

aris [KN], an edging of cord or rattan to a sail or net.

Aristu [KN], Aristotle.

arit [KN], Jav. a curved knife used for tapping trees; a sickle; Ked. *meng~*, to tap a toddy-palm or cut *nipah*.

Arjuna [KN], Skr. sl. for *Ranjun~* q.v.; (sl.) a jocular description of a handsome youth.

arkeologi [KN], archaeology.

arkib [KN], Eng. archives.

arloji [KN], small clock; watch.

armada [KN], armada.

arnab [KN], Ar. a rabbit, hare.

arpus [KN], resin for rubbing catgut.

aruan = haruan [KN], a coarse fresh-water fish *(Channa striata)*, much caught for food, esp. in rice-fields; also **ruan.**

arung [KK], wading, fording; *meng~*, to wade through water, to ford; to traverse; *belayar meng~*, to put out to sea; *meng~*

darah, to wade through blood (a metaphor for great slaughter); ~*an*, a crossing, a channel (a metaphor for the deep central part of the sea); *sekali* ~, making one journey of it, doing it in one go.

arus [KN], current as of water, air, electricity, stream, flow; ~ *sungai*, the river's current; *menentang* ~ *lalu-lintas*, against the flow of traffic.

arwah [KN], Ar. the vital elements in a man; the soul; the spirits of the dead; *kenduri* ~, a feast in honour of the dead; *terbang* ~, loss of consciousness; *doa* ~, prayers for a deceased person, esp. at his grave; *menjadi* ~, to part from the body, to die; ~ *tuan* ... while Mr ... was still alive; is also used for 'the late Mr ...'; *alam* ~, the world of spirits; also *ruah.*

asa [KN], Skr. hope; *putus* ~, disappointed; *hilang* ~, id.

asah [KK], grinding down, filing (the teeth); *mengasah pisau*, to sharpen a knife; *batu* ~, a whetstone; ~*kan*, to whet, to grind down; *meng~ otak*, to exercise one's brain.

asai [KN], a fruit-weevil or wood-weevil.

asak [KK], pressing in or down, ramming into a small space, cramming in, stuffing in; *ber~-~*, crowded together, 'jam-packed'.

asal [KS], Ar. origin; ~ *usul*, history, origins, lineage; ~*nya*, originally; ~*kan* (or simply ~), if, provided that, if only; *biar lambat* ~ *selamat*, let it be late provided that it is safe, i.e., safety first; *ber~*, ancient, that has existed long; *raja ber~*, a *raja* by descent; *pulang ke* ~, back to where one started, i.e., ruined or dead.

asam [KN], acid, sour; acid fruits, esp. the tamarind; *laksana* ~ *dengan garam*, like acids and salt (which go well together), (prov.); *limau* ~, the lime; ~ *sendawa*, nitric acid; ~ *belerang*, sulphuric acid; ~ *samak*, tannic acid; ~ *garam*, acids and salts; viewed as indispensable flavourings for a meal; so, sometimes used, in effect for 'varied experiences', 'one's lot'; ~- *garam sudah dia telan selama itu* (such had been his lot for all that time); ~ *garam yang tidak terpisah dari keluarga petani yang miskin itu,* such is the inevitable lot of the families of poor cultivators; cf. **garam.**

asap [KN], smoke, vapour; ~*kan,* to fumigate, to perfume with incense; *per~an,* a censer; *rumah meng~ getah,* rubber smoke-house; ~ *naik berpayung,* smoke rising into a mushroom (lit. an umbrella).

asar [KN], Ar. the afternoon, with special reference to the afternoon prayer *(sembahyang asar),* i.e. about 4 p.m.

asas [KN], 1. Ar. foundation, establishment; *batu* ~, foundation stone; *tidak ber~,* groundless; ~~, basic principles (of one's faith, etc.); *persetujuan pada ~nya,* agreement in principle; ~*i,* basic; *hak-hak ~i manusia,* basic human rights; *peng~,* the founder member. 2. *Asas,* see **kutu.**

asin [KN], 1. salted; *ikan* ~, salted fish. 2. ~-~, a shrub, the leaves of which are eaten as vegetables, = *cekur manis.*

asing [KS], distinct, separate, apart; *orang* ~, a different person; a foreigner; ~*kan,* to set apart, to discriminate; *per~an,* segregation; *ber~an,* separate; *per~an,* separation; *kurungan ber~,* solitary confinement; *ber~ dari,* to separate from, withdraw from; *bantuan* ~, foreign aid; *ter~,* separated; *peng~an,* act of separation, dissociation; *peng~an Singapura dari Malaysia,* the separation of Singapore from Malaysia; *tidak* ~, nothing new; *itu tidak* ~ *bagi kami,* it's nothing new to us.

askar [KN], Ar. soldiery, a soldier; ~ *berjalan kaki,* infantry; ~ *upahan,* mercenaries; ~ *bayaran,* id.; ~ *biasa,* regulars; see **tentera.**

asli [KN], Ar. original, primal; genuine, not synthetic, not adulterated; *getah* ~, natural rubber; *orang* ~, aborigines;

ke~an, natural state; authenticity; *saya meragukan ke~an dokumen ini,* I question the authenticity of this document; original state; (fig.) originality (of a writer, etc.).

asmara [KN], Skr. love, sexual love; *ber~,* to make love.

aspal [KN], resurfaced road.

aspek [KN], aspect.

asnaf, plural of sinf, q.v.

Asrafil [KN], Ar. the archangel Israfel.

asrama [KN], Ind. hostel, boarding-house, esp. for students.

astagfirullah, Ar. an exclamation denoting amazement and, often, horror: 'Lord have mercy upon us!'

astaka [KN], a dais; a (royal) pavilion.

astakona [KN], Skr. an octagonal pattern, a large receptacle for rice of that pattern used at weddings.

astana [KN] = **istana.**

asu [KN], *gigi* ~, the canine teeth.

asuh [KK], *meng~,* to nurse; ~*an,* upbringing; *peng~,* a nurse.

asuk [KN], Ked. male dancer at a *ronggeng.*

asut = *hasut* [KK], *meng~,* stirring up enmity, egging on to a quarrel; to incite, abet; *hasutan,* incitement, esp. to sedition; *tukang hasut,* trouble-maker, troubler of the peace.

asyik [KS], Ar. enamoured, in love, wrapt up in (any work), passionately addicted to, fond of (doing); owing to a misconception the passion fruit is often called *buah* ~.

asyura [KN], feast of 10th Muharram in honour of Hassan and Hussin; so, the porridge-mixture eaten on that day.

atap [KN], roofing; thatch of palm-leaf usually made of leaves of the *nipah* palm, but those of the *rumbia* (sago) palm are most esteemed and in the jungle inferior leaves such as those of the *bertam* palm have to serve; ~ *ayan,* a corrugated-iron roof; ~ *batu,* ~ *genting,* or ~ *sisek tenggiling,* a tiled roof; ~ *zink,* corrugated iron.

atar [KN], *minyak ~,* attar of roses.

atas [KN], position above, with reference to, about; *di ~,* above; *ke ~,* upward, to a place above; *meng~i,* to overcome; to surmount; to surpass; *orang ~an,* the top people, the 'high-ups'; *~ angin,* the windward; *~ dasar kemanusiaan,* on humanitarian grounds; *~ nama,* on behalf of.

atau [KPhbg], Skr. or, or else.

athar [KN], Ar. survivals, antiquities (e.g. buildings or traditions).

atma [KN], Skr. spirit, = **utama,** used for, e.g., the 'spirit' of imperialism.

atung [KK], *ter~-~,* becalmed (of sailing-ships), drifting (of steamers broken down); *meng~,* to be carried by current.

atur [KK], *meng~,* to arrange; *~an,* arrangement; *per~an,* method or scheme of arrangement; rules and regulations; *dengan ter~,* in a regular, orderly manner; *secara ter~,* in accordance with a regular plan, organised; *jalan-jalan yang berper~an,* regular methods, standard methods.

atus [KK], Ked. to filter; to rinse.

aulia [KN], Ar. *sanits;* a holy man, a saint of Islam.

audit [KN], audit.

auditorium [KN], auditorium.

aum [KN], (onom.); *meng~,* to growl (as a tiger), to murmur (as a crowd).

aur [KN], a generic name given to many large bamboos; *kehidupan ~ di tebing,* the life of a bamboo on the bank of a river, a simile for a precarious existence, dependent on others.

aurat [KN], Ar. those parts of the body which should not be exposed (between the knees and the navel for men and the whole body except the feet and hands for [Muslim] women); *menutup ~,* to keep the person covered; *mendedahkan ~,* to uncover the person; also **urat.**

auta [KN], Tam, lying, boasting, exaggeration, humbug.

autobiografi [KN], autobiography.

awak [KN], body, person; self; contents; you, thou (Joh., Pah., N.S., Sel.); *~ perahu,* the crew of a ship; *per~an,* posture, carriage disposition; *berper~an,* having 'presence', of imposing appearance; having a good physique; *pisang ~,* an inferior kind of banana.

awal [KS], Ar. beginning, first; *~ musim,* the beginning of the season; *~-~,* early (before time); *ter~ daripada,* earlier than; *~an,* primary, first; *kenyataan ~,* examination-in-chief (in Court); *~an,* a prefix (gram.).

awam [KN], Ar. civilian; *kepentingan ~,* public interest; *kenderaan ~,* public transport; *perkhidmatan ~,* civil service.

awan [KN], cloud, cloud-like pattern; *~ mengandung hujan,* a raincloud; *~ timbul,* pattern in relief; *~ tenggelam,* an incised pattern; *~ pengarak angin,* driving clouds, *meng~,* to rise skywards; *tinggi meng~,* sky-high; *terbang meng~,* to soar right up into the sky.

Awang [KN], 1. young fellow; a familiar and rather contemptuous form of address to any unknown youth. 2. *awang-awang* or *awang-awangan,* the lower heavens; *terawang,* suspended in the middle air; *menerawang,* rising to high heaven, as a piercing voice.

awas [KS], keen sight; second sight; a view (scenery); *meng~i,* to superintend, to supervise; *Pengawas Kewangan,* Auditor; *~! ~!,* observe! take heed!; used as a heading to notices and advertisements; *~i!,* look out for!; beware of, usually as a heading; *peng~an,* surveillance; *~ dan waspadalah,* keep your eyes open, be on the alert, be on guard.

awat [KS], 1. = *apa buat?,* why? [KKtr]. 2. ridge between plough-furrows; *memecah ~,* to cross-plough. 3. *~-~,* N.S. rattan lashings of an adze; cf. **perawat.**

awet muda [KS], to stay young;

meng~kan makanan, to preserve food.

aya [KN], *ikan ~,* Treng. the tunny fish; usually *ikan tongkol.*

ayah [KN], 1. father; ~ *bonda,* parents. 2. Hind. an Indian nurse.

ayahanda [KN], sire (in courtly language).

ayak [KK], *meng~,* to pass through a sieve; *~an,* a sieve.

ayam [KN], 1. a generic name for fowls; ~ *Belanda,* a turkey; ~ *peru,* a turkey, also a guinea-fowl; ~ *katik,* a bantam; ~ *panggang-perenggi* or *peranggam-perenggi,* a pullet or cockerel; ~ *dara,* pullet; ~ *denak* or ~ *hutan,* a jungle-fowl; ~ *itik,* poultry; ~ *jantan,* a cock; ~ *sabungan,* fighting-cock; ~ *kasi* or ~ *kembiri,* a capon; ~ *mutiara,* a guinea-fowl; ~ *pegar,* the fire-back pheasant *(Lophura rufa); ~-~,* a watercock; *anak ~,* a chicken; *berkaki ~,* barefooted, shoeless; ~ *tambatan,* pet fighting cock, so (met.) local champion; *bapa ~,* a cock; also (met.) a pimp, procurer; *ibu ~,* a hen; also (met.) the 'madam' of a brothel; ~ *bapa,* daddy fowl, cock, the old rooster; *membawa perangai* ~ *betina,* behave like a hen, i.e. be obsequious, fawning, fail to stand up for oneself; ~ *betina,* a hen *(ibu* ~ rather implies a hen with chicks); ~ *babun,* Ind. is sometimes used 2. N.S. = **anyam.**

ayan [KN], Eng. corrugated iron.

ayapan [KN], victuals.

ayat [KN], Ar. verse, esp. of the Koran; a sentence (grammar).

ayu [KS], Jav. beautiful (elder sister).

Ayub [KN], Ar. the patriarch Job. Used as a proper name by Malays.

ayuk [KK], (coarse) sexual intercourse.

ayun [KK], to rock, to sway, *ber~* or *meng~,* id.; *~an,* a hammock, a cradle; *matahari ber~,* *~-tem~,* afternoon; *meng~ kaki,* to swing the legs, trudge along; *meng~ betis, meng~ tunjang, meng~ langkah,* id.

ayut [KK], (coarse) sexual intercourse.

azab [KN], Ar. sorrow, pain, trouble torture, punishment.

azal [KS] Ar. the beginning of time, the endless past; in contrast to *abad,* the endless future.

azam [KN], Ar. intention, purpose, resolution; *ber~ nak,* to make up one's mind to —.

azan [KN], Ar. the call to prayer, = **bang;** ~ *disuarakan,* the call to prayer was uttered.

azim [KS], Ar. august, exalted, great, *sultanul-~,* the august *sultan.*

azimat, [KN] Ar. a talisman.

aziz [KS], Ar, dear, darling; *Abdul Aziz* is a common proper name, meaning Servant of the Loved One, i.e. God.

azmat [KS], Ar. awe-inspiring (especially of sounds); also *adzmat;* cf. **hadamat.**

azza [KS], Ar. honoured; ~ *wa jalla,* honoured and illustrious (of God).

B

ba [KN], the name of the second letter of the Arabic alphabet.

bab [KN], Ar. 1. gate, door. 2. a chapter, a main division of a book, a paragraph.

baba [KN], a Straits-born Chinese, a foreigner born in Malaya.

babad [KN], history, chronicle.

babak [KN], Ind. section; episode or act of a play; scene, ~-~ *perjuangan*, fighting scenes; in the sense of 'period', ~ is sometimes used for a 'half' at football: ~ *yang pertama*, first half.

babang [KS], gaping wide, agape, of an opening (of mouth, wound, abyss).

babar [KK], *mem~*, lay out; *mem~kan barang-barang dagangannya di tepi jalan*, to lay the merchandise at the roadside; *mem~kan layar*, to spread one's sails.

babas [KK], *ter~*, blown completely off course, esp. of a ship not merely deflected (bias); *hujan ter~*, rain blown away before reaching one.

babat [KN], Ind. category, set, type; *se~*, alike, of the same type; *kalau bersahabat cari sama ~*, if you want a friend choose someone of your own type (prov.).

babi [KN], a pig, hog, pork, pig as a term of abuse; ~ *buta*, recklessness; ~ *hutan*, a wild pig; ~ *kawan*, the half-grown wild pig; ~ *nangui*, the bearded pig *(Sus barbatus)*; ~ *tanah*, Kel. the bamboo rat (us. *dekan*); *bulu ~*, a sea-urchin; *burung ~*, the adjutant bird; *gila ~*, epileptic; *mem~ buta*, to attack furiously without a plan, to act blindly.

babil [KN], quarrelsome; *ber~*, squabble, quarrel; *per~an*, squabble, row, ruckus.

babit [KK], implicate third parties in a dispute; 'to drag in'; *mem~-~*, keep bringing up irrelevant or stale matters; *~an*, implications, connections (with a problem).

babu [KN], 1. a Javanese nurse. 2. Hind.

'Mr.'.

babut [KN], rug, carpet; *mem~i*, carpet (a room).

baca [KK], reading; the utterance of formulae, prayers or incantations; *mem~*, to read; *tanda ~an*, vowel-points; diacritical marks; *bahan ~an*, reading materials; *mem~ erti tersembunyi sesuatu tulisan*, to read between the lines; *pem~*, reader.

bacang [KN], see **macang** or **embacang**.

bacar [KS], leaky; ~ *mulut*, glib in speech, loquacious, garrulous, talkative.

bacin [KS], Sum. stinking, fetid.

bacuk [KN], a section of a large bamboo used as a water-vessel.

bacul [KS], timid, spiritless; *ayam ~*, a cock that will not fight.

bada [KN], Pk. a sort of puff, made of flour, mashed bananas and spices.

badai [KS], 1. *ter~*, driven together, adhering, of flotsam on the surface. 2. [KN], a sudden severe squall; *ribut mem~*, a storm working up.

badak [KN], 1. a generic name for the rhinoceros and tapir; ~ *api*, a fabulous rhinoceros; ~ *himpit* = ~ *kerbau*; ~ *kerbau*, the Sumatran rhinoceros; ~ *raya*, the Java rhinoceros (R. sondaicus); ~ *tampung*, the tapir, = *tenuk*; ~ *murai*, Kel. Treng. Pah. the tapir; used as a simile for blind stupidity. 2. = **bidak.**

badam [KN], Pers. the almond.

badan [KN], Ar. the body — cf. *tubuh*; used generally for 'body' and, e.g. for the hull of a ship; *ber~ dua*, (sl.) pregnant; *orang berisi ~nya*, stout, of full figure; used for a political body; *per~an*, body, corporation; *per~an bandar*, municipality; *gerak ~*, to do exercise; *tidak sedap ~*, not feeling well.

badang [KN], a round bamboo winnowing tray; *Badang*, a giant of legend.

badar [KN], Ar. 1. the moon. 2. the name of a plain near Mecca. 3. Kel. free and easy, = **bebas.**

badi [KN], see **bahadi.**

badik [KN], a small, straight dagger.

Badui [KN], Ar. a Bedouin; a wandering scoundrel.

baduk [KS], clumsy, bulky.

badut [KN], a clown, buffoon.

bagai [KN], Tam. kind, species, variety; like, = *seperti; ~-~,* sorts, kinds; also *pelbagai; ber~-~,* of different sorts; *se~,* like, resembling, as, in the function of, in the form of; *~kan,* just as if; *se~ imbalan,* in return; *apakah yang kita perolehi se~ imbalan?,* what do we get in return?

bagaimana [KKtr], how?, in what way?; *~ pun,* anyhow, anyway; *walau ~ pun,* somehow or other; *se~ mestinya,* the way it should be done.

bagal [KS], 1. clumsy, big (of a cock). 2. = **baghal.**

bagan [KN], 1. a platform for drying fish; a scaffolding; open space as for landing-ground or as a field for cattle. 2. *mem~,* to sketch, draw in outline; *~an,* a sketch, diagram.

bagau [KN], a plant (Xyris Indica); a kind of rush.

baghal [KN], Ar. a mule.

bagi [KKtr], 1. to, for, for the use or purpose of. 2. divide, *~ dua,* divide into two. 3. allotment, *pem~an harta pusaka,* the allotment of the legacy... 4. *~ pihak* (b.p.), for, on behalf of, esp. in signatures; *~ pihak Pengetua,* on behalf of the Principal.

bagimana = **bagaimana.**

baginda [KN], king, prince, ruler; *Baginda King,* H.M. the King, *Baginda Kuin,* H.M. the Queen; *Seri Paduka Baginda,* His Majesty. It seems that strictly speaking the title should be used only by a Ruler who has been victorious in war.

baguk [KS], Pk. big for one's age, overgrown and clumsy; a variant of **bagur.**

bagung [KS], 1. clumsy (as of the build of a boat). 2. huge and heavy (as of chop-

per). 3. wild boar.

bagur [KS], big for one's age, overgrown; ponderous; massive.

bagus [KS], fine, handsome; *~!,* well done, that's fine!

bah [KN], *ayer ~,* flood water, inundation.

bahadi [KN], = **badi,** supernatural influences believed to haunt a place where there has been a killing, particularly of a deer in the jungle; *buang ~,* to perform a ceremony to exorcise such influences.

bahaduri [KS], Pers. knightly, gallant; heroic; chivalrous.

bahagi [KK], Skr. to divide, to allot; *~an,* a division, a share; *ambil ~an,* to take part (in an action); *pem~an,* portion; dividend; *memb~ berekor,* to divide by long division; *~an terpenting,* the most significant part; highlights; *pem~an kerja,* division of labour; *~an* is also a department of a business or government; *~an badan,* parts of the body.

bahagia [KS], Skr. blessing; *ber~,* fortunate, blessed, happy; *yang ber~,* the Blessed, as opposed to yang *celaka,* the damned; *ber~lah,* long life and happiness! *ke~an,* happiness, contentment.

bahak [KKtr], Ind. guffaw; *ter~-~,* guffawing long and loud.

bahalan [KN], a blind bubo or swollen gland in the groin.

baham [KK], to crunch; to gobble up; *mem~ tanah,* to bite the dust (fall flat) or to be starving (reduced to eating earth).

bahan [KN], 1. chips, splinters, esp. of bits of wood which fly during felling; *besar kayu, besar ~nya,* the bigger the timber, the bigger the chips (i.e., the bigger the business, the bigger the expenses). 2. drubbing, thrashing. 3. Ind. raw materials; stores, supplies; basis, subject; *~ pembakar,* fuel; *~ makanan,* food-stuffs; *~ mentah,* raw materials; *~ cerita,* the subject of a story, *~ jenaka,* the butt of jokes.

bahana [KN], Skr. noise; the confused murmur of many sounds; echo.

bahang [KN], the glow of fire; glowing hot; radiant heat; blast; *mem~*, to blaze fiercely as fire or the sun; *~- ~*, (bad) effects.

bahar [KN], Ar. the sea; *bintul-~*, a mermaid.

bahara [KN], a load, a weight of materials, usually 3 pikuls.

bahari [KS], 1. Pers. ancient, antique; *zaman ~*, the 'good old days'. 2. maritime, nautical, *sejarah ~*, maritime history.

baharu [KS], new, newly; just, just then; not till then; *tahun ~*, the new year; *~ dia datang*, he has just come; *~ lagi*, quite recently; *gadis ~ naik*, a girl nearing maturity; *~ saat-saat*, just a moment ago; *pem~an*, an innovation; *per~i*, to renew; also **baru.**

bahas [KK], Ar. *ber~*, debate, to discuss; *pem~*, the opposer (of a motion), in contrast to *pencadang*, the proposer.

bahasa [KN], 1. Skr. language; fitting language; politeness; manners; *~ Melayu*, the Malay language; *jalan ~*, idiom; *tata ~*, grammar; *juru ~*, an interpreter; *tidak tahu ~*, not to understand etiquette or to lack manners; *peri~ = jalan ~*; *bahasa asing*; foreign language; *~ rasmi*, official language; *~ daerah*, local dialect; *~ pasar, ~ kacukan*, 'bazaar language' (spoken by foreigners); *~ persuratan*, literary language; *~ cakap mulut*, colloquial language; *~ halus*, refined language; *~ dalam*, high-flown language, esp. of Court; *~ ibunda*, mother tongue; *~ perantaraan*, language used as a means of communications; *~ pengantar*, language normally used, esp. for educational purposes; *per~an*, way of speech; *~ jiwa bangsa*, language is the soul of the nation; *ber~*, courteous; to express oneself, speak; *tak ber~*, lacking the

refinements of good manners, brash; *mem~kan*, to style, describe in specific terms; *mem~kan dirinya aku*, refer to oneself as *aku* (rather than, e.g., *sahaya*). 2. an attenuant, carrying the idea of 'slightly': *gila ~*, slightly mad, eccentric; *juling ~*, slightly squinting, having a cast in the eye.

bahawa [P], Skr. the story is, that, the facts are namely, to wit — a word used to open a paragraph or an asseveration; *~ sanya* or *~ sesungguhnya*, id.

bahaya [KN], Skr. danger, peril; *mar~*, also *mer~*, id.; *mengisytiharkan keadaan ~*, to proclaim a state of emergency (i.e. martial law); *mem~kan*, to endanger, to imperil as *mem~kan nyawa penumpang*, to imperil the passangers' lives.

bahkan [KKtr], of a truth; verily, in fact.

bahlul [KS], Ar. a fool, esp. a dotard; as a term of abuse, 'booby'.

bahtera [KN], Skr. a vessel; an ark; an argosy — a poetic equivalent for a ship.

bahu [KN], 1. Skr. shoulder; *tercabutlah sendi ~nya*, his shoulder was put out of joint; *~-mem~*, shoulder to shoulder; *bertemu ~*, id. 2. (Dutch) a measure of superficies (a bouw).

Bai [KN], Hind. brother, a term of address used to Bengalis; *~ serbat*, a Northern Indian soft-drink seller.

baid [KKtr], Ar. far, distant; *karib dan ~*, near and far; relatives and strangers.

baiduri [KN], Skr. an opal; a generic name for a number of precious stones — such as opals, cat's-eyes etc.

baik [KS], good, excellent; useful; well; *tuan ~kah?*, are you well?, how are you?; *~-~*, carefully; *jaga ~-~*, take care; *~ ... ~ ...*, both ... and ... , e.g., *~ lelaki ~ perempuan*, both men and women; *~ ... mahu pun*, Ind. *= ~ ... ~ ...*; *~lah!*, all right! very well!; *~ kita*, let us ...; *~ buruknya*, the good and bad points, the pros and cons, the rough and the smooth (of life); *se~-~*, however well, as well as possible; as soon as; *se~ sahaja,* id.; *se~-~nya,* the best course is; *ber~ dengan,* on good terms with; *per~,* to put right, to 'fix'; *baiki* or *mem~i,* to repair, mend; *mem~kan,* to reform, improve; *mem~i duduk,* to shift one's (sitting) position, make oneself comfortable; *anak orang ~,* of gentle birth; *ke~an* or *budi ~,* good deeds.

bairup [KN], Eng. a beacon; a buoy; a trigonometrical station.

bait [KN], Ar. house; *~ulmal,* the treasury; *Baitullah,* God's house, an honorific for Mecca; *Baitul-Mukadis,* Jerusalem; *Baitulaham,* Bethlehem.

baja [KN], 1. steel; the process of tempering; manure; *membaja,* to manure (land), to temper (steel); *~ tahi lembu,* cattle manure; *~ tahi kuda,* horse manure; *~ tahi kelawar, batguano; ~ buatan,* artifical manure; *~ urea,* a chemical manure used in rice-fields; *~ yang tidak berkarat,* stainless steel; *kalau asal ~ yang baik,* if of good steel to start with; *tanah yang tiada ber~,* unmanured land. 2. a preparation of burnt coconut shell used for staining the teeth.

bajak [KN], Sp. a plough; = Pen. *tenggala; mata ~,* the ploughshare; *bersifat seperti ~ bangkang, makan diangkat,* the type of man who is like a wide ploughshare which won't bite unless it is lifted continually, i.ê., the sort of man who has to be coaxed and 'jollied along' to get him to work, a person who likes to be praised.

bajan [KN], Skr. a bowl or basin described in literature; used for mixing; also **bajana.**

bajang [KN], 1. an evil spirit; a familiar spirit. 2. *ber~,* dovetailed.

bajau [KN], *orang Bajau,* a tribe in North Borneo; *orang ~* is sometimes used for 'sea-gipsy' and for 'pirate'.

baji [KN], a wedge; *~ belah,* a wedge for forcing open a fissure; *~ rapat,* a wedge for filling an interstice so as to keep an object in position or steady; *kenakan ~,* to drive in a wedge.

bajik [KN], advantage, profit, meritorious actions; *kebajikan,* welfare, prosperity; *ke~an am,* public welfare; *ke~an masyarakat,* social welfare, welfare work; *alamat ke~an,* a good omen (for prosperity).

bajing [KN], Jav. a squirrel.

bajingan [KN], Ind. ne'er-do-well, rascal.

baju [KN], Pers. outer garment, a coat, jacket, a tunic; *~ dalam,* a singlet; *~ hujan,* a mackintosh, a rain-coat; *~ panas,* sweater, an over-coat; *tangan ~,* the sleeve of a coat; *~ kurung,* the ordinary Malay *baju,* not open at the front; *~ tekua (takwa),* an old-fashioned tight jacket; *~ layang,* long loose coat; *~ belah,* jacket open at the front; *ukur ~ di badan sendiri,* measure the coat on your own body, undertake what is within your own capabilities.

bak [P], like, just like.

baka [KN], 1. heredity; inherited character, breed, stock; *ber~,* to copulate (of animals); *membuang ~,* to give up heritage; *belum bercampur ~,* thoroughbred (opposed to *kacuk ~); ~ dia begitu sahaja,* that's just like him, it runs in the blood. 2. Ar. eternal, lasting; *dari negeri yang fana ke negeri yang ~,* from a perishable to an imperishable country (from earth to heaven); *alam ~,* the world of eternity.

bakai [KK], Ked. *mandi ~,* to wash in fresh water after bathing in the sea; washing from the waist downwards.

bakal [KN], 1. prospective, future, would-be; *~ menantu,* future son-in-law; *~ Laksamana,* the future *Laksamana; ~* also = original, the first; *peperiksaan ~,* entrance examination; *~* is often used now with verbs to denote the future tense, and in that sense tends to oust *kelak,* q.v. 2. Jav. materials for construction.

bakap [KN], *ikan ~,* a dark murrel (*Channa gachua* and *C. melasoma*).

bakar [KK], *mem~,* to burn, to roast, to

bake; *ter~*, burnt; *ter~ habis,* completely burnt; *ke~an,* a fire (building, etc., on fire); *~ hangus-hangus,* to burn to ashes; *tempat pem~an,* incinerator; *orang yang melakukan pem~an (rumah, hartabenda) dengan sengaja,* arsonist.

bakarat [KN], baccarat, a kind of card game.

bakat [KN], signs, traces, esp. of tide-rip and high-water mark; signs of talent, aptitude; *ber~,* talented; *~ semula jadi,* natural talent.

bakau [KN], mangrove-swamp, a generic name for mangroves; *ular ~,* a species of viper (*Lachesis purpureo-maculatus*).

bakhil [KS], Ar. mean, stingy, miserly.

bakhtiar [KS], Pers. fortunate; corresponds to Felix as a name in romance.

baki [KN], Ar. balance left over, surplus; *caki-~,* last remnants.

bakik [KN], a pepper (*piper chaba*),

bakir [KS], sour (of milk).

bakteria [KN], bacteria.

bakti [KS], Skr. meritorious service; *berbuat ~,* to show devotion to God, to earn merit; *ber~,* devout; *ke~an,* devotion, loyal service.

baku [KS], basic, genuine *(yang pokok, yang dasar, yang benar); tata-bahasa Melayu ~,* standard Malay grammar.

bakul [KN], a basket, a hamper; *menjunjung ~,* to carry a basket on the head; *~ jahitan,* sewing-basket; *masuk ~ angkat sendiri,* (prov.) sit in a basket and lift yourself up (in it), an impossible task; so the saying is used as a simile for extravagant and silly boasts; *~ kepasar,* shopping-basket.

bakung [KN], a large white-flowered lily-like plant (*Crinum Asiaticum*).

bakup [KS], closed by inflammation (of the eye); 'bunged up'.

bala [KN], 1. Ar. misfortune, injury; *tolak ~,* a propitiatory offering or sacrifice; to exorcise evil spirits or influences; *jangan cari ~,* don't look for misfortune, i.e., don't run into dangers unnecessarily. 2. Skr. soldiery; *~tentera,* an army.

balah [KK], *ber~,* disputing, quarrelling; *per~an,* argument, at logger heads, dispute.

balai [KN], 1. a hall of audience; the court of a *penghulu;* Pen. a police-station; in some states the Ruler's palace, is referred to as the *~; ~ raya,* Community Centre; *~ angin,* summer-house; *~ menghadap,* audience hall; *~ is* used also for a gallery (for pictures, etc.) and for a lecture hall; *orang ~,* (sl.) a male, esp. of the sex of a baby (a female being *orang dapur*). 2. Kel. to treat with indifference, leave alone; also **belai.**

balairong [KN], a hall of assembly; *~ agung,* id; a hall of audience.

balak [KN], (Dutch) a baulk, a large piece of timber; felled timber generally.

balam [KN], 1. a spotted dove, especially a brownish variety found in Siam. 2. dimly visible, hazy (as distant hills); *~~,* id.; *air mata mem~kan pandangannya,* tears dimmed his vision; *gambar ber~~ hitam,* an indistinct picture; *ber~~,* looming, as through a mist. 3. *mem~~,* to paddle with short quick strokes.

balang [KN], 1. a bottle with a long narrow neck, jug, decanter; sometimes used for a bowl. 2. a missile; to hurl a missile. 3. Jav. mournfulness, = *walang.* 4. to paddle quickly = **balam.**

balar [KS], albino, whiteness, pinkness; *kerbau ~,* a pink buffalo.

balas [KK], 1. sending back, return; requite, revenge; *~i,* to require; *mem~,* to send back, e.g., *~ tabik,* to return a salutation; *~ surat,* to reply to a letter; *~ dendam,* avenge, to vent one's spite; *~ kebaikan,* return the favour; *sebagai ~an,* as (an act of) retaliation or requital; *ber~~ kata,* exchanging 'words'; *jahat di ~ baik,* returning good for evil; *hari pem~an,* the day of requital, esp. the Day of Judgement. 2. Kel. = *macam; ~ mana,* how?

balau [KN], 1. *pokok ~,* a large tree (Swintonia sp.) 2. to pare off, as prickles from a durian or pineapple. 3. *ber~,* con-

fused, chaotic; *kacau* ~, id.
Balci [KN], Baluchi; *negeri* ~, Baluchistan.
baldi [KN], Hind. a horse-bucket, pail.
balgham [KN], Ar. mucus, phlegm.
bali [KN], 1. Ch. the cabin of a junk. 2. Bali, Balinese; *Pulau Bali*, Bali; *limau* ~, pomelo.
baligh [KS], Ar. adult, mature; *akil* ~, years of discretion, puberty; *belum akil* ~, a minor.
balik [KN], position behind, in rear of; the reverse; *di-*~, behind; ~ *adab,* disrespect; *bolak* ~, backwards and forwards; ~, to return; *ber-*~, to turn back; *mem-*~*kan,* to turn (something) over; *ter-*~, upside down, reversed; *menter-*~*kan,* to turn upside down; ~*-bokong*, upside down, inverted; *se*~ *nya*, on the other hand, on the contrary; *ada udang se*~ *batu*, I smell a rat; ~*-sana*, beyond; ~*-kuang*, upside down, flat on the back; ~ is often used in the sense of re- (connoting return to previous state): *tangkap* ~, to recapture; *bayar* ~, to repay; *mem*~*-*~, to turn over and over, as when riffling through the pages of a book; *main* ~ *mata*, to do conjuring tricks; ~*-pungkang*, upside-down, head-over-heels; ~ *belakang*, behind one's back (not openly; *bagitulah se*~ *nya*, and vice-versa.
baling [KK], to hurl; to whirl; ~ *peluru*, to put the shot; ~ *cakera*, to throw the discus; ~*-*~, *be*~, a toy windmill, a weathercock; *peluru bulang-*~ chain-shot; ~ *lembing*, to throw the javelin.
balu [KN], 1. widow or widower. 2. immune (from a disease).
baluarti [KN], Port. bulwark, rampart.
baluh [KN], the wooden frame of a drum; Kel. a rice-bin; ~*an*, the skeleton of a howdah.
balun [KK], to beat with a stick, to drub.
balung [KN], 1. the comb of a cock; ~ *kulit*, patches of bark sticking out loosely from the truck; *bunga* ~ *ayam*, the flower called love-lies-bleeding. 2. ~ *bidai*, an evil spirit of the water.

balur [KN], hard skin, such as that which forms under the yoke on a bullock; untanned hide; jerked meat; *bangsa* ~ *liat*, a 'hard customer', either because of pig-headedness or meanness; ~*-*~, weals, wales on skin.
balut [KN], 1. enwrapping, enwinding; *membalut*, to bandage; *jururawat mem*~ *lengannya yang luka itu*, the nurse bandaged his injured arm; ~ *rokok*, to roll up a cigarette; *di*~*nya surat*, he wrapped the letter in the envelope. 2. inflamed, red (of the eyes).
bam [KN], cross-tree; cross-piece; the bar of a bullock-cart; shaft of cart; tiller of helm.
bambang [KS], flat and broad (as a mirror; as the moon); *ter-*~, looming large; *bulan mengambang nampak ter-*~, the moon looming large just above the horizon.
bambu [KN], bamboo; *senapang* ~, a bamboo gun, i.e. an empty threat, mere bluff; better **buluh** and **aur**.
bambun [KN], the Malayan mongoose.
bami [KN], Ch. a dish of vermicelli, prawns and pork; also **mami**.
ban [KN], Eng. an embankment, a causeway.
banang [KN], large (of the *duku* fruit, a shell and some fishes).
banat [KK], 1. *mem-*~, to thrash. 2. [KN], wild, forest-covered, = **belentara**.
bancah [KK], perplexed, 'in a fix'.
banci [KN], 1. roll, census, enumeration per capita. 2. hermaphrodite; sometimes used to mean congenitally impotent.
bancuh [KK], mix, knead.
bancut [KS], 1. projecting, *ter-*~ *mata*, with the eye thrust out intently (of a lizard on a wall). 2. to frustrate, = **bantut**. 3. Hind. sodomite.
bandang [KN], *ikan* ~, a kind of sea-bream.
bandar [KN], 1. Pers. a sea-port; a town serving as a trade centre, normally situated by the sea or a river, so, in effect, often used to mean harbour; ~ *raya*, a city; *shah*~, harbour-master; *majlis*

per~an, municipal council; *luar bandar*, outskirts of a city; *Datuk Bandar*, mayor. 2. *~an*, a water-course; *~ air*, id. 3. the furrow between nostrils and upper lip.

bandarsah [KN], a prayer house or religious school.

bandela [KN], a bale; a measure for thread, = 40 *bantal*.

banding [KN], comparison; *tiada se~*, incomparable; *~kan*, to compare; *per~an*, comparison; proportion; a simile; *di~ tak bertukar, diukur sama tinggi*, a well-matched pair, compare them, they are very much alike, measure them, they're the same height.

banduk [KS], nervous, self-conscious.

bandung [KN], a connected pair, e.g, *balai ~*, two halls connected by a passage; *telur dua se~*, two yolks in one egg; *rumah se~*, semi-detached house (two houses with a common roof).

bandut [KK], to fasten, to bind up what is cracked, e.g. top of spear shaft.

bang [KN], 1. Pers. the call to prayer. 2. Jav. red; *batik ~*, a pattern of a *sarong* in which red predominates; *tukang ~ = bilal*, q.v. 3. = **abang**.

bangai [KS], *ter~*, abandoned (of a person or corpse, of saucepans left unlidded or on a dead fire, of dishes left uncovered, of work); cf. **bengkalai**.

bangar [KN], putrid (of drains, stagnant water).

bangat [KS], speed, quick; *~-~* or *~ amat*, very quickly.

bangau [KN], the Malayan egret (Bulbulcus coromandus and Herodias intermedia); *berkaki ~*, spindle-shanked.

bangbang [KN], Jav. red; *ketara ~ wetan*, the eastern glow appeared.

bangelas [KS], not cut up into sections, not partitioned, wide, not obstructed (of view).

bangelo [KN], Eng. bungalow.

bangga [KS], proud, exultant; *ke~an*, pride; *mem~kan*, to pride oneself on; *ber~ dengan*, proud of.

banggi [KS], perverse, disloyal; *zaman ~*

ini, this degenerate age.

banggul [KN], Kel. a low hill, = **cangkat**.

bangka [KS], useless, good-for-nothing; *orang tua ~*, useless old dotard.

Bangkahulu [KN], Bencoolen, the port in Sumatra given to the Dutch by the British in exchange for Malacca; also *Bangkulu* and *Bangkulun; memberi ketupat ~*, to give a Bangkahulu rice-packet, i.e., a clump over the head (play on words; *~* and *bengkak hulu*).

bangkai KN], a dead body, a carcase — cf. **mayat** (which is respectful); sometimes used of the remains or wreckage of a ship or crashed plane.

bangkang [KS], 1. wide apart (of the points of horns, etc.); wide and broad, as a blade; *tanduk ~*, horns, the points of which are wide apart; *kala ~*, the black forest scorpion. 2. contradicting, disputing; *~an*, objection, protest; *puak pem~*, the Opposition. 3. unfinished, left incomplete.

bangkar [KS], 1. tough, hard, stiff; rigid, of a corpse. 2. snags in a river.

bangkas [KN], yellow flecked with black (as the colour of a fighting-cock).

bangking [KS], a large round urn-shaped lacquered box for clothes.

bangkit [KK], rising up; *~ berdiri*, to rise and stand erect; *ber~*, to rise; *mem~kan semangat*, to motivate, to inspire; *ber~lah ketakutan*, a panic arose; *mem~-~kan*, to keep bringing up (stale subject); *kuih ~*, a sort of cake, made with sago-flour.

bangku [KN], Port. a bench, a stool, a seat without arms or back; *~ gereja*, a pew; *kaki ~*, clumsy, leaden-footed (particularly as a reproach to a footballer).

bangkung [KN], *parang ~*, a short broadbladed Bugis chopping-knife.

bangkut [KS], stunted in growth; stumpy.

bangsa KN], Skr. race, family, good birth; *bahasa menunjukkan ~*, a man's manners show his descent (prov.); *~ Cina*, the Chinese; *ber~*, of birth; nobly born; *~-~ Bersatu*, the United Nations; *Majlis Keselamatan ~-~*

27

Bersatu, the U.N. Security Council; *ke~an,* national; *Parti Kebangsaan Melayu,* Malay Nationalist Party; *bahasa ke~an,* the national language; *gila ke~an,* ultra-nationalist, chauvinist; *bangsa* is sometimes used now for 'nation', irrespective of race.

bangsai [KS], decayed, rotten (of wood).

bangsal [KN], a shed; *~kuda,* a stable or stall.

bangsat [KS], vagrant, mean, despicable; *orang ~,* a vagabond.

bangsawan [KN], Skr. 1. of good birth, noble. 2. the old-time Malay opera.

bangsi [KN], a Malay flute or flageolet; a mouth-organ.

bangta [KN], *anak ~,* a child born to a (Perak) ruler after his accession — cf. Ach. *abangta.*

bangun [KK], to rise, to get up; shape, bearing; *jatuh ~,* falling and rising; stumbling along; *terlalu takut ~nya,* bearing himself like a man in great fear; *~an,* an erection, building; *~~an,* a turret or crow's nest in a stockade; a scaffolding; *mem~kan,* to construct, erect; *pem~an,* construction, building-up, development; *bingkas~,* to spring to one's feet; *~ dara,* to reach maidenhood; *~ tidur,* to 'get up', get out of bed; *~kan,* to 'call' (to get up); *~ tubuh,* physique, bodily structure.

bani [KN], Ar. *~ Adam,* the children of Adam, mankind; *~ Israel,* the children of Israel.

baning [KN], a tortoise (Testudo emys).

banir [KN], a buttress-like projection at the base of the trunk of certain trees; in folk-lore the pig is reputed to have got its flat nose from colliding with such a projection.

banjar [KN], rank, file; *ber~,* in rows; *taman ~an sari,* the old Javanese garden of the Hesperides; *~an gunung,* a range of mountains; *mem~kan,* to align, form up in lines.

banji [KN], Ch. glazed earthenware latticework.

banjir [KN], Ind. floods, inundations.

bantah [KK], *ber~,* to dispute; *~an,* objection, quarrelsome, given to contradicting; *per~an,* an altercation; *~ hukum,* to disobey an order, esp. of contempt of court; *~an,* a protest.

bantai [KK], *mem~,* cutting up a slaughtered animal, quartering (sl.) (1) 'cut and run'; (2) to belabour; *pem~,* a butcher; *~* is used vulgarly for 'to guzzle'.

bantal [KN], a pillow, a cushion; *~ guling,* a bolster; *~ peluk,* long bolster, 'Dutch wife'; *~ pasir,* sand-bag; *salah ~,* having a stiff neck; *~ sandar* (specifically), a cushion; *~~,* a short horizontal patch of rainbow light; a bundle of yarn; a measure of yarn 1/40th of a bandela, equivalent to 16 skeins (*tukal*); *ber~kan lengan,* to use one's arms as a pillow; *orang mengantuk disorongkan ~,* (prov.) a sleepy man has a pillow pushed under his head [good luck],.

banteras [KK], Ind. to combat, struggle against, do away with; a variant of *berantas; mem~ jenayah,* to eradicate crimes.

banting [KK], 1. dashing down, beating together; threshing padi against the sides of a wooden tub; *mem~,* to dash against; *seperti ombak mem~ dirinya,* like waves dashing into each other; *~ tulang,* to 'sweat one's guts out' esp. on someone else's work; *mem~ kepala,* to rack the brains. 2. the small wild ox (bos sondiacus).

bantu [KN], aid, assistance; *mem~,* [KK], to succour, to help; *~an,* assistance, backing, esp. financial; *wang ~an, ~an kewangan,* financial aid; *~an kebendaan,* material help; *~an asing,* foreign aid; *bala ~an,* auxilliaries; reinforcements; *per~kan,* to supply — as aid.

bantut [KK], *ter~,* frustration; rendering abortive; *mem~kan,* to nip in the bud, abort, foil (as a plan); *~kan hati,* to discourage, lower morale.

banu = **bani.**

banyak [KS], much, many, a quantity; ~ *orang,* many people, a number of persons; *orang ~,* the populace; *se~,* the same number as, as many as, as much as; *ke~an,* most, the majority; *orang ke~an,* a commoner; *ke~an orang,* most people, the majority of people; *orang ter~,* the (definite) majority; *per~kan,* to increase numbers of; *tidak ~ waktu,* pressed for time.

bapa [KN], father; *mak ~* or *ibu ~,* parents; also *bapak; ~ angkat,* adopted father, ~ *ayam,* father who does not discharge his duty to take care of his children.

bara [KN], 1. embers; ~ *api,* live coals; *hati mem~,* hot with anger. 2. *tolak ~,* ballast; see **bahara.** 3. *sara-~,* higgledy-piggledy, chaos. 4. Hind. big, great, main (in certain nautical expressions).

barah [KN], abscess, tumour; internal ulcer; ~ *darah,* leukaemia.

barai [KN], 1. an edible salt-water shellfish. 2. = **burai.**

barak [KS], vicious, as a domesticated elephant or bull.

baran [KN], 1. N.S. low swampy undergrowth; *babi ~,* wild pig infesting such undergrowth. 2. [KS], hot-tempered, quick-tempered.

barang [KN], things in general; luggage; commodity; one's belongings; anything; any; would that in some way; ~ *apa,* whatever; ~ ~, (1) things, belongings, luggage; (2) ordinary, common; ~ *bila,* whenever; ~ *kali,* perhaps; ~ *siapa,* whoever; *se~,* whatever; any, anything; *bukan se~,* no common ...; no mean ...; ~ is also used in the sense of 'some' (approximately), with figures; ~ *duapuluh,* some twenty; sometimes ~ is used in the sense of, would that, may it be that; ~ *kiranya,* would that perchance....

baras [KN], Ar. leprosy.

barat [KN], 1. west; ~ *tepat,* due west; *orang ~,* westerner; ~ *daya,* S.W.; ~ *laut,* N.W.; *utara ~ laut,* N.N.W; *ke~-b~an,* westernized. 2. *sesat ~,* very much astray, confused.

barau [KN], *ikan ~-~* a carp, = **sebarau**; a freshwater fish with a broad black stripe on each side (Cyprinid genus (Hampila macrolepidota); *burung ~-~,* the yellow crowned bulbul (Trachycomus ochrocephalus).

bari-bari [KN], fruit-flies.

barik [KS], mottled, veined, variegated, marbled.

baring [KK], lying down at full length; *ber~,* to lie down; ~*kan,* to place in a recumbent position; ~*kan diri,* to lay oneself down.

baris [KN], a line, a row; ~ *sipahi,* a line of troops; *ber~,* to drill; ~*an,* ranks; ~*an kehormatan,* guard of honour; ~ is also used for a political 'front'; *per~an,* parade; *per~an pentadbiran,* a review; *memeriksa per~an,* to inspect the parado; *perbarisan tamat latihan,* 'passing out' parade; *mem~,* to 'fall in'; *masuk ~an,* id.; *pem~,* a (school) ruler; ~ *depan,* front line, esp. of battle.

baru [KS], 1. new, = **baharu.** 2. a seashore tree (Hibiscus tiliaceus); *ikan daun ~,* a fish (Drepane punctata).

barua [KN], Hind. a pimp; ~ *babi,* pig pimp, jocular appellation for a Chinese who goes round with a stud boar.

baruh [KN], the land lying between a Malay house and shore or riverbank, land in the flood-channel of a river; generally, coastal or river-side land, as opposed to land upcountry

Barus [KN], *kapur ~,* camphor (from Barus in Sumatra).

barut [KN], a long bandage; a bodice worn by children; to bandage or swathe in cloth.

barzakh [KN], *alam ~,* Purgatory, where sinners await Judgement Day.

basah [KS], wet, moist; *ikan ~,* fresh ('wet') fish, i.e. not dried; *beras ~,* wet rice, met. for something spoilt and useless; ~ *kuyup,* wringing wet; *kain ~an,* clothes used for bathing in, old clothes; *kain* *jadi* ~*an,* the cloth which is being used as a bathing cloth, met. for someone who has come down in the world; *tertangkap* ~, caught red-handed, caught in the act; ~*kan,* to wet; ~*!,* first blood! (in cock-fighting), that went home!; *perkara* ~*an,* an everyday occurrence, commonplace; *bahasa-*~*an,* everyday language; *mem*~ *tekak,* to wet the gullet, i.e. have a drink, 'wet one's whistle'; rarely is ~ used in the sense of 'successful, prosperous', possibly because the cry *b*~*!* (above) may be a cry of victory.

basal [KN], beri-beri; dropsy; puffy, as a result of beri-beri, etc.

basau [KS], hard (of a boiled potato).

basi [KS], 1. musty, stale, mouldy; *mem*~*kan semangat,* to depress, make despondent. 2. something extra; in such expressions as *mengambil* ~ *arus,* to make allowance for the current; ~*kan sikit,* chuck in a little more (as on a sale); *doa* ~, an extra prayer said for some special object.

basikal [KN], bicycle.

basing [KN], (Borneo) a squirrel.

basmi [KK], Ind. *mem*~*kan,* to exterminate, put an end to, liquidate; stamp out; *mem*~ *buta-huruf,* to wipe out illiteracy.

basuh [KK], washing; *seperti air* ~ *tangan,* like water for washing one's hands (a cheap and little prized article), prov; *tak payah* ~ *tangan,* no need to wash your hands (after it), 'an easy job'; ~*kan,* to wash; *mesin pem*~ *pakaian,* washing machine.

basung [KN], 1. a pointed excrescence near the root of a tree. 2. a mould of light wood on which an *upih* bag for *damar* is made. 3. light easily cut, e.g., of *pulai* wood. 4. N.S. the handle of a Malay adze.

basut [KN], fountain, jet.

Batak [KN], an aboriginal tribesman, a Battak; *mem*~, to lead a nomadic life; to live from hand to mouth, have no settled job.

batal [KS], Ar. futile, useless; *mem*~*kan,* to bring to nought, abrogate, cancel, repeal; *hak mem*~, right of veto; *mem*~*kan air sembahyang,* to render nugatory the water for ritual ablutions, i.e., to do something necessitating further ablutions in due course.

batang [KN], a tree-trunk; a shaft; a handle; a rod; ~ *air,* a watercourse; ~ *hidung,* the bridge of the nose; ~ *hidung dia tak nampak sudah dua tahun,* haven't seen the bridge of his nose for two years (haven't seen hide nor hair of him for two years), i.e., he has completely disappeared; ~ *joran,* a fishing-rod; ~ *tubuh,* the trunk of the body; ~ *kayu,* a tree; ~ *leher,* the neck; ~ *pengayuh,* the handle of a paddle; *mem*~, read without spelling out the letters; *menjadi* ~, to be killed stone-dead; ~*an,* a bar or boom across a river; ~ is used as a numeral coefficient for long objects such as sticks and, often, for rivers; *se*~ *kara,* without any relatives.

batas [KN], a boundary, esp. a boundary marked by a bank; the low bank separating rice-plots; a bank generally; a bed for planting or sowing; *daerah per*~*an,* borderland, frontier area; *ter*~, limited (as a Company); *mem*~*i,* to limit, keep within bounds; *di*~*i bumi,* banked up by earth, i.e., dead and buried; *mem*~*kan ... dengan,* to separate from; *pem*~*an,* restriction; *pem*~*an anak,* contraception.

bati [KS], *se*~ inseparably connected (of soldered things, milk and water mixed, etc.); (of a person) *se*~ means 'grown accustomed to a place or position or intimately associated with another person'; *saya dengan dia se*~, he and I are one.

batik [KN], = *batik,* printed patterned fabric usually worn by Javanese women.

batil [KN], a metal bowl; ~ *azimat,* a bowl inscribed inside with verses from the Koran; used as a medicine bowl.

batin [KN], 1. a tribal chief (of

aborigines, *orang Laut,* etc.); in Trengganu used for 'headman' of the (Malay) islanders. 2. Ar. esoteric; inner; hidden; *~nya,* inwardly, as opposed to *lahirnya* (openly, outwardly); *kehidupan ~,* mental and emotional life; *lahir ~,* with all one's heart; *sokongan ~,* moral support; *kepercayaan ~,* spiritual faith; *santapan ~ = nafkah ~,* see **nafkah;** *~ ~ kata,* unexpressed meaning in spoken words, hints; *~* is sometimes used to mean mind, as opposed to body or to heart.

batir [KN], *~-~,* a cord fastening a *keris* scabbard to its belt.

batu [KN], stone, rock; milestone, mile; stone used as anchor; *~ api,* flint; (fig.) mischief-maker, scandal-monger; *~ loncatan,* stepping-stone; *~ timbul,* pumice stone; *~ arang,* coal; *~ asah,* whetstone; *~ bata,* brick; *~ Belanda,* a bath brick; *~ berani,* magnet; *~ peringatan,* a stone memorial; *~ besi,* granitic rock; *~ canai,* grindstone; *~ dacing,* the weight on a balance; *~ duga,* a plummet; *~ geliga,* a bezoar; *~ kail,* the weight on a fishing-line; *~ karang,* coral; *~ kepala,* crown of the head; *~ las,* emery; *~ lintar,* fossil stone implements; *~ nisan,* tombstone; *~ petir,* id.; *~ sauh,* a Malay anchor; *~ sempadan,* boundary-stone; *~ uji,* touchstone; *air ~,* ice; *cap ~,* lithography; *gula ~,* loaf-sugar; *~ bipang,* Treng. a brick; *~ hidup,* a megalith; *~ merah,* laterite; *~ asas,* foundation stone; *meletakkan ~ asas,* to lay a foundation stone; *diam mem~,* to preserve a stony silence; *~-~an,* small stones, esp. gall-stones, 'gravel'; *mem~,* to be petrified; *mem~-batang,* (fig.) to be tongue-tied, to be perversely stubborn, to 'stonewall', esp. of a person refusing to listen to or answer arguments.

batuk [KK], a cough; *~ kering,* tuberculosis, phthisis; *~ lelah* or *~ sisik, ~ rejan, ~*

kukuk, whooping-cough; *~ darah,* to cough up blood; *melepaskan ~ ditangga,* to cough before entry (not so much carrying the idea of giving warning of approach as of doing something to satisfy public opinion), pay lip service to.

bau [KN], smell, odour; *~-~an,* perfume; *ber~,* to be scented, to smell of; *tuah dan malang tidak ber~,* good luck and bad luck have no smell, i.e., you can't foretell your fate.

baucar [KN], voucher.

bauk [KN], a beard under the chin; *cambang ~,* a full beard, beard and whiskers; *janggut ~,* id.

baulu [KN], = **bolu.**

baung [KN], 1. (Dayak = plantain) curved (as a plantain or chairback, i.e., concave on one side, convex on the other). 2. *ikan ~,* a freshwater catfish *(Mystus planiceps).*

bawa [KK], conveying; *mem~,* to bring, to carry; *~ diri,* to take oneself off, to be off; also hold oneself aloof, and see below; *~ mulut,* to 'carry tales', *kaki ~ mulut,* tale-bearer; *~ nyawa,* to run for one's life, escape with one's life; *~ hati,* to depart in distress as an exile; *~ rezeki,* to bring luck; *~ sial,* to bring bad luck; *~* is sometimes used to mean, in effect, behave, bear oneself; *masuk ke kampung, ~ perangai ayam betina,* if you visit someone else's homestead, behave like a hen, i.e., in a timid, self-effacing manner; *baik-baik mem~ diri,* i.e., mind how you behave; *~ iman,* to accept the Islamic faith; *~ jalan,* to lead the way; *~ lari,* to carry off, to run away with; *~ mati,* to retain till death; to carry to one's grave; *~ pergi,* to take away; *pergi ~,* to fetch; *~an,* that which is carried, burden, esp. the 'weight' on a racehorse; *~an* and *pem~an,* also used to convey the idea of that which is congenital in one's body or mind, constitutional; *kecacatan ~an,* congenital weakness or deformity; *~* at times conveys the idea of 'bringing about', 'causing'; *sokongan mem~ rebah,* the support brought about the fall (met. for 'let down by friends'); *pem~ usul* is used for the proposer of a motion; *mem~kan lagu,* to present a tune to (the public).

Bawean [KN], *Pulau ~,* Boyan.

bawah [KKtr], below, under, the bottom of an article; *ke ~,* downward; *di ~,* below; *dari ~,* from under; *orang ~han,* the underdogs, 'the lower classes'; *~ angin,* leeward; *yang terke~,* nethermost, at the bottom (of pile).

bawal [KN], *ikan ~,* the pomfret (Stromateus sp.).

bawang [KN], a generic name for onions, leeks, etc.; *~ Benggala* or *~ Bombai,* imported onions; *~ putih,* garlic; *~ merah,* the shallot; *~--~, be~,* bulbs of all sorts.

bawasir [KN], Ar. piles, haemorrhoids; also **wasir.**

bawat [KS], drooping; *mata ~,* drooping eyelids, sleepiness.

baya [KN], 1. age, *se~,* of the same age, esp. of playmates; *ada ~ juga orangnya,* he is not as young as he was. 2. Skr. danger, = **bahaya.**

bayak [KS], bulky, 'tubby', fat, corpulent.

bayam [KN], spinach; *pokok bunga ~,* amaranthus.

bayan [KN], 1. *burung ~,* the paroquet *(Paloeornis longicauda); ikan ~,* a kind of wrasse (red and green). 2. Ar. clear, obvious; *ter~lah nyata,* id., 3. Jav. a waiting-maid at a court.

bayang [KN], shadow, image, vague outline, silhouette; *ter~,* imaged vaguely, shadowed forth; *~kan,* to suggest, foreshadow; *mem~-~kan,* to picture to oneself, conjure up the image of; *gila ~,* unrequited love, love for the unattainable; *~an,* vague mental images; *Kabinet ~an,* Shadow Cabinet. The general idea conveyed by *~* is that of uncertainty of outline, instability, lack of clarity or certainty, mere reflection of an object: thus (in an extreme instance), *berdiri ~,* standing feebly and tottering, as if about to fall.

bayar [KK], paying; *mem~,* to pay; *~an* [KN], payment; *~ tunai,* to pay in cash; *mem~ kembali,* to pay back, refund, to reimburse; *~ pukal,* to pay in a lump sum; *~ lebih dahulu,* to pay in advance; *~ beransur-ansur,* to pay by instalments; *~ niat,* to fulfil a vow; *askar ~an,* mercenaries.

bayas [KN], *pokok ~,* a jungle fan-palm, the leaves of which irritate the skin *(Onchosperma horrida).*

bayi [KN], Ind. a baby.

bayu [KN], 1. Skr. the wind, the breeze, Vayu, the Aeolus of the old Javanese mythology; *di puput ~,* waving in the breeze. 2. a slave; a submissive pronoun of the first person.

bayung [KN], *pisau ~,* a small knife.

bayur [KN], a name given to several trees of the genus Sterculiaceoe.

bazir [KS], waste; *jangan mem~kan air,* don't waste water; *mem~kan wang sahaja,* it's a waste of money.

bea [KN], Ind. customs dues; *pe~n,* a customs-station.

bebal [KS], stupid, dull, dense; *orang yang ~,* a dullard; sometimes, surly, but the basic idea generally conveyed by the word is that of dullness and lack of imagination; cf. Munshi Abdullah's heart-cry: *orang putih ~ belajar dan orang Melayu ~ mengajar,* Europeans can't learn and Malays can't teach.

beban [KN], a burden, a load; *mem~i keluarganya,* to be a burden to his family; *kuda ~,* pack-horse.

bebang [KS], a stoppage (as in the anus or uterus); *anak ke~an,* a still-born child.

bebar [KS], *ber~,* rushing here and there (as frightened poultry); *ter~,* running wild, unrestrained.

bebas [KS], free; familiar; independent; *mem~kan,* to discharge; to set at liberty; *ke~an,* liberty, liberation; *ke~an akhbar,* freedom of the Press; *ke~an beragama,* religious freedom; *ke~an berbicara,* freedom of speech; *~ dari* *semua tuduhan,* the suspect has been cleared of all charges; but *ke~an* is also used of licence and immunities (to favourites).

bebat [KN], band, bandage, ligature; to bind round, (fig.) to block (a passage); *~kan pinggang,* to gird up the loins.

bebawang [KN], bulb.

beber [KK], Ind. *mem~kan,* to expound, to set forth in detail, elucidate.

bebek [KN], 1. Jav. duck, = (Malay) *itek; mem~,* to quack; to bleat. 2. to purse the lips, of a child.

beca [KN], trishaw; *~ roda tiga,* trishaw.

becak [KS], muddy, slushy.

becuk [KS], noisy, heated, as an argument; *becang-~,* the sound of quarrelling; *mem~,* to speak angrily and noisily.

beda [KN], Ckr distinction, difference; *sekarang ini terlalu ber~,* things are very different now; *mem~kan,* to distinguish between, to differentiate; *per~an,* distinction, difference; *ber~ pendapat,* to differ, still at odds about certain issues; *per~an warna kulit,* colour discrimination; *dasar mem~~kan kulit,* apartheid; also **beza** and **bedza.**

bedah [KN], Ind. to operate surgically; *doktor ~,* surgeon; *per~an,* an operation; cf. **belah.**

bedak [KN], cosmetic powder, esp. rice-powder; *ber~,* powdered with cosmetic.

bedal [KK], 1. *mem~,* beat, whip, thrash, s.o. 2. [KS] run wild, bolt (of a horse).

bedan [KN], heat-spot, spots due to nettlerash.

bedar [KN], an East-coast fishing boat of some size; *anak ~,* a smaller boat of the same type.

bedara [KN], also *bidara,* Skr. a name given to several trees; *~ Cina,* the jujube; *buah ~,* (1) the fruit of this tree; (2) a name of a Malay sweetmeat.

bedebah [KS], Pers. ill-starred, accursed.

bedek [KK], *mem~,* to look fixedly through one eye; to aim; to examine, esp. a small object, with close attention; also *belek.*

bedil [KN], Tam. a gun; *mem~,* to shoot with a gun; *ubat ~,* gunpowder; *~ buluh,* bamboo gun, fig. for empty threats.

beduk [KN], a big drum used to call people to the mosque; = Ked. *gendang raya.*

bedukang [KN], *ikan ~,* a freshwater catfish; = *belukang,* q.v.

bedung [KN], a sort of apron worn by a child; *bedungan,* (fig.) bonds, restrictions imposed on the young, (fig.) swaddling-clothes.

beg [KN], bag.

bedza = **beda.**

bega [KN], pointing at; *mem~,* to aim at; to poise and aim, e.g., a spear; *lang mem~,* a hawk poised for a swoop.

begak [KS], foppish, dandified.

begal [KN], highway robbery, *pem~,* hijacker, robber.

begap [KS], robust; square-set.

begar [KN], Ar., hard, tough, esp. as insufficiently cooked; so, 'a tough nut', difficult to deal with; refractory, rebellious.

begawan [KN], Skr. blessed (a title given to minor deities and to heroes who have given up kingship for asceticism).

begini [KKtr], in this way; thus.

begitu [KKtr], in that way; so; *~ sahaja,* 'just like that' (e.g., without effort, without protest, without obvious reason); *~ hal sahaja,* not bad, fair to middling, so so; *~lah keadaannya,* precisely, that's the way it is.

beguk [KN], goitre; swellings in the throat generally; mumps.

behena [KS], Pers. excellent, important; *tiada ~,* not to attach importance to; *mem~kan,* to pay attention to, to care about; also **bina.**

beka [KK], *ber~,* to gossip, to discuss.

bekal [KN], supplies for a journey; stores, provisions; *mem~i,* to provide with; *per~an,* id.; *~ mati,* provision against one's death — i.e., for funeral expenses and necessary rituals; *~an air,* water-supply; *pegawai per~an,* Supply Officer, Purser.

bekam [KN], a slight bruise or discoloration of the skin; to cup with a heated glass.

bekas [KN], impression, trade-mark; the wrapper, garment or receptacle in which a thing is contained; ~ *menangis*, traces of weeping; ~ *bau-bauan*, a scent-bottle; ~ *pinang*, a sirih box; ~ *tubuh*, a keepsake garment; ~ *tangan*, handiwork, creation; ~ *kaki*, ~ *tapak*, footprint; used for ex-, e.g., ~ *penghulu*, the ex-penghulu.

bekat [KS], tightly filled up; *penuh* ~, id.

beku [KS], coagulated, congealed, frozen; *air* ~, ice; *darah* ~ *di dalam hati*, one's heart standing still, one's blood running cold; ~ is also used (fig.) to mean stiff, formal, in manner, esp., from shyness.

bekukung [KN], *ikan* ~, a marine fish *(Chrysophrys calamara)*.

bela [KK], *mem*~, to bring up (a child); to support (a relative); to keep (a familiar spirit); to tend (a plant); *kucing* ~*an*, a pet cat (esp. if bred in the house); Kel. to copulate.

bela [KN], atonement by blood; suttee, vengeance, revenge; *menuntut* ~, to seek revenge; to champion, uphold, esp. of patriotic support; to defend; *pem*~, defender (esp. of defending counsel); *peguam*~, attorney.

belacan [KN], a paste of prawns and small fish (used as a relish); *kertas* ~, paper in which~ has been wrapped, useless; used esp., of hoarded money; 'might just as well throw it away'.

belacu [KN], unbleached calico.

beladau [KN], a curved dagger.

belah [KN], splitting in two, cleaving, halving; side; *se*~, a side; *se*~ *sana*, on that side, in that direction; *se*~ *tangan*, one hand; *se*~ *menye*~, on both sides; side by side; *menye*~*i*, to side with; *se*~ *ka-nan*, on the right-hand side; *se*~ *kiri*, on the left-hand side; ~ is the word used to describe surgical operations; *doktor* ~, a surgeon; ~*an*, a slit, opening; *pem*~*an*, an incision; *lahir dengan pem*~*an*, born by Caesarean operation; ~*an jiwa*, lover,

sweetheart, wife; *mem*~-*bahagi,* to partition, divide up; *retak menanti* ~, the crack awaits the split, a way of saying that the situation is precarious and ominous of disaster; so *hanya menanti* ~ *sahaja,* on the point of breaking up, e.g. of a political party; *pecah*-~, to create friction; *ikan se*~, a flat-fish; *se*~*kan,* to side with.

belahak [KK], see **labak**.

belai [KN], 1. dalliance; to caress. 2. Kel. = **balai**.

belajar [KK], see **ajar**.

belak [KN], mottled (as the grain of certain timbers or as spotted shabby fabrics); ~ *yang bulat,* the rings of a tree-trunk.

belak [KN], opening out folds or creases; holding the fold open.

belaka [KKtr], altogether, quite, without exception; *semuanya Melayu* ~, all were Malays without exception.

belakang [KN], back, behind; *di* ~, in rear, subsequent; *di* ~ *hari*, in the future, in later days; *mem*~, to turn one's back, have one's back turned; *mem*~*kan* to turn one's back on, (fig.) to slight, treat discourteously, *di* ~ *mata*, behind one's back, unseen; *di* ~ *layar*, behind the curtain, i.e. behind the scenes (not generally known); *bertemu* ~, to stand back to back; *gaji ke*~*an,* back-pay; *tulang* ~, the spine; *latar* ~, background; *ter*~, out-of-date, old-fashioned; sometimes, backward; *ke*~*an,* lately.

belalai [KN], trunk, proboscis; the spur of a hill running down into a plain; sometimes used for 'tentacles'.

belalak [KS], to have a fixed look about the eyes; *mem*~*kan mata,* to glare (with protruding eyes); cf. **beliak**.

belalang [KN], a generic name for grasshoppers, stick-insects, leaf-insects, etc.; *mata* ~, prominent eyes; ~ *kunyit,* the locust; ~ *ranting,* the stick-insect; *Pak 'Belalang,* Daddy Grass-hoppers, an old humbug of folk-lore continually lucky; *nujum Pak 'Belalang,* a forecast, the success of which depends on luck.

belam [KS], *ber~-~*, indistinct (as the colour of a cloud or of one fabric covered by another); cf. **balam** 2.

belambang [KN], a truss; a lath; polles or trunks, esp. of palms used for rough flooring.

belanak [KN], *ikan ~*, a grey mullet (Mugil sp.).

belanar [KN], in swarms, e.g., as ants, in 'heaps', 'galore'.

Belanda [KN], Dutch; *orang ~*, a Dutchman; *negri ~*, Holland; *ayam ~*, a turkey; *kucing ~*, a rabbit (better **arnab**).

belang [KS], 1. striped; *~ cicak* or *~ berintik*, spotted; *Pak 'Belang, Tok 'Belang, Sang Belang*, the tiger. 2. *~ ...-~*, Treng. at the same time; *~ berjalan, ~ berkata*, walking and speaking; *hidung belang*, a flirt.

belanga [KN], earthenware cooking-pot.

belangkas [KN], the king-crab; *bagai ~*, like king-crabs, i.e. inseparable (because a pair of king-crabs walk about clinging to each other).

belanja [KN], expense, cost of sustenance; *~kan*, to expend; money for expenses; *ber~*, to do the shopping; *putus ~*, expense-money finished: *~an*, things purchased; *~ hidup*, cost of living; *~wan*, budget; *memakan ~*, *per~an*, to involve the expenditure of; *~ tata usaha*, overhead expenses.

belantan [KN], a club or cudgel, a truncheon.

belantara [KN], (Kawi) *hutan ~* or *rimba ~*, the wilds of the forest.

belantik [KN], see **lantik**.

belar [KK], *mem~*, swarming, teeming, over-running everywhere, as ants, mob, children; *selar-~*, id.

belas [KN], 1. a word utilised in forming the numerals from eleven to nineteen; it suggests that having counted all the fingers, the counter goes back *(balas)*, counting them over again; *se~*, eleven; *dua ~*, twelve; *budak-budak ~an tahun*, teenagers. 2. pity, mercy, sympathy; *~ kasihan*, id.

belasah, see **lasah**.

belasungkawa [KN], Ind., condolences, expressions of sympathy; *menyatakan ~*, to express condolences.

belat [KN], a large screen of bamboo or *bertam* used in fish-traps; fish-traps in which such screens are used.

Belati [KS], 1. Hind. European (of goods); imported from afar; *tali ~*, hempen rope; *tembakau ~*, cake tobacco, plug. 2. broad-blade knife.

belatuk [KN], a generic name for woodpeckers; also **pelatuk**.

belau [KS], 1. (Dutch) blue. 2. *~-~*, blinking, shimmering, trying to the eyes.

belebas [KN], a lath laid horizontally along ataps, a ruler; a cross-piece in a loom; a lath nailed across the inside of a plank wall as a stay, often used for hanging things on.

belebau [KK], Pen. belabouring, swishing.

belebir [KK], Kel. to chatter, blather.

beleda [KN], a sweet gruel made from Indian beans *(kacang hijau)*.

beledu [KN], Port. velvet; *~ benang*, velveteen.

belek [KK], 1. looking closely into anything, examining carefully (as a watchmaker examines the works of a watch). 2. turning the upper eyelid up or the lower eyelid down.

belenggu [KN], shackles, fetters.

belengkok [KS], bent, curved; a bend, e.g., in a river.

belengset, see **lengset**.

belera [KN], a weaver's 'sword'; *ular ~*, a sea-snake; also *ular belerang*.

belerang [KN], sulphur; *asap ~*, sulphur fumes used (medicinally); *ular ~*, a sea-snake.

beletir [KK], Ked. to chatter, nag; = **merepet**.

beli [KK], buying; *mem~*, to purchase; *~an*, things bought; *mem~-belah*, to do one's shopping; *tak ter~*, unobtainable, not on offer; *~ Haji*, to perform the pilgrimage vicariously by paying for someone else to go.

belia [KS], Skr. a youth; *muda ~*, young and fresh, in the bloom of youth; *per-*

himpunan ~ sedunia, World Youth Congress.

beliak [KS], *ter~ mata,* exposing the whites of the eyes; protruding eyes; *mem~kan mata,* to glare, opening the eyes wide.

belian [KN], 1. *hantu ~,* the tiger-spirit in incantations. 2. *pokok ~,* the Borneo iron-wood tree *(Sideroxylon schwageri).*

beliau [KGN], 'what's-his-name', 'so-and-so' (when speaking of someone whose name one knows but does not wish to utter); often used in newspapers respectfully to 'he': 'the gentleman already referred to'.

belibis [KN], the whistling-teal *(Dendrocygna javanica).*

belida [KN], 1. *ikan ~,* a marine fish *(Notopterus chitala).* 2. isinglas.

beligu [KN], Jav. the wax gourd *(Benincasa cerifera).*

belikat [KN], the space between the shoulder blades; *urat ~,* the dorsal muscles; *tulang ~,* the shoulder-blades; *~ panjang,* lazy-bones.

belimbing [KS], ridged longitudinally; a descriptive name given to the leathery turtle, *(Dermochelys coriacea),* and also to a well-known fruit, (star fruit).

belit [KN], twining round, coiling round; *mem~,* to coil round; *ber~-~,* twisting, turning; complicated; *cakap ber~-~,* to talk round and round a subject, indulge in circumlocution; *se~-~,* a coil, e.g., of a chain.

beliung [KN], an adze; *puting ~,* a waterspout.

belok [KS], luffing; going about; turning, wheeling; to change course, to turn (a corner); *mem~kan,* to divert, e.g., the course of a ship or of a stream; *mem~kan kembali,* to turn around; *mem~kan kuda,* to wheel a horse; *~an,* a corner, turn in a road; *jalan ber~-~,* the winding road; *selok-~,* ins-and-outs, subtleties, quirks (esp. of a language).

belon [KN], balloon.

belongkang [KN], barge, river freighter.

belongsong [KS], wrapper.

belontok [KN], a kind of fish, large goby.

belot [KK], to desert to the enemy, betray.

belu [KK], Jav. *~-belai,* to chatter, to converse.

beluam [KN], a mendicant's wallet, esp. that of a Buddhist priest.

belubur [KN], a round rice-bin.

beludak [KS] outburst (of laughter, applause).

beludar [KN], a dry, crisp Malay cake.

beluduh [KS], *ter~,* filing the landscape; looming large, = Pen. *beleduh.*

beluduk [KS], projecting (of the eyes); [KN], *ikan ~,* the mudfish (also *ikan tembakul).*

beloh [KS], stupid.

Beluka [KN], *orang ~,* an aboriginal tribe in Northern Malaya.

belukang [KN], a freshwater catfish; it is notorious as a coarse and omnivorous feeder; so (fig.) *~ darat,* a keen and indiscriminate womaniser; also **bedukang.**

belukap [KN], a mangrove *(Rhizophora mucronata).*

belukar [KN], secondary jungle; *~ muda,* land that has been cleared, but is reverting to jungle; *~ tua,* land long abandoned and overgrown, though not like real jungle *(rimba); tinjau ~,* beautiful only from a distance, of a view or object.

belulang [KN], a dry pelt, a patch of hardened skin.

beluluk [KN], 1. young coconut. 2. fallen in quantities (of fruit).

belum [KKtr], not yet; *~ lagi,* not yet, *~ pernah,* never yet; *se~,* before (conjunction); *~ ada,* unheard of; *waktu itu kemudahan demikian ~ ada,* at that time, such facilities were unheard of.

belung [KN], 1. *belah ~,* an insect which makes a loud noise at night and is believed to bring bad luck; also *belah belum.* 2. large for age, overgrown.

belungkang [KN], a river-boat in use at Palembang.

belungkur [KN], *ikan ~,* the Queensland smelt.

belungsong [KN], a cloth fabric of mixed silk and cotton.

belunjur, see **lunjur.**

beluntas [KN], a sea-shore shrub with lilac flowers *(Pluchea Indica* or *Conza Indica).*

beluntuk [KN], *ikan ~,* a large freshwater goby *(Oxyeleotris marmoratus).*

belus [KS], free to go in and out, unobstructed, loose in a socket.

belut [KN], *ikan ~,* an eel.

bembam [KK], to roast in hot ashes.

bemban [KN], a shrub *Clinogyne* (sp.); its wiry stems are used for stitching ataps and for basket making; *se~ bunga,* a bouquet of flowers; *se~ kayu,* a bundle of kindling wood.

bembet [KK], lifting a light object in the hand; cf. *bimbing,* but the usage of the two words seems to differ slightly.

bembereng [KN], *ikan ~,* a fish *(Platax vespertilio).*

bena [KN], 1. a tidal bore. 2. *anak ~,* N.S., the child of a raja father and commoner mother. 3. [KS] *~ tak ~,* unconcerned, indifference.

benah [KN], an insect-pest; a blight.

benak [KS], 1. making a dull sound, as a false coin when rung; so dull, slow of apprehension. 2. marrow, brains.

benam [KK], *ter~,* buried in sand or mud; (more rarely) immersed in water, drowned; generally used for 'stuck' in mud, as a car; *mem~kan,* to push down into water or mud, and so, drown; (fig.) to drown a voice, as does a storm; *ter~* is also used to mean sunk out of sight, as the sun or the blade of an axe in the object struck.

benang [KN], thread, yarn; a thread-like line; *~ emas,* gold thread; *~ arang,* a charcoal line drawn by carpenters to guide them in their cutting or carving; (fig.) a boundary line beyond which one should not go; *memijak ~ arang orang,* to encroach on the rights or privacy of others, 'tread on people's toes';

ikut ~ arang, keeping close to the rules; *~ bulu,* wool yarn; *menegakkan ~ basah,* to (try to) make wet cotton stand on end, met. for a hopeless task, sheer waste of time.

benar [KS], right, accurate; *~lah seperti kata tuan,* what you say is true; *ke~an,* verification, approval; truth; *mem~kan,* to approve; to confirm; *se~ nya,* in fact, actually; *yang ~,* yours truly, yours faithfully or yours sincerely.

benara [KN], a washerman, a dhoby.

bencah [KN], a morass; swampy.

bencana [KN], Skr, mischief-making, trouble; (fig.) affliction, disaster; *hari ~,* a day of disaster; *~ alam,* natural disaster, 'act of God'; *mem~kan,* to slander; *~ peperangan,* the curse of war.

benci [KS], hatred, to hate; *~ dan marah dan dengki,* hate, anger, spite; *~kan* or *mem~kan,* to hate, (rarely) to arouse hatred in another; also *saling mem~; pem~,* a talisman or charm to cause another person to hate a third party, e.g. to cause a girl to hate a rival suitor.

benda [KN], Skr. thing, article; *mata ~,* things of value, gems, curios; *tak jadi ~,* does no good, useless; *harta ~,* goods and chattels; *~ berharga,* valuable articles; *~ ayat,* the subject of a sentence in grammar; *ke~an,* material wealth; materialism.

bendahara [KN], Skr. the title of a very exalted Malay State official, usually ranking next to the heir-apparent in old time Malaya; in effect, the Prime Minister; *per~an,* treasury; *ketua per~an,* Chancellor of the Exchequer; *per~an kata,* vocabulary.

bendahari [KN], 1. Hind. a treasury officer. 2. = **bendari.**

bendalu [KN], a mistletoe shrub.

bendang [KN], a wet rice-field; sometimes a 'swamp' generaly; *~ air hangat,* a hotspring (which always creates a little swamp); *buat ~,* to plant padi.

bendari [KN], Hind. a sea-cook, sometimes a palace-cook; also **bendahari.**

bendawat [KN], a stay, a lashing; cordage

in a ship.

bendera [KN], Port. a flag; *tiang ~,* a flag-staff; *~ separuh tiang,* flag at half-mast; *~ tapak catur,* chequered flag; *~ kapak,* the ordinary oblong flag; *~ tiga warna,* tricolour; *~ corak tiga, ~ berpelang tiga,* id.; *~ takuk,* swallow-tailed flag; *~ ular-ular,* pennant, pennon; *naikkan ~ putih (tanda tunduk),* to hang out the white flag (as a sign of submission).

benderang [KS], 1. *terang ~,* all-pervading (of brilliant light). 2. *tombak ~,* a spear with a tuft of horse-hair attached to it; a spear of state.

benderung [KN], a passage in a prince's audience-rooms.

bendi [KN], Hind. *sayur ~,* the okra, 'ladies' fingers'; *kacang ~,* id.

bendir [KN], a gong used by hawkers.

benduan [KN], Hind. a transported convict.

bendul [KN], the cross-beam supporting the floor or the threshold.

bendung [KN], a dam, a dyke; *mem~,* to dam up; (met.) to check advance; *mem~ inflasi,* to curb inflation.

bengah [KS], holding one's head up; stuck up, conceited.

bengal [KS], temporarily dull of hearing, e.g. when water gets into the ear; *kepala terasa ~,* feeling fuzzy in the head, confused.

bengang [KS], singing noise in the ear; *ter~,* knocked silly, 'laid out'; *mem~kan telinga,* to deafen the ears.

bengap [KN], artifically dull of hearing, e.g. when cotton is put in the ear; ringing dully, as a bad coin, or a human voice; muffled, deadened, of sound.

benggal [KS], knobbly; *~ benggul* or *~ benggil,* covered with bumps.

Benggala [KN], Bengal.

Benggali [KN], a native of Bengal, but Malays also use the word for Punjabis.

benggil [KS], 1. a small knob or swelling, esp. on the forehead. 2. *ber~,* be bumpy (of road).

benggul [KN], a large bump or a hump.

bengih [KK], Ked. to hiss (of a cat).

bengik [KN], 1. asthma. 2. asthamatic.

bengik [KS], *tetek ~,* insignificant, trivial matter.

bengis [KS], cruel, heartless; *ke~an,* cruelty; *pem~an,* indifference to the sufferings of others.

bengkah [KN], to strike and let go one's weapon; to hit an opponent's top with one's own; also **pangkak.**

bengkak [KS], inflamed, swollen; a swelling; *~-bengkil,* covered with bumps.

bengkalai [KS], *ter~,* incomplete (of work); *~kan,* to neglect, esp. of leaving work half-done.

bengkang [KS], 1. out of alignment, out of tune, as warped; twisted this way and that (as a bicycle that has been run over); *~ bengkok,* zigzag, 2. a Malay cake.

bengkar [KK], Pk. opening out, expand; *jagung ini mem~ kalau digoreng,* this corn expands when fried.

bengkarak [KN], bare bones (of skeleton), nothing but bones; so, unfinished, of a job (only useless bits and pieces left).

bengkarung [KN], the skink, grass-lizard; also **mengkarung.**

bengkawan [KN], a lath, used to fasten thatch; a numeral coefficient for ataps.

bengkayang [KS], gorged, glutted, stuffed (from overeating).

bengkel [KN], Ind. foundry, workshop, machine shop.

bengkeng [KS], angry, irritable, peevish; savage (of an animal).

bengkerap [KS], Eng. bankrupt; also (fig.) spoiled, ruined beyond repair; *jatuh ~,* to go bankrupt.

bengkil [KS], a small swelling, e.g. a boil.

bengkok [KS], crooked, bent; *~ akal,* 'crooked', as a cheat.

bengkong [KS], crooked — cf. **bengkok** and **bengkang.**

bengkuang, see **mengkuang.**

bengkudu, see **mengkudu.**

bengkunang [KN], a name for the napoh

(tragulus napo).

bengkung [KN], a girdle.

bengsit [KK], (vulg.) to make improper advances to a woman, to behave indecently to a woman.

benguk [KN], swollen in the neck; *sakit ~,* mumps; *ter~,* humped up and dejected-looking; probably akin to *beguk,* q.v.

bengung [KS], confused — cf. **bingung.**

bengut [KS], twisted, awry.

benian [KN], 1. a coffer. 2. Hind. a trader or merchant from India. 3. Hind. a banyan or singlet.

benih [KN], seed from small fruit.

benin [KN], seed; grain for use as seed; (fig.) *~ cacar,* vaccine; (fig.) *~ tiram, kerang,* a bed of oysters, cockles; *~ bunga,* pollen

bening [KS], clear, limpid, = **hening.**

benjing [KK], *mem~,* to carry hanging from the hand, as a bag; *ber~,* in a trailing line, as a concourse of people.

benjol [KS], a slight bump or swelling, a bulge in the cheek; berbenjol, bumpy, not smooth.

benok [KK], turning aside, swerving.

bensin [KN], gas, gasoline, also **benzin.**

benta [KN], 1. a small ulcer. 2. a kind of grass, us. growing in marshy land.

bentak [KK], N.S. *mem~,* to adress sharply, 'snap at'.

bentala [KN], Skr. the earth (poet).

bentan [KS], 1. relapse; the return of sickness. 2. N.S. *mem~,* to hold a fertility ceremony.

bentang [KK], 1. *mem~* and *mem~kan,* to spread out (a carpet); to pitch (a tent); to bring forward (as a proposal). 2. a rough sledge for transport of timber in the jungle; *ter~,* to lie; *saya tidak gentar apa yang ter~ di depan saya,* I'm not afraid of what lies ahead.

bentangur [KN], a name given to a number of trees yielding good timber *(Calophyllum* sp.).

bentar [KKtr], *se~,* a moment, an instant; *se~ di sini, se~ di sana,* one moment here, another moment there; *dengan se~,* in a moment, at once; *tunggu se~,*

one moment, please!, just a moment!.

bentara [KN], Skr. herald, court-marshal.

bentas [KK], to tear up and dash down; *di ~ nya sebuah bukit kepada hulubalang,* he (a giant) tore up a hill and dashed it on the troops.

bentat [KS], lacking lightness, stodgy (of cake).

benteng [KN], an embankment, dyke; a stronghold, strong-point; (fig.) a shield; a breastwork, a parapet; *~ sasaran,* the mound behind targets on a range; *~ tua,* an old fortress.

benteh [KK], to lock shins, to trip up; *ber~,* to engage in a sort of wrestling, each of two persons trying to lock shins and throw the other; also **bintis.**

bentrok [KK], *per~an,* clash, fight; *melerikan pem~an,* to avoid clashes.

bentuk [KN], a curve, a ring-shaped object; shape, form, framework; a numerical coefficient for curved objects such as rings, fish-hooks, etc.; *sepuluh ~ cincin,* ten rings; *mem~,* to set up, to establish; to keep in shape, keep in order, as hair; *pem~an,* formation, *pem~an pemerintah baru,* the formation of a new government.

bentur [KN], 1. bending, 'giving'; = **lentur.** 2. a lift-net for crabs; 3. [KK], *ter~ dengan,* to knock up against, stumble against (e.g., some unseen person in the dark).

benturung [KN], the bear-cat *(Arctictis binturung).*

benua [KN], a large expanse of country, an empire, a continent, the mainland, as against an island; *~ Cina,* China.

benuang [KN], *rusa ~,* a variety of the deer Cervus unicolor; also (Ked.) *genuang; Kerbau ~,* a large variety of buffalo.

benum [KS], untrodden (as distant jungle).

benyai [KS], soppy, too watery, of cooked food, esp. rice.

benyut [KS], twisted, awry.

beo [KN], the name given (in Java) to the *tiung,* or mynah.

bera [KN], changing colour, red or pale,

inflamed (of brown faces); dull brown as weather-worn roof-tiles; a face-ache, neuralgia.

beragan, see **agan**.

berahi [KN], Skr. love, lustful; ~*kan,* to be in love with.

Berahman [KN], *Berahamana,* Skr. a Brahmin.

berak [KS], 1. flushed — a variant of *bera,* q.v. 2. *ber~,* to sink in, as into water or mud; to work in, of roots.

berak [KK], to ease oneself, defecate; *dia mem~kan periuk nasi dia sendiri,* i.e., he fouls his own nest; sometimes used simply for excrement.

berakah [KS], self-important, stuck up.

beraksa [KN], 1. *kuda ~,* or *burung ~,* a legendary Pegasus. 2. *pokok ~,* a tree *(Cassia fistula); buah ~,* Pk. bullock's heart fruit.

beram [KN], a generic name for liquors made of fermented rice-spirit — cf. **peram**.

beramin [KN], *bakul ~,* a basket of the 'loop' pattern.

beranda [KN], Port. veranda.

berang [KN], ~-~, the otter *(Lutra sumatrana);* also *memerang.*

berang [KS], 1. angry, wrath; *hati yang ~,* angry feelings, passion; *naik ~,* to get fierce, to be in a fury. 2. *ular ~,* a venomous sea snake.

berangai [KN], *perahu ~,* a piratical prahu furnished with a boarding gangway and grapping irons.

berangan [KN], 1. realgar; = **warangan**; ~ *putih,* white arsenical oxide. 2. a generic name for oaks and chestnuts; *buah ~,* a chestnut; *buah ~ babi,* an acorn.

berangas [KN], barnacles.

berangus [KN], muzzle, a covering round an animal's mouth, to prevent it from biting.

berani [KS], courage, brave; to dare; *batu ~,* or *besi ~,* magnetic iron; steady, a 'sticker', Kel. (of a fighting bull); *mem~kan diri,* to brace oneself (in face of danger); ~ *bersumpah,* to swear; ~

bertaruh, willing to bet.

berantas [KK], Ind. to combat, to seek to get rid of (esp. as disease or ignorance); also **banteras**.

berapa [P], how much?, how many?; ~ *harga?,* how much? (what is the price?) us. shortened to simply ~*?* ~ *ekor anjing?,* how many dogs?; *be~,* some, a quantity (us. shortened in speech to ~*);* ~ *besar,* what's the size?; *tak ~,* not very; see **apa**; ~ *kali,* how often.

beras [KN], rice (without the husk, but uncooked); ~ *kunyit,* rice stained yellow with saffron; ~ *Belanda,* barley; ~ *hancur,* broken rice; ~*-petas,* all kinds of rice, food-stores generally; cf. **padi** and **nasi**.

berat [KS], heavy, weighty; ~*nya,* weight; *kepala ~,* heavy, dull-witted; ~ *kaki,* slow-moving, sluggish (esp. as a reproach to a footballer); ~ *siku,* lazy; ~ *nak,* disinclined to; *mem~kan,* sometimes, to make a great point of; *ke~an,* pregnancy; burden; *mem~kan,* to hinder, to handicap; ~ *telinga,* hard of hearing; also, wearisome to listen to; ~ *sebelah,* weighted down on one side, so not impartial; *ke~an* is also used for obstacle, objection, scruple; *kalau anda tidak ke~an,* if it's okay with you; *berke~an datang,* to have scruples about coming, to object to coming; *mengambil ~,* to take seriously; *pengangkat ~,* a weight-lifter; *denda ~,* severe penalty.

berata [KN], an idol; *memuja ~,* to worship idols.

berdikari [akr], independent, to stand on one's own feet; *wang ini membolehkan saya ~ dari keluarga saya,* this money gives me independence from my family.

berdus [KS], corpulent, obese.

berek-berek [KN], *burung ~,* the bay-backed bee-eater *(Merops sumatranus);* in speech us. **beberek**.

beremban [KN], 1. Pk. a padi barn. 2. the cross-bars in a fence.

berembang [KN], *pokok ~,* a seaside tree

(Sonneratia acida).

beremi [KN], the local water-cress *(Herpestes monniera)*.

berenang [KK], to swim; see **renang**.

bereng [KN], ~-~, a small Chinese gong.

berenga [KN], larvae of insects, e.g., as visible on decayed animal matter.

berenggil [KS], serrated, of a mountain range.

beres [KS], Ind. correct, in good order, well-balanced, straightened out; *mem~kan*, to put in order, reorganise, 'tidy-up', clear up; *jualan mem~*, clearance sale.

berguk [KN], Ar. a veil worn by a woman performing the pilgrimage.

berhala [KN], an idol.

beri [KK], *mem~*, to give, to bestow, to allow; *mem~tahu*, to inform; *mem~ tabik*, to greet, to salute; *mem~ kesempatan*, to give an opportunity, *mem~ isyarat*, to give a signal, to give a cue; *pem~tahu*, a notification; *pemberian*, gift, grant, dowry; *pem~an hidup*, voluntary conveyance inter vivos; ~ *muka*, to 'spoil', encourage to be cheeky; ~ is also used for 'give', in the same way as 'bending under pressure' In English.

beriang [KN], the large monitor-lizard *(Maranus salvator)*.

beringin [KN], the waringin tree *(Ficus Benja mina)*.

berita [KN], Skr. news, information; = *warta*, *pem~*, a reporter; *berita utama*, headlines, ~ *kilat*, bulletin.

berkas [KN], a tied bundle; a bale of otherwise disconnected objects; to tie together, e.g., sticks, horns; to round up, as criminals.

berkat [KN], Ar. blessing (divine favour bestowed directly or through the intercessory power of someone); *dengan ~ ...*, thanks to ..., owing to the good offices of...; *mem~i*, to bless, *Mudah-mudahan Tuhan mem~i anda*, may God bless you; ~ is also used of favours given to guests at a wedding.

berkik [KN], *burung ~*, (Singapore Malacca) the snipe; = (Penang) *burung tetiruk*.

berkuk [KN], *burung ~*, the large green pigeon (Sutreron capelli).

berlian [KN], Eng. a diamond, a brilliant.

Berma [KN], 1. Skr. Brahma. 2. redness, especially when caused by suffusion of blood. 3. Burma; *orang ~*, a Burmese.

bernas, see **renas**.

berniaga [KK], see **niaga**. (Wilkinson says that *berniaga* (or *beniaga*) is a Sanskrit word meaning trade, commerce, i.e. 'not a root *niaga* with the prefix *ber-*. But the origin of the word is practically lost now and it seems better to treat *niaga* as being the root word.).

beroga [KN], *ayam ~*, a name for the junglefowl *(Gallus ferrugineus)*.

berombong [KS], funnel-shaped.

beronok [KN], a name given to several edible sea slugs, e.g. *Colochirus anceps, Haplodactyla molpadisides*, etc.

berontak [KK], *mem~*, rebel, to take up arms; *pem~an*, rebellion, uprising, coup.

beroti [KN], a lath, a rung, a batten.

bersat [KS], gone astray (of food which gets into the windpipe).

bersih [KS], clean, free from impurities; net, clear (of profit); ~ *belanja pos*, postfree; *ke~an*, cleanliness, hygienic; *pem~an*, cleaning out, purging, introducing sanitary measures; used (fig.) for a political purge; *~-hati*, happy, contented, with unclouded mind; *pasukan pom~ bom*, bomb disposal squad; ~ *daripada tuduhan*, be exonerated from the chargo.

bersin [KK], to sneeze.

bersut [KS], scowling, frowning.

bertam [KN], a well-known palm *(Engeissona tristis)* used in thatching; *burung ~*, a black wood-partridge.

bertih [KN], to toast rice in the husk; *beras ~*, toasted rice; used esp. in magical ceremonies.

beruang [KN], the Malayan bear *(Ursus*

malayanus).

beruas [KN], a wild mangosteen.

berudu [KN], a tadpole, usually *anak ~*

beruk [KN], the pig-tailed monkey *(Macacas nemestrinus); serah ~* or *~ menghantar hasil,* the mumps; *~ Cik Mat Arif,* sometimes used as a derisive nickname for Japanese.

berus [KN], Eng. a broom.

besan [KN], the relationship between people whose children have married.

besar [KS], large, great; grown-up; *masalah ~,* an enormous problem; *hari ~,* festival, holiday; *~ hati,* elated; *tuan ~,* the head of an office; *~kan* and *mem~kan,* to enlarge; *mem~-~kan,* to exaggerate; *mem~kan diri,* to be pompous, give oneself airs; *per~kan,* to enlarge, expand; *kaca pem~,* magnifying glass; *alat pem~ suara,* microphone; *corong pem~ suara,* id., *ke~an,* grandeur, greatness; pride; *dengan segala ke~an,* with great pomp; *pem~,* official, dignitary; *pem~ suara,* megaphone, loud-speaker; *se~ dirinya,* life-size; *~nya,* size; *secara ~-~an,* on a grand scale.

beser [KS], incontinence of urine.

besi [KN], iron; *~ berbaja,* tempered steel; *~ berani,* magnetic iron; *~ batang,* bar iron; *~ kawi,* manganese; *~ lantai,* sheet iron; *batu ~,* granite; *tukang ~,* a blacksmith; *pukul ~,* to shoe a horse; *tahi ~,* rust; *~ buruk,* scrap-iron; *~ tuangan,* cast iron; *~ tempawan,* wrought iron; *kikir ~,* iron file; *bijih ~,* iron ore.

besing [KN], whizzing (of a projectile).

Besisi [KN], *orang ~,* an aboriginal tribe, probably akin to *Jakun,* found in small numbers in the southern parts of the Malay peninsula.

besit [KK], to beat (as with a light cane).

besok [KN], tomorrow; also esok; *~ pagi-pagi,* first thing in the morning.

bestari [KS], well-bred, accomplished.

beta [KN], Skr. slave, your servant, I (in old-fashioned and formal correspondence).

betah [KS], convalescent, recovered.

betak-betak [KN], a skin disease.

betapa [KKtr], how?, in what manner?, what?, why?; *~ pun,* no matter.

Betara [KN], Skr. a title given in old Java to major divinities and to reigning princes of great power.

betari [KN], a kind of cereal *(Sorghum saccharatum).*

betas [KS], ripping open, splitting open (as seam gives way under strain).

beti [KN], Hind. a female slave; a palace attendant — the female of *beta.*

betik [KN], 1. *buah ~,* the papaya fruit *(Carica papaya); ~ semangka,* the red-fleshed papaya; *timun ~,* the squash-melon. 2. announced (of news etc).

betina [KN], female, feminine (of animals), and (familiarly) of human beings; *kuda ~,* a mare; of inanimate objects *~* means flat or rounded, not pointed *(jantan); embun ~,* light flat drops of dew; also the lower of two objects: *kasau ~,* the lower rafters.

beting [KN], a sand bank or mud bank; *membeting,* to dart along the surface on its tail (of a gar-fish).

betis [KN], the leg (between knee and ankle); *buah ~,* or *jantung ~,* the calf; *beri ~, dia hendakkan paha,* give an inch and he wants an ell.

betul [KS], correct, true, straight; *~kan,* to correct, to set right; *mem~kan,* id.; *ber~an dengan,* corresponding to (in meaning or date); *~an,* what is right; acceptable, of a price; *pem~an,* correction; *~-~,* extremely; *anda ~-~ gila,* you're utterly mad!.

betung [KS], 1. large (in certain connections only), e.g., *katak ~,* a large species of frog; *buluh ~,* a large bamboo; *tebu ~,* a large sugar-cane; and *rumput ~,* a large grass. 2. Ind. a flood-gate; *pem~,* Joh. a culvert.

beza [KS], difference; = **beda**.

bi [KDpn], 1. Ar. with, in; *~'smi'llah,* in God's name; *~-ni,* on him, with him. 2. Used with colour in such expressions as *~-ka-merah,* a great mass of red.

biadab [KS], Pers. disrespectful, discourtesy; *bangsa yang* ~, an uncivilised race.

biak [KS], 1. prolific, reproductive; *mem~kan,* to breed (as poultry); *mem~kan jenis,* to reproduce one's species. 2. N.S. muddy, slushy.

biang [KS], 1. lascivious; on heat. 2. ~-*biut,* all awry; hanging badly, of clothes; bristling this way and that irregularly; (fig.) intractable; ~ *keladi,* ringleader.

biaperi [KN], Pers. a merchant, a trader.

biar [KK], 1. to permit, to allow, to let it alone; ~ *putih tulang jangang putih mata,* let the bones whiten but not the eyes (better death than shame), prov.; ~*kan,* to permit, to concede, to allow; ~ *pun,* granted that, even allowing that; ~ *bagaimana pun,* however, despite all that may be said; *terbiar,* neglected, abandoned; *ter~ dengan bagitu sahaja,* completely neglected. 2. *cacing* ~-~, intestinal worms (ascaris?); ~-~, *naik ke mata,* the *biar-biar* worm reaches your eyes (a play on the meanings of *biar* 1. and *biar* 2., conveying the warning 'If you are not on your guard, you will have reasons to regret it').

biara [KN], convent, monastery.

bias [KK], *ter~,* deflected from course, as a ship by wind or current or rain falling at an angle; less strong than babas, cf. **tempias.**

biasa [KS], Skr. accustomed to, practised in; ordinary; ~*nya, seperti* ~, as usual, *ter~,* accustomed to, usually; ~*lah tanganku memegang kalam,* my hand became accustomed to holding a pen; custom, habit; *luar* ~, extraordinary; *orangnya luar* ~, an oustanding person.

biasiswa [KN], Ind. a scholarship.

biawak [KN], a generic name for monitor and other large lizards.

biaya [KN], Skr. cost, expenses; outlay; special allowances; *mem~i,* to provide funds for, defray cost of; *Lembaga Penggalak Pelancong akan mem~i,* The Tourist Promotion Board is going to foot the bill.

bibi [KN], Hind. lady, mistress; the queen in cards.

bibir [KN], lip, edge, rim; ~*mata,* eyelids; ~ *sumbing,* hare-lip.

bibit [KK], 1. to carry a light object in the hand; also *bimbit.* 2. seed; germ, sperm; *mem~kan,* to sow.

bicara [KN], Skr. opinion; discussion; deliberation; a judicial proceeding; concerns, business; *ber~,* to discuss, to debate about; *per~an,* Court proceedings, the hearing; ~*kan,* to concern oneself about, see to, deal with; *ber~,* Ind. to speak, to talk; *sedang* ~, Ind. line engaged; *juru* ~, spokesman; *pem~,* a speaker, as in a debate; *mem~kan,* to hear, deal with, as a Court case; *habis* ~, that's the end of it, no more to be said; *pem~an,* hearing (of a trial); *banyak* ~*nya,* he talks too much; *tidak banyak* ~, he was habitually taciturn.

bidadari [KN], Skr. nymph; fairy.

bidai [KN], long narrow strips of rattan or bamboo, esp. for making screens, etc.; chicks, jalousies.

bidak [KN], Ar. a pawn at chess; ~ *dilantik,* a crowned pawn.

bidal [KN], a maxim, an old 'saw'; also **bidalan.**

bidan [KN], Skr. a midwife; *penempah* ~, a midwife's retaining fee; ~ *terjun,* the plunging midwife (summoned at the last moment), met. for extreme haste; ~ *tarik,* id.; *upah* ~ *pun tak terbayar,* not worth the price of the midwife's fee (of a useless child); *ilmu per~an,* midwifery.

bidang [KN], a broad, flat piece (e.g., of thatch); *se~ tanah,* a stretch of land; spacious; a numerical coefficient for things that are spread out e.g. sails, mats, etc.; field, area of action, sphere; broad (as of chest or shoulders).

bidas [KK], springing forward (of a flexible body when tension is removed); *mem~,* (met.) to criticise sharply, attack verbally.

biduan [KN], Skr. a musician, a singer.

biduanda [KN], 1. Skr. a royal musician. 2. original inhabitants, a pagan Malay tribe. 3. a royal messenger; (Johore) Malay police cadets.

biduk [KN], a fishing-boat or river cargo-boat of some bulk and draught; *kutu ~,* the beetles infesting ill-kept lockers, etc., in boats.

bidur [KN], a slab (of tin); formerly of recognised weight (about 3 lb.) and used as a medium of exchange.

bijak [KS], Skr. learned, sage, intelligent, prudent; *~ laksana,* id.; = *~sana.*

bijaksana [KS], Skr. learned, sage, prudent; wisdom; *Penghulu itu terkenal kerana ke~an-nya,* the village headman was well-known for his wisdom.

bijan [KN], sesame *(Sesamum Indicum),* yielding gingerly oil.

biji [KN], Skr. a seed, a grain, a pip; sometimes used (sl.) for testicles; numerical coefficient for small objects; *~ mata,* eyeball; *~-~an,* seeds, grain, generally; *~ darah merah (putih),* red (white) blood corpuscles.

bijih [KN], grains of alluvial tin; ore, esp. tin ore; *~ besi,* iron ore.

bijirin [KN], cereal; *gandum adalah termasuk ~,* wheat is a cereal.

bikin [KK], to make; to do.

bikini [KN], bikini, *pakaian mandi wanita terdiri dpd. dua potong kain;* very small two-piece bathing suit for women.

bikir [KN], Ar. virginity.

biku [KN], 1. a saw-edged pattern, a zig-zag pattern; lace-edging. 2. (Pali) a Buddhist priest.

bila [KKtr & KPhbg], when?, used in speech as a relative; *apa~,* id. (relative); *~ mana,* whenever; *barang-~,* as often as; *~ ~ sahaja,* any time, 'any old time'.

bilah [KN], a thin strip or lath; a bar of a cage; a numeral coefficient for knives, chisels, daggers, hatches, needles, etc.

bilai [KN], a weal.

bilal [KN], Ar. muezzin,

bilang [KK], recounting, enumeration, to repeat, to say, to tell; *se~,* each, every; *~an,* enumeration, tale; *cukup hari ~an,* when the tale of days was complete; *mem~,* to count, to number; *ter~,* fa-

mous; talked about; *ber~,* numerous; *se~an orang,* a number of people; *~ bini,* (sl.) to change wives frequently; *per~an,* N.S. a traditional saying; *kepercayaan ber~ Tuhan,* polytheism; *dasar ber~ bahasa,* multi-lingualism; *negeri ber~ bangsa,* a multi-racial state; *~an surat,* reference number (in correspondence); *~an penduduk,* the number of population; *~ hari,* to 'count the days' (while waiting); *tidak ter~,* countless; *se~an besar,* a large number; *penjodoh ~an,* numeral coefficient.

bilas [KK], 1. to wash in clear water, to rinse. 2. dim of sight, owing to disease.

bilik [KN], room, apartment; *~ air,* lavatory, bathroom; *~ bersekat,* cubicle; *berkongsi ~,* to share a room; *~ rihat,* recreation room; *~ gerakan,* operation room, *~ kuliah,* lecture room; *rumah pangsa 5 ~,* 5-room flat.

bilis [KN], 1. *mata ~,* bleary-eyed. 2. *ikan ~,* anchovies, whitebait.

bi'llahi, Ar. by God.

bilur [KN], a scar, a weal; *~ rotan,* weals left by the cane.

bimbang [KS], anxious, worry, concern, fearful.

bimbing [KK], Ind. to lead by the hand; *berbimbing tangan,* hand-in-hand; *~an,* guidance; *kelas ~an,* tuition class.

bimbit [KK], to carry lightly in the hand; *radio ~,* portable radio; also **bibit**.

bin [P], Ar. son of; *Putih ~ Mat,* son of Mat.

bina [KK], 1. Pers. caring about, taking to heart = *behina,* q.v. *~ta'~,* not paying full attention, showing half-hearted interest. 2. to build; *Persatuan Pembina Badan,* Body-building Association; *kritik mem~,* a constructive critic; *alasan mem~,* constructive arguments; *seni ~,* architecture; *pem~an negara,* nation building; *~ bahasa,* language development.

binasa [KS], Skr. ruined, destruction; *ikut rasa ~,* to give way to one's passions is destructive, (prov.);

~*kan* or *mem~kan*, to destroy.

binatang [KN], an animal, creature; ~ *yang liar*, wild animals; ~ *yang jinak*, domestic animals; ~ *yang buas*, beasts of prey; ~ *yang melata*, creeping creatures; ~ *yang merayap*, id., esp. insects; ~ *maging*, carnivorous; ~ *maun*, herbivorous; ~ *maserba*, omnivorous.

bincang [KK], *ber~-~*, discuss, talk about; *per~an*, discussion, meeting.

bincul [KN], a slight protrusion or bump, esp. of the 'bumps' on a person's head.

bincut [KN], a variant of *bincul*.

bindu [KN], a turning-lathe.

bingas [KS], fierce, fiery.

bingit [KS], ~ *kepala*, deafened by noise or by a stream of talk; confused, half-stupified.

bingka [KN], *kuih* ~, a Malay cake, made of rice-flour, coconut-cream, eggs and sugar.

bingkah [KN], clod; *se~ tanah*, a clod of earth.

bingkai [KN], rim, border; rattan binding on edge; ~ *cerminmata*, frame of spectacles; ~ *gambar*, picture frame; ~ *adat*, the bonds of custom; *~kan*, to bind, as a cracked staff.

bingkang, Pen. = **bingka**.

bingkas [KK], *mem~*, springing back (of a spring); sprung (of a trap); rising to attention; resuming a proper position.

bingkis [KN], 1. a complimentary gift accompanying a letter; *surat ~an*, id. 2. *bungkus* ~, all kinds of parcles and packages.

bingung [KS], mazed, disconcerted; dull, muddle-headed; *mem~kan*, to bewilder, confused, dazed; *gambaran yang mem~kan*, a misleading description.

bini [KN], wife (less courteous than isteri); *anak* ~, family; *ber~*, to be married; *ber~kan*, to marry, to take to wife; *ber~an = bilang* ~, see **bilang**.

binjai [KN], the name of a common fruit-tree (*Mangifera coesa*).

bint [KN], Ar. daughter; ~ *l-bahar*, mermaid — cf. **binti**.

bintang [KN], a star, a heavenly body; a decoration; ~ *berasap* or ~ *berekor*, a comet; ~ *beredar*, a planet; *tahi* ~, a meteor; ~ *dua belas*, the signs of the Zodiac; ~ *temabur*, a galaxy, esp. the Milky Way; ~ *bima-sakti*, the Milky Way; *rangkaian* ~, *susunan* ~, constellation; ~ *pari*, ~ *tohok*, the Southern Cross; ~ *ketika*, the Pleiades; ~ *biduk*, ~ *jong*, the Great Bear; ~ *belantik*, Orion; ~ *Marikh*, Mars; ~ *utara*, the Pole Star; ~ *musytari*, Jupiter; ~ *timur*, ~ *kejora*, Venus; ~ is also used for 'star' of a film or play; ~ *undangan*, guest star; ~ *kebesaran*, the star of an order of knighthood; *ber~-~*, full of small holes (through which light penetrates, of a roof); ~ *tiga*, a nickname for Communists; *ilmu* ~, astronomy.

bintangur, see **bentangur**.

hintat [KN], spots of a rash or caused by bite of insect.

binti [P], 1. Ar. daughter of; *Baidah ~ Hasan*, Baidah, daughter of Hasan — cf. *bin* and *bint*. 2. *~-~*, a small species of kingfisher.

bintik [KN], *ber~-~*, covered with small spots as of prickly heat; spotted, speckled.

bintil [KN], a stye in the eye.

bintis [KK], ~ *kaki*, to trip up; also **benteh**.

bintit [KN], a small swelling (such as that caused by the bite of a mosquito).

biografi [KN], biography; a person's life-history (written by someone else); *kami lebih meminati puisi dpd.* ~, we prefer poetry to biography.

biola [KN], Port. a violin; *menggesek* ~, to play a violin.

birah [KN], a name given to a number of aroids (chiefly wild), proverbially itchy to the touch; ~ *keladi (Colocasia antiquorum)*; *sakit ~ keladi*, lascivious.

birai [KN], a low parapet, balustrade, flange, gun-wale of a boat; brim (of a hat); Kel. edge.

biram [KN], 1. a poetic word for an elephant; ~ *berjuang*, a war-elephant. 2. a mythical snake with a head at both ends; *cincin patah* ~, a puzzle-ring joining at the heads of this snake.

biras [KN], the relationship between two men who have married sisters or two women who have married brothers.

birat [KN], a mark left by, e.g., a blow, causing contusion and discolouration of skin.

biri [KN], 1. *kambing* ~-~, a sheep. 2. *sakit* ~ ~, beri-beri.

birih, = **birai**.

biring [KS], 1. light red or yellow (of a fighting cock). 2. [KN], a skin eruption causing itchy spots.

biru [KS], blue; ~ *pekat,* deep blue; ~ *tua,* dark blue; ~ *muda,* light blue; ~ *langit,* sky-blue; ~ *lebam,* livid blue (as of a bruise); *ke*~-~*an,* bluish; ~ *kehitam-hitaman,* blue verging on black.

bisa [KS], 1. venom, blood-poison; *ular* ~, a venomous snake. 2. Ind. skill, can, able to; = **boleh**.

bisai [KS], dandified, dainty.

bisik [KK], *ber*~, to speak in whispers; ~*kan,* to whisper to, to prompt in a whisper; ~*an hati, (kata hati)* conscience.

bising [KS], chatter, noise, tiresome noise.

bismi [P], Ar. in the name of, esp. in the expression ~*llah,* in the Name of God, a pious utterance and a conventional heading to a treatise; it is supposed to be uttered when killing an animal for food; ~*llah al rahman al rahim,* in the name of God, the Merciful, the Compassionate; *baca* ~*llah, mengucap* ~*llah,* to utter *bismillah; tak dan baca* ~*llah,* before you could say Jack Robinson; ~*llahkan,* to kill (for food) with the proper utterances.

Bisnu [KN], Skr. Vishnu.

bisu [KS], dumb, mute; *mem*~, silent, mute; *mulutnya mem*~ *seribu bahasa,* he held his peace in spite of a thousand utterances (struggling to come out), i.e. managed to refrain from saying what he might have said; *mem*~ *mayat,* as silent as the grave, 'not a word'.

bisul [KN], a boil, a superficial abscess; ~

lada, a small boil, esp. as one of a crop of small boils; *punat* ~, the core of a boil.

biuku [KN], a sp. of water-tortoise *(Notochelys platynota).*

biung [KS], Pk., curved (of the cutting edge of areca-nut scissors).

bius [KN], Pers. *ubat* ~, a stupefying drug; an anaesthetic; *ber*~, anaesthetised; *mem*~*kan,* to administer an anaesthetic.

biut [KS], disobedient; hanging badly (of clothes); worsening, not responding to treatment, of a disease.

blok [KN], Eng. a (pulley) block.

bobok [KK], *mem*~, 1. to gurgle; to bubble up (as a spring); 2. *memina*~*kan,* to put the baby to sleep.

bobos [KS], leaking through one big hole; suffering from diarrhoea; *mem*~, bursting out through a hole, esp. of water; (fig.) of flying ants emerging in swarms from the ground after hatching out.

bobrok [KS], Ind. rotten, dilapidated, useless; *bangunan* ~, dilapidated building.

bocok [KN], awning over a cradle.

bocong [KN], an earthenware vessel shaped like an hour-glass; a jug.

bocor [KK], leaky (not as strong as *bobos);* ~ *mulut,* babbler, loose-tongued; ~ *bacir,* continually leaking, as a tank; (sl.) of the bowels; ~*kan rahsia,* to let the cat out of the bag.

bodek [KN], testicles.

bodoh [KS], stupid, dull, simple; *orang* ~, a fool; *ke*~*an,* stupidity; *mem*~*kan diri,* to make oneself look silly, to make a fool of oneself.

bodok [KN], Eng. a gaff, a boat-hook.

bodong [KN], 1. a squall. 2. a lean-to.

boga [KN], 1. Skr. *sempana pergam* ~, a kind of pleasure-boat. 2. Skr. *anta*-~, a great serpent.

bogam [KN], 1. pieces of gold or silver leaf on a head ornament *(tajuk).* 2. great — a rare equivalent of *besar.*

bogang [KS], *telanjang* ~, stark naked.

bogel [KS], stark, naked, bare; featherless; *mem*~*kan,* to strip s.o. of his or her clothes, ~ *dada,* 'topless' (of dresses).

bogot [KS], horrid, ugly — in the expression, *hitam* ~, horridly black (of Papuans).

bohong [KS], lie, lying, false; ~ *semata-mata,* altogether untrue; *pembohong,* a liar; *ber~, mem~,* to tell lies; *mem~i,* to tell lies to, deceive; *mem~kan,* to give the lie to, denounce as a liar.

boikot [KK], *mem~,* boycott.

bok [KN], 1. Jav. mother; = **embuk,** 2. Ked. a mattress, = **tilam.**

bokong [KK], *mem~,* worn the wrong way; front and back interchanged; also *balik* ~.

bokop [KS], swollen, closed by inflammation (of the eyes); = **bakup.**

bokor [KN], a metal bowl (like a soup-plate) with a flat rim, used as a stand for water-vessels.

bola [KN], Port. a ball, a cricket ball, football, billiard or tennis ball; ~ *sepak,* football; ~ *tampar,* volley-ball; ~ *jaring,* netball; ~ *keranjang,* basket-ball.

bolak [KKtr], ~ *balik,* there and back, backwards and forwards; alternating; *karan ~-balik,* alternating current; ~ *cakap,* going back on one's word, prevarication; *mem~-balekkan mata,* to roll the eyes.

boleh [KKtr], able to, can, power to; *se~-~ nya,* the best of his ability; *mana ~?,* how can this be so?, impossible; *apa ~ buat?,* how can this be so?, impossible; *apa ~ buat?,* what is to be done?, there is an end of it; ~ *jadi,* possibly, 'could be'; *mem~kan, memper~kan,* to empower, to enable; *ke~an,* ability; in Kel. ~ is often used to mean simply `obtain, get'.

bolos [KS], 1. fallen off, as wrapping, leafless; stripped of clothes, feathers, hair; deprived, e.g., of a bargain. 2. *ter~,* stumbling, e.g., into a hole. 3. Ind. *mem~,* to break out, to escape, 'make oneself scarce', truant.

bolot [KK], roughly or hastily wrapping up a parcel — cf. **balut**; grabbing, making off with; *mem~,* to win, carry off, as a

prize; to grab everything, monopolize.

bolu [KN], Port. sponge-cake; ~ *gulung,* sponge-roll; also *buah hulu* and *baulu.*

bom [KN], 1. the shafts of a carriage; the boom of a ship. 2. Eng. bomb; ~ *lempar,* hand-grenade; ~ *zarah,* atom bomb; ~ *jangka,* time bomb.

bomantara [KN], also **bumantara,** Skr. the firmament, the vault of heaven.

bomba [KN], Port. a pump; the hose of a fire-engine; a fire-engine; *pejabat* ~, fire-brigade; *balai* ~, fire station; *ahli* ~, firemen.

bomoh [KN], a Malay medicine-man; also *bomo* and *bomor.*

bonceng [KK], *mem~,* to carry at the back of the bicycle or motorcycle.

boncol [KN], a knob-like protuberance.

bonda [KN], mother (in respectful language), = *ibunda, ayah* ~, parents.

bondong [KN], *ber~,* [KK], to depart bag and baggage; *ber~ ke sana ke sini,* hustled from pillar to post; *ber~-~,* bustling about.

boneka [KN], Port. a puppet, a doll.

bongceng [KK], Ind. *mem~,* to get a lift to sit behind; to sit pillion; *mem~ di belakang,* id.; *tukang* ~, parasite.

bonggol [KN], a dome-shaped protuberance; a hump on a camel's back; a knoll; also **bongkol.**

bongkah [KN], a piece, a block; ~ *ais,* iceberg; *ber~-~,* lumpy, bumpy.

bongkak [KS], proud, arrogant.

bongkal [KN], a measure of weight for precious articles (1 oz. approximately); also a lump generally; *mas ber~,* gold in the form of nuggets.

bongkang [KS], ~ *bangking,* spread out to its full length (of a dead body), in contradistinction to being huddled up; *ter~,* id.

bongkar [KK], heaving up, turning up the soil, weighing anchor; ~ *kota,* to blow up a fort; *mem~,* to heave up; ~ *sauh,* to weigh anchor; ~ *bukit,* to dig up a hillock; ~ *mayat,* to exhume a corpse; ~ *rahasia,* to discover a secret, or reveal a secret; ~ *barang-barang,* to unpack

47

goods or articles; ~ is also used generally for breaking up, putting an end to; ~ *bangkir,* turning everything topsy-turvy; ~ is used for 'getting-up', of a bird from the ground.

bongkas [KS], rising up (as the roots of a tree when the tree is blown down; or as the buried portion of a stake or pile when the pile is knocked down); heaved up; thrust up; to start up, jump up.

bongkeng [KS], lying forward, face downwards and knees drawn up (of a dead body).

bongkok [KS], hump-backed; ~ *baharu betul,* 'the hump-back who has just become straight' (a beggar on horseback), prov., ~ *udang,* slightly stooping; ~ *sabut,* bowed, but still tough; *mem~,* to stoop, to humble oneself; to bend right over, as when riding a bicycle; *hidung ~,* a hooked nose; *ter~-~,* continually stooping, as persons planting seedlings.

bongkol = **bonggol**.

bongkong [KS], 1. ~ *kayu,* a parasitic growth on the trunk of a tree. 2. a Malay cake made in a wrapper of a banana leaf.

bonglai [KN], a ginger used in medicine *(Zingiber cassumunaar).*

bongok [KS], 1. heavily built, clumsy. 2. stupid.

bongsu [KS], youngest-born; *gerham ~,* wisdom-tooth.

bonjol [KS], projecting outward — cf. *bujal benjul; mem~,* to bulge.

bonus [KN], bonus, an additional payment beyond what is usual or expected.

bonyor [KS], soft and bad, of fruit, fish, meat; sloppy, also **bonyok**.

bopeng [KS], pock-marked; also **mopeng**.

borak [KN], 1. Ar. a mysterious flying animal; the animal upon which Mohammad made his journey to heaven. 2. to chatter, converse; *tukang ~,* a chatterbox.

borang [KN], a form (as of application).

bordu [KN], Port. the gunwale (sometimes the hatches).

borek [KS], spotted (with fairly large spots); *ayam ~,* a spotted fowl.

boria [KN], Hind. bands of minstrels who go round serenading in the month of Muharram, esp. in Penang.

borong [KK], *mem~,* wholesale; by the gross; *mem~* or *membeli ~,* to buy up wholesale, esp. when trying to 'corner' a product; *pem~,* a contractor; a tenderer, wholesaler; *pem~an,* a tender.

boros [KS], prodigal, extravagant; *pem~,* extremely wasteful; *ayahnya kedekut, tetapi dia pem~,* her father is stingy, but she herself is extremely wasteful.

bosan [KS], 1. annoyed, irritated, bored, 'browned-off'; *mem~kan,* to bore, *pekerjaan yang mem~kan,* a monotonous job. 2. Kel. = **bising**.

bosor [KS], gluttonous.

bota [KN], Skr. a goblin, an evil spirit.

botak [KS], bald; *burung ~,* the adjutant stork.

botok-botok [KN], a dish of salted and spiced fish cooked by steam.

boya [KN], 1. Port. a buoy; also **bairup**. 2. Pen. Ked. = **buaya**.

boyak [KS], 1. tasteless, insipid; dull, uninteresting. 2. Pk. unwieldly (of men, boats).

Boyan [KN], the isle of Bawean, between Java and Borneo; *orang ~,* a 'Boyanese'.

b.p. = *bagi pihak,* see **bagi**.

buah [KN], fruit; a spherical or nearly spherical object; a descriptive prefix or numeral coefficient for objects of a more or less spherical or cubical appearance such as houses, hills, baskets, stones, countries, towns, etc.; ~ *catur,* chessmen; ~ *dadu,* dice; ~ *hati* (especialy as a term of endearment); ~ *keras,* the candle-nut *(Aleurites moluccanus);* sometimes means nuts generally; ~ *Melaka,* a sweetmeat of soft dough; ~ *pala,* nutmeg; ~ *pelir,* the testicles; ~ *pinggang,* the kidneys; ~ *timbangan,* weights; ~ *guli,* a marble; ~

tangan, a small gift; ~ *mulut,* a popular topic of conversation, 'the latest scandal'; ~ *kalam,* written work, opus; ~ *fikiran,* an idea; ~ *ulu* = *bolu;* ~ *di hujung,* aftermath, = *ceding;* ~ *sulung,* firstfruits; ~ *bibir,* much talked about, having name on everyone's lips; ~ *dada,* breasts (of a woman), ~ *susu,* id.; ~ *butir,* details; ~ *rindu,* object of longing; *anak* ~, (1) dependants, people under a penghulu, (2) lineal descendants; ~-~*an,* fruits in general, fruits of all sorts; *ber*~, to bear fruit.

buai [KK], rocking, swaying, swinging (as a cradle); *ber*~, to swing; *buaian,* a swinging cradle; *ter*~-~, swinging to-and-fro.

buak [KK], bubbling up, surging up, piling up (as water under a ship's bows).

bual [KK], bubbling up; *ber*~-~, to chatter; *per*~*an,* conversation.

buana [KN], Skr. the world, the universe; *paku* ~, nail from which the universe hangs (a Javanese royal title); *sangga* ~, prop sustaining the universe (a similar title); *seri teri*-~, light of the three worlds (another title).

buang [KK], throwing away, discarding; *mem*~, ~*kan* or *mem*~*kan,* to expel, to get rid of; ~ *air,* to obey a call of nature; ~ *air darah,* dysentery; ~ *ingus,* to blow the nose; ~ *nyawa,* to give one's life; ~ *undi,* to cast lots; ~ *negeri,* to banish; *orang* ~*an tempatan,* person whose area of residence is restricted; ~ *padang,* to 'send off' (a player); ~ *diri,* to withdraw into solitude; sometimes, to commit suicide; ~ *hidup,* to banish for life; *kerajaan dalam* ~*an,* Government in exile; *mem*~-~, to waste, fritter away; ~ *mata pada,* to keep an eye on; ~ *atau melontar lembing,* a javelin; *para* ~, window or aperture (in a house) through which rubbish is thrown out; *ter*~, wasted, abandoned, discarded; *anak* ~*an,* a discarded child, a foundling; *mem*~ *muka* (fig.), to cast one's face, to look away.

buapak [KN], N.S. head of a family in a community governed by the *Adat Perpatih;* see **adat.**

buas [KS], wild, fierce (of animals), *singa yang maha* ~, a most ferocious lion; naughty (of children); *binatang (yang)* ~, a beast of prey; *mem*~, to act wildly, 'go off the rails'.

buat [KK], doing, making; *ber*~ or *mem*~, to make; ~-~, to feign, pretend, shamming; ~-~ *nak,* to make as if to; ~ *sesuatu,* to do something; *buatan,* make, e.g. ~*an Inggeris,* of English make; *buatan* is also used for 'synthetic', not natural (= *tiruan,* as opposed to *asli*); *buat* is also used for 'for the purpose of' or simply 'for'; *ambil kayu ini* ~ *tongkat,* take this bit of wood as a walking-stick; ~ *sementara,* for the time being; ~ *saya sendiri,* for my part, as far as I am concerned; *per*~*an,* act, deed; *bukan* ~*an!,* amazing!, like nothing on earth!; ~*an sendiri,* home-made; *mem*~ *huru-hara,* to turn into a complete fiasco.

buaya [KN], a crocodile; ~ *tembaga,* the common crocodile *(Crocodilus porosus);* ~ *katak,* another species with protruding eyes; ~ *serunai,* ~ *jenjulong,* ~ *nyenyulung* or ~ *julung,* the gavial *(Tomistoma schlegeli);* the crocodile is a symbol of pitiless greed, e.g., as a money-lender or a dishonest trustee; but ~ *darat,* land crocodile, may also be used to denote a 'wolf', who is after the girls; *ikan korek telinga* ~, the fish *(Castroceus biaculeatus); lidah* ~, the aloe *(Aloe ferox);* ~-~, stem and stern pieces of a boat.

bubar [KK], Ind. ~*kan,* to dissolve *(kerahan) tentera,* to demobilize; *mem*~*kan Parlimen,* that Parliament be dissolved.

bubu [KN], Pk. Ked. a river fish-trap of bamboo and rattan; = **lukah.**

bubuh [KK], to put, set, affix or deposit anything in the position in which it is meant to stay (as opposed to *letak* — to set down casually); *mem*~ or *mem*~*kan,* to lay, to affix; ~ *tanda tangan,* to attach one's signature; ~ *chap,* to seal; *mem~ hati pada,* to set one's heart on.

bubuk [KN], 1. a weevil, a wood-maggot; *dimakan ~,* worm-eaten. 2. to boil in water.

bubul [KK], 1. *mem~,* to mend (a net). 2. tertiary yaws on feet.

bubur [KN], rice-broth, gruel; ~ *susu,* rice boiled in milk; *nasi sudah menjadi ~,* the rice has turned to gruel — too late! the milk is spilt.

bubut [KN], 1. a name for coucals and crowpheasants *(Centropus eurycercus* and *Centropus pengalensis); also but-but.* 2. the throat-halliards (in rigging); *~an* id. 3. *mem~,* to force way violently, burst through, e.g., of the concentrated force of a stream or of wind; cf. **bobos**.

bucu [KN], a corner or angle, a projection in basketry patterns.

budak [KN], a young boy or girl; used loosely both for children and for unmarried young people; ~ *pejabat,* office-boy; *~-~ makan pisang,* a mere child (eating a banana); *memper~-~kan,* to treat as a mere child; ~ is used (Ind.) to mean slave; *memper~kan,* to enslave.

budaya [KN], *ke~n,* culture; *ke~n kuning,* 'yellow culture', a term applied in modern times to activities, particularly literary, regarded as anti-social, pornography; *pertukaran ~,* cultural exchanges; *Anugerah Pingat Budayawan,* Cultural Medallion Award.

budi [KN], 1. Skr. wisdom; kindness; understanding, mental disposition, charm, high character; *akal ~,* or ~ *bicara,* id.; *hilang ~,* loss of discretion; throwing discretion to the winds; ~ *bahasa,* tact courtesy; *~-perkerti,* nature, disposition; *ber~,* discreet, considerate; *berhutang ~,* to be under an obligation; *balas ~,* to repay an obligation. 2. Skr. the peepul-tree *(Ficus religiosa); daun ~,* the leaf of that tree (a name given to a fig-leaf-like pattern or border).

budiman [KS], Skr. wise, prudent, kind — cf. **budi**, 1.; *penulis ~,* an unpaid con-

tributor to a paper.

budu [KN], 1. a pickle (small fish preserved in brine with their scales and entrails). 2. = **berudu**.

Bugis [KN], the name of a people from the Celebes.

buih [KN], foam, froth; *ber~,* to froth.

bujal [KS], projecting outward (esp. of a navel).

bujam [KN], an envelope-shaped bag of *mengkuang* leaf for carrying *sirih,* etc.

bujang [KS], single, unmarried (used of widows, widowers and divorced persons as well as of persons who have never been married); ~ *talang,* childless widower; *hidup membujang,* to live a bachelor life; *orang ~ sarang fitnah,* unmarried people are a nesting-place for slander, i.e. are apt to be slandered; ~ *serong,* a bachelor or girl single in name only; *kopi ~* to serve coffee only (without providing cakes etc.); *rumah ~,* Pen. a house without a porch; ~ is sometimes used to mean servant.

bujangga [KN], man of learning, sage; also *pujangga.*

bujuk [KK], 1. coaxing, soothing — better *pujuk;* to persuade; *mem~ dengan kata-kata manis,* to sweet-talk. 2. *ikan ~,* a fresh-water fish, a murrel *(Channa lucius); also ikan ubi.*

bujur [KN], extension of length relative to breadth; long, straight, vertical; longitudinal; *mem~,* stretching lengthwise; ~ *lalu, lintang patah,* those that go straight get through, those that fall across (the channel) get broken (one must follow customary procedure), prov.: but this saying sometimes means, 'everything goes', of an unscrupulous or greedy person; ~ *bulat,* elliptical; ~ *telur,* oval; *lintang ~,* diagonal; *ter~,* stretched out, e.g., as a corpse; ~ *sirih* is used to mean oval, esp. of the face of a pretty girl.

buka [KK], *mem~,* to open, unharness, untie, unfold or undo; *alat pem~,* opener, ~ *jalan,* to open out a road; ~ *kain,* to take off one's clothing, ~ *layar,* to un-

furl sails; ~ *pintu,* to open a door; ~
puasa, to end a fast; ~ *rahsia* to reveal a
secret; ~ *topi,* to take off one's hat; ~
tanah, to open up land for cultivation;
~*nya,* extent, width, as of an orifice;
bercakap secara ter~, to speak openly
(not in camera); *bersikap ter~,* to keep
an open mind; *ter~ kepada orang ramai,*
open to the public.

bukan [KSer & KKtr], no, not; there is not;
it is not; ~ *sebarang perempuan,* no ordinary woman; *yang ~-~,* that do not
really exist, impossible, wrong, nonsensical; foolish, groundless; ~ *apa,* it's
nothing, it's all right; ~ *waktunya untuk
bergurau,* this is no time for jokes.

bukat [KS], troubled, disturbed, turbid, of
water; thick and billowing, of smoke;
mem~, to grow turbid, of water; to
thicken, of smoke.

bukau [KN], *bukit-~,* wilderness, wildwood.

bukit [KN], a hill; *anak ~,* a hillock; *kaki ~,*
the foot of a hill; *kawasan berbukit,* a
hilly area, *orang ~,* aboriginal tribes
dwelling in the mountains; *penara ~,*
the level ridge at the crest (of a range);
~ *berapit,* hills connected by a low col;
~ *bukau,* hilly land, broken country;
peminggang ~, flanks of a hill; *tujuh ~,
tujuh lurah jauhnya,* seven hills and
seven valleys away, i.e. far from it!;
Bukit Bendera, Penang Hill; *Bukit Tur
Sina,* Mount Sinai.

bukti [KN], evidence, proof; *buktikan,* to
prove true; *mem~kan kebenaran kata-
katanya,* to verify his statements; to
accomplish; *ter ,* proved; come to pass.

buku [KN], 1. a joint (in a finger, on the
ankle, wrist, etc.); a knot (in wood); a
lump; the lumpy or disagreeable part
of anything; (met.) the sting of a remark; the pith or substance of anything;
tak ada ~, there's no sense in it; ~ *lima,*
the knuckles, a 'bunch of fives'; ~ *jari,*
id.; *kena ~,* to come across the nasty
part of anything, to run up against the
wrong spot; *pilih ruas terkena pada ~,*
choosing the inter-space (of a bamboo)
and running up against the node, i.e.

however carefully you plan you may
run against difficulties; *bertemu ~ dengan ruas,* well-matched; ~ *lali,* ankle;
ber~, clotted, in lumps; *ter~ hati,* downcast, grieved; *ada suatu ~ dalam perut,*
I have a 'lump' in my belly, i.e. I have a
worry, something sticks in my gullet; ~
benang, a bobbin of thread; ~ *sabun,* a
cake of soap. 2. Eng. a book; ~ *rampaian,* book for odd notes; ~ *teks,*
textbook; ~ *catatan harian,* diary; ~
kenang-kenangan, memoirs; ~ *pegangan,* handbook; *di~kan,* to make into a
book.

bul [KN], globular; bubble-like; *jambu ~,*
guava *(Eugenia malaccensis).*

bulai [KN], 1. albino. 2. = **belalai.**

bulan [KN], the moon; a month; the period
of gestation; *setelah genap ~nya,* when
her period of gestation was complete;
sehari ~, the first day of the month; the
one-day-old moon; *empatbelas hari~,*
the fourteenth day of the month; the
full moon; ~ *pernama,* id.; ~ *timbul,*
next month, new moon; *terang ~,*
moonlight; ~ *setempik,* crescent moon;
~ *sabit,* id.; ~ *kahwin = Rejab; datang ~,*
women's monthly course; *anak ~,* new
moon; ~ *tua,* full moon; ~ *bertanduk,*
new moon; ~ *bertambah,* waxing moon;
~ *susut,* waning moon; ~ *tengah naik,*
waxing moon or rising moon; ~ *nahas,*
the unlucky month, i.e. the month of
Safar, q.v., ~ *sakit,* eclipse of the moon;
~ *puasa,* Ramadan, the month in the
Muslim calendar when Muslims must
observe fasting; ~ *naik,* the moon rises;
~ *masuk,* the moon sets; ~ *mengambang,* moon appearing to hang just over
the horizon; ~ *kesiangan,* (pallid) moon
seen in daylight; ~ *gelap,* period when
the moon is invisible; ~ *bunting pelanduk,* half moon; ~ *rekaan,* ~ *tiruan,* artificial moon, Sputnik; *ber~ madu,* to have
a honeymoon; ~ *jatuh ke riba,* the moon
falling into one's lap, amazing good
luck.

bulang [KN], 1. enwinding, enwrapping; ~
luar, to wrap the *sarong* outside the

coat or over trousers; *mem~ taji,* to bind on the spurs of a fighting-cock; ~ *hulu,* head-cloth (of a prince). 2. generic name for a number of thorny shrubs *(Canthium* sp., etc.); *bulangan,* id. 3. *~-baling,* rolling over and over; a whirligig; *peluru ~baling,* a name given to chain-shot; also *bulang-baling.*

bular [KS], whitish discoloration of the eye, esp. due to cataract; *buta ~,* blind with such discoloration.

bulat [KS], round; smooth of surface; free from angularities; ~ *bujur* or ~ *panjang,* elliptical; ~ *pipih,* flat and round (as a coin); ~ *torak,* cylindrical; *kayu ~,* round logs stripped of branches; *masak ~,* cooked whole; *pusat ~,* the centre of a circle; *seluar ~,* pyjamas; *telanjang ~,* stark naked; *se~-~,* altogether; *dengan se~-~ suara,* with one voice, unanimously; *telan ~,* to swallow whole; *dengan se~-~ hati,* with my whole heart; N.S. *ke~an,* unanimity; completion, rounding off; *~-kata,* a variety of word-puzzles; ~, to swallow up, submerge (fig.); *~an,* a circle; *mem~kan,* to concentrate, e.g. one's strength; *angka bulat,* a whole number.

buli [KN], *~-~,* a small flask or bottle; so, a small gland or body-cell.

bulir [KN], ear (of padi); cluster.

bulu [KN], wool; feathers; the hair of the body; ~ *kening,* the eyebrows; ~ *landak,* the quills on a porcupine; ~ *liang roma,* the fine hairs on the body; ~ *roma,* id.; ~ *tengkuk,* the mane (of a horse); ~ *kapas,* down; *ulat ~,* the hairy caterpillar; ~ *sua,* hackles on neck (of cock); ~ *tangkis,* Ind. badminton; *~-~ remang,* bristles; *hati berbulu,* angry; *memilih ~,* to show partiality, discriminate; *memandang ~,* id.; *mendirikan ~ roma,* to make the hair stand on end; *tidak se~,* disagree, be contrary to.

buluh [KN], bamboo; a generic name for many bamboos; ~ *bangsi,* a reed pipe; ~ *perindu,* (1) a sort of Jew's harp; (2) a singing bamboo, Aeolian harp; *seperdu*

~, a clump of bamboo; *pem~,* a tube or piping; *pem~ darah,* an artery; *pem~ nafas,* windpipe.

bulur [KN], starvation; *mati ~,* to die of hunger; *ke~an,* famine; *ke~,* hunger;

bulus-bulus [KN], the Australian whiting; also **bebulus.**

bumbu [KN], Jav. condiments; = **rempah.**

bumbun [KN], 1. a hut in which a hunter hides when decoying game. 2. overfilled (as a plate with rice). 3. *lang ~,* the honey-buzzard.

bumbung [KN], the ridge of a roof, rooflike; *~an,* a roof; *tulang ~,* the ridgepole; *mem~,* to swell up; to describe a trajectory; to swell up, rise high, as fire or thick smoke, or (fig.) as hopes or prices; *ber~,* roofed, covered; ~ is sometimes used for the 'hood' of a car.

bumi [KN], Skr. the earth, the soil, the ground; *jatuh ke ~,* to fall to the ground; *petala ~,* the folds or layers of which the earth is said by Malays to be formed; *mangku ~,* a regent; *bawa ke ~,* to bury (a corpse); *ke~kan,* id.; *kerja ke~kan mayat,* a funeral; *perke~an,* id.; *~putera,* sons of the soil.

bun [KN], 1. (Dutch) a metal pail. 2. *setali ~,* a string (of *pantuns).*

buncit [KS], corpulent, round, of the stomach.

bundar [KS], rounded, globular, e.g., of breasts.

bunga [KN], a flower; an ornamental pattern or design; ~ *api,* sparks, fireworks; ~ *air mawar,* the rose; ~ *karang,* a coralline sponge; ~ *kutu,* the base (of the finger-nail); ~ *pala,* mace; ~ *rampai,* flower-petals mixed with scented leaves; pot-pourri; ~ *raya,* the scarlet hibiscus (created the national flower of Malaya in 1960); ~ *pukul lapan,* the morning glory flower; ~ *mas,* a tribute of a golden flower formerly sent to the King of Siam triennially by the Rulers of Kedah, Kelantan and Trengganu; ~ *telur,* coloured boiled eggs, stuck on sticks, given to guests at a wedding; *~-~ percakapan,* (fig.) flowers of speech;

~ is used to describe 'flower-like' eruptions on a sore, e.g., that of yaws; ~ is used for 'tails' when tossing a coin (as opposed to *kepala*); ~ *wang,* interest on money; ~ *wang tercampur,* compound interest; *pokok ~ kertas,* the bougainvillea; ~ *air,* minute fishfry, also plankton; *de~,* pollen; *pende~an,* pollination.

bungar [KS], first, earliest, esp. of growths; *buah ~an,* first fruits.

bungkam [KS], *mem~,* quiet, cause to become silent.

bungkam [KK], *mem~,* to keep one's mouth shut, to stay mum; *azimat pem~,* a drug or talisman to silence a hostile witness; *kena pem~,* to be struck dumb (either by magic or fig.).

bungkus [KK], to wrap, rolling up a thing; *~an,* a bundle, package; *mem~,* to make up a parcel; ~ *tikar,* to 'pack and go' (= *gulung tikar*).

bungsil [KN], a very young coconut (used as a plaything by children).

buni [KN], *orang ~an,* invisible elves (of the forest).

buntak [KS], stumpy, beamy (as a boat); tubby, of a person.

buntal [KN], the box-fish, sea-porcupine; the name is also applied to freshwater puffer-fishes *(Tetraodon* sp.).

buntang [KS], 1. wide open (as the eyes of a man who is being strangled); staring; stiff and stark, of a corpse. 2. a weaver's rod.

buntar [KS], dome-shaped; roughly hemispherical; ~ *bayang-bayang,* round, of shadows at noon.

buntat [KN], a gall-stone; a petrified substance found in animal or vegetable substances; a bezoar; without the talismanic qualities of the *guliga;* ~ *masyarakat,* the cream of society (opposed to *sampah masyarakat,* dregs of society).

buntil [KN], a clothes-bag, a kitbag.

bunting [KS], pregnant; ~ *sarat,* advanced pregnancy; ~ *bantang,* id.; ~ *kecik,* in the early stage of pregnancy; *padi ~,*

rice-grain in the ear.

buntu [KS], filled, of a well, cutting or belly; restricted, stopped; *jalan ~,* a cul-de-sac; *berhati ~,* depressed, bored; *ke~an,* a deadlock; frustration; *berhati ~,* having a feeling of frustration.

buntut [KN], the posterior, the stern, the fundament; the base of a sheath; the butt of a gun; the bottom of a bottle; ~ *kereta,* the boot of a car; ~ *kapal,* the stern of a ship, *ber~~,* in single file; *mem~,* to follow closely; *men~i,* to keep closely behind (someone).

bunuh [KK], killing; *mem~,* to kill, to put an end to; *mati di~,* murdered, destined to a bad end; *pem~,* a murderer; *pem~an,* killing, slaughter; *pem~an beramal-ramai,* a massacre; *mem~ diri,* to commit suicide; *mem~ perbualan,* to cut short a conversation.

bunut [KN], *hujan ~,* drizzle.

bunyi [KN], sound, noise; meaning, accent, intonation; *demikian ~nya,* of the following tenor; ~~an, strains of music; *ber~,* to sound; *mem~kan,* to enunciate; to pronounce; to sound, to cause to ring (as a bell); *mem~kan radio,* switch/turn the radio on; *ber~ batu ber~lah dia,* when a stone sounds, he will sound, i.e. can't get a word out of him.

bupati [KN], Skr. a Javanese title; lord of the earth.

bura [KN], spitting out, ejecting, pillorying; *ular naga ~,* a snake (probably *Naia sputatrix,* the black cobra).

burai [KS], *ter~,* gushing out (as entrails), or as contents of a cut sack.

burhan [KN], Ar. demonstration, proof.

burit [KN], posterior, stern; ~ *an,* the stern of a ship; *mem~,* to commit an unnatural offence.

buru [KK], hunting, the chase; *mem~,* to hunt; *pem~,* hunter; *hantu pem~,* the wild huntsman, an evil spirit; *per~an,* sport, the game hunted; *orang ~an,* an outlaw, a hunted, 'wanted' man; *orang per~an* id.; *ter~~,* acting hastily, rushing in like a bull at a gate; *ter~nafsu,* acting in rash haste (yielding to emotions); *jangan ter~-~*, don't rush, take your time.

buruh [KN], labour; *kaum ~*, labourers; *Parti Buruh*, the Labour Party; *~ kasar*, an unskilled labourer; *~ paksa*, forced labour; *pejabat pendaftaran ~*, Labour Exchange, *pusat mencari pekerjaan; Kesatuan ~*, Trade union; *Kesatuan Sekerja* id.

buruk [KS], worn, decayed (of vegetable and manufactured articles, but not of animal matter — cf. **busuk***; ~ siku*, (fig.) shabby, mean (e.g. as a person reclaiming a gift); *~-baiknya*, ups and downs (of fortune), good and bad points; *mem~kan nama*, to defame; *mem~-~kan*, to 'run-down', speak ill of; *cuaca ~*, inclement weather; *bertabiat ~*, nasty, wicked, bad-mannered; *ke~an*, weakness.

burun [KN], *kambing ~*, the serow (Nemorrhoedus swettenhami); a type of wild goat.

burung [KN], a bird; *~ dewata*, the bird of paradise; *tembak ~*, bird-shooting; *~* is used (fig.) for the hammer of a gun and for a child's penis.

burut [KN], hernia, rupture, hydrocele.

busa [KN], Ind. foam, froth.

busar [KN], a bow, an arc; a bow-shaped attachment to a kite, emitting a humming sound in flight; the bow for cleaning cotton; *seperti kapas di ~*, like cotton after cleaning (pure white), prov.; *seperti ~ Ranjuna*, like the bow of Arjuna (a simile for a beautiful arm); also *busur*.

busi [KN], Hind, rice-bran; Ind. Spark plug.

bustan [KN], Pers. a garden; a plleasaunce (poet.).

busu, = **bongsu**.

busuk [KS], decayed (of animal matter), putrid, stinking; *bau ~*, a bad smell; *hati ~*, a bad disposition; *nama ~*, an extremely bad name; *mayat yang sudah ~*, decomposed body.

busung [KN], dropsical inflammation; *~ darah*, an aneurism; *~ pasir*, a mound of sand, dune; *mem~*, to swell, grow larger; *mem~kan dada*, to swell out one's chest (as with pride).

busut [KN], an ant-hill, a small mound; *~ jantan*, a tall, pointed ant-hill; *~ betina*, a rounded ant-hill.

buta [KN], 1. blind; *~ larangan*, myopia; *~ tuli*, blind and deaf; *pukul ~ tuli*, striking recklessly; *mem~*, (vulg.) to sleep soundly; *~ perut*, (course) blockhead; *makan gaji ~*, to have a soft job, a sinecure; *pagi-pagi ~*, the grey of dawn; *~ huruf*, illiterate; *~ kayu*, completely illiterate; *~ bahasa Inggeris*, knowing no English; *orang ~ kehilangan tongkat*, a blind man who has lost his stick, met, for helplessness and bewilderment; *~ ayam*, night-blind; *~ ragi*, having pattern washed out, of cloth; *~ politik*, not politicaly minded; *~ sebelah*, blind in one eye. 2. = **bota**. 3. *~-~*, a seashore tree *(Cerbera odollam)*. 4. *Cina ~*, (corruption of Skr. word) a *muhallil*, q.v.; *menembak secara membabi ~*, to fire at random.

butang [KN], Eng. a button; *~ dasi*, a stud.

but-but [KN], the crow pheasant.

butir [KN], a grain, particle; a numeral coefficient for small round objects (such as gems), also for nuts; *~-~*, details, minutes of meeting; *buah ~*, details, items; *~an*, a fragment, flake.

butuh [KN], 1. penis. 2. Ind. *mem~*, to require, need; *ke~an*, requirements.

buyung [KN], 1. a round-bottomed earthenware water-jar, 2. a boy, youth; *si-Buyung*, nickname for a lad, 'Master So-and-so'.

buyut [KS], 1. flabby of flesh; *perut ~*, flabby obesity, also used for pregnancy. 2. [KN], ancestor in the fourth or fifth generation (the first three being *bapa, nenek, moyang*).

C

cabai [KN], Skr. long pepper (*piper longum*); capsicum; covers peppers and chillies of various kinds.

cabak [KN], a gaping tear or wound.

cabang [KN], branch, bough, prong, bifurcation, the main branches of a tree; *ber~*, forked (as the tongue of a snake); *besi tiga ~*, a trident; *ber~ hati*, wavering between different courses, undecided; also **cawang**.

cabar [KS], faint-hearted, timid; *~ hati*, pusillanimous; *men~kan hati*, to reduce to timidity, discourage, dishearten; *men~*, to taunt as a funk, so, to challenge; *~an*, a challenge; *pen~*, a challenger, contender.

cabik [KS], torn, rent; *cabak-~*, tattered; *~-~kan*, to tear to tatters.

cabuk [KN], 1. a whip. 2. gangrene, ulcer (especially in the lower leg).

cabul [KS], outrageous behaviour; licentious violence; unseemly language; *berbuat ~*, to commit an outrage (esp. rape); *men~ hak-hak peri-kemanusian*, to violate human rights; *ber~*, raging (as a disease or a fire); *~-mulut*, dangerous babbler; *pen~an*, an outrage, gross affront, violation (esp. of rights); *men~ kehormatan*, to outrage the modesty or honour of; *men~ maruah*, id; *gambar-gambar ~*, pornographic; *gambar-gambar lucah*, id.

cabut [KK], plucking out; a royalty; commission; *~ lari*, to clear off, 'bolt'; *men~*, to pull out, *men~ gigi*, to have bad tooth extracted; to drag out, to uproot; *ter~*, pulled out; drawn (of a knife); *~an*, the draw (e.g., in a race); an extract from a writing; *~an bertuah*, lucky draw.

cacah [KK], *men~*, 1. pricking a pattern; *ber~*, tattooed. 2. a Malay soup. 3. Ind. number, quantity; *~ jiwa*, a census.

cacak [KK], *men~*, implant; sticking s.t. upright into the ground; *~ lari*, (sl.) to make a bolt of it; *ter~*, erect (of a pole, an animal's tail).

cacar [KN], small-pox; *~ air*, measles or chicken-pox; *menanam ~*, to vaccinate; *bertanam ~*, to be vaccinated; *surat ~*, *sijil pengimunan* id., vaccination certificate; *benih ~*, vaccine.

cacat [KN], a flaw, a defect, a blemish; *~kan*, to find flaws in, to criticise adversely; *orang ~*, disabled persons or deformed persons; *~ badan*, a disability or deformity; *~ rupa*, a deformity or unsightly physical blemish; *~ bawaan*, a congenital disability, etc.; *~ cedera*, a disability, etc., esp. of such a nature as to invalidate a contract of marriage.

cacau [KS], to confuse, disorder, fickle, inconstant; *men~*, to be delirious, capricious.

caci [KN], 1. a lever used to roll up a sail, 2. [KK], to abuse, name calling, vilify; to express disapproval of, criticise adversely, censure, 'run down'.

cacil [KN], small for its purpose, very small.

cacing [KN], a worm; *~ pipih*; *~ pita*, the tape worm; *~ kerawit*, pin worms, thread worms; *~ gelang*, round worms; *~ biarbiar*, (probably) ascaris; *~ kerawit*, also used for hook worms; *~ halus*, id.

cadang [KK], a stand-by; a reserve fund or war-chest; *~kan*, to deposit as security; to plan, propose; *~an*, 1. deposit, pledge. 2. a proposal, a suggestion; *tentera ~an, tentera simpinan* id., reserve troops; *ber~ nak*, to propose to, intend to; *~an nafsu*, a proposal based rather on sentiment or hope than on reason; *pen~*, the proposer (esp. of a motion), as opposed to the opposer (*pembahas* or *pembangkang*).

cadar [KN], Hind. a sheet; bedsheet, bedspread.

cagak [KN], the forked stick used as a stand for a swivel-gun (*lela*) or a telescope.

cagar [KN], surety; a Malaccan form of mortgage in which the mortgagee is given the usufruct of land in lieu of interest; ~*kan,* to deposit as security.

cagu [KN], a disease of the toes due to leprosy.

cagut [KK], *men~,* to bite (as fish), peck.

cahar [KS], diarrhoea, purging; *pen~,* purgative, laxative.

cahaya [KN], Skr. lustre, brilliancy, light, glow; ~ *mata,* light of the eyes (a term of endearment); esp. to a baby; ~ *mata* is sometimes used simply for 'baby'; *ber~,* to glow, to shine; *mengeluarkan* ~, to radiate light; ~ *buatan,* artificial light; *injap* ~, light valve.

cair [KS], thin (of liquids), watery; *lumpur* ~, very watery mud; *bubur* ~, thin broth; ~*an,* a liquid; *men~,* to melt, liquify; *cair* is also used for pale, 'watery' (of colour); *teh* ~, weak tea.

cak [KN], ~ *padang,* the Malayan meadow pipit; ~ *padi,* the munia; ~-~, Kel. the tailor-bird.

cakah [KS], wide (of an angle), obtuse.

cakap [KK], speech; *ber~,* to speak; *dia tahu* ~ *Melayu,* he can speak Malay; ~ *angin,* mere talk, empty boasting, idle talk; *ber~-~,* to talk about, to have a conversation; *bahasa per~an,* conversational language.

cakar [KK], scratching; ~ *balar,* scratched all over; *men~,* to scratch (as a fowl); ~ *ayam,* met. for bad hand-writing; ~ *ayam* is also the name of a cake made of sweet potato; *pen~,* a rake; *bangunan pen~ langit,* sky-scrappers; *men~* is also used for 'to rake'; *ber~an,* (fig.) on bad terms, 'at daggers drawn', quarrel.

cakat [KS], brisk, alert; ~*an,* briskness, also **cekat**.

cakera [KN], Skr. a discus, a quoit.

cakerawala [KN], Skr. the revolving vault of heaven; the firmament; a planet.

cakuk (cangkuk) [KN], hook; pointed, hook-like, of a weapon; *golok* ~, a curved chopper.

cakup [KN], 1. catching in the open mouth (as a dog catches a biscuit); so, to snap up, grab; 2. to cover, *men~i banyak hal,* covers all kinds of subjects.

cakus [KK], *men~,* to carry a burden suspended from a stick that rests on the shoulder; take a little at a time (of food).

calak [KS], 1. Pk. affectation, airs, smartness; wild and ill-considered, of statement; *men~,* to talk wildly. 2. ~ *gobek,* pestle of areca-nut pounder, whetstone. 3. *men~,* to spread forth, flame forth, of rays of rising sun, shining, splendid; cf. **carak**.

cak-pong-pong [KN], onom, for the sound of a band; also *cak-lempong*.

calang [KS], ~-~, mediocre, not of first quality; cf. **alang**.

calar [KN], a long scratch on the skin; *ber~,* scratched; ~-*balar,* covered with scratches.

calat [KS], *ter~,* 'cleaned-out', as in gambling (very coarse).

calit [KK], smearing, smudging on, smudging slightly; dabbing on (as eye-black); *ter~,* slightly smudged, of writing; *sudah* ~ *jangan palit,* when you have smudged it, don't go smudging it more (i.e., in particular, apply your eye-black judiciously, but also carrying the general idea, don't overdo it); *men~ arang ke muka,* to soil one's face with charcoal (met) to besmirch s.o's. reputation.

calon [KN], a candidate for election or for an examination; sometimes, a representative; *men~kan,* to put up as a candidate; *pen~an,* candidature.

calung [KN], 1. a small ladle; a small cup, esp. one made from the bamboo. 2. *pisau* ~, a small knife resembling a *pisau wali*.

cam [KN], recognition by sight; ~*kan,* to recognise; to identify; *menge~kan,* to recognise (and understand) a sign.

camar [KN], *burung* ~, a tern; also *cen~*.

camau [KN], a generic name for tree *(dra-*

coenas).

cambah [KK], *ber~*, to germinate (of seed); germination, *per~an*, germinating, sprouting.

cambai [KN], a coarse leaf used as inferior *sirih*.

cambang [KN], side-whiskers, moustache; ~ *bauk*, a full beard.

camcha [KN], a tea-spoon.

campah [KS], insipid, tasteless, flavourless.

campak [KK], 1. *men~kan*, discarding; to throw, cast; ~ *buang*, to throw away; also used to mean a javelin; *ter~*, thrown, as from a horse; *~kan*, to throw away, e.g., a cigar-end; *duit ~*, wedding present (i.e. money thrown down in front of the newly wedded couple as they sit in the *bersanding* ceremony). 2. measles.

campang [KK], *men~*, sculling or paddling from the bows of a boat.

camping [KS], Pen. flawed (of material used, not of appearance); *campang-~*, tattered and torn.

campung [KK], *men~*, 1. shattered at a stroke (as a man, or tree, struck by lightning), to cut off the end of something, in ruins; *~-campang*, thunderstruck, dumbfounded. 2. Ind. = **cebur**.

campur [KK], *men~*, mixing, mingling; ~ *baur*, utterly mixed up, in confusion; ~ *gaul*, id.; ~ *aduk*, id.; *~an*, components of a mixture; mixed (as a coalition Government or combined team); ~ *tangan*, to interfere; to take part; *ber~ dengan*, to associate with; ~, to total up, *men padukan*, *men~adukkan*, to blend.

camur [KK], *men~*, scatter about, throw here and there; *berke~*, scattered about.

can [KN], 1. Ch. a Chinese conical basket. 2. a 'bit of fluff'; or, as e.g., ~ *kopi*, good for a drink of coffee. 3. chance, opportunity.

canai [KK], *men~*, to whet; smoothing or polishing or grinding by means of a roller; cutting and polishing (gems); (fig.) 'working on', wheedling; *keris baharu di~*, a newly sharpened *keris*;

kena ~, (sl.) to be outwitted, be cheated; ~ *fikiran*, refers to printed materials such as books etc. as a source of knowledge.

canang [KN], a gong with a shallow rim and no hemispherical nob in it; *~kan*, to proclaim by beat of gong.

canar [KN], a generic name for the plants known as smilax.

cancang [KN], *ter~*, sticking up, erect, upright, rising to a point (as certain forms of head-dress or a crag).

canda [KK], 1. *tak ~*, to care nothing about; = *tak endah* (ignore). 2. the strip of wood at the stern of a boat to which a rudder is attached. 3. [KK] to joke, clowning. q.v. 4. [KN] *~-peti*, a secretaire, a box divided into compartments, a cabinet (for keeping jewllery, money).

candal [KS], 1. difficult; = **sukar**. 2. Hind. loose, foul-mouthed, ribald. 3. jarring; = **janggal**, q.v.

candan [KN], a variant of **cendana**.

candang [KS], *berani ~*, not knowing when one is beaten, obstinately courageous.

candat [KN], a kind of hook with several unbarbed points sticking out in different directions; a grapnel; it is used to fish up sunken cables; or, in small size, for catching cuttlefish.

candi [KN], Jav. a monument, a memorial pillar or building, a shrine, a temple. 2. Tam. (Pen.) incorrigible, restive (of a horse). 3. Tam. (Pen.) a street-corner prostitute.

candik [KN], a recognised concubine of a prince — as distinct from an inferior wife (*gundik*) or casual mistress (*ja mah-jamahan*). 2. a fixed riverine purse-net.

candu [KN], prepared opium, *menghisap ~*, to smoke opium; *hasil pajak ~*, revenue from an opium-farm; *pemakan ~*, *pen~*, one who takes opium; *ketagih ~*, an opium addict; ~ *gelap*, smuggled opium; *tahi ~*, opium dross; also used to describe an opium addict; *~kan*, to deceive, as with drugs; ~ is also used by extension to mean simply, addicted: ~ *perokok*, cigarette-addict; ~ *main judi*, gambling-fiend; *ber~ di darah daging,* to 'get under the skin', become part of one, as some superstitious belief.

candung [KN], *parang ~,* a chopper in which the handle and blade are in one piece, and not fastened together.

cang [KK], 1. carrying pick-a-back 2. C. a square lift-net. 3. Ked. panniers for an elephant. 4. taut, not pendulous (as cheeks or breasts).

cangak [KK], *men~,* to look round hastily (as a frightened man), *ter~--~,* look uncertainly in all directions.

cangap [KN], a notch or dent for fitting together two pieces of wood.

canggah [KN], a forked punting-pole (used for propelling a boat up-steam by pushing against tree-boughs, snags, etc.); (fig.) to probe, consider in detail (as a report); *ber~,* forked; branching off; (fig.) in disagreement.

canggal [KN], metal nail-protector (worn as an ornament).

canggung [KS], 1. inharmonious, incongruous; out of place; unnatural; gauche, awkward in behaviour, esp. owing to shyness; discordant, jarring of speech; *berasa ~ berkerja di pejabat baru,* to find it awkward working in a new office. 2. a snag in a river; *seperti kera dapat ~,* like a monkey which has found a snag in a river, i.e. eager to snatch at any means of safety, but sometimes used to mean, looking silly and helpless. 3. astonishment; better **cengang**.

cangkat [KS], 1. a low hillock, a piece of rising ground. 2. shallow.

cangking [KK], to seize and pick up, as when greeting a child.

cangkir [KN], a small glass cup of Arab make.

cangkuk [KN], a crook; a hook (e.g., at the end of an elephant goad); *penyangkuk,* a hooked coupling; *~ tingkap,* a jemmy.

cangkul [KN], a hoe or heavy mattock used for digging; *men~,* to dig with this instrument.

cangkung [KK], squatting,

cangkup [KK], *men~,* scooping up food

into the mouth with the palm of the hand.

canguk [KK], *men~, ter~,* to peer down (as a hawk on a bough), sit with head bowed.

cantas [KK], *men~,* to sever by a single blow from a heavy cutting instrument; lopping, pruning.

cantik [KS], pretty, good-looking; neat, nicely got up, well-groomed; *ber~--~,* to 'pretty oneself up'; *ke~an,* beauty; *men~kan,* to decorate.

canting [KN], a sort of bamboo bucket (used for getting water out of a ship's well).

cantum [KK], *ber~,* folding again, as bird's ruffled feathers; joined as a collar by a pin; used for 'splicing', for 'budding' (in grafting), and for 'amalgamating', 'combining'; *men~,* to join up, bring together (severed parts); *per~an,* merger, amalgamation, union; *pokok ~,* a grafted or budded tree; *anak getah baka ~,* rubber seedlings of bud-grafted stock.

cap [KN], 1. Ch. printing; 'chopping'; a Chinese chop or seal for use with ink; type used in printing; a trade-mark; business name, 'chop', of a Chinese firm; *cincin ~,* a signet ring; *~ Sulaiman,* Solomon's seal; *membubuh ~,* to affix a seal; *syarikat ~,* printing firm; *~kan,* to print; *perkakas ~,* apparatus for printing, a press; *tukang ~,* a printer; *~ batu, ~ jari,* fingerprint, lithography; *~ mohor,* government seal; *~ timah,* printing in metallic movable type; *~,* Kel. a legal document; *~* is also used for 'to brand as', 'stigmatise'; *dia di~ pendusta,* he was branded a liar; *tukang ~ duit,* one who prints money; *aku bukan tukang ~ duit,* I am not a printer of money, a retort to someone asking for monetary assistance: 'I can't make money'. 2. C. to shuffle (cards).

capah [KN], a rough, unpainted, shallow washtub (of Burmese make); a wooden plate.

capai [KK], *men~,* to grasp; to attain to; to

reach; to grip; to pick up, take in one's hand; *hendak men~ bulan,* to wish to get hold of the moon (a proverbial description of mad ambition); *tak ter~,* out of reach; *dapat di~,* within reach; *pen~an,* achievement.

capak [KK], *men~,* to overlook unintentionally; to slight, show disdain for, be indifferent to, take no heed of, ignore.

capal [KN], Hind. a leather sandal.

capang [KS], wide (of nostrils or horns or ears), long and curved (of moustache).

capik [KS], lame, limping, halt; ~ *riuk,* lame on account of a twisted foot.

caping [KN], a metallic plate (used to cover the nudities of a very young female child); used for flat covers, e.g., over key-holes and for, e.g., shin guards.

capuk [KS], pock, spot on the skin.

cara [KN], way, custom, manner, style, method; *memakai ~ perempuan,* to dress as a woman; ~ *Cina,* in the Chinese language or in the Chinese way; *se~ besar-besaran,* on a large scale; *se~ kecil-kecil,* on a small scale; *se~ kebetulan,* a coincidence; *tata~,* procedure, programme; *tidak se~ langsung,* indirect (indirectly); *se~ damai,* peacefully; *se~ perdamaian,* by way of peaceful settlement; *se~ mengejut,* in a startling way; *se~ resmi,* officially; ~ *hidup,* way of life.

carak [KK], to become visible, display oneself; *men~ sinarnya,* to show its rays (of the rising sun).

carang [KN], the minor boughs and branches of a tree; a spray, sprig, leaf-bearing twig.

cari [KK], *men~,* seeking for, looking for; *carikan,* to search for anything; *men~,* to seek, N.S. seek a livelihood; *perempuan men~,* (Pen.) a prostitute; *mata pen~an,* a source of livelihood; *sepen~an, se~an,* the joint earnings of husband and wife; ~ *salah,* to look for trouble, 'pick on' someone; ~ *fasal,* id.; ~ *hal,* to seek a living; ~ *undi,* to canvass for votes; *men~ akal,* to come up with something; *men~ penjelasan,* to

seek clarification.

carik [KN], tearing; a rent; *corak-~,* frayed, tattered; *~kan,* to tear up; *men~-~,* id.; *se~ kertas,* a scrap of paper.

caruk [KN], a runnel, a running ditch, the long incision on a rubber tree.

carum [KN], *ber~,* Pen. to club together; *pen~,* contribution to a fund, e.g. a provident fund.

carut [KS], obscene language; *men~,* to use obscene language; *~-marut,* filthy language.

cas [KN], charge; ~ *nukleus,* nuclear charge.

cat [KN], 1. Ch. paint; *sapu ~,* to paint; the process of painting. 2. Kel. exactly; apparently used only in the expression *matahari berdiri ~,* exactly mid-day.

catat [KK], Ind. to note down, to enter up; *~an,* a note; N.B.; *buku ~an,* a notebook; *~an kaki,* footnote; *~kan,* to note down; to register, enter in a record.

catu [KN], Pen. ration, allotment, doling out; *catuan,* a ration, fixed quantity of food etc. allowed to a person.

catuk [KK], *men~,* 1. the blow of a pick; the peck of a bird. 2. sitting on the hunkers with knees up; *pelita ~,* a table-lamp. 3. = 1/4 leng, a measure of capacity, roughly a tablespoon full.

catur [KN], Skr. chess; *main ~,* to play chess; *buah ~,* chessmen; *tapak ~,* chequered; *loh ~* or *papan ~,* a chessboard; *teka-teki ~,* a chess-problem; *penekaan ~,* solution; *per~an politik,* political game, manoeuvre.

catut [KN], tweezers (for pulling hairs etc.), pincers, instrument for pulling nails.

caung [KS], sunken — of the cheeks (through loss of teeth).

cawan [KN], Ch. a tea-cup.

cawang [KN], bifurcation, branching off; a branch; sometimes, a clause in a sentence; *~an kedai,* a branch shop — cf. **cabang.**

cawat [KN], a loin-cloth; *ber~,* to wear as a loin-cloth is worn, to wear a loin-cloth; *kemudi ~,* a rudder (on European lines); ~ *kanak-kanak,* a 'nappy', *men~kan ekor,* to put the tail between the legs.

cawai [KN], 1. *burung* ~, the drongo; also ~-~ and *ce*~. 2. the linch-pin of an axle; also **cabi**.

cebak [KK], *men*~, to excavate (in quarry work); digging out by side-long blows; turning over the earth; *pen*~, long-handled spade.

cebik [KK], ~-*cebai*, pouting, making a wry face; *mencebik*, to make a wry face, sneer; *ter*~, id.

cebis [KN], *se*~, a tatter, a shred; ~-~*an*, shreds, tattered pieces.

cebuk [KN], 1. a coconut scoop with handle thrust through the shell; ladling up water with this scoop; 2. *men*~, cleansing from faecal defilement; *tak ber*~, a term of abuse; 'dirty beast'.

cebul [KN], 1. Ind. dwarfish; a dwarf, midget, extremely small person.

cebur [KN], plunging heavily into water or flame; *men*~*kan diri*, to plunge, to cast oneself into; *men*~*kan diri dalam bidang politik*, to get oneself involved in politics; *ter*~, ruined, 'done for', involved.

cecah [KK], *men*~, just touching, barely reaching (as in dipping a pen in ink or the tip of one's finger in gravy); *seelok-elok ter*~ *di tanah*, just touching the ground; *men*~ *lapangan terbang*, to touch down on an airfield (of a plane); ~ *hujung jari ke tanah*, to touch the ground with the tips of one's fingers; ~*kan cawan ke bibir*, to put a tea-cup to one's lips; *se*~, a tiny bit; a moment; also **cicah**.

cecair = **cair**.

cecap [KK], touching (food) with the finger and then applying the finger to the lips; tasting; *ter*~ *air*, just touching the water, as a bridge in a flood.

cedera [KS], Skr. a flaw, a defect; injury, casualty; *mendatangkan* ~, to injure (somebody's) reputation; *ke*~*an*, damage, losses in war; casualties, injury, wound; *menyebabkan* ~ *parah*, to cause grievous hurt; *tidak* ~, unscathed.

ceding [KS], 1. thin and out of condition, (of children, trees, etc.). 2. aftermath.

ceduk [KS], *men*~, sunken (of the cheeks and eyes).

ceduk [KK], to scoop, ladle out; *men*~ *jasa orang*, to scoop the credit for what someone else has done; *men*~ *ciptaan orang*, to steal from the works of others, to plagiarize; ~*an*, a plagiarism; *hasil* ~*an*, the fruits of plagiarism.

cedung [KK], *men*~, to plant wet padi, *padi* ~ wet padi.

cega [KS], *ber*~-~, wary, cautious, careful, esp. of 'shy' game.

cegah [KK], *men*~, to hinder, prevent; *pasukan pen*~ *rusuhan*, anti-riot squad; *pasukan pen*~ *maksiat*, anti-vice squad; *ubat pen*~ *penyakit*, prophylactic medicine; *alat pen*~ *pencuri*, anti-burglar contrivance; *pil pen*~ *beranak*, a pill to prevent birth; *men*~ *hamil*, to prevent conception; *men*~ *kelaparan*, to free from hunger; *bahagian pen*~ *penyeludupan*, anti-smuggling division; *langkah-langkah pen*~*an*, preventive steps.

cegak [KS], erect; = **tegak**; *ter*~, standing erect; also **cegat**, strong and active.

cegar [KN], a shallow rapid, a water-race; *burung* ~, the fork-tail.

ceh [KSn], fie!

cekah [KS], *ber*~, split open; splitting under pressure (as a mangosteen); cf. **cekih**.

cekak [KK], 1. holding between the thumb and fore-finger; *se*~, a small handful, as much as one can pick up with thumb and fingers; *ber*~ *pinggang*, with arms akimbo; but *ber*~ *pinggang* is sometimes used with the meaning of 'having a fight', probably with the idea of wrestling, gripping each other's waist; *men*~ *dahi*, to clasp the forehead, as in thought; ~ *rambut*, a fillet for the hair, a snood. 2. reliable (of a workman); *ber*~, to strive hard.

cekal [KS], staunch, steadfast, courageous, stout-hearted.

cekam [KN], a sharp-pointed stick (used for making holes in the ground for hill padi cultivation); *sakit* ~, a festering sore under a toe-nail; *tilam* ~, a mattress stabbled and sewn, i.e. tufted.

cekang [KS], tight; tightly stretched; taut; stiff; *rangak* ~, a shell (*Pteroceras chiragra*).

cekap [KS], skilful, efficient, expert; *kerja suatu tak boleh* ~, he is not good for any work; ~*-tangan*, dexterous, deft; *ke~an*, capability, competence, skill, efficiency.

cekau [KK], *men*~, to hook (as with a crook); to reach for, try to grab (esp. at end), esp. something overhead, clutch at.

cekcok [KK], Ind. *per~an*, dispute, difference of opinion, altercation.

ceki [KN], Ch. small Chinese playing-cards, 'chicky-cards'.

cekih = **cekah**.

cekik [KK], *men*~ *leher*, to seize by the throat; to garotte; *mati ter*~, death by choking; ~ *kedadak*, violent vomiting (invoked as a curse on an enemy); *ter*~, choked; *men*- (fig.) to sneak, pilfer, pinch.

cekit [KK], *men*~, to pick away small morsels; to pick to pieces.

ceku [KK], *men*~, denting with the finger-nail.

cekuh [KK], *men*~, Pk. to pick up with the finger and thumb.

cekuk [KK], *men*~, to seize by the throat; ~*-cekik*, the struggle for breath by a choking man, administer medicine forcibly.

cekung [KS], cunken concave; *kanta* ~, concave lens.

cekup [KK], *men*~, 1. covering with the hands. 2. = **cakup**.

cekur [KN], ~ *manis*, a shrub (*Sauropus albicans*), the leaves of which are eaten as vegetables (= **asin-asin**).

cekut [KK], *men*~, to pick up between the tips of the thumb and three fingers.

cela [KN], censuring, criticise, finding fault; a defect; damage, loss; ~*-men*~, [KK], to abuse; *nama yang ke~an*, a bad name; *ke~an*, censure, adverse comment; *perbuatan* ~, a disgraceful

act.

celadang [KN], Pen. a square basket for padi; cf. **cenangau**.

celah [KN], crevice, fissure, crack, cleft; ~ *batu*, the space between two boulders; ~ *dinding*, a crevice in a wall; ~ *gigi*, the line between adjoining teeth; ~ *gunung*, a gully or ravine; ~ *jari*, the space between two fingers; *men*~, (met.) to slip in, infiltrate; to interpose a remark, to 'put in'; *hilang* ~ *gigi pun tidak*, a skimpy meal (not filling the gaps between teeth).

celak [KN], antimony-powder (used to darken the fringe of the eye); kohl, eye-black; *ber*~, using mascara; *men*~, put on or apply mascara.

celaka [KS], ill-starred, ill-omened, bringing bad luck; a term of abuse; *orang* ~, a scoundrel; *yang terlalu besar* ~ *ku lihat*, the greatest infamy of all that I saw; *yang* ~, the damned (as opposed to *yang berbahagia*, the blessed); *dia ditimpa ke~an*, he was involved in an accident.

celana [KN], trousers (loose above but tight round the calf); ~ *dalam*, drawers, briefs, panties; ~ *paip*, jeans.

celapak [KKTR], astride, sitting on the fork, sitting astride; *jatuhlah ter*~ *pada belakang ikan alu-alu*, he fell astride on a barracuda's back; also **celepak**.

celari [KN], *kain* ~, a thin fabric of shining silk with gold thread.

celaru [KS], Ked. disorderly confused.

celatu [KN], the flying ant; better **kelekatu**.

cele [KN], *kain* ~, a cloth fabric imported from Southern India.

celedang [KS], ~*-celeduk*, a swaggering, rolling gait (affected by abandoned women).

celempong [KN], a musical instrument, a set of gongs.

celeng [KN], 1. Jav. a pig; = **babi**, ~ *alas*, a wild pig, = **babi hutan**. 2. a money-box made of a bit of bamboo closed by its nodes, the money being dropped in through a slit in one node.

celiguri [KN], a shrub (*Clerodendron dis-*

parifolium); also **seliguri**.

celih [KS], idle, lazy, sluggish.

celik [KK], lifting the eyelid, seeing; *si buta baharu* ~, a blind man who sees for the first time (a beggar on horseback), prov.; *hujan tak boleh* ~ *mata*, raining 'cats and dogs'.

celepik [KN], (onom.) the sound made by mud bespattering a surface.

celepuk [KN], (onom.) the sound of a heavy mass of mud falling on anything.

celici [KS], covetous, mean.

celingkang [KS], ~-*celingkuk*, curved and bent this way and that.

celipa [KS], a round (Pk.) or octagonal (N.S.) watchlike box for tobacco, suspended by chain from belt or kerchief.

celipak [KKTR], sitting astride; = **celapak**.

celis [KK], chopping into small pieces.

celoteh [KK], *ber*~, to chatter, blather, talk idly or aimlessly.

celuk [KK], to cheat by small tricks (e.g. by giving short weight); to sneak, pinch.

celum [KN], (onom), ~-*celam*, sound of walking through marshy ground with squelchy noises; ~-*belam,* sound of noisy tramping.

celung [KN], a stall for an elephant or buffalo.

celup, [KK], steeping in, dyeing; *di*~ *merah,* dyed red; ~*kan*, to dip, to dye; *air* ~, *pen*~, a dye; *pen*~ *tak lekat,* the dye won't take.

celupar [KS], garrulous — cf. **cupar**.

celur [KK], *mencelur,* immerse in boiling liquid, scalding, e.g., fowl to remove their feathers; *ter*~, scorched, scalded.

celus [KS], slipping on and off readily (of a ring); easily passed through, as a gap; ~-*celas*, passing in and out freely, as person on intimate terms with a household; *celum-celam* id.

cemak [KS, KN], Treng. many, much; ~ *mana*, how many?

cemamai [KS], *ber*~, tattered and torn; in a hopeless state of disrepair and disorder.

cemar [KS], pollution, dirt; *ber*~ *kaki,* to deign to proceed (honorific, of a Ruler's progress); sometimes used, esp. sarcasticaly, in the meaning, to deign, lower oneself to a course of action, condescend; *men*~*kan kaki,* id.; *men*~*kan nama,* to defame; *men*~*kan nama keluarga,* to bring disgrace to his family, to besmirch your family's name.

cemara [KN], Skr. a pendant of horsehair (under the blade of a spear); yak-tail; a chignon; a wig; a fly-whisk; *kayu* ~, a name sometimes given to the casuarina.

cemas [KS], anxious, nervous; *janganlah* ~, don't be nervous; *masa ke*~*an,* crisis, danger; *pertolongan* ~, first-aid; *menaruh* ~, to feel apprehension; *men*~*kan,* disturbing; *insiden yang men*~*kan,* a worrisome incident; ~ is sometimes used in the sense of almost, of narrow escapes; ~ *kena peluru,* almost hit by a bullet; cf. **nyaris**.

cemat [KK], 1. fastening together with a pin or spike; fastening ataps. 2. to wrap in, to kedge. 3. N.S. to beat, whip.

cembang = **kembang**.

cembul [KN], 1. a casket; a small box, us. of metal; a knob; *laksana* ~ *dengan tutupnya,* like a casket and its cover (exactly suited one to another), prov.; *si Cembul,* appellation of a very short person, 'Shorty'. 2. *men*~, to be aghast, flabbergasted.

cembung [KS], rounded, convex; *lensa* ~, a convex lens.

cemburu [KS], suspicious, jealous; *kekasih yang* ~, a jealous lover.

cemer [KS], extremely dim-sighted, nearly blind; *men*~*kan mata,* to shut one's eyes, esp. of deliberately ignoring something; *cemeh* id.

cemerkap [KS], rough, careless, of work; rash, thoughtless, of action.

cemerlang [KS], glittering, radiant, splendid, excellent; *lulus ujian dengan* ~, passed the test with flying colours, passed with distinction.

cementi [KN], Tam. a whip.

cemik [KK], *men*~, to show disgust, make a wry face, sneer.

cemingkian [KN], a fruit (used medicinally as an laxative).

cempaka [KN], Skr. the champak tree (*Michelia champaca*); ~ *biru,* the frangipanni (*Plumiera acutifolia*); ~ *tanjung,* the gardenia.

cempedak [KN], a jack-fruit (*Artocarpus polyphema*); *a. air,* a tree (*Artocarpus Maingayi*).

cempelik [KN], pitch and toss.

cempelung [KN], (onom.), the sound of a heavy body falling 'plump' into water.

cemperai [KN], a generic name given to a number of sea-shore shrubs, notably *Champereia Griffithii* and *Cansjera Rheedii*.

cemperling [KN], the tree-starling (*Calornis chalybeius*); *mata* ~, very red eyes; also **perling**.

cempiang [KN], Ch. a gang-robbery.

cemping [KN], *se*~, a very small bit, a morsel.

cempira [KK], *ber*~, broken, scattered, as a crowd by rain or by police; *men*~*kan,* to break up, cause to scatter (abruptly).

cempua [KN], Ch. an abacus = **sipuak**; *pukul* ~, to reckon with an abacus.

cemuas [KS], dirty of the face (after a meal); greasy, also **jemuas**.

cemucup [KN], love-grass; burrs.

cemuh [KK], Ind. ~*an,* taunts; *men*~, to taunt, to sneer at; *men*~ *pendapat orang lain,* to scoff at other people's ideas.

cemuk [KK], *men*~, 1. to prod. 2. Ked. to quarrel. 3. to shake to-and-fro, to brandish, boat, strike.

cempung [KK], *men*~, carrying between both arms (as a bale of firewood is carried).

cemus [KS], sick of, sated with — stronger than **jemu**.

cena [KN], old and hardened (of a fighting-cock); *muda* ~, arrived at puberty.

cenangau [KN], a malodorous flying bug very destructive to padi, = **pianggang**.

cenangga [KN], Skr. a birth-mark, a congenital deformity.

cenangkas [KN], a heavy cutlass.

cenayang [KN], the medium or interpreter at a *berhantu,* seance (Kedah).

cencala [KN], a Kedah name for the fantail fly-catcher *(Cipadura* sp.); elsewhere *murai gila.*

cencaluk [KN], a relish made of small prawns; a derisive nickname for locally-born persons of mixed blood.

cencang [KK], *men*~, slashing hacking, as with a cutlass. (This appears to be a different word from *cincang.*)

cencaru [KN], a horse-mackerel (*Caranx boops*); also *jaru-jaru;* ~ *makan petang,* the ~ feeds in the evening, met. for work that is slow but sure.

cencawan [KN], the socket of the knee; *minyak* ~, the oily matter in the patella.

cenceng [KK], *men*~, running as hard as one can, tearing away — cf. **kengkeng**.

cencudak [KN], the Kedah and Penang name for the fish *(Belone strongylura);* elsewhere **todak.**

cencurut [KN], the musk-rat = **tikus turi**.

cendala [KN], Skr. hariot, profligate, immodest.

cendana [KN], Skr. sandalwood (*Santalum album*); *air* ~, water scented with sandalwood, used at interments; *sudah gaharu* ~ *pula,* we have had eagle-wood and now comes sandalwood, a saying implying, by sound-suggestion, *sudah tahu bertanya pula,* i.e., I have told you, don't keep questioning me.

cendawan [KN], a generic name for fungi (mostly *Agarici*); a mushroom; *mabuk* ~, poisoned by fungi; (by metaphor) love-sick — of a woman; *merecup bak* ~, to spring up like mushrooms.

cendekia [KS], fraud, deceit; also Ind. Intelligence, acuteness, intellect; *wan,* an intellectual; also *candakia.*

cendekel [KS], tricky, slippery, mean.

cendera [KN], 1. Skr. a race of fairies. 2. deep (of sleep); = **nyedar**; ~ *mata,* souvenir.

cenderai [KN], a generic name given to several plants, viz., one croton (*c. argyratus*) and three *Grewia.*

cenderamulia [KN], Skr. a tree bearing an edible fruit (unidentified).

cenderawasih [KN], the bird of paradise; used loosely for many birds known only by their bright plumage; also (fig.) for a lovely woman.

cenderus [KK], (Penang), removing rancidity from oil.

cendol [KN], a kind of thin broth with cakes of dough floating in it.

cenduai [KN], *minyak ~*, oil made from a flower and used for enticing women by magic art; also **cenuai**.

cendurung [KS], declivitous; of a track down to a river; also *cenurung, cenderung, chenerung; ~ pada,* inclined towards, having a sympathy with; *~ mengikut jejak orang tuanya,* an inclination to follow in his parent's footsteps.

cengal [KN], the name of a tree (*Balanocarpus maximus*); Ked., Pk. *cengai* = Pah., N.S. *penak.*

cengang [KK], *tercengang,* bewildered with surprise; *~-bengang,* thunderstruck.

cengeng [KS], whining continually (of young children).

cenggek [KK], *ber~,* to perch; = **bertenggek**.

cengil [KS], cantankerous, harsh and sharp.

cengis [KN], stinking, as a strong scent, rotten fruit.

cengkadak [KN], Pk. the praying mantis.

cengkam [KN], gripping between finger and thumb; *~ penjajahan,* the grip of imperialists.

cengkang [KS], 1. wakeful, sleepless. 2. wooden bar (to fasten the door) — cf. **sengkang**.

cengkaruk [KN], a sweetmeat made of boiled rice.

cengkau [KN], broker, middleman; *men~* [KK], grab, seize with the hand or claws.

cengkeh [KS], walking on the side of one's foot; unevenly balanced, of gait or posture.

cengkera [KS], hollow-eyed, sleepless-looking.

cengkeram [KN], earnest money, an advance.

cengkerik [KN], a cricket; *beradu ~,* to make crickets fight.

cengkering [KN], an abscess.

cengkerama [KN], Skr. moving over an area; spreading as news; wandering; promenading; *ber~,* (fig.) to play round and have a fine time; also *cengkerma.*

cengki [KS], Ch. a run of luck, good luck.

cengkih [KN], the clove-spice (*Eugenia caryophilla*); *buah ~,* a clove.

cengkik [KS], thinner at the centre than at the extremities (as a post); shaped like an hour-glass.

cengkok [KS], 1. twisted; bent at the end, like a hockey-stick; *~ beledok,* zigzag. 2. a leaf-monkey (*Semnopithecus pruinosus*).

cengkolong [KK], *mencengkolong,* withdrawing a small amount from a large, drawing on a deposit; also *cengkelong,* reduce, decrease.

cengkuas [KS], 1. shaggy, unkempt. 2. to carry on a stick over the shoulder; to make off with.

cengkol [KS], twisted, deformed, of the arms, or, e.g., the tail.

cengkung [KS], sunken (of the eyes or cheeks); *~-mengkung,* haggard and drawn.

cengkurai [KN], 1. (? from Skr. *kurai*) a silk fabric. 2. *berengkurai,* crumbling to fragments, breaking up into pieces.

cengung [KK], *ter~,* gazing in open-mouthed astonishment — cf. **cengang**.

cenok [KN], *burung ~,* a malkoha (*Pamphococcyx erythrognathus* or *Rhopodytes symatranus*); *burung ~ menyebut diri,* the malkoha repeats its own name, a sneer at someone who 'blows his own trumpet'.

cenuk [KN], *minyak ~,* a vegetable oil obtained from the tree *Diplocnemia sebifera*; also *minyak kawang.*

cenung [KK], *ter~,* to look fixedly at anything, contemplative.

cenunut [KN], *~ ayam,* 'parson's nose' in fowl; *tulang ~,* the coccyx.

centung [KN], 1. a ladle (of bamboo with a

handle rising vertically up from it); used locally as a measure: 4 *centung* = 1 *cupak*. 2. an erectile tuft of feathers on a bird's head, an erectile crest.

cepak-cepak [KN], lapping noises; *minum ~-~*, to drink noisily.

cepak-pong [KN], (onom), the sound of a band.

cepat [KS], speedy, quick rapid; *~ kiri*, left-handed; *se~ kilat*, as quick as lightning; *seberapa ~*, as quickly as possible; (*berjalan*) *sama ~ dengan*, to keep up with, not lag behind; *~kan jam*, to put the clock forward; *~-ligas*, agile; *ke~an yang betul*, correct speed (for camera); *siapa ~ dia dapat*, first come, first served; *lebih ~ daripada yang dijadualkan*, ahead of schedule.

cepiau [KN], Port. a hat; *~ lipat*, a cocked hat.

cepih [KS], soft and pendent (of buffalo horns or of a broken arm).

cepir [KN], a metal saucer or plate on which a bowl (*batil*) rests; a small metal tray, e.g. a card-tray.

cepit [KK], to nip, as tongs; a spring clip; a variant of sepit; *ter~*, nipped; (fig.) in a fix.

cepu [KN], a flat round box of wood (used as a receptacle for toilet requisites) or of metal, for betel; *~-~*, the trunk of the mast; *puting ~-~*, the foot of the mast; *~* (Kel. Treng.) is used for a 'travelling-case' for clothes; *~ debunga*, anther; *cepu* is used locally for the box in which fishermen take their food when they go to sea.

cepua [KS], a blush of shame, a guilty look.

cepuh [KK], *men~*, to dip s.t. in hot liquid.

cerabah [KS], grubby, untidy; also **cerebih**.

ceracak [KN], sticking up in points; bristling; *men~*, to bristle with spikes; cf. **cerancang**.

ceracap [KN], Malay castanets (bamboos beaten against each other.)

cerah [KS], light (as opposed to dark), daylight; *cuaca ~*, clear daylight; *~ is* also used of 'bright' colours; and for a 'clear' skin; sometimes used to mean transparent.

cerai [KK], severance, separation, divorce; *ber~*, to separate from, to be divorced from; to part in two, as giving passage, of a crowd; *ber~ mati*, to be divorced by death, to be a widow or widower; *~ susu*, weaned, *~ sendi*, dislocated; *~kan*, to separate (one person from another); *~-berai*, broken up, scattered (of a defeated army); *~an*, section, paragraph; separation, divorce; *per~an*, a divorce; *ber~ hidup*, to be divorced by a living spouse.

cerakin [KN], 1. a sort of Malay medicine chest. 2. analyse, *~an statistik*, statistical analysis.

ceramah [KN], talkative; a talk or discussion, esp. on the radio; *menyampaikan ~* to give a talk; *pen~*, lecturer.

cerana [KN], Skr. a salver on which are placed the various vessels used for holding the requisites for betel-chewing; *menyorongkan ~*, to pass round this salver to allow guests to help themselves; *menerima ~*, to receive a tray, i.e. (fig.) to receive a marriage-proposal, cf. **pinang**.

cerang [KN], an abandoned and partly overgrown clearing in the jungle; *~ rimba*, id.

ceranggah [KK], *ber~*, branching into points; *rusa ber~*, a deer of many tines; *ber~-ceranggih*, bristling unevenly, as teeth.

cerap [KS], Kel. to take note of, be cognisant of; *tak ~*, I do not know (in courtly language).

cerat [KN], a plug-hole.

ceratuk [KK], *ber~*, squatting, perched in a row (as birds on a telegraph wire), sit together.

cerca [KN], Skr. abuse, insult, reviling; *kena ~*, to be reviled.

cercak [KN], 1. slightly pockmarked—cf. **cecak**. 2. = **cerca**.

cerdas [KS], 1. intelligent, smart; *darjah ke~an*, intelligence quotient (I.Q.), *angka* *ke~an,* id. 2. a buffalo-whip.

cerdik [KS], cunning, sharp-witted; bright, intelligent; *mendatangkan ~,* to sharpen the wits; orang *~-pandai,* the intelligentsia; *ker~an,* shrewdness; *ke~an pencuri itu,* the thief's cunningness.

cerek [KN], a kettle; a vessel for boiling water.

cerewet [KS], fussy, annoyances, petty difficulties; tiresome, of work; *orang banyak ~,* fussy, hard to please; *burung ~,* the Burmese wattled lapwing; also *burung duit-duit; jangan ~,* don't be fussy, stop complaining.

cergas [KS], reliable (of work), energetic, capable; active competent.

ceri [KN], Hind. *gelang ~,* a bangle.

ceri [KN], a gong, the sides of which slope inwards.

ceria [KS], Skr. clear, pure, fidelity; *men~kan,* clean, purify, cleanse; *men~,* rear, faster (*memelihara, mendidik*). 2. cleared, brightened (of the countenance).

ceridau [KN], cries, shouts in unison, vocal music, chorus singing.

ceriga [KS], 1. being on one's guard, wary, watchful; *mencerigai,* to be suspicious of, suspect; also **curiga**. 2. a type of short sword.

cering [KS], dry (of skin), goose-flesh.

cerita [KN], 1. Skr. story, a narrative; *~ zaman dahulu,* a tale of old times; to narrate, recount; *~ bersambung,* serial story; *~ dongeng,* fiction; *~ benar,* a true story; *~ pentas,* stage play; *~ warisan,* traditional story; *~ sebelum tidur,* bed-time story; *men~kan satu jenaka,* to tell a joke or funny story. 2. (onom.), *ber~,* to twitter (of the magpie robin).

cerlang [KN], 1. shining, resplendent — cf. **cemerlang.** 2. *men~kan biji mata kepada,* to glare at (so as to alarm) with rolling eyes.

cermai [KN], a tree (*Phyllanthus distictous*); it yields a small round acid fruit.

cermat [KS], 1. careful, cautious; *berfikir dengan ~,* to think carefully; care; neat, neatness in appearance or dress; *~ dan*

bersih, spick and span. 2. *menjimatkan,* to be thrifty, economical; *menjimatkan wang belanja,* to take care in the use of money.

cermin [KN], a mirror; *~ mata,* the pupil of the eye; an eye-glass, spectacles; *~ teropong,* the lens of a telescope; *~ lekat* (*khas*), spectacles with contact lenses; *~ solek,* mirror for dressing-table; *men~kan,* to reflect, throw back (light); *men~kan keperibadiannya,* to reflect his personality.

cerna [KK], Ind. *men~kan,* to digest.

ceroboh [KS], rough, rude, coarse, violent, vulgar; *men~,* to act violently, esp. of high-handed trespass; encroach upon; *pen~an,* outrages, breaches (of a treaty), aggression; *men~i,* to violate, assault violently (esp. a woman).

cerobong [KN], a chimney, a funnel; a variant of *ceropong; ~ penyulingan minyak,* an oil-distillation column.

ceropong [KN], *cerompong* id., a chimney, a funnel.

cerpelai [KN], Tam. the imported Indian mongoose.

cerpen [KN], = *cerita pendek,* a short story.

cerpu [KN], Tam. sandals, clogs; *bawah ~,* position beneath the sandals (of a prince), the position of a subject — cf. **kaus** and **duli**; *menjunjung ~,* to acknowledge the rule of a prince.

cerucup [KN], burrs, love-grass.

ceruh [KS], a second pounding of rice (to whiten it).

ceruk [KN], 1. a corner; an out-of-the-way part of the room where things are placed that one does not need; the space under a wardrobe or between it and the wall; a hidden nook; a niche; *~ gunung,* a glen; *merata ~ rantau,* every nook and corner of the country. 2. a bamboo funnel used in milking.

cerul [KS], friable, loose on top, as sand (if deep, *gembur*).

cerun [KN], sloping, a slope.

cerup [KN], to lap up water; the sound of lapping water.

cerut [KK], *men~,* to compress on all sides,

as a tight belt or as a python constricting to crush its prey; *ber~*, closely fitting, clinging; to get tight; *cerutan*, close-fitting; *men~kan*, to tighten, as belt. 2. cheroot; also *cerutu*. 3. Kel., Treng. a sickle; *men~*, to cut (grass) with a sickle.

cerutu [KN], Tam. a cheroot.

cetai [KS], *ber~-~*, tattered; *men~-~*, picking to pieces.

cetak [KK], *men~*, to print, the work of a compositor; Pen. a cake-mould; *~an* [KN] edition; *pen~*, a printer; *~an ulangan*, a reprint.

cetek [KS], shallow; *ilmunya ~*, his learning was shallow.

cetera [KN], 1. Skr. *payung ~*, an umbrella with a hanging fringe. 2. Skr. a story; = **cerita**.

ceteri [KN], Hind, tent, awning, canopy.

ceteria [KN], Skr. a kshatriya; a member of the princely or warrior caste; ceti [KN], Tam. a chettiar; a money-lender.

cetrawara [KN], Ind. a play, esp. a 'straight' play without musical interludes; one-act play.

cetuk = **catuk**.

cetus [KN], (onom.), *~ api*, to strike a light; and so, (met.) to precipitate, set off (as a crisis); *men~kan rusuhan*, to incite a riot; *~an*, an explosion, a blast; *men~*, to explode; (fig.) to break out (into a rage).

cewe [KN], Treng., Pah., Pat., Kel., a *pawang* — name for four-footed animals and snakes, esp. at sea; *~ menggaum*, a tiger; *~ deras*, a horse.

ci [KN], Ch. a measure of weight used in weighing opium; a tenth of a tael.

ciak [KN], a sparrow; a finch; *~ raya*, Kel. the weaver-bird.

ciar [KK], *men~-~*, *ter~-~*, crying continually (of a child).

ciau [KK], *men~*, 1. Pen. *ter~*, disarranged (of dress). 2. a long oar (worked standing).

cicah [KK], = **cecah**.

cicak [KN], a lizard; *~ rebeng*, the flying lizard; *~ kubin*, id.; the lizard is used as

a simile for extreme thinness; *kurus kering macam ~ di-salai*, as skinny as a dried-up lizard.

cicik [KS], Pen. feeling a strong aversion to, looking upon with disgust.

cicir [KK], dropping away in driblets; *ber~an*, dribbling away, leaking, as rice from a cut sack or (fig.) as money pilfered; *sengaja ~kan permainan*, to 'throw' a game deliberately, lose on purpose.

cicit [KN], 1. great-grandchild. 2. *men~*, to cheep, to twitter; to squeak, screech, as brakes.

cik [KN], 1. = **kecik**; used esp. with the meaning of 'minor': *mak ~*, the younger of two aunts or a maternal aunt, as opposed to a paternal aunt. 2. 'Mr.—', 'Mrs.—' or 'Miss—', a title given to otherwise untitled Malays; a variant of *ence* or *encik*, which are more formal.

cika [KN], colic; also the something in shellfish causing colic (e.g., *~ kerang, ~ tiram*).

ciku [KN], the sapodilla.

cili [KN], cilli, red pepper; *~ padi, ~ burung*, small varieties of chillies; *kecil-kecil ~ padi* (idiom), small but courageous.

cilik [KS], Jav. small.

Cina [KN], Chinese; *orang ~*, a Chinese; *negeri ~* or *benua ~*, China; *~ buta*, the *muhallil* or intermediate husband necessary to make the remarriage of divorced persons legal; *main ~ buta*, blind man's bluff; *lada ~*, capsicum *(Piper caba)*, also called **cabai**; *bunga ~*, a name given to gardenias and sometimes to cultivated varieties of the Ixora.

cincang [KK], = **cencang**, to mince; *~ lumat-lumat*, to mince finely.

cincau [KN],Ch. a cold sweet jelly.

cincin [KN], a finger-ring; *~ tanda*, a keepsake ring; an engagement ring; *~ tanda pertunangan*, an engagement ring; *~ cap*, signet ring.

cincu [KN], Ch. the owner's agent on a ship.

cinda [KN], great-grandson; a polite variant of **cicit**.

cindai [KN], (? = from Sind) *kain* ~, a silk fabric made by the tie-and-dye process; reticulated, having a net-work pattern.

cingam [KN], a sea-shore plant *(Scyphiphora hydrophyllacia)*.

cingge [KN], *Chingay*, a type of Chinese procession with colourful attire during Chinese festival.

cinta [KN], Skr. loving desire; regret, longing; *ber~*, to be in love; *ber~kan*, to pine for; ~ is the word generally used for 'romantic love', and sometimes for 'sweetheart'; *per~an*, longing, 'wild regret', love; *buku per~an*, a novel about love; ~ *berahi*, passionate love; *pantai ~ berahi*, the Beach of Passionate Love; *jatuh* ~, to fall in love, *teman ter~*, a dear friend.

cintamani [KN], Skr. (the Hindu philosopher's stone), a fabulous gold-yellow snake the finding of which betokens good fortune in love; *ular ~ gajah*, a name given to light forms of the viper *(Lachesis wagleri)*.

cipai [KN], a monkey *(Semnopithecus melalophos)*.

cipan [KN], 1. a battle-axe. 2. Pk. a tapir.

cipta [KK], *men~*, to found, create, bring into being; to compose, construct (e.g., music, a story); *daya* ~, creative; *~an*, a creation, work; *pen~ fesyen*, dress-designer.

ciri [KN], Skr. the coronation formula used in certain Malay States; a distinguishing mark, characteristic sign; *mengenali ~~~*, to identify the characteristics.

cirit [KN], diarrhoea; ~ *birit*, running continuously.

cis [Kseru], exclamation showing feeling of anger, hate — stronger than *cih*.

cita [KN], Skr. feeling, emotion, yearning, aspiration; *suka~*, joy; *duka~*, sorrow; *men~*, to fix one's thoughts upon a talisman in order to get its magical aid, to call into existence by will-power; *men~kan*, to fix one's heart on, wish for; *ber~-~ tinggi*, ambitious; *untuk*

mencapai *~-~anya*, to achieve one's aspirations. 2. Port. *kain* ~, chintz, printed cotton cloth.

ciu [KN], 1. a state cushion, a mat for a royal divan. 2. Ch. spirituous liquor.

cium [KK], *men~*, to smell; to kiss (in the Malay way); id.; *pen~*, the sense of smell; *~kan ... ke hidung*, to apply (e.g., a bottle to be sniffed) to the nostrils.

ciup [KN], ~ *tembolok*, a bladder made by blowing out of a fowl's crop.

cuba [KK], *men~*, attempting, trying, testing, 'please', 'just'; ~ *tanya guru*, please ask the teacher; *~i*, to hold a test; *~kan*, to put to the test; *pen~, pen~an*, a trial or test; *kebun per~an*, experimental plantation; *~an berat*, an ordeal; *per~an membunuh*, an assassination attempt.

cobak [KS], *~-cabik*, tattered or torn at the edge; frayed.

cobar [KS], tattered, torn; ~ *cabir*, much torn.

cobek [KN], saucer like utensils used for crushing spices and chillies; a bit, a little, a pinch.

codak [KK], *men~*, to hold the head aloft (as a swimming snake); *men~kan kepala*, to raise the head (as a snake or as an awakened sleeper).

coek [KN], a soup-plate or bowl of Chinese make.

cogan [KN], Pers. an ensign — better **jogan**; a portent in the heavens; a standard; Pah. a trowel-shaped royal spear; ~ *kata*, a motto, slogan.

cok [KN], E.C. a spade, shovel.

coakar [KN], a game resembling draughts.

cokelat [KN], Eng. chocolate (the sweet and the colour).

cokin [KN], a bathing-cloth (used by Chinese labourers).

cokmar [KN], Pers. a mace.

cokok [KK], *men~*, 1. the cry of a *latah* subject when excited. 2. Kel. pensive, absent-minded; *duduk ter~*, to sit with one's mind a blank. 3. *pak pen~*, a swindler, so, a traitor, fifth columnist.

cokol [KK], *ber~*, to squat; (fig.) to 'stay put', refuse to move, as trespasser.

colak [KS], ~-*caling,* confused, entangled.

colang [KS], ~-*caling,* confused, entangled; not keeping time, out of step; disorganised, 'at sixes and sevens'.

colek [KK], *men~,* 1. prizing out with a point; digging out with a pin; to scrape out with a pointed instrument; *pen~ api,* a lucifer match; *men~ hati,* to 'tickle', cause to laugh. 2. Ind. to kidnap, abduct; to hijack.

coli [KN], Hind. a tight-fitting bodice worn next to the skin by Indian women; ~ *dada,* a brassiere.

colok [KN], 1. match for a fuse; a wick; a primitive oil-lamp; joss-sticks. 2. = **jolok.**

combol [KN], the knob on a door.

comek [KN], small cuttle-fish — cf. **sotong.**

comel [KS], 1. dainty, pretty. 2. babbling, unable to hold one's tongue; muttered grumbles.

comot [KS], defiled with dirt.

compang [KS], ~-*camping,* torn, tattered at the edge, frayed.

compes [KS], chipped at the edge (plate, saucer).

cenderung [KS], inclining, leaning; ~ *hati,* mental leanings, inclinations; ~ *kepada,* having an inclination towards, biased towards; also **condong.**

condong [KS], leaning to one side, out of the perpendicular; ~-*hati,* personal inclination; ~ *ke-perut,* greedy (esp. of a grasping official); ~ *mondong,* leaning this way and that, as trees in a wood, stakes; ~-*kepada* = *cenderung kepada.*

conek [KN], a boy's penis; probably a variant of **conet.**

conet [KS], a slight upward projection of the tip of anything, e.g. a moustache; tip-tilted; also **cotet.**

cong [KN], N.S. a river-pool, water-hole.

congak [KS], turned upwards (of the face); holding his head up (of a buffalo sniffing when alarmed); pointing up (of the beak of a bird); *men~,* to work out mentally, e.g., a sum; *kira dengan ~,* to do mental arithmetic; ~-*cangit,* restless up-and-down movement of the head.

conggang [KS], ~-*congget,* bobbing up and down (as a sand-piper picking up food, or as a man climbing a difficult hill).

congkah [KS], jagged, uneven, in disarray, sticking-out unevenly; *men~,* to break up, break into pieces (as a hard surface); ~-*mangkih,* sticking out in an irregular way, e.g., of bundled sticks; not aligned; of buildings.

congkak [KN], 1. a generic name for cowrie shells *(Cyproea); main ~,* a game played with these shells; *papan ~,* the board used for playing this game. 2. proud, haughty.

congkang [KS], ~ *kelalak,* topsy-turvy', 'at sixes and sevens'.

congkar [KS], *ter~,* sticking out, protruding; ~-*cangkir,* sticking out here and there untidily, as bundled sticks.

congkeng [KS], sticking out in all directions (as the points of a caltrop).

congok [KS], *men~, duduk ter~,* to squat (esp. in the sense of just sitting or standing erect without helping).

congsam [KN], Ch. one-piece Chinese woman's dress with high neck and us. slit to the thigh.

conteng [KK], *men~,* smearing (anything) on a surface; *muka ter arang,* a face smeared over with charcoal; (fig.) disgraced.

contoh [KN], a model of an object to be copied, a sample, a specimen, *men~i,* to take as an example, model oneself on; ~ *tingkah laku yang baik,* an examplary conduct.

copet [KK], *men~,* Ind. to pilfer, 'pinch', esp. of pick-pockets.

corak [KN], the general colouring (of a cloth), the prevailing hue in a design, pattern; *saya tak suka ~ dia.,* (fig.) I don't like the cut of his jib; *bendera ~ tiga,* a tricolour flag; *radio ber~ perniagaan,* commercial radio; *radio ber~ kebangsaan,* national ratio; ~ *dunia,* the way of the world; ~ *fikiran,* mental attitude.

corat-coret [KN], Ind. outlines, sketches, notes.

corek [KN], the long linear markings in the grain of certain woods.

coreng [KN], streaked with long vertical streaks (as a man on whom paint has fallen); *~-moreng,* covered with streaks.

coret [KK], *men~,* Ind. to sketch, depict in outline, make notes of.

corong [KN], 1. a metal vase for *sirih* leaves, = **jorong**. 2. a cylindrical funnel, the chimney of a lamp; *~ radio,* a radio microphone; *~ pentis,* dropping-funnel.

corot [KS], 1. bringing up the rear; *pen~,* the hindmost, last, as in a race; 2. *men~,* to spout, gush out; (vulg.) to pass water; (met.) to declaim, 'spout', of an orator.

cotet [KN], *se~,* a very small portion; a pinch; a bite.

cotok [KN], 1. a small fleshy protuberance at the base of a bird's beak. 2. projecting above the surface (of a low flat rock).

cua [KS], not pleasing, unsatisfactory.

cuaca [KN], Skr. clear (of the atmosphere); *terang ~,* bright daylight; sometimes, weather, generally *pangkalan menyukat ~,* Weather Bureau; *carta ~,* weather chart (map); *ramalan ~,* weather forecast; *laporan ~,* weather report; *penerbangan peninjauan ~,* weather reconaissance flight; *tahan ~,* weather resistant.

cuai [KS], to hold in little esteem, make light of; to act carelessly; *men~kan,* to neglect; *secara ~,* negligently.

cuak [KS], Pen., Pk. nervous (as a player before a match).

cuat [KS], *men~,* sticking up, rising high.

cubit [KK], *men~,* pinching, pressing between finger and thumb; *se~,* a pinch.

cuca [KK], abasing or silencing one's foe (especially by magic arts); so, soothing a person, calming him down.

cuci [KK], *men~,* cleansing; *ber~,* to clean, to cleanse; *~an,* laundry; *ketam ~,* a

plane; *~* is used for 'developing' a film and (sl.) for to circumcise; *~ lantai,* to clean the floor, a ceremony supposed to be performed after a birth; *~ muka,* to clean the face; often used of shaving rather than washing.

cucu [KN], grandchild; *anak ~,* descendants; *~ cicit,* id.

cucuh [KK], setting anything alight; putting fire to anything.

cucuk [KK], *men~,* 1. piercing; driving a point into something; threading a needle; piercing with a needle; perforating; injecting (medicinally); *manik tanggal daripada ~nya,* pearls fallen from their strings, *~ kajang,* making *kajang* mats by running a piece of bamboo through pandanus leaves to hold them together; *rambut ~ senjata,* the leader of a charge; *ber~~,* in strings; *men~,* to pierce, to perforate; *~ tanam,* agriculture; *~ hidung,* to 'lead by the nose'; *men~~,* to 'pinprick', annoy with remarks, harass in a petty manner; *men~~ sakitnya,* to have 'stabbing' pains; *se~ ikan,* a string of fish; *surat ~,* vaccination certificate. 2. Ind. agreeable, suitable; *se~ dengan,* in conformity with.

cucunda [KN], grandchild — a respectful form of **cucu**.

cucur [KN], 1. trickling, flowing in small quantities; to 'make up' an amount, Ked.; *~an atap,* the edge of a roof; *~i,* to let water fall or drip on anything, to anoint; in Kel. *~* is used for 'change' (balance due); *men~kan,* to sprinkle; *men~kan air mata,* tears well up in one's eyes. 2. a generic name given to cakes of hard-baked pastry.

cucut [KN], Jav. the shark.

cuit [KK], *men~,* a playful tap or blow with the finger; a movement of the finger hinting 'go away'; a slight nudge; the wagging of a bird's tail; *ber~-gamit,* to gesticulate; to fiddle and meddle.

cuka [KN], Hind. vinegar; *makan ~,* (fig.) to get a dressing-down; *~ di-minum pagi ini,* he has drunk some vinegar this morning, i.e. has 'got out of bed the wrong side', is in a bad mood; ~ *getah*, acid used to coagulate rubber (acetic acid).

cukai [KN], Hind. toll tax, impost, duty; ~ *rumah*, rates on houses; ~ *kepala*, poll-tax; m*elarikan* ~, to avoid the payment of an impost; ~ *pendapatan*, income tax; *men*~, to tax; *dasar* ~, tax policy; *tahun* ~, tax year; *undang-undang* ~, tax law.

cuki [KN], a game resembling draughts.

cuku [KN], Tam., dried gambier-root.

cukup [KS], complete, sufficient; quite; fully; full; ~ *seratus hari*, a full hundred days; *sudah* ~, it is enough; *beranak belum* ~ *bulan*, premature birth; *ke*~*an sendiri*, self-sufficiency, esp. in food-supplies; ~ *makan*, enough to live on; ~ *pakai*, enough (e.g. materials) to go on with; ~ *umur*, come of age, to attain adulthood.

cukur [KK], shaving; *tukang* ~, a barber; *men*~, to shave (someone); *ber*~, to shave (one-self); shaven; *pisau pen*~ or *pisau penyukur* or *pisau* ~, a razor; *pisau* ~ is also used (sl.) for a tricky person, 'smoothie'.

cula [KN], Skr. the horn of a dragon; magical or supernatural horn; the penis of a squirrel (believed to be a powerful aphrodisiac).

culan [KN], *bunga* ~, a flower *(Aglaia odorate?)*.

culas [KS], 1. inert, sluggish, slow, idle—a stronger expression than *malas*. 2. Kel. shy (of game), = **cega**.

Culia [KN], a name given to a class of Muslim traders from the Malabar coast.

culim [KN], Hind. a pipeful of tobacco or opium.

cuma [KS], vain; useless; idle; gratuitous, gratis; ~-~, uselessly; *per*~, id.; *dengan per*~, free, without payment; *tendang per*, free kick.

cumbu [KN], coaxing; love-making, verbal endearments, ~*an*, loving words; *ber*~-~*an*, flirting, exchanging endearments; *dilarang ber*~~*an di de-* *pan khalayak ramai*, you're not supposed to caress in public.

cunam [KN], 1. long, delicate pincers for extracting wax from the ear, for working in precious metals, etc. 2. Hind. prepared lime used in the betel-quid.

cunda [KN], grandchild— a respectful equivalent of **cucu**.

cundang [KN], *ke*~ or *per*~, conquest; the position of the defeated relative to the victor —cf. **kundang**.

cungap [KS], ~-*cangip*, panting, short of breath; *men*~-~, panting, out of breath.

cungkang-cungkit [KS], jerking up and down.

cungkil [KK], *men*~, to extract with a pointed instrument (e.g. as a toothpick is used), gouging; *pen*~ *gigi*, a toothpick; *men*~-~, to make pointed remarks about, criticize.

cupak [KN], 1. a measure of capacity; a quarter of a *gantang*, or, approximately, the capacity of a half-coconut-shell; *seperti* ~ *hanyut*, like a floating ~-measure — a half-coconut shell (which rocks greatly when it floats) — a simile for loose swagger; ~ *gantang*, measures, generally; (fig.) local customs. 2. the bowl of a mortar or opium pipe or rice-pounder.

cupar [KS], garrulous — cf. **chelupar**; *men*~, to belittle, speak lightly of.

cuping [KN], the lobe (of the ear or nostril); ~ *telinga*, the lobe of the ear; *ter*~, projecting (as a stick out of a bundle).

cupil [KS], N.S. close to the edge; so, in a precarious position; *duduk* ~, sitting on the edge of a chair.

cupul [KS], not long enough (for the purpose in view); inadequate owing to shortness, e.g., of a bit of string or a sum of money.

cura [KS], jesting, joking, not taking seriously.

curah [KN], emptying out; ~*kan*, to pour out; *men*~-~, to pour, of rain; *men*~*kan isi hati*, to confide.

curai [KS] loose, severally, one at a time; [KK], to separate (of things sticking or mixed together).

curam [KS], sloping, precipitous; *lereng bukit yang ~,* a steep hill.

curang [KS], Ind. false, dishonest; *ke~an,* fraud, dirty trick; *berlaku ~,* to behave dishonestly; to be unfaithful, esp. of husband and wife.

curat [KN], gushing out (of liquid) in a thick stream.

curi [KK], Hind. theft, stealing; stealthy removal, stealth; *~-~,* stealthily, surreptitiously; *men~,* to steal; *men~-~,* to do something secretly; *pen~,* a thief; *ke~an,* theft; *barang ke~an,* stolen property; *~ masa,* to shirk on the job or to snatch a moment to do something, to 'make time', *men~ naik kapal,* to stow-away on a ship; *pen~ dalam*

selimut, a thief in the blanket, i.e. an inside job.

curiga [KS], = **ceriga**.

cus [KN], hush!, 'dry up'!

cutam [KN], a black-and-gold 'niello' ware made at Ligor, a black sulphide being fused into the hollows of the pattern on a silver vessel and the high relief gilded wholly or partly.

cutap [KN], a waist-buckle of shiny black material.

cuti [KK], Hind. leave of absence, vacation, holiday, furlough; *ber~,* to be on leave; *~ sakit,* sick leave; *~ bersalin,* maternity leave; *~ penggal,* school holidays (at the end of term); *per~an,* time spent on leave, period of holidays.

D

d.a. = *dengan alamat;* see **alamat**.

dabak [KKtr], *men~,* (approach) suddenly; *hujan men~,* a sudden downpour.

dabal [KN], pouch fixed to a belt for putting cartridges.

dabik [KK], to smack, as with flat of hand; *men~-~ dada,* to beat the breast.

dabung [KK], *men~,* to file the teeth.

dabus [KN], Ar. a broad round shaft of wood with a short spike set like a spearhead at its end; *main ~,* a quasi-religious dance in which the self-stabbings of devotees are imitated.

dacing [KN], a steel-yard of Chinese type; *anak ~, batu ~,* or *buah ~,* the weight on a steel-yard; *batang ~,* beam of scales; *lidah ~,* tongue marking weight; *menipu ~,* to give false weight, fake the scales.

dada [KN], chest; *tepuk ~,* to beat the breast; *berperang ber~,* to fight hand to hand; *buah ~,* the bust; *tulang papan ~,* the breast-bone; *membusungkan ~,* boastful, brag; *belah ~ melihat hati,* cleave my breast and look at my heart, (provb.) to speak the truth.

dadah [KN], a Malay medicine-box; medicines, drugs.

dadak [KS], 1. *cekik ke~,* violent vomiting (often invoked upon the head of a scoundrel); choking and vomiting. 2. *men~,* to act hurriedly, abruptly; *secara men~,* abruptly, violently, at a moment's notice.

dadar [KN], a thin pancake or omelet of Malay make.

dadih [KN], curds; *air ~,* whey; *men~,* to curdle.

dadu [KN], 1. Port. a die, dice; *main ~,* to play with dice. 2. roseate; *mega ~,* the roseate clouds. 3. *ber~,* to gossip. 4. *seri ~,* a variant of **soldadu** q.v.

daduk [KK], *men~,* to beg, to solicit alms.

dadung [KK], 1. Ked. crooning a child to sleep. 2. Joh. exposing for fermentation.

daerah [KN], Ar. circuit; district, outlying area; region, area, generally; *~ padat,* thickly populated area; *~ hukum,* area of sovereignty; *faham ke~an,* provincialism, narrow views; *bahasa ~,* dialects.

daftar [KN], Ar, a tabular list, a roll, a register; *~ istilah,* glossary of terms.

daga [KK], *men~, ~-dagi,* an act of insubordination, to rebel against authority.

dagang [KN], a stranger, a foreigner; *perahu ~,* a vessel from elsewhere, a trading ship; an, commercial products; *~ senteri,* a stranger student — a depreciatory description of himself often used by a writer; *~ piatu, ~ yang miskin* and *~ yang hina,* id.; *~ yang rawan* and *~ yang rayu,* id. (in love poetry); *per~an,* commerce; *siaran per~an,* commercial broadcasting; *ber~,* to travel in a foreign land; to go trading; *per~kan,* to commercialize; *per~an bebas,* free trade; *utusan ~,* trade envoy; *imbangan per~an,* trade balance; *pusat ~an,* trade centre, *persuruhjaya per~an,* trade commissioner.

daging [KN], flesh, meat; *~ ular sawa,* the flesh of the python; *~ kambing,* mutton; *~ babi,* pork; *~ lembu,* beef; *~ baru,* fresh meat; *~ darah* or *darah dan ~,* flesh and blood (close relationship or intimate friendship, such as 'blood-brotherhood'); *sudah menjadi darah ~ pada dia,* it has become flesh and blood to him, i.e. second nature.

dagu [KN], the human chin, the 'chin' or corner near the handle of certain Malay knives and choppers; *ber~,* to sit chin in hand (in despondency); *duduk bertopang ~,* id.

daguk [KN], *hantu* ~, clouds on the horizon of weird and changing form (believed by some Malays to be ghosts of murdered men).

dah [abbrv.], finished, done — a coll. abbreviation of **sudah**, q.v.

dahaga [KS], 1. thirst, thirsty; *lapar* ~, hunger and thirst; *menghapus* ~, to assuage one's thirst; *mati* ~, to die of thirst. 2. N.S. ~ *dahagi*, lese-majeste and insubordination.

dahagi [KS], 1. extreme covetousness. 2. difficult work; *men*~, to work under difficulties, toil, as when rowing upstream.

dahak [KN], phlegm, mucus (from the mouth); *ber*~, to clear the throat noisily.

daham [KN], (onom.); *ber*~, to hum and haw; to clear the throat; *ber*~ *nyanyi*, to hum a tune; also *dehem*.

dahan [KN], a minor bough or branch of a tree; *harimau* ~, a larger tiger-cat or small leopard *(Leopardus macrocedus)*.

dahi [KN], the brows, the region of the eyebrows; *sehari bulan* ~*nya*, her brow was as the new moon.

dahsyat [KS], Ar. dreadful, frightful, terrible; horrifying; *bencana alam yang* ~, a devastating natural disaster.

dahu [KN], *burung* ~, Kel. the adjutant bird.

dahulu [KKtr], before; *zaman* ~, past ages; *adat* ~ *kala*, customary law; ~ *daripada Masihi* D.M., B.C.; *ter*~, previously, already; in advance of due time; *sehari ter*~, a day early; *men*~*i*, to get ahead; *sudah* ~, has 'passed on', died; *ber*~-~*an*, pressing on, one trying to get in front of the other; *lebih* ~, well in advance, ahead of time; *pen*~*an*, an advance (as on a contract); a deposit; an introduction (as to a book); cf. **hulu**.

daif [KS], handicapped, disabled, weak, despised.

daing [KN], 1. dried fish; *minta darah pada* ~, to ask dry fish for blood (to get blood out of a stone), prov. 2. a Bugis. title of distinction.

Dajal [KN], Ar. Antichrist, the false Messiah; the word is sometimes used as equivalent to 'Father of Lies'; *membuat* ~, to play mischievous tricks; *orang dajal*, a scoundrel.

daka, dakah [KN], *tiang* ~, the wooden supports upon which rests the plank hiding away the body in a Malay grave.

dakap [KK], *men*~, embracing; *berdakan*-~*an*, exchanging embraces; *ber*~ *tangan*, to clasp the hands.

dakar [KS], perverse; obstinate in doing wrong; offensive arrogance; *ber*~-~, boasting, bragging.

dakhil [KS], Ar. inner, inward, intimate.

daki [KK], 1. dirt on the person; *membuang* ~, to clean, to wash. 2. *men*~, to ascend, climb up; *jalan men*~, a road going uphill; *pen*~ *gunung*, mountain climber.

daksina [KN], Skr. the south (poet).

daku [KN], a form taken in literature by the word *aku* after the words *akan* and *dengan*, and verbs ending in *kan*.

dakwa [KK], *men*~, accuse, bring charges, sue, make a legal claim against; ~*an*, [KN], accusation, a lawsuit; *ter*~, defendant, suspect.

dakwah [KK], *ber*~, to preach.

dakwat [KN], ink, *bekas* ~, an ink-stand.

dal [KN], Hind. split peas.

dalal [KN], Ar. a middleman; *potongan* ~, a middleman's commission.

dalam [KS], 1. interior, inside, in, while, during; *ke* ~, inward; *di* ~, inside, position in; *di* ~ *hati*, mentally, to oneself; *daerah pen*~*an*, the interior, hinterland; ~ *itu pun*, nevertheless, even so. 2. deep; *terlalu* ~ *air-nya;* its waters were very deep; ~*nya*, depth; *men*~*kan*, to deepen; *men*~*i*, to delve deeply into; *secara men*~, deeply, thoroughly. 3. Jav. princely dwelling, Court; *bahasa* ~, the language of the Court; *orang* ~, a man of the Court; ~ *banyak hal*, in may cases; ~ *ingatan*, in one's mind.

dalang [KN], the story-reciter (who also works the figures) at a Malay shadow-show; the author (in stories written for use in a shadow-show); *men*~*i*, mastermind; *siapa men~i rusuhan ini?* who's masterminding this riot?

dalih [KN], quibble, equivocation; *ber~*, to put forward an excuse; *sekarang apa pula ~mu*, now, what's your excuse.

dalil [KN], Ar. the elucidation of the Koran by commentaries; the whole of the standard commentators; clarification (generally); proof.

dalung [KN], a large platter.

dam [KN], 1. (Dutch) *main ~*, draughts; *papan ~*, a draughts board; *buah ~*, the pieces. 2. Ar. a religious penalty; *kena ~*, to be fined for a religious offence. 3. a whiff or puff at a pipe.

damai [KS], peaceful, calm, quiet; bringing about a good understanding; *~kan*, to effect a settlement; to reconcile; *minta ~*, to sue for peace; *menurung ~*, to make overtures for peace; *ber~*, to be at peace; to be reconciled; *per~an*, a settlement of differences; a treaty of peace; *per~an sementara*, armistice; *secara ~*, in a peaceful way; *Pasukan Pendamai PBB*, U.N. Peace Keeping Force.

damak [KN], the dart of a blow-pipe; usually *anak ~*; *tabung ~*, the quiver for such darts.

damal [KS], slow to move; difficult to sail or row (of a boat).

daman [KN], Hind. the sheet of a large sail.

damar [KN], resin, 'dammar'; a torch of resinous wood; *~ ke lulut, ~ seraga, ~ daging*, low-grade kinds of resin; *~ penak, ~ cengal*, resin from the cengal tree.

damba [KS], desire for, wish to possess; yearning for; *men~kan cinta*, to reach out for love.

dampar [KK], cast ashore; being aground; *ter~*, stranded.

dampil [KS], contiguity; *ber~-~*, in close proximity — cf. **damping**.

damping [KN], juxtaposition, contiguity, contact; *ber~*, to be hard by; to come next.

Damsyik [KN], Damascus.

dan [Kphb], 1. and, furthermore, 2. time to manage anything; *tak ~*, it cannot be done in the time; *tak ~ sehari*, within a day, before a day is out; *~-~*, instantlly. 3. N.S. (polite), your servant, I; *~ lain-lain lagi*, et cetera, *~ sebagainya*, and so on, and so forth.

dana [KN], Skr, gift, charity; a fund; *merayu ~*, to go a-begging — cf. *dahana;* also *danai.*

danau [KN], a mere, a pool, a lake; *~ buatan*, a reservoir; *men~*, perform immoral act.

dandan [KN], 1. the projecting platforms or galleries on a local ship; *~ haluan*, the prow platform. 2. decoration, adornment; *ber~* [KK], dress up, get dressed; *kedai men~ rambut*, women's hair dressing saloon.

dandang [KN], a large copper boiler, used esp. in Jav. for steaming rice.

dandi [KN], 1. small Tamil kettledrum (a musical instrument often mentioned in literature). 2. spotted, mottled; *rusa ~*, a deer with spotted markings.

dang [KN], a title given in old romances to ladies about a Court — cf. **dayang**.

dangau [KN], a temporary hut erected when camping out to watch padi-fields.

dangdut [KN], popular music with strong beat reminiscent of Hindi or Arabic music.

dangkal [KS], dry, lacking in juiciness; shallow; arid; (flg.) dull, lacking vividness; futile.

danguk [KK], *men~*, to have the head thrust forward; to sit with chin in hand, sit slumped idly; *ter~*, aground with bows high on reef and stern in water.

dansa [KN], Ind. *ber~*, to dance.

danta [KN], Skr. ivory; a poetical word = **gading**; *asmara ~*, beautifully, white, of teeth.

danu [KN], a mere, pool; *ular ~*, Ked. a rainbow.

danur [KN], putrid emanations from a dead body; a putrefying corpse.

dap [KN], 1. Pers., a tambourine. 2. a sword with a long blade and a bamboo hilt covered with skate-skin.

dapa [KN], a slave-messenger sent as a gift with a proposal of marriage.

dapat [KKtr], obtaining, getting, acquiring, managing to; *hutang mas ~ dibayar,* a debt in money may be paid; *lemak ~ ke orang,* the fat goes to others; *~i,* to discover, to conclude, to infer; *ke~an,* the acquisition of anything; that which is discovered or obtained; *ke~an akal,* a special phrase meaning, to get a lesson, learn by bitter experience, to 'burn one's fingers'; *pen~an,* the thing acquired; the proceeds; a profit, income; *cukai pe~an,* income tax; *pen~,* conclusion, finding, opinion; *pen~ umum,* public opinion; *men~kan,* to obtain, to reach (a point aimed at); to approach (a person, as for advice); *tak ~ tidak,* it must be, must; *tak ~ tidak dia menolong,* he is sure to help you; *~ kejar,* to overtake; *se~-~nya,* as far as possibles; *ter-di,* found in, occurring in (as, e.g., some species of animal); *berpen~,* of the opinion; *berpen~ sebaliknya,* to think otherwise.

daperas [KS], Hind. a ship's fender.

dapur [KN], 1. a Malay kitchen; an oven; a brick-kiln; *rumah ~,* a cookhouse; *ceruk ~,* nook in which cooking is done in a house; *juru ~,* a cook; *~ tanah,* a mud-oven; *~* is used (sl.) for 'pipe': *membakar ~,* to smoke a pipe; *orang ~,* (sl.) (my) wife; sometimes used simply to mean a female, esp. a female baby. 2. *~-~ susu,* the outer portion of the breast; *~-~ kubur,* the grave mound (in contradistinction to the headstone).

dar [KN], Ar. abode (in compound words); in Malay letters, the following are conventional; *Perak darulridwan,* Perak, the abode of grace; *Kedah darul-aman,* Kedah, the abode of peace; *Selangor darul-ihsan,* Selangor, the abode of mercy; *darul-ihsan* is sometimes used for a charitable institution e.g. an orphanage.

dara [KN], Skr. maiden, the hymen; *bini dan ~,* matrons and maids; *anak ~,* a

virgin; *ber~,* virgin; *anak ~ sunti,* a young girl barely nubile, 'flapper'; *selaput ~,* membrane of hymen; *pecah ~,* having lost virginity; *~ tua,* old maid; *~* is used to mean young, immature; *buah ~,* first fruits.

darab [KK], Ar. to multiply arithmetically.

darah [KN], blood; *buang ~,* blood-letting; *buang air ~,* dysentery; *~ putih,* 'white blood', i.e. royal blood; *ber~,* bleeding, suffused with blood; *se~ se-daging,* one's own flesh and blood; blood relation; *~ gemuruh,* very nervous, all in a dither; *tetak tak ber~,* deathly pale; *tempat tumpah ~,* birth-place; *kurang ~,* anaemic; *penyakit ~ tinggi,* high blood pressure; *pecah ke ~,* bruised with effusion of blood; *mabuk ~,* faint at the sight of blood or from loss of blood; *datang ~,* to have menses; *putus ~,* to cease to have menses (on change of life); *tabung ~,* blood-bank; *mendermakan ~,* to donate blood for transfusion; *memindahkan, ~,* to transfuse blood; *menyalurkan ~,* id.; *berlumur ~,* blood-stained; *~ sudah kering,* blood seeming to flow slowly, either because of weakness or because it 'congeals in the veins' (from horror or shock); *sudah menjadi ~ daging padanya,* has become second nature to him; *tersimbur ~ di hati,* having a rush of blood to the heart, in a flurry of emotion; *~ diraja,* of noble descent.

darai [KS], Ked. impotent.

darang [KN], a hole, cavity; *ber~-~,* full of holes (as a dam or a mosquito-net).

daras [KK], *men~,* recite the Koran, to study diligently.

darat [KN], land; dry land (as opposed to water); the interior (as opposed to the coast); *naik ke ~,* to land (from a vessel); *turun ke ~,* to land (from a vessel or of a plane); *pen~an,* a landing-place; a landing; *pen~an terpaksa,* forced landing; *tali pen~,* a hawser; *orang ~,* upcountry people, people living far from the sea or from large riverine settlements, esp. aboriginees; *~an,* dry land;

men~, to go inland; to land (as troops or a plane); *ber~*, (sl.) immersed in speculation, forgetful of reality; beside oneself (with emotion); *hilang ~an*, id; *angkatan ~*, = *tentera ~*, the arm.

dari [Kdpn], from; out of; of (in the sense of 'made of'); in the matter of; than; ~ *sini*, hence; ~ *situ*, thence; *~pada*, from, out of, regarding; than; ~ *hal*, concerning; ~ *sekarang*, from now on;~ *hari ke hari*, day by day.

dari-dari [KN], Ked. a small hill-tortoise.

darjah [KN], 1. Ar. grade, rank; class or standard (school); ~ *ulangkaji*, refresher course; ~ *peralihan*, intermediate class, 'remove'; an Order of Chivalry, of which there are two modern (1958) creations: i. *Darjah Utama Seri Mahkota Negara*, the Most Exalted Order of the Crown *(D.M.N.)*, ii. *Darjah Yang Mulia Pangkuan Negara*, the Most Distinguished Order of the Defence of the Realm—it has four grades: a. *Seri Maharaja Mangku Negara*, Grand Knight of the Most Distinguished Order of the Defence of Realm *(S.M.N.)*, b. *Penglima Mangku Negara*, Commander of the etc. *(P.M.N.)*, c. *Johan Mangku Negara*, Member of the, etc. *(J.M.N.)*, d. *Ahli Mangku Negara*, Member of the, etc. *(A.M.N.)*; *Darjah Kerabat*, Family Order, an honour in the bestowal of the Sultan of Brunei; ~ *hidup*, standard of living. 2. a degree (unit of measurement); also *darjat*.

darma [KN], Ind. righteousness.

darmawisata [KN], Ind. excursion, trip, expedition.

darurat [KS], Ar. necessity; serious trouble, time of stress, time of emergency; *undang-undang ~*, emergency regulations; *bekalan ~*, emergency rations.

darwis [KN], hermit, dervish.

das [KN], a shot; *raja ini datang, berapa ~ tembak*, when this prince arrives how many 'guns' are we to give him?

dasar [KN], bottom (as of sea); basis, method, ground-work; prevailing element in a design; ~ *hidup*, way of life; ~ *luar*, foreign policy; *ber~kan*, based on, grounded on; *ber~kan pilih kasih*, on a basis of favouritism; *atas ~ perniagaan*, on a commercial basis; *lima ~ = panca sila*, see **panca**; ~ *negara*, form of constitution, principle; *persetujuan pada ~nya*, agreement in principle.

dasau [KN], Pk., small coconut-shell bowl.

dasawarsa [KN], decade period of ten years.

dasi [KN], Ind. necktie.

dastur [KN], *layar ~*, a studding-sail.

datang [KK], coming, approch; *daripada Allah ~ nya*, it comes to us from God; *men~kan*, to cause to come, bring about; *awan men~kan hujan*, clouds bring rain; *men~kan sembah*, to bring respectful greetings (to a Ruler); *men~kan fikiran*, to invite reflection, make one think; *ke~an maut*, the coming of death; *men~i*, to approach, draw near to; formerly used to mean to assault, attack, esp. a fort; ~ *bulan*, woman's 'periods'; ~ *kotor*, id.; *~~*, Treng. suddenly, = **tiba-tiba**; *ke~an*, arrival; *Jadual Kedatangan*, Register of Attendance; *selamat ~*, welcome.

datar [KS], smooth, level; = **rata** and **natar**; *~an*, a plateau, level tract.

datin [KN], female of datuk (as a title).

datu [KN], a Malay herbalist, = **bomoh**.

datuk [KN], grandfather; a senior; a title of distinction; a joss or idol; the tutelary spirit of a *keramat* or wonder-working spot; ~ *nenek*, ancestors; ~ *kayu*, Pen. land bailiff; ~ *bandar*, mayor; also *dato'*.

Daud [KN], Ar. David, author of the Psalms *(kitab zabor)*; a Malay proper name.

daulat [KN], Ar. majesty; the sanctity which invests the office of a king; the mysterious kingly power which does not die with a sovereign, but abides so as to punish any degenerate successor (according to Malay belief); ~ *tuanku*, your majesty! — an exclamation of homage; *ditimpa ~*, struck down by the power of offended majesty; *~*, sovereignty; *negeri yang ber~*, a sovereign state; *kedualatan*, suzerainty.

daun [KN], a leaf, blade of grass or oar; the submerged screen in an outshore fishtrap *(jermal); ~ buntut,* the short outer pocket of this screen; *~ penjarang,* the long inner pocket over which the fish first pass; *~ ceki,* 'chicky' cards; *~ teh,* tea, tea-leaves; *~ pintu,* the leaf or flap of a door; *~ dayung,* the blade of an oar; *~ telinga,* lobe; *~ terup,* playing cards; *~-~an,* herbs, generally; *~ kayu,* the leaf of a tree; *men~ kayu,* as the leaves of the forest in number; *burung ~,* the green leaf-bird; *naik ~,* to prosper, get ahead; *tak dapat naik ~,* to be kept under, to have no scope; *bertukar ~,* to turn over a new leaf; *ikan ~,* a small fish of the family *Cyprinidae* inhabiting mountain streams; *bersifat naik ~,* self-assertive, 'uppish'.

daup [KN], beamy and heavy (of a boat), heavy and sullen (of a face).

dawai [KN], wire; *~ gelang,* very thick wire; *~ duri,* barbed wire; *~ beranyam,* wirenetting.

dawas [KK], Treng. faded; also exhausted, of soil.

daya [KN], 1. resource, capacity, energy; *~ upaya,* resources, means; *apakah ~?* what can one do?; *memper~kan,* to deceive by a stratagem, to outwit; *tak ber~,* feeble, unable to help oneself; *tak ter~,* helpless; exhausted; *se--upaya,* with all one's might; *terpe~,* deceived, outwitted; *~ utama,* the ultimate moving force; the initiative. 2. *barat ~,* the south-west; *daya tarik,* apppeal, physical attraction.

Dayak [KN], Dyak.

dayang [KN], a damsel, a young girl; *awang dan ~,* young men and maidens; *~-~,* attendants in a Court.

dayu [KK], *men~-~,* to rumble in the distance.

dayung [KN], an oar; the breast fin of a fish; *anak ~,* an oarsman; *batang ~,* the shaft of an oar; *daun ~,* the blade of an oar; *ber~,* to row.

dayus [KS], Ar. a despicable coward, unmanly, esp. as a cuckold or hen-pecked husband.

debak, *debak-debuk* [KN], (onom.) a smacking sound.

debap [KN], (onom.) a slapping sound; plong!; *ber~ jatuh,* to fall with a thud or to flop down.

debar [KK], beating of the heart; *ber~-~lah rasa hatinya,* he felt his heart throb violently; *men~kan hati,* to cause the heart to beat fast, to thrill with emotion or excitment.

debas [KN], (onom.) the hiss of rushing air.

debat [KN], Ind. debate; *per~tan,* subject of debate, argument, deliberations; *mempe~kan,* to take issue.

debik [KN], *~-~,* a slapping sound; *men~-~ dada,* to beat the breast; also **debak**.

debu [KN], dust; haze; *ber~,* dusty or hazy to the view, as if obscured by dust; *~,* atom, atomic fall-out — cf. *lebu.*

debum [KN], (onom.) a thumping sound.

debung [KN], (onom.) a thumping sound.

debunga [KN], pollen, a type of fine powder, usually yellow, formed on flowers which fertilizes other flowers.

debur [KN], (onom.) the sound of a landslip or heavy crumbling fall.

debus [KS], = **debas**.

decing [KN], (onom.) a chinking sound.

decit [KN], (onom.) a twittering or squeaky sound; berdecit, to squeak.

dedah [KK], *ter~,* open, of a door, of the bosom of a dress; *men~,* to expose for sale; to open up; open to the sky, uncovered; *tidur ter~,* to sleep in the open; *men~kan,* to disclose; *perahu ter~,* an open boat; *pen~an,* exposure.

dedai [KS], *ber~-~,* in long, straggling, disorderly lines — cf. **derai**.

dedak [KN], 1. bran; padi husk; rice polishings; 2. *men~,* crowded. 3. revengeful.

dedalu [KN], the mistletoe, a type of parasitic plant that grows on trees (it is considered by some unlucky to bring it into a house).

dedam [KK], *ber~,* crowded together.

dedap [KN], a generic name given to a number of trees (*Erythrina* sp.) that bear very bright scarlet flowers and are used to provide supports for the pepper plant; *ikan pari ~*, a ray *(Eurogymnus asperrimus)*.

dedar [KS], feverish, out of sorts.

dedau [KK], *men~*, to shout, to cry out in distress.

dedaunan [KN], edible leaves.

degam [KN], (onom.) a slamming sound.

degan [KN], young coconut.

degap [KK], *ber~-~*, to heave quickly (of the breast); panting heavily.

degar [KS], *cakap ber~-~*, boastful talk, esp. of guns; *~-degam*, booming away; *bunyi ber~-~*, reverberation.

degil [KS], stiff-necked, obstinate, stubborn, difficult to persuade or deal with.

Degul [KN], Pulau, East Indian island used by the Dutch as a penal settlement.

degum [KN], (onom.) 1. a booming sound, esp. of guns; *~-degam*, booming away. 2. mumps.

dekah [KN], (onom.) the sound of loud laughter; *tertawa ber~* or *tertawa ber~-~*, to laugh heartily.

dekak [KN], 1. a variant of **dekah**. 2. *~-~*, Sum. abacus. 2. clever, lucky.

dekan [KN], 1. the bamboo-rat *(Rhizomys sumatrensis)*; *~ air* is sometimes used for beaver. 2. dean, head of a department of studies in a university.

dekar [KS], [KS], lucky, effective (e.g., as a fishing rod).

dekar [KS], artful, clever, esp. at a game; *pen~*, a fencing-master; swash-buckler; gang-leader.

dekat [KKtr], near, hard by; *~ ke darat*, near the shore; *~i* and *men~i*, to approach; *men~kan*, to bring close; *ber~an*, close to each other; *pen~an*, an approach; *jangan ~-~*, stay away; *ter~*, nearest.

deklamasi [KN], poetry recital, formal speech, speech full of strong feelings.

dekor [KN], Ind. stage scenery; *papan ~*, scenic 'flats',=; also *decorasi*.

dekus [KN], *men~*, *ber~*, the blowing of a porpoise.

dekut [KN], (onom.) calling pigeons; *bu-*

luh ~; the bamboo instrument used to call pigeons for snaring.

delah [KN], a sea-bream *(Caesio* sp.)

delan [KN], 1. snag. 2. small ripples in the water caused by fish.

delapan [KN], eight, the number eight; *~ belas*, eighteen; *~ puluh*, eighty; in speech *lapan* is used.

delik [KK], Ind. *mata men~*, staring.

delima [KN], Skr. the pomegranate; *batu ~*, the ruby; *~ merekah*, a split pomegranate (showing its red contents), a simile for ruby lips.

dema [KN], Pk. they; Kel. also, you.

demah [KN], dry-poulticing; hot dry applications to a diseased part.

demak [KN], stumpy, not tappering (as a nib or fingers).

demam [KN], fever; *~ gigil*, fever with ague; *~ kepialu*, any violent fever, e.g. typhoid; *~ kepialu ketulangan*, rheumatic fever; *~ berlat* or *~ berselang*, intermittent fever; *~ selsema*, influenza; *~ rabu kembang*, fever in lung disease; *~ kura*, fever with enlarged spleen; *~ tarik ruas*, a touch of fever; *~ panas*, high fever; *~ ketulangan*, dengue; *~ meroyan*, puerperal fever; *~ kepialu ketulangan*, high fever with rheumatic pains.

deman [KK], like, glad, willingly.

demap [KS], gluttonous, voracious, greedy *(gelojoh, rakus, pelahap)*.

dembal [KK], *berjalan ber~-~*, to slouch along, to shamble.

dembarangan [KN], a resounding crash.

demi [KP], by, with, on, at (when); in relation to, so as to; *seorang ~ seorang*, one by one; *~ berbunyi genta*, when the bell rang; *~ Allah*, by God; *~ kepentingan generasi muda*, for the sake of younger generation.

demikian [KKtr], thus, so, in this way; *kalau memang ~*, if that is the case indeed; *~ rupa*, in such a way.

demit [KS], 1. young; [KN] child (an expression often used by medicine-men to describe the patient). 2. a ghost.

dempak [KS], broad, beamy (of a boat), blunted, squared (of the end of a stick cut in two).

dempang [KN], 1. hollow-sounding, resonant; *cakap ber~-~*, boastful talk. 2. going across to; visiting; stopping at (of ships).

dempir [KN], cracked-sounding (of a gong); Ked. depir; shrill, strident.

dempuk, *ber~* [KK], Pk. to approach close to; *ter~ pada*, bumping up against, colliding with.

dempul [KN], a sort of putty made of tree-cotton, chalk and oil, used for caulking boats.

demukut [KN], Ked. broken pieces of rice-husk; chaff; = **lemukut** and **melukut**.

den [KN], N.S. I, me.

denah [KN], an evil-spirit causing diseases in the feet.

denai [KN], a wild-beast track.

denak [KN], decoy; *ayam ~*, a jungle-fowl *(Gallus ferrugineus)*.

dencing [KN], (onom.) the chink of a coin.

denda [KN], Skr. a fine; *kena ~*, to incur a fine, to be fined; *~kan*, to fine; *pen~an*, penalty, punishment.

dendam [KS], 1. longing; *rindu ~;* loving, longing. 2. a grudge; = **damdam**; *melepaskan ~*, to vent one's spite; *membalas ~*, to get even; *~ kesumat*, revenge and deep hatred.

dendang [KN], 1. a name sometimes given to the crow *(Corvus macrorhynchus); ~ air*, a bird *(Phalacrocorax carbo); burung pen~*, a bird *(Heliopais personata); ~ laut*, the brown gannet. 2. *timun ~*, a bitter inedible gourd. 3. Spanish fly.

dendang [KN], the droning chorus to a Malay quatrain; *ber~*, to croon, chant; *men~kan*, to chant.

dendeng [KK], *men~* 1. to display prominently, as with the whole flat side showing. 2. [KN], dried meat, biltong.

dengak [KK], *terdengak*, a variant of *dongak* or *danguk*.

dengan [Kdpn], with; along with; in conjunction with; in accordance with; by means of; on, by (in imprecations); *~ nama Nabi Allah*, by the name of the Prophet; *~ suruhan raja*, in accordance

with the prince's order; *masing-masing ~ kehendaknya*, everyone as he pleased; *~ tiada*, without; *~ sendirinya*, spontaneously; *~ alamat* (d/a) in care of; *~ potongan harga*, at discount.

dengang [KN], loud laughter; = **dekah**.

dengar [KK], listening to, hearing; *cuba ~*, please listen; *di~nya*, in his hearing; *men~*, *men~kan*, to listen to, to hear; *pen~an*, the sense of hearing; *alat pen~*, a hearing aid; *memper~kan*, to cause to be heard (i.e., play music, sing a song, utter a speech, present to the ears of an audience); emit (an alarm, etc.); *dapat di~*, audible; *pen~*, listener; *~ kata enggang, makan buah belolok*, if you listen to a hornbill, you'll eat *belolok* fruit: rhyming slang for *~ kata orang, terjun lubuk*, if you listen to people, you'll fall into a deep place in the river; a warning against paying heed to idle talk.

dengeng [KN], jerked meat; cf. **dendeng**.

dengkam [KN], *hati men~*, despondent, depressed.

dengkang [KK], *ber~*, to croak.

dengkat [KS], 1. limping (less strong than *dengkut*). 2. N.S. shallow.

dengkel [KS], dry, lacking in juice; *ke~an hati*, mean-spiritness, lack of generosity; a variant of **dangkal**.

dengki [KS], envious hatred; *menaruh ~*, to nurse a grudge; *berasa ~*, to feel spiteful.

dengking [KK], *men~*, to howl, to yelp.

dengkung [KN], bay, sound like the barking of dogs, croaking of frogs or other deep gutural sound.

dengkur [KN], snoring; *ber~* or *men~*, to snore; to purr, of a cat.

dengkut [KS], Pk. halt, lame; *jalan ber~-~*, to limp along.

dengu [KK], 1. *ber~* or *men~*, to draw in one's breath before muscular effort. 2. dull, stupid; also **dungu**.

dengung [KN], (onom.) humming; the sound of a Jew's harp or of a bumble-bee; the twang of a bow-string; droning or buzzing in the ear; the hum of a kite or top; *ber~*, to give out a humming sound; *~an*, reverberation, boom, rumble.

dengus [KN], *men~*, to snort, to sniff.

dengut [KN], *ber~*, to emit a low throaty noise, as a quail or a 'grunting' fish.

denih [KS], to run (as ice, paint, colour, also eyes); *warna turun ber~*, the colour is running.

dening [KN], Treng. pair (as of bullocks).

dentam [KN], (onom.) a slamming sound; *~-kentamkan*, to boast about, 'make a great song' about; also **dentum**.

denting [KS], *ber~*, taut, as a rope; stiff (not drooping), as a moustache.

dentum [KN], (onom.) a deep booming sound, a thud; *ber~*, to strike with a booming sound, of a big clock; *berdentam-~*, sound of banging or slamming one after another.

denyut [KN], throbbing (of a boil), beat of the heart; impulsion, impulse (electrical); *~ nadi*, pulse.

depa [KN], a Malay fathom, the span from finger-tip to finger-tip of the outstretched arms; taken as roughly six feet, though actually often less; *men~*, to fathom, gauge depth — cf. **depang**; *men~kan tangan*, to spread one's arms.

depa [KN], they; = *diapa*, see **dia**.

depan [KN], front; *di hadapan, di ~*, in front; *di ~ umum*, in public; *bor-~*, openly, not in secret; *ber~an dengan*, face to face with; *dike~kan*, bring forward.

depang [KK], *men~*, to stretch out the arms in a cruciform position; *dengan tangan ter~*, with arms spread wide, as to embrace or as a person lying spreadeagled; *(naik) men~*, to climb by clinging, swarm up.

depun [KN], the lining or border of a garment; hem, edge.

depus [KN], *ber~-~*, coming in puffs, of heavy breathing.

dera [KN], Ar. chastisement, punishment esp. physical punishment or torture.

derai [KN], *ber~-~*, in long straggling line; trailing away; sometimes, trickling, as tears or sand; sometimes, lying untidily about; *roboh ber~*, to crash in ruins (the idea seems to be that of the sight of a building disintegrating into a 'straggling line' as if falls) — cf. **dedai**.

derajat [KN], = **darjah**.

derak [KN], (onom.) a cracking or creaking sound; also **derik**.

deram [KN], (onom.) a rumbling sound; *men~*, to rumble (as thunder); to growl.

derang [KN], (onom.) a clanging sound (such as that of a bell); *ber~*, to tinkle, to chink; to clang.

derap [KN], (onom.) a crackling or rapping sound; the sound of small-arms firing; *~ tangan*, the sound of clapping; *~ kasut*, the tramp of boots; *se~*, sounding or moving in unison.

deras [KS], 1. speedy, rapid of motion; *terlalu ~ larinya*, he ran very fast. 2. Ar. *men~*, to revise one's study of the Koran.

derau [KN], (onom.) 1. the sound as of a heavy shower approaching; *ber~*, murmuring, buzzing, rustling. 2. *men~*, to work in cooperation, esp. in rice-fields.

derawa [KN], Skr. *gula ~*, syrup; (~ is often pronounced di-rawa).

deret [KN], a row, a long line, as of teeth, seats or persons; *ber~-~*, in long lines (as people fleeing along the road from a stricken city); *se~ rumah*, a row of houses; *men~kan*, to put in a row.

derhaka [KS], Skr. traitorous; treason, betrayal; disloyalty or undutifulness generally; *anak ~*, an undutiful child; *adakah patut kita akan dia?* is it right that we should betray their confidence?; *men~* or *berbuat ~*, to turn traitor, to betray.

derham [KN], Ar. a small silver coin or gold coin from Turkey or Persia.

dering [KN], (onom.) a ringing sound; *ber~*, to ring (of a telephone); to trumpet (of an elephant); to jingle (money); to tinkle (glass).

derita [KN], Skr. to endure; *tidak ter~*, insupportable, unbearable; *pen~*, suffering.

derma [KN], Skr. alms, gifts to the poor, charity; favour; gift to a subordinate; *memberi ~,* to distribute charity; *jikalau ada ~ kurnia tuanku,* by the favour and kindness of my lord; *~-bakti,* charitable works; *pen~ darah,* blood-donor; *men~kan,* to donate.

dermaga [KN], Ind. a quay; a sea-wall, wharf.

dermawan [KN], Skr. charitable, philanthropist.

derni [KN], the threshold or sill of a door; *pintu ~,* a light screen-door.

deru [KN], (onom.) the roar of a storm, or of a crowd, or of an inundation, or the deep note of engine; *men~,* to roar; *angin men~,* the howling wind.

derum [KN], 1. (onom.) the sound of a tree falling heavily. 2. a word of command to make an elephant kneel; *~kan,* to make an elephant kneel.

derung [KN], (onom.) a sonorous clang (as of a deep-toned bell).

derut [KN], 1. (onom.) a dull scraping sound. 2. Pk. sinking in, as post or grave.

derwis [KN], Pers. a dervish; mendicant friars.

desa [KN], Skr. region, country; country as opposed to town; a village; *se~ negeri,* every country and town, everywhere; *mendesa negeri,* id.; *bertandang ~,* to go wandering from place to place; *anak ~,* country boy; *gadis ~,* country girl.

desak [KK], *men~,* to harass; urge; press; keep in subjection; *masa ter~,* an emergency, crisis, time of stress; *waktu sudah men~,* time is running out.

desar [KN], (onom.); *ber~,* to hiss (as water falling on hot iron), or to rustle.

desas-desus [KN], whispers, esp. of discontent; *~~ mengenai,* there has been talk of.

desau [KN], (onom.) the swish of rain, esp. of rain falling through leaves, or of a broom on a wet pavement.

desigram [KN], unit of weight, decigram; 1/10 gram.

desiliter [KN], unit of capacity, 1/10 litre.

desimeter [KN], units of length, 1/10 metre.

desing [KN], (onom.) the whizzing sound made by a projectile; *ber~,* to buzz; to hiss; to chirp, as a cricket.

desir [KN], desiran, a faint hissing or buzz; *~an orang,* a buzz of conversation.

desis [KN], *ber~,* to rustle.

destar [KN], Pers. an unstarched headcloth, a turban.

detak [KN], *ber~,* sound like heart-beat; *~ jantung,* throb of the heart.

detar [KN], N.S. (= **destar**) Malay headkerchief.

detas [KN], (onom.) the rustle of paper.

detektif [KN], detective; *cerita detektif,* detective stories.

detik [KN], (onom.) 1. the cracking of a twig. 2. Ind. a dot; a second; a tick (as of a clock); the tap of a typewriter; also *detap; ~* is sometimes used for details, points, incidents; *pada ~~ terakhir,* at the last minute.

deting [KN], (onom.) the twang of a stretched string when struck.

detup [KN], small cracking sounds.

devaluasi [KN], devaluation, a reduction in the exchange value of money.

dewa [KN], Skr. a 'deva', a Hindu divinity; a fairy, a demi-God; generally any deity not recognised by Islam; *memper~kan,* to defy; *men~kan wang,* money-mad.

dewan [KN], Pers. a council chamber, a court, a public hall; *~ bandaran,* Town Hall; *~ rakyat, ~ orang ramai,* House of Commons; *~ pertuanan,* House of Lords; *~ perwakilan,* House of Representatives; *~ rendah,* Lower House; *~ undangan,* Legislative Council; *~ negara,* Council of State, Senate; *~ negeri,* State Council; *~ perniagaan,* Chamber of Commerce; *~ putih,* Whitehall; *~ menari,* dance-hall; *~ bahasa dan pustaka,* language and literacy agency; also **diwan**.

dewasa [KS], Skr. *~ ini,* now; *sikap ke~an,* a mature attitude; time, period, date; age; *orang ~,* adults.

dewata [KN], Skr. godhead, divinity; *~ mulia raya,* the greatest of gods; *burung ~, unggas ~, manuk ~,* or *paksi ~,* the bird of paradise.

dewi [KN], Skr. a goddess; a fairy.

di [Kdpn], 1. at, in; ~ *sini*, here; ~ *sana*, there; ~ *dalam*, inside; ~ *luar*, outside. [By an idiomatic use of this word, it forms a passive, e.g., *kapal ~tunda jongkong*, a ship in tow of a dinghy, i.e., a ship towed by a dinghy; *~dengarnya*, in his hearing; heard by him.] ~ is often used in modern writing of time as well as space; ~ *waktu itu*, at that time. 2. Skr. noble — an abbreviation of *adi* in certain titles, e.g., *~pati* for *adipati*, *~raja* for *adi-raja*, etc.; *~raja*, Royal; *angkatan udara ~raja*, R.A.F.; *ketua panglima ~raja*, Chief of the Imperial General Staff.

dia [KGn], he, him, she, it; they (if clear from the context); ~ *orang*, they; *~ma*, *~pa*, id.

diafragma [KN], diaphragm.

dialek [KN], dialect.

dialog [KN], dialogue.

diam [KK], 1. being silent; *~lah dia*, he was silent; *~~*, silently; *men~kan*, to silence; *ber~ diri*, to preserve silence, say not a word; ~ *menunggul*, to keep stupidly silent (when speech is needed); ~ *ubi*, to be silent, but mentally active (for a potato is progressing underground); ~ *seribu bahasa*, to keep silent in a thousand languages, i.e., to keep mum in spite of many words struggling for utterance; ~ *berisi*, to preserve a pregnant silence; *dengan ~~*, quietly (whether lit., i.e., making no sound or fig., i.e., not attracting attention). 2. residence, abode, dwelling; *~lah dia di Melaka*, he lived at Malacca; *~i*, to inhabit; *ke~an*, abode; *tempat ke~an*, place of abode, home; *~!*, shut-up!, silence!, hold your tongue!; *pen~*, quiet, *orangnya pen~*, he has a quite disposition; *ter~*, speechless, *secara ~~*, quietly, secretly.

dian [KN], a candle; *kaki ~*, a candle-stick; *sinar ~*, the light of a candle; *lilin ~*, the wax of a candle; *burung kaki ~*, the redshank; *puntung ~*, a candle-end.

diang [KK], 1. toasting, heating before a fire; *ber~*, to heat at a fire (used remedially after a confinement); *api ~an*, fire for warming. 2. *men~*, to become a disembodied spirit; the late, the deceased.

diat [KN], Ar. blood-money; expiatory payment; a fine for violating some religious injunction.

diayah [KN], propaganda.

didih [KN], effervescing; *men~* or *menidih*, to boil up; to be boiling hot; *air men~*, boiling water; had mendidih, boiling point; darahnya mendidih, furious, enraged.

didik [KK], *men~*, nurturing, fostering, bringing up (used of men bringing up animals); often used as a term of endearment to the animal — 'my pet'; *~an*, *pen~an*, education, training; pedagogy, *pen~an semula*, rehabilitation (moral); *pen~an otak;* mental training; *pen~an jasmani*, physical education, gymnastic instruction.

didis [KK], *men~*, to hash; slice thinly.

diesel [KN], *minyak ~*, diesel oil, *injin ~*, diesel engine.

diet [KN], *ber~*, to go on a diet.

dif [KN], Ar. Treng. a guest.

dik [KN], 1. = **adik**, 2. by (agent).

dikau [KN], a form of *engkau* — you, thou, thee.

dikir [KK], Ar. *ber~*, to chant religious verses.

dikit [KS], a tiny bit; *se~*, a little; somewhat; *se~ sebanyak*, a fair amount; to some extent; *ber~~*, bit by bit; *ber~~ jadi bukit*, i.e., many a mickle makes a muckle; *se~ sekali*, of very small amount, very few; *secara ber~*, in small quantities; in speech *sedikit* is normally conracted to *sikit*.

diktator [KN], dictator.

din [KN], Ar. faith; the faith of Islam.

dina [KS], despised, miserable, poor, humble.

dinar [KN], Ar. a coin (usually of gold); ~ *mas*, id.

dinamik [KS], dynamics.

dinas [KN], Ind. department, one of several divisions of a government.

dinda [KN], short for *adinda*; a term of endearment for a girl; cf. **kanda**.

dinding [KN], screening; a light partition; a party-wall; a wall, generally; ~ *hari*, a sun-sail; ~*an*, serving as a screen or partition; ~*kan*, to screen off; *pen*~, screening; *doa pen*~, prayers protective against evil spirits; *men*~, to 'intervene', as, e.g., a 'screen' of trees shutting out a view.

dingin [KS], cold, chilly; ~*kan*, to chill; *men*~*kan badan*, to cool off; never used of pleasant coolness as *sejuk* may be; *ke*~*an*, feeling chilly.

dinihari [KS], daybreak, dawn.

dipati, see **adipati**.

diraja, see **raja**.

dirgahayu [KS], Skr. long life, majesty and dominion (an expression of homage addressed to a ruler).

diri [KN], 1. self; *seorang* ~, all by oneself; ~*ku*, I myself; ~*nya*, himself, herself, itself, themselves; *di dalam* ~, to oneself, mentally; *bawa* ~, to run away; *buang* ~, to commit suicide; *minta* ~ or *mohon* ~, to beg leave to depart; ~ is sometimes used as a pronoun of the second person; ~ *yang ketiga*, the third person (as sometimes used in place of the first and second persons in letter-writing); *memakai* ~ *yang ketiga*, to use the third person — cf. **sendiri**; *pada* ~ *saya*, for my part, as far as I am concerned. 2. ~*kan*, to erect, to put up; to found, to build up, to establish; *men*~*kan*, id.; *ber*~, to stand erect; to get up; *ter*~, set up; upright; *ter*~ *dari*, composed of, made up of; *pen*~*an*, process of erection; policy, stand-point, attitude; *ber*~ *di atas kaki sendiri*, to stand on one's own feet.

dirus [KK], irrigation; the flowing of water; *men*~ *air*, to water; to flush with water; also **jirus**.

diwal [KN], Pers. a wall; the thick outer wall of a palace or fortress.

diwan = **dewan**.

diwani [KK], Pers. authorised by government; minted; a minted coin.

dll. [abbrev.], etc., et cetera; = *dan lain-lain*.

doa [KN], Ar. prayer, incantation, magical formula; ~ *pengasih*, a charm to arouse love; ~ *pendinding*, a formula protective against evil spirits; *minta* ~, to pray; ~ implies prayer for a specific purpose, as opposed to ritual prayer *(sembahyang)*; ~ *selamat*, a blessing; *membaca* ~ *selamat*, to invoke a blessing.

dobi [KN], Hind. a dhoby; laundryman.

dobrak [KK], Ind. *men*~, to break up; to infringe; *men*~ *pintu*, to force the door open.

dodoi [KN], cradle-song, lullaby; *men*~*kan*, to croon to sleep; also **dodol**.

dodol [KN], *kueh* ~, a cake made of glutinous rice-flour, molasses and fruit. It often accompanies an invitation to dinner in Kelantan.

dodor [KS], *ke*~*an*, all awry, fitting badly, of a garment.

dogang [KN], support by a rope, e.g., as a rope is tied to a tree when the tree is felled to prevent it falling on the woodsmen, or as Malays hang out to windward in a racing boat by holding on to ropes *(tali* ~*)* attached to the mast.

dogol [KS], 1. hornless. 2. stupid; *ke*~*an*, stupidity.

dok [KK], 1. a coll. shortening of *duduk*. 2. dry-dock; ~ *apung*, floating dock.

dokoh [KN], Jav. a set of gold crescentic breast-ornaments worn at marriages and ceremonies.

doktor [KN], Eng. a doctor of Western medicine; ~ *gigi*, dentist; ~ *haiwan*, ~ *binatang*, veterinary surgeon; ~ *bedah*, surgeon; ~ *pakar kanak-kanak*, pediatrician, ~ *bahasa* and *kesusasteraan*, doctor of philosophy; *ilmu ke*~*an*, medical knowledge; ~ *biasa*, general practitioner; ~ *yang pakar (kulit)*, (skin-) specialist.

dolak [KS], ~-*dalik*, shilly-shallying.

dolar [KN], dollar.

domah [KN], *pen~*, a gift (sent by a *raja*).

doman [KN], 1. see **pedoman**. 2. Skr. *hantu ~*, a dog-faced spirit; a (Kedah) survival of the Hanuman legend.

domba [KN], sheep; *mengadu--~*, to play off one against the other.

domol [KN], snout, nose of an animal; often used to describe the distance by which a horse has won a race; by a short head.

dompet [KN], Ind. a small bag, a handbag, a purse.

dondang [KN], a lullaby; *~-sayang*, id.; *kain ~* or *kain ~an*, a swinging cradle.

dondon [KN], pattern or colour in clothing; *se~*, of similar pattern (of a *sarong* and *baju*).

dongak [KK], *men~*, tilting the head skyward, as a buffalo; sloping, as a drain; gazing with raised chin.

dongeng [KN], berdongeng, intoning, chanting, as in reciting a romance; so, fictional; *cerita ~*, a fictional story; a tale, legend; *~ sahaja*, mere fiction; *ber~* is also used fig. for the whining of importunate children.

dongkang [KS], *~-dangking*, emaciated.

dongkol [KS], 1. hornless or with downward curving horns (of a bullock), combless (of a cock); bare-headed; featherless. 2. Ind. mendongkol, to get excited, 'worked-up', annoyed.

dongkor [KS], *~-dangkar*, bundling out bag and baggage.

dongok [KS], disproportionately broad; uncouth; badly proportioned.

donor [KS], Treng. boggy, as land after rain.

doran [KN], a net on a rod, a sort of lift-net.

dorong [KK], 1. stumbling forward; *ter~*, fallen forward; tripped up, *khabar ter~*, indiscreet disclosure, 'blurted out'; *kata ter~*, slip of the tongue, spoken without thought. 2. Ind. *men~*, to urge on, encourage, stimulate, motivate, impel; *~an*, motivation.

dosa [KN], Skr. a sin; an offence against religion or morality, but not necessarily an offence against statute law; *ber~*,

sinful.

doyak [KN], (Riau) a large cuttle-fish.

doyan [KS], to like, to be fond of.

dsb. [KKtr], and so on, and such and such; = *dan sebagainya*.

dua [Kbil], two; *~ belas,* twelve; *~ puluh,* twenty; *~-~* two by two; *ke~,* both; *yang ke~,* the second; *men~kan,* to have two of, e.g., *men~kan laki,* to commit bigamy; *men~kan Allah,* to worship more gods than one; *ber~,* in a party of two; *ber~ dengan,* in company with (someone else); *ber~an dengan,* alone with (one other person), forming a 'twosome'; *ber~-~an,* in pairs, in couples; *pen~,* a fellow or match; *ambil per~,* to buy, esp. cattle, on a share basis (sharing profit with the vendor); *ambil per~an,* id.; *peraturan berpe~ (ternak),* such an arrangement; *~ kali lima jadi sepuluh,* twice five makes ten, i.e. just the same, no difference; nothing outstanding, much of a muchness; *awak ~ kali lima dengan dia,* you are twice five with him, i.e. you're just as bad; *seper~,* (exactly) one half; *dibuka ~ puluh empat jam,* open around the clock, night and day; *tiada ~nya,* has no equal or match; perduaan, duplication.

duai [KN], *ipar ~*, a brother-in-law or sister-in-law.

dubur [KN], Ar. the anus.

duda [KN], Ind. widower.

dudu [KK], *men~*, following a course unswervingly, keep straight on.

duduk [KK], sitting, to sit; to reside; situation, position; *~kan,* to seat; fig. to give in marriage; *ke~an hal,* state of affairs; *~ perkara,* id.; *ke~an,* position; *tempat ke~an,* residence; *ter~,* seated; *pen~,* inhabitants; *pen~an Jepun,* Japanese occupation; *~ laki isteri,* to live as man and wife; *berseke~an,* to be associated with, euphemistic for having sexual intercourse with; *bangun ~,* to sit up, as a person in bed; *~ bersandar,* to recline, sit with support for the back, lounge; *jatuh ter~,* to fall in a sitting position; *~* is commonly used coll. to give the effect of -ing: *dia ~ menangis,* she was weeping, and even *dia ~ berdiri,* she was standing; *mengambil tempat ~,* please be seated.

duga [KK], probing, fathoming, sounding; *laut yang dalam dapat di~, hati manusia siapa tahu?,* a deep sea may be sounded, but who can fathom a man's thoughts?; *batu pen~,* the lead on a sounding-line; *ter~,* under test, in danger; *men~,* (fig.) to expect, anticipate; *men~ bijih timah,* to prospect for tin; *~an akal,* intelligence test; *tak ter~,* fathomless; *seperti telah di~,* as expected; *~an,* test, trial; ordeal; *salah ~,* miscalculation.

dugal [KS], *men~,* to have a feeling of nausea.

duit [KN], (Dutch) a cent, a doit; *~ sen,* copper coins; *~* is very often used simply to mean money; *ber~,* to have money; *burung ~~, burung minta ~,* the Burmese wattled lapwing; *mata ~an,* having an eye only for money; *perempuan mata ~an,* 'golddigger'; *~ ayam* is sometimes used for small bribes; *~ teh,* tea-money (a sort of commission given esp. to landlords); *~ pasar,* housekeeping money.

duka [KS], Skr. grief, sorrow, mental anguish; *men~kan,* to grieve, to distress, suffer unhappiness; *hati yang ~,* a sorrowful heart; *suka dan ~,* happiness and grief; *tanggung ~,* to suffer sorrow; *~-cita,* feelings of sorrow; *ke~an,* id.

dukana [KS], sensual, lascivious.

dukat [KN], ducat, gold coins formerly used in many European countries.

duku [KN], a well-known fruit *(Lansium domesticum);* it has a yellow-brown skin and so is used to describe such a colour; *kera ~,* the slow loris *(Nycticebus tardigradus).*

dukun [KN], a Malay herbalist, medicine-man.

dukung [KK], carrying on the hips (as a Malay woman carries her child); *men~,* to carry in this way; *~an,* a support for

the child; *men~,* is used fig. to mean 'to support', 'work to effect'; *men~ peranan,* to support (perform) a role in a play or (fig.) as a task.

dulang [KN], a wooden platter or tray; *~ mas,* a platter used in washing for gold; *men~,* to wash for ore; *lain ~ lain kakinya,* everyone has his faults, peculiarities or idiosyncracies.

Dulfakar [KN], Ar. a Malay proper name, but not common; see **Dzulfakar**.

duli [KN], Skr. dust; the dust under a sovereign's feet; (met.) the position which a subject occupies and to which he can address himself; *Ke Bawah ~,* the form of address of a subject to a sovereign; *Duli Yang di-pertuan,* a royal title; *bawah Duli* (coll.) the Sultan, H.H.

dumpu [KS], blunted, not having a sharp point.

dundun [KS], *ber~-~,* pressing on (of a crowd).

dungu [KS], dull-witted, dense, stupid; also **dengu**.

dunia [KN], Ar. the world; this world below; *peredaran ~,* the chances and changes of mortal life; *~ akhirat,* this world and the next; *harta ~,* the riches of this world; *ke~an,* the things of this world, material things; *se~,* world-wide, existing all over the world.

duniawi [KS], worldly, material.

dupa [KN], Skr. incense; *bakar ~* or *pasangkan ~,* to burn incense; *~* is also used for censer.

dura [KS], 1. anxious; mental restlessness; disturbed; *berhati ~,* disquieted. 2. distant, far.

Durga [KN], Skr. the goddess Durga; *Dewi ~ Sakti* or *Dewi ~ Kesuma,* id.

duri [KN], a thorn; a prickle, as of a porcupine, a spine, sting, as of a fish; *terasa ber~-~,* to have a pricking pain; *adakah ~ dipertajam?* does one sharpen thorns?; *kawat ~,* barbed wire; *~ pandan,* a barb.

durian [KN], the well-known fruit, the 'durian'; *~ Benggala,* the sour-sop; *~ runtuh,* a windfall, stroke of luck; *~ tem-*

baga, a yellow variety, reckoned the best; *macam timun dengan ~, menggolek pun luka,* the cucumber alongside the durian gets pricked if it only rolls over, 'uneasy bedfellows', 'next to a dangerous neighbour'.

durja [KN], Skr. countenance, visage—a poetic equivalent for face *(muka); ~ berseri,* a bright countenance; *~ muram,* a clouded visage; *jamjam ~,* expression; a poetic equivalent for *air muka.*

durjana [KS], evil, wicked; *menteri ~,* a traitorous minister; *durjana* is often used for Evil, as opposed to Good *(mulia); si ~,* the villain, the 'baddy'.

dusi [KK], *men~,* to be perpetually crying (of young children); not fully awake.

dusta [KS], Skr. a lie, lying; *berbuat ~,* to deceive, to tell a lie to; *ber~, i~; men~,* false, e.g., *cemara men~,* false hair, *pen~,* a liar.

dusun [KN], an orchard, a fruit-grove without a dwelling-house; *orang Dusun,* a name given to an aboriginal tribe in North Borneo, now generally known as *orang Kadayan.*

duta [KN], a messenger, an envoy, an ambassador; *ke~an,* an embassy.

duyun [KS], *ber~~,* crowding forward, pressing forward; *~an orang,* a stream of people.

duyung [KN], 1. the dugong *(Halicore dugong); ekor ~,* the tail of the dugong; forked, treacherous; *minyak tangis ~,* the tears of the dugong (a potent love-philtre). 2. *men~,* to totter when about to fall; to hover when about to perch.

dwi [Kbil] Ind. dual (in such expressions as *~-kewarga-negaraan,* dual nationality); *~-warna,* the bicolour flag of Indonesia *(Sang Merah Puteh); ~bahasa,* bilingual; *ke~bahasaan,* bilingualism.

E

eban [KK], flinging out of the way; to chuck away.

ebek [KN], a sun-sail; a wooden, propped shutter; also embik.

ebeng [KK], meng~, to sway the body (as a dancing-girl).

ebro [KN], four-wheeled carriage.

endah [KK], meng~kan, pay attention to.

edan [KN], Jav. mad; = **gila**; ~ kesmaran, madly in love; = gila berahi.

edar [KK], to go round, to wander, revolve, to ramble; zaman ber~, times are changing; meng~kan, to circulate; peng~, distributor.

edisi [KN], edition.

egah [KK], 1. walking with a waddling or affected gait. 2. to control, guide, as bicycle or vehicle.

egeh [KS], berjalan ber~-~, swaggering along; ter~-~, swaying to-and-fro, waddling; a variant of **egah**; also hegeh.

eja [KK], Ar. spelling, to spell; meng~, to spell; to read slowly, spelling out the words; ~an, spelling; ~an Melindo, a new system of spelling adopted in 1972; ~an menurut bunyi, phonetic spelling.

ejek [KK], meng~, to tease, to mock at, scoff at, jeer; memper~kan, to hold up to ridicule; menjadi ~-~an orang, to be a laughing-stock, a butt for ridicule; suara ~an, cries of derision; nama ~an, nickname, byword.

eka [Kbil], one, sole.

ekabahasa [KN], monolingual.

ekonomi [KN], Eng. economy (management of resources); per~an, economic state; ~ teratur, planned economy.

ekor [KN], tail, end, final part, a numeral coefficient for animals; ~ mata, the corner of the eye; ~ pulau, the point (of a riverine island) that is farthest downstream; ber~-~, in Indian file, one holding on to the other (as children in certain games); bintang ber~, a comet; tunggu ber~-~, to queue up; meng~, (fig.) to follow (behind a leader), to be in a dependent position, to 'tag along'; jangan men~, don't follow the crowd; meng~ angin, to go downwind, keep to the lee; meng~(i), to follow, to trail; meng~i dengan mata, to follow with the eyes; menjadi ~an, to be an imitator; ~an, consequences.

ela [KN], 1. an ell, a yard. 2. a variant of **hela**.

elah [KN], helah, Ar. strategem, contrivance, device; habis daya tipu ~, at the end of his wiles, tricks and resources; olah-~, extreme duplicity; full of dodges; also elat and helat; it is often used of 'not playing fair', e.g., as a referee; ~ is often used for 'excuse', pretext': suatu ~, a mere excuse.

elak [KK], evasion, getting out of the way; ber~, to get out of the way; ~kan, to dodge (a blow); (derog.) meng~ dpd. membayar cukai, to evade paying one's taxes.

elok [KS], handsome, fine, orang yang ~ rupanya, a man of handsome appearance; maha-~, very beautiful or fine; ke~an, beauty; excellence; se~-~, just, barely; se~-~nya, just as, just when; but, yang se~-nya, best of all, the best way is; meng~kan, memper~kan, improve, beautify.

emak [KN], see **mak**.

emas [KN], see mas.

embacang [KN], the horse-mango (Mangifera foetida); also **macang** and **bacang**.

embak [KN], case, instance, time; se~, once; dua ~, on two occasions, simultaneous.

embal [KS], still damp, moist.

embalau [KN], lac; solder; sealing-wax.

emban [KN], an arrangement of ropes enabling a porter to secure a burden borne on the back; a girdle, a broad band or belt; a baldric.

embara [KK], = **kembara**.

embarau [KN], an artifical embankment; also *embarang*.

embas [KS], like; resembling; ~ *tupai*, like a squirrel.

embat [KK], a long swishing stroke; *kena ~*, to be caned.

embek [KN], a sun-sail; also **ebek**.

embih [KN], 1. *ber-*, shaking to-and-fro (as twigs in a tree in which a bird is moving). 2. form of address to girls.

embik [KN], *meng~*, to bleat (as a sheep or goat).

embuh [KK], *rebus tak ~*, unwilling; no; I won't; *~-~an*, although; admitting that; yet.

embuk [KN], 1. Jav. mother, a respectful designation for old ladies. 2. *meng~*, to throb; also *mengembut*.

embun [KN], dew; ~ *asap*, haze; ~ *betina*, dew in small drops; ~ *jantan*, dew in large drops; *kering ~*, when the dew dries up, i.e. about 7.30 a.m.; *ber~*, to be falling (of dew); *meng~*, to fall in thin drops (of spray); *ber~*, Pk. to expose oneself to the elements; *seperti ~ di hujung rumput* (prov.), transitory, momentary, fleeting (love).

embus [KK], *hembus*, to blow (of wind); *~an*, bellows; *~an udara*, a current of air, a draught; *ber-*, to blow, of wind; to puff, as a runner; *ber-~*, to puff and snort; *meng kan api*, to breathe fire, as a dragon; *meng-kan hidung*, to blow the nose; *meng~kan ingus*, id., also *hembus; menghembuskan nafas terakhir*, (fig.), to pass away, expired.

embut [KK], *ber-~*, pulsating, flickering, showing fitful vibration; a variant of **embuk** 2.

emosi [KN], emotion; *ucapan yang penuh ~*, an emotional speech.

empai [KN], = **ampai**, *emparan*, an arrangement of poles for drying nets.

empang [KK], *meng~*, barring; damming, stopping the course or flow of anything — a weir, a dam; *~an*, a large dam, a barrage; and so, the reservoir impounded by it.

empap [KN], (onom.) the sound of a flat object falling on a soft surface; *sepel~*, the width of the hand when the palm is laid flat on the table; *meng~*, to fall on and cover (e.g. of a collapsed tent); *ter-*, to sit, fall, or be let down, with a bump, flop down.

empat [Kbil], four; *~-belas*, fourteen; *yang ke~*, the fourth, also **ampat**.

empedal, = **pedal**.

empelas, = **mempelas**.

emper [KN], Jav. a pent-house, a shed.

emping [KN], 1. rice plucked, crushed and cooked before it has attained maturity; *peng~* or *lesung peng~*, a pounder for young rice; *masak per-*, just ripe enough to be cooked, as *emping*. 2. feeble; ~ *tubuhnya*, of poor physique.

empis [KN], covering fences (to lead driven animals into a trap).

empu [KN], *perempuan*, a woman.

empuh [KK], overflowing; *rebus tak ~*, boiling without overflowing (playing with fire yet escaping unsinged), prov; *~kan*, to inundate.

empuk [KS], a soft spot in fruit; tender from boiling; soft, of voice or of a cushion.

empul [KK], *meng~*, to beat about against adverse winds (of a ship).

empulur [KN], pith; the core (of fruit); ~ *rumbia*, a tree *(Randia anisophylla)*.

empunya [KN], *yang ~*, whose; *m~i*, to possess, to own; *tuan ~*, owner, proprietor.

emul [KK], officious questioning; *meng~*, to importune, to intrude.

enak [KS], delightful, enjoyable; *ber-~*, to enjoy oneself; *se~nya*, to take one's sweet time.

enal [KN], = *nal*, plug, stopper (bottle).

enam [Kbil], six.

enap [KN], *tanah ~*, soil washed down by a river, banked-up tailings.

enau [KN], *nau*, sugar palm.

enca-benca [KS], in disorder, higgledy-piggledly.

encal [KS], ~-~, descriptive of up and down movement; jerking alternately up and down.

encang [KK], 1. an equivalent of **encal**. 2. ~-*encok,* crooked, awry, zigzag.

encat [KS], *ter~,* checked, as utterance; stunted, of growth.

encik [KN], an honorific prefix; often written *cik;* ~ *puan,* an honorary title given to the commoner wife of a prince.

encer [KS], watery.

endal [KK], 1. *meng~,* rebound, to walk with the head and shoulders held back and the breast and stomach thrust forward. 2. stuffing in = **asak**.

endang [KN], female ascetic.

endap [KK], 1. crouching; keeping oneself concealed while watching; *meng~,* to spy, to lurk on the watch; to lay an ambush; N.S. to abet; *ter~,* crouching, watching; *serangan ~,* an ambush; *berjalan ter~-~,* to proceed stealthily. 2. *mendak,* sinking in, subsiding, esp. as soil under the weight of a building; *ter~-~,* gradually subsiding, settling.

endil [KN], *buang ~,* a sweep of the right arm in dancing; a sign indicating rejection.

endul [KN], a swing support, a hammock, a cradle, a sling for an injured arm.

endung [KK], to complain, protest, esp. as a child.

endus [KK], *meng~,* to sniff, snuffle up (a scent or smell).

engah [KS], *ter~-~,* puffing and blowing; *ter~-~ kerana bermain badminton,* he's panting from playing badminton.

enggak [KN], 1. a basket, shaped like a bird; made of matwork; for holding *emping*. 2. no, not.

enggan [KS], unwilling; ~ *bercerai,* unwilling to separate; ~ *menonton filem yang demikian itu,* he's reluctant to see such kind of films.

enggang [KN], a generic name for large hornbills (esp. *Dichoceros bicornis* and *Buceros rhinoceodes);* ~ *papan,* the great hornbill.

enggat [Kphb], as far as; ~ *ini,* thus far.

enggil [KN], ~-*ber~,* serrated (of a mountain ridge).

engguk [KK], 1. to nod the head; also angguk; ~-*enggal,* pitching of a ship; bobbing up and down; continuallly nodding. 2. hump (of a bullock).

enggut [KK], *ber~,* swaying from side to side; rocking; rolling, as a boat; (fig.) swaggering along.

engkah [KN], a gum, glue; 2. ~-~, ~-~an *(mengkal)* half-ripe (of fruits).

engkap [KS], ~-*engkip,* rising and falling, up and down, ~-~ *bagai rumput di tengah jalan,* now up, now down, like grass in the middle of a road (a hard life).

engkar, = **ingkar**.

engkau [KGN], you; little used except in literature and anyway should not be used except to inferiors; but it is sometimes used in addressing God, Who is above such distinctions; abbreviated coll. in the North to **hang** and **kau**.

engkol [KN], crank, L-shape arm and handle used to start a machine.

engku [KN], a title of high rank; in Perak a form of address to members of the Royal House other than the *Sultan, Raja Muda* and *Raja Bendahara* (who are *tuanku*)— practice varies in different States; in some parts *tengku* has replaced *engku,* on the East Coast a *Syed* is often called *Engku.*

engsel [KN], (Dutch) a hinge.

engsut, = **esut**.

enjak [KK], *meng~,* to tread down; *peng~,* the sole of the foot; *jalan meng~,* to walk in a springing manner; *mengikut meng~ kuda,* to rise in the stirrups on a horse; *ke mana meng~ itu?,* Pk. where are you lolloping off to?; cf. **kinja**.

enjal [KK], to give a sudden push or jerk.

enjelai, = **jelai**.

enjut [KK], *meng~,* to tug (as a fish tugs at a line); to beat up, as an egg; *ber~-~,* bobbing up and down; springly, as a mattress; *main ~-~,* to play at see-saw; *meng~kan bahu,* to shrug the shoulders; *meng~kan* is also used for pressing on, as on a pedal.

entah [Kktr], an expression of doubt and interrogation; perhaps; I do not know; I cannot tell; *jawab-ku, ~lah,* I replied, I do not know, sir; ~ *bertemu, ~kan tidak,* perhaps we shall meet, perhaps not; ~ *macam mana,* somehow or other; ~ *apakah sebab-nya,* for some reason or other; *negeri ~-ber~,* fairy-land; *zaman ~-ber~,* once upon a time, no one knows when, in the remote (and romantic) past; cf. **antah** 3.

entak [KK], = **hentak,** ramming down, pounding down; *~-anti = untak-anti; pengentak,* pounder.

entang [KK], 1. Pk. *tak ~,* I don't care, I'm indifferent; = *tak endah.* 2. = **tang.** 3. to set down; = **letak.**

entek [KK], *meng~,* to winnow rice by shaking it in a sieve and giving occasional front and back jerks.

enten [KK], to graft (plant).

enteng [KS], Ind. light, not severe; easy; *ini perkara ~,* this is a trivial matter.

enyak [KK], = *hemyak,* to stamp down, force down; ~ *dengan tumit,* to crush with the heel; *ter~,* falling with a bump, 'plumped down'; (fig.) thunderstruck; also **henyak.**

epeh [KS], continually talking; *orang ~,* a chatterbox; a variant of **repek.**

epek [KN], outer posts used to keep the screens in position against the skeleton framework of a large fish-trap (*belat*).

epok [KN], 1. a small envelope-shaped bag for carrying the requisites for betel-chewing, = **bujam.** 2. *~-~,* to cuddle up, as a child or cat. 3. a sort of pastry-puff.

erak [KK], edging away slightly; making a slight movement.

eram [KK], = *ram,* to sit on (eggs); *telur-telur itu hendaklah diramkan,* those eggs must be hatched.

erang [KK], *meng~,* to groan loudly.

erang [KN], 1. Jav. black, blue-black; extremely dark red. 2. *~-erot,* twisted;

awry, distorted. 3. *meng~,* groan, moan.

erat [KS], Ind. firm, tight; *meng~kan,* to tighten, esp. (fig) as *meng~kan pertalian muhibbah,* to tighten the bonds of friendship (between States); *memper~,* to strengthen, *memper~ persahabatan,* to strengthen friendship.

ereng [KS], a variant of **erang.** 2. *meng~,* to twist oneself round (as when trying to look at something).

erik, see **panas.**

erong [KN], 1. a small cup of Chinese porcelain. 2. ~ ~, the scupper holes in a ship. 3. slanting askew; *pahat ~,* a chisel (the edge of which is cut at an angle).

Europah [KN], Europe.

erot [KS], twisted, bent, awry; ~ *hujung hidungnya ke kiri,* the point of his nose pointed slightly to the left.

erti [KK], Skr. meaning, signification; ~ *kitab,* meaning of a book; ~ *perkataan,* the meaning of a word; *~nya,* that is to say; its meaning is; *~kan,* to interpret, to explain; *ber~,* to bear a meaning; *meng~,* to understand; *~-kata,* significance, meaning, way of expression; *kata-kata se~,* synonyms; *peng-an,* definition, explanation, interpretation; *dalam ~-kata yang sebenarnya,* in the true meaning of the word (or expression).

esa [KN], a variant of *se,* one (in certain expressions, e.g., *yang ~,* the one, the only); *kepercayaan ke~an Tuhan,* monotheism. (As a numeral and article, the form *sa* is used.)

Esah [KN], Ar. a proper female name from *Ayesha; Ayesha* was the favourite wife of the Prophet and daughter of Abu Bakar, the first Caliph. 2. legal, legitimate; *peng-an,* legitimation, confirmation; *meng~kan,* to legitimize, confirm.

esak [KN], = **isak;** to sob.

esang [KK], *meng~,* to blow the nose.

eseh [KS], *ter~-~,* sidling up, as a shy child; also **esek.**

esei [KN], essay, a piece of writing, not poetry, usually short and on one subject.

esek [KN], a disease causing the skin to become dry and scaly.

esok [Kktr], tomorrow, in future, 'one day'; ~ *lusa,* tomorrow or the day after; *ke~an hari,* the morrow, also **besok**; ~-~, 'one of these days'; often contracted to *sok.*

esut [KK], *meng~,* sidling along, edging along; also *hesut* and **engsut**.

etiket [KN], etiquette.

F

faal [KN], 1. deed, act, good works. 2. sign, omen, prophesy.

fadilat [KN], Ar. virtue, excellence.

faedah [KN], Ar. profit, advantage, gain, benefits, *ber~*, useful, profitable; *tidak ber~*, it's useless, esp. material; Kel. euphemistic for interest on money.

faham [KK], to understand, take note; *salah ~*, misunderstanding; *~ tua*, Conservative; *~an*, ideology, doctrine; *se~an*, mutual understanding; *ber~ kolot*, having old-fashioned ideas, ultra-conservative.

fahrasat [KN], Ar. index to book, list, catalogue.

failasuf [KN], Ar. a philosopher (plural *falasifah*).

fajar [KN], Ar. dawn (poet); *~ sidik*, bright day light; *harian ~*, morning paper.

fakir [KN], Ar. a needy man, a mendicant (esp. a religious mendicant); *~ miskin*, the poor and needy; also *pakir*.

faktor [KN], factor.

falak [KN], Ar. the vault of heaven; astronomy, see **ilmu**.

falsafah [KN], Ar. philosophy; *ahli ~*, philosopher.

fana [KS], Ar. mortal; corruptible; to die; *dari negeri yang ~ ke negeri yang baka*, from a perishable to an imperishable world — from earth to heaven; also (coll.) *pana*.

faraid/faraiz [KN], Ar. religious obligations, esp. regarding the division of intestate property; *faraizkan*, to divide such property in accordance with Islamic law; so (fig.) to divide up property.

faraj [KN], Ar. vagina.

fardah [KN], Ar. the veil covering head and face, supposed to be worn by Muslim women.

fardu [KN], Ar. a religious duty; *menuna-*

ikan ~ Haji, to fulfil the duty of pilgrimage; often corrupted to *perlu*; cf. **rukun** for the five duties which are regarded as the 'pillars' of Islam; *~-kifayat*, collective religious obligation, *~-ain*, individual religious obligation.

Farsi [KN], Ar. Persian; *bahasa ~*, the Persian language.

fasakh [KN], Ar. divorce by judicial decree under Islamic law; also *fasah* and *pasah*.

fasal [KN], Ar. paragraph, article, section, chapter, minor sub-division; concerning; *apa ~*, why?; *~ itu*, for that reason, therefore; *cari ~*, to look for trouble, 'trail one's coat', try to get someone into trouble; *buat ~*, to make trouble, to 'make something of it'; *ber~-~*, in sections, in clauses.

fasih [KS], Ar. fluent; *berlidah ~*, glib; *~ berbahasa* Melayu, she's fluent in Malay.

fasik [KS], Ar. ungodly, sinful; notorious evil-doer from the religious point of view.

fatihah [KN], Ar. the confession of faith; the first *sura* of the Koran.

Fatimah [KN], Ar. the favourite daughter of the Prophet; a common proper name for women, us. abbreviated to *Timah* or *Mah*.

fatwa [KN], a legal ruling by a jurist, esp. on a question of Islamic law.

Feringgi [KN], Ar. Frank, Portuguese.

fesyen [KN], Eng. fashion, style.

fi [Kdpn], Ar. in, at, upon, regarding; *fil-alam*, on earth; in the world.

fiil [KS], Ar. deed, work, behaviour, conduct; character, as shown in manner; *~nya seperti pencuri*, he behaves like a thief; *membuat ~*, to behave petulantly, show temperament.

fikah [KN], doctrine of duties.

fikir [KK], Ar. to think, have an opinion;

ber~, to ponder, think it over; *~an*, an opinion; *pada ~an saya yang bodoh ini,* in my humble opinion; *ber~an luas,* broad-minded; *ber~an sempit,* narrow-minded; *ber~an jauh,* sagacious, to have foresight; *ber~ masak-masak,* to think hard; *pemikiran,* thinking, thought; also **pikir**; *ahli ~,* thinker, philosopher.

Filipina [KN], *negeri ~,* the Philippines.

filsuf [KN], Ar. a philospher; = **failasuf**.

firasat [KN], Ar. a horoscope; a book of astrology; astrological work; divination.

Firaun [KN], Pharaoh.

firdaus [KN], Pers. Paradise; fairyland; *taman ~,* the Paradise.

firma [KN] business firm.

firman [KN] Ar. order, command; the word of God; *be~,* to speak (of God); *seperti ~ Allah,* in accordance with God's word; also **perman**.

fitnah [KN] Ar. calumny, slander; *kena ~,* to be slandered; *~ yang disengajakan,* deliberate slander; also **petenah**.

fitrah [KN], Ar. 1. a tithe of 1 *gantang* of rice per head paid in the annual fasting month; *tiga gantang ~ umurnya,* he is three years old. 2. natural ability; *mem~kan,* to pay the tithe for someone.

fonim [KN], Eng. phonetic, word spelled phonetically.

foya [KK], Ind. pleasure, fun; *ber~-~,* to enjoy oneself, make merry.

fuad [KN], Ar. heart; the seat of the feelings, = **hati**.

fulan [KN], so-and-so; *si ~,* id.; us. pronounced *si pulan.*

fulus [KN], Ar. a small copper coin; used (sl.) for 'money', generally, 'lolly'.

futur [KK], Ind. break a fast.

G

gaba [KN], ~-~, arch which is decorated with palm fronds.

gabak [KK], Pk. *cari ter~-~,* to search all over the place, search eagerly.

gabal [KS], Sol. = **gabas**.

gabas [KS], coarse; roughly done (of work).

gabuk [KS], bulky; *besar* ~, big without strength, as a person or a plant; *biawak* ~, a variety of monitor lizard.

gabung [KK], to affiliate; *ber~,* affiliated; *meng~kan,* to combine, join, bind together; *~an,* combination, group, federation, association; *ber~* is also used for, run together, telescoped, of words: e.g. *cerpen* for *cerita pendek; ~an usaha,* a collective effort.

gabus [KN], 1. easily cut (of wood; sharpened (of a knife), to sharpen; *pe~,* a strop. 2. *ikan* ~, a freshwater fish *(Ophicephalus, sp.).* 3. covered with gold (of the corss-piece of a *keris* sheath); *keris terapang ~ hulu,* a kris with sheath entirely covered with gold. 4. ~ *kaki,* a Malay doormat. 5. cork (the substance).

gadai [KN], mortgage; *ber~,* to pawn; *pajak* ~, a pawn-shop; *meng~kan nyawa,* to risk one's life.

gading [KN], ivory; the tusk of an elephant; ~-~, the ribs of a boat; *aur* ~ or *buluh* ~, the large bamboo *(Bambusia vulgaris); punai* ~, the pink-headed pigeon *(Ptolopus jambu); bila ada ~ bertuah, tanduk tidak berguna lagi,* when you have some luck-bringing ivory, horn ceases to be useful, i.e. the new drives out the old; *tak ada ~ yang tak retak,* nothing is perfect.

gadis [KN], a maiden, = *anak dara.*

gado-gado [KN], Ind. a dish made from vegetables and fried groundnuts, = **rojak**.

gaduh [KS], tumult; loud dispute; *berbuat* ~, to create a disturbance; *per~an,* an altercation; *ber~,* to take part in a row; ~-~, to clamour, make a fuss.

gagah [KS], strong, mighty, forceful; capable, reliable (in physical activities); *orang* ~, a handsome man, 'fine-looking chap'; ~ *perkasa,* valiant and strong; to make an effort, e.g., as a sick man trying to walk; ~*i,* to force by menaces, to threaten; ~*lah!,* make an effort!; ~*kan diri,* to brace oneself, control oneself.

gagak [KN], the Malayan jungle crow *(Corvus macro-rhynchus).*

gagal [KS], failed, frustrated; *ke~an,* failure, fiasco; unsuccessful (negotiations); *meng~kan,* to frustrate; *dia mencuba meng~kan perjanjian itu,* he tried to sabotage the agreement.

gagang [KN], the stalk or stem of a flower or leaf; a handle; ~ *telefon,* telephone receiver.

gagap [KS], stuttering; *orang* ~, a stammerer.

gagasan [KN], Ind. scheme, plan, concept.

gagau [KK], groping about for anything, searching with hand (of an elephant); picking up with the trunk.

gah [KN], dignity, fame, importance, distinction, greatness, a sense of greatness, pride; renowned; *megah,* id.

gahara [KN], Skr. of royal birth on both sides; *anak* ~, *raja yang* ~, a prince of fully royal descent.

gaharap [KN], = **amber**.

gahari [KS], = **ugahari**. moderate, equal.

gaharu [KN], Skr. *kayu* ~, agila wood, eagle-wood; a name given to several fragrant woods; ~, (China) joss-sticks; *sudah ~ cendana pula,* to ask what one knows already (prov.).

gahir KS], Ked. lust, covetousness.

gaing [KK], 1. N.S. *ber~,* to cluster round. 2. a shallow fin-keel of wood.

gairat [KN], = **ghairah**.

gajah [KN], the Indian elephant *(Elephas maximus);* a descriptive epithet meaning 'large'; ~ *berjuang,* a fighting elephant; ~ *lalang,* a tame elephant; ~ *menyusu,* a covered way between a Malay house and its kitchen or outhouses; ~ *mengkuna,* a tuskless elephant; ~ *meta,* a rogue elephant; ~ *mina,* (literally) a 'fish-elephant'; (in Javanese design) a monster with the head of an elephant and the body of a fish; a name given to the whale when it is met with — one specimen locally obtained is the hump-backed whale *(Megaptera boops);* also used for the seal and the walrus; *badak ~,* the large rhinoceros *(Rh. sondiacus);* the bishop in chess; *main ~,* to play chess; *burung ~,* the Malayan whimbrel; *mati ~,* (fig.) dead but hard to forget (esp. of a man who has left a lot of property).

gajai [KK], N.S. *ter~,* loosened, forced open (as a door).

gaji [KN], 1. wages, pay; *orang ~,* a paid employee; *~an,* id.; *hari ~an,* payday; *makan ~,* to be in the pay of; *makan ~ buta,* to have a paid sinecure, soft job; *~ pokok,* basic salary. 2. *~-~,* a saw — usually *gergaji.*

gajus [KN], *buah ~,* the cashew *(Anacardium occidentale).*

gak [KN], Kel. a common particle, sometimes used as a virtually meaningless 'pillow-word', sometimes meaning 'methinks', 'maybe' (from agak?); also *gat.*

gala [KN], 1. *tidak ber~,* unbounded. 2. Skr. *~-~,* a mixture (pitch and resin) used for caulking boats — more commonly *gegala.*

galah [KN], a pole (for poling a boat); a mooring-pole; a long pole (one of a pair) for thrusting down the submerged screen in a *jermal;* a stick for knocking down fruit from trees; ~ *pasir,* the short poles used for punting a boat over shallows; ~ *lubuk,* long poles for use in deep places; ~ *bujang,* ordinary punting-poles of medium length; ~ *canggah,*

punting-poles provided with a forked end for resting against snags, treetrunks, etc.; *matahari tinggi sepeng~,* when the sun is low on the horizon (as it were, the height of a punt-pole); about eight o'clock in the morning; *lompat ~,* pole jumping.

galak [KK], 1. menacing, threatening; uxorious, lascivious; ardent, 'worked-up', excited; *dia ~ dan kata-katanya sangat jijik,* he's belligerent and foulmouthed; *~an,* encouragement. 2. ~ *kali,* again and again, often.

galang [KN], a bar or roller laid athwart the path; *~an (Perahu),* a slipway (for boats); ~ *perahu,* the rollers on which a boat rests when hauled ashore; ~ *temalang,* such rollers when resting on others, to which they are at right angles; *tupai ~ perahu,* a squirrel *(Sciurus rafflesii); jalan ~,* a corduroy road; *~an,* an obstacle, objection; *~kan,* (i) to lay a boat on rollers; (ii) to interpose a bar to a descending blow; *meng~,* to be in the way, to obstruct; *ter~,* aground, of boats; *~-kepala,* stubborn, unyielding; *lidah ter~,* struck dumb; — cf. **alang, palang** and **malang**.

galas [KN], *meng~,* carrying on the back by means of a sling or support; *meng~, ber~,* used esp., of hawkers carrying round their wares, and so may mean just, hawking.

galat [KN], aversion, objection, demur; *dia tidak ~ memberi dua tiga-puluh sen,* he did not mind giving 20 or 30 cents; a variant of **ghalat** 2.

gali [KK], digging; *meng~,* to dig; galian, a surface-mine, also minerals mined; *peng~,* a spade; *peng~an,* excavations, diggings; *sungai ~,* a canal made by making a river-cutting; *cara hidupnya dahulu, gali lubang, tutup lubang,* his way of life before was robbing Peter to pay Paul.

galir [KS], 1. flowing or running rapidly but evenly; *perkataan yang ~,* fluent but foolish talk — cf. **alir.** 2. *kain ~,* the curtain used in a puppet show. 3. loose, not fitting closely, as a fitting.

galuh [KN], silver, gem (a term of endearment to a princess).

galur [KN], connecting, tracing back (as origins); *menyusur-~*, to trace back history or pedigree; *ombak-~*, a receding wave (appearing to join up with the others).

gamak [Kktr], 1. *meng~*, take s.t. in hand to feel size or estimate its weight. 2. guessing. 3. put o's hand threateningly on the hilt of a dagger; *~-~*, approximately; *tak ter~ nak*, cannot venture to, feel unequal to (when facing a task); *dia ter~ membunuh tiga orang*, he could bring himself to kill three men; *ter~-~*, hesitating, uncertain.

gamam KS], *ter~*, flustered, esp. used for 'put off one's stroke' at games, shocked and unable to do anything; *gopoh ~*, eagerly hurrying.

gaman [KN], = *ge~;* weapon.

gambar [KN], 1. representation, picture, statue, model; *~ dilarik*, a polished image; *~ tulisan*, a sketch; *ter~*, imaged, pictured, represented; *~ rajah*, diagram, drawing, design; *~ timbul*, bas-relief; *~* is often used by children for 'doll'; *~ bisu*, silent films; *~ bercakap*, 'talkies'; *ber~*, illustrated (as a book); to have one's photo taken; *ber~-ramai*, to have a group photo taken; *tukang ~*, a photographer; *~an*, an illustration; (fig.) a mental picture, image, description, impression; *meng~kan*, to make a picture of, to film (fig.) to depict, illustrate; sometimes, *tidak ter~kan*, indescribable; *meng~kan dalam hati*, to depict in one's mind, imagine; *meng~kan sebagai hal yang diidamidamkan*, to idealize.

gambir [KN], gambier *(Uncarid gambir).*

gambuh [KN], a professional dancing-girl from Java or Madura; *ber~* or *bermain ~*, to dance (of such girls).

gambus [KN], an Arabian six-stringed lute.

gambut [KN], *tanah ~*, fibrous, peaty soil.

gamgam [KK], Ked. *naik ~*, to get angry, to flare up.

gamelan [KN], a set of musical instruments making up a Javanese band.

gamit [KK], *meng~*, to beckon with the fingers; to solicit (of a prostitute); to sway inwards, of a pendulous body; *~an*, laughing stock, topic of conversation.

gampang [KS], light; of little account; *~kan*, to render easy, simplify; *anak ~*, a child of doubtful paternity.

gamuh [KN], a large water-vessel.

gana [KN], 1. Skr. *sang yang Gana*, Ganesha, the Hindu deity; 2. *guna-~*, confused, mentally befogged.

ganal [Kktr], alike, almost the same; *~-~*, closely resembling, almost identical; *~- ~ mati*, practically dead.

ganas [KS], fierce (of animals); *harimau ~*, a man-eating tiger; *meng~*, to be fierce, to rampage, as predatory animals or bandits; *peng~*, terrorist; *ke~an*, cruelty, violence.

gancang [KS], nimble, agile, lively.

gancu [KN], a long crook for pulling down fruit or branches, or for hooking out crabs; hooks for holding open a mosquito net; *ter~*, hooked, (fig.) as a man in love.

ganda [KS], 1. fold (in expressions such as 'two-fold', 'three-fold'); *sekali ~*, once; *~ ber~*, time after time, over and over again; *~kan*, to repeat, to double; *meng~-~kan*, to cause to increase many-fold; *melipat~kan*, id.; *naik sekali ~*, to be doubled; *dua kali ~ lebih (mahal)*, twice as (expensive); *per~an*, multiplication; in bull-fighting, Kel. *ganda* = the favourite; *makan ~*, the non-favourite; *ganda* also = the 'odds'; *sali ~*, 'evens'; *beri ~*, to back a favourite; *ambil ~*, to back a non-favourite. 2. Skr. perfume, fragrance — a component part in the name of many plants.

gandam [KN], coloured by betel-chewing (of the teeth).

gandar [KN], the lever of a rice-pounder *(Lesung hindik); ~ cincin*, the claws (in a ring) which hold the gem in position.

gandarusa [KN], a medicinal plant *(Justi-*

cia *gandarusa).*

gandasuli [KN], a plant *(Hedychium coronarium).*

gandi [KN], Skr. a bow; also *gandewa; main* ~, archery.

gandik [KN], a frontall ornament worn by a bride; a tiara.

ganding [KK], rubbing up against; *ber~,* alongside; *ber~ dengan,* side-by-side with; *ber~ tangan,* arm-in-arm; *meng~kan,* to place by the side of; *ber~an,* (lying) side by side; *meng~i,* to equal, 'keep up with'.

gandu [KN], *buah* ~, a hard black fruit (unidentified) used as a ball or marble in some children's games.

gandum [KN], Pers. corn, wheat, *tepung* ~, flour.

gandung [KN], light logs attached as outriggers to a boat to give it greater steadiness.

gang [KN], 1. a brazier's chisel; ~ *bulat,* id., with a rounded edge; ~ *rancung,* id., with a sharp-cut point. 2. alley, narrow street.

Gangga [KN], Skr. the deified Ganges; a fabulous monster; *Betara* ~, the deified Ganges.

ganggang [KK], roasting above a fire — cf. **pang-gang.**

ganggu [KK], importunate; worrying, interfering, molesting; *kata-kata meng~,* interruptions (as to a speech); *~an,* interruption, disturbance (including 'interference' on the radio); *tidak ter~,* imperturbable.

ganggut [KK], *meng~,* to graze, grazing.

gangsa [KN], Skr. bell-metal, bronze.

gangsi [KK], Ked. *meng~,* to perfume cloth with incense-smoke; = **mengukup.**

ganja [KN], 1. bhang, or Indian hemp *(Cannabis sativa); mabuk* ~, intoxicated by Indian hemp. 2. the guard at the top of a *keris* blade; *keris* ~ *iras,* a *keris* with the guard and blade in one piece.

ganjak [KK], *ber~,* edging forward or backward slightly; shifting one's seat or position; to give ground, 'budge'; cf. **anjik;** *tidak ber~ dari,* not to budge.

ganjal [KN], wedge, support, base, *meng~* [KK], keep in place with a wedge, to fasten.

ganjar [KK], Ind. *~an,* reward, payment; gratuity.

ganjil [KS], uneven, odd (of a number), unusual, bizarre; *orang empat genap lima* ~, to him four is an odd number, five even, i.e. he is contrary, perverse, can't argue with him; *pakaian* ~, fancy dress; *ke~an,* remarkableness, peculiarity.

gantang [KN], 1. measure of capacity; gallon; as a measure of capacity, = 5 katis. 2. *guling-~,* rolling over and over; *meng~ asap,* to build castle in the air.

ganti [KK], substitute, changing the one thing for another, stead, instead; ~ *rugi,* compensation for injury, reparations; *~an* or *per~an,* a substitute; *~kan* or *meng~kan,* to substitute, to replace; *ber~,* in place of; *ber~-~,* in turns, successively replacing; *~-nama,* pronoun; *ber~ tikar,* to marry late wife's sister; *hari ber~ hari,* day after day.

gantih [KN], 1. N.S. barrel-shaped, thick in the centre (of pillars), the horns of cattle and cupolas. 2. to spin, [KK], = **antih;** *~-~,* a daddy-long legs, crane-fly.

gantung [KK], suspension, dependence, hanging; *~kan,* to hang anything up; *ber~,* in dependence on; hanging; *ber~ rambut sehelai,* hanging by a single thread; *tempat boleh ber~,* home, a place to which one can attach oneself; *ber~ hidup kepada,* to depend for one's livelihood on; *ber~ kepada dirinya sendiri,* self-supporting; *nyawa ber~ di hujung kuku,* life hanging on the point of a finger-nail, i.e. in a precarious position; *ber~ kepada banyak sedikitnya,* it depends on the amount of; *ber~ tak bertali,* a dependant without legal rights, e.g. a mistress; *kena* ~ *kerja,* to be suspended from duty; *di~ jawatannya,* id; ~ *bicara,* to adjourn a case; *tiang per~an,* gallows.

ganyah [KK], *gonyoh-~,* to rub down, to scrub vigorously; *ber~,* (fig.) quarrelling, 'getting up' against one another; *meng~*, to denounce, inveigh against.

ganyang [KK], Jav. *meng~*, to chew up, devour; (fig.) to overthrow, crush; this is the word often used by the Indonesian authorities in the early 60s as descriptive of what they were going to do to Malaysia, and so has crept into the Malay language: it is now sometimes used jocularly as a synonym for, to eat.

ganyut [KS], half-cooked, hard inside (as yams, potatoes); *orang tua ~*, withered old man.

gapai [KK], *meng~*, to reach out and touch; to grab at.

gapil [KK], *meng~*, to meddle with things, pick at things.

gapis [KN], a tree with tawny blossoms (*Saraka* sp.).

gapura [KN], Ind. an archway, gateway.

gara-gara [KN], Ind. 1. troubles, evil results; difficulties; causes, reasons. 2. ber~, to bustle about.

garam [KN], salt; *~ angin*, effervescent salt; *ibu ~*, brine, coarse-grained salt; *bubuh ~*, to flavour with salt; *belum banyak makan ~*, (met.) young and inexperienced; *~~ galian*, mineral salts; *meng~i*, to salt, pickle; (fig.) to encourage, play up to; *kurang ~*, tasteless, insipid; *membuang ~ ke laut*, to carry coals to Newcastle.

garang [KS], fierce, savage, quick-tempered; *men~*, to fly into a passion; *~* is used for glaring, of lights or bright colours.

garap [KK], Ind. a harrow; *meng~*, to work, to cultivate.

garau [KS], 1. hoarse, raucous (of the voice). 2. *tembak ~*, shooting at random, or merely so as to frighten.

garfu [KN], Port. a table-fork.

gari [KN], 1. handcuffs; *pasang ~*, to handcuff. 2. Port. *malau ~*, (Kedah) sealing-wax.

garing [KN], 1. a kind of satchel or basket. 2. crisp and dry (of food); to grill; clear and 'clinking', of a sound.

garis [KN], scratching; *ber~*, scratched;

~an, a line (long narrow mark); *~an lintang*, line of latitude; *~an bujur*, line of longitude; *~ tanda air*, Plimsoll mark; *~ tengah-tengah*, diameter; *~~ kasar*, rough outlines (as of a plan); *penjaga ~an*, linesman at a game; *peng~*, a (school) ruler; *~an Sartan*, tropic of Cancer; *~an jadi*, tropic of Capricorn; *~an air*, water-line; *~an peperangan*, front line.

garit [KK], *ber~*, to make a slight movement, to stir.

garu [KK], = **garuk**; *meng~-garukan pisau cukur pada*, to scrape with a razor.

garuk [KK], 1. *meng~*, to scratch; also *garu*. 2. hoarse, raucous.

Garuda [KS], the eagle of Vishnu; the fabulous roc.

gas [KN], Eng. *minyak ~*, kerosene oil; *~ pemedih mata*, tear-gas.

gasak [KK], to do anything vigorously; to hit; to eat gluttonously; *~ lari*, (sl.) to abscond, to 'clear out'; *ber~*, to have a fight, exchange blows; *~~lah!* a very coarse expletive, carrying the idea of, 'as you wish!' or 'do as you like!'

gasal [KS], Ked. odd, uneven, of numbers; = **ganjil**.

gasang [KS], incontinent, lustful, passionate.

gasing [KN], a spinning-top.

gatal [KS], itchy; lustfull; *sakit ~*, the itch (as a disease); *miang ~*, extremely itchy or lascivious; *~ keladi*, lustful, esp. of a woman; *~ tangan*, (fig.) can't leave things alone, must fiddle with things, as a mischievous child; *~ mulut*, garrulous, fault-finding.

gatih [KK], to press down with the foot, as in pedalling; *peng~*, a pedal; *meng~*, also, to spin, = **gantih** 2.

gatik [KKtr], together.

gaul [KK], *campur ~*, very much mixed or confused; = *campur baur; per~an*, society, social intercourse.

gaung [KN], 1. sound dulled or confused by echo; reverberation. 2. a ravine; *ber~*, over-hanging (of cliffs).

gawai [KN], 1. a tool or instrument; *pe~*,

an agent; a civil or military officer; see
pegawai. 2. Hind. from Port. a topsail.
gawang [KK], waving about (e.g. as a stick
to keep off an attack), brandishing. 2.
goal-posts, *penjaga* ~, goal keeper.
gawar [KN], a token or mark placed across
a road to signify that passage is prohibited; ~-~ or *ge~*, quarantine; *tembak* ~,
to fire in the air so as to warn robbers
off the premises.
gaya [KN], strength, bearing, spirit, mode
of action; commanding air, 'presence';
meng~kan, to show off, esp. one's
charms; to 'go through the motions' (in
imitation) of some action; to perform
(e.g., a dance); *dengan* ~-*nya*, proudly;
penuh ~; swankily; full of swank; *ber~-
~*, acting affectedly; ~ *berjalan*, gait,
carriage; ~ *bahasa*, style of language; ~
tulisan, literary style; *ber~*, (moving)
proudly, 'swanking'; *tak ber~*, feeble,
lacking, vigour.
gayam [KN], *buah* ~, the Otaheite chestnut.
gayang [KS], swaying, uncertain in one's
movements (as after a debauch).
gayat [KS], giddy from looking down a
great height.
gayung [KN], 1. a ladle of half a coconut
shell with a handle attached; ~ *bersam-
but (kata berjawab)*, to accept a challenge. 2. a kind of quarterstaff or single-
stick.
gayu [KN], N.S. old, of persons and trees.
gayut [KK], hanging from a rope or bough
(as a monkey).
gebar [KN], a counterpane; a blanket; ~
gandam, a richly-embroidered coverlet.
gebeng [KN], 1. a long boat with a rudder
of the European type. 2. Eng. cabin.
geberau [KS], Pk. sad, anxious.
gebu [KS], delicate in texture, loose (of
soil); ~ *cantik*, daintily pretty; *pasir* ~,
fine light sand; ~ is also used for, soft,
delicate, of skin.
gecar [KN], dribbling saliva, watering of
the mouth; *meng~kan*, making the
mouth water (of an enticing dish). 2. to

frighten, scare.
gedabir [KS], loose folds of skin (the dewlap of an ox, the gills of a cock); also
gelambir.
gedak-geding [KN], (onom.) sound of
band.
gedang [KS], 1. N.S. great, large; = **besar**.
2. ~*kan tangan*, to stretch out the arms
at right angles.
gedebung [KN], 1. a sort of bamboo box
or receptacle. 2. envelope-shaped
pouch.
gedik [KK], men~-ngedik, Pk. to exhibit an
article for sale.
gedempol [KS], obese; *gemuk-~*, id.; *Si-
Gedimpul*, Fatty; also *gedempul* and
gedempong.
gedoboh [KS], big and loose (of garment,
clothing etc.).
gedubil [ ], Ked. *muka* ~, brazen-faced.
geduk [KN], 1. Ked. = **beduk**. 2. ~-*gedak*,
bumping, of the noise of a rumbling
cart.
gedumbak [KN], a single-membrane
drum.
gedung [KN],1. an office, store or magazine; a 'godown'. 2. (in the North) a
main (artificial) watercourse, a conduit.
gedut [KS], puckered, crumpled.
gegai [KS], Pk. weak in construction (of
houses, boats).
gegak [KS], 1. noise, uproar (esp. the din
of battle); ~ *gempita*, extreme uproar.
2. to drop off (as ripe fruit).
gegaman [KN], Jav. weapons, armed
soldiery; forces; munitions; also **gaman**.
gegap [KS], = **gegak**.
gegar [KS], quivering, shaking; *ber~*, to
vibrate, to shake; ~*an bom*, bomb blast.
gegas [KN], 1. a movable hatch or planking in a Malay boat. 2. haste, hurry,
excitement; *dalam ke~an aku*, in my
eager haste; *ber~-~*, to hurry along.
gegat [KN], a small insect which bores
holes in clothes, books etc., the 'silver-
fish'.
gegepi [KN], Pah. a malodorous bug.
gejala [KN], Ind. symptoms, appearances,

signs; so, mannerisms, peculiar behaviour; odd happenings.

gejolak [KN], *ber~*, to flare up (of fire, feelings, etc.), heaving violently.

gelabir [KS], = **gelambir**.

gelabur [KK], to fall 'plump' into water.

geladah [KK], Ind. to raid, make search (esp. of police); also **geledah**.

geladak [KN], 1. the deck of a ship; *pintu ~*, a trap-door. 2. Ind. *(anjing) ~*, stray dog; wild dog.

geladir [KN], a large movable piece of planking in a ship's side — removed to facilitate loading.

gelagah [KN], a wild sugar-cane *(Saccharum glaga)*.

gelagak [KN], blustering, talking big.

gelagat [KN], Ind. signs, distinguishing marks; odd behaviour, odd happenings; *~ baik dan ~ buruk,* good and bad symptoms.

gelak [KK], to laugh; *tertawa ~~,* to laugh peals of laughter; *~ sumbing,* sly laugh, snigger.

gelakak [KK], a chuckling laugh.

gelam [KN], 1. a tree *(Melaleuca leucodendron)*. 2. the name of a tribe of the *Orang Laut*. 3. *burung ~*, the chestnut bittern.

gelam [KN], paper bark tree.

gelama [KN], a generic name given to a number of jew-fish, including *Gerres oyena* and *(~ panjang) Otolithus argenteus*.

gelambir [KN], the dewlap of an ox, the gills of a cock; *meng~*, to hang in folds, of skin; also **gelabir**.

gelandang [KK], Ind. *ber~*, to wander about, to loaf, lounge; *orang ~an,* tramp, loiterer, idler; *perempuan ~an,* nightbird.

gelang [KN], a bracelet or anklet; *~ ceri,* a bangle; *~ kaki,* an anklet; *~ kana* (Jav.) an armlet; *~ kunci,* a key-ring; *dawai ~,* wire wrapped round a cylindrical surface, e.g. the neck of a bottle; *peng~,* the wrist; *peng~an kaki,* the ankle; *~~ tanah,* earth-worm.

gelanggang [KN], cockpit; an arena, a

sports-ground; *~ politik,* (fig.) the political arena; a circular space; *~ ayam,* a cockpit; *~ susu,* the dark circle round the teat.

gelangsar [KK], *meng~,* to slip, slide, glide.

gelap [KS], dark, obscure; surreptitious, secret; *~ katup,* pitchy dark; *~ gulita,* id.; *pasar ~,* black market; *mata-mata ~,* a detective; *~ mata,* mental derangement, mad, go berserk, run amok; *~ samar,* dusk (when it is hard to distinguish faces); *meng~kan,* to make away, embezzle; to 'keep dark', conceal; *~~ lagi,* while still dark, very early in the morning; *~* is sometimes used for dark, of colour; *menjalankan keadaan ber~,* to enforce a black-out.

gelapung [KK], Pk. *meng~,* to float about, drift.

gelar [KK], *~i,* to bestow a title or designation; *~an,* a title; *ber~,* entitled; possessing a title; *~* is sometimes used for nickname; *di~ tuan penyapu,* he was nicknamed Mr. Broom.

gelas [KN], Eng. a drinking glass, tumbler; *tali/benang ber~,* Sp. to make kites fight — powdered glass being stuck on the strings.

gelasar [KK], *meng~,* to slip, (forward), slide, as a man on slippery ground.

gelatik [KN], = **jelatik**.

gelatuk [KK], *meng~,* to chatter (of the teeth); to tremble (with fear).

gelebar [KS], to flap continuously, to flutter — cf. **kibar**.

geleber. [KS], to hang down, hang loosely, sloppy (of clothing), hang in folds (of skin).

gelecek [KK], *meng~,* to slither, slip (away); *ter~,* slip accidently.

gelecok [KS], *ter~,* strained, as after making a false step.

geledah [KK], = **geladah**.

geledang [KK], *meng~,* to stretch out the arms at right angles to the body.

geleding [KN], *meng~,* to become warped (of wood).

geleduh [KS], looming large = **beluduh**.

gelegak [KN], 1. boiling up, bubbling (of

hot water); of a crowd of chickens. 2. a heavy wooden sounding-block.

gelegar [KN], 1. a girder on which floor-joists rests; 2. *meng~*, to quiver, to shiver.

gelegata [KN], nettle-rash.

gelegut [KK], = **gelugut**.

gelek [KK], to roll over, as the wheel of a vehicle over a man; to roll from side to side, as a boat, to get it off the mud-bank; *ber~*, rolling gently from side to side; *meng~kan leher*, to arch the neck, as a horse or heron, *ter~*, ran over; *peng~*, roller — cf. **golek**.

gelekak [KK], *meng~*, to crumble away (as the plaster on a wall).

gelekek [KN], *meng~*, to chuckle.

gelema [KN], phlegm, mucus in the throat.

geleman [KN], *geli~~*, on edge, of nerves at rasping noise, shuddering, wincing.

gelemat [KN], decking over the bows and stern of a boat.

gelembung [KN], a bubble; anything blown out with wind; *~an*, a blown-out bladder made of a chicken's crop; *meng~*, to be puffed out (of the cheeks).

gelempang [KN], lying outstretched (as a man on the ground with arms extended); also **gelimpang**.

gelempuk [KS], *~-gemuk*, extremely fat.

gelempung [KN], 1. a spongy kind of lint used for staunching the flow of blood. 2. *~-gelampang*, sound of drums.

gelendong [KN], a reel, a bobbin; a roller.

geleng [KK], to shake the head (in denial); also *geling*.

gelenggang [KN],a medicinal plant *(Cassia alata);* the leaves are supposed to be a remedy for ringworm.

gelentang [KK], *guling-~*, rolling over and over; = *guling-gantang*.

gelentar [KK], *meng~*, to quiver, to tremble — cf. **ketar**, *gemetar, gegetar.*

gelenyar [KS], *meng~*, to tingle, unable to sit quietly.

gelepar [KK], *meng~*, to writhe, to quiver; *meng~kan*, to excite (as a writer, by sensationalism); *meng~kan sayap*, to flutter, as a dying fowl.

gelepek [KK], to lie slackly upon anything (as a sail against a mast).

gelepung [KN], *meng~*, to fall heavily into water.

geletar [KK], *meng~*, to quiver, to tremble — cf. *ketar, gemetar, gelentar.*

geletek [KK], *meng~*, to be ticklish, restless as fish in a basket; to wriggle, as worms or snakes; *meng~ hati,* to amuse, 'tickle'.

geleting [KN], = **leting**.

geli [KN], ticklish; desiring to laugh; *~ hati,* tickled, amused; *~ geman* or *~ geleman,* on edge, of nerves from a rasping or scraping noise; *peng~ hati,* things that rouse mirth, humorous tales.

geliang [KN], *~-geliut,* to writhe, to wriggle, as a snake.

geliat [KN], *ter~,* twisted, as ankle; *meng~,* to wriggle and writhe, as a landed fish; to turn and twist, as a sleeper.

gelibat [KN], = **kelibat**.

gelibir [KS], *ber~*, hanging, pendulous.

gelica [KN], Hind. a light quilt-mattress.

gelicau [KK], *meng~*, chirping (of birds).

geliga [KN], a bezoar-stone; *batu ~,* it is supposed to be talismanic and to have the property of sucking venom out of wounds; *ber~,* of outstanding excellence, 'a jewel'.

geligin [KN], a cross-rod holding the cloth against the yard-beam in a weaver's loom; also *geliging*.

geligis [KK], *meng~*, to shudder (because of fever, fright etc.).

geligit [KK], to keep biting, cf. **gigit**.

gelimang [KS], Ind. smearing; *ber~ dengan,* smeared with.

gelimpang [KK], *ter~,* lying stretched out, sprawling.

gelincir [KK], *meng~, ter~ lidah,* to make a slip of the tongue; slipping away to the side, skidding; *ter~,* slipped, e.g. *ter~ kakinya lalu jatuh,* his foot slipped and he fell.

gelincuh [KK], *ter~,* to stumble.

gelingsir [KK], *meng~*, side-slip; to slide; also *gelinsir*.

gelinjang [KK], to prance about, cut capers;

used fig. for 'antics', esp. of political opponents.

gelintir [KN], a particle, pellet; *se~*, a minute fraction, a title; *se~ orang hadir dalam mesyuarat*; a small group of people showed up at the meeting.

gelisah [KS], *meng~*, to fidget, to move restlessly; *ke~an* (political) unrest; worry, anxiety, emotional upset; *itu pengumuman yang meng~kan*, it was a disturbing announcement.

geliung [KN], 1. a galleon. 2. see **geliang**.

gelitak [KK], *meng~*, to tickle, to stimulate.

gelobok [KK], *meng~*, to gurgle, as water when a bottle is filled.

gelodak [KN], trouble, worry; *meng~*, to disturb, annoy; *meng~ perasaan orang*, to upset people's feelings.

gelodar [KS], turbid, troubled; of water; *meng~*, to thrash about wildlly in the water, flounder about.

gelogok [KN], to menace; bluff; *salah ~*, do something hurriedly (without due consideration).

gelohok [KK], *ter~*, broken in continuity, gapping, as a seam; planed boards; scanty eye-brows; also *tergelehok*.

gelojoh [KS], gluttonous, greedy of.

gelombang [KN], long, rolling waves, rollers; *~ bunga lepang*, rollers with white crests; *~ kepala kera*, choppy rollers; *~ mangkuk*, an eddy, a whirlpool; *hempasan ~*, breakers, the surfline; *~*, wave-length (radio); *~ sederhana*, medium wave; *ber~an*, in waves (as flights of aircraft); *main ~*, surfbathing; *lembah ~*, trough of wave; *puncak ~*, crest of wave; *lautnya agak ber~*, the sea is rather choppy.

gelomor [KK], *meng~*, to dirty, besmear.

geloneng [KN], a small gong forming a part of the Javanese *gamelan*.

gelongsor [KK], *meng~*, to slide down, to slip down.

gelopak = **kelopak**.

gelora [KN], Ar. stormy, troubled; trouble, care; *ber~*, (fig.) seething, storming (with excitement, enthusiasm, etc.);

musim ~, E.C., the stormy season (November and December); also *gelurat* and *gelora*; *~ hati*, restlessness, anxiety, passions; *meng~kan*, to stir up, incite, spur on.

gelosok [KK], to scrub vigorously, an intense form of **gosok**.

gelotak [KK], *mang~*, to remove a hard husk.

geluga [KN], a red dye; *kayu ~*, the tree (the arnotto, *Bixa crellana*) from which this red dye is obtained.

gelugur [KN], *asam ~*, a tree with orange acid fruits used in flavouring curries *(Garcinia atroviridis)*; a fluted pattern in art.

gelugut [KK], *meng~*, to shiver; to quiver; to chatter (of the teeth).

geluh [KN], clay, mud.

geluk [KN], a water-vessel made of coconut shell.

gelulur [KK], *meng~*, to slip and roll, as a person at football; to slip off, as a garment.

gelumang [KS], *ber~*, to roll one's wet body in dust, flour, etc.; smeared with (mud, blood, etc.); *meng~*, to wallow in (mud, etc.); also *bergelomang*.

geluncur [KK], *meng~* = **gelongsor**.

gelung [KN], 1. a cutting or channel; the navigable channel for entering a river. 2. a loop (of rattan); a coil, as of hair; *ber~*, in loops, in coils; curled up. 3. Ked. an elephant track; = **denai**.

gelungsur [KK], *meng~*, to slip vertically down a chute or pole — cf. **gelincir** (which is a sideslip); also *geluncur*; *papan ~*, a chute (for play).

gelupar = **kelupar**.

gelupas = **kelupas**.

gelupur = **kelupur**.

gelut [KK], *ber~*, to strive, to contest, to compete, e.g., in boat-racing *(ber~ lancang)*; *bergelut benak*, to match brains; used of 'struggling' (of people in a crowd); milling about; *per~an*, wrestling, fight.

gema [KN], echo, reverberation; so, repercussions (esp. political); *ber~*, to resound; *meng~kan,* to re-echo.

gemak = **gemap.**

gemal [KN], a clump, a cluster; *ber~-~,* in clusters (of small stalks); ~ *padi,* a cluster of rice (on stalks).

gemala [KN], a talisman; a luminous bezoar; ~ *hikmat,* a magic gem; also **kemala.**

gemalai [KS], *lemah* ~, graceful movement, swaying gracefully, willowy (as a dancer); delicate, fine; also *kemalai.*

geman [KK], *geli* ~, repulsion at the sight of filth; feeling of nervous irritation, as at an unpleasant noise.

gemang [KS], thick; barrel-shaped.

gemap [KK], tergemap, taken aback, thunderstruck.

gemar [KK], *gemari,* to like, to take pleasure in; *ke~an,* delight; *suatu ke~an,* something which provides a special delight, such as a hobby or one's favourite relaxation; *peng~,* fan; *dia peng~ tennis,* he's a tennis fan.

gemas [KN], anger, envy, annoyance; annoyed.

gemaung [KS], murmur (of a crowd).

gemawan [KS], thin clouds.

gembak [KN], a tuft of grass; a lock of hair; also **gombak.**

gembal = **kembal.**

gembala [KN], Skr. a man employed to look after animals; ~ *anjing,* a dog-boy; ~ *ayam,* a poultry-tender; ~ *gajah,* a mahout; ~ *kambing,* a shepherd or goatherd; ~ *kuda,* a groom; *burung* ~ *kerbau,* the buffalo mynah; *burung* ~ *rimau,* the orange-breasted trogon; *tanah peng~an,* pasture, grassland.

gembar-gemburkan [KK], Ind. to brag loudly about, to harp on, to boost.

gembira [KS], passion, fire, enthusiasm, keen interest, excitement; happiness; *ber~,* to be happy or thrilled; to have a good time; *naik* ~, to become excited; *suara* ~, a rousing voice; *secara* ~, enthusiastically; *dengan* ~, with pleasure.

gembling [KK], Ind. *meng~,* to combine, weld together.

gembul [KN], a hemispherical excrescence; a knob on a tree-trunk.

gembung [KS], 1. = *kembung.* 2. = *gelembung;* ~ *politik,* political personages, 'big noises'.

gembur [KS], loose (of earth), friable; ~ *lagi,* not settled, not firmed up, of a new road; soft, pliant, elastic, of hair.

gembut [KN], 1. surface motion (the agitating cause being below the surface); the movement of sand when an animal is digging underneath; the movement of bed-clothes over a sleeper; the throbbing of the fontanel; *meng~,* to pulsate. 2. a canopy borne by an elephant.

gemelatuk [KK], shaking with cold or fear or with laughter.

gemeletap [KN], (onom.) continuous tapping — cf. *gemeteretap.*

gemelugut [KK], continuous shivering and trembling.

gementam [KN], (onom.) a crashing sound.

gementar [KS], trembling all over; *badan* ~ *kedinginan,* shivering with cold; ~ *(sebab) ketakutan,* trembling with fear; also *gemetar —* cf. **gentar, ketar,** etc.

gemerecak [KN], (onom.) the splash of oars or paddles.

gemerecang [KN], (onom.) continual clanking or clashing or jingling; sound of a tinkling crash, as of crockery.

gemerecik [KN], (onom.) a slight splashing sound.

gemeresik [KN], (onom.) continual rustling or crackling.

gemerlap [KS], glittering, (eyes) shimmering, sparkling (diamonds); *gemerlapan,* id.

gemerutuk [KN], (onom.) a continuous chatter.

gemetar [KS], trembling all over; also *gementar —* cf. **ketar, gentar** etc.; *badannya* ~ *kerana diserang sakit malaria,* she's shivering with malaria.

gemi [KN], *ikan* ~, the sucking-fish.

gemilang [KS], shining, dazzling, glittering; *gilang-~,* resplendent, radiant.

gempa [KN], an earthquake, us. *gempa*

bumi; a cataclysm; *gerak* ~, an earth-quake shock.

gempal [KS], average (in size or build); ~ *tubuhnya,* he was of average build.

gempar [KS], noise, clamour; ~ or *buat* ~, to bluff (by hectoring manner); disturbing rumours or sounds; *persidangan ter*~, extraordinary meeting; *lawatan ter*~, surprise visit; *meng~kan,* to alarm, frighten away; to shock, startle, cause sensation; *ke~an,* a sensation, startling occurrence.

gempita [KS], Skr. noise; *gegak* ~, extreme uproar.

gempur [KK], Ind. *meng*~, to attack, storm, assault; *askar peng*~, shock-troops.

gemuk [KS], fat, plump; rich (of soil); *gelempuk-*~, extremely fat; ~*-gempal,* plump, nicely rounded, as a girl; *bertambah* ~, to gain weight, *meng~kan,* fattening.

gemulah [KN], Ke. the late; ~ *Haji Ali,* Haji Ali deceased.

gemuruh [KS], the roll of thunder; the roar of many waters; the murmur of an angry crowd; thunderous; *tepuk sorak ber*~, thunderous applause.

genahar [KN], a furnace; the crater of a volcano.

genang-genang [KN], a kind of sweet-meat made of glutinous rice.

genang [KK], flooding, irrigating; to flow, as tears; *ter*~ *air,* flooded; *meng~i,* to irrigate, to inundate.

genap [KS], 1. complete, full, even; *dua puluh* ~, a full score; *se*~, every; *setelah* ~, on the completion of. 2. Kel = *tiap.*; *masuk tak* ~, *keluar tak ganjil,* an insignificant looking person; to be considered a nobody.

gencat [KS], *ter*~, 'put off', frustrated (as plant put in at wrong season), made backward in growth; ~*kan,* to check (progress or development); ~*an senjata,* cease-fire, armistice.

gencok [KK], keeping time, as by tapping foot.

gendala [KN], hindrance, obstruction, difficulty; *aral* ~, id.; *ter*~, held-up, ob-

structed, as a plan.

gendang [KN], a drum; ~ *Batak,* a name given to certain instruments of the monochord and primitive zither type; ~ *Keling,* a drum (both sides of which are beaten by the drummer); ~ *melela,* a drum (one side of which is beaten with the hand and the other with a drum-stick); ~ *raya,* a large drum used to summon people to mosque; ~~ *telinga,* ear-drum; *juru* ~, a drummer; *memalu* ~, *memukul* ~, to beat a drum; *menitir* ~, to beat a drum with swift rapping motion; *se*~, a large bundle (of cigarettes).

gendeng [KS], slanting, crooked, oblique; *ber*~~*an,* walk one behind the other.

gendap [KN], *juru*~, the leading drummer in a Malay band.

genderang [KN], a war-drum, state drum or processional drum — cf. **gendang**.

gendit [KN], a belt, a girdle; also *kendit*.

gendung = **kendung**.

gendut [KS], heavy and pendulous (of the stomach); pot-bellied.

genggam [KN], grasp, to seize in the closed hand; *se*~, a handful; ~*kan,* to seize in the closed hand; to seize in its talons (of a bird); *meng~kan tangan,* to clench the fist; *meng~kan penumbuk,* id.; ~*an,* grip.

genggang [KN], 1. striped gingham cloth; but *ber*~ is sometimes used to mean simply, striped, of cloth and sometimes covers checked cloth. 2. cleft, crevice, ajar (of door); *ter*~, ajar (door), open.

genggeng [KK], to carry an object by seizing a small portion of it between the teeth; *siput* ~, a shell *(Nautilus pompilius).*

genggong [KN], a sort of Jew's harp made of bamboo.

gengsi [KN], Ind. prestige, honour; social status.

genggulang [KN], an altar used by Malay *pawang.*

genih [KN], the teeth in a cow-elephant corresponding to the tusks in the male; also *genis.*

genit [KS], charming (of a girl); cute, petite, sexy; alluring; *ke~an*, allure.

genjala [KN], lamp-black.

genjang [KS], Pen. awry, crooked; aslant, not parallel; out of line; *~-genjut*, zigzag.

genjur [KS] ,= **kejur.**

genjut [KKtr], 1. aslant, awry — cf. *genjing.*

genta [KN], Skr. a bell, esp. a cattle-bell; *anak ~*, the clapper; *goyang ~*, to ring a bell.

gentala [KN], a magic wheeled car (in contradistinction to flying chariot); *naga ~*, a fabled dragon of monstrous size.

gentang-genit [KS], wavy and tapering to a point (as a kris).

gentar [KS], quivering, shaking, trembling — cf. **ketar** and **gementar.**

gentas [KK], 1. to pluck (a flower); to snap off, as a flower. 2. Ind. finished, ended.

gentat [KS], shrunken or withered on one side (of bones, of a fruit).

gentel [KN], a pellet; to roll up a pellet between thumb and finger-tips; *meng~-~*, to finger between fore-finger and thumb; to roll a ball along; (fig.) to control (a football) with tricky footwork.

genting [KS], 1. slender in the middle, as a very slim waist; *~ tanah,* isthmus; *~ bukit,* pass between hills, also *se~; pinggang ~,* a slim waist; so, delicate, crucial, critical, of a situation; *per~an,* narrow part of pass, narrow passage; *ke~an,* critical situation; *~ membawa putus,* the thin part (of a cord) brings a break i.e. a critical situation or an illustration of the fact that 'a chain is only as strong as its weakest link'. 2. *atap ~,* a tiled roof; *~ putus, biang menanti tembuk,* s.t. definite and conclusive, irrevocable.

gentung [KN], a large earthenware tub or jar.

genyeh [KK], to rub roughly, but less strongly than *gonyoh; meng~ mata,* to rub the eyes; *ber~-~ tangan,* to rub the hands together.

genyit [KK], *ter~,* twitching spasmodically;

meng~kan ekor, to twitch the tail; *meng~kan mata,* to blink, to wink; a variant of **kenyit.**

genyut [KS], not parallel; out of line; awry.

gepuh [KN], *~-~,* Ked. a padlock.

gepuk [KN], a small watch-shaped tobacco-box.

gera [KK], reminding, drawing attention to; *tembak ~,* Kel. to fire shots as a warnin~

gerabak [KN], a railway truck or coach.

gerabang [KS], *~ pari,* strips of salted skate preserved for food; *meng~,* in strips (of a wall with several planks out, of tattered fabrics).

geragas [KK], clawing, pawing, scrambling; *meng~,* to run (o.'s fingers through o.'s hair).

geragau [KN], a small shrimp; *Inche Geragau,* derisive nickname for Portuguese Eurasians.

geraham [KN], molar; *~ bongsu,* wisdom tooth.

gerai [[KN], a sleeping-dais or platform, or place for *bersanding;* a stall or stand at a sale or show.

gerak [KN], motion, movement; *~ hati,* impulse; intuition, presentiment; *ber~,* to move, to stir; mobile, not static; *~kan (dari tidur),* to awaken (someone) from sleep, to 'call'; *meng~kan,* to give motion to; *tenaga ~,* working power, kinetic (dynamic); *~an, per~an,* political movement; *~ angkatan muda,* Youth Movement; *~ bumi,* an earthquake, = *gempa bumi; pelajaran ~ badan,* physical training; *~ geri,* bodily or other movements; *~-langkah,* gait, movements; (fig.) actions; *~ balas,* reflexes, reaction (physical, as to a stimulus); *~an polis,* a police operation; *~an tentera,* military operation; *bilik ~an,* operations room.

geram [KS], 1. Pers. warm (of anger, courage or passion); *memberi ~,* to excite; *naik ~,* to become excited; used esp. in relation to children; a child is said to be *geram,* i.e. exciting to affection, cute, cuddlesome; conversely, a person seeing a child may feel *geram*, i.e. keenly affectionate. 2. acronym of *gerakan angkatan muda*, see under **gerak**.

gerang [KN], 1. an oily cosmetic obtained by burning coconut-husks and other vegetable substances; used in old-fashioned teeth-blackening; *meng~*, to blacken (the teeth). 2. see **gerangan**.

gerangan [Kktr], perchance, perhaps — or expression suggesting doubt or interrogation; *bulan pernama ~ jatuh daripada langit yang ketujuh?*, can it be that the full moon has fallen from the seventh heaven?; see also **gerang**.

gerapai [KK], *meng~*, to fumblle with the hands, to feel about; to clutch at.

gerapak [KK], to bluff, attempting to frighten; *ter~*, 'put off' (from some action) through fear.

gerat [KK], *meng~kan*, a corrugation (on hard substances, esp. horn).

gerapu [KS], *ber~*, rough to the touch, as the skin of a toad.

gerau [KN], Ked. a palace cook.

gerayang [KK], *meng~;* 1. to go about picking up odds and ends; foraging around, gleaning. 2. to run one's fingers over.

gerbak [KN], to spread (of an odour).

gerbang [KN], spread out extended; *pintu ~*, the main gate; also an arch; *meng~*, to open or spread out; to be dishevelled (of hair).

gerbung [KN], railway coach or truck.

gerebak [KN], a noisy clapper used to frighten squirrels and birds from fruit-trees.

geredak [KN], (onom.) a heavy bumping sound — cf. **geduk**.

geredam [KN], (onom.) a heavy repeated slamming sound.

geregak [KK], 1. *~-geregau*, clawing at, grabbing at, as when searching for food. 2. a bamboo clapper = **gerebak**.

gerehak [KK], (onom.) coughing up phelgm.

gereja [KN], Port. a church.

gerek [KK], 1. *meng~*, to bore; *ber~*, perforated; *peng~, seng~*, awl. 2. ea-

ger, keen; = **gerang**.

geremut [KK], *meng~*, to throb (of a boil); to crowd (of persons, insects); *meng~-menggeramat*, seething, 'boiling', as ants or a vast crowd.

gerencang [KN], (onom.) a continually repeated clanging noise.

gerendek [KN], tremulous and low (of a voice).

gerendeng [KS], snappish, irritable.

gerendik [KN], a small fitting; *ber~*, full of gadgets.

gerengau [K], clawing, scratching; scraping (a hard surface).

gerenseng [KN], 1. a large pan for boiling rice. 2. Jav. *kain ~ wayang*, a pattern of *sarong* much referred to in literature.

gerentam [KN], (onom.) *meng~*, to stamp the feet; also **geretam**.

gerenyau [KS], restless (of children); skittish, forward, of a girl; unmannered (usually of girls).

gerenyot [KK], 1. *meng~*, to wriggle about, esp. from discomfort. 2. [KS], crooked (of the mouth).

geretak [KN], a type of tree, *Turpinia pomifera*.

geretam [KN], (onom.) *meng~*, to stamp in anger; a knocking or bumping sound; also **gerentam**.

gergaji [KN], a saw; *yu ~*, the large sawfish; *~ tangan*, pad saw, fox saw; *penggergaji kayu*, sawyer; *habuk ~*, sawdust; *serbuk ~*, id.; *seperti ~, dua mata*, like a saw with two blades, i.e. something that catches you both ways, 'coming and going'; *seperti ~, sorong makan, tarik makan*, id.; also *gaji-gaji*.

gergasi [KN], Skr. a tusked man-eating demon; a name given to the aborigines of Kedah; a giant of legend.

gerham [KN], a molar tooth; *~ bongsu*, a wisdom tooth.

gerhana [KN], Skr. eclipse; *kena ~*, to suffer eclipse — a metaphor for great man under calamity.

geri [KN] *gerak-geri*, involuntary movement or unconscious gesture.

geriang [KN], iguana, monitor lizard.

gericau [KN], *meng~,* to chatter (of a shrilly twittering bird).

gerigi [KN], tooth-edged; regularly serrated; a ratchet; *peng~an,* the milling on a coin — cf.**gigi** and **gerigis**; *daun-daun ber~,* these serrated leaves.

gerigis [KS], jagged; irregularly serrated — cf. **gigi** and **gerigi**.

gerila [KN], guerrilla, *terlibat dalam kegitan ~,* his involvement in guerrila warefare.

gerim [KN], *kain ~,* a coarse flannel cloth.

gerimis [KN], Ind. drizzling, of rain.

gerinda [KN], *batu ~,* a whetstone; a stone used for filing teeth.

gering [KS], sick (of a prince); *~ ulu,* a prince's headache; *~ tengah,* stomach-ache.

gerit [KK], 1. (onom.) the gnawing of a mouse, screech (of pencils, pens) — cf. **kerit**. 2. *akar ~~,* a generic name for a number of rubbervines belonging to the order *Apocynaceoe.*

gerlap [KK], *meng~,* to glitter, sparkle.

gerling = **kerling**.

germang [KS], *meng~,* to bristle up (of short hair); from fear, nausea etc.

germit [KN], Pen. an auger; a drill.

gerobak [KN], truck, wagon, coach; *~ lembu,* bullock cart; *~ roda,* wheelbarrow; *~ sorong,* handcart.

gerobek [KS], full of holes.

gerobok [KN], 1. Jav. a crockery chest, a cupboard; sometimes used for 'railway trucks', as opposed to a passenger coach, cf. **gerabak**. 2. *meng~,* to bubble up (of boiling water).

gerodak [KN], (onom.) *meng~,* to rumble, to rattle.

gerogoh [KN], a barrel-like trap for prawns and crabs.

gerombolan [KN], Ind. a group, a band; gang.

gerombong [KN], *~an,* group, party, troop.

gerondong [KN], goitre, *gondong,* id.

geronggang [KN], hollow; lacking in kernel or core; a deep hollow, a chasm.

geronggong [KN], 1. the name of a tree *(Cratoxylon arborescens).* 2. a stinging

medusa or jelly-fish much feared by Malays.

gersang [KS], dry, barren; (fi~) vain, barren, unfruitful, as a way of life; a variant of *kersang.*

gersik [KN], gravel, coarse sand; also *kersik.*

gertak [KK], 1. to bully, to intimidate, to browbeat, display a threatening attitude; *meng~,* bluffing; *meng~kan,* to urge on (a horse); *main ~ sambal,* to make empty threats. 2. a bridge; also **geretak**.

geru [KK], *meng~,* to trumpet (of elephant).

gerudi [KN], Tam. an auger; a boring drill; also **gurdi**.

gerugul [KN], *hantu ~,* an evil spirit of the forest.

geruh [KS], constitutional bad luck; persistent misfortune; *buat ~-gerah,* to 'ask for' trouble.

geruit [KK], *meng~,* to wriggle, to squirm.

geruk [KN], a wrapper used to prevent a heavy fruit (such as *nangka* or *cempedak)* from falling to the ground through its own weight.

gerun [KS], 1. panic, alarm; *peng~,* formidable in appearance or manner; *meng~kan,* to terrify, scare, commanding respect. 2. Sum. jungle; *kambing ~,* the Malay serow *(Nemorhoedus swettenhami).*

gerung [KN], (onom.) *meng~,* to growl (of a wild beast).

gerunyut [KK], giving a twinge (of pain).

gerup [KN], a portion of a Malay loom in which the comb *(sisir)* is fixed.

gerupuh [KN], (onom.) *meng~,* to splash about.

gerus [KK], sand-papering, polishing; *di~,* polished (of certain Bugis fabrics); the big cowrie used for such polishing; *kain ~an,* glossy cloth.

gerut [KN], *ikan ~~,* a fish *(Pristipoma hasta),* the grunter; *meng~,* to emit grunting noises.

gerutu [KS], 1. rough to the touch, as a badly tapped rubber tree (stronger than *gerapu).* 2. *meng~,* to grumble, grouse, 'belly-ache'; *kena* ~, to get grumbled at, nagged; cf. **kerutu.**

gerutup [KN], (onom.) the noise of artillery fire; *meng*~, to crackle and bang, as a fusillade.

gesa [KK], impulse, urge; *ter*~-~, much moved, impulsively, hastily; *meng*~, to urge; *jangan ter*~-~, take your time.

gesek [KK], rubbing or scraping a sharp edge against anything; scour; ~ *api*, Kel. matches; *meng*~ *biola,* to play the violin — cf. **gesel** and **geser.**

gesel [KK], rubbing two sticks or other light bodies together e.g., in ignition by friction; *ber*~ *bahu,* to rub shoulders, be next to one another; *meng*~-~, to rub up against — cf. **gesek** and **geser.**

geser [KK], scraping past each other (as two ships striking each other at an extremely acute angle); *ber*~ *bahu,* to rub shoulders — cf. **gesek** and **gesel.**

geta [KN], Skr. a dais, a sleeping-platform; a broad sofa or couch; ~ *kerajaan,* a royal divan; ~ *peraduan,* a state bed; *per*~*an,* basis, foundation, 'platform'.

getah [KN], sap; latex or gum produced by trees, gutta, caoutchouc; bird-lime; gum; *pokok* ~, a caoutchouc-yielding tree; ~ *ipuh,* the poisonous sap of the ipoh *(Antiaris toxicaria)* used as dart-poison; ~ *jelutung, (Dichopsis obovata);* ~ *keping,* sheet-rubber; ~ *tarik,* scrap-rubber; ~ *busa,* foam-rubber; ~ *padu,* coagulated rubber; ~ *cair,* uncoagulated rubber; ~ *asli,* natural rubber, plantation rubber; ~ *tiruan,* synthetic rubber; *meng*~, to collect latex, catch birds with rubber; *pokok (~) kawin,* a bud-grafted rubber tree; *susu (pokok ~)* latex; *Institusi Penyelidikan* ~, the Rubber Research Institute.

getak [KK], to drop off (= **gegak**, but used of lighter objects).

getang [KN], = **ketang.**

getar [KK], *meng*~, to shiver, to vibrate; to shudder (with horror), ~*an jiwa,* emotion(s).

getas [KN], brittle, crisp, as a biscuit; *meng*~, to snap off, as a stalk; ~-~, a

Malay cake.

getek [KS], 1. loose in gait or manner; *menunjuk* ~, to assume a 'fast' manner; loose conduct (woman); *meng*~ *ikan,* to fish using rod and line with a live fish as bait. *ter*~-~, moving pompously. 2. Kel. = *juga.*

geti [KN], 1. *pokok* ~ = **turi** 2. 2. ~-~, a Malay cake.

getik [KK], 1. Pk. to loathe, abominate. 2. ~*kan,* to pick at, esp. a sore.

getil [KK], pinching, nipping — cf. **ketip, ketam, getu** etc.

getir [KS], Ind. bitter,; also **getar.**

getis [KK], 1. *meng*~, to break the stalk of a flower; to pinch off, as a bud. 2. fragile, delicate, brittle.

getu [KK], nipping between the finger-nails; breaking off; *meng*~ *tangkai padi,* to break off the ear of a rice-plant from the stalk; *meng*~ *kuman,* to kill a louse or flea; to squeeze (between o's nails) — cf. **getil, ketip** etc.

gewang [KN], mother-of-pearl.

ghafur [KS], Ar. very forgiving, all merciful (of God); *ya Ghafur al-Rahim,* oh, most forgiving and merciful One! (a common superscription to old-style letters).

ghaib [KK], Ar. hidden, concealed, obscure; super-natural; *kuasa* ~, occult power; *ilmu* ~, spiritualism; occult power; the Unseen, esp. the world of spirits; vanished; ~*lah dia,* he vanished; *perkataan yang* ~, mysterious words; *rijal ul*-~, spirits presiding over good and evil fortune; *sembahyang* ~, prayer for the absent dead; also (coll.) **raip.**

ghairah [KS], Ar. 1. envy, emulation, enthusiasm. 2. delight, rapture, thrill; *men*~*kan,* to stir, rouse to delight; also *ghairat, gair* and *gairat; ke*~*an,* longing, desire, passion, jealousy.

ghalabah [KS], 1. Ar. melancholy, anxious. 2. ascendance, success, cf. **ghalib.**

ghalat [KS], 1. Ar. mistake, error. 2. aversion, dislike; also **galat.**

ghalib [KS], 1. Ar. victorious, conquering. 2. normal, usual.

gharib [KN], Ar. foreign; a stranger.

ghulam [KN], Ar. a slave; servant; serf.

ghusul [KN], Ar. ritual washing, esp. of the dead.

gi [KN], 1. Hind. ghee; clarified butter. 2. Kel. = *pergi*.

gian [KS], exhausted (of money); penniless.

giang [KS], = **miang**.

giat [KK], 1. *meng~*, to taunt, mock at, 'get a rise' out of. 2. Ind. to show enthusiasm, to do all one can; *secara ~*, eagerly; *ber~*, active, zealous; *meng~kan kembali*, to revive; *meng~kan usaha*, to intensify one's efforts; *ke~an*, zeal, activities; *ke~an subersib*, subversive activities.

giang [KS], indecent, lustful, lewd.

giau [KN], *pisau peng~*, a bill-hook; a sickle; *meng~*, cutting rice crop with a sickle.

gibas [KN], fat-tailed sheep.

gigi [KN], tooth; the serrated or rippling edge of anything; *~ anjing* or *~ asu*, the canine teeth; *~ air*, the rippled surface of water; the edge of the sea (on the beach); *per~an air*, the brink of sea or other water; *per~an pantai*, the (seaward) edge of the beach; *~ berdukung*, overlapping teeth; *~ hutan*, the uneven fringes of the jungle; *~ jentera*, the teeth of a toothed wheel; *~ kapak*, large front teeth; *~ laut*, high-water mark; *~ manis*, the incisor teeth; *~ taring*, eye-tooth; *~ asu*, *~ siung*, id.; *~ gerham*, molar; *~ tua*, wisdom tooth; *~ bungsu*, id.; *salut ~*, enamel of teeth; *~ kena makan dek ulat*, a decayed tooth; *~ parang-parang*, small separated teeth; *~ sisir*, the teeth of a rake or comb; *~ sulung*, the four front teeth; *~ tikus*, small regular teeth; *pencungkil ~*, a toothpick — cf. **gigit, gerigi, gerigis**; *~ buatan*, artificial tooth, denture; *doktor ~*, dental surgeon, dentist; *sakit ~*, toothache; *tinggal ~ dengan lidah sahaja*, to be utterly destitute; *tidak ber~ lagi*; spineless, powerless.

gigih [KS], Ind. persevering, steadfast; *pejuang yang ~*, a determined fighter.

gigil [KS], *meng~*, to shiver; to tremble, to quiver; to shake (with laughter, etc.); to quaver, be tremulous, of the voice.

gigit [KK], *meng~*, biting; to bite; *ter~ jari* (fig.) all the efforts were in vain, to look foolish; — cf. **gigi**.

gila [KS], mad, insane; *~ babi*, epilepsy; *~ bahasa*, cracked, eccentric; *~ berahi*, madly in love; *~ isim*, religion mad; *~ ekor*, *~ urat*, amative, salacious; *~ talak*, a sort of nervous breakdown sometimes affecting a man after divorce; *~ angin*, mentally unbalanced; *~ kebangsaan*, ultra-nationalistic, chauvinist; *~ bayang*, infatuated, esp. for the unattainable; *ayam ~ mengeram*, broody hen; *~ hormat*, (fig.) ambitious, status conscious; *~ kuasa*, power hungry; *anyam ~*, pattern in *mengkuang* work; *murai ~*, a fantail flycatcher (*Rhipadura* sp.); *yu ~*, a fish (*Chyloscillium indicum*); *meng~kan*, to be mad after (with love); *ter~~ pada*, *meng~i*, id.; *main ~*, to play the fool — cf. Jav. *edan*.

gilang [KS], shining; *~ gemilang*, radiant, dazzling, resplendent — cf. **gilap**.

gilap [KS], lustrous (of a polished surface); reflected (of light); to polish, rub up — cf. **gilang**; *pe~*, a hone, strop; *peng~*, id.; *perut kosong peng~ otak*, an empty belly sharpens the brains.

gilas [KK], Ind. *meng~*, to run over, knock down, collide with; *peng~ jalan*, steam roller.

gilau [KN], = **kilau**.

giling [KK], *meng~*, to roll into a spherical or cylindrical shape; rolling up a cigarette; grinding curry-stuff, etc.; *batu ~*, a roller for grinding curry-spices; *~an*, N.S. axle of water-wheel; *peng~*, a steamroller.

gilir [KK], *ber~*, occurrence in succession; turn; *ia duduk sampai ~an tarinya*, he sat down till it came to his turn to dance; *ber~~*, in succession, in turn; *~an*, one's turn; the word is also used to describe the rule of succession by which two or more families take it in turn to provide the successor to an office or title: the rule is almost confined to Negri Sembilan.

gilis [KK], 1. Sel. = **linggis**. 2. = **gilas**.

gincah [KK], = **kincah**.

gincu [KN], Ch. rouge; ~ *bibir*, lipstick.

ginjal [KN], the kidneys; *anak* ~, adrenal, the upper portion of the kidney, *batu* ~, stone in the kidney.

ginjat [KK], *ter~-~*, moving about on tiptoe; pottering about, fussing about.

girang [KS], glad, delighted, merry, elated; *ber~ (hati)*, to be cheerful; *ke~an*, happiness, gladness, joyously.

girap [KS], quickening, as of a stroke or heart; to accelerate the stroke while rowing; *~-gemirap*, beating fast, of heart; — cf. **kirap** and **perap**.

giri [KN], Skr. mountain — in compounds such as *Indera-~*.

giring [KK], 1. *meng~*, to drive (wild animals); *gembala itu meng~ kambing-kambingnya ke padang rumput*, the shepherd led his goats to the pasture. 2. *~-~*, a sort of bell made out of seashell.

gisal [KK], to rub, e.g., a seed-pod or a powder in the palms of the hands; to rub gently (something on to a surface, as lipstick on lips); to rub down; to massage (the body etc.).

gisar [KK], *meng~*, to twist, to give a twisting motion to anything — cf. **kisar**.

gitar [KN], Eng. a guitar; *tubuh potongan* ~, a shapely body (curved in the right places).

giur [KK], Ind. *meng~kan*, to delight, enrapture, thrill; *menimbulkan ke~an*, to give a thrill, arouse a thrill; *ter~*, charmed, enchanted.

gua [KN], 1. Skr. a cave; *kelawar* ~, a bat *(Chiromeles torquatus); kambing* ~, the Malayan serow; *burung* ~, the whistling thrush; *ibu* ~, Treng. the swallow which makes edible nests. 2. Ch. I, me.

gobar KS], 1. Ar. gloomy, sombre, overcast (as a sky when a storm is brewing); ~ *hati*, depressed, worried. 2. spreading (of a rumour).

gobek [KN], an areca-nut pounder (used by the toothless); ~ *api*, a fire-syringe; *anak* ~, *calak* ~, pestle; *tombong* ~, removable base of pounder; *meng~*, to pound.

gobok [KN], a primitive house, esp. of bamboo, a shack.

goblok, [KS], Ind. dull, stupid; *si-~*, a fool; *ke~an*, stupidity.

gocoh [KK], 1. to punch with the fist; *~i*, to so strike (a blow) (especially woman); *meng~*, to strike (a person). 2. hurrying; *ber~-ganyah*, in frantic haste; a variant of *kocoh*.

goda [KK], spurring on; harassing; *meng~*, to urge on; ~ *angin*, Treng. a whirlwind; *~an nafsu*, the urge of the senses, temptations; *meng~i*, also (fig.) to tempt; to seduce.

godak [KK], *meng~*, to stir up, esp. as to stir so as to mix ingredients; used particularly of stirring herbs so as to mix with rice; *nasi* ~, such a mixture.

godam [KK], *meng~*, to strike a heavy blow (e.g., with a mace); *peng~*, a club or knuckleduster.

godar [KN], *kayu* ~, driftwood on the edge of the sea.

godek [KK], 1. *ter~-~*, wagging, like a dog's tail. 2. whisker(s).

godok [KK], *meng~*, to boil; ~ *kepala*, the occipital bone.

gogoh [KS], shivering with extreme cold.

gogok [KK], to gulp down, as a pill; also *ogok*.

gogol [KN], a long-handled chisel used by braziers.

gok [KN], 1. Siam., Kel. jail. 2. hump of cattle — cf. **enggok**.

golak [KK], *~-galik*, topsy-turvy — cf. *bolak-balik; per~an*, movements, agitation, disturbances; *ber~*, in a disturbed state; *hati ber~*, 'upset'.

golang [KK], *~-golek*, to sway (of a spherical or cylindrical body).

golek [KK], 1. easily swaying; easily shaken or rolled; rolling, rocking; *ter~-~*, rolling along; *tahan* ~, (of a boat) not easily upset; *golang-~*, swaying or rocking;

hantu ~, a sheeted ghost believed to propel itself by rolling along the ground; *sampan* ~, (Pen.) the common Chinese *sampan*. 2. *wayang* ~, puppet show.

golok [KN], a chopper for clearing jungle; ~-*galar*, Pk. covered with scratches; ~ *kayu*, charlatan, empty braggart; *dapat juga berhutang ber*~, to get it by borrowing the money or by using a chopper; i.e., by hook or by crook.

golong [KK], *meng~kan*, to group, to classify, form into several parties etc., *ter*~, included, incorporated, to belong to; ~ *bangsa*, population group, ~ *terbesar*, majority; *peng~an*, classification.

gomba [KN], Skr. the frontlet of an elephant.

gombak [KN], a tuft (of grass); a lock (of hair); crested (of birds).

gombang [KN], an anchored purse-net; *ber*~, wearing a *sarong* without garment underneath it; also *pompang*.

gomol [KK], *ber*~, to wrestle, come to grips; not used of wrestling as a sport (*gusti*).

goncang [KK], to cause anything to rock or sway, to shake, e.g., a bottle or a branch; ~*kan* and *meng*~, id.; *ber*~, shaky, unstable; *ter*~, tremble, shake violently; ~ *otak*, a concussion of the brain.

gondang [KN], *siput* ~, a generic name for several marine shells of the genus *Dolium*; ~ *bukit*, a land shell (*Cyclophorus* sp.).

gondok [KS], squat (of the neck); *leher* ~, bull-necked.

gondol [KS], bare; hairless; treeless; stripped bare; *ber*~, hatless; *meng*~, to carry off, make off with, as, esp. swag; the underlying idea seems to be that of stripping.

gondong [KN], Pat. goitre; mumps.

gondrong [KS], long-haired.

gong [KN], 1. a gong (with a hemispherical protuberance, while the *canang* has not); *pemukul* ~, the striker of a gong. 2. Kel. a ridge between rice-fields, = *permatang*. 3. Kel. eccentric, stupid.

gonggong [KK], 1. seizing and carrying off in the mouth (as a dog or bird). 2. a generic name for a number of shells (mostly of the genus Strombus). 3. *meng~*, to bark.

gonjak [KK], to make fun of; *kena* ~, to 'have one's leg pulled' by a flatterer.

gonjing [KK], *ber*~, to wrangle; to abuse, speak ill of.

gonjong [KS], acute-angled (of a woman's coiffure {*sanggul*}).

gonyeh [KK], to chew between toothless gums.

gonyoh [KK], to rub out impurities, scrubbing (when bathing); ~-*ganyah*, scrubbing vigorously.

gopoh [KS], to hurry; ~-*gapah* or ~ *mamang*, hurry-scurry; *ke~an*, hastiness.

gopong [KN], N.S. a coconut-shell bowl in rattan holder, = **sekul**.

goreng [KK], frying in a pan; Pen. to 'butter up', flatter; *(laris) seperti pisang* ~, (selling freely) like banana-fry (i.e. like hot cakes); ~, a fry, a fried dish.

gores [KN], a scratched line; ~ *api*, matches; *ter*~ *di hati*, engraved on the heart, unforgettable.

gosok [KK], ~*kan*, to scrub, rub; *meng*~, id.; to stroke; *meng*~~, (fig.) to arouse anger, incite; *meng*~ *gigi*, to clean the teeth.

gosong [KN], a shoal, submerged bank.

gotong [KK], Ind. *ber*~-*royong*, co-operating, helping one another; *secara ber*~-*royong*, collectively, in mutual co-operation.

goyah [KS], loose, shaky, as a tooth.

goyang [KS], *ber*~, to shake, to sway; *duduk ber*~ *kaki*, to sit and swing one's legs, i.e. to be at a loose end, to twiddle one's thumbs, esp. of a person who can afford not to work — cf. **goncang**.

gu [KN], 1. a (double) yoke for bullocks; (fig.) a match (able to contend); a pair; *ber*~ *dengan*, paired with (as in a doubles match; = *igu* — cf. **kok**. 2. *Cik'Gu*, common appellation for a schoolmaster (= *guru*).

guam [KN], 1. thrush in children. 2. *pe~*,

Kel. a lawyer, pleader; *pe~ agung,* the Attorney-General.

guar [KN], Ked. hillock, rising ground.

gubah [KK], wearing in the hair (as a flower or jewelled ornament is worn); *di~,* pressed into a flower-like pattern (of slices of boiled egg); *meng~,* arrange; gubahan, (poet.) a posy; a composition; arrangement; *peng~,* a composer; *peng~ lagu,* a composer of music; *~-~,* decorative arrangements.

gubal [KN], the portion (of a tree-trunk) immediately under the bark; *nyiur ~,* a coconut with the husk off; *~an,* prospective, likely candidate for; *~an undang-undang,* a Bill, proposed law; *meng~kan,* to draft (as a Bill); *peng~,* legislator; *peng~an,* legislation.

gubang [KN], 1. a one-masted sea-going *perahu* of a Bugis type. 2. a notch cut in a tree-trunk to facilitate climbing.

gubar [KK], *meng~kan,* to liquidate, to wind up, dissolve; a variant of **bubar.**

gubuk [KN], hut, shelter, shed (in a rice field).

guci [KN], a vessel of glazed earthenware.

gudang [KN], a store-house; a godown; *~ senjata,* arms-magazine.

gudu [KN], *~-~,* a hookah; a hubble-bubble.

gugah [KK], *meng~,* to awake; *ter~,* moved, stirred by emotion.

gugat [KK], Ind. 1. to criticise adversely. 2. to make claims, to make demands, agitate.

gugup [KS], 1. booming, pealing; a confused noise. 2. nervous, agitated; *ter~-~,* nervous, faltering, of speech; *ke~an,* nervousness, panic; *peng~,* a nervous person; —cf. **gagap.**

gugur [KK], to miscarry; premature fall (of fruit); a sudden and unnatural fall; to drop; *ke~an kanak-kanak,* miscarriage; *~ pengsan,* to fall in a faint; *bintang ~,* a falling star; to crash (of a plane); *musim ~,* autumn *ber~an,* to fall off; *daun-daun ber~an,* the leaves fell off in heaps; *meng~kan,* to drop, as a bomb; *meng~kan anak,* to abort a child.

gugus [KN], patchy; *~an pulau-pulau,* an

archipelago; *ber~-~,* in patches, in clusters, e.g., of *rambai, langsat,* of football players in a scrimmage.

guit [KK], a gentle sidelong push with the foot — cf. **kuit.**

gula [KN], sugar; sugary substances obtained from plants; *~ batu,* loaf sugar; *~ tepung,* finely sifted sugar, caster sugar; *~ nyiur, ~ tuak,* palm sugar made from juice obtained from the coconut-palm; also called *~ Melaka; ~ kabung,* palm sugar obtained from the juice of the sugar-palm; *~ nipah,* palm sugar made from the juice of the nipah-palm; *mati semut kerana ~,* ants die for the sake of sugar, i.e. tempting objects may lead into danger; *penyakit ~,* diabetes; *~ pasir,* granular sugar; *meng~kan,* flattering, 'buttering up'; *~ kabung* and *~ batu* are used for 'sweetheart'.

gulai [KN], currying; curried food; *meng~,* to prepare curry; *~kan,* to curry, make into curry (fig.) to make things hot for a person, castigate.

gulana [KS], *gundah ~,* despondent, sad.

gulat [KK], Ind. bergulat, to struggle, strive; *ber~ demi penakatan,* struggling to survive; *per~an,* struggle, conflict.

guli [KN], *buah ~,* marbles; *main ~,* to play marbles.

guling [KK], to roll, revolving; *~ gantang,* rolling over and over; *~-garak,* rolling uneasily; *~kan,* to roll (a cylindrical object); *ter~-~,* rolling about; *~-tahi,* the dung-beetle; *meng~kan,* (fig.) to subvert, overthrow; to throw (in wrestling), 'floor'; *ber~,* to have a roll, as a horse; *bantal ~,* Dutch wife (a long round pillow).

gulita [KS], *gelap ~,* pitch dark.

gulung [KK], *meng~,* rolling up; *tikar dua ~,* two mats; *~ tikar,* to roll up the mat (the last thing done before moving house), so (fig.) to 'pack up' (having lost everything or as giving up the struggle); *~an,* a community, a circle; a class of society; *~an yang kecil,* minorities; *meng~ perdebatan,* to wind up a debate; *ber~,* to roll (self) into a ball.

gumal [KK], *meng~*, to rumple, crumple; *meng~ tanah*, (fig.) to grub up the earth (in agriculture); a variant of *kumal.*

gumpal [KN], spherical lump or clod; a ball, e.g., of thread; *ber~*, clotted, coagulated; (fig.) to grapple; *~an orang*, a small crowd of people; *~an awan*, a mass of clouds; *~an rambut*, a mass of (dressed) hair, coiffure; *~kan*, to roll up, as cloth; also *gumpil.*

gun [KN], Ked. gently rising ground.

guna [KN], Skr. use, utility; magic art; *ubat ~*, a philtre; *apa ~?*, why?, for what purpose?; *membalas ~*, to show one's gratitude; *~kan*, to make use of; *ber~*, useful; *ber~ sekali*, to serve well.

gunawan [KN], Skr. skilled in magic art — cf. **guna**.

gundah [KS], sad, despondent; *~ gulana*, id.; *~kan*, to sorrow after.

gundal [KN], a knob, e.g., on a stick.

gundi [KN], decorated with coloured paper; *kembal ~*, Pk. baskets so decorated and used at weddings. 2. = **guni**.

gundik [KN], an inferior wife of a prince, i.e. a wife married formally to his *keris* or to his *bulang hulu*, but not to the prince himself.

gunggang [KS], Pah. hollow — cf. **geronggang**.

guni [KN], Hind. a sack, a 'gunny-bag'.

gunjai [KN], a fringe or ornamental tassel at the end of a puggaree.

guntai [KS], wide, of stride; *melangkah ~*, to stride along, walk with wide strides, stalk along.

guntil [KN], a small sack.

gunting [KN], shearing; shears, scissors; the 'cut' of clothes; *meng~*, to cut with a pair of scissors; to 'cut' clothes; *ber~ rambut*, to have a hair-cut; *tukang ~ rambut*, hair-dresser, barber; *meng~ dalam lipatan* (prov.) to cheat one's close associates; *~an surat khabar*,

newspaper cutting.

guntung [KS], 1. stumpy through the removal of a projection; cutting short; *tiang ~*, a mast when the topmast has been removed. 2. a hill-locked basin.

guntur [KN], thunder.

gunung [KN], a mountain; *ber~-ganang*, mountainous; *pekakian ~*, foothills; *pe~an*, highlands; *~ berapi*, volcano.

gurau [KK], sporting; jesting; flirting; *~ jenaka*, quips and cranks; *senda ~*, dalliance, flirtation; *ber~*, to flirt; to sport; to jest; *secara ber~*, sportively.

gurdi [KN], = **gerudi**.

guri [KN], 1. a small vessel of earthenware, larger than *takar*, smaller than *tempayan*. 2. a slipway; a dry dock.

gurindam [KN], Tam. a proverbial verse; a well-known saying appositely quoted.

guris [KK], scratched; *meng~ hati*, offend, give offence.

guru [KN], Skr. a teacher; *mak ~* or *siti ~*, a school-mistress; *Betara Guru*, Siva; a teacher is generally addressed as *Cik Gu — Mr Teacher*; *per~an*, the art of teaching, pedagogy; *~* is also used to mean familiar spirit, 'guide'.

guruh [KN], thunder - -cf. **gemuruh**.

gus [Kktr], together, all the time, collectively; *ditembaknya tiga kali ~*, they all fired together three times, i.e. they fired three volleys.

gusar [KS], Hind. taking offence; *jangan ~*, do not be offended; *~i*, to become angry; *~* is sometimes used to mean excited, upset.

gusi [KN], 1. the gums; *tinggal ~ sahaja*, only gums left, i.e. toothless. 2. bran.

gustan [KK], Eng. to go astern, to reverse (a car).

gusti [KN], 1. Jav. a title of some distinction; master, lord. 2. Pers. wrestling; *bermain ~* or *ber~*, to wrestle; *ahli ~*, a wrestler. 3. Hind. instalments of loan.

H

haba [KN], heat, warmth of the air, hotness.
habia [KN], Kel. court fees.
habib [[KN], Ar. a title of respect given to Syeds.
habis [KK], done, finished; entirely; the end of; *belum* ~, not yet finished; *se*~-~, utterly, completely; ~*i*, to come to an end of; *peng*~*an*, termination, end; *ke*~*an wang*, he's gone broke; *per*~*kan*, to finish; *yang peng*~*an sekali*, the last; *se*~-~*nya*, to the fullest extent; ~-~*an*, id.; *meng*~-~*kan*, to squander; ~-~*kan waktu*, to idle away o's time; ~ *perkara*, no more to be said, that's the end of it, period! *tak* ~-~*nya*, to keep on.
habluk [KN], Hind. piebald (of a horse).
hablur [KN], = **abelur**.
Habshah [KN], Abyssinia.
Habshi [KN], Ar. Abyssinian, Ethiopian, Negro; *orang* ~, a Negro.
habuan [KN], a share, portion.
habuk [KN], 1. = **abuk**; ~ *gergaji*, sawdust. 2. Pk. traps, belongings; share, possession. 3. Kel. strengthens a negative; *tak ada seorang* ~, not a single man was there.
had [KN], Ar. up to, as far as, also *hat*; *ber*~, limited; ~*laju*, speed-limit; *papan tanda* ~ *laju*, speed-limit sign.
hadar [KK], *mati* ~, death without a just cause, an unwarranted death.
hadam [KN], Ar. digestion; also **hajam**.
hadap [KN], position in front of, facade (of house); *raja di* ~ *menterinya sekelian*, a prince with his ministers before him; ~*an*, front, portion in front; *ber*~ *dengan*, to face, to stand directly opposite; *meng*~*i ajalnya*, to be about to die; *di* ~*an*, in the presence of, in front of; *us* shortened to *depan*; *ke ha*~, to the front; forward; *meng*~*i*, to face; *meng*~*i jalan buntu*, we're getting nowhere, at a dead end; *meng*~*kan*, to set in front, to place

in front; *meng*~ or *mengadap*, to enter the presence of (a prince); to have an audience of a superior; ~*kan*, to put forward (as a proposal); *ter*~, relative to, regarding; facing; in relation to, in face of.
hadas [KK], Ar. *mandi* ~, ablution after menstruation or defecation; ~ *besar (kecil)*, great (small) impurity.
hadiah [KN], Ar. a gift; a prize, a reward; ~ *harijadi*, birthday presents.
hadir [KN], Ar. presence, to be present; *meng*~*i*, to attend, be present; *orang* ~*an*, those present, the audience; *meng*~*kan diri*, to present oneself; *para* ~*an*, all those present.
hadis [KN], Ar. the traditional sayings and deeds of the Prophet, not contained in the Koran; sometimes used for moral sayings, logia, pious tags, generally; also *hadith*.
hafal [KK], Ar. well versed in the Koran; also *hapal* and *hafaz*; the word is also used generally for 'to learn by heart'; ~*an*, a lesson for learning by heart; *mengucapkan* ~*an*, to repeat such a lesson.
haflah [KN], Ar, social gathering, at home.
hai-hui [KSrn], exclamation denoting sorrow; so, groans, woes.
hairan [KS], Ar. astonished, to wonder, wonderful; also *heran*.
haiwan [KN], Ar. animals; living creatures; also *hewan*.
haid [KN], Ar. the menstrual flow; *ber*~, to menstruate; also *haiz* and *hel*.
haj [KN], pilgrimage to Mecca.
hajat [KN], Ar. wish, desire, intention; *sembahyang* ~, to perform a special prayer; *ada* ~, to hold a religious thanksgiving meal to ask for safety.
Haji [KN], Ar. a man who has made the pilgrimage to Mecca; *naik* ~, to perform

this pilgrimage; *hari raya ~,* the festival following the annual pilgrimage; *bulan ~,* the month of the pilgrimage (*Zulhijjah*); *menunaikan fardu ~,* to fulfil the duty of the Pilgrimage; *beli ~,* to go on Pilgrimage through the medium of a (paid) deputy.

Hajjah [KN], female of *Haji.*

hajrat [ ], Ar. = **hijrat.**

hajar [KN], stone.

hak [KN], 1. Ar. truth; due, rightful claim; rights of property; description of property; *kaul-ul-~,* the writing is true — a superscription to Malay epistles; *~ mana?,* of what description?; *~ membatal,* the right of veto; *undang-undang ~ cipta,* law of copyright; *~ istimewa,* privilege; *~ pengarang terpelihara,* copyright reserved; *~ mendahulu,* special privilege or precedence; *~ milik,* proprietary rights; *~ mutlak,* absolute possession; *tidak ber~,* illegal, unlawful; *ber~,* having the right to. 2. Kel. = *yang.*

hakap [KS], greedy, covetous.

hakikat [KN], Ar. truth; esp. Divine Truth; actuality; a fact; *pada ~nya,* in truth, actually; *satu agama yang benar-benar ~nya,* the True Faith.

hakiki [KS], Ar. true, real.

hakim [KN], Ar. a judge; a judge of the supreme court; *~ pembantu,* an assistant judge; the judge advocate at a court martial; *meng~kan,* to sit in judgement on; *ke~an,* judicature.

hakis [KK], *meng~,* erode, wear away, gradually.

hal [KN], Ar. state, condition, position, case; *mengadu ~,* to lay one's case (before any person); *dari~,* concerning, regarding; *~ ehwal,* circumstances, facts of the case; *orang ~,* Kel. a poor, hardworking man; *~-ehwal luar,* foreign affairs; *pada ~nya,* in fact, as it turned out; *tidak menjadi ~,* it did not matter, had no ill effect; *ada ~,* there is something going on; *dengan ~ yang demikian itu, maka...*in this way, thus; *~kan,* N.S. to describe; *belum tahu ~,* young and simple; *ter~,* Kel. in difficulties, 'in a

fix'; *kalau ada apa-apa ~,* if anything crops up, in case of need.

hala [KN], direction; *tak tentu ~,* aimless; *meng~kan,* to direct, point (a weapon); *jalan se~,* one-way street.

halaju [KN], speed, velocity, quickness, rapidity.

halai [KS], *~ balai,* confused, disorderly.

halal [KS], Ar. legitimate; permissible according to divine law, e.g., of food; *anak ~,* a legitimate child; *~kan,* to waive (a claim, esp. a debt), to forgive an action; to give authority for an action, to make lawful; to justify; *~ nikah = ajnabi;* cf. **haram**; *mencari wang dengan cara ~;* to make an honest living.

halaman [KN], a courtyard; a lawn; a page of a book; a column of print; *kampung ~,* a homestead (i.e. a house with its immediately surrounding open space); *~ tempat bermain,* a playground (attached to a building); *membaca ~ demi ~,* to read (magazine etc.) from cover to cover.

halang [KK], to obstruct, handicap; *lari ber~an,* obstacle-race; *peng~ kemajuan;* a barrier to progress; *~an,* stumbling block, hindrance; *meng~i,* to get in the way, obstruct.

halau [KK], *meng~kan,* to drive away, expel; *~ mentah-mentah, ~ tegak-tegak,* to drive away brusquely, unceremoniously; *peng~,* driver, beater; *ubat peng~ serangga,* insect repellant.

halba [KN], Ar. an aromatic plant *(Foenum groecum).*

halban [KN], *kayu ~,* a plant *(Vitex pubescens);* also *leban.*

halia [KN], ginger *(Zingiber officinalis).*

halilintar [KN], = **halintar.**

halimun [KS], invisible or transparent through magic art; *~an,* the magic art of making oneself invisible; also *limun.*

halintah [KN], a horse-leech; also **lintah.**

halintar [KN], a thunderbolt; *panah ~,* id.; *batu ~,* fossil stone implements (believed to be bits of a thunderbolt); a meteorite; also **lintar.**

halipan [KN], a centipede; *~ bara,* a centipede with a dark back and light legs; ~ *laut, nereis, jari* ~, a pattern made by cutting trailers diagonally from the midrib of a palm-leaf; also **lipan**, q.v.

halkum [KN], Ar. throat, gullet; *buah* ~, Adam's apple.

haluan [KN], the bows of a boat; (met.) aim, object; *se*~, having the same aim; ~ is used fig. to mean course, policy; *ber*~ *kiri,* having a Left Wing policy.

haluba [KS], covetousness; also *luba; tamak* ~, extreme covetousness.

halus [KS], fine in texture; delicate; minute; *pisau* ~, a lancet-like knife; *tangan yang* ~, a delicate hand; *bahasa* ~, refined language; ~*i,* to investigate thoroughly, go into carefully; *orang* ~, a class of invisible elves or fairies, who can make themselves visible and pass for human beings; *sindiran yang halus,* indirect hint.

halwa [KN], Ar. a generic name for preserves in sugar; ~ *telinga,* musical treat, something that is delightful to the ears; ~ *mata,* something that is delightful to the eyes.

hama [KN], a gnat; a very small insect; a microbe; a minute particle, an atom; ~ *penyakit,* germs of disease.

hamak [KS], disobliging; gruff and ill-tempered.

hamba [KN], slave; your servant; I; ~ *Allah,* God's poor; ~ *kompeni,* Indian convicts; ~ *sahaya,* slaves generally; ~ *hutang,* a debt-slave; ~ *tebusan,* a bought slave (i.e. bought from his original creditor); *tuan* ~, (polite for) you; *per*~*an,* slavery; *ber*~, (i) to be possessed of slaves; (ii) to serve; *memper*~*kan diri,* to give oneself to, to marry; *minta per*~, to offer oneself in marriage; *burung* ~ *kera,* the racquet-railed drongo; also *cawi-cawi.*

hambal [KN], carpet; *ambal* id., rug mat.

hambar [KS], tasteless; ~ *hati,* dejected; also **ambar**; *ucapannya agak* ~, his speech was rather dull and insipid.

hambat [KK], *meng*~, to pursue, chase; to run; *meng*~ *hati,* to win over, persuade;

tindakan mereka meng~ *kemajuan projek itu,* their unusual reactions stalled progress on the project.

hambur [KK], 1. ~-~, largesse; ~*kan,* to scatter; *ber*~*an,* strewn or scattered about; *meng*~*kan wang dengan membeli sesukanya,* to go on a buying spree. 2. to curvet, to prance; to plunge, lurch forward; to spring, as a tiger; *meng*~*kan kuda,* to make a horse rise to a jump or to curvet.

hamil [KS], Ar. pregnant (more polite than *bunting*); *meng*~*kan,* fecundate, impregnate, cause to be pregnant.

hamis [KS], fish-scented; malodorous (less strong than *cengis*).

hampa [KS], lacking contents, empty; fruitless; unfulfilled; ~ *hati,* disappointed; *meng*~*kan angan-angan,* to disappoint aspirations; *ke*~*an,* failure, frustration.

hampar [KK], spreading out, flat; *batu* ~, bedrock; *batu ber*~, flat rock formation; ~*an,* a carpet, a mat; ~*kan,* to spread out; ~ *khemah,* to pitch a tent.

hampas [KN], dregs, dross; waste products (left after processing); *pasir* ~, sand-tailings (from a mine); ~ *tebu,* megass; ~ *sutera,* silk dross.

hampir [Kktr], near, nearly; ~ *serupa,* nearly identical; ~-~, very nearly; *meng*~*i,* to approach; ~*kan,* to get close to; *ber*~*an,* in close touch with, in proximity to.

hampu [KK], intens. of *ampu,* in the sense of 'sucking up'.

hamun [KK], to abuse; reviling; wild abuse; *maki*-~, all sorts of abuses.

hamzah [KN], Ar. the *Spiritus lenis;* punctuation mark (application to certain Jawi words).

hancing [KS], rank, foul (of smell, e.g., of urinal); ~ *pering,* overpowering stench, esp. of urinal.

hancur [KS], melting, crushed, dissolving; ~ *hati,* broken-hearted; ~ *luluh,* utterly crushed; *meng*~*kan,* to crush to pieces; *ke*~*an, peng*~*an,* destruction.

handai [KN], associate, comrade; companion, ~-*tulan, sahabat*-~, colleagues, companions.

handal [KS], trusty, reliable, successful; also ~an.

hang [KN], 1, you, thou; Ked. = engkau. 2. an obsolete Malay title; Hang Tuah, a semi-legendary Malay hero. 3. Ked. a tree-shelter.

hangat [KS], hot, warm; ~ hati, angry; sambutan ~, enthusiastic reception; bendang air ~, a hot spring; per~, to heat up (water or food); ~-~ kuku, lukewarm; ~ is not generally used of sun-heat (panas); in regard to air, it means overwarm, stuffy; ~ ~ tahi ayam, temporary in nature, half-hearted (prov.).

hangit [KS], rank smelling, as burned rice or something singed or as sweat.

hangus [KS], burn, scorch; ~kan, to consume by burning; belanja ~, expenses for feast, etc. (esp. at wedding, as opposed to dowry); ~ hati, anger, annoyed; ke~an, burning, scorching.

hantam [KK], Jav. ~-kromo, (acting) wildly indiscriminately, at random; a variant of hentam.

hantar [KK], 1. conveying; sending in a person's charge; meng~kan, to accompany away; to escort, to see off; wang ~an, gift (by the man) on betrothal; pengantar, the sender of a letter (but see bahasa); malam ~ tanda, the night of formal betrothal; bola ~an, a pass (at football); temasya ~ curi, a custom prevalent in parts of Perak: young men at night in the Fasting month place plates of cakes in front of girls' houses: if any girl so desires, she emerges and pelts the men or man with cakes — bucolic flirtations; also **antar** 2. 2. ter~, stretched out; stranded and helpless, = telantar.

hantu [KN], an evil spirit; a ghost or goblin; a police informer; wild (of fruit, i.e., planted by ghosts, not men); ~ bangkit, the ordinary sheeted ghost risen from a grave and making its way by rolling along on its side, as the fastenings of the winding-sheet prevent its walking; ~ belian, the tiger spirit; ~ bungkus = ~ bangkit; ~ golek = ~ bangkit; ~ jamuan,

a familiar spirit; ~ kocong = ~ bangkit; ~ orang mati dibunuh, the revengeful spirit of a murdered man; ~ pemburu, the spectre huntsman; also ~ raya; ~ pari, a fairy; ~ rimba, the demon of the woods that preys on lonely travellers; ~ wewer, the invisible ghosts which causes travellers to go astray; ~ tanah, the gnomes of the soil; ~ mengamuk, a mischievous spirit, a poltergeist; ~ baling-baling, a similar spirit, fond of throwing stones at night; ~ toyol, a familiar spirit acting as thief, etc., on behalf of the person to whom it is attached; sudah kenaikan ~, possessed by an evil spirit; burung ~, the Malayan orchard owl; dirasuk ~, to be attacked by an evil spirit; jari ~, the middle finger; kapal ~, a model ship laden with offerings and let go in a river to propitiate spirits; rumah ~, Masonic Lodge; rumah ber~, a haunted house; ber~, to hold a seance (of a sorcerer); naik ~, to go into a mediumistic trance; sometimes, to be beside oneself with rage, cf. **syaikh**; kena lintasan ~, to fall ill from having a spirit cross one's path, particularly, of having a stroke; ~ is used to convey the idea of 'extreme addition to' (haunting); ~ judi, habitual gambler; ~ bola, football enthusiast; meng~i, haunt, terrify, torment, to frighten; takut akan ~ terpeluk bangkai, he that always fears danger always feels it (prov.).

Hanuman [KN], Skr. the Hindu monkeygod; an evil dog-faced spirit (in Kedah); Sang Seri ~, the god Hanuman in romance.

hanya [Kktr], except, unless, only; anakku ~ lah seorang, my child is an only child.

hanyir [Kktr], stinking (of fish, eggs or water); fetid.

hanyut [KK], drifting, floating; hanyutan, floatsam; ~kan, to set adrift; ber~, adrift; ber~-~, drifting about; orang ~, a waster, 'drifter'; a waif; air tenang meng~kan, still waters run deep.

hapak [KS], = **apak**.

hapal [KK], Ar. = **hafal**.

hapus [KK], to expunge, wiping out; ~kan, to stamp out, to do away with; peng~an, writing off, abolition, eradication; ~kan riwayat, (sl.) to end (life-) story of, finish off, 'do in'; ~kan arang di muka, avenge an insult, wipe out the memory of a disgrace, etc.

haram [KS], Ar. unlawful, forbidden by religious law; a strong expression of negation; ~ zadah, born out of wedlock; ~ tak-dapat, he utterly failed to get; ~kan, to declare unlawful (e.g., a Society), to ban; secara ~, illegally; peng~an, a ban.

haram [KN], Ar. a pyramid; al-~, the Great Pyramid.

harap [KK] to hope, expect confidence, trust; ~lah engkau kepada Allah, put your trust in God; ~an, trusted, trusty; a trusted retainer; hope, expectation, trust; seperti di~kan, as expected; tak ter~, unreliable; past hoping for; meng~kan hati, to raise hopes; yang ber~, yours hopefully; pecah ~an, breach of trust; masih ada ~an, all is not lost; jangan meng~kan yang belum pasti, don't count your chickens before they are hatched.

harau [KK], to haul in a line; also **karau**.

harbab [KN] = **rebab**.

hardik [KN] abuse, scolding.

harga [KN] price, monetary value; ber~, invaluable; ~ mati, fixed price, bed-rock price; tarik ~, to 'jockey up' prices (e.g., by pretending that an article is hard to get); buat-buat tarik ~ sikit, to make a show of exclusiveness, play 'hard to get'; per~an paun, the exchange rate of the pound; ~ tukaran wang, the rate of exchange; ~ baku, standard price; ~ langganan, subscription; ~ runcit, retail price; ~ pokok, cost price; ~ pasaran, market price; ~ rata, average price; ~ diri, self-respect; meng~kan, to appreciate, value; peng~an, appreciation; also **rega**; tidak ber~, worthless.

hari [KN], day (both the day of twenty-four hours and the daylight hours by themselves); siang ~, daylight; tengah-~, midday; malam ~, night-time;

sepanjang ~, all day; keesokan ~, the morrow; selang se~, every alternate day; lat se~, id.; se~-~, every day; ~raya, holiday; ~ besar, id.; ~ bulan, day of the month; ~an, daily; akhbar ~an, daily paper; ber~-~an, for days and days, day in, day out; se~-~an, all day long; hal se~-~an, daily events; buku per~an, diary; buku pendapatan ~an, day-book of sales; ~ depan, the future; ~ lahir, birthday; ~ peringatan, anniversary; pekerja ~an, day-labourer; sari-sari, normally, on most days; zaman sari (sehari), N.S. the good old days; perempuan dalam ~, a woman who has recently given birth (and is still within the 40-day-period of conventional 'uncleanness').

harimau [KN], tiger; leopard; any of the larger felidae, a type of the strong and unscrupulous; ~ belang ceclak, kucing hutan, the leopard-cat (Felis bengalensis); ~ anjing, ~ telap, ~ compok, N.S. the golden cat (Felis temminckii); ~ belang, the tiger; ~ belang kasau, the tiger (Felis tigris); ~ belang tebuan, ~ bintang, ~ akar, the common leopard (Felis pardus); ~ burung, Pat. the flat-headed cat (Felis marmorata); ~ daun pinang, ~ sipahi, names given to the tiger when the black markings are not extensive; ~ jadi-jadian, a were-tiger; ~ kumbang, the black panther (Felis pardus, var. niger); ~ lalat, a jumping spider; ~ tarum, a large black panther; ~ terung kasau, the royal tiger (Felis tigris) when of very large size; tulang ~ menangis, the manubrium; uban tahi ~, the colour of the hair when either black or white largely predominates; also rimau.

harta [KN], property, wealth, goods; ~ benda, goods and chattels; ~ used for assets; ~ dunia, worldly wealth; ~ pusaka, heirlooms; ancestral property; ~ sepencarian, joint earnings of husband and wife (shared on divorce); ~ si mati, estate of a deceased person; ~ karun, treasure.

hartal [KN], 1. Hind. a yellow face-powder, orpiment; saffron; also *retal*. 2. a general strike.

hartawan [KN], wealthy.

haru [KS], uproar, disturbance; *~-hara*, a noisy disturbance; *~ biru*, id.; *di-~ syaitan*, plagued by an evil spirit; *ter~*, much moved, moved, upset, grieved, amazed; *ke~an*, emotion; *keter~an*, deep emotion; *meng~kan*, to move, stir the emotions.

harum [KS], fragrant, perfumed; *~an*, perfume; *~ sekampung*, perfuming the whole kampung, i.e., the village belle; *~ nama*, famous, renowned, to be of good repute.

Harun [KN], Ar. Aaron; a Malay proper name.

harung [KK], = arung.

harus [Kktr], proper, fitting, right, probable; *se-~nya*, properly if rightly (treated or arranged); *meng~kan*, to enjoin, lay down as fitting, prescribe (line of conduct); *ke~an*, necessity, essential, requisite.

hasad [KS], Ar. envy, jealousy, spite.

hasil [KN], Ar. outcome, return, rent, products, revenue; *~ tanah*, land-rent; *~ pokok*, land assessment; *membayar ~*, to pay land-rent to Government; accomplished; *tidak ber~*, in vain; *semua usaha kita tidak ber~*, all our efforts were in vain; *meng~kan*, to bring to pass; *~* is used for 'results' generally; *~ penamat*, final results; *~-mahsul*, produce generally, sources of revenue; *ber~*, to succeed, show results; *~ padi*, rice-crop; *~ bumi*, natural products, esp. minerals; *~ pecahan*, by-products; *~ ikutan*, id.; *~ cipta*, creations, esp. literary; *peng~an*, products, production, economic resources.

hasrat [KN], strong desire.

Hassan [KN], Ar. the eldest son of Ali and Fatimah, daughter of the Prophet; a common Malay name.

hasta [KN], Skr. a Malay cubit (from the elbow to the finger-tips); *lengan ~*, forearm; *tulang ~*, ulna; *beroleh se~ hen-*

dak sedepa, give him an inch and he'll take a yard (prov.); pronounced rather *seta* and sometimes so written.

hasut [KK], *meng~*, instigate, incite, goad, to pit against each other; *jangan meng~*, don't make inflammatory remarks; *peng~*, agitator.

hasyiah [KN], edge, margin, marginal note.

hatam [KN], Ar. end, finish, termination, *sudah ~*, it is finished, used esp. of the completion of studies; also *khatam*.

hati [KN], the heart and liver; the interior portion of anything; the seat of the feelings; *ambil di ~*, to store up a grudge; *baca di dalam ~*, to read to oneself; *bakar ~*, wrath; *belas ~*, compassion; *berbalik ~*, suffering evulsion of the feeling; *berdebar ~*, to beat (of the heart), from excitement, fear; *berkata di dalam ~*, to say to oneself; *besar ~*, elated; *buah ~*, heart — as a term of endearment; *condong ~*, inclination towards; *gerak ~*, emotion; *hancur ~*, heart-broken, despair; *hulu ~*, the pit of the stomach; *tulang hulu ~*, the xiphoid process; *jantung ~*, the heart in its anatomical sense; *jauh ~*, offended; *~ jelemput*, deeply depressed; *karat ~*, malicious; *kecil ~*, hurt feelings; *keras ~*, obstinate; *keruh ~*, malicious ill-feeling; *kurang ~*, spiritless; *lebur ~*, crushed in spirit; *lembut ~*, soft-hearted; *makan ~*, to brood; *mata ~*, inward perception; *mengambil ~*, to captivate; *panas ~*, angry; *pilu ~*, melancholy; *puas ~*, satisfied; *putih ~*, sincere; *putus ~*, in despair; *rawan ~*, melancholy; *sakit ~*, angry; *sangkut ~*, lovingly attached; *sayup ~*, melancholy; *sebal ~*, disappointed; *sedan ~*, gratified; *sejuk ~*, contented; *suci ~*, pure of motive; *susah ~*, sorrowful; *tawar ~*, disinclined; *terang ~*, clear-sighted; *tinggi ~*, proud, elated; *waswas ~*, anxious; *memper~kan*, to grasp, to understand, to realise; *tertarik ~*, moved, touched, interested; *~-~ hari*, capricious, temperamental; *dalam ~ kecilnya*, in his innermost heart; *per~an*, supervision, keeping an eye on; *memusatkan per~an*, to focus one's attention; *pemer~*, an observer; *memer~*, to observe; *per~an*, attention, interest, attentiveness; *kata ~*, conscience; *suara ~*, id; *sagu ~*, gift made a way of compensation or compassion; *ber~-~*, gingerly, carefully, attentively; *memper~kan benar-benar*, to take a hard look at; *secara ~-~*, carefully; *~ perut*, basic moral character, esp. in regard to finer feelings; *tidak ber~-perut*, devoid of finer feelings, incapable of decent behaviour; *~ roboh*, full of suppressed rage; *~ nurani*, the mystically enlightened soul; *~ sanubari*, the human heart; *dengan segala senang ~*, with the greatest pleasure.

hatta [Kktr & Kphb], (*maka*) then, further, next, thereupon.

haus [KS], 1. reduced by friction, worn away; *~-~*, having surface rubbed off; rubbed sore. 2. thirst; *ke~an*, suffering from thirst.

hawa [KN], 1. Ar. breath, air; climate; affection; lust, desire; *~ nafsu*, carnal lusts; the passions; *~ api*, the hot breath of a furnace; *kawasan ~ panas*, the tropics; *~ sederhana*, a temperate climate; *peng~ dingin*, cooling system (in air-conditioning). 2. Ar. *Siti Hawa*, Eve; *kaum Hawa*, womankind; women generally.

hawar [KN], a pestilence, an epidemic, a murrain.

hayat [KN], Ar. life; *dalam masa ~ kita*, in our life-time; *selama ~ dikandung badan*, as long as one lives; *ilmu ~*, biology.

hayun [KK], intens. of *ayun*.

hazrat [KN], Ar. presence, the royal presence; majesty; *ke~*, to the Presence of, form of words used in old-style letters to magnates.

hb. [abbrv.], = *haribulan*, day of the month.

hebah [KN], 1. Ar. a gift, esp. a voluntary conveyance of land. 2. [KK], to announce; *juru~*, an announcer.

heban [KK], = *eban*, hurl violently, toss away.

hebat [KS], Ar. terrible, awe-inspiring, grand; also *haibat; per~kan*, to press an action vigorously, to intensify; *meng~kan diri*, make oneself look impressive; *~ pada pandangan*, impressive to the eye; *ke~an*, greatness, intensity, strength.

heboh [KS], agitated, in an uproar, in a tumult; *~-~kan*, to publicise, make a great to-do about, 'trumpet'; *ke~an*, sensation, manifestation of strong emotion; *apa yang di~kan?* what's up; what's going on; *perkara yang sangat meng~kan*, a very controversial issue.

hela [KK], drawing over the ground; dragging; *meng~*, to pull after one; *peng~*, a puller, a drawer; *meng~ nafas*, to breathe deeply.

helai [KN], a numeral coefficient for tenuous objects such as sheets of papers, garments, leaves, blades of grass, etc.; also *lai; se~, sepinggang*, one cloth for each waist, met. for extreme poverty; *bawalah, biar se~ sepinggang*, bring him, even if he has only the clothes he stands up in.

helat [KN]. foreign; *orang ~*, foreigner.

heman [KN], Jav. affection; interest; care; devotion to.

hemat [KS], Ar. careful consideration, solicitude; *pada ~ saya*, in my considered opinion; *tidak sampai ~nya*, calculated that the task was beyond him; *meng~kan perbelanjaan*, to cut down on expenditure; *pandai ber~*, a good saver; *peng~an*, economy, care with money; *tinggi ~*, ambitious, planning ahead; also *hemmah* and *himmah*.

hembus [KK], *meng~-~kan nafas*, to snort violently, as a horse; a variant of *embus*.

hempang [KK], dammed, blocked off; stopped in motion; *peluru tidak ter~ dik lalang*, lalang grass won't stop a bullet; a variant of *empang*.

hempap [KK], = **empap**.

hempas [KK], *~kan*, to dash down violently; *meng~kan*, id.; *~-pulas*, dashing wildly about, helterskelter; *jatuh ter~*, to crash, as a plane; *meng~ tulang urat*, (sl.) to slog and slave; *~an ombak*, place where waves break, surf; *~kan pintu*, to slam a door.

hempedal [KN], = **pedal**.

hempedu [KN], the gall; brownish-yellow bitter liquid produced by the liver; *pundi-pundi ~*, the gall-bladder.

hempis [KN], fence built an wings to converge on a trap; also *empis*.

hempit [KK], 1. wedging or squeezing between two surfaces; *ber~-~*, huddling together (e.g., on account of the cold). 2. *badak ~*, (Ked.) the two-horned rhinoceros *(Rh. sumatrensis)*.

hempuk [KK], to strike a heavy 'swashing' blow, to 'slosh'.

hendak [KK], wish, intention, purpose; *~kan*, to desire; *ke~*, desire, wish; *seperti ke~ tuan*, as you please; *berke~*, to wish for; *seke~*, in accordance with one's wishes; *~ tak ~*, half-hearted; in speech *hendak* is normally shortened to *ndak* or *nak*; in practice there is a slight difference in meaning between the two; *ndak* implies rather desire, *nak*, intention, 'going to'; *meng~i*, want, need, to be willing; *kalau ke~nya tidak terkabul*, if things don't go his way.

hendap [KK], = *endap*; conceal oneself; *serangan ~*, an ambush.

henggung [KK], *meng~*, to waddle along, esp. of a very fat person.

hening [KS], 1. limpid, clear, transparent. 2. Ind. still, silent; *meng~-ciptakan*, to honour (esp. the name of a dead person) by a silence in an assembly (the idea being to wish peace to his soul).

hentak [KK], striking downwards as with a perpendicular rod; (met.) striding swankily along; clumping along; used for 'dash' and 'show-off': *membuat besar ~*, to 'cut a dash', 'make a splash', e.g., by lavish expenditure; *~ sahaja!*, just bluffing!, just bragging!; *meng~ meja*, to bang on the table; *meng~kan kaki*, stamp the feet.

hentam [KK], stamping with the foot; to bang against, bump against.

henti [KK], stopping; *ber~*, to come to a stop; *ber~kan* to put a stop to; *per~an*, an ending a place to stop at; *ter~*, interrupted, stopped; *meng~kan perkelahian*, to break up a fight; *Pulau Perhentian*, stopping-place islands; two islands off the coast of Kelantan with a strait in between, which used to serve as a shelter for sailing vessels in bad weather.

henyak [KK], *meng~kan bandan ke kerusi*, to plump oneself down in a chair; a variant of *enyak*.

hep [KN], Ked. pretext, excuse for quarrel; *mencari ~*, to seek to pick a quarrel.

herbab [KN], = **rebab**.

herdik [KK], *meng~*, scold, revile, abusive language.

hereng [KS], crooked, slanting.

heret [KK], to drag along; to lead (an animal).

herik [KK], *meng~*, to shriek, to cry out with pain.

herok-herok [KS], noisy quarrelling, sounds of strife (esp. of rows which offend the neighbours).

herot [KS], intens. of *erot*; *~-merot*, all twisted up, awry.

hewan [KN], = **haiwan**.

hias [KK], *meng~i*, to adorn; *ber~*, decorated; *per~an*, ornament, decoration; *~an pentas*, stage scenery; *almari ~*, show case; *janda ~*, a childless widow.

hiba [KS], 1. pity, compassion. 2. moved, touched, compassionate; also *iba*.

hibur [KK], *meng~*, *~kan* or *meng~kan*, to allay sorrow, to calm, to console; to entertain; *peng~*, a comforter; *wang ~an*, entertainment allowance; *ber~*, to amuse oneself, enjoy oneself; *tidak ter~*, inconsolable; *taman ~an*, amusement park, play-ground, recreation park.

hidang [KK], placing in a dish; dishing up; *~an*, a plateful; *ter~*, served up; *~kan*, to present a programme; *~an ringan*, light refreshments.

hidayat [KN], Ar. right guidance, esp. in

religion.

hidu [KK], *meng~*, to be on the scent of; to smell.

hidung [KN], the nose; *~ mancung,* a sharp-cut nose; *~ kemek,* a flat nose; *batang ~,* the bridge of the nose; *liang ~,* the nostril cavity; *daun ~,* the nostrils (viewed from the outside); *cucuk ~, tanjul ~,* to 'lead by the nose'; *lelaki ~ belang,* a seducer; a procurer; *ber~ tinggi,* stuck-up, conceited; *sudah dua tahun tak nampak batang ~ dia,* haven't seen the bridge of his nose for two years, i.e. haven't seen hide nor hair of him for two years; *beroleh ~ panjang,* to be embarrassed, (met.); *potong ~ rosak muka,* if one cuts off one's nose, one hurts only oneself (prov.).

hidup [K], live, alive; *gajah ~,* a live elephant; *seumur ~,* as long as I live; *matahari ~,* the rising sun; *meng-hidupkan,* to bring to life; to light (to be lighted) (lamp); also to keep alive; *ke~an,* life, means of livelihood; subsistence; *~--an,* livestock; *keba-hagian ~,* a happy life; *~-~,* in person, 'in the flesh'; *~-~ lagi,* while still alive; *hal ke~an,* condition of life; *~* is used for 'fresh' (not preserved); *susu ~,* fresh milk (as opposed to *susu tin*); *~* is used for 'Long live', 'Vive'; *~ Melayu,* 'Long live the Malays!'; *perjuangan ~ mati,* life and death struggle; *~ bersama se-cara damai,* peaceful co-existence; *meng~kan* is sometimes used for, starting (an engine); *jalan ke~an,* way of life, occupation; *riwayat ~,* biography; *pandangan ~,* philosophy; *teman ~,* partner in life; *~ sendiri,* to make it on one's own.

hijab [KN], Ar. curtain, veil; berhijab, to veil oneself (of women before men).

hijau [KS], green; *~ pucuk pisang,* bright light green; *~ tua,* dark green; *~ muda,* light green; *~ daun,* jungle green; *ke~-~an,* greenish; *~ kekuningan,* green tending to yellow, as fading leaf; *~* is also used, as is green in English, to mean, young and raw; Malays often

call an object *hijau* which would be described as blue in English; *naik kuda ~,* drunk.

hijrat [KK], Ar. the hegira, i.e. the flight of the Prophet from Mecca to Medina in 622 A.D.; *tahun ~* or *sanat al'~,* the year of the flight, from which the Islamic calendar starts, each year being A.H.; *ber~* is sometimes used to mean, to go on a journey or to change one's place of residence; also *hijrah* and *hajrat.*

hikayat [KN], Ar. a romance.

hikmat [KN], Ar. wisdom; knowledge; magic art; supernatural power; *gemala ~,* a wonder-working talisman.

hilang [KK], to be lost, to disappear; to die; *~ akal,* to lose self-restraint; *~ arwah,* or *~ semangat,* to lose consciousness; *~lah dia,* he died; *meng~kan,* to cause to disappear; *ke~an,* loss; *~kan diri,* to disappear, 'make oneself scarce'; *~-pin-tang,* lost and gone, disappeared; *~-~ timbul,* lost to view or absent, frequently and suddenly reappearing unexpectedly; *meng~kan kepercayaan rakyat,* to erode the confidence of the people; *meng~kan tanggapan yang ke-liru,* to set the record straight.

hilap [KN], Ar. error; better *khilaf.*

hilir [KN], to go downstream; the lower waters of a river; *hulu-~,* top and bottom; beginning and end; upstream and downstream; *~-mudik,* to go up and down river; (fig.) to bustle about here and there; *meng~kan,* to set adrift in a river so as to float downstream, as, e.g., a *lancang* or *kapal hantu,* see **lan-chang**.

himpit [KK], = **hempit**.

himpun [KK], *ber~,* to meet together; *meng~kan,* to bring together; to mass (troops); *per~an,* a gathering, a meeting; association, society.

hina [KS], Skr. mean, poor, contemptible; *~ dina,* the poor and lowly; *meng~kan,* to disdain, to insult; to abase; *ke~an,* degradation, abasement; *terasa ~,* to feel inferior; to feel slighted; *meman-dang ~,* to despise; *peng~an,* insulting behaviour; *menelan peng~an,* to swallow an insult; *menjadi ke~an kalau bekerja,* it was looked upon as a degradation to work; *meng~,* insulting, offensive; humiliate.

hincit [KK], to depart, exit, quitting; *~-lah,* be off with you!, beat it!

hindar [KK], Ind. *meng~kan,* to hinder, avert, prevent; *ter~ dari bahaya;* escaped from a danger; *meng~i,* to stay out of.

Hindi [KN], Indian.

Hindu [KN], Hindu.

Hindustan [KN], India.

hingar [KS], intens. of *ingar; ~-damat,* rowdy disturbance, noise, commotion.

hingga [Kdpn & Kphbg], up to; as far as; until; *~ pada masa ini,* up to the present time; *se~,* until; *per~an,* boundary, limit; also *perenggan; tiada ter~,* boundless; *~kan,* until it came to pass that.

hinggap [KK], to perch; settling, alighting (of a bird); *~ api,* to catch fire; *~i,* to infect, of a disease.

hinggut [KK], to shake to-and-fro, as in shaking down fruit; cf. **enggut.**

hirau [KK], *~kan,* to care, trouble about.

hiris [KK], slicing, slitting, ripping up; *se~,* a slice.

hirup [KK], = *irup; ~an,* liquid food, broth.

hisab [KN], Ar. enumeration, calculation; *ilmu ~,* mathematics, accounts, commercial arithmetic; *tiada ter~kan banyaknya,* innumerable.

hitam [KS], black; very dark in coloration; *~ bogot,* hideously black; *~ legam,* pitch black; *~ manis,* dark brown; *~ muda,* deep blue; *~ tua,* very dark brown; *~ pudar,* pale brown; *~ putihnya,* certainty, definite answer; *ke~-~an,* darkish; *Hitam* is a not uncommon name, esp. for a younger child in a family.

hitung [KK], calculate, to reckon; *ilmu ~an,* arithmetic; *per~an,* calculation, a taking into account, reckoning; *salah per~an,* miscalculation; *~ panjang,* average; *memper~kan,* calculate, enumerate, give attention to, heed, consider; *setelah diper~kan,* taking everything into account.

hoe [KN], Ch. a 'hoey', a secret society.

Hokiang [KN], Ch. appertaining to the Fukien province (esp. the Amoy and Chang-chow divisions, not Fuhchau itself).

Holanda [KN], Dutch; also *Belanda.*

Holi [KN], Hind. a spring festival of the Hindus in honour of Krishna; also a name given to the dancers at this festival.

homam [KN], Tam. a burnt sacrifice.

honar [KK], Pers. discredit; a subject of reproach or censure; a queer trick; *khabar ber~,* a scandal; a tale to somebody's discredit; also *onar.*

hong [KN], the Sanskrit and Buddhist 'om', a word signifying the Hindu Trinity, used by Malay medicine-man.

hongah [KK], Kel. *~-~,* going straight on.

horloji, horologi [KN], Eur. a watch, a clock.

hormat [KN], Ar. respect; reverence — esp. with the idea of respectful behaviour; *memberi ~,* to pay respect to; *yang ber~,* the Honourable; *yang ke~,* the Honorary; *dif ke~,* guest of honour; *anggota ke~,* an honorary member; *barisan ke~an,* guard of honour; *dengan segala ~,* with all due respect; *untuk meng~i,* in honour of; *dipandang ~,* respected; *di~,* id.; *peng~,* respectfull; *peng~an,* an honour, a distinction, esp. a medal; *ke~an,* id.; *senarai ke~an,* Honours List; *menembak tabik ke~an,* to fire a salute; *dengan ke~an tentera yang lengkap,* with full military honours; *berbaring dengan ke~an negara,* to lie in state.

hu [KN], Ar. the possessive pronoun (third singular masculine) in its genitive and acusative forms.

Hua [KN], Ar. He, i.e. God.

hubaya [KN], *~-~,* warning!, take head!, beware!; *~-~ pengurus Majalah Guru berkuasa menahan kiriman ke mana-mana cawangan yang tidak taat dengan pembayarannya,* warning! the Manager of the 'Mujallah Guru" has power to stop despatch of the magazine to any branch falling behind in payments; ~-~ *terhadap*, beware of.

hubbu [KK], Ar. love; hardly used except in the Arabic saying, ~*'l watani mina'l imani*, love of one's native land is part of the Faith; this saying, attributed by some to the Prophet, is often quoted in newspapers.

hubung [KK], to connect, to link; ~*an*, link; *ber*~, united; ~*kan* or *meng*~*kan*, to unite, to connect; ~*an baik*, good relations (as between States); *per*~*an*, communications; *jalan-jalan per*~*an*, means of communication (roads, airlines, etc.); *ber*~ *surat dengan*, to communicate with by letter; *per*~*an baik sangka*, friendly relations; *per*~*an diplomatik*, diplomatic relations; *menjalin* ~*an*, to have a relationship; *memutuskan per*~*an diplomatik*, to break off diplomatic relations; *memutuskan* ~*an dagangan*, to break off trade relations; *alat peng*~, (mechanical) means of communication; *mengadakan* ~*an jenis dengan*, to have sexual relations with; *per*~*an jenis sesama jenis*, homosexuality; *ber*~ *dengan*, in connection with; *putus* ~*an*, to lose contact; ~*an nyawa*, darling.

Hudai [KN], *orang* ~, the name of a tribe of aborigines in the Malay Peninsula.

hudar [KK], Ked. to bolt, to abscond.

hudhud [KN], Ar. the hoopoe; in Arabian fables; the hoopoe is unknown in the Malay Peninsula except for rare visits from the North; when seen, it is called *belatuk* (woodpecker).

hujah [KN], questioning, cross-examination, contentions, proofs, arguments; *ber*~, to contend, maintain; also *hujja*h.

hujan [KN], rain; ~ *deras*, pouring rain; ~ *lebat*, rain in large drops; heavy rain; ~ *renyai*, drizzle; ~ *rintik-rintik*, a few drops of rain only; ~ *batu*, hail; ~ *lari*, a shower, sporadic rain; *ke*~*an*, drenched with rain, caught in the rain, *air* ~, rain-water; *musim* ~, the rainy season; *teduh* ~, stopped (of rain); *ber*~, rained upon;

rainy (of a place); ~ *panas*, rain during sunshine; ~*i*, to rain down upon; *meng*~*kan*, id.; *burung* ~, the broadbill; ~ *emas di negeri orang*, ~ *batu di negeri sendiri, baik juga di negeri sendiri*, though it rains gold in a foreign land and stones at home, it is better to be at home; East or West, home is best.

hujat [KK], reviling; to abuse.

hujung [KN], end, point, extremity; ~ *telunjuk*, the tip of the index finger; ~ *tanah*, a headland; Land's End; *ber*~, pointed; *peng*~, the 'tail-end' of a period (e.g. the last few days of a month); ~-*pangkal*, the prime cause; the person having the prime responsibility for an event; ~*an*, an end; a tip; (fig.) an appendix to a writing.

hukah [KN], Ar. a hookah; a water pipe, also *ogah*.

hukama [KN], Ar. the plural of *hakim*; learned men, authorities on law and theology.

hukum [KN], Ar. order, command, judicial decision, sentence; law, legal rules; *beri* ~, to give an order; *jatuh* ~, to give a judicial decision; *kena* ~, to suffer a penalty; ~ *paksa*, a strict order; ~*an*, punishment; ~ *adat*, customary law; ~ *alam*, natural law; ~*an mati*, capital punishment; ~ at card-games means 'good', e.g. as a king when the ace has been played; ~ is also used for government, governmental control; *negara* ~, constitutional State; *ahli* ~, lawyers, legal officers; *bilik* ~*an*, orderly room; *meng*~, to sentence; *melanggar* ~, illegal.

hulam [KN], uncooked vegetable foods (served as side-dishes); *pucuk dicita*, ~ *mendatang*, I hoped for a shoot and vegetables came (all hopes exceeded).

hulu [KN], head, upper portion; beginning; hilt, handle; the upper waters of a river; the interior of a country; ~ *hati*, the pit of the stomach; ~ *keris*, the handle of a kris; *gering* ~, a headache (when speaking of a prince); *orang* ~, dwellers up-country; *da*~, before; *peng*~, headman, chief; Muhammad (as chief of Muslims); also *ulu*.

hulubalang [KN], 1. a leader in war; a captain; a royal guard. 2. Ach., Pk. a territorial chief.

hulur [KK], 1. letting go, slacking; ~*kan*, to slacken, to pay out rope; ~*kan lidah*, to put out the tongue; ~*an*, varicocele; ~*kan tangan*, to stretch out the hand; ~*kan derma*, to proffer or bestow charity. 2. Pah. a debt slave (to a *raja* for non-payment of fine).

huma [KN], 'dry' or 'hill' padi, a padi-clearing on high ground; *ber~*, to plant hill padi.

humban [KK], intens., of *umban*, to hurl, cast (some heavy object); *meng~kan (penunggang)*, to throw (rider), of a horse.

humbas [KK], Ked. *meng~*, to 'make onesellf scarce', bolt.

hun [KN], 1. Ch. a Chinese measure of weight, one tenth of a mace (chi). 2. Ch. a share in a business.

hungap [KK], *ter~-~*, panting, gasping.

hunggah [KK], Kel. to run, rush.

huni [KK], Ind. to inhabit; *peng~*, inhabitants.

hunus [KK], drawing off; in effect, unsheathing; ~*kan cincin*, to draw off a ring; ~*kan pedang*, to draw a sword; *di~nya kerisnya*, he drew his kris; *ter~*, bare, naked (of a weapon); *pedang ter~*, drawn sword.

Hurmuz [KN], Ar. Ormus; on the Persian Gulf.

huru [KN], ~-*hara*, uproar, tumult; public disturbance, riot.

huruf [KN], Ar. letters; an alphabetical symbol; ~-*pangkal*, initials; ~ *baluk*, block letter; ~ *Jawi*, Arabic letters used for writing; ~ *harkat*, vowels; *buta huruf*, illiterate (idiom.); ~ *besar*, capital letters; ~ *condong*, italics; ~ *hidup*, vowel; ~ *mati*, consonant; ~ *bercerai*, block letters; *pengatur ~*, compositor.

Hussain [KN], Ar. grandson of the Prophet and brother of Hassan, q.v.; a common Malay name.

hutan [KN], jungle, forest; wild; *anjing ~*, the wild dog *(Cyon rutilans)*; *ayam ~*, the jungle-fowl *(Gallus ferrugineus)*; *babi ~*, the wild pig *(Sus cristatus)*; *orang ~*, a wild man, aborigine, a jungle-dweller, a boor; *ke~an*, forestry; ~ *larangan*, forest reserve; ~ *lepas*, ~ *rimba*, virgin jungle; ~ *belukar*, wilderness; *pulau ~*, a patch of forest in the middle of cultivated land; also *utan*.

hutang [KN], debt; owing, due; ~ *kepala*, a debt on the repayment of which one has staked one's liberty; ~ *piutang*, debts; *ber~*, to owe; *orang ber~*, debtor; *banyak ter~ wang*, heavily indebted; *lekat ~ orang*, to get into debt; *per~an*, debts, amount due; *orang ~an*, a debt slave.

huyung-hayang [KS], staggering, reeling; also *huyu-hayang* and *huyung-huyung*.

I

ia [KGn], 1. he, she, it and, sometimes, they; often used in writing as the subject of a verb; ~itu, that is, i.e. 2. meng~kan, to assent to; = ya, q.v; se~ (sekata), unanimous; ber~-berbukan, to consider.

iang [KK], meng~, to emit small, vague continuous noises, buzz, whirr, esp. as insects in the jungle; terng~-ng~, so buzzing unceasingly; also used of continued whining of children; also ngiang.

iau [KK], meng~, to mew (of a cat).

iba [KN], Ar. yearning, passionate regret, loving, longing; also hiba.

ibadat [KK], Ar. service to God; pious duties; religious duties; beramal ~, to perform one's religious duties.

Iban [KN], orang ~, a Borneo tribe, formerly notorious for head-hunting.

ibar [KN], ~-~, a small river dug-out.

ibarat [KN], Ar. metaphor, parallel; analogous case; an example of the fact that, like; ambil ~, to take a parallel case; to illustrate a point by a parable or fable; certia ~, a fable; ber~, parabolical; ~ is occasionally used in the sense of 'so-called': racun ~, the so-called poison.

ibau [KN], an edible mussel.

Iblis [KN], Ar. the devil; diharu ~, harried by Satan.

ibni [KN], Ar. son of; = bin (but ibni is used more politely or ceremonially than bin).

Ibrahim [KN], Ar. nabi ~, Abraham; a Malay proper name.

ibu [KN], mother, dam (of animals), source, matrix; saudara se~, a uterine brother; ~ bapa, parents; ~ suri, royal mother; ~ jari, thumb; ~ kaki, big toe; ~ pasir, gravel; ~ pertiwi, native country; ~ tangan, thumb; ~ telur, Treng. turtles generally; ~ kota, capital of a State; ~ pejabat, head office; ~ tiri, step-mother;

ibu is the leader or 'he' in children's games; playing at chasing the 'he', such as hide-and-seek; sometimes used for prophylactic; serum ~ kolera, cholera serum; ~ susu, wet-nurse; ke~an, motherhood.

ibul [KN], a palm (Orania macrocladus); its fruit is poisonous.

ibunda [KN], mother (honorific); (fig.) motherland.

ibus [KN], a palm (Corypha sp.).

idam [KK], ~kan, to long for anything (esp. when pregnant); ~-~an, the things so longed for.

idap [KK], chronic (of sickness or malancholy); meng~, to linger on in illness; dia meng~ lukanya kira-kira dua bulan, he continued to suffer from his wound for about two months.

idar [KK], meng~i, to wander round; meng~kan, to send round, to pass or hand round; beredar, in revolution; to circulate; also, to depart, leave; bintang beredar, a planet; peredaran, a revolution, a turn; peredaran dunia, the chances of this mortal life; pengedaran, Kel. a (Government) circular; peredaran, departure, movement.

iddah [KN], Ar. the period wherein a Moslem widow or divorcee may not remarry, i.e., 3 full menstrual periods or 40 days after child-birth; also edah.

Idil Adha [KN], Ar. the festival following the annual pilgrimage to Mecca, held on the tenth day of the month Zulhijjah; see **Haji**.

Idil Fitri [KN], Ar. the festival held on the first day of the month Shawal, following the Ramadan Fast; see **puasa**.

igal [KK], meng~, to strut, posture, show off, esp. of birds 'displaying', e.g. of the peacock spreading his tail.

igama, = **agama.**

igap [KK], Kel. Treng. to catch, arrest.

igau [KN], a double yoke (for oxen); also *gu* — cf. **kok.**

ihram [KN], Ar. devotional, sacred; a name given to the seamless wrapper worn by pilgrims.

ihsan [KN], Ar. beneficence, kindness; *dengan ~,* by courtesy of.

ihtiar, = **ikhtiar.**

ihtifal [KN], Ar. party, social gathering.

ijab [KK], Ar. consent, approval; ~ *kabul,* marriage ceremony; *meng~kan,* to perform a wedding ceremony.

ijabat [KN], Ar. the granting of prayer.

ijazat [KN], Ar. diploma, certificate, licence; a degree; also *ijazah.*

ijma [KN], Ar. agreement, consensus of opinion, esp. on a religious point.

ijmal [KN], Ar. general description, summary; opposed to *tafsir,* q.v.

ijtihad [KN], Ar. conclusion formed after careful study of evidence, conviction so formed; cf. **zan.**

ijuk [KN], fibre resembling horse-hair got from the sugar-palm; *tali ~,* rope made of this fibre.

ikal [KS], curl (of the hair); ~ *manis,* slightly curly; ~ *mayang,* more tightly curled, in ringlets (like the curl of palm blossom).

ikan [KN], a generic name for fish; ~-~, ship's log; ~ *kering,* dried fish; *nyawa ~,* the life of a fish on shore ('at the last gasp'); ~ *sempilai,* the gifhting fish; ~ *belalang,* flying fish; ~ *paus,* the whale; *per~an,* fisheries; ~ *air tawar,* freshwater fish.

ikat [KK], binding, fastening; *~an perang,* the line of battle; ~ *pinggang,* a belt; ~ *rumah,* to build a house; *~an,* bonds, fastenings, ties; *meng~kan,* to fasten, to put together; *ter~,* bound, attached; *meng~ kontrek,* to enter into a contract; *ter~,* in bonds, tied up; *~an, per~an,* association, league, alliance; *per~an Muslim India,* the Indian Moslem League; *per~an khidmat,* Service League; *kuasa-kuasa ber~,* Allied Powers; *per~an Atlantik,* Atlantic pact.

ikhlak [KN], Ar. morals, moral character; also *akhlak.*

ikhlas [KS], Ar. sincerity, sincere; *surat ul-~,* the letter is sincere (a common exordium to an old-style epistle); *ke~an,* integrity; *dengan ~nya,* yours truly.

ikhtiar, Ar. elected action, plan, course; *dengan ~nya sendiri,* by his own choice; *mencari ~,* to think out a plan; *pulangkan ~ kepada,* to leave the decision to (another); *bagaimana ~ kamu?,* what is your proposal?; *~kan,* to 'fix' something, make the necessary arrangements; also *ihtiar.*

ikhtifal, = **ihtifal.**

ikhtilaf [KN], Ar. inconsistent, misunderstanding; discord, lack of unanimity; the converse of *ijma.*

ikhtisar [KN], *meng~kan,* summarize; Ar. definition; summary, synopsis.

ikhwan [KN], Ar. brothers; *~-ul-muslimin,* Islamic brethren; a Wahabi community, considered fanatical by some.

iklan [KN], Ar. *meng~kan barang,* to advertise goods.

iklim [KN], Ar. a region or zone of the earth; clime, climate; ~ *panas,* tropics; *~-~,* climatology.

ikrar [KN], Ar. a promise, pledge, attestation; *surat ~,* Ked. an affidavit; *ber~,* to vow, solemnly declare, pledge oneself; ~ *taat setia,* to take the oath of allegiance.

iktibar, Ar. example, model.

iktikad, Ar. will, determination, set purpose; also *tekad.*

iktiraf, Ar. to recognise (e.g., a Government).

iktisad [KN], Ar. economy; *hukum ~,* economic sanctions.

ikut [KK], *meng~,* to follow (in point of space, not time); *peng~,* a follower, a disciple; *~an,* a pattern to follow; *~-~an,* follow blindly; imitator, lacking originality; henchman; *meng~,* in accordance with; *ber~an dengan,* as a result of, following (some event or action); ~ is also used in the sense of taking part in, joining in: ~ *tertawa,* to join in a laugh; ~ *serta dalam —*, id.; *yang ber~*, next (who is next); *seperti ber~*, as follows; *~-~an*, to keep up with the Joneses; *meng~ jejak*, to follow suit; *tidak meng~i perkembangan zaman*, does not keep abreast of the times.

Ilaha, Ar. God; *la ~ illallah*, there is no God but God.

ilahat [KN], Ar. Godhead.

Ilahi [KN], Ar. the Lord; *menyambut seruan ~*, to receive the call ofthe Lord, i.e. to die.

ilai [KK], *meng~*, to laugh loudly, 'cackle'.

ilam [KS], *~-~*, dimly or intermittenly visible.

ilham (il-ham) [KN], Ar. divine inspiration.

ilmiah [KN], Ar. scientific, pertaining to science.

ilmu [KN], Ar. science; special systematic knowledge; higher education sometimes including what in English are regarded rather as arts; also *ahli sains*, a scientist; *ahli ~ ...*, a man learned in the science of ...; *~ pertanian*, science of agriculture; *~ l athar*, archaeology, including the study of ancient traditions; *~ purbakala*, *~ barang-barang kuno*, archaeology; *~ hisab*, *~ kira-kira*, arithmetic; *~ manusia*, anthropology; *~ perbintangan*, *~ nujum*, astrology; *~ l hayah*, astronomy; *~ falak*, *~ falakiah*, astronomy (usually confined to calculation of the first day of the lunar month, eclipses, etc.); *~ kaji logam*, mineralogy; *~ kuman*, bacteriology; *~ perolekan*, science of beauty treatment; *~ hayat*, *~ kaji hayat*, biology; *~ jahat*, the black art, black magic; *~ kimiahayat*, biochemistry, *~ kimia*, chemistry; *~ tumbuh-tumbuhan*, botany; *~ penyakit kulit*, dermatology; *~ ekonomi*, economics; *~ juruteraan*, engineering; *~ batin*, esoteric learning; *~ bumi*, geography, sometimes geology; *~ batu*, geology; *i hasil bumi*, mining geology; *~ ukur*, *~ handarsah*, geometry; *~ kebidanan*, *~ penyakit kandung*, gynaecology; *~ lambang*, heraldry; *~ sejarah*, *~ tawarikh*, history; *~ hukum*,

jurisprudence; *~ bahasa*, linguistics; *~ pesawat*, mechanics; *~ pasti*, mathematics; *~ bentuk*, morphology; *~ jamur-jamur dan lumut*, mycology; *~ kedoktoran*, science of medicine; *~ perubatan*, id.; *~ udara*, meteorology; *~ pelayaran*, navigation; *~ penyakit saraf*, neurology; *~ alam*, *~ kejadian*, physics; *~ pemulih*, physiotherapy; *~ hukum*, political science; *~ faal*, physiology; *~ falsafah*, philosophy; *~ tengkorak*, phrenology; *~ penyiasatan jiwa*, psychoanalysis; *~ jiwa*, *saikology*, psychology; *~ kesihatan*, sanitary science; *~ kemasyarakatan*, sociology; *~ ghaib*, spiritualism; occult power; *~ mendidik*, science of teaching. pedagogy; *~ agama*, *~ ke-Tuhanan*, theology; *~ yogi*, yoga (Hindu system of philosophic meditation); *~ haiwan*, *~ binatang*, zoology.

imalat [KK], Ar. joining two letters in pronunciation, e.g. *insyallah* for *insya Allah*.

imam [KN], Ar. president or a mosque.

iman [KN], Ar. faith, creed, belief, religion; the true faith; *membawa ~*, to accept the true faith; *ber~*, religious; *rosak ~*, irreligious, back-slider; *ke~an*, basic faith, creed.

imbal [KS], one-sided, as the uneven work of a grindstone, or of a lathe, e.g. a table-leg, a badly ground blade; of a judge's decision; of an affected gait; not uniformly level or flat; cambered, of a road; *~an*, something in return; *mereka mengharapkan ~an*, they always expect something in return.

imbang [KS], 1. conveys the idea of uncertainly, doubt; 'hanging about'; *hati di dalam ~-~an*, heart full of uncertainty; *~an bayu*, (poet.) fitful gusts of wind. 2. *~an*, balance, proportion; *ber~*, well-balanced; *menurut per~an*, prorata; *kese~an*, balance, steadiness; *~an kekuasaan*, balance of power; *se~*, proportionate; *perwakilan per~an*, proportionate representative; *mense~kan*, to make proportionate.

imbas [KN], 1. the aura, subtle emanation, influence, effect, 'atmosphere', diffused by a noxious person or object; *kena ~an hantu,* to be affected by a passing spirit of disease; *pandang sekali ~,* to glance at. 2. *~-meng~,* swaying to-and-fro, as a pendulum or a tree in the wind.

imbau [KK], 1. N.S. hailing, addressing; *meng~,* to hail. 2. *meng~,* to be tossed up, rise, swirl up, as a skirt in the breeze; *suaranya meng~ tinggi,* his voice rose high (of a singer); *~kan,* to toss upwards, lob upwards.

imbuh [KN], making up the balance; additional payment; contributing; *rial ~,* Ked. money paid above the assessed value in compensation for land reclaimed by the State.

impi, Ind. = *mimpi.*

imsak [KN], Ar. the time at which the Fast starts daily in the Fasting month, *Ramadan.*

inai [KN], Ar. henna; a red dye obtained locally from a shrub *(Lawsoniaalba); ~ batu,* a pink balsam *(Impaticus Griffithii); ~ paya,* the water balsam *(Hydrocera triflora); malam ber~,* the night on which the bride's fingers are stained with henna, i.e., the commencement of the wedding festivities; some believe that painting the nails with henna averts evil spirits; *siput ~,* a shell *(Mitra episcopalis); kaki terdorong ~ padahnya,* he who has made his bed must lie on it.

inal [KN], a wad (as in a cartridge); also *nal.*

inang [KN], a nurse, a duenna, a chamberwoman to a princess.

inangda, (polite) = *inang;* wet nurse of a royal child.

inap [KK], Ind. *meng~,* to spend the night; *peng~an (rumah),* hotel, inn, night's lodging.

inas [KN], 1. the humming apparatus on a Malay humming-kite. 2. *pekung ~,* a malignant tumour.

inayat [KN], Ar. favour, bounty, aid.

incang [KKtr], *~-incut,* awry, askew.

incar. [KN], a drill, bore.

inci [KN], Eng. inch.

incut [KKtr], *incang-~,* awry, askew; *terincut-~,* swaying from side to side; unsteady.

indah [KS], beautiful, attractive, handsome; *~ sekali pemandangan di sini,* what a spectacular view! what a sight!; *ke~an,* beauty; *perasaan ke~an,* aesthetic sense; *~ permai,* beautiful, magnificient; precious, important, fine, handsome; *~ khabar dari rupa,* report is fairer than reality; *apa ~nya?,* of what value is it (to me)?, what does it matter?; *~kan,* to consider important, to care about; *per~kan,* to decorate, embellish; *buat ~ tak ~ (terhadap),* to behave in an offhand manner (to), to be indifferent.

indang [KK], to winnow with a side jerk.

Indera [KN], Skr. the Sanskrit divinity Indra; a name given to a class of minor divinities inhabiting Indra's heaven; a royal title; royal; *ke~an,* the heaven of Indra; *meng~,* royal; *panca~,* five senses.

indik [KK], to lever by pressure with the foot; *lesung ~,* a padi-pounder worked with the foot; *lang ~,* the changeable hawkeagle.

inding [KK], *meng~,* watching constantly like an inquisitive or hungry child; *ter~-~,* eyeing covetously.

induk [KN], mother, dam; *~ kerbau,* a milchbuffalo; *induk ayam,* clucking hen/ mother hen; *~-semang,* landlady, female employer; *~ goa,* (Borneo) the cave-swallow or swiftlet which makes edible nests; *perindukan* or *perindun,* brood — cf. *indung.*

indung [KN], mother (this world is rare); *~ mutiara,* mother-of-pearl — cf. **induk.**

ing, Jav. of, for — cf. **yang.**

inga-inga [KK], abstracted, in a brown study, stupefied.

ingar [KK], brawling, noisy disturbance; *~ bangar,* very great uproar; also *hingar.*

ingat [KK], recollect, remember; to give attention; to have in mind; *~-~,* take care, look out; ~an, attention to one's surroundings; recollection; ~i, to remember; ~kan, to remind; to call to mind; per~an, reminder; memper~i, to commemorate; buku per~an, diary, memorandum; dalam per~an, to be kept in view (of a file in an office); yang saya ~, as far as I remember; se~-~ saya, to the best of my recollection; ter~kan, to call to mind; — yang di~i, my dear — (at the start of a letter to a friend).

ingau [KK], ~-~, dozing, half awake, talking in one's sleep — cf. **igau**.

Inggeris [KN], English.

inggih [KN], Jav. yes; tukang ~, a yesman; also enggih.

inggu [KN], Skr. asafoetida; ikan ~, a generic name given to a large number of fish of the genera Pempheris, Pomacentrus, Pterois, Amphihrion, Stolocentrum, Stolacanthus and Pseudoscarus.

ingin [KK], longing, strong desire; ke~an, main ambition, what is desired; ~ tahu, curious, inquisitive; dia tetap ~ tinggal, he insisted on staying; tidak ~, to have no desire; dia ~ sekali meneruskan perjalanan, he feels very strongly about continuing the journey.

ingkar [KK], Ar. breaking a pledge; to disobey (an order); ~ kepada sumpah, false to an oath; meng~i, to disobey; to break (a promise).

ingsang [KN], = isang, the gills of a fish.

ingu, = **inggu**.

ingus [KN], mucus from the nose; buang ~, to blow one's nose; budak ~, snotnosed, child too young to wipe its own nose; nyiur ber~, young coconut with flesh just beginning to firm up.

ini [KKtr], this, these; aku ~, I who stand here, I myself; sekarang~, at this very moment; ~ juga bererti, this also means; ~ dia, here she is; ~kan pula, how much the more; much less, so much the less (in accordance with the context) — cf. **sini**.

injak [KN], = **enjak**.

injap [KN], the inturning spikes which permit entrance into a basket-trap for fish but prevent egress; a constricted entry generally; sometimes used for valve.

injil [KN], Ar. the New Testament; ~ Lukas, the gospel according to St. Luke.

insaf [KN], Ar. justice, equity; sympathy, consideration, appreciation, realisation, thoughtfulness; meng~i, to realise, to appreciate; meng~kan, to bring awareness to, to convince; to arouse sympathy.

insan [KN], Ar. a human being; ~ ulkamil, perfect, ideal man.

insang [KN], = **isang**.

insut [KK], meng~, to edge towards or away; bejalan ter~-~, to proceed with painful slowness, inch one's way along; also kesut, esut, ingsut and engsut.

insya, Ar. ~ Ilah, if God wills it.

intai [KK], meng~, to peep, to spy on; tukang ~, Paul Pry; peng~an, spying surveillance.

intan [KN], a diamond; used as a term of endearment; often shortened to tan; ~ mentah, uncut diamond, rough diamond.

inti [KN], 1. nucleus, essence; ~ sari, quintessence, gist, basis; ~sanggul, false addition to hair, switch of hair; gist of (a letter); stuffing in, e.g., a fowl. 2. Pk. star performer (theatre).

intikad [KN], criticism; dispute, oppose.

intip [KK], Ind. to peer at, watch closely, spy on; snoop; peng~an, a reconnaissance; peng~, a spy; pihak meng~ rahsia, Intelligence officers.

inu [KN], Jav. a title of distinction, princely.

ipar [KN], brother-in-law; sister-in-law.

ipil [KN], a tree (Intsia sp.).

ipuh [KN], the poison tree or upas (Antiaris toxicaria); the poison obtained from it; dart-poison generally.

iradat [KN], Ar. will; the will of God.

iram [KN], 1. ~-~, the fringe round a State umbrella. 2. change of colour; blushing.

irama [KN], rhythm, tempo, measure (as in music, to dance, esp. solo); musik yang ber~ pantas, music with a fast beat.

irap [KKtr], *se~,* alike; *~-~,* very much alike.

iras [KKtr], similar; *se~,* alike, of the same material, blood, or character; *~-~,* similarities; *keris ganja ~,* a kris of which the blade proper and the aring (or guard) are in one piece.

iri [KS], *~ hati,* envious, jealous; *meng~kan,* to admire enviously.

Irian [KN], Western New Guinea.

irik [KK], *~kan,* to tread down, to stamp on padi that is too short for threshing; *pelantar peng~,* threshing floor.

iring [KS], processional following; Indian file; one after another; accompanying; *ber~-~an,* in long succession; *meng~, meng~i,* to follow in procession; to escort; *di~kan,* to be followed by; *meng~jalan,* in line with the road; *~an,* accompaniment, esp. muscial; *lagu peng~,* the tune forming the accompaniment; *peng~,* escort; *peng~raja,* royal guards; *~-~an kapal,* a convoy of ships; *se~,* accompanying, together; *ber~an,* together, one following the other; *se~ bertukar jalan,* to disagree.

iris [KN], slice fillet (of fish); mengiris, to cut off, to slice.

irup [KK], to suck up liquid from a spoon or cup; to lap up; also *hirup.*

Isa [KN], Ar. Nabi Isa, Jesus Christ.

Isahak [KN], Ar. *nabi ~,* the patriarch Isaac; a Malay proper name, often shortened to *Sahak.*

isak [KN], *ter~-~,* sobbing; asthmatic coughing.

iseng [KK], Ind. pastime; *meng~,* to while away the time; *~-~,* miscellaneous; heading to 'Notes' in newspaper.

isi [KN], contents; that which fills; flesh (as opposed to bones or skin), of fish or fruit; *~ negeri,* the inhabitants of a settlement; *~ rumah,* the household; *~ dunia,* mankind; *~ hati,* what's on your mind; *~ surat,* the contents of a letter; *~ kahwin,* the marriage settlements on a bride; *se~nya,* lock, stock and barrel, *bagai kuku dengan ~,* like the nail and

the flesh within it — inseparable except at great pain, (prov.) *meng~kan,* to fill; *meng~ kedahagaan,* to quench thrist; *ber~,* filled with, containing; *badannya sudah ber~,* she is with child; *ber~* is sometimes used to mean fulfilled, of hopes; *~ lemak dapat ke orang, tulang bulu pulang ke kita,* we sow but others reap (prov); *~ ada bekal berjalan,* knowledge is power (prov).

isim [KN], Ar. name, esp. of the 99 Names of God; plural *~-~* or *asma,* used in incantations by sorcerers; the word also occurs in Arabic phrases, e.g. *bismillah* (= *bi-ismi-Allah*), in the Name of God.

Iskandar [KN], Ar. Alexander; *~ duzul.-Karnain,* Alexander the Great.

Iskandariah [KN], Alexandria.

Islam [KN], Ar. salvation; peace in God; the Muslim religion; *meng~kan,* to convert to Islam.

Isnin [KN], Ar. *hari ~,* Monday.

Istambul [KN], Constantinople.

istana [KN], Pers. a palace; *~ rupa,* flawless beauty, beauty needing no adornment; *~ hinggap,* a palace intended for occasional residence; also *astana.*

istanggi [KN], Skr. incense; also *setanggi.*

isteri [KN], Skr. wife (more respectful than *bini*); *ber~,* to be married (of a man); *ber~kan,* to marry (a woman); *memper~kan,* to marry off, esp. one's son.

istiadat [KN], Ar. ceremonial custom; ceremony; *Datuk ~,* Chamberlain at Malay Court.

istilah [KN], Ar. term, expression, phrase, terminology.

istimewa [KS], more especially; above all; special, notable, as an event; *satu ke~an,* a special feature, special point; if with a negative, it means 'much less', 'even less so'; *ter~,* special, exclusive.

istinggar [KN], Port. a matchlock.

istinja [KK], Ar. ablutions prescribed by Muslim custom, consisting of ritual cleansing of the body after relieving the bladder or bowels or after sexual intercourse.

istirahat [KN], Ar. repose, rest, peace; *ber~*, to rest.

istislam [KN], Ar. acceptance of the Muslim faith.

istiwa [KN], Ar. parallel; *khattul ~*, the equator; *per~*, important event or place; an occurrence, event.

istizah [KN], Egypt., Ar. Mrs. or Miss.

istrika [KN], a smoothing iron; to iron; *~ karant*, electric iron; also *seterika*.

isya [KN], Ar. *sembahayang ~*, the evening prayer.

isyarat [KN], Ar. signal, sign; *memberi ~*, to give the signal; *~-~ tangan,* gestures; *pasukan ~*, Signals Unit.

isytihar [KN], Ar. proclamation, announcement; *per~an perang*, declaration of war.

itarad [KK], Ar. to criticise, stand out against.

ittifak [KN], Ar. concord; decision; faith.

itik [KN], duck; *~ air*, a grebe, the masked fin-foot; *~ Surati, ~ nila,* the Muscovy duck; *pelir ~*, an auger; *ular ~*, a fabulous duck-billed snake (the finding of which brings luck in money matters); *berdayung cara ~ berenang*, to feather in rowing; *berdiri ~*, to stand on one leg.

itu [KS & Kgn], that, those; *~ pun,* even so; — cf. **situ**.

izin [KN], Ar. permission; also; *surat ~*, written permission.

Izrael [KN], Ar. Azrael, the Custodian of Death.

J

Jaafar [KN], Ar. a cousin of the Prophet; a Malay proper name.

jabar [KN], Ar. omnipotent; *Malik ul-~,* the Almighty King, God; *Khalik ul-~,* the Almighty Creator.

jabat [KK], grasping in the hand, holding; *~an,* (1) the sense of touch; (2) occupation, profession, = *jawatan; ber~,* to hold; *~ tangan, ~ salam,* to shake hands; pe~, office; *Pe~ Jajahan Takluk,* Colonial Office; ~an, department of government; *~an Kawalan Harga,* Price Control Department; *~an Kawalan Makanan,* Food Control Department; *~ Negara,* State Department; *~an Perhubungan Raya,* Department of Public Relations; *~an Perhubungan Luar,* Department of Foreign Relations; *~an Maklumat,* Department of Information; *~an Kebajikan Am,* Public Welfare Department; *Menteri tidak ber~an,* Minister without portfolio; *~an Haiwan,* Veterinary Department; *~an Kerja Raya* (J.K.R.), Public Works Department; *~an Kaji Cuaca,* Meterological Department.

jabing [KS], prominent (of the ears).

jabu [KK], Ked. *ber~,* rising in clouds (of smoke, dust, etc).

jabut [KN], hairy; *ketam ~,* the boring crab.

jadah [KN], Pers. son, born of; *baram ~,* bastard, ill-begotten; better *zadah.*

jadam [KN], 1. an extract of ales used as medicine. 2. a Sumatran ware made by filling the hollows of a pattern traced on a brass or silver article with a sulphide or pitch.

jadi [KK], coming into existence; becoming; turning out satisfactorily; accomplishing its purpose; *aku pun ~lah,* I was born; *kerja itu tak ~,* that work will not do; *~~an,* a supernatural creation; *harimau ~~an,* a were-tiger; *men~,* to become; *men~kan,* to create; *ke~an,* creation; *men~~,* abounding (as crops), continually occurring, rife (as crimes or diseases); popular, much in vogue, as forms of entertainment; *boleh ~,* perhaps, 'could be'; *semula ~,* natural, innate, provided by nature; *pelabuhan semula ~,* a natural harbour; *bakat semula ~,* natural talent; *bagaimana jadinya?* what will be the outcome of it?; *hari~,* birthday; *men~~,* increase, lengthen; *rusuhan para pelajar men~~,* the students' riot is getting worse.

jadual [KN], Ar. a tabular statement, a schedule; *~ waktu,* time-table; *di~kan akan dilangsungkan pada,* scheduled to take place on; *lebih cepat dari yang di~kan,* ahead of schedule.

jaga [KK], Skr. to be awake, to be watchful; *orang ~,* a watchman; *~ daripada tidur,* to awake from sleep; *men~kan,* to wake (a person); *ber~,* to be awake; *ber~~,* to keep open house day and night (in marriage festivities); to be on the watch, alert; *ter~ dari tidur,* woken up, disturbed from sleep; *pen~an,* precautions; *men~,* to watch; *men~ kebersihan,* to keep clean; *men~ berat badan,* watch your weight; *pen~ harta musuh,* custodian of enemy property.

jagat [KN], Skr. the world; *~ buana,* id.

jagla [KK], Pk. amusing.

jago [KN], Ind. a cock; also *jaguh;* used for 'local champion', 'cock-of- the-walk'.

jagung [KN], maize, Indian corn; *men~,* sprouting of rice, pustules, breasts; *setahun ~,* the period needed for a crop of maize, about 100 days, so, a short period generally; *umur baharu setahun ~,* ' a mere kid'; *men~,* to begin to swell, as a young gilr's breasts, as young plants; *baik ber~~ sementara padi belum masak,* live on maize till the rice ripens (make do).

jaguni [KN], Skr. spirits of good fortune.

jagur [KS], massively built, burly.

jagut [KN], Jav. chin — cf. **dagu** and **janggut**.

jahan [KN], Pers. the world.

jahanam [KN], Ar. gehenna, hell; destruction; *men~kan,* destroy, wreck, ruin; *sudah ~,* (sl.) it's ruined, spoilt.

jahang [KK], 1. violent abuse. 2. [KS], *merah men~,* a deep red.

jaharu [KN], Hind. a pariah, a low scoundrel.

jahat [KS], wicked, evil, immoral; naughty, of a child; mischievous, dangerous, of an animal; *dengan ~,* with evil intent; *perempuan ~,* a prostitute; *ke~an,* wickedness; *pen~,* bad characters; *ber~,* to go to the bad, become wicked; *~ baiknya,* the good and bad points of a person, the varying behaviour.

jahil [KS], Ar. ignorant of God's word; irreligious; so, bone-headed, crassly ignorant, uncultured; *~ murakkab,* utterly and hopelessly ignorant; *murakkab* means 'compound', and the idea is, 'ignorance on top of ignorance', and so invincible ignorance.

jahiliat [KN], Ar. the general ignorance of God's word that prevailed before Muhammad enlightened mankind with the *Koran.*

jahim [KKtr], Ar. fiercely blazing (of hellfire); *neraka ~,* the hottest hell.

jahit [KK], needlework, sewing; *tukang ~* or *orang pen~,* a tailor; *~an,* sewing, article being sewn; *mesin ~,* sewingmachine; *bakul ~an,* sewing-basket.

Jahudi [KN], Jaudi, Jew, Jewish.

jais [KS], *kalis ~,* id., very unreceptive or inattentive.

jaja [KK], *ber~,* to hawk about; *men~,* id.; *pen~,* a hawker.

jajah [KK], to travel about; *men~i,* to travel about, tour; *~han,* a district, province; *pen~an,* imperialist; imperialism, colonialism; *pen~an pemeras darah,* bloodsucking imperialists; *~an amanah,* a Trust Territory.

jajan [KN], Ind. a snack; *wang ~,* pocket money.

jajang [KN], *burung ~,* Kel. the broadbill.

jajar [KN], a row, a line; *ber~,* drawn up in a row, stretching out in a line; *menye~kan,* make in line, make parallel; *~an genjang,* parallelogram; *se ~,* parallel — cf. **janjar** and **banjar**.

jajat [KK], Pen. to mimic; ridiculing by mimicry; to argue hotly.

jaka [KN], Jav. a young unmarried man — cf. **bujanggal.** 2. also *jejaka.*

jakas [KN], a kind of *mengkuang.*

jaksa [KN], Jav. an officer of Justice in Indonesia; *~ agung,* Attorney General; *ke~an agung,* the Department of the Attorney General; *~ pendamai,* Justice of the Peace.

Jakun [KN], a name given to aboriginal Malayan tribes in the south of the Malay Peninsula.

jala [KN], Skr. 1. a casting-net; *men~,* to fish with a casting-net; *je~,* anything that resembles a net; *pen~,* a person who catches fish with a net; *pen~an,* fishing with a net. 2. *akar ~~,* a climbing plant of the fig family.

jalad [KN], executioner.

jalak [KN], 1. a one-masted or two-masted sailing vessel peculiar to Pahang (it is built up fore and aft and is not decked except for a loose framework of split *nibungs* or planks). 2. *ayam ~,* a black cock with white markings.

jalan [KN], road, way; movement in a definite direction; the course taken; *~ bahasa,* idiom; *~ ugama,* theology; *~ raya,* the main road; *mata ~,* a scout; *membawa ~,* to lead the way; *ber~,* to be in motion; *ber~ kaki,* to walk; *ber~ kereta,* to travel by carriage; *men~i,* to travel over, traverse; *men~i hukum,* to undergo a sentence; *men~kan,* to set in motion; to put into effect, to carry out (e.g., a command, plan, law); *per~an,* journey; route; *ber~ terus,* to go straight on; to continue (of actions or events); *~ buntu,* a cul-de-sac; *~ mati, ~ sekerat (sahaja),* id.; *~ tembok* or *~ tambak,* a made road, a causeway; *~ bertar,* tarmac road; ~ *satu hala,* a one-way street; ~ *berkeliling,* a roundabout; ~ *batang,* a main road; ~ *gua,* a tunnel; ~ *pendek,* ~ *singkat,* short cut; ~ *masuk,* entrance; ~ *keluar,* exit; *per~an darah,* circulation of the blood; *dia sekadar men~kan tugas,* he's only doing his duty; ~ *tengah,* a compromise; *selamat ~!,* goodbye!, go in peace!

jalang [KS], 1. running wild; (fig.) lecherous; *kucing ~,* a domestic cat run wild; *perempuan ~,* a loose woman. 2. to approach, draw near, esp. as a date; *menjelang Hari Raya,* by the time Hari Raya comes; also *jelang.*

jalar [KK], *men~,* to creep (as a snake or creeping plant); *ter~,* widely extended, spreading far; lengthily; *menjalar* is also used to mean to spread wide, as a curtain or as weeds or vapour; (fig.) to prowl about.

jali [KS], Ar. evident, clear; *ter~,* revealed, inspired.

jalibut [KN], Hind. a jolly-boat.

jalil [KS], Ar. noble, honourable; *Abdul Jalil,* a Malay proper name.

jalin [KK], tied parallel by means of string or rattan (as the strips of bamboo in chicks or fish-screens); *men~,* so to tie; (fig.) to compose, to build up, to put together (as a story); *men~ hubungan diplomatik,* to establish diplomatic relations; *ber~~,* involved, intricate; *~an,* complication; composition; *~an bahasa,* syntax.

jalis [KK], Ar. *se~,* sitting together, in company.

jalu [KN], the natural spur of a fighting-cock; *ikan ~,* a fish *(Lutianus sp.).*

jalur [KN], lane; *memandu di ~ kiri,* drive on the left lane; also *lorong;* 1. a band or stripe of colour; broad stripes separated by lines; a strip of padi-field as marked by the lines of padi-stalks; a river-boat of shallow draught (the ribs of which give it a striped appearance); sometimes used for wrinkles — cf. **lajur.** 2. ~ *(serempu),* a dug-out canoe.

jam [KN], Pers. a watch; a clock; an hour;

the time; *sudah ~ berapa?,* what is the time?; ~ *pukul berapa?,* id.; ~ *tangan,* wrist-watch; ~ *saku,* pocket watch; *setengah ~* half-an hour; *se~ dua,* an hour or two; *sikit ~,* (sl.) a short time; ~ *rasmi,* official time; ~ is also used for 'mater'; ~ *bayang matahari,* a sun-dial; *pesawat ~,* the works of a watch or clock.

jamaah [KN], delegation, body, assembly.

jamah [KK], physical contact or handling; actual (even if temporary) possession; to feel with the fingers (as when testing the sharpness of a blade); to handle; *men~,* to have sexual intercourse; *~~an,* an occasional mistress of a prince.

jamang [KN], a gold or silver frontlet worn by a woman.

jambak [KN], a (double) handful, a bunch, e.g., of fruit; ~ *kunci,* a bunch of keys; ~ is also used to mean a flowertuft; *rosak bawang ditimpa ~,* an onion is ruined by its flowertuft falling on it (and rotting), i.e. a man is ruined by excessive display.

jamban [KN], a privy; ~ *tarik,* a water-closet; but normally, though not necessarily, a *jamban* is made over a stream; hence the simile for persons thriving on filth, i.e. dirty deeds; *seperti lampam di olak ~,* like *lampam* fish on the down-river side of a privy.

jambang [KN], 1. a flower-pot or stand for flower-pots; *~an,* id.; also 'flower-bed'. 2. whiskers, a full beard.

jamber [KN], 1. *se~,* a plateful. 2. Pk. a rough temporary hut built by travellers camping in the jungle.

jambatan [KN], a bridge; a pier; a way with a hand-rail; a variant of *jabatan* (from *jabat*); ~ *angkat angkat,* a drawbridge; ~ *gantung,* suspension bridge.

jambiah [KN], Pers. a curved dagger.

jambu [KN], Skr. a generic name for a number of fruits of the rose-apple class; ~ *air, Eugenia aguea;* ~ *bersin = ~ biji,* the guava *(Psidium guava);* ~ *bul,* a common red guava *(eugenia*

malaccensis); ~ keling and *~ merah,* id.;
~ golok, Treng. the cashew-nut; *merah
~,* a shade of deep pink; *padi ~,* Kel.
early varieties of rice; *~ mawar (Eugenia jambos); ~ monyet,* the cashew
(Anacardium occidentale); ~-~, the lume
or crest on a helmet; the ornamental
top of a standard; *jambu* is used in sl.
for pretty, (as rosy-cheeked or smooth-skinned or both).

jambua [KN], a shaddock.

jambul [KN], a tuft of hair; the crest of a
bird; the queue of a Chinese; the tassel
of a fez; the long lock left on a boy's
head prior to circumcision; *~ merak,*
the crest of a peacock; a plant *(Poinciana pulcherrima);* a common grass
(unidentified, but not a *selaginella);
merbah ~,* the Southern, red-whiskered
bulbul.

jamhoriah [KN], republic.

jamin [KK], Hind. bail, security, to go bail;
pen~, a bailor, a surety; *mengikat ~,* to
enter into a bond, esp. a bail-bond;
~an, a guarantee, a security, a bond, an
assurance; *~an hak,* patent; *di~,* under
warranty *(kenderaan baru).*

jamjam [KN], water of the Zamzam well in
Mecca, and so, water (very poetically
expressed); *~ durja,* complexion, expression; = *air muka; ~ mas,* gold paint.

jampang [KK], Sel. light, of little account,
easy; *~kan,* to make easy — cf. **gampang.**

jampi [KK], Skr. incantation; *men~,* to practise magic by incantation.

jampuk [KN], 1. the Scops owl. 2. *men~,*
interrupt, break into a conversation.

jamu [KK], *men~,* to entertain (a guest); to
keep (a familiar spirit); *hantu ~an,* a
familiar spirit; *per~an,* entertainment,
dinner; *~an teh,* a tea-party; *~an berselerak,* a buffet party; *~an mata,* a feast
for the eyes; *men~ mata,* to feast with
the eyes in pleasure or gloating; *men~
selera,* to indulge one's appetite; *men~
nafsu,* to indulge one's desires, esp.
one's lust; *~-~,* a plant *(Aporosa microcalyx); bahan ~,* medicinal herbs.

jamung [KN], Ked an extemporised torch,
= *andang.*

jamur [KN], Ind. fungus, esp fungoid
growths on plants.

janabat [KS], Ar. cf. **junub.**

janda [KN], a widow; a divorced woman; *~
sekali kirai,* a widow who has been
married only once; *~ sat lekuk,* (sl.)
lonely widow (only one heart); *~ berhias,* childless widow; *lenggang ~,* Pk.
a small curved knife broadening and
fretted at the point.

jangak [KK], abandoned; *pen~,* profligate,
immoral, dissolute; *men~,* to lead a licentious life; *penyangak,* Pk. sneak-thief, petty criminal.

jangan [KK], don't; lest; *~ lah,* do not;
supaya ~, lest; *~kan,* so far from ; not to
mention; *~ tidak,* don't fail to ...; *~~,*
N.S., I fear that, don't tell me that, it
may be that; *~ sampai,* lest, don't get to
the point; *~-~, dia dah dapat kerja,* don't
tell me that he has got work!; *~~ dia
kena pergi sekolah,* it may be that he
has to go to school.

jangat [KN], 1. a process of splitting
rattans; *pisau pen~,* the knife used in
this process; *perekat ~,* glue. 2. N.S. a
patch of hardened skin, e.g., on the
foot, a callus.

jangga [KN], a variant of *jaka.*

janggal [KS], discordant, inharmonious,
awkward; *tingkah laku yang ~,* an awkward manner.

Janggi [KN], 1. Pers. Zanzibari; African;
pauh ~, a tree supposed to grow in the
centre of the great ocean; *buah pauh ~,*
shells of the coconut *(Cocos maldiva),*
believed to be the fruit of this tree. 2.
Pers. warrior-like.

janggus [KN], *buah ~,* the cashew *(Anacardium occidentale).*

janggut [KN], the beard; *ber~,* bearded; *~
bauk,* a full beard; *~ beramus,* a bristling beard; *~ diurut,* a forked or pointed
beard; *~ kambing,* goatee; *~ jarang,* a
sparse beard; *~ tebal,* a full beard; *pak
~,* Bengali.

jangka [KN], compasses; measurement as

with compasses; measure of time; ~nya, apparently, as far as one can estimate; ~kan, to anticipate; pinjaman ~ pendek, a short-term loan; tiada jangkanya, unlimited; pinjaman ~ panjang, a long-term loan; pinjaman ~ jauh, id.; ~ waktu, a period of time, a distinguishable amount of time; bom ~, time-bomb; ~ lukis, drawing compasses.

jangkah [KK], stepping over an obstacle; more commonly langkah.

jangkang [KN], 1. ter~, spread widely, as limbs; gaping widely, as a door; men~, to walk with one's legs wide apart; jatuh ter~, to fall with limbs spread wide, spread-eagled. 2. a generic name for a number of trees with stilt roots.

jangkar [KN], a grapnel; an anchor; ~kan, to reach out and clutch at something; branching, visible roots (e.g., of the roots of the mangrove).

jangkau [KK], men~, to reach out to, to attain; = jengkau; di luar ~, beyond one's power, beyond the reach of.

jangki [KN], a basket or wicker knapsack.

jangkih [KS], ~-mangkih, bristling, disorderly, projecting irregularly, like a chevauxde-frise.

jangkil [KK], morose, ill-tempered.

jangkit [KN], 1. to hop across a gap, jump across, as a squirrel crosses from tree to tree; so, ber~, to spread, as disease or fire; penyakit ber~, infectious or contagious, of a disease; ~kan, to cause to spread, to extend (e.g. as wind spreads a fire); ~-kena, to make contact (of an electrical circuit). 2. pierced by a barbed thorn or point.

jangut [KS], Kel. smart, well-dressed.

janik [KK], radiating from a common centre; ringgit ~, the Mexican dollar, so called because it depicts a rising or setting sun.

Janin [KN], a proper name; jadi Mat ~, to build castles in the air (from a story that a man of this name, when climbing for coconuts, day-dreamed about his profits and fell); angan-angan Mat ~, castles in the air.

janjar [KN], a row or line; ber~, in rows.

janji [KN], contract, agreement; to agree; minta ~, to request the fulfilment of an agreement; sudah ada ~ yang lain, (I) have previous engagement; pegang ~, to observe an agreement; mungkir ~, belot ~, break an agreement; ber~, to agree, to contract; per~an, a contract; per~an tiada membuat pelanggaran, non-aggression pact; ber~an tidak serang-menyerang, id.; luar ~, not covered by an agreement (i.e., an event or circumstance which will nullify it); ~ itu harus dipenuhi, an obligation to fulfill o.'s promise; a promise is a promise; ~ is sometimes used to mean appointed hour of death; sudah sampai ~, his hour had come; in this sense ~ = ajal.

jannat [KN], Ar. (a garden); ~ al naim, the Garden of Delights (in Paradise).

jantan [KS], male (usually of animals), masculine; anak ~, a manly person; ke~an, manliness, courage, bravery; tunjukkan ke~anmu, be a man, be a gentleman; ~ is used fig. for the long and narrow and the big, as opposed to the short and squat (betina); busut ~, a tall ant-hill; garam ~, coarse salt; embun ~, dew in heavy drops; ketam ~, a plane; pahat ~, a narrow deep chisel; main berjantan, to commit unnatural offences (between males).

jantina [KN], sex; kedua ~, both sexes; this seems to be one of the 'telescoped' words popular in modern times, = jantan-betina.

jantung [KN], core, heart; the heart is us. ~ in the anatomical sense, and hati (anatomically liver and heart) in the sense of 'seat of the feelings'; penyakit lemah-lemah ~, having a weak heart; debar ~, heartbeat; serangan ~, heart attack; ~ paha, the fleshy portion of the thigh; ~ tangan, the triceps; burung ~, spider-hunter, sun-bird; si ~ hati, ladylove.

jantur [KN], Skr. sorcery.

jap [KK], come together, collected; sudah ~, it is complete, it has come about; sej-

~, each and every.

jara [KN], an instrument for cleaning coarse cotton-wool; a drill; a churning instrument for milk; any instrument worked by a revolving shaft; *kepala* ~, buttermilk.

jarah [KK], 1. *men*~, prowling about as plunderer; ~*an*, a slave carried off by raiders; *pen*~, a bandit. 2. Ar. a mite; a particle; an atom; *bom* ~, atom bomb; also *zarah*. 3. Ar. a pilgrimage; better *ziarat*.

jarak [KN], 1. distance between; ~*nya*, interstice, intervening space; distance of a course or between racers at finish; ~ *dekat*, short distance; ~ *umur*, difference in ages; *men~kan*, to move away from; *kalah ~ kepala*, beaten by a head; *ber~* to spread out, open out, as troops in open order. 2. the caster-oil plant (*Ricinus communis*) or plants looking like it; *minyak* ~, castor-oil; *pokok daun* ~, a shurb (*Plumbago zeylanica*) which has a habit of springing up on abandoned clearings; *padang* ~, a desolate place.

jaram [KN], *pen*~, a cooling lotion for the head.

jarang [KS], scarce, rare, separated by wide intervals; seldom; diaphanous; widemeshed; (*cara*) *men~kan beranak*, (method) of birth-control; *ubat pen~ beranak*, birth-control drug; *dia ~ membuat kesilapan*, he rarely makes mistakes.

jaras [KN], 1. a creel. 2. a handful (when the stalks or strings only are held in the hand); a bunch.

jari [KN], a finger; a toe; ~ *hantu*, the middle finger; ~ *kaki*, a toe; ~ *kelingking*, the little finger; ~ *manis*, the ring-finger; ~ *telunjuk*, the index-finger; *anak* ~, a finger; *buku* ~, the knuckles; *celah* ~, the cleft between two fingers; *ibu* ~, a thumb; *sarung* ~, a thimble; ~~, spokes; rays (of light); *jari-jari* is sometimes used for the legs of a centipede; see *lipan*.

jariah [KN], 1. Ar. *amal* ~, a charitable

work of permanent utility. 2. Ar. a slave-girl.

jaring [KN], a wide-meshed drift net; used for tennis 'nets'; *men*~, to fish with a net; ~ *angin*, to do unproductive work; ~ *laba-laba*, spider's web; ~*an*, Ind. tissue; ~*an tubuh*, bodily tissue; *memindahkan ~an tubuh*, to transplant bodily tissue.

jaru [KN], *ijkan* ~-~, a fish (*Caranx boops*); also *cencaru*.

jarum [KN], a needle, the hands of a clock; ~ *cucuk*, a bodkin; a surgical probe; a syringe for inoculation, etc.; sometimes, a probe; ~ *penunjuk*, an indicator, sign, a pointer; ~ is used (vulg.) for penis; *lubang* ~, the eye of a needle; *mata* ~, id.; ~-~ or ~*an*; (fig.) intrigues, underground activities; *menjalankan* ~-~, to intrigue, *men*~ to sprout up; as grass.

jasa [KN], Skr. meritorious service; deserts; loyalty; *buat* ~ or *ber*~, to do one's duty loyally; beneficent, actively kind; ~ *baik*, to do a person a good turn; *memakan* ~ —, profit by kindness or good work of —; *memberi* ~ *baik*, to give one's good offices (assist, e.g., in settling a dispute); *lupakan* ~, to be remiss in one's duty; *hilang* ~, wasted effort, good work done for nothing.

jasad [KN], the material and visible body (as opposed to the soul); a living creature.

jasmani [KN], = *jismani*.

jati [KKtr} 1. Ar. true, real; *Melayu* ~, a real Malay; *timur* ~, due east; *kayu* ~, teak (*Tectonia grandis*). 2. *pe~an*, titbits, esp. of meat; *pe~an awak kepantangan orang*, what are titbits to you are forbidden food to others, i.e. one man's meat is another man's poison.

jatuh [KK], to (accidentally) fall; to happen, to occur; ~ *sakit*, to fall sick; ~ *cinta*, to fall in love; ~ *tersungkur*, to fall, flat on one's face; ~*kan*, *men~kan*, to let drop, to over-throw; *ke~an*, fall; *te*~, Kel. the West, i.e. the region in which the sun sets; ~ *hati kepada*, to be keen on, take a fancy to (esp. of a lover);

the basic idea of ~ is falling from or off, as opposed to falling from a position standing on the ground, which is *rebah,* but even Malays do not always adhere to this basic idea.

Jaudi [KN], Ar. a Jew, Jewish.

jauh [KS], distance, far; *dari ~,* from afar; *~lah malam,* the night was far spent; *men~i,* to keep off (at a distance); *men~kan,* id.; *men~kan diri,* to avoid company, to keep apart; *ber~an,* far apart; *men~kan diri dari,* to shun; *di~kan Allah,* God forbid!; *~ sekali* !, far from it!; *dike~an,* in the distance; *~ di mata ~ di hati,* out of sight, out of mind.

jauhar [KN], Ar. gem, jewel, essence, embryo.

jauhari [KN], Ar. a jeweller.

jauk [KN], a small tortoise (unidentified).

Jawa [KN], Javanese; *Tanah ~,* Java; *orang ~,* a Javanese; *asam ~,* tamarind; *~ demam,* fevered Javanese, name given to the crude figure usually forming the handle of a kris.

jawab [KK], Ar. answer; *minta ~,* to request a reply; *beri ~, ber~* or *men~,* to reply.

jawat [KN], *~an,* an office, a post; *~ankuasa,* a committee; *~ankuasa am,* General Committee; *~ kuasa tadbir,* Central or Executive Committee; *~ankuasa kerja negeri,* Executive Council; *pegawai per~an,* Establishment Officer; *per~an berpencen,* pensionable establishment; *rakan se~,* colleague; 'our contemporary' (newspaper).

Jawi [KN], 1. Ar. Malayan; Sumatran and Javan; *huruf ~,* the Arabic character; *~ pekan,* a term applied to Indian Muslims who are partly Malay. 2. Jav. an ox. 3. *~-~,* a large fig-tree *(Ficus rhododendrifolia).* 4. Kel. spiritless in appearance, of a fighting bull (from 2.?).

jaya [KK], Skr. to succeed, to 'come off'; *ber~,* successful; *men~kan,* to make a success of (e.g., a plan, meeting); *~* is used in titles of honour carrying the idea of triumphant, victorious, prosperous.

jaying [KS], Jav. and Skr. victorious, = *jayaing; ~ seteru,* conquering all foes.

jazirah [KN], Ar. a peninsula, esp. the Arabian Peninsula.

jebah [KS], broad and full (of the face).

jebah [KS], *ber~,* lying about in profusion, in abundant supply.

jebak [KN], a trap. esp. a cage-trap for birds; *men~,* to lure into a trap.

jebang [ ], 1. an oblong shield. 2. rather prominent (of ears).

jebat [KN], 1. Ar. civet; *Musang jebat,* the Indian civet *(Viverra zibetha).* 2. Kel. a colour of cattle, black with a touch of white under the belly.

jebuh [KN], *ikan ~,* a fish *(Dussumiera sp.).*

jebung [KN], *ikan ~,* a leatherjacket.

jeda [KN], Ar. pause, break; *tak berjeda,* without a break.

jegang [KS], stiff, esp. of rigor mortis; *keras ~,* id.

jegil [KS], *ter~,* prominent (of the eyeball); glaring with protruding eyes.

jegung [KN], stern-lockers.

jejak [KN], mark, footprint, mark serving as a clue; treading on, (fig.) reaching down to; *rambut ~ ke bahu,* hair reaching the shoulders; *mencari ~,* to trace, to track down; *men~kan kaki,* to put down o.'s foot; also *jijak;* cf. **cecah.**

jejal [KK], *men~,* to close a crack; to force food into a child's mouth (sl.); *ber~-~,* crammed, packed (as cars in a traffic jam); *ber~an kereta,* traffic jam.

jejas [KK], to abrade, scratch, graze; *tidak ter~,* invulnerable — cf. **relas, lelas.**

jejeh [KK], slightly spilling, slopping over.

jejek [KK], *men~,* N.S. to mock at, ridicule.

jejer [KN], row, line; *ber~,* in lines, lined up.

jekera [KN], assistant to a *batin* (see **batin** 1.); *Bukit Jekera* or *Jegera,* Jugra Hill; also *juru kerah.*

jela [KN], 'gadding about' (of a woman).

jela [KK], berjela, trailing slackly or loosely; *ber~-~,* id.; (fig.) rambling on and on, as a speech.

jelah [KS], clear, unobstructed (of the

view).

jelabak [KK], *ter~*, Pk. to collapse (as a building).

jelaga [KN], soot.

jelai [KN], a millet *(Aphania paucijuga)*.

jelajah [KK], *men~*, to travel about, tour round; *pen~an*, exploration; *kapal pen~*, cruiser.

jelak [KK], sated, glutted; *jemu ~*, sick of.

jelanak [KK], advancing under cover, wriggling through long grass.

jelang [KK], Ind. *men~*, to approach, of a date; draw near, come round, of a future event; *men~ pertemuan puncak*, prior to the summit; also *jalang.*

jelantah [KN], 1. insufficiently cooked (of rice); under-done. 2. small remainder of coconut oil which has been used for frying.

jelapang [KN], a paid-barn.

jelar [KK], extended at full length (of a long-bodied animal or creeping plant).

jelas [KK], settled; wound up; made plain; *~kan*, to settle accounts; *pen~an*, explanation, clarification.

jelat [KK], *ter~*, carelessly thrown down (as, e.g., a coat).

jelatang [KN], the tree-nettle *(Laportica crenulata);* a deadly poison can be made from it, so that word is sometimes used for 'poison'.

jelatik [KN], the Java sparrow.

jelau [KK], *jenguk ~*, to peer at anything.

jelawat [KN], *ikan ~*, a sp. of carp *(Leptobarbus hoeveni); krai ~*, id.

jelebau [KN], a kind of river-turtle.

jelebut, = **kelebut**.

jelejeh [KK], *ber~*, dribbling, watering at the mouth.

jelek, Ind. unpleasant.

jelekit [KK], adhering, as gummy eyelids.

jelempah [KK], *ter~*, lying strewn about and neglected, as fallen fruit.

jelepak [KN], (onom.) the sound of a book (of any similar body) falling on the ground; flopping.

jelepang [KK], cross-gashes; cross-cutting with a sabre.

jelepuh [KK], *ter~*, falling in a heap, lying

huddled up; also *jeleput.*

jelibir [KK], Kel. to talk nonsense, blather.

jelimpat [KK], *men~*, to break a journey at, visit; to branch off.

jelinap [KK], *men~*, to shoot ahead (as a horse in a race).

jeling [KK], a sidelong languishing look; *men~*, to look at anyone through the corner of the eye.

jelingar [KK], *men~*, to pay little attention to a fact; to half-remember, half-forget.

jelir [KK], *men~*, to project the tongue; *lidahnya ter~~*, continually shotting out its tongue (of a snake).

jelita [KS], beautiful, pretty, charming.

jelma [KK], Skr. incarnation; *men~*, to assume human form; to be re-incarnated; *men~ menjadi harimau*, to be transformed into a tiger; *pen~an*, an incarnation; metamorphosis; apparition; *men~*, to materialise (as hopes); to appear, as a ghost; to become visible; to come into being, as a new State.

jelojoh, = **gelojoh**.

jelu [KN], 1. *~ masak pisang*, the weasel *(Putorius nudipes)*. 2. resentful, annoyed.

jeluak [KN], hawking before expectoration.

jeluang [KN], tissue-paper.

jeluat [KK], *jeling-~*, to give a long sidelong look — cf. **jeling.**

jelujur [KK], 1. loose sewing, temporary stitching. 2. horizontal bars shot into sockets to close a cattle-pen.

jeluk [KS], 1. deep (of a bowl). 2. Kel. a basin.

jelum [KK], to wet without actual immersion; *ubat ~*, a lotion.

jelungkap [KK], *men~*, to rebound (of an elastic body released from strain).

jeluntung [KN], chicken-pox.

jelutung [KN], 1. a leaf-monkey (esp. *Semnopithecus obscurus*). 2. a kind of wild rubber tree; its rubber is used in making chewing-gum.

Jemaah [KN], congregation, pilgrims, crowd, audience; *~ haji*, Mecca pilgrim; *~ Menteri*, the Cabinet; *ber~*, to attend mosque, to form part of a congregation or assembly, = **Jumaat**.

jemah [KKtr], there or thereabouts, perhaps, sooner or later, an idiomatic word used in literature lessening the precision of a statement; *esok* ~, one day perhaps; *kelak* ~, will be perhaps.

jemala [KN], the crown of the head.

jemawa [KS], strong desire, determination; sometimes, headstrong behaviour; *ke~an*, naughtiness, conceitedness.

jemba [KN], 1. a measure of length equal to about 12 feet. 2. Kel. to press onwards; *men~*, to seize, to pull, to stretch out the hand.

jembak [KK], *ter~--*, flapping up and down as a child's locks when the child runs.

jembalang [KN], an evil spirit of the soil; a gnome of disease; Treng. mischievous, as an animal or child, 'regular imp'.

jembel [KS], Ind. *orang* ~, the poorest classes, the depressed classes.

jemerang [KK], Kel. = *menyeberang*; see **seberang**.

jempana [KN], Hind. a state litter.

jempu [KS], Jav. rotten, friable; *men~kan*, to dishearten.

jempul [KN], Ind. 1. thumb; *isapan* ~, a sucking of the thumb, (fig.) sheer nonsense. 2. first class, A1; big, lusty; so, *~an*, champion.

jemput [KK], 1. gripping between forefinger and thumb; *se~--~*, a pinch; *men~*, to invite (to a a feast, etc.); to greet (a visitor); to invite in; *~lah* ..., please ... (from host to guest, inviting to eat, etc.). 2. *~--~*, a cake of fried bananas with egg and sugar.

jemu [KS], sated; weary of; ~ *jelak*, sated, wearied, 'fed up to the teeth'; *dengan tidak mengenal ~--~*, insatiably, unweariedly; ~ *daripada hidup*, sick of life; *men~kan*, to bore, to tire, to be distasteful to.

jemuas [KS], besmeared; dirty.

jemuju [KN], caraway-seed.

jemur [KK], drying by exposure to the sun's rays; *men~*, to put a thing out to dry; *ter~*, put to dry; *ber~*, sun oneself; *~an*,

Kel. a sort of veranda or landing in the front part of peasants' houses.

jenak [KN], a short space of time; a pause.

jenaka [KS], Hind. a farce, practical joke; farcical; wily; *bergurau ber~*, with quips and jokes; *buat* ~, to play jokes, esp. practical jokes; *pelanduk* ~, the jesting mousedeer of folklore, always playing tricks on other animals.

jenakarama [KN], a stage comedy.

jenalik [KN], a favourite resort (e.g. a hot spring) of wild animals — cf. **sira** and **jenut**.

jenang [KN], prop, support, aid; coadjutor; the chief assistant to a *Batin* or headman of *Jakun* tribes; ~ *pintu*, the uprights of a door.

jenawi [KN], *pedang* ~, a long rapier.

jenayah [KN], criminal (matter); *kesalahan* ~, criminal offence; *perbuatan* ~, crime.

jenazah [KN], Ar. a royal hearse (by metaphor); the body of a deceased prince or other great person; also the coffin containing the body.

jendala [KS], Skr. scoundrelly, low, mean.

jendela [KN], Port. a window, esp. a French window.

jendera [KS], Kel. fast asleep.

jendul [KS], prominent, protruding; *muka yang panjang dengan tulang yang men~*, a long bony face; *perut men~*, protruding belly.

jengah [KK], to have a quick look at, glance at; *men~kan kepala*, to poke the head out.

jenggala [KN], Skr. wild, untamed; appertaining to the forest.

jenggi [KK], *ber~*, N.S. to expose oneself to the elements.

jenggir [KN], Jav. the comb of a cock.

jenggul [KS], *jenggal-~*, covered with notches; gnarled.

jengkal [KN], a span (between thumb and finger); ~ *telunjuk*, the span between the thumb and index-finger; ~ *kelengkeng*, the span between the thumb and little finger; *se~* is used fig. for a very small space or distance; *men~ muka*, humiliate, degrade somebody.

jengkang [KK], drawing out a leg; extending a leg — cf. **kengkang.**

jengkang [KK], on its back with legs in the air (of a carcass or of a dead insect).

jengkau [KK], stretch to pluck or grasp an object above one; to erect its head (of a leech); *tinggi se~*, as high as a man can reach; *~ ulat*, fingers which arch backwards; cf. **jangkau.**

jengkel [KS], Ind. cross, irritated, annoyed.

jengkeng [KK], moving about on tiptoe — cf. **jengket.**

jengkerik [KN], = **cengkerik.**

jengket [KK], walking on tiptoe — cf. **jengkeng.**

jengking [KN], raising the tail aloft; *kala ~*, the common house-scorpion.

jengkolit [KK], tilted to one side (as a man's head when he goes to sleep on a chair, as a boat in a storm).

jengkul [KN], the span between the thumb and the joint of the bent index-finger.

jenguk [KK], *men~*, to peer, to peep; *ter~*, peeping out, protruding; *men~kan kepala*, to poke one's head out (or in).

jengul [KK], *men~*, to emerge above the surface (as the snout of a crocodile); to poke out.

jenis [KN], Ar. kind, species; *ber~~*, of all kinds, various; *men~kan*, to classify; *pen~an*, classification; *se~*, of the same kind, esp. of the same sex; *berahi ke~an*, sexual desire; *~ lawan (nya)*, the opposite sex.

jenojenah [KN], tittle-tattle; malicious gossip.

jentaka [KS], Skr. ill-luck.

jentat [KK], *men~*, to leap (of a flea, or of any other creature with great jumping powers).

jentera [KN], Skr. a wheel, spinning-wheel; machine; the comb of a loom; *ber~*, to rotate; to move in waves (of light); to be on wheels; *pesawat ber~*, machinery; a clockwork appliance; *tanglung ber~*, a rotating Chinese lantern.

jentik [KN], jerking so as to propel (as a marble); jerky or wriggling motion; *~~*, mosquito-larvae, 'wrigglers'; *men~*, to

flick, fillip sharply, to nip; *men~kan abu rokok,* to flick away the ash of a cigarette.

jenuari [KN], Eng. a non-religious festival or celebration; *~ Raja*, Kel. the Sultan's birthday; this usage sprang up in some East Coast areas as a result of a regatta which used to be held in Singapore each January; the usage naturally tends to die out.

jenuh [KS], to the full; *makan ~*, to eat one's fill; *~ saya mencari*, I have done my best to find him; *~~*, thoroughly; *men~kan*, cause to be satisfied, satiated.

jenut [KN], Pah. salt-lick.

jepang [KN], a sea-weed from which jelly is made.

Jepun [KN], Japanese; *orang ~*, a Japanese; *Maharaja ~*, the Mikado.

jera [KS], taught caution; *tiada ~*, he has not yet learnt by experience.

jerabai [KS], tattered; also *jerambai.*

jerah [KS], plentiful (of a crop); numerous (of cases of illness in an epidemic).

jerahak [KS], *men~*, to neglect, abandon (a task).

jerahap [KK], falling prostrate (with limbs outstretched).

Jerai [KN], *Gunung ~*, Kedah Peak.

jerait [KK], interlinked as the links of a chain, or strands of a net or cobweb; *ber~an*, all stuck together, all linked together.

jeram [KN], 1. rapids in a stream. 2. *kakap ~*, Sel. a fishing-boat.

jeramah [KK], seize with claws and teeth (of a tiger or any similar beast); to fight (of a woman).

jerambah [KN], a platform outside a Malay house for water-jars, etc.

jerambai [KS], tattered; also *jerabai.*

jerambang [KN], St. Elmo's light; an *ignis fatuus* taken by sea-faring Malays to be an evil spirit.

jerami [KN], stubble, after-grass, straw.

jeran [KS], deterred, intimidated.

jerang [KK], warming at a fire; *~kan ke api,* put on the fire; to warm up (as food gone cold).

jerangau [KN], a medicinal plant (*Acorus calamus*).

jerangkah [KK], = **ceranggah**.

jerangkang [KS], spiky, sticking out; *ter~ kaki empat,* falling on back with legs in the air (of an animal); *ter~,* thin with protruding bones; *tulangnya ber~,* his bones are sticking out, he is a 'bag of bones'.

jerangkung [KN], bony framework of the body of a human being.

jerap [KK], saturated (till drops begin to fall); thorough steeping (as a wick is steeped in oil); *men~,* absorb.

jerat [KN], a running noose, a lasso, a noosetrap; *mata ~,* the loop of a noose; *menahan ~ di pergentingan* (or *di tempat genting*), to set a noose at a narrow place; used met. of seizing an opportunity to work a squeeze, e.g., by getting a 'corner' and putting up prices; *men~ leher sendiri,* to put a rope round one's own neck (by rash action); *~ semata bunda kandung,* the apple of one's eye; *~ semata,* a certain covert; a 'deadsnip' (of a place to find game).

jerau [KS], deep red.

jeraus [KS], agile, sprightly.

jerawat [KN], pimples on the face.

jerbak [KK], *men~,* to pervade; = *menyerbak.*

jerbu [KN], *laut ~,* the sea out of sight of land or when the land is only a dim haze on the horizon.

jerejik [KN], *burung ~,* Kel. the sun-bird, or spider-hunter.

jereket [KS], adhering, e.g., of eyelids.

jereluk [KN], *mangkuk ~,* a deep bowl or cup — cf. **juluk.**

jeremang [KN], short props or buttresses, esp. for boats on the beach; *men~,* so to prop.

jeremba [KK], meeting suddenly and unexpectedly, bumping up against; also *jerempak.*

jerembap [KK], *men~,* to fall to earth in a prone posture.

jerembit [KS], interlinked, intertwined; = *jerait.*

jerembun [KS], heaped up all together.

jerengkah [KS], swollen with milk (of the udders).

jerengkik [KS], very thin, emaciated.

jerepet [KS], interlinked but capable of independent movement (as two links in a chain), drooping (of eyelids) — cf. **sepet.**

jeriat, = **seriat.**

jeriau [KN], small joists.

jerih [KS], exhausted; done up; *~-payah,* hard work, great efforts; *~-pereh,* id.; *~ titik peluh,* all one's efforts, all one has worked for; *ber~-~,* completely exhausted.

jerimpit [KK], *ber~,* to huddle together.

jering [KN], a tree with evil-smelling pods (*Pithecolobium lobatum*).

jeringai [KK], *men~,* to grin; also *jeringing.*

jeringing [KK], *men~,* to grin; also *jeringai.*

jerit [KK], *men~,* to shriek; *ber~an,* with shrieks; shrieking.

jerjak [KN], small, vertical timber strips, set parallel and close to one another in basket-work, thatch, carpentry, etc.; *~ tingkap,* bars of a window.

jerkah [KN], menacing gesture, to menace; *men~,* to heckle, address roughly, threateningly.

jermal [KN], a marine fish-trap (in which fish are herded by means of converging rows of stakes over a submerged screen; there they are caught by the borders of the screen being raised).

Jerman [KN], German; *negeri ~,* Germany.

jernang [KN], the vegetable products known as 'dragon's blood', a red resin used in making dye.

jernih [KS], clear, limpid, transparent; *hati yang ~,* heart free from guile; *men~kan suasana,* clear the air; *kenyataan ini bertujuan men~kan suasana,* this statement is intended to clear the air.

jerobong [KN], an awning for deck-cargo.

jerohok [KK], stumbling into a hole concealed by long grass.

jerojol [KK], = **rojol**.

jeronging [KS], grinning broadly.

jerongkah [KS], uneven, jagged (of teeth).

jerongkis [KS], aslant, as a post in a rapid.

jerongkok [KS], *duduk ter~*, to sit huddled up.

jerongkong [KK], knocked on one's back.

jerpak [KK], *men~*, to fall over.

jeruh [KS], very steep and sloping (of a declivity — esp. of a roof).

jeruju [KN], a flowering shrub with holly-like leaves *(Acanthus ebracteatus)*.

jeruk [KN], a generic name for fruits of the citron class and for acid pickles preserved in salt; *men~*, to pickle, preserve; (sl.) to take a snack; *daging ~*, preserved meat; *ber~*, Kel. wet through; also cleaned out, ruined.

jerukup [KK], joining, of boughs overhead; over-arching; *men~*, to over-arch, as trees covering the passage underneath — cf. **rungkup**.

jerumat [KK], darning.

jerumbai [KN], dangling (of a tassel-fringe).

jerumbung [KN], a permanent awning in a Malay boat — cf. **jerobong**.

jerumbun [KN], the lair of a wild boar; the hut of a fowler.

jerumun, Ked. = **jerumbun**.

jerumus [KK], *ter~*, sprawling; *men~kan*, to send sprawling, cast headlong; (fig.) to ruin; *dia men~kan saya ke dalam sengketa itu*, he got me into big trouble.

jerung [KN], a man-eating shark (esp. the ground shark).

jerungkau, = **rungkau**.

jerunyas [KS], rough-surfaced.

jerupih [KN], *men~*, to add a and or layer to the top of anything so as to increase its height.

jerut [KK], to draw a slip-knot or noose; to pull tight; tight-fitting, as jeans.

Jibrail [KN], Ar. the Archangel Gabriel.

jidar [KN], Ar. the 'walls' within which type is confined on some printed pages.

jihad [KN], Ar. Holy War to protect Islam; *ber~* is now sometimes used of 'striving for the Faith' (peacefully).

jijak [KN], step., tread; bearing; *ber~*, to step on, to touch (with the lower extremities); also *jejak*.

jijik [KS], shame, disgust; *ter~*, put to shame; *memandang ~*, to scorn; *~!*, nasty!, disgusting!, exclamation, esp. as a warning to children; a variant of *cicik*.

jika [Kphbg], if; supposing that; = *jikalau*.

jikalau [Kphbg], if; supposing that; = *kalau* (*lau* being an Arabic equivalent of *jika*).

jilak [KK], a ship's lockers.

jilat [KK], *men~*, to lick, to lap up.

jilid [KN], Ar. a volume; binding; *men~*, to bind; *tukang ~*, a book-binder.

jilit, = *jilid*.

jimak [KK], Ar. sexual intercourse; berjimak dengan, to have sexual relations with.

jimat [KS], 1. Ar. a talisman; = *azimat*. 2. Ar. careful, economical; economy; *ber~*, thrifty; *men~kan perbelangaan*, to cut down expenditure, to economise; *~-cermat*, economical saving.

Jimbam [KN], N.S. *si-~*, nickname given to a lazy man, Lob-lie-abed.

jimbit [KK], to lift an object with the fingers.

jin [KN], 1. Ar. wonder-working spirit; *~ Islam*, a good *jin*; *~ kafir*, an evil *jin*. 2. Hind. a saddle.

jinak [KS], tame, docile, familiar; *~ hati*, familiarised; *~kan*, to tame; *per~kan*, to tame, to break in; *~ merpati*, tame as a pigeon is tame, met. for a simple-seeming person, who neverless 'knows his way about'; *ber~-~ dengan*, to associate intimately with, be on familiar terms with.

jingga [KS], dark yellow; yellow mixed with red, orange; *~ muda*, pale yellow.

jinggang [KS], slender; thin.

jinggi [KN], tutelary spirit (as of a cave).

jingkit [KK], tilting; *~kan kaki*, tilting the feet (with heel up), so as to walk on tiptoe; *~kan telinga*, to prick up the ears, as a dog; *kakinya ter~-~*, tip-toeing painfully or walking on the heel (the foot being tilted in either case).

jingkir [KN], a platform on which a newly-confined woman is laid so that she may be warmed.

jinjal [KN], hardship, trouble.

jinjang [KS], 1. narrow and tapering, but not too long (of the neck). 2. attachment; continuity; attachment for duties, role, mission, position, assignment, task; *~an,* person attached for duties, person with a mission; an attache; *hantu tak ber~,* homeless spirit; *se~ sawah,* N.S. a stretch of rice-fields; *ber~,* continuous, of rice-fields; *~ pelamin,* the bridal couch.

jinjing [KK], carrying a light burden, using the fingers only; so the children's song beginning, *~-~ tikus, sana genting, sana putus,* carry, carry the rat (by the tail in the tips of the fingers), it has got thin there and broken.

jinjit [KK], picking out, pinching out, pulling out (a loose body), carrying by fingers; *ter~-~,* walking on tiptoe; *orang tua saya sudah tidur, saya harus ber~ masuk ke bilik tidur,* my parents were asleep, I had to tiptoe into the room.

jintan [KN], caraway-seed *(Carum carui); ~ hitam,* the seeds of *Nigella sativa,* fennel; *~ manis,* anise seed *(Pimpinella anisum); ~ putih,* cumin seed, dill *(Cuminum cyminum).*

jintang [KN], a disease causing splitting in feet.

jintih [KN], a generic name for several trees; *~ merah, (Baccaurea Wallichii* and *Baccaurea Griffithii), ~ putih, (Urophyllum sp.).*

jir [KN], target; the point aimed at in a game.

jirai [KN], *se~,* a strip, a small quantity.

jirak [KN], a tree *(Eurya acuminata).*

jiran [KN], Ar. relatives; one's family; also neighbours; *negeri-negeri yang ber~,* neighbouring countries.

jirat [KN], Ar. a non-Muslim cemetery.

jirim [KN], Ar. matter; that which occupies space.

jirus [KK], sprinkle with water — cf. **dirus**.

jismani [KN], Ar. bodily (as against spiritual); also *jasmani.*

jitu [KS], Ind. precise, exact; clear.

jiwa [KN], Skr. life; the spirit of life; soul; *bahasa ~ bangsa,* language is the soul of a people; *ke~an,* spiritual; *~* is also used for souls in the sense of units of the population; *~ raga,* body and soul; *berhutang ~,* incur blood-guilt; *sakit gangguan ~,* mental trouble, nervous breakdown; *doktor ~,* psychiatrist; *serahkan ~,* to give up one's life; *utama ~,* the breath of life; *air utama ~,* the water of life; *air merta ~,* id.

jodoh [KN], Tam. match; a pair; *~an,* counterpart; twin-soul; *ber~,* to take as one's mate; well-matched; *~ pertemuan,* fitting mate; *~kan,* to match; also *kodo.*

jogan [KN], Pers. a standard with metallic emblems like the Roman signum; also *cogan.*

joget [KN], a dancing-girl.

jogi [KN], Skr. a religious ascetic; *mengamalkan ilmu ~,* to practise yoga.

johan [KN], Pers. a champion; *~ pahlawan,* a warrior champion; *~ arifin,* a champion of learning; used for, e.g., boxing champion; *naib ~,* runner-up; *~ tinju dunia,* world boxing champion; *peraduan sukan ke~an,* sports championship meeting.

johong [KN], a charm to counteract the machinations of others; *men~,* to baffle with such a charm.

jojol [KK], 1. sticking out prominently, protruding, as teeth or eyes; so, a bundle of cross-pointed sticks used in making barriers or chevaux-defrise across a river. 2. caption, title, heading; *~an,* id.; a variant of *judol.*

jokir [KN], Kel. a corner.

jokoh [KN], coin used by unofficial (e.g., gambling farmer) as a token in former days.

jokong [KN], a variant of *jongkong.*

joli [KK], Eng. 1. *buat ~,* to have a good time, enjoy oneself; *kaki ~,* a playboy; *~kan wang,* to fritter away money on amusements, etc. 2. *se~,* a pair.

jolok [KK], *men~,* poking with a stick at an

object above one; to project upwards, as crag; *rumput ~-~,* a coarse thrust-grass; *men~-~,* to 'nose round', make inquiries; *menyolok (men~) mata,* to strike the eye, leap to the eye; hurt one's feelings; *~an,* nick-name, title; *sarang tebuan jangan di~,* don't poke a hornets' nest, i.e. let sleeping dogs lie.

jolong [KN], 1. tip, point, a projecting prow, nose or snout; *buaya ~-~,* the gavial *(Tomistoma schlegi); ikan ~-~,* a sword-fish; a gar-fish. 2. = *julung.*

jong [KN], a junk.

jongang [KS], projecting, prominent (as the teeth).

jongit [KS], curving up (of the upper lip).

jongkah [KS], lagged and projecting (of a tooth).

jongkang [KS], *~-jangking,* rising and falling irregularly (as the points of the picks of a party of workers).

jongkar [KS], sticking out, as a long object amid short objects; *~-jongkir,* bristling with projecting points.

jongkat [KK], *~-jongkit,* see-sawing, unsteady.

jongkir [KN], edge, rim.

jongkit [KK], to tip up; *jongkat-~,* see-sawing, unsteady; *ter~-~,* jerking up and down, as a loose plank when trodden on; *~-~an,* id.; *bermisai tebal men~ ke atas,* having a thick moustache twisted upwards.

jongkok [KK], to squat; to stoop down to pick up something.

jongkol [KN], a tin Trengganu coin.

jongkong [KN], 1. a dinghy; a short beamy boat; *sampan ~,* id.; *tampang ~,* a tin slab, cast roughly in the shape of a boat and formerly used as currency; *timah ~,* block tin. 2. a type of cake made from flour and eaten with sugar.

jongol [KS], *ter~,* sticking out, protruding; *~kan kepala,* to poke the head out; (fig.) cropping up, as a subject for talk, coming to mind.

jongor [KN], snout, nose; projection (such as the bowsprit of a ship or the sword of a sword-fish).

jonjot [KK], picking out (as a man picks hemp or oakum).

joran [KN], a fishing-rod.

jorang [KN], a narrow channel, a water-course, a gully, a ravine; (fig.) a dividing gulf.

joreng [KN], 1. a shred; *tanah se~,* a small patch of land. 2. sharp-nosed.

jori [KN], Hind. a pair of horses; *kuda ~,* id.; *kereta ~,* a carriage and pair.

jorong [KN], 1. a metal vase for *sirih* leaf. 2. a section, a division, a corner, 3. a conical funnel or tube.

jose [KN], Ch. silk crepe.

jua = **juga**.

juadah [KN], Pers. cakes, provisions.

juah [ ], curling of the lower lip; *mulut yang ~,* coarse-mouthed; *~-juih,* sulky-looking.

juak [KN], 1. a raja's retainer; an attendant generally; so, a spoilt darling, minion. 2. to thrust outwards; to boom out a sail.

jual [KK], selling; *~-janji,* a conditional sale; *ber~-beli,* trading; *~an,* a thing for sale; *men~,* to sell; (fig.) to betray; *~ nama orang,* to talk scandal; *~(an) murah,* a cheap sale; *~an sapu,* a clearance sale; *ter~,* sold; (fig.) beguiled, 'sold'; *ter~ dek janji-janji,* beguiled by promises; *~ muka,* (sl.) to get oneself stared at, become a public show; *men~ bangsa,* traitor; *khusus men~,* to specialize in; *kedai ini khusus men~ barang-barang pakaian wanita,* this store specializes in women's accessories.

juang [KK], *ber~,* to fight — of large animals (esp. elephants); *biram ber~,* fighting elephant; *per~an,* battle, heavy fighting; (fig.) struggle; *teman seper~an,* comrade in arms; *pe~,* warrior, fighter, champion; *per~an hidup mati,* life and death struggle.

juar [KN], *pokok ~,* a shade tree *(Cassia siamea); kayu ~,* a black ebony-like wood used for making plain furniture, but not suitable for carving.

juara [KN], 1. a trainer of fighting animals; *bujang ~,* id., *ikan ~,* a river cat-fish. 2.

Ind. an arbiter, an umpire; an entrant; a champion; ~ dunia, world champion; ke~n terbuka, open championship.

jubah [KN], Ar. a long robe worn by hajis; a cassock; a long gown, such as a surgeon's.

jubin [KN], batu ~, floor-tiles.

jubung = jerobong.

jubur [KN], Ar. the anus; also dubur.

judi [KN], 1. gambling; main ~ or ber~, to gamble; ~ bola golek, roulette; pen~, gambler; tahi ~, habitual gambler; kaki ~, id. 2. Bukit Judi, the hill in Arabia believed to be Mount Ararat.

judul [KN], title, name of literary work.

juga [KKtr], and yet; all the same; still; to some extent; mahu tak mahu naik ~, willing or not, up they went all the same; intan itu batu ~ adanya, a diamond is a stone for all that; tuan ada baik? — baik ~, are you well? — yes, fairly well; kau tidak senang terhadapnya? aku ~, you dislike him, same here.

jugak = juga.

juita [KN], Skr. and Kawi, a term of endearment; precious, of great price, rare; ratna ~, pearl of price; mas ~, gold of fineness; tali ~, an ornamental girdle.

jujat [KN], Ar. mulut ~, a slanderer.

jujuh [KS], ber~, continuous (of water, rain from eaves) or in unbroken line, e.g., of marching ants, crowds, logs in river; in abundant supply, as fruit.

jujur [KN], 1. marriage by purchase (one of the three Sumatran forms of marriage). 2. ber~an, sticking out, projecting. 3. [KS], Ind. honest, sincere; secara tidak ~, dishonestly; ~ is often used as the opposite of curang; ~ adalah sikap terbaik, honesty is the best policy.

jujut [KK], = jonjot.

juku-juku [KN], a hard-shelled water-tortoise.

julai [KN], 1. projecting, overhanging (as branches); men~, to project, esp. as branches projecting over a boundary. 2. ~ julita, neat, pretty, graceful.

julang [KK], lifting up aloft; carry on the shoulders; 'chair', carry in triumph; ~an,

a seat on the shoulders; pen~, a nurse; menulang is also used to mean, rise high, as flames or as tall grass; men~-~, to extol, hero-worship.

julap [KN], Ar. aperient.

julat [KN], range, reach; sepen~ peluru meriam, the distance a cannon can carry; tikam men~, stabbing as far as one can reach.

juli [KN], Hind. a dhooly or litter.

julik [KK], wrapped in a single petal (as a very young bud seems to be).

juling [KS], a cast in the eye; squinting; mata ~, cross-eyed; ~ bertangkap, cross-eyed; ~ bahasa, having a slight cast in the eye; ~ air, id.

julir [KN], a fish-spear or harpoon with a detachable barbed head to which a long rope is attached.

julita [KN], jelita, pretty, graceful, dainty.

julung [KN], Ind. the first; ~ kali, the first time.

julur [KK], men~, emerge (of a long body); dart out (or a snake's tongue); ter~, hanging out (as the tongue of a corpse), or hanging down, as hair; men~ is also used to mean to crawl along slowly, to slide along on stomach.

Jumaat [KN], Ar. hari ~, Friday; se~, a week.

jumbai [KN], pendent, dangling — cf. jerumbai.

jumhur [KN], Ar. the righteous, the learned in God's way.

jumlah [KN], Ar. sum total; se~ wang, a sum of money; ~kan, to add up; to amount to; hutangnya ber~ beribu-ribu dolar, the debts amount to thousands of dollars.

jumpa [KK], encountering, coming across; ber~, to meet; per~an, a meeting; an interview.

jumpul [KN], ikan ~, a grey mullet.

jumpung [KN], ikan ~, a parrot-fish (Cheilissus chlorurus).

junam [KK], downward motion; diving head foremost, swooping; used of planes 'diving'; men~kan bendera, to dip a flag in salute.

junjung [KK], *men~,* carrying on the head; (fig.) obeying a raja's order; ~ *sirih,* the post on which the *sirih* vine is trailed; *Junjungan,* He Who must be obeyed, i.e. the Prophet; *men~,* heaped (of a brimming measure); *men~ duli,* to perform a homage ceremony (before a Ruler); *men~ tinggi,* to exalt; to deem of great importance; *men~ tinggi hak asasi manusia,* to uphold human rights.

juntai [KK], ber~, to dangle; *duduk ber~,* to sit with the feet dangling in the air; *ber~* also means to hang down, as hair, as dead fronds.

junub [KS], Ar. *mandi ~, mandi ~ janabat,* ablution after coition; *ber~,* in a state of major ritual impurity, esp. after coition.

juragan [KN], the master of a fishing boat or *perahu.*

jurai [KN], *ber~,* hanging down loosely in tatters or a fringe; *se~,* a strip (of ricestalks); also, a slice.

juring [KN], a segment of a fruit or gourd.

jurit [KN], Jav. *pen~, para~* or *pera~,* a warrior; a roving plunderer; now used generally for, a soldier, esp. a private.

juru [KN], 1. a skilled workman other than a handicraftsman; ~ *bahasa,* an interpreter; ~ *batu* and ~ *tinggi,* petty officers on a ship; ~ *masak,* a cook; ~ *tulis,* writer, a clerk; ~ *cakap,* spokesman; ~ *bicara,* id.; ~ *hebah,* radio-announcer; ~*tera,* engineer; ~*tera perlombongan,* mining engineer; ~ *rawat,* nurse (in hospital); ~ *terengkas,* stenographer; ~ *latih,* trainer; ~ *kira-kira,* accountant; ~ *ubat,* dispenser; ~

ulas, commentator; ~ *iring,* aide-decamp; ~ *wata,* male nurse, ~ *wati,* female nurse; ~ *urut,* masseur; ~ *lukis,* artist, painter; ~ *lukis bangunan,* architect; ~*acara,* compere; ~ *terbang,* airman, pilot; ~ *kerah = jekera,* q.v.; ~ *selam,* diver; ~ *gendang,* drummer; ~ *letrik,* electrician; ~ *lampu,* man in charge of lighting. 2. *pen~,* a corner, an angle; *institut ke~an,* vocational institute.

jurus [KN], 1. a pause; a very brief interval of time; *se~ lamanya,* for a second or two. 2. dragging, pulling, hustling. 3. = *dirus.* 4. Kel., Treng. *ber~,* good, successful; striving hard, doing one's best; 5. Ind. *men~kan,* to direct, aim; ~*an,* angle of vision, side from which one gets the best view; field, sphere; *usaha ini men~ ke arah penghuraian masalah secara damai,* these efforts are geared toward a peaceful solution; lines (as of education); branch of education; *sekolah aneka ~an,* comprehensive school. 6. = *jirus.*

justru [KN], Ind. verily, actually; in fact.

jut [KN], 1. *tali ~,* a trace in harness. 2. a riverine fish-trap. 3. a fish-basket.

juta [KN], Skr. a million; ~*wan,* millionaire.

juz [KN], Ar. a section of the Koran (which is divided into thirty such); *ber~~,* interminable, of a writing; *demi Allah dan Rasulnya dan Kuran tigapuluh ~,* by God and His Apostle and the thirty chapters of the Koran, an exclamation emphasising a statement.

K

ka [KN], Kel. *tanah* ~, land broken up by the plough, a ploughed land.

Kaabah [KN], Ar. the *Caaba* or cube-shaped stone building found in the great mosque at Mecca.

kabam [KN], a basket fish-trap used in streams; also *kebam*.

kabar [KN], = *khabar*.

Kabil [KN], the Biblical Cain.

kabin [KN], Eng. a cabin.

kabir [KS], 1. Ar. great, mighty. 2. [KK], to back water; backing with a single paddle so as to bring a boat round.

kabisat [KN], Ar. leap-year; *tahun* ~, id.

kabu [KN], ~-~, a coarse tree-cotton; *pokok* ~-~, the tree (*Trevesia sondaica*) from which this cotton is obtained; also *kapuk*.

kabul [KN], Ar. approval, confirmation; ~*kan*, to confirm; *jika segala permintaannya tidak ter~, dia marah,* if things don't go his way, he gets furious.

kabung [KN], 1. the sugar-palm (*Arenga sacharifera*); also *nau* and *enau*. 2. a white band worn as a symbol of mourning; *per~an*, mourning; *ber~*, to wear mourning; *hari ber~ ditetapkan selama tiga hari,* they observed a three-day period of mourning; *tertawa dalam per~an,* to laugh amidst one's mourning, jibe at the heir of a rich man.

kabur [KS], 1. dim-sighted from age or infirmity; obscure to the eye or the understanding; fogged, of a film; *mengabur,* to become misty; (fig.) to be bewildered; *banyak hal mengaburi kehidupannya pada masa lampau,* a lot of things obscure his past life. 2. a beetle, esp. the coconut-beetle; also *ke~*. 3. Kel. colour of cattle, grey generally with brownish shoulders.

kabus [KN], dimly visible, as objects in smoke, haze or twilight; mist, haze.

kabut [KN], cloudy, misty, indistinct; mist; *hilang* ~, clear away, of mist; *kelam* ~, confused, chaotic; *mata* ~, dim-sighted, unable to see distant objects.

kaca [KN], Skr. glass (the material); *roda* ~, a glass-wheel; ~ *pembesar,* magnifying glass; ~*mata,* spectacles; ~ *cermin, papan* ~, plate-glass; *serbuk* ~, powdered glass; *ber~-~,* glistening with tears, of eyes.

kacak [KS], 1. smart, dandified, handsome. 2. *ber~, ter~-~,* stepping gingerly along, walking quietly on tiptoe, mincing along; *mengacak,* to lift, to feel with o's hand (the weight, size of a thing); *mengacak galas,* to try one's luck in trade.

kacang [KN], a generic name for beans; ~ *bendi,* the okra or beni fruit (*Hibiscus esculentus*); ~ *buncis,* French beans; ~ *Cina,* the peanut (*Arachis hypogoea*); ~ *goreng,* id.; ~ *hijau,* the small bean which produces tauge; ~ *hantu,* corner-boy, scalywag; ~ *cindai* (*Phaseolus mungo*); ~ *Jepun,* ~ *Kedelai,* the soya bean (*Soya hispida*); ~ *kara* (*Dolichos lablab*); ~ *kayu,* the Indian dall (*Cajanus indicus*); ~ *lendir,* the common Chinese bean (*Hibiscus esculentus*), okra; ~ *putih,* peas; *ikan* ~-~, the barracuda; also *alu-alu;* ~-~, small-shot; ball-bearings; ~ is used Ind. as a derogatory epithet for locally-born persons of mixed blood; 'peanut'; ~ *melupakan kulit,* the bean forgets its pod; i.e. a man who has been successful forgets his origins and his old friends.

kacapuri [KN], the capital of a column; the heart or centre of a building; *durian* ~, a durian that has some flesh at its very centre.

kacar [KN], 1. *siput* ~, a shell (*Voluta pulchra*). 2. fussy; bustle; *ter~-~,* fussing about, bustling about.

kacau [KS], stirring; confusing, mixing up; disturbed; a mess; ~ *bilau*, extremely confused; ~ *birau*, id.; ~*kan*, to upset, to throw into disorder; to stir; *membuat ~ balau*, to turn into a complete fiasco; ~!, what a nuisance!; *pengacau*, a nuisance (person); *mengacau-ngacau*, to confuse, to muddle up; *jangan mengacau kehidupan orang lain*, don't mess around with anybody else's life.

kaci [KN], Ch. wolfram.

kacip [KN], betel-nut scissors; *mengacip*, to cut up into slices.

kacuk [KN], impure, unidiomatic (of language); mixed, esp. of breed; ~-*baka*, cross-bred; ~*an*, impure, esp. of language, mongrel, as opposed to *jati*.

kacung [KN], Jav. 'youngster'.

kada [KN], Ar. fate, destiny; God's ordinance; so, *meng~*, to fulfil, make good, an ordinance hitherto unfulfilled; e.g. *meng~ puasa*, to fast so as to make up for a fast previously not duly kept; ~ *hajat*, (sl.) to ease oneself; also *kadha* and *quadha*.

kadal [KN], Jav. the grass-lizard, = *bengkarung*.

kadam [KN], Ar. the sole of the foot; *di bawah ~*, below the sole of the (prince's) foot — the position of the subject; *ber~ kaki*, to trudge along.

kadang [Kdpn], 1. ~-~, at times; occasionally; *ter~* or *ter~-~*, id.; ~ *kala*, id. 2. ~ *kedayan*, followers or retainers of a Javanese chief; a prince's suite. 3. Treng. but.

kadar [KN], Ar. power, ability; *se~*, as far as one can; as far as one's ability goes; about, more or less; merely; *se~ dua bulan*, about two months; ~ *namanya*, in name only, nominally; *se~ nya*, in proportion to, up to the ability; *seberapa ~*, as much as one can afford; as far as one is able; *mengikut ~*, in proportion to, proportionate to; ~*kan diri*, to realise one's limitations; *se~kan*, save only, allowing for; *lailat al-~*, the Night of Power, i.e. the 26th Ramathan, when the Koran was sent to the Prophet; *kur-*

ang ~nya, his standing (prestige) has lessened.

Kadi [KN], Ar. a registrar of Muslim marriages and divorces, who has some judicial powers.

Kadiani [KN], *kaum ~*, a sect formed by Ghulam Ahmad Qadyani, claiming to be Islamic, but considered unorthodox by some; also called *Ahmadiah*.

kadim [KN], Ar. ancestry, family, descent; *se~*, of common descent; *saudara ~*, next of kin.

kadir [KN], Ind. a cadre, small body forming a nucleus of staff.

kaduk [KN], a vine, the leaves of which resemble those of the *sirih* vine; *pak-Kaduk*, unlucky Juggins or Mutt of Malay folk-tales.

kadut [KN], *kain ~*, a coarse sacking made of rami fibre.

Kadyan [KN], *orang ~*, a Borneo tribe, formerly called *orang Dusun*.

kaedah [KN], aim, object; method.

Kaf [KN], Ar. *Bukit ~*, Mount Kaf (the king of mountains according to Muslim tradition).

kafan [KN], = *kapan*.

kafarah [KN], Ar. a fine for breach of religious observance.

kafarat [KS], cursed, damned, also **keparat**.

kafilah [KN], Ar. a caravan.

kafir [KS], Ar. an unbeliever, a non-Muslim; *meng~kan*, to cause to become or to deem to be or denounce as an infidel, i.e. other than People of the Book; see *kitabi* and *ahad*.

kaget [KS], Ind. nervous, alarmed; *mengagetkan*, to frighten, to startle.

kagum [KS], Ind. amazed, astonished; *meng~kan*, to arouse admiration, *meng~i*, to admire.

kah [P], an interrogative suffix; *sungguh~?*, is it true?

kahak [KN], phlegm; *ber~*, to clear the throat.

kahat [KN], Ar. scarcity, esp. of food, famine.

kahin [KN], Ar. astrologer, mage, wizard.

Kahirah [KN], Cairo.
kahwa [KN], Ar. coffee.
kahwin [KK], = *kawin.*
kaifiat [KN], Ar. manner, way, mode.
kail [KN], line-fishing; *mata ~,* a fish-hook; *mengail,* to fish with a hook and line; *pengail,* a line-fisherman; *ter~,* (to be) hooked.
kain [KN], cloth; a sarong, a generic name for patterns of sarongs and kinds of cloth; *~ baju,* sarong and baju, clothing generally; *~ basah* or *~ basahan,* old clothes used as bathing clothes or clothes used for daily wear; *~ batik,* Javanese painted sarongs; *~ belacau,* unbleached calico; *~ cita,* flowered chintz; *~ kadut, ~ rami* or *~ rawa,* coarse sacking made of rami fibre; *~ mastuli,* a heavy silk fabric; *~ songkit,* a silk fabric heavy with gold thread; *~ telepuk,* a gilded silk; *~ lilin,* waxed cloth; *~ pelekat,* the common cotton sarong, see *pelekat; kepala ~,* a portion of the sarong differing in pattern from the rest; *~ basah kering di pinggang,* to be in dire necessity (prov.), as poor as a church mouse.
kais [KK], scratching up (as a fowl scratches up the earth); drawing anything towards one with a stick, crook, etc.; scrabbling; *seperti ayam, ~ pagi, makan pagi, ~ petang, makan petang,* like fowls, scratch in the evening and eat in the evening, i.e. living from hand to mouth; *pengais,* a sort of light rake.
kait [KK], hooking; catching (of thorns); *di~ onak,* caught by thorns; *ber~ kelengkeng,* with little fingers interlinked (as bride and groom) at the *bersanding* ceremony; *ber~ dengan,* relative to..., connected with...; involved in; *jangan ~kan hal ini dengan perkara peribadinya,* don't link this matter with his personal affairs; *ber~ rapat,* closely involved; closely connected; *mengait* is used for 'knitting'; *jarum pengait,* knitting-needle.
kajai [KN], *tali ~,* a halter for a horse.
kajang [KN], waterproof matting of *pandan* or *mengkuang,* used on boats and

carts; *ter~,* in shelter, protected from the rain; *se~ kertas,* a (complete) sheet of foolscap paper; *lipat ~,* double, folded.
kajar [KS], Ked. stinking, = *aring.*
kajau [KK], *mengajau,* Sum. to head-hunt.
kaji [KN], *mengaji,* to read the Koran; to study; *mengaji sekolah,* to attend school; *meng~,* to scrutinize, make a study of; *Badan Peng~ Getah,* Rubber Research Institute; *~an,* study, consideration; *di~,* under study; *syor-syor itu sedang di~,* the suggestion is under scrutiny; *meng~ semula,* to scrutinize afresh, review; *~ jiwa,* psychiatry; *~ balik,* to reconsider.
kak [KN], = *kakak.*
kakak [KN], 1. elder sister; *adik ~,* younger and elder brothers and sisters; near relatives; *~ kandung ibu,* half-sisters (by mother). (In some works and on East Coast ~ is used of elder brothers). 2. (onom.) *mengakak,* to quack (of ducks), to cackle (of a hen about to lay an egg); *adik-~,* brothers and sisters; *kami adik-~, satu laki-laki, satu perempuan,* there are two of us, a brother and a sister.
kakanda [KN], elder brother, or sister; a politer variant of *kakak,* often used, esp. in poetry, as a mode of address by a girl to her lover or by wife to husband; sometimes used of a close friend or, e.g., a half-brother.
kakang [KN], Jav. elder brother or sister.
kakap [KN], 1. *perahu ~,* a river boat with a lofty prow and stern but a low waist. 2. *ikan ~,* a fish (*Lates nobiles*); also *siakap.* 3. *mata ~,* a plug-hole in a boat's bottom. 4. *mengakap,* to stalk, scout, reconnoitre; *budak pengakap,* boy scouts; *pengakap wanita, (pandu puteri),* girl guide; *Perkumpulan Pengakap Sedunia,* International Scouts Association.
kakas, see *perkakas.*
kakatua [KN], the cockatoo; a nail-extractor, pincers (from resemblance to a cockatoo's beak).
kaki [KN], foot, leg, base, lower extremity,

pedestal; a foot as a measure of length; ~ *lima,* the five-foot way, side-walk; ~ *segi,* square foot; ~ *padu,* cubic foot; ~ *bukit,* the foot of a hill; ~ *dian,* a candlestick; ~ *langit,* the horizon; ~ *tembok,* the foundations of a wall; *bekas* ~, footprint; *jalan* ~, to go on foot; *mata* ~, ankles; *tapak* ~, sole of the foot; *kura-kura* ~, instep; *pe~ layar,* the boom (of a sail); *~tangan,* staff; *burung ~ dian,* the redshank; ~ is used as a numeral coefficient for things with stems, such as flowers and umbrellas; ~ is used fig. for 'addict', 'slave to'; ~ *minum,* drunkard; ~ *rokok,* cigarette-fiend; ~ *judi,* gamester; ~ *gaduh,* quarrelsome, a rowdy; ~ *bual,* chatterbox; ~ *borak,* id.; ~ *joli,* playboy; ~ *bola,* mad on football; ~ *betina,* womaniser; ~ *bawa mulut,* tale-bearer; scandalmonger; *pe~an gunung,* the foothills; ~ *buatan,* artificial leg, ~ *tiga,* tripod.

kaku [KS], hard, e.g., of corpses; stiff, tough; 'fig,' hard, awkward, of situation; lacking ease, stiff in manner, as a bad actor; *ter~,* immobile, `rivetted to the spot'; ~ *mulut,* lock-jaw.

kal [KN], a measure of capacity; half a *cupak.*

kala [KN], 1. Skr. time, epoch, period, age; *apa~,* when; *barang* ~, whenever; *dahulu* ~, past ages, the past; *purba* ~, id.; *sedia* ~, the time that has just gone by; *senja* ~, evening; *ada ~ (nya),* sometimes; *ber~,* occurring periodically; seasonal; *(penerbitan) ber~,* a periodical (publication); *angin ber~,* seasonal winds. 2. a scorpion; ~ *bangkang,* the black forest scorpion; ~ ~ and ~ *lotong,* id.; ~ *jengking,* the common house-scorpion; ~ *lipan,* the centipede — cf. *halipan;* ~ *mayar,* the luminous millipede; better *kelemayar.* 3. Skr. the Hindu divinity (*Kala*); *Betara Kala,* id.; Siva as the destroyer.

kalah [KS], 1. defeat, being worsted — cf. *alah; mengalah,* to yield (the right of way); *tak ter~kan,* unbeatable, invincible; *pertandingan secara ~mati,*

knockout competition; ~ *suara,* outvoted; ~ *undi,* id.; *tak ~ dengan,* just as good as, up to the standard of. 2. (Jalor) a bamboo gong; *menyerah ~,* surrender; ~ *membeli menang memakai,* (prov.), cheap goods are dearest in the long run.

kali [KN], 1. a venomous insect; a sort of water-hornet. 2. [KK], to clean by scraping.

kalak [KS], *songsang-~,* upside down, topsy turvy, as a child nursed anyhow.

kalakian [Kktr], moreover; further.

kalalawar = *kelawar.*

kalam [KN], 1. Ar. a pen. 2. word, saying, speech; *akhirul ~,* at last; eventually. 3. a flaw in a gem, in a metal.

kalang [KN], something lying across the way; a bar, a roller; a ship-yard, slipway; *~an,* Ked. hen-roost; *~an,* area, region, sphere, 'circles'; *~an politik,* the sphere of politics; *~an* is also used for class, of society; *~an menengah,* the middle classes; ~ *terpelajar,* in intellectual circles; *~an perniagaan,* business circles; *mati ber~ tanah,* dead and buried (i.e., with the earth mounded over him).

kalas [KN], 1. a thole strap (of rattan). 2. Ar. *habis ~,* utterly exhausted, quite finished.

kalat [KN], remnants, dregs, what is left over.

kalau [Kphbg], if; supposing that; used in speech instead of *jika* and *jikalau;* ~ *begitu,* in that case, *~~,* just in case; ~ *boleh memilih,* if given the choice.

kalbu [KN], Ar. heart; often used in literature for the heart as the seat of emotions.

kaldai [KN], Tam. donkey, ass.

kaldu [KN], Port. meat broth, esp. chicken broth.

kali [KN], 1. time, occasion, instance; *barang* ~, perhaps; on some possible occasion; *berapa ~?,* how often?; *se~,* (1) once; (2) altogether; very; *dengan se~ gus,* all at once; *baik se~,* altogether good, excellent; *se~~~,* most, exceedingly; *se~ pun,* even; *se~an,* all; *se~ se~,* now and then, very occasionally; *se~,* even though; *tak se~ se~,* sooner or later (if not at one time, then at another); *ber~-~,* frequently; *dua ~ lima se puluh juga,* twice five is ten, just the same (six of one and half a dozen of the other); *awak dua ~ lima dengan dia,* i.e. you're just as bad, etc., as he is; *se~ sekala,* from time to time. 2. Ind. ~, a river.

kalian [KN], N.S. you.

kalih [KK], shifting, to change position; *ber~ tidur,* to turn over, change position in bed; *ber~,* to shift, of the wind; = *alih.*

Kalikausar [KN], Ar. a pool in paradise.

kalimah [KN], Ar. a syllable, an expression, a short statement, a sentence; *dua ~ syahadat,* the two statements of the Creed.

Kalimantan [KN], *orang ~,* an aboriginal tribe inhabiting Western North Borneo; hence that area is often called Kalimantan.

kaling [KN], Ind. tin; tinned iron sheeting; *tukang ~,* a tinker.

kalis [KS], inadhesive; irreceptive; impermanent; weak, failing to hold, as brakes; *dendam tak ~,* love that does not pass away; *~ bagai air di daun keladi,* nonpermeating, as water on a calladium leaf (rolling off like water on a duck's back).

kalkalah [KN], Ar. inflexions, modulations, of voice.

kalpat [KK], Hind. caulking.

kalu [KK], (from Ar. owing to a misconception), dead, to die; *~ inna,* a pious ejaculation uttered on hearing of a death, meaning, in effect, 'may he rest in peace'. (*~ inna* are the first two words of the Koran which is supposed to be recited on hearing of a death; actually, they mean 'they said verily').

kaluk [KS], 1. hook-shaped; *tongkat ber~,* a stick with a crooked handle. 2. a fine sieve, or strainer, esp. for coconut milk.

kalul [KN], *ikan ~,* a kind of carp (*Osph-*

ronemus gorami).

kalung [KN], 1. a fruit-bat; = *keluang.* 2. a neck-chain, e.g. a Mayor's chain of office; *~ bunga,* a wreath, garland; *meng~kan, meng~kan bunga di leher,* to garland with flowers; *~ leher,* necklace; *asap ber~-~an,* smoke rising in rings; 3. *akar ~,* a wild pepper (*Piper caninum*). 4. Ked. *teng~, meng~,* to hurl vigorously.

kalut [KS], *ber~,* to fuss round, bustle about; *meng~kan,* to confuse, cause disorder; *~ fikirannya,* entirely confused, hopelessly lost.

Kama [KN], Skr. *Betara ~ Jaya,* the victorious god of love.

kaman [KS], 1. Eng. common; N.S. lines, barracks. 2. common, second-rate (of goods).

kamar [KN], 1. Hind. room; a cabin in a ship. 2. Ar. the moon.

kamat [KN], Ar. the final words of the call to prayer, by which the faithful are called upon to 'stand up and pray'.

kambau [KN], the large leathery turtle (*Dermochelys coriacea*).

kambeli [KN], rough blanket cloth; a woollen blanket or rug.

kambi [KN], a thin light planking; a sort of dado; *pintu ~,* a light door made of a wooden framework covered with cloth.

kambing [KN], a sheep; a goat; *~ biri-biri,* a sheep; *~ jati,* a goat; *~ Benggala,* a large imported goat; *~ gerun, ~ hutan, ~ bukit, ~ gua, ~ burun* or *~ gunung,* the Malayan serow (*Nemorhoedus swettenhami*); *~ perahan,* a milchgoat; *~ randuk,* a rank of old he-goat; *kuku ~,* (1) the trotters of a sheep; (2) the feet of a salver; (3) a peculiar forked instrument for planting padishoots taken from the nursery; *~ hitam,* scapegoat (fig.).

kambu [KN], the block at the end of a pistonrod; *kayu tiga se~,* a sort of crude 'three-card-trick' based on guessing which of three sticks is the shortest.

kambus [KK], chocked up, e.g., of a drain; to fill up (as a hole); *ter~,* buried, as by falling earth; a local variant of timbus.

kambut [KN], a large padi-basket.

kamera = *kamar* 1.

kami [Kgn], 1. we — the speaker's party and not including the person addressed; nous autres. 2. the royal or editorial 'we'. 3. *Kami,* the Indonesian Students' Action Society (*Kesatuan aksi maha-siswa Indonesia*); ~ *setuju untuk ber-beza pendapat,* we agreed to disagree.

kamil [KS], Ar. perfect; fulfilled; used esp. in the expression *Orang Kamil,* the Per-fected One, an appellation of the Prophet; sometimes used as a Malay proper name.

kamir [KN], Ar. leaven fermentation.

kampil [KN], 1. a heavy, pointed sword used by the Lanun pirates in old days; also ~*an.* 2. = *kampit.*

kampit [KN], a plaited *mengkuang* sack for flour, rice, clothes; also a small bag or pouch.

kampuh [KN], a thin strip of something serving as binding; *ber~,* bound or sewn together, as two strips of cloth (side by side); a numeral coefficient for pieces of *terubuk* roe, the Malay caviare.

kampung [KN], assembling, grouping, a cluster of houses, a hamlet; the build-ings (with out-houses, etc.) making up a dwelling; used adjectively for domes-tic, of animals or birds commonly kept or found near houses; *tanah per~an,* residential land; ~ *halaman,* one's home; *rumah* ~, homestead; ~*kan,* to collect (people) together; *ber~,* to come together (of people); *semangat per~an,* group loyalty, cliquism; *pulang ke* ~, to go back to one's home, town.

kamu [Kgn], you; ~ *sekelian,* you all.

kamus [KN], Ar. a dictionary, an encyclo-paedia.

kan [abbrv], 1. = *akan.* 2. a causal suffix to verbs.

kana [KN], 1. Jav. *gelang* ~, large hollow armlets. 2. Ch. an olive.

kanaah [KS], Ar. contentment with one's lot; *perasaan* ~, id.

kanak [KN], 1. ~*~,* a child, a very young boy or girl. 2. *Orang Kanak,* a small

tribe of aborigines in Johore; *bahasa* ~-~, child's language; *keanak-anakan,* childish, infantile.

kanan [KN], the right-hand side; *tangan* ~, the right hand; *sebelah* ~, on the right; ~ is used for 'senior' in rank; *langkah* ~, to be lucky.

kancah [KN], a large cooking-pot, cauldron.

kancang [KS], Ind. smooth, full, of cheeks.

kancap [KS], flush with, on an exact level; full to exactness.

kancil [KN], a name given to the small chevrotin (*Tragulus pygmoeus*) on account of its size — cf. *kecil* and *pelan-duk.*

kancing [KN], a bolt; a rivet; a buckle; a stud; links; ~*kan* or *mengancingkan,* to bolt (a door); to buckle up; *ter~,* secure, fastened up; ~ *tarik,* a zip-fastener; ~ *mulut,* lock-jaw.

kancung [KN], Pk. a section of a large bamboo used as a water-vessel.

kancut [KN], Ked. a loin-cloth. 2. foiled, unsuccessful (of work).

kanda [KN], an abbreviation of *kakanda,* used specifically of a child chosen to act as an elder brother or sister to a newly born prince.

kandang [KN], an enclosure; a sty; ~ *kuda,* a stall for a horse; ~ *babi,* a sty; ~ *ker-bau,* a pen for buffaloes; ~ *gajah,* an elephant corral or pen; ~ *saksi,* wit-ness-box; *ter~,* penned.

kandar [KK], carrying on a pole (a burden being hung at each end); *kayu* ~, such a pole.

kandas [KK], running aground; *ter~,* stranded.

kandi [KN], a purse or small satchel; ~-~, id.

kandis [KN], 1. a tree with an edible fruit (*Garcinia nigrolineata*). 2. Jav. sweets; a type of sweetness.

kandul [KN], folding up in a cloth, curtain or net; the bunt of a net.

kandung [KN], carrying in a sack or enclo-sure; carrying in the womb; *mengan-dung,* to be pregnant; containing (a clause, section, meaning; of clouds holding rain); *mengandungi,* to contain; *buah ini banyak mengandungi vitamin C,* this fruit is rich in vitamin C; *~an,* contents, esp. of book; that which is in the womb, i.e. the unborn child; the womb itself; *mati dalam ~an,* still-born; *abang (adik) ~,* brother of the same mother, generally meaning full brother, i.e., *abang (adik) seemak sebapa; anak ~,* own child (not adopted).

kandut [KK], *~i,* to stow away in the lap; to take on the lap; *seluar ~,* drawers.

kang [KN], 1. a bit; *~ kuda,* id.; *tali ~,* reins; *mengulum ~,* to champ the bit. 2. *Kang Senohong,* a Javanese title of the highest rank used in addressing royalty or divinity.

kangcu [KN], Ch. the owner of a *kangka,* q.v.

kangka [KN], Ch. an old form of land concession in Johore, being the area between the water-sheds of two rivers.

kangkang [KK], wide apart (of the legs); *celah ~,* the perineum; *mengangkang,* to step out; *ter~,* extended (of the legs), open (of a door); *tanah selebar se~ kera,* land as broad as a monkey's straddle, i.e. a tiny piece; *mengangkangi,* to bestraddle.

kangkung [KN], a white or pink flowered convoluvulu—commonly used as spinach (*Ipomea aquatica*).

kangsa [KN], 1. = *angsa.* 2. = *gangsa.*

kanguk [KN], a brown eagle.

kanjal [KK], worsted unexpectedly, as a clever person by a fool; *~kan,* to fool, deceive.

kanjang [KS], persevering, persistent.

kanjar [KN], 1. Pers. a broad dagger. 2. [KK] tearing at anything; tugging and running.

kanji [KN], 1. Hind. rice-gruel; 'congee'. 2. Tam. starch; *~kan,* to starch; *patah ~,* baggy, of clothes; *tak patah ~,* uncrumpled; *huruf ~,* Chinese characters.

kanjiprak [KN], a singlet.

kanjus [KN], Hind. (congee-house), the lockup at a police-station, gaol.

kanta [KN], lens, piece of glass with one or both sides curved for use in eye glasses, cameras, telescopes etc.

kantan [KN], a large wild ginger (*Nicolaia imperialis*).

kantang [KN], a mud-bank at a river mouth.

kantuk = *antuk* 1.

Kantung [KN], 1. Ch. the Canton province; *orang Cina ~,* Muslim Chinese from Yunan. 2. *kantung,* a fish-creel worn at the waist, so, pouch, purse; also *keruntung.*

kantur [KN], Ind. office, bureau; *~ berita,* news-agency.

kanun [KN], Ar. laws, rules (civil).

kap [KN], 1. the roof of a palanquin; the hood of a carriage. 2. *kain ~,* a kincob, gold brocade cloth.

kapa [KN], Skr. nervous trembling; *ter~-~,* in a quiver.

kapah = *kapa.*

kapai [KK], *ter~-~,* nervously moving about the arms (as a bad swimmer) or a foot (as an elephant on soft ground); flapping (as a flag); struggling (with threshing limbs), as a drowning man.

kapak [KN], an axe; *~ bungkus, ~ kecik,* a sort of lethal cosh used by criminals in Kelantan; *bendera ~,* a broad ensign; *gigi ~,* large front teeth; *ular ~,* a generic name for viperine snakes, notably *~ bakau* (*Lachesis purpureo-maculatus*), *~ rimba* (*L. wagleri*) and *~ daun* (*L. gramineus*); *seperti ~ naik pemidangan,* (prov.), doing something without enough knowledge or tools

kapal [KN], Tam. a ship; *~ api,* a steamer; *~ hantu,* see *lancang; ~ layar,* a sailing-ship; *~ belangkas,* stern-wheeler; *~ roda lambung,* a paddle-wheeler; *~ muatan,* a merchant ship; *~ (pengangkut) minyak,* a tanker; *~ calu,* a ship on a regular run; *~ liar,* a tramp steamer; *~ tumpang,* passenger ship; *~ tunda,* a tug; *~ peronda,* a patrol boat; *~ pengemas,* Ind. a salvage vessel; *~ pecah,* a wreck; (fig.) woman's menstruation; *~ pendaratan,* landing-craft; *~ perang induk,* mother-ship; *~ pem-*

bawa ~ terbang, aircraft carrier; *~ terbang,* an aeroplane; *~ terbang pelawan,* a fighter plane; *~ terbang penyerang,* id.; *~ pejuang,* id.; *~ pemburu,* id.; *~ terbang pengebom,* a bombing plane; *~ terbang penambang,* a passenger plane; *~ pembinasa, ~ penjahanam,* a destroyer; *~ penjajah,* a cruiser; *~ pengangkut,* a transport; *~ selam,* a submarine; *~ penyapu periuk api,* a minesweeper; *~ penyapu ranjau (periuk api),* id.; *~ pengorek,* a dredger; *~ bijih,* id.; *~ penggali, id.,* but also used for a drilling vessel; *~ meriam,* gun-boat; *tubuh ~,* hull; *badan ~,* id.; *per~an,* shipping.

kapan [KN], 1. Ar. a winding-sheet; *ter~,* shrouded, sheeted; *mengapani,* to shroud (a corpse). 2. Ind. [Kktr], when.

kapang [KN], 1. the *Teredo navalis;* a barnacle. 2. excretions adhering to a newborn child; *ber~,* dirty, smeared, e.g., of a glass.

kapar [KN], lying strewn about without order or method; *ber~an,* scattered about; *~an,* flotsam; *mengaparkan badan,* to stretch oneself out; *~an tanduk,* the 'body' of a horn (not the point); *~an pisau,* the flat side of the blade of a knife.

kapas [KN], Hind. cotton; a generic name for cultivated cottons (esp. *Gossypium herbaceum*); *kain ~,* cotton cloth; *limau ~,* the common lime (*Citrus acida*).

kapi [KN], a pulley; *pecah ~ putus suai,* irreparable (loss, disaster).

kapir [KN], Ar. = *kafir.*

kapis [KN], a generic name for shells of the genus *Pecten.*

kapit [KN], support on each side; *pengapit,* a supporter, a second; *pengapit bicara,* assessor — cf. *apit.*

kapitan [N], Port. a headman of a racial division of the population.

Kapri [KN], Caffre, African Negro.

kapri [KN], a type of bean.

kapu [KN], *~~,* water lettuce.

kapuk [KN], 1. tree-cotton; the cotton of *Eriodendron anfractuosum.* 2. *ber~,* to enfold in the arms and climb, e.g., a tree; embracing from behind, as a bad rider at horse's neck; *ter~ pada,* clinging to, e.g., the side of a tree; stuck to, as a picture on a wall.

kapung [KN], = *apung.*

kapur [KN], 1. Pers. camphor; chalk; the lime eaten with *sirih; sirih se~,* a quid of betel; *~ Barus,* camphor; *~ Belanda,* chalk; *~ masak,* plaster; *~ tohor,* whitewash; *~ mentah,* quick-lime; *~ mati,* slaked lime; *mengapur sirih,* to prepare a quid of betel and lime; *baharu se~ sirih sahaja,* just the time in which to prepare a quid, i.e. a very short time; *ke~,* Treng. a sort of sandfly. 2. *mengapur,* to seal up.

karah [KN], 1. spotted, variegated; *kulit ~,* tortoise-shell, *sisik ~,* id.; *penyu~,* the turtle yielding the best shell. 2. *sebatang ~,* alone; by oneself or without family ties (*kara* being a shrub which is said always to root wherever thrown).

karak [KK], 1. Pah. *ber~,* to fight, of dogs. 2. Kel. a torch made of coconut fronds.

karam [KK], to founder (of a ship), to be wrecked; *~ berdua, basah seorang,* both were ship-wrecked, but only one got wet, there's no justice!

karang [KK], 1. a reef, a coral bank; coral-line sponge; *kena ~,* to run on a reef; *batu ~,* (1) coralline rock; (2) galena ore; *bunga ~,* a sponge; coralline growths; *isi ~,* shells, corals, etc. (picked up on the shore); *~~an,* id.; *penyakit ~~,* diseases of the urethra; *ber~,* to hunt for shells; *~* is also used generally for ore-bearing stratum; also for the roughest method of stitching thatch. 2. literary composition; *pe~an,* Ind. an ordered garden; *~an,* composition, setting; *~mengarang,* to do literary work; *~kan,* to arrange flowers; to compose; *~ bunga,* bouquet, floral tribute; *pengarang jantung,* darling; *pe~an,* yard; *pengarang,* an author; *pengarang akhbar,* editor; *pengarang berita,* newseditor. 3. an instant; *se~ ini,* now; also *se~* and *se~~lah!,* one moment!; presently;

soon.

karan [KN], Eng. electric current; *barang-barang ~,* electro-plated goods; *rambut terkerinting dengan ~,* 'permed' hair; *meja judi ~,* pin-tables; *barang-barang (celup) ~,* electro-plated articles; *~ searah,* direct current; *~ bolak-balik,* alternating current.

karap [KN], a weaver's comb, the heddles of a loom.

karas [KN], *ke~,* a Malay sweet cake.

karat [KN], 1. rust; deterioration; *~ di hati,* malice; *ber~,* to rust; *diam penggali ber~, diam ubi berisi,* when a spade is silent (i.e. put away), it rusts; when a potato is silent (in the earth) it grows (some people sit vacantly when silent, others are thinking). 2. *ber~,* to fight with claws (as cats) or pincers (as crabs); *~ gigi,* to grind the teeth.

karau [KK], 1. disturbing; stirring up the oil when frying. 2. to haul in a line, = *harau.*

kari [KN], Hind. 1. curry; *~ nasi,* curry and rice; *~pap,* Eng. curry-puff. 2. *~ Kuran,* a Koran reader.

kariah [KN], 1. Malacca, a district. 2. a female Koran reader.

karib [KS], Ar. near (esp. of relations); intimate (of friends).

karih [KK], stirring rice with a spoon when boiling the rice.

karim [KS], Ar. merciful, generous, esp. as an epithet of God; *al-Karim,* the Bountiful.

karkus [KN], Pen. a privy.

kartu [KN], Ind. a playing card; a card; a ticket; *~ nama,* business card.

kartus [KN], Hind. from Eng., a cartridge; *~ hampa, ~ kosong,* blank cartridge.

karuk [KN], a torch of dry fronds.

Karun [KN], Ar. Korah (the enemy of Moses), believed by Malays to have been of enormous wealth, whose treasure is now buried in the earth for wizards to find; and so, *harta ~,* treasure trove.

karung [KN], a coarse matting sack; sometimes any small bag; *~ perkakas,* toolbag; *~ kosong,* a windbag; an irresponsible and credulous person; *mendirikan ~ kosong,* to make an empty bag stand up, met. for 'hopeless task'.

karut [KS], involved, self-contradictory, obscure; muddled rigmarole; *mengarut,* to talk nonsense, *~* is also used as an expletive — nonsense!: *ka~an,* a piece of nonsense; *~-marut,* in confusion, mixed up.

karya [KN], a literary or artistic work.

kasa [KN], Ar. a fine muslin.

kasad [KN], Ar. wish, intention, resolve.

kasap [KS], 1. rough to the touch (as coarse paper or coarse wool). 2. a sailor whose duty it is to attend to the lamps, flags, cordage, etc., of a ship.

kasar [KS], coarse or rough in texture; coarse in manner; hefty, of build; 'heavy', of a fish; *~-tangan,* clumsy, 'ham-fisted'; *~* is also used for gross (of takings or profits); *mengasari,* to treat rudely.

kasau [KS], a rafter, a cross-beam; *~ jantan,* the main rafters; *~ betina,* the subsidiary rafters; *belang ~,* striped, esp. as a tiger.

kasi [KK], 1. give = *beri.* 2. Hind. castration, gelding; *lembu ~,* a bullock; *ayam ~,* a capon; *~kan,* to castrate.

kasidah [KN], Ar. Arabic chants.

kasih [KN], affection, love, strong liking; *terima~,* 'there is receipt of favour', i.e. thank you; *terima ~ daun keladi,* rhyming sl. for *kalau boleh, hendak lagi,* of gratitude given only in expectation of further gifts; *~an,* kindness, favour; pity; an unfortunate thing; *~ani,* or *mengasihankan,* to show pity for, to pity; *mengasihi,* to love; *mengasih,* to be in love with; *pengasih,* a creator of love — e.g., a love-philtre; *ke~,* the beloved, lover; *pengasihan,* merciful, esp. of God; see *kasi.*

Kasim [KN], Ar. 1. a common Malay name. 2. *orang ~,* a eunuch.

kasrah [KN], Ar. the name of one of the vowel-points, *e* or *i.*

kasta [KN], Ind. caste.

kasteria [KN], = ceteria.

kasur [KN], Ind. a light mattress.

kasut [KN], shoes, boots; pakai ~, to wear boots; ~ kayu, clogs; tapak ~, the sole of a shoe; ~ tumit tinggi, high-heeled shoes; ~ runcing ke hujung, pointed shoes; ~ seret, 'mules'; ~ sambau, grass slippers; sepasang ~, a pair of shoes; kayu sengkang ~, shoe-trees; tukang ~, a shoe-maker, a cobbler.

kata [KN], saying, utterance; ber~, to say, to speak; ber~~, to keep talking; mengatakan, to utter, to mention; per~an, a word; ~-dua, an ultimatum; ~-~, a phrase, an idiom; mengata-ngata, to revile, 'tell-off'; ~ pengantar, a foreword; se~, agreement, unanimity; ~ sepakat, mutual agreement; seia se~, unanimous agreement; ~ putus, a definite decision; memper~kan, to expound, set forth; make mention of; to talk about, talk of; tak ter~~, unspeakable; ~ sifat, an adjective; ~ kerja, a verb; ~ benda, a noun; ~ seru, an exclamation; ~ pengganti, a pronoun; ~-~ perbandingan, a simile; ~ dasar, root word, basic root of word; ~-~ perintah baris, words of command.

katak [KN], a frog, a toad; ~ betung, the bullfrog; ~ lempung, a frog (Oxyglossus sp.); ~ pisang, a green frog with great leaping powers (Rana erythroea or Rhacophorus leucomystax); ~ puru, a toad; buaya ~, a broad-bodied variety of crocodile; meriam ~, a squat cannon, e.g. a howitzer; ~ di bawah tempurung, a frog under a coconut-shell, met. for a simple person, knowing nothing of the outside world; ~ hendak jadi lembu, pride will (must) have a fall.

katam [KK], meng~kan, to cut up into short lengths; se~ tebu, a (cut) section of sugarcane.

katang [KN], 1. ~-~, a small mengkuang pouch. 2. ~-~, runners; rattan rings allowing a pole to have free play up and down, e.g. the poles forcing down the submerged screen in a large fish-trap of the jermal type. 3. ular ~ tebu, the

banded karait (Bungarus fasciatus).

kati [KN], a 'catty', = 1-1/3 lb.

katib [KN], Ar. a writer, a scribe.

katik [KN], stunted, dwarf (of a cock or person); ayam ~, a bantam fowl.

katil [KN], Tam, a bedstead; ~ kelamin, a double bed.

katir [KN], perahu ~, a catamaran; kolek ~, a light racing catamaran.

katuk [KK], to knock, tap; ~ pintu, to knock or tap on a door; ~-mengatuk, name given in Kelantan to the knock by which users of the kapak bungkus despatch their victims, see kapak; a variant of ketuk.

katung [KN], 1. the king turtle, 2. ter~~, swinging to-and-fro, as a boat not under control. 3. = kotong.

katup [KK], closing up tightly; ter~, closed; mulut ter~, silenced.

kau [Kgn], thou; you; = engkau.

kaul [KN], Ar. ber~, to offer prayers (e.g., at a shrine) with the object of bringing about some special event; membayar ~, to pay a vow when event fulfilled; ~ tak sampai, vow unfulfilled or fruitless vow.

kaum [KN], Ar. crowd, multitude, family, people; ~ keluarga, family; community, group, faction, party; ~ buruh, workers; ~ tua, the older generation or old people with conservative ideas; ~ kerabat, family circle; ~-~ kecil, minorities; ~ tani, peasants; ~ bangsa, one's race (as opposed to one's family); ~ ibu, womenfolk; per~an, racialism; kebencian ~, racial hatred; ~ atasan, elite, upper classes; ~ marhaen, the proletariat.

kaup = kaut.

kaus [KN], 1. Ar. shoes; di bawah ~, below the sovereign's foot; the position of a subject; ~ kaki, Ind. socks. 2. Eng. couch, sofa.

kaut [KK], scraping towards oneself, scooping up (earth) with the hands; ladling out (e.g., rice).

kawad [KK], Ar. drill; ber~, to drill.

kawah [KN], a cauldron; the crater of a volcano; makan nasi ~, to have meals in a group.

kawal [KN], Tam. watching; the work of a sentry or watchman; ~an, a watch, a guard; *mengawal* or *ber~*, to be on the watch; *mengawal* also means to regulate, control, keep in order; *mengawal perasaan*, to control one's feelings; ~an harga, price-control; ~an, a safeguard; ~an dalam negeri, internal security; *pengawal peribadi*, personal bodyguard; *asykar sebagai pengawal*, id.; *kapal pengawal pantai*, coastguard vessels; *pengawal kampung*, Home Guard; *pengawal asrama*, warden of hostel; ~an kehormatan, guard of honour.

kawan [KN], a company, a party; a herd or flock; a swarm; a companion, a friend; ~ gajah, a herd of elephants; ~ penyamun, a band of robbers; ~ perahu, the crew; in Kelantan ~ is often used for 'I'; tiga se~, a trio, esp of performers; *mengawan*, to pair, mate, of animals; ~ dan lawan, friend and foe; ~ sekerja, colleague.

kawang [KN], *minyak ~*, the fat of the tree (*Diplocnemia sebifera*).

kawasan [KN], sphere, demesne, area (as of jurisdiction); electoral division; ~ rumah, grounds of a house; ~ khas Melayu, Malay Reserve; ~ larangan, closed area, area to which entry is forbidden.

kawat [KN], wire; *surat ~*, a telegram; ~ tak berdawai, wireless telegraphy; ~ berduri, barbed wire; ~ beranyam, wire-netting.

kawi [KN], 1. *bahasa ~*, the old poetic language of Java; *kekawin*, a poetic narrative. 2. *batu ~*, cinnabar, manganese. 3. Ar. *besi ~*, iron of supernatural hardness, manganese.

kawin [KK], 1. Pers. to marry, wedding; *mas ~*, the settlements on a bride; ~ lari, elopement; to elope; ~ gantung, child marriage (in which consummation is postponed); ~kan, to cause to be married, to give in marriage; ~kan pokok, to graft trees; ~ campuran, mixed marriage; ~~mawin, marriages generally; per~an, wedding; ~ paksa, forced marriage; *mengawini*, to take in marriage; ~ durian (sl.) trial marriage: *menggoncang, mencium, kemudian mengopak, dan dirasanya sikit, kalau tidak baik dibuangkan*, you shake it and smell (kiss) it, then you open it and taste it a little; if it isn't good, you throw it away; also *kahwin* and *kahawin*. 2. *tombak pengawinan*, a State halberd.

kaya [KS], 1. rich, powerful; *menjadi ~*, to become rich, *orang ~*, a rich man; ~ melangit, as rich as Croesus; ~-raya, wealthy, affluent; *orang ~-raya*, the rich; ~ baru, parvenu, upstart; *ke~an alam, ke~an Allah*, wonder, miracle (of nature, God); but ~ is also used in what is probably its original sense, that of 'powerful' or 'pre-eminent', as a title of Malay dignitaries and also of God: *Tuhan Yang Kaya*, God Almighty: *ke~an Tuhan*, the power of God. 2. *buah seri ~* or *buah sirih ~*, the bullock's heart fruit (*Anona squamosa*).

kayak [KN], Ind. like, just as.

Kayang [KN], a place in Perlis where royalties are buried; said formerly to have given its name to the State.

kayap [KN], an eruptive disease; herpes; also used for other swellings with a rash.

kayau [KN], 1. Dyak head-hunting. 2. over-flooding; inundation. 3. a snag.

kayu [KN], wood, wooden; ~~an, timber of all sorts; ~-kayan, id.; ~ balak, trees suitable for cutting as timber; ~ api, firewood; ~ arang, ebony; ~ gaharu, eagle-wood; ~ manis, cinnamon; *akar ~*, a creeping or climbing plant; *mata ~*, a knot in wood; ~ bongkok, a bent branch; (fig.) easily led or an easy mark; *tukang ~*, a carpenter; *air ~*, wood and water; ship's stores; *batang ~*, a log, a tree-trunk; *buah ~*, fruit; *daun ~*, a leaf; *kulit ~*, bark; *pokok ~*, a tree; *buat ~ tiga*, to bamboozle (of two parties conspiring to trick a third).

kayuh [KN], a paddle; *ber~*, to paddle

(intransitive); ~*kan*, to paddle (transitive); *pengayuh,* a paddle; also used for 'pedal'; also for the man who pedals; *pengayuh beca roda tiga,* a trishaw driver; *mengayuh,* to pedal; *pengayuh di tangan, perahu di air,* paddle in hand and boat on the water, i.e. all ready to go, 'raring to go'.

ke [Kdpn], 1. to; ~ *atas,* upwards; ~ *sana,* thither; ~ *dalam,* into; ~ *mana,* whither; ~*pada,* to (a person).

kebabal [KN], the young half-grown nangka or cempedak fruit.

kebah [KS], 1. breaking into perspiration during fever. 2. ~ *raksa,* rubbing quicksilver into the body (to render a man invulnerable).

kebahi [KN], a Javanese village official.

kebak [KN], gaping (of a deep cut).

kebal [KS], impenetrable, of the flesh; invulnerable; *kereta* ~, a military tank; ~*kan (terhadap),* to immunize (against).

kebam [KK], 1. to suck, as a sweet; ~ *bibir,* to turn in the lips till they cease to be visible. 2. [KN], leaden-coloured (of the sky). 3. = *kabam.*

keban [KN], a work-basket (of *mengkuang* leaf) made at Malacca.

kebas [KK], 1. (onom.) shaking out a cloth vigorously; to flick, jerk away, shake out; *ber-,* a ritual 'flicking away' of evil by a *bomoh* (medicine-man), esp. in cases of sickness; ~*kan,* to brush off, brush away; (sl.) to snatch, 'pinch'; ~*kebus,* the sound of cloth being shaken; rustling, as stiff clothing. 2. deadened, paralysed temporarily (of a limb), e.g., by a blow on the funny-bone or the attack of an electric ray; numbed, having a feeling of 'pins and needles'; *buang* ~, to 'stretch the legs'.

kebat [KK], = *bebat.*

kebaya [KN], Port. a long outer garment worn by Malay and Straits Chinese women.

kebayan [KN], Jav. an order; a village regulation; a village headman; *nenek* ~, an old woman who plays a great part in Malay romance as the complaisant guardian of princesses.

kebek [KS], awry, of the mouth; having one's tongue in one's cheek.

kebil [KS], *ter~-~,* blinking (of an absent-minded man); inattentive, absent-minded.

kebin = *keban.*

kebirah = *kembiri.*

kebun [KN], a plantation; a garden; an estate; *tukang* ~, a gardener; ~ *binatang,* zoological garden; ~ *bunga,* flower garden, esp. botanical garden; *pe~,* a planter; ~ *percubaan,* experimental garden, *ber~,* to work in the garden.

kebuk [KN], a hollow cylinder used in making vermicelli, sometimes used for cylinder of an engine.

kebur [KK], to clean a well by agitating the water; to agitate water, stir up, e.g., with a stick in order to drive fish.

kecai [KS], *ter~,* smashed to atoms; in pieces, shattered.

kecam [KK], 1. Ind. to criticise; ~*an,* criticism, *rancangan pembangunan itu di-~,* the development plan is under attack. 2. = *kejam* 2.

kecamuk [KK], *ber~,* to spring up, shoot up; to occur suddenly; to come into action; to leap, of the heart, from excitement or alarm; mentally agitated, 'upset'.

kecap [KN], (onom.) *mengecap,* to taste, try the taste of; smacking the lips; the sound made by a lizard; *makan ter~-~,* eating with loud smacking noises.

kecapi [KN], Skr. a mandolin or lute with four strings; *buah* ~, the fruit of *Sandoricum radiatum.*

kecek [KN], 1. wheedling, to worry by importunity; *kena* ~, to be taken in. 2. a game played with coins. 3. Kol. *ber~,* to converse.

keceng [KK], to close an eye.

kecewa [KS], injured; put to shame; disappointed; *mengecewakan,* to cause to fail, to foil; to prejudice (impair the prospects of).

keci [KN], Eng. a ketch; a square-rigged ship; a sailing vessel of small tonnage and light draft.

kecicak [KK], Pk. *ber~*, trampling all round; stamping in a dance.

kecik = *kecil.*

kecil [KS], small inferior; younger; lesser in rank; *tuan ~*, assistant manager; *~ molek*, daintily pretty; *dari ~*, from youth up; *~ hati*, hurt, wounded in the feelings; *jangan ber~ hati*, cheer up, take heart; *mengecilkan*, to reduce in size; *per~- ~kan*, to belittle, disparage; *tanpa berasa ~ hati*, undaunted.

kecimpung [KK], plunging in; (fig.) immerse in; to involve oneself; *mereka ber~ dalam bidang politik*, they involve themselves in politics.

kecoh [KN], *~-kecah*, uproar; *mengecoh*, to make trouble, brawl; *ke~an*, uproar, commotion, brawl, confusion, state of chaos.

kecoh [KK], cheating at cards, swindling by giving false weight, etc.

kecong [KK], swindling by denying a debt incurred; repudiating a fair claim; *~- kecoh*, all sorts of fraud.

kecubung [KN], 1. the datura (*Datura metel* and *D. fatuosa*); *mabuk ~*, intoxicated by datura poisoning; (fig.) lovesick; *batu ~*, the amethyst. 2. a dome.

kecundang see *cundang.*

kecut [KS], shrunken, shrivelled up; *pengecut*, timid; coward, fainthearted; *~ perut*, alarmed, 'having the wind up'; *~ hati*, fearful, afraid; *mengecut*, to contract.

kedadak [KN], a choleric attack; only used in the expression *cekik ~*, an imprecation calling down a horrible death upon a person.

kedah. [KS], 1. exposed, wide open; *mangkuk ~*, a bowl with a wide mouth. 2. Kedah. 3. Hind. a corral.

kedai [KN], Tam. a shop; a selling-booth; *ber~*, to keep a shop; *~ ramsum*, *~ rempah-cabai*, a general (grocer's) shop; *rumah ~*, a shophouse; *~ layanan sendiri*, a self-service shop.

kedak [KN], 1. (onom.) *~-~*, the noise made by a rickety cart on a bad road. 2. *lin- tang ~*, lying across each other confusedly; at sixes and sevens, criss-cross.

kedal [KN], a disease causing peeling, cracking and dirty-white discoloration of the soles of hands and feet.

kedam [KS], staunch, weatherproof.

kedang [KK], stretched out, with limbs extended; *mengedangkan tangan*, to stretch out the arms; *ter~*, stretched, as skin of drum.

kedangsa [KN], *limau ~*, a cultivated lime (*Citrus acida*).

kedap [KS], 1. close, almost waterproof (of sail-cloth, meshing); *~ udara*, airtight. 2. *se~*, a handful (of stalks, esp. padi stalks).

kedau [KK], 1. *mengedau*, to cry out loudly, e.g., for assistance. 2. *~-~*, flickering (of light).

kedaung [KN], *pokok ~*, a large tree (*Parkia Roxburghii*).

kedayan [KN], Jav. servants, followers of a prince.

kedek [KS], *ter~-~*, walk like a duck.

kedekik [KN], a greenish medicinal compound resembling salt.

kedekut [KS], mean, stingy; *~ tangkai jering*, as mean as cats' meat (because the stalk carrying the *jering* fruit is very tough and 'parts' with difficulty).

kedelai [KN], *kacang ~*, the soya bean.

kedempung [KS], 1. blown out, swollen, of rotten fruit; sometimes of obesity. 2. a tobacco-pouch made of *mengkuang* leaf. 3. (onom.) sound of a soft thud, plop.

kedengkik [KS], extremely emaciated.

kedera [KN], 1. *ikan ~*, a grey mullet. 2. *burung ~*, Kel. a sort of plover.

kedewas [KN], *ikan bawal ~*, a sort of pomfret.

kedi [KN], 1. congenitally impotent. 2. Kel. a Siamese wat.

kedidi [KN], a generic name for small sandpipers (*Totanus*) and plovers (*Aegialitis*); *~ bukit*, the water-wagtail; *~ padang*, the collared pratincole; the meadow-pipit (also called *cak padang*).

kedih [KK], *mengedih*, Pk. to lessen (of

sickness).

kedik [KS], slight bent; *duduk ter~*, sitting with shoulders bent.

kedip [KN], wink (of the eye), *ber~, ter~*, blink o's eyes, to flicker; *mengerdipkan mata*, to blink one's eyes.

kedondong [KN], a generic name for a number of trees mostly of the genus *Canarium*.

kedu [KS], a slight stoop (such as that of a writer at a desk or of a shy person); *duduk ter~*, sitting hunched up.

keduduk [KN], a generic name for a number of plants with showy pink flowers (*Melastoma polyanthum* and allied sp.); also *senduduk*.

keduk [KN], *ber~*, mask, disguise.

kedumpas [KN], a cheat, trickster.

kedut [KN], a crease, a wrinkle; *ber~*, crumpled (of a dress); wrinkled (of face); *ber~ kening*, frowning.

kehel [KS], *ter~*, dislocated (of a limb); inharmonious, out of place; out of its course (of a ship), kinked (of wire); twisted, as wire or string.

kehendak, see *hendak*.

kejam [KK], 1. closing (the eye) for some time; keeping (the eye) shut; *mengejamkan*, to close (the eyes); ~ *kejip*, blinking ? cruel, heartless, devilish; also *kecam*.

kejan [KK], 1. Pen. inciting, stimulating. 2. to urge, to hurry a person to do something.

kejang [KS], stiff, of muscles; *ber~~*, stretched out stiff (of legs); *membuang ~*, to stretch oneself, to take exercise; ~ *mulut*, tetanus, lockjaw; *ke~an*, cramp.

kejap [KN], closing (the eye) for a moment; winking; *se~*, the time it takes to wink; an instant only — cf. *kejip*.

kejar [KK], *mengejar*, to pursue; *ber~*, to rush; *ber~~an*, chasing one another, as children; *~kan*, to 'rush', carry hastily, transport hurriedly, as a sick person to hospital; *mengejar-ngejar*, to pursue unceasingly, to harry, to persecute; *dapat ~*, to overtake; *mengejar ke depan*, to come from behind and take the

lead; *di~ waktu*, pressed by time.

kejat [KS], firm (of made earth), things embedded; definitely settled.

keji [KS], discreditable, disgraceful, infamous; *nama yang ~*, infamy; *mengeji*, to disparage, 'run down', show contempt; *perkara ~*, scandalous incident; *memandang ~ pada*, to look with contempt on.

kejip [KN], a wink; = *kejap* (but even shorter in duration); *~an mata*, a wink.

kejora [KN], Ar. the morning star, Venus; also *Zuhrah*.

keju [KN], Port. cheese.

kejur [KS], stiff, unpliable, inelastic of dried betel-leaves; person's carriage, hair; also *genjur* and *kenjur*.

kejut [KS], *~kan*, to startle; to awaken; *ter~*, startled; *melakukan serangan mengejut*, to make a sudden attack.

kek [KN], 1. a hand-loom. 2. Eng. cake.

kekah [KN], the banded leaf-monkey (*Presbytes femoralis, Semnopithecus femoralis*).

kedah = *akikat*.

kekal [KS], enduring, lasting; *akhirat yang ~*, eternal life; *~kan*, to perpetuate.

kekang [KN], a bit for a horse; = *kang*; *mengekang*, to curb, (fig.) to hamper; *dia harus mengekang nafsu makan*, he has to curb his appetite.

kekar [KS], to separate; e.g., rice-grains to dry; or, fruit, to keep.

kekas [KK], *mengekas-ngekas*, to scratch, scrabble, as a fowl; (fig.) to scrabble for something unseen with one's foot.

kekasih, see *kasih*.

kekat [KN], scum and drifting matter on tidal river; *mati ~*, dead low water; *balik ~*, to turn, of the tide.

kekau [KS], starting out of sleep in terror.

kekek [KN], 1. a gusset. 2. *ter~~*, (onom.) a giggling laugh. 2. *burung ~*, the black hornbill.

kekel [KS], extremely stingy.

kekok [KS], awkward, blundering, clumsy; *ter~*, showing clumsiness, making a blunder.

kektus [KN], Eng. *pokok ~*, a cactus plant.

kekura [KN], a tortoise; see *kura* 1.
kekwa [KN], Ch. *bunga* ~, a chrysanthemum.
kelabu [KS], grey or ash-coloured; *mata* ~, a film over the eye; *mengelabukan mata,* to deceive, cast dust in the eyes; ~ *kehitam-hitaman,* very dark grey.
Kelabit [KN], *orang* ~, an aboriginal tribe in Sarawak.
keladak [KN], dregs, refuse; the last and worst of anything.
keladau [KK], 1. to look after, watch over, take care of. 2. bitts, posts on deck for fastening cables.
keladi [KN], a common name for a number of aroids (notably *Colocasia antiquorum*); ~ *bunting,* water hyacinth; *biang* ~, very lustful; sometimes used for instigator, source of trouble; *anak* ~, a child who is too small to keep up with his mates, a 'runt'; *ibu* ~, an adult person who behaves childishly, fails to be his age; some of the aroids are itchy to the touch: hence the saying, ~ *kata kemahang gatal,* the ~ calls the *kemahang* itchy, i.e. the pot calls the kettle black; *daun* ~ *dimandikan,* a person who is difficult to teach or advise; *tua-tua* ~, physically old but young at heart.
kelah [KN], *ikan* ~, a species of carp (*Tor tembroidos* and *Tor douronensis*) said to be related to the Indian mahseer.
kelah [KK], *ber~,* to picnic.
kelahi [KN], *ber~,* to quarrel; *per~an,* a quarrel.
kelak [Kktr], an adverb indicative of future possibility; may; possibly; perhaps.
kelakar [KN], joking, jesting, comic, as film or actor; *orang* ~, a comedian, esp. of the slapstick kind.
kelalut [KS], twisted; involved; incoherent, of speech.
kelam [KS], dark, obscure; ~ *kabut,* confused, chaotic; *pening* ~, dizziness affecting the optic nerve.
kelambit [KN], the large fruit-bat (*Pteropus edulis*); also *keluang.*
kelambu [KN], a mosquito-curtain; *cangkuk* ~, hook for holding the net open.
kelambur [KS], wrinkled.
kelamin [KN], a pair (male and female); a married couple; *per~an,* pairing, mating; married state; *ber~,* to pair, mate; *mengelamini,* marry, wed; *jenis* ~, sex; *penyakit* ~, euphem. for veneral disease.
kelamkari [KN], an Indian painted fabric.
kelamun [KK], Ind. = *lamun* 2.
kelana [KN], wandering; a vagabond; ~ *yang hina papa,* a miserable wandering wretch. 2. a Bugis title given in Sungai Ujong to a ruling chief.
kelangkabut [KS], = *kelam kabut,* see *kelam.*
kelangkang [KN], the perineum; also *kelengkang.*
kelanit [KK], unpick stitches.
kelanjar [KS], rheumatic pain (after a massage).
kelantang [KK], set to dry in the sun; bleach.
kelap [KK], ~-*kelip,* to sparkle, sparkling (eyes, stars).
kelapa [KN], the coconut (*Cocos nucifera*); ~ *hijau,* the young coconut, ~ *muda,* id.; ~ *kering,* copra; ~ *bali,* the oil-palm; ~ *sawit,* ~ *sabit,* id.
kelapu [KS], *mengelapu,* to bustle in agitation.
kelar [KN], incision, nick, esp. the nicks made on a fish prior to salting, or, sometimes, cooking; to slash, to gash.
kelara [KN], *ikan* ~, the young *sembilang* fish.
kelarah [KN], a maggot which eats into wood and fruit; *dimakan* ~, worm-eaten (of fruit or roots).
kelarai [KN], diamond-shaped (of patterns); *mengelarai,* to plait basketwork in such patterns.
kelas [KN], Eng. a school class; sometimes, class of society; *perjuangan antara* ~, class struggle; ~ *pimpinan,* tutorial classes, esp. extra-mural; ~-*kambing,* cheap seats, gallery; ~-*satu,* first class.
kelasa [KN], a hard, protuberant mass of

flesh; muscular tissue; any protruding lump of muscular tissue, such as a camel's hump; *cucuk ~,* to give an intramuscular injection.

kelasak [KN], 1. a floor-mat. 2. a long, light shield of leather or wood with a handle in the centre.

kelasau [KN], Pah. a species of bat.

kelasi [KN], 1. Pers. a sailor. 2. the long-nosed Borneo monkey (*Hylobates leucicus*).

kolat [KS], 1. astringent (of taste), setting the teeth on edge. 2. *tali ~,* the shoot of a small boat. 3. a generic name for a number of trees (mostly of the genus *Eugenia*).

kelatl [KN], 1. betel-nut scissors. 2. = *keliti.*

kelau [KS], *kelip-~,* glistening (as the surface of the sea), alternatively bright and dark (as when shadows chase each other).

kelawan [KN], the cord holding the nose-rings of a buffalo; *menjilat ~,* to be reduced to licking this cord, met. for a person who has missed his opportunity.

kelawar [KN], 1. a generic name for bats; *~ gua,* a name given to the bats *Chiromeles torquatus* and *Nycticeiu kuhli.* 2. the Clubs suit in cards.

kelebak [KS], gaping, widely opened (of wounds), a big tear.

kelebat [KK], *ber~ ,* to move swiftly as in *silat* [Malay art of self defence], *se~ mata,* a glimpse.

kelebang [KK], *ber~,* dancing in swarms, as midges (or planes), flying around.

kelebek [KS], to scrabble round for something, to pick at (as a scab).

kelebet [KK], *mengelebet,* to turn up the edge, tip or fold of anything.

kelebur = *kelebang.*

kelebuk [KN], (onom.) the sound of a heavy body falling on a flat surface.

kelebur [KK], giving way under weight; *~an,* abyss, pit.

kelebut [KN], Pers., Hind. a fez-rest.

kelecek [KK], a variant of *lecek; mengelecek bola,* to control the ball (in foot-

ball), to dribble.

keledang [KN], a large tree (*Artocarpus lanceoefolia*).

keledar [KK], precautionary measures or preparations; schemes; careful surveillance; *ber~an,* bustling around busily with intent to act, e.g. as sharks around a boat; watching over like sentinels or watch-dogs, *topi ~,* crash helmet.

keledek [KN], *ubi ~,* the sweet potato; *loyar ~,* a cheap lawyer.

keledut [KS], crumpled, ruffled — cf. *kedut.*

kelek [KK], carrying anything under the arm without using a cloth or sling, as a gun.

kelekati [KN], 1. = *kelekatu.* 2. Tam. are-canut scissors.

kelekatu [KN], the flying ant; the Malay equivalent for the proverbial moth which is attracted by flame and perishes in it; *seperti ~ masuk api,* lured to destruction (to pursue one's object resstlessly)

kelelap [KK], drowned, submerged, sunk.

kelelut [KK], *kata ber~,* broken (of dying speech).

kelemayar [KN], the luminous millipede; phosphorescence.

kelembahang [KN], a wild aroid (the leaves of which give a sort of itch to the hand that clasp them); *anak ~,* a term of abuse; a variant of *kemahang,* q.v.

Kelembal [KN], *Sang ~,* the name of a wonder-working wizard in Malay folklore; in some parts, supernatural giants.

kelembak [KN] a fragrant wood.

kelembuai [KN], a species of snail; it is amphibious, and so is used as a simile for people who are capricious in temper and, eg., for politicians who waver in their loyalties; in context it may mean 'turncoat' or 'deviationist'.

kelembung [KS], blown out with wind; a blister.

kelemoyang [KN], a name given to a number of plants, including *Homolomena coerulescens, H. rostrata,* and others.

kelemping [KS], flabby and pendulous

(of the breasts).

kelemumur [KN], scurf, dandruff.

kelendara [KN], the ring or fastening connecting a boom with the mast.

kelengar [KS], fainting, unconscious; knocked 'silly'.

kelengkang [KN], 1. a perineum; also *kelangkang*. 2. a key-ring; also *gelang kunci*.

kelengkeng [KN], 1. *burung* ~, the small southern hornbill (*Anthracoceros convexus*); also *langling*. 2. *jari* ~, the little finger; *kurung* ~, the innermost chamber in a fish trap.

kelengkiak [KN], = *kongkiak;* a type of large, black ant which bites.

kelengkuk [KN], Ked. = *kelongkong;* young coconut (fruit).

kelenjar [KN], *buah ~an* or *biji ~an*, the lymphatic glands; *sakit ~an*, bubonic inflammation.

kelentang [KN], 1. (onom.) the clanging of a gong. 2. *buah* ~, the horse-radish (obtained from the plant *Moringa pterygosperma*).

kelenting [KN], (onom.) tinkling (of a bell).

kelentit [KN], the clitoris; used as a term of abuse among women.

kelentong [KN], (onom.) a Chinese hawker (so called from the gong-like instrument he uses to draw attention of his presence).

kelentung [KN], (onom.) booming (of a gong).

kelenung [KN], (onom.) the booming of a gong.

kelenyar [KS], restless, on the move.

kelepai [KS], broken but not sundered, as, e.g.; a cluster of coconuts — cf. *kelepet*.

kelepat [KK], Hind. caulking (of boat); also *kalpat*.

kelepet [KK], turned down (of the corner of a page); a turned over part, a flap; flapping, as pendulous (as a broken wing or horn); also *kelepek*.

kelepir [KN], the testicles.

kelepit [KN], *kelepai-~* = *kelepai*.

kelesek [KN], the thin skin or coating on a

banana-stem or aloe-leaf.

keletah [KK], manner, idiosyncrasy, mannerism; *banyak* ~, capricious, uncertain of temper; *ber~*, to pose, play up, act with an eye to effect.

keletak [KN], (onom.) continuous rapping — cf. *ketuk*.

keletang [KN], (onom.) the clang of metal falling on the ground.

keletar [KS], quivering, trembling — cf. *ketar*.

keletik [KN], (onom.) the sound of continued ticking.

keleting [KN], (onom.) the sound of continuous tickling.

keletok [KN], (onom.) continuous rapping or knocking — cf. *ketuk*.

keletung [KN], (onom.) a thumping sound.

kelewang [KN], a heavy chopper of sword.

kelewar [KN], (Dutch) a foresail.

keli [KN], *ikan* ~, a freshwate cat-fish (*Clarias majur*).

kelian [KN], 1. a surface mine; = *galian*. 2. = *kalian;* see *kali* 2.

kelibat [KN], 1. a double-bladed paddle; *mengelibat*, to paddle using this form of paddle. 2. *ter~-~*, wriggling forward (of leeches, catepillars). 3. *~an*, glimpses, indications, signs; *se~*, a glimpse.

kelicap [KN], a name applied to various small passerine birds, esp. sunbirds and, in some places, tailor-birds.

kelici [KN], a hard fruit (unidentified — used in children's games).

kelih [KS], to see, noticing, glancing at.

kelik [KK], Kel. = *balik*.

kelikir [KN], 1. a loop of rattan; a nose-ring for cattle; a thole-strap; *kena* ~, to be led by the nose. 2. *batu* ~, gravel.

keliling [KN], position round; the part around; *ber~*, around, encircling; *mengeliling* or *mengelilingi*, to encircle, to travel round; *~kan* or *mengelilingkan*, to whirl round, to bear round; *belayar mengelilingi dunia*, to sail round the world; *Jalan Pekeliling*, Circular Road; *keadaan se~*, environment.

kelim [KN], a small seam; hemming;

mengelim, to hem.

kelincir = *gelincir*.

kelincung [KK], Pk. to diverge (of a road, a traveller).

kelindan [KN], 1. strong sewing-thread. 2. *ter~*, full of regrets, worrying. 3. lorry-driver's helper.

Keling [KN], 'Kling', a name formerly applied to all immigrants from the Coromandel coast (but sometimes limited to Muslim immigrants from that coast, the others being called *orang Hindu*); *orang ~*, a Tamil or Telugu; *negeri ~*, the Madras Presidency; the name is now regarded as derogatory, though it was not so originally.

kelingsir = *gelingsir* and *gelincir*.

kelip [KK], a twinkle; the appearance and disappearance of light; *~-~*, fireflies, spangles; *~ kelau*, shimmering; *ter~-~*, twinkling (of light), blinking (of eyes); *se~ mata*, a moment.

kelipat [KN], hem; cf *lipat*.

keliru [KS], confused of thought; muddle-headed; flustered; *pikir ~*, id.; *barang ~*, a thing difficult to grasp (mentally); *mengelirukan*, to deceive, to lead astray, to bewilder; *ter~*, struck with bewilderment; led completely astray; *ke~an*, mistake; *kau tidak akan ~*, you can't miss it.

kelisa [KN], 1. Hind. a church. 2. *kacang ~*, a plant (*Psophocarpus tetragonolobus*).

kelit [KK], *ber~*, dodging, e.g., behind a tree, avoiding, getting out of the way; *ber~~~*, dodging from side to side.

keliti [KN], a thole-pin.

kelmarin [Kktr], yesterday; *~ dahulu*, the day before yesterday; also *kemarin*.

kelocak [KK], broken (of water); choppy (of the sea).

kelodak [KN], thunder — cf. *kelodan*.

kelodan [KN], *panah ~*, a thunderbolt — cf. *kelodak*.

kelok [KN], a curve; an arc; *ber~*, curved; *ber~-~*, cut in semi-circles (of a border) — cf. *lok, telok*, etc.

kelola [KK], 1. manage; superintend, supervise. 2. steel; also *keluli*.

keloloh [KS], scatter-brained.

kelompang [KS], the broken egg-shell when the chicken has been hatched.

kelompok [KN], a cluster, a collection, a group of persons; a clump (of trees); *se~ awan*, a mass of clouds; *mengelompokkan*, to group, to combine.

kelonet [KS], *se~*, a little; a tiny piece.

kelong [KN], a large marine fish-trap of several compartments: fish are hustled from the outer into the inmost and smallest, where the entrance is closed, and the fish caught.

kelongkong [KN], the soft-shelled young coconut.

kelongsong [KN], 1. a cone-shaped wrapper such as the tissue-paper cover of a fez; the leaf enfolding maize, the slough of a snake or the 'cup' made by a tailorbird; the 'bag' of the belly. 2. a metal vase for *sirih* leaf; *~ jagung*, sheath of maize.

kelongtang [KN], a noisy clapper scare-crow.

kelopak [KN], a sheath, covering; calyx; *~ mata*, the eyelid; *~ salak*, the calyx of the *salak* (*Zalacca edulis*); *~ bunga*, a petal; *bunga yang ber~ dua lapis*, double flower; *mengelopak, ter~*, to loosen, to get loose, to open.

kelorak [KN], *rumput ~*, a grass (*Lophaterium gracile*).

kelorek [KS], mean, stingy.

keloyak [KS], tattered and torn — cf. *koyak*.

kelu [KS], = *koyak*.

kelu [KS], dumb, speechless; terkelu, struck speechless, losing power of speech

keluak [KN], a type of nut with a hard shell.

keluang [KN], the flying fox; *siku ~*, a very acute angle.

keluar [KK], motion outwards, to go out; *mengeluar* or *mengeluari*, to sally out against; *mengeluarkan*, to drive out, to remove out; to issue, to emit; *pengeluar kelapa kering*, an exporter of copra; *~ ~ masuk*, in and out; *pengeluaran*, export, expenses.

keluarga [KN], Skr. family, kinsfolk, circle

of relations; *kaum ~,* id.

kelubi [KN], a plant (*Zalacca conferta*): it is a thorny stemless palm and bears a sour fruit (*asam ~*), reputedly loved by orang-utangs and porcupines: its leaves can be used for thatching and matmaking.

kelubung [KN], veiling; to veil — cf. *selubung;* veiling so as to cover both shoulders (*selendang* may cover only one).

keluh [KN], *~ kesah,* sighing and restless (as a lover or an anxious person); *mengeluh,* to sigh; *~an,* a complaint, protest.

keluli [KN], steel; also *kelola.*

kelulu [KS], decent, proper.

kelulut [KN], a small bee (Trigona sp.).

kelum [KS], curved inwards.

kelun [KK], *ber~,* to rise in spirals (of smoke) — cf. *lok, telum, kelung* 1., etc.

keluna [KN], a climber with green berries (*Smilax megacarpa*).

kelung [KS], 1. curved, arching, concave — cf. *keluk.* 2. a wooden shield large enough to protect the whole body. 3. *tikam ~,* to turn on its keeper (of an elephant).

kelupas [KK], *mengelupas,* (1) to keep peeling off; (2) to waste away — cf. *kupas.*

keluping [KN], a small scabby sore; cf. *kuping* 2.

kelupur [KS], *menggelupur,* to struggle and sprawl or wriggle (as a slaughtered fowl or a stranded fish).

kelur [KK], Kel. *ber~,* to call, hail; = *laung; ber~ dengar,* within hailing distance.

kelurut [KS], a gathering of pus, festering sore; *naik ~,* to 'gather'; *jari naik ~,* a whitlow.

kelus [KN], 1. an edible sea-slug. 2. [KK], *mengelus-ngelus,* to touch lightly; to caress.

kemahang [KN], an aroid, ·notorious for its itchy leaves; a variant of *kelembahang.*

kemala [KN], a talisman; a luminous bezoar; also *gemala.*

kemam [KK], mouthing, but not swallowing — (e.g., a quid of tobacco).

kemamam [KS], weak after illness.

kemamar [KS], dazzled, blinking wildly, aghast.

keman [KN], the sensitive plant.

kemanakan [KN], nephew, niece; see *anak.*

kemang [KN], an evil spirit affecting newborn children.

kemangi [KN], *medang ~,* a tree (*Cinnamomum parthenoxylon*).

kemarau [KS], a drought; *musim ~,* the dry season.

kemaruk [KS], ravenously hungry.

kemas [KS], packed close; tidy, storing away in limited space; *~kan,* to pack; to tidy away; *ber~,* to tidy up; to pack one's things, pack up; tidied up; neat, in order; *ber~ diri,* to huddle oneself up (into a small space, as when hiding); *per~kan,* to put in order, establish on a sound footing, reorganize, reconstitute; *barang ~,* valuables, esp. jewellery.

kemasai [KS], miserable object, feeble-looking.

kematu [KS], hard, as a corn or boil or the sole of the foot.

kembal [KN], a basket made of *mengkuang* leaf; Pen. = *rombong.*

kembali [Kktr], return to the point of original departure; *hidup ~,* to come to life again; *~ ke rahmat Allah,* to return to God's mercy; to die; *~ kan,* to give (anything) back; to restore; *se~,* on one's return; *terima kasih ~,* you're welcome.

kemban [KN], fastening the *sarong* round the bosom; *ber~,* so fastened; wearing a *sarong* so fastened; *ber~ tuala,* wrapped in a towel (so as to cover up the breast).

kembang [KK], 1. opening out (of a flower); *kain ~,* a *sarong* worn without trousers underneath; *~ hati,* exulting; *ber~,* to blossom out; to expand, to develop; to swell out; to rise, of dough; to fill, of sails; *ber~ biak,* to spread, to multiply, of population, livestock, etc.; *~ kempis,* expanding and contracting like a jellyfish; *per~an,* development; *ter~,* expanded, spread out; *pengembang agama,* a missionary; 2. Ind. a flower; ~ *malam,* a prostitute; ~ *kuncup,* to open and shut.

kembar [KS], twin; duplicated; *anak* ~, twin children; *saudara se~,* twin-brothers; *mengembari,* to duplicate; to rival in contest; *senapang* ~, double-barrelled; *injin ber~,* twin-engine; *anak* ~ *tiga,* triplets.

kembara [KK], *mengembara,* to wander; *pengembara,* traveller, explorer; nomad; vagabond.

Kembayat [KN], *kain* ~, cloth from Cambay in India.

kembili [KN], a tuber (*Coleus tuberosus*).

kembiri [KK], gelding, castrated; *ayam* ~, a capon.

kemboja [KN], 1. frangipanni (*Plumiera acutifolia*), associated, like the cypress in England, with graveyards. 2. *negeri Kemboja,* Kampuchea.

kembung [KS], 1. inflated, blown out; *perut* ~, inflated after meals; *ter~,* swollen out, puffed out; ~ *kempis,* to pant, going up and down panting. 2. a large rice tun. 3. *ikan* ~, a kind of mackerel.

kemelut [KN], the crisis in certain diseases, esp. fevers; ~ *naik,* the approach to the crisis; ~ *turun,* the following period.

kemendalu [KN], a mistletoe, a tree-parasite; also *bendalu* and *dedalu.*

kemendikai [KN], a water-melon; also *mendikai* and *temikai.*

kemendit = *kendit.*

kementam [KS], (onom.) the tramp of many feet; *ber~ gemuruh bunyinya,* the thunderous tramp of a host.

kemenyan [KN], benzoin; incense; *kayu* ~, the tree (*Styrax benzoin*); *pasang* ~ or *bakar* ~, to burn benzoin; ~ *hantu,* jocular euphemism for *bau kentut.*

kemering [KN], a were-tiger.

kemeruk [KS], addled egg, when the chick is not yet formed; also *kemuruk* — cf. *tembelang* and *kemungkus.*

kemetut [KS], dwarfed, stunted.

kemih berkemih, [KK], to pass urine.

kemik [KS], dented, as wood, metal; *hidung* ~, a snub nose; *kemek-~,* covered with dents.

kemirau [KS], Pah. half-ripe (of fruit).

kemiri [KN], the candle-nut (*Aleurites molluccanus*); also *buah keras.*

kemis [KK], Ind. = *Khamis; ber~,* to beg for alms; *pengemis,* a beggar.

kempang [KN], Pen. a river dug-out.

kempas [KN], a large tree (*Cumpassia malaccensis*).

kempik [KS], restless from curiosity.

kempilur [KN], a wicker-work case divided into compartments.

kempis [KS], shrinking, shrunk (as a sack, abscess, breasts); or a deflated tyre; ~ *perut,* ravenous, nearly starving.

kempu [KN] a large-lidded lacquer round box with handle and trays, for clothes.

kempul [KS], *ter~--~,* slow and laborious (of progress).

kempunan [KS], a calamity, misfortune; unfortunate, owing to not having satisfied an urgent desire to eat some particular thing, e.g. a pregnant woman desires to eat a cuttle-fish: she does not get the cuttle-fish, and dies in childbirth from having neglected to satisfy her desire; so *kena* ~, to fail in one's ambition; *sudah lepas* ~, succeeded his ambition.

kempung [KS], shrunken, esp. about the cheeks (as a toothless man); ~ *pipi,* haggard.

kemudi [KN], a rudder; *ber~,* to steer; ~ *cawat,* a rudder of European type; ~ *sepak,* a paddle-rudder of Malay type; *mengemudikan,* steer, guide; *pengemudi,* helmsman, steerman, pilot; ~ *di haluan,* the rudder in the bows, i.e. in the wrong place; met. for the wrong person in control, esp. of a woman 'wearing the trousers' — cf. *kemudian* and *mudik.*

kemudian [Kktr], after, afterwards, subsequent to; ~ *daripada itu,* subsequently; *hari yang* ~, days to come; *yang ter~,* the last, e.g., in a queue.

kemuk [KS], ~-*kemek,* covered with dents

— cf. *kemek*.

kemumbu [KS], over-full (as mouth).

kemuncak [KN], top, summit, crest.

kemuncup = *cemucup*.

kemungkus [KN], 1. cubebs; medicine made from a sp. of pepper plant *(Piper cubeba)*; a diuretic used to treat dysentery and gonorrhoea. 2. *telur ~*, addled egg, when the chick is formed.

kemuning [KN], a tree yielding a veined yellow wood (*Murraya exotica*), valued for making *kris* handles and scabbards and also furniture.

kemunting [KN], the rose-myrtle (*Rhodomyrtus tomemtosa*); also *kermunting; ~ Cina*, a pink or white periwinkle (*Vinca rosea, Vinca rosea alba*).

kemuruk [KS], Pk. in heaps, in swarms.

kemut [KK], throbbing motion; rising and falling, of a surface; bulging out and deflating; *mulutnya ter~-~*, cheeks bulging and deflating, while eating; *~ lumpur*, partially stuck in the mud, of a boat.

Ken [KN], Skr. a title of Javanese ladies; also *Kin*.

kena [KK], contact; the basic meaning conveyed by this word is 'to come into contact with' or 'have something come into contact with one'. From this basic meaning come almost innumerable 'facets' of meaning in accordance with the context. So, besides mere contact, *~* carries the idea of 'to experience', 'to incur', 'to touch the right spot', 'to hit off exactly'; in the sense of 'incur' it often, in effect, creates what in English is the passive voice; examples: *~*, to hit (a mark); *tak ~*, missed; *~ denda*, to incur a fine; *~ sakit*, to fall ill; *~ tangkap*, to be arrested; *~ tembak*, to be shot; *~ dah itu!*, that went home, that touched the right spot, of a blow, of a smart repartee, of some arrangements that just fits; *jangkit-~*, to make contact (in an electrical circuit); *besok saya ~ pergi Ipoh*, tomorrow I have to go to Ipoh; *duduk salah, berdiri tak ~*, can't sit right and can't stand properly, i.e. all in a

fluster; *tiket saya sudah ~*, my ticket has 'touched' (of a winning ticket in a lottery); *betul-betul ~ pada batang hidung dia*, that hit him right on the bridge of the nose, i.e. touched him on a sore spot, 'went home'; *ter~*, to come sharply or unexpectedly into contact; *kaki ter~ pada batu*, foot knocked against a stone; sometimes *ter~* by itself conveys the idea of 'caught out', e.g. got cheated, ran into trouble; but, *undi ter~ pada dia*, the lot fell on him; *mengenakan*, to affix, to fit on; to impose (a tax); sometimes, to deceive (put it over someone); *ber~an dengan*, connected with, relating to; *perkara ini tidak ber~an dengan agama*, this matter has nothing to do with religion; *tidak ~* can mean, unsuitable; *tidak ~ pada tempat dan saatnya*, unsuitable to the place and the occasion.

kenal [KS], *mengenal* or *mengenali*, to recognise; to identify, establish the identity of; *~an*, an acquaintance; *pengenalan*, introduction (as to book); *ter~*, celebrated, well-known; *per~kan*, to introduce; *kad pengenalan*, identity card; *~-~ Cina*, to know someone very slightly; *mengenalkan diri*, to introduce oneself; *~ dirinya sendiri*, to know oneself; *ber~an dengan*, to get acquainted with; *~ biasa*, to know intimately; *ter~ jahat*, notorious; *tidak ter~*, unknown.

kenaling [KS], shaky with fear.

kenan [KS], 1. *ber~*, to take kindly to something; *memper~kan*, to approve, to assent to. 2. congenital deformity or weakness.

kenang [KK], *~an*, loving recollection; *~-~an*, keepsake; memories; *~kan*, to regret; to recall affectionately; to recall and ponder over (an event or subject); to recollect, call to mind; *mengenang budi*, to feel grateful.

kenanga [KN], a tree with scented green flowers (*Cananga odorata*).

kenantan [KS], white all over (of a fighting-cock); also *Sinantan*.

kenap [KN], servant, waiter.

kenapa [Kktr], why?, for what reason? = *kena apa?*

kenari [KN], 1. Eng. canary-seed (*Canarium commune*); *burung ~*, the canary. 2. *pokok ~*, a shade tree, the Java almond.

kenas [KN], shell-fish preserved in brine (with rice, sago, etc.).

kencana [KN], Skr. gold (in lit. language); = *mas* (in coll. language).

kencang [KS], stiff (of a breeze); blowing freely; vigorous, of movement; *se~*, a force, impetus, of wind; *ribut taufan se~ 120 batu sejam memukul Hongkong*, a typhoon of a force of 120 miles per hour struck Hongkong.

kencar [KS], *ter~~*, hurriedly, to and fro, flurried.

kenceng [KN], 1. a Chinese drill worked with a bow. 2. a kettle.

kencing [KK], passing urine; *sakit ~*, gonorrhoea or other urethral trouble; *cakit ~ manis*, diabetes; *sakit ~ batu*, gallstone, calculus; *sakit ~ nanah*, gonorrhoea; *air ~*, urine; *ter~*, to wet oneself; *ubat melawaskan ~*, a diuretic; *kalau guru ~ berdiri, murid ~ berlari*, i.e., pupils are apt to carry the results of their teaching to extremes; *seperti kuda ~ depan*, a blather-sklte.

kencong [KN], 1. *kasut ~*, a kind of slipper with upturning toes. 2. *akar ~*, a large climbing plant (*Melodorum manubriatum*). 3. = *mengencung*, to deviate from the course; to go in another direction; *mengencungkan*, to distort (facts, discriptions etc.).

kencup [KS], coming to a point; budding; folded up, like a bud.

kendak [KN], mistress or guilty lover; *ber~*, to commit adultery or fornication.

kendali [KN], Jav. the bridle of a horse; *~kan*, to control, to manage, to restrain.

kendara [KK], Skr. *kenderaan*, a mount, a steed, a vehicle, a carriage; *mengendarai*, to ride, to be mounted on, to be borne on.

kendati [KN], 1. desire, wish; = *kehendak hati*. 2. *kendatipun* [Kphbg], although, though.

kenderi [KN], Tam. a measure of weight, a 'candareen'.

kendi [KN], 1. *burung ~*, a name sometimes given to the curlew (*Numenius arquata*), to the whimbrel (*M. phoeopus*) and to the large sandpiper (*Limosa limosa*), and sometimes limited to the *limosa*. 2. Skr. gem; *nila-~*, the sapphire. 3. Malayalam, a water vessel with a spout, a water kettle.

kendiri [Kgn], self, oneself; = *sendiri*.

kendit [KN], a narrow belt, often of coins; also *gendit*.

kendung [KK], carrying in a small fold or wrapper — cf. *kandung* (which refers to carrying on a large scale); *mengendung* is used esp. of carrying a baby in a sort of sling formed by a scarf or sarong tied round the neck; cf. *ambin*.

kendur [KS], loose, slack, not taut; relaxed, of tension; *ghairahmu ~*, your enthusiasm is slackening.

kenduri [KN], Pers. a feast; *~ arwah*, feast in honour of the dead; *~ meniga, ~ menujuh*, feasts held on the third and seventh day after a death.

kengkang [KS], walking with the knees wide apart; the walk of a bowlegged man; not apparently merely a variant of *kangkang*, which conveys the idea of having the feet wide apart.

kengking [KS], *ter~~*, the legs apart (as a dog running or of a man disabled).

kengkeng [KN], 1. raising a foot or paw; resting one knee on the other. 2. the yapping, 'tonquing' of dogs.

kening [KN], the brows; *bulu ~*, the hair on the eyebrows; *belum terangkat ~nya*, before 7 o'clock in the morning; *sudah terangkat ~*, about 8 a.m.; *angkat ~*, look of mutual understanding.

kenit [KS], tiny, of a person; *Awang Kenit*, Tom Thumb; also *kenik*.

kenjang [KK], *mengenjang*, to dig.

kenjur [KS], erect, stiff (of leaves).

kental [KS], thick (of a fluid); only slightly viscous; firm, as a sound potato;

mengental, to congeal, congealing; ke~an, viscosity; darah itu mudah mengental, blood clots easily.

kentang [KN], ubi ~, the potato (*Solanum tuberosum*).

kentung [KN], ~-~, a wooden sounding-block used at a private mosque.

kentut [KN], ber~, to break wind; fart; ter~, to let a fart by accident.

kenung [KN], a small copper gong forming part of the *gamelan*.

kenyal [KS], pliable to the touch; resilient, elastic.

kenyam [KK], N.S. tasting by touching the lips.

kenyang [KS], satisfied, sated; mengenyangkan, filling; makanan ini tidak akan cukup mengenyangkan kamu, this food won't be sufficient to satisfy your hunger.

kenyir [KS], lusting after; = *ingin*.

kenyit [KK], spasmodic, of movement of the lips or eyelids, hence, 'summer lightning'; mengenyit, to flash (briefly); ter~-~, blinking rapidly; mengenyit mata (pada), to wink at; mengenyit also means to twitch, pull slightly.

kenyut [KK], sucking movement.

kepada [Kdpn], to (a person); telah diberikan ~nya, it has been given to him.

kepah [KN], a generic name for a number of bivalve shells (esp. of the genus *Capsa*).

kepak [KN], the wing of birds; mengepak-ngepak, to flap the wings.

kepak [KK], to break off (as a branch from a tree or a piece from a stick of sugar).

kepal [KN], a lump; a clot; a coagulated mass (of cooked rice); ais ~, balls of crushed and flavoured ice, sold by hawkers; mengepalkan tangan, to clench the fist.

kepala [KN], Skr. head; (by metaphor) fountain, source; ~ angin, empty-headed, frivolous; flighty, feckless, irresponsible; tunjukkan ~ batu (kepada), to present an unyielding front (to), behave icily (to); be pig-headed; ~ besar, conceited, arrogant, proud, to

act big; ~ kampung, headman (of village); mengepalai, to be in charge; menjadi ~ berita, to make headlines; ~ keretapi, the locomotive, engine, of a train; ~ kain, the narrow strip of a sarong worn at the back; ~ berat, heavy-witted, dull; ~ kongsi, the head of a secret society; ~ ringan, intelligent; ~ surat, the heading to a letter; ~ susu, cream; batu ~, the cranium; pening ~, dizzy; sakit ~, headache; ~ mayat, an offering of money (N.S.), or a weapon (Pah.), made to the ruler by a chief elected to succeed a chief deceased; tak ada ~-ekor, confused, no head or tail (of a story).

kepalang [KS], of little account; ordinary; bukan ~, out of the common; alang ~, id.; sometimes the bukan is omitted so that ~ alone may mean, out of the ordinary; alang-~, half-hearted; sudah ~ sekarang, it's too late now; bukan ~, tremendous, extraordinary.

kepam [KS], bleached by the sun; faded, sub-fusc through age.

keparat [KS], Ar. unbelieving, infidel (as a term of abuse).

kepari [KN], daun pokok ~, mint.

kepatil [KN], small adze for planing.

kepaya [KN], buah ~, the papaya fruit; better buah betik.

kepayang [KN], a tree (*Pangium edule*); its fruit is proverbially pretty but dangerous to eat; hence the saying, buah ~, dimakan mabuk, dibuang sayang, the ~ fruit — if you eat it, it makes you dizzy, but you are loth to throw it away [esp. (fig.) dangerous love-affairs].

kepeng [KN], a small coin; a 'cash' or fractional part of a cent.

kepet [KS], unwashed (of the abaimana) — a term of abuse.

kepialu [KN], demam ~, fever with delirium; a severe type of fever, typhoid.

kepil [KS], adjoining, alongside; ber~-~, in line side by side, ~kan, to draw up alongside.

keping [KS], a fragmentary portion, a piece; a numerical coefficient of flat objects; e.g., planks; ~an, pieces; in pieces (not a solid whole); a portion; a wad; a flake; a particle.

kepingin [Kktr], Ind. longing, yearning.

kepir [KK], a jerk with the hand or finger; to shake out (as a pipe).

kepiran [KS], scored off, diddled, neglected.

kepit [KK], to press between connected surfaces, e.g., between the arm and the body; *mengepit,* to carry under the arm — cf. *apit, sepit,* etc.; *ber~ tangan,* arm-in-arm.

kepiting [KN], an edible marine crab; (fig.) a miser.

kepompong [KN], a chrysalis.

kepudang [KN], Ind. *burung ~,* the golden oriole.

kepuh [KS], 1. full (as the sails of a ship); bulging out; *mengepuh,* to fill, of sails, to belly out. 2. *gantung ~,* Pk. to put up hangings in a raja's court. 3. whitish-grey.

kepuk [KN], a large round tun for storing rice; *berdoa sampai dua ~ banyaknya,* to pray at great length (viewing each extension of the hands as a handful); sometimes used for a small box or case; cf. *gepuk.*

kepul [KN], closely packed; clotted; thick (as smoke); *mengepul,* to rise in thick clouds, as dust or smoke.

kepulaga [KN], cardamon (*Amomum cardamomum*).

kepum [KS], shrunken (of the cheeks); hollow and drawn; also *kempung.*

kepung [KK], 1. *ber~,* to patrol round and round; to blockade; *mengepung,* to besiege, to surround, to cut off retreat, to outflank, to make a pincer-movement; *ter~,* invested, hemmed in; *~an,* brackets. 2. *pokok ~,* a tree (*Shorea sp.*).

kera [KN], the common long-tailed monkey (*Macacus cynomolgus*); *periuk ~,* the 'monkey cup' or pitcher plant (Nepenthes); *~ duka,* the slow loris (*Nycticebus tardigradus*); *gembala ~,* a bird (*Eupetes macrocercus*); *hamba ~,*

the racquet-tailed drongo (*Dissemurus platurus*); *~ sumbang,* (met.) an unsociable person, a 'lone wolf'; a 'leper'; *kalau bunga diberikan kepada ~, hancurlah bunga itu,* if you give flowers to a monkey, they will be destroyed, i.e. don't cast pearls before swine; *hanya segenggam ~,* only as much as a monkey could hold in its paw, i.e. skimpy, esp. of food supplied; *selebar sekangkang ~,* as much as a monkey could straddle, i.e. a tiny piece (of land); *sebagai ~ kena belacan,* to be very restless.

kerabat [KK], 1. climbing up, swarming up, clinging (as a climber to a tree); *ikat ~,* a knot in several coils. 2. Ar. relations; *kaum ~,* id.; in some parts used only of Royal families; *~ diraja,* royal family.

kerabik [KS], *kerobak~,* picking or plucking to pieces.

kerabu [N], 1. a tiny 'stud' earring. 2. a sort of salad made of fish, prawns and cucumber. 3. a tree (*Xanthophyllum refum* or *Lophopetallum fimbriatum*).

keracak [KN], ripples, 'cat's-paws' on the water.

keracang = *kerajang.*

keracap [KN], a wooden musical instrument used in menora performances.

kerah [KK], to call people together for forced labour, mutual defence, etc.; *juru ~,* an official sub-ordinate of the *batin* or chief of *Jakun* tribes; *ju-~,* id.; *gong pengerah,* a gong used for summoning people to meet; *~an,* conscription, general call-up; *~an umum,* id.; *menerima ~an,* to be called up, mobilization.

kerai [KN], *rotan ~,* a valuable rattan (*Doemonoropus geniculatus*). 2. = *gerai.* 3. *ikan ~,* a freshwater fish (*Cyprid genus*).

kerajang [KS], *mass ~,* tinsel, gold foil.

kerak [KN], 1. the scorched bits of food adhering to the sides of the saucepan; refuse in cooking; crusted dirt; *burung ~ nasi,* Treng. the malkoha — cf. *cenok; besar periuk, besar ~nya,* i.e. the bigger the income, the bigger the expenses or debts. 2. (onom.) a crackling sound.

kerakal [KN], *batu* ~, pebbles, coarse gravel (bigger than *kelikir*).

kerakap [KN], 1. *sirih* ~, the larger (and coarser) *sirih* leaves; inferior *sirih* leaf. 2. a plant growing near water; *macam* ~ *tumbuh di batu*, like a ~ plant growing on stone, i.e. a hard life, to live miserably.

keram = *ram*.

keramat [KS], Ar. miracle-working; invested with supernatural power (of a place, object, or person); *wali* ~ or *datuk* ~, the saint buried in a wonder-working shrine; a genius loci; *di timpa* ~, slain by unseen powers for sacrilege at a sacred spot; an animal, e.g. a tiger or a crocodile, which frequents a locality without doing any harm is often looked upon vaguely as ~ (and should not be shot).

karambit [KN], a narrow-bladed curved dagger.

kerampang [KN], the fork; the point of junction of the lower limbs.

keran [KN], a small portable brazier.

kerana [Kphbg], Skr. because; owing to; for the sake of; ~ *Allah,* for God's sake; better ~.

keranda [KN], Skr. a three-plank coffin.

kerang [KN], 1. a generic name for a number of shell-fish (*Arca sp.*), esp. cockles; *kulit* ~, sometimes used for sea-shells generally and ~-~*an* for shell-fish generally. 2. (onom.), *ber*~, to clang; *kerung-* ~, a clanging sound.

kerang [KS], ~-*keruh,* uneven, irregular (as writing on unruled paper).

kerangka [KN], basic framework; *tulang* ~, skeleton; cf. *rangka*.

kerani [KN], Hind. a clerk, a writer; ~ *besar,* chief clerk; ~ *kiriman,* despatch clerk.

keranjang [KN], a coarsely made basket, hamper, crate; *tali* ~, a specious rogue; *mata* ~, a roving eye (for women); *bola* ~, basketball.

keranji [KN], a generic name for a number of trees (*Dailium sp.*)

kerap [KS], frequent, close of texture; ~

kali, often; ~*i,* to repeat, e.g., a dose of medicine.

kerapu [KN], a kind of sea-perch, a grouper; *muka* ~, ugly and grubby-looking.

keras [KS], hard, stiff; obstinate; rigid, inelastic; loud of voice; ~ *kepala,* stubborn; ~-~ *kerak nasi,* as stubborn as rice-crust is stubborn, i.e. can be softened (cf. *kerak*); ~ *lembut,* tempo and stress, of a tune; ~ *hati,* obdurate (not necessarily cruel); *kotak (alat) pengeras suara,* loudspeaker; *buah* ~, the candle-nut (*Aleurites moluccanus*); *minuman* ~, strong drink; ~*i,* to press for, to insist; ~*kan,* to stiffen, to harden; ~ *kematu,* hard, of fruit which refuses to ripen; *ber*~ *nak,* to insist on (doing something); *ber*~ *tekak,* stubborn and vociferous; *menggunakan ke*~*an jenayah,* to use criminal force; *dasar ke*~*an,* a policy of force; *jangan bertindak dengan ke*~*an,* don't resort to violence.

kerat [KK], 1. sever, cut off; *se*~, a portion cut off, a line of a poem; ~ is also used for giving a decision; ~*an,* a piece cut off; *anak* ~*an,* a (plant) cutting; *se*~ *jalan,* half-way; *jalan se*~ *(sahaja),* a cul-de-sac; *dengan tulang dua* ~, with nothing but o's pair of hands. 2. Ar. a carat, a measure of weight for diamonds. 3. *mengerat,* to gnaw, esp. noisily; *mengerat gigi,* to grind the teeth.

keratun [KN], Jav. the abode of a prince (*ratu*); a palace.

kerawai [KN], a large wasp making its home in the ground.

kerawak [KN], *tupai* ~, a squirrel.

kerawang [KN], open-work, fret-work; *ber*~, fretted, e.g., of pierced brass-work; having open-work, e.g., of lace, etc.

kerawat [KN], a rattan fastening connecting the iron of an adze with the handle.

kerawit [KN], *cacing* ~, intestinal worms, pin-worms; thread-worms; also used for hook-worms.

kerayau [KK], to wander about; cf. *rayau*.

kerbang [KN], a tree whose bark is used for cording.

kerbas [KK], to shake vigorously; a frequentative of *kebas*.

kerbat [KN], enfolding in many folds; winding round, binding (as a cricket bat).

kerbau [KN], a buffalo; ~ *balar*, a pink buffalo; ~ *China*, ~ *pendek*, euphem. for 'pig'; ~-*jalang*, wild buffalo; *membeli ~ di padang*, to buy a pig in a poke.

kerbuk [KK], boring into; gnawing into; *nyiur sudah di~ tupai*, the coconut has been gnawed by the squirrel, i.e. the maiden is a maiden no longer, a gibe at an unmarried girl.

kercut [KN], 1. a common sedge used in mat-making and for sails (*Scirpus mucronatus*). 2. a sack of that sedge.

kerda [KN], a curry-comb; also keruk.

kerdam [KN], (onom.), *kerdum-~*, a continuous thumping sound.

kerdil [KS], undersized (of men, animals).

kerdip [KN], ~*an mata*, wink of the eye.

kerdut [KS], wrinkled, crumpled, creased.

keredak [KS], dirty, caked with filth (of person's crockery).

kerek [KN], the tyre of a wheel; the small wheel inside a pulley; *se~*, a 'round' (as of palm-sugar).

kerekot [KS], shrivelled up into a coil; curling (as paper exposed to heat); curling up (as a dog); *orang ~*, a miser (who 'coils round money'); *tidur mengerekot*, to sleep curled up.

kerenah [KS], caprice; *ada banyak ~*, capricious.

kerencang [KN], (onom.) chinking, clinking, clanking.

kerencat [KS], dwarfed (of men, trees).

kerencing [KN], the triangle (musical instrument).

kerengga [KN], the red ant or tailor ant (*Decophylla smaragdina*).

kerengkil [KK], to spread (of skin disease).

kerenyang [KS], *ter~-~*, snarling, showing teeth in nervous anger, of a dog; also *kernyang* and *kernying*.

kerenyih [KS], *ter~*, smiling broadly.

kerepek [KN], tapioca or banana which has been thinly sliced and fried.

kerepes [KK], feeling about for something

(with the fingers only).

kereput [KS], shrivelling up round a central point (as a boil), wrinkled, shrunk.

keresek [KN], sand, gravel.

keresing [KS], just revealing the interior (as parted lips or as a crack in fruit).

keresut [KK], puckering the forehead.

kereta [KN], a carriage; a generic name for wheeled vehicles; a car; ~ *sorong*, a wheelbarrow; ~ *keranda*, a hearse; ~ *mayat*, id.; ~ *kanak-kanak*, a pram; ~ *tolak*, a wheeled chair; ~ *angin*, a switchback railway; (sometimes) a bicycle; ~ *api*, a railway; *landasan ~ api*, a railway sleeper; also, the track generally; *jalan ~ api*, the railway line; ~ *api mel*, the mail train; (see *gerabak* and *gerobok*); ~ *becak*, a jinrikisha; ~ *lanca*, Pk., Pen., id.; ~ *kerbau*, a buffalo-cart; ~ *lereng*, a bicycle (semi-obsolete); ~ *sewa*, a hackney carriage; *pasang ~*, to harness the horses to a carriage; the original meaning was probably simply 'wheel'; a child's hoop is still called ~.

keretapi [KN], = *kereta api*.

keretut [KS], crinkled, uneven.

keri [KN], a small sickle for cutting out weeds from a field of growing padi.

keriat [KN], (onom.), ~-*keriut*, creaking (of rowlocks or of a door).

keriau [KK], to cry out; clamouring.

keribas [KK], shaking vigorously — cf. *kibas*.

kerical [KN], the slave of a slave; a term of extreme self-abasement.

keridik [KN], the mole-cricket.

kerikal [KN], a large salver or tray.

kerikil [KN], *batu ~*, flints, pebbles, gravel.

keriling [KS], Pah. *ber~*, twisted (of branches).

kerimah [KN], a princess (in high-flown language).

kering [KS], dry; *batuk ~*, consumption, phthisis; *ikan ~*, dried fish; *tulang ~*, the shin; ~ *kuntang*, completely dried up; *alat pengering rambut*, a hair-drier; *pengeringan*, drainage (of marsh land); *musim ~*, dry season; *tanah ~*, dry land.

keringat [KN], Ind. sweat; (in Malaysia)

us. refers to 'the sweat of one's brow' rather than physical sweat).

kerinting [KN], 1. shellfish dried for preservation. 2. = *keriting*.

kerip [KK], (onom.), *mengerip,* to gnaw (as mice).

keris [KN], a 'kris' or Malay dagger; ~ *alang,* a straight kris of medium length; ~ *cerita,* a long kris with fifteen or seventeen curves in the blade; ~ *coban,* a kris with a piece running down the centre of the blade; ~ *lendayan,* a long kris with a sword-handle; ~ *pandak,* a short straight kris; ~ *panjang,* a kris with a long and narrow blade used for executing criminals; ~ *picit,* a kris of a type believed to have been worked by mere finger-pressure; ~ *sepukal,* the common straight kris (intermediate in length between the ~ *alang* and ~ *pandak*); ~ *berlok,* ~ *berkaluk,* a sinuous, wavy kris; ~ *sempana,* the common sinuous-bladed kris (with seven curves in the blade); ~ *silam upih,* a kris like the ~ *sepukal* but with a narrower blade; ~ *sonak udang,* a Raman type of the ~ *sempana;* ~ *tajang,* a straight-bladed Patani kris with the typical 'kingfisher's head' handle; *buntut* ~, the ferrule at the base of the kris-sheath; *hulu* ~, the kris-handle; *sampir* ~, that portion of the kris-sheath which covers the guard of the kris; *sarung* ~, the kris-sheath; *ukas* ~, a shell (*malleus*) resembling a kris-sheath.

kerisi [KN], *ikan* ~, a sea-bream (*Synagris sp.*); *ikan* ~ *bali,* another var. (*Scolopsis bilineatus*).

kerisik [KK], *berkerisik,* to rustle; *daun-daunan ber*~ *kerana ditiup angin,* the leaves rustled in the wind.

kerit [KN], (onom.) a scraping or scratching sound; ~*an api,* matches — cf. *gerit.*

kerita [KN], *ikan* ~, an octopus.

keritik [KN], Eng. criticism, esp. literary; *peng*~, a critic.

keriting [KS], *rambut* ~, curly hair; extremely curly; *kedai* ~ *rambut,* women's hair-dressing saloon; *meng*~*kan rambut,* to curl (perm) the hair; ~ *asli,* naturally curly.

kerja [KN], Skr. work, business, profession; *pe*~*an,* work, occupation; ~*kan,* to effect, to do the job thoroughly; (fig.) to 'put it across someone', 'give him the works'; to deal with (some article); process it; ~ *biasa,* usual work, routine; ~ *keras,* hard work; ~ *berat,* hard labour, esp. in jail; *be*~, usually means 'to celebrate', 'have a feast', e.g., for a wedding; *be*~ *sama,* co-operative; *pe*~, a worker; *pusat mencari pe*~*an,* Labour Exchange; ~ *lambat-lambat,* a 'go slow' (cf. *mogok*); ~ *mengikut peraturan,* a 'work to rule'; *pe*~*an sepenuh masa,* a full time job; *pe*~*an sambilan,* a part-time job; *be*~ *mati-matian,* to work himself to death; *be*~ *lembur,* to work overtime; *teman se*~, colleagues; *sedang be*~, to be at work; *mengerjakan,* to perform; *apa pe*~*anmu datang ke mari?* what do you want here?

kerjang [KK], 1. kicking out with the hind-legs (of a horse); *ter*~-~, prancing; galloping along; the basic meaning appears to be, stretching out the legs — cf. *rejang.* 2. = *kerajang.*

kerkak [KN], (onom.) crunching (of an animal crunching a bone); ~-*mengerkah,* crunching and munching.

kerkau [KK], clawing, lacerating.

kerkut [KN], a chain for closing a door.

kerlap [KK], 1. glistening; *mengerlap,* to glitter. 2. *ter*~, twisted, turned over (as foot).

kerling [KN], a side-glance; *mengerling,* to give a side glance at a person.

kerlip [KN], flickering — cf. *kelip; mengerlip,* to twinkle; ~*an bintang-bintang,* twinkle of the stars.

kerluk [KK], feeling with fingers; e.g., for a bone in the throat.

kerma [KN], Skr. a curse; *jatuh* ~, the falling of a curse; *papa* ~, an accident. 2. Skr. *Betara Kerma,* or *Kerma Wijaya,* the Hindu Cupid (*Kama*) or conquering god of love.

kermah [KN], *siput* ~, a shell (*Oliva subu-*

lata or *nobilis*).

kermak [KN], a plant, the leaves of which are eaten (*Staurogyne setigera*).

kermangka [KN], a plant (*Aracoena Maingayi*).

kermunting [KN], the rose-myrtle (*Rhodomyrtus tomentosa*); also *kemunting*.

kernai [KK], Kel. slicing into small pieces.

kernying [KK], angry, snarling.

kernyit [KN], *mengernyitkan alis*, knitting or raising the brows (as a signal or hint).

kernyut [KN], 1. *kernyat-~*, throbbing convulsively. 2. *kernyat-~*, creaking.

kerobang-kerobek [KS], Pk. dilapidated, broken down; (fig.) untidy, shabby.

kerobek [KS], *~-kelebek,* a pinch of anything; picking out a very small portion of anything; *mengerobek*, to tear off a piece from; to tear to pieces.

korobok [KN], a provision-hamper.

kerocap [KK], to crunch

kerocok [KN], a sort of rattle used to attract the *parang-parang* fish, etc.

kerodak [KN], dregs, sediment.

keromong [KN], a series of gongs forming part of a Javanese orchestra.

kerompang [KS], missing, of a tooth; showing a gap; a variant of *rompang*.

keroncong [KN], 1. a large tinkling anklet. 2. a rough bell or clapper, e.g., for bullocks. 3. a kind of plaintive Malay song. 4. bunt or inmost pocket of seine-net. 5. *ber~*, to rumble, as an empty stomach.

keroncor [KN], the male king-crab; *seperti ~ dengan belangkas*, like the male and female king-crabs, i.e. inseparable (because a pair of king-crabs habitually walk clinging together); also *keronco* and *konco.*

kerong [KN], *~-~*, ship's scuppers; *ikan ~-~*, a fish (*Sebastes stolizkoe*).

kerongkong [KN], the gullet; *~an*, id.; *pemasah ~*, a 'nip', a 'wet'; *sakit ~*, sore throat; *penyakit ~*, soreness of throat, generally meaning diptheria.

kerongsang [KN], = *kerosang*.

kerontang [KS], parched, extremely dry; *kering ~*, id.

keropas [KN], *~-kerapis,* odds and ends.

keropok [KN], a crisp wafer made of flour and mashed fish or prawns.

kerosang [KN], a Malay brooch.

kerosek [KK], (onom.) to wash rice; to scrape the scales of fish — cf. *kosek.*

kerosok [KN], (onom.) rustling and crackling (of dry leaves).

kerotong [KK], *mengerotong*, swarming (as ants).

keroyok [KK], Ind. to attack simultaneously, mob.

kerpai [KN], a powder-flask.

kerpak [KN], (onom.) the sound of crackling; so, a bird-scarer, acting by crackling and waving about.

kerpas [KN], 1. (onom.) rustling. 2. dregs, sediment, lees. 3. to dust.

kersai [KS], crisp (of cooked rice).

kersang [KS], 1. dry and stiff (of the hair), arid (of the soil); cf. *gersang*. 2. = *kerosang.*

Kersani [KN], besi ~, Khorassan iron; iron of proof.

kersik [KN], 1. (onom.) a rustling sound. 2. gravel, coarse sand; also *gersik.*

kertak [KN], 1. a bridge; also *gertak*. 2. (onom.) a dull, cracking sound; *~-kertuk*, cracking (rattling), sound of shoes, door; *ber~ gigi*, to grind the teeth.

kertang [KN], 1. covered with dirty sores. 2. *ikan ~*, a sp. of perch.

kertap [KN], (onom.) a sound such as that of a door being closed; *mengertap*, to close or come together with a crash; *~-kertup*, to give a slap sound.

kertas [KN], Ar. paper; *~ kembang* or *~ tekap*, blotting-paper; *mas ~*, gold leaf; *~ papan*, cardboard; *~ lap*, blotting paper; *~ jeluang*, tissue paper; *~ khabar*, a newspaper; *wang ~*, paper money, notes; *~-kerja*, written dissertation, 'paper'; *penindih ~*, paper-weight; *~ belacan*, paper wrapped round belacan; (fig.) only fit to be thrown away (said esp. of hoarded wealth).

kertau [KN], 1. a small insect destructive to cloth. 2. an evil spirit dangerous at child-birth.

kertuk [KN], 1. (onom.) the sound of rapping. 2. a cattle-bell. 3. Kel. a kind of drum.

keruan [KS], Jav. *tiada ~,* indescribable; in utter confusion; and so, rotten, useless; = *tak ketahuan.*

kerubung [KK], 1. gathering together of people; mobbing; = *kerumun; ~i* or *mengerbungi,* to mob, to overwhelm by numbers. 2. a padi barn built of pandan leaves.

kerubut [KN], 1. a plant (*Thottea grandiflora*). 2. a padi barn. 3. *mengerubut,* to crowd round in a disorderly manner, to mob.

kerucut [KN], a cone.

kerudut = *kerdut.*

keruh [KS], 1. turbid (of water); troubled, glum (of face); ~ *hati,* malicious; *ke~an,* (fig.) bad feeling, trouble; *suasana keruh,* time of confusion; *menangguk di air ~,* to fish (with a lift-net) in troubled waters. 2. (onom.), *mengeruh,* the sound of snoring; snoring.

keruing [KN], a generic name for a number of trees yielding a special kind of oil (*Dipterocarpus sp.*); *minyak ~,* the oil so yielded.

keruit [KN], 1. wagging (of the tip) (e.g. of the tip of a cat's tail). 2. *burung ~,* the Eastern golden plover.

keruk [KN], 1. (onom.) a dull, cracking sound; the croak of a frog. 2. scrapping, rasping; *~~,* a curry-comb. 2. a fruit-fly; = *bari-bari.* 4. to eat away, erode, as water eats away a bank; as expenses eat away profits; to burrow.

kerukut [KK], curling round; curling up; warping or shrivelling, as a leaf.

kerul [KS], trimmed or barbered (of the hair).

kerulit [KN], twinkling.

kerumit [KK], 1. to gnaw. 2. crawling progress; *jalan ter~~,* id.

kerumun [KK], *ber~,* to mass together; *~i,* to mob; *lalat-lalat mengerumuni makanan yang terdedah,* the flies swarmed on the uncovered food.

kerumus [KK], wild hugging; *ber~,* hugging and kissing wildly, as persons meeting after long parting.

keruntil [KS], abundant (of hanging fruit).

kerunting [KN], a wooden clapper.

keruntung [KN], = *kantung.*

kerup [KN], (onom.) sound of munching.

keruping [KN], the scab over a healing wound — cf. *kuping.*

kerusi [KN], Ar. a chair; a seat generally; ~ *panjang,* a long chair; ~ *malas,* id.; ~ *lunjur,* id.; ~ *ungkang-ungkit,* a rocking chair; ~ *bertilam empuk,* a well-padded chair; *terlucut dari ~nya,* unseated, of a elected member; *pengerusi,* chairman.

kerusut [KS], very much entangled — cf. *kusut.*

kerut [KS], 1. creasing up, puckering up, frowning; *ber~,* wrinkled, lined; *~~an,* wrinkles; *ber~~,* wrinkled; corrugated. 2. (onom.) a rasping sound.

kerutu [KS], wrinkled, lined, creased, rough to the touch; like the skin of a toad; *ber~,* gnarled.

kerutup [KN], 1. (onom.) a crakling sound. 2. Pen. assault by a gang.

keruyup [KS], uxorious.

kesa [KN], first, the first (from *sa*).

kesah [KS], restless; *keluh ~,* sighing and restless (as a lover).

kesah [KN], Ar. narrative; alk., 'the story runs' — a common exordium to a paragraph; ~ is sometimes used to mean events, affairs; *mengesahkan,* to tell the story of, recount; sometimes, N.S. to busy oneself with, look after.

kesak [KK], edging about, shifting uneasily in one's seat — cf. *kesah.*

kesal [KS], Jav. repentant, feeling regret or concern, = *sesal.*

kesambi [KN], a tree (*Antidesma ghoesembilla*).

kesan [KN], = *berkasan,* the footprint of an animal; a dent or mark left by pressure; (fig.) effects, consequences; *ber~,* effective leaving its mark; *secara ber~,* in an effective manner; *~-balas,* repercussions; *pengesan, pengesan jejak,* a tracker; *mengesan,* to track; (fig.) to seek traces of (e.g., tin).

kesang [KK], 1. = *esang; mengesang,* to blow the nose. 2. an insect destructive to crops; apparently = *kesip* 4.

kesat [KS], 1. rough to the touch; coarse of surface-texture. 2. to wipe moisture off the smooth surface; *mengesat mata,* to wipe the eyes; *pengesat kaki,* door mat.

kesbih [KN], *pokok* ~ = *pokok tasbih,* the canna.

kesek [KK], rubbing or scraping a sharp edge against anything (used esp. of playing the violin); also *gesek.*

kesel = *gesel.*

kesian [KS], what a pity!, pity (him)!; a variant of *kasihan;* see *kasih.*

kesik [KN], (onom.) ~-~, rustling, whispering — cf. *kesu-kesi.*

kesing = *kesang.*

kesip [KS], 1. lacking kernel (of fruit); pipless; wizened; *buta* ~, blind when the eyeball is destroyed. 2. gone down (of a boil). 3. to suck the fingers, fruit, etc. 4. Kel. = *piang-gang.*

kesmak [KN], dried parsimmons imported from China.

kesmaran [KS], Skr. and Jav. in love, love; = *berahi; edan* ~, madly in love; = *gila berahi,* anxious, perplexed; (from asmara).

Kesna [KN], Skr. *Betara* ~, the Hindu divinity Krishna.

Kesturi [KN], Skr. musk; a type of small lime.

kesu [KN], (onom.), ~-*kesi,* the sound of whispering — cf. *kesik.*

kesuari [KN], *burung* ~, a cassowary; may be used of any bird of the ostrich family.

kesuir [KS], hairy in the nostrils.

kesuma [KN], Skr. a flower; (fig.) a beautiful woman or youth.

kesumat [KS], grudge; *dendam* ~, rancour.

kesumba [KN], Skr. the arnotto (*Bixa orellana*); a red dye; red; dyed red; *burung* ~, the trogon.

kesup [KN], 1. (onom.) a sucking sound. 2. bowed with head between shoulders.

kesut [KS], = insult; move slowly and quietly.

ketagih [KK], crave, yearn, see *tagih.*

ketai [KS], *ber*~, crumbling to pieces.

ketak [KN], 1. a crease, a fold, a wrinkle; *ber*~, crinkled (of the hair); in folds. 2. *ber*~, to cackle, of a hen; *leher ber*~ *tiga,* a throat with three creases (beauty idea).

ketam [KN], 1. a plane; planing; *tahi* ~, shavings. 2. a small reaping knife; *mengetam,* to harvest; (*alat*) *pengetam rambut letrik,* an electric hair-cutter. 3. a generic name for crabs; ~ *batu,* the stone crab (the crab us. eaten); ~ *angin,* the sand-crab; ~ *jabut,* the boring crab; *lumpur* ~, caked mud (in which boring crabs make their holes); ~ *bersepit,* bepincered crabs, derisive nickname for Chinese; ~ *nak mengajar anak berjalan betul,* the crab (which walks sideways) wants to teach its child to walk straight: presumption, 'look who's talking!'

ketan [KN], Jav. dry glutinous rice.

ketang [KS], taut, astretch; ~ *ke dada,* tight over the breast (of a garment); ~ is also used for a tight band or cover, esp. a rubber band.

ketap [KK], *mengetap bibir,* to bite the lips; *mengetapkan gigi,* to set the teeth (determinedly); *mengetapkan gerham,* id.

ketapang [KN], the Indian almond (*Terminalia Catappa*); the tulip tree.

ketar [KS], to quiver; *terketar*-~, trembling all over; quavering, of voice.

ketara [KS], visible; obvious.

ketat [KS], tight, as a stopper or cork; strict; *peraturan di kampus ini* ~, we have strict rules around this campus; *memper*~, to tighten; *mereka memper*~*kan langkah-langkah keselamatan,* they tightened security measures.

ketawa [KK], Ind. to laugh; ~ *tidak bersuara,* to laugh silently; ~ *merendah,* to have a quiet laugh; ~*kan,* to laugh at; a variant of *tawa.*

ketaya [KN], a torch-holder.

ketayap [KN], 1. a small white skull-cap worn under a turban; ~ is sometimes used as a symbol of excessive devotion to the letter of religious rules, 'clericalism'. 2. = *ketiap.*

ketegar [KS], obstinate; (fig.) stiff, as in death.

ketek [KS], *berjalan ter~-~,* strutting (of a short-legged person or animal).

ketela [KN], = *keledek.*

ketelum [KN], Tam. a bastion; also *ketlum.*

ketemu [KK], Ind. = *temu; ~ lagi,* au revoir.

ketengga [KN], *kayu ~,* a very pretty light-coloured veined wood.

keti [Kbil], 1. hundred thousand; *se~,* a hundred thousand; *ber~-~,* in hundreds of thousands. 2. *anak ~,* a ball (used in playing certain obsolete games; and, in literature, a simile for the heads of the slain rolling about a battlefield); also *kuti.*

ketiak [KN], the armpit; *tongkat ~,* a crutch; *seperti ~ ular,* long winded, tedious.

ketial [KS], difficult to remove (as a cork from the mouth of a bottle); *ber~,* in a fix.

ketiap [KN], Pk. *perahu ~,* a house-boat used on rivers.

ketik [KN], the long pair of legs in grasshoppers or crabs; feelers, antennae.

ketika [KN], Skr. time; division of time; period; *pada ~ itu,* at that time; *dengan se~,* immediately; *~ lima* and *~ tujuh,* the division of time into five or seven periods that are lucky or unlucky as the case may be; *bintang ~,* the Pleiades; *temu ~,* Kel., Treng. the period is complete — e.g., of a one-year-old baby.

ketil [KK], a pinch, nipping, *ber~-~,* in tiny pinches, *mengetil,* to cut off a piece.

ketimbal [KS], crawling (of maggots on dead flesh).

ketimpung [KN], (onom.) making a splashing sound (of bathers).

keting [KN], the tendon Achillis.

ketip [KN], 1. the biting of leeches, mosquitoes, ants, nipping slightly between the teeth as a man biting his lips. 2. a very small silver coin; a five-cent piece.

ketipung [KN], a small hand-drum (musical instrument); *ber~,* to splash one's hand on water.

ketiri [KN], Kel. *buah ~,* the cashew nut.

ketis [KK], 1. to jerk off something adhering to a finger or limb. 2. the immediate stalk of a fruit that grows in clusters. 3. N.S. the long legs of a grass-hopper or prawn — cf. *ketik.*

ketitir [KN], *burung ~,* Kel. the barred ground-dove, = *merbuk.*

ketola [KN], a generic name for a number of pumpkins, e.g., *Lua cylindrica* and *Trichosanthes anguina.*

ketoprak [KN], popular stage show of song and dance which is popular in central and east Java.

ketopong [KN], a helmet or shako mentioned in old romances; the air funnel of a ship.

ketua [KS], see *tua;* chief, leader, head; *ber~kan,* to have as leader; *mengetuai,* head, lead, preside.

ketuat [KN], a large wart.

ketubung [KN], the swarming and stinging of hornets; to attack in swarms; *kena ~,* to be attacked by a swarm (of hornets).

ketuit [KN], a wart; *~ nasi,* a tiny wart.

ketuk [KN], (onom.) tapping, rapping; the note of certain birds; a small sounding block; *mengetuk pintu,* to knock on a door; *mengetuk-ngetuk,* to make the sound *tok, tok, tok,* as do nightjars; also *katuk.*

ketul [KN], a thick piece; a clot; a hardish lump; a loaf; *mengetul,* to curl up (as a sleeper).

ketulul [KN], a confederate in an offence; a thieves' spy; a go-between in dealings in stolen property; a procurer.

ketumbar [KN], Tam. coriander (*Coriandrum sativum*).

ketumbit [KN], 1. a herb used in the treatment of skin diseases (*Leucas zeylanica*). 2. a stye in the eye.

ketun [KN], *ringgit ~,* the 'pillar' dollar.

ketung [KN], 1. (onom.) to give out the sound 'tong'; the sound made by a

drum. 2. the stump left when a limb,
tail or branch is cut off; *mengetung,* to
cut so as to leave a stump, as when
cutting *mengkuang.* 3. *semut ~,* a large
black ant.

ketungging [KN], a big black scorpion.

ketup [KN], *~-ketap,* a tapping noise.

ketupat [KN], square or polygonal packet
of cooked rice; *belah ~,* lozenge-shaped.

ketur [KN], 1. Hind. a spittoon for betel
chewers. 2. *ber~,* to croak (of frogs).

ketut [KS], warped, stunted.

kewik [KS], Kel. splay-toed (i.e. with big
toe splayed like a thumb).

khabar [KN], Ar. news; *apa ~?,* what news?,
= how do you do?; *kertas ~,* or *surat ~,* a
newspaper; *tidak ~kan dirinya,*
unconscious; *~ angin,* rumour.

khadam [KN], Ar. a servant, personal attendant.

Khadijah [KN], Ar. *Siti ~,* the first wife of
the Prophet; a Malay female proper
name, commonly shortened to *Tijah*
and *Jah.*

khairat [KN], Ar. charity, alms-giving.

khalayat [KN], Ar. the world of creation
and created things; mankind; the multitude, the public; *di ~ ramai,* in public.

khali [KS], Ar. empty, void; omitting, failing to do.

Khalifah [KN], Ar. Deputy, i.e. Successor,
of the Prophet; *~ almuminin,* Caliph of
the Faithful, i.e. Head of the Muslim
world; *~* is used for 'leaders' of Islamic
or quasi-Islamic movements generally.

Khalik [KN], Ar. God the creator,

khalka [KN], Ar. the creation; *Khalik-ul-~,*
the Creator of created things; God.

Khalkum = halkum.

khalwat [KN], 1. Ar. hermitage; *ber~,* to
go into retreat or seclusion. 2. = *kheluat.*

khamir [KN], Ar. yeast, leaven.

Khamis [KN], Ar. the fifth day of the week;
Thursday; also Ind. *Kemis.*

khanah [KN], Ar. storehouse; *ajaib ~,* museum.

khas [KN], special, reserved for a particular service, opposed to *am; ~kan,* to set
aside for a special purpose, reserve.

khasah [KN], *kain ~,* gauze, muslin.

khasiat [KN], Ar. property, virtue, special
qualities (e.g., of a medicine); *ilmu ~
ubat,* pharmacology.

khat [KN], Ar. handwriting.

khatam [KS], Ar. ended, concluded (esp.
of studies).

khatan [KN], Ar. circumcision.

khatib [KN], Ar. the reader in a mosque;
the chief mosque official after the imam;
the preacher.

khattul-istiwa [KN], Ar. the equator;
daerah ~, the tropics.

khalwat [KK], Kel., Treng., Pah, to associate with a woman in an improper or
indiscreet manner, contrary to Muslim
law; also *keluat.*

khaur, Ar. *~ ul umani aw-satu-ha,* moderation is best in all things; a saying of
the Prophet, often quoted in the newspapers.

khayal [KN], Ar. vision, trance; *~an,* imagination, hallucination, day-dream; *cerita ~an,* a fantasy, fanciful story;
meng~kan, to entrance; *ber~~,* to indulge in daydreams, build castles in
the air; *mabuk ~,* light-headed through
drink, though not drunk.

khazanah [KN], Ar. treasury, strong-room.

khemah [KN], Ar. a tent; *ber~,* to encamp;
menghampar ~, to pitch a tent; *papas
~,* to furl a tent; *tiang ~,* a tent-pole; *tu
mang ~,* a tent-peg.

kherajat [KN], 1. Ar. land-tax; expense; *~
mati,* N.S. funeral expenses. 2. Pk. trim-
mings of bride's hair.

kheranda [KN], a coffin; also *keranda.*

khianat [KN], Ar. deceit, treachery, abuse
of confidence, breach of trust; *orang ~,*
a traitor; *~* is used now for 'sabotage';
membuat ~, to do some treacherous or
harmful action; *peng~,* saboteur; vandal; traitor.

khidmat [KS], Ar. service, obedience;
duties; *ber~,* to serve (as in the Army);
per~an, service, task; government services generally; *per~an kesihatan,* health
service; *per~an perubatan,* medical
service; *per~an gaji,* pay corps; *per~an*

awam, civil service; per~an (negara) kebangsaan, national service; per~an rahsia, secret service.

khilaf [KS], Ar. error, mistake, blundering.

Khizir [KN], Ar. nabi ~, a legendary prophet, said to wander round the world; sometimes alleged to be the wandering Jew; if one meets him on the 27th Ramadzan, one will obtain great good fortune.

khuatir [KS], Ar. fear, apprehension, fancy; also kuatir; meng~i, meng~kan, be worried; ke~an, worry, apprehension.

khula [KN], Ar. divorce from a husband granted on a wife's application.

khurma [KK], Ar. buah ~, a date (fruit); also kurma.

khusus [KS], Ar. particular, special; Treng. settled, decided; meng~kan, to specialize.

khususa [KS], Ar. in particular, particularly.

khusyuk [KS], Ar. devotion; rapt attention; meng~kan, to hold, compel, rapt attention (as a lecture).

khutbah [KN], Ar. the formula of a prayer; a sermon; ~ nikah, the marriage service; membaca ~, to preach a sermon or perform a religious service.

kia [KN], yu ~-~, species of ray (Rhyncobatus) which suggests a shark at one extremity of its body and a ray at the other; a type of double-faced person.

Kiai [KN], Jav. a title given to religious teachers.

kial [KK], ter~-~, making a supreme effort; putting out one's full strength; doing one's best under difficulties, struggling laboriously to succeed.

kiamat [KN], Ar. hari ~, the Day of Judgement; ber~, making a great noise, clamouring.

kiambang [KN], duck-weed — symbol of fleeting love in verses; biduk lalu ~ bertaut, cat's fighting, quarrel and ill feeling when ended is swiftly mended.

kian [P], a word hardly translatable by itself, basically conveying the idea of progression; ~ bertambah,

increasing(ly); this way, this direction: berlari ke ~ ke mari, running this way and that; 'time' in such expressions as 'five times'; as much; se~, once; this much, so much; so much and no more; se~lah dahulu, so much for now; ~ lama ~ besar, the longer (the time), the bigger (it gets); ~ hari ~ nyata, becoming clearer each day; kese~ kali, umpteenth time; demi~, to this extent, so; ara~, accordingly; kala~, next, afterwards, then.

kiap [KN], the trunk of a mast or flagstaff.

kias [KN], Ar. analogy; innuendo; veiled hint, hidden meaning; mengambil ~, to draw an analogy; kata-kata ber~, hints, innuendoes; mengiaskan, to insinuate; to symbolize.

kiat [KS], out-of-joint, not meeting exactly; stiff, strained; tulang ~, a dislocated joint of a limb; leher ber~, a stiff neck.

kibar [KK], ber~-~, 1. flapping in the breeze; ber~an, to be waving (of flags, pennons, etc.); ~kan, to wave (transitive); to fly (a flag); mengibar-ngibarkan bendera, to wave a flag; ber~-~, waving (in the wind). 2. (sl.) Ked. — to bolt.

kibas [KK], mengibas-ngibas, 1. holding a fan or any similar object in the hand and shaking that object vigorously; to brush off, shake off, as dust; mengibas-ngibaskan tangan, to wring the hands (as in pain); mengibas-ngibaskan ekor, to wag the tail vigorously; mengibas-ngibaskan, to wave to-and-fro, e.g., a fan, to encourage a flame, or an elephant flaps its ears. 2. Ar. kambing ~, the Arabian sheep.

kiblat [KN], Ar. the direction in which Mecca lies and so the direction to be faced when praying; cf. mihrab; sometimes used for, goal, aim; also kiblat.

kicak [KN], 1. (onom.) the note of the magpie-robin; also cerita mengicak, to twitter. 2. (coll.) a sponger; dead-beat; mengicak, to sponge, beg.

kicap [KN], soya-bean sauce.

kicau [KN], = kicak.

kicu [KN], a deceitful trick; mengicu-ngicu

orang, to swindle people.

kida [KN], ~-~, thin, lozenge-shaped spangles; ~-~ *mas,* gold lace.

kidal [KS], left-handed.

kidap [KN], rubbish, dirt.

kidat [KS], *ter~-~,* lolloping about.

kidul [KN], Jav. the south; *segara ~,* Indian Ocean (South of Java).

kidung [KN], *mengidung,* to intone (an address or a tale); to chant; ~ *gereja,* church hymn, ballad; *mengidungkan,* to sing (a child) to sleep.

kifayah [KN], ~ *fardu,* collective religious obligation (in Islam).

kijai [KN], *ter~-~,* quivering with pain (as a man stung by an insect).

kijak [KK], to tread on (less strong than *pijak*).

kijang [KN], the barking deer (*Cervulus muntjac*).

kijing [KN], an edible freshwater mussel (species unidentified).

kikir [KN], a file, a grater; miserly; *meng ikir,* to file; (fig.) to gnaw

kikis [KK], scraping, e.g., the paint off wood; to rasp off, abrade, erode; to erase; to scour out, as a swift current.

kilah [KN], trick, deception, ruse.

kilan [KN], 1. Jav. the span of the hand; = *jengkal.* 2. N.S. *ter~,* [KS], aggrieved.

kilang [KN], the rollers or crushers of a mill; a mill; a factory; pivotal arm for supporting infants learning to walk; ~ *ubi,* a tapioca-mill; ~ *tapisan minyak,* an oil-refinery; ~ *mengetin nanas,* a pineapple factory; ~ *penyaringan mlnyak,* oil-refinery; ~ *masak bir,* brewery; ~ *peluru,* ammunition factory; ~ *besi,* steel mill; ~ *padi,* rice-mill; *pengilang padi,* miller; *sudah mengilang membajak pula,* (prov.) working ceaselessly to make ends meet.

kilap [KN], shine, sheen; *mengilap,* to shine, glisten.

kilas [KN], a thong; a strap for pinioning; to tie in the fold of one's *sarong; mengilas,* to bind, to lash up with thongs; *mengilas tangan ke belakang,* to pinion hands behind back. 2. *se~,* an instant;

se~ pandang, at a glance; *itulah se~ mengenai hidup saya,* that was the story of my life in a nutshell.

kilat [KN], scintillation, flashing; lightning; *petir ~,* thunder and lightning; *ber~,* to flash; *(dawai) penangkap ~,* a lightning conductor; *disambar ~,* struck by lightning;; *mengenal ~ di air,* to recognise lightning (reflected) in the water, i.e. be able to take a hint; *mengilatkan,* to polish up; *hilang ~ dalam kilau,* (prov.) a person's wisdom is no longer seen when he is surrounded by wise people.

kilau [KN], brilliancy, glitter, radiance; *ber~-~,* sparkling; *air danau itu ber~-~,* the lake water sparkled; *~-~an,* flashing at intervals; *~-kemilau,* shining bright.

kili [KN], ~-~, the reel on a fishing-rod; the ring through a buffalo's nose; *mengili layang-layang,* to overtake a kite.

kilir [KK], *mengilir,* to sharpen; whetting; *~-an,* grindstone; *~an budi,* sharpener of the intellect; *~an taji,* the sharpened tip of a cock spur.

kima [KN], *siput ~,* the clam.

kimbah [KK], to clean with sand and water.

kimbang [KK], *ber~,* wheeling about in the air (as a hawk or eagle); *ter~,* to hesitate, perplexed, wavering.

kimbul [KN], the latrine (in a ship).

kimia [KN], Ar. alchemy, chemistry.

kincah [KK], cleaning by scraping or rubbing; *tempat pengincah,* scullery.

kincak [KK], *ter~-~,* pantomime accompanying singing; violently gesticulating.

kincang [KN], ~-~, gadding about; rushing wildly, darting away; *kecoh~-~,* all kinds of excuses or pretext.

kincar [KK], Sp. to wash clothes by rinsing.

kincir [KN], a water-wheel turned by the pressure of the current against the paddles of the wheel (the revolving wheel raises water up in bamboo cylinders and pours it into a conduit at a higher level); ~ *air,* id.; ~ *angin,* windmill; ~ *padi,* rice huller.

kingkap [KN], Hind. a 'kincob', or piece of

gold brocade.

kini [Kktr], modern (opposed to *kuno*); now, at the present time; ~ *begini nanti begitu,* now he is so, then again he is another.

kinja [KK], *ter~-~,* jerking about; hopping along, prancing, like, e.g. a kangaroo; cf. *enjak.*

kinyang [KN], rock-crystal.

kipan [KN], Pk. the young tapir (showing striped markings and believed by Malays to be a different animal from the adult); also *badak ~.*

kipas [KN], a fan; *tingkap ~,* venetians; *~i, ~kan,* to fan; ~ *angin,* a cooling fan (esp. electric); ~ is also used for 'propeller'; *ber~,* to fan oneself; *mengipas-ngipaskan,* to use as a fan; *mengipas-ngipas,* to swing to-and-fro in fan-like motion, as a swing-door when passed through.

kira [KK], 1. estimating, to calculate; to arrange, negotiate; *~-~,* accounts; about, approximately; *ilmu ~-~,* arithmetic; *jikalau ~nya,* if by any chance; *se~ nya,* perchance; if; *per~an,* arrangement; running account; *pengiraan,* counting, a count, as of votes; *tidak ter~,* uncountable; indescribable. 2. Ind. opinion; *saya ~,* in my opinion (view).

kirai [KK], 1. *ber~-~,* marbled (of markings). 2. shaking out water from a wet cloth or moisture (as a wet dog) or dust; *~kan* and *mengiraikan,* to cleanse by shaking. 3. *roti ~,* a preparation resembling macaroni.

kirap [KK], *ber~,* flapping (of a sail); bustling (of a man); darting (of a fish); *mengirap,* disappear, vanish; *lambat laun peristiwa itu mengirap daripada ingatannya,* the unfortunate incident will gradually fade from his memory.

kirau [KS], hard and unripe (of fruit).

kiri [KN], left; left-hand side; *cuba ~kan,* please pass the ... (i.e., don't trouble to be formal — the right hand being the proper hand to use); ~ is also used fig. for 'junior' in rank; *terus ke ~ sahaja,* keep left.

kirim [KK], sending (things, not persons); *di~nya surat,* he sent a letter; *~i, ~kan* and *mengirimkan,* to send; *~an,* a thing sent; the essential idea is of sending by someone: *saya nak ber~,* I want you to take for me; in Kelantan ~ is often used simply as meaning 'to entrust' (e.g. land); *pengiriman,* sending, despatch; *sipengirim,* sender; *~an,* shipment.

kisa [KN], a small drag-net or seine used by Malacca fisherman.

kisah [KN], = *kesah.*

kisar [KN], revolution; motion round a central point; *~an,* anything that does its work by revolution, e.g., a lathe, grindstone, or mill-wheel; *~an air,* whirlpool; *~an angin,* whirlwind; *pengisar,* id.; *ber~,* to turn over (as a sleeper); to centre; *perbincangan itu ber~ soal-soal peluang pekerjaan,* the discussion centred upon job opportunities; to veer, of wind; *angin bertiup ber~-~,* wind veering continually; *~an padi,* a mill for grinding rice.

kisas [KN], *~kan,* exact an eye for an eye.

kisi [KN], *~-~,* lattice-work; a lattice; window-bars.

kisit [KS], shrunken (stronger than *kecut*).

kismis [KN], Pers. raisins, currants.

kisut [KS], crumpled, wrinkled.

kita [Kgn], we (includes the person addressed; *kami* does not).

kitab [KN], Ar. a writing; a book (esp. a religious book); scripture, ~ *khanah,* a library; *Al-~,* the Koran; ~ *hukum,* code of law.

kitabi [KN], Ar. 'scriptural' — name given by Muslims to Christians and Jews who accept biblical books revered as authorities but who do not accept the Koran; they, as well as Muslims, are *ahli al-~,* People of the Book.

kitang [KN], the spotted butter-fish (*Scatophagus sp.*) notorious for its poisonous dorsal fin.

kitai, [KS], *ter~-~,* quivering.

kitar [KK], to move in a circle, to revolve; *se~,* all round the place; the entire situation; *di se~ bandar,* in the environs of the town; *alam se~an*, environment — cf. *kisar.*

kiuk [KN], 1. *ber~*, the cackling of a fowl picked up or of a defeated cock; so, ~ is used (sl.) for 'defeated' (with a suggestion of K.O.). 2. = *kiat.*

kiut [KK], *ber~*, to creak.

kiwi [KN], 1. a supercargo in a Malay *perahu.* 2. fond of showing off one's possessions; *si ~-~*, an ostentatious person, a show-off'.

kobah [KN], Pers. a kettle-drum.

kobak [KK], *~kan*, to peel, husk; gaping (as wound).

kobar [KK], Ind. *ber~*, to flare up, to flame high; *semangat yang ber~-~*, burning enthusiasm; *mengobarkan*, to inflame; *mengobarkan semangat*, to motivate; *berilah bantuan moral untuk mengobarkan semangatnya*, your moral support is needed to motivate him.

kobel [KK], *ter~-~*, munching, chewing.

kobis [KN], Hind. a cabbage.

kobok [KN], a party; *duduk ber~-~*, to sit about in groups.

kocah [KS], *~-kacih*, fiddling about with things.

kocak [KN], *ber~*, be stirred (of water) and so, rough (of sea); *~kan*, to shake up, as a bottle; to churn up.

kocek [KN], a pocket in a garment.

Koci [KN], 1. Cochin-China. 2. a water-jug. 3. = *kuaci.*

kocoh [KS], *ter~-~*, in a haste, hurry.

kocok [KK], *mengocok*, shake, shuffle the cards.

kocong [KN], a long, pyramidal cap; *hantu ~*, a sheeted ghost which progresses over the ground by rolling along sideways; *labu ~*, a gourd with a long, narrow neck; *ber~*, swathed from head to foot; e.g. in a blanket or a shroud.

kodi [KN], 1. Tam. a score; twenty. 2. Ind. ready-made; also *~an; barang ~an*, mass product.

kodian [KN], Eng. an accordian: see *kodi* 2.

kodok [KN], 1. Jav. a frog or toad; = *katak.* 2. *kuih ~*, a pancake of sugared and mashed bananas dippped in boiling fat.

kohong [KS], stinking; putrid.

kohor [KS], Kel., Pat., Treng., slowly, carefully; *~...~*, the more...the more. 2. faint, soft (voice).

kohut [KS], Pah. stiff from exercise or remaining in one position.

kojah [KN], Pers. a name given to Indian traders; also *khojah.*

kojol [KS], stiff in death.

kok [KN], 1. a single yoke — cf. *igu* (a double yoke). 2. *pokok ~*, a tree found in Ulu Kelantan, the large leaves of which are used as thatch.

kokak [KK], to bite, as a dog.

kokok [KN], 1. (onom.) the crowing of a cock; *ber~*, to crow; *seekor ayam tak ber~ hari tak siangkah?*, if one fowl does not crow, will the day not dawn?, a saying ridiculing someone who flouts the will of the majority. 2. to carry pick-a-back.

kokol [KK], 1. *ter~-~*, huddled up, not spry. 2. *batuk ~*, a deep, 'whooping' cough; *duduk mengokol*, to sit hunched up; *demam ter~*, shivering fever.

kokong [KS], claw-shaped; claw, clutches; to abduct.

kokot [KS], shaped like a claw; clawing; scraping up or off.

kolah [KS], a tank for ablutions at a mosque; sometimes used for a tank generally.

kolak [KS], 1. *~-kalik*, up and down or backwards and forwards; shaky, not fitting in firmly. 2. [KN], a dish of ba nanas and sweet potatoes boiled with sugar and coconut cream; *~-~*, a game with dice.

kolam [KN], Tam. a pond, reservoir, tank; *~ berenang*, swimming pool.

kolang [KS], *~-kaling*, topsy-turvy; whirling helpless (as a boat in a torrent).

kolek [KN], a Malay canoe; locally a small sailing boat, usually sailed for pleasure.

kolong [KN], a hollow, e.g., under a table or under a bungalow; *di ~ rumah*, under the bungalow sometimes used for a space generally; ~ *flat,* void deck; ~ *langit,* here below; *anak* ~, soldier's child.

kolot [KS], old-fashioned, out-of-date.

koma [KN], 1. Skr. ~-~, saffron. 2. Pah. a familiar pronoun for the first person. 3. Eng. a comma; ~ *bernoktah,* semicolon.

komat [KK], ~-*kamik,* mouthing; the movement of the mouth when speaking or eating; to mumble, to chew.

komeng [KS], small of its kind, dwarf; congenitally impotent (of the male); failing to mature.

komentar [KN], commentary.

komidi [KN], comedy.

kominis [KN], communist.

komisen [KN], Eng. commission, brokerage.

kompang [KN], a small tambourine.

Kompeni [KN], Eng. the government; *hamba* ~, convicts (in the East India Company's days); *jalan* ~, the public road.

kompleks [KN], complex; *ada* ~ *perumahan baru di kawasan itu,* there's a new housing complex in that area.

komplot [KN], Ind. a plot; conspiracy, intrigue.

kompong [KN], maimed (by the lopping off of a limb), if a stump is left.

kompot [KS], maimed (by the lopping off of a limb), if no stump is left; clipped; *si misai* ~, Hitler.

kompromi [KN], Ind. a compromise.

konco [KN], Ind. comrade, partisan.

koncor [KN], the male of the king-crab (*Limulus moluccanus*); see *belangkas.*

kondangan [KN], visitor to a feast.

kondor [KN], ~*an,* hernia, hydrocele.

konek [KN], a child's penis.

konfrantasi [KN], Jav. confrontation; term which came into use in 1963 when Indonesia opposed the formation of Malaysia.

kong [KN], 1. the rib of a boat. 2. *siput* ~, a shell (*Cassis cornuta*). 3. a deep resonant sound, esp. the exact note which is the mark of a pet dove of the *merbuk*

sp.; *bersuara* ~, to utter or possess this note.

kongkalikung [KS], Ind. hanky-panky; *main* ~, to indulge in hanky-panky, to prevaricate, intrigue, behave in a devious and underhand way.

kongkang [KN], 1. a name sometimes given to the slow loris (*Nycticebus tardigradus*) and sometimes to the tarsius. 2. [KK], to bite, as a dog.

kongkeng [KN], altercation, snarling.

kongkiak [KN], a large, black, biting ant.

kongkong [KN], 1. baying (of dogs). 2. a block suspended from the neck to impede an animal's movements; ~*an,* (met.) handicap, burden, 'mill-stone round neck'; (fig.) fetters, as of a prisoner or of a subject country; *ter*~, so fettered; (*gadis*) *si* ~ *dapur* (a girl), enslaved to the kitchen.

Kongres [KN], congress; ~ *Watania Indonesia,* Indonesian National Congress.

kongsi [KN], Ch. an association; a society; *kepala* ~, the head of a Chinese secret society; ~ *gelap,* a secret society; *rumah* ~ or, simply, ~, a communal labourers' dwelling; *per*~*an,* business association, financial combine; *ber*~, in partnership, sharing; *ber*~ *bilik,* sharing a room; *ber*~ *hidup dengan,* to share one's life with.

konon [KKt], it is said; the story goes; forsooth, methinks; 2. [KK], *mengononkan,* to inform, to relate the story with examples or references.

kontal [KK], ~-*kantil,* pendulous and swaying (of short thick objects).

kontan [KS], (French) ready money.

kontang [KK], ~ *kanting,* dangling and swaying (of a long pendant).

kontol [KS], short, stumpy and pendulous.

kontot [KS], stumpy, clipped (as moustache); maimed, short of a limb.

konyong [Kktr], 1. *se*~-~, all of a sudden, unexpectedly. 2. *jalan ter*~-~, to walk about stiffly erect.

kop [KN], 1. dome, cupola, the howdah of an elephant; *ber*~, domed. 2. a Siamese tical. 3. Siam. (from Pali) a cycle of years, the 12-year cycle of the rice *pawang*, the years of which are designated by animal names in Siam, Cambodia, China, Japan and Malaya.

kopah [KK], a mass, a lump, a clot, a quantity; *darah ber~-~*, blood in great clots.

kopak [KS], 1. *~-kapil*, very limp and pendulous (of the breast) — cf. *kopek; ~-kapik* also slovenly, untidy; tattered. 2. plucking out a small piece of anything; breaking open (as a box); *~-apik*, pulled to pieces, scattered, dispersed, dilapidated. 3. *senapang ~*, a breech-loading gun.

kopek [KS], 1. limp, long and pendulous (of the breasts). 2. [KK], *mengopek,* to cut open, force open.

kopi [KN], 1. Eng. copy. 2. Eng. coffee; *~ o*, Ch. black coffee; *~ kosong*, id.; *~ bujang*, coffee alone (without bread or cake); *~ kosong, ~-o*, coffee without cream or milk; *~-o-beng*, iced coffee without cream or milk; *serbuk ~*, ground coffee; *duit ~*, a tip, a gratuity; *wang ~*, id. 3. a round oval-lidded metal casket for betel, tobacco.

kopiah [KN], Ar. a cap; a hood.

korban [KN], Ar. a sacrificial offering; a victim; *bulan ~*, the pilgrimage month (*Zulhijjah*); *pengorbanan,* sacrifice.

korek [KK], boring or digging a hole; *mengorek,* to dig; *~kan,* to dig up; *ikan ~ telinga buaya*, a fish (*Gastroloceus biaculeatus*); *kapal ~*, tin dredger; *pengorek telinga,* ear-pick.

koreng [KN], 1. a scurfy skin disease. 2. streaky, striped.

koret [KN], (Singapore), dregs, sediment; *~-~*, last romnants.

Korinci [KN], *orang ~*, the inhabitants of an area in Sumatra who are believed by some to have the power of turning themselves into tigers; *belanja ~*, 'Dutch treat' (each person paying his own share).

korma [KN], 1. = *khurma*. 2. Hind. meat stewed with spices.

korok [KK], 1. to dig a broad hole through,

as in making a canel. 2. *mengorok,* to grunt.

korupsi [KN], Ind. corruption; *wang yang di~*, embezzled money.

kosa [KN], 1. Skr. an ankus or elephant-goad; *~i*, to prod with the ankus; also *besi kuasa; burung ~*, the Indian darter, the cormorant. 2. a variant of *kuasa; memper~kan,* to seize violently; to overpower, subdue; to oppress; to overpower in the course of rape; perkosaan, control, mastery; oppression; *~kata,* vocabulary

kosak [KN], (onom.), *~-kasik,* fidgeting.

kosek [KN], 1. (onom.) the sound of washing rice or scraping the scales off fish. 2. to interfere with, fiddle with.

kosol [KK], fidgeting, pottering; *ter~-~*, pottering about (instead of getting on with the job).

kosong [KS], empty, hollow; *cek ~*, (1) a blank cheque, (2) a 'dud' cheque; also (fig.) plain, as coffee without milk; vacant, of land or houses; idle, of talk; *tempat ~ tidak berudara*, a vacuum; *rumah ~*, the abandoned house; *biliknya ~, tanpa perabot*, his room is bare of furniture; *janji ~*, it's an empty promise; *mengosongkan,* to clear out; *kekosongan,* lonely, emptiness.

kota [KN], Skr. a fort; *~i*, to fortify; *~ mara*, the casement or breast-work protecting gunners (in a pirate ship), in contradistinction to the movable gun-shields (apilan); *~ raya*, a city; *~ praja*, a municipality; *di pinggir ~*, in the suburbs; *di pusat ~*, downtown.

kotai [KS], 1. *pinang ~*, dried betel-nut; *nyiur ~*, an old dried coconut. 2. hanging by a thread, not quite severed; hanging precariously, as a leaf or fruit on a stalk; sometimes (fig.) 'left', be deserted or worsted by fate, e.g., as a 'choosey' person who puts off marriage until too late.

kotak [KN], a chest, a locker, a packet (e.g., of matches); a space, as in a printed form; a cubicle; *~ sorong-sorong*, a drawer; *sampan ~*, a Chinese shoeboat with lockers in the stern; *tidak terdengar ~-katiknya, semuanya membisu,* to have heard no more of a thing.

kotek [KN], 1. tail, caudal projection, (vulg.) the penis; *ter~-~,* wagging the tall. 2. Sp. *ter~,* cackling (of a hen that has laid an egg). 3. *mengotek,* playing about at a thing, not doing it seriously; *~-katikkan,* to interfere with, mess about.

koteng [KS], *parang ~,* a chopper without a handle; *ter~-~,* alone, solitary.

kotes [KS], *se~,* a pinch, a very small quantity.

kotong [KN], *baju ~,* a jacket with short sleeves or no sleeves; *seluar ~* or *celana ~,* short trousers like bathing-drawers, but looser.

kotor [KS], dirty, filthy; *~an,* dirty marks, smears, dirt; *ke~an,* filth, esp. sewage; *datang ~,* woman's 'period'; *pengotor,* dirty fellow.

koyak [KS], tear, rending; torn; *~-rabak,* much torn, ragged; *~kan,* to tear; *~-~kan,* to tear to pieces, to keep tearing up.

koyan [KN], a measure of 40 *pikul* or about 800 *gantang.*

koyo [KN], Ch. sticking-plaster.

koyok [KN], cur, pariah dog.

krisis [KN], Ind. crisis.

ku [Kgn], 1. I, me; = *aku.* 2. 'your highness'; an ejaculation made by a subject on hearing a prince's words; = *tengku* or *tuanku.*

kuaci [KN], Ch. dried melon seeds; also *koci.*

kuah [KN], sauce, gravy; *tuang ~,* to pour out the gravy; *makan ber~ air mata,* (prov.) to flavour one's food with tears (a life of sorrow); *~ tumpah ke nasi,* as it ought ot be; normal course; marriage with one's own cousin.

kuak [KK], 1. to part a crowd, a pair of curtains, one's hair; *ber~,* to part, to disperse, as clouds. 2. *menguak,* to croak (as a bull-frog); to low; to bellow. 3. *burung ~,* the tiger bittern.

kuala [KN], estuary; the point where a main stream falls into the sea or a tributary into the main stream; often in effect used to mean harbour, since seagoing vessels us. have to enter an estuary to anchor; *musim tutup ~,* the season when the estuaries are closed, i.e., the monsoon period (November, December, Janaury), when fishing-boats cannot put out to sea.

kuali [KN], a wide shallow pan for frying.

kuang [KN], 1. a generic name for pheasants; *~ raya,* the argus-pheasant (*Argusianus argus*); *~ ranggas* or *~ ranting,* the peacock-pheasant (*Polyplectron bicalcaratum*) — cf. *kuau.* 2. Ch. *bijih ~,* wolfram; *mati ~ kerana bunyi,* pride will have a fall (prov.).

kuang-kuit [KN], the cuckoo-shrike.

Kuantung [KN], Ch. *orang Cina ~,* Muslim Chinese from Yunnan.

kuap [KN], *menguap, ber~,* [KK], to yawn.

kuar [KK], 1. *~-~kan,* to wave to-and-fro, as a stick to clear the way or to feel for something — cf. *kuak.* 2. *siput ~,* a large land snail.

kuaran [KN], *burung ~,* a sort of bittern.

kuas [KK], 1. *~-kuis,* scratching up the earth (of a hen). 2. Kel. the ground-squirrel.

kuasa [KN], 1. Skr. power, strength, might; an attorney; a power of attorney; letters of administration to the estate of a deceased person; *ber~,* possessed of power or authority; *tak ~,* emphatic for 'don't want to'; (lit.) have no power to; *~-ramai,* democracy; *pihak yang ber~,* the authorities; *menguasai,* to control, to govern, to manage, to rule; *maha ~,* omnipotent, almighty; *penguasa lembaga perniagaan,* controller of the board of trade; *ke~an,* powers (as of authorities); *kuat-~,* operation (of a law); *kuat-~ undang-undang itu mulai berlaku pada,* that law comes into effect on ...; *~-kuat,* the Executive; *~-usaha,* Ind. Government Agent, charge d'affaires; *penguasaan diri,* self-control; *meng~i,* to control; to subdue; cf. *kosa* 2. 2. Skr. *besi ~,* an ankus or goad; = *kosa.*

kuat [KS], Ar. physical strength; vigorous,

strong; ~*i*, to exert strength, to wrest by force; *ber~*, to exert oneself to, be determined to; ~-*kuasa*, authority, power to enforce rules; cf. *kuasa; ke~an*, strength ~-~*kan*, to make stronger; turn up (as sound of radio); ~ is used (sl.) to mean 'great on', 'a one for'; ~ *minum arak*, a great drinker of spirits; *ubat ~*, tonic.

kuau [KN], (onom.) the argue-pheasant (*Argusianus argus*); ~ *cermin*, the peacock-pheasant (*Polyplectron bicacaratum*) — cf. *kuang*.

kubah [KN], Ar. a vaulted building or hall; a vaulted roof; a cupola, a dome.

kubang [KN], a wallow, a mud-pool; *ber~*, wallowing in mud or water; ~ *nadi*, the hollow at the base of the throat.

kubin [KN], the flying lizard; *cak ~* or *cicak ~*, N.S. id.

kubu [KN], a stockade, an entrenchment of earth and wood; ~ *gajah*, a large enclosure for catching elephants; ~ is sometimes used for castle at chess; cf. *tir* and *rukh; per~an*, fortress, rampart; *mengubui*, to entrench.

kubung [KN], the flying lemur (*Galeopithecus volans*).

kubur [KN], Ar. a tomb; ~*kan*, to bury, to inter; *bunga ~*, the cemetery flower, the frangipanni; *tanah per~an*, graveyard; *ber~*, buried, lit. and sometimes fig. as of a document buried under a pile of papers.

kucai [KN], Ch. a leaf vegetable (*Allium sp.*).

kucar-kacir [KS], disorder, disorderly, *menimbulkan ~-~*, to foment disorder; *habis ~-~*, complete disorder, 'regular shambles'.

kucil [KK], 1. *ter~*, slipping out of position (as a mast out of a badly fitting truck). 2. a chancre.

kucing [KN], a cat; a generic name for the smaller *felidae*; ~ *Belanda*, the rabbit; ~ *hutan*, the leopard cat (*Felis bengalensis*); ~ *jalang*, a name sometimes given to the flat-headed cat (*Felis planiceps*) and sometimes to domestic cats that have run wild; ~-~, the triceps muscle; ~ *negeri*, the domestic cat; ~ *pekak*, a Malay rat-trap; *anak ~*, a kitten; *ekor ~*, a small plant with spikes of flowers suggesting a cat's tail (*Uraria crinita*); *mata ~*, a well-known fruit-tree (*Nephelium Malayense*); *damar mata ~*, the cat's-eye dammar (*Hopea globosa* or *Pachynocarpus Wallichii*); *kalau ~ bertanduk, barangkali*, when cats have horns, perhaps ...,i.e. when pigs fly; ~ *kurap*, mangy cat, a term of abuse; *malu-malu ~*, quasi shy.

kucir [KN], 1. a short queue such as that worn by a Tamil. 2. a pig-tail (Chinese).

kucup [KK], a smacking kiss — cf. *kecup; ber~an bibir (dengan)*, exchanging kisses on the lips (with); kissing with the lips (and not in the Malay way — cf. *cium*); ~*i*, to kiss; *mengucupi*, id.

kuda [KN], a horse; the knight in chess; an old Javanese title; *kereta ~*, a vehicle drawn by a horse (as opposed to a cart or jinrikisha); ~ *beraksa*, a pegasus; a magic steed; ~ ~, (1) trestles, clothes' horse, (2) the bridge (of a violin); ~ *laut*, an insect that runs about on the surface of water; ~ *semberani*, a pegasus, = ~ *beraksa*; ~ *tezi*, an Arab steed; *bangsal ~*, a stable; *gembala ~*, a groom, a syce; *ikan ~-~ laut*, sea-horse (*Hippocampus trimaculatus); kandang ~*, a horse-stall; a stable; *sepatu ~, ladam ~*, a horse-shoe; *ber~*, mounted on a horse; ~ *kasi*, a gelding; ~ *Deli*, a Deli pony; ~ *belang*, a zebra; *per~kan*, to overwork; to illtreat; to 'ride roughshod over'; *naik ~ hijau*, to be tipsy; *ber~*, on horseback.

kudai [KN], 1. a pouch, a rattan bag. 2. the female of the *mawas*.

kudap [KN], a snack, light refreshments.

kudis [KN], skin disease; the itch; scabby sores generally; mange; *perkara itu 'menjadikan ~*, (sl.) 'that's no skin off my nose', 'I couldn't care less'.

kudrat [KN], Ar. power, might (of God); *dengan ~ Ilahi Rabbi*, the power of our Lord God.

kudu [KN], 1. a folded bud. 2. (Singapore)

a Hindu image.

kudung [KS], stumpy, maimed, docked — cf. *kotong; perahu* ~, a vessel with a square stern; *sampan* ~, a boat with a broad stern and narrow bows; ~ *telunjuknya,* short of his index finger; ~ *sebelah kakinya,* having lost one of his legs.

kudup [KN], = *kudu* 1.

kudus [KS], Ar. holy (esp. in the expression *roh-ul-*~, the Holy Ghost); *ajaran* ~, holy teachings.

kufur = *kupur.*

kui [KN], 1. a brazier's mould. 2. N.S. a ricebin.

kuih [KN], a generic name for cakes and puddings; ~ *pulang hari,* any cake intended for consumption on the day of baking (being too stale next day); ~ *lipat,* a sort of pancake; ~ *bangkit,* pastry; ~*-muih,* cakes and sweet puddings generally; *tepungnya pun dia mahu, ~nya pun dia mahu juga,* he wants the flour and also the cake, i.e. he wants to eat his cake and have it.

kuik [KN], Pah. a small fishing-boat.

kuil [KN], a Hindu temple.

kuing [KN], 1. Siam. a superintendent of a raja's corvee; in Kelantan under the Siamese, = *penghulu.* 2. *pokok* ~ (*Diplocnemia sebifera*), a tree yielding a resinous oil; also *minyak kawang.*

kuini [KN], a type of mango which has a strong smell (*Mangifera foetida*).

kuis [KK], ~*kan,* to push aside or draw towards one with stick or foot; also *kais.*

kuit [KN], jerky movement of hand or tail; *jangan menguit,* Pk. keep quite still; ~ is sometimes used to mean to pull gently or twitch; ~*-gamit,* gesticulation.

kujau [KN], Ar. a jug, a water-jug.

kujur [KN], a spear with a broad blade and long handle; *se*~ *badan,* all over o's body.

kujut [KK], strangling, garrotting.

kuku [KN], nail, claw, hoof, talon; *seperti* ~ *dengan isi,* like the nail and the quick (separation causes intense pain), prov.; *bergantung di hujung* ~, hanging from

the tip of the finger-nail (a very precarious position), prov.; ~ *kambing,* a peculiar instrument for planting padi; ~ *sauh,* the claw of an anchor; *bunga* ~, the light patch at the base of the finger-nail; *pahat* ~, the round chisel; *penyirat* ~, the skin covering the base of the finger-nail; ~ *besi,* an iron hook; a staple; ~ *bercabang,* a cloven hoof.

kukuh [KS], firm, strong, steady; ~ *setia,* firm loyalty; *ber*~, to adhere obstinately to; ~*kan,* to strengthen, to fortify; to stablize.

kukup [KN], alluvial flats at an estuary.

kukur [KN], 1. a rasper; to scrape, to rasp; ~ *nyiur,* a coconut scrapper; *nyiur tahan* ~, a young coconut just before the water begins to collect in it; ~*an* is sometimes used (vulg.) for penis. 2. (onom.) the murmuring note of the dove.

kukus [KK], cooking by steaming; ~*an,* a steamer, i.e. cooking utensil; *air yang di*~, = *air suling,* distilled water.

kula [KN], 1. Jav. I, me. 2. Skr. race, people, family; ~ *sentana,* id.

kulah [KN], 1. Pers. a helmet. 2. a kind of mango.

kulai [KN], 1. hanging down slackly (as a broken branch or limb); *ter*~, drooping, as from weakness; ~*-balai,* swaying, dangling loosely, waggling about. 2. a shell (*Turbo marmoratus*).

kulak [KN], a cubic measure for cereal like rice equivalent to about one *gantang,* to buy (in order to sell it again).

kulasentana [KN], relations (of the prince).

kulat [KN], 1. a fungus, a mushroom. 2. *ber*~~, mumbling, as an old woman; licking the lips nervously in disappointment or embarrassment.

kuli [KN], Hind. a coolie labourer; *ber*~, *menguli,* to work as a coolie.

kuliah [KN], Ind. educational discourse, lecture.

kulim [KN], a large tree (*Sorodocarpus borneensis*).

kulit [KN], skin, peel, crust, shell, rind, husk, bark, leather; ~ *babi,* pigskin; (by metaphor) defilement, dishonour; ~

buku, cover of a book; *berniaga peti* ~ is sometimes used for 'trafficking in women'; ~ *samak,* dressed hide; ~ *karah,* 'tortoise-shell'; *tali* ~, a strap; *menguliti,* to peel; to flay; *buang* ~, id.; ~ *tiruan,* imitation leather; *kebal* ~, invulnerable; *penyakit* ~, skin disease; *wayang* ~, Javanese shadow-play.

kulum [KK], *mengulum,* to chew, to mouth, masticate; *mengulum senyum,* to smile broadly tight-lipped; *mengulum lagam,* to champ the bit.

kulun [KN], Jav. the west, occident.

kulup [KN], Ar. foreskin; a name given to the young, i.e., 'boy'; Pk. a name for men; *ber~,* uncircumcised.

kulur [KN], a cultivated variety for the bread-fruit (*Atrocarpus incisa*).

Kulzum [KN], *laut* ~, the Red Sea.

kumai [KN], an ornamental line, either ooiled (as paper).

kuman [KN], a very small insect; a louse (as a type of the insignificant); atom, bacteria, parasite.

kumandang [KN], Ind. reverberation; *ber~,* to reverberate, resound.

kumba [KN], 1. Skr. a frontlet worn in the state trappings of an elephant. 2. pot; ~ *mayang,* pot decorated with coco palm-leaves (at wedding).

kumbah [KK], *ber~,* to rinse roughly; to slosh water about; *air ~an,* slips; *beras* ~, wet (spoilt) rice; a type of the valueless.

kumbang [KN], a generic name for bumble-bees, coconut beetles, etc.; the bee as the assiduous lover of the flower; *belat* ~, a peculiar Penang type of large fish-trap (a sub-variety of the *belat* Kedah), black (of dogs, cats and bulls); *harimau* ~, the black panther; *main* ~, a game played with *perah* or *belolok* fruit, something like the British game conkers played with chestnuts; ~ *bertanduk,* horned beetle, sometimes used for the coconut beetle, = *kabur;* ~ *tidak seekor,* there are as good fish in the sea as ever come out of it (prov.), there are more pebbles on the beach, there are more

men in the world.

kumbar [KN], 1. a large and almost stem-less palm (*Zalacca Wallichiana*). 2. *sampan* ~, a Kedah type of fishing-boat.

kumbas [KK], *ber~,* Pk. to skedaddle.

kumbu [KN], a basket used by anglers.

kumbuh [KN], seed-bud in coconut; also *tombong.*

kumin [KS], *se~,* a minute portion, a particle.

kumis [KN], Sum. a moustache.

kumpa [KN], *rumput* ~, a swamp grass the pith of which used to be used as a wick (*Panicum myurus*).

kumpal [KN], a clot, a lump.

kumpar [KK], Ind. to wind up, coil up; *~an,* a coil, esp. an electrical coil.

kumpul [KK], *ber~,* assemble, gather, meet together; *se~,* in one gathering, together; *~an,* a gathering; an organisation, society; a group, e.g., of performers; ~ *sulit,* secret society; *~an lebah,* a swarm of bees; *guru ~an,* group teacher; *~kan,* to gather (people) together; to collect (objects); to muster, esp. troops; *hak ber~,* the right of assembly; *per~an,* an association, esp. for social or sporting activities; *per~an perempuan,* women's group; *per~an wanita,* id.; *pengumpulan,* raising; *pengumpulan dana itu hendaklah dipergiat,* the fund raising must be intensified.

kumur [KK], to gargle, to rinse the mouth.

kun [KS], 1. cone-shaped. 2. Ch. a border to a garment when that border is of a different colour.

kunang [KN], *~~,* a firefly; *~~ sekebun,* a garden of fireflies (a name given to a ring in which a large gem is set in a circle of smaller ones); *ber~,* to sparkle; *mata ber~~,* to see stars.

kunca [KN], Skr. a bale; a measure for straw, grass or anything easily made up into bales; = 1/5 of a *koyan; padi* ~, a system of borrowing money on a crop prior to harvest.

kunci [KN], Hind. a lock; locking up; a key (but *anak* ~ is more correct in this sense);

temu ~, a ginger (*Koempferia pandurata*); ~*kan*, to lock (a door), to wind up (a clock); *jambak* ~, bunch of keys; *ter*~, locked; ~ *kira-kira*, winding-up of accounts; balance sheet; *gelang* ~, a key-ring; ~ *air*, water gate, sluice-gate; ~ *mati*, deadlock, impasse (unsolvable) secret.

kuncit = *kucir*.

kuncup [KK], closing up or folding up (of an umbrella or of any object which shrinks on itself and is not rolled round itself like a flag); *kembang* ~, opening and shutting; expanding and contracting; *menguncupkan payung*, to close an umbrella; (fig.) to give up one's royal position, as when a Malay princess marries a commoner; see *payung*; *menguncup*, to bud; *bunga ini menguncup*, the flower is budding; *hatinya menguncup*, afraid, fearful.

kundai [KN], Tam. the short queue of a Tamil; *rambut anak* ~, the short hair at the top of the neck.

kundang [KK], 1. control, command, authority; (in magic) influence of the nature of hypnotic influence; ~ *semangat*, hypnotic love-charm; *budak* ~, personal attendants or orderlies to a prince, pages; *budak* ~*an*, id. 2. *tali* ~, a bandage used on wound after circumcision.

kundi [KN], a small, red and black pea (used as gold-weight).

kunding [KS], Pk. (sl.) rotter, no-good.

kundur [KN], the wax gourd (*Benincasa cerifera*).

kungkum [KK], N.S. conveys the idea of concentric pressure, as by a band; folded, as the wings of a bird when not flying; *mengungkum*, to close in upon, to press in upon; to fold (the wings).

kuning [KS], yellow; *putih* ~, pale yellow; a much-admired colour of the complexion (whence it has become a term of endearment, 'my fair one'); *mambang* ~, the sunset glow; *ke*~*an*, the royal colour — yellow; *ke*~-~*an*, yellowish; ~ *jingga*, orange; ~ *(me)langsat*, creamy,

(beautiful colour of the skin); ~ *emas*, golden; ~ *telur*, yolk (of egg); *nasi* ~, yellow (saffron) rice; ~ *lesi*, pale yellow; ~ *air*, clear light yellow; *menguning*, to turn yellow, as ripening grain; *sakit* ~, jaundice.

kunjung [KK], *mengunjung*, to visit; *tanpa diduga, dia mengunjungi saya*, he paid us an unexpected call; *tak* ~, not lightly, not quickly.

kuntau [KN], 1. Ch. fist; *ber*~, to box.

kuno [KS], ancient (opposed to *kini*); old, old-fashioned; orthodox, of opinions; conservative; *Bahasa Jawa* ~, Old Javanese.

kuntum [KN], a bud, a blossom; *menguntum senyum*, to break into a smile.

kunut [KN], Ar. *doa* ~, a special prayer said in the night of the 15th *Muharram* and in the last *rakaat* of early morning prayer.

kunyah [KK], chewing, ruminating; *mengunyah*, to gnaw.

kunyit [KN], turmeric, saffron; *temu* ~, turmeric (*Curcuma longa*); *burung* ~, the common iora; the oriole; *umpama* ~ *dengan kapur*, like turmeric and lime, i.e. closely intimate (indissolubly blended as are turmeric and lime in a quid of *betel*); *umpama* ~ *dengan seti*, id. (because a tumeric stain on satin is deemed unremovable); ~ is often coupled with the names of birds showing a tinge of yellow.

kupang [KN], 1. a coin or measure of value (equal in Penang to 10 cents, in Kelantan to 12 cents); ~ *tembaga*, a brass (so, worthless) 10 cent piece; met. for a useless person, a bad lot. 2. a marine mussel (*Mytilus*).

kupas [KK], peeling, husking; ~*kan*, to skin; *ter*~, skinned, shelled; *mengupas*, (fig.) to disclose; to expose; to criticize; to analyse, to examine minutely; *mereka telah mengupas masalah kewangan itu*, they have analyzed the financial problem.

kuping [KN], 1. Jav. the ear. 2. a scab over a sore — cf. *keruping*.

kupu [KN], 1. Ar. equality (of rank), parity. 2. ~~, butterfly; ~-~ *malam,* a nightwalker, prostitute.

kupur [KS], Ar. blasphemy, heresy, carrying, esp. the idea of ingratitude to God; so *orang ~,* an atheist; *mengupurkan,* to denounce or treat as an atheist; cf. *neemat.*

kur [KN], a cry for calling fowls and birds; *~ semangat,* come, my life! — a term of endearment; also an exclamation of astonishment, esp. admiring astonishment; *perempuan berbadan ~ semangat,* (sl. and vulg.) a woman with a gosh-and-God-bless-my-soul figure.

kura [KN], 1. ~-~, a generic name for a number of tortoises (other than *Testudo emys*); in speech us. *ke~; ke~ katup,* box tortoise; *ke~ kaki,* the instep; *seperti ~-~ telentang,* like a tortise on its back, met. for helplessness. 2. spleen; *demam ~,* low fever, ague, fits; *seperti ~-~ memanjat kayu,* when pigs fly; it is impossible to reach.

kurai [KN], straight broad lines in the veining of wood or the damescening of a keris.

Kuran [KN], 1. Ar. the Koran; *~ al aazim,* the Sublime Koran. 2. ~, Ind. a newspaper.

kurang [Kktr], reduction; less; (by extension) a negative adverb; *~ hati,* lacking in spirit, spiritless; *ke~an,* lack; fault; *kita semua mempunyai ke~an,* we all have our faults; *~kan,* to reduce; *pengurangan,* depreciation in value (term used in accounts); *ber~,* to diminish, lessen; to be in short supply; *makan ber~,* to suffer from malnutrition; *ke~an zat makanan,* malnutrition; *tak ~ apa-apa,* it is quite all right; *~ ajar* (met.), impolite; *se~-~nya,* at least; *mengurangi berat badan,* to slim down.

kurap [KN], 1. ringworm; mange. 2. a shell (*Capsa deflorata*).

kuras [KN], quire (of paper) *menguras,* to wash out (a drain pipe).

kurau [KN], a fish (*Polynemuss sp.*); a thred-fin.

Kuripan [KN], an old kingdom in Java, the home of Sira Panji.

kuris [KK], *menguris,* to scratch; a variant of goris.

kurnia [KN], Skr. favour, kindness, gift (from a superior to an inferior); *jikalau ada ~ tuanku,* if your highness pleases; *~i or mengurniai,* to confer a favour or gift; to bestow.

kursus [KN], Ind. course; *~ melalui pos,* correspondence course; *~ kilat,* intensive course; *mengikuti ~,* to attend a class.

kurun [KN], a century.

kurung [KN], enclosing; shutting up; an enclosure; the compartments of a large Malay fish-trap (*jermal* or *kelong*); a room a cabin; *ber~,* to be enclosed or shut up; *ter~,* shut up; *perintahan ber~,* curfew order; *perintahan ber~ dikenakan,* a curfew order was imposed; *baju ~,* overdress, a skirt with shoulder straps.

kurus [KS], thin, lean, attenuated; *~ kering,* withered and bony; *ubat (untuk) meng~kan badan,* slimming drugs; *~ ceding,* puny; *~ melidi,* thin as a lath; *~* is sometimes used to mean poor, of oil.

kus [KN], a sound to frighten away cats.

kusal [KK], rolling up by friction between the palms of the hands.

kusam [KS], lustreless, dull.

kusar = *gusar.*

kusi [KN], *rumput ~,* a grass (*Poa cynosuroides?*).

kusta [KN], *sakit ~,* leprosy.

kusu [KK], 1. a small group; *ber~-~,* In knots, in clusters. 2. ~-~, the vetiver or cuscus grass (*Andropogon muricatus*).

kusut [KS], matted, confused; *hati ~,* perplexed; *rambut ~,* tangled hair; *berbulu panjang ~,* shaggy; *~ masai,* in complete disorder, dishevelled, as hair.

kut [Kktr], perhaps, possibly.

kutang [KN], Jav. a thin bodice, = coli; (*baju*) ~, a brassiere.

kutat [KS], pimply.

kuti [KS], 1. ~-~, nagging, petty annoyance. 2. *~kan,* to 'send to Coventry'.

kutik [KK], *tidak ber~-~,* motionless; *mengutik-ngutik,* to pick (o's teeth); *sebagai ular di~ ekor* (prov.) being compelled to move or to shift position due to fright, inconvenience etc.

kutil [KN], 1. a wart. 2. to pick to break off a small piece of anything.

kutip [KK], *mengutip,* to collect, esp. in the sense of collecting here and there, as, e.g. taxes or stamps; *mengutip hasil tanah,* to collect land revenue; *~-katip,* oddments, bits and pieces, esp. of a collection of such things; *~an,* a collection; an extract (from a writing).

kutu [KN], 1. a skin parasite, generally; a nit; *~ anjing,* a flea; *~ biduk,* the beetles infesting dirty lockers in boats; *~ busuk,* a bug; *telur ~,* a nit; *tindas ~,* to kill lice (on the thumb-nail); *~ bandar,* gutter-snipes, corner-boys; *~ embun,* 'night-birds' (people who stay out late for dubious reasons); *mengutu,* to be a parasite, cadge round. 2. Tam. a sort of lottery, each subscriber drawing the pool in turn; an association; *se~,* a federation; *persekutuan,* id.; an association, esp. political or economic; *perse~an negara-negara Asia Tenggara (Asas),* an alliance for co-operation between Malaysia, Thailand and the Philippines (not connected with military or political action) — Association of S.E. Asia States; *berse~ bertambah mutu,* i.e. Unity is Strength (motto of Malaysia); *berse~,* federated; *Negeri Malayu yang berse~,* the Federated Malay States; *Perse~an tanah Melayu,* Federation of Malaya; *Perse~an Asykar tua,* Ex-Servicemen's Association; *perse~an dagang,* commercial combine.

kutub [KN], pole, *~ janubi (selatan),* South-pole; *~ syamali (utara),* North pole.

kutub [KN], Ar. centre, axis; geographical pole.

kutub-khana [KN], = *kitab-khana,* library.

kutuk [KN], a curse, accursed; *si~,* a wretch, a scoundrel; *~i* or *mengutuki,* to curse; *mengutuk,* id.; also to denounce; *~lah atas mu,* a curse on you; *di~ Allah mati terdiri,* may you be cursed by God and die standing up (i.e. not on your bed), may you die with your boots on!

kutur [KN], *burung ~,* Kel., Treng. the buffalo egret, = *bangau.*

kuyu [KS], 1. melancholy, rueful-looking, out of sorts or ill; *bermata ~,* heavy-eyed. 2. Pk. a side-bet, esp. at billiards; *ber~,* making a side-bet; *makan ~,* accepting a side-bet; a handicap, start (in a race).

kuyup [KS], 1. *basah ~,* sopping wet. 2. = *kuyu* 1.

kuyut = *kuyu.*

L

la [Kktr], ~ *ini*, now; ~ *itu*, then (short for *kala*).

laba [KN], 1. Hind. (from Skr.) profits, rich returns; *beroleh* ~, to profit greatly; ~ *dan rugi*, profit and losses; *mendatangkan* ~, profitable. 2. ~-~, a spider; ~-~ *beruk*, the large venomous bird-spiders; ~-~ *lotong*, a large black well-spider; also *lelaba* and *labah-labah*.

laberang [KN], stays at right angles to the mast of a native ship.

labi [KN], ~-~, turtle.

labu [KN], 1. Skr. a generic name for gourds, pumpkins; a calabash; a pipkin; ~ *air*, a pumpkin (*Cucurbita peop*); ~ *batu*, an earthenware pipkin; ~ *jantung*, the bottle-gourd (*Legenaric vulgaris*); ~-~ an earthenware water calabash modelled on the gourd; ~ *manis* = ~ *air*; ~ *merah*, a gourd (*Curcurbita maxima*); *siput* ~, a shell (*Murex haustellhm*); *tampuk* ~, the small stalk left on a gourd when it is plucked; (fig.) clitoris. 2. come up!, cry used by sorcerers to bring a crocodile to the surface.

labuh [KS], 1. lowering by means of a rope, string or cable; letting down blinds or curtains; ~*an*, an anchorage; ~*kan*, to lower; *ber*~, to moor, to anchor; *pe~an*, anchorage, harbour. 2. flowing (of robe); loose, overlarge; *lepas* ~, flowing, hanging low, of hair.

labun [KK], *ber*~-~, to gossip.

labur [KK], 1. smearing, daubing; *me~ putih*, to whitewash; ~*kan minyak*, to smear on oil. 2. *pe*~, rations supplied to troops or labourers; *tauke* ~, the Chinese capitalist financing e.g. a tin mine. 3. to invest.

labut [KS], certain, definite; *tak* ~, not accepted as true, not believed (as news or a complaint); also *labud*.

lacak [KS], 1. *be*~ or *me*~, to be abundant (as fruit). 2. drag (of an anchor).

laci [KN], (Dutch) a drawer; a chest of drawers.

lacur [KS], Ind. obscene, immoral; *pe~an*, prostitution; *me~kan diri*, to prostitute one-self; *pe~an adalah pekerjaan yang tertua di dunia*, prostitution is the oldest profession in the world.

lada [KN], pepper; *pipis* ~, to grind pepper for cooking; ~ *berekor*, cubebs (*Piper cubeba*); ~ *China*, a pepper (*P. chaba*); ~ *hantu*, a wild pepper (*P. canium*); ~ *hitam*, black pepper (*P. nigrum*); ~ *merah*, red pepper, capsicum (*Capsicum annuum*); ~ *sulah*, white pepper; *serbuk* ~, ground pepper; *siapa memakan* ~, *dia berasa pedas*, he who eats pepper tastes its pungency, i.e wrong-doing rebounds on your head, or, your sins will find you out.

ladam [KN], Tam. a horse-shoe; *me*~, *pukul* ~, to shoe (a horse).

ladan [KN], *minyak* ~, a strong oily preparation used in caulking native boats; *setanggi* ~, joss-sticks.

ladang [KN], planting on high dry ground in contradistinction to planting on low swampy ground (*sawah*); ~ *padi*, 'hill-padi'; ~ *gambir*, a hill-clearing for planting gambier; ~ *lada*, a pepper-clearing; ~ *getah*, a rubber estate; *tikar* ~, a coarse type of mat; *ber*~, to plant on dry soil; the original meaning of ~ was probably 'smooth', 'level': *betisnya se*~, *tidak berporut*, his legs were of the same level without protrusion, i.e. were of the same thickness throughout their length with no protrusion at the calf; *pe*~, farmers.

laden [KK], to serve.

lading [KN], 1. *parang* ~, a long chopper, the blade of which tapers towards the handle; *perahu* ~, a heavy cargo-boat.

2. *ikan ~-~*, a fish (*Pellona* sp.); *~ tajam sebelah*, (prov.) greedy, covetous.

ladu [KN], Hind. sugared rice-flour cakes.

ladung [KN], 1. *batu ~*, a plummet; *~ kail*, a lead on a fishing-line. 2. inundated, under flood water; *ber~*, stagnant; *ber~an*, id.; *ber~ air mata*, wet with tears.

lafaz [KN], Ar. the spoken word; *~kan*, to utter, express (as feelings); to propose (a motion).

laga [KN], the fighting of large animals — such as buffaloes, bulls, rams and chevrotins; the fighting of quails (but not cocks); *ber~*, to collide; to fight (of animals); *~kan*, to pit against one another; (met.) to stir up trouble between; to set (thing or person) against another; *me~ ayam*, to have a cock-fight; *~kan kepalsuan dengan kepalsuan*, to fight falsehood; *ikan pe~*, the fighting fish; *ikan sempilai*, id.

lagak [KN], affectation, swank, studied airs; manner, mannerisms; *menjual ~* (of women), to coquet, 'play-up' (to attract men); *ber~*, to pose, act with an eye to effect; to play one's part; *banyak ~nya*, he has many pretensions; *ber~ sebagai*, to act as; to pose as, pretend to be; take part of (in a play); *gaya yang harus di~kan*, how to comport oneself; *ber~ irama*, to dance a rhythmic dance (particularly solo); *me~-~*, to attitudinize; *~-lagu*, mannerisms, ways of behaviour.

lagam [KN], Hind. the bit (of a horse).

lagang [KK], *me~kan*, the first steps in weaving a mat; starting to weave; starting any task; so, *~an*, the first steps in a task.

lagi [KS & Kgn], more, yet more; still, also, moreover; *dan ~*, furthermore, besides; *se~*, so long as; as long as; while; *~ pun*, moreover; *hujan ~, gelap ~*, not only was it raining, but it was dark; *~kan*, even; not to say; *ke~-~*, yet once more, again and again, proceeding yet.

lagu [KN], 1. tune; *menurut ~*, in time with the music; *~ kebangsaan*, national anthem; *~ kalimat*, intonation; *~ berentak*, a 'march'. 2. like, similar to; *membawakan ~*, to lead or conduct the singing.

lagut [KS], Pk. to gaze fixedly; used generally as a variant of *leka*.

lah [P], a particle emphasising the word to which it is appended, e.g.; *orang itu-~ yang pergi*, it was that man who went.

lahad [KN], Ar. *liang ~*, an excavation dug into the left side of the grave and used for the actual reception of the dead body; used often simply for the grave (as the end to which all must come).

lahak [KN], *be~*, to belch loudly, hawk deep in throat.

lahap [KS], *pe~*, gluttonous, voracious.

lahar [KN], 1. a pool, a mere, a patch of water in the jungle; also *wilahar*. 2. revenous. 3. Ind. lava.

lahir [KK & KS], Ar. clear, plain, visible, born into the world; *~kan*, to reveal; to give birth to; *pada ~nya*, obviously; as far as appearance goes; openly; *~ dan batin*, both open and hidden; outwardly and inwardly; also *zahir; hari ~*, birthday; *ke~an*, birth; *tanah ke~an*, native country; *tempat ke~an*, birth-place.

lai [abbrv.], *sehelai*, a numeral coefficient for tenuous objects — such as sheets of paper, garments, leaves, blades of grass, etc.; also *helai*.

laici [KN], Ch. a well-known Chinese fruit (*Nephelium litchi*).

Laila [KN], see *Majnun*.

lain [KS], different; other than; exclusive (of); some other...; *~ diminum, ~ disapu perut*, some were portions, some were lotions; *~ orang ~ hati*, different men have different hearts; *mencari ~*, to seek a new love; *~-~kan*, to sort; *ber~an*, differing from; apart from; *me~kan*, but, nevertheless, except; *se~ daripada itu*, besides that; *~ padang ~ belalang*, so many countries so many customs; *~ dahulu lain sekarang*, other times, other manners; *~ kali*, another time; *ke~an*, difference, dissimilarity, exception.

lais [KK], 1. *me~*, to back water with oars.

2. *ikan* ~, the glass catfish (*Kryptopterus* sp.).

lajak [KS], quick; quickly; *te*~, travelling on of own momentum, as a braked car on a slippery road; ~ *perahu dapat dikayuh balik,* ~ *perbuatan dan perkataan tak dapat ditarik balik,* if a boat overshoots the mark, it can be paddled back, but nothing can recall a deed or a word which overshoots the mark (think well before you act or speak).

laju [KS], rapid, swift, fast; speed, velocity; *had* ~, speed limit; ~ *awal,* initial velocity, as of a projectile; *me~kan,* to accelerate; *ke~an,* speed; swiftness.

lajur [KN], a band, a broad line, a furrow — cf. **jalur.**

lak [KN], 1. Hind. (from Skr.) sealing-wax. 2. Treng. let be, allow.

laka [KN], 1. *kayu* ~, a tree (*Phyllanthus* sp.?). 2. Kel. black, with a little red (colour of bull).

laki [KN], husband; ~~, male, masculine; manliness; *le~,* id.; *ber*~, to have a husband; to be married (of a woman); *ber~kan,* to take as one's husband, to marry (of a woman); *burung* ~ *padi,* name applied to various warblers; sometimes, to the tailor-bird.

lakin [Kktr], Ar. well, so, yet, but; *wa*~, and yet; and still.

laknat [KN], Ar. curse; ~ *Allah,* the curse of God; ~*an,* accursed; *me*~, to curse.

lakon [KN], Jav. a stage play (esp. a classical play in ancient Java); ~*kan,* to present (such a play) on the stage; *pe*~, an actor; *ber*~, to act, take part in a play.

lakri, Port. = *lak* 1.

laksa [Kbil], 1. Skr. ten thousand; *se*~, a myriad; *ber*~, in myriads; in countless numbers. 2. Pers. vermicelli.

Laksamana [KN], Skr. admiral; commander of the fleet; *Dewa* ~, the hero Laksamana, the half-brother of Rama; *baris* ~, the double triangle; the magic figure drawn by the hero Laksamana to protect Sita, Rama's wife, from Rawana; admiral generally.

laksana [KN], 1. like, similar to; resemblance; = *seperti* or *bagai,* but lit. in use; ~*kan,* to imitate, to equal, to compare with, to rival; to effect, to put into effect, to accomplish; *pe~an,* fulfilment, accomplishment, settlement of; *pe~an rancangan,* fulfilment/implementation of a plan. 2. *bijak* ~, wise, prudent; = *bijaksana.*

laku [KN], manner, behaviour; to act or behave; to take effect; to pass current; to be saleable, to attract buyers; ~ *mahal,* fetching a good price; *rosak bangsa kerana* ~, (prov.) good birth is wasted by bad manners; *seperti* ~ *orang gila,* like the conduct of a madman; *ringgit ini tak* ~, this dollar will not pass current; *tingkah* ~, general deportment; ~*nya seperti pisang goreng,* selling like fried bananas, 'like hot cakes'; *me~kan,* to perform, as a duty or part; to put into effect; *me~kan sendiri,* to manage (singlehandedly), he said he could manage; *se*~, as, in the capacity of; *ber*~, to take effect, to prevail, to pass current, to occur; *ke~an,* bearing, behaviour; *berke~an seperti,* to behave like, act like; *langkah* ~, behaviour, actions; *buat ke*~, (sl.) to make a scene, put on an act, play up; *lepas* ~, uninhibited, poised, mentally matured; Pah. married (of a girl); sometimes, uninhibited, behaving indiscreetly, of young people; ~ is sometimes used to mean like, similar to.

lakum [KN], a generic name for a number of wild vines, e.g., *Vitis diffusa, V. mollissima* and *V. novemfolia.*

lakur [KN], to fuse metals into an alloy.

lala [KN], 1. *siput* ~, a salt-water bivalve resembling a mussel, eaten as a tonic by pregnant women. 2. *me*~, to swim on one's back.

lalah [KS], gluttonous eating.

lalai [KS], 1. careless, sleepy, listless, negligent; ~*kan,* to forget, to lose interest in; *ilmu pe*~, a spell to render people careless or forgetful; *ter*~, dozing off. 2. halliards.

lalak [KN], 1. the touch-hole of a cannon; to ignite, take fire, as gunpowder. 2. [KK], screeching; *ter~-~ ke sana ke mari,* screeching up and down, as cats at night, and fig. as roisterers.

lalang [KN], 1. the well-known 'lalang' long grass (*Imperata cylindrica*); *gajah ~,* a tame elephant; ~ *laut,* Treng. a coarse thrust-grass, = *jolok-jolok; bunga ~ di kepala,* lalang flowers on the head; i.e., grey hairs; ~ is sometimes used as simile for a person who is a pestilential nuisance; ~ *berduri,* dangerous nuisance; *tanam ~ tak akan tumbuh padi,* if you plant lalang, you can't expect rice to come up, i.e. don't expect figs of thistles. 2. *lalu-~,* going and coming; passing to and fro.

lalat [KN], the common fly (*Musca*); ~ *hijau,* the 'bluebottle' fly; ~ *kerbau,* the oestrus; ~ *kuda,* the horse-fly (which flies away for a moment but returns) — courage that is discreet but persistent; *harimau ~,* the common small jumping spider; *tahi ~,* a freckle, a small mole; spots of mildew on cloth; *tepuk ~,* the peculiar flap used by Malays to catch grasshoppers; *belum terbang ~,* very early in the morning.

lalau [KK], *me~,* to make marks, e.g., by 'blazing' trees to warn off trespassers; *hikmat pe~,* a charm to hinder a girl from marrying.

lali [KN], 1. *buku ~,* the projecting portion of the ankle-bone. 2. *ikan ~,* a sort of loach (*Botia hymenophysa*). 3. insensitive to pain, as after an injection; *ter~,* made impervious to sensation; *ubat pe~,* opiate, pain-killing drug.

lalu [KK], past, after, afterwards; elapsing; traversing; moving past; *ber~,* to pass on; to elapse, of time; *alangkah cepatnya waktu ber~,* how time flies; *tahun ~,* past year; *~lah kami,* we passed by; *orang masuk ~ duduk,* they entered and then sat down; ~ *lalang,* passing to and fro; *se~,* always, continually; *~i,* to traverse, to override, to disobey; *me~i,* id.; by way of, via; *~!,* move on!, out of

the way!; *~-lintas,* moving to-and-fro; traffic; *ter~,* surpassingly, very; *jangan ter~ mengharapkan,* don't expect too much; *keter~an,* exaggeration; excess; sometimes, grossly offensive, of behaviour of words; ~ Is also used, generally with a negative, of physical ability to do something; *saya tak ~,* I can't do it (e.g. lift a log).

lalut [KS], rambling, inconsequent; cf. **kelalut**.

lam [KN], a marine worm from which an oil, minyak lam, is obtained.

lama [KS], long (of time); ancient; former; *orang ~,* the ancients; *berapa ~?,* how long?; *rumahnya yang ~,* his former house; *~-~,* in the end; finally; *se~,* while; as long as; *se~-~,* forever; *tak ~ lagi,* shortly; *se~nya,* always, continuously; *~-ke-an,* as time goes on.

lamar [KK], Ind. *me~,* to seek in marriage, to woo; *me~kan diri,* to offer oneself (for a task); *me~ pekerjaan,* to ask for a job.

lambai [KK], *me~,* to wave, to beckon (e.g., to a friend on a departing ship); *me~-kan,* to wave (a flag, weapon, etc.); *me~-~,* to flutter, as a flag; *~an,* fluttering, as a flag.

lambak [KN], a heap; *me~, ber~ ~,* to lie in heaps.

lambang [KN], Ind. symbol, emblem, insignia; ~ *negara,* the coat-of-arms of a State; *me~kan,* to symbolize; *pe~,* symbolic of; *pe~an,* symbolization, symbolism, representation; ~ is sometimes used to mean a symbol of quality and in this shade of meaning approaches very closely to 'status symbol'; *di berberapa negara warna hijau dianggap me~kan kemakmuran,* green supposedly sumbolizes prosperity in some countries; ~ in the sense of symbol is sometimes used of a mere figurehead, nominal leader.

lambar [KN], layer, lining.

lambat [KS], slow; ~ *belajar,* slow to learn; ~ *sampai,* slow to arrive; *~-bangatnya,* sooner or later; *~-launnya,* id.; *ter~,* too late, belated; *per~kan jam*, to put the clock back, retard it.

lambing [KS], coming to a point; pricked up (of the ears).

lambuk [KN], 1. *bubur ~*, a soup of prawns, fish, ginger, etc. 2. = *lambur.* 3. [KK], *me~*, to dig, break ground; *jentera pe~*, mechanical digger or plough.

lambung [KN], 1. side, flank; *roda ~*, a paddle-wheel. 2. swelling up (as a wave); bouncing up (as a ball); *me~*, to surge; to rebound; (fig.) to boast; to 'go up in the air' (as with astonishment); *di~ ombak*, wave-tossed; *di ~ angan-angan*, in the clouds.

lambur [KN], a large jelly-fish; notoriously poisonous.

lamin [KN], *ke~*, a pair (male and female), a married couple; *pe~*, the bridal bed; or dais on which bride and bridegroom sit.

lampai [KS], slender, lissom, svelte; *me~*, to hang down; *panjang ~*, willowly — cf. **ampai.**

lampam [KN], a fresh-water carp of the genus *Puntius;* it is a very foul feeder.

lampan [KN], four-sided wooden tray with holes in the sides for the fingers; *me~*, [KK], to use a wooden tray in washing for tin.

lampar [KK], spread flat over; *tidur be~*, to sleep sprawling — cf. **hampar.**

lampas [KK], *me~*, polishing, smoothing.

lampau [KS], excess; surpassing, exceeding; *ter~*, too much; *me~*, to go too far; *me~i*, to overdo; *me~i kemampuan*, beyond the reach of, *pe~*, extremista; *pada masa ~*, in the past.

lampin [KN], a swaddling-cloth for a newly born child.

lampir [KK], Ind. to add, to supplement, append; *~an*, appendix; supplement; *surat ~an*, covering letter.

lampit [KN], Jav. a sleeping-mat.

lampu [KN], Port. a lamp; *~ picit*, *~ petik*, an electric torch; *~ pam*, pressure lamp; *~ isyarat*, signalling lamp; traffic lights; *~ colok*, an oil lamp, esp. of a primitive kind.

lampung, [KS], light in weight (of wood); *pe~* or *te~*, a float for a line or net — cf. **ampung, apung,** etc.; *ke~*, a lifebelt; *gertak ~*, a pontoon bridge; *dok ~*, a floating dock.

lamun, [KPhbg], 1. provided that; if only. 2. Ind. *me~* [KK], to meditate, cogitate; *~an*, meditation; *ini ~an yang menjadi kenyataan*, this is a dream come true.

lanang, [KN], 1. Jav. man, male, manly; = *laki-laki*. 2. twining by twisting.

lanar [KN], mud, slime.

lancang [KN], 1. Port. a swift Malay war vessel. 2. a model ship laden with offerings, set adrift to propitiate demons. 3. hasty; ill-considered, of action or speech; *me~*, to dash ahead, dash forward.

lancap [KS], smooth and slipery; *me~* [KK], to masturbate.

lancar [KS], quick; fluent; without a hitch; *latihan kecemasan berjalan ~*, the Emergency Exercise was conducted without a hitch; *~ membaca*, fluent in reading; *perahu ~an*, a swift cruiser; *me~*, to dart along (as a snake, boat); to glide along, slip along; *me~kan*, to launch; *dengan ~nya*, quickly, without hesitation, smoothly; *ke~an*, smooth working, as of an organisaton; *tempat pe~an roket*, rocket launching-site.

lancing [KN], Jav. trousers (of the type worn by Javanese).

lancong [KS], 1. false, counterfeit, debased (of currency). 2. Ind. *me~*, to go on a sightseeing tour; *pe~*, tourist; *pe~an*, tourism.

lancuk [KN], a pool; a puddle.

lancur [KK], gushing out violently; emptying tin-bearing earth into a mining-washer; *me~*, to spurt out — cf. **pancur.**

lancut [KK], *me~*, to gush out, spurt out in large jets.

landa [KK], 1. *me~ mas*, to wash for alluvial gold. 2. *me~*, to bump into, knock up against; *me~ masuk*, to intrude, to 'barge in'; *sebagai benang di~ ayam*, (prov.) entirely confused.

landai [KS], gently sloping; *me~*, to slope,

of land or path.

landak [KN], a porcupine; ~ *raya,* the large porcupine (*Hystrix longicauda*); ~ *batu,* ~ *kelubi* or ~ *ubi,* the brush-tailed porcupine (*Atherura macrura*); *duri ~,* quills of porcupine.

landar [KS], slightly sloping.

landas [KN], 1. *~an,* an anvil; a chopping block; a railway sleeper; a railway track; *terkeluar dari ~an,* derailed. 2. (Borneo) the stormy season, monsoon.

landuh [KK], *me~,* increasing in breadth (as a cone).

landung [KS], long (of a rope) — cf. **lanjar**.

lang [KN], a generic name for hawks, kites and eagles; ~ *merah,* the Brahminy kite (*Haliastur* sp.); ~ *rajawali,* a generic name for small hawks, e.g., *Tinnunculus alaudaris;* ~ *sewah,* the sparrowhawk; ~ *kanguk,* the brown eagle; ~ *belalang,* the black-legged falconet; ~ *hindik,* the changeable hawk-eagle; ~ *tikus,* the black-winged kite; ~ *lebah,* the crested Malayan honey-buzzard; *~ling,* the Southern pied hornbill (also *lilin* and *kelengkeng*); ~ *ayam* = ~ *merah;* ~ *siput,* the white-bellied sea-eagle; *di mana tiada elang, kata belalang akulah elang,* (prov.) in the country of the blind, the one-eyed man is king.

langah [KK], *ter~,* gaping wide (as door or cave); *terbe~,* id.

langau [KN], the bluebottle fly; ~ *mengerumun bangkai,* bluebottles flock to carrion, i.e. people flock to a centre of attraction; esp. a vicious one; *sebagai* ~ *di ekor gajah,* (prov.) always running after those in authority.

langgai [KN], a triangular push-net worked by one man; *belat ~,* a fixed (estuarine) purse-net (also **ambai**).

langgak [KS], open, easily visible; *ter~,* scattered about, wide-apart.

langgam [KN], N.S. manner, style; *lagu ~,* stylised (modern) tunes, as opposed to *lagu asli,* which are ancient tunes, suiting folk-songs.

langganan [KN], subscription to newspaper; *pelanggan,* a subscriber; a customer.

langgang [KS], *tunggang ~,* topsy-turvy, upside down.

langgar [KK], 1. knocking up against; ~ *bahasa,* a breach of etiquette; *~i,* to attack; *me~,* to knock against, come into collision with; *pe~an,* a collision; *ter~kan,* to run into, crash into. 2. Jav. a small private mosque; = *surau* or *bandarsah.*

langgung [KK], to put down athwart something else, e.g. a gun against a log.

langir [KN], materials such as bark and fibres used for cleaning the person in the old days; sometimes used for modern cosmetics.

langit [KN], the sky; the heavens; *tujuh petala ~,* the seven folds of heaven; *kaki ~,* the horizon; *~~,* a canopy, a ceiling; *~~ kerongkong,* the roof of the mouth; *tinggi me~,* sky-high (lit. and fig.); *di mana bumi dipijak, di situ ~ dijunjung,* (prov.) when in Rome, do as the Romans do.

langkah [KN], a pace, a stride; *salah ~,* a false step; *~i, ~kan,* to step over; *me~,* to travel, to set out; to stride; *me~ guntai,* to walk with long strides; *me~ kata-kata adat,* to commit a breach of customary rules or etiquette; *angkat ~ seribu,* (sl.) to 'beat it', skedaddle; helter-skelter; *buka ~ seribu,* id.; *membuka ~,* to quicken one's pace; *cepatkan ~,* id.; *me~ perut isteri,* to step over one's wife belly; an old-time custom by which a husband was supposed to relieve his wife's labour pains; *~nya sebagai diatur,* a measured stride; ~ *kanan,* to arrive opportunely, esp. for a meal; ~ *sumbang,* false step; ~ *baik* (met.), a good opportunity; favourable prospect; *(taip)* ~ *sebaris,* double spaced (typing).

langkan [KN], Ch. a balustraded terrace in a Chinese house.

langkap [KN], *pokok ~,* a palm tree (*Arenga obtusifolia*).

langkas [KS], 1. fiery (of a steed). 2. over

(as a fruit season); *se~ betik berbuah*, (met.) a short time.

langkat [KN], three days hence; the morrow of the day after tomorrow.

langkau [KK], skipping; omitting a little and resuming farther on; *~ sehari*, every other day; Pah. planted too late (of rice); passing over, e.g., other boys in a class when going higher.

langkup [KK], *te~*, capsized (of a boat); upside down (of a cup); face downwards.

langlang [KN], Jav. travelling round; *~ buana*, wandering over the earth.

langsai [KS], winding up; *habis ~*, quite finished; settled (of debts).

langsar [KS], long in proportion to width (as a flagstaff); tall and straight.

langsat [KN], 1. the well-known fruit (*Lansium domesticum*). 2. fawn-coloured.

langsi [KN], 1. shrill (of the voice); *me~*, to give out a shrill note. 2. drapery, hangings.

langsing [KS], 1. = *langsi* 1. 2. slender, willowy; also *lansing; menjaga agar bandan tetap ~*, to stay slim.

langsir [KN], hanging curtains for door or window.

langsuir [KN], a vampire.

langsung [KS], moving on to, proceeding to; forthwith, next; *berjalan dia ~ ke pekan*, they went straight to the market; *ter~*, (1) gone forth; issued; (2) too much; *jangan ter~*, do not go too far; *~kan*, to execute, perform (as a ceremony); *ber~*, to take place (as a ceremony); to continue in operation or existence; *hari ~*, day of fulfilment, day on which an event is due to take place (used esp. of a wedding); also *lansung; siaran ~ dari Stadium Negara*, direct telecast from National Stadium; *dia kemukakan saranan itu secara tidak ~*, he made the suggestion in a subtle way.

langut [KK], *me~*, to look longingly at anything.

lanjam [KN], a ploughshare.

lanjar [KS], long (of a rope) — cf. **landung**.

lanjung [KN], *tebu ~*, a long, thin variety of the sugar-cane.

lanjur [KS], *te~*, protracted, dragging on, going too far; *kata sudah te~*, I spoke hastily, spoke 'out of turn'; *dia te~ mengatakan terang-terang*, he openly blurted out — cf. **lanjut, anjur**, etc.

lanjut [KS], long, lengthy, prolonged; *me~kan* or *memper~kan*, to lengthen; *se~nya*, furthermore, in continuation; *dengan ~nya*, in full detail; *pelajaran lanjutan*, extension course, continuation course; *~ umurnya*, old, ancient; no longer young; *ber~an*, prolonged, esp. as a war; *~kan umur*, to prolong life; *se~nya*, furthermore, in continuation; at length, in full.

lansing [KN], 1. wooden brake for bullock-cart; also *lasing*. 2. [KS], slender.

lansir = *langsir*.

lantai [KN], a floor.

lantak [KK], ramming down, hammering down; *luluh ~*, crushed under heavy blows or weights, *~ lari*, 'skedaddle'; *pe~*, a ramrod; a paramour; *~* is also used for a pile (timber) and, as a verb is used (vulg.) for guzzling and for having sexual relations (of a man).

lantang [KS], clear, open, plain, distinct (as view or sound).

lantar [KN], *pe~*, a flooring without a roof; a piece of scaffolding; an open-air theatre-stage; *pe~an*, id.; *te~*, lying stretched on the floor; stranded (as a stranger); *ramai penduduk ter~ di situ*, a large number of the residents were not properly taken care of.

lantaran [KN], Ind. concerning; by reason of; on account of; reason, cause; *melantarkan*, to cause, to be responsible for.

lantas [Kktr], forthwith; thereupon; passing right through, straight through; *setelah datang lalu naik ~ ke peraduan*, on arriving he went promptly to bed.

lantik [KK], 1. *me~*, to install; to crown. 2. *be~* or *pe~*, a spring-gun or spring-bow.

lanting [KN], 1. *se~* and *sering-~*, long-billed partridge (*Rhizothera longiros-*

tris). 2. ~ Pk. a small raft. 3. Pah. a framework for carrying loads on the back; the carrier at the back of a bicycle. 4. a lantern; a street lamp. 5. *me~,* to throw, hurl.

lantun [KK], *me~,* to ricochet; to fly of course; to diverse sharply; to give a sudden violent start, as from pain; *me~-~,* to reverberate, echo and re-echo.

lantung [KS], strong (of smell); putrid; *busuk me~,* putrid and stinking.

lanum [KN], Treng. a rainbow.

Lanun [KN], Ilanun (the name of a piratical tribe from Mindanao); piratical; a pirate.

lanyak [KK], treading down (esp. of soil being trodden by buffaloes as a way of preparing it for cultivation); to beat violently.

lanyau [KN], mud with a hard crust or mud mixed with decayed vegetable matter.

lap [KK], to mop up; *kain ~,* a dish-cloth; *kertas ~,* blotting paper; *menge~,* to mop up, to wipe.

lapah [KK], stripping, skinning; to flay (esp. used of skinning animals for the market or kitchen).

lapan [Kbil], eight (used in speech instead of de~).

lapang [KS], empty, vacant, open; *bilik di atas itu ~,* the room upstairs is spacious; *~ hati,* contented, care-free; relieved; *~ rasa dadanya,* he felt relieved; *me~-~kan fikiran,* to clear one's head, e.g., by having a holiday; *me~kan masa,* to find time (to do something); *ke~an,* complete leisure; *tanah ~,* an open space; *~an udara,* an airfield; *~an,* (met.) field, sphere; *~ politik,* the field of politics; *~-luas,* roomy (as a car); *~an lumba,* a race-track; *~an* or *tempat ~* is used for a square (space enclosed by houses); *~an (gelanggang) tenis,* tennis-court; *~* is used for roomy and for comfortable, of clothes.

lapar [KS], hungry; *~ dahaga,* hunger and thirst; *~ susu,* hungering for milk (of a baby); *~ air,* thirsty; *~kan,* to keep hun-

gry, to starve; *ber~,* to go hungry.

lapik [KN], base; the surface on which a thing rests; a rug, mat, mat or doyly; *~ kaki,* sandals; *~ punggung,* a mat for sitting on; *tak ber~,* Pk. unreservedly; *kain ~ (piring),* a doyly; *me~ perut,* to 'have a bite', get something in one's stomach.

lapis [KN], layer, stratum; *ber~,* in layers; *kuih ini ber~,* this cake is in layers; in coats; *segala ~an bangsa,* all classes.

lapor [KK], Ind. *me~,* to make a report; *~an,* a report; *me~i diri,* to report oneself (for duty).

lapuk [KS], mould; decayed by the action of damp; mildew, fungoid growths; (fig.) out of date; *tak ~ dik hujan,* not damaged by rain; *tak ~ dik zaman,* ageless, unaffected by the passage of time.

lapun [KN], a kind of net-snare for birds.

lar-lar [KN], 1. Kel. dazzled. 2. a species of insect.

lara [KS], 1. disquietude; anxiety, care; the solicitude of love; *orang yang ~,* they who pine; *penglipur ~,* a soother of cares; a storyteller. 2. to wander about; *kaum me~,* nomads.

larah [KN], *ber~-~,* one after another, in succession; taking turns, esp. in drinking, each person calling on another to drink; very nearly, toasting one another.

larak [KS], 1. close together (as the seeds of a durian which has very little pulp). 2. *akar ~,* a kind of liana containing water.

laram [KK], *me~,* to display one's attractions, to 'set one's cap', show off (to the opposite sex).

larang [KK], prohibited; *~an,* a thing prohibited; *hutan ~an, (simpanan),* a forest reserve; *~kan,* to forbid, to prohibit; *kawasan ~an,* a prohibited area; *Bukit Larangan,* the Forbidden Hill (because it contains some ancient royal graves), Fort Canning, Singapore.

larap [KS], 1. readily saleable; = *laris.* 2. to open out, e.g., *me~kan tali,* to separate the strands of a rope.

laras [KS], 1. smooth and cylindrical; the

stem of a tree; the barrel of a gun; *senapang dua ~,* a double-barrelled gun; *yu ~,* a dog-fish (*Mustelus manazo*). 2. Ind. conformity, agreement; *se~ dengan,* in conformity with, in line with; *pe~an,* adjustment (of accounts); *menye~kan,* to make go well together; to bring into agreement with; to synchronize; to coordinate.

larat [KK], 1. dragging on slowly; lengthy; *tahun-tahun ~ dia mengaturnya,* he spent long years in arranging them; to drag (of an anchor); *me~,* to spread, as fire or disease; see *melarat.* 2. *tak ~,* unable to, lacking power to; *tak ter~,* tired out, unable to make an effort, miserable, poor.

larau [KN], annoyance; *me~,* to worry (as a child); *membalas ~,* to pay out a man for disturbing you.

lari [KK], running (not of liquids running); fleeing; *~ mengaji,* to play truant; *me~kan diri,* to abscond; *me~kan cukai,* to evade Customs duty; *ber~,* to run; *le~,* Pah. the platform between a Malay house and its kitchen or its *balai; ~ berganti-ganti,* a relay race; *orang pe~an,* refugees; displaced persons; *~an, course* (as of a river or range of mountains); *kawin ~,* to elope; *ber~ anak,* to scamper along; to trot, to jog; *pe~ jarak pendek,* sprinter; *pe~ jarak jauh,* long distance runner; *ber~ anjing,* to go at speed; to gallop, *se~ dengan,* running parallel with (as, e.g., a road with a river).

larik [KS], turning (with a lathe); polishing and rounding; *gading di~,* polished ivory.

laris [KN], in demand; selling well (of goods); *pe~,* a charm to secure good business, or to make a woman attractive; *me~kan jualan,* to increase one's sales, to push one's sales.

larung [KN], a coffin (without bottom).

larut [KS], 1. to drag (of an anchor); *~ malam,* far into the night; *~ petang,* far into the evening; *ber~~,* to drag on and on, as a task; *usia sudah me~,* old

age creeps on, advanced in years. 2. Ind. soluble; *me~,* to dissolve; *~an,* a solution.

las [KN], *batu ~,* a hard mineral substance used as emery stone.

lasa [KS], numb; paralysed; insensible; *anggota yang ~, menjadi lagi rasa,* the numbed limbs regained the power of sensation.

lasah [KK], striking, switching; *be~,* to thrash, to beat up.

lasak [KS], industrious, 'on the go'; in everyday use; *pakaian pe~,* everyday wear; working clothes; *tahan ~,* to wear well; *membuat ~ tangan,* to fiddle, meddle, unable to keep hands to oneself; *tentera ~,* experienced, trained troops.

Lasam [KN], a place in Java celebrated for its painted cottons (*batik Lasam*); *laksana batik ~,* the older the better.

lastik [KN], Eng. a catapult.

lasu [KS], stale, musty (of food) but not spoilt; esp. used of fruit; overripe.

lasykar [KN], Per. soldiery.

lat [KN], alternate; = *elang; ~ sepintu,* every alternate door; the next door but one; *~ sehari,* every other day.

lata [KK], crawling; *me~,* to creep; *pokok me~,* a creeper (plant); *air me~,* a waterfall.

latah [KS], a nervous paroxysmal disease aroused by suggestion and often taking the form of hysterical mimicry; *me~,* to suffer from *latah;* to get frantically excited; to get hysterical.

latam [KK], pressing or stamping down; rolling earth to harden its surface; to prepare rice-fields by making buffaloes trample them.

latar [KN], basic colour, basic design; *~ belakang,* background; *ber~ belakang politik,* politically motivated.

latih [KK], to train; *me~ mulut,* to speak coherently; *~kan,* to practise; *~an,* training; practice; performance, as of a rite; course of instruction; *pe~,* a trainee; *ber~,* to train, undergo training; to rehearse; *tentera ter~,* trained (i.e. regular) troops.

latuk [KN], 1. *parang* ~, a chopper, the tip of which turns downwards. 2. *me*~, to quiver, to chatter (of teeth) — cf. **gela-tuk**.

lau [Kphbg], 1. Ar. if, *wa*~, and if; although; *jika*~, if. 2. Ked. a fowl-house.

lauk [KN], materials cooked for consumption with rice; ~ *pauk*, all kinds of food (other than rice); solid food (fish or meat).

laun [KS], protracted, dragging on; *jangan ber*~, do not spin it out; *lambat-*~, at last, eventually.

laung [KN], a loud call; *ber*~ or *me*~, to cry out loudly; to hail; ~*kan*, to call loudly to (a person); *sepe*~ *jauhnya*, hailing distance; *pe*~ *suara*, a loud-hailer, megaphone; public address system.

laur [KS], a curve; the numeral coefficient for rings; bracelets, etc.; *me*~, to curve.

laut [KN], sea; ~ *madu*, a sea of honey (a symbol of sweetness); ~ *lepas,* the open sea; ~ *api*, hell; *barat* ~, N.W.; *utara barat* ~, N.N.W; *timor* ~, N.E.; *ikan kuda-kuda* ~, a sea-horse (*Hippocampus trimaculatus*); ~*an*, the seas, the ocean; *me*~, to travel seawards; *me*~*i*, to navigate; *orang ke*~, Kel., Treng. a fisherman; ~*an teduh*, the Pacific; *pe*~, a seaman; *Orang* ~, Sea Gipsies; *bahasa* ~, language of sea nomads; *angkatan* ~, navy.

lawa [KN], 1. a cross-bar in a fish-trap; *me*~, to stop the way, e.g., of a bridal party pending the payment of a fee; *upah pembuka* ~, the fee so paid. 2. *pe*~, to invite (informally). 3. = *lawah*.

lawah [KS], smart, chic.

lawak [KS], Hind. ~-~, poking fun, jesting; *pe*~, humbug; Kel., Treng. to tell lies; *orang* ~, a clown, 'funny man'; *ahli* ~, a comedian; (film) ~ *jenaka*, a comedy (film); *pe*~ *orangnya*, he is a witty chap.

lawan [KN], opposition, rivalry, competition, contest; a rival, a foe; ~*i*, to contend against; *ber*~, to be engaged in a contest, to be in rivalry or contrary to; *tak* ~, incomparable, unequalled; *tak*

ter~, id.; *tak boleh* ~ ..., not up to the standard of ...; *per*~*an*, contest, match; *ber*~*an dengan,* inconsistent with, contrasting with; *ini ber*~*an dengan harapan saya,* this is contrary to my expectation.

lawang [KN], 1. *bunga* ~, mace; *kulit* ~, an aromatic bark (*Cinnamomum culit lawan*). 2. a great gate, a main entrance; ~*an*, id.

lawar [KN], 1. a preparation of roasted mincement with raw chillies and onions. 2. = *laram*.

lawas [KS], 1. *me*~, no longer bearing well, of a tree; past its best; 'turned' (of milk). 2. clear, unobstructed, as view; *berak* ~, to have a good 'motion'; *ubat me*~*kan kencing,* medicine to promote the flow of urine; a diuretic.

lawat [KK], *me*~, to visit.

lawi [KN], *bulu* ~, the long feathers in a cock's tail; ~ *ayam*, a curved dagger with a hole in the handle.

layah [KK], 1. *me*~, to bend over backwards; to sway; to bend; to rise and fall, of a singer's voice; *te*~, swaying as if to fall (as, e.g., in crossing a plank). 2. [KN], a loose outer garment worn by women on the Mecca pilgrimage.

layak [KS], 1. Ar. right suitable, proper, appropriate; *diperlakukan se*~*nya,* treat him accordingly; *bukan* ~ *kita memakainya,* it is not fitting that we should wear it; *ke*~*an*, qualification. 2. cutting up a fish (longitudinally) to preserve it.

layam [KK], *be*~, to brandish, wave about (as a weapon), esp. in a sword-dance.

layan [KK], ~*i* or *me*~*i,* to wait on; to attend on, pay attention to, treat with due consideration; entertain; *pe*~, a waiter; a waitress; Treng. an orderly; ~, to entertain, serve; ~*an*, reception, service, due attention; treatment, e.g., by superiors.

layang [KK], 1. soaring in the air; *me*~, to fly; *me*~ *jatuh,* to flutter down, as a leaf; *jiwa me*~, to die; *me*~*kan*, to fly away with; blow away; *ter*~ *sekejap,* dozing off for a moment: ~-~, (1) a generic name for swallows and swifts; (2) a generic name for children's kites; *se~ pandang*, a fleeting glance. 2. *~kan*, to slice up finely; *burung ~~*, swallow.

layap [KS], *me~*, to skim the surface.

layar [KN], sailing; a sail; a cloth used as a screen; *~ agung*, the mainsail; *~ apit*, a lug-sail; *~ dastur*, a studding-sail; *~ penyorong*, a mizzen; *~ tupang*, a foresail; *ikan ~*, a fish (*Histiophorus gladius*); *pasang ~*, to set the sails; *perahu ~*, the yard; *pekaki ~*, the boom; *~ perak*, the silver screen (of the cinema); *di belakang ~*, in the background, under the surface; *be~*, to sail; to travel by water; to set sail; *pe~an*, a sea-voyage; *be~ simpang-siur*, to cruise around; *kaum pe~an*, sailors, sea-faring men; *~ timpa tiang*, friends become enemies.

layat [KK], to tear off (a bit of something).

layon KN[], Jav. the dead body of a prince; *layunan*, id.

layu [KS], faded, withered (of a tree or flower).

layur [KS], 1. parch, scorch up with fire. 2. *ikan ~~*, a scabbard fish (*Trichiurus savala*). 3. *~ daun*, dark patches on the skin, due to illness.

lazat [KS], Ar. delightful to the senses; delicious, pleasure-giving.

lazim [KS], Ar. usual, ordinary; *~ disebut*, generally called.

lebah [KN], the honey-bee; *sekawan ~*, a swarm of bees; *kumpulan ~*, id.; *sarang ~*, a bees' nest; *~ bergantung*, bees hanging in a cluster from a branch.

lebai [KN], a mosque official who attends to the order of the service; any pious elder; often used satirically for a person who pretends to be 'very good'; cf. **ketayap**; *Lebai Malang*, a legendary figure who always missed his opportunities.

lebak [KN], (onom.) a thud.

lebam [KS], 1. livid (of a bruise); used fig. of a cloth to mean dingy; *kelam-~*, pitch dark. 2. [KN], (onom.) a banging noise.

leban [KN], a plant (*Vitex pubescens*); also *halban*.

lebang [KS], *~ pinggang*, weak after illness (esp. after child-birth); lumbago.

lebap [KN], (onom.) a dull thud.

lebar [KS], wide, broad; *~nya sedepa*, it was six feet broad; *terbuka ~*, wide-open, as a door; *me~kan*, to widen, to extend; *pe~an*, expansion, extension; *me~kan bibir*, to pout; *se~ dua kali katak melompat*, as wide as two frog-jumps, i.e. very narrow, 'hardly room to swing a cat'.

lebaran [KN], Ind. a festival, esp. Hari Raya Puasa.

lebat [KS], dense (of foliage, hair or rain); close, thick; *hujan ~*, heavy rain; *bulu keningnya ~*, his eyebrows were bushy.

lebih [KS], more, superior, greater; *~~nya*, the surplus; *dan se~nya*, and the remainder and the surplus; *yang ~*, the most; the more; *~ kurang*, more or less; *~kan*, or *me~kan*, to augment; in favour, indulge, give preference to; *ber~ ~an*, going on increasing; boasting; exaggerating; *ter~*, much more, most, excessively; *ber~kurang*, to compromise; *me~~kan*, to exaggerate; *ber~an*, superfluous; *jangan ber~an*, be moderate; *ke~an*, an advantage, favourable circumstances; *ke~an suara*, a majority of votes; *me~i kuasa*, to exceed one's authority; *~ lama ~ baik*, the longer the better; *~ buruk*, inferior; *~ dahulu*, ahead; *me~i yang lain*, to excel.

lebu [KN], also *debu*, dust; *~ duli*, 'dust below the royal feet' — a humble way of indirectly addressing a prince.

lebuh [KN], 1. a broad street. 2. in the dim distance—cf. **sayup**.

lebum [KN], (onom.) a thumping noise.

lebun [KN], fraud by adulteration or by specious appearance.

lebur [KS], smelting; the molten state; solution, liquefaction; destruction; *hati ~*, a crushed spirit; *me~ bumi*, to 'scorch the earth'; *me~* is used met. for 'to liquidate', 'put an end to'; *pe~*, a chemical solvent; *kilang pe~*, tin-smelting works; *titik* ~, melting point; *hancur* ~, thoroughly devastated.

leca [KN], 1. Pah. a mattress — cf. **geleca**. 2. necklace of beads.

lecah [KS], muddy (of the ground); wet (of walking); also *lecak*.

lecak [KN], ~-~ (onom.) a splashing noise.

lecak [KS], *ber*~, in abandance, 'heaps'.

lecap [KS], saturated; wet through (as a handkerchief).

lecat [KS], smooth and slippery.

leceh [KS], 1. *me*~, to coax, to wheedle. 2. dawdling, lazy, scamping work; dissipated, idle, useless; also *kerja* ~, a long job, can't be hurried, troublesome; time-consuming.

lecek [[KK], to beat up with a spoon; mash; e.g. *me*~ *kentang rebus,* to crush or press boiled potatoes to a soft consistency; hitting with the flat side of the foot, as when dribbling to make into pap, crush into pulp.

lecer [KS], 1. *me*~, to be moist (as a sore or abrasion); to suppurate. 2. = *leceh* 2.

lecet [KS], blistered, abraded — cf. **lecer**.

lecing [KN], *me*~, to whizz (as a bullet).

lecit [KK], 1. *me*~, to shoot out (as water from a leak)—cf. **lecut** and **lencit**. 2. ~ *ingus,* to blow one's nose. 3. (onom.) twittering (of birds); = *decit.*

lecok [KS], smooth, oily or polished; *terpe*~, sprained.

lecuh [KS], sodden (of cooked food); withered (by heat).

lecup [KS], blistered.

lecur [KS], *me*~, scalded; blistered; crinkled by heat.

lecut [KK], *me*~, to ooze out (as the contents of some fruits when squeezed); ~*kan,* to squeeze out, as juice.

ledak [KK], Ind. *me*~, to explode; to erupt, of a volcano; *bahan pe*~, explosive; ~*an,* explosion.

ledang [KS], conspicuous, standing out; *me*~*kan diri,* to show oneself off (esp. in a new suit); *Gunung Ledang,* Mount Ophir.

leding [KN], *me*~, to warp; to become convex; to sag (of plank under weight);

me~-~, to bend this way and that — cf. **ledung**.

ledok [KK], *ber*~-*ledak,* hanging with waving fins.

ledung [KS], *me*~, to give (under a weight) — cf. **leding**.

lega [KS], broad, wide; easy, comfortable; in easy circumstances; feeling better (of a patient), feeling comfortable; ~ *dada,* relieved; *tak* ~, disquieted, uncomfortable; *rumah* ~, a spacious house; *me*~*kan fikiran,* to 'ease one's thoughts', relax; *me*~*kan badan,* to have a rest, esp. in the sense of having a rest-cure.

legam [KS], *hitam* ~, coal-black; pitch-black.

legar [KK], *me*~, *ber*~, to make a circuit, to circle, as a hawk or a plane.

legas [KK], to 'snick' off a projection.

legat [KS], keeping steadily on the same course (of a ship); looking fixedly, of eyes.

legih [KN], a dividing line, watershed.

legir [KN], Treng. a cask; floor beam.

legu [KK], *me*~, to weave the selvedge or border of a mat.

legum [KN], (onom.) thumping.

legung [KN], (onom.) the booming of a gong.

leher [KN], the neck; *batang* ~, the column of the neck; ~ *baju,* collar; *kerat* ~, to cut the throat; *penggal* ~, to behead; *pulaskan* ~, to wring the neck; *ber*~ *lembut,* obsequious; ~ *berkiat,* a stiff neck.

lejang [KN], to dart out (as a spear); *me*~, to kick; *se*~ *terbang,* in a flash, as quick as lightning.

lek [KS], Treng. assuredly, certainly.

leka [ ], *ter*~, straightened out under pressure, e.g., as a soft-metal hook taken by a big fish.

leka [KS], dwelling on; dawdling over; busy on; ~ *bermain,* lingering over play; ~ *menangis,* continuous weeping; ~ *burung,* mad on birds; *ber*~-~, to dawdle about, to dally.

lekah = *rekah.*

lekak [KS], *me*~, to whirl or buzz round

and round a spot; ~-*lekuk,* bumpy, uneven, full of hollows.

lekang [KS], shelling off (as plaster from a wall); *rambutan* ~, a rambutan fruit whose flesh is separable from the pip; me~*kan,* to unfasten, to peel off; *tak lapuk dek hujan, tak ~ dek panas,* (prov.) lasting, constant, invariable.

lekap [KK], cleaving to; flattened on; to cling to (a flat surface); *biawak me~ pada batang pokok,* an iguana clinging to a tree-trunk; me~*kan pipi ke dada,* to press one's cheek against the breast of...; cf. **lekat;** ~-*lekup,* to crack, to snap.

lekar [KN], a rattan frill for lifting pots off the fire without burning the fingers.

lekas [KS], quickly, promptly; *nanti* ~, *rosak mata,* your eyesight will soon be spoilt; *se~-~nya,* as soon as possible; *ber~-~,* hastily, hurriedly; *memper~,* quicken.

lekat [KS], pasted on; ~*kan,* to stick (a thing) on; me~, to adhere to; *ter~,* stuck on; ~ *api,* to strike a light; *tak* ~, to fail (of a scheme), 'didn't stick'; ~ *hutang orang,* to get into debt; *tak ~ buruh,* can't keep his labour force; me~*i,* to cling to, adhere to (as dust to a wall); *pakaian yang me~ di badan,* the clothes one has on; me~*i,* stick to; *pe~,* gum, glue.

lekeh [KS], low, mean, despicable.

lekir [KS], *panau* ~, a disease discolouring the skin; *ular awa* ~, a snake with curious white markings suggesting the disease (*Coluber melanurus*); [KS], streaky, having white streaks.

lekit [KS], slightly sticky; thick, not clear, of liquid; me~, to stick, adhere.

lekoh = *selekoh.*

lekor [KN], a numeral which when occurring after the numbers one to nine signifies that twenty is added, i.e., *se~,* twenty-one; *dua* ~, twenty-two.

leku [KK], *berte~,* to lean on one's elbows.

lekuk [KS], 1. a hollow; a puddle; ~ *mata,* eye-socket; ~ *dada,* the cleft between the breasts, 'cleavage'; ~-*lekak,* full of little indentations or puddles; *lekak-~,*

id. 2. the Hearts suit in cards; *ber~,* dimpled.

lekum = *halkum.*

lekung [KN], a hollow, cleft, cavity.

lela [KN], 1. a swivel-gun. 2. Ar. beloved, darling. 3. *Maharaja Lela,* the title of a chamberlain at a Malay court; *bermaharaja-~,* to act arbitrarily. 4. to disport oneself; me~*kan* to brandish, wave about. 5. *besi me~,* steel; *keris me~,* an undamascened keris; *muda* ~, young and smart.

lelah [KS], weary, exhausted; *penat* ~, extremely weary; *sakit* ~, asthmatic; *melepaskan* ~, to take a rest.

lelak [KK], to slip down, fall (of fruit or a garment). 2. [KS], in disarray (of weaving etc.).

lelaki [KN], = *laki-laki,* see *laki; ke~an,* manliness, virility; *menunjukkan ke~an,* to show one's manliness.

lolangun [KN], Jav. a pleasure garden; = *taman.*

lelap [KK], deep (of sleep); forfeited (of a pledge); *pajak* ~, shop in which forfeited pledges are sold; me~*kan mata,* to close the eyes in sleep, get to sleep; *makan tak kenyang, tidur tak* ~, (prov.) to be very restless.

lelar [KK], *per~,* to drag about, draw after one, particularly of household objects continually and thoughtlessly used.

lelas = *relas.*

leleh [KK], me~, to trickle gently.

leler [KS], 1. careless, solvenly (of work), sluggish. 2. = *leleh; tua* ~, very old, dilapidated; *ke~an,* slovenly, neglected.

lelewa [KN], Jav. behaviour, conduct; *tingkah* ~, id.; = *tingkah laku.*

lelong [KN], 1. Port. sale by auction. 2. a measure of length and area; a quarter of an orlong in area. 3. me~-~, to totter along, stagger along, as a wounded man.

leluasa [KS], Ind. freedom from restraint; *ber~,* doing as one pleases, acting without restraint.

lelucon [KN], Ind. jokes, drollery; *jaguh* ~, champion jester; *bahan lucon,* laughingstock.

lemah [KS], weak, soft; lacking firmness or rigidity; ~ *lembut*, gentle, mild; ~-*liat*, supple; ~ *semangat*, to have a weak spirit (mind); ~*kan*, to enfeeble, to weaken, enervate; *ubat pe*~, a stupefying drug.

lemak [KN], fat, grease; rich, of voice; run to fat; *isi ~ dapat ke orang, tulang bulu pulang ke kita*, others get the flesh and fat, we get the bones and bristles; *cakap* ~-*manis*, oily talk, wheedling; *naik* ~, to be cheeky, uppish; ~-~ *santan berlada*, rich though the coconut-cream is, it is peppered; of flattery with an edge to it or of pleasure tinged with bitterness; *nasi* ~, rice cooked with coconut milk.

lemang [KN], 1. *me*~, to cook glutinous rice with other ingredients in a bamboo lined with plantain leaves. 2. *me*~, to bend over backwards and pick up a coin with the lips (as is done occasionally by Malay dancers).

lemar = *almari*.

lemas [KS], 1. suffocated, drowning, stifling; ~ *fikir*, confused thought. 2. = *lemah; mati* ~ (died from) asphyxiation, suffocation.

lemau [KS], weak, sleepy, apathetic; spiritless; damp, not crisp.

lemba [KN], a plant (*Pothomorpha subpeltata*).

lembab [KS], 1. damp. 2. Ked. slow at work; feeble, spiritless, inactive; *hari* ~, overcast (sky).

lembaga [KN], 1. mould, matrix; rough shape, rudimentary figure; embryo, beginnings; primeval (customs); ~ *bisul*, the early stages of a boil; *adat* ~, customary laws handed down from prehistoric times; a commission, board; ~ *perlabuhan*, Harbour Board; ~ *perniagaan*, Board of Trade; *per*~*an*, constitution; ~ *bangsa-bangsa*, the League of Nations; ~ *amanah*, Board of Trustees; ~ *pemegang amanah*, id.; ~ *letrik pusat*, Central Electricity Board; ~ *pemasaran*, Marketing Board; *dengan cara yang berper*~*an*, in a constitutional

manner. 2. N.S. a tribal chief.

lembah [KN], low-lying land, meadow; ~*kan*, to irrigate (of rivers); ~*an*, valley floor; ~ *gelombang*, trough of a wave.

lembak [KK], *me*~, to boil over.

lembam [KS], slow, dull, 'wet'; *ke*~*an*, inertia, slowness.

lembang [KS], 1. soft-spoken, plausible. 2. [KK], depressed, indented, as soft soil.

lambap [KS], 1. moist, clammy, wet; 2. humid; *ke*~*an*, humidity.

lembar [KN], a thread, a strand, a piece of string; a numerical coefficient, = *helai*; ~*an*, a sheet (of paper); a page.

lembayung [KN], a name given to several plants with red or purple flowers; *merah* ~, crimson.

lembek [KN], a light mattress.

lembik, [KS], pulpy soft; *penyakit* ~, rickets, beri-beri.

lembidang [KN], a flat rim, brim or edge (of plate, saucer).

lembing [KN], a spear; ~ *buang-buangan*, a dart, a light javelin; ~ *tikam pari*, a spear with three barbs; ~ *patung*, Kel. a special spear used as a symbol of the Royal authority; *me*~, to throw (to hit with) a spear.

lembu [KN], an ox; ~ *jantan*, a bull; a cow; ~ *kasi*, a bullock; ~ *tanah*, a large beetle; ~ *hutan*, the smaller wild ox (*Bos sondiacus*); *ikan* ~, the box-fish; also the leather-jacket; *memper*~, treat like a cow.

lembung [KK], *me*~, to be blown or puffed out; to expand into globular shape, as a box-fish; to rise, as leavened bread; *me*~*kan dada*, to expand the chest.

lembur [KN], overtime work, night work.

lembut [KS], soft, delicate, weak, flexible; ~ *hati*, softened (of angry feelings); *lemah* ~, extremely soft or delicate; gentle; ~*i* or *me*~*kan*, to soften; ~-*lunak*, smooth-running, as a car; ~ *pinggang*, supple in body; *ke*~*an*, softness, gentleness.

lempah [KK], *me*~, to spill out, overflow.

lempai [KS], *me*~, to curl up at the edge

(as a leaf); to droop (as a branch).

lempam [KK], *me~*, to falter in spirit; *semangat sudah me~*, morale has fallen.

lempang [KK], 1. lying athwart or across anything; *me~*, to lie outstretched; *apit ~*, garboard strake. 2. to slap.

lempar [KK], throwing, casting; *~i* or *me~*, to pelt; *me~kan*, to throw (anything); *me~kan bola besi*, to put the shot; *~ batu sembunyi tangan*, (prov.) not to admit a thing frankly; to cause trouble secretly to a person.

lempedal = *pedal; mempedal; empedal*.

lempedu = *hempedu*.

lempek [KN], *berlempil-~*, in coats or layers.

lempeng [KN], name given to light flat cakes; made of pulut flour.

lempoyan [KN], a fishing-reel.

lempoyang [KN], a ginger (*Zingiber casumunaar*).

lempuk [KN], 1. cooked sugared durian. 2. a poultice; a plaster.

lempum-lempang [KN], the sound of fruit falling.

lempung [KS], light (as wood, pumice, etc.); spongy; *kayu ~*, light timber (of little value); *katak ~*, a frog (*Oxyglossus* sp.).

lemuas [KK], *ber~*, smeared with dirt.

lemukut [KN], broken grains of husked rice; also *melukut*.

lemusir [KN], shoulder (of meat); sometimes, loin.

lena [KS], sound (of sleep); *tidur ~*, to sleep soundly; *~kan*, to put to sleep; *~ pelanduk*, sleeping with one eye open.

lencana [KN], Ind. a badge.

lencas belencas, [KN], hairy caterpillar.

lencit [KK], springing forward (as a slippery body squeezed between the fingers — cf. **lecit**).

lencong [KK], swerving, deviating; *terpe~*, deviating widely, esp. from policy; *me~kan*, to divert (road or traffic).

lencun [KS], dripping; soaked; *~ basah*, soaking wet.

lendat [KK], Pen. *me~*, beat down, e.g., grass; to rub against; *ter~*, pressed

down, as trodden grass.

lendih [KK], *me~*, nestling up.

lendir [KN], viscous secretions of all sorts; greasy matter; matter from a boil; the runnings in certain diseases; *duit ~*, 'dirty' money; *makan duit ~*, to live on dirty money, esp. the proceeds of prostitution.

lendung [KK], *me~*, to be dented or knocked in (of convex surfaces).

lendut [KS], 'giving', as a plank under a heavy weight.

leng [KN], a measure of capacity; half a *cupak*.

lenga [KN], *minyak ~*, gingelly oil — cf. **bijan**.

lengah [KS], dawdling, wasting time; *~ mata*, to droop with sleepiness (of the eyes); also *longah; ber~~*, loitering.

lengai [KS], listless, careless.

lengan [KN], arm; *~ baju*, the sleeve of a garment; *pangkal ~*, the upper arm; *berbantal ~*, (prov.) to be homeless.

lengang [KS], sparse (of population or of the attendance at a festival); forlorn; quiet, of business.

lengar [KS], dizzy (from a blow); *ter~*, 'knocked silly'; *si kepala ~*, a man of giddy conduct.

lengas [KS], clammy, moist; *me~*, to become clammy or moist; *pengukur ~*, hygrometer.

lengat [KK], Pen. to cook in a steamer, = *kukus*.

lenggak [KK], leaning the head back and looking skyward.

lenggang [KS], rocking, swaying; swinging the arms; *ber~*, to swing one's hips; *lenggok-~*, id.; *~ yang lemah-lembut*, a slow, undulating motion; *~ janda*, a small curved knife broadening towards the point and fretted at the broad end; *mandi ~ perut*, ceremonial bathing in the seventh month of pregnancy; *me~*, walking with a swagger, swinging the hips; *ber~-lenggok*, to sway back and forth; *tak juah ~ dari ketiak*, empty swagger, bluster (swinging from the armpits only, not a natural swing); *ber~*

kangkung, to indulge in empty swagger.

lenggar [KS], wide apart (of packages in a receptacle).

lenggara [KK], *me~kan,* to manage, look after; also *ke~, menye~kan.*

lenggok [KS], swaying the body, posturing, esp. as a dancer; *ber~,* swaying in dance; *me~kan tarian,* to perform a dance; *~-lenggang,* rocking to-and-fro; *~-lenggang bagai cupak hanyut,* rocking like a floating half-coconut shell.

lengguak [KN], *burung ~,* the large thick-billed green pigeon.

lengguh [KK], *me~,* to sit resting one's arms on a table, = *berteleku.*

lenggundi [KN], a small tree with violet flowers and aromatic leaves (*Citex trifolia*).

lenging [KS], *ber~,* not wearing a shirt; bare from the waist up.

lengit [KS], beaten badly at a game.

lengkai [KS], *panjang ~,* tall and willowy (of the figure).

lengkang [KS], ring-shaped; a circumference; a numeral coefficient for bracelets, anklets, etc.; *ber~,* curved; *~-lengkok,* winding, meandering; (fig.) loafing about.

lengkap [KS], complete; fully equipped; sufficiently supplied; *cukup ~* or *~ genap,* id.; *dengan se~-nya,* in full; *me~i, me~kan,* to fit out; *ke~an,* equipment; *~an,* an expeditionary force; *se~,* a set, a batch; *se~ pakaian,* a suit of clothes.

lengkar [KN], coil, rim, circular framework.

lengkara [KS], Skr. miraculous, fabulous.

lengkayan [KN], a 'crow's-nest' in a Malay stockade.

lengkiang = *rengkiang.*

lengking [KN], *me~,* to ring out; to tinkle; to emit a high-pitched sound.

lengkok [KS], *me~,* to bend, wind or curve (as river or road); *lengkak-~,* winding, meandering.

lengkung [KS], 1. bow-shaped; curved; circular; encircling; *me~,* to bend, as a tree in the wind; to curve; *bengkok me~,* curved; *me~i,* to encircle, to enclose, to

include; *belat ~,* a long, movable line of screens laid to shut in a large portion of water between it and the shore; as the tide recedes, the fish in that area are left high and dry; *~an,* a frame (as for a picture); 1. circles (social or political); a group (number of persons classed together as regards age, views, etc.), a class; *~ yang berketanggungan,* responsible circles; *duduk me~,* to sit in a circle; *~an bandar,* town limits. 2. a kind of jelly, generally sold by hawkers.

lengkor [KS], *me~,* to be slightly bowed or bent.

lengkoyan = *lempoyan.*

lengkuas [KN], a kind of wild ginger (*Alpinia galanga*); it is very hot, esp. when old; *tua ~, makin tua semakin buas,* old as wild ginger is old, the older the 'hotter' (the 'old dog').

lengos [KK], *me~,* to turn the head away, esp. in order to show anger or disapproval; cf. **lingas**.

lengsan [KS], listless, idle, dawdling, unreliable.

lengser [KK], sliding sideways, side-slipping; *kain ter~,* sarong slipped down; *me~(kan),* to slide something up and down.

lengset [KK], *be~,* turned inside out; having the inside exposed; bent out of true.

lenguh [KS], 1. *me~,* to feel weak and tired in the joints; *~-lumpuh,* stiff all over. 2. *me~,* [KN], to low, of cattle.

lengung [KK], *me~,* pensive; thoughtful, = *temenung.*

lening [KN], (onom.) tinkling (of a little bell).

lenja [KK], 1. running (of the saliva); foam at the mouth; *sawan ~,* fits accompanied by foaming at the mouth; *me~,* to run (of the saliva). 2. a coarse sack of netting (in which things are hung from the roof to protect them from mice); Kel. a basket frame for carrying grass or cut padi.

lenja [KK], 1. *me~,* be brazen, become bold. 2. ring, hoop.

lenjan [KK], stamping down (as buffaloes,

a rice-field).

lenjar [KN], *biji ke~,* the glands; *sakit ke~an,* glandular swellings; cf. **kelenjar**.

lenjuang [KN], the dracoena; ~ *bukit* (*Dracoena congesta*) and ~ *merah* (*Cordyline terminalis*), plants whose roots and leaves are believed to be of medicinal value; also *senjuang*.

lenjun = *lencun*.

lentam [KN], (onom.) the sound of stamping.

lentang [KN], 1. (onom.) a clanging sound. 2. *te~,* lying on the back; *duduk te~,* spending one's time on one's back, bedridden; *mene~,* to turn over on to one's back. 3. *lenting 2.*

lentera [KN], Ind. a lantern, lamp.

lentih [KS], *per~,* lustful, lascivious.

lentik [KS], curling back, concave surface, of eyebrows, Chinese roofs, etc.); *per~an,* (fig.) a concession, special privilege.

lenting [KN], 1. (onom.) a tinkling sound; *me~,* to screech, raise voice (from excitement or as an angry woman). 2. *me~,* to warp (of wood exposed to heat); to curl up, as a dried leaf or a worm in the sun, shrivelling up; *me~~,* wriggling, as a newly caught fish. 3. to dart about, as an insect; to slip away; *kekuatan pe~,* elasticity.

lentuk [KS], *me~,* to sway from side to side; *ter~,* incline the head to one side.

lentuk [KS], supple, flexible; = *lentur*.

lentul [KK], *me~,* to feel empty (of the stomach); to be flabby, of flesh.

lentum [KN], (onom.) a thumping sound.

lentung [KN], (onom.) a deep booming sound; *~an,* a thud.

lentur [KN], flexible, yielding (as a bough); *~i,* to give a twist, or bend to anything; *me~,* [KK], to bend (intransitive); *me~kan panah,* to bend a bow; *lembut me~,* flexible; *me~ jari,* to twiddle one's thumbs.

lenung [KN], (onom.) the booming of a gong or big bell.

lenyak [KS], deep (of sleep).

lenyap [KS], disappearing; *me~kan,* to

cause to vanish.

lenyek [KS], to mash, crush; *ubi ~,* mashed potatoes.

lepa [KS], Skr. careless, negligence; also *alpa*.

lepa [KK], 1. *ter~,* sprawling from fatigue; trailing loosely; thrown away, discarded. 2. Hind. (from Skr.) *me~,* to plaster.

lepah [KK], *ber~-lepuh,* huddled, slouched; slumped down, e.g., in a chair.

lepak [KK], 1. *me~,* to whiten, become white; *putih me~,* snow-white. 2. a dull smacking sound; *me~,* to smack, pat.

lepak [KS], 1. beetling, overhanging. 2. *ber~~,* abundant, esp. as food; overflowing.

lepan [KN], N.S. a swampy plain.

lepang [KN], a creeper (unidentified); *ombak bunga ~,* white-crested billows.

lepap [KN], flat-bottomed (boat).

lepas [KS], escaped, starting, quitting; past, ago, since; ~ *sembahyang,* after prayers; ~ *itu,* after that; *sudah ~ masa,* too late (the time for that has passed); *belum ~,* young and unmarried, esp. of a girl; *(se)~,* after (the time at which); *se~ sahaja,* immediately after—; *se~,* Kel. a bout in bull fighting; *me~kan tembakan,* to open fire, *me~kan tangan,* to abandon an enterprise, 'drop it', 'wash one's hands' of it; *di bawah kuasa pe~,* under starter's orders; *tahun ~,* last year; *tidak ~~,* continuously; ~ *laku,* see *laku; me~kan nyawa,* to escape with one's life; *ter~ keretapi,* missed the train (left behind by the train); *me~kan hajat,* to fulfil one; purpose, (fig.) to relieve oneself; *kain ~,* a loose garment worn as a plaid; *~i,* to free from, to release; *~kan,* id.; *ter~,* having escaped, free; *ber~,* to start; to depart; *ber~ diri,* to get clear away; *hari ke~an,* a holiday; *hari ke~an umum,* public holiday; *~an,* discharged (as from Forces); *budak-budak ~an kolej,* former college-students; *le~,* a sort of fan used in certain magical ceremonies; *me~ cakap,* to boast.

lepat [KN], *kuih ~,* glutinous rice cooked in

leaf-packets, esp. to be eaten on a journey; cf. **ketupat**; *pergi ~ balik lemping*, to go trading and return with less than your capital (*lemping* being only a snack).

lepau [KN], a kitchen balcony in a Malay house.

lepek [KK], *me~*, to be flattened; to fall flat.

leper [KS], 1. turned up vertically (of the edge of anything); *~-~*, the raised edge of a coaming, the gunwale. 2. provincial accent, brogue. 3. shallow (of boat or cup); flattened; *~kan*, to flatten out, as a sheet of corrugated iron; *bulat ~*, flat and round, as a disc or a coin; *ter~*, crooked (of a limb); twisted, bent.

lepu [KN], a generic name given to a number of fish, e.g., *Antennarius mummifer, Synnancidrum horridum* and *(~ panjang) Pelor didactylum;* these fishes are notorious for their poisonous dorsal fins: hence, *diam ~*, a person who is outwardly good and honest but is really mean and dangerous.

lepuh [KS], *me~*, to be blistered.

lepuk [KN], (onom.) pattering (as rain); a thump; *mencangkul dua tiga ~*, to thump a cangkul down two or three times.

lepung [KN], (onom.) a thumping noise.

lepur [KK], *mati ~*, dead by suffocation in mud.

lerah [KK], *ter~*, knocked out (as fruit blown down by a storm or as a book knocked out of its binding).

lerai [KK], *me~kan*, to separate (as persons fighting).

lerak [KN], 1. *buah ~*, a fruit (*Sapindus rarak*). 2. [KK], to burst open, burst through.

lerang [KN], strip, slip, the strips in a sail; *kain se~*, a sarong woven in one piece and not in two.

lerap [KN], a game of pitch-and-toss; *main ~*, to play this game.

lesang [KK], *me~*, to sting.

lesap [KN], 1. disappearing; = *lenyap; ~-pantat*, Kel., Treng. (vulg.) completely

disappeared; *hilang-~*, completely disappeared. 2. *me~*, to make a swishing noise.

lesar [KN], sound like that of a mat being pulled.

lesau [KN], sound like that of rain falling on leaves.

lesen [KN], licence.

leser [KK], *me~*, to drag along the ground (as a garment); *pukul ~*, to drive (a ball) along the ground.

leser = *peleser*.

leset [KK], Ind. *me~*, to slip, slip up; *sangkaan me~*, a slip in anticipation; see *meleset*.

lesi [KS], *pucat ~*, extremely pale, haggard.

lesing [KN], (onom.) to whizz.

lesir [KN], 1. a sword-dance. 2. *tawar ~*, insipid; *~kan*, to hurl a stone along the surface of water.

lesit [KK], *me~*, to emit a whistling or buzzing noise.

lesok [KN], (onom.) *~-lesak*, to rustle.

lestari [KS], eternal, perpetual; *me~kan*, [KK], to perpetuate.

lesu [KS], utterly tired out; completely exhausted; *letih ~*, id.; drawn, of face.

lesut [KS], shrunken, shrivelled, esp. of limbs; atrophied.

leta [KS], mean, low, base, despicable; *me~kan*, to detest, despise.

letak [KK], to set down, to place; *~kan*, id.; *me~kan*, id.; *me~*, to lie prostrate (without a pillow); *ter~*, laid down, set down; *ter~ di*, situated at; *me~kan jawatan*, to resign; *me~kan berat pada*, to lay great stress on; *me~kan calun*, to propose a candidate; *me~kan senjata*, to lay down arms.

letam [KN], (onom.) sound of slamming.

letang [KN], (onom.) sound of clanking.

letap [KN], (onom.) the sound of tapping or rapping.

leter [KN], chatter; *me~* or *be~*, to chatter; *ber~kan*, to nag at.

letih [KS], weary, fatigued, tired; *~-lesu*, exhausted.

letik [KN], (onom.) the sound of ticking.

leting [KN], (onom.) sound of chinking.

letis [KN], (onom.) the sound of 'whisking' along.

letum [KN], (onom.) a thumping or drumming sound.

letung [KN], (onom.) sound of thumping.

letup [KK], *me~*, to go off with a bang, explode; to crackle and pop, as coral under water; *~-~*, physalis, sometimes called the Malayan Cape goosberry; *bahan-bahan ~an*, explosives.

letus [KN], burst; *me~*, to burst (of a boil); to break out (as war); *~an*, a burst (as of machine-gun fire); eruption.

lewa [KK], *me~*, to move slowly, to dawdle; *me~-~kan*, to wave slowly to-and-fro (as a fan); *~-tak-~*, casually, unhurriedly.

lewar [KK], *me~*, to fly in coveys; to swim in shoals; to swarm.

lewat [KK], 1. to exceed, pass; end of period; *~ tahun ini atau awal tahun depan*, the end of this year or the beginning of next; *~ pukul enam*, after 6 o'clock; *ter~*, too late; *me~i tebing*, to overflow its banks, of a river in flood. 2. hurry, speed.

leweh [KS], careless, proud, snobbish.

liang [KN], 1. a small aperture; *~ cincin*, the hole in a ring; *~ luka*, the orifice of a wound; *~ kubur*, grave; *ke ~ kubur*, to die; *~ mata*, the eye-socket; *~ roma*, the pores of the skin; *~ kumbang*, scuppers; *~ lahad*, see lahad; *ber~-~*, full of tiny holes; porous. 2. *~-liuk*, rolling of gait, swaying from side to side; *me~-liuk*, to twist to-and-fro, as a loosening a nut.

liar [KS], wild, disorderly, undomesticated; of eyes, restless, looking this way and that; *orang ~*, wild aboriginal tribesmen; *berke~an*, running wild all over the place; *me~-~*, to run wild, be out of control; *lari me~*, to run away, of a horse.

lias [KN], *penge~*, *pe~* or *penge~an*, a charm for invulnerability (so that the enemy's weapon fail to touch).

liat [KS], tough, leathery, lithe; *tanah ~*, clay; *~* is sometimes used to mean stiff, sluggish, of movement, as of a person going unwillingly; *me~*, to firm up, acquire consistency, as flesh of fruit or jelly; *~-liut*, to twist, to wind.

liau [KK], *me~*, to fester, to run (of a sore).

libas [KK], N.S. *me~*, to flash by, as a bird past a window; *me~-~*, flapping and jerking spasmodically, as a newly caught fish.

libat [KK], *ter~*, involved, concerned; *keter~an*, involvement; *apakah keter~an anda dalam hal ini?* what is your involvement in this case?

libur [KS], Ind. *hari ~*, a holiday; *~an*, holidays.

libut [KN], cork (substance).

licau [KS], glossy, shiny, oily-looking.

licik [KS], smart, clever sly, cunning, tricky.

licin [KS], smooth, slippery, bare; (fig.) 'cleaned-out', 'broke'; *~ licau*, glossy, sleek; *sapu ~*, to make a clean sweep of; *membayar ~*, to pay in full; *~* is sometimes used (fig.) to mean an easy mark, a 'push-over', esp. of a woman; *minyak pe~*, lubricating oil.

lidah [KN], tongue; *~ api*, a tongue of fire; *~ badak*, rhinoceros-tongue, a name given to an aroid (*Pothus latifolius*); *~ bahu*, a shoulder-strap; *~ bercabang*, a forked tongue, duplicity of speech; *~ biawak*, a monitor's (forked) tongue; *~ buaya*, crocodile's tongue, a name given to the aloe (*Aloe ferox*) (the crocodile itself is believed to have no tongue); *~ gajah*, the elephant's tongue, a name given to a plant (*Aglaonema oblongifolium*); *~ jin*, the 'spirit's tongue', a plant (*Hedyotis congesta*); *~ keling*, unreliable; *akar ~ jin*, a plant (*Hedyotis capitellata*); *~ kerbau*, buffalo-tongue, a plant (*Clerodendrum deflexus*); *~ kucing*, the cat's tongue, a plant (*Turneria ulmifolia*); *~ lembu*, the ox-tongue, a plant (*Aneilema nudiflorum*); *~ manis*, sweet-tongued; smooth-spoken; *~ panjang*, loquacious; *~ rusa*, deer's tongue, a small tree (*Fagroea racemosa*); *~ tak bertulang*, inconstant, changeable; *anak ~*, the uvula; *anak ~ timbangan*, the tongue of a balance; *tatang di anak ~,* to support on the uvula (to take the greatest care of a beloved person); *ikan ~* or *ikan ~-~,* a generic name for flat-fish; *~ pengarang,* editorial, leader.

lidas [KS], smarting, of the taste in the mouth after smoking or eating acid fruits.

lidi [KN], the veins of a plam-leaf; midrib; *sapu ~,* sweeper (broom); *ular ~,* a small snake *(Dendrophis pictus);* (fig.) the the spoke of a wheel.

ligan [KK], (coll. and common in familiar or childish talk) to drive out, to expel, e.g., a wife; *pe~,* to shoo away.

ligat [KK], *me~,* whirling round (as a top), twirling.

lihat [KK], Ar. *me~,* seeing; to see; *~i,* to inspect, to look over; *me~i,* id.; *ke~an,* visible; *pe~,* the sense or power of sight; *peng~an,* vision, view; a sight, a scene; *ter~,* striking the eye, came into sight; *memper~kan,* to display, manifest; *tukang me~,* an onlooker (taking no part), a rubber-neck; *ke~an,* there came into view, (we) saw; *ke~annya,* apparently.

lik [KN], Kel. the 'young flood', preceding the main flood *(bah).*

likas [KN], a small wheel on which the skein is wound when weaving.

likat [KS], sticky, adhesive, syrupy — cf. **lekat**.

liku [KN], 1. Jav. royal title. 2. Ked. lonely (of a place). 3. an angle, sharp corner; *ber~-~,* turning sharply this way and that, as a path.

lilah [KK], *be~,* retching; *muntah be~,* vomiting and retching.

lilang [KN], = *lilin.*

lilau [KK], *me~,* to totter (of a stricken man); also *melelung-me~.*

lilin [KN], wax; a taper; *~ lebah,* bee's wax; *kain ~,* waxed cloth; *burung ~,* the small southern hornbill *(Anthracoceros convexus).*

lilit [KN], *~nya,* circumference; *me~,* to coil round; *me~,* Kel. to have an 'affair'.

lima [Kbil], 1. five (originally, the hand of five fingers); *buku ~,* the knuckles; *ke~,* all five; *yang ke~,* the fifth; *pang~,* a leader in war, commander, warrior; *kaki ~,* pavement; 2. a generic name for a number of plants *(Xanthophyllum* sp.).

limas [KN], pyramidal; *atap ~, a* pyramidal roof (viewed from the ends); *kuang ~,* = *buang ancak,* q.v. (under *ancak).*

limau [KN], a generic name for oranges, limes, lemons, etc., *~ kapas,* the common lime *(Citrus acida); ~ nipis,* id.; *~ manis,* the orange *(Citrus aurantium); ~ kesturi,* the little musk-lime; *~ asam, ~ telur buaya, ~ puting,* the lemon; *~ Langkat,* Treng. a tangerine; *~ Haji Abdullah,* Treng. a thick-skinned sweet orange; *~ kedangsa,* a sp. of bitter lime used medicinally; *~ jambu* is sometimes used for grape-fruit; *ber~,* to use lime-juice in washing.

limbah [KN], a cess-pool, a drain; *~an* or *pe~,* id.

limbai [KK], *me~,* to wave about an object; to sway the arm; to brandish a whip or switch; *membuang ~,* to wave the arm (of a dancer); to suggest a negative or rejection.

limbang [KK], 1. *me~,* to wash (gold in washing trough); 2. *~ tengahari,* noon.

limbuk [KN], *burung ~,* a pigeon, generally in the language of sorcerers only; in some localities = *punai tanah,* the bronze-wing dove.

limbung [KN], *~an,* a dry dock; *~ kapal,* a dock; a dockyard.

limpa [KN], the liver.

limpah [KN], overflowing; *~ kurnia,* overflowing generosity; *me~,* to overflow; *maha ~,* ever-flowing, freely poured, esp. of the Mercy of God; *me~ ruah,* to overflow copiously.

limun [KS], = *halimun; orang ke~an,* the Invisible Man; *ilmu ~an,* the art of making oneself invisible.

linang [KS], 1. gathering (as tears or as water on porous stone or sweat on body); *ber~,* to ooze out, slowly drip out; gleaming, shimmering; *ber~ air mata,* tears slowly dropping. 2. Treng.

still, calm (of water).

linau [KN], the sealing-wax palm.

lincah [KS], active, nimble, restless; ~ *ke sana ke mari*, bustling here and there; *ter~-~*, always on the move.

lincin [KS], = *licin*.

lincur [KS], slippery.

lindap [KK], Pk. abated (of fever); to lessen, diminish, as youth, strength.

lindung [KK], protective cover, shelter; *me~i* or *me~kan*, to shelter, to protect, to hide by covering; *ber~*, to take shelter; *ber~ panas*, to shelter from the heat of the sun; *per~an*, a place to shelter, protection; *pe~*, a guard, a defence; a screen (from the elements); a safeguard; *per~an undang-undang negeri (suaka politik)*, political asylum.

lindur [KK], *me~*, to talk in one's sleep.

lingar [KK], *me~*, to look at anything with a sidelong look — cf. **jeling**.

lingas [KK], turning the head to look sideways; *terbe~*, turning the head this way and that, as when looking out for danger.

linggam [KN], Tam. red; red-lead.

linggi [KN], the covered or decked portions at the prow and stern of a boat.

linggis [KN], 1. *~an dayung*, the long pole fastened to the thole-pins and running parallel to the gunwale of a Malay boat. 2. a crowbar.

lingkap [KS], 1. spent, destroyed, wasted; forfeited (as a pledge); swallowed up (by misfortune), ruined. 2. *me~i*, to veil, to hang down so as to cover; *rambut disikatkan me~i dahi sikit*, hair combed down a little over the forehead.

lingkar [KN], a coil (of a snake, rope, or anything similar); *ber~*, in coils, rolled up; *~an*, a circlet; a halo; *me~i-~i bukit*, to follow the contours of a hill; *ber~-~*, encircling; *me~i*, to encircle; *me~i angkasa*, to encircle the stratosphere; *~an syaitan*, vicious circle; *~an hukum*, jurisdiction.

lingkung [KK], *me~*, surround, encircle, cover, enclose.

lingkup [KK], hanging down to one side, as a veil or tablecloth; a variant of lingkap 2; *bertudung ~*, veiled (entirely); *ruang ~*, scope.

linsang [KN], Ind. a sp. of civet-cat; see *musang*.

lintah [KN], a horse-leech; ~ *darat*, land-leech, fig. for bloodsucker (e.g., a money-lender); also *halintah*.

lintang [KS], lying athwart or across; horizontal; ~ *bujur*, diagonal; *balai ~*, a reception-hall built at right angles to the main building; *palas ~*, a sort of platform or bridge on a Malay ship; *~i*, to thwart, to cross; *me~kan*, to lay athwart; *me~*, to move across (a path); *me~i*, obstruct, hinder, impede; *terbang me~*, to fly across the sky (in front of the spectator); *me~ dengan*, broadside on to; *berlari ~-bujur*, to run, scattering right and left ([lit.] sideways and straight on).

lintap [KS], lying one on another or in strata (of flat objects — such as books).

lintar [KN], a thunderbolt; *batu ~*, a celt (prehistoric tool) such as a spear-head or arrow-head; also *halintar*.

lintas [KK], dashing past, flashing by; *me~*, to dart across; *me~i*, pass by, cross, overcome; *jin ~an*, an evil spirit darting like a comet or meteor in front of a man; a will-o'-the-wisp; *~an*, a crossing (of a wild animal over a path); a stroke (as of apoplexy); *ter~ (di hati)*, to have a sudden idea; *ter~ dalam fikiran*, to cross one's mind; *dengan se~*, suddenly; *tanda ~an jalan*, marked road crossing; *lalu ~*, traffic.

lintuh [KS], dizziness, loss of consciousness; *ilmu pe~*, magic art to deprive a person of consciousness so as to facilitate theft or abduction.

lintuo = *litup*.

linyak [KS], stamped flat, *ber~*, quarrel.

linyar [KK], smooth-sailing (of a boat); gliding through the water.

lipan [KN], a centipede; *jari ~*, used fig. for, insidious subversive activities, poisonous influences; see *halipan*.

lipas [KN], a cockroach; *seperti ~ kudung,* like a maimed cockroach, i.e. never still, bustling abbout, always on the move; *mata ~,* dull eyes.

lipat [KK], to fold up (e.g., a piece of cloth or garment); *~an,* the folds of anything; a crease caused by folding; *~ dua,* folded in two, (fig.) double; *me~gandakan,* to (cause to) increase many-fold; *pisau ~,* clasping knife.

lipis [KN], *pe~* or *pe~an,* the temples of the forehead.

lipit [KN], a narrow fold (of thread, etc.); a hem; *~an,* folds, a folded cloth; *menggunting kain dalam ~an,* to cut cloth under the folds, i.e. (fig.) to act secretly, work underground; *kala ~,* the common slender-bodied house-scorpion.

lipur [KK], calming; *peng~ lara,* a 'consoler of cares', a story-teller or story; *me~kan,* to soothe, to allay.

liput [KK], flooding, swamping, overcoming; covering; *cahaya me~ serata dunia,* her brightness permeates the world; *di~i oleh pembujuk,* overborne by endearments; *me~i* is used as an adjective, meaning 'universal'; also, to include, to comprise.

lira [KS], smooth, level.

lirik [KK], glance, look aside, to steal a look at (a person); *me~,* to glance stealthily.

lis [KN], 1. (Dutch) a cord, a twist (of cord-like patterns in carving); ornamental edging, moulding. 2. Eng. list.

lisah [KS], restless; *menge~,* to fidget; = *mengge~.*

lisan [KN], Ar. the tongue; us. in the sense of speech; *ujian ~,* oral test; *jangi ~,* verbal pledge; *bahasa ~,* spoken language; *dengan ~,* orally, by word of mouth.

litah [KS], *~ mulut,* loose-tongued, garrulous.

liter [KN], litre.

litmas [KN], litmus.

litup [KK], covering and concealing; completely overshadowing; *habis ~, dunia*

ini banyaknya, their numbers were such as to hid the world under them — cf. **liput.**

liu [KN], *~-~,* a stern-paddle.

liuk [KN], a twist or turn; the movements of a fencer or dancing-girl; *~an api,* a wavering tongue of flame; *me~-~,* to sway to-and-fro, as a tree in the wind; *me~-lentur,* id.

liung [KN], *tali ~,* a sort of belt for carrying a kris.

liur [KN], *air ~,* saliva.

liut = *liuk.*

liwat [KN], 1. Ar. sodomy. 2. = *lewat.*

loba [KS], Hind. (from Skr.) greed, covetousness; also *haloba.*

lobak [KN], the Chinese radish (*Raphanus caudatus*); used for 'turnip'.

loban [KN], Ar. *~ Jawi,* gum benjamin.

lobok [KN], a deep pool in a river or in the sea; *galah ~,* the longest kind of punting-pole; *~ kawah,* crater of an extinct volcano.

locak [KK], *me~,* to be abundant; to be plentiful (as fruit).

loceng [KN], Ch. a bell; *~ gila,* alarm-bell; *~ kecemasan,* id.; *tempat yang jauh dari ~,* a remote place.

locok [KK], *me~,* to give a push; to push up and down, as a piston; (fig.) to masturbate.

lodak [KN], mud, silt.

lodan [KN], *ikan ~,* the whale or leviathan of Malay romance.

lodeh [KN], *masak ~,* cooked to pulpiness; *sayur ~,* a vegetable soup — cf. **lodoh.**

lodoh [KS], very soft and plpy, as rotten fruit.

loga [KN], 1. Skr. abode: place; *syurga~,* heaven; also *loka.* 2. = *duga.*

logam [KN], Tam. mineral; *panca~,* an alloy of five minerals or a stone of five colours; *berma~,* a red talismanic stone; *mata air ~,* mineral springs.

logat [KN], vocabulary, = *loghat.*

loghat [KN], Ar. precise meaning, literal translation; *kitab ~,* a vocabulary; also *logat* — cf. **makna.** 2. dialect, accent.

loh [KN], Ar. slate; tablet; *~ mahfuz,* the

Tablet of Fate.

loha [KN], Ar. the forenoon; *sembahyang* ~, a morning prayer.

lohok [KS], rotten through and through.

lohor [KN], = *zuhur*, Ar. the name of midday prayer, so, midday; *lepas* ~, afternoon.

lok [KN], a curve or bend in a kris.

loka [KN], Skr. abode, place; *syurga*~, paradise, heaven; ~-*antara*, Ind. international, overseas; also *loga*.

lokan [KN], an edible bivalve found in mangrove swamps.

lokcuan [KN], Ch. smooth shining silk.

lokek [KS], stingy, mean, miserly; also *kelokek*.

loki [KN], Ch. a Cantonese prostitute.

loklok [KN], a trochus shell (from which buttons are made).

lokos [KS], bare, denuded of hair, leaves or feathers; dishevelled, not fully dressed; *basah* ~, bed-raggled; ~ *berlumus*, id.

loleh [KS], casual, carefree; ~-~, unguardedly, unconscious of danger.

lolo [KN], Ar. a pearl; probably ~ and *loklok* are really the same word, *loklok* being used as a variant to describe the pearly-looking trochus shell

lolok [KK], 1. *mo* ·, to spy upon. 2. pond, midden-hole. 3. Pah. muddy, slushy. 4. *buat* ~, to chaff, pull the leg.

lolong [KN], (onom.), *me*~, to howl.

lomba [KN], billowy motion; cantering or galloping (in a horse); the play of porpoise; *tempat ber*~ *kuda*, a racecourse; ~-~, a porpoise or dolphin; ~-~ *alur*, a porpoise (*Arcella brevirostris* and *Phocoena phocoenoides*); ~-~ *sungai*, the dolphin (*Steno plumbeus* and, rarer, *Delphinus delphis*); ~ *lari*, a footrace; ~ *merebut kerusi*, musical chairs; *perlumbaan berjalan*, walking race; *perlumbaan jarak juah*, long distance race; *perlumbaan jarak dekat*, short distance race; *perlumbaan merentas desa*, cross-country race; *perlumbaan*, races, race-meeting; *perlumbaan lepas beramai-ramai*, an open race-meeting; *temasya*

perlumbaan, race-meeting.

lombong [KN], a cavity in the ground; a surface mine; the chasm left after a volcanic explosion; a pond (old mining hole filled by rain); *tahi* ~, mining tailings; *syarikat per*~*an*, mining company.

lomis-lomis [KK], wheedling.

lompat [KK], leaping; ~*i*, to jump upon; *me*~, to spring; ~ *tinggi*, high jump; ~ *jauh*, long jump; ~ *bergalah*, pole-vault; *lari* ~ *pagar*, hurdle-race; ~ *kijang*, hop-step-and-jump; ~-*hambur*, to plunge and buck; ~ *katak*, leap-frog; *me*~ is used of 'crossing over' from one political party to another; *me*~-~ *anak*, to skip in childish excitement.

lomrah [KS], Ind. logical, natural; common, regular; *seperti* ~, as usual.

loncat [KN], jumping with both feet together, leaping (as a fish out of water); *ter*~-~, hopping about, springing about; *batu* ~*an*, (idiom) stepping stone, spring board.

loncos [KS], Ked. stark naked; bare.

londang [KN], a mud-hole.

londeh [KK], *me*~, insecurely fastened (of a sarong).

long [KN], 1. *papan* ~, a simple bier, often only two or three planks. 2. – *sulung*.

loggak [KK], looking upwards with head bent right back; *hantu* ~, a name given to the spectre huntsman from his appearance.

longgar [KS], loose-fitting; *me*~*kan*, to loosen; to relax (rules, etc.); *pe*~*an*, relaxation.

longgok [KN], a mould or heap; ~*kan*, to stack; *ber*~-~, in stacks.

longkah [KS], loosened, easily separated or loosened as of flesh from the seed.

longkai [KK], Pah. ~-~, tapering, of fingers — cf. *lengkai*.

longkang [KN], a ditch, a drain.

longlai [KS], bent, bowed; drooping, of head, from weariness; feeble, of movements; *berjalan* ~, to walk feebly; *lemah* 1., swaying, willowy.

longok [KK], *me*~, to gape (with astonishment).

longot [KS], N.S. dun-coloured, blotchy (of skin).

longsor [KK], slipping forward, sliding down; *tanah* ~, a land-slide; *me~ dalam salji,* to toboggan.

lonjak [KK], *me~,* to rise on the toes, as when looking over a wall; to bob up and down; *cakap me~,* to boast; *me~~,* to jump with excitement; *ber~ dalam hati,* to occur suddenly (of an idea); *ter~ rasa hatinya,* to jump up with joy; *me~kan,* to raise, to brandish; *me~kan tangan,* to shake one's fist; to make sparring motions.

lonjong [KS], long, straight and slender (as a tree); *tinggi me~,* lanky; ~ is used to describe the appearance of a rugby football and of a long cucumber.

lonta [KK], *ter~~,* struggling violently; showing great agitation; jumping about excitedly, as a child; a variant of *ronta;* *hidup papa ter~~,* struggling in great proverty.

lontar [KK], 1. hurling; *~kan,* to throw, to bowl a ball; *pe~,* a missile; ~ *duit,* to toss a coin; *sepe~ran batu,* a stone's throw; *ter~,* cast out. 2. a palm (*Borasssus flabelliformis*), the leaves of which were used as paper; the Palmyra palm.

lonteh [KN], Jav. a harlot.

lontok [KS], short and thick, stumpy; *orang tua* ~, a broken-down old man.

lontong [KN], cooked rice wrapped in banana leaves.

lontos [KS], smooth and cylindrical (column, pillar).

lonyai [KS], crumpled, rumpled, limp.

Lop [KN], Pk. a common Perak name; = *Kulup.*

lopak [KN], 1. a shallow puddle; a water-logged patch of ground. 2. *~~,* a pouch of *mengkuang.* 3. *~-lapik,* confused, in disorder, inconsistent.

lopek [KN], *perahu* ~, a small flat-bottomed boat.

lopong [KS], *ter~,* gaping wide, as the mouth of a cave; (fig.) agape, all agog, as at a piece of news.

lopor [KK], Ind. *me~,* to lead, to promote, to champion, *pe~,* leader, pioneer.

lorah [KN], = *lurah.*

lorat [KS], very busy, harassed.

lorek [KS], delicate graining or markings.

lorong [KN], a lane, a road or street, alley; *~an,* an opening serving as a path; *~-~kan,* to lead, induce to, esp. a wrong action.

lorot [KK], *me~,* to slide away, to descend; *me~kan,* to lower.

loseng [KN], the warp in weaving; *belah* ~, split bamboos; cf. **pakan**; also *lungsin.*

losong [KS], a white scaly eruption; ichthyosis; *sakit* ~ and *kurap* ~, id.

lotar = *lontar.*

lotek [KN], a kind of pitch for caulking boats.

loteng [KN], Ch. upstairs, the upper floor or floors.

loteri [KN], Eng. lottery.

lotong [KN], black; a name given to 'leaf monkeys' of the genus *Semnopithecus;* also *jelutung;* ~ *kelabu,* the silvered leaf-monkey (*Semnopithecus cristatus*); ~ *cangkau,* the dusky leaf-monkey (*S. obscurus*); *ekor* ~, 'monkey's tail', a name given to a swivel gun or jingal with an iron 'tail' to fix in the ground.

lowong [KS], Ind. vacant; opportunity, vacancy; *~kan,* to open out (as an opportunity); ~ *perkerjaan,* vacancy.

loya [KS], *me~,* to feel squeamish; *me~kan tekak,* to fill with disgust, make feel squeamish.

loyak [KS], soft (as overboiled rice).

loyang [KN], bell-metal; copper, brass; a copper tube; a copper mould.

loyar [KN], 1. *pinang* ~, cudgels known as 'Penang lawyers', made from the *pinang liar.* 2. Eng. lawyer; ~ *buruk,* a hedge-lawyer or sea-lawyer; a person who likes to argue and makes empty talk; ~ *keledek,* a qualified practitioner with a pettifogging practice.

loyong [KS], *me~,* to walk with tottering gait.

lu [KGn], Ch. you.

luah [KK], spitting out (food, etc., but not saliva) from the mouth.

luak [KS], 1. disgusting; *me~*, to feel nausea — cf. *loya*. 2. N.S. the territory ruled by a tribal *penghulu*. 3. *me~*, to have decreased in quantity; as shown by the lowering of the level in the container.

luan = *haluan*.

luang [KS], abated (of storms); *pe~*, (1) a calm after storm, (2) leisure after toil, opportunity, chance, *berilah dia pe~*, give her a chance; *waktu yang ter~*, spare time; *me~kan waktu*, to give time, find time; *~* is sometimes used for vacant (place).

luap [KK], *me~*, to swell, to expand; to swell high, as a body of water or a conflagration; to boil up, of anger; *kemarahannya me~*, his anger flared up.

luar [KN], outer portion; the part beyond or outside; *di ~*, outside; *di ~ dugaan*, to one's surprise; *ke~*, outwards; *tanah ~*, foreign countries; *ke~an*, outer, strange, foreign, common; *ke~an*, an issue (of a newspaper); *~-biasa*, extraordinary; *hal ehwal ~*, foreign affairs; *menteri hal ehwal ~, menteri ~*, Foreign Minister; see *keluar; menge~kan*, to produce.

luas [KS], spacious; *dahinya ~*, his forehead was broad; *per~kan*, to broaden, to extend; *~nya*, area, extent; *me~*, to extend, spread; *berke~an*, widespread; *pe~an*, expansion.

luat [KS], = *luak* 1.

lubang [KN], hole, hollow, aperture; a business opportunity; *~ tikus*, a name given to the side-cavity in which the body rests in a Malay grave; *duit ~*, Sarawak cents; *pukul ~*, to act as a broker; *~ pot*, a port-hole; *pe~*, a pitfall; *tutup ~ gali ~*, to close a hole and dig a hole, i.e. to pay a debt with borrowed money, 'borrowing from Peter to pay Paul'; *~ periksa*, man-hole.

lubuk [KN], depth (under water), *di dalam ~ hati*, deep in one's heart; *lain ~ lain ikannya*, (prov.) so many countries, so many customs.

luca [KS], Hind. obscene, low; also *lucah*.

lucas = *luncas*.

lucu [KS], bright, merry, funny; *orang pe~*, a wit; *lelucon*, farce.

lucut [KK], 1. slipping off, down or away; dropping and being lost; *me~kan jawatan*, to resign; *me~kan senjata*, to disarm; *me~kan kerakyatan*, to deprive of citizenship; *ter~ dari kerusi*, unseated (of an M.P.). 2. abrasion; scraping off skin.

ludah [KN], spit, spittle; *~i*, to spit at; *me~*, to spit; *~kan*, to eject from the mouth; to spit out; *sudah di~ dijilat balik*, (prov.) to take back what one has despised.

lugu [KS], satisfied, 'fed-up'; *tak ~*, insatiable.

luhur [KS], Ind. exalted, noble; *ke~an*, high standard; exalted position.

lui [KS], farthest from the goal; last in a race.

lujur [KK], sewing roughly together; tacking.

luka [KN], a wound; *mata ~*, or *liang ~*, the orifice of a wound; *me~kan* or *me~i*, to wound; *~ parah*, badly wounded.

lukah [KN], 1. a generic name for small riverine fish-traps, *~ bubu*, Ked., Pk. 2. to expose, uncover (as camera-films).

lukis [KK], draw; *~an*, drawing, sketching, tracing; *me~kan*, to draw; *pe~*, artist, painter; *~an cat*, a painting; *seni ~*, the art of painting or drawing.

luku [KK], *me~*, to rap the head (as in punishing a boy).

luli [KN], *ikan ~*, a fish (*Harpodon* sp.) from which 'Bombay duck' is made — cf. **keropok**.

lulu [KN], 1. crack, split (on the bark of mangrove trees); 2. *me~* [KK], to swallow without chewing; so, (fig.) generalised, indiscriminate, uncompromising; *tuduhan me~*, a sweeping accusation; *percaya me~*, blind belief.

luluh [KS], powdered, crushed to powder; *hancur ~*, crushed to pieces.

lulum [KK], sucking at (sweets, chocolate, etc.).

lulur [KK], *makan me~,* to swallow whole (as a python); also *lulu.*

lulus [KK], just slipping through, getting through; pasing (an examination); *me~,* to pass (an examination), to pass through (a crowd); *yang berke~an,* qualified (by examination); *me~kan diri,* to squeeze oneself (through); *~ benang, (jarum) ~ kelindan,* if the cotton will go through, thick thread will go through (the thin end of the wedge); *~ kehendak,* realising one's wish; *~kan,* to put through (a task); *orang ke~an universiti,* persons with University degrees.

lulut [KN], to rub the body; *pe~,* masseuse.

lumang [KK], *be~,* smeared with mud; also *ge~.*

lumat [KS], fine, soft (of earth); crushed, ground or chopped to pieces; *me~kan,* to pulverize; *pipis ~-~,* minced quite fine; *me~kan,* to mince up; to break up (soil) into a fine tilth, to pulverize.

lumayan [KS], Ind. moderate, not considerable, reasonable; comfortable in amount, as pay.

lumba = *lumba.*

lumi [KN], *ikan ~-~,* a fish (*Echineis*); also *luli.*

lumpang [KN], 1. a pounder. 2. a gap, an aperture.

lumpuh [KS], lame (from oedema or peripheral neuritis); *penyakit ~,* paralysis; polio; *me~kan,* to paralyse; (fig.) to disable, put out of action; also *lumpuk.*

lumpur [KN], mud; *~ ketam,* an area of mud caked on top, such as frequented by boring crabs; *takut akan ~ lari ke duri,* from the frying pan into the fire.

lumu = *lumut.*

lumur [KK], besmearing; *ber~,* polluted; *~kan,* to smear.

lumus [KS], 1. smeared — cf. **lumur.** 2. deep in, esp. work or trouble; cf. **tungkus.**

lumut [KN], lichen; mosses generally; algae; surface scum; *ber~,* moss-covered.

lunak [KN], soft, fleshy (as fruit); smooth-running (as oil); mellow (of voice); soft to the teeth; pulpy; mild, as policy or voice; *me~kan suara,* to adopt a mild tone, speak softly; *dengan ~nya,* without friction; amicably.

lunas [KN], 1. the keel of a boat; the main point, source; basic principles, esp. of a doctrine. 2. Ind. payment; *me~kan hutan,* to settle a debt.

luncai [KS], misshapen, fat and clumsy; *si Luncai,* a comic figure in some folktales.

luncas [KK], failing to hit, missing the mark or goal.

luncur [KK], slipping forward or downward; forfeited (as a pledge); (fig.) to slip out, as an indiscreet remark.

lundu [KN], 1. generic name given to a number of fish (*Bagrus gulioides* and *Drius* sp.). 2. *pokok ~,* a plant (*Antidesma bunias*).

lungkum [KS], dome-shaped; covering like a dome.

lungkup [KK], *te~,* capsized, overturned; = *langkup* and *lukup.*

lungsin = *loseng.*

lunjur [KK], *be~,* to stretch out the legs; *belum duduk, sudah be~,* stretching out the legs before sitting down (hasty, ill-considered action); also *unjur.*

luntang [KN], 1. *pe~,* a float (used with nets or lines). 2. *~-lantang,* loafing about.

luntur [KS], 1. *pe~,* opening medicine, whether to promote the flow of urine or the menstrual flow (*p. darah*); *ubat pe~,* bleaching chemicals. 2. to fade, lose colour (as dyed cloth or metals); (fig.) dull, dispirited, of mind; dampened, of enthusiasm.

lunyai [KS], worn thin (as a broom); also *lenyai.*

lup [KN], the rod through which the threads pass in weaving.

lupa [KK], 1. forgetting; *~kan,* to forget; *pe~,* a forgetful person; *~kan daratan,* to be immersed in thoughts, forgetful of reality; *~kan diri,* to be unconscious, to 'wander'; sometimes, to lose one's head. 2. *~-~,* fishmaws; isinglas.

lupas, see *kelupas.*

lupat [KN], a shell-fish (*Hippopus maculatus*).

lupi [KN], *papan* ~, a piece of decking flush with the gunwale in a Malay boat.

lupuh [KK], *me*~, to hammer bamboo flat; *pe*~, bamboo so flattened.

luput [KS], slipping away from; lost; passing away (as bad times or hope); ~ *daripada kejahatan,* escaping from evil; *hilang* ~, lost and gone; *tidak* ~ *dari ingatan,* unforgotten; to cease, die out, as a custom; to slip away; *dunia ini* ~ *daripada genggaman,* this world is slipping from my grasp.

lurah [KN], 1. Jav. district or division of a country; = *daerah; se*~, the entire division, all — us. pronounced *selurub,* q.v. 2. a valley; a groove, a depression; also *lorah.*

lurik [KN], (finely striped) textile.

luru [KK], *me*~, to dash forward, to charge.

luruh [KS], 1. dropping; being shed (as leaves); *ber*~, to be falling (of flowers, etc.); *se*~, whole, entire; 2. see *lurah.*

lurup [KS], *susup-*~, helter-skelter (of running).

lurus [KS], straight, smooth and straight, regular; ~*kan,* to straighten; ~ *akal,* straightforward; *lapangan* ~, the 'straight' in horse-races.

lurut [KK], 1. running a chain through the fingers; drawing one's hand over a rope, a man's arm or any similar object; to pass fingers through (hair) — cf. **urut.** 2. N.S. to flow down (of a river); to slip off, as a bracelet; *ke*~, whitlow.

lusa [KN], the day after the morrow; *besok atau* ~, in due time, shortly.

lusuh [KS], well-worn; shabby, dowdy; trite, platitudinous, stale (of joke or plot); antiquated, out-of-date.

lut [KS], penerating, effective; *tak* ~, it did not penetrate (of an arrow or bullet); *batu* ~, sounding-lead; ~ *cahaya,* translucent; ~ *sinar,* transparent.

luti [KS], ruffled, crumpled; spoilt by use but not worn out; ~*-lenyai,* id.

lutu [KK], *me*~, to attack in swarms (as wasps).

lutut [KN], the knee; *kepala* ~, the forepart of the knee; *pelipatan* ~, the intercondyloid fossa; *tempurung* ~, the knee-pan; *ber*~, to be on one's knees; *berte*~, id.; *bertindih* ~, *bertemu* ~, to sit side by side; Kel. *beralas* ~, id.

luyu [KS], *mata* ~, drooping eyelids; sleepy.

luyut [KK], *me*~, bending, drooping; *me*~ *dik buah,* heavily laden with fruit, of branches.

M

ma [KN], 1. Pk. a plural pronominal suffix; *saya~*, we; *dia~* (or *de~*), they; (= Ked. *pa*) 2. mother (familiar), = *mak*, q.v.

maa [KN], Ar. water; *~! hayat*, water of life.

maaf [KN], Ar. pardon, forgiveness; *minta ~*, to ask for pardon; to ask to be excused; to apologize; *~kan*, to forgive; *~ lahir dan batin*, pardon inward and outward, i.e. pardon for both intentional and unintentional offences; it is customary for friends to ask each other for this on the occasion of the festival at the end of the Fast (*hari raya puasa*); *saling me~kan*, to forgive and forget.

mabuk [KK], intoxicated; *~ berahi*, intoxicated with love; *~ darah*, see *darah; ~ kecubung*, dazed by datura poisoning; *~ ombak*, seasick; *~ pinang*, lightheaded (from drink or amorousness); *~ asmara*, love-sick; *~ kepayang*, intoxicated with vain (and dangerous) desire; *~ khayal*, light-headed through drink, but not drunk; *~kan*, to be mad with desire for; *pe~*, drunkard.

mabung [KS], porous, cellular, not solid (in these senses opposed to *pukal*); also *mambung*.

macam [KKtr], sort, type; as, *~-~*, of sorts, different kinds; *~ ini*, this way, thus; *~ mana?*, how?; *apa ~?*, how is it?, what's all this?; *satu ~*, (sl.) a derogatory epithet implying that the person referred to is 'a nasty piece of work', 'a type'; *se~*, a kind of, of the same kind.

macang [KN], the horse-mango (*Mangifera foetida*); also *embacang*.

macis [KN], (Eng.) matches; *anak ~*, id.; *anak ~ yang bersepuh lilin*, wax vestas; *~ minyak*, sometimes used for cigarette-lighter; also *mancis*.

macet [KS], Ind. stopping, failing to work (as an engine); *ke~an kenderaan*, traffic-jam; *me~kan*, to check, to hold up; *ke~an hidup*, life's handicap.

macuk [KS], 1. *kaki ~*, lame. 2. Ch. a gambling game.

madah [KN], 1. Ar. saying, utterance; *ber~*, to say, to speak, eulogy, high praise. 2. Ar. the vowel point marking the long alif.

madal [KS], N.S. stupid, dull, dazed.

madam [KS], depressed.

madang [KKtr], Ind. always, continually.

madat [KN], 1. Hind. prepared opium; candu; *pe~*, opium addict, drug addict; sometimes used for addicts generally. 2. a turret, a watch-tower, battlements.

Madinah [KN], Ar. Medina.

madrasah [KN], Ar. a school attached to a mosque.

madu [KN], 1. Skr. honey; *air ~*, honey; *laut ~*, an ocean of sweetness. 2. fellow-wife; *ber~*, two women sharing a husband; *me~kan*, to give one's wife a fellow-wife, to marry again; *per~an*, polygamy; *bulan ~*, honeymoon.

mafhum [KK], Ar. understood, comprehending; *tiada ~ akan makna bahasa Melayu*, he had not grasped the spirit of the Malay language.

magang [KS], overripe (of fruit).

magrib [KN], Ar. the west; the time for evening prayer; sunset time; *negeri Maghrib*, Morocco; also *maghrab*.

Magindanau [KN], Mindanoa in the Philippines; associated in Malay history with pirates.

magun [KN], fixed, esp. of awnings and skylights on a Malay boat; *kajang ~*, the shelter for the steersman, 'deck-house'.

maha [KS], Skr. great (used in compounds only); *~ besar*, very great; *~-mulia*, Highness; *~-tinggi*, most exalted; *~siswa*, university student, undergraduate; *~guru*, professor; *~ kuasa*, Almighty.

mahal [KS], costly, dear, rare; ~ *dibeli, sukar dicari,* dear to buy and hard to get for oneself; *membuat ~,* to 'make oneself expensive', sep. by being niggardly of information; *menjawab ~,* id; *jual ~,* to play hard to get.

Mahameru [KN], *Gunung ~,* a legendary mountain used as a symbol for giant size; identified with several peaks in the Himalayas and in Indonesia.

mahang [KN], a generic name for a number of trees *(Macaranga sp.).*

mahar [KN], Ar. the settlement on a bride by the bridegroom; = *mas kawin.*

mahir [KS], Ar. experienced, skilled, master of one's art; *me~kan,* practise, train; *ke~an,* skill, capability.

mahisa [KN], Skr. a buffalo; a title in ancient Java; also *misa.*

mahkamah [KN], Ar. a court of justice; ~ *jenayah,* Treng., Kel. criminal court; ~ *mal,* civil court; ~ *tengah,* a Sessions Court; ~ *tentera,* a court martial; ~ *tinggi,* high court; ~ *rayuan,* court of appeal.

mahkota [KN], Sr. a crown; *perayaan hari ke~an,* coronation celebrations; *putera ~,* crown prince.

mahligai [KN], Tam. a palace; us. applied to the house or chamber of a Royal lady.

Mahmud [KN], Ar. (= *belauded*), a common Malay name.

mahsul [KN], result, product.

mahsyar [KN], Ar. meeting, assembly; *Padang Mahsyar,* the Plain of Assembly, where the dead will be judged on the Last Day.

mahu = *mau.*

main [KK], sport, play, amusement; ~ *judi,* gambling; *ber~,* to play, to play at; *ber~ mata,* to cast amorous glances; *per~an,* an amusement; *barang ~an,* toys; *budak seper~an,* a playmate; ~ is used as the equivalent of the English 'play' (of loose bearings); ~ *muda,* to be a playboy (with special reference to womanising); ~-~, to play about, not be serious; *bukan ~,* no joke!, terrific!, very; *memper~kan,* to 'fool', make game of; *memper~kan*

jari tangan, to make play with fingers (in dances); to gesticulate; *me~-~kan,* to finger, play with; ~ *tutup ibu,* to play hide-and-seek; *~kan lagu,* to play a tune; ~ *pantai,* Treng. a sort of harvest festival held on the beach (not to be confused with *puja pantai*); *pe~,* a player; ~ *tangan,* to gesticulate.

maisir [KN], ar. gambling.

maja [KN], a generic name for a number of plants, e.g., *~kani, ~pahit,* etc.

majakani [KN], imported gall-nut, used medicinally.

majal [KS], 1. blunt; dull of hearing. 2. unlucky; *sial-~,* very unlucky.

majallah [KN], Ar. magazine, periodical; ~ *penggalan,* school magazine (issued each term).

Majapahit [KN], 1. a famous Javanese city and empire founded A.D. 1294, overthrown after A.D. 1400. 2. a small tree *(Aegle marmelos).*

majhar [KS], Kel. absurd, nonsensical.

majikan [KN], Ind. employer.

majlis [KN], Ar. assembly, gathering; a party; a council; *di tengah ~,* in public; ~ *agama,* Kel. the Department of Religion; ~ *undangan,* Legislative Council; ~ *pentadbir,* Executive Council; ~ *Islam tertinggi Malaya (Mata),* Supreme Council of Islam, Malaya; ~ *bandaran,* Town Board; ~ *Perhimpunan Agung Bangsa-bangsa Bersatu,* General Assembly of the United Nations; ~ *Mesyuarat,* Council of State; ~ *Perhimpunan Kebangsaan,* National Assembly; ~ *Keselamatan Bangsa-bangsa Bersatu,* Security Council of the United Nations; ~ *jamuan,* a (social) party; *di tengah ~,* before others (i.e. in semi-public); ~ *makan malam,* a dinner party, esp a banquet; ~ is also used in such polite expressions as *kehadapan ~,* into the presence of, when addressing a person, esp, in formal letters.

majmuk [KS], Ind. plural; compound, complex; also *mankuh; kalimat ~,* compound sentence.

majnun [KS], Ar. 1 possessed by a jin;

frenzied; used esp. of those mimicking frenzy in Hassan-Hussain processions. 2. *Majnun*, the 'frenzied' lover of Laila in certain Eastern romances; he and Laila symbolize lovers, like Romeo and Juliet.

maju [KK], progressive, prospering, improving; *ke~an*, improvement, progress; *me~kan*, to promote (as a scheme); to proposed (a motion); *berke~an*, improved; *bergerak ~*, to progress; *~-mundurnya*, the successes and set-backs, of, e.g., a scheme; *~lah*, (slogan) onwards!, forward!, may ... prosper!

majuh [KS], gluttonous in eating.

Majuj [KN], Ar. the giant, Magog.

majum [KN], oakum; used in caulking boats; also *majun.*

Majusi [KN], Pers. Magian; connected with the Zoroastrian religion; used for 'heathen' generally.

majzub [KN], Ar. religious frenzy.

mak [KN], mother; also *ma*; *~ saudara*, (Pen.) *~ penakan, ~ sepupu*, aunt; *~ angkat*, foster mother; *~ sulung*, eldest aunt; *mak tua*, id.; *~ ngah, ~ utih*, intermediate aunt; *~ bongsu, ~ busu, ~ kecil, ~ muda*, youngest aunt; *~ cik*, 'aunty'; *duduk di bawah ketiak ~ lagi*, living under mother's armpit, i.e. tied to mother's apron-strings; also *emak.*

maka [P], a moment of time; used in writing as a punctuation word and translatable as 'and', 'then', 'next', further'.

makalah [KN], Ar. an article (newspaper).

makam [KN], Ar. 1. a grave with a small pavilion over it; a grave- shrine; *~kan*, to entomb, enshrine. 2. foundation, place, site. 3. rank, position; *pe~an*, burial; *upacara pe~ah*, funeral services.

makan [KK], to eat, to consume, to wear away; (in such games as chess) to take a piece; (of weapons) to take effect; food, a meal; *~ nasi*, to dine; *~ jenuh*, to eat one's fill; *di~ karat*, eaten into with rust; *~ suap*, to take bribes; *~ gaji*, to receive regular pay; *~an*, things eaten; diet; *~ masa*, to take up time, spend

time; *tidak ~ tua*, unaffected by old age; *~-tanggung*, 'all found' (receiving food as well as wages); *brek tak ~*, the brakes don't bite; *~ sumpah*, to suffer the effects of a curse or of the breaking of an oath; *~ diri*, to waste away with worry, sorrow, etc; *~ masak-mentah*, to eat indiscriminately, 'all is fish that comes into his net'; *~nya dalam air*, the draught of a ship; *~ berkurang*, to suffer from malnutrition; *~ modal*, to live on capital; *~ dik hari*, weather-beaten; sun-burned; *ter~*, using a bit too much or a bit too little; *ter~ hari*, to fail to complete on a fixed date (whether by being too early or too late); *ter~ bulan*, starting the Fast a few days late; *~ hati*, to eat one's heart out (with resentment); *di~ umur*, stricken in years; *~ hasil perempuan*, to live on a woman's earnings (generally, but not necessarily, immoral earnings are implied); (reput) *di~ zaman*, (crumbling away) owing to the passage of time; *ter~ kata-kata orang*, taken in by people's talk; *~ berlebih*, to over-eat; *~pakai*, food and clothing, esp. as part of earnings or result of earnings; *~ tanggung berak cangkung*, (vul. sl.) pungent description of 'an easy life'; *ter~* in the sense of exceeding or falling short (*vide supra*) is sometimes used to mean, in effect, error, breach of etiquette or good manners; *khilaf dan ter~ maaf halalkan*, I ask pardon for mistakes and shortcomings; *~ dengan tahi sekali*, pungent equivalent of 'make mincemeat of'; *~ sambil-sambil*, to eat at odd times, between meals; *~ hati berulam jantung* (prov), to eat one's heart out.

makar [KS], 1. hard, stony (of fruit). 2. tricks, wiles.

makbul [KK], Ar. confirmed, approved, agreed to; granted, of a prayer.

maki [KK], 1. abuse, bad language; me-maki, to revile; *~ hamun*, reviling and insulting; *~an*, abuse. 2. Ar. sena *~*, 'senna of Mecca' (*Cassia angustifolia*).

makin [KKtr], the more; *~~*, the more ...

the more; ~-se~, id,; ~ lama ~ baik, the longer the better.

makjun [KN], Ar. compounded medicine.

Makkah [KN], Mecca.

makhluk [KN], Ar. created things; a creature, mankind, humanity.

maklum [KK], Ar. known, understood; ~kan, to inform; lebih ~, you are aware; ~-lah, y'know; harap di~i bahawa..., please be advised that....

maklumat [KN], Ar. notice, information.

makmal [KN], Ar. a laboratory.

makmum [KN], Ar. the followers of the imam at the mosque; the congregation.

makmur [KS], 1. Ar. prosperous, populous, abounding; plentiful, of money; ke~an, prosperity. 2. Pk. a sort of mince-pie.

makna [KN], Ar. meaning, real meaning, as opposed to literal translation (lughat).

makrifat [KN], perfect knowledge, wisdom.

makruh [KS], Ar. hateful, detestable, esp. of food which is not yet haram.

maksiat [KN], sin, wickedness, act of breaking God's laws, vice.

maksud [KN], wish, desire, intention; what the speaker is 'getting at', purport, meaning; ~kan, to mean (intend to indicate), hint, imply.

maksyuk [KN], Ar. the beloved one, mistress; loved.

maktab [KN], Ar. a college; ~ tentera, military college.

maktub [KK], Ar. ter~, written.

makyung [KN], a theatrical performance met with in the Northern States of the Peninsula.

makzul [KK], Ar. ~kan, to depose, degrade.

mal [KN], Ar. property; baitul-~, the treasury; bicara ~, a civil case.

mala [KN], 1. Skr. accursed; a curse; misfortune; ~ pestaka, extreme ill-luck; disaster; ~ petaka, id. 2. faded, withered (of flowers).

malah [p], Ind. nay rather; furthermore; also ~an, instead.

malai [KN], Sk. a flower worn in the hair; sunting ~, id.

malaikat [KN], Ar. an angel; the principal angels are Mikail, Izrail, Munkar and Nakir, q.v.

malak [KN], 1. Ar. angel; ~ulmaut, the angel of death — us. pronounced malikulmaut. 2. king; Al Malak Farouk, King Farouk.

malakat [KN], Ar. a mart; hence probably the name of Malacca.

malam [KN], night; the darkness of night; tengah ~, midnight; siang ~, day and night; se~, one night ago, yesterday; ~ tadi, last night; ber~, to pass the night; ke~an, benighted; se~-~an, all night long; sepanjang ~, id.; ~ buta, a pitch-dark night, the dark of night.

malan [KS], drunk, amazed, perplexed.

malang [KS], 1. adverse (of fortune); unlucky; ke~an, ill-luck; an accident. 2. a submerged reef.

malap [KS], flickering (of a light); dulled (of radiance) or of paint; pe~, to turn down, dim, a light; ~ is also used to mean gloomy, somber, (of fate).

malar [KKtr], constantly, steadily; ~ pucat kurus, always pale and thin; air ~ dua depa, water with a constant depth of two fathoms.

malas [KS], Skr. idle, lazy, sluggish; Kel. reluctant; pe~, habitually lazy; ke~an, laziness.

malau [KN], ~ gari, Ked. sealing-wax; also embalau.

malaun [KS], Ar. accursed, evil.

mali [KK], 1. pe~, tabooed, forbidden. 2. tali te~, cordage; rigging; me~, to twine string. 3. ~-~, a generic name given to several plants (esp. to Leea sambucina). 4. Tam. (Penang) = malai, a garland.

maligai [KN], Tam. a palace; also mahligai.

malik = malak.

malim [KN], Ar. a learned person (esp. one learned in navigation); a navigating officer or first mate.

maling [KN], Jav. a thief; thieving; pintu ~, a side or back entrance to a Malay house.

malis [KS], faded, dulled (of bright colour).

malu [KS], modest; bashful; *menaruh ~,* to feel shame; *mendapat ~,* to be put to shame; *dengan tak ~,* shamelessly; *ke~- ~an,* feelings of modesty or feeling very shy; *rumput si ~,* the sensitive plant; *tak tahu ~,* shameless; *me~kan,* to put to shame, disgrace, defame; *pe~,* shy, retiring; *~-~ kucing,* pretend to be shy; *~-~ asam,* affecting shyness; *wang tim- bang ~,* damages for loss of reputation; *saman ~,* case for such damages; *~kan,* to look up to; *bahagian ke~an,* private parts.

Maluku [KN], *Pulau ~,* the Moluccas.

malung [KN], a conger eel.

mam [KK], to suck at the breast.

mamah [KK], masticating, crushing in the mouth; *~-biak,* to chew the cud.

mamai [KS], of clouded mind, not quite right in the head.

mamak [KN], Skr. uncle, aunt; uncle (a form of address from a prince to an aged minister); also an address to uncles generally and elder non-rela- tives, esp. Indians.

mamanda [KN], uncle; a respectful vari- ant of *mamak.*

mamang [KS], 1. looking but not perceiv- ing (as an absent-minded man). 2. *gopoh ~,* extreme haste.

mambang [KN], a spirit, the personifica- tion of the sunset glow.

mambu [KN], Tam. (Penang) the nim tree.

mambung [KS], = *mabung.*

mami [KN], Skr. an aunt.

mamik [KS], slightly changed or gone off (of taste or flavour), overripe.

mampat [KS], 1. tight, densely packed, sunk, settled down (of earth); com- pressed. 2. *~-~,* a name given to some plants (*Cratoxylon sp.*).

mampir [KK], Ind. to pay a short visit, 'drop in'.

mampu [KS], means, resources, capable; *tidak ~,* (I) can't afford (to buy); = *upaya; se~-~-nya,* as far as (my) resources permit; *ke~an,* ability, wealth, prosperity, capability.

mampus [KS], dead (vulgarly expressed); wiped out; 'kicked the bucket', 'croaked'; *pergi ~ dengan,* to blazes with.

mamu [KN], Skr. uncle; a variant of *mamak.*

mamun [KS], in a daze; half-asleep; wool- gathering.

mamung [KS], dull, unseeing (of the eyes) — cf. *mamang.*

man [KN], Hind. a measure of weight; a maund.

mana [KKtr], 1. where, which, what, how, why? *di ~?,* in what place?, where?; *ke ~,* whither?; *dari ~?,* whence? *~ saja,* whichever, whatever; *di~-~,* every- where. 2. = *makna.* 3. *~kan (~ akan).* how can it be that?

manah [KN], see *mas.*

manai [KS], pale, anaemic; *pucat ~,* id.

manau [KN], *rotan ~,* thin rattan (sp. un- identified).

mancis [KN], Eng. matches, = *macis; ~i,* to put a match to.

mancit [KK], to spout or gush out.

mancung [KS], clear-cut, sharp-angled (of the profile, esp. the nose).

manda = *mamanda.*

mandah [KN], rice barn.

mandam [KS], dizzy, intoxicated; *~ khiali,* id.

mandang, 1. to see; to gaze at, = *meman- dang* (from *pandang*); *tak ~,* Pk. expres- sion of strong negation; 'certainly not!' 2. *te~,* aspect; imposing appearance.

mandarsah = *bandarsah.*

mandi [KK], bathing; to bathe; *batu ~,* a rock that is just awash; *tempat ~,* a bathing-place; *me~kan,* to give a bath to; *~ laut,* to bathe in the sea; *~ Safar,* a festival held on the last Wednesday of the month *Safar* for the purpose of purfying oneself so as to avert future disasters *(menolak bala)*; in practice, an excuse for bathing picnics; *~-manda,* bathing, ablutions; *~ peluh,* bathed in sweat; *batu ~, ombak,* sea-washed rock; *per~an,* baptism; *tempat per~an,* bath- ing-place, esp. swimming pool; *~ biar basah,* if you bathe, get wet, i.e. be thorough; *~ wajih,* to perform ritual ablutions.

mandul [KS], childless, unfruitful, barren, us. of females, rarely of males; *me~kan,* to sterilize; *pe~an,* sterilization.

mandum [KS], Tam. (Penang) sluggish, quiet, e.g., of a horse.

mamdung. [KN], a cock.

mandur [KN], Port. an overseer.

manera [KN], Jav. 1. we, your servant; also *mendera.*

manfaat [KN], Ar. = *munafaat.*

mangap [KK}, Java. agape; with jaws wide open — cf. *mangau.*

mangau [KK], agape (esp. with astonishment); all in a dither; *mengap-~,* wide-agape; *ter~,* id.; also *mangu* — cf. *mangap.*

mangga [KN], Skr. the mango — us. *mempelam;* a padlock; *me~,* to fasten with a padlock; sakit ~, suffering from bubo.

manggan [KN], manganese.

manggar = *mangkar.*

manggis [KN], the mangosteen *(Garcinia manggostana).*

manggista = *manggis.*

manggul [KN], *tanah ~,* high land, hillock.

manggustan = *manggis.*

mangkar [KN], 1. *mayang ~,* the opening blossom of the coconut (a simile for curly hair). 2. unripe, hard; also *makar.*

mangkat [KK], 'to be borne aloft' (a euphemism for death when speaking of a prince); *ke~an,* the death.

mangkin [KN], 1. = *makin.* 2. any substance used with the effect of a catalyst to dilute or thin out another substance, e.g., in cooking or making cosmetics.

mangku [KK], to nurse, to control, to guard; a variant of *pangku,* nearly obsolete except in titles of honour; *~bumi,* guardian of the realm; see also under *darjah.*

mangkuk [KN], bowl; a cup; *pinggan ~,* crockery; *~tingkat,* a tiered tiffin-carrier, = *siak;* ~ *som,* a small Chinese bowl.

mangli [KS], Pen. bold, unafraid (as of a wild animal which is semi-tame).

mangsa [KN], Skr. flesh, food; prey (of animals), victim.

mangsi [KN], Skr. a compound of burnt tamarind bast used for staining the teeth.

Manguni [KN], a name of a revolutionary organisation in Indonesia, said to be allied to Permesta, q.v.

mani [KN], Ar. the seminal fluid; *memasukkan ~ seorang lelaki ke dalam rahim seseorang isteri kerana berkehendakkan anak,* to practice artifical insemination (for humans).

manik [KN], Skr. a bead; *se utas ~-~,* a string of beads.

manikam [KN], Tam. gem; essence; embryo; *jauhar juga yang mengenal ~,* it takes a jeweller to pronounce upon a gem (prov).

Manikul [KN], Ind. short for *Manifesto Politik Sukarno,* the political manifesto of President Sukarno, setting forth his system of administration.

Manila [KN], the capital of the Philippines; *orang ~,* Manila man, is often used simply to mean a Filipino; *tali ~,* Manila hemp.

manis [KS], 1. sweet; (in colour) light; *adas ~,* aniseed; *gigi ~,* incisor tooth; *hitam ~,* fine light brown (complexion); *jari ~,* ring finger; *kayu ~,* cinnamon; *ke~an,* sweetness; *pe~,* a charm to render attractive; *~an,* sweets; *~an lebah,* honey; ~ *buah,* as sweet as fruit, i.e. sweet, but not as sweet as sugar, fairly sweet; *tidak ~,* not sweet; (fig.) in bad taste; *lagi ~,* sweeter, (fig.) in good taste; ~ is used for charming, attractive, of a girl; ~!, sweetie!; ~ is also used as an attenuant with adjectives; *Ikal ~,* wavy. 2. *penyakit kencing ~,* diabetes; *habis ~ sepah dibuang* (prov), ingratitude is the way of the world.

manja [KS], 1. conveys the idea of clingingly affectionate, esp. that of a child for its parents; so, a darling, a pet; *~kan,* to indulge, to 'spoil'; so, ~ often means spoilt; ~ *dengan,* on familiar, affectionate terms with (a superior); *ter~,* over-indulged, spoilt; *ke~an,* favoured position. 2. (Punjabi) a string-bed, charpoy.

manjang [KN], *hantu* ~, the familiar spirit of a wizard.

manjapada [KN], Skr. the earth; the abode of mortals.

manjung = *anjung.*

manora = *mendora.*

mansuh [KK], Ar. cancelled, repealed, abolished.

mantap [KS], steady, calm.

mantera [KN], Skr. a magical formula.

mantik [KN], Ar. logic.

mantul [KN], Ind. past thinking, mind in a whirl, as from worry.

manuk [KN], bird; = *unggas;* ~ *dewata,* the bird of paradise.

manusia [KN], Skr. mankind, man; *orang* ~, a human being; *nyawa* ~, the human life; *lidah* ~, the human tongue; *ke*~*n,* humanity; natural justice; *perike*~*n,* humaneness.

manyan = *kemenyan.*

mapan [KS], established.

mapar [KN], gang, a flat-ended brazier's chisel — cf. *papar.*

mar [P], Ar. word of warning in chess, when one's opponent's queen is en prise.

mara [KN], 1. Skr. danger, misfortune; ~-*bahaya,* danger, risk, peril. 2. *kota* ~, the breastwork protecting the gunners in the battery of a local pirate-ship. 3. to advance, esp. as an army.

marah [KK], angry; wrath; ~ *angin,* idle threats; ~*kan,* to show anger to; to rebuke, ~*i,* id,; *pe*~, irascible.

marak [KK], to flare up (of a flame); *se*~, light, glow; *me*~*kan,* light up, kindle.

marga [KN], Skr. a wild animal; ~*setua,* wild animals generally; *Pejabat Pelindung* ~*setua,* Wild Animals Protection Department; *pengawal* ~*setua,* game warden.

marhaban [KN], Ar. the singing of the praises of the Prophet.

marhaen [KN], Ind. the proletariat.

marhum [KN], Ar. that has found mercy; *al-*~, the late (prince).

mari [KK], 1. here, come here; *ke* ~, come here; *bawa ke* ~, bring here; *pergi* ~,

going and coming. 2. (coll.) come; ~ *sini,* come here; *dia sudah* ~, he has come.

Marikh [KN], Ar. (the planet) Mars.

markah [KN], Port. the mark on a sounding line; school marks; stripe denoting rank; ~ *kepujian,* marks earning distinction.

markas [KS], Ind. headquarters, esp. of troops; ~ *besar,* G.H.Q., but often used simply for H.Q.

marmar [KN], Hind. *batu* ~, marble.

martabat [KN], Ar. a rung of a ladder; a grade in the scale of rank; prestige.

martil [KN], Port. a hammer; Pen., Pk. a police truncheon.

maruah [KN], Ar. self-respect, manhood; dignity; *menjatuhkan* ~, to humiliate publicly; *hilang* ~, to lose face, to loose one's dignity; *menjaga* ~, to keep up one's dignity, preserve one's self-respect; *memelihara* ~, id.; *ber*~, dignified (of behaviour); *menjual* ~, to demean oneself, esp. for money.

maruas [KN], Ar. a small hand drum to accompany a gambus.

mas [KN], gold, golden; a term of endearment; a Javanese title; a weight, = tahil; ~ *kawin,* the settlements on a bride; ~ *tempawan,* hammered gold; a term of endearment; ~ *urai,* ~ *biji hayam,* ~ *pasir,* alluvial gold; *anak* ~, a born slave; (fig.) opportunists; people who curry favour; *air* ~, gilding; gold paint; *benang* ~, gold thread; *kertas* ~, gold leaf; ~ *tua,* pure gold; ~ *muda,* alloyed gold; ~ *telerang,* reef-gold; *tongkol* ~, a nugget, *jongkol* ~, id.; ~ *urung,* iron pyrites; ~ *sejati,* genuine gold; ~ *lancungan,* false or imitation gold; see *mutu;* ~ *juita,* darling; ~ *lantak,* bar-gold; ~ *bertitik,* hammered gold; ~ *tuangan,* moulded gold; ~ *kerajang,* gold foil; *tukang* ~, goldsmith; ~ *manah,* N.S. a ceremonial gift of gold made by the four *Undangs* to the Ruler (*Yang Di pertuan*) on the occasion of his enthronement; also *emas.*

masa [KN], Skr. season, period, epoch;

pada ~ itu, at that time; *~ lalu,* old days, the past; *~ percobaan,* probationary period; *pada tiap-tiap ~ dan ketika,* at all times and seasons; *~ mana,* when?; *dari ~ ke se~,* from time to time; *se~,* while, throughout the time of, during; *~ depan,* the future; *curi ~,* to find time, make time or to slack on the job; *separuh ~,* half-time; *bila-bila ~ sahaja,* at all times, always, 'any old time'; *~ perubahan,* period of transition.

masalah [KN], Ar. a thesis; a puzzling question; an enigma; an interrogatory; the knack of doing something, the 'hang of it'; a problem.

masak [KS], ripe, mature, cooked; (fig.) experienced; to cook, to smelt; *~ mentah,* food cooked and raw; *juru ~,* a cook; *kapur ~,* plaster; *tengah ~,* 'half-baked'; *~an,* a method of cooking; a 'dish'; *~lemak,* to cook in coconut cream; *~* is used with the meaning of treating (material), processing, esp. under heat; *me~kan perjanjian,* to fix up an agreement, make a firm agreement; *fikir ~-~,* to think carefully.

masakan [KS], (in literature) is it likely?, what though?; can it be that?, incredible!

masulla [KN], Ar. a prayer-mat.

masam [KS], acid, sour; *~ muka,* sour-faced; *~-manis,* bitter-sweet — cf. *asam.*

maserba [KS], omnivorous

masih, 1. still; while still; *~ lagi,* id.; *dilihatnya ~ ada lagi baginda sedang berkata-kata dengan seorang temannya,* he saw that the king was still conversing with one of his companions; also *masi.* 2. *masikan,* to win over, induce.

Masih [KN], 1. Ar. *Al-~,* the Messiah, Jesus. 11. = *masi.*

Masihi [KN], Ar. Christian, Protestant; *tahun ~* (T.M.), the Christian era, A.D.; *dahulu daripada ~* (D.M.) before Christ, B.C.

masin [KS], salt, briny, brackish — cf. *asin;* (fig.) piquant, not boring, (of a speech); pungent, effective; *~ mulut,* what has

been said has come true, wise in speech; *garam kami tidak ~ padanya* (prov.), our word does not count with him.

masing [KKtr], separate, singly (of persons only); *~-~, kan,* to insert; *ter~,* including; *~ sojar, ~ tentera,* to enlist in the army; *~ angin,* to catch a cold; *ter~akal,* reasonable, acceptable, plausible; *ke~an pencuri,* to have one's house broken into; *tidak ter~,* excluding.

Masir [KN], *negeri ~,* Egypt.

masjid [KN], Ar. a mosque; *~-ul-Haram,* the great mosque at Mecca.

masuk [KK], enter; join; *dibawa ~,* carried in; *~ keluar,* going in and out; *~ Islam* or *~ Melayu,* to become a Muslim; *~i,* to enter into; *~kan,* to insert; *ter~,* including; *~ sojar, ~ tentera,* to enlist in the army; *~ angin,* to catch a cold; *ter~akal,* reasonable, acceptable, plausible; *ke~an pencuri,* to have one's house broken into; *tidak ter~,* excluding.

masta [KN], *buah ~,* Kel. the mangosteen.

mastautin [KK], Ar. to live, reside — of chiefs and officials; in epistolary language; *ber~,* to settle (in a country), be domiciled.

mastuli [KN], *kain ~,* a heavy cloth of rich silk.

masya, Ar. *~ Allah,* God's will be done, as God wills.

masyarakat [KN], Ar. society; *~ pelbagai bangsa,* multi-racial society.

masygul [KS], Ar. sad, sorrowful, depress.

masyhadat [KN], Ar. assembly, meeting.

masyhur [KS], Ar. famous, well-known; *~kan,* to spread news; *pe~an,* declaration, proclamation.

masyrik [KN], Ar. the east.

mat [KN], 1. Pers. mate (at chess); *sa~,* checkmate. 2. *Mat,* a common Malay proper name, short for Muhammad or Ahmad or Mahmud.

mata [KN], 1. eye, focus, centre; the blade or point of a weapon; a point of the compass; points (in a competition); *~ wang,* currency, legal tender; *kaca ~,* spectacles; *~ kasar,* the unaided eye; *~ kepala sahaya sendiri,* my own eyes; *~ pencarian,* means of livelihood; *~ pelajaran,* educational subject; *~ jerat,* the loop of a noose; *~ dacing,* the marks on a steel-yard showing the various weights; *mengenal ~ dacing,* (fig.) not easily misled, knowing what's what; ~ *duitan* (fig.), greedy, money-grubbing, money-mad; ~ *keranjang,* a flirt; ~ *air,* a spring; ~ *bisul,* the head of a boil; ~ *cas,* a roving eye; ~ *gobek,* the blade of a betel-nut pounder; ~ *gunting,* the point of a pair of scissors; ~ *hari,* the sun; ~ *hati,* mental perception, the mind's eye; ~ *hidung,* used idiomatically as *batang hidung,* see *hidung;* ~ *jalan,* an outpost, a scout; ~ *juling,* squint-eyed; ~ *kail,* a fish-hook; ~ *kaki,* ankle; ~ *kakap,* the plughole; ~ *kayu,* a knot in wood (fig. an illiterate); ~ *keris,* the blade of a kris; ~ *kucing,* 'cat's-eye', a well-known fruit *(Nephelium Malayense); damar ~ kucing,* a valuable damar obtained from *Hopea globosa;* ~ *liar,* wild-eyed; ~ *luka,* the orifice of a wound; ~~, (in old-time Malaya) a satellite of the *syah-bandar* or harbour-master; (in Malacca) a penghulu's assistant; a policeman; *se~ ~,* only, merely, wholly; ~ *panah,* the point of an arrow; ~ *pedang,* the blade of a sword; ~ *piano,* the keys of a piano; ~ *pedoman,* the needle of a compass; ~ *punai,* 'green pigeons' eyes', the lozenge-shaped apertures in a grille or cross-grating; ~ *sabun,* pale-eyed; ~ *susu,* the nipple of the breast; ~ *tong,* the bung-hole in a cask; *anak ~,* the pupil of the eye; *air ~,* tears; *bermain ~,* eye-play; *biji ~,* the eyeball; *bulu ~,* eyelashes; *cahaya ~,* light of the eyes; a term of endearment; *cermin ~,* eye-glasses, spectacles; *ekor ~,* the corner of the eye; *kelopak ~,* the eyelid; *liang ~,* the eye-socket; *orang-orangan ~,* the image in the pupil of the eye; *putih ~,* being put to shame; *silap ~,* conjuring, magic show; legerdemain; *terus ~,* (1) clear of vision; (2) second sight; *ber~kan tongkat,* having a stick for eyes, i.e. blind; *hilang di ~ hilang di hati,* out of sight out of mind. 2. Ar. things of value; gems, etc., which represent great value in small compass; ~ *benda* and ~ *dagangan,* id; *se~~,* pure, solely.

matab [KN], Hind. (from Pers.) blue-lights; Roman candles.

matahari [KN], the sun; ~ *hidup,* ~ *naik,* ~ *terbit,* sunrise; ~ *turun,* ~ *mati,* ~ *jatuh,* ~ *masuk,* ~ *tenggelam,* sunset; ~ *tinggi,* the sun high in the heavens; ~ *rembang,* the meridien; ~ *condong,* the sun declining; *kena panah ~,* sun-stroke; ~ *sakit,* ~ *kena gerhana,* eclipse of the sun; *burung ~,* Wray's minevit; *bunga ~,* sunflower.

matan [KN], Ar. original text; so, gist, purport (as of a speech).

matang [KN], 1. *per~* or *pe~,* a hog's back, rising ground in alluvial flats. 2. Ind. ripe, mature.

matari = *matahari.*

mati [KK], 1. dead; ended; ~ *dibunuh,* dead by violence; 'a bad end'; ~ *beragan,* a natural death, to die not because of disease (but because of yearning, sadness, etc.); ~ *lemas,* dead from suffocation or drowning; ~ *pucuk,* impotent; *belanja ~,* fixed allowance; *grant ~,* a freehold grant of land; *harga ~,* a fixed price, or bedrock price; *hukum ~,* sentence of death; *jalan ~,* blind alley; *ber~ ~,* earnestly, assiduously; ~ is used for the 'running down' of a clock, the 'dying out' of a fire, the 'closing' of a business and the 'dying away' of a wind; *ke~an angin,* a dead calm; *me~kan,* to put to death; (fig.) to turn off, e.g. the radio; *me~kan diri,* to cause one's own death; (fig.) to 'freeze', keep quite still; ~~, insistently, persistently; ~~ *tak mahu,* absolutely refuse, 'rather die'; *bekerja ~~,* to work earnestly, whole-heartedly; *berjuang ber~~an,* to be engaged in a struggle to the death; *surat ke~an,* death certificate; *perjuangan hidup ~,* a life and death struggle. 2. ~~, if you are going to, taking it that you mean to; *simpul ~,* a knot which is not a slip-knot or running knot; *burung ~ anak,* the brain-fever bird; *burung ~ sekawan,* the bushy-crested hornbill.

matlamat [KN], Ar. objective.

mau [KK], wish, intention, will; ~ *tak ~,*

willy-nilly; *kemahuan,* desire; also *mahu.*

maudhuk [KN], Ar. title (as of a book).

maujud [KS], Ar. life, existence; *~kan,* to give life to.

maujudat [KN], Ar. existing things, all creation.

maulud [KN], Ar. birthday; *bulan Maulud,* the month commemorating the Prophet's birthday, the month *Rabial awal.*

maun [KS], herbivorous.

maung [KN], unpleasant in taste, nasty; *pahit-~,* very bitter, all kinds of hardships.

maut [KN], Ar. death; the hour of death; *malak ul ~,* the angel of death; *membawa ~,* fatal.

mawa [KN], a leaf-monkey *(Semnopithecus sp.),* believed by Malays to live on dew.

mawar [KN], Ar. rose-water; *air ~,* id.; *bunga air ~,* the rose.

mawas [KN], Sum. the *mias* or *orang-utan (Simia satyrus),* an animal known to Peninsular Malays only by tradition and so endowed with miraculous attributes; *tulang ~,* prehistoric iron tools, supposed to be the forearm of the mawas.

maya [KS], 1. Skr. unsubstantial, illusory; outward appearance; brightness; illusion; *tak ber~,* listless, spiritless; exhausted; *ketawa tak ber~,* to laugh quietly; *~pada,* this transitory earth; = *manjapada.* 2. *umor ~,* trickiness - a corruption of the name of Omar Ommaiya, the Ulysses of the Hikayat Amir Hamza. 3. *~ perahu,* wood-louse.

mayam [KN], a goldsmith's weight, = of a *tahil* or *bungkal.*

mayang [KN], the blossom of a palm; *seperti ~ mengurai* or *seperti ~ mekar,* like the unfolding blossom of the palm — a symbol for beautiful curling hair; *~kan,* to slice up finely.

mayapada, see *maya* and *manjapada.*

mayas [KN], (Borneo) = *mawas.*

mayat [KN], Ar. a dead body (expressed respectfully) — cf. *bangkai; bamar ~,*

morgue.

mayau [KS], absent-minded.

mazhab [KN], Ar. a sect, a school (of thought).

mazkur [KK], Ar. mentioned, stated; *seperti yang ter~,* as stated.

medan [KN], Pers. a plain, an open field, a field of battle.

medang [KN], 1. a generic name given to trees of the order *Laurineoe,* and to others which have a timber of similar appearance. 2. *batu ~ sila,* a kind of gypsum used medicinally.

medit [KS], stingy.

medu [KS], 1. squeamish, feeling nausea. 2. *Meduwangsa,* a complimentary epithet occurring in Malayo-Javanese romances.

mega, 1. [KN], Skr. white fleecy clouds, cirrhus; *~ berangkat,* rising white cirrhus; *~ berarak,* white clouds chasing each other across the sky; *~ dadu,* a rose-tinted sunset sky. 2. = *mika,* you; *~ mendung,* raincloud.

megah [KS], famous, glorious; proud, exultant; *me~kan,* to show off, show to advantage; *me~kan potongan badan,* to show off the figure (as does a close-fitting dress); — cf. *gah.*

megak [KS], disrespectfully, taking liberties.

megan [KN], a sweetmeat made of rice suet and eggs.

Megat [KN], Skr. a hereditary title borne by men of royal descent on the mother's side.

meh [KN], face; facial appearance.

meja [KN], Port. a table; *~ solek,* dressing-table; *~ tulis,* writing table; *kain ~,* table-cloth; *daun ~,* table-top or leaf of table; *~ bundar,* a round table.

mejal = *majal.*

mejam [KS], to rotate round a motionless centre; the rotation of a wheel in an engine-room.

mejelis [KS], 1. fair, pretty, handsome. 2. = *majlis.*

Mek [KN], pat. a prefix to the names of girls of good family; a nickname for girls generally.

meka = *mega* 2.

Mekah [KN], Mecca; = *Makkah*.

mekar [KK], to open out (of a bud or blossom); blooming; blossoming; (fig.) blossoming, of an adolescent girl; *mayang ~,* the opening blossom of the palm — a simile for curling hair.

mekis [KK], defiance; memekis, to utter defiance; also *mengkis*.

mel [KN], Eng. mail; *~ udara,* air mail; *~ laut,* surface mail; *keretapi ~,* mail train, express train.

melaka [KN], 1. Skr. a tree (*Phyllanthus pectinatus*), possibly giving its name to the well-known town of Malacca; but some think that the name is derived from *malakat,* q.v. an Arabic word for 'mart'; *gula Melaka,* see *gula; buah Melaka,* a Malaya dumpling — dough filled with sweets. 2. *bandar Melaka,* the town of Malacca.

melarat [KS], 1. = Ar. *mudarat,* difficulty, loss, injury; in poor circumstances, 'under-privileged'; *hidup ~,* a miserable life. 2. see *larat.*

melas [KS], badly fitting; not coinciding.

melati [KN], Skr. a name for the jasmine — us. melur (*Jasminum sambu*).

Melayu [KN], Malay; Muslim; *bahasa ~,* Malay language; *anak ~,* a Malay; *orang ~,* id; *masuk ~,* to become a Muslim; *~ jati,* a true Malay.

meleset [KN], (Dutch) slump, business depression; *ke~an,* id.

Melindo [KN], *ejaan ~,* a unified system of Malay spelling for Malaysia and Indonesia.

meling [KK], to turn away; look in another direction; *pe~,* Kel. ring-shy (of a bull).

melit [KS], inquisitive.

melodi [KN], melody.

melongo [KS], with wide open mouth, agape with wonder.

melukut [KN], broken grains of husked rice, broken rice; also *lemukut.*

melung [KS], 1. over-developed, over-big for the age. 2. a large, scented lily.

melur [KN], the Indian jasmine (*Jasminum sambu*).

mem [KN], Eng. a European lady.

memang [P], as a matter of fact, of course, indeed, naturally; *~ jahat,* notoriously wicked; *~ dia pandai cakap Melayu,* of course he knows Malay.

memar [KS], bruised, crushed (of a fruit).

membacang = *embacang.*

membalau = *embalau.*

membazir = *mubasir.*

memberang = *berang=berang.*

memek [KK], 1. whining, fretting (as a young child); *membuat ~ mulut,* pursing up the mouth; pouting. 2. soft (as a tyre).

memerhati, see *hati.*

memerang = *berang-berang.*

mempas = *mepas.*

mempedal = *pedal.*

mempedu = *hempedu.*

mempelai [KN], Tam. bride, bridegroom; *naik ~,* to ascend the bridal dais; to be married.

mempelam [KN], Tam. the mango (*Mangifera Indica*).

mempelas [KN], a plant (*Tetracera assa*); the leaves are very rough; hence sandpaper is called *~.*

mempelasari [KN], a name given to two plants (*Alyxia stellata* and *A. lucida*).

mena [KN], 1. calculation; = *kira; se~~,* about, approximately; *tidak berse~* or *tiada teper~i,* incalculable; without cause, inexplicably. 2. see *semena.*

menalu = *bendalu.*

menang [KK], to win; to prevail; to be successful; *~kan,* to give victory to, to support; *~ dengan tidak payah bertanding,* to get a walk-over; *~ sabung, kampung tergadai,* to win the cock-fight, but have your home still under mortage, a 'Pyrrhic victory'; *~, ~i (hadiah),* to win (a prize); *ke~an,* victory; *pe~,* winner.

menantu [KN], son-in-law, daughter-in-law.

menara [KN], ar. a minaret; a tower; a derrick; a pylon.

menasabah [KS], reasonable; *~ pada akal,*

agreeable to reason.

mencak [KN], ability to use weapon to defend oneself; = *main pencak*.

mencil [KN], solitary, unfriended.

mencing [KS], a full stretch, fully distended, taut (as a sail or paper).

mendak [KK], curdled, 'stood' (of water which has settled); settling, as small objects in water or raisins in a cake; also *mendap*.

mendeleka [KN], a tree yielding a kind of bread-fruit.

mendera [KN], I, we; your servant.

menderung [KN], a sedge used in mat-making (*Scirpus grossus*).

mendikai [KN], a water-melon.

mendora [KN], a threatical performance of Siamese or Buddhist origin.

mendung [KN], gloomy, overcast (of the weather) or (fig.) of faces; *awan ~* or *~*, dark clouds.

mendusta [KK], to tell lies.

menerung = *menderung*.

mengah [KS], panting; puffing; *sakit ~*, asthma.

mengapa [KKtr], why?; see *apa*.

mengerna [KS], gay with colour; pretty —. cf. *warna*.

menggul-menggul [KS], knotted, gnarled, as a badly tapped rubber tree; less strong than *monggul*.

mengih [KS], panting, after exercise.

mengkal [KS], half-ripe (of fruit); just beginning to soften; soft but firm, of lips.

mengkalai, = *bengkalai*.

mengkarung, = *bengkarung*.

Mengkasar, *Macassar*.

mengkawan, = *bengkawan*.

mengkelan [KK], *ter~*, stuck in the throat (of food; fig.) revolting.

mengkin, Pk. = *makin*.

mengkis [KS], defiant, also meis; *me~*, to utter defiance.

mengkona [KS], Skr. tuskless (of elephants).

mengkuang [KN], the common screwpine (*Pandanus atrocarpus*) and other sp. of *Pandanus*; used for mat-making, etc.,

when a stronger leaf than that of the smaller pandan plants is needed.

mengkudu [KN], a generic name for a number of plants used in dyeing (esp. *Morinda tinctoria*); a red dye is obtained from its roots.

mengkunang [KN], Pah. a napoh, mousedeer.

mengkunit, = *merkunyit*.

mengsu [KN], *bulu ~*, the fine hairs round the forehead.

mengut [KS], ill-fitting, unsuitable, inharmonious.

meniga, see *kenduri*.

menjangan [KN], the barking-deer (*Cervulus muntjac*); us. *kijang*.

menjelai, = *jelai*.

menora, = *mendora*.

mensiang [KN], a triangular rush in rice-fields; used in mat-making.

menta [KS], rutting, of an elephant; *gajah ~ turun menyak*, a rutting elephant having its discharge; also *mota*.

mentah [KS], raw, uncooked; *masak ~*, food cooked and uncooked; crude, untreated, of materials; *susu ~*, fresh (untreated) milk; *kain ~*, unbleached cloth; *budak ~*, (fig) raw youth.

mental [KN], 1. mental. 2. resilient.

mentang [P], even though; see *sementang*.

mentari [KN], (poet) = *matahari*.

mentat [KK], just protruding (e.g. baby's teeth, mushrooms).

mentega [KN], Port. butter; *~ laut*, jocular for *belacan*; *~ hidup*, fresh butter; *~ tin*, tinned butter; *~ buatan*, margerine.

mentelah, = *sementelah*.

menteri [KN], Skr. minister, vizier; *Perdana ~*, Prime Minister; *~ Hal Ehwal Luar*, Foreign Minister; *~ Hal Ehwal Dalam*, Home Secretary; *~ utusan*, envoy; *~* is used for the queen at chess; *Ke~an Penerangan*, Ministry of Information; *~ Pertahanan*, Minister of Defence; *~ Keselamatan Dalam Negeri*, Minister of Internal Security; *~ Pelajaran*, Minister of Education; *~ Tanah dan Galian*, Minister of Lands and Mines; ~ *Kewangan,* Finance Minister; ~ *Pertanian dan Perikanan,* Minister of Agriculture and Fisheries; ~ *Buruh dan Kebajikan Masyarakat,* Minister of Labour and Social Welfare; ~ *Perdagangan dan Perusahaan,* Minister of Trade and Industry; ~ *Kerajaan Tempatan dan Perumahan,* Minister of Local Government and Housing.

mentibang [KN], N.S. millipede.

mentimun [KN], a generic name for gourds, pumpkins, passion-flowers, cucumbers, etc.; normally used to mean cucumber, but also used in Kelantan for melon; also *timun; seperti ~ dengan during,* (prov.) unequal conflict (adversary).

mentua [KN], parent-in-law; *pak ~,* father-in-law; *mak ~,* mother-in- law; ~ *taya,* in-laws generally; *burung tebang ~,* a sp. of hornbill (*Rhinoplax vigil*), also *mertua.*

menung [KK], *ter~,* sunk in thought.

menyelangan [KN], N.S. bast on coconut branch; = *sampil.*

mepas [KK], fly-fishing.

meragi [KS], variegated in colouring — cf. *ragi; burung ~,* the painted snipe (*Rostratula capensis*).

Merah [KN], an old Sumatran title borne by chiefs and headman.

merah [KS], red; ~ *tua,* dark red; ~ *merang,* bright red; ~ *muda,* light red; ~ *padam,* lotus-red, fiery red — as the face of an angry person; ~ *menyaru,* blazing red; ~ *jambu,* deep pink; ~ *menyala,* scarlet (as a hibiscus flower); *ke~-~an,* reddish; *ikan ~,* the red snapper; *Palang Merah,* Red Cross.

merak [KN], a peacock (*Pavo muticus*); ~ *mas,* a 'golden peacock', a type of beautiful bird; *jambul ~,* 'the peacock's crest', a name given to a plant (*Poinciana pulcherrima*).

merakap [KS], Ar. see *jahil; jahil ~,* extremely ignorant in religious matters.

merangas [KS], spoilt by air-bubbles (in smelting).

meranti [KN], a name given to a number

of trees (*Shorea sp.*) which yield a good soft wood.

merawan [KN], 1. a tree (*Hopea mangarawan*). 2. = *berawan* (from *awan*).

merayan, = *meroyan.*

merbah [KN], the yellow-vented bulbul (*Pycnonotus analis*); ~ *jambul,* the Southern red-whiskered bulbul; ~ *sampah,* the red-winged babbler.

merbau [KN], the well-known hardwood tree (*Turtur tigrinus*).

merca [KK], skr. to faint, to swoon.

mercapada [KN], Skr. the earth; = *manjapada.*

mercu [KN], summit, crest, pinnacle; ~ *pulau,* highest point on an island.

mercun [KN], crackers, fireworks; *membakar ~,* to let off crackers.

merdeka [KS], Skr. free; independent; *~kan,* to liberate; ~ *ayam,* fowls' freedom, i.e. incomplete independence.

merdu [KS], Skr. soft, sweet (of the voice or of music), melodious.

merebu [KK], Pk. bristling.

mereka [KN], 1. they; ~ *itu,* id.; common in formal writing. 2. see *reka.*

merela [KS], improperly suggestive (of behaviour).

merelang [KS], smooth-edged; without a rim or raised border.

mereng [KS], to keel over (of a boat); to lie on the side; *otak ~,* not right in the head.

merguk [KN], = *berguk;* praying-veil.

meriam [KN], 1. a cannon; *pasang ~,* to fire a cannon; *pedati ~,* the gun-cariage; *ringgit ~,* the pillar-dollar; ~ *penangkis,* A.A. guns; ~ *katak,* a howitzer; a mortar; ~ *peminggang,* broadside guns; ~ *haluan,* bow-guns; ~ *turut,* stern-guns; *kapal ~,* gunboat; *pasukan ~,* artillery; *tembakan ~,* gun salute. 2. *Meriam,* a woman's name; *Siti Meriam,* the Virgin Mary.

merih [KN], Ar. = *amris;* also *meris.*

Merikan [KN], Tam. an honorific in use among Muslim settlers from Southern India.

merinyu [KN], Port. an overseer; an

inspector of police; a municipal inspector; a land bailiff.

merjan [KN], Ar. red coral beads.

merkubang [KN], a tree (*Mezzetia Herveyana*).

merkunyit [KN], *akar ~*, a plant (*Coscinum blumeanum*).

merlimau [KN], *akar ~*, a scandent thorny wild orange (*Paramignya monophyllia*).

merombong [KN], a small tree (*Timonius janbosella*); also applied to *Adina polycephala, Vernonia arborea* and *Vatica pallida.*

merosot [KN], to fall, to drop, to go down (price).

merpati [KN], Skr. a domestic pigeon; *sekawan ~,* flock of pigeons; name for a wavy pattern on sarongs; *jinak ~,* tame as a pigeon, description of a man who is simple and docile, yet not so simple as he seems; in modern writing ~ is used for 'young lovers', like turtledoves in English; ~ *sejoli,* a pair of young lovers; ~ *sepasang,* id.; ~ *pos,* carrier-pigeon.

merpisang [KN], a palm (*Polyalthia Jenkinsii*).

merpuing [KN], a plant (*Carallia integerrima*).

mersawa [KN], *pokok ~,* a tree providing a light, but hard timber.

merta [KN], 1. *serta, merta,* instantly. Skr. 2. *air ~-jiwa,* the water of life; = *air utama jiwa.*

mertabak [KN], Ar., Pen. a meat omelet.

mertajam [KN], a tree (*Erioglossum edule*).

mertua [KN], = *mentua;* parents-in-law.

merual [KN], a long oblong flag or pennon with two metal balls on the farther end.

merunggai [KN], the horse-radish (*Moringa pterygosperma*); also *remunggai.*

mesarong [KN], a shell (*Pinna*).

mesem [KK], grinning, smiling; *ber~-~,* to keep grinning.

mesin [KN], Eng. a machine; ~ *jahit,* sewing-machine; ~ *kira,* calculating-machine; *secara ~,* mechanical.

mesiu [KN], saltpetre.

meski [KPhbg], Port. although, even though; ~ *berbisik, saya pun tahu,* even though you speak in whispers, I can tell what you are saying; *~pun begitu,* nevertheless.

mesra [KS], Skr. completely assimilated or absorbed through and through; to soak in (as water or advice); *~kan,* to absorb; intimate of relations, friendly; *ber~ dengan,* on intimate terms with, sympathetic to; *suasana ~,* friendly atmosphere; *kasih ~,* deep affection; *ke~an,* affection; *dengan ~,* lovingly.

mesteri [KN], a master-workman.

mesti [KKtr], Jav. needs must; must; *ter~,* compulsory (as service or education); *se~nya,* necessarily; *sudah se~nya,* as a matter of course, naturally; *ke~an,* necessity.

mestika [KN], a bezoar; a tallsman; a term of endearment; (fig.) a jewel, a gem, a precious thing; ~ *embun,* a bezoar of (petrified) dew, having magical powers; there is a crystal ball in the Perak regalia believed to be such a bezoar; ~ *hati, darling, beloved.*

Mesuara [KN], Skr. Maheswara; Siva.

mesui [KN], a tree with a fragrant bark used medicinally (*Cortex* sp.).

mesum [KS], Ind. dirty, grubby, of person; obscene.

mesyuarat [KN], Ar. counsel, conference; meeting; *ber~,* to take counsel; hold a meeting, confer; ~ *negeri,* State Council; *ahli ~,* Member of Council; ~ *agung biasa,* Ordinary General Meeting (as opposed to Extra-ordinary Meeting, *persidangan tergempar*); see *sidang.*

meta, Skr = *menta.*

meterai [KN], Tam. see *tera;* seal, *me~, me~kan,* seal, brand, stamp; *ter~,* sealed, branded stamped.

mewah [KS], plentiful, abundant, prosperous, *ke~an,* prosperity, plenty; luxury; a glut; sometimes, special privileges or benefits; *barang ~,* luxury articles; *serba* ~, luxurious, as, e.g., an hotel; *hidup* ~, life of luxury.

mewek [KK], pursing up the mouth to cry; pouting.

mi [KN], Ch. = *mihun* and *miswa*.

miang [KN], the fine hair-like pieces of bamboo seen when a bamboo is split; the smart created by them or by a nettle; ticklisth itchy; lascivious; ~ *gatal*, extremely lustful or itchy; *orang tua* ~, 'dirty old man'.

miap [KKtr], ~-*tiap*, every, each — cf. *tiap*.

midar [KK], = *megidar* (from *idar*, q.v.); [KK], to go about, to walk about.

mihrab [KN], Ar. the niche in a mosque indicating the direction in which Mecca, i.e. (in Malaysia) the West.

mihun [KN], Ch. vermicelli.

mika [KN], 1. = *mega*. 2. Pk. thou, thee, you — a term of intimate or affectionate conversation.

Mikael [KN], Ar. the Archangel Michael.

mikraj [KN], Ar. Prophet Muhammad's journey to heaven; the golden stairs; *bulan* ~, a name given to the month *Rejab*.

milik [KN], Ar. property, possession; *grant* ~, a freehold title; *me*~, to own; *pe*~, owner; ~*negara*, state or government property.

mimbar [KN], Ar. a sort of pulpit or lectern in a mosque.

mimpi [KN], dream, dreaming; *ber*~, to dream; *tabir* ~, interpretation of dreams; ~ *tercipta*, dream come true; ~ *terbukit*, id.; ~ *syahwat*, to have a voluptuous dream; ~ *buruk*, bad dream; *impian*, dream vision, illusion.

mina [KN], Skr. the sea; *gajah* ~, the sea-elephant of leviathan; the whale; the seal; the walrus.

Minangkabau [KN], a Malay territory in the highlands of Sumatra with a matriarchal system of law; Malays from it colonised Negeri Sembilan.

minat [KN], *ber*~, to have a fancy for, to like, to have an interest in; *pe*~, enthusiasts, 'fans'.

minduk [KK], Kel., Treng. to hold a seance

to summon spirits; *tak* ~, a shaman.

Minggu [KN], Port. week; *hari* ~, Sunday; ~*an keselamatan*, Safety Week; *hujung* ~, week-end.

minhaj [KN], Ar. road, path; the Way of Truth.

minta [KK], *me*~, requesting, applying for, asking for; ~ *ampun*, to beg pardon; ~ *tabik*, to ask to be excused; ~ *doa*, to pray for any person; ~ *diri*, to take one's leave; *me*~, to request; *me*~ *maaf*, to apologize; *per*~*an*, a request; ~~, N.S. used (coll.) like *moga-moga*, in writing; may it be that; ~~ *ada hujan hari ini*, let us hope that it will rain today; *orang pe*~~~ *damai*, to sue for peace; ~ *perhatian*, to call for attention; also *mintak* and *pinta*.

minum [KK], drinking; *makan dan* ~, eating and drinking; ~*an*, a drink; *me*~, to drink; *pe*~, a man given to drink; ~ *kerana keselematan*, to drink to the health of; ~*an keras*, strong drink, alcohol, spirits.

minyak [KN], oil, fat, ointment; ~ *babilard*, grease; ~ *gas*, kerosene oil; ~ *ikan*, fish-oil; ~ cod-liver oil; ~ *jarak*, castor-oil; ~ *kacang*, ground-nut oil; ~ *kelapa*, coconut oil; ~ *sapi*, suet; ~ *tanah*, crude petroleum, kerosene oil; ~ *saitun*, olive-oil; ~ *tar*, tar; ~ *wangi*, scent, perfume; ~ *serai*, citronella oil; ~ *pelumur*, lubricating oil; ~ *pasang*, illuminant oil; *stesen* ~, petrol station; *turun* ~, to be 'must' or rutting, of an elephant; *ada banyak* ~, lustful, nymphomaniac, of a woman.

mipat [KK], Treng. to take the wrong turning.

mipis, = *nipis*.

mirah [KN], *batu* ~, a ruby, a carbuncle, a jacinth.

miring [KS], Ind. = *mereng;* sloping; slanting; (lying) on o's side; *me*~*kan*, to tilt.

mirip [KS], Ind. like, similar to; ~ *kepada*, id, to bear a slight likeness, identical to.

misa, Skr. buffalo; an ancient Javanese title; = *mahisa*.

misai [KN], moustache; ~ *bertaring*, a

moustache with fiercely turned-up ends; ~ *lebat,* a heavy moustache; ~ *kompot,* a clipped moustache; ~ *kucing,* bristling moustache, *ber~ tebal berjonkit ke atas,* having a heavy moustache with the ends pointing upwards.

misal [KN], Ar. example, instance; *~nya,* for instance; *~kan,* supposing, taking it that; also *misalan.*

miskal [KN], Ar. a weight of about 1 1/4 *drachms.*

miskin [KS], Ar. poor; *ke~an,* poverty, destitute; *daerah ~ di kota,* slum, ghetto.

misoa [KN], Ch. a kind of vermicelli.

misru [KN], Pers. (= lawful) silk or satin with a cotton back, an old trade fabric.

mistar [KN], Ar. a ruled line; a line, as of poetry.

mobil [KN], Ind. a motorcar.

modal [KN], capital (for business); *makan ~,* to live on one's capital; *kaum ~,* capitalists; *pe~,* id.; *~ pusingan,* working capital.

modar [KK], *mati ~,* to die an unholy death; of a beast slaughtered otherwise than in the ritual way (*sembeleh*), but also used to imprecate a bad death on a person.

moden [KN], Eng. modern.

modin [KN], Ar. a circumciser.

moga [KKtr] 1. *~~,* would that; might it be; *se~,* may it be; *se~ Tuhan memberkatimu,* May God bless you; given that. 2. Kel. a thing. article, = *benda.*

mogok [KK], a strike (or workers); *pe~an,* a state of strike; *tabung ~,* strike fund; *pe~an timbangrasa,* sympathetic strike; *~ simpati,* id.; *~ berlapar,* hunger strike; *~ tergempar,* lightning strike; (*~*) *kerja lambat-lambat,* a 'go slow'; (*~*) *bekerja mengikut peraturan,* a 'work to rule'.

moh [KK], 1. = *embuh.* 2. Pk. come along.

mohon [KK], to apply for, beseech; *ber~,* to take one's leave; to depart; to ask to be excused from doing something, to 'beg off'; *per~an,* petition, application; *me~kan,* to ask humbly for, esp. in asking for pardon; also *pohon.*

mohor [KN], Pers. the stamp or die-mark

on a coin; a seal; *cincin ~,* a signet ring. esp. a royal signet ring.

molek [KS], charming, pretty.

molong [KN], *buah ~,* a sweetmeat resembling the buah Melaka.

momok [KN], 1. blunt. 2. bogey-man; *~-~kan,* to make a bogey of, scare people with; to pour scorn on.

moncong [KN], snout-shaped; a snout; ~ *cerek,* the spout of a kettle; *~kan mulut ke arah,* to point with one's mouth (i.e. chin) at, direct one's gaze at; ~ is used (sl.) for 'face'; *menarik ~ panjang,* to pull a long face.

mondok [KS], short and thick; stumpy — cf. *montok; parang ~,* a short chopper; *tikus ~,* mole.

mongel [KS], N.S. dainty, as a girl or a vessel.

monggok [KS], rising in the form of a dome; protuberant (as a small mound); a small hillock; *batu ~,* a cairn.

monggol [KS], knotty, gnarled (or a tree).

mongmong [KN], (onom.) a small brass gong (laid on the ground and beaten).

montel [KS], well-fleshed, svelte, buxom.

montok [KS], short in proportion to its length; stumpy; full and firm, of woman's breasts or figure generally; svelte, plump, cf. *mondok.*

monyet [KN], a monkey; 'monkey' (as a term of abuse); *baju ~,* an overall; *kera menjadi ~* (prov.), it is quite the same.

mopeng [KS], pock-marked; also *bopeng.*

moreng [KS], *coreng-moreng,* smeared with dirt.

morfin [KN], morphine.

mori [KN], white, fine cloth for making batik.

mota [KN], Hind. a coarse sail-cloth.

motar [KN], mortar.

motobot [KN], motor-boat.

motokar [KN], motor-car.

moyang [KN], great-grandfather or great-grandmother; *nenek ~,* ancestors.

moyangda [KN], a respectful form of moyang, great-grandfather.

moyok [KS], rueful, dejected.

mu [KGn], you; = *kamu.*

mua [KS], 'difficult', obstructive; cheeky, pert, of children; ~kan, to spoil, to over-indulge.

muafakat [KN], Ar. agreement, arrange-ment, consensus, settled plan; ber~, to meet in conference; to settle by discus-sion; to agree upon; also mupakat and pakat; se~, unanimous.

muai [KK], me~, rise, swell, expand.

muak [KS], disgust, nausea; feeling of satiety as from continually eating the same food; ~ melihat, detest; me~kan, disgusting.

mual [KS], a variant of muak; me~kan, to fill with disgust, nauseating, sickening.

mualap [KN], Ar. proselyte, convert to Is-lam.

mualif [KN], Ar. editor of a paper.

mualim [KN], Ar. a learned man; an ex-pert; a navigator — cf. **malim**.

muara [KN], the estuary of a river; = kuala; hidup dua muara (prov.), to run with the hare and hunt with the hounds.

muat [KK], loading cargo; containing, having withing itself; ~an, cargo; ber~, to be laden with; ~kan, to load with; tanah ini boleh ~ ditanam seratus batang pokok, this land can carry 100 trees.

muazam [KN], Ar. awe-inspiring, majes-tic, sublime; sultan al-~, the august sul-tan, i.e. the Sultan of Turkey.

muazin [KN],, summoner to prayer.

mubah [KS], Ar. permitted by religion but not meritorious.

mubaligh [KN], Ar. religous propagandist, missionary, particularly of Islam.

mubarak, Ar. blessed.

mubazir [KS], Ar. to waste; wasted; often corrupted (coll.) to membazir.

mubut [KS], fragile, weak.

muda [KS], young, unripe, light (of colour-ing), much alloyed (of metals); Raja Muda, the heir-apparent; mas ~, much-alloyed gold; merah ~, light red; main ~, to run after women; muda is com-mon in titles in the sense of 'junior' or 'future' or deputy, e.g., Raja Muda, the heir-apparent; menteri ~, the Deputy

Minister; leftenan ~, second lieutenant; pe~, young man; awet ~, to stay young; kawin ~, to marry young; pemudi, girl.

mudah [KS], easy, light, trivial; also used in Perak for cheap; dengan ~nya, easily; ~-~an, perhaps, possibly; would that; me~kan, to render easy, painless, or light; per~kan, to treat as of little ac-count, to slight; under-estimate; buat ~, id.; dengan ~ sahaja, quite easily; tidak se~ dua kali dua empat, it's not as easy as twice two is four; ~ tersinggung, sensitive; ~ dipujuk, vulnerable to flattery; ~ lupa, prone to forgetfulness, absent-minded; ke~an, facilities, ameni-ties.

mudarat [KS], Ar. loss, disaster, suffering; often corrupted to melarat.

mudi [KN], rear, stern, rudder; juru~, the steersman; ke~, a rudder; ke~an, after-wards, subsequently.

mudif [KN], Ar. a host (of a guest).

mudik [KK], travelling upstream.

mudun [KN], Ar. culture; civilisation; ke~an, state of culture; orang ber~, cultured people; civilised people; cf. **tamaddun**.

muflis [KS], Ar. (sl.) insolvent, 'broke'.

mufti [KN], Ar. a specialist in law and theology; a doctor of Muslim law; a sort of chief justice.

muhalil [KN], Ar. an intermediate husband required by Muslim law to legalise the remarriage of fully divorced persons.

Muhammad [KN], Ar. the name of the Prophet; a Malay proper name.

Muhammadiah [KN], Ar. Islamic, pertain-ing to Islam.

Muharram [KN], Ar. the first month of the Muslim year.

muhibbah [KN], Ar. affection, friendship; in such expressions as salam ~, friendly greetings; utusan ~, goodwill mission.

mujarab [KS], Ar. tried, tested by experi-ence, trusty; efficacious, esp. of medi-cine.

muhrim [KN], Ar. relatives within the pro-hibited degrees of marriage; cf. **ajnabi**.

mukjizat [KN], Ar. a miracle; miraculous power.

mujtahid [KN], Ar. legal expert on Muslim law who interprets the Quran and the Traditions according to his own opinion.

mujur [KK], fortunate, lucky.

muka [KN], Skr. face, countenance, visage, front; ~ *papan*, brazen- faced; ~ *manis*, pleasant-looking; ~ *surat*, a page; *di ~ pintu*, in front of the door; *air ~*, expression, look; *cahaya ~*, id.; *seri ~*, the charm of the countenance; ~ *air*, surface of the water; *ke~kan*, to bring forward (e.g., a proposal); *dike~kan*, brought forward (as a proposal); *per~an*, surface, superficial area; *menarik ~ duabelas*, to pull a long face; *ber~~*, to put on hypocritical airs, to 'pose'; play the humbug; *bertemu ~*, face to face, tete-a-tete; *berse~*, id.; *cari ~*, to seek to ingratiate oneself, try to get into favour; *beri ~*, to countenance, 'encourage', allow to take liberties; *buang ~*, to turn away one's face. (as a portrait); *orang pe~ negeri*, prominent citizens; *terke~*, prominent, leading; *ber~ dua*, double-tongued, unreliable.

mukaddis [KN], Ar. *baitul ~*, the heavenly city; Jerusalem.

mukadimah [KN], Ar. preface, prologue, peramble.

mukah [KN], fornication, adultery, also *moqah*.

mukallaf [KN], Ar. fit for religious duties, i.e., of age and of sound mind.

mukarram [KN], Ar. honourable, distinguished.

Mukha [KN], Ar. Mocha in Arabia.

mukim [KN], Ar. a parish; a territorial division; the area served by one mosque of general assembly.

mukmin, Ar. devout, religious, God-fearing; *Amir ul muminin*, Commander of the Faithful, Caliph.

muktamad [KS], Ar. conclusive, final.

muktamar [KN], Ar. congress, conference.

mukun [KN], a bowl or cup with a cover.

mula [KN], Skr. commencement, beginning, source; *ber~*, to make a beginning, *~~*, to begin with; firstly; *se~*, as at first; all over again; but also used to mean original; *niat se~*, the original intention; *se~ jadi*, natural, innate; *bakat se~ jadi*, natural talent; or provided by nature, not the work of man; *pelabuhan se~ jadi*, a natural harbour; *seber~*, in the first place; *~i*, to commence, to begin; *me~i*, id.; *per~an*, commencement, beginning.

mulas [KS], ~ *perut*, griping pains in the stomach — cf. **pulas**.

mulia [KS], Skr. illustrious, glorious; noble; of high quality; precious (of metals); *kain yang ~*, mantle of splendid appearance; *yang maha ~*, His Highness; *yang teramat ~*, His Highness (the son of a Ruler); *yang ~*, a non-royal person of high position; *per~kan*, to honour; to treat with distinction; *ke~an*, a mark of honour or distinction; glory; ~ is often used for 'good' in stories (as opposed to villainous [durjana]).

muluk [KS], Ind. lofty, uplifted; *jani-janji ~*, golden promises.

mulut [KN], mouth; *manis ~*, soft-spoken, gentle in speech; *panjang ~*, loquacious; *sedap ~*, fair-spoken; *bawa ~*, to sneak, carry stories; *buah ~*, general topic of conversation; 'talk of the town'; ~ *terkunci*, lock-jaw; ~ *panisl*, warning cry, esp. to children for indiscreet or dangerous remarks; ~ *terlanjur semas tentangannya*, (prov.) a promise is a promise, in for a penny, in for a pound.

mumbang [KN], a very young coconut; proverbially useless; ~ *jatuh kelapa jatuh*, (prov.) death keeps no calendar.

mumbung [KS], loaded above the gunwale (of a ship or boat); brimful.

mumut [KS], worn out, mouldering.

munafaat [KN], Ar. profit, benefit, advantage; also *manfaat*.

munafik [KS], Ar. hypocritical, dissembling; a hypocrite; esp. a person who merely pretends to accept the Faith.

munajat [KN], Ar. private devotions.

muncih, Sel. = *rincih*.

muncul [KK], Ind. to come into sight, appear; a variant of *timbul*.

mundam [KN], Ach. a bowl for water (of

metal or glass), used in certain ceremonial ablutions.

mundar-mandir [KK], Ind. to move this
way and that; to walk up and down.

mundur [KK], to retreat; = *mengundur*
(from *undur*), so, to decline (as opposed
to *maju*), backward, under-developed
(country); *langkah ~,* retrogressive step;
ke~an, set back.

munggur [KN], wintering or dying (of a
tree).

mungkin [KS], likely, possibly; *secepat ~,*
as quickly as possible; *tidak ~,* not a
chance; *ke~an,* possibility; *me~kan,* to
make possible.

mungkir [KK], Ar. to deny, to repudiate a
statement, to refuse, to break a promise;
me~i, deny, disavow, break a promise.

mungkum [KS], dome-shaped, covering
like a dome.

mungkus [KS], miserable in appearance,
looking half-dead.

mungut [KN], to totter.

Munkar [KN], 1. Ar. one of the angels that
examine the dead in the grave. 2.
munkar, evil actions, mischief.

munsyi [KN], Hind. a teacher of languages.

musykil [KS], Ar. Kel., Treng. dissatisfied,
having a grievance (possibly a corruption from *masygul*), doubt.

muntah [KN], vomiting; *~kan,* to vomit
up; *~kan darah,* to vomit blood — believed to be the result of an evil spirit's
work and so imprecated as a curse; *~
kedarahkan,* (vulg.) to gobble up; *sakit
~ berak,* cholera.

mura [KN], *ular ~,* a venomous snake
(*Lachesis purpureomaculatus,* black
variety, or *Anaia sputatrix*) — cf. **bura**.

murad [KN], Ar. intention, purpose.

murah [KS], generous, good-hearted,
liberal; cheap; *lagi ~, lagi ditawar,* the
more I reduce, the more he bargains!,
maha-~, all-generous (of God); *ke~an,*
generosity; *pe~,* generous; *~ di mulut
mahal di timbangan* (prov.), apt to
promise, apt to forget; easier said than
done; quick to promise, slow to perform.

murai [KN], 1. *burung ~,* the magpie-robin

(*Copsychus saularis*); *~ batu,* the shama
(*Cittocincla macrura*); *~ gajah,* the fairy
blue-bird (*Irene cynanaea*); *~ gila,* a
name given to fantail-fly-catchers
(*Rhipadura* sp.); *~ ekor gading,* the Paradise fly-catcher. 2. Pah., Treng. *badak
~,* a tapir.

murakkab [KS], compound, mixed; *jahil
~,* an arrogant blockhead.

muram [KS], sombre, paling (of moon);
not lustrous, of surface; dismal, of face;
to go downhill, diminish (as business);
ber~ durja, to look surly; *ke~an,* gloomi-
ness, melancholy.

murang [KN], Port. the match (applied to
a cannon).

murba [KS], Ind. common, ordinary; esp.
rakyat ~, the common people, the proletariat.

muri [KN], 1. Pers. a flute or clarionet of
metal. 2. Jav. white calico. 3. religious
feast.

murid [KN], Ar. pupil, disciple; *anak ~,* id.;
ber~kan, take as a pupil.

murka [KK], Skr. wrath, anger (of God or
of a prince); *me~i,* to be angered; *~kan,*
to be angry with; *ke~an,* anger, wrath.

murni [KS], Ind. pure, undefiled, noble;
refined, purified; *ke~an,* purity of blood
(unmixed); *me~kan,* purify, cleanse;
pe~an, purification; sometimes *~* is used
to mean 'of high quality', of material.

mursal [KN], Ar. one sent, an apostle.

mursyid [Kn], religious teacher, spiritual
guide.

murtad [KK], Ar. renegade; the abandonment of the true faith.

murung [KS], dejected, downcast; *duduk
~ sahaja,* to mope, depressed; *ke~an,*
depression.

murup [KS], fiery (of colouring); brilliant.

Musa [KN], Ar. *nabi ~,* Moses.

musabab [KN], Ar. reason, basic reason.

musafir [KN], Ar. a traveller, wanderer.

musang [KN], a generic name for civets; *~
akar,* the small-toothed palm-civet
(*Artogalidia leucotis*); *~ babi,* the otter
civet mongoose (*Herpestes
brachyurus*); *~ batu,* the zebra civet-cat

(*Artogale leucotis*); ~ *batu*, ~ *belang*, the slender banded civet (*Hemingale hardwickei*); ~ *akar*, id.; ~ *buah*, the tiger-civt (*Prionodon gracilis*), = *lisang*, Ind.; ~ *bulan*, the white whiskered palm-civet (*Paradoxurus leucomystax*), the smaller civet (*Viverra malaccensis*); ~ *jebat*, the Indian civet (*Viverra zibetha*), the Burmese civet (*Viverra megaspila*); ~ *mengkuang*, ~ *ayam*, ~ *pandan*, the palm civet (*Paradoxurus hermaphroditus*); ~ *teverau*, a dark civet (probably *Paradokurus niger*); ~ *tenggalung*, the Burmese civet (*Viverra megaspila*); ~ *pulut*, the small palm civet (*Paradoxurus minor*); ~ *pisang*, the Malayan marten; ~ *babi*, the mongoose; *Pak Musang*, a legendary person whose good luck always got him out of the scrapes into which his folly plunged him; ~ is often used fig. for 'big bad wolf' where girls are concerned; *rezeki* ~, an easy mark for wolves (of an unprotected girl); ~ *berbulu ayam*, wolves in sheep's clothing.

musibat [KN], Ar. an affliction, calamity; as a term of abuse; you plaque!

musim [KN], Ar. season; monsoon; ~ *hujan*, the rainy season; ~ *kemarau*, the dry season; ~ *utara*, the north-east monsson; ~ *tengkujuh*, season of heavy rain; ~ *bunga*, (European) spring; ~ *buah*, (European) autumn; ~ *gugur (runtuh, rontok)*, autumn; ~ *dingin*, winter; ~ *turun*, time of scarcity, bad times; ~ *tutup kuala*, the season of the closing of the river-mouths, i.e. November-January, on the East Coast, when the sea is too rough for fishing-boats to put to sea.

muslihat [KN], Ar. resource, stratagem, means, object, policy; deceit; deceitful.

Muslim [KN], Ar. Muslim.

Muslimat [KN], Ar. Muslim woman.

musnah [KK], to destroy; *pe~an*, annihilation; *ke~an*, destruction.

mustaid [KS], Ar. in working order; ready for use; ready; *me~kan*, to make ready, to prepare.

mustahak [KS], Ar. important; *me~kan*, to necessitate.

mustahil [KS], Ar. incredible, ridiculous; ~ *pada akal*, utterly absurd, rejected by the intellect, by extension ~ is sometimes used to mean impossible, cannot be done; *ke~an*, impossibility.

mustajab [KS], Ar. efficacious; sure to act (of a medicine).

mustakim [KS], Ar. upright, sincere.

Mustakman [KN], Ar. non-Muslims sojourning in a Muslim State.

musuh [KN], a foe; *ber~*, to be enemies; *per~an*, a state of war, enmity; Kel. an armed disturbance; ~ *dalam kelambu*, ~ *dalam selimut*, an enemy in the house-hold; often used jocularly of one's wife, now sometimes used to mean 'Fifth Columnists'; *saling ber~~an*, at enmity with one another, at 'daggers drawn'; *me~i*, to fight against, to be hostile; *jangan mencari* ~, don't seek enemies.

musykil [KS], thorny, ticklish, very difficult to solve.

musyawarah [KN], Ind. a conference; a variant of *mesyuarat*.

musyrik [KN], ar. polytheist, pagan.

Musytari [KN], Ar. *bintang* ~, Jupiter.

mutakhir [KS], recent, modern.

mutaliah, Ar. readers (of a newspaper).

mutia [KN], Skr. pearl; *siput* ~, mother-of-pearl shell; *intan* ~, diamonds and pearls — cf. *mutiara*.

mutiara [KN], Skr. a pearl; *indung* ~, the pearl oyster; mother-of- pearl; *ayam* ~, a guinea-fowl.

mutlak [KS], Ar. unconditional, absolute; complete, final; *wakil* ~, plenipotentiary; *larangan* ~, a total prohibition.

mutu [KS], 1. melancholy, brooding; *ber hati* ~, id. 2. pearl [KN], *ratna* ~ *man-ikam*, all sorts of precious stones. 3. Tam. a measure of the purity of gold, = 2.4 carats; *mas sepuluh* ~, 24 carat gold; ~ is used for 'quality' of goods; high standard; *~-nilai*, value, standard of value; *rendah ~nya*, of low quality.

muzakarah [KN], Ar. convocation of religious leader.

N

nabi [KN], Ar. prophet; ~ *Ibrahim,* Abraham; ~ *Idris,* Enoch; ~ *Isa,* Jesus; ~-~, the starfish of seven points — cf. *tapak Sulaiman;* the plural of *nabi* is *anbia; Mohammad ialah penghulu segala anbia,* Mohammad is Head of all the prophets; *ke~an,* prophetic.

nada [KN], tone, pitch (in music); *dengan ~ suara yang menurun,* with a low voice; *dengan ~ suara yang meninggi,* with a high voice; *dengan ~ yang mengejek-ejek,* in the mocking tone; ~ *darah,* pulse; *nada* is also used for stress, beat (in music); ~ *utama,* key note; ~ *tambahan,* overtone; *tangga ~,* scale.

nadi [KN], Skr. the arterial pulse; *pegang ~,* to feel the pulse; *tinggal ~ sahaja,* only the pulse left, i.e. nearly dying; *pembuluh ~,* artery.

nadir [KN], 1. *perahu ~,* a Malacca type of large sea-going fishing-boat. 2. Ar. inspector, supervisor; = *nazir.*

nafas [KN], Ar. breath, respiration; *menarik ~,* to breathe; *ber~,* id.; *membuang ~,* to breathe out, exhale; *menarik ~,* to breathe in; *tahan ~,* to hold one's breath; *sesak ~,* short of breath; *putus ~,* out of breath; *per~an,* breathing; *pembuluh ~,* the larynx; also *napas.*

nafi [KS], 1. absent-minded, unconscious of one's surroundings; *ter~,* lost to sight or memory. 2. Ar. *me~kan,* to deny, repudiate.

nafiri [KN], Pers. a long, narrow trumpet blown at a coronation, one of the appurtenances of Malay royalty.

nafkah [KN], Ar. means of livelihood; a living, alimony; *mencari ~,* to seek a livelihood; *sumber ~,* means of livelihood; ~ *batin,* conjugal rights (as opposed to ~ *zahir,* mere maintenance); *tidak menyempurnakan ~ batin,* to refuse conjugal rights; *menunaikan ~*

batin, to fulfil conjugal duties.

nafsu [KN], Ar. lust, the promptings of the flesh; *hawa ~,* the emotions, the passions; *menahan ~,* to bridle one's passions; *menjamu ~,* to indulge one's passions; ~ *makan,* appetite; ~ *makan bertambah kurang,* increasing loss of appetite; ~ *marah,* feeling of anger; *menimbulkan ~,* to excite the passions; *ubat ~ berahi,* an aphrodisiac; *terburu ~,* actuated by mere emotions.

naga [KN], Skr. dragon, a snake of supernatural size, *cula ~,* the horn of a dragon; *gemala ~,* the luminous bezoar with which a dragon lights its way; ~ *balun,* a dragon that kills by lashing with its tail; ~ *berapi,* a fire-breathing dragon; ~ *bura,* a snake that spits out venom on its foes (*Naia sputatrix?*); ~ *gentala,* a gigantic dragon that lies still and sucks its prey into its mouth — see also below; ~ *umbang,* a huge marine dragon; ~ *berjuang,* ~ *berseru* and ~ *gentala,* names of patterns (converging, diverging and parallel lines, respectively); ~-~, (1) a dragon-shaped figurehead; (2) the keelson; *perahu kakap ~,* a boat with a dragon-shaped figurehead.

nagasari [KN], a tree yielding a pretty flower (*Messua ferra*).

nah [KSr], there!, take it!.

nahak [KK], *ter~,* excited (of appetite, lust or desire).

nahas [KS], Ar. ill-starred, foredoomed to misfortune; *saat yang ~,* an unlucky hour; *nahas* is used sometimes for 'disaster'; accident; *bulan ~,* the month *Safar;* see *Safar;* also *naas.*

nahi [KN], Ar. the forbidden; ~ *Allah,* what God has forbidden.

nahu [KN], Ar. grammar, i.e. Arabic inflexions.

naib [KN], Ar. deputy; ~ *kadi,* a kadi's

deputy; ~ *raja,* a viceroy; ~ *yang diper-tua,* vice-president (as of a club); ~ *johan,* runner-up.

naik [KK], ascent, motion upwards; ~ *raja* or ~ *kerajaan,* to ascend the throne; ~ *kereta,* to get into a carriage; ~ *ke darat,* to go ashore; ~ *haji,* to go on the pilgrimage to Mecca; *tengah* ~, half-grown; *ke~an,* a mount; a steed or vehicle; a rise, e.g., in taxes; *ke~an hantu,* possessed by a devil; ~ *saksi,* to go into the witness-box; *matahari* ~, sunrise; ~ *tangan,* to get the upper hand; ~ *daun,* to prosper, get ahead; sometimes, to get 'uppish'; ~ *rumah,* to enter a house (on piles); to commit house-trespass; to hold a house-warming in a new house (in accordance with the context); ~ *angin,* to get excited, to get above oneself, 'throw a temperament'; ~ *darah,* to grow angry; ~ *kepala,* to get 'swell-headed'; ~ *lemak,* to be 'uppish', cheeky, provocative, esp. as a girl; ~ *pangkat,* to get promotion; ~ *turun,* fluctuations, as of prices; ups and downs, as of a road; ~*i* is sometimes used to mean to go up against, attack, esp. a fort.

najis [KS], Ar. filth; things which defile; ordure; faeces; *kena* ~, to incur pollution; *kelakuan yang* ~, filthy habits; *me~kan,* soil, defile, make dirty or impure.

nak [KK], going to, intending to; short for *hendak*

naka [KK], part-singing; singing in alternation.

nakal [KS], mischievous, naughty; *ber-* or *me~,* to commit mischief in sheer wantoness; *ke~an,* a prank, an escapade; *per~kan,* to play a prank on, do some mischief to.

nakas [KN], Ar. a motive in art, where figures face one another, e.g. dolphins.

nakhoda [KN], Pers. the master of an Arab or Persian trading-ship.

Nakir [KN], Ar. one of the angels who examine the dead in the grave.

nal [KN], (Dutch) wad; also *enal.*

nalar [KKtr], regularly, frequently.

nali [KN], 1. a turn to play, an innings in a Malay game. 2. = *nalih.*

nalih [KN], a measure of capacity, = 16 *gantang.*

naluri [KN], Ind. instinct.

naluriah [KS], Ind. instinctive.

nama [KN], Skr. name, designation, renown; reputation; ~*nya Muhammad,* he was named Muhammad; *beroleh* ~, to obtain renown; ~*i* and ~*kan,* to name; *ber~,* by name, named; *ter~,* famous; *atas* ~ *sahaja,* nominally; ~ *tubuh,* personal name (as opposed to title); *orang ke~an,* notables; ~ *samaran,* pseudonym; ~ *pena,* pen-name; *hari pe~an calun,* candidates' nomination-day; ~ *keluarga,* family name; ~ *keturunan,* id.; ~ *kecil,* first name, familiar name; *daftar* ~, nomenclature, list of names, register.

nambi [KN], an ulcerating disease of the feet.

namnam [KN], a fruit tree (*Cynometra cauliflora*).

nampak [KK], to be visible, come into view; to espy, see; ~*nya,* apparently; *ter~,* seen, appearing, to be found (as a rare sp.); *me~kan,* to display, make visible; ~ *sekali,* conspicuous; ~~*kan,* to make (something) appear what it is not; ~~*kan susah,* to make something appear very difficult; cf. *tampak.*

Namrud [KN], Ar. Nineveh.

namun [KKtr], Ind. 1. = *lamun.* 2. still, nevertheless; ~ *demikian,* notwithstanding.

nan [Kg], who, which, that — a poetic equivalent of *yang.*

nanah [KN], matter, pus; *me~,* to suppurate; *kencing* ~, gonorrhoea.

nanai [KN], a monkey (in the language of magic).

nanar [KS], giddy; silly (as the result of a blow); wild behaviour (as the result of illness).

nanas [KN], Port., Hind. the pineapple (*Ananassa* sp.); also *lanas* and *nenas.*

nandung [KN], 1. *tupai* ~, the large squirrel (*Sciurus bicolor*). 2. a large cock-roach.

nang = *nan* and *yang.*

nangka [KN], the jack-fruit (*Artocarpus integrifolia*); ~ *belanda,* soursop.

nangui [KN], 1. *babi* ~, the bearded pig (*Sus barbatus*). 2. *anak* ~, dwarf in puppet show.

naning [KN], a large blue ground-wasp; also *aning-aning.*

nanti [KK], awaiting, to await; shall, will; ~*kan,* to await, to wait for; *me*~, to sit waiting; *me*~*kan hari,* to await the day (esp. of expectant mothers and dying persons); *ter*~--~, waiting and waiting, kept waiting; *seperti bumi me*~*kan hujan,* as the earth awaits the rain.

napal [KN], an edible earth; marl; also *nampal.*

napuh [KN], the larger chevrotin (*Tragulus napu*).

nara [KN], Skr. hero, man (in titles).

narwastu [KN], spikenard, frankincense.

nas [KN], Ar. dictum, legal opinion (esp. on a point of religious law); *di*~*kan,* authorized by the *Koran.*

nasab [KN], Ar. race, family, origin.

nasar [KN], Ar. *burung* ~, the vulture.

nasi [KN], 1. boiled rice; *makan* ~, to dine; ~ *hadap-hadap,* the rice consumed at a wedding feast; ~ *damai,* id.; ~ *Kabuli,* ~ *pulau,* 'pillau' rice; ~ *kukus,* steamed rice; ~ *kuning,* glutinous rice cooked with saffron; ~ *lemak,* rice cooked in coconut milk, us. with fish and chilli paste; ~ *minyak,* rice cooked in oil or mutton-fat; ~ *pelabur,* rations; ~ *tambah,* a second helping of rice; ~ *tanak,* plain boiled rice; ~ *beriani,* an Indian dish of rice and meat, us. mutton; ~ *kepal,* rice-balls; ~ *goreng,* fried rice; ~ *sudah menjadi bubur,* (prov.) what is done cannot be undone, it is no use crying over spilt milk. 2. ~--~ [KN], a generic name for many plants.

nasib [KN], Ar. fortune, luck, lot in life; *sudah untung* ~, it is my destiny; ~ *malang,* extreme bad luck; *membawa* ~, to trust to luck; to risk one's all; *buang*

~, to 'have a shot', have a try.

nasihat [KN], Ar. advice; the moral of a story; *me*~, to advise; *tak ter*~, impervious to advise, pig-headed; *pe*~, adviser; *atas* ~, on the advice of.

nasional [KN], *nasionalis,* nationalist; ~*isma,* nationalism; *me*~*isasikan,* to nationalize.

naskah [KN], Ar. original text (*Editio princeps*); a copy (as of a newspaper, manuscript).

Nasrani [KN], Ar. 'Nazarene'; Christian (esp. Roman Catholic); also *Serani.*

Nasurah [KN], a Christian.

nasyid [KN], Ar. Arabic song or recitation.

nata [KN], Skr. lord, prince; *sang* ~, the king.

natang [KN], Siam. a French window.

natar [KS], smooth, level; = *rata;* also *datar.*

natijah [KN], Ar. results, consequences.

nau [KN], a sugar-palm (*Arenga saccharifera*); ~ *sebatang dua sigai,* one sugar-palm and two ladders, met. for 'unfaithful spouse'; *seperti* ~ *dalam belukar melepaskan pucuk masing-masing,* like a sugar-palm in a thicket which lets go all its shoots, met. for extreme selfishness and disregard for others (because the tough, spreading fronds of this palm work upwards and outwards, smothering the growth of neighbouring trees); also *enau* and *kebung.*

naung [KK], shade, shelter from the sun, shelter generally; ~*i* or *me*~*i,* to give shelter to; *ber*~, to take shelter; ~*an,* protection, patronage; shade (of a tree); *negeri* ~*an,* a Protectorate; *pe*~, protector; patron.

nayam [KN], the blade of a ploughshare.

nazam [KN], Ar. order, composition, arrangement; = *karangan.*

nazar [KN], Ar. a vow, a promise made to God; *ber*~, to vow; *menyampaikan* ~, to fulfil a vow; *melepaskan* ~, id.

nazir [KN], Ar. an overseer, a superintendent, an inspector; also *nadir.*

negara [KN], 1. Skr. city, town — a poetic

variant of *negeri;* a State; *menjadikan hak* ~, to nationalise; *menjadi warga* ~, to be naturalised; ~ *hukum,* a constitutional State; ~*ku,* title of Malaysian national anthem; *kesedaran ber*~, sense of citizenship. 2. ~ *bergunung-ganang,* mountainous country. 3. Ar. a kettle-drum (included among the insignia of Malay royalty).

negerawan [KN], Ind. statesman.

nagatif [KS], negative, word or statement that denies.

negeri [KN], Skr. town, city, state, settlement; *ber*~-~*an,* parochial; *membuat* ~, to make a settlement; *ber*~, having a state or country.

nek [KN], 1. a titular prefix indicating high rank in a commoner. 2. short for *nenek.*

nekad [KS], Ind. fixed determination; headstrong; bold, determined; *kenekatan,* recklessness.

nelayan [KN], Tam. a fisherman.

nenas = *nanas.*

nenda [KN], a respectful variant of *nenek.*

nenek [KN], grandmother; ~ *moyang,* ancestors, forefathers.

nenenda = *nenda.*

nenes [KK], *ber*~, to ooze out (as pus).

neraca [KN], Hind. a balance; a sensitive pair of scales; ~ *kira-kira,* balance-sheet.

neraka [KN], Skr. hell; *api* ~, hell fire; ~ *dunia,* hell upon earth; *me*~*kan* [KK], cause ruin, disaster.

nesan [KN], gravestone.

nescaya [KKtr], Skr. certainly, surely, inevitably.

nestapa [KS], Jav. and Skr. sorrowful; misfortune, suffering; *duka*-~, wretched.

ngah [KN], (short for Tengah) common appellation for a younger (but not youngest) son.

nganga [KK], *me*~, open, agape (of the jaws); ~!, open wide!

ngangut [KK], *me*~, to mutter to oneself.

ngap [KN], (onom.) 1. 'snap', as a cat catching its prey. 2. ~-~, panting, catching at one's breath; hard breathing; *ber*~-~, panting; *tempoh melepas* ~, breathing-space.

ngarai [KN], ravine, valley.

ngaung [KK], *me*~, roar.

ngelu [KN], aching (of the head); *penyakit* ~, heavy head.

ngengap = *ngap-ngap.*

ngening [KK], *me*~, to tighten, lose slackness, as skin after fattening.

ngerang [KK], *me*~, to groan from pain; annoyed, angry.

ngeri [KS], fearful, alarmed; horrifying, shocking; shocked, horrified; *me*~*kan,* horrible, abominable, terrify; *ke*~*an,* extreme fear.

ngeriap [KK], *me*~, to swarm; to teem, crawl about everywhere, as ants.

ngering [KN], (onom.) sound of ringing.

ngerung [KN], (onom.) the sound of beating gongs.

ngiang [KK], a variant of *iang; rasa ter*~-~ *di telinga,* having a feeling of buzzing in the ears.

ngiau [KK], *me*~, to mew (of a cat).

ngilu [KS], unpleasant to the ears, *ke*-*an.*

ngobrol [KK], Ind. *me*~, to chatter, gossip; also *obrol.*

ngungap [KK], (onom.) to pant, puffing, gasping for breath.

ngunyap [KK], to water (of the mouth).

ni, an abbreviation of *ini.*

niaga [KN], *ber*~, to trade; *per*~*an,* trading, commerce; *memper*~*kan,* to trade in; *pe*~, trader; *hukum per*~*an,* commercial law; *penguasa lembaga per*~*an,* President of the Board of Trade; see *ber*~.

nian [KKtr], Ind. very, extremely; *apa* ~ *yang dimaksud,* whatever can he mean.

niat [KN], Ar. desire, wish, longing, vow, aspiration; ~*kan,* to will; *ber*~ *nak,* to make a resolution to; *putus* ~, desire satisfied; ~ *tak sampai,* desire unfulfilled; *membayar* ~, to fulfil a vow, by, e.g., making gifts at a shrine in gratitude for success; *adat minta* ~, a quasi-religious ceremony still performed in some parts before padi-planting to ensure good crops.

nibung [KN], 1. the well-known palm (*Oncosperma tigillaria*). 2. brindled (of dog).

nidera [KK], Skr. sleepy, fast asleep.

nifas [KN], Ind. childbed; *perempuan ~*, woman in childbed; *darah ~*, secondary hemorrhage (after delivery).

nihil [KS], nothing, nil.

nika [KN], Skr. kinds, species; *serba ~*, various; also *anika*.

nikah [KN], Ar. wedding, marriage ceremony; *me~kan*, to wed two other people together; *ber~*, to be married oneself; *membaca kutbah ~*, to read the marriage-formula; *~ taklik*, a marriage subject to a conditional divorce; see *taalik; ~ gantung*, marriage in which consummation is postponed, child marriage.

nikmat [KS], Ar. a delight, a pleasure, a joy; anything pleasant to the taste; *me~i*, to enjoy; *kupur ~*, ungrateful for God's blessings (as opposed to *syukur ~*); *ke~an*, enjoyment, pleasure, comfort.

nila [KN], Skr. deep blue indigo; indigo dye; blue for laundering; *permata ~* or *~ kendi*, the sapphire; *sebab ~ setitik, rosak susu sebelanga*, a whole pot of milk spoilt by one drop of indigo, i.e. a little carelessness may ruin everything.

nilai [KN], value, worth; *~kan*, to appraise, value; *tak ter~*, priceless; *ber~*, valuable; *~-seni*, artistic value, charm; *~ batin*, inner value (not materialistic); *~an*, worth, quality; *pe~an*, assessment, valuation, judgement.

nina bobok [KN], lullaby; *me~kan*, to lull.

nilam [KN], 1. the patchouli (*Pogostemon patchouli*). 2. Tam. the sapphire; *batu ~*, id.

nin [KS & Kgn], this — a poetical variant of *ini*.

ningrat [KN], Ind. *kaum ~*, the aristocracy, elite, bourgeoisie; *ke~-~an*, snobbish.

nipah [KN], the well-known truckless palm (*Nipa fruticans*); its leaves are the commonest material for thatch; *seperti daun ~*, like nipah leaves (which sway with every breeze), vacillating, continually changing, of feelings, thoughts.

nipis [KS], tenuous, thin; *limau ~*, the lime

(*Citrus acida*); *~ melayang*, so thin that it seems able to float in air, gossamer-thin; see *tipis*.

nira [KN], Skr. the fresh juice of the palm (from which spirit is made by fermentation and also palm-sugar).

nirmala [KS], stainless, immaculate.

Nirwana [KN], Skr. *alam ~*, the Abode of Bliss, Nirvana (of the Buddhists); (fig.) seventh heaven of delight.

nisan [KN], Pers. a grave-stone; *~ bulat*, rounded headstone for males; *~ pipih*, flat headstone for females.

nisbah [KN], Ar. ratio, similar relationship, capacity, function; true comparison, real difference.

nista [KS], insult, abuse; *me~i, me~kan*, to revile, to scoff at; *ke~an*, indignity.

nobat [KN], Pers. royal band of nine items; specifically, the principal drum (*gendang ~*) of the band; *me~kan*, to inaugurate; *pe~an*, an inauguration.

noda [KN], Ind. a spot of dirt, a stain; *ter~*, stained, esp. of reputation; *~i*, to defile (esp. a virgin); disgrace, shame.

noga [KN], a shell (*Turbinella conigera*).

Noh [KN], Ar., *nabi ~*, Noah; *bahtera nabi ~*, Noah's ark.

noja [KN], a servant or caretaker in a mosque; *daun ~*, a herb used in dyeing (*Peristrope montana*).

noktah [KN], Ar. a diacritical mark, a vowel-point, a dot, a full-stop.

nomad [KN], nomad.

nombor [KN], number, figure.

nona [KN], 1. Jav. an unmarried daughter of a European or Chinese; Miss. 2. *buah ~*, the custard-apple (*Anona squamosa*); *~ kapri*, the 'bullock's heart fruit (*Anona reticulata*).

nonam [KN], a shell (*Murex sp.*)

nong [KN], a title given to distant descendants of a prince.

nonong [KK], menonong, to walk straight ahead without noticing surroundings.

nonton [KK], Ind. *me~*, to go and see a sight, a play, etc.; a variant of *tuntun* 2.

noreng [KN], a vulture.

nota [KN], Eng. notes; *~ isi keterangan*

saksi, notes of evidence.

nujum [KN], Ar. astrological tables; *ahlin-~,* astrologers; *membuka ~,* to work out a horoscope; *surat ~,* a horoscope; *me~kan,* to prophesy.

nukil [KK], Ar. a narrative, tradition; copy, translation; nukilkan, to narrate.

nun [KN], 1. Ar. *ikan ~,* the 'whale' that swallowed Jonah. 2. yonder.

nur [KN], Ar. light.

nurbisa [KN], an antidote to venom.

nuri [KN], a parrot, a lory.

nus [KN], the sepia or cuttle-fish.

nusa [KN], Ind. an island, but generally used for 'fatherland'.

nusantara [KN], Ind. archipelago, esp. the Indonesian archipelago.

nusus [KN], Ar. recalcitrant, of a wife who, if pronounced nusus by the Court, loses her dower (*mahar*) and right to maintenance (*nafkah zahir*) without being di vorced.

nutfah [KN], Ar. semen; the germ of life.

nya [KS & Kgn], its, his, her — a possessive pronoun of the third person.

nyah [KK], be off!, get away!; *~kan,* to drive away; *me~,* to run away, 'scarper'.

nyai [KN], Jav. a term of endearment; (in Deli) a mistress.

nyala [KS], flaming, glowing; *me~,* to burst into flames; *lampu letrik itu me~,* the electric light is on; *ber~,* blazing; *me~i,* light, kindle; *me~kan,* ignite, arouse.

nyalang [KS], wide open (of eyes); *me~ng* [KK], to open wide.

nyaman [KS], fit; healthful; comfortable; having a feeling of euphoria;; nice and cozy.

nyampang [KKtr], perchance, just in case; *~~ kalau lalu ...,* if you happen to be passing.

nyamuk [KN], a mosquito; *~ tiruk,* the anopheles mosquitoe; *~ harimau,* the Stegomyia mosquito; *tamparan ~,* the space between the shoulder blades.

nyanyi [KK], singing; *ber~,* to sing; *me~,* id.; *tarikkan ~,* id.; *pe~,* a singer; *peti ~,* a musical box; a gramophone.

nyanyuk [KS], dull, in one's dotage.

nyarap [KK], to plug or cork up.

nyaring [KS], clear; distinct (of utterance); shrill (of a voice).

nyaris [KKtr], nearly, all but; used of 'nearly' having an accident; *~ jatuh,* nearly fell; in the North *tak* is added; *~ tak jatuh,* nearly fell.

nyata [KS], Skr. obvious, plain, manifest; *me~kan,* to make clear, to show; to declare; *me~kan prihatin,* to express concern; *pe~,* report, statement; *ke~an,* declaration; manifesto; reality statement; plain fact; *per~an perang,* declaration of war; *ke~an rasmi,* official statement; *ke~an perubatan,* medical bulletin; *pe~an,* a declaration or expression; *pe~an kapal,* a ship's manifest; *pe~ kemajuan pelajaran,* school report.

nyatuh [KN], a valuable timber-tree (*Payena costata*).

nyawa [KN], soul, life, spirit; 'my life' (as a term of endearment); *me~,* breathing heavily, of animals; *ber~ ikan,* more dead than alive; *ber~ rapuh,* having a frail hold on life; *minta ~,* to ask for quarter; *se~kan,* to graft (a tree); *tiga se~,* Ind. a Trinity; *membuang ~,* to risk one's life; *tidak ber~,* lifeless.

nyedar [KS], Skr. sound (of sleep).

nyeyai [KS], coarsely woven (of cloth).

nyenyeh [KK], *me~,* to talk wildly and inconsequently, as a drunken person.

nyenyen [KK], teasing, worrying.

nyirih [KN], a mangrove tree.

nyiru [KN], a basket-tray, used for winnowing; sometimes a sieve.

nyiur [KN], a coconut; *pokok ~,* a coconuttree; *setandan ~,* a cluster of coconuts; *sabut ~,* husk or fibre of coconut; *~ ladih,* a coconut, the water of which has coagulated into a pulp; *~ dimakan bulan,* a coconut without water in it; *~ mumbang,* the very young coconut; *~ semantan,* the coconut when the water can be heard on the nut being shaken; *~ muda,* the 'green' coconut (at the stage when it is just ready for opening to drink); ~ *sungkuran,* the nut before the shell has commenced to harden; ~ *tahan kukur,* the nut when the shell is hardening but the water cannot be heard; ~ *gubal,* a husked coconut; also *kelapa;* ~ *gading,* ivory coconut palm.

nyolo [KN], Ch. an incense-burner.

nyonya [KN], a designation given to Chinese married women; the queen, at cards; also *nonya.*

nyonyeh [KS], *me~,* to mumble indistinctly, as a toothless person.

nyonyong [KS], blown out, swollen up, inflamed.

nyonyot [KK], *me~,* pulling at something that gives, as at the breast (of a baby), or at a piece of elastic or at an ice-cream.

nyut [KS], the throbbing of a boil or of the fontanelle; ~-~, continually throbbing.

O

O, the fifteenth letter of the Roman alphabet.

O [KSn], Oh, exclamation of surprise etc.; interjection used to call somebody.

oasis [KN], oasis.

oat [KN], oats.

obari [KN], ovary.

obiul [KN], ovule.

objektif [KS], objective.

obor [KN], Jav. a torch; used esp., of the Olympic torch, ~ *Olimpik; meng~*, to smoke out or fumigate with a torch.

obral [KK], *meng~*, to sell off at a cheap price, clearance sale.

obrol [KK], Ind. = *ngobrol; meng~*, to chat, to chatter.

ocak [KN], ~-~, source (of a stream).

ocok [KK], 1. stirring up by teasing or talebearing; exciting; mischief-making. 2. a rattle for driving fish.

ogah [KK], 1. Hind. a hookah, a hubble-bubble; also *hukah* and *hogah*. 2. to shake to-and-fro, as in loosening; unwilling, reluctant.

ogam [KN], *peng~*, a scraper; *peng~ may-ang*, a borer or cutter for extracting palm sap; *peng~ sampah*, a sort of broom; *meng~* [KK], urge on.

ogoh [KK], to shake (as a monkey) a branch, or as a child shakes a thing without violent commotion.

ogok [KS], 1. stingy. 2. to gulp down.

Ogos [KN], Eng. *bulan ~*, the month of August.

ohm [KN], ohm, unit of electrical resistance.

oja [KK], mengoja, to excite to attack, esp. of bulls and fighting-cocks; in Kel. used esp. of exciting a beaten bull to fight again.

okid [KN], orchid.

oksid [KN], oxide; *peng~an*, oxidization.

oksigen [KN], oxygen.

olah [KN], 1. way of doing things, manner, method; excuse, attitude taken up; *banyak ~*, capricious, variable; *~-elah*, duplicity; *~-~*, tricks, diversions; *se-~-~*, about the same as; similar to, as though, just as if; *meng~*, to show temperament; 'play-up'. 2. *~-raga*, Ind. sports, games; *ber~raga*, play games; *~raga-wan*, sportsman, athelete. 3. = *kelola; peng~an*, direction, management; method of doing something, treatment of a problem, 'handling'.

olak [KN], 1. an eddy or agitation on the water; *~-alik*, backwards and forwards. 2. down-stream; *sebelah ~*, down-stream, i.e. where the ripples are below a stake, on the down-stream side.

oleh [KD], 1. by means of, through the medium of, owing to; used in writing for 'by' (agent) instead of *dek; per~an*, revenue; *ber~*, to obtain — cf. *boleh*. 2. *~-~*, Ind. keepsake, memento, parting gift; *diper~ dengan susah payah*, hard earned; *memper~ kembali*, to regain; *memper~ kesan*, to get the impression.

oleng [KS], *meng~-~*, to rock to-and-fro, as a tub in rough water; *~-aling*, id.; also used for backwards and forwards; *~-~*, a crank, windlass; *~-alingkan*, to waggle (something) to-and-fro, e.g., as cleaning it in water; to work-to-and-fro, as a stake in order to loosen it.

olok [KN], joking, jesting; *meng~-~*, to chaff; *burung ~-~*, the booby (*Sula leucogaster*); *~* is used for 'mock' in such expressions as *serangan udara ~-~*, mock air-raid; *perkhabaran ~-~*, spoof report; *memper~-~kan*, to play the fool with, trifle with; travesty.

omah-omah [KN], Kel. mosquito larvae, = *jintik-jintik*.

Omar [KN], Ar. the second Caliph; a Malay proper name.

ombak [KN], a wave, a billow; *ber~*, to roll in waves; to surge; *mabuk ~*, seasick; *~ menyorong*, a following sea; *~ pengundak*, a head sea; *~ bunga lepang*, white-crested waves; *batu mandi ~*, a sea-washed rock.

ombang-ambing [KK], *ter~*, to drift about (on water), rock to and fro.

omboh [KN], a piston.

ombong [KK], N.S. *meng~*, to wheedle, 'butter-up'.

omel [KK], Ind. *meng~*, to grumble, grouse.

omong [KN], 1. a mark to indicate that a place is reserved by a man for the erection of fishing-stakes. 2. [KK], *meng~*, to meet together; to gossip, to chat; *~-~ kosong*, idle chatter.

ompang [KN], *~-~*, miscellaneous articles carried about by a trader (as gifts to chiefs).

ompok [KN], 1. a method of printing on cloth. 2. a border sewn on to a piece of embroidery or on to a mat.

ompong [KS], Ind. toothless.

onak [KN], a curved thorn.

onang-aning [KN], the seventh generation.

onar [KN], noisy, in commotion, to make trouble.

ondeh [KN], *~-~*, sweetened dumplings of dough rolled in coconut scrapings.

oneng [KN], *~-~*, remote descendants.

ong = *hong*.

onggok [KK], 1. *~-onggol*, swaying, rocking. 2. *ber~-~*, [KN], in small heaps or clusters or groups.

ongkak [KN], posts (in a boat's bows) to which the cable is secured, bitts.

ongkos [KN], (Dutch) outlay, expenses, charges (esp. travelling expenses).

onis [KS], pale; *pucat ~*, id.

onyak [KS], *~-anyik*, vacillating, undecided; shaking (as a loose tooth).

opah [KN], granny (as mode of address).

opau [KN], Ch. a purse-pouch attached to the waist-belt.

opor [KN], Ind. cooking without vegetables or condiments; plain roasting or stewing.

orak [KK], unloosing, unwinding, uncoiling, undoing; *meng~*, to unfasten, to unfold, to untie; *meng~ langkah*, to 'stir one's stumps', to make the first move.

orang [KN], a human being; a man or woman; people generally (esp. in the sense of other people); *~ Melayu*, a Malay; *kata ~*, people say; it is said; *~ banyak*, the multitude, the people; *~ hutan*, *~ liar* or *~ bukit*, aboriginal tribesmen; *~ asing*, foreigner; *~ baru*, a new comer, novice; *~ besar*, authority, an important person; *~ tengah*, a middleman; *~ rumah*, 'my wife'; *perse~an*, individual, personal; *sifat perse~an*, egotism; individualism; *berse~*, single (meant for one person); *usaha secara perse~an*, private enterprise; *se~ diri*, all alone, without a companion; *bercakap se~ diri*, to talk to oneself; *kese~an*, loneliness; lonely, left alone; *~-~*, a figure like a man, e.g., a scarecrow; *~-~an mata*, the pupil of the eye; *~-nya*, the character or attributes of a person; *baik ~-nya*, he's a good chap.

ordi [KN], Port. commands, instructions, orders; also *rodi*.

organ [KN], organ; party paper.

orlit [KN], earring of diamond, with nut and screw behind the ear.

orok [KN], (onom.) *~-~*, a number of perforated objects strung on a stick so as to rattle when the stick is shaken; used to drive fish; cf. *ocok* 2; *anak ~*, new born child; *meng~*, to snore.

otak [KN], brains, marrow; *~ tulang*, the marrow; strictly speaking *~* applies to the physical brain, but is often used for the intelligence also; *~ mereng*, not quite right in the head; *~-~*, a type of food made of fish etc. mixed with spices and toasted wrapped in coconut leaves; a kind of Malaysian food.

otek [KN], 1. an edible salt-water fish (Arius sp.); a sp. of catfish. 2. working slowly.

Othman [KN], Ar. the fourth Caliph; a Malay proper name, also written as Osman.

otot [KN], Ind. muscle.

P

pa [KN], father (expressed familiarly); *pak penakan,* uncle; *pak long,* eldest uncle; *pak busu,* youngest uncle; *pak cik,* id.

pabrik [KN], Ind. a factory, a mill.

pacai [KN], sandalwood dust sprinkled on a dead body to prepare it for the grave.

pacak [KK], 1. *memacak (kan), ter~,* planted or driven into the ground, to spit; sticking a sharp-pointed stick through something else. 2. accustomed to, experienced in, versed in.

pacal [KN], 1. slave of a slave; the humblest of the humble (a very self-depreciatory expression used as a pronoun of the first person). 2. Treng. a mark designating ownership made on a fruit tree; = *pacau.*

pacar [KN], 1. Ind. a plant bearing a red flower; a kind of henna; ~ *Merah,* the Scarlet Pimpernel (the fictional character, well known in literature). 2. (Ind.) lover; ~ *pria,* boyfriend; ~ *wanita,* girlfriend.

pacat [KN], a leech; *burung ~,* the pitta; ~ *kenyang,* thick ring worn as a fingerguard when using a *keris.*

pacau [KN], a talisman hung on a tree to make the fruit of that tree disagree with anyone who steals and eats it.

paceli or **paceri** [KN], Tam. brinjal or pineapple condiment.

pacih [KN], *main ~,* Ach., Pen. a children's race-game played with cowries on a cross-shaped board.

pacu [KK], goading on or spurring on (a horse); *memacu,* to spur on; *memacukan,* make to race or compete; *~an,* race, race course.

pacul [KK], squeezing or pressing out (as one presses matter out of a sore); crushing in fingers.

pada [KD], 1. Skr. *seri ~,* the holy feet of a prince; a royal title. 2. sufficient, adequate, enough; *ber~lah,* enough to go on with, it will do; *memadai,* to suffice; *asal ada kecik ~,* a little is better than nothing; *dalam ~ itu,* still, nevertheless, however that may be. 3. by, at, near, in according to, than; *ke~,* to; *dari~,* from; ~ *akhirnya,* finally; *~hal,* whereas.

padah [KN], 1. *memadah,* to invite. 2. result, effect (us. bad); *ber~,* bringing disaster, so, ominous; *~nya,* the consequence.

padam [KK], 1. *memadamkan, memadami,* extinguishing; putting out (a light); (by metaphor) putting an end to evil feelings; rubbing out (a mark, etc.); *pemadam kebakaran,* extinguisher. 2. Skr. a lotus; *merah ~,* lotus-red, fiery red.

padan [KS], adequate, fitting well, congruent; *~kan,* to fit together; to harmonize, to adapt (modify so as to make suitable for a particular purpose); ~ *dengan muka dia,* (sl.) serves him right!

padang [KN], a plain; an open space; a field, esp. a playing-field; ~ *tembak,* a shooting-range; ~ *saujana,* a stretch of open country; ~ *belantara,* desert steppe; *lain padang lain belalang,* (prov.) so many countries, so many customs; ~ *jarak,* ; *tekukur,* a tract of waste land.

padat [KS], *memadat, memadati,* cramming, crushing into a small space, stuffing; compact, solid; well-knit, terse, of style; *pemadatan,* compression.

padau [KN], *layar ~,* a storm-sail.

paderi [KN], Port. a Christian priest; a clergy-man.

padi [KN], rice in the husk; *semangat ~,* the spirit of life in the ~; ~ *ringan,* varieties of quick-growing rice; ~ *berat,* slow growing rice; ~ *Taiwan,* a variety of ~ obtained from Formosa which can be sown twice a year; ~ *bunting,* rice in the ear; ~-~*an,* grasses similar to ~.

padu [KS], welding together, hammering together; coagulated (or rubber); *ber~,* to unite, mix, fuse, combine; *menyatu~kan,* merge, unite; *memadu~kan,* to blend; *ber~an,* union, unity; *~an suara,* vocal harmony; *tayar getah ~,* solid tyres; *per~an nasional,* national unity; *pertubuhan per~an Afrika,* Organisation for African Unity.

paduk [KN], a crease or starting line used in playing Malay games.

paduka [KN], Skr. a royal title derived from the fact that the subject addresses the raja's feet, being unworthy to address the price himself; ~ literally means 'shoe'.

padung [KN], a short shoot or projection from the stem of a creeper; a tendril.

pagan [KS], solid; sturdy; strongly built.

pagar [KN], a fence, a palisading; a row of stakes or palings; *memagari,* to fence in, to enclose; ~ *duri,* barbed wire; ~ *anak,* (1) the palings leading to an elephant corral; (2) a tree (*Ixonanthes obovata); bunga ~,* the common lantana (*Lantana camara); ~ hidup,* a hedge; *~an,* fencing; fenced area; *jimat pemagar diri,* a protective talisman; *pemagar,* a guard-rail; ~ *makan padi,* the fence eats the rice, i.e., the trustee or guardian is dishonest.

pagi [KN], morning, in the morning; early , a.m.; ~-~, early in the morning; ~-~ *buta,* the grey of dawn; ~ *muda,* morning before the sun is high; *se~, se~an,* throughout the morning; *besok ~-~,* first thing in the morning.

pagu [KN], a ceiling; a loft or attic; *di atas ~,* in the loft; *arang ~,* soot in the kitchen.

pagut [KK], *memagut,* the peck of a bird, the bite of a small fish or snake; to peck.

paha [KN], the thigh of a man; the ham of an animal; a quarter (= *pauh* 2); *jantung ~,* the fleshy part of the thigh; *pangkal ~,* the upper portion of the thigh; *lipat ~,* the groin; *pangkal ~,* id.

pahala [KN], Skr. gain, esp. as the reward of virtue; merit, virtuous actions (as opposed to *dosa); mencari ~,* to seek ot acquire merit.

pahar [KN], a large salver of metal resting on a stand or on legs.

pahat [KN], a chisel; *memahat* [KK], carving with a chisel; ~ *jantan,* a chisel with a narrow deep blade; ~ *kuku,* a gouge; ~ *lebar,* a chisel with a flat broad and shallow balde; *pemahat,* a sculptor.

pahi [KN], *mata ~,* the iron tip of a Malay ploughshare.

pahit [KS], bitter; *memahitkan,* make bitter; *ke~an,* bitterness; *kita tahu ~ maungnya,* we know how unpleasant he is; but this also may mean, 'we know the worst of him', i.e. 'we can put up with him'; ~ *getir,* of bitter flavour; *kalau ~-~ darahnya,* i.e. if he is bold, if he is a red-blooded man.

pahlawan [KN], Pers. leader in war; *johan ~,* world-champion; *ke~an,* courage.

pain [KN], pint, pine.

paip [KN], Eng. a pipe for liquid; *tukang ~,* a plumber.

pais [KN], *ikan ~,* fish cooked in banana leaves.

pajak [KN], (Dutch) farm, monopoly; ~ *candu,* the opium farm; ~ *gadai,* the pawnbroking firm; a pawnshop; ~ *dusun,* to let out (or rent) an orchard; ~ *potong,* an abattoir; *memajaki,* pay tax for; *memajakkan,* lend, loan; *~kan,* to let on lease, give the right to take produce; *~an,* such a lease.

pajuh [KS], gluttonous, guzzling.

pak, 1. father; = *pa.* 2. packing-case.

pakai [KK], *memakai,* using or wearing anything; assuming, adopting, employing; putting on (clothing); *memakai,* to wear; to use; to act on take as correct; *didengar ada, di~ tidak,* he hears (my advice), but won't act on it; *~an seragam,* a uniform; *tak ber~ lagi,* no longer in use; *ber~ benar!,* (sl.) really dressed up!, 'sharp!'; *~an,* clothes, garments; *ber~,* to dress oneself; *sepemakai,* normal, of usual type; *tak* *ter~*, past using, unserviceable; *pemakaian*, the using of, the practice of using.

pakak [KN], *ulun ~*, a name given to a class of shells imported from Celebes (*Conus* sp.).

pakal [KK], caulking.

pakan [KN], 1. the woof; *tirai yang berpakankan mas*, curtains shot with gold. 2. a compound smeared on the heads and necks of fighting bulls to render the skin impervious to wounds.

pakar [KN], Ar. expert, expert knowledge.

pakat [KN], Ar. arrangement by conference; agreement; settlement; *ber~*, [KK] to agree; to conspire to; *~an*, a pact; corrupted from *muafakat; menyepakati*, to agree on.

pakau [KN], 1. a cross-piece in a bucket or well. 2. *daun ~*, Ch. playing cards.

pakih [KN], Ar. a jurisconsult, learned in religious law.

paksa [KK], 1. compulsion, force; *memaksa*, to compel; *memaksa wang*, to extort money; *wang ~an*, money extorted; *memaksakan*, to enforce; *buruh ~*, forced labour; *pendaratan ~*, forced landing. 2. auspicious, lucky; a bit of luck; *~ tekukur padi rebah*, felled rice is a bit of luck for the turtle-doves.

paksi [KN], 1. Skr. a bird (expressed poetically). 2. = *paksa* 2.

paksina [KN], Jav. the north; *dari daksina datang ke ~*, from the south to the north; (poet. – *utara*).

paku [KN], 1. a spike, a nail; *ter~*, nailed, firmly affixed; (fig.) confined, unable to get about; *ter~ di pejabat*, stuck in the office; *~ Belanda*, met. for fixed, immovable; *memulangkan ~ buah keras*, to cast some action in a person's teeth, to say, 'I told you so!'. 2. a generic name for the fern *Filex*, and for plants resembling it.

pal [KN], 1. a tack (in sailing); *ber~*, to beat about, to tack. 2. (Dutch) the Dutch 'pole' as a measure of length.

pala [KN], 1. Skr. *buah ~*, the nutmeg (*Myristica fragrans*); *halwa ~*, nutmegs in syrup. 2. *~~*, genuinely, properly; *se ~*, as thoroughly as possible; *se~ mencuri jangan tanggung-tanggung*, if you must steal don't take half-measures. 3. *burung ~*, a crane.

palam [KN], to plug up, e.g., a leak or the mouth of a bottle or the lower orifices of the body *(abaimana)* before burial; *pemalam*, to fill in (a crack) by pushing in, e.g., a rag.

palang [KN], position across or athwart; *kayu ~*, the cross-bar on a buffalo's horns; used to mean a cross, us. not in the religious sense *(salib); Palang Merah*, the Red Cross; *Palang Merah Antarabangsa*, International Red Cross.

palas [KN], a generic name for the fan-palms known as *licualas* (the leaves of which are sometimes used by Malays as cigarette wrappers).

palat [KN], *tahi ~*, smegma.

palau [KN], a cicatrix or other mark facilitating identification.

paldu [KN], Hind. side-awning of a ship.

paling [KK], 1. *ber~*, to look aside, to turn one's head; *~ kepala*, id.; *ber~ tadah*, to change one's loyalty; *ber~ arah*, to change direction; *~ tiak*, the least; *~~*, at most; *~ buruk*, worst. 2. Ind. very, exceedingly. 3. Kel. = *tukar*.

palis [KK], turning away the head, e.g. as a modest girl when compliments are paid her; *memaliskan muka*, id.; cf. **paling**.

palit [KK], *memalit*, to smudge or smear.

palsu [KS], Port. false, forged, counterfeit (of money, notes, etc.); *gigi ~*, false teeth; also *falsu; memalsukan*, forge, fake; *ke~an*, forgery, deception.

paltu [KN], Hind. a deputy.

palu [KK], *memalu*, striking with a stick or bar or other rigid cylindrical body; *ber~*, *ber~~an*, beaten.

paluh [KN], a hollow filled with stagnant water, a pool; Sel. a navigable channel.

palut [KS], enwrapping, = *balut; ber~*, wrapped in (e.g., a rind or a cover); *memalutkan*, to enwrap.

pamah [KS], flat, low-lying (of land).

paman [KN], maternal uncle; a familiar

form of address to persons a good deal older than oneself.

pamir [KK], *mem~kan,* Ind. to show, display; *~an,* a show, an exhibition.

pamitan [KK], Ind. *ber~ (pada),* to take one's leave (of).

pampang [KK], stretching out before the eye; *ter~,* clearly visible; *memanpangkan,* to display.

pampas [KN], *memampas,* to compensate; *~an pekerja,* Workmen's Compensation.

pamur [KN], the damascening on a *keris.*

panah [KN], a bow; the use of a bow; (better *anak ~*) an arrow; *~ liang,* a black wasp that lives in holes in the ground; *~an,* archery; the shooting of arrows; *memanah,* to shoot with a bow; to direct an arrow or, (fig.) a spotlight, to 'pick out' with light, to pierce darkness; *~an matahari,* the fierce rays of the sun; *kena ~(an) matahari,* to get sunstroke.

panas [KS], heat, esp. solar heat; hot; *~ cing,* Kel. swelteringly hot; *~ egat, ~ erik, ~ gekja,* N.S. id.; *tengah-tengah ~,* in the sun (not in the shade); *ber~,* be in the hot sun; *memanaskan,* warm, heat up; *pemanas,* heater, hot tempered; *hujan ~,* (idiom) rain during sunshine; *ke~an,* to be over-heated (mobil); *~ tidak sampai ke petang,* (prov.) good luck (fortune) is not everlasting; *~-hati,* angry, 'worked-up'; *heboh macam cacing ke~an,* all hot and bothered like a worm out in the sun, 'like a cat on hot bricks'; *ber~ berembun,* in the sun and in the dew, i.e. exposed to all weathers; *~ baran,* hot tempered, (*baran* here = *bara* 1); *~ lembab,* humid heat.

panau [KN], discoloured light patches on the skin.

panca [KBil], Skr. five, multiple, varied; *~ indera,* the five senses; *~ logam,* an alloy of several metals; *~ persada,* temporary stucture for the celebration of a bathing-ceremony; *~ roba,* uncertain, fickle, changeable; *~ rona* or *~ warna,* of many colours; *~ bicara,* Pah. a five-pronged gold head-ornament (like a small flat fork) thrust into the kerchiefs

of the Ruler and his consort after they have partaken of the *nasi adap-adap* at installation; Pk. the lustration water used at installations; *~ ragam,* a band; *~ sila,* Ind. the Five Principles of the Indonesian Republic, also called *lima dasar; peri ke-Tuhanan, peri kemanusian, peri kebangsaan, peri kerakyatan (demokrasi), peri keadaan sosial,* recognition of Divine Omnipotence, humanity, national consciousness, democracy and social justice. (Not to be confused with the *~sila* of the pact between India and China regarding international relations.)

pancang [KN], a pole, pile, or stake; *~ silang,* cross-cross stakes used esp. in scaffolding for building; *memancang,* to drive (piles); *memancangkan,* to drive (piles) into the ground; *ter~,* driven into the ground.

pancar [KK], flowing out violently; gushing out; pouring out; *kilat memancar,* the lightning flashing; *ter~ otaknya,* his brains gushed out; *~an air,* a hydrant; a fountain; *~ radio,* a broadcasting station; *~kan,* to broadcast; *pemancar radio,* radio transmitter.

pancing [KK], angling, to fish with hook and line; *~ ikan,* id.; *~ tunda,* to troll; *ter~,* baited, hooked; *ke~an,* pharyngitis, laryngitis.

pancit [KK], to ooze out, to gush forth in a thin stream; *~kan,* to squirt (e.g.,) insects; to spray.

pancung [KK], cutting off a projection; *memancung,* to lop off, to prune, to mutilate; *~kan kepala,* to behead.

pancur [KK], *memancur,* to flow (of water in pipes and conduits), flowing from the end of a pipe; *~an air,* a conduit; *pemancur api,* a flame-thrower; a cigarette-lighter; *ter~ otaknya,* his brains were blown out.

pancut [KK], spouting or gushing out (of water); *ter~,* spout out under pressure; *memancutkan air racun,* to spray poison (over insect pests or fungoid growths); *(jentera) pemancut air,* a water-pump, monitor for emitting a jet of water.

pandai [KS], skilled, versed in, proficient, smart, intelligent; Kel. a type of fighting bull that uses rushing tactics, a hustler; *ke~an*, knowledge, skill; *memandai-mandai,* to show off, show how clever one is; *memandai sendirinya,* id.; *~-~lah!,* carefully!, make a job of it!

pandak [KS], short (in a limited number of expressions, the usual word being *pendek*); *keris ~*, a short dagger.

pandam [KN], fixing jewellery in resin to keep it steady while being worked at.

pandan [KN], a generic name given to the smaller screw-pines *(Pandanaceoe),* the leaves of which are used in making mats.

pandang [KK], *memandang,* gazing, to look fixedly at, seeing and observing (as opposed to merely glancing at); *~an,* observation, notice; a look, a glance; *memandang rendah,* to look down on, despise; *memandang serong pada,* to look askance at; *pemandangan,* views, sights; power of sight; *membuang ~an pada,* to cast a glance at; *sekali ~,* at first glance; *memandang berat pada,* to take a serious view of; *memandang tinggi,* to respect, look up to, *mencuri ~an pada,* to steal a glance at; *ber~an,* exchanging looks; *ber~an luas,* have an open mind.

Pandir [KN], Pk. *Pak ~,* the name of a legendary fool.

pandu [KK], *memandu,* to guide, pilot; lead a dance; to test, have a try; *pemandu kapal terbang,* an air pilot; *peluru ber~,* guided missile; *peluru ber~ antara benua,* inter-continental guided missile; *ber~kan pada,* to take guidance from; *buku ~an jalan,* road-guide-book; *buku-buku sebagai ~an,* authorities consulted (by an author); *~,* Ind. a boy-scout; *~ puteri,* a girl-guide.

pangan [KN], extensive tracts of forests; *orang ~,* a name given to some aboriginal tribes.

panggak [KS], N.S. swagger, pride; *~-~kan,* to pride oneself one, give oneself airs

about.

panggang [KK], 1. roasting, toasting; *pemanggang,* the roast; *roti ~,* toast; *seperti kucing dengan pemanggang,* like the cat and the roast (they must not be left together); a way of warning about dangerous proximity between youths and young girls. 2. *ter~,* gripped, clipped, crosswise; *ter~ ke mulut buaya,* (falling) into the grip of the crocodile's mouth.

panggar [KN], a scaffolding.

panggau [KN], a light raised framework used for drying fish; or any framework supporting flooring, etc.; cf. **panggar**.

panggil [KK], *~kan,* to have a man summoned, to send for; *memanggil,* to summon, to call; to name; *kata-kata ~an,* vocative mode of address, name normally used; *nama ~an,* a nick-name; *surat ~an,* an invitation; a letter sending for someone.

panggu [KN], Pen. a share.

panggul [KK], Ind. *memanggul,* to carry across the shoulder (as a gun).

panggung [KN], an erection on pillars, a stage, a raised flooring; *~ wayang,* the stage of a theatre, now us. the theatre itself; *seri ~,* the leading lady in a theatrical cast, the principal actress in a Malay play; *duduk bersila ~,* to cross one leg over the other — cf. **panggar** and **panggau;** *~* is also used locally for scaffolding and, in the North, for a brushwood dam. 2. to raise the head after prostration in prayer *(sujud).*

pangkah [KN], 1. the mark of a cross; a caste-mark; to mark with a cross; *tanda ~,* the mark of a cross, esp. on a ballot paper. 2. Hind. a punkah.

pangkal [KN], beginning; commencement, first stage or initial portion of anything; *ber~,* originate; *memangkalkan,* beach a boat; *~ bahu,* the shoulder; *~ lengan,* the upper arm; *~ jalan,* starting point of a journey; *~an,* a landing place; the point where a traveller leaves the sea for a land journey or vice versa; pier, quay, base of operations; *~an terbang,* an airport; ~an angkatan laut, naval base; ~an peluru berpandu, guided missile launching-site; ~an asing, foreign bases.

pangkas [KK], to crop the ends of anything; memangkas, trim or cut hair; cut the top of grass; memangkas jambul, to cut off the long lock left on the head of a small boy prior to circumcision; tukang ~, sometimes used for 'barber'.

pangkat [KN], degree, rank, stage; se~, of the same rank, status, social position, grade or degree; ber~-~, in grades, in stages; naik ~, to be promoted; turun ~, to be demoted; ber~ lebih tinggi (daripada), to out-rank.

pangking [KN], Ch. a sleeping-bed platform.

pangku [KK], holding between the breast and the forearm; fostering; defending; ~an, the upper portion of the lap; memangku, to hold to the breast; to nurture; pemangku, a regent; pemangku raja, id.; pemangku is also used generally for deputy (for a high official); memangku is also used for to take on one's lap; se~an, an armful; ~ tangan, to sit with one's hands in one's lap, i.e. sit idly; asyik dengan memangku tangan, mati dalam angan-angan, if you are set on sitting with your hands in your lap, your day-dreams will ruin you, i.e. get a move on!

pangkung [KK], to pommel or pound with a heavy stick.

pangkur [KN], an instrument for scraping sago out of the tree-trunk.

panglima [KN], executive officer; military leader; ~ often forms part of a title of honour; ~ agung pihak terikat, Supreme Allied Commander; ketua ~ diraja, Chief of the Imperial General Staff; ~ agung, General Officer Commanding; ~ tertinggi tentera-tentera bersenjata, Supreme Head of the Armed Forces; ~ agung angkatan bersenjata, id.

pangling [KS], 1. failing to recognise or notice; over-looking. 2. Ked. the purple moorhen.

pangsa [KN], the carpel or hollow in a durian in which the 'pip' (ulas) is found; a natural 'slice' of an orange; a natural division in fruit; rumah ~, a block of flats or tenements, a multiple dwelling; ~ menunjukkan bangsa, a tree is known by its fruit.

pangsi [KN], 1. the peg of a top. 2. the sepia of a cuttlefish.

pangus [KK], to spout, to blow (of a porpoise).

panitia [KN], Ind. a committee, board.

panja [KN], Pers., Pen. the figure of a hand used at the Muharram.

panjak [KN], a drummer at a makyung.

panjang [KS], long; umur ~, long life; se ~, all along; ~kan, diper~, extend, to lengthen; ber~-~, continous, endless; berke~an, long, dragging; se~ pengetahuan saya, to my knowledge; ~kan kalam, to write at length; ~kan leher, to stretch out the neck (to see); ~ mata, flirtatious, fond of 'giving the eye'; ~ lebar, in detail; memanjang, lengthways (opposed to melintang — horizontal).

panjar [KN], Jav. earnest-money; = cengkeram, deposit.

panjat [KK], to climb; ascend, memanjati, climb on; memanjatkan, lift up something; pemanjat, climber.

panji, 1. ~-~, a pennon, colours, a streamer. 2. Jav. an ancient Javanese military grade; Sira Panji, the nom de guerre of the great Javanese hero Radin Inu Kertapati, Prince of Kuripan.

panjut [KN], 1. tipped with white (a lucky marking) — of an animal's tail, a kris' damask. 2. a torch used at festivals.

pantai [KN], a beach; the sea-shore; pasukan kawalan ~, the coastguard.

pantak [KK], to drive nails, peg. etc; memantak, to penetrate (sharp object).

pantalun [KN], Eng. trousers.

pantang [KN], prohibited; forbidden (by custom or doctor's orders, not by law or religion); ber~ undur, determined not to retreat; no retreat! ber~, abstaining, dislike, unwilling; ~ menyerah!, no surrender!; ber~ nikah, celibate; ber~

kalah, invincible; *ber~ di gambar,* not to be photographed; *makan ber~,* to be on a diet; *~kan,* to forbid; *~ pemali* or *~ larangan,* tabooed; *~ larang,* rules (of custom or tribal law) forbidding certain acts; *memantangi,* to avoid, hold aloof from, treat as taboo; *~ tersinggung,* won't stand interference, touchy.

pantas [KS], 1. agile, swift, speedy; *memantaskan,* accelerate, quicken; *~ berlari,* a fast runner; *~ mulut,* ready-witted; *seperti kilat ~nya,* swift as lighting; *~ tangan,* deft; *kepantasan* (rate of) speed. 2. Ind. proper, becoming.

pantat [KN], the base, the fundament, the buttocks; the pudenda.

pantau [KK], *memantau,* to look up a person, to visit.

pantik [KK], striking together two hard substances; to produce fire; *pemantik api,* a flint and steel.

pantis, [KN] to touch up (with colour or rouge); *memantis gincu,* to apply rouge to cheek.

pantuk [KN], the coaming on a Malay half-decked boat.

pantul [KK], *~ balik,* to rebound — cf. **antul**; to ricochet; *~an,* reflection; *~an cahaya,* reflection of light.

pantun [KN], 1. a quatrain, the first line of which rhymes with the third, and the second with the fourth; *ber~,* to extemporise a quatrain. 2. *se ~,* like, similar to; = *seperti.*

panus [KN], Ar. a candle-bracket, a lantern.

papa [KS], Skr. penniless, destitute; *~ kelana,* a pauper vagabond; *~ kerma,* a pauper by misfortune.

papah [KK], prop, support; *berjalan ber~,* to wall with support (as a cripple); *memapah,* to support, to help someone along.

papak [KS], 1. flat, eve, without cavities or prominences; *rumah ~,* flat-roofed house. 2. a hermaphrodite. 3. crunching, mastication; to crunch, bite up; also *pepak.*

papan [KN], a plank, a board, flooring; *~*

batu, a slate; *~ catur,* a chessboard; *~ mistar,* a ruling-board; *muka ~,* brazen-faced; *tulang ~ pungkur,* the lumbar vertebrae; *~ punggung,* the small of the back; *~ tanda jalan,* road signposts; *~ tulis,* blackboard; drawing-board; *~ notis,* notice-board; *~ tanda kedai,* a shop sign; *~ nama,* id.; *bukan memapan, menarah,* not making planks, rough-hewing, rhyming sl. (somewhat vulgar) for *bukan makan, muntah ke darah,* not eating, guzzling (see **muntah**), i.e. golly, what a spread!

papar [KS], flat, smooth; the blunt side; the back (as opposed to the edge) of a blade; the flat of a horn (as opposed to its point); *~kan,* to set forth, recount, consider; to display, e.g., banners.

papas [KK], 1. removing or taking off — clothes, mats, *kajang* roofs, etc.; *memapas khemah,* to furl up a tent. 2. *ber~an (dengan),* to encounter, come face to face (with).

para [KN], 1. a shelf, rack, attic or framework of any sort raised above the flooring; *~~ buku,* book-shelf; *arang ~,* soot. 2. a collective prefix in expressions — such as *~ pembaca,* 'our readers'; *~juri,* members of the jury. 3. Hind. sentry-go; *orang ~,* a sentry; a constable on duty at a door; *ber~,* to be on duty at a door; to be on guard.

parabola [KN], parabola.

parafin [KN], paraffin.

parah [KS], severe, deadly (of a wound); *luka ~,* mortally wounded.

parajurit [KN], a warrior, soldier; see *jurit.*

parak [KN], Ar. 1. separation, barrier (esp. between the male and female guests at a wedding); *ber~,* to separate, as when dissolving intimacy; to be kept apart, as sexes; *memarakkan,* to divide, separate; *~ siang,* shortly before daybreak. 2. Kel. much, in quantities.

param [KN], *~~* (or *pe~*), a medicinal ointment used after a confinement.

paran [KN], direction, aim; *memarani,* to go to, to approach, head for (a place).

parang [KN], 1. a chopper; *memarang,*

chopping, cutting at; ~ *candung,* a cleaver (the handle and blade of which are in one piece); ~ *puting,* a very sharp chopper; ~ *jenguk,* Kel. a lethal stabbing weapon; ~ *belitung,* a big heavy parang; ~ *Panjang,* Malay Defence forces against Chinese terrorists after the Japanese surrender. 2. *ikan* ~-~, the wolf-herring.

parap [KK], 1. to strike hammer-wise with the side of the fist; *pemarap,* the lower part of the fist; *bertumbuk-ber~,* punching and slogging; 2. initials; *memarap,* initial.

parasit [KN], 1. parasite, animal or plant living on or in another and getting its food from it. 2. person supported by another and giving him nothing in return.

parau [KS], harsh, hoarse of the voice, e.g., after much talking — cf. **garau.**

pari [KN], 1. a generic name for fish of the skate and ray type; ~ *punai,* a ray with green flesh, reckoned the best eating; *kikir* ~, a skate-skin grater; *menikam* ~, to spear the ray; *sengat* ~, the sting of the ray; the plaint, rough tail of a ray is sometimes used as a weapon in brawls, hence *ekor* ~ is sometimes used for 'cat-o'-nine-tails'. 2. a fairy, us. *hantu* ~, also *peri.*

pariah [KN], Hind. a pariah, outcast.

parih [KK], *memarih,* deal (cards); cast (lots); throw (dice).

parit [KN], a trench, a moat, a ditch, a drain, a canal for drainage; ~ *buang,* outlet drain.

pariwisata [KN], tourism.

parlimen [KN], parliament; *ber~,* having a parliament.

Parsi [KN], *negeri* ~, Persia.

parti [KN], Eng. party, faction; body of persons united in opinion in support of a course etc.; *ber~,* to join a political party; ~ *Islam Se-Malaya (P.A.S.),* the Pan-Malayan Islamic party. [P.A.S. because in the Jawi script the first letter of Islam is the Arabic *a (ain).*]

paru [KN], 1. ~-~, the lungs; the gills of a fish. 2. ~-~, sweet fritters sold by streethawkers.

paruh [KN], 1. the beak of a bird. 2. *se* ~, a half; *berair se* ~, half-full of water.

parung [KN], *keris* ~, a kris with an exceptional number of curves.

parut [KN], 1. a scar; *ber~,* scarred; a cicatrix. 2. the process of rasping; *memarut,* [KK] to rasp, to grate, e.g. a coconut.

parwah [KN], care, anxiety.

pasah [KN], Ar. = *fasah;* divorce (by the judge at the wife's request); *minta* ~, to demand divorce.

pasak [KN], a peg, nail, or wedge; (fig.) a prop, a strong support; wedging in; ~ *seribu,* the thousand grains of cramming, i.e. rice; so, (fig.) wealth; ~*kan sepatu kuda,* to shoe a horse; ~ *negeri,* supporters of a country, good old families; ~ is used for 'stopping' a tooth; ~, the Axis (political); *kuasa-kuasa* ~, the Axis Powers; *pihak melawan* ~, opponents of the Axis; *besar* ~ *dari tiang,* (prov.) to live above one's social position.

pasang [KN], 1. pair; *se~,* a couple; ~*an,* id.; *ber~,* in pairs; *memasang,* kindle; assemble, set a trap. 2. the tidal flow; *air* ~, the rising tide; *penuh* ~, the full rush of the tide; *air ada* ~ *surutnya,* the tide flows and also ebbs, i.e. life has its ups and downs; *air* ~ *penuh,* high tide. 3. *sakit* ~-~, hydrocele. 4. fitting on, putting into working order, motion, or use; to light (a lamp); to harness (a horse to a carriage); to fire (a cannon); to hoist (a flag); to put together, assemble (a machine); to set a trap, esp. an elaborate apparatus; ~ *badan,* (sl.) to 'doll oneself up'; ~ *telinga,* to prick up the ears, listen attentively. 5. to be effective (of a blow); to penetrate or produce the intended result; *kena* ~, hitting a vital spot or hitting 'full'; also *pepat;* opposed to *menyipi.*

pasar [KN], Pers. a bazaar; a market-place; also *pekan;* ~ *gelap,* ~ *belakang,* black market; ~ *ria,* fun-fair; ~ *gembira* is sometimes used for a Scots' jàmboree;

pasaran, markets, outlets, openings for trade; pemasaran, marketing; memasarkan, to market.

pasi [KS], *pucat* ~, very pale, as white as a sheet.

pasif [KS], passive; *ke~an*, passivity.

pasik [KS], 1. wrong-headed; unwilling to behave properly (of a child) or to listen to reason (of an adult). 2. = *fasik*.

pasir [KN], sand; the sands by a sea; the beach; ~ *panjang*, a long stretch of sandy beach; *galah* ~, a short pole for punting over shallows; *gula* ~, sugar in minute grains; *ibu* ~, coarse-grained sand; *mas* ~, gold dust (better *mas urai*); ~~ *buangan lombong*, sandy tailings from mines; *kertas* ~, emery paper; *rumput* ~, a common weed *(adenostema viscosum)*; ~ *muda*, sandy soil (mixed with earth); *ikan* ~, a kind of loach *Cobitiae* (sp.); *bantal* ~, sand-bag; ~ *apung*, quicksand; *busung* ~, sandhill; *hujan jatuh ke* ~, rain on sand — all wasted.

Paska [KN], Easter.

pasmat [KN], Spanish dollar.

pasport [KN], passport.

pasrah [KK], to surrender, to leave.

pasti [KE], = *pasti; oure, undoubted) mo mastikan*, determine, ascertain; *ke~an*, certainty, determination.

pasu [KN], a basin or bowl; a flower-pot; a vase; a tub; ~ *bunga*, a flower-pot; or vase; ~~, the cheek-bones.

pasuk [KN], a troop, a body of men, a company; a squadron; a squad; *~an*, a troop; a team; a side in a game; a guncrew; a contingent; an organised corps; *ber~~an*, in groups, teams, etc.; ~ *palang merah*, Red Cross Squad; *~an pelopor*, shock troops; *~an berani-mati*, suicide squad; *~an pendamai*, the 'Peace Corps'.

pasung [KN], stocks, shackles, fetters; *memasung*, to handcuff; *~an*, id.; *rumah* ~, a police station; also Pen. and Pk. *balai*.

patah [KS], 1. fractured, broken, snapping asunder (used only of rigid objects being broken); ~ *tebu*, broken but not

snapped off (as a 'green-stick' fracture); *kayu* ~ *tulang*, a plant *(Euphorbia tirucalli* or *Moesa ramentacea)*; *~an*, a broken fragment; *~an bengkarung*, cramp; *mematahkan*, to break; (fig.) to overpersuade, to convince; ~ *masuk*, to cut in, turn in sharply; *mematah selekoh*, to cut a corner; *selekoh* ~, a sharp corner, L-turn; *mematah lagu*, to modulate, vary pitch of voice in singing; patch is sometimes used (sl.) to mean smashed up, disabled, as in an accident; ~ *arang*, definitely divorced; ~ *hati*, become dejected, indifferent; *~ layak*, to lose power, weaken (as tired limbs); *~riuk*, compound fracture; ~ *balik* to break back (as driven game). 2. a numeral coefficient for sayings, pieces of advice, etc.; *tutur se~*, a single saying; *pematah*, a piece of warning or advice.

patar [KN], a wooden rasp.

pateri [KN], *mematerikan*, join edges of hard metals with easily melted metal; Hind. solder.

pati [KN], 1. Skr. a high officer of state; a term used as a component part of many old names and dignities, e.g., *adi~*. 2. finest portion; 'cream' of anything; essence; *mengambil* ~, to make a precise; ~ *santan*, the milk first extracted from the coconut; next comes *kabar* or *kemancar* (Pen.) and finally *hampas*; ~ *ayam*, essence of chicken; ~ *arak*, alcohol. 3. death — the old root of *mati*.

patik [KN], 'humble slave', a term of self-depreciation used as a pronoun of the first person when addressing a prince.

patil, [KN] 1. a small adze for roughly planing what has been rough-hewn with a hatchet; also *ke~*. 2. the feeler or antenna of an insect.

patin [KN], *ikan* ~, a large freshwater catfish *(Pangasius ponderosus)*.

pating [KN], 1. a stone-hewer's chisel. 2. a peg (used esp. of pegs driven into a tree to facilitate climbing, or into the gunwale of a boat so as to allow of a temporary gunwale (rubing) being affixed to them).

patuh [KS], obedient; to obey; ~*i,* id.; *mematuhi,* follow, observe, obey; *ke!~an,* obedience, loyalty.

patuk [KN], 1. the peck (of a bird); the bite (of a snake); the nibble f a fish; *mematuk,* to bite, to peck; *ayam mematuk anaknya,* a fowl pecks its chick, simile for rebuke not intended to hurt; ~*an,* (fig.) criticisms, 'digs'; *bunyi ~an,* sound of continuous tapping, as of typewriters. 2. Ind. a peg. picket.

patung [KN], 1. an image, statue, figure, a doll; *wayang ~,* puppet-show; *umpama ~,* statuesque; *ringgit ~,* the pillar-dollar; *kerajaan ~,* puppet government. 2. *ikan ~,* a freshwater perch *(Catopra fasciatus).*

patut [KS], right, fitting, proper, suitable; *tak ~,* unfair, improper; *mematutkan,* to settle, to put right; *mematutkan diri (di hadapan cermin),* to titivate, primp oneself (before a mirror); ~ *lah,* often used to mean, ah! that explains it, or that's what one would expect; *se ~nya,* properly; if due action were taken.

pauh [KN], 1. a species of wild mango; ~ *janggi,* a tree *(Cocos Maldiva)* (believed by Malays to grow in the centre of the great ocean upon a bank which represents all that is left of a submerged continent); *buah ~ janggi,* a fruit (the shell of which is used as a beggar's bowl by Hindu mendicants); *tasik ~ janggi,* the great ocean round the sunken bank above referred to; ~ *kijang,* a large tree *(Irvingia Malayana);* ~~, a name sometimes given to trees of the *Evodia* class. 2. a quarter; a quarter-*cupak* as a measure of capacity.

pauk [KN], *lauk-~,* all sorts of side dishes.

paung [KN], Port. bread (esp. Chinese bread or biscuits, the usual word, for ordinary bread being *roti).*

paus [KN], the whale; *ikan ~,* id.

paut [KK], clinging and pulling, heaving at; ~*lah,* heave ho!; hauling in; to be drawn to anything; to be attached, or attracted, or bound; *ber~ pada,* to cling

to (as a drowning or struggling man clutches and clings); *bersangkut-~,* connected (with); *tempat ber~,* something to cling to, something to reply on; *gadis ~an hati,* girl to whom one is attached, lady-love.

pawah [KN], pay (esp. according to profits or by piecework and not as a daily wage, *upah);* ~ *tanah,* to work land on a profit-sharing basis; *se cara ~,* on a profit-sharing basis, e.g. of working of loaned animal or farming a fruit-orchard; ~*kan,* to lease, let out, on such a basis; *rempah ~,* all kinds of spices.

pawai [KN], the suite or train of a *raja;* the followers in a bridal procession; insignia bearer; (the insignia are *alat ~;* a rally; a procession; *ber~,* to go in procession.

pawang [KN], a man who practises some primitive industry (such as hunting, fishing or agriculture) by the aid of the black art; a witch-doctor; a man who combines magic and skill in the exercise of his profession; ~ *belat,* ~ *jermal,* ~ *kelong* and ~ *pukat,* practitoners of magic in connection with various kinds of fishing; ~*gaharu* and ~ *kapur,* collectors of scented woods and comphor; ~ *gajah,* an elephant-trapper.

paya [KN], as swamp, a marsh, a morass.

payah [KS], difficult (of work); serious (of illness); hard (of times); *tak ~,* don't trouble to; *jangan ber~~,* don't go to a lot of trouble.

payang [KN], a large East Coast sea-going fishing-boat or small trading-boat; *pukat ~,* large seine-net used on these boats.

payar [KN], *perahu ~,* a small warship (such as a revenue-cutter or port-guardship).

payau, 1. brackish (of water); insipid, tasteless. 2. Borneo (from Dyak?) a sambhur deer, = *rusa.*

payu [KN], price, sale-price; precious; *tiada ter~,* priceless, invaluable; ~*dara,* breast, bust.

payung [KN], an umbrella; the head of a nail; shelter under a heavy-fringed umbrella; ~ *ubur-ubur,* a heavy-fringed

umbrella; ~ *berapit,* two small unbrel-
las borne side by side in the train of a
prince; ~ *cetera,* a canopy; *paku* ~, a
drawing-pin; *pokok* ~, the travellers'
palm; ~ *terjun,* parachute; *ber~ sebelum hujan,* get an umbrella before it
rains, i.e. a stitch in time saves nine;
naik ber~, to rise in umbrella-shape
(mushroom-shape), of smoke, esp. from
an explosion; *memayungkan,* (fig.) to
shelter, to cover; *memayungkan bibir,*
to put one's hand over one's mouth; an
umbrella, esp. a yellow umbrella or, in
some localities, a black umbrella, is a
symbol of royalty.

pecah [KK], broken into fragments;
wrecked; breaking open, breaking out,
burst, breaking up, spreading (of news);
~ *perang,* the breaking of a line of battle;
breaking out of war; ~ *peloh,* breaking
out into perspiration; ~ *khabar,* the news
spread; *memecahkan,* to break anything
up; *ber~,* broken up, divided; *memecah-
belahkan,* to cause divisions, impair
unity; ~ *lerai,* fallen to pieces, fallen
apart; *duit* ~, small change; *~an,* a fraction; breaking into pieces; division, partition; *pemecahan,* the subdivision of
property, esp. land; *~an ombak,* the surf;
~ *ke darah,* bruised with effusion of
blood; *~an batu,* rubble; *memecah suasana dingin,* to break the ice.

pecak [KK], crushed flat or sunken in (of
roundish objects); *mata* ~, one-eyed; ~
*boleh dilayangkan, bulat boleh digul-
ingkan,* to be absolutely unanimous.

pecal [KN], = *pacul,* a vegetable dish; *me-
mecal,* [KK] to press with the fingers or
hands.

pecat [KK], to remove from office; to get
rid of; to dismiss; to deprive; *di~kan
Allah makanan mu,* may God deprive
you of food; *lembaga pemecatan,* dis-
ciplinary Board (dealing with expul-
sions, esp. from a party).

pecuk [KS], Kel. = *kecok,* lame.

pecut [KK], a whip; whipping up; *memecut basikal,* (fig.) to speed up a bicycle;
memecut kereta, to accelerate, 'step on

it'.

peda [KN], perserved fish, — *budu.*

pedada [KN], a tree *(Sonneratia acida);*
also *berembang.*

pedaka [KN], Skr. a collar ornamented
with pendants.

pedal [KN], the gizzard.

pedang [KN], a sword; a scythe; ~ *kerajaan,* a sword of state; *~kan,* to sabre; to
mow with a scythe; *sarung* ~, a scabbard.

pedap [KK], suck up moisture, absorb; *kertas* ~, blotting-paper.

pedar [KS], hot (as ginger or lemon).

pedas [KS], hot, pungent (as curry); (fig.)
pungent, or criticism; *~hati,* heart-burn,
indigestion; (fig.) annoyed.

pedati [KN], a wheeled vehicle, a waggon
of any sort; ~ *meriam,* a gun-carriage.

pedena [KN], a large wide-mouthed jar or
tub (us. of earthenware).

pedendang [KN], 1. *kain* ~, braid. 2. *burung* ~, a bird *(Heliopais personata)* —
cf. **dendang.**

pedewakan [KN], a Bugis trading ship.

pedih [KS], smarting (in the eyes, or nose,
or of a wound); *hati* ~, feeling angry;
gas pemedih mata, tear-gas.

pedoman [KN], a compass; *jarum* ~, a
compass-needle; ~ is used (fig.) for a
guide, serving to direct the eye; a
directing principle.

pedukang [KN], a fish; generic for many
Ariidae; also *bedukang.*

peduli [KK], Ar. to care, concern oneself;
saya tak ~, I don't care; *mem~kan,* never
mind that; *tidak mem~kan,* to show no
consideration.

pedur [KS], lameness from a bent shin-
bone.

pegal [KS], Ind. stiff, esp. of limbs.

pegan [KS], = *pegun; ter~,* silent and bewildered.

pegang [KK], hold, grasp, control; *di~nya
tangan,* his hand was grasped; *kata tidak di~nya,* he does not keep to his
promises; *~an,* hold, control, occupation; handle; fief; accepted doctrine;
faith held; *ber~-~ tangan,* holding

hands; *pemegang,* a handle; a hand-hold; *ber~,* to hold, to grasp; *memegang kuasa,* in charge; *memegang peranan,* to play a role.

pegar [KN], *ayam ~,* the fireback pheasant *(Lophura rufa).*

pegari [KK], to be visible, come into view, to espy.

pegas [KN], a spring, as of a watch.

pegawai [KN], an officer or government agent; *~ daerah,* District Officer; *~ kerajaan,* Government officers, officials; *~ rendah,* Petty Officer; minor official; *~ awam,* civil servant; *~ staf,* staff-officer; *~ turus,* id.; *~ menjaga,* duty officer; *~ perisik,* intelligence officer; *~ pemerintah,* officer commanding; *~ pinjaman,* seconded officer; *~ perantara,* liaison officer; *~ perbekalan,* supply officer; *~ margasetua,* game warden; *~ penjaga daerah polis,* officer commanding police-district; *ke~an,* ruling body, ruling class, controllers; in some contexts, the Establishment, official.

Pegu [KN], Lower Burma; *beras ~,* Rangoon rice.

peguam [KN], lawyer, barrister; *~cara,* solicitor.

pegun [KS], *ter~,* silent in meditation; aghast, stunned into silence; also *pegan.*

pejabat [KN], office.

pejal [KS], firm (of flesh); not easily pressed or pinched; not crumbly, of stone.

pejam [KK], closing the eye; *~ celik,* continuously blinking, of a person, or (fig.) of a light.

pejar [KS], Pah. incessant (of rain).

pejera [KN], the sighting-bead of a gun.

peka [KS], sensitive, thoughtful; *dia ~ terhadap perasaan orang lain,* he's thoughtful of others.

pekaca [KN], *ratna ~,* a term of endearment; = gem of purity.

pekak [KS], hard of hearing , deaf; less strong than *tuli; ~ badak,* deaf to all but loud sounds (the rhinoceros is notoriously deaf); *memekak,* deafen.

pekak [KN], the knave (cards).

pekaka [KN], a generic name for kingfishers, and also (*~ hutan* or *~ rimba*) for barbets; (the king-fisher is also called *raja udang* in the south.)

pekan [KN], 1. a market; town; *bunga ~,* a flower *(Jasminum grandiflorum); ~ ahad,* Sunday fair; *~ sehari, ~ sari,* id. 2. Ind. a week; *ber~~,* several weeks.

pekap [KK], 1. to dab lightly, as when staunching a wound or applying liniment. 2. *menekap,* to cover with the hand; *menekap telinga,* to cover the ears with the hand (to shut out noise); also *pekup* and *tekup.*

pekasam [KN], a strong-smelling preserve of fish.

pekat [KS], sticky and thick (of liquids); strong (of coffee); *memekatkan,* thicken, condense.

pekau [KK], *ter~,* a (meaningless) cry of excitement.

pekembar [KN], = Umno, see **tubuh.**

pekerti [KN], Skr. nature, character; *budi ~,* id., esp. of good disposition.

pekik [KK], a shrill cry or scream; *jerit ~,* screams and shrieks; *memekik,* to scream out; *memekikkan,* yell, shriek; *ter~,* suddenly yell; *~an,* scream, shout.

pekin [KK], pondering, puzzling a thing out — cf. **pegun.**

pekuk [KS], twisted (of an arm); malformed (of a limb).

pekong [KN], 1. Ch. a joss. 2. Kel. to hurl; *pemekong,* a throwing stick.

pekung [KN], a syphilitic ulcer.

pekur, *terpekur* = *tefekur,* q.v.

pelabur, see **labur.**

pelaga [KN], 1. *buah ~,* the cardamon *(Amomum cardamomum).* 2. *ikan ~,* the fighting-fish; see *laga.*

pelahap [KN], gluttonous, voracious.

pelajar [KN], pupil; *~an,* lesson, education.

pelak [KN], a malignant spirit; a noxious aura.

pelamin [KN], see *lamin; ~an,* bridal dais.

pelampung [KN], a floating mark; the floats of a net; a float marking the position of an anchor.

pelan, = *perlahan*.

pelana [KN], Pers. a saddle; *alas ~*, a saddle-cloth; a numnah; *ber~*, saddled.

pelancar [KN], a joist or cross-beam joining together the foundation pillars of a house.

pelanduk [KN], the smaller chevrotin *(Tragulus kancil);* the mouse-deer; *lena ~*, easily awakened, a cat-nap; *~ dua serupa,* two people who look alike.

pelang [KN], stripe (of colours); *bendera ber~ tiga,* a tricolour.

pelang [KN], 1. an old type of trading-ship. 2. the crupper in the harness of an elephant.

pelangah [KK], *ter~*, wide open (door), agape.

pelangi [KN], a rainbow; *~ minum,* id.; *~ membangun,* a short rainbow.

pelantar [KN] flooring, staging; a platform, e.g., of a railway station or a jetty.

pelanting [KK], *ter~*, hurled sprawling; *ber~an,* rolling over and over, falling and rebounding.

pelasari [KN], a medicinal shrub *(Alyxia stellata).*

pelasuh [KN], a ne'er-do-weel, a worthless idler.

pelat [KS], accent, brogue, inability to pronounce correctly.

pelata [KN], *ikan ~*, a kind of mackerel *(Scomber microlepidotus).*

pelatuk [KN], a generic name for wood-peckers; also *belatuk.*

pelaut [KN], seaman.

pelawa [KK], *mem~*, invite; *~an*, invitation.

pelawak [KN], clown, comedian.

pelawat [KN], visitor.

pelayan [KN], waiter, waitress.

pelbagai [KBil], varied, of different sorts.

pelebaya [KN], an executioner, = *pertanda.*

pelecok [KK], *ter~*, a strain caused by a false step.

pelekat [KN], 1. (Dutch) a placard; sometimes a notice-board. 2. to caulk a ship.

Pelekat [KN], *kain ~*, an Indian cotton fabric from Pulikat.

pelkoh [KS], awry, twisted out of true; also *pelonoh.*

pelempap [KN], *se~*, a hand's-breadth (as a unit of measurement); also *satelempap.*

pelencit [KK], *ter~*, forced out by pressure (as matter from a boil); to slip away.

pelepah [KN], a frond, the branch-leaf of the trees of the palm type; *~ bawah luruh, ~ atas jangan gelak* (prov.), one man's fault is another man's lesson.

peleset [KK], *ter~*, to slip; = *tergelincir; ter~ lidah,* a slip of the tongue.

pelesir [KK], Ind. pleasure; to enjoy pleasure; *~an,* a delightful time, esp. a honeymoon; an idyll.

pelesit [KN], a familiar spirit, believed to be in the form of a cricket.

peleting [KN], *buluh ~*, a weaver's spool.

peletok [KN], to twist out of true, distort; a variant of *pelecok.*

pelihara [KK], Skr. cherishing; bringing up; protecting, guarding; *memeliharakan,* to nurture, to look after; *~an,* that which is reared; *pemelihara,* breeder; *pemeliharaan,* nursing, care, fostering; *~kan cakap,* to act so as to avoid adverse criticism or a scandal; also *peliara* and *piara.*

pelik [KS], 1. curious, out of the common; strange, odd; *barang yang ~,* curious; *~* is used (rarely) to mean 'surprised'. 2. lacking in breeding; deficient in character; *ke~an,* strangeness.

pelinggam [KN], marble or stone, the veining of which offers a contrast of colour with the rest.

pelipir [KN], Pah. a kitchen.

pelipis [KN], the temples of the forehead; also *pelipisan.*

pelir [KN], *batang ~*, the penis; *buah ~*, the testes; *~ itek,* a screw.

pelit [KS], stingy.

pelita [KN], Pers. 1. a lamp; *~ gantung,* a hanging lamp; *~ catuk,* a table lamp; 2. something that gives guidance.

pelohong [KS], gaping open (as a badly decayed tooth).

pelong [KS], bent, warped.

pelontang [KN], a float for nets.

peluang [KN], still, calm (of wind and weather); leisure, opportunity; *merebut ~*, to seize an opportunity; *terlepas ~*, opportunity missed.

pelubung [KN], a culvert.

peluh [KN], perspiration, sweat; evaporation on glass; *ber~*, to perspire; *pecah ~*, to burst into a perspiration; *mandi ~*, to be bathed in sweat; *merecik ~*, lightly bedewed with sweat.

peluit [KN], a whistle, esp. a ship's siren.

peluk [KK], *ber~*, *memeluk* or *~kan*, to embrace; *sepemeluk*, an armful; as much as the arms can encompass; *bertubuh*, to fold the arms; *ber~-~an*, hug or embrace each other; *ter~*, accidently embrace; *bantal ~*, Dutch wife; *pemeluk agama*, religious adherent.

pelukis [KN], artist.

peluncur [KN], glider.

pelung [KN], Pen. a small dug-out used in fishing with *pukat*.

pelupuk [KN], *~ mata*, the eyelid; = *kelopak mata*.

peluru [KN], Port. shot, bullets, connonballs; *~ besi lantai*, cylindrical shot; *~ bolang-baling*, chain shot; *~ jantung*, shot with a cylindrical body but rounded or pointed at the end; *~ kendali*, guided missile; *~ berpandu*, id.

pelusuk [KN], remote corner, far places (of a country); *ke seluruh ~ dunia*, to every corner of the earth.

peluwap [KK], *memeluwapkan*, condense; *~an* [KN], condensation.

pemabuk [KN], drunkard.

pemadam api [KN], fire extinguisher.

pemadat [KN], opium addict.

pemajangan [KN], a state bed (esp. a bridal couch).

pemali [KN], forbidden, tabooed; *pantang ~*, id.

pemangku [KN], deputy.

pemanis [KN], a charm for beauty.

pematang [KN], a long stretch of high sandy soil in a rice-swamp or on a shore, a 'hog's back'; a hummock; see *matang*.

pematung [KN], N.S. a bamboo conduit-pipe.

pembekal [KN], petty official.

pembakaran [KN], process of burning.

pembalikan [KN], return, reverse.

pemerhati [KN], an observer; see *hati*.

pemidang [KN], a frame for embroidery or for stretching and drying hides; a banner (of the sort tied on two poles).

pempan [KK], *ter~*, 'winded', gasping; aghast.

pemuras [KN], a blunderbuss.

pena [KN], 1. a pen; *sahabat ~*, pen-friend; *~ tabung*, foutain-pen. 2. *~*, short for *Persatuan penulis-penulis Melayu*, the Association of National Writers of the Malayan Federation; *buah ~*, one's pen product.

penaga [KN], a generic name for a number of trees (esp. *Calophyllum inophyllum*); they are good timber trees; the promontory on which the business quarter of Penang is built is called *Tanjung ~*; hence the town (officially Georgetown), is generally called *Tanjung* by Malays.

penak [KN], *pokok ~*, a local name for the chengal tree.

penaka [KKtr], so to speak, as it were, if by any chance.

penanak [KN], *se~ nasi*, as long as it takes rice to boil.

penanggah, see **tanggah**.

penanggalan [KN], a vampire; sometimes identified with the langsuir.

penara, see **tara**.

penaram [KN], Malay pastry containing meat or prawns.

penat [KS], weary; exhausted, fatigued; *ber~-~*, making great efforts, exerting oneself; *memenatkan*, tire; *ke~an*, exhaustion; *buat ~sahaja*, just a waste of time and effort.

pencak [KN], a sword-dance, art of self-defence; *silat ~*, id.; *memencak*, *ber~*, to dance his dance (fencing with an imaginary opponent), perform an art of self defence.

pencalang [KN], a sea-going type of ship used by Bugis traders.

pencar [KK], Ind. divergent, diverging; *memencar*, to spread everywhere, to scatter everywhere; *ter~*, scattered, dispersed.

pencen [KN], pension.

pencil [KK], *memencil*, detach, separating from the main body; *terpencil*, separated, detached, remote.

pencung [KS], out of line, crooked; swerved; *~-mencung*, planless, haphazard, orderless.

pendahan [KN], a javelin; a dart hurled by hand.

pendam [KK], *terpendam*, concealed, hidden.

pendap [KK], to preserve, salt away (as fish); so, (fig.) to salt away money or to 'sit on' a file of papers; sometimes, *(duduk) ~*, to stay away from company, live in solitude.

pendar [KN], phosphorescence in the sea; the glow of a firefly or luminous millipede; also *pebar*.

Pendawa [KN], Skr. a hero of the Mahabharata; any one of the five sons of Pandu; a pattern of sword named after these heroes.

pendek [KS], short; *panjang ~*, tall and short; *memendekkan*, to shorten, to abbreviate; *akal ~*, short-sighted; *bekerja panjang ~*, to do odd jobs; *~nya, ~kata*, in short, to sum up.

pendekar [KN], see *dekar*; one who is skilful in fencing, expert in the art of self defence.

pendeta [KN], Skr. a learned man, great scholar, 'pundit'; used of persons who exercise semi-priestly functions in non-Islamic faiths or cults; *~ Yahudi*, a Rabbi.

pendiat [KN], a corral for elephants.

pending [KN], a waist-buckle; *tali ~*, a girdle for use with a buckle.

pendongkok [KN], a metal ferrule between the blade and handle of a keris.

penduk [KN], a wrapper of thin metal halfway up the sheath of a kris.

penebat [KN], insulator.

pengakap [KN], Boy Scout.

pengalaman [KN], experience.

pengalan [KN], N.S. a long pole for knocking fruit off the tree.

pengalir [KN], conductor.

penganan [KN], a cake, a sweetmeat.

pengangguran [KN], unemployment.

penganjur, [KN] promoter.

pengantin [KN], 1. a party to a marriage, bride or bridegroom; *~ baru*, newly married couple; *senapang ~*, a double-barrelled gun. 2. the player of the viol *(rebab)* at a *makyung* performance.

pengap [KK], cover up, seal from intrusion, hermetically closing.

pengapuh [KN], *layar ~*, a topsail or topgallant-sail.

pengar [KS], heavy-witted (as a drugged man).

pengarang [KN], author, writer.

pengarah [KN], director.

pengaruh [KN], influence; *ter~*, influenced, affected; *ber~*, influential.

pengat [KN], a sweetmeat made of fruit cooked in coconut milk and sugar.

pengawal [KN], guard, sentry.

pengawinan [KN], *tombak ~*, a spear of state.

pengecut [KN], coward.

pengembara [KN], wanderer.

Pengeran [KN], a title of nobility in use in Java and Borneo.

pengerek [KN], awl; also *sengerek*.

pengerma [KN], incubator.

pengerusi [KN], chairman.

pengetahuan [KN], knowledge.

pengerih [KN], a fish-trap of the *lukah* type.

pengga [KN], deep (of a bowl or dish).

penggaga [KN], a creeping herb (*Hydrocotyle Asiatica*); it is used as a salad and a decoction made from its leaves is said to be good for tuberculosis.

penggal [KK], to break off, cut out (as a page); a part, e.g. an act of a play; a term (school); *cuti ~*, school holidays; *ber~-~*, in sections, portions or divisions; *memenggal*, cut.

penggawa [KN], an officer in charge of a district; Kel. = *penghulu*, as meaning 'head-man'.

penghulu [KN], a headman; a local chief; also used of Muhammad as the Head of Islam; ~ *istana,* palace caretaker.

pengit [KS], fetid, reeking.

pengkalan, = *pangkalan;* see **pangkal.**

pengkar [KS], bow-legged or bandy-legged; ~ *ke dalam,* knock-kneed.

pengkeras [KN], a fee, as to a *bomoh* or an astrologer; also *pengeras.*

pengkis = *mengkis* [KK], to defy.

pengsan [KK], fainted.

pening [KS], dizzy, headache; ~ *kepala,* suffering from vertigo; ~ *kelam,* id.; ~ *lalat,* slightly dizzy; esp. from drink or drugs.

peninggir [KN], the confines of a country; the outlying portions — cf. **pinggir.**

peniti [KN], Port. a pin.

penjajap [KN], an ancient Malay type of fighting-ship.

penjara [KN], Skr. a large cage, jail, prison; ~*kan* or *mem~kan,* to imprison; *ter~,* imprisoned.

penjuru [KN], an angle, a corner; *pe~,* di-ogonal.

pensil [KN], pencil.

penta [KBil], *ber~-~,* in crowds, in groups, in quantities.

pentas [KN], a platform, esp. a sleeping platform; a stage; *pementasan,* staging, putting on the stage; *cerita ~,* a stage-play.

penting [KK], 1. to test a coin by chinking; to tinkle, strum (as stringed instrument); to 'toss' (a coin). 2. [KS] Jav. important special; *ke~an,* needs, interests; *me-mentingkan diri sendiri,* to place one's own interests first; *ke~an umum,* the public interest; *ke~an sendiri,* personal interests; *menganggap ~,* to attach importance to. 3. to twist upwards, as a moustache.

pentung [KK], to club or cudgel.

penuh [KS], full; ~ *sesak* or ~ *pepak,* chockfull, crowded; ~*i* or *memenuhi,* to fill up, to complete, to accomplish, to fulfil; *dengan se ~-~,* with full, with all, with every.

penyap [KK], to 'keep dark', 'keep under cover', 'sit on', conceal.

penyengat, see **sengat.**

penyek [KS], flat, flattened out (as a frog under a wheel).

penyu [KN], the green turtle *(Chelone mydas).*

peon, Hind. (from Port.) an orderly, a mes-senger.

pepah [KK], *memepah,* striking with a stick or pole.

pepak [KS], 1. complete; in full; fully attended; in full state; *penuh ~,* quite full; chock-full. 2. to bite or tear at, to maul with the teeth, crunch up; *buah rambu-tan kena ~ dek keluang,* the rambutans were mauled by flying foxes; a variant of *papak* 3.

pepat [KS], smooth of surface; flattened; direct, of a question; *kena ~,* to hit full.

pepatah [KN], adage, maxim, aphorism (from *patah).*

pepatur [KN], the extreme outer plank on which a roof rests.

pepaya [KN], papaya.

pepejal [KS], solid.

peper [KK], edging sideways; to be driven aside (as a boat with a heavy sea on its beam).

pepet [KN], mark indicating a short 'e', not generally used now.

pepijat = *pijat.*

pepuah [KS], fizzled (of the hair); *negeri Pepuah,* Papua.

per [KN], Ind. a spring, as for a watch.

perabot [KN], Ind. equipment, materials, furniture; ~*an,* id.

perada [KN], Port. gold or silver leaf cut into patterns; tinsel; gold leaf.

peragawati [KN], Ind. a clothes-model; see *raga.*

perah [KK], 1. to express; wring out; to milk; *kambing ~an,* a milch-goat; ~*kan,* to press out. 2. large forest tree *(Elaterio-spermum Tapos).*

perahu [KN], a boat or ship; *awak ~* or *anak ~,* the crew; *galang ~,* the rollers on which a boat rests when hauled ashore; *tupai galang ~,* a descriptive name given to Raffles' squirrel *(Sciurus* *rafflesi).*

perai [KK], 1. *ber~-~,* breaking up (of a crowd); scattering — cf. **berai.** 2. *kain ~,* a black silk cloth of Siamese origin. 3. turning about, from one side to another; *membuang ~,* to tack.

perajurit, see **jurit.**

perak [KN], silver; *wang ~,* silver coinage; *~ campur, ~ asam,* alloyed silver; *~lancungan,* counterfeit silver; *~ tulin,* genuine silver.

perak [KS], a nervous start, a hasty glance to right and left; shy and bewildered; looking this way and that, as a countryman in town; apt to gape foolishly or rudely; *~ siang,* [KN] daybreak.

peraksi, see **rakai.**

peram [KK], 1. *memeram,* to store fruit, esp. bananas, until ripe; to store liquid until fermented; to store manure until it is rotted down; generally, to put a product away until natural changes make it ready for its desired used; so *memeram* can be used of seasoning timber; *nira ber~,* fermented palm-juice; *baja yang sudah lama ter~,* well-rotted manure. 2. *memeram,* to coo.

perambut [KS], 1. invulnerability against weapons. 2. the trace of a fishing line.

peran [KN], a clown in a makyung; *~an,* a part in a play; a role; *mendukung ~,* to sustain a role; *memainkan ~,* id.

perancah [KN], the wooden framework of a house; a scaffolding, a painter's 'cradle'; also *peranca.*

Perancis [KN], Port. French.

perancit [KK], to splash up in all directions (as water or mud when a stone is dashed into it).

perang [KN], war, battle; *ikatan ~,* the line of battle; *mengikat ~,* to draw up troops in array; *panglima ~,* a leader in war; *gendang ~,* a war-drum; *ber~,* to go to war; to be at war; *pe~an,* a state of war; *~ dingin,* cold war; *~ sabil Allah,* a Holy War; *~ saudara,* civil war; *~ mendada,* hand-to-hand fighting; *~ urat saraf,* war of nerves; psychological warfare; *medan ~,* battle-field; *~ mulut,* war of

words; *pe~an salib,* the (Christian) Crusades; *memerangi,* to make war against; *pe~an terang-terang,* open warfare.

perang [KN], brown; *~-perus,* [KS] very pale, very wan; sallow, of a man naturally dark.

perangai [KS], nature, disposition, innate character; *membuat ~,* to show temperament, behave petulantly; *~ baik,* good conduct.

peranggu [KN], *se~an,* a set, e.g., of buttons; a suit (of clothes).

perangkap [KN], a cage-trap for birds or mice; *memerangkap,* to trap; *tahan ~,* to set the trap.

peranja [KN], a scaffolding in successive tiers; the seating arrangements in an amphitheatre; a dove-cot or pigeon-house.

peranjat [KK], *ter~,* startled, suddenly alarmed.

perap [KK], 1. to fly at an enemy (as a fowl); to be touchy (of a disposition); to be anxious always to have the last word (or women); to 'fly out' (at a person) in sudden rage. 2. *memerap,* to stay quiet, 'stay put'; *memerap sahaja di rumah,* be a stay-at-home.

perap [KK], to quicken the stroke when rowing; cf. **girap.**

perapatan [KN], cross-roads.

peras [KK], 1. (onom.), *~-~,* rustling (of garments or of paper) ? = *perah; memeras wang,* to extort money, 'squeeze'; *permeras,* an oppressor; *pemerasan,* pressure, extortion, blackmail.

perat [KS], acrid, sour; *terung ~,* a small brinjal *(Solanum aculeatissimum).*

perata [KN], Hind. *roti ~,* unleavened bread of flour and ghee, a chupatti.

perawan [KN], a maiden; virgin; *~ tua,* spinster, old maid.

perawas [KN], a medicinal plant *(Lindera* sp.).

perawis [KN], ingredients, factors, materials.

perban [KN], Ind. a bandage.

perbani [KS], neap tide; *bulan ~,* the

waxing moon.

perbu [KN], Jav. a prince; ~ *jaya*, the conquering prince (Panji).

perca [KN], 1. Hind. (from Pers.) a rag; remnants, a piece of cloth; *se ~ kertas*, a scrap of paper. 2. *Pulau Perca*, Sumatra.

percambahan [KN], germination.

percaya [KK], *mem~i*, Skr. trusting, believing in; *mem~kan*, entrust; *harap ada, ~ tidak*, there is ground for hope but not for confident expectation; *~ dengan tiada dicuba*, trust without testing, faith; *ke~an*, trust, trusty; belief, confidence; *orang yang ke~an*, a man who can be trusted; *mengemukakan usul tidak ~ kepada kerajaan*, to propose a vote of no confidence in the Government; *tiga perkara jangan di~, pertama laut, kedua api, ketiga raja-raja,* three things should not be trusted, first, the sea, second, fire, third rajas, (put not your trust in princes).

percik [KK], *memercik,* to splash, to spatter, to sprinkle; *ber~an*, splashed; *memercikkan,* cause to spatter or splash.

percit [KK], squirting out (of water).

percubaan [KN], experiment.

percul [KK], *ter~*, protruding (of animal's head).

perdah, 1. the handle of a chopper or hatchet. 2. N.S. large adze for planning; *sanggul ~*, the socket for the tang of the adze. 3. Hind. an awning, screen.

perdana [KN], Skr. surpassing, excelling, supreme in merit; *~ menteri*, prime minister.

perdata [KK], careful, accurate.

perdu [KN], the base of a tree-trunk, the visible part of the root; *se~ buluh*, a clump of bamboos.

pereh [KS], worn out by a struggle or sustained effort; exhausted (as a fighting cock or fencer).

perekat [KN], lime, mortar, gum, cement, glue; any sticky compound for holding materials together — cf. **lekat**.

perenggan [KN], 1. a boundary; border, = *perhinggaan.* 2. paragraph.

perepat [KN], a tree (unidentified), closely resembling *Sonneratia acidia; ~ bukit,* a tree *(Cupania lessertiana).*

pergam [KN], the green imperial pigeon; *~ bukit,* the mountain green imperial pigeon.

pergi [KK], to proceed; to go; *~lah dia ke Riau,* he went to Riau; *permergian,* departure.

pergul [KN], (Dutch) gilt; gilding.

peri [KN], 1. Pers. a fairy; *dewa syah ~,* the king of the fairies; *dewa ~ mambang,* fairies of all sorts, i.e. Indian, Persian, Indonesian; more often *pari* or *hantu pari.* 2. way, manner; *~ hal,* matters, details, circumstances; *memerikan,* to describe, to tell; *~ bahasa,* an idiom; *~kan,* to describe; *ber~~,* in various ways; persistently; *tidak ter~,* indescribable; *~ kemanusiaan,* humanity.

peria [KN], 1. bitter gourd *(Momordica charantia); sudah tahu ~ pahit,* (prov.) to have learned by bitter experience. 2. Ind. a man; male, esp. a young man.

periai [KN], Jav. a minor noble, a local notable.

perian [KN], 1. N.S. a section of a large bamboo used as a water-vessel. 2. Pah. the monkey-jack fruit, = *temponek; bagai ~ pecah,* (idiom)], grating (voice).

periang [KN], 1. the proper moment for doing anything; the most auspicious time. 2. see *riang.*

peribadi [KN], personality; *kata-mengata yang menyentuh ~,* personal remarks; *wakil ~*, personal representative; *pengagungan ~,* Ind. 'cult of personality'; *doktor ~,* personal physician; *ke~an,* characteristic.

peribahasa [KN], proverb.

peridi [KN], Skr. prolific; fast growing; fertile; fecund (of human and the animal kingdom).

perigi [KN], a well; a spring.

perih [KS], smarting (of wound), worn out (of strength), staggering.

periksa [KK] Skr. investigate, enquire; *~i,* to enquire into, to examine; *pe~an,* an examination; *kurang ~*, I don't know; *pemeriksaan awal*, preliminary inquiry (prior to committal to a higher Court); *masuk pe~an*, to enter for an examination; *menduduki pe~an*, id.; *pe~an bertulis*, written examination; *pe~an bertutur*, oral test; conversation examination.

periman [KN], Eng. a civilian; *kain ~*, mufti.

perimbon [KN], astrological tables.

peringkat [KN], tier, grade, stage (as of journey); phase (of events); class (of society); standard of merit or importance; *mem~kan*, classify, grade; *pertemuan pada ~*, tertinggi, a meeting at the highest level; *~ akhir*, the last stage; the final (of a competition).

pering [KS], a repulsive smell; fetid.

Peringgi [KN], Pers. Frank, European, Portuguese.

perintah [KK], govern, rule, order; command; *datanglah ~*, an order came; *-- Inggeris*, British rule; *memerintah*, to govern; *pemerintah*, a government, a ruler; *pemerintahan*, government.

perisa [KS], nice, delicious.

perisai [KN], a shield, a buckler; *kereta ~*, armoured vehicle.

peristiwa [KN], episode, happenings, event.

perit [KS], 1. tingling, as when a hair is pulled out; smarting; (fig.) unpleasant to the feelings; *~ kerongkong*, feeling of tickling in the throat; *panas ~*, scorching heat; also *~* 2. = *pering*.

periuk [KN], a cooking-pot; *~ api*, mine; *~ kera*, the pitcher-plant *(Nepenthes)*; *~ belanga*, pots and pans; pottery, earthenware; *~ nasi*, rice pot; (fig.) means of livelihood; domestic establishment; *simpan dua ~*, to keep up two establishments; *mencari ~ nasi (dia) sendiri*, looking to (his) own interests, self-seeking.

perkakas [KN], instrument; tool; appliance; *~ cap*, apparatus for printing; *~ perang*, war-material; *~ rumah*, furniture; *~ tubuh*, an organ of the body; *~an*, varied appliances, tools, devices, etc.

perkara [KN], Skr. a matter; an affair; a concern; a section, an item (as in a document); *~ panjang*, serious matter, likely to be a cause of trouble; *tidak jadi ~*, a mere nothing, no one thinks anything of it, won't cause trouble; *~ hidup mati*, a matter of life and death; *habislah ~*, there is an end of the business.

perkasa [KS], Skr. brave; gallant; valiant; esp. used in titles of honour.

perkutut [KN], Jav. the dove; = *tekukur*.

perlahan [KS], slowly, quietly; *berkata dengan ~*, to speak quietly; *berjalan ~*, to move slowly; *~-~*, slowly, carefully; also *pelan-pelan*; *mem~kan*, slow down, delay, diminish.

perlang [KS], glittering, flashing.

perlenteh = *lenteh*.

perling [KN], 1. *burung ~*, starling. 2. sparkling (of the eye).

perlu [KKtr], Ar. compulsory; obligatory; necessary; used esp. of bounden duty under religion, in contrast to what is merely commendable *(sunat)*; *ke~an*, necessities; *ke~an dapur*, kitchen requisites; *memerlukan*, to need, require; to deem important.

perlus [KK], *te~*, putting one's foot into a hole or place where the soil gives way.

permadani [KN], Jav. a rug.

permai [KS], 1. fair, pretty, lovely, beautiful. 2. = *~suri*.

permaisuri [KN], Skr. a queen; *~ kuin*, H.M. the Queen; *Raja ~ Agung*, official title of the consort of the Yang DiPertuan Agung; see **tuan**.

permana [KBil], Skr. *tiada te~i lagi*, innumerable, incalculable.

permata [KN], skr. a gem, a precious stone.

permatang [KN], rising ground between rice-fields; see *matang;* in N.S. used for the low bank between rice-plots (= *batas*).

Permesta [KN], name of a revolutionary organisation in Celebes and Sumatra.

permisi [KN], (Dutch) a permit, a pass.

pernah [KKtr], ever; at times, on occasion; *belum ~* or *tak ~*, never.

perniagaan [KN], business, trade.

perohong [KS], *ter~*, gaping, wide open.

perosok [KK], to thrust into; to be thrust into; to stumble into; *barang siapa menggali lobang, ia juga ter~ ke dalamnya*, who so diggeth a pit, the same shall fall into it; *mata ter~ ke dalam*, deeply sunken eyes; also *persuk*.

perpatih [KN], customs of the Minangkabaus.

persangga [KN], Pers. a parasang as a measure of length.

persetua [KS], Skr. *sekali ~*, 'once upon a time'—a common exordium to a story.

persih [KS], clean, clear, pure, bright, frank — cf. **bersih**.

persil [KN], *te~*, forced almost out, e.g., as an eye or a pip.

persis [KS], Ind. exactly, exact; just like.

persuk [KK], a variant of *perosuk; ter~ ke-dalam*, pushed in, staved in, as a hat.

pertala [KN], a magic steed; *burung ~ Indera*, a figure of a large grotesque bird, formerly carried in procession, esp. during royal circumcision ceremonies in Kelantan.

pertama [KBil], Skr. first; *yang ~*, the first; *buat ~ kalinya*, for the first time.

pertiwi [KN], Skr. the earth (deified); *Dewi ~*, id.; *ibu ~*, Motherland.

peruan [KN], Hind. the yard of a ship.

peruang [KN], 1. *ilmu ~*, a magic art to protect oneself from drowning by creating an air-cavity around one — cf. **ruang**. 2. Kel. a magic compound smeared on the horns of fighting bulls.

perui [KK], crumbling (as earth or rotten wood); 'crumby' (of boiled rice).

peruk [KK], nervous, jumpy; pungent (as ammonia).

perum [KN], Hind. (from Port.) the sounding-lead; *membuang ~*, to cast the lead.

perun [KN], second burning when clearing land; buring what is left after the first burning (*bakar*).

perunggu [KN], bell-metal.

perunjung [KN], *se~*, a measure of depth; the length of a man with arms raised as far above his head as possible.

perupuk [KN], 1. a kind of rush (*Hemigyrosa longifolia*). 2. *ikan ~*, a sp. of herring.

perus [KS], gruff, unfriendly.

perusah [KS], headstrong, wilful, domineering.

perut [KN], the stomach; the womb; *~ besar*, pregnant; *mandi lenggang ~*, to take a ceremonial bath during the 7th month of pregnancy; *~ pukat*, the centre or belly of a seine-net; *~ sungai*, the bed of a river; N.S. *~* is used for a family unit, clan; *bawa ~*, to cadge for a meal; *kirim ~*, to bespeak a midwife; *selaput ~*, the membrane of the stomach, the peritoneum; *tali ~*, viscera; *isi ~*, entrails; *lapik ~*, a snack; *tidak ber~*, having no 'bowels'; *~ tidak bertelinga*, the belly has no ears, i.e. a hungry man won't listen to arguments; *~ kosong penggilap otak*, an empty belly sharpens the brains; *dasar berperut ~*, greedy, selfish policy; *~ betis*, the bulge of the calf; *sakit ~*, stomach-ache; *segah ~*, feeling of 'fullness' in the stomach.

perwara [KN], Skr. the damsels of a court (spoken of collectively); the retinue of a princess.

perwira [KN], Skr. a hero, a warrior; heroic; a military man, esp. an officer; military; *~an*, martial valour.

pesa [KN], a roller of rod on which cloth is wound up as it is woven.

pesai [KKtr], *ber~-~*, crumbling (as the mortar on an old wall).

pesak [KN], a gore; a piece of cloth let in on purpose in making a garment; a gusset.

pesam [KS], *~-~*, lukewarm; warm, of body; *~-~ kuku*, just hot enough to allow tip of finger to be dipped in; pesam is sometimes used of normal blood-heat.

pesan [KN], 1. order, command, direction; *~i*, to give instructions; *ber~* [KK], to commission a person, order a thing; *~an*, reminder, request; *pemesan*, customer, buyer. 2. *~-~*, a large and venomous spider (*Poecilotheria*).

pesantren [KN], a hostel for students

taking up religion.

pesara [KN], bazaar.

pesat [KS], Ind. speedy, hasty; ke~an, haste; *maju ~*, to make quick progress.

pesawat [KN], an instrument; a machine; a tool; ~ *berjentera*, machinery; ~ *senapang*, the bolt of a rifle; ~ is used for the mechanism actuating any instrument, the 'works'; also vulg. for penis.

peseban [KN], a broad gangway round the *seri balai*.

pesek [KS], Ind. flattened out, snub, pug, of nose.

pesiar = *bersiar* — cf. **siar**.

pesing [KN], (onom.) whzzing (of a projectile through the air); stinking (of urinals).

pesirah [KN], a district official (in Palembang).

pesisir [KN], the shore, sands.

pesona [KN], Pers. a spell, a magical incantation, the effects of a spell, witchcraft; insidious mischief-making, slander; ter~, spell-bound; entranced; deceived; 'flummoxed'; mem~ [KK], to cast a spell on, bewitch; influence.

pesong [KK], ter~, altered (of a course); changed (of direction in motion); breaking (of a direction of a ball); deviated from the way.

pesta [KN], Port. a tesival; a celebration; a carnival, ber~~, feast, celebrate; ~ *menari*, a ball, a dance.

pestaka [KN], book of astrology, incantations etc., spell, charm.

pesuk [KS], broken to pieces, crumbled away, much battered (of a hard substance, such as timber or masonry); ber~~~, pitted with holes.

peta [KN], a plan, map, sketch, drawing or design; ~kan, to a make a picture or sketch-plan of anything.

petah [KS], well-spoken; having a ready tongue, fluent in speech.

petai [KN], a tree yielding a pod which is very offensive in smell *(Parkia biglandulosa, ~ Roxburghii); ~ belalang (Pithecolobium microcarpum); ~ laut (Desmodium umbellatum).*

petak [KN], a compartment; a division of a padi field; a locker in a boat; the hold in a ship; a cubicle; ~ *kedudukan*, starting position drawn in race; ~ *keretapi*, railway compartment.

petaka [KN], *mala~*, disaster, catastrophe, calamity.

petala [KN], Skr. a fold; layer; a stratum; *tujuh ~ langit*, the seven firmaments.

petaling [KN], a tree yielding a good timber *(Ochanostackys amentacea).*

petam [KN], a frontlet or browband worn by a bride.

petang [KN], evening, afternoon; ~ *hari*, late in the day; *pukul empat ~*, 4 p.m.; ~ *yang tua*, the late evening.

petar [KK], taking a true aim, training a gun on to anything.

petarang [KN], *pukat ~*, a deep-sea net used on the east coast of the Peninsula.

petas [KN], Hind. crackers, noisy fireworks; *memasang ~*, to discharge crackers.

peterana [KN], Skr. a seat near the throne (used by princes of the blood), the seat of the bride and bride-groom at a Malay wedding.

potorae [KS], Tam. *tunjuk ~*, to 'put on side', behave in a conceited way; arrogant.

peterum [KN], *ubat ~*, powder in packages or cartridges.

peti [KN], Tam. a box, a case, a chest; ~ *nyanyi*, gramophone.

petia [KK], Pk. to notice, observe.

petik [KK], *memetik*, to pluck, to pick, to play on a stringed instrument; to strike (a match); to press, flick, a catch or a trigger; *alat pemetik api*, a lighter, as for cigarettes; *pemetik senapang*, a trigger; *memetik urat*, to make a small incision in the veins, as when bleeding or transfusing blood; *memetik*, to collect by picking out (e.g., passages from books of reference).

peting [KK], jerk with the thumb and finger.

petir [KN], a clap of thunder, thunder; *bunyi ~*, the sound of thunder; ~ is the Malay title of the Singapore People's Action

Party — *Parti Tindakan Rakyat; batu ~,* 'thunder stones', i.e., fossil stone implements.

petis [KN], a sauce containing tiny prawns and fish.

petis [KS], talkative, esp. of a child; c.f. **petah**.

petola [KN], Skr. a generic name given to a class of pumpkins (also *ketola); ~ hutan (Luffa acutangula), ~ manis (L. cylindrica), ~ ular (Trichosanthes anguina);* esp. the snake-gourd; when desiccated, it can be used as a flesh-brush *(loofah).*

petua [KN], Ar. a precept; a traditional rule; an authoritative ruling; advice by one who knows; magical formula, spell; recipe.

petur [KN], Port. a factor, a minor official.

petus [KN], thunderclap; *~ tunggal,* a single violent thunderclap; *sebagai ~ tunggal,* (prov.) like a bolt from the blue.

petutu [KN], a tree *(Hibiscus floccosus).*

pi [KN], Ch. a gambling counter; *main ~,* to gamble with such counters, redeemed on settlement.

piagam [KN], Jav. register; charter; *~ Atlantik,* Atlantic Charter.

piai [KN], a common swamp plant *(Acrostichum aureum).*

piak [KN], a quid of betel-leaf; a fold; a strip.

pial [KN], 1. the wattles on the comb of a cock. 2. *memial* [KK], to twist, esp. of twisting a child's ear as a punishment.

piala [KN], Pers. a cup or goblet; a phial; *~ cabaran,* challenge-cup; *~ pusingan,* challenge cup; sometimes, league cup.

pialing [KN], *burung ~,* the little Malay parroquet; also *puling.*

piama [KN], Ked. the rainy season.

piang [KN], 1. mother (in Boyanese). 2. a preparation of *pulut* rice.

pianggang [KN], a green bug destructive to growing rice *(Leptocorisa acuta);* in Perak it is known as *chenangau* and in Kelantan as *kesip.*

pianggu [KN], a tree yielding a red fruit *(Clerodendron nutans).*

piatan [KN], opportune, of time for planting, for one's fortunes.

piarit [KN], a fish-spear with a double barb.

pias, 1. a strip (of material). 2. a fish *(Chatoessus sp.).*

piat [KK], 1. twisted, oblique, out of line; *memiat,* to twist, to twitch, to nip. 2. a remote descendant; *~-piut,* remote descendants.

piatu [KN], desolate; having no relatives; *anak ~,* an orphan; alone in the world.

piawai [KN], Ind. verified, standard, esp. as weight.

picagari [KN], syringe.

picik [KS], narrow, confined, limited in means of money; *ke~an,* straitened circumstances; *~ pengetahuan,* of limited learning.

picing [KK], Ind. *memicing mata,* to close the eyes.

picis [KN], Ind. a small coin worth 10 cents; *~an,* (fig.) of trifling value, cheap and basty, est of literary works.

picit [KK], *memeit,* to pinch pressure between finger and thumb; to massage.

picu [KN], the trigger of a gun.

pidal [KS], Treng. stingy, 'tight-wad'.

pidana [KN], Ind. punishment; criminal (case or law).

pidato [KN], Ind. a speech, an address; *ber~,* to make a speech.

pidi [KN], throw (marbles).

pigura [KN], portrait, picture.

pihak [KN], side; *~ kepala,* the side of the head; *~ ugama,* on the side of religion; in the matter of faith; *ber~,* to take sides, form factions; *ber~ kepada,* to side with; *dari ~,* on behalf of, as representative of; *bagi ~ diri saya,* as far as I am concerned; *bagi ~,* (in signatures) on behalf of, per pro; *~ berkuasa,* the authorities, esp. the Government; *~ yang tertentu,* certain 'parties' (persons).

pijak [KK], *memijak,* to step on, tread on; *dapat ter~,* dirt-cheap; *~ bumi,* an old-time ceremony to celebrate the first time a baby 'sets foot on earth'.

pijar [KS], 1. a resinous substance used by goldsmiths in their work. 2. hot (of body in fever); to heat up on the fire; *memijar* [KK], to glow (with heat).

pijat [KN], a bed-bug.

pikat [KN], 1. a horse-fly. 2. [KK] *memikat,* to snare, esp. by liming; *burung pemikat,* a decoy bird; *memikat,* (fig.) to allure, entice; *ter~ hati dengan,* to 'fall for', be attracted by.

pikau [KK], *ter~,* confused; dull from sleep; *burung ~,* the blue- breasted quail *(Excalfactoria chinensis).*

piket [KN], picket; *ber~,* [KK] to stage a picket.

piknik [KN], picnic.

pikrama [KN], a respectable title.

pikul [KK], to carry a load on the shoulder; to lift a heavy weight; to weigh; a weight equal to 133 pounds; *memikul,* to carry; *~an,* a burden; the 'weight' on a race-horse.

pilak [KS], Ked. impishness, petulance.

pili [KN], p. ayer, a water-tap.

pilih [KK], *memilih,* to select, *~an,* choice; selection; *orang ~an,* picked men; *~an (suara) ramai,* an election; *~ raya,* id.; *~anraya kecil,* a by-election; *~anraya umum,* general election; *~anraya setempat,* local elections; *panitia pemilih,* selection committee, *tak ~,* not particular, not fastidious; *pemilihan,* choosing, selection; *memilih kasih,* to show favouritism; *sangat pemilih,* 'choosey', over-fastidious; *ber~~~, orangnya yang ada berperahu,* people with boats were hard to come by; *~anraya negeri,* State Elections; *melakukan ~ kasih,* to pursue a policy of favouritism; *memilih sangat, terkena pada buku,* if you are too 'choosey', you'll find that you have chosen the wrong thing; see *buku.*

pilin [KK], twining; plaiting; making a rope of several strands.

pilis [KN], a mark traced on the forehead as a protection against evil spirits.

pilu [KS], 1. sympathy, sensibility; melancholy, regret; *memberi ~,* to inspire tenderness; *berasa ~,* to feel melancholy; to feel tender solicitude. 2. an

old-time type of ship; also *pilau.*

pimpin [KK], *memimpin,* to lead by the hand, conducting, guiding; *pemimpin,* a guide; a chairman, leader; *demokrasi ter~,* guided democracy; *kelas ~an,* tuition classes; *memimpin pancaragam,* to conduct a band; *pucuk ~an,* the leaders, the governing body.

pimping [KN], a grass.

pinak [KN], *anak-~,* descendants, family, the children, the kids.

pinar [KS], *mata ber~,* dazzled, blinking; *pandangnya ber~-~,* his eyes were swimming (with dizziness).

pinang [KN], the areca-nut or betel-nut, *(Areca catechu);* the use of the areca-nut in a proposal of marriage; *~ muda,* a pimp; *~ raja,* the red-stemmed palm *(Cyrtostachys lacca); ~kan,* to betroth one's daughter; *meminang,* to ask in marriage; *ber~,* betrothed; *(seperti) ~ belah dua,* (like) a betel-nut spilt in two, (fig.) a perfect match, made for each other; symmetrical; *rombongan ~an,* the marriage-proposal group.

pinas [KN], Treng. a type of cargo-carrying lugger.

pincang [KS], 1. irregular; askew; *ke~an,* irregularities, defects; *ke~an hidup,* life's difficulties, awkward problems; *~-pincut,* irregular, halting, of a gait. 2. Ind. lame, crippled; (met.) defective.

pincuk [KK], slicing sour fruits and vegetables and cooking them in sugar.

pinda [KK], amending, improving; *~an,* an amendment.

pindah [KK], transition, movement from one place to another; transference; *~kan,* to transfer; *ber~,* to move house; *ber~-randah,* to be constantly on the move; *ber~ tangan,* to change hands, of property; *kampung pemindahan,* New Villages (under the Emergency Regulations); *pemindahan,* evacuation, of people; *orang ~an,* emigrants; *pemindahan darah,* blood transfusion; *cakap. ~,* indirect speech (as opposed to direct speech — *cakap ajuk).*

pindang [KN], fish cooked with a piquant

sauce containing *asam gelugur* and other ingredients.

pinga [KS], *ter~-~*, distracted, bewildered; astonished.

pingat [KN], a medal, a badge (as of rank); *~ kebaktian*, Order of Merit; *~ bakti setia*, long service medal; *~ perangai baik*, good conduct medal.

pinggan [KN], Hind. (from Pers.) a plate; a dish; *~-mangkuk*, crockery.

pinggang [KN], waist; middle of the body; amidships; *~-ramping*, a slender waist; *~ genting*, wasp-waisted; *ikat ~* or *tali ~*, a girdle; *peminggang*, the midmost portion; the waist, of a ship; *dayung peminggang*, the oars amidships; *kain sehelai se ~*, one sarong per person, sign of great poverty or scarcity.

pinggir [KN], edge, border, boundary, limit; *~an negeri*, frontier; *~an bandar*, suburban area.

pinggul [KN], the pelvis.

pingit [KK], confine to the house, keep under lock and key; *ter~*, jealously shut up; *gadis ~an*, a girl brought up in seclusion, a 'carefully brought up girl'; *lepas ~an*, freed from such restraints, (fig.) emancipated.

pinjam [KK], a transaction of the nature of a loan; borrowing, lending; *~an*, a loan; *beri ~*, giving a loan; lending; *minta ~*, borrowing; *meminjam* or *~kan*, to borrow.

pinta = *minta*.

pintal [KK], *memintal*; 1. twining (as in making rope); *ber~-~*, tangled (hair), twisted; *pemintal*, spinning-wheel; *awan ~*, a rope-like spiral pattern. 2. keen (of intellect).

pintang [KK], *hilang ~*, lost for ever; altogther gone; wholly disappeared.

pintar [KS], clever, wily, sharp; *ke~an*, cleverness, capability, skill.

pintas [KK], to cut across, taking a short cut, intercepting by cutting across, to make a detour; *se~ lalu*, at first glance; *~-memintas*, making detour after detour, (met.) intriguing; *jalan ~an*, a detour; a short cut.

pintu [KN], a door, a gate, an entrance; numeral coefficient for houses or buildings; *di muka ~*, in front of the gate, *penunggu ~*, a porter; *~ ambang*, a light screen-door not touching the ground; *~ air*, a water-gate; *~ gerbang*, a main gate or door; an arch; *~ kambi*, a light screen-door reaching down to the ground; *~ lawang*, an outer gate; *~ maling*, a side-door or back-door; *~ mati*, a door nailed up or permanently closed; *jenang ~*, the door-posts; *ambang ~*, lintel of door; *~ gol*, the goal in football; *~ sekerat berdaun dua*, half-door opening in the middle; *daun ~*, panels, etc., of door, body of door; *~ rangkup*, double door; *~ sorong*, sliding door; *~ memantul*, id.; *~ pelapas perlumbaan*, starting-gate (for race-horses).

pipa [KN], 1. a barrel. 2. Eng. a pipe (for liquid).

pipi [KN], the cheek; *kedua ~*, both cheeks; *merahkan ~*, to rouge the cheeks.

pipih [KS], flat, not rounded; *cacing ~*, the tapeworm.

pipis [KK], 1. pound between two hard substances, mash; grind curry-stuff with a heavy pounder or roller; *burung terbang, di~kan lada*, grinding the spices while the birds are still on the wing, i.e. counting your chickens before they are hatched. 2. = *pipih*.

pipit [KK], 1. a generic name for small sparrows and finches, in particular, the Malayan tree sparrow; (fig.) a child's penis; *~ uban*, the white-headed munia; *sarang ~*, a dimple. 2. a bird or animal call (whistle).

pirai [KN], *penyakit ~*, a rheumatic or gouty complaint causing pain in the joints.

pirik [KK], to crush small, to grind to atoms.

piring [KN], saucer; *~ peti nyanyi*, gramophone record; *~ hitam*, id.; *~ aneka lagu*, long-playing record.

piru [KN], Hind., Pen. *ayam ~*, guinea-fowl; in some parts, the turkey.

pirus [KN], Pers. *permata ~*, a turquoise.

pisah [KK], put asunder; severing; divorcing; *ber~,* to be separated; to disperse, depart; *per~an,* departure; *memisahkan,* to segregate, to isolate, to separate.

pisang [KN], a banana, of which there are many varieties, ~ *mas,* ~ *raja* and ~ *rastali* being perhaps the most popular dessert varieties and ~ *udang* the most used for cooking; *seper~,* as much time as it takes to eat a banana — a minute or two; ~ *kaki,* a persimmon; *katak ~,* a kind of tree-frog; *jantung ~,* the blossom of the banana; the banana tree *(pokok ~)* is remarkable for bearing only once and for having a very soft trunk, hence: *jangan terkena pokok ~ berbuah dua kali,* don't let the banana tree fruit again, i.e., don't be caught that way again; and *lawan batang ~, menikam batang ~,* fighting a banana trunk, stabbing a banana trunk, i.e., attacking a person who can't retaliate or picking out the easiest task; *setandan ~,* a mainbunch of bananas; *sesikat ~,* a layer in a bunch of bananas; *pondok ~ sesikat,* a pent-house, a lean-to; *pokok pe- (~-~),* name given to several trees whose leaves give them a superficial resemblance to a banana tree.

pisat [KS], *ter~-~,* dizzy with sleep.

pisau [KN], a generic name for knives of all sorts; ~ *cukur,* ~ *pencukur,* or *penyukur,* a razor; ~ *daun padi,* a lancet; ~ *wali,* id.; ~ *lidah ayam,* an office-knife (with a small blade which does not fold); ~ *lidah ayam lipat,* a penknife; ~ *lipat,* id.; ~ *raut,* a small paring knife; *mata ~,* the blade of a knife; *punggung ~,* the blunt side of a knife-blade; ~ *cukur* is also used (fig.) for 'a smooth worker', tricky.

pisit [KK], *~-~,* ask persistently; *memisit,* interrogate, a spy, informer.

Pit [KN], a nickname meaning 'slit-eyed', from *sepet.*

pita [KN], Port. a tape, ribbon; *~kan,* to record on tape (of a tape-recorder).

pitam [KS], a rush of blood to the head causing dizziness; *naik ~,* to have a rush of blood to the head.

pitis [KN], a very small denomination of coin something like Chinese cash; 480 to the dollar; ~ is used in Kelantan for 'money' generally.

pitu [KBil], seven; a rare equivalent of *tujuh.*

piuh [KK], *ter~,* knotted (of roots or branches); involved or complicated (of a business).

piut [KN], a descendant in the fourth or fifth generation.

piutang [KN], debts receivable, money due; *si-~,* a creditor.

plagiat [KN] Ind. plagiarism; *mem~,* to plagiarize.

plonco [KN] Ind. novice, 'greenhorn', esp. freshman at college; *per~an,* ragging of freshman; *mengadakan ~,* to hold such a rag; *mem~kan,* to rag.

po [KN] Ch. a sort of die-box used by Chinese gamblers; *main ~,* to gamble by guessing the position of the hidden die.

podak [KN] *pandan ~,* a plant *(Pandanus inermis).*

podi [KN], 1. Tam. the dust of gems; very small gems mounted in large numbers to make a glittering sholo. 2. limewhisk.

pohon [KN], 1. a tree, ~ *kayu,* id.; ~ *kelapa,* a coconut tree. 2. *pulang ~,* the first anniversary of a death; *dua kali pulang ~,* the second anniversary of a death. 3. = *mohon, memohon,* to beg, to ask (for).

pojok [KN], Ind. corner, margin; *penulis ~,* columnist.

pokah [KS], to become bent; to give way; twisted; to snap; *orang ~,* a broken-down wastrel.

pokeng [KS], tailless (of fowls).

pokeri [KN], Telegu (Penang.) a blackguard.

pokok [KN], a tree, a bush, a plant; the nucleus of a storm; the capital for working an undertaking; the butt of a counterfoil book; main point, fundamental principle, basis; ~ *kelapa,* a coconut tree; ~ *angin,* a gathering cloud presaging wind; ~ *ribut,* a storm-cloud; *makan ~,* to sell at below cost price; ~

tahun, a perennial tree; ~ *tahunan*, an annual; *soal* ~, the main question; *tujuan* ~, the main aim; ~ *perdebatan*, subject of debate; *gaji* ~, basic salary; *harga* ~, cost price; ~ *perselisihan*, matter in dispute; *pulang* ~, not to make profit; *mengalihkan* ~ *perbualan*, to change the subject.

pokrol [KN], advocate.

pola [KN], design, pattern, model.

polang-paling [KK], veering (of wind).

polan [KN], Ar. *si* ~, so-and-so.

polis [KN], Eng. police.

politik [KN], politics; *ber*~ [KK], to be involved in politics.

polok [KK], to swallow a large mouthful; to swallow greedily.

polong [KN], a familiar spirit, a sort of bottle-imp.

polos [KS], plain and simple.

pompa [KN], (Dutch) a pump, spout, or hose; = *bomba*.

pompang [KN], an anchored purse-net; also called *gombang Cina*.

pompong [KN], an inedible cuttle fish.

pondok [KN], a shed, a lean-to, a temporary shelter; *kepala* ~, Sp. a Boyanese headman; used in particular of the huts in which religious students live near their teacher's house; ~ *telefon*, telephone-box; ~ *pancaragam*, bandstand.

pondong [KK], *memondong*; 1. carry in the folds of a scarf slung over the back. 2. N.S. = *pondok*.

ponen [KN], Tam., Pen. impotent.

pong [KN], *buluh* ~, a toy, the paper membrane which bursts with a bang under air pressure; *burung* ~-~, the Malayan fluffy-backed babbler.

pongah [KS], proud, cocky.

pongkes [KN], a shallow rubbish-basket.

pongsu [KN], a hillock or mound; an ant-hill — cf. **busut**; *merak* ~, the peacock pheasant *(Polyplectrum bicalcaratum)*.

ponok [KN], Pah. a hump on cattle.

pontang [KKtr], ~-*panting*, topsy-turvy; helter-skelter; scattered about.

ponteng [KK], Sp. to swindle; esp. ~ *sewa*, to bilk (e.g., a taxi- driver); ~ *belajar*, to

skip one's lessons; to play truant; ~ *sekolah*, id.

pontianak [KN], vampire; evil spirit preying on women in labour and on children.

popia [KN], a type of food which consists of vegetables with a thin piece of dough.

popok [KN], *kain* ~, diaper, baby's napkin.

porak [KS], ~-*parik*, helter-skelter; in confusion; ~ *peranda*, disturbance, choatic conditions.

porok [KN], a game resembling quoits.

poros [KN], 1. the vertex of a cone; the top of a mast; the point of a spear. 2. porous, allowing liquid to pass through.

pos [KN] *buah* ~, (Riau) the testes. 2. post, *menge*~ [KK], post, send by post.

pot [KN], Eng. a latex cup; earthenware etc. for cooking things in; etc., flower pot, vessel for urine.

potong [KK], cut off; a piece cut off; *se*~ *(tanah)*, a piece (of land), a pack (of cards); *memotong*, to cut off; slice, chop, deduct, overtake, interrupt; ~ *nama*, to transfer property (by deed); to cut out, cancel; to 'scratch' (from contest); ~*an*, cut (of clothes); shape (of manufactured articles generally); ~*an badan*, figure; ~ trip, to get ahead of someone by trickery, to 'steal a march'; ~ is used by foreigners instead of *sembelih* to mean cutting the throat (when slaughtering for food); *saya berani* ~ *ayam*, I am prepared to kill a fowl while taking an oath; a method of truth-testing considered binding by old-fashioned Chinese.

poyang [KN], a Sumatran word sometimes meaning 'ancestor' — cf. **moyang**; and sometimes a magician (= *pawang*).

pramugari [KN], Ind. air-hostess, air stewardess.

prasangka [KN], Ind. prejudice.

prima [KS], prime.

primadona [KN], primadonna, leading woman, singer in opera.

prinsip [KN], Eng. principle(s), rules.

protes [KN], Ind. *mem*~ [KK], to protest (against).

puadai [KN], Tam. cloth laid down for a procession to pass over; sometimes a mat to be sat on by royalty on certain ceremonial occasions.

puah [KK], N.S. blowing away evil (after reciting a charm); ~-*peralih*, to renounce, abjure; (~ may be connected etymologically with *puar,* q.v.).

puak [KN], tribe, a family in the widest sense, or clan; ~ *kiri,* the Left Wing; *ber~,* to gather together to form a clique.

puaka [KN], a spirit of the earth; a genius loci; a spirit haunting a spot.

pualam [KN], Tam. marble.

puan [KN], 1. a large metal or wooden caddy for betel requisites, smaller at the top than at the bottom. 2. a lady; used now as a polite equivalent of Mrs or Miss; in particular, *Toh Puan* is the title which may be used by holders of the Order S.M.N. and their wives — see **darjah**.

puar [KK], N.S. *ber~,* a mimic fight held triennially in Rembau to propitiate the spirits *Tok Sayat* (upstream) and *Tok Manggan* (downstream) in order to ensure a good rice-crop; *melepaskan batang ~,* id.; is the name given to several plants believed to have a medicinal value; stalks of ~ are used in the mimic fight.

puas [KK], satisfied, sated; ~ *hati,* satisfied; *memuaskan,* to satisfy; *(dengan) se~~~nya,* to heart's content; *ke~an,* satisfaction, contentment; *ketidak~an,* discontentment.

puasa [KK], Skr. a fast; fasting; *bulan ~,* the fasting-month Ramadan; *ber~,* to fast; *buka ~,* to break one's fast; *ibadat ~,* the performance of the fast; *hariraya ~,* the festival at the end of the fast; *berniat ~,* to vow (to oneself) to fast.

pucat [KS], pale; ~ *lesi,* pale through anaemia; ~ *perang,* pale brown; wan; the pallor of a dark skin; ~ *pudar,* pale and tired-looking.

pucik [KN], the principal post or pile in a marine fish-trap.

pucuk [KN], a sprouting-branch, a shoot; *ber~,* budding, sprouting; ~ *api,* a darting point of flame; ~ *rebung,* (1) the edible young shoots of the bamboo; (2) chevrons (in art); *ular ~,* the common green tree-snake *(Dryophis prasinus);* used for 'penis'; *mati ~,* sexually impotent; ~ is used as a numeral coefficient for letters and firearms. (In the case of letters the reason probably is that the old-time letter took the form of a rolled paper, for which 'a shoot' fitted well.)

pucung [KN], a generic name given to bitterns, e.g., to *Dupetor flavicollis, Ardetta cinnamonea, Ardetta sinensis* and *Butorides javanica;* ~ *bakau,* the little green heron; ~ *batu,* the Eastern reef-heron; ~ *gagak,* ~ *hitam,* the black bittern; ~ often = *burung gelam.*

pudar [KS], faded, dim, 'washed out'; *pucat ~,* pale and tired-looking.

pudat [KS], crammed full; packed.

puding [KN], the garden croton *(Codioeum variegatum);* ~ *hutan,* a wild var. *(Tabernoemontana Malaccensis).*

pugal *memugal* [KK], (coarse) to have sexual intercourse.

pugar [KK], repair, restore, renew, do up, recover; *ber~,* rehabilitate.

puhu = *puih.*

puih [KS], *reput ~,* crumbling to pieces; rotting.

puing [KS], ruin of a house, debris.

puisi [KN], Eng. poetry.

puja [KK], Skr. prayer, adoration; *memuja,* to adore, address prayers to — used of Hindu rites and of the prayers to spirits of the jungle and not of a service in a mosque; *memuja berhala,* to worship idols; ~ *pantai,* (Kel.) a triennial propitiation ceremony for the spirits of the sea, similar to *semah,* q.v.; *perayaan ~ umur,* birthday celebrations (of a Ruler); *~an hati,* adored one; *~an ramai,* popular idol, e.g. film-star; *pemujaan tokoh,* cult of personality; *pemuja,* worshipper, adorer.

pujangga [KN], man of letters, philosopher.

puji [KN], 1. praise, laudation; ~-~*an,*

praises, the complimentary phrases at the beginning of a letter; *memuji* [KK], to praise; to declare praise-worthy; *ter~*, belauded; *~ melambung,* to praise to the skies; *surat ~an,* testimonial. 2. = *puja.*

pujuk [KK], coaxing, flattery, blarney; *~-rayu,* blandishments; *~kan* or *memujuk,* to coax, to clatter; to persuade; also *bujuk.*

pujur [KS], fast, loose, licentious, dissolute.

pukal [KN], a lump or clod of anything solid, compact (of texture or body-substance), (in this sense opposed to *mabung); keris se~,* a straight-bladed *keris; bayar ~,* to pay in a lump sum.

pukang [KN], the fork; the junction of the lower limbs; *lintang ~,* higgledy-piggledy; *ter~,* thrown (wrestling).

pukas [KN], *ber~* or *ber~-~an,* in a state of nudity, as bathers; used esp. with the implication of indecent behaviour.

pukat [KN], a generic name for large nets (esp. drift-nets and seines); *memukat,* to catch fish with a ~; *pemukat,* fisherman who uses *pukat* to catch fish; *~ tarik,* the common seine; *~ hanyut,* the common drift-net; *~ takur,* a lift-net; *~ tunda,* a trawl.

pukau [KN], a narcotic (used by thieves to drug their victims to sleep); *ber~,* drugged.

puki [KN], the female genitals; *~ mak,* coarse imprecation.

pukul [KK], *memukul,* beat, strike, knock, hammer; *~ lima,* five o'clock; *~ cap,* printing; *~ ladam,* to shoe a horse; used for 'to multiply' (arithmetic); *~ rata,* to strike an average; on the average; *~-cabut,* to hit-and-run; *~ curi,* id.

pula [KKtr], also; likewise; again; too; furthermore; *demikian ~,* and so once more; *siapa ~?,* who then?; *mengapa ~?,* why then?

pulai [KN], a large tree *(Alstonia scholaris).*

pulak = *pula.*

pulan [KS], crisp (of well-cooked rice); firm and clear, of writing.

pulang [KK], return to the point of original departure, e.g. to one's country, to one's home, etc.; *berjalan ~,* to return; *modal pun tak ~,* I didn't even get my capital back; *ter~ pada,* it depends on, it is left to; *~kan pada,* to leave (decision) to; *ke~an,* return; *pemulangan,* repayment.

pulas [KK], twist, wring, wringing out; *~ leher,* to wring the neck; *memulas,* to twist (used of griping pains in the stomach); *pemulas,* a twister, a screwdriver, Kel. a 'locker', a fighting bull which always tries to lock horns.

pulasan [KN], 1. a fruit — closely resembling the rambutan *(Nephelium mutabile).* 2. the Malay weasel *(Putorius nudipes).*

pulau [KN], 1. an island; an isolated piece of rising ground in a sea, river, swamp or rice-field; *~kan,* to boycott, isolate; to ostracize; *ke~an,* archipelago. 2. *nasi ~,* pillau rice.

puli [KK], *ber~-~.* 1. struggling (as flies in a web). 2. rubbing legs together.

pulih [KS], return, recovered, restored; *pulang ~,* to be restored to an original state; *simpul ~,* fastening which is easily undone; *~kan,* to bring back; to restore; *~ air mandi,* the (ceremonial) corpse-washing water receded, of a recovery from near death; *pemulihan,* recovery, generally; *tempat pemulihan orang yang berpenyakit —,* place for the treatment of persons suffering from —; *memulihkan nafas,* to revive by artificial respiration; *memulihkan akhlak,* to reform (character); *rumah pemulihan,* rehabilitation centre; *beransur ~,* getting better, improving.

puling, Kel. = *pialing.*

puluh [KBil], a group of ten; *se~,* ten; *dua ~,* twenty; *per~an,* decimal point; *2 per~an 5,* 2.5; *dua-~an,* the twenties.

pulun [KK], *memulun,* gathering up in folds; *ber~-~,* gather up on one side (as a sarong).

pulur [KN], 1. = *empulur.* 2. [KK], to roast in ashes.

pulut [KN], adhesive, sticky; glutinous varieties of rice; a generic name for cakes made out of glutinous rice; ~! is sometimes used as an exclamation of pleasure on seeing an easy task, e.g., a ball just over a pocket: Jam!; ~-~, a generic name given to a number of plants, e.g., *Mallotus* sp. and *Urena lobata.*

pumpun [KN], a harmless sea-millipede much used as bait.

pun [P], an inseparable particle suffixed to a word or clause that is intended to emphasise; *itu~,* that also; *se kali ~,* yet; *ada~,* now — introducing a parenthesis; *dia ~ pergi,* he too went; *datang keretapi dia ~ naik,* the train came and he (on his part) got in.

punah [KS], *habislah ~,* utterly destroyed — a strong form of *habis;* *~-ranah,* utterly ruined, in ruins.

punai [KN], a generic name for many green pigeons; *burung ~,* the common green pigeon *(Osmotreron vernans);* ~ *daun (Osmotreron nipalensis),* ~ *gading* or ~ *jambu (Ptilopus jambu),* id.; ~ *rimba,* the cuckoo-dove *(Micropygia ruficeps);* ~ *siul (Osmotreron olax),* id.; ~ *tanah,* the bronze-wing-dove *(Chalcophaps indica);* ~ is sometimes used in salacious conversation to mean a girl (a 'bird').

punat [KN], nucleus, control element; (fig.) main actuating device; ~ *(bisul),* core of a boil; *budak ~,* (fig.) young rascal.

punca [KN], Skr. the loose end or fag end of anything — such as a piece of rope or cloth; the pendent extremity; source; the start, cause, e.g., of an incident; *ber~,* originate; *hilang ~, tengelam ~,* to loose one's head; ~ *yang boleh dipercayai,* reliable source.

puncak [KN], top, summit, crown; the knob on a flagstaff; ~ *gunung,* the summit of a mountain; *memuncak,* to reach its peak, rise to highest point; (fig.) zenith, e.g., of power; climax of events or story; ~ *ombak,* crest of a wave; also *kemuncak; sidang ~,* summit meeting.

pundak [KN], Ind. shoulder.

pundi [KN], *~-~,* a satchel, a bag, a purse; *~-~ hempedu,* the gall-bladder; *~-~ kencing,* urinary bladder.

punding [KK], to twist or ravel up (of a rope or thread).

pungah [KS], Kel. arrogant, fierce.

punggah [KK], *memunggah,* unload, discharge; remove goods from one place to another; *~an,* [KN] dock, discharging, berth; ~ *angkat,* to pick up and remove; to transport; to unpack (goods, articles); (fig., sl.) to evacuate heavily, as after taking an aperient.

punggal *memunggal* [KK], to throw, hurl.

pungguk [KN], stumpy, dumpy, squat; *ekor ~,* stumpy tail, as of a woodpecker or snipe; *ter~,* crouching low, hunched; *burung ~,* the Malayan hawk-owl; a proverbial simile for a despairing lover, as this owl is believed to pine for the moon.

punggung [KN], the fundament; the buttocks; the seat; ~ *pedang,* the dull side of a sword; *papan ~,* the small of the back; *lapik ~,* something to sit on, as a cushion; *~-memunggung,* back to back.

punggur [KN], a standing, dead tree-trunk.

pungkah [KN], a fragment, a large piece of anything.

pungkur [KN], the posterior, the fundament; the rimmed base of a saucer; ~ *siput,* the heart of the whorl in finger impressions; *tulang papan ~,* the lumbar vertebrae.

pungut [KK], picking up, collecting; *memungut,* to gather; to take in, adopt, a foundling; *anak ~an,* foundling; *pemungut,* collector, picker; *pemungutan,* collection.

punjung [KN], an arched framework on which plants are trailed; arbour; pergola.

punjut [KK], *memunjut,* to tie up sackwise, to fold up; a bag formed by tying together the ends of some material.

punpun [KK], *~kan,* to draw forward in a bunch, e.g., the end of a shawl.

puntal [KK], *memuntal,* to coil rope round the hand so as to get a good grip of it;

to wring; to twist round, wind round; ~*an*, a spool; a rolled up edge, e.g., of a sarong; *ber*~-~, in coils.

puntang-panting [KS], topsy-turvy (of things).

punti [KN], *ular* ~, a name given to the snake *Dipsadomorphus dendrophilus*; also called *ular tiung*.

puntuh [KN], an armlet worn by heroes of romance, by Malay princes at marriage in Perak, and by Javanese brides and bridegrooms.

puntung [KN], a stump, a half-burnt log; the fag-end of a cigar; used as a numeral coefficient for teeth.

punya [KK], possession; a word used to form a possessive or genitive, e.g., *saya* ~ *rumah*, my house; *ke~an*, property of, owned by —; *mem~i*, to own; sometimes ~ alone is used in writing with this meaning; *tuan* ~ *rumah*, the owner of a house, but generally this would mean, your house.

punyat [KK], Pen. to steal.

pupu [KN], a grade or degree of relationship; a generation; *saudara se~*, a first cousin; *saudara dua* ~, a second cousin.

pupuh [KK], *memupuh*, to fly at each other (of fighting cocks); *ber*~ *ayam*, to set cocks on to each other (without artificial spurs); *ayam* ~, a fighting cock — cf. **sabung**.

pupuk [KK], 1. to apply plasters and poultices to the body. 2. Ind. manure, fertiliser; *memupuk*, to fertilise with manure; (fig.) to promote, further, help forward; to nurture, cultivate; (fig.) blow up, fan (flames); *masih berbau pupuk jeringau*, (prov.) to be still a baby; very young; inexperienced.

pupur [KN], a face-powder made of rice-meal scented with herbs; ~*an* or *tepung* ~, id.; *ber*~, to apply such powder to the face; ~*an ayam*, the nest a fowl makes in the dust.

pupul [KN], (Borneo) crop; *memupul*, to harvest, gather; ~ *tahun*, the first harvest (of edible birds' nests); ~ *merai*, the second harvest.

pupus [KS], blighted (of plants, men's fortunes); left desolate (of human beings).

puput [KK], *ber*~, blowing, swaying (anything) of the wind; *di*~ *bayu*, swayed about by the breeze; ~*an angin*, a gust of wind; a squall.

pura [KN], 1. Skr. a city (only in compounds -

such as Singa-~). 2. ~-~, feigning, pretence; *menangis* ~-~, shedding crocodile's tears; *ber*~-~, to make pretence; *orang* ~-~, humbug, hypocrite. 3. ~ *peranda* = *porak peranda*; see *porak*. 4. waist-cloth, waist-belt (used as a receptacle for money); *membuka* ~, (fig.) to loosen one's purse-strings; *membuka* ~, *hutang langsai*, when you open your waistbelt, settle your debts, i.e., when you do a job, do it thoroughly.

purba [KS], Skr. ancient, former; ~ *kata*, days of old; ~ *sangka*, old-fashioned ideas; also *perba*.

purbawara [KN], a play with an old-time theme.

puri [KN], Skr. the residential portions of a palace.

puris, Ked. = *lidi*.

purnama [KS], Skr. full (of the moon); a full moon as a measure of time; a month.

puru [KN], yaws *(Framboesia tropica)*; ~ *tak jadi*, suppressed yaws; *bunga* ~, the eruptions of yaws; *katak* ~, a toad.

purun [KN], a rush used in basket-making; = *memderung*.

purut [KS], rough-skinned, esp. of the rough-skinned bitter lime *limau* ~ *(Citrus papeda)*.

pusaka [KN], heirloom, family property (esp. quasi-entailed property); *adat* ~, Malay customary law regulating succession; ~*i*, to inherit (by right of birth); also sometimes used to mean to create as family property, nearly meaning to entail.

pusar [KN], a spiral motion, to roll in the hands (as a swizzle); ~*an air*, a whirlpool; ~*an angin*, a whirlwind; ~*an* is also used as a whorl in a growth of hair (used in

Kelantan as an identification mark of cattle); also for the grooves on a gramophone record.

pusara [KN], Ind. sleeping-place; grave, graveyard.

pusat [KN], the navel, the centre; *se~*, concentric; *ber~*, all centred on; *memusatkan*, to concentrate; centre; *~ bulat*, the centre of a circle; *~ tasik*, the centre of the great ocean; the navel of the seas; *tali ~*, the umbilical cord; *~ is used for a 'a centre'* — e.g., for registration; *kerajaan ~*, Central Government; *garisan ~*, circumference; *~ pendaftaran buruh*, Labour Exchange.

pusi [KN], *bulu ~*, a kind of lint formerly used for dressing wounds.

pusing [KK], revolve, rotate; (coll. fig.) to cheat; *~ kepala*, vertigo; *ber~-~*, revolving; *ambil ~*, to worry about, take seriously; *~an*, a round (as in boxing); *pertandingan secara ~an*, league competition; *~ belakang*, to turn about; *memusing-musingkan badan*, to pirouette.

puspa [KN], Skr. a flower, flowery, variegated; *~-ragam*, variegated; sometimes, variety show.

pustaka [KN], Skr. a book, a book of divination or spells; literature; *balai ~*, library; literary academy; *per~an*, literary studies; a library; *taman ~*, reading room.

pusu [KN], 1. *ber~-~*, surging to and fro (of a crowd of people); jostling in a mad rush; in thick clouds, of smoke. 2. tangled (hair); in large numbers; in heaps, in groups.

putar [KK], rotate, motion on an axis; *~an* [KN], a windlass; *~an air*, a whirlpool; *menjalankan ~-belit*, to work a swindle; prevaricate; twist, distort (words); *jarum ~-belit*, a swindle; *~ is* also used for 'stirring briskly'; *memutarkan*, to cause to revolve, so, to run (a film); to turn, as a handle or winder; *pemutar*, a winder, key; *pemutar paip*, a tap; a lever for controlling water; *jam ber~ dengan sendirian*, a self-winding watch; *memu-*

tar nombor telefon, to dial a number on the telephone; *memutar-balik*, to try tricks; to twist (statement, words) so as to misrepresent, to garble; *memutar misai*, to twirl one's moustache.

putarwali [KN], Jav. *akar ~*, a medicinal creeper *(Lepidagatis longifolia?)*, with medicinal value; also called *seruntun;* it is proverbial for its bitterness.

putat [KN], a generic name for a number of plants *(Rarringtonia* sp.).

putera [KN], Skr. a prince; the child of a prince; *ber~*, to bear a child; *~ garam*, water-shy; *~ lilin*, afraid of the sun, shirking outdoor work; *hari ke~an*, birthday, esp. of royalty; *menyambut hari ke~an*, to celebrate such a birthday.

puteri [KN], Skr. a princess; the daughter of a prince; a fairy; *~ malu*, a name given to the sensitive plant; *burung sepah ~*, a bird *(Dicoeum cruentatum);* *main ~*, Kel. a performance of the black art to cure the sick or effect some other purpose; *~ Gunung Ledang*, the Fairy Princess of Mount Ophir; *~ is* sometimes used politely for girl.

putih [KS], white, pure, clean, pale; *~ kuning*, cream; *~ mata*, put to shame; 'scored off'; *tulang*, the whitening of the bones — death; *kayu ~*, kajeput; *Orang ~*, a white man; a European (esp. an Englishman); *memutih*, to become white; *memutihkan*, to whiten; *~ bahana*, sallow, dead-white; *~ telur*, the white of an egg; *~ kuning*, pale gold colour (the colour of the skin most admired by Malays); *~ kapas*, white as cotton cloth, esp. of skin; *~ sabun*, milky white; *~ melepak*, snowy white; *~ kekuning-kuningan*, yellowish white; *tak ada ~ hitamnya*, I haven't got it in black and white; *memutih tapaknya lari*, to 'hare off' (soles white with dust); *biar ~ tulang, jangan ~ mata*, (prov.) rather dead than ashamed.

putik [KN], the fruit as it appears immediately after the falling of the blossom; *ber~*, to set, of fruit-blossom.

puting [KN], the part of a knife-blade which

is buried in the handle; a pointed projection; a fag end or stump; shank, helve; *ribut ~ beliung,* a whirlwind; *~ (hisapan kanak-kanak),* a baby's 'comforter', 'titty'; *~ beliung,* a water-spout; *~ cepu-cepu,* the foot of a mast; *~ susu,* the nipple; *parang ~,* a handleless chopper; *memuting,* to swing at anchor; with the tide, anchored at one end.

putu [KN], a generic name given to a number of cakes.

putus [KK], severed; broken off; (fig.) to settle, to decide, to put an end to; *~ asa,* hopeless; in despair; *~ harga,* to settle a price; *~ hati,* heartbroken; *~ makan,* exhausted (of supplies); *~nyawa,* dead; *~kan,* to settle, to terminate, to break; *ke~an,* severance, termination, settlement, decision; *yang tidak berke~an,* endless; *tak ~,* incessantly, without a break; *memberi kata ~,* to give a definite answer; *~ berlanja,* run out of cash; *ber~ arang,* to break off relations, 'part brass rags'; *~ ikhtiar,* at wits' end; *ke~an,* result, decision, verdict; *dengan suara ter~-~,* with broken utterance; *jangan mudah ~ asa,* don't give up easily.

puyu [KN], *~-~,* the climbing perch, *(Anabas tetudineus); dah menangkap ikan pe~!,* jocular cry of women when cooking, as the water begins to bubble in the pan (because this fish betrays itself by agitating shallow water); also *pepuyu.*

puyuh [KN], common bustard quail *(Turnix pugnax).*

R

raba [KK], feeling about with the hands; *me~*, to grope; to fondle; *me~-~*, fumbling, guessing; *me~i*, grope; caress, fondle; *~an*, feeling, groping; *pe~*, sense of touch.

rabak [KS], gashed, rent, torn lengthwise; *me~*, tear; rip; *parang itu tiba pada mulutnya ~ sampai ke telinga,* the chopper landed on his mouth and there was a gash extending to his ear.

raban [KK], *me~*, to 'wander' in speech, to be delirious, to read incoherently, to walk unsteadily.

rabas [KK], drip, fall (of raindrops, tears).

Rabbi [KN], Ar. Lord (of God); *Ilahi ~,* the Lord God.

Rabbul-alamin [KN], Lord of the Universe (God).

Rabbul-izzati [KN], Lord of Glory.

Rabi [KN], Ar. *~-al-awal,* the third month of the Muslim calender; and *~-al-akhir,* the fourth month of the Muslim calendar; names of months known (coll.) as *bulan maulud* and *adik maulud* respectively.

rabit [KS], 1. gashed or rent (of the edge of a cloth, mat, etc.); *bibir ~,* a hare-lip. 2. to drag third parties into a suit.

rabu [KN], 1. the lungs; = *paru-paru; kembang ~,* exulting; *demam ~ kembang,* pneumonia. 2. Ar. *hari Rabu,* Wednesday; coll. for *Arbaa.*

rabuk [KN], tinder, touchwood; *seperti rabuk dengan api* (prov.), dangerous (to leave, to be left) together.

rabun [KS], fumigation; *me~* [KK], to send smoke into a house so as to drive away mosquitoes or evil spirits; *pe~* [KN], leaves etc. which are burned to drive away evil spirits. 2. dim of sight; *mata ~,* id.; *~ ayam,* night-blind.

rabung [KN], swelling or mounting up; brimming over; summit-dome; summit-ridge; *air naik me~,* very high tide; *~* or *pe~,* ridge-covering of a house, us. made of double row of pieces of thatching.

rabut [KK], pulling out, forcibly extracting; *me~,* to tear out.

racau [KK], *me~,* delirious, raving (of persons in high fever); to talk wildly, to rant.

racik [KN], 1. snare of hanging nooses for catching birds; *me~,* to snare birds. 2. to slice up; *se~ ikan,* a slice of fish.

racun [KN], poison (esp. stomach poisons in contradistinction to blood poisons — *bisa*): *penyakit ~ darah,* blood-poisoning; *kematian termakan ~,* death from poison; *me~* is used (sl.) as a strong negative: *seorang pun me~,* not a single blasted man!

radai [KK], 1. Sp. *me~,* to beg from door to door = Pen. *rawai.* 2. Pah. a rain gutter under eaves.

radak [KK], *me~,* to spear or stab from below; (sl.) to guzzle.

radang [KS], *me~,* to become angry, to rage; to flare up (of a disease); to be inflamed; *me~kan,* annoyed with; *ke~an,* anger, rage; *pe~,* hot tempered; *~ paru-paru,* inflammation of the lungs, pneumonia; *~ usus buntu,* appendicitis.

radas [KN], apparatus.

radi [KK], Ar. may (God) bestow favour in the expression *~ Allah an-hu* (may God show him favour) — an exclamatory remark when the names of the early Caliphs are mentioned.

radif [KN], Ar. the burden of a song; the rhyme.

radin [KN], 1. Jav. a princely title. 2. a kind of rice, a quick-growing variety.

radio [KN], Eng. radio; *alat pemancar ~,* radio transmitter; *alat penerima ~,* radio receiver; *tempat pancaran* ~, broadcasting station; *rangkaian* ~, radio network; ~ *bercorak kebangsaan,* national radio; ~ *bercorak perniagaan,* commercial radio.

radup [KK], to put in a stitch (as to a tear).

Radfidi [KN], Ar. (lit.) 'foresakers' — the name used by Sunnites for the Shi'ah sect.

raga [KN], 1. a coarsely-plaited creel; a basket; *buah* ~, a sort of football of basketwork; *main* ~ or *sepak* ~, a primitive Malay football. 2. Jav. the body (in opposition to the soul). 3. *mempe~kan,* to show off; *pe~,* a dandy; *me~-~,* to 'play to the gallery'; *pe~wati,* Ind. mannequin, model; also *pergawati.*

ragam [KN], Tam. modes in music; variety in sound, colouring, or disposition; entertainments, varieties, amusements; *banyak orang, banyak ~nya,* there are as many temperaments as there are men, (prov.); *se~ sebau* (idiom), unanimous; harmonious (married couple); *me~,* to 'play up', show temperament, of persons and (fig.) of engines, etc.; *membuat* ~, id.; *se~,* of a similar type, colour-scheme, pattern; *pakaian se~,* uniform, livery; *kese~an,* uniformity; *penye~an,* standardization; ~ is now used for mood (gram.): ~ *cerita,* the indicative mood; ~ *lepas,* the infinitive mood; ~ *perintah,* the imperative mood.

ragang [KK], *me~,* to scale a wall; to climb a tree; pulling oneself up by the arms.

ragas [KK], *me~,* to pull at or tear at, e.g., the hair (but not to tear out).

ragi [KN], 1. essence, alloy, colouring matter; leaven, yeast; *buta* ~, with the pattern washed out (of cloth); *burung me~,* the painted snipe (*Rostratula capensis*); *be~,* fermented with yeast. 2. the grain, ~.

ragu [KS], ~ *hati,* doubtful, uncertain; ~-~, hesitatingly; hesitating; *tak* ~-~, without hesitation undoubtedly; *ke~-~an,* suspense, anxiety, uncertainty; *me~kan,* suspicious of, be doubtful about.

ragum [KN], a vice or clip worked with a screw.

ragun [KK], *teragung-~,* knocking against one another (of heavy bodies hanging in a bunch).

ragup [KK], snatching and carrying away.

ragus [KS], *me~,* greed, gluttony; also *rakus.*

ragut [KK], *me~,* to tear out with violence (esp. hair); to drag at, pull at; *me~-~ rumput,* to crop grass.

rahang [KN], the jaw; *tulang* ~, the jawbone.

rahap [KN], *kain* ~, a pall cast over a body at a funeral but not buried with it.

rahat [KN], 1. a winder used in spinning. 2. *gugur* ~, a sudden and general (but untimely) fall of durians.

rahib [KN], Ar. a monk.

rahim [KS], 1. Ar. merciful, compassionate. 2. Ar. the uterus; also *raham.*

rahman [KS], Ar. merciful, compassionate, esp. of God.

rahmat [KS], Ar. mercy (esp. the mercy of God); *suatu* ~, a blessing, bit of luck, aid; *pulang ke* ~ *Allah,* to go home to the mercy of God, i.e. die; *moga-moga Allah limpahkan* ~ *ke atas rohnya,* may God have mercy on his soul.

rahsia [KN], Skr. a secret; 'information received'; *buka* ~, to reveal a secret; *taruh* ~, to keep a secret; ~ *sudah bocor,* the secret has leaked out; *polis* ~, the Special Branch of the police; *me~kan,* to keep secret, to suppress (news); also *rahasia.*

Rahu [KN], Skr. the dragon which is believed to attempt to swallow the moon (at eclipses); *bulan dimakan* ~, an eclipse.

rai [KK], *me~kar,* entertain guests, celebrate, have a gathering.

raih [KK], 1. to draw towards oneself; taking (as opposed to giving); *mujur tak dapat di* ~, *malang tak dapat ditolak,* we cannot draw good luck towards us nor can we avert bad luck. 2. Kel. to hawk, peddle; also, to buy here and there; *pe~,* dealer, middleman (esp. of fish-dealers: *pe~ ikan,* fish-dealer); also *rais.*

rais [KK], 1. to sweep off (as one sweeps crumbs off a table). 2. = *raih* 2.

raja [KN], Skr. prince, ruler, monarch; the king (in chess); ~ *berasal,* a prince by descent; ~ *bintang,* the principal heavenly bodies; ~ *digelar,* a prince by virtue of office; *Raja Muda,* a title given to the heir-apparent; ~ *sehari,* a bridegroom; ~ *udang,* (Southern part of Peninsular Malaysia) a kingfisher; (Northern part of Peninsular Malaysia) a large sandpiper; *anak ~,* a prince; *budak ~,* courtiers; retainers at court; *hamba ~,* menials about a court; *penyakit ~,* a malignant ulcer on the neck or shoulders; *pinang ~,* the red-stemmed palm (*Cyrtostachys lacca*); *ke~an,* rule, government, dominion, empire; *alat ke~an,* regalia; *burung ~,* Kel. the house-sparrow; *berke~an sendiri,* autonomous; *be~ di hati,* to act according to one's whims and fancies; *be~ di hati, bersultan di mata,* monarch of all one surveys.

Rajab [KN], Ar. the seventh month of the Muslim calendar; also *Rejab.*

rajah [KN], probing; groping for anything with a stick; tattooing; a design, geometrical sketch, diagram; *~kan,* to draw such a design.

rajalela; *me~; bermahrajalela* [KK], tyrannical; do something according to one's liking.

rajang [KN], N.S. a rope of rattans serving as a sort of bridge or as a line for a ferry.

rajau [KN], Pk. aftermath of rice-fields; *me~,* to glean such aftermath.

rajawali [KN], Skr. an eagle; *lang ~,* a name given to small hawks, e.g., *Tinnunculus alaudaris.*

raji [KN], *talak ~,* first and second divorce.

rajin [KS], persistent, frequent, diligent; assiduity; ~ *berbuat jahat,* persistent in doing wrong; ~ *dan usaha,* assiduity and diligence.

rajuk [KN], *me~,* to sulk; *pe~,* sullen; (person who) likes to fret, sulk or complain.

rajut [KN], knitting, darning; network; ~ *rambut,* hair-net.

rak [KN], 1. Kel. physical ability, physical well-being; *tak ~,* I can't manage it. 2. Eng., a kitchen shelf; *~~,* id.; also used for a book-case and a mantelpiece.

raka [KS], fragile, brittle, worm-eaten; esp. a fragile through damage, near breaking-point.

rakaat [KN], Ar. the series of ritual movements which follows a Muslim prayer; *sembahyang empat ~,* four prayers.

rakam [KK], Ar. *me~,* to inscribe indelibly, as on stone or by painting on cloth; so, to record; *~an,* a recording; *alat pe~ suara,* tape-recorder; *te~,* printed, imprinted, engraved.

rakan [KN], associate, companion, comrade, partner; *~an,* a partner in business; *buat ~,* to accompany; ~ *sekerja,* fellow worker; ~ *sejawat,* colleague.

rakap [KK], 1. *me~,* to creep at a snail's pace; to crawl; *orang hina me~,* a beggar crawling from door to door. 2. a stirrup; a pedal.

rakat [KN], a performance (with dancing and playing jokes).

raket [KN], racquet.

rakit [KN], arrangement side by side; the construction of a raft or of the framework of a house; a raft; *se ~,* a pair, e.g., two *sirih* leaves one over the other; *be~,* to sail with a raft; *be~~ ke hulu, berenang-renang ke tepian,* (prov.) after rain comes sunshine.

rakna = *ratna.*

raksa [KN], Skr. mercury, quicksilver.

raksamala [KN], a tree (*Altingiana excelsa*), yielding a perfumed gum.

raksaksa [KN], Skr. a ogre; a goblin; a giant generally; giantic; *rapat ~,* mammoth meeting.

raksi [KS], 1. yielding fragrance; *me~,* to perfume; *pe~,* flower petals and scented leaves used for perfuming a bed. 2. a person's star, i.e., the astrological force affecting his fortune; so, *se~,* harmonising; affinities; suiting one's constitution; lucky.

rakus [KS], greed, gluttony; *dengan ~nya,* greedily; also *ragus.*

rakut [KK], *me~,* to deceive, to set a snare, to weave a web (of a spider).

rakyat [KN], Ar. subject; the common people; the rank and file of an army, troops; *ke~an,* nationality; citizenship; *~ jelata,* the masses; *~ murba,* id.

ralat [KN], Ar. error (in writing); mistake; regret (for not having done something better).

ralip [KS], in a brown study, absorbed in something so as to be unconscious of one's surroundings. 2. usual, normal; *pada ~nya,* normally; also *ghalip.*

ram [KK], 1. *menge~,* brooding, sitting on eggs (of a hen); crouching over, e.g., prey. 2. *tingkap ~,* venetian blinds. 3. to coo.

Rama [KN], 1. Skr. *Seri ~,* the Hindu demi-god Rama. 2. *rama-rama,* a butterfly, a moth; *ringgit rama-rama,* the Mexican dollar. 3. Jav. father — *rama aji,* princely father; sire.

Ramadan [KN], Ar. the fasting-month or *bulan Puasa.*

ramah [KS], *pe~,* friendly; affable, gracious; *be~ dengan,* on friendly terms with; *pe~ mulut,* well-spoken, charming to talk to; *~ mesra,* friendly; *suasana ~ mesra,* friendly atmosphere; *be~-tamah,* mixing cordially; *~-mesra,* intimate.

ramai [KS], crowded, populous; numerously attended (of a festival); festive; joyous; *be~-~an,* attended by a large following; *me~kan,* to give population and prosperity to a place, enliven; *orang ~,* the public; *be~-~,* in crowds, en masse; *terbuka kepada ~,* open to the public; *di tengah ~,* in public; *ke~an,* a festivity, popular occasion.

ramal [KN], 1. Ar. soothsaying, horoscopic calculations; *me~kan,* to forecast, foretell; *memasang ~an,* to divine, practise divination; *~an,* a forecast; *tukang ~,* soothsayer, one who predicts the future; *~an pakar-pakar cuaca,* weather-

forecast. Pers. a scarf, a kerchief.

ramas [KK], *me~,* to knead; to massage; to squeeze.

rambah [KS], 1. moist, damp (of the ground). 2. *me~* [KK], to chop down, clear away; *me~ jalan,* to clear a way through.

rambai [KN], 1. a common fruit-tree (*Baccaurea Motleyana*). 2. *bulu ~,* short feathers on either side of the tail of a fowl.

rambaian [KN], hairy, bushy.

rambak [KK], extending in every direction (as a creeper); flourishing, prosperous; merambak, to spread in all directions; to do well, to prosper.

rambang [KS], extensive, wide, broad; *jala ~,* a casting-net without bait; *lela ~,* a wide-mouthed swivel-gun; *mulut ~,* erratic in talk; *~ mata,* roving (of wanton eyes); *me~,* to take a wide sweep (of a river); do something blindly; *tembak ~,* to shoot 'into the brown'.

rambas [KK], *me~,* exorcise evil spirit.

rambat [KK], *me~,* spreading in all directions (of plants).

rambih [KK], *be~* or *me~,* to go on an excursion with one's family.

rambu [KN], 1. a thick post; *~ perahu,* bitts. 2. a hanging fringe; *~-~,* id.; *tombak ~,* a spear with a hanging fringe under the spearhead; to wander about, forage round; *kaki ~,* a gadabout; rover, wanderer; *pandai me~-~,* id.

rambun [KN], tangled undergrowth; roots; climbers and creepers.

rambut [KN], hair; *~ ikal,* curly hair; *~ keriting,* curly or waved hair; *~ terurai,* dishevelled hair; *anak ~,* short hair round the central growth; *gigi ~,* the hair just as its junction with the forehead and neck; *kaki ~,* the hair on the neck; *suak ~,* the parting; *~ jejak ke bahu,* shoulder-length hair; *anak ~,* a ringlet; *be~ lepas labuh ke belakang,* with hair flowing loose down the back; *~i,* woollen cloth; *pe~,* the trace at the end of a fishing-line; *~ sama hitam, hati masing-masing berlainan* (prov.), we all have black hair but each of us has his own disposition.

rambutan [KN], the well-known fruit *Nephelium lappaceum;* a fruit with a hairy integument; cf. **rambut**; *rambutan lekang,* rambutans whose flesh comes easily away from the pip — a desirable attribute.

rambuti [KN], *kain ~,* woollen cloth.

rami [KN], 1. the rhea of China grass (*Boehmeria nivea*); hemp; *kain ~,* a coarse sacking made of *rami* fibre. 2. but *kain ~* is also used for linen.

rami, *~ bukit, ~ bulan, ~ hutan, ~ jantan* [KN], a type of shrub (*Alchornea villosa*).

ramik [KN], N.S. *~-~,* oddments, bits collected here and there, titbits of meat.

ramin [KN], loop-work in basketry; *bakul be~,* a basket of loopwork; *~kan,* to twist in loops.

rampai [KN], *~-~,* miscellaneous; of a mixed character, varied; also used for general or informal (as opposed to *tertentu* — definite, certain); *buku ~an,* miscellaneous book; notebook; *me~,* do various written exercises; *me~kan,* mixed different kinds of flowers; *bunga ~,* a fragrant preparation made by scattering pandan and other flowers; *~kan,* to scatter, to spread news, etc.

rampak [KS], spreading horizontally (of a tree); umbrageous.

rampas [KK], seizing, carrying off; *barang ~an,* booty, plunder; *me~,* to take by force, to confiscate.

rampat [KK], *me~,* sweeping about a long pole (or similar object) so as to strike all within a certain radius; giving sweeping blows instead of deliberately aimed blows; *memaki me~ papan,* abusing everybody who comes near; sweeping abuse; to abuse indiscriminately.

ramping [KS], 1. slender; lissom (of the waist); *~ sedang naik,* slender and just blossoming into full womanhood, to an adolescent girl; slender, but not thin, svelte; *manis ~,* id. 2. *~-rompang,* in torn rags.

rampok [KK], *me~,* to filibuster, to go plundering, as a brigand; *pe~an,* plundering, pillage.

rampus [KS], 1. *me~,* to be in a violent rage, fly into a rage. 2. = *rapus.*

ramput [KK], coarse, vulgar; not refined.

ramu [KK], *me~,* to collect materials of all sorts; *pe~ kayu,* a wood-gatherer; *~-~an,* miscellaneous material, odds and ends; ingredients; *~an,* ingredients generally; *sukatan ~an,* recipe; a collection (oddments picked up here and there); *me~,* to pick up what one can here and there.

ramus [KS], excessive hairiness; *be~,* overhairy (of the face); *buang ~,* to get rid of superfluous hair.

ran [KN], a tree-hut, a shooter's platform.

rana, 1. *me~* [KK], to pine; to languish; to be ailing, in distress; depressed; *sakit me~,* a wasting disease. 2. = *ratna.*

ranah, *punah-~* [KS], utterly destroyed.

ranak [KK], *be~-~,* to play in a swift tremolo; quivering and trembling (of voice, sound).

ranap [KS], *me~* [KK], to crumble under great pressure, flattened out (as bombed buildings); beaten down (of a crop of rice, grass, etc.), fallen (as a house after a hurricane); clean gone, disappeared.

rancah [KK], to mark a track by cutting down an occasional sapling.

rancak [KS] gay; continuous and lively (of music, dancing, etc.); *ke~an,* activeness.

rancang [KN], pointing upwards; a pointed stake stuck in the ground as a rude caltrop; *~an,* Ind. programme, plan; *~ Marshall,* the Marshall Plan; *me~,* to plan, scheme; *~an bandar,* town-planning; *~an jangka panjang,* long-term planning; *~an jangka pendek,* short-term planning; *(pe)~an keluarga,* family planning; *~an beranak,* id.

rancap [KK], *me~,* to masturbate (of males).

rancu [KS], mixed of dialects, confused, *me~kan,* to confuse.

rancung [KS], sharp cut; cut at a sharp

angle (of a pencil or quill pen); to sharpen to a point, as a pencil; cf. **runcing**.

randa [KK], *me~*, to wander about wildly; going here and there.

randai [KK], *me~*, to wade through shallow water.

randi [KN], a silk fabric of Chinese or Siamese make.

randu [KK], to stir liquid round and round with the arm.

randuk [KN], 1. *kambing ~*, a rank old he-goat. 2. *me~* [KK], treading down, wade, treading under-foot grass, crops, water; crashing through, e.g., a crowd.

randung [KK], *me~*, treading down; trample on — cf. **randuk** and **serandung**.

rang [KN], 1. *tanah ~*, a rice-field banked and previously cultivated, but lying fallow. 2. grade, rank. 3. the draft (of a letter); *~ undang-undang*, Bill of Rights.

rangah [KS], haughty, supercilious; *me~*, to swagger.

rangai [KS], 1. obstinate or chronic (of a disagreeable, but not dangerous disease). 2. Pk. *me~* [KK], to forage about like a thief; to ransack.

rangga [KN], 1. pointed projections; *me~*, sticking up in points (as the tine of a deer). 2. Jav. a title of inferior distinction.

ranggah [KK], 1. *me~*, to strip a tree of fruit. 2. to stab upwards, = *radak*.

ranggak [KK], hauling a boat ashore; to steal, pilfer.

ranggas [KN], a mass of twigs or fallen branches; a spiky mass of brushwood or fallen branches forming an abattis; *~ kayu*, id.; *be~--~*, bristling, of a obstruction; *me~*, bristling leafless (of trees).

ranggi [KS], Tam. smart in dress; attractive, 'putting on side'; spirited, lively, of a horse; *me~kan*, show off, brag.

ranggit [KS], *te~--~*, making convulsive movements.

ranggu [KK], *me~*, mix.

ranggul [KK], *me~*, to dip (of a boat's

bows); lifted up; raised — cf. **anggul**, **tanggul**.

Ranggun [KN], Rangoon.

ranggung [KK], *me~*, to crawl laboriously along (as infant or wounded man); to squat with the knees wide apart; *burung ~*, a long-legged water-bird; *kail ~*, fishing when two sticks project from the lead, a hook being suspended from the extremity of each stick; the paternoster on a fishing line; the basic idea seems to be, 'with trailing or outstretched legs'.

rangin [KN], Jav. shield.

rangka [KN], skeleton, framework; outlines (as of a scheme); a rough draft; *~kan* [KK], to frame, draft outlines; *be~*, possessing or serving as a framework.

rangkai [KN], strung or fastened together; *me~*, learning how to arrange flowers; *~an*, a string of, a combination; an expression, combination of words; a radio network; *be--~*, in strings or clusters (used of the 'strings' of maidens carried off by Siamese with a long thin rotan through the lobes of their ears); *tiga se~*, a trio, a trinity; *~ hati*, darling; *~-kata*, a phrase; *~ huruf*, the arrangement or method of joining letters.

rangkak [KK], *me~*, to crawl on hands and knees; to make slow progress; *me~--~*, (fig.) halting, of speech or reading.

rangkap [KN], 1. pair, set of two; a verse of a poem; *se~*, a pair, a verse; *be--~an*, in couples; *te~*, combined, e.g., fine and imprisonment; *pengerusi Umno me~ Menteri Besar*, combining the posts of Chairman of UMNO and Prime Minister; *me~*, to superimpose a thin flat object on another, as when sticking them together. 2. *pe~*, a trap; probably from 1., the idea being that the cover of the trap is superimposed on its floor; but *pe~* has come to be virtually a word on its own right; see *perangkap*.

rangkiang [KN], a rice-barn.

rangkik [KN], a generic name for shells of the genus *Canus*.

rangkul [KK], *me~*, to seize, to grip with

the arms and pick up (as in wrestling or as one picks up a child); to hold on to, hold in one's arms, support.

rangkum [KK], grasping between the hands; clasping (fig.) grabbing, gripping; *se ~*, as much as one can so grasp; (fig.) a part, a portion; *se ~ kata,* an extract from a speech; *me~,* to grasp; (fig.) to include; *~an,* grip.

rangkung [K], *me~,* to squat; *~an, kerongkongan,* throat.

rangkup [KK], *me~,* the formation of a cavity or channel between two sides which slope to meet each other; *me~ tangan,* to form a cup with the hands.

rangrang [KN], red ant.

rangsang [KK], *me~,* to stimulate, esp. in the sense of making pugnacious; *pe~,* an exciting drug, a stimulant; *memberi pe~,* to excite to passion; *buat pe~,* serving to stimulate, make keen, e.g., hunting dogs.

rangum [KK], snatching; grabbing at.

rangsum [KN], rations for soldiers.

rangup [KS], crisp (as a biscuit).

rani [KN], Hind. the wife of a prince or governor.

ranjang [KN], 1. a pallet bed; plaited work, basketwork.

ranjau [KN], a caltrop; *~ cacak,* pointed stakes driven into the ground with the points uppermost; difficulties; trials; *me~,* drive stakes into the ground; *~ mata parut,* a plank with nails projecting out of it; *~ mata satu,* a caltrop consisting of a plank and a spike; *~ mata tiga,* the common caltrop, *~* is used for a military mine, esp. a seamine (*~ laut,* id.); *kapal ponyibar ~,* a mine-layer, *kapal penyapu ~,* a minesweeper.

ransun [KN], rations; *nasi ~,* a mass meal, meal in a mess; *kedai ~,* a general (grocer's) shop; *perempuan ~,* a Japanese army prostitute; also *ramsum.*

Ranjuna [KN], Skr. also *Sang ~,* the hero famed in Indian and (later) Javanese legend; noted for his beauty and skill in archery; often corrupted to Arjuna, q.v.

rantai [KN], a chain; of metal or as a measure of 22 yards; *be~,* wear a chain, necklace etc.; *pe~an,* chained convict; *~an,* a chain, as of mountains; *baju ~,* a coat of chainmail; *~kan,* to put in chains.

rantam [KK], *be~,* clubbing together for a common purchase, e.g., of villagers, to purchase a buffalo to slaughter, or cooperating in work.

rantang [KN], a basket or hamper for provisions, crockery, etc.

rantau [KN], a reach of a river or of the seacoast; *teluk ~,* bights and reaches; entire territory; *di ~ orang,* abroad; *me~,* to go wandering; to emigrate; *~ orang,* foreign parts; *pe~,* expatriate, one who adventures abroad; *pe~an,* far journey; emigration; foreign parts.

ranting [KN], a minor branch, a twig; *belalang ~,* a stick insect; *kuang ~,* the peacock pheasant (*Polyplectron bicalcaratum*); sometimes used for a small branch of a society.

ranum [KS], *masak ~,* fully ripe (of fruit).

ranyah [KK], *me~,* to pick small pieces of food here and there out of a dish.

rap [KN], 1. Ked. *tanah ~,* land cleared, weeded and banked, and ready for cultivation. 2. (onom.) the sound of rapping or stamping.

rapah [KK], 1. to walk roughly over anything, blunder over felled logs; to force a way through; e.g., a thicket, Pk. to go over a rice-field and weed with the *keri* a month after planting. 2. Jav. a meeting; *~ raksasa,* a mammoth meeting; *~ umum,* a public meeting.

rapai [KK], *me~,* to fumble with, to grope for, to fondle — cf. **gerapai.**

rapang [KN], *ikan ~,* a fish (Mugil bleekeri).

rapat [KS], 1. continuous; to approach close to; *sahabat yang ~,* close friends; *me~kan,* to move closer; to fit two things together (as a joiner); *me~i,* approach, draw near, often visit; *tutup ~,* to shut tightly; *pe~an,* the joining point of, e.g., floor-planks. 2. = *rapah* 2.

rapi [KS], Ind. neat, well-finished; tidy;

me~kan, to fix; *dia me~kan sanggulnya,* she fixed her hairdo; *kawalan ~,* strict guard.

rapih [KK], pull down, haul in; draw towards oneself, as when shortening a line.

rapik [KK], *me~,* to talk nonsense; *me~!,* nonsense! — cf. **apik**.

rapu [KK], *me~,* to pick up trifles — cf. **ramu;** *me~ dana,* to beg.

rapuh [KS], 1. brittle, fragile; *~ mulut,* unable to control one's tongue; *bernyawa ~,* very feeble, near to death; *~ hati,* tender/soft hearted, weak willed; spineless. 2. *terung ~,* a green brinjal (unidentified).

rapung [KK], Ind. *me~,* to rise upwards, rise to the surface.

rapus [KK], *me~,* to pinion; to throw, e.g. a buffalo, for slaughter.

ras [KN], 1. Hind. the reins. 2. (onom.) a rustle. 3. race.

rasa [KN], 1. Skr. taste, flavour, perception, sensations, feeling; *~ hati,* perception; *~nya,* it seems, it appears; as it were; *putus ~,* forgetful, unsympathetic; *se~,* resembling (in taste); like; *timpa ~,* to bear the brunt of anything; *timbang ~,* to show sympathy; show consideration; be tolerant; *lari timbang ~,* consolation race; *me~,* to feel; *be~,* feeling; *pe~an,* perception, impression, feeling, opinion; also *perasan; hati be~ nak,* to feel inclined to...; *te~-~,* continually irritating (of a nagging pain, such as caused by a thorn in the flesh or by something in the eye); *~kan,* used (sl.) with the idea of feeling something by way of punishment; *~kanlah!,* take that!. 2. Skr. mercury, quicksilver; also *raksa.*

rasai [KK], *me~kan,* to experience (painfully); *pe~an,* painful experience, blow, ill-luck.

rasau [KN], 1. wild growing, screw-pine (*Pandanus russow*). 2. *me~,* to make a swishing noise (of branches moved by the wind).

rasuah [KN], Ar. bribe; an illegal gratification.

rasi [KN], constellation, star(s); *se~,* suitable, belonging together, right.

rasional [KS], rational.

rasmi [KS], 1. Ar. natural, characteristic, the adjective of *resam* official; *jam ~, waktu ~,* official time; *ahli yang bukan ~,* Unofficial Member; *dengan ~nya,* officially; *me~kan,* to make official; to inaugurate (as a public building) with ceremony, open; sometimes = *resam.* 2. *secara separuh ~,* semi-officially.

rasuk [KK], 1. the attack of an evil spirit; *di~, kena ~,* or *di~, hantu,* to be possessed of a devil; to be affected by some spirit of disease; *ke~an,* being possessed by evil spirit. 2. cross-beams from pillar to pillar. 3. *se ~,* suitable, adapted to (as a particular kind of manure to a plant).

rasul [KN], Ar. apostle; one sent by God; *~ Allah,* God's apostle, Muhammad; also *Rasulullah; kisah segala ~,* the Acts of the Apostles; *ke~an,* apostolate.

rasyid [KN], Ar. orthodox, *Harun al-~,* the famous Caliph of Baghdad, sometimes used as a Malay proper name.

rat [KK], 1. constricted; *segenggam ~,* a tight handful; *menge~,* to squeeze. 2. (kawi) the earth; *jaya ning~,* conqueror of the world. 3. Kel. tame, docile.

rata [KS], 1. (1) level, even, flat (of surface); *~-~,* on the average; *sama ~,* the same level; equally; *pe~kan* or *me~kan,* to smooth; *menye~kan,* spread or scatter everywhere; (2) on the level of the ground, prostrate; *jatuhlah dia ~ ke bumi,* he fell flat on the earth; (3) bringing everything to the same level; completing; 'rounding off'; *~-~,* everywhere; *se~,* all over; *me~,* to spread over; *pukul ~,* to strike an average; *hitung ~,* id. 2. Skr. a chariot (esp. the winged chariots of the gods).

ratah [KS], plain (of food when eaten without rice or vegetables); *me~* [KK], to eat food without rice.

ratap [KK], loud mourning; *me~,* to wail, bemoan, keen, lament; *~kan,* to lament over; *me~i*, cry for; *~an*, lament, cries.

ratib [KN], Ar. the constant repetition of the name of Allah, creating a sort of ecstatic trance; wild devotional cries accompanied by shaking of the body.

ratna [KN], Skr. a jewel; a princess (in titles).

ratu [KN], Jav. a prince, a princess; *Sang Ratu*, the king; *Ratu Kuripan*, the Prince of Kuripan, Panji; ~ is used for 'queen' in certain contexts: ~ *lebah*, queen-bee; ~ *cantik*, beauty queen.

ratus [KBil], hundred; *se* ~, one hundred; *be~~*, in hundreds; *~an*, hundreds, in hundreds; *pe~*, per cent; *pe~an*, a percentage; *upah mengikut kira pe~an*, payment on a percentage basis; *menye~i*, hold a religious feast In remembrance of a person, a hundred days after his death.

rau [KN], 1. (onom.) a sound — such as that of rushing water; *~~*, a clapper-rattle or sistrum. 2. Pah. ~, *erau*, *menge~*, to fish by dragging a rope across a stream — cf. **relap**.

raum [KN], (onom.) a deep crooning moaning sound; *me~ dan meratap*, to moan and lament.

raun [KK], Eng. rounds (as of police).

raung [KN], (onom.) a roar of agony; *me~* [KK], to cry out in pain.

raup [KK], *me~*, to scoop up with both hands; to put the hands together cupwise; to take up, e.g., water, in the cupped hands, *be~*, in double handfuls.

raut [KN], smooth, cut off asperities; clear-cut, of features; *mukanya bagai di~*, his features were clear-cut; *~an tubuh*, shape of figure; sometimes *~an* is used of the cut of dress; *pisau* ~, a small sharp knife for whittling a stick.

rawa [KN], 1. *burung* ~, the pied imperial pigeon (*Myristicivora bicolor*). 2. a marsh. 3. a tree with edible fruit (*Mangifera microphylla*). 4. a shrimpnet, = *sungkur; kain* ~, coarse sacking. 5. *orang* ~, the name of a race in Sumatra.

rawai [KN], a line of unbaited hooks intended to foul-hook fish; *me~*, (1) to fish with this contrivance, (2) Pen. to beg from door to door.

rawak [KK], *me~*, to fire aimlessly, random.

rawan [KS], 1. emotion (esp. tenderness); *memberi* ~, to stir the emotions. 2. numeral coefficient for articles made of cordage or string. 3. *tulang* ~, the sternum; also cartilage. 4. *me~*, in the clouds, berawan, melancholy, low spirited; *me~*, *me~i*, troubled or disturbed about. 5. Pers. *takhta* ~, a vehicle mentioned in romance.

rawang [ ], 1. a hole or orifice, a gap; *ke~*, fretwork; *berke~*, fretted (of wood or metal work, e.g., of a brass tray, having open-work, of lace). 2. a morass. 3. *me~*, to wash a body for burial.

rawat [KK], 1. to attend, wait on, treat; *~an*, medical treatment; *juru~*, a hospital nurse. 2. *me~*, to resume one's original form after a transformation; *pe~an*, nursing, care.

rawi [KN], Ar. a narrator, a story-teller; the author.

rawit [KK], 1. *me~*, to drag fresh people into a scandal — cf. **babit**. 2. Jav. small; *cabai* ~, a capsicum (*Capsicum fastigiatum*).

raya [KS], great, large; *badak* ~, the large variety of rhinoceros (*Rhinoceros sondaicus*); *bulan pernama* ~, the full moon at its brightest; *bunga* ~, the cultivated hibiscus; *dewata mulia* ~, the most high gods; *hari~*, a holiday; *berhari~*, to make a holiday of an event; *hantu* ~, an evil spirit of great power and savagery; *Jalan~*, the high road; *landak* ~, the large porcupine (*Hystrix longicauda*); *rimba* ~, primeval jungle; *tanah* ~, the mainland, the continent; *me~kan*, to celebrate; to entertain; *pe~an*, celebration, festivity; *ini harus di~kan*, this calls for a celebration; *elaun ke~an*, entertainment allowance.

rayan-rayan [KN], a sort of influenza (particularly a children's ailment).

rayang [KS], dizzy, light-headed.

rayap [KK], 1. *me~*, crawling, creeping (of insects); *me~i*, to creep over, crawl over, esp. as a plant over a wall; also of a hand; *tangannya me~i tubuh gadis itu*, he pawed the girl. 2. the white ant, = *anai-anai*.

rayau [KK], *me~*, to wander along at random; to prowl.

rayu [KS], plaintive melancholy, stirring the emotions, rousing pity or allying wrath; *me~* [KK], to influence, to affect (as notes of music affect the hearer), to appeal (to), petition, to sweet talk; *~ hal*, a petition (to authorities); *~an*, petition, appeal; *lembaga ~an*, Appeals Board.

reaksi [KK], Ind. reaction, responsive effect.

reba [KN], fallen timber, felled masses of brushwood and undergrowth; an abattis.

rebab [KN], a Malay viol; a mandolin; cf. **kecapi**; *tempurung ~*, the drum of a viol.

rebah [KK], falling (through weakness, not violence); *~ pengsan*, falling in a faint; *~kan*, to let fall aslant, as when felling a tree; *~kan diri*, to throw oneself down; *~-rempah*, to have a big fall, e.g. sprawling and rolling; *dapat tebu ~*, (idiom) to be lucky; *sokong membawa ~*, to be betrayed by one's own friend.

rebak [KK], *me~*, to spread, as perfume or as a sore or as disorder, extend, satter.

reban [KN], a fowl-house; *~ ayam*, id.; *me~kan*, coop up.

rebana [KN], Hind. tambourine.

rebang [KK], *me~*, let tresses loose; *me~kan*, loosen, spread out (hairs).

rebas [KK], 1. falling into decay (of a wooden building); pouring down, as rain or tears; *hujan ~*, a heavy shower of rain. 2. to throw away, so (sl.) to ease oneself.

rebat [KK], *me~*, to block an entrance or exit; to barricade; to put, e.g., barbed wire or thorns as a barrier; to close (a road).

rebeh [KS], 1. injured on one side only (as a bird with a broken wing); so, wobbling. 2. [KS], *~-rebek*, tattered and torn (of clothes etc.), old, worn-thin.

rebis [KK], to fall, slip down, e.g., as sand on the side of a pit; *te~* (or *terbis*), slipped down.

rebuk [KN], *me~*, to fester (of a sore).

rebung [KN], the edible young bamboo shoot; *pucuk ~*, chevrons (as a design in art).

rebus [KK], boiling in and with water (as distinct from boiling by immersion in boiling water); *ayam ~*, boiled fowl; *~an*, a (boiled) decoction.

rebut [KK], snatching, tearing away; *be~*, to snatch, to struggle for anything; *me~*, to try to seize, to struggle to get; *pertandingan me~ piala*, Cup-competition; *me~ peluang*, to seize the opportunity; *me~ kerusi*, to contest a seat at an election; *main me~ kerusi*, to play musical chairs; *menjadi ~an antara*, to be a bone of contention between; *pe~an kuasa*, (violent) seizure of power, coup d'etat.

recak [KN], 1. *~-~*, slightly pock-pitted. 2. [KK], *me~*, to sit astride.

recik [KK], *me~*, to splash up; to show drops of water or mud (as one who is splashed); *jamjam me~*, a euphemism for perspiration; *pe~*, splashed, dotted, speckled; splashes; (fig.) chips, flying fragments; *~an air*, spray, splashed water; *pe~kan*, to sprinkle (as water, salt).

recup [KN], to appear just above the surface; to begin to sprout up; *me~ bak cendawan*, to spring up like mushrooms.

reda [KK], abating, lessening (of rain, waters, nuisance, crime); *me~kan*, to calm down, soothe.

redah [KK], 1. *me~*, cutting a track through the jungle; to force one's way through; *me~ paya*, to force one's way through a marsh. 2. = *redih; anak ~an*, seedlings.

redaksi [KN], Ind. editorial staff.

redam [KS], 1. *~-~*, *me~*, faintly visible, e.g., of ships; or faintly audible. 2. *re-*

muk ~, crushed to atoms; ~ *padam,* completely extinguished.

redan [KN], a large tree (*Nephelium Maingayi*).

redang [KN], Ked. a deep swamp.

redap [KN], 1. a small hand-drum or tabor. 2. *me*~, to spring up plentifully (of pustules); to spread, as an ulcer; tumor, rash.

redas [KK], making straight for a point; *me*~, (i) to make one's way through the jungle; cf. **redah** 1.; (2) to fell fruits by throwing sticks etc. (esp. children).

redi [KN], a sort of hammock-litter (much used in the past by Straits-born Chinese women).

redih [KK], *me*~, to plant out rice in a secondary nursery before planting out in the field; *anak* ~*an,* seedlings; also *redah.*

redik [KK], *me*~, to threaten or scold; cf. **hardik.**

redum [KS], 1. obscure, gloomy; the darkness that precedes a storm — cf. **redup.** 2. closing a road to traffic — cf. **rebat.**

redup [KS], dimmed, obscured (of the rays of the sun); overcast, gloomy weather; also, dull of colour; *me*~*kan,* cloud, make gloomy; ~*kan lampu,* to lower the light, to dim a light; cf. **redum**; *ke*~*an,* cloudiness.

regang [KS], stretching to full length; so, to put up (a tennis net); taut; tight; *me*~ *layar,* to boom out a sail to its full stretch; *me*~ is sometimes used now of 'holding up' (by robbers); ~*kan,* to pull taut; *be*~~~, stretch the limbs of the body; *berse*~, quarrel, dispute; *me*~ *nyawa,* to be dying, to be in o's death struggle; *me*~ *telinga,* to teach a person a lesson.

regas [KK], to cut with a saw.

regat, meregat [KK], to take a short direct cut.

regu [KN], Ind. a plough; a team, a pair (in doubles).

regut [KK], a variant of *renggut;* ~*kan bibir,* to kiss passionately (as if tearing at the lips).

rehat [KK], Ar. a rest; *be*~, to rise for recess (of Parliament); *bilik* ~, recreation room; ~ is sometimes used for halftime, at a match.

reja [KN], Hind. (from Pers.) scraps left over; leavings; ~~~ *kain,* the bits of cloth left over when garments are made.

Rejab [KN], Ar. the name of a Malay month; often called *bulan kahwin* because it is a popular month for weddings.

rejah [KK], *me*~, thrust oneself foward without caring for others; *pe*~ [KN], unmannerly and self-assertive.

rejam [KK], Ar. stoning; thrusting down and suffocating under mud, water, etc.; to throw (a missile); *me*~, to pelt.

rejan [KK], *me*~, pain in evacuations; painful straining, e.g., in child-bearing; *batuk* ~, deep coughing, as in whooping-cough.

rejang [KN], 1. a spring forward; *se*~ *kuda berlari,* as far as a horse can gallop at a stretch. 2. a name given to a series of symbols, one for each day of the month; these symbols are believed to affect the 'luck' of the day; astrological calendar. 3. a tree (*Alstonia scholaris* or *Acronychia laurifolia*).

rejeh [KS], blear-eyed; looking askew.

rejuk [KN], a standing jump (as opposed to the running jump); *me*~, to spring or leap in this way.

reka [K], Skr. composition, stringing together, = *karang;* ~*an,* a narrative, a tale; an invention; design, invent; *me*~ [KK], to invent; *pe*~, an inventor; *pe*~ *fesyen,* dress-designer.

rekah [KK], splitting, cracking; *saga me*~, *delima me*~, similes for a beautiful red mouth; ~*an,* a crack, a split opening; ~*an dada,* the cleft between the breasts.

rekam [KN], *hati* ~, sullen with concealed anger.

rekat [KN], adhesion, cleaving, sticking; *pe*~, glue, gum; *me*~, to gum together, to paste.

rekod [KN], Eng. a record, best performance, limit hitherto attained; *mencipta*

~, to set up a record; *membuat* ~, id.; *menyamai* ~, to equal a record; *mengatasi* ~, to beat a record.

rela [KK], Ar. willing, consenting; *me~kan*, to please, to give satisfaction to; *be~-~*, to be submissive, subservient, esp. in face of threats; to 'lump it'; *me~kan diri*, to resign oneself, accept the inevitable; *ke~an*, permission.

relah [KK], *me~kan*, ripping, splitting along a seam.

relai [KK], crumbled to pieces (as very rotten wood); *reput* ~, id.; to fall to pieces, disintegrate.

relang [KN], a ring of rattan, e.g., a collar for a dog.

relap [KN], a flash; *me~*, to flash; *tali* ~, Pk. a thick rope of *ijuk* hung with rushes and used for driving fish towards a trap of the *belat* type.

relas [KK], the scraping off of skin, abrasion; ~ *jagung*, to strip the sheath off maize grain; *me~*, (1) to trim a cock's comb; (2) abraded, e.g., from the scratch of thorns; variant = *melelas*.

relau [KN], a smelting-furnace; so, glaring (of lights).

reluh [KN], (onom.) a low grunting sound; *me~*, to snore; to grunt.

relung [KN], 1. a Malay measure of area; 1-1/3 acres in Penang, 1/10 acre in Kedah. 2. a cavity, hollow; *me~* to overarch so as to create a hollow.

remaja [KN], Skr. adolescent, just ripening into full maturity; *putera* ~, a prince just before he attains a marriageable age; *puteri* ~, a princess at a similar age.

remak [KKtr], liefer, better, rather it were better that; it were preferable; ~ *mati haram tak lari*, better die; never, never run away!

remang [KS], 1. a thick, cloudy (of weather). 2. stiff, stiffly erect (of coarse hair); *me~ bulu roma*, having goose-flesh (as from horror); *me~ bulu*, to bristle up, as hair of dog or feathers of cock.

remba [KS], Pen. *jalan be~-~*, walking in pairs.

rembah [KK], *me~*, to trickle (tears); *~-rembih*, slipping down, as a sarong badly fastened; streaming down, as tears.

remban [KK], Pk. to hack, slash.

rembang [KS], 1. the meridian; *matahari sedangnya* ~, the sun at its zenith, high point, *be~*, *me~*, reach its zenith; *hari sudah be~ petang*, late in the afternoon. 2. Ked. *pe~*, to aim at, = *tuju*.

rembas [KS], 1. utterly disappeared or destroyed; *habis* ~, completely gone — a strong form of *habis*. 2. Pk. to display anger by action or words.

rembat [KN], 1. a cross-bar, the bars across a fence or gate; the bar holding together the upright stakes in a fish-trap, a long pole fixed parallel to the gunwale of a boat; *~i*, to strengthen with a cross-piece. 2. *me~*, beat, whip.

rembet [KK], 1. encumbrance, e.g., from dependents; obstruction; anything which interferes with motion. 2. *me~-~*, to spread wide, as a plant (fig.) to digress.

rembia [KN], the sago palm.

rembih [KK], trickle (of tears).

rembulan [KN], (poet.) the moon; *Sang Rembulan*, Mr. Moon.

rembung [KN], Treng. sea-anemone.

rembunai [KS], average (of height); fair or medium size.

remeh [KS], Ind. trifling, unimportant; *ini soal* ~, this is a matter of little consequence.

remis [KN], a tiny bivalve edible shellfish.

rempah [KN], drug, spice; ingredient; currystuff; *inilah ~nya*, these are the ingredients; this is the recipe or prescription; *~-ratus*, mixed spices (fig.) miscellany, jottings; *~-pawah*, mixed spices.

rempak [KS], *se~*, in unison, in harmony; simultaneous, running concurrently.

rempang [KS], ~ *bahasa*, slightly mad; eccentric.

rempat [KK], blown aside (e.g., on a lee shore) by bad weather; drifting helplessly; *me~ ke sana ke sini*, drifting about (esp. as a vagrant).

rempih [KK], Pk. to clear weeds with a *tajak.*

rempit [KK], Pk. to strike with a stick or cane, to swish.

rempuh [KK], *me~,* knock over, upset, barge through; to collide, clash (as rival gangs); to head into the wind; to charge into, e.g., a fence; to break through; barging against one another, as ships adrift or as persons in a crowd; *be~--an,* rush; *~an,* charge, scramble.

rempung [KK], *me~,* pinion (a man); tie the legs (as of a fowl) together.

remudu [KN], Ked. = *berudu.*

remuk [KS], smashed or dashed to pieces; *~ redam,* crushed to atoms.

remunggai [KN], the horse-radish (*Moringa ptergosperma*); also *merunggai.*

remunia [KN], a fruit-tree (*Bouea macrophylla*), bearing a small acid fruit.

remut [KK], *me~,* to throb, pulsate; so, to swarm in a mass, as ants.

renang [KK], *be~,* to swim; *be~ katak,* to swim breast-stroke; *be~ belakang,* to swim on the back; *be~ rayap,* to do the 'crawl'; *pelampung be~,* water-wings; *ahli be~,* a swimmer (esp. in a race).

renap [KK], breaking in (as elephants).

renas [KK], *be~,* sprouting well, established (of young plants); of a speech, lively, spirited.

rencah [KK], 1. *me~,* to plough through thick and thin; to travel through jungle and swamp without stopping to choose the easiest way, to wade through the mud. 2. pe~, flavouring; spicy or salted titbits; *~-~,* id.

rencoak [KN], a large kind of cauldron.

rencam [KK], not fixed, not conforming to any set pattern; *me~,* confused (for the eye); *hati ~,* fancy-free and fickle; *duta ~,* ambassador-at-large. 2. bristling, as seedlings or as spikes.

rencana [KN], 1. narrative; precis; transcription; account; dictation; article (in newspaper); *~kan,* to relate; to dictate. 2. Ind. plan, programme; *~ lima tahun,* five year plan; *me~kan,* to plan; *pe~an,*

planning; the plot of a story.

rencat [KK], *te~,* checked in growth or progress.

renda [KN], Port. lace (esp. gold lace and silver lace).

rendah [KS], 1. low; short; of limited height; low of voice; *me~kan diri,* to assume a humble tone, to abase oneself; *~ hati,* modest, humble; *ke~an hati,* humility; *dengan segala ke~an hati,* with all due respect; *me~kan suara,* to lower the voice; *me~-~kan,* to disparage, 'run down'. 2. *riuh-~,* in an uproar, tumultuous — stronger than *riuh; me~,* to resound.

rendam [KK], immersion in water or mud; *ular sawa ~,* the reticulate python when aquatic in its habits; *be~,* to wallow (of a buffalo); to plunge into water; *me~kan,* to immerse, to submerge.

rendang [KN], baking or frying; *me~* [KK], to bake, to fry; esp. when making a dry curry; to fry with oil or fat, frying away the oil so that dry food is left; *me~ pedas,* to 'devil'.

rendang [KS], umbrageous; leafy; *pohon kayu ~,* a shady tree; *pokok ~ melempai,* a tree with thick drooping branches, a weeping tree.

reneh [KK], *me~,* to bubble out, exude.

renek [KS], tremulous (of the voice when singing); *menge~,* to make the voice quaver over a succession of notes.

reng [KN], 1. *burung ~* a vulture (of which three var. are known in the Northern part of Peninsular Malaysia). 2. Kel. backbone, staying power; *tak ada ~,* he can't stay.

renga [KS], *be~,* maggoty.

rengang [KN], Ked. throbbing pains in the head.

rengap [KN], (onom.) *be~,* to puff out (a flame).

rengas [KN], a generic name given to some trees which yield fine timber, but whose sap is virulently poisonous (*Melanorhoea Curtisii, M. Wallichii* and *Gluta rengas*).

rengat [KN], griping pain, colic; *~ hati,* intensely angry — a stronger expression than *sakit hati*.

rengau [KS], opening wide; *pe~*, wide open.

rengek [KK], *me~*, to whine or cry for something (of a child); to whimper.

rengga [KK], Ked. = *rengka;* [KN], howdah; seat fastened to the back of an elephant.

renggah [KK], to pull down roughly, as fruit.

renggam [KN], Ked. a sickle; = *tuai*.

renggang [KS], distant, apart; asunder, showing an opening, as a developing crack; *te~*, gaping open; *saudara ~*, a distant relative; *~kan*, to open out; to create a gap between; *~kan pintu sikit*, to open a door slightly, so that it is ajar; *~* may be said to be the opposite of *rapat*; cf. the saying, *kalau tak ada rial di pinggang, saudara yang rapat menjadi ~*, if you have no dollars at your waist, your near relatives become distant.

renggik [KK], *me~*, to be protracted; to drag on.

renggis [KS], thin; with few branches and leaves (of a tree); scraggy; also *ringgis*.

renggut [KK], *me~kan*, to tear down or tear away, e.g., a nest, tug at oars, tear greedily at food; to snuff out; *kecelakaan itu me~ nyawanya*, the accident snuffed out his life.

rengit [KN], a kind of sand-fly.

rengka [KN], the saddle on which a howdah rests; sometims, the howdah itself; cf. **kop**.

rengkah [KK], 1. to crack, split; *me~*, to gape open; a variant of *rekah*. 2. swell (of breast from milk).

rengkam [KN], 1. a growth (*Sargassum* sp.) found on coral rock. 2. not opening properly, as a casting net. 3. uncomfortable (of stomach).

rengkang [KK], arguing hotly.

rengkat [KS], *kaki ~*, one leg shorter than the other, unequal in length of legs, the halting gait caused thereby.

rengkeh [KK], *me~*, to bow or stoop under a burden.

rengkiang [KN], a granary, a barn on posts; also *lengkiang*.

rengkuh [KK], 1. *me~*, to tear violently at, e.g., food; to push or pull violently at, to wrench; *biar cermat, jangan ~*, let it be done carefully (don't wrench at it, go at a job gently). 2. *~an*, griefs, woes.

rengkuk [KK], *me~*, to crouch huddled up (fig.) to lie helpless, as a prisoner, to 'languish'.

rengkung [KN], = k*erongkung; biji ~*, tonsils.

rengsa [KS], listless, apathetic; of a disease, obstinate, persistent.

rengus [KS], *pe~*, gruff, surly; *me~* [KK], to speak in a surly way.

rengut [KK], *me~*, to murmur, to grumble.

renik [KS], fine, delicate, minute.

renjak [KK], *me~*, to walk along springily.

renjas [KK], *me~*, (Pen.) to bounce in anger, to flounce away, show anger by action; *me~ keluar*, to flounce out.

renjis [KK], *~kan, me~kan*, to besprinkle, to dash drops of water over; used esp. of dribbling water from the mouth on to a pet bird in order to wash and tame it; *~ minyak*, to baste.

renta [KK], *me~*, to speak angrily or in high tones.

renta [KS], *tua ~*, old and weak; decrepit.

rentak [KK], 1. *me~*, to stamp the foot in excitement or anger; *me~kan kaki*, id. 2. haul, tug at chain or rope; *se~*, co-ordinated; simultaneous; *hukuman berjalan se~*, running concurrently (of sentences for two offences); *~* is also used for 'tempo' in music; *~ irama*, rhythm of music; *mengikut ~*, in time with; *mengikut ~ kaki*, to keep in step; *~ suara*, intonation.

rentaka [KN], a small swivel-gun.

rentan [KS], a weak state of health predisposing to disease (but not actual disease), low (of vitality).

rentap [KK], *me~*, pulling, hauling, tugging, e.g., of a motor engine running badly and spasmodically; to snatch roughly.

rentas [KN], a path cut through the jungle; a short cut; *me~*, to take a short cut, take the direct route.

rentung [KS], scorched and blackened by fire.

renung [KK], a fixed and steady look at anything, to look searchingly at; the idea is of a fixed yet somewhat abstracted gaze, as opposed to keen minute scrutiny (*bedek* and *belek*); *me~i*, observe, gaze at; *me~kan*, contemplate, reflect.

renut [KN], *tali ~*, the belly-band in the harness of an elephant.

renyah [KS], 1. troublesome, 'ticklish' (of a job); *be~* [KK], to take great pains, to be meticulous; *me~*, to pester, to annoy. 2. = *renjas*.

renyai [KN], drizzling (of rain); *peluhnya be~an*, dripping with perspiration.

renyak [KK], *me~*, to press with one's weight, come down heavily; bear with weight on, press hard down.

renyap [KK], *me~*, hit (especially on the mouth).

renyeh [KK], *me~*, to behave in an ill-humoured way.

renyih [KK], *me~*, flounce with anger.

renyuk [KS], 1. crumpled, crushed, pounded to pieces; = *remuk*. 2. = *renjas*.

renyut [KK], 1. = *denyut*. 2. *be~*, seething (as ants).

repak [KN], (onom.) a 'slapping' noise.

repang [KS], smoothed; cut, trimmed or filed to the same level, levelled; *me~*, to trim; level, as hair or a hedge; *pe~*, diameter of a tree, (lit.) the smooth sawn end of a felled stump; *~(an)*, a cross-section.

repas [KS], fragile, crumbling; *~ layu*, withered to fragility (of a flower).

repek [KK], 1. = *repet*. 2. Kel. to chide, rebuke; talk nonsense.

repes [KK], *me~*, to fidget.

repet [KK], *me~*, to chatter.

repih [KK], *me~*, to pluck a little at a time; to pick away.

repis [KN], *se ~*, a chip.

repuh [KN], first growths on abandoned land; an overgrown clearing.

repui [KS], crumbling, extremely decayed.

reput [KS], rotting.

resa [KN], internal motions — such as digestive motions, motions in child-birth, etc.

resah [KS], restless, fidgeting; a feeling of discomfort, *buat ~*, to keep on the move, not lounge about; *ke~an*, anxiety, restlessness.

resak [KN], a generic name given to several timbers used in boat-building, e.g., *Shorea barbata, Castanopssiss nephelioides*, and other woods.

resam [KN], 1. bracken (*Gleichenia linearis*); *kalam ~*, the old-time pen made from a bracken stalk. 2. Ar. custom, constitution, habit; *~ tubuh*, bodily constitution.

resan [KK], taking as personal, taking offence.

resap [KK], *me~*, to permeate or percolate gradually; to merge slowly into surroundings (as water seeping in or out, as dew vanishing, as propaganda making headway); *me~kan*, absorbed, take in.

Resi [KN], Skr. a 'Rishi'; a sage, a Hindu hermit.

resip [KK], to seep slowly in or out; to ooze in or out; *angin me~ sahaja*, the air is just slowly oozing out (of a slow puncture).

resit [KN], Eng. receipt.

restung [KN], syphilitic ulceration of the nose, lupus.

restu [KN], a blessing or curse; a spell; *doa ~*, id.; *me~kan*, to cast a spell on for good or evil; to curse or bless; memberikan doa *~*, to invoke a blessing (curse); *mohon doa ~*, wish me luck.

reta [KK], *me~~*, to chatter inconsequentially, to talk wildly; *ke~an*, wild, irresponsible talk; also *retak*.

retak [KS], a crack; a line, the result of a crack; the lines on the hand; *~-belah*, deficiences, weak points; *~ menanti belah*, the crack awaits (i.e. heralds) the split; a dangerous situation.

retal [KN], saffron; also *hartal.*

retas [KS], breaking or giving way (as a fragile seam); *me~,* to unpick, to rip open; *me~ jalan,* to clear a way.

retik [KK], *me~,* 1. to crackle and splutter in the fire. 2. to hop about, as prawns in a net. 3. to form blisters or watery pustules; also *retih.*

retin [KN], diamonds (in cards).

retuk [KK], *me~,* to shirk one's share of work.

rewak [KK], *me~,* to become known, be spread abroad; as news or troubles; cf. **rebak.**

rewang [KK], *me~,* 1. to yaw (of ship), to change course; to fall off-course; to swing, of a ship to wobble; *fikiran me~,* anxious, confused. 2. act at random.

rewel [KS], troublesome, tiresome, of behaviour; *ke~an,* trouble, difficulty.

rezeki [KN], Ar. food, daily bread, livelihood, source of income; 'jam', a bit of luck; *~ mata,* a delight to see, a sight for sore eyes; *~ musang,* an easy prey for 'wolves', of an unprotected girl; see *musang.*

ria [KS], joy, pleasure, noisy enjoyment; *be~,* joyful; also *riah; me~kan,* delight.

riah [KS], *me~,* exciting, merry; *meme~kan,* make happy; *keme~an,* joy, grandeur.

riak [KN], 1. ripples of water; *dada me~-~ cemas,* breast heaving with anxiety. 2. *~-~,* creaking. 3. pride, vanity.

rial [KN], Kel. a dollar.

riam [KN], a small waterfall or rapid.

rian [KN], a measure of thread; = 1/16 of a *tukal;* a parcel of skeins.

riang [KN], 1. *~-~,* a cicada. 2. [KS], dizzy with excitement, light-headed or feverish with pleasure; *me~kan,* gladden; *pe~,* happy, joyful. 3. a motion on the surface of a stream caused by the presence of a snag or rock. 4. flute or cry of birds.

riap [KK], *me~,* to spread; to sprout up; to grow apace (as weeds).

rias [KN], the soft trunk of trees — such as the banana.

riau [KK], *me~,* to wash for gold.

riba [KK], 1. *me~,* to support on one's lap. 2. Ar. usury.

ribu [KBil], 1. thousand; *se~,* a thousand; *be~,* in thousands; *~an,* a thousand. 2. *~-~,* a plant (*Lygodium scandens*).

ribut [KN], storm; *pokok ~,* a storm-cloud; *~ turun,* a storm came down; *~ perubahan,* wind of change; *ke~an,* uproar, disturbance.

ricau [KK], *me~,* to chatter (of a child or bird).

riding [KN], 1. toils for large game; a line of rattan nooses — cf. **siding.** 2. *me~,* to just appear above the surface.

ridip [KN], Pk. dorsal fin (e.g., of a shark).

rigap [KS], 1. Pk. deft of hand. 2. Kel. to catch, arrest.

rihal [KN], Ar. a Koran-stand or lectern.

rihat = *rehat.*

rijal [KN], Ar. *~-ul-ghaib,* spirits presiding over good or evil fortune.

rimah [KN], crumbs left on the table after a meal; also *remah.*

rimas [KS], feeling physically uncomfortable (from heat or other cause); feeling 'hot under the collar' (from annoyance or embarrassment); *me~kan,* to cause discomfort, as tight clothing.

rimau [KN], a tiger; see *harimau.*

rimba [KN], primeval jungle; *~ raya,* the great forests; *ular kapuk ~,* the viper (*Lachesis wagleri*).

rimbas [KN], 1. an agricultural instrument resembling the adze (*beliong*). 2. Kel. to gore (of cattle).

rimbun [KS], bosky, spreading; a thicket, umbrageous; *~an belukar,* id.; *me~,* to grow thickly, as scrub.

rimpi [KN], dried banana.

rimping [KS], *pe~,* the last of a row.

rinah [KK], *me~,* to shed drops of water.

rincik [KK], slicing, cutting into minute portions; in bits, in small pieces; *be~-~,* bit by bit, item by item; *pe~an,* details; also *rincih, rinci* and *runcit.*

rincing [KS], thin, slight of build.

rindu [KS], loving, longing; yearn; *~ dendam,* id.; *me~kan,* to pine for; *seperti pungguk me~kan bulan,* as the owl pines for the moon; *berasa* ~, to feel nostalgic; *ke~an*, longing; *pe~*, person who longs or yearns for lover.

ringan [KS], light, of little weight or little account; light, not severe, of sentence; ~ *tulang*, very helpful, quick in doing things, active; ~ *kepala*, quick-witted; ~ *mulut*, friendly, fluent; *me~kan*, to alleviate, mitigate; *pe~kan*, to treat lightly; ~ *mulut, berat punggung*, quick with his mouth and slow with his behind, more talker than doer.

ringgi [KN], *pe~*, roasted young padi; *padi panggang-pe~*, padi ripe enough to be roasted; see *ayam*.

ringgit [KN], a dollar; ~ *besar*, a Spanish dollar; ~ *burung*, ~ *janek*, ~ *lang* or ~ *rama-rama*, the Maxican dollar; ~ *kepala* or ~ tengkorak, the 2-pound guilder piece; ~ *meriam*, the pillar dollar; ~ *patung*, id.; ~ *tongkat* or ~ *orang bertongkat*, the British dollar; *ber~~*, crenellated, milled, serrated.

ringin [KN], *sapu-sapu* ~, the name of a game for children.

ringis, = *rengis* [KK], to grin.

ringkai [KS], emaciated, thin.

ringkas [KS], brief; cut short; concise; *~an*, a summary, a precise, *~kan*, to summarise, to cut short; *tulisan* ~, short-hand, generally shortened to *trengkas; Jalan* ~, a short-cut; ~ is also used of clothing in the sense of 'trim' (not over-loose or fussy); *~an berita*, news-summary.

ringkik [KK], *me~*, neighing (of a horse).

ringkuk [KK], *me~*, bent, stooping, ducking; *me~ dalam penjara*, to be in prison.

rintang [KK], 1. stretching out or extending (of object like nets and not things like mats which are spread on the ground) — cf. **bentang**; *me~kan*, to stretch out, e.g., a tape, rope, esp. as a cord across a street to carry banners, etc.; *kain* ~, a banner; *gertak me~i sungai*, a bridge across a river; *me~*, to stretch, run, as a mountain range; *~an*, barriers; difficulties; *~an jalan*, street-barricades. 2. a main in cock-fighting.

3. *~an*, difficulties; obstructions; worries, a barricade, barrier; *pe~ waktu*, a way of passing the time.

rintih [KK], Ind. *me~*, to groan, lament; *~an*, lamentations.

rintik [KN], a speck; speckled markings; *be~*, speckled; *hujan ~~*, drops of rain just sufficient to make a few specks on the ground.

rintis [KN], *me~* [KK], to clear (a way), to pioneer, to open up a country.

rinih [KK], *~-rayu*, coaxing, cozening — a strong form of *rayu*.

ripai [KS], *te~~*, smashed; broken off.

ripang [KN], Treng. star-fish.

ris [KN], a bolt-rope.

risa [KN], a painless wen or bump; a gland.

risalah [KN], Ar. pamphlet, leaflet, brochure; also *risalat*.

risau [KS], anxious, uneasy; ~ *hati*, id.; sometimes used of disturbances of the peace; *orang yang* ~, rowdies; *~kan*, to worry; *~an*, something that worries.

risik [KK], *me~*, making private inquiries, esp. as to the prospects of a proposal of marriage; *~~*, confidential inquiries; covert talk; 'whispers'; *pegawai pe~*, intelligence officer; *pe~ rahsia*, secret agent; *sumber-sumber pe~an*, sources of investigation, 'intelligence'; *pusat pe~ Amerika*, the Central Intelligence Agency; *anak kita sudah di~*, our daughter has been inquired for (with a view to marriage); *me~~*, to make covert inquiries; to put out feelers (with a view to agreement); *mengirim ~ untuk berunding*, to put out feelers with a view to talks. 2. shrill, piercing; *me~*, id.; also, resounding (as a drum); Intense, of heat.

riuh [KS], noise, clamour; ~ *rendah*, uproar, tumult; ~ *mulut*, vociferous; *menjadi ~ heboh*, to be in an uproar.

riuk [KS], *patah* ~, compound (of fractures).

riung [KN], 1. a very tall grass (*Antistiria gigantea*). 2. N.S. curved (of the cutting edge of arecanut scissors).

riwayat [KN], Ar. a narrative, a story; a formal statement; ~ *resmi*, official statement; ~ *hidup,* a biography, resume; *pendekkan* ~, (sl.) to finish off (a person), 'do for'; *hapuskan* ~, id.

rizwan [KN], Ar. 1. grace, favour. 2. the angel guardian of the gate of Paradise.

robak [KS], ~*-rabik,* in tatters; in a ruinous state, of a building, dilapidated.

robek [KS], worn through, perforated; torn; ~*kan,* to tear up, to destroy; as a slogan, down with!

roboh [KK], falling (of heavy or massive bodies); ~*kan,* to demolish; *ke~an,* ~*an,* ruins; *batu* ~, a land slip.

robok [KN], (onom.) *me~* [KK], to give out a bubbling sound; to bubble up (as a spring).

rocah [KS], dirty and untidy-looking, unwashed.

rocoh [KK], prodding.

rocok [KK], *me~,* to peel off, flake off.

roda [KN], Port. a wheel; ~ *lambung,* a paddle-wheel; *bingkai* ~, felloe of wheel; ~ *air,* water wheel; *beca* ~ *tiga,* tricycle.

rodak [KK], *lari me~,* to rush, clattering; *me~,* to clatter, as stones in a box; *hati* ~, agitated.

rodan [KS], injury in a tender spot; very painful.

rodat [KN], Ar., Treng. a semi-religious dance with chanting, performed by boys.

rodi [KN], Port. order, command, instructions; also *ordi.*

rodok [KK], *me~,* to stab from below; ~ *rambut,* locks curled upwards, 'flick-ups'; *me~kan,* to thrust (e.g., a spear), = *meradak.*

rodong [KK], *me~,* doubtful or uncertain wandering; *me~ sana, me~ sini,* running round in circles; *me~* (of two persons or a group); to 'knock about together', be on friendly terms; *sahabat* ~, travelling companion.

rogol [KN], rape; *me~* [KK], to ravish; to outrage.

roh [KN], Ar. spirit, soul, life; *Roh ul-kudus,* the Holy Ghost.

rohani [KN], Ar. spiritual (opposed to *jismani*).

rojak [KN], 1. fruit or vegetables served up with vinegar and flavoured with spices; salad. 2. Pk. *pe~ (sirih),* areca-nut pounder; *me~,* to pound up (acrea-nut) for chewing; cf. **gobek.**

roji [KN], Pers. daily bread.

rojol [KK], *me~,* to emerge from a hole; to stick out.

rokok [KN], 1. a (Malay) cigarette; ~ *kertas,* a (European) cigarette; *dua batang* ~, two cigarettes; *menghisap* ~, to smoke a cigarette; *me~,* id.; *pe~,* person who smokes a lot of cigarette.

roma [KN], Skr. *bulu* ~, the down on the human skin, fine hair on the body; *liang* ~, the pores.

roman [KN], 1. shape, figure; ~ *muka,* looks, face; *dagangan berbagai* ~, goods of various types; *pe~,* general appearance. 2. padi straw. 3. *buku* ~, novel.

romantik [KS], romantic.

romba [KN], a mark placed in the sea to guide fishermen in the erection of stakes; a fisherman's beacon.

rombak [KK], taking down, taking to pieces; unravelling; *me~kan,* to unloose, to undo, to alter, to reshuffle, to untie; *te~,* undone, untied, loosened; *pe~an,* overhaul.

rombong [KS], 1. piling or heaping up; *penuh me~,* full till the contents appear over the top (e.g., of clothes in a box, rice in a measure, etc.); ~*an* [KN], party (as of travellers), group. 2. a round lidded basket of *mengkuang.*

romok [KK], physical depression; *me~,* to feel out of sorts; to look seedy or depressed.

rompak [KK], rob; *pe~,* a robber; Kel. also a robber; ~*an,* robbery.

rompang [KS], ~*-ramping,* tattered and torn; jagged, uneven (of teeth).

rompeng [KS], defective; partly eaten away or destroyed, e.g., of fruit, damaged, injured.

rompis [KS], chipped at the tip or at the edge.

rompong [KS], destroyed or eaten away (of a prominent feature — such as a nose or ear); ~kan, to cut off (as nose, an ear, or other feature), to mutilate.

rona [KN], Skr. colour; = warna; panca~, of many colours; gay, bright with colouring.

ronda [KK], Port. military rounds; be~, to go on patrol; pe~, a patrol.

rondah [KS], ~-randih, in disorder, dishevelled, in confusion.

rongak [KS], broken by gaps; gigi ~, gaptoothed; pagar ~, a fence from which palings are missing here and there.

rongga [KN], hole, cavity, hollow; be~, hollow; ~ dada (hidung, mulut), chest, cavity (nasal ..., oral ...); ~ roma, a pore.

ronggah [KK], pe~, use filthy language.

ronggang [KS], broken by gaps; = rongak.

ronggeng [KN], a square dance; anak ~, a danseuse.

rongkal [KK], te~, loose, come to pieces; unloosed (as a shoe-lace).

rongkas [KK], taking to pieces (with a view to reconstruction and not destruction).

rongkok [KK], me~, bowed with hands on knees; to stoop.

rongkol [KN], a cluster or bunch; ~ kunci, a bunch of keys; be~-~, in large clusters.

rongkong [KN], see ke~.

rongkok [KS], chipped off; 'gapped'; stronger than rongak, which is stronger than sompek.

rongos [KS], merongos, to be short-tempered; perongos, peevish; an intens. of rengus.

rongrong [KK], Ind. me~, to destroy, to eradicate; to undercut; mereka me~ kepentingan negara, they're undercutting the interest of the country.

ronta [KK], me~, to struggle (to free oneself from the clasp of someone else or from bonds); to make a violent scene.

rontak [ ], = ronta; pembe~an, revolution; rebellion; gerakan be~ di laut, mutiny.

ronyeh [KK], me~, to talk indistinctly (as a toothless man).

ronyok [KS], much dented, knocked in, crumpled; me~, to crumple; terpe~, crumpled up.

ropak [KS], disordered, slovenly untidy; ~-rapik, id.; ~-rapikkan, to mess up (a job), make a much of it.

rosak [KS], spoilt; violated; damaged, out of order; ~ mata, injured (of the eyesight); ~ iman, corrupted (of religion); ~ hati, heartbreak; ~ tabiat, depraved; me~kan, to injure; to damage, spoil; to ruin morally.

rosok [KS], dismantled, worn with age, used up, see merosok [KK], to grope for.

rosot [KK], Ind. me~, to fall off, decline; to depreciate in value.

rotan [KN], a generic name for rattans, i.e., plants belonging to the genera Calamus and Doe monorops; among the best-known is Rops geniculatus; ~ sega (Calamus ornatus); ~ semambu, the 'Malacca cane' (Calamus scipionum); belum be, berakar dahulu, a liana will serve until you can get a rotan (do your best with what resources you have).

roti [KN], Hind. bread; tukang ~, a baker; ~ kirai, a preparation of dough resembling macaroni; sebantal ~, a roll of bread; seketul ~, a loaf of bread; a hunk of bread; ~ canai, a pancake; ~ perata, a cuppati.

rotok [KK], me, to mutter angrily.

royak [KK], me~, to spread (as an ulcer or skin disease, news). 2. Kel. to tell, inform; also royat.

royan [KN], N.S. me~, to be very sick and suffer from hallucinations; esp. of woman suffering from complications following child-birth; demam me~, puerperal septicaemia.

royat [KN], Ar. aspect, vision, observation.

ru [KN], the casuarina-tree (Casuarina equisetifolia); ~ bukit, a tree resembling the casuarina (Dacrydium elatum); being easily swayed by the wind, this tree is used as a simile for a vacillating person or one with no fixed principles.

rua [KK], me~, to expand, to open out (as the neck of a cobra).

ruadat [KN], Ar. ceremonial etiquette.

ruah [KK], 1. *me~*, to call a person from a distance; *ke~*, as far as the sound of a cry can carry. 2. *tumpah ~*, poured out en masse; *melimpah ~*, abundant, filled to overflowing; *me~*, Pen. to defecate. 3. *bulan ~*, a popular name for the month *Syaaban:* here *~* = *arwah:* the name given because an 'All Souls' festival is held during the month.

ruai [KS], disproportionate in length, causing weakness; over-tall; too thin in comparison with height or not thick enough for some purpose.

ruak [KK], 1. *me~*, to spread (as the contents of an egg when the shell is broken). 2. *burung ~-~*, the white-breasted moorhen.

ruam [KN], pimples in thrush; a rash; *~ saraf*, shingles; prickly heat; *me~*, to pustulate.

ruan, = *aruan* [KK], a murrel (fish).

ruang [KN], hollow space; well of ship; a space, bay; a chamber, enclosed space, such as a store-room; *~ kapal*, the hold of a ship; *air ~*, bilge-water; *~(an) tengah rumah*, the central room of a house; *~ tamu*, guest parlour; *~ rumah sakit*, the ward of a hospital; any large camber or space or hall; *~ belakang*, the hollow of the back; *~ susu*, the hollow between the breasts; *be~-~*, full of holes; *~an akhbar*, a newspaper column; *me~*, disembowel a corpse; *di ~ mata*, before one's eyes.

ruap [KK], *me~*, to seethe up, to boil up, to foam up; to erupt, of a volcano; *minuman me~*, aerated waters; *darah me~*, rush of blood to the head or heart.

ruas [KN], interspace or segment between, esp., the nodes of a bamboo; *be~*, segmented, having parts marked as if separable, as bamboos, fingers, some worm and some stalks; *~ tulang belakang*, vertebrae; *se~ jari*, a section of the finger from joint to joint; *pe~an*, joints.

ruat [KK], 1. fallen, of anything that is not broken, e.g. of an uprooted tree. 2. *me~*, to resume human shape (of a were-tiger or *hantu jadi-jadian*); = *rawat.*

rubah [KN], 1. = *ubah.* 2. Hind. a jackal; a fox.

rubai [KS], N.S. *me~*, to be dishevelled, untidy. 2. quatrain.

ruban [KN], *air ~*, the watery scum in the preparation of coconut oil; *me~*, to purify oil.

rubin [KN], = *ubin* [KN], *batu ~*, floor tiles.

rubing [KN], a temporary light gunwale to increase the freeboard of a Malay boat; the wash-strake.

rubu [KK], *me~-~*, roam aimlessly, grope in the dark.

rubung, see *kerubung.*

rudu [KS], drooping (of the eyelid from sleepiness).

rudul, Ked. = *rudu.*

rugi [KS], Skr. loss, injury (other than physical injury); *ke~an*, id.; *kena ~*, to incur losses; *ganti-~*, compensation, reparations.

ruing [KN], a large winder used in spinning; the revolving frame used in weaving.

ruit [KS], 1. bent but not broken (of a branch); *capik ~*, lame through a bent limb. 2. a barb.

rujah [KK], *me~*, stabbing at, thrusting downwards, e.g., a spear at a foe under the house.

ruji [KN], Ind. a metal bar or grill.

rujuk [KK], Ar. to withdraw from a position taken up, to recant; esp. of taking back a divorced wife after the first or second *talak*; so, reconciliation, composition of quarrel; *me~i*, remarry; *~ kepada*, to rejoin, revert to, make one's peace with (e.g., a political party which one has left); *nombor ~*, reference number; *buku ~*, a reference-book; *me~kan*, to refer (a matter) to (some authority).

rukam [KN], a name given to a number of trees (*Flacourtia cataphracta* and other sp.), esp. a thorn-tree with red cherry-like fruit.

rukh [KN], Pers. the rook at chess; better *tir.*

ruku [KN], a generic name for a number of

plants, esp. (*ruku-ruku*) the basil (*Ocimum basilicum* and *Ocimum album*).

rukuk [KK], Ar. to bow the head in prayer — cf. **sujud**.

rukun [KN], Ar. fundamental doctrine; commandment; principle, basic rule; essential part of a religion; *lima ~ Islam*, the Five Pillars of Islam (confession of faith, prayer, fasting, obligatory tithe, the Haj); *~ hidup*, a rule of life; *~ is* used (fig.) for law-abiding, peaceful; *ke~an*, orderly behaviour; *~egara*, principles or rules which serve as guide to good citizenship.

Rum [KN], Ar. Rome; the Byzantine empire; *~i*, romanised characters (as opposed to *jawi*).

rumah [KN], a dwelling-house; *~ sakit*, hospital; *~ monyet*, sentry-box; *~ gambar*, museum; *~ pasung*, police-station; *~ sakit otak*, *~ sakit orang gila*, mental hospital; *~ api*, lighthouse; *~ miskin*, poor-house; *~ sunyi* (euphem.) latrine; *~ kembar*, semi-detached house; *~ pangsa*, a block of flats or other multiple dwellings; *~ terasing*, detached house; *~ papak*, flat-roofed house; *~ kotak*, shanty made of packing-cases etc.; *~ amal*, a (charitable) Home; *~ bertiang*, house on piles, bungalow; *~ tambahan*, outhouse; *~ tumpangan*, a hostel; *tambahan ~*, extension, annexe; *tapak ~*, a house site; *~ tangga*, a homestead; *~ household*; wedded state; *be~tangga*, to set up house, to be married; *soal ~ tangga sahaja*, a purely domestic problem; *pe~an*, housing.

Rumawi [KN], Roman.

rumbai [KN], tassel, tuft, pendant; *be~umbaikan*, dangle with.

rumbia [KN], a type of palm tree that yields sago.

rumbun [ ], a fire of piled logs, etc., a bonfire; *me~*, to pile up a bonfire.

rumenia = *remunia*.

Rumi [KN], Roman; *me~kan*, romanize.

rumit [KS], fine, delicate; intricate, involved complex; *ke~an*, difficulty,

inconvenience; *me~kan*, to complicate.

rumpun [KN], clump, cluster, a numeral coefficient for grasses; *se~ serai*, a clump of lemongrass; *se~*, of the same family stock; *~ bangsa*, racial stock; *berasal dari satu ~ bangsa*, descended from the same racial stock.

rumput [KN], grass; herbage generally; *me~*, to weed, to plant grass in patches; *~ tahi babi*, the plantain; *~ minyak*, Serangoon grass; *~ simalu*, sensitive plant (also *keman*); *~ kemuncup*, love-grass; *~ jolok-jolok*, a sp. of thrust grass; *~ rantai*, weedy growths of all sorts; *~ rampai*, id.

rumrum [KK], to coax a girl with flattery.

rumus [KN], Ind. *~an*, a formula; *me~kan*, to formulate, to put into words.

runcing [KS], sharp, tapering to a point; *ke~an*, difficult situation, crisis; *me~*, to sharpen to a point; (fig.) to become delicate, of a situation; *me~kan*, to sharpen, aggravate.

runcit [KN], *be~~*, in instalments; bits, petty items; a bit by bit; *kedai ~*, retail shop; a variant of *rincik*.

runding [KN], calculation, making up accounts; *be~* [KK], to discuss, deliberate; *~an*, negotiations, consultations, 'talks'; *mengadakan ~an*, to hold talks.

rundu [KS], *~-randa*, erratic, capricious, following in crowds.

runduk [KK], lowering the head — cf. **tunduk**; *me~*, to bend one's course to a point, to bow.

rundung, [KS], *me~*, 'cadging' from a person; 'sponging'; dogging and pestering; *di~ malang*, to be dogged by ill-luck.

runggu [KS], *~-rangga*, bristling with points.

runggun [KK], *me~*, banking a fire with logs; *me~ cinta*, to bank the flame of love.

rungkap [KK], *me~*, to speak in a surly tone.

rungkau [KK], *me*, to hang down over the face (of hair).

rungkup [KN], over-arching (as eaves);

over-spreading; *me~*, to overhang.

rungsung [KK], *me~*, to be querulous or peevish; to grumble; also *runsing* and *rusing*.

rungut [KK], *me~*, to grumble, to murmur; to mutter.

runjang [KK], *me~*, to poke around with a stick (as in feeling for something under water).

runjau [KS], *me~*, lanky.

runjung [KS], *me~*, to be piled up (of rice on a plate); rising to a cone; *pe~*, a measure of depth — a man's length (with arms raised above his head).

runsing [KS], a variant of *rungsung; me~kan* [KK], to worry, to cause anxiety, fretful, troubled; *ke~an* [KN], worry, anxiety; also *rusing*.

runtai [KS], dangling loosely — cf. **juntai;** *se ~*, a dangling cluster (e.g. of fruit).

runtas [KK], *me~*, to break by a pull or jerk as, e.g., a flower.

runti [KK], *me~*, rubbing asperities off the common rattan of commerce (*rotan sega*).

runtih [KK], *me~*, to pluck (leaves, flowers).

runting [KS], fragile, weak looking.

runtuh [KK], a heavy fall, a crash, collapse; *tebing ~*, the sunken bank, the Malay Atlantis; *~kan*, to overthrow, ruin, topple; *tanah ~*, landslide; *membakar ~*, to burn to the ground; *~an bangunan*, ruins; debris; *~-rantah*, to crash in ruins; *anjing menyalak, bukit mahukah ~*, just because a dog barks, will a hill collapse? i.e., a trifle, not worth taking notice of.

runtun [KK], *me~kan*, to tug down, to pull down (rope, branch); dragging (by the hand or by a chain or rope) — cf.

tuntun; ~an suara, intonation, articulation.

runut [KN], a track, spoor; *me~*, to track down, to search out; (fig.) to pester.

rupa [KN], Skr. appearance, form, looks; *indah khabar dari ~*, the report is fairer than the reality — not up to expectations; *~nya*, it appears; *~~*, id.; *~-nama*, adjective; *~-kata*, adverb; *me~*, to open out (of a flower-bud); *se ~*, similar; just like; *~~*, id.; *~-bangsa*, race, racial stock; *me~kan*, to display, *be~kan*, be in the shape of; *menye~i*, to resemble; *menye~kan diri sebagai*, to assume the appearance of; to impersonate; *tak te~ dek akal*, inconceivable.

rupawan [KS], Skr. handsome, beautiful.

rupiah [KN], Hind. a rupee, a guilder.

rupul [KN], a frill, a ruffle; *be~*, frilled.

rusa [KN], the sambhur deer (*Cervus unicolor*); *~ bintang*, the (imported) deer (*Cervus axis*); *~ senggirik*, the unicorn; *babi ~*, the well known 'deer-hog' of the Celebes (*Babirusa alfurus*); *seperti ~ masuk kampung*, like a deer entering a homestead, simile for 'bewildered stranger'; *pipit ~*, a deer-call.

rusuk [KS], side, flank, rib; *~ surat*, the marginal space in a letter, *tulang ~*, the rib-bone; *tumbuk ~*, a 'dig in the ribs', a quiet bribe.

rut [KN], 1. power of endurance; able to tolerate, *tak ada ~*, unable to stand it. 2. pressure, squeezing, crushing. 3. Pk. = *renut*.

ruwit [KS], confused, puzzled; *ke~an*, complication.

ruyung [KN], outer and harder portion of a palm-trunk; when dried, it can be cut up and used as rough material or to make a stockade.

S

s.a.w., see *sallahahu*.

saadat [KN], Ar. fortune, happiness; highness, majesty (as a title); *Baginda Saadat*, H.M. the King.

saat [KN], Ar. time, moment; a second; *dengan se ~ ini juga*, at this very moment; *~ yang nahas*, inauspicious moment; *~ yang sempurna*, auspicious moment; *~-~ terakhir*, the last minute.

saba [KK], *ber~*, to mix with, to visit.

Sabah [KN], a Malaysian state in northeast Borneo, formerly British North Borneo.

sabak [KK], *menyabak*, 1. boiling palm-sap (in the making of sugar). 2. *meratap-berbiji ~*, to weep copiously.

saban [KS], Ind. every; *~ hari*, daily, day in and day out.

sabar [KS], Ar. patient; moderate, tolerant; forbearance; *~lah dahulu*, be patient awhile; *tak tahu ~*, impatient (by nature); *tak boleh ~*, losing patience; *penyabar*, patient; *menahan ~*, to keep one's patience; *hilang ~*, to lose one's patience, *menyabarkan*, to put up with, endure; but sometimes, to soothe, to pacify; *tidak ter~kan lagi*, could stand it no longer, patience exhausted.

sabas [KS], Pers. bravo, excellent, capital.

sabda [KN], Skr. saying, utterance (esp. of words of the prophets); more generally also in literature the equivalent of *titah*, the word of a prince; *~* is used of a chief (e.g. the Penghulu of Rembau), while *titah* is used of the suzerain (the *Yam Tuan*).

sabil [KN], Ar. way, road; *perang ~ Allah*, a war in God's cause; a holy war; *ber~*, (sl.) to quarrel.

sabit [KN], 1. a sickle; *menyabit*, to reap with a sickle. 2. Ar. revealed (of truth); fixed, constant, proved; *bulan ~*, crescent (moon); *berthabit dengan*, con-

nected with, related to. 3. *pokok ~*, Ind. an oil-palm also *sawit*. 4. = *sebab*.

Sabtu [KN], Ar. *hari ~*, Saturday.

sabuk [KN], a sort of kerchief or plaid worn over the shoulder.

sabun [KN], Ar. 2. soap; *tepung ~*, soapflakes; *~ tepung*, id.; *~ serbuk*, id.; *~ buku*, soap in cakes; *~ kepingan*, id.; *~ air*, liquid soap; *~ cuci*, washing soap; *~ mandi*, toilet soap; *~ ubat*, medicated soap; *air ~*, soap-suds; *~ wangi*, scented soap; *buku ~*, a cake of soap; *ketul ~*, id. 2. near-white, light-coloured (of certain objects): of dogs; of blue or grey eyes (in this sense opposed to *cokelat*); *orang ~*, an albino.

sabung [KK], *menyabung*, darting at each other (of cocks); cock-fighting; *ayam ~an*, a fighting-cock; *menyabung*, to fight (of a cock); *~-menyabung*, flashing of forked lightning; *menyabungkan jiwa*, to risk one's life; *ber~ mata*, looking each other in the eye, eyes meeting squarely; *menyabung kaki*, to kick the legs about, of an uneasy sleeper (deemed unlucky).

sabur [KS], 1. a confused melee, wild scurrying, not to be able to distinguish well; *di dalam ~ itu*, in the crush; *semut ~*, a stinging ant (*Sima rufonigra*). 2. *layar ~*, a top-gallant-sail.

sabut [KN], the fibrous part or wrapper of a fruit like the coconut; coconut fibre; *bungkuk ~*, bent with age; *untung ~ timbul, untung batu tenggelam* (prov.), it is kill or cure, neck or nothing, nobody can get away from his destiny; *tali ~*, a rope of coconut fibre; a coir rope; *kering ~*, (fig.) getting on in years.

sadah [KN], lime for betel-chewing.

sadai [KK], *ter~*, lying at length, particularly in the sense of being beached, of a boat which has been run on to the beach, but not hauled up away from the water; so, used of a crocodile similarly 'beached', having pulled itself partly out of the water.

sadak [KS], sloping (of masts), raking, leaning (of pillars).

sadap [KN], *penyadap,* a knife; *menyadap,* to use this knife for extracting toddy; Kel. a sickle.

sadik [KS], Ar. upright, true (of friendship); *~-amanah,* truthful and honest.

sadikit see *dikit.*

sadin [KN], sardine; *muka ~,* poker-faced.

sadir ⌈KN⌉, salt ammoniac.

sadung [KK], *ter~,* tripping, stumbling, e.g., on a creeper — cf. **seradung**.

sadu [KS], Skr. excelling; *~ perdana,* first, foremost.

sadur [KN], plating, overlaying with shining metal; *menyadur mas,* to plate with gold; *~an,* plating; (fig.) an adaptation (lit); an interpretation; so, *menyadur,* (fig.) to adapt; to transcribe; *cerita itu sudah di~,* the story has been adapted.

saf [KN], Ar. rank, file of soldiers; *ber~-~,* in rows.

Safar [KN], Ar. the second month in the Muslim calendar; *ber~, merayakan hari ~,* to celebrate the *~* festival (by bathing picnics, cf. **mandi**); *~* is also called *bulan nahas,* the unlucky or disastrous month becuase it contains the anniversary of Hassan's death; the festival is, it appears, a sort of memorial to him and his brother Husain.

saga [KN], 1. the Indian pea, the seed of *Adenanthera pavonina; biji ~,* id.; *ber~,* red, bloodshot, of the eyes; *matanya ber~-~,* his eyes blazed red; (the pea was also used as a small measure of weight.) 2. old story of heroic deeds.

sagang [KK], *menyagang,* 1. buttressing (used when the prop is at an angle with the ground). 2. a sort of prawn-net, set in a channel.

sagai [KN], *ikan ~,* a sea fish.

sagar [KN], Pers. sugar; also *sakar.*

sagat [KK], *ter~,* jammed, scraped (as a wheel against a post).

sagu [KN], mealy pith, esp. that of the sago-palm (*rembia*); *untung ~,* the lot of the second best (rice being preferable); *hadiah ~ hati,* consolation prize; *bayaran ~ hati,* compassionate allowance; solatium, gratuity; sometimes 'sweetener', small bribe.

sagun [KN], a Malay dish made of rice-flour, rasped coconut and salt; also *~~.*

sagur [KN], a river dug-out; *perahu ~,* id.

sah [KK], 1. Pers. check! — in playing chess. 2. approved, in order, admissible; confirmed (as news); valid (as law or coinage); made out (of a case); *tidak ~,* the charge has not been substantiated; illegitimate, null and void; *~!,* done! (in striking a bargain); *~kan,* to confirm (as news); *penge~an (rasmi),* (official) confirmation; ratification; *tidak ~ di sisi undang-undang,* illegal, unconstitutional; *tukang ~,* person having nominal authority, a 'rubber-stamp'.

sahabat [KN], Ar. friend, comrade, *~ beta* or *~ kita,* 'my friend'; the person written to (in a formal official letter); often used for 'accomplice'; *peraduan secara per~an,* a 'friendly' match; *ber~ erat,* on terms of close friendship; *~ handai,* one's circle of friends.

sahaja [KN], 1. only; merely; just; *begitu ~,* just like that (e.g., without inquiry or protest, without waiting for orders); *dengan ber~,* id.; *ber~,* simple, plain, not affected; of face, expressionless, showing no emotion. 2. = *sengaja.*

saham [KN], Ind. a share, a portion, as in an undertaking; *ahli ~,* a shareholder; *pemegang ~,* id.

sahang [KN], pepper.

saharah [KN], a large box or chest.

sahaya [KN], Skr. slave; humble servant; 1. *~ semua,* we all; *hamba ~,* slaves and serfs; now us. written *saya.*

sahi [KS], careless, thoughtless.

sahih [KS], Ar. true, clear, correct; definitely proved; valid, reliable, esp. of traditional sayings of the Prophet not contained in the Koran; see *hadis.*

sahib [KN], Ar. master, owner of; *~-ul-*

hikayat, the author of the story; the author's 'we'.

sahur [KK], Ar. the meal taken before dawn in *Ramadhan.*

sahut [KK], replying, answering; ~-~*an,* in continual response (as salutes after salutes); ~*i, menyahut,* to make reply; to answer; to give an answering call; *burung ber~-~an,* birds calling to one another.

sahwi, see *sujud.*

Said [KN], Ar. a title given to male descendants of the Prophet; ~ *itu keturunan daripada Rasul Allah,* the ~s are descended from the Apostle of God; also *Syed.*

Saidi [KN], Lord (God); *ya* ~, Lord!

sain [KN], Eng. signature; *menyain,* to sign.

saing [KK], travelling in company; Kel. a companion (= *kawan*); a rival, Ind.; *per~an,* competition, rivalry; *menyaingi,* to compete with; *per~an senjata,* arms race; *ber~,* to accompany; to compete, be in rivalry.

sair [KN], Ar. hell-fire.

sais [KN], 1. Hind. a syce, a groom. 2. Eng. size, esp. of articles of commerce, e.g. shoes.

sait [KS], trim, well-pressed (of clothes), a neat crease; *jangan patah* ~, (of dandies) don't let your clothes get baggy.

saja = *sahaja.*

sajadah [KN], Ar. a prayer-mat.

sajak [KN], Ar. assonance, harmony, rythm, cadence; rhyme; ~*nya janggal,* the rhythm is faulty, *ber~,* rhyming, assonant, harmonious; ~ is also used for a poem; *ahli* ~, a poet.

saji [KN], Skr. serving up (a dish); dressing food; *tudung* ~, a dish-cover; *ber~,* to dress food; to serve up food; ~*an,* a dish of dressed food; an offering of food in a temple; *nasi ter~ di lutut,* rice served at the knee (said of a woman who does not have to cook for herself; 'on easy street'); *penyajian,* presentation; *penyajian acara itu sangat baik,* the presentation (of the show) was great.

saka [KN], 1. Ind. the pillars of a house, = *tiang.* 2. N.S. female line of descent; ~ *baka,* on both sides of descent; also used to describe 'ancentral' property. 3. a legendary King of Java; *Sang* ~, the Indonesian flag; it is also called *Sang Merah Putih.*

sakai [KN], dependants, retainers, subjects; *orang* ~, a name given to 'subject' aboriginal tribes by Malays; the term is derogatory and it is better to call them *orang darat,* upcountry people.

sakal [KN], knocking against; knocking back; *angin* ~, a contrary wind; *menyakal,* to knock up against; to use violence; *kena* ~, mishandled, maltreated.

sakan [KN], Kel. much, a considerable amount; much (of things), serious (illness), heavy (rain).

sakar [KN], Pers. sugar; also *sagar.*

sakat [KK], 1. to vex; trouble, annoyance; ~*an,* mischievous; *hantu* ~*an,* malignant spirit. 2. a generic name given to many epiphytes, esp. aroids and orchids. 3. *suku~~,* a genealogical tree; relations generally, kith and kin. 4. *ter~,* aground (of boats). 5. up to, as far as; ~ *lutut,* up to the knee.

sakhlat [KN], Pers. broad-cloth.

saki [KN], 1. Pers. a cup-bearer, comrade. 2. Kel., Treng. a shallow rubbish-basket, = *pongkis.* 3. ~-*baki,* see *baki.*

sakit [KS], sick, diseased, in pain; *mendapat* ~, to fall ill; ~ *hati,* resentful, angry; *menyakiti hati,* to offend to hurt one's feelings; ~ *hidup,* ill without apparent cause (attributed by some Malays to evil spirits); ~ *orang baik,* a euphemism for small-pox; ~ *teruk,* seriously ill; *menyakiti,* to injure; to afflict with pain or sickness; *penyakit,* to disease; *ke~an,* illness, pain; ~ *perempuan,* venereal disease; ~ *kelamin,* id.; ~ *pinggang,* lumbago; *tahi penyakit,* valetudinarian; *berpenyakitan,* liable to illness, delicate; ~ *menahuan,* chronic illness; ~ *tersalah makan,* food-poisoning; *pe~,* patient, an invalid; *menanam benih penyakit,* to inoculate.

sakrat al-maut [KN], Ar. the death-agony.

saksama [KS], Skr. just, impartial, careful, thorough; impartial justice.

saksi [KN], Skr. witness, evidence, testimony; *memanggil* ~, to call witnesses (in a case); *naik* ~, to give evidence; *menyaksikan*, to witness (as a spectator); also, to consult, as authorities; *kandang* ~, witness-box; *ber~ ke lutut*, calling relatives, i.e. partial persons, as witnesses.

sakti [KS], Skr. supernatural power; magical; *dewa yang* ~, a wonder-working divinity; *ke~an*, supernatural power.

saku [KN], a small canvas bag, a satchel, a pocket; *wang* ~, pocket money; *menyakukan*, put in one's pocket.

sal [KN], Hind. a shawl.

salah [KS], fault, error, flaw, discrepancy; being out of place or going wrong; ~ *kena*, tactless of words; ~ *seorang*, one or the other (person); ~ *suatu*, one or the other (thing); ~ *urat*, dislocated or strained (of a sinew); *orang* ~, an accused person; a convict; *serba* ~, puzzled, wrong, at a loss; *menyalahi*, to vitiate; to blame; to act contrary to; ~-*silih*, faults and errors of all kinds; *menyalah-gunakan*, to misuse; *di~gunakan*, open to abuse; *ke~an*, an error, a fault, a mistake; *se~an*, N.S. a custom by which an unmarried couple found indiscreetly associating can be compelled to marry; *cari* ~, to find fault; to pick holes; *sepenuh-penuh* ~, guilty without extenuation; *ber~*, at fault; *ber~an dengan*, contrary to, inconsistent with; *ter~ langkah*, to miss one's footing; *ter~, letak*, put away in the wrong place, mislaid; *apa ~(nya)?*, what's wrong (with it)? (i.e., what's the matter with it? or why not do it?); ~ *nama* is used sometimes as a polite way of referring to some creature or place with a 'rude' name and so 'unmentionable'; *~kan*, to blame; *menyalahertikan*, to misinterpret; *perasaan ber~*, guilty feelings.

salai [KK], 1. heating over the fire; smoking; fumigation or curative heating; *menyalai*, to heat in this way; to preserve by smoking; *rumah* ~ *getah,* rubber smoke-house; ~ *setambun,* a grid forming a sort of altar used in *bersemah* ceremonies in Pahang (see *semah*); *~an,* a rack, a grid; *~an kelapa,* a copra-drying rack. 2. N.S. *ter~,* caught up, as an object in the branches of a tree.

salak [KN], 1. a stemless thorny palm *(Zalacca edulis),* producing an edible fruit. 2. the barking of a dog; *menyalak* [KK], to bark.

salam [KS], Ar. peace; a greeting salutation; blessing; used in the salutation, ~ *alaikum,* peace be with you; *berjabat* ~, to touch hands in greeting; *ber~an,* exchanging greetings; *sang* ~ *di rimba,* emperor of the jungle, a name used in folk-tales for the mousedeer.

salang [KK], *menyalang* 1. to execute by the kris; done by driving a long rapier-like kris down past the collar-bone to the heart; *keris penyalang,* the kris so used; *mati di~,* condemned to death. 2. a rope basket as used for cargo by ships.

salangkan [KPhbg], Ind. even though.

salap [ ], Ind. ointment, salve.

salasilah [KN], Ar. genealogical tree.

salatin [KN], Ar. sultans — the plural of sultan.

salih [KN], 1. motion, approach; ~ *kembali,* to return. 2. Ar. pious, godly.

sali [KS], strength, power, *sama* ~, of equal might; *berhati* ~, with a pure heart, honestly; *~ganda,* Kel. evens (in betting); *ke~an,* congruity, aptness.

salib [KN], Ar. a cross; crucifixion; *menyalibkan,* to crucify; *tanda* ~, the sign of the cross; *perang* ~, crusade.

salim [KN], good and pure.

salin [KK], change of garb or of food or outward form; *~an,* a translation; copy; *~i,* to bestow garments upon anyone; *ber~,* to be confined (of a woman); to put on other clothes; to assume a different form by metamorphosis; *per~* or *per~an*, a change of clothing; a robe of honour; ~ *tak tumpah*, exactly alike, 'spit'n image'; *~an bersih*, fair copy.

saling [KS], Ind. in turn, in succession, mutually; ~ *mengerti*, mutual understanding; ~ *bertalian*, mutual ties; ~ *bertentangan (antara satu dengan yang lain)*, mutually opposed.

salir [KK], *menyalir*, drain, lead off liquid by means of drain.

salji [KN], Ar. snow.

Sallalahu alaihi wassalam, may God bless and save Him; an ejaculation which should be uttered after the name of the Prophet; usually abbreviated in writing to *s.a.w.*

Sallih [KN], a common proper name; *Mat ~*, derisive nickname for European; 'John Willie'.

saluk [KN], *destar ~*, a twined handkerchief.

salung [KN], a kind of flute.

salur [KK], *~an*, [KN], a channel, a gully; a gutter; a conduit; *~an isi perut*, the colon; *~an peranakan*, the vagina; *~an suara*, a voice-pipe (e.g., on a ship); *~an radio*, a radio channel.

salut [KN], to enwrap, enfolding; *kertas ~*, a wrapper; ~ is also used for plating — cf. **balut**.

sama [KKt], Skr. 1. identical, same; ~ *besar*, of equal size; ~ *tengah*, in the very centre; *~kan*, to rank as equal; *ber~*, along with; *ber~an*, similar, identical; *ber~~an*, coincide with, resemble; *~~*, together; *menyamai*, to attain equality with; *menyamaratakan*, to treat impartially; ~ *sekali*, wholly; ~ *ada ... mahupun*, Ind. both ... and; *~ada ... atau*, whether...or; ~ *lalu*, while passing, on the way; ~ *semasa itu juga*, at the same time; ~ *sehari*, on the same day; *per~an*, equality; *per~an gaji*, equal pay; *hidup ber~*, co-existence; *maksud ber~*, common purpose (as of conspirators); *se~ sendiri*, among them (selves). 2. 'to', 'with'; *bilang ~ saya*, tell me.

samak [KN], Ar. tanning; material, esp. bark, used for preserving cordage or leather; *kulit ~*, dressed hides; a generic name for trees, the bark of which is used for tanning; the word is also used of the 'ceremonial cleansing of that which is defiled'.

samal [KN], water-weeds.

saman [KN], 1. Ar. *ratib ~*, the name given to a peculiar ratib or mystical religious performance. 2. Eng. legal summons.

samar [KS], conceal, hiding one's identity; personating someone else; *~kan*, to pretend, to affect; *menyamar diri*, to disguise oneself; *menyamar diri sebagai*, to disguise oneself as; *nama ~an*, a pseudonym; *~~*, vague, not clear; obscure, vague to the eye; *waktu ~ muka*, dusk (when it is hard to distinguish faces); *warna ~*, pale, dull, of colour; *dun; penyamaran ~an*, camouflage; *ke~an*, ambiguity, vagueness; *~kan*, to dim (a light).

sambal [KN], a generic name for cold condiments served with curries; *membuat ~*, (fig.) to make mincemeat of.

sambalewa [KKtr], half-heartedly (of workers).

sambang [KS], 1. empty (in the sense of being devoid of expected contents); failing to form (as grain); non-fertile (as eggs); devoid of honey (as a bees' nest). 2. a round; *ber~* [KK], to visit a sacred spot for a ceremony (perhaps from an old usage meaning 'to patrol', 'to guard').

sambar [KK], *menyambar*, carrying off in the talons (esp. of a bird of prey swooping and carrying off its victims); to snatch up, to grab, to pounce; to strike (of lightning); *kena ~an kilat*, struck by lightning; *yu ~an*, a man-eating shark.

sambat [KK], to splice together; *menyambat*, to connect, to bind together.

sambau [KN], a coarse, thick grass (*Eleusine indica*); *kasut ~*, grass slippers; *macam ~ di tengah jalan*, like ~ grass on a path, simile for 'struggling for existence'.

sambil [KPhbg], with, together with, simultaneously with; *kerja ~an*, a side-line job, a job additional to regular work; ~ *menyelam minum air,* drinking while diving, i.e., killing two birds with one stone, used of a man who, while doing a job, makes a bit 'on the side'; *secara ~an,* part-time (as opposed to *sepenuh masa,* full-time); ~ *lalu,* incidentally, on the way, while passing; so, transient, trifling; *secara ~ lalu,* casually, cursorily; cf. **sambilewa.**

sambilewa [KKtr], Ind. hesitating, half-hearted; *secara ~,* cursorily, casually.

sambung [KK], to add in prolongation; joining on; *menyambung,* lengthen, extend, continue, join; *ada ~an lagi,* 'to be continued'; *cerita ber~an,* serial story; *menyambung hidup (nyawa, umur),* to keep alive.

sambur [KKtr], *~-limbur,* intermittently visible; appearing and disappearing.

sambut [KK], to receive (of a person standing to receive one coming to him, and not of a person going to meet his guest); *ber~,* answered, replied; *gigi ~,* overlapping teeth; *menyambut,* to stand and receive; *menyambut baik,* to think well of; *~an,* a (social) reception; *majlis ~an kahwin,* wedding reception; *kata-kata ~an,* words of welcome; *penyambut tetamu,* receptionist; *~an dagangan,* a consignment of goods; *penyambut,* (gram.) the object of a verb.

samfu [KN], Ch. woman's dress of jacket and trousers, us. worn by poorer people.

sami [KN], 1. a Buddhist priest. 2. Tam. a Hindu sacred image.

samir [KN], the natural undried leaves of the *nipah* (stitched together as a rough protection against rain).

sampah [KN], rubbish, dry dirt, filth; ~ *itu ke tepi juga,* rubbish always finds its way to the side; the poor are always shoved aside; *~-sarap,* rubbish generally, refuse; *menyampah,* like rubbish, dislike; ~ *masyarakat,* scum of society, off-scouring.

sampai [KK], 1. to arrive, arrived, to come to, attaining to, reaching; as far as; *~kan,*

to cause to attain to, or to cause to extend to; to deliver, e.g. *~kan khabar,* to convey news; *~kan hadiah,* to present the prizes; *tak ~ hati nak,* cannot bring (myself) to; *sudah ~ hukum,* has received the Command, i.e. has died; *sudah ~ janji,* id.; *tak ~-~,* failed, as a plan, an aspiration; *~-~ sahaja dia,* as soon as he arrived; *penyampaian,* presentation, delivery, transmission. 2. hanging loosely (as a garment on a clothes-line); *~an kain,* a towel-horse or clothes line.

sampak [KN], 1. the metal ring or band at the base of the shaft of a weapon (it serves to keep the haft *(puting)* from splitting the shaft). 2. *main ~,* heads or tails. 3. *seluar ~,* trousers worn by Malays in padi fields and swamps

sampan [KN], Ch. a generic name for large number of types of boats, esp. the Chinese shoe-boat; ~ *cedok ikan,* a boat in use with large fish-traps; ~ *golek,* (Pen.) the common Chinese ~; ~ *kotak,* the Chinese ~ with stern lockers (much used in Singapore); ~ *kudung,* a heavy beamy Chinese ~; ~ *itik,* small flat-bottomed ~ for use on mudbanks; ~ *selit,* a dug-out; ~ *mengail,* the canoe-like boat in which fishermen visit their traps; ~ *panjang,* a long narrow canoe-like passenger-boat; ~ *tunda,* a dinghy; ~ *pukat China,* Chinese seine boat (formerly used for coastal trading).

sampang [KN], 1. a Malay varnish. 2. Pk. = *sempat.*

sampar [KN], plague, murrain.

sampat [KN], *mandi ~,* Pk. ceremonial bathing on the third day after marriage.

sampean [KN], Jav. a title used in addressing a prince.

sampil [KN], the bast or husk at the lower end of a palm-branch.

samping [KN], 1. *kain ~,* the sarong, worn over trousers. 2. Ind. side; *di-~ itu,* besides; *di ~,* next to; by the side of; *mengke~kan,* to push aside, make light of; *ber~an,* close together; *~an,* by-product.

sampir [KN], 1. the upper portion of a kris-sheath — the part that covers the *ganja; ~an keris,* id. 2. *~an kain = sampaian kain,* clothes line.

sampu [KN], decline, emaciation; *demam ~,* a wasting fever in children.

sampuk [KK], *menyampuk,* to intrude; to interfere (in other people's affairs); to interrupt; to put in a remark; to 'run up against'; *sakit ter~ hantu,* ill from coming into contact with an evil spirit.

sampul [KN], a covering or wrapper — such as a pillow-case; (book) jacket; a caul (but *tembuni* is more technical in this sense); *sampul surat,* envelope.

Samsam [KN], a name given to a mixed half-Siamese race inhabiting the northern parts of the Peninsula.

samseng [KN], ch. a rowdy, professional bully, hooligan.

samsu [KN], Ch. Chinses alcoholic spirit.

samudera = *semudera.*

samun [KK], robbing; theft accompanied by violence; *menyamun,* to rob; *penyamun,* robber; *~-sakal,* robbery, generally.

sana [KKtr], yonder; the farther, in contradistinction to the nearer; there; *di ~,* there; *di seberang ~,* on the opposite side; *tidak ke ~, tidak ke sini,* neutral; impartial.

sanak [KN], Ar. kindred, blood relations, one's whole family; *~ saudara,* id.

Sanat [KN], Ar. year of the Hegira; see *hijrat.*

sanbal [KN], Per~ spikenard.

sandang [KK], wearing a band over the shoulder and across the body (as the cordon of a knightly order is worn); *menyandang pesaka,* N.S. to wear the insignia of a hereditary office; *menyandang, menyadangkan* or *memper~kan,* to carry (a sword or kris suspended from a cross-belt or a gun slung over the back by a strap); *sayap ~,* a sort of cross-belt; *menyandang* is used in the general sense of being invested with an office or an Order; *~ kartus,* a bandolier, cartridgebelt; *tuala ter~ di*

bahunya, with a towel over his shoulder; *menyandang jawatan,* to hold an official post; *menyandang johan,* to hold a championship.

sandar [KK], 1. resting the back against any surface; *ter~,* leaning back upon; *~an, per~an,* something to lean gainst; *~an kerusi,* the back of a chair; *~an papan tulis,* an easel; *titik ~,* a fulcrum; *bertumpang ~ di lengan,* to lean on someone's arm for support; *ber~ bermalas-malas,* to lounge; *duduk ter~,* id. 2. mortgaging, pledging.

sandarmalam [KN], a name given to the tuberose which flowers at night; also *sundal malam.*

sandera [KN], hostage, debt-slave.

sanding [KKtr], 1. *ber~* [KK], to be set next to one another (as a bride and bridegroom), side-by-side; *upacara per~an,* the *ber~* ceremony; sitting on a dais (of a bride and bridegroom). 2. a corner; a projection; *tak ber~,* smooth, globular; *ber~,* angular.

sandiwara [KN], a play, esp. a play combined with music and dancing; *dia pandai ber~,* he's a great pretender; *pentas ~,* stage.

sandung [KK], stumbling against; *ter~ kakinya pada,* he caught his foot against — cf. **serandung** and **sadung.**

Sang [KN], an honorific prefix applied, (1) to the names of heroes and minor divinities — such as *Darmadewa, Kelembai, Nila Utama* (the founder of Singapore), *Arjuna,* and others; (2) to the titles of kings, e.g., *~nata, ~aji, ~ratu,* etc., (3) in the expression *~ Yang* only, to the names of major divinities, e.g., *~ Yang Tunggal;* (4) to the names of animals in fables, e.g., *~ tupai, ~ kancil, ~ nyamuk;* (5) *~ Merah Putih,* the flag of the Indonesian Republic; *~ Saka,* id.; *~ Dwiwarna,* id.

sanga [KN], 1. the scum or dross in smelting. 2. Pk. *penyanga,* a rascal, bad lot; also *sangak.*

sangai [KN], a rough dish-cover of *nipah* or *mengkuang* leaf.

sangaji, see *sang* and *aji*.

sangat [KS], extremely, very; *amat* ~, id.; *ke~an*, excess; *ter~*, surpassingly.

sangga [KK], holding up, propping up, sustaining; shielding from a downward blow; the stout post at the side of a Malay fishing-boat where the net is secured; ~ *buana*, 'prop of the universe', a Javanese title; ~ *layar*, small props for holding up the boom; ~ *mara*, a projecting knob or guard on a blade; ~ *tembok*, abutment of a wall; ~ *gerigi*, the stop on a ratchet.

sanggah [KK], N.S. *menyaggah*, to contradict; to protest, to object; to withstand; *~an*, an opposition.

sanggam [KK], Sel. *menyanggam*, to borrow articles for temporary use.

sanggama [KB], sex, coitus, coition; *ber~*, to have sex.

sanggan [KN], a metal bowl with a rough milled edge.

sanggar [KN], family altar, studio, gallery; ~ *seni*, art gallery.

sanggang = *sagang*.

sanggat [KK], running aground (of a boat).

sanggatuas [KN], fulcrum.

sanggerah [KK], to bleed.

sanggit [KK], rubbing two hard bodies against one another; *ber~*, rubbing against one another, as crossing branches; *menyaggit gigi*, to gnash the teeth; also *singgit*.

sanggul [KN], the coiffure; *cucuk* ~, hairpins; ~ *terlepas*, with hair down, streaming unconfined; *ber~* [KN], to wear a bun; *menyanggulkan*, make or twist into a bun.

sanggup [KK], accept responsibility for; acknowledge; to undertake to, be ready to; ~ *membayar wang*, accepting responsibility for a payment; *pak* ~, a putative father; also a person claiming the merit for what someone else has done; *ke~an*, capacity, sense of responsibility, readiness; *menyanggupi*, to promise to give an under-taking.

sangir [KN], dog-tooth, canine tooth; *ter~*, showing the teeth, as in a snarl.

sangka [KK], 1. Skr. think, expect, fear; suspicion; *~kan*, to suspect or think anything; *tak di* ~, unexpected; *di luar* ~, id.; *salah* ~, misconception; *baik-~*, good feeling; *per~an*, suspicion; *~kala*, trump of doom, a trumpet. 2. Skr. a triton shell used as a trumpet, a splayed-out bamboo cup-like basket to hold incense or offerings to spirits.

sangkak [KS], 1. hinder, resist; *raja di* ~, a ruler who should be risen against; *~i*, to obstruct, hinder, or resist; *ter~*, in a fix; *penyangkak*, obstructive. 2. a fowl's nesting-place.

sangkal [KK], disavow, repudiating; to object, protest, deny; *~i*, to deny (one's faith); to repudiate knowledge of; to rebut.

sangkar [KN], 1. a coop; a cage (esp. a bird-cage); *~an*, an enclosure serving as a cage. 2. ~ *bidang*, thwarts in a boat.

sangkil [KS], to the point; doing exactly what is wanted, e.g., of medicines which work perfectly or a boat which floats exactly right.

sangku [KN], a large metal bowl or basin for washing the hands after a meal.

sangkur [KN], a bayonet.

sangkut [KK], stopped; not getting past; adhering to or remaining in; *ber~an*, connected, related; *menyangkut-paut*, involve, implicate; ~ *di-dalam hati*, sticking in the memory; *penyangkut*, a hook, holder, rack; *~an*, to hang up (as on a nail); *ter~*, stuck fast; *ter~ pada*, devotedly attached to, 'stuck on'; *wang ter~*, (fig.) piled up arrears of money; *yang ter~ ialah ...*, the crux is that ...; the difficulty is that ...; *wang langganan sudah banyak ter~*, many subscriptions are in arrears; *motor-~*, outboard motor.

sangluk [KN], miscarriage (of animals).

sangsang [KK], N.S. *menyangsang*, to rebut, to refute, to obstruct, to hinder.

sangsi [KS], Ind. to doubt, feel uncertain; *ke~an*, doubt, uncertainty.

sangulun [KN], Jav. a royal title.

Sangyang, see *Sang*.

sanjai [KS], tall and well-built.

sanjung [KK], Ind. to praise, flatter; ~*an,* praise adulation flattery.

santak [KK], 1. *menyantak,* to strike with the fist or knuckles; *ter~ (pada),* bumping into; obtruding. 2. Ind. up to, until.

santan [KN], the milk or cream expressed from the flesh of the coconut; *kepala ~, pati ~,* the first pressing (yielding the best cream); *kemancar ~,* the second pressing; *pati ~,* may be used (fig.) for 'virginity'.

santap [KK], to regale oneself, partake of food (as opposed to mere eating); ~ *sirih,* to chew *sirih* (of a prince chewing *sirih*); ~*an* or *per~an,* a royal repast; ~*an rohani,* spiritual (mental).

santau [KN], a slow and sure poison; not a specific drug, but a compound of several poisons.

santun [KS], sedate, polite, courteous, well-mannered.

sanubari [KN], the human heart, feelings, mind, soul.

sanuk [KN], Joh. *burung ~,* the malkoha.

sap [KN], 1. a piece of cloth or fibrous material placed in an inkstand as a pad for seals; *kertas ~,* blotting-paper.

sapa [KN], 1.mode of address, courtesy; *tegur ~,* id., *menyapa,* to address politely, greet. 2. = *siapa.*

sapai [KK], 1. *ber~,* to hang about exposed to the elements; also *sapau.* 2. *angin si ~~,* gentle breeze.

sapi [KN], an ox, a bull or cow; *minyak ~,* suet; ~ *hutan,* a name given to the *Anoa* of Celebes (*Anoa depressicornis*), (which is well known to maritime Malays); also, in the interior of the Malay Peninsula, to a local wild ox, either a small *Bos gaurus* or a separate sp. (*Bos sondaicus*).

sapu [KK], wiping; sweeping off; smearing off or on; ~ *cat,* painting; ~ *minyak,* varnishing; ~ *kapur,* whitewashing; ~ *tangan,* a handkerchief; Kel. Treng. a head-cloth; us. contracted to *setangan;* ~*kan, menyapu,* to sweep, to pass a

cloth or broom over; *penyapu,* a broom; *penyapu lidi,* a hard broom; *menyapu bersih,* to make a clean sweep; *teksi ~,* a pirate taxi.

saput [KN], a thin fleecy or cloth-like covering; a film; clouding over; *di~ awan,* clouded over (as a mountain).

sara [KN], 1. *ber~, menyara,* to join in an under-taking; to 'chip in.' 2. ~ *bara,* in confusion; helter-skelter; topsy turvy. 3. *ber~,* to retire from service), the implication being, to go on a pension, ~ here signifying means of support; *masukkan dalam lingkungan ber~,* to place on the pensionable establishment; *biaya ~ hidup,* cost of living allowance; *elaun ~ hidup,* id.; *menyara hidup,* to earn a livelihood; *menyarai,* to finance, support with funds.

saraf [KN], Ar. 1. *ilmu ~,* etymology. 2. nerve; *perang urat ~,* psychological warfare; ~ *tunjang,* spinal cord.

sarak [KK], *ber~,* parted, parting; divorced.

saran [KK], Ind. *menyarankan,* to suggest; ~*an,* proposal, suggestion.

sarang [KN], a nest; ~ *lebah,* a bees' nest; ~ *tebuan,* a hornets' nest; ~ *burung,* the nest of a bird; *ber~,* to nest; *telur se~,* a nest of eggs, a 'clutch', ~ *laba-laba,* spider's web; *ber~~,* full of cobwebs, mason-bees' nests, etc. (as a deserted house); (fig.) riddled, as with bullets; ~ *pipit,* a dimple; in Trengganu ~ is also used for 'bird-cage'.

sarap [KN], 1. dust, fine dirt; *penyapu ~,* a sweeper; ~ *sampah,* sweepings, refuse generally.

sarapan [KN], breakfast.

sarat [KS], heavily laden; of full burden; *bunting ~,* in the last stage of pregnancy; ~ *dengan muatan,* full of cargo (of a ship).

sarau [KN], 1. the groove between two parallel bones — for instance, along the tibia. 2. a creel used by collectors of agar-agar. 3. unlucky, unfortunate.

sarbat [KN], Ar. sweet, cooling drink; also *serbat.*

sardi [KN], Hind. glanders.

sari [KN], 1. length of cloth draped round the body worn by Indian women. 2. Jav. a flower; beautiful or delicate; a common expression in the names of fair ladies, e.g., *Bida~, Puspa-~, Tunjung-~,* etc. 3. *timah ~,* zinc. 4. essence, extract; *inti~,* gist, main points; ~ *berita,* news headlines; *~pati,* essence; ~ *bunga,* pollen, corolla; *taman ~,* flower garden; *menyari madu,* to sip honey, as a bee. 5. = *sehari;* see *pekan.*

saring [KK], Ind. to sift, filter; (met.) to investigate, to 'screen' (investigate antecedents); *~an, penyaring, penyaringan,* filter, sieve.

sarik [KN], a type of bamboo with slender stem.

Sarip [KN], = *Syarif.*

Saripah [KN], Ar. a title given to female descendants of the Prophet; a sort of feminine of *Syed;* abbreviated *Cik Pah.*

sarjan [KN], sergeant.

sarjana [KN], Ind. a scholar, a graduate, a M.A.; ~ *muda,* a B.A.

sarsi [KN], Eng. sarsaparilla.

saru [KS], Kel. *ber~,* confused, not clear, vague, dim (of sight, sound); *menyaru,* to disguise; *menyarukan,* to become dim.

saruk [KK], *ter~,* put one's foot into a noose, or trap, or hole; being tripped up — cf. **sadung;** *ter~,* fluke.

sarun [KN], Jav. a musical instrument, a sort of xylophone with metal keys.

sarung [KN], sheath, covering; *kain ~,* a sarong; ~ *jari,* to thimble; ~ *kaki,* socks; ~ *keris,* a kris-sheath; ~ *tangan,* gloves; *menyarung* or *menyarungkan,* to sheathe; to put on, as a coat; to encase; *ter~,* sheathed; *kepala ~,* the strip of different colour at the back of a sarong.

sarut [KK], scraping up against anything; gnawing.

sasa [KBil], Skr. strong, sturdy.

sasak [KN], 1. wattles; *pagar ~,* a wattled fence. 2. crammed tight; a variant of *sesak.*

sasap [KK], *menyasap,* to weed, to pull

up; *susup-~,* to creep under everywhere.

sasar [KN], 1. dazed, confused, astray, offcourse, eccentric, odd; *bom ke~an jatuhnya,* a stray bomb (not a 'bomb on the target'!); *anak ke~,* a muddle-headed fool. 2. *~an,* target; *mata ~an,* bull's eye; *benteng ~an,* the mound behind the target; *menembak ~an,* to shoot at a target.

sasau = *sasar* 1.

sastera [KN], skr. sacred books; astrological tables, divination; pure literature, belles lettres; *ke~an,* literary studies.

sasterawan [KN], Skr. one versed in sacred books; an astrologer; a literary man.

sasteria [KN], knight = *kesateria.*

sasul [KK], *ter~,* gone past, gone too far, = *terlangsung.*

sat [KN], 1. measure of capacity, = 5 *gantangs.* 2. the ace (at cards); *janda ~ lekuk,* (sl.) lonely widow (only one heart).

satah [KN], plane, flat, level surface which has length and width but no thickness.

satar [KN], Ar. = *syatar;* a line (of writing, print).

sate [KN], Tam. kebabs; pieces of meat or fish cooked on a skewer; *secucuk ~,* a skewer of kebabs.

satu [KBil], one; = *suatu; ber~,* united; *ber~ padu,* firmly united; *ke~an,* union, unity; *per~an,* id.; *ke~an buruh,* labour union; *ke~an pekerja,* id.; *ke~an sekerja,* id.; *negara ke~an,* a unitary state; *menyatukan,* to unite; *menyatu-padukan,* to unite firmly, to integrate; *penyatuan,* consolidation, amalgamation; ~ *per~,* one by one; *~-~,* one at a time; *~-~nya,* only.

satwa [KN], *marga~,* a (wild) animal.

sau [KN], (onom.) rustling, soughing.

saudagar [KN], Pers. a merchant, a trader, a wholesale dealer; ~ *wang,* a financier.

saudara [KN], Skr. brother, sister; an intimate friend whom one calls a brother or sister, now also used in a semi-political sense of comrade; ~ *sepupu,* a cousin; ~ *sejalan sejadi,* a full brother or sister; ~ *bau bacang,* very distantly related; ~ *jauh,* ~ *renggang,* id.; ~ *daging,* ~ *sedarah,* blood relation; ~ *rapat,* nearly related; ~ *kadim,* next-of-kin; ~ *mara,* relatives generally; *per~an,* comradeship; brotherhood; *mengambil akan ~,* to break off a love-affair by agreeing to be 'brother and sister'.

saudari [KN], sometimes used as female of *saudara.*

sauh [KN], 1. an anchor; *campak ~,* to cast anchor; *bongkar ~,* to haul up the anchor; ~ *cemat,* an anchor fastened ashore for mooring a boat to; ~ *larat,* anchor that is dragging; ~ *terbang,* a light grapnel used for scaling a wall; *batang ~,* the shaft of an anchor; *batu ~,* the stone or weight in it; *kuku ~,* the blade. 2. a fruit-tree (*Mimusops kauki*).

saujana [KKtr], Skr. far, distant, as far as; ~ *mata memandang,* as far as the eye can see; *padang ~,* a wide plain.

sauk [KN], 1. a landing-net; a scoop; *men-yauk,* [KK], to scoop up in a landing-net; *ter~,* scooped up; (fig.) to steal, 'pinch'; *pak ~,* daddy sneak-thief. 2. the lid of a pot. 3. (onom.) sighing; *dengan ~ tangis,* with sighs and tears.

sauku [KN], Tam., Pen. a whip.

sawa [KN], 1. a generic name for snakes considered by Malays to belong to the python class; *ular ~ batu,* the reticulate python when living on rocky soil; *ular ~ burung,* the long snake (*Dipsadomor-phus cynodon*); *ular ~ cindai,* the reticulate python when its coloration is very brilliant; *ular ~ lekir* (*Coluber melanurus*); *ular ~ rendam,* the reticulate python when dull in colouring and aquatic in habits; *ular ~ tekukur,* a name for Coluber melanurus. 2. *buah ~, buah sawanilla,* the sapodilla; also *ciku.*

sawab [KN], Ar. the exact truth; *wallahu aalam bi~,* god knoweth what the real truth is!

sawah [KN], (= *bendang,* Ked., Pk.) an irrigated padi-field; *membuat ~,* to plant rice (on swampy ground); *per~an,* an area planted with wet rice; *ber~,* hav-

ing padi fields; *menyawah,* work in a padi field; *pe~,* padi planter.

sawan [KN], convulsions; ~ *babi,* epilepsy; ~ *bangkai,* apoplexy; *orang ~ gila,* a maniac; *terkena ~,* to have an attack of convulsions.

sawang [KN], 1. a plant (unidentified), used as a remedy for skin disease. 2. Pk. cobwebs.

sawar [KN], a barrier-fence; cf. **gawar-ga-war**; a fence to trap fish, deer and other animals.

sawat [KN], 1. a sort of plaid; ~ *sandang,* a sort of cross-belt. 2. *pe~,* a tool; an implement or appliance; the penis.

sawi [KN], 1. a leaf vegetable known from its flower as the Chinese mustard plant. 2. = *senawi.*

saya [KN], = *sahaya.*

sayak [KN], a plaited basket-work tray.

sayang [KS], 1. regret, pity, sorrow for; affectionate pining; love; *menaruh ~,* to be in love; *~kan,* to regret, to love; *merasa tidak di~i,* (he) feels unwanted; *~!,* what a pity!; as an address, dearie!; *~nya,* unfortunately; ~ *duit,* to be over-fond of money, close-fisted; *penyayang,* affectionate; compassionate; *ke~an,* favourite, affection. 2. *tombak ~,* a sort of gaff used with a coil.

sayap [KN], wing, pinion; ~ *kumbang,* a bumble-bee's (shiny black) wing; *baju ber~,* a coat with pendulous sleeves; the mudguard of a car; ~ *kiri,* the left wing.

sayat [KK], slicing off the skin, top, or cover of anything, or any projecting portion — such as a nose or ear; *men-yayatkan hati,* to tear the heart; heart-breaking.

sayembara [KN], Ind. contest.

sayidina [KN], leader in the Faith, a title of Muslim missionaries and Sayids and of certain Javanese rulers.

sayu [KS], sad, melancholy; plaintive, lifeless.

sayung [KS], uneven or crooked, not evenly cut (e.g., a divided fruit); not frank (of speech).

sayup [KS], faintly visible or audible; just noticeale (stronger than *lebuh*, less strong than *riam*); ~ *mata memandang*, so far as to be only indistinctly seen; ~ *piama*, Ked. the close of the rainy season.

sayur [KN], vegetables in general; green food; ~*kan*, to cook as a vegetable; to serve up as a vegetable; ~*-mayur* or ~-~*an*, all kinds of vegetables; *membuat* ~ *mentah*, (sl.) to make mincemeat of.

sdr [KN], = *saudara;* not infrequently written before a man's name in the sense of 'Comrade' or 'Mr'.

se, a prefix expressing or suggesting unity, one, a; forming or constituting one, i.e., making up a whole; forming one in some particular, i.e., alike in some one respect; ~*umurku*, in all my life; as long as I live — life being considered as a single item though made up of many years; ~*rasa*, forming one in taste; alike in taste; ~*bagai*, one in type, of one type, like; as in the function of, in the form of; ~*belah*, one side, on one side; in the direction of, towards; *dan* ~*bagainya*, and so on; ~*belah menyebelah*, on both sides; ~*belum*, while as yet not; before, previous to; ~*hingga*, until; ~*kali*, at one time, all at one time, altogether; ~*kali-kali*, altogether; ~*kali* ~*kali*, occasionally, every now and then; ~*kali* ~*kala*, id.; ~*kian*, so much; ~*kian jauh*, thus far; ~*kian lama*, so long; ~*lagi*, while still; ~*lalu*, always; continually, frequently; ~*mata-mata*, clearly, obviously; wholly; ~*orang*, one man; alone; ~*orang diri*, quite alone; without assistance; ~*orang-orang*, quite alone; ~ ~*orang*, each person; ~*suatu*, each; ~*telah*, when (a thing), was over, after; ~*telah ia pergi*, when he had gone; ~*tuju*, in harmony, harmonious.

sebab [KKr], Ar. cause, reason; (better *dari* ~), because; ~*itu lah*, therefore, for that reason; *apa* ~*?*, why?; ~*-musabab*, the causes, all the various reasons; ~*-akibat*, cause and effect.

sebai [KN], a scarf worn on the shoulders; *menyebai, menyebaikan,* wind (a shawl round the neck.)

sebak [KS], 1. *air* ~, an inundation; water lying on ground us. dry. 2. short of breath, gasping; ~ *dada,* id.; ~ *hidung,* feeling of choking in the nose; ~ *air matanya,* to shed tears.

sebal [KS], angry, sulky; ~ *hati,* id.

sebam [KS], losing brightness of colour, dull.

sebar [KS], numb, having lost sensation; 2. *menyebar, menyebarkan,* [KK], scatter, strewn, spread; *penyebar,* distributor.

sebarau [KN], a kind of carp; = *barau-barau.*

sebasah [KN], a generic name given to a number of trees or shrubs of the order Euphorbiaceae, e.g., *Glochidium desmocarpum.*

sebat [KK], 1. to switch; to flog; (fig.) to 'pinch', make off with. 2. a shiver caused by the taste of something extremely acid. 3. choked (of the nostril).

sebekah [KN], *ikan* ~, a kind of sea-perch (*Apongon* sp.).

seberang [KN], the opposite side; *di* ~ *sana Sungai Singapura,* on the opposite bank of the Singapore River; *Seberang Perai,* Province Wellesley (from Penang); *menyeberang,* to cross over; ~ *laut,* overseas; *menyeberangi,* to cross, (be laid across, as a bridge).

seberhana [KN], Skr. full (of full dress); *memakai* ~ *perhiasan,* to wear all one's jewellery or decorations.

sebik [KK], to purse up the lips; *ter*~, making a wry face.

sebit [KK], a dish of buffalo meat and vermicelli.

sebu [KS], filled up, choked up (of a well, nostril or stomach, or silted drain).

sebuk [KK], *menyebuk,* to intrude on a company.

sebun [KS], 1. protracted (of labour); refusing to come to a head (of a boil). 2. = *sebu.*

sebung [KN], a single division (from node to node) of the bamboo.

seburut [KN], a plant *(Thottea grandiflora).*

sebut [KK], ~*an* the thing said; the drift or tenor of remarks; pronunciation; ~*kan, menyebutkan,* to utter; to repeat; to pronounce; to mention; *ter~,* said; *seperti yang ter~ di bawah ini,* as follows; *jadi ~an,* to get talked about (for good or evil); ~-~*an,* much talked about; *nama di~ orang,* to get talked about, esp. in disparagement.

sedak [KN], *ter~,* choked.

sedak [KK], to tighten with rattan a tambourine *(rebana); perutnya macam rebana di~,* his stomach was like a tightened tambourine, 'as tight as a drum' (from over-eating).

sedal [KK], *menyedal,* drying clothes on a line inside a house.

sedan [KN], *ter~-~,* sobbing.

sedang [KS], medium; intermediate; during, while; ~ *masak,* just ripening; ~*kan,* although; even though; whereas; while.

sedap [KS], pleasant, nice, agreeable; ~ *hati,* satisfied; *berasa tak berapa ~ badan,* not feeling very well.

sedar [KK], alive, to, awake to, conscious; realize; *tiada ~,* to be unconscious (of a fact); ~ *daripada bius,* to recover consciousness after being drugged; ~*kan,* to be conscious of; *tidak ~kan diri,* (1) to be unconscious; (2) not to know one's self or one's place; *ter~,* roused to consciousness; *dia sudah ~ tepi kainnya,* he knows the end of his sarung, i.e. he realizes his limitations; (as to this use of *tepi kain* see *tepi); menyedari,* realize; *menyedarkan, awaken; ter~,* remembered, awaken, regain consciousness.

sedari Ind. since, from the time when.

sedawa [KK], to belch.

sedawai [KN], *akar ~,* a plant *(Smilax calophylla).*

sedekah [KN], Ar. alms, charity; *ber~,* donate.

sedelinggam [KN], Tam. minium, red-lead.

sederhana Skr. medium, average; moderate; temperate, of climate; simple; tolerant; *tubuhnya ~,* he was of average height and build; *menyerdehanakan,* moderate, simplify; *ke~an,* moderation, temperance.

sedia [KS], 1. Skr. ready, in readiness, prepared; already present, already in position; *ter~,* ready to use, ready-made; *ber~,* prepared, ready for action; *siap ~,* everything ready, 'ready, aye, ready' ; *per~n,* stocks; arrangements, necessary measures; ~*kan,* to get (things) ready, to prepare; to lay in a stock of. 2. Skr. former, ancient, original; *rupanya yang ~,* his original form; ~*-kala,* days of old; always, at all times, immemorial.

sedih [KS], sad, sorrowful, unhappy; *ber~,* sad, depressed; *tahan ~,* to control one's grief; *menyedihkan,* sadden; *ke~an,* sadness, sorrow.

sedikit, see *dikit.*

sedingin [KN], a common succlent herb *(Bryophyllum calycinum).*

sedu [KS], short broken sobs; sobbing; *ter~-~,* id.; ~ *katak,* short quick breathing after violent exertion; ~*-sedan,* sobs and moans; also *sendu.*

seduayah [KN], a medicinal plant (unidentified).

seduh [KK], *menyeduh,* to soak in warm water; to infuse in water.

sedut [KK], to sniff up the nostril; *hati ter~,* sullenly angry; used also of sucking up generally, e.g., by a vacuum cleaner; ~*an,* (fig.) an extract, e.g., from a speech; inhalation; *menyedut,* to sniff up; to sip or suck up, a drink; (fig.) to filch, pilfer; *penyedut,* inhalator, straw.

sega [KS], smooth; shining on the surface; *rotan ~,* the common rattan of commerce.

segah [KS], full (after meals); a sense of distension; flatulence.

segak [KS], gorgeously got up, dressy; *memakai ~-begak,* all dressed up.

segala [KBil], Tam. all, every; the whole of; ~ *tubuh,* the whole body; ~ is sometimes prefixed to a word merely to show that it is in the plural.

segan [KS], reluctant; slow; *penyegan,* a sluggard; *burung ~,* the night-jar *(Ca-*

primulgus macrurus); lepat ~, a Malay sweetmeat of banana and pulut rice; hidup ~, mati tak mahu, reluctant to live, but won't die, i.e. listless, won't make an effort; tak ~-~, boldly without hesitation; ~i, to respect, look up to; jangan ~, to feel free; penyegan, shy, unsociable.

seganda [KN], Skr. a name, or introductory name, of several fragrant plants, e.g., ~-puri, ~-mala.

segani [KN], helmsman.

segar [KS], feeling fit, healthy and strong, well; refreshed; revived; ~-bugar, fit and fresh, in fine shape; yang menyegarkan badan, refreshing; berasa ~, to feel fit; penyegar, stimulating, tonic, stimulant.

segara [KN], 1. Skr. the ocean. 2. Pers. sugar, = sagar. 3. Jav. a flower, = sekara.

segel [KN], a Malay basket of rattan or wood for keeping captured animals.

segera [KKtr], Skr. speedily, promptly; menyegerakan, to expedite, to hurry up; used for 'urgent', e.g., on telegrams.

segi [KN], side, corner, angle; aspect; empat ~ or empat per~, four-sided, square; ~ tiga, a triangle; triangular; per~ memanjang, oblong; ~ tiga sama panjang, equilateral triangle; ~ is used in the sense of 'angle of vision', 'viewpoint'; dilihat dari ~ itu, anda benar, you have a point there.

seguk [KS], bad (of work that offends the eye), jarring, inharmonious.

seh [KN], Ch. clan, family; the first word in order in a Chinese name is the clan name, in effect, the surname.

sejahtera [KS], Skr. peace, tranquillity, ease; selamat ~, id.; ke~an, welfare, prosperity.

sejak, since; = semenjak.

sejarah [KN], Ar. annals; pedigree, history, genealogy; hari ber~, historic day.

sejat [KS], to get rid of water (by filtration or evaporation); rinsing or steaming out; to evaporate.

sejati [KS], real, true, genuine.

sejuk [KS], cold, cool; ~ hati, calm;

menyejukkan, cool off; penyejuk, cooler; penyejukan, cooling; Jawa ~, a name given to the pattern of the ordinary kris-handle, which is really the Garuda bird, whereon Vishnu rode; ~ hati, calm, cool; menyejukkan hati, to pacify; console; ~ in some contexts means fortunate; tanganku ~, I was in luck.

seka [KK], menyeka, to wipe away, as tears.

sekah [KS], broken but not broken off; fractured but not severed.

sekah [KS], 1. active, nimble. 2. Ar. the mint-impression; the 'guinea- stamp' on a coin.

sekala [KKtr], Treng. formerly, hitherto.

sekali [KBil], once, altogether, very; se~, very seldom.

sekaliah, see kali.

sekam [KN], rice-husk, chaff.

sekarang [KKtr], now, at present; ~ ini, now at this very time; just now; also ~; see karang 3.

sekat [KK], 1. opposing; intercept, obstruct, block, bar; cutting off (as supplies by blockade); ~an, a bar, an obstruction; restrictions, controls; menyekati, to hinder, to obstruct; menyekat beranak, birth- control; undang-undang ~an tempat, law regarding restriction of places of residence; bilik ber~, a cubicle; ~ jalan, to seal off a road. 2. a clod (of earth).

sekeduduk = senduduk.

sekedup [KN], Ar. the litter-like saddle on a camel's back; sometimes used to describe rail-trolleys worked by hand.

sekendi [KN], the white ibis.

sekedup [KN], (Dutch) screw.

sekian see kian.

sekin [KK], menyekin ronggeng, to join the dancers at a ronggeng (as is commonly done by spectators).

sekoci [KN], (Dutch) a ship's cutter; a gig.

sekoi [KN], Italian millet (Panicum Italicum).

sekolah [KN], Port. school; ~ tumpangan, boarding-school; ~ ulangan, day-school; ~ umum, standard school; ~ rendah, primary school; ~ menengah, secondary school; ~ *bantuan,* aided school; ~ *bebas,* independent school; ~ *budak-budak nakal,* reformatory; ~ *pembentuk akhlak,* id.; ~ *perdangangan,* commercial school; ~ *perguruan,* teachers' training school; ~ *pertanian,* agricultural school; ~ *perubatan,* medical school; ~ *pertukangan,* technical school; ~ *jurutera,* engineering school; ~ *gambar,* museum; ~ *malam,* night-school; ~ *lanjutan,* school for extension courses; ~ *yang berasrama,* school with a hostel attached; ~ *anika jurusan,* comprehensive school; ~ *latihan jasmani,* 'Outward Bound' school; *mengaji* ~, to attend school; *ber*~, id.; *wang per*~*an,* school-fees; *menyekolahkan,* enroll in a school; *kawan seper*~*an,* schoolmate.

sekopong [KN], (Dutch) the suit 'Spades' in playing cards.

seksi [KN], Ind. section, small party, e.g. sub-committee.

sekul [KN], Pers. a water vessel made of coconut shell; a beggar's bowl.

sekup [KN], (Dutch) a spade, a shovel.

sekut [KN], 1. a drug or charm used by thieves to stupefy people whom they intend to rob. 2. stingy, miserly.

sekutu [KN], associate, accomplice, association.

sela [KN], interval between; interstice; *tiada bor*~, continuous, unbroken; ~ *batu,* a shell *(Pholas)* — cf. **celah, selang,** etc.

seladang [KN], the wild ox of the Peninsular *(Bos gaurus).*

selagi [Kktr], as long as.

selak [KN], a door-bolt, any sort of cross-bar.

selak [KK], lift up a curtain or garment; *kain ter*~, with the sarung drawn up high; ~*kan kain,* to pull up a garment; *menyelak-nyelakkan,* to turn over, turn up, as when riffling through the leaves of a book or examining articles in a box.

selaka [KN], 1. a bamboo frame on which garments are placed to be perfumed by burning fragrant wood inside the frame. 2. Jav. silver.

selalu [KKtr], 1. always; ~*nya,* usually. 2. Pah. at once, immediately.

selam [KK], diving; plunge; *juru*~, a diver; ~*kan,* to give (a person) a ducking; *menyelam,* to dive; *menyelam mutiara,* to dive for pearls; *ter*~, immersed; *penyelam,* diver; *penyelaman,* diving, immersion.

selamat [KS], Ar. peace, security, safety; *menyelamatkan,* save, protect; *ber*~*an,* have a religious feast to ensure safety; ~ *jalan,* bon voyage; ~ *tinggal,* goodbye (from a traveller to those who stay behind); ~ *berpisah,* farewell; ~ *berbahagia,* long life and happiness to ...; ~ *belayar,* goodbye (to a person sailing); *ke*~*an umum,* public safety; *langkah ke*~*an,* security forces; *majlis ke*~*an dalam negeri,* Internal Security Council; *majlis ke*~*an bangsa-bangsa bersatu,* Security Council of the United Nations; *raja pun* ~*lah sempai ke Melaka,* the prince reached Malacca safely.

selamba [KS], rough, coarse of words; *muka* ~, shameless, pocker-faced, brazen; expressionless.

selampai [KN], wearing a thing loosely suspended over the shoulder; *menyelampai,* to wear in this way; *ter*~, draped, hanged.

selampit [KN], 1. a travelling story-teller or rhapsodist; also *selapit.* 2. to braid (hair); tie up (cloth); *ber*~*kan kainnya,* with his sarong tied up like a loin-cloth.

Selang [KN], Ceylon; *batu* ~, the sapphire.

selang [KN], 1. alternate, at intervals; ~ *dua pintu,* every third door; ~ *tiga empat bulan,* every three or four months; *sudah* ~ *dua bulan,* after an interval of two months; ~*i,* to alternate; *ber*~, ~*seli,* alternating; ~*an,* an interval, an intermission. 2. ~*kan,* a variant of *sedangkan* — cf. **sedang.**

selangat [KN], a fish *(Dorosoma* sp.), the bony bream or hairback.

selangin [KN], = *senangin.*

selangka [KN], *tulang* ~, the collar-bone; *kena* ~, to be executed (with the kris).

selanting [KN], the long-billed partridge.

selap [KK], *menyelap,* to have hysterics; *di~,* in hysterics, in a fit; *menyelap,* Kel., Treng. to be unconscious, to faint; *menyelapi,* to enter into, to penetrate, to take possession of (by evil spirit).

selapit, Kel. = *selampit* l.; *orang tarik ~,* id.

selaput [KN], 1. a film, a guazy covering; *~ mata,* the film in a cataract; *~ lendir,* mucous membrane; *penyakit radang ~ perut,* peritonitis. 2. Pen. mace.

selar [KK], 1. to brand; *~ dengan besi,* id.; (fig.) to stigmatise, cast opprobrium on; *menyelarkan,* to brand; to scorch; to cauterize; *~an,* attack, severe criticism. 2. creeping along the ground like a snake; *ular tedung ~,* the hamadryad *(Naia bungarus); menyelar,* to creep; *akar menyelar,* a creeping root (above ground). 3. *ikan ~,* a generic name given to a number of fish, e.g., *Caranx cambon* and *C. gymnos-tochrides.*

selara [KN], 1. fine thorns like thistledown found on the skin of some plants. 2. *anak ~,* the young sembilang fish.

selarung [KN], a wild-beast track.

Selasa [KN], Ar. *hari ~,* Tuesday.

selasar [KN], a side-gallery or balcony in a house, *~ dandi,* a little shrub *(Stachytarpheta Indica); mabuk bunga ~,* drunk from wine, or love-sick; stupefied, stunned; *ayam ~,* a black fowl.

selat [KN], a strait; *Selat Singapura,* the Straits of Singapore; *Selat Teberau,* the Johor straits.

selatan [KN], the south; *jauh ke ~,* far away to the south; *~ daya,* S.S.W.; *~ menenggara,* S.S.E.

selawat [KN], *membaca ~,* to pray to God to bestow peace on the Prophet Muhammad.

selayar [KN], 1. an edible jungle fruit, also called *kembang semangkuk;* see *semangkuk.* 2. *ikan ~,* a sailfish.

selayun [KN], a scarecrow of rags hung on strings — cf. **selayut.**

selayur [KN], *ikan ~,* a fish *(Trichiurus savala?);* also *ikan layur-layur;* see *layur* 2.

selayut = *selayun.*

selebaran [KN], Ind. a hand-bill.

selebu [KN], *laut ~,* the open sea.

seleguri [KN], a shrub *(Clerodendron disparifolium); ~ padang,* a small shrub *(Sida rhombifolia);* it has yellow flowers — simples are made from its roots.

selekeh [KN], a stain, smeared, smudged, a splash of dirt; *ber~,* bespattered.

selekoh [KN], a bend or twist in direction; a turn in a road; salient angle; *~ kota,* a bastion.

selekor [KN], *ikan ~,* Singapore name for large horse-mackerel *(cencaru).*

selembada [KN], *semut ~,* a large unidentified ant.

selembana [KK], *menyelembana,* to lay to (of a ship).

selembayung [KN], an arm a cross-bar, or yard from which decorative streamers are suspended; an emblem of royalty; also *sulur bayung.*

selembubu [KN], *angin ~,* an eddying wind, whirlwind.

selempang [KN], cross-wise; *~kan,* to wear a garment cross-wise over the chest. 2. afraid, frightened, anxious; *menyelempangkan,* to worry about; *ter~,* fall down with legs astride.

selendang [KN], shawl worn by women over the shoulders; *kain ~ merah,* a red cloth carried into battle by the superstitious as a charm.

selenggara [KK], to look after, attend to; to maintain, to upkeep; *menyelenggarakan,* manage.

selepa = *celepa.*

selepang [KN], thrown on and over the shoulder (as a shawl) — cf. **selempang.**

selepat [KK], besmeared, bedaubed.

selepung [KS], *ber~,* dirtied.

selera [KN], Skr. 1. body; a very poet. equivalent of *badan.* 2. appetite, enjoyment of eating; *~ tiada,* to have lost one's appetite; *yang membuka ~,* appetising; *tepuk perut tanya ~,* pat your stomach and inquire of your appetite (before embarking on a big meal); a saying meaning, don't undertake a task before you are sure that you can do it; don't bite off more than you can chew;

look before you leap.

selerak [KS], *ber~*, scattered about, dotted here and there; *jamuan ber~*, buffet party (tables dotted here and there).

selesa [KS], uncramped, spacious, with ample accommodation; comfortable (as roomy), of clothes.

selesai [KS], settled, completed, finished, terminated; *setelah ~ daripada belajar*, when his education was finished; *~kan*, to wind up, to terminate, to settle (a dispute or debt); to straighten out; *~lah!*, that's torn it!, that finishes it!

selesema [KN], a cold in the head; influenza; also *sema-sema*.

seleweng [KN], *penyeleweng*, mischievous busybody, meddler; *bawa menyeleweng*, to lead astray; *menyeleweng*, to deviate; *penyelewengan*, deviation from the straight path.

selia [KK], to inspect, watch over; *penyelia*, inspector, overseer, supervisor.

seliap [KN], a kind of mackerel *(Chorinemus moadetta)*.

seliat [KK], a skin; to strip off skin or bark.

selidik [KK], make diligent enquiry or investigation — cf. **sidik**; *menyelidiki*, examine thoroughly, study, research; *penyelidikan*, investigation, research, esp. Governmental.

seligi [KN], a short light bamboo, or wooden dart, or pointed stick; *menyeligi*, hurl a ~.

selilir [KK], Pk. *ber~*, to overflow.

selimbar [KN], a large wild gambier *(Un caria sclerophylla)*.

selimpat [KN], plaited work; wicker; *~ air*, a small aroid *(Aglaonema minus)*; *ular ~*, a generic name for sea-snakes owing to their flattened tails (the name is applied sp. to *Enhydris hardwickii)*; *ular ~ katang tebu*, a name for broad-banded sea-snakes, e.g., *Distira stokesii* and *Chersydrus granulatus*; *ular ~ sungai*, a small sea-snake without distinctive markings *(Enhydrina valakadyen)*.

selimut [KN], *kain ~*, a blanket; *~i*, to cover with, to wrap up in a blanket; *~kan*, to use as a sheet.

selinap [KK], 1. tearing off the skin of anything, e.g. of a fowl, to avoid the trouble of plucking the feathers. 2. to scuttle along, slip through, to sneak off e.g., long grass (opposed to *rapah* 1).

selindar [KN], Eng. a cylinder (of an engine); *berjalan tiga ~*, (sl) to limp.

selindung [KK], hiding, veiling; *ber~*, concealed, veiled; *tak ber~*, openly — cf. **lindung**; *ter~*, covered, concealed.

seling [KN], 1. Jav. glazed earthenware, chinaware, porcelain. 2. Eng. small silver. 3. Ind. = *selang*; *~an*, an interlude; a variety entertainment.

selingsing = *singsing*.

seliput [KK], *menyeliput*, to cover all over (as a creeper); cf. **liput**.

selirat [KS], mesh-work; ordered entanglement; *ber~*, complicated, reticulate — cf. **sirat**.

selisih [KK], to disagree; *ber~*, (of things); to fail to meet (of joinery); to pass one another (as vehicles going in opposite directions); to be separated; *per~an*, a dispute; *per~an faham*, misunderstanding; difference of opinion; ~ is also used in the sense of differing, showing disparity; *dia ber~ sikit mata sahaja*, he had a difference of only a few marks.

selisik [KK], picking out fleas of lice from the hair; preening the feathers (of a bird); *menyelisik*, to cleanse the hair or feathers.

selisip [KK], *menyelisip*, to slip in, to insert (a th.) secretly somewhere.

selisir [KK], walking round the edge of anything; see *sisir* 2.

selit [KK], to trust in between; *ter~*, stuck or jammed between two surfaces; (fig.) in a fix, in a jam.

selitar [KKtr], 1. all round, = *keliling*; *~ alam*, all over the world; (by extension) of a ruler or spirit whose power is felt all over the earth. 2. a community of Sea Gypsies living on Singapore Island in the time of Raffles.

seliuh [KS], *ter~*, twisted, wrenched, esp. of a joint, sprain.

seliwir [KK], *ber~an*, to loiter about.

selodok [KK], *menyelodok,* to worm one's way through jungle.

selofen [KN], cellophane.

selok-belok, see *belok.*

seloka [KN], Skr. verses, rhyme; ironical or satirical poetry when not in the form of the *pantun.*

selomor [KN], the slough of a snake.

selompot [KN], mace.

selongkar [KK], *menyelongkar,* to search a man's belongings, e.g., for stolen property; to rummage; to pillage, sack — cf. **bongkar.**

selongsong [KN], wrapper.

selonok-selanak [KS], intermittently visible (as an animal running in tall grass).

seloroh [KN], droll; *ber~,* to joke, jest; also *selurau.*

seluang [KN], *ikan ~,* the slender carp. *(Rasbora* and *Basilicus* sp.); this fish is used as a simile for 'home-loving' because it haunts the mouths of rivers without going to sea.

seluar [KN], Pers. trousers, breeches; *se helai ~,* a pair of trousers; *~ bulat,* pyjama trousers; *~ China,* Chinese trousers; *~ kotong,* short trousers — such as those worn by rikisha pullers; *~ sampak,* trousers worn by Malays in the rice-fields; *~ katuk,* Jav. shorts.

selubung [KK], veiling, covering; overshadowing, enveloping; *~kan diri,* to cover oneself with a veil; *ber~ baik-baik,* to wrap up well (as on a cold day); *di~ oleh hutan rimba,* covered with jungle.

seludang [KN], the sheath or outer covering of a palm blossom; *~ mayang,* id.; *seperti ~ menolak mayang,* to make known (to bring to light) the hidden truth (beauty).

seludip [KN], the sheath or outer covering of a young palm.

seludu [KN], a catfish *(Arius gagora).*

seludup [KK], Ind. to smuggle; also s*elundup; penyeludup,* smuggler.

seluk [KK], to grope after something hidden, e.g., as a man in his pocket for a coin; used of skirmishing through a jungle, infiltrating; *menyeluk,* to grope about with the hand; *~ kocek,* to pick pockets.

selukat [KN], a musical instrument forming part of the *gamelan* or Javanese orchestra.

seluloid [KN], celluloid.

selumar [KN], a tree *(Mussoendopsis beccariana).*

selumbar [KN], long thorns — such as those of the *nibung;* splinter; also *selimbar.*

selupat [KN], a natural thin filmy covering, such as the almost transparent skin under the shell of an egg — cf. **selaput.**

selurai [KN], a kind of vermicelli.

selurau Pk. = *seloroh.*

seluruh [KBil], *menyeluruhi,* universal, covering all fields or aspects; (fig.) to cover the whole area (with eyes), look (a person) up and down; *ke~an,* the whole, unity made up of parts; *pada ke~annya,* on the whole; taken as a whole; *secara ke~annya,* id.; cf. *lurah* 1.

selusuh [KN], a generic name for all drugs, medicines and charms used for facilitating delivery in childbirth; *~ beranak,* id.; *~ uri,* a drug for getting rid of the after-birth.

selusur [KN], Pah. the hand-rail of a bridge.

selut [KN], mud, slush, slimy mud.

sema [KN], *~~,* a cold in the head; also *selesema.*

semadi [KK], *ber~,* to dwell, esp. as a recluse, to rest; to meditate.

semah [KN], a propitiatory offering to evil spirits, a sacrifice; *jin yang kurang ~,* a hungry ghost; *penyemah,* a sacrifice; *tempat ~,* hut for spirits, to keep them off, e.g., mine-workings; *ber~,* to hold a propitiatory ceremony, e.g., at a rivermouth at the opening of the fishing season.

semai [KN], *~an,* a nursery for rice-plants; *menyemai, ~kan,* to plant in a nursery; (fig.) to sow the seeds of, e.g., discontent.

semaja [KKtr], only; = *sahaja.*

semak [KN], thick undergrowth, scrub;

jalan yang ~, a road that has become overgrown; ~ *samun,* extremely overgrown; (fig.) in a mess, untidy, as a room; ~ *sangat ini!,* what a mess!

semak [KK], to compare, esp. in checking; *penyemak,* a proof-reader; ~ is also used to mean, 'to consider, review'; *menyemak kertas jawapan,* to mark the papers of answers in an examination.

semalu [KN], sensitive plant (mimosa).

semambu [KN], *rotan* ~, the Malacca cane *(Calamus scipionum);* ~ *bangkut,* a Malacca cane of which two or more joints occur exceptionally close to one another, a peculiarity believed to bring luck.

semampai [KS], 1. loosely lashed together (as the component parts of a raft). 2. tall and graceful (fig.); hang loosely.

seman [KS], fruitless, abortive; coming to nothing; spoilt, failed, futile (of a petulant child who will not eat or obey orders).

Semang [KN], a name given to Negrito aborigines in the country near the headwaters of the Perak river; *anak* ~, N.S. a child by tribal adoption under special tribal system; *rupa nenek* ~, like an old woman of the woods (reproach to a child with untidy hair).

semangat [KN], the spirit of life; the soul in the ancient Indonesian sense; a term of endearment; *ambil* ~, to capture another person's ~ and so render that person subject to your will; *buah* ~, special padi-stalks used as an offering at the harvest rites; *hilang* ~, *kurang* ~ or *lemah* ~, faint, weak; *kur* ~, an expression used in invoking a ~ because of its bird-like character; *terbang* ~, to depart (of the spirit of life, resulting in temporary unconsciousness); ~ *padi,* the spirit of life in the padi; ~ is also used for 'zeal', 'morale'; *tinggi-*~, of high morale; *lemah-*~, of low morale; *memberi* ~, to raise morale; *hilang* ~, to be dispirited; *tak ber-*~, listless, spiritless; *ber-* *perang,* warlike.

semangkuk [KN], a plant *(Stercaleia*

scaphigera); kembang ~, id.; the seeds of this plant swell in water and fill a small bowl; see *selayar.*

semanja [KKtr], a variant of *semaja* and *sahaja.*

semantan [KN], *nyiur* ~, a coconut at the stage when the water inside can just begin to be heard when the nut is shaken — cf. **santan.**

Semar [KN], 1. a comic character in a Javanese play. 2. as far as, up to, until.

semarak [KS], showing brightly, shining, burning bright; *ber*~, to cast rays afar; *menyemarakkan,* to brighten, light up; (fig.) to enliven, animate.

semat [KN], a sort of lath used for pinning pieces of atap together in making roofing; *per*~*kan,* to pin together, e.g., sheets of paper; *penyemat atap,* a thatch-pin.

semata [KKtr], Skr. quite, utterly.

semayam [KK], 1. sitting enthroned; *ber*~, to sit on the throne in state; (fig.) to reside (of a prince); *per*~*an,* royal residence. 2. *kaum Semayam,* a tribe of aborigines living in the Malacca district.

sembah [KK], a salutation suggestive of deep respect or homage; (fig.) the speech of a subject to a prince; an offering by a subject to a prince; *demikianlah* ~*nya,* thus he (the subejct) spake; *membawa* ~ *daripada buah-buahan,* bringing offerings of fruit; ~*kan,* to convey (a message or offering) to a prince; to represent (facts) to a prince; *memper*~*kan,* id.; *menyembah,* to perform the salutation of homage; to do obeisance; *berdatang* ~, id.; *per*~*kan,* an offering; *per*~*kan,* to persent (as a play); *ber*~, address respectfully.

sembahyang [KN], to worship God; to pray; cf. **sembah** and *yang; air* ~, water for ceremonial ablution; ~ *hajat,* to pray for a particular object, as opposed to ritual prayers; ~ *lima waktu,* the five compulsory times of prayer (of Muslims).

sembam [KK], 1. falling face foremost;

ter~ *sungkur* ~, id.; *menyemban muka ke...*, burying one's face in.... 2. cook fish over embers.

sembang [KK], *ber~*, to gossip, chit chat.

sembap [KS], swollen with dropsy; bloated, puffy, as with beri-beri.

sembarangan [KKtr], Ind. indiscriminately, carelessly; haphazardly.

sembari [KKtr], Ind. while.

sembat [KK], throwing with a jerk (e.g., a casting-net); springing back with a jerk (e.g., as a branch); *tali* ~, the cord that jerks and closes a trap; *ter~*, caught up (as foot in wire).

sembawang [KN], a tree *(Kayea ferruginea)*.

sembelih [KK], to slaughter by cutting throat, killing; *mati ber~*, slaughtered by cutting of throat, i.e. duly slaughtered under Islamic law.

sembelit [KS], costive, constipation.

semberani [KN], (? Tam. = bay), *kuda* ~, a Pegasus; a steed of supernatural power; *besi be~*, magnetic iron.

semberap [KN], a complete set of articles; a *sirih*-box with its requisites.

semberip [KN], a brass pedestal tray or stand for one plate.

semberono [KS], Ind. careless, not serious; *menyemberonokan,* to treat lightly, disrespectfully.

sembeta [KN], props to keep a boat upright when hauled ashore or steady in a surf or a shallow.

sembilan [KBil], nine; one taken from ten *(se ambilan); Negeri Sembilan,* the Nine States (a name given to a confederacy of Menangkabau States).

sembilang [KN], *ikan* ~, a generic name for some marine catfish with very poisonous fins *(Plotosus canias, P. unicolor, P. lineatus* and perhaps, *P. horridus)*.

sembilu [KN], a bamboo knife, a sharpened splinter of bamboo.

sembir [KN], 1. the edge or rim of a plate. 2. 'to show wrong' (of the compass).

semboyan [KN], a tocsin; an alarm-gun, or alarm-bell, or gong; a siren; *pasang*

~, to fire a signal-gun; *memberi* ~, to signal a warning; *ber~kan,* use something as an alarm; e.g. sound a siren; *pasukan* ~, signal corps; a signal, signalled message; slogan; motto.

sembuang [KN], 1. an offering cast away in the jungle for evil spirits. 2. a mooring-post or winning-post.

sembuh [KK], healing, getting well, recovering; *~kan,* to heal, to cause an illness to end in recovery.

sembul [KS], protuberant, prominent (of the breasts, a bruise), etc.; *ter~*, projecting, bulging out.

sembulu [KS], rough-hewn, unplaned, in the rough (of timber).

sembung [KN], 1. a strongly scented herb *(Blumea balsamifera).* 2. splashing up (e.g., as when a shell strikes water).

sembuni = *sembunyi.*

sembunyi [KN], concealment; *~kan* [KK], to conceal; *ber~*, in hiding; *ter~*, hidden; *~-~*, stealthily; *per~an,* hiding place.

sembur [KN], ejecting forcibly from the mouth; spitting out; (the word is not used of actual spitting *(ludah),* but of a snake spitting out venom or of a man spitting out a mouthful of water); *~kan,* to spit out; *menyembur ubat,* to spray chemicals; *menyembur,* to bespatter; to pour out (as blood); *(alat) penyembur api,* a flame-thrower; a blow-torch; *ber~an,* bespattering all around; *pecah ber~,* to break in spray; *kena* ~, to get splashed; (fig.) to get a reprimand, to be 'told off' ~ is used for the ceremonial spitting out of water, in magical incantations.

semburit [KN], sodomy.

semburna [KS], Skr. gold-coloured; aureate.

semedang [KKtr], Pk. always.

sememeh [KS], besmeared, befouled, dirty (of the face).

semena [KKtr], *tiada* ~, without reason; suddenly, unexpectedly; often written *tiada ~-mena*

semenanjung [KN], peninsula; ~ *Melayu,* the Malay Peninsula.

semenda [KN], N.S., Pah., the transference of a man's residence to the home of his wife's family; *orang ~*, a man who has married into his wife's tribe; *tempat ~*, a married man's wife's relations; *ber~*, to intermarry.

semendal [KN], mica.

semenderasa [KN], Jav. a name for the *cempaka* flower.

semenggah [KS], harmonious, fitting, proper; *tak ~*, unbecoming.

semenjak [KPhbg], since; *~ perang China*, since the war in China.

semenjana [KKtr], mediocre, middling.

sementang [KPhbg], although; granting that; while; = *sungguhpun*.

sementara [KKtr], while, during, for a time, temporary; *~ dia lagi kecil*, while he was still young; *buat ~*, temporarily.

sementelah [KKtr], the more; the more so; esp.; all the more; *~ pula*, furthermore.

sementung [KS], blunt, simple, dull-witted.

semerbak [KS], diffused, as odour, pervasive, fragrant.

semerdanta [KN], Skr. white pearly teeth; often written *asmara danta*.

semesta [KS], Skr. all, entire; *alam ~*, the whole world; *sarwa ~ sekalian*, the universe; all and everything.

semur [KN], (Dutch) to stew.

sempada [KN], *ketam ~*, a kind of crab.

sempadan [KN], boundary; *batu ~*, a boundary-stone; so, a warning example; *kalau elok, jadi tauladan; kalau tak elok, jadi ~*, if it is good, it is an example to follow; if it is bad, it is an example to avoid.

sempak [KS], chipped, notched, injured along the edge.

sempal [KK], jutting out; *menyempal*, to jut out; *ter~*, prominent, projecting slightly, as breasts.

sempalai [KS], lying about (as corpses after a battle, trees after a storm).

sempana [KS], *keris ~*, sinuous kris with three, five or seven curves *(lok);* a kris with more curves is *keris cerita*.

sempat [KKtr], able to do anything; having time to; *aku tak ~ lari*, I had no time to get away; *ke~an*, opportunity; *se ~ sahaja*, at the very moment that....

sempelah [KN], accursed, good for nothing; *anak ~*, a term of abuse, rubbish, dregs (of society).

sempelat [KS], *ber~*, begrimed, dirty (of the skin).

sempena [KS], a lucky mark, peculiarity that brings luck, e.g., on a weapon; blessing or auspiciousness brought by an object or a name; a sign or omen, esp. of success; (fig.) an opportunity, a favourable moment; a proptious symbol; *ber~ dengan*, in honour of, in celebration of, e.g., a date.

sempilai [KN], *ikan ~*, the fighting-fish.

sempit [KS], narrow; confined (cf. space); *ke~an*, a shortage; *ke~an belanja*, narrowness of means.

sempudal [KS], *ber~*, dirty, filthy (of clothes, crockery, the person); also *sempedal*.

sempuh [KK], to gore.

sempul [KK], *ter~*, sticking out, markedly prominent; cf. **sembul** and **sempal**.

sempuras [KS], dirty, unwashed (of the food).

sempurna [KS], Skr. complete, realised, perfect; intact; *~-akal*, level-headed; *~ pengetahuan*, his knowledge is perfect; *~kan*, to complete, to perfect; *menyempurnakan mayat*, to perform the due rites for a corpse; *ke~an*, entirely; un impaired state.

semput [KN], short of breath; *~-~*, in gasps; *sakit ~*, asthma.

semu [KN], deceit; *bermain ~*, to play a deceitful game; *ter~*, deceived.

semua [KKtr], Skr. all; the whole; every one of; *ke~nya*, all of them.

semudera [KN], Skr. 1. the ocean. 2. possibly the name of an extinct state in Acheen, which gave its name to the island of Sumatra; but see *Sumatera;* also *samudera*.

semugut = *senggugut*.

semut [KN], a generic name for ants other

than the white ant *(anai- anai)* and the tailor-ant *(kerengga);* ~ *api,* a long black ant which stings badly *(Nobopelta distinguenda);* ~ *sabun*g, a black and red ant found in boats and sandy places *(Sima rufonigra);* it also stings badly; in Malay the ant typifies insignificance, not industry; hence; *datang ribut, keluar* ~, came as a storm, went out as an ant, (in like a lion, out like a lamb — but of persons, not the month of March, as in England); (a protest) *disifatkan seperti kentut ~ sahaja,* treated as being no more than *kentut semut* (extract from leading article); *berasa diri se kecik ~,* to feel no bigger than an ant, i.e. thoroughly humiliated; *rasa ~-~,* a pringling, tingling feeling.

sena [KN], 1. Ar. ~ *maki,* 'Mecca senna'; the true senna obtained from the tree *Sassia angustifolia.* 2. *pokok ~,* [KN], the angsana tree *(Pterocarpus Indicus);* also *angsana.*

senai [KK], to rest (of a Malay medium).

senak [KS], griping pains in the stomach; a sharp pain, pang; *ter~,* winded; choked, as an air-locked pipe; ~ *nafas,* id.; *menyenakkan,* make too full or congested; *ke~an,* congestion, tightness.

senam [KN], 1. the dark colour visible when plated ware is scratched; *hilang sepuh nampak ~,* he is seen in his true colours. 2. *ber~,* to stretch oneself on waking; to do physical drill, physical exercise.

senandung [KN], Ind. humming a tune; crooning, also *sinandung.*

senang [KS], comfortable, easy; ~ *menipu dia,* it is easy to deceive him; *ke~an,* comfort; *~kan diri,* to make oneself comfortable; *ber~ diri,* to take a rest, *ber~-lenang,* in comfortable circumstances; *ber~-~,* in comfort, without difficulty; *~hati,* happy.

senangin [KN], *ikan ~,* a thread-fin *(Polynemus tetradactylus).*

senapang [KN], (Dutch) a musket, a gun; ~ *batu,* a flintlock; ~ *'cap',* a muzzle-loader, ~ *kembar,* a double-barrelled gun; ~

kopak, ~ patah, a breech-loader; ~ *terkul,* a rifled gun; *mengisi ~,* to load a gun.

senarai [KN], Kel. a list.

senawat [KK], Pk. to whip. swish.

senawi [KN], a passenger who works his passage.

Senayan [KN], Ar. *hari ~,* Monday; also *hari Isnin.*

senda [KN], 1. a joke, a jest; *gurau ~,* id.; *ber~-gurau* or *bergurau-~,* to flirt; *memper~kan,* to make a joke of, treat lightly. 2. Skr. 1, myself; = *salyanda.*

sendal [KK], 1. to insert, e.g., a stick under a door; *penyendal,* packing (e.g. shavings); to wedge (something) in. 2. surreptitious theft; to pick a pocket.

sendalu [KN], *angin ~,* a moderate breeze.

sendar [KK], to snore lightly.

sendat [KS], *ter~,* wedged in; nipped; jammed in.

sendawa [KN], Skr. saltpetre; nitrates; *asam ~,* nitric acid.

sendayan [KN], a coarse sedge.

sendel [KK], leaning against; *ber~ bahu,* shoulder to shoulder.

sendeng [KK], heeling over; laid against anything at an angle; *tèr~-~,* leaning first to one side, then to another; tilting this way and that; *~-mendeng,* id.; *~kan,* to turn over (e.g., a boat) on its side; ~ *senjata* is sometimes used for sloping arms.

senderung [KN], *ikan ~,* a sea-perch *(Plectropoma maculatum).*

sendi [KN], Skr. sinew, joint; *tercabutlah ~ bahunya,* his shoulder was put out of joint; *ber~,* with a hinge or fastening; mounted in; *ber~kan,* mounted in —; (fig.) based on, connected with; *sakit ~,* arthritis; *cerai ~,* dislocated; *ber~,* jointed, articulated.

sendikata [KPhbg], a conjunction (gram.).

sendinama [KDpn], a preposition.

sendiri [KS], self; *saya ~,* I myself, personally; *ber~,* individual, separate, independent; *dengan ~nya* of (its) own accord, spontaneously; automatically; *~an,* individual, personal, isolated; *tertawa ~an,* to laugh inwardly; *ber~an,* alone, unaccompanied; *ter~*, individual, of distinct character; *secara per~an*, *ke~an*, solitary, alone, without outside help; *hal per~an*, personal affairs; *surat per~an*, personal letter; *dengan ber~*, unilaterally, acting on one's own; *alat bertukang ~*, 'do it yourself' kit; *sesama (sama-sama) ~*, among (them)selves, limited to (them)selves.

sendu [KS], depressed, serious, melancholy — cf. **sedu**.

senduduk [KN], a rhododendron-like shrub *(Melastoma polyanthum)*; also *keduduk*.

senduk [KN], a large spoon, a ladle; *siput ~*, a shell *(Patella* sp.); *menyenduk*, to eat anything with a spoon, ladle up; *hidup gantung ~*, precarious livelihood (esp. of 'spongers').

sendung [KN], a narrow pen to confine a buffalo for milking.

senantiasa [KKtr], Skr. always, perpetually; also *sentiasa*.

sengaja [KK], deliberately, on purpose; *bukan ~*, I did not do it intentionally; *~kan*, to do on purpose; to 'put on', pretend, as emotion.

sengal [KS], 1. rheumatic or gouty twinges; *~ tulang*, id. 2. Pen. = *senyar*.

sengam [KK], *menyengam*, to gorge.

sengap [KK], holding one's tongue, to 'shut up'; quiet, noiseless; *menyengapkan*, silence, quiten.

sengat [KN], a sting; the venomous 'bite' of an insect; *menyengat* [KK], to sting; *penyengat*, a wasp.

sengau [KN], talking through the nose, nasal; speak nasally.

sengerek = *pengerek*, *senggirik*.

senget [KS], keeling or leaning over; *ter~*, set at an angle, inclined; *~-menget*, keeling this way and that.

senggak [KK], to sing loudly in chorus.

senggam [KK], *menyenggam*, to devour.

senggang [KS], an interval, a period; *~ dua bulan*, after two months.

senggau [KK], rising on tiptoe and stretching out to draw something towards oneself; reaching (of fire across an intervening space).

senggayut [KK], dangling (a man, or ape, hanging by the hands, or a bat).

senggeh [KK], *ter~*, grinning so as to show the teeth; also *senggek* and *sengeh*.

senggirik [KN], an auger.

senggugut [KN], dysmenorhoea.

sengguk [KK], nodding; *ter~-~*, continually nodding the head, as in weariness (basically, shake up and down, esp. head); hence, *senggukkan kepala*, to bump someone's head (against the ground or wall).

senggulung [KN], a millipede that rolls itself up into a ball when touched.

senggut [KK], *menyenggut*, a sidelong blow with the head; to butt with the horn — cf. **sengguk**.

sengit [KS], pungent (of odour), causing the nostrils to curl up; bitter, as fighting.

sengkak [KS], nauseated from over-feeding.

sengkalan [KN], a wooden slab on which curry-stuff is pounded; *seperti ~ tak sudah*, like an unfinished curry-board, ugly and unsightly; *muka ~*, shameless, unabashed.

sengkang [KN], thwart; position across; crossbar; *ter~*, jammed across; *kayu kasut*, boot-trees; *~ merah*, the Read Cross; *~ pintu*, the bolt of a door; *~ roda*, a chock for checking the motion (of a wheel).

sengkang [KK], *jalan menyengkang*, to walk unevenly.

sengkar [KN], a crossbar or thwart in a boat.

sengkarut [KK], interlacing; *ber~*, in a tangle; involved (of a story, of debtors).

sengkau [KN], *~ perahu*, the Malay weasel *(Putorius udipes)*.

sengkayan [KN], a watersprout.

sengkela [KN], Skr. shackles, fetters, hobbles.

sengkelang [KS], crossed (of the arms or legs).

sengkelang [KS], a slanting cross; an irregular figure; bad (of work).

sengkelat = *sakhlat.*

sengkelat [KN], filthy; unwashed (of the *abaimana*) — a term of abuse, dirty, unwashed.

sengkeling [KK], crossing the legs slightly by laying one just over the other or the hand across the back.

sengkelit [KN], a band into which the feet are placed when climbing a tree.

sengkenit [KN], a tick.

sengker [KN], confine, lock in.

sengketa [KN], a feud, friction; *ber~,* to be at loggerheads; *tanah ~,* territory in dispute, *terra irridenta.*

sengkona [KK], Sel. to scold, reproach severely.

sengkuang [KN], the yam-beam *(Pachyrrhizus angulatus).*

sengkuap [KN], a canopy; a kitchen adjunct.

sengkul [KN], difficulty in swallowing (due to an inflamed or sore throat).

sengsara [KN], Skr. pain, agony, torture; *azab ~, seksa ~* or *susah ~,* id.; hardship, life of hardship; *menyengsarakan,* torment; *ke~an,* misery, suffering.

sengsat [KK], to put end by end (as in eking out a short strand in weaving a mat); to add what is missing.

sengse [KN], ch. a Chinese medicine-man.

sengsut [KN], a fabulous man-eating ape that walks with its head between its legs.

seni [KN], delicate of texture; clear in tone; thin and fine; *intan yang ~,* diamonds of fine water; *air ~,* urine; *ke~an,* art; *~man,* artist (generally, e.g., actor); *~wati,* female artiste; *~ suara,* singing, the art of song; *~ lukis,* the art of painting; *~ kata,* lyrics; *~ rumah-tangga,* domestic science; *~ tari,* the art of dancing; *~ tulis,* calligraphy; *~ cipta,* works of art (of all kinds).

senja [KN], Skr. evenfall; *~ kala,* dusk; *awal ~,* the early part of the evening, twilight.

senjah [KK], to grab, to bite (of a fish).

senjak, since, = *semenjak.*

senjata [KN], Skr. instrument of warfare; weapon; *alat ~,* war- material; *~ api,* fire-arms; *~* is used (vulg.) for penis; *ber~,* armed; *ber~kan,* armed with; *ke~an,* armaments.

senjolong [KN], having a long projecting snout — a descriptive name given to the gavial *(Tomistoma schlegeli),* to garfish, and to certain types of boats — cf. **jolong.**

senjuh [KN], Ind. style (lit.).

senjuang, = *lenjuang; Bukit Senjuang,* St Paul's Hill, Malacca.

senjung [KN], the bar of a pair of scales.

senohong [KN], *ikan ~,* a large thread-fin *(Polyemus paradiseus).*

senok [KN], tapir.

senonggang [KN], *main ~,* somersault.

senonggeng [KK], inverted.

senoman [KN], rural association for mutual assistance; pooling of money by a group of people where members collect their savings in rotation.

senonoh [KS], becoming; fitted; suitable; *tak ~,* improper (esp. of conduct); *kelakuan yang tidak ~,* improper behaviour.

sensasi [KN], sensation.

sensitif [KS], sensitive.

senta [KN], the horizontal supports for the thwarts in a boat.

sentada [KN], a tree resembling the yew *(Podocarpus neglectus).*

sentadu [KN], *ulat ~,* a large green caterpillar.

sentak [KK], a jerk, a pull; *menyentakkan,* to give a sudden tug; *ter~,* to start (make a slight involuntary movement).

sental [KK], to rub vigorously with a hard surface, scrubbing; (fig.) to gobble up.

sentana [KN], Jav. family, kindred; *kula ~,* id.

sentap = *sentak.*

sentir [KN], Ind. flash, as of lamp; *lampu ~,* flashlight.

senteri [KN], Tam. a wandering student, a wanderer, a stranger generally; *dagang ~,* id.

sentiasa [KKtr], Skr. always; also *senentiasa.*

sentil [KN], *ter~*, to stick out of a hole partly in and partly out, e.g. a quid of tobacco in the mouth so that the protrusion so caused is visible through the cheek.

sentolar [KN], plaiting or twisting an extra strand into a rope; adding a lash a whip.

sentosa [KS], Skr. rest, peace; tranquil; *ke~an*, id.; selamat ~, 'peace and happiness'.

sentuh [KK], *ter~*, collide, knock up against (of persons); to come into contact with, touch; *kaum yang tidak boleh di~*, the Untouchables (of India); *menyentuh*, to touch; (fig.) to touch on (a subject); to affect (esp. adversely).

sentul [KN], 1. a fruit tree *(Sandoricum Indicum)*. 2. stocky, sturdy; also *sintul*.

sentung [KN], a ring, a circle, a circular enclosure, the bunt of a net; *kain ~*, a sarong that has been sewn ready for use; *baju ~*, a jacket with oval opening for head.

senuh [KS], feeling of repletion after meals.

Senuhun [KN], Jav. a royal title; a monarch; *Sang ~*, His Majesty.

se nya, of a truth; = *se sungguhnya; bahawa ~*, verily, verily.

senyap [KS], 1. *sunyi ~*, extremely quiet; deserted — a strong form of *sunyi; ~~*, quietly, stealthily. 2. = *lenyap*. 3. = *sengap*.

senyar [KN], tingling, the sensation caused by a blow on the funny-bone; also *sengal*.

senyawa [KS], *ber~*, fertilize, unite.

senyum [KN], smiling; a smile; *~an*, id.; *~ simpul*, a quizzical uncertain smile; *~ kambing*, a supercilious smile; *~ monyet*, a toothy grin; *~ raja*, a hypocritical smile; *~ mekar*, a slight smile; *~ tawar*, a vague smile; *~ pahit*, a bitter smile; *~ suming*, a sly smile, a leer; *~ tauke*, an ingratiating (shopkeepers') smile; *~ selamba*, a pretending smile; *~ kemanja- manjaan*, a saucy smile; *dengan ~ tak menjadi*, with an attempt at a smile; *ter~*, with a smile on the face; *melebarkan ~*, to

smile broadly; *mengorak ~*, to smile brightly; *senentiasa mengorak ~*, always smiling; *mengulum ~*, to smile a tight-lipped smile.

sepah [KN], a quid (of betel); *~ bulan*, a hazel-worm or filbert-worm; *~ puteri*, a name given (1) to several small pretty birds with red in their colours, esp. the scarlet sunbird; (2) to a large tree *(Pentace triptera); ~ raja*, the bird of paradise; *menyepah*, to chew up, to devour.

sepah [KK], *ter~*, littered about, abundant; *~kan*, to scatter about; (fig.) spend profusely.

sepai [KK], *ber~*, scattered about in bits; *ter~*, smashed to pieces.

sepak [KK], a slap, blow with the flat of the hand or a racquet; *menyepak*, to slap. 2. to kick with the side of the foot; spurning; *~ raga*, a Malay game which uses a rattan ball; *kemudi ~*, a paddle-rudder, in contradistinction to a hinged rudder of the European type; *~ raga jaring*, netball.

sepam [KN], a large wild mango *(Mangifera Maingayi)*.

sepan [KN], a tree *(Dialium patens)*.

sepanduk [KN], Ind. a poster; a banner.

sepang [KN], the 'sappan' tree whose wood can be made into dye, *(Caalpinia sappan)*.

Sepanyul [KN], Spanish.

sepat [KN], *ikan ~*, a freshwater fish of the genus *Trichogaster;* a common cheap food.

sepatu [KN], Port. shoes; *~ kuda*, horse shoe.

sepegoh [KN], a marine mussel yielding pearls of little value.

seperai [KN], (Dutch) a counterpane or coverlet.

Seperba [KN], Skr. the name of a nymph of Indra's heaven, whose two companions were *Nila Utama* and *Maniaka; Sang ~*, the legendary founder of the Malayan Empire, according to the confused Malay tradition.

seperti [KKtr], like; similar to, as to, as for, according to; such as; *dengan ~nya*, as a thing should be; appropriately; *yang tidak ~nya*, inferior, not 'up to scratch', 'poor effort', generally used deprecatingly of some work of one's own; *~kan*, as though about to; also *saperti*.

sepet [KS], half-closed (of the eyes); almond-shaped; *buta ~*, blind — so that the eyes become closed as well as sightless; *mata ~*, slit-eyed.

sepi [KS], Ind. still, quiet, calm; lonely.

sepi = *sipi*.

sepiar [KN], sphere.

sepit [KK], nip, confine, squeeze or press between two surfaces; *kuih ~*, a wafer-like Malay biscuit; *ber~*, possessing claws (as a crab); *~ rambut*, a hair-clip; *~* is used for the claws of crustaceans; chop-sticks; a loop; the fork of a bicycle; the latter also *~ udang; ~* is also used for tongs; *ter~*, nipped in between, squeezed; (fig.) fallen between two stools (having failed to satisfy either side).

sepoi [KS], gently blowing; soft (of the breeze).

sepuh [KN], gloss, glaze; veneer, patina; *mas yang sudah ter~*, burnished gold; *menyepuh*, to burnish, i.e., with a preparation of alum and saltpetre; *intan yang tidak ber~*, a rough diamond (lit.) and (fig.); *macis ber~ lilin*, wax vestas; *~an* is sometimes used to mean not genuine (polished up so as to deceive).

sepuk [KK], *ter~*, cast carelessly aside, as clothes, or of a person fallen and 'lying in a heap'.

sepung [KN], Treng. a hen-coop.

seput [KS], dull (of colours), speedy, fast (of trains).

sera [KK], 1. *ter~-~*, rushing frantically about. 2. bright, glowing. 3. a midge.

serabai [KN], *kuih ~*, a cake made of flour and coconut-milk, supposed esp. to be given to mourners and helpers at a funeral.

serabut [KN], shaggy, fibrous; confused, tangled; *perkara ini ber~an kepada kira-kira*, this will mess up the accounts.

seradung [KK], *ter~ kaki*, to have one's

foot caught in anything, to trip.

seraga [KN], *bantal ~*, a large round cushion used at weddings.

seragam [KN], uniform.

serah [KK], or *menyerahkan*, to hand over, surrender; *~ diri*, to surrender; to give oneself up; *~kan diri*, to submit oneself to another's control; *ber~*, id.; *ber~ sahaja*, offering no resistance; *ber~ kepada Allah*, in the hands of God; *menyerah kalah*, to surrender; *perjanjian (teriti) saling ~-menyerahkan orang salah*, extradition treaty; *~* is also the name of a custom in N.S. by which a man can get engaged to a girl by more-or-less invading her house and claiming her; she is then said to *kena ~ atau merumahan; ter~*, given over, surrendered.

serah [KS], glowing red, fiery red.

serahi [KN], Ar. a wine-bottle or flask.

serai [KN], lemon grass *(Andropogon schoenanthus); minyak ~*, citronella oil.

serak [KS], 1. hoarse; mucus in the throat and nostrils; *tertawa sampai ~*, to laugh oneself hoarse; *~-~ basah*, deep, of voice. 2. a little loose (of a fastening).

serak [KK], 1. scattering in disorder; *~-~kan*, to disperse; *ber~, ter~-~*, scattered about, dotted here and there, strewn; cf. **selerak**. 2. *tumbuh ~*, young sprouts in water.

serakah [KS], greedy.

seram [KS], to stiffen (of the muscles); to stand on end (of the hair); *~-kulit*, gooseflesh; *berasa ~ sejuk*, to have cold shivers, esp. from fright; *~ bulu tengkoknya*, to get goose flesh on one's neck.

serama [KS], Skr. in time, in measure, rhythmical; *gendang ~* [KN], a drum (one side of which is beaten by the hand, the other by a drumstick); *menyerama*, to beat time.

serambi [KN], (malayalam), a Malay open veranda, balcony; *~ gantung*, Pen. a veranda on a lower level than the main room (in contrast to *~ sama-naik*).

serampang [KN], 1. a barbed trident for

spearing fish; a fork. 2. Ind. *menyerampang*, to harpoon. 3. *~an*, Ind. haphazard, slipshod, inaccurate; *ter~*, speared.

serampin [KN], 1. refuse sago flour. 2. a mat for collecting sago.

seran [KN], *ber~*, striped (of materials).

serana [KN], 1. Skr. style, fashion; general effect. 2. *menyerana,* to pine away; also *merana.*

seranah [KN], curse, cursing; imprecations; *sumpah ~*, id.

serandang [KN], a prop formed by crossing two sticks.

Serandib [KN], Pers. *Pulau ~*, an old name of Ceylon (Sri Lanka).

serandung [KK], tripping or stumbling over = *seradung; kakinya ter~kan tunggul kayu,* he tripped over a stump.

serang [KK], 1. assault, attack, charging, onslaught; *menyerang,* to assail, make adverse criticism; *penyerangan,* aggression. 2. Hind. a 'serang' or petty officer on a ship; a quartermaster. 3. *~menyerang,* wavy (of colouring); changing tint according to light.

serang [KN], wide-meshed (of baskets, nets, etc.).

serangga [KN], Ind. insect.

seranggung [KK], *menyeranggung,* to sit with one's elbows on the table; to crouch (as a tiger); to squat with the knees wide apart — cf. **ranggung**.

serangkak [KN], a girdle of thorns put round a tree to prevent thieves climbing it; *~ payung,* the little bars (of an umbrella, sunshade).

serangsang [KK], *menyerangsang,* to be excited and abusive, esp. of women.

Serani [KN], Ar. 'Nazarene'; Christian (esp. Roman Catholic); Eurasian; also *Nasrani.*

seranta [KK], *menyerantakan,* advertising a fact, letting everyone know, publicity.

serap [KK], absorb, sponge up, suck up; *embun di~ panas,* dew sucked up by heat; *kain penyerap kotoran,* sanitary towel; *di~ hantu,* possessed by an evil spirit.

serap [KN], 1. a wooden dado or planking along the base of a wall. 2. a Javanese sleep-producing spell. 3. *ter~ darah* [KK], having the feeling of a sudden rush of blood to the heart from astonishment or excitement; *menyerap darah,* blood runs cold; *mukanya menyerap merah,* (she) flushed red. 4. Ind. a reserve, something kept back; *~an,* penyerapan, absorption, pervasion.

serapah [KN], Skr. a curse, an imprecation; *~ jampi,* a magic imprecation, esp. as used by a *pawang.*

serapih [KK], *kena ~,* to be chipped or abraded by a blow.

serasa [KN], a name for *sirih.*

serasah [KN], Ind. manure.

serasi = *seraksi* [KS], suitable, efficacious.

serat [KK], 1. jammed, held fast in an aperture, tight, stuck or firmly embedded 2. Ind. fibre.

seratung [KN], a small tree *(Tabernoemontana corymbosa).*

serau [KN], 1. noise (e.g., of water). 2. cellular tissue of teeth, ivory; net-like stuff.

seraup [KN], a kind of rice.

serawa [KN], a fritter made of banana and flour.

Serawak [KN], Sarawak.

serawan = *seriwan.*

seraya [KKtr & KPhbg], 1. with, while, along with, during, as; *bertanya ~ tersenyum,* to ask with a smile. 2. a generic name for timbers obtained from trees of the genera *Shorea* and *Hopea.* 3. Skr. *menyeraya,* give co-operative help, aid in numbers, e.g., to plant rice.

serba [KS], Skr. of all sorts; various; all kinds of; *~ nika* or *~ serbi,* id., *~ salah,* confused; *~ salah fikiran,* at one's wits' end; *~ sikit,* a little of all kinds; a small amount; *~ putih,* all white (e.g., of the various garments that make up a costume); *~ tahu,* all-knowing.

serbah [KS], *~-serbih,* slovenly, improperly fastened (of dress), untidy.

serbak [KK], *menyerbak,* to spread; to be diffused (of an odour), to prevade.

serban [KN], 1. Pers. a turban. 2. numbed.

serbat [KN], Ar. a cooling drink of any sort; also *syarbat.*

serbit [KN], (Dutch) serviette, napkin.

serbu [KK], to dash forward, charge; to raid, esp. of police; ~*an,* a raid; *perahu* ~, assault-craft; *menyerbukan diri,* to throw oneself upon the enemy.

serbuk [KN], powder, fine dust; ~ *kikir,* filings; ~ *kaca,* powdered glass.

serdadu [KN], Port. = soldado.

serdak [KN], 1. fine dust — such as collects on furniture. 2. Pen. crumbs of food.

serdam [KN], a fife of bamboo.

serdang [KN], a tall fan-palm *(Livistona Cochinchinensis).*

serdih [KS], sticking out (of the stomach or chest, when a man does not sit upright), protruding (of chest); *duduk menyerdih,* to loll, lounge, with the stomach sticking out.

serelum [KK], slipping down (e.g., as a spoon into jam).

seremban [KN], 1. a game played by children; like knuckle-bones, but played with pebbles or seeds. 2. wearing the sarong high in front and low behind; of women when bathing; cf. **kemban.**

serembap [KK], to fall face downwards.

serempak [KK], *ter~,* meeting by chance, 'knocking up against'; *kerja* ~, work down 'anyhow', haphazard and roughly.

serempu [KN], a rough keel shaped like a dug-out; *jalur* ~, a dug-out.

serendah [KN], 1. the dwarf banana. 2. a variety of rice.

serendeng [KK], heeling over, aslant; *menyerendeng,* to list, heel over to one side; ~*kan,* to turn over one side; to careen (a ship); cf. **sendeng.**

serengam [KS], *ber~,* over-abundant, excessive (as hair in nostrils, ants in sugar).

serenjang [KS], (of a flag-staff, tree, etc.), towering skywards.

seresah [KN], rubbish, offal.

seret [KK], *menyeret,* to trail behind; to drag over the ground behind one; *menyeret-nyeret, menyeretkan,* involve, mention; *kasut* ~, grass slippers; 'mules'.

sergah [KK], *menyergah,* to startle anyone with a sudden sound or movement; to address harshly, 'fly out at'; to make a threatening movement.

sergam [KS], *ter~,* standing out, in bold relief, conspicuous, prominent.

sergap [KK], *menyergap,* to surprise with a sudden onslaught, to take by surprise, startle.

sergut [KS], roughly finished; coarsely done (of bad work).

seri [KN], 1. Skr. charm, beauty, glory; brilliance, brightness; the best of anything; an honorific prefix; ~ *negeri,* the pride of the city; ~ *balai,* the heart of the audience hall; ~ *menanti,* N.S. the waiting hall in a palace; ~ *muka,* the light of the countenance; ~ *panggung,* the 'star' of a play; *tiang* ~, the main post of a house; *ber~,* to brighten up (as the countenance); radiant; of good colour; *menyerikan,* to enliven (as a ceremony with music); to grace with presence; *penyeri,* a decoration, ornamentation; *per~an,* dignitaries; ~*kaya,* a sort of sweet pudding. 2. drawn (of a game). 3. *menyeri bunga,* to buzz round a flower, taking the honey; = *sering* 3.

seriap [KN], a grey heron.

seriat [KN], 1. a large shrimp-net. 2. Pk. abated (of rain).

seriau [KK], Pk. shuddering (sight of blood etc.).

seriawan [KN], a sort of sprue, scurvy.

seriding [KN], side, border, edge, fringe.

serigala [KN], Skr. a jackal; *anjing* ~, the wild dog *(Cyon rutilans); anak* ~, used for cubs in Boy Scout movement.

serik [KS], 1. deterred, frightened off; amending one's ways through a bad fright. 2. (onom.), *seruk-~,* cracking (of the finger-joints). 3. Kel. stopping (of rain).

Serikandi [KN], a heroine of legend; so, a heroine generally.

serikat [KN], Ar. = *syarikat.*

serindai [KN], an evil spirit attacking women in labour.

serindit [KN], the love-bird *(Loriculus galgulus).*

sering [KS], 1. stiff (of cloth or paper). 2. the feeling of 'goose- flesh'; ~ *seram,* id. 3. (onom.) humming (of a bee); *bunga di~ kumbang,* a flower an insect has buzzed round; (fig.) a maid deflowered. 4. Jav. ~ *kali,* often.

seringai [KN], *menyeringai* [KK], to grin; *menyeringaikan gigi,* to show one's teeth in a grin; also *seringing.*

seriosa [KN], musical beat or rhythm.

Seriwa [KN], part of the title of a *Bendahara,* i.e., *Bendahara ~ Raja.*

serkah [KS], torn apart, split.

serkai [KK], rinsing or wringing out; sieving (of flour).

serkap [KN], a coop-shaped fish-trap thrust down over a fish; *buang ~ jarang,* to make a wild guess; a ~ is often used as a coop for fowls for sale; *menyerkapi,* coop up, put in a conical coop; *ter~,* suddenly, unexpectedly.

serkup [KN], enclosing under a dome or cupshaped surface; to catch with a *serkap; cahaja,* (fig.) to have no settled policy, to be an opportunist; *menyerkupkan,* cover, put over.

serlah [KS], *ter~,* glowing bright; showing clearly and brightly; *menyerlahkan,* to display, show clearly.

serling [KN], a pitfall for game.

sermangin [KN], a kind of drum.

serobeh [KS], dishevelled (of the hair); *ber~,* unkempt.

serobot [KN], Ind. *menyerobot* [KK], to penetrate, to force one's way into; to reach.

seroda [KN], a belt of thorns (also *serangkak)* placed round a tree to stop thieves climbing.

serodi [KN], filing down precious stones.

seroja [KN], Skr. the lotus *(Nelembium speciosum).*

serok [KN], a fish-trap (better known as *kelong).*

seroka [KK], *menyeroka,* N.S. to open up a new country, esp. rice-fields; *penyeroka,* a colonist, settler.

serokan [KN], a water-course; a stream; a creek, a gulf.

seroloh [KK], sink through mud.

serombong [KN], a funnel, a hollow cylinder; a chimney; a guard on the tips of the horns of fighting bulls; *pahat ~,* a round chisel; a gouge.

serompok [KS], *ter~,* to come suddenly on; a variant of *serempak.*

serondong [KK], to bend the head and butt.

serong [KS], askew, at an angle; *~-merong,* much askew; *berjalan ~,* to incline to left or right when proceeding; ~ is sometimes used (fig.) for crooked, dishonest, of an action; *ke~an,* crookedness, dishonesty.

seronggong [KN], cross-beams used in mining.

seronok [KS], Ked., Pk. pleasant, agreeable, entertaining; *ber~~,* to amuse oneself, have a good time; *menyeronokkan,* please, delight, gratify; *ke~an,* pleasure, enjoyment.

seronot [KK], to slip through (as a small animal through a thicket); to cower, crouch low; also *serunup.*

serpih [KS], or *serpis,* = *serepis,* q.v. used as one word for 'chipped'; *~an,* chips.

serta [KDpn], Skr. with, together with, accompanying; while, and; *rajin ~ usaha,* diligently and industrious; *~-merta,* at that very moment, immediately; on the spot; *be~,* along with, together with; *menyertai,* to join, participate; *pe~,* a participant, an entrant; *penyertaan,* participation.

sertu [KK], ceremonial ablution after defilement, e.g. after touching a pig; *ber~,* so to cleanse oneself.

sertup [KK], closing, shutting up.

seru [KN], 1. Skr. all; ~ *sekalian,* id.; ~ *semesta sekalian,* id.; better *sarwa.* 2. *ber~,* to call out loudly; *menyeru,* id.; *~an,* appeal (public); *penyeru agama,* a missionary; *menyeru-nyerukan,* spread, propagate; *tanda ~an,* (gram.) an exclamation mark. 3. Ind. profit; dividend.

seruh [KS], shrunken, reduced (of a boil).

seruk [KN], a large bin used as a rough measure of capacity, = about 10 *gantang.*

serul [KS], Pen., Pk. crumby, not sticky, of boiled rice; sometimes, of soil.

seruling [KN], = *suling.*

serun [KN], Ked. a fowl-house.

serunai [KN], a name given to a number of musical instruments (esp. to a wooden whistle with a slide for varying the pitch); *buaya ~,* a name given to the gavial.

serunda [KK], *menyerunda,* to drag boats overland.

serundang [KK], rooting (of a pig).

serunding [KN], a Javanese preparation of ground coconut and spices.

seruntun [KN], *akar ~,* a kind of derris, a creeper, also *putarwali.*

serunup [KK], = *seronot.*

serupa [KS], similar, alike, looking the same.

sesah [KS], to beat with a cane.

sesak [KK], closely pressed, packed tightly; busy, overwhelmed with work; hardpressed, in difficulties; *sakit ~ dada,* suffering from bronchitis or asthma; *penuh ~,* full to crowding; *kawasan ~,* a built-up area; an over-crowded area; *ber~~,* jammed, over-crowded.

sesal [KK], sorrow, repentant, *~kan,* to regret (anything); *menyesal,* to feel regret; *menyesal sambal belacan,* to feel a prawn-paste repentance, i.e., a short-lived one; (the idea perhaps is that this paste is very pungent and puts off an eater at first, but he comes back for more); *~ dahulu pendapatan, ~ kemudian apa gunanya?,* repentance before the action is profitable, but what's the use of repenting afterwards?

sesap [KK], lapping up water (of animals); *di~ lembing,* stabbed; run through by a lance; *~an,* salt-lick; N.S. abandoned lands; *~ burung,* a pool frequented by birds.

sesar [KK], to push or shove aside; *~kan,* to push (people) aside, thrust aside when making one's way; *yang hidup ~kan mati,* the living displace the dead; *menyesar,* to sidle to and fro.

sesat [KS], straying from the right path; *menyesatkan,* mislead, deviate; *ter~,* lost, stray from; *ke~an,* error, mistake, losing one's way; *~ jalan,* astray; *~ barat,* confused; *diper~,* lead astray; *ter~ langkah,* to get out of step.

sesawi [KN], mustard.

sesuai [KS], matching, suitable, in conformity with, fitting; *ber~an,* to agree with; *menyesuaikan,* adjust, adapt; *penyesuaian,* adjustment, modification; *per~an,* agreement, harmony, concord.

setail [KN], Eng. style (smartness); *lebih pada ~ sekoyan dah,* it's more than a *tahil,* it's a *koyan,* i.e., very, very smart (play on words — setail and *se tahil).*

setak [KN], Pah. a small fishing-boat.

setambun [KN], a small tree with edible fruit *(Baccaurea parvifolia).*

Setan [KN], Ar. a devil, an evil spirit, Satan; *pesetan kepada,* to the devil with ...; better *Syaitan.*

setangan [KN], Kel., Treng. a head-kerchief, = *sapu tangan.*

setanggi [KN], Skr. incense; also *istanggi.*

setarang [KK], Treng. strengthens a negative; *tak embuh ~,* quite unwilling.

setawar [KN], the name of some medicinal herbs *(Costus speciosus* and *Forrestia* sp.).

setela [KN], Kel. the sweet potato.

seteren [KN], Eng. (steering) wheel of a car.

Seteria [KN], Skr. a Kshatriya, a member of the warrior-caste; = *ceteria.*

seterika [KN], an iron; *~ karan,* an electric iron; also *istrika.*

seteru [KN], Skr. a personal (not national) enemy; *ber~,* to be at enmity with; *per~an,* a feud; *ber~-meru,* at loggerheads; *memper~kan,* to be hostile to.

seterup [KN], (Dutch) syrup.

seti [KN], (Dutch) satin.

setia [KS], Skr. loyal, fidelity, faith, constant; ~ *teguh,* firmly loyal; ~ *usaha,* secretary; ~ *usaha rendah,* undersecretary; ~ *usaha sulit,* confidential secretary; ~ *usaha peribadi,* personal secretary, ~*kawan,* (political) solidarity; *majlis* ~*kawan rakyat Afrika-Asia,* Africa-Asia Peoples' Solidarity Council; ~ *usaha tetap,* Permanent Secretary; ~ *usaha agung,* General Secretary.

setiawan [KS], Skr. loyal, faithful, constant — cf. **setia**.

setim [KN], Eng. *naik* ~, (idiom) to get 'all steamed up', wild with anger or excitement.

setimpal [KS], fitting, matching, balance.

setinggan [KN], Joh. unlawful occupants of land, 'squatters'.

setinggi [KN], a reef in a sail.

setoka [KN], *ikan* ~, a kind of small ray.

setokin [KN], stocking.

setolop [KN], (Dutch) a wall-lamp.

setu [KN], 1. Jav. blessing, favourable influence (of a Hindu divinity or ascetic blessing a devotee); laying a transformation on a person; ~*i,* to bless; to lay a spell on. 2. a green ribbon seaweed.

setua [KN], Skr. an animal; *marga* ~, animals generally; *angkara,* a fabulous wild beast.

setuju [KK], to agree.

sewa [KK], hire, hiring, leasing; rent; ~*kan,* to lease, to let; *rumah* ~*an,* a house held on or intended for leasehold tenure; *menyewa,* to hire; to rent; *menyewakan,* to let out on hire or rent; *penyewa rumah,* the tenant of a house.

sewah [KN], 1. a short curved dagger. 2. a generic name given to a number of birds of prey; ~ *belalang,* the Malayan black and white falconet; *lang* ~, the Japanese sparrow-hawk; ~ *tekukur,* the hawk-cuckoo.

sewajarnya [KS], of course, naturally.

sewal [KS], misfortune — cf. **sial**.

sewan [KK], a sort of mime, performed by Pangan in Ulu Kelantan.

sewemamg-wenang [KS], arbitrary.

si, a prefix (half contemptuous) to the names of persons and personified animals or things; ~ *anu,* so-and-so; ~*apa,* who, what person; ~*engkau* ~ *aku,* a person with whom you can take liberties (using familiar words such as *aku* and *engkau).*

sia [KS], ~-~, idle, useless, futile; *se*-~, id.; *dengan* ~-~, uselessly; ~-~*kan,* to waste, make of no avail, spend to no purpose; *mense-kan diri,* to waste oneself, waste one's abilities, chances; *ke*-~-~*an,* fruitless, futility, trivality, frustration.

siah [KK], 1. *ber*~, bustling; ~ *layah,* swaying about. 2. N.S. to cause to deviate, avert; ~ *peralih,* God forbid; *barang di* ~*kan oleh Tuhan,* id.; *menyiah,* to move slightly (out of the way); cf. **puah**.

siak [KN], 1. the caretaker of a mosque. 2. *akar* ~, a slender climber with white flowers *(Physostelma Wallichii).* 3. *Siak,* a state in Sumatra. 4. Ked. to pour out. 5. Ch. a tiffin-carrier.

siakap [KN], a kind of sea-perch.

sial [KS], ill-omented, ill-starred, unlucky.

sialang [KN], N.S. = *tualang*.

siamang [KN], Skr. the well-known long-armed ape *(Symphalangus syndactylus).*

siang [KN], 1. daylight; ~ *hari,* during the daytime; *bulan ke*~*an,* the moon in daylight — a symbol of pallor; ~-~, in broad daylight; (met.) in the open, without secrecy; ~*nya,* while still daylight; so sometimes, early, before expected time; straightaway. 2. to scrape off projections (e.g. to scrape a fish, or a weedy drain).

siap [KS], ready; *sudah* ~, it is ready; ~*kan,* to get ready; *ber*~, to make ready; *ber*~ *nak,* ready to; *per*~*an,* preparations.

siapa [KGn], who? see *si;* ~-~, whoever; *barang* ~, id.

siar [KK], 1. Port. *ber*~, to stroll about; *pe*~*an,* a walk, place to stroll, etc. 2. welding together pieces of heated metal. 3. ~*kan,* to make known, publish; *per*~*an,* proclamation; *ber*~, to circulate; *penyiar,* announcer, broadcaster; ~*an radio,* a broadcast; *penyiaran,* broadcasting. 4. Kel. recovered (from sickness).

siasah [KN], politics; *ke~*, political situation.

siasat [KN], 1. Ar. management, control, discipline; *~ perang*, strategy, tactics. 2. [KK], to investigate; *penyiasatan*, research; *ahli penyiasatan ilmu sains*, scientific investigators; *penyiasatan kematian*, an inquest.

siat [KK], 1. *siatkan*, to tear to pieces, rip, rend. 2. Kel = *usah*.

siau [KK], cooled to a bearbale temperature (of water, metal, etc.).

sibak [KK], to part, divide; parting of hair.

sibang [KS], *~sibuk*, hustling about; bustling.

sibar [KK], to distribute, to supply, to propagate (as doctrine); to extend; *~~*, a border sewn on to embroidery; *kapal penyibar ranjau*, a minelayer; *penyibaran*, distribution (different places in which, e.g., a species of animal, is found).

sibuk [KS], *ber~*, in a whirl (of work or amusement), active, busy, activity; *ke~an*, rush, bustle; state of confusion; *menyibukkan*, to get excited about; *menyibuk*, to spy on, to peep.

sibur [KN], a ladle of coconut shell; *~~*, *se~*, a dragon-fly.

sida [KN], *~~*, a class of functionaries at an old-time Court; sometimes translated as 'eunuchs', though that meaning is doubtful.

sidaguri, = *seleguri*.

sidai [KK], to hand clothes to dry; *penyidai kain*, a clothes' line or rail; *ter~*, hung to dry.

sidang [KN], 1. a gathering, a council; *~ mesyuarat*, members of council; *~ Jumaat*, the Friday meeting for congregational service; *ber~*, to sit, as a Council; *per~an akhbar*, news-conference; *per~an kemuncak*, Summit conference; *per~an tergempar*, Extraordinary Meeting; *per~an agung*, General Meeting; *~* is also used as a collective prefix; *~ pembaca*, all our readers. 2. the sharpened edge of a knife (show-

ing the scraping of the grindstone). 3. Pk., Pah. stopping (of rain). 4.(Malacca) a local headman.

sidi [KS], Skr. effective (of incantations).

sidih [KK], swank; swanky.

sidik [KK], to investigate — cf. **selidik**, also *~ jari*, finger print.

siding [KN], a sharply defined edge; a low dyke or fence; a long rattan with nooses used in catching deer.

sifat [KN], 1. attributes, qualities; appearance, look, nature, character, disposition; *~ dua-puluh*, the Twenty Attributes of God; *~kan*, to deem to be, consider as; *~-lembaga*, manners and customs; *men~kan sebagai*, to describe as, characteristics as 2. *ber~ menyerang*, aggressive, offensive; *ber~ tetap*, lasting, permanent; *kata ~*, adjective.

sifir [KN], Ar. cypher, arithmetical symbol; multiplication table.

sigai [KN], *tangga ~*, a ladder made by lashing short pieces of wood to a tree-trunk.

sigap [KS], 1. bearing, pose; = *sikap*. 2. readiness, briskness; *dengan ~*, briskly, promptly; *ber~*, ready, esp. for fight. 3. efficient, *dia pekerja yang ~*, he is an efficient worker; *ke~an*, efficiency.

sigar [KN], *kain ~*, a head-dress worn by a bridegroom.

sigi [KK], 1. pointing the finger at any person or thing. 2. [KN], a band of thin metal round the sheath of a *keris*. 3. a torch of resinous wood.

sigia [KS], right, proper (= *sayugia*).

sigung [KK], *menyigung*, to jerk slightly, to prod, to nudge.

sihat [KN], Ar. health, fit, sound; recover from illness; *~ dan afiat*, id.; *pegawai ke~an*, health officer.

sihir [KN], Ar. *ilmu ~*, the black art; *ahli ~*, a sorcerer; *menyihir* [KK], to practise black magic on; *tukang ~*, id.; *tukang ~ ular*, a snake-charmer.

sijil [KN], Ar. a scroll, certificate; a diploma.

sikap [KN], 1. manner, bearing, pose, attitude, position, disposition; *~ orang tengah*, position of intermediary; also *sigap;* ~ *hidup,* attitude to life; *ber~ pesimistis,* pessimistic attitude. 2. *lang* ~, the crested goshawk. 3. *baju* ~, a jacket with tight sleeves.

sikat [KN], a comb, a harrow; *ber~* [KK], combed, to comb, combing; *pisang se~,* (1) one row in a bunch of bananas, (2) a penthouse kitchen adjunct, any shed with sloping roof; ~ is used (fig.) to mean to steal, to 'pinch'; to diddle.

sikit [KS], a little, somewhat; used in speech for *sedikit*—see dikit; *se~s-nya,* at least, at any rate.

siku [KN], the elbow; a sharp angle; ~ *jalan,* a sharp turn in the road; ~-~, a set square; *se~,* id.; *menyiku,* to nudge.

sil [KK], Eng. to attach (property by Court order).

sila [KK], 1. Skr. 'welcome'; 'please' (in 'please sit down', etc.); ~ *duduk,* please be seated; *~kan,* to be pleased to; kindly agree to; *ber~,* to sit down with legs crossed tailor-fashion; *memper~kan,* to invite; *membaiki* ~, to alter one's (sitting) position, shift in one's seat. 2. *batu medang* ~, a kind of gypsum used medicinally. 3. *benang* ~, a thick white thread.

silah [KN], Ar. ~-~, a genealogical tree.

silam [KS], 1. gloom, darkness; *ter~,* benighted. 2. Ind. past; *lapan tahun yang* ~, the past eight years.

silang [KN], cross-wise; *ber~,* crossed, marked with cross-cuts; *~-menyilang,* lying across each other; *besi* ~, expanded metal screen; *ber~-siur,* traversing to-and-fro, shuttling this way and that; criss-cross; *~kan,* to cross, to place so as to be across one another; *penyilangan,* crossbreeding; *ber~ kaki,* to cross the legs.

silap [KS], Ar. an error, a mistake; *ter~,* making a mistake unintentionally; *main* ~ *mata,* to do conjuring tricks; *tukang* ~ *mata,* a conjuror; *per~nya,* a catch, the trick of a device.

silasilah, see *silah.*

silat [KN], Malay art of self defence; *main* ~, a sword-dance; *ber~,* to fence; *mem-*

buka ~ *seribu,* N.S. to 'beat it', make oneself 'scarce' (probably because of the active movements of fencers); *membuka* ~, to perform fencer's steps.

silatul rahim [KN], Ar. the tie of blood-relationship; *menghubungkan* ~, to renew or strengthen such ties; by extension, to establish friendly relations.

silau [KS], dazzled; dazzling, glaring; *lampu itu sangat menyilaukan,* it was such a glaring light.

silih [KKtr], replacing; to repair a loss; ~ *mata,* making good to the eyes, i.e., publicly paying a large sum only to have it quietly returned later; *~-ganti,* in turns, alternating, as events; *~-rugi,* reparations; *ber~-ganti,* to replace, to substitute one thing for another; to be passed from hand to hand; to follow one after the other, as events; *kami menghadapi masalah* ~ *berganti,* we had endless problems.

siling [KN], Eng. a ceiling.

silir [KK], *~-semilir.* 1. waving (as the loose end of a garment). 2. *angin ~an,* a gentle breeze.

silu [KS], shy, retiring, modest, subdued; *tidak ~-~,* shamelessly.

siluman [KN], Ind. elves.

simbah [KS], besprinkling; watering, e.g., dusty floor; *menyimbah* [KK], splash, spatter, sprinkle; *ter~,* spilt; shed, as blood.

simbai [KS], smart in carriage, well-dressed.

simbal [KN], grit, sandy tailings.

simbang [KN], 1. *burung* ~, the frigate bird. 2. unreliable; *musim* ~, the uncertain weather at the change of monsoon. 3. = *sembang.*

simbur [KK], to spatter, to splash, to sprinkle with water; *ter~ darah di hati,* having a rush of blood to the heart in a flurry of emotion; cf. **sembur** and **simbah.**

simpai [KK], 1. fastening in a band; a band or hoop; the 'rings' on the horns of a bull; ~ *mulut,* a muzzle; a rattan fastening on the handle of a chisel or similar object; *rotan* ~, a piece of very flexible rattan used for this purpose; to bind with bonds. 2. a sp. of monkey *(Semnopithecus melalophos)*.

simpan [KK], retaining in one's possession; to put away; kept, preserve; to save; *menyimpankan*, keep for, entrust with; ~ *di hati*, to remember; ~ *hati*, id.; but these expressions are often used for remembering something against someone, harbouring resentment; *menyimpan diri* (sl.) to escape, make off; *menyimpan*, to keep; to preserve; Kel. *ber*~, ready to, about to; *ber*~ *lari*, about to bolt; *Bank* ~*an Pejabat Pos*, Post Office Savings Bank; *perempuan* ~, a kept woman; *pemain* ~*an*, a reserve player.

simpang [KN], crossing, cutting across one another, junction, turning aside; ~ *empat*, intersection; ~~*perenang*, confused, 'at sixes and sevens'; *jalan* ~*an*, a by-pass road; *menyimpang*, turn, diverge, swerve; *menyimpangkan*, cause to deviate; *penyimpangan*, deviation; *per*~*an*, junction, place where roads unite (and divide); *jalan* ~~*siur*, a zigzag road; a road branching this way and that; a network of roads; *berjalan* ~~*siur*, to proceed without any fixed destination, diverging this way and that; ~~*siur* is also used (fig.) of a speech, not keeping to the point, rambling; of news being contradictory; ~*kan*, (fig.) to controvert, to call in question.

simpir [KK], to extend the wings sideways (as a peacock).

simpuh, = *timpuh* [KK], *menyimpuh*, kneel and pay respect to; *ter*~, kneeling, knelt.

simpul [KN], a knot; to tie, fasten; ~ *mati*, a fast knot; ~ *pulih*, a slip-knot; *senyum* ~, a quizzical, uncertain smile; ~*an*, a fastening, *menyimpul*, to fasten; ~ *teguh*, a tight knot; ~*an bahasa*, idiom; *ke*~*an*, gist, conclusion, synthesis (not knotty point); *menarik ke*~*an*, to come to a conclusion, to infer; *ke*~*annya*, to sum up; ~ *mengkarung*, cramp; ~ *hidup*, a slip-knot.

sinambung [KK], to continue; *ke*~*an*, continuity.

sinar [KN], ray of light, radiance, beam, gleam; *menyinari*, to shine on; *ber*~, to shine; *matahari ber*~, the sun is shining; *kena* ~ *matahari*, to be struck by the sun's rays; ~~*menyinar*, to keep flashing, as a jewel or a lighthouse; ~~*banar*, radiant, brightly shining.

sindir [KN], sarcasm; ~ *nyanyi*, teasing in song; *menyindir*, to make sarcastic remarks; ~*an*, satire; a piece of sarcasm, a sly dig; insinuation, hint, jibe; *secara menyindir*, sarcastically; *menyindirkan*, to cast reflections on, have a sly dig at; *pukul anak* ~ *menantu*, to beat one's daughter as a hint to one's son-in-law (of action by way of an oblique hint or warning).

sindura [KN], Hind. e.g. minium, red lead.

sinf [KN], Ar. category (plural *asnaf*); used esp. of the eight categories of persons entitled to receive *fitrah*, (q.v.); viz. the poor, the needy, the executives who collect and distribute it, debtors, those whose minds are inclined towards Islam, prisoners needing ransom, stranded travellers and charitable works generally.

singa [KN], 1. Skr. a lion; *menyinga*, to become angry; *mata menyinga*, glaring ferociously. 2. *raja* ~, syphilis.

singar [KS], N.S. ferocious, man-eating (of tigers).

singga, = *sehingga*.

singgah [KK], to stop over for a while, visiting; breaking a journey; ~ *menyinggah*, to keep stopping at places, e.g., as a pedlar; *per*~*an*, place of call, sojourn, stop.

singgang [KN], 1. fish cooked in salt. 2. to bob up and down as in Swedish drill.

singgasana [KN], Skr. a throne or royal dais, ~ *kerajaan*, id.

singgir [KK], *menyinggir*, to open and reveal.

singgit [KK], to scrape up against; to show to be on rival terms; *per*~*an*, friction; *ber*~~, rubbing up against one another, as crossing branches.

singgul [KK], to hit or knock with the side of the head, to butt.

singgung [KK], to give a side-thrust; to interfere with, encroach, to nudge, brush against; *menyinggung*, to allude to; to affect; *menyinggung perasan*, to give offence, to hurt feelings; *ter~*, hurt, moved (as by a remark or an insinuation); *ter~ pada*, to come into contact with (e.g., a live wire).

singkap [KK], *menyingkap*, to open or draw aside a curtain or mosquito net; to turn over a page.

singkat [KS], succinct; short (not long); limited; abbreviated; *~-umur*, short-lived; *dengan ~nya*, briefly, curtly; *~an*, an abbreviation.

singkik [KN], Ch. a 'new-comer'; a contract-labourer fresh from China.

singkil [KN], 1. *~ gigi*, 'on edge' (of teeth). 2. *tali ~*, a cord holding up curtains.

singkir [KK], to push aside, draw aside; to remove, 'weed out'; sometimes, to 'put out of the way', to liquidate; *menyingkirkan*, to bar, to shun, to avoid; to purge; *kami berjaya menyingkirkan pasukan lawan*, we succeeded in eliminating the opposing team; *dasar menyingkirkan kaum*, apartheid; *menyingkirkan diri*, to 'stand aside' (as in a dispute), to stand down (as in a competition), to hold aloof.

singkur [KK], 1. kicking aside, pushing aside, knocking out of the way. 2. Pah. to pole, using either end of the pole alternately.

singsing [KK], rolling up (as the sleeves); pulling up, as a sarung; lift, pass away, disappear (as of clouds, fog, etc.); *fajar menyingsing*, the day is breaking.

sini [KKtr], here; this way, this direction; *di ~*, here, in this place; *ke ~*, hither; *dari ~*, hence; *di seberang ~*, on the nearer bank; *dike~kan*, brought here.

sinis [KS], Eng. cynical; *~ma*, cynicism.

sinjuh [KK], to elbow a man out of the way.

sintar, [KN], the blue-breasted banded rail

(Hypotoenidia striata).

sinting [KS], 1. *seluar ~*, short trousers. 2. a thin shell *(Placuna sella).*

sintir [KN], Ind. dice, = *dadu.*

sintuk [KN], a tree *(Cinnamomum sentu),* of the fibre of which a kind of soap can be made; *menyintuk*, to use this fibrous stuff for washing one's person.

sipahi [KN], Hind. a sepoy; a soldier.

sipat [KN], Ar. to measure, a measured line; *tali ~*, a line drawn by a carpenter to guide him to his work; a plumb-line; *batu tali ~*, a plumb-bob; = *sifat.*

sipi [KS], off the centre; wide of the bull's-eye; not direct; *belah ~*, not cutting directly down the middle; *kena ~*, to strike a glancing blow; cf. *pasang 5*; also *sepi*; *biar ~ jangan sesat*, it is better to stop half way than to persevere in an error.

sipolan [KN], Mr So and So.

sipu [KS], *ke~~an*, *ter~~*, abashed, coy, affecting modesty; looking sheepish, to blush.

sipuak [KN], Ch. an abacus.

siput [KN], a generic name for many shells, esp. snails; the whorls, loops, lines and markings on the hand; a chignon, 'bun'; other shells have generic names of their own, e.g., *rangkik*, *congkat*, etc.; *~ babi*, the giant snail; *~ limau purut*, a style of hair-dressing (two plaits and a bun).

sir [KS], 1. Ar. secret. 2. Ar. desire; the promptings of lust; *~ berahi*, id.; 3. *tak ~*, Kel. unwilling, don't want to.

sira [KN], 1. Jav. a title of distinction; *~ panji*, the nom de guerre of the famous Javanese hero *Radin Inu Kertapati*, Prince of Kuripan. 2. a resort of wild animals such as a salt-lick.

sirai [KS], dressed (of the hair).

siram [KK], besprinkling; watering; *ber~*, to bathe (of a prince or princess); *~kan*, to pour (a liquid over anything), to water.

sirat [KN], netting together; *mata ~*, a mesh; *~an gigi*, the mesh-like appearance of regular teeth; *penyirat kuku*, the thin edge of skin covering the edge of the finger-nail; *~an*, a reticulated design, like a net-work; *ber~*, so designed, as lace; *ter~* (fig.) wrapped up, veiled, as by innuendo; *~ ul-mustakim,* the razor-edged bridge over which the true believer passes into heaven; *menyirat jaring,* to weave a net; cf. **selirat**.

siri [KN], Ind. a series.

sirih [KN], the betel-vine *(Piper betle); ~ dara,* the first pickings from a *sirih* vine; *~ carang,* soft new shoots on the vine; *~ kaduk,* a sp. of the *sirih* vine *(Piper longum); ~ kerakap,* coarse leaves from the vine; *unjung ~,* the pole or support of the *sirih* vine; *makan ~,* to chew betel; *santap ~,* id. (of princes chewing betel); *tempat ~* or *bekas ~,* a betel-box; *per~an,* id.; (The use, of *~* in the betrothal formalities has given rise to the following expressions; *~ bercakap,* the *~* sent to typify the formal proposal of marriage; *~ meninang,* the *~,* typifying the formal acceptance; *~ lelat, ~ genggam,* the best man at a wedding); *~ kuning,* a golden *~-*leaf, used (sl.) for a pretty girl, nice little bit of stuff; *~ dara,* ornaments made with *~* leaves for weddings.

siring [KN], 1. a large shrimp-net handled by one man. 2. to pour off water by turning the container on its side.

sirip [KN], the fin of a fish; *ber~,* overlapping, as tiles.

sisa [KN], Skr. surplus, residue; remains (esp. of a meal); *~ Nabi,* a freshwater flatfish; so called because of the story that the prophet *Khizir* (q.v.) threw a half-eaten fish into the river and it came to life and swam away; *~ mati, ter~,* left aside; a survivor (of a massacre or other disaster).

sisi [KN], brink, edge; side; *di~ puteri,* by the side of the princess; *di~* is used (fig.) to mean 'in relation to', 'in connection with', 'in the view of, ' in the opinion of'; *di~ Tuhan,* in the sight of God; *di~ undang-undang,* from the legal standpoint; *ber~,* side-by-side.

sisih [KK], *ber~,* to move away a little; so, to have a difference of opinion, to

dispute; *menyisihkan,* to segregate, to separate; *menyisihkan diri,* to isolate oneself.

sisik [KN], the scale of a fish, or armadillo, or dragon; the bars in the plumage of a dove; the scraping off of the scales of a fish or of leaves or bark from a branch; the shell of turtles, 'tortoise-shell'; *ber~-~,* scale-like; *~ tenggiling,* the scales of the armadillo — a description of a shingle roof; *batuk ~,* whooping cough; sometimes used for turtles generally, esp. *~ lilin (Chelone imbricata)* and *~ tempurung (Thalassochelys caretta).*

sisil [KK], turning up the ends of the sleeves or trousers — cf. **singsing**.

sisip [KK], to insert between two flat surfaces, e.g., a paper-knife between the leaves of a book; *menyisipkan,* to slip in; *ter~ di pinggang,* stuck into the waist (i.e. belt), as a knife or pistol; *~an,* infix.

sisir [KN], 1. a comb (resembling a comb of bananas), a harrow, a toothed instrument of any sort; *menyisir,* to harrow, to comb; to rake up. 2. fringe, border; *pe~an pantai,* coast-line, littoral.

siswa [KN], Ind. pupil; *maha~,* graduate; *bia~,* scholarship; *~zah,* graduate; *~ti,* female student.

sita [KN], Ind. *menyita* [KK], to seize, to confiscate.

sitar [KN], Hind. an Indian three-stringed guitar.

siti [KN], 1. Ar. lady; *Siti Hawa,* Our Lady Eve; *Siti Mariam,* the Virgin Mary; *~ guru,* a lady teacher. 2. a whistle; *tiup ~,* to blow a whistle.

sitin [KN], Eng. satin.

siting, = *sinting.*

situ [KKtr], that place, there; *di ~,* in that place; at that place; *dari ~,* thence; *ke ~,* thither.

situn [KN], a pot of glazed earthenware.

siuh [KK], *menyiuh,* to make a warning noise, shoo off.

siul [KN], whistling; *ber~,* to whistle; *~an melangsi,* piercing whistle; *menyiuli,* to wolf-whistle at; *burung ~,* the crested wood-quail *(Rollulus roul-roul)*; *punai* ~, the small green pigeon *(Osmotreron olax)*.

siuman [KN], recovered (from a fainting fit or drunken debauch); fit, well; having all his senses; *kurang* ~, not right in the head; *fikiran tidak* ~, id.

siung [KN], 1. tusks, large canine teeth; *gigi* ~, the canines; *ber*~, tusked. 2. Pah. an eddy in a river due to a rock or snag. 3. *ber*~, to whizz, as a bullet; cf. **ceong**.

siur [KN], Pk. *tak* ~, not to care about; cf. **sir 3**.

siut [KN], 1. singeing. 2. whistling; = *siul*.

soal [KN], a question; to question, esp. to cross-examine; *ber*~-*jawab*, to exchange questions and answers; to take part in a dialogue; ~*an jawab mulut*, viva voce examination; *kertas* ~*an*, examination paper; *per*~*an*, problem, matter for discussion; ~ *hidup mati*, a question of life of death; *memper*~*kan*, to take into account, consider; to talk over; *penyoalan*, interrogation.

sobat [KN], Ar. friendship, friend.

sobek [KS], a pinch of anything; to nip off a piece; ~-~, frayed at the edge, having little bits torn out; *menyobekkan hati*, to tear the heart.

sobok [KN], *penyobok*, a night-prowler, a sneak-thief who steals under cover of the darkness.

sodok [KK], shovelling up, ladling up; a shovel; *jentera penyodok*, a bull dozer; *menyodok*, to bull-doze; cf. **sudu**.

sodor [KK], Ind. *menyodorkan*, to hold out, to offer; to put forward, present, as ideas; to serve (food); also *sogoh*.

soga [KN], a tree *(Ormosia venosa)*; from its bark a red dye is made.

sogang [KN], palisades, fencing.

sogeh [KK], 1. attempting work for which one lacks experience; the bungling of a beginner. 2. a quid (of, e.g., tobacco).

sogoh, = *sodor*.

sogok [KK], 1. *menyogok*, to direct with a nod, e.g. to gesture a visitor towards a betel-box; to direct, guide; to poke; ~*kan kepala*, to poke the head out. 2. Ind. to

pierce; (met.) to bribe; *dia cuba menyogok saya*, he tried to bribe me.

soh [KK], to slack off (a rope), (nautical).

sohor [KS], Ar. *ter*~, famous; cf. **masyhur**.

soja [KK], *ter*~-~, kowtowing.

sokma [KN], Skr. the soul (in contradistinction to the body); *raga dan* ~, body and soul (the soul in the Hindu sense).

sokom [KK], Ar. smearing with paint or colouring; clouded-white (as a colour of a dog); ~*kan*, to besmear.

sokong [KK], propping up, buttressing, sustaining, supporting; corroborating (witness); *penyokong (usul)*, the seconder (of a motion); ~ *membawa rebah*, one's hopes are deceived (disappointed).

solak [KK], pen. inclined to, liking.

soldadu [KN], Port. a soldier.

solek [KS], fashion, mode, style; *ber*~, all dressed up; to do one's toilet (of a woman); *pe*~, foppish; *alat pe*~, toilet requisites; *kedai pe*~, beauty parlour; *per*~*an*, beauty treatment; *ber*~ *muka*, to 'make up'; ~*i muka*, id.

solir [KS], Pk. soft, out of training.

solok [KN], 1. *pe*~, a gift to be returned in kind, e.g., a contribution to a feast to which one is to be invitied. 2. N.S. small isolated communities and the places where they live.

som [KN], 1. *akar* ~, a Chinese tonic. 2. *tulang* ~, a pubic bone.

sombong [KS], arrogant, proud; *menyombong* [KK], to boast, to brag; *penyombong*, braggart, swanker.

sompek [KS], jagged at the edge (through injury).

sompoh [KK], carrying on the neck and shoulders.

sonak [KN], 1. the 'thorns' on a 'thornback' fish; the barb-like sting of a ray. 2. N.S. = *senak*.

sondeh [KN], a tree *(Payena Leerii)*; *getah* ~, gutta from this tree.

sondol [KK], *menyondol*, to lower the head for a charge; *ter*~-~, rubbing with lowered head (of a cat); jostling in a crowd; bumping against; *menyondol tetek ibu*, nuzzling mother's teats, as kids.

sondong [KN], 1. a kind of push-net used in Singapore for prawns. 2. a sort of hybrid of *sungkur* and *sondol; menyondong*, lowering the head, as a bull; *menyondong muncung pada*, nosing in, rooting in (e.g., rubbish); nuzzling at.

songar [KS], Jav. affected in dress or manner.

songel [KK], sticking out (as the cheek, when a quid of betel is in the mouth).

songkak [KN], bitts, = *ongkak*.

songkok [KN], a small cap worn by devout Malays; in many parts the word is also used of the Malay coloured velvet cap *(kepiah)*.

songkom [KK], *menyonkom*, to bury the face in mother's lap (as a child); to cuddle up against.

songkong = *sokong*.

songsang [KS], reversed, turned upside down; 'the wrong way', 'against the grain'; *beranak menyongsang*, birth by breech-presentation (feet first); *~-kalak*, at sixes and sevens, topsy-turvy; *seperti aur ditarik ~*, like a bamboo pulled the wrong way (i.e., against the direction of the thorns sticking out of it); of a difficult or painful task; also *sungsung*.

songsong [KK], 1. making way against; *menyongsongi*, to meet when coming from the opposite direction; *~ arus*, a name given to a shell *(Murex ternispina); menyongsong*, to make head against (as an eagle flying against the wind). 2. to hail, call to action; *~an*, Joh a 'hurry-up' call.

sontot [KS], short and stumpy.

sopak [KN], a skin disease, causing white patches on the hands; a form of psoriasis.

sopan [KS], modest, of a self-contained but respectful demeanour; courteous, *~la kepada siapa sahaja*, be courteous with everyone; demure; *~-santun*, respectable, well-behaved; *dengan ~-santun*, courteously, respectfully; *~-santun* is also used to mean 'recognised code of behaviour', esp. professional, 'the decencies', accepted code of behaviour.

sopoh [KK], *menyopoh*, to carry pick-a-back.

sorak [KN], cheering; cries of elation; *ber~*, to cheer; *tiga kali ~*, three cheers; *~-sorai*, general cheering; *~-seranah*, derisive cheering; *menyoraki*, to boo; *para penonton menyoraki penceramah itu*, the audience booed the speaker.

sorang = *seorang*.

sore [KN], Ind. evening.

sorok {KK], 1. conceal by withdrawal; *harimau menyorokkan kuku*, a tiger hiding its claws; *main menyorok*, to play hide and seek; *penyorok makanan*, a food-hoarder; 2. *~-~*, a grub destructive to padi.

sorong [KK], *menyorong*, to push forward, shoving forward; surreptitously offer a bribe; *~ dayung*, backing water; *angin ~ buritan*, a following wind; *~kan*, to push forward from behind; to pass (a dish); *~-tarik*, to push and pull, as when sawing; (met.) to vacillate, fail to stick to a decision or promise; *~ sentak*, id.; *kereta ~*, wheel-barrow.

sorot [KN], Ind. *~an*, a reflection, so, views; a review (of a book); *menyorot*, to reflect; to throw light on; to consider, review, to focus on.

sotoh [KN], Ar. the flat roof of a house.

sotong [KN], a cuttle-fish; they are (in descending order of size) *maban, sotong, torak* and *comek*, but to the man in the street *sotong* will do for all.

soyak [KK], to tear down (e.g., a poster); to rend, tear in two.

soyok [KN], N.S. a projection from the roof, esp. from the kitchen, serving as a cover from weather.

spida [KN], Ind. a bicycle.

spidu [KN], dynamite.

sponsori, *men~* [KK], to sponsor; *siapa mensponsori program ini?*, who sponsors this program?

su [KS], youngest, = *bong~* (in certain expressions, *pak ~, mak ~*).

sua [KK], pushing an object towards an-

other, e.g. holding a fighting-cock towards his rival; *bulu* ~, the feathers on
the neck of a fighting-cock; *pagar* ~, the
paling separating two buffaloes which
are being matched against one another;
ter~, coming across, 'knocking up
against'; faced with 'as danger';
memper~kan, cause to meet or encounter, confront.

suai [KS], 1. fitting, matching; *ber*~, be in
accord; *se*~, in harmony (with), fitting
with; *menye~kan diri*, to accustom oneself (to), habituate oneself (to); *tidak
se~ dengan*, incompatible with. 2. Eng.
tali ~, sway-ropes.

suaji [KN], the breech of a flag.

suak [KN], an indentation, a slight hollow;
the parting of the hair; a creek; the
hackles, of a cock, cf. **sua**.

suaka [KN], Skr. a place of refuge, a
lodging; *orang ber*~, dependants; N.S.
one's mother, as opposed to one's
wife's relations; ~ *politik*, political asylum.

suam [KS], lukewarm; ~ *kuku*, just hot
enough to dip one's finger in.

suami [KN], Skr. husband (more respectful than *laki*); lord (in the sense of
husband); *ber*~, to be married (of a
woman); *ber~kan*, to be married to.

suang [KS], *se~-~*, lightly, easily.

suap [KN], a mouthful; *menyuap* [KK], take
a mouthful; *biarlah saya menyuap bayi
itu*, let me feed the baby; *~kan*, putting
in the mouth; feeding a child; (by metaphor) bribing; *se ~ dua*, a mouthful or
two; *makan* ~, to take bribes.

suar [KN], a fire-signal; a torch or lantern
used to convey a message.

suara [KN], Skr. voice, vocal sound; *dengan ~ yang lemah lembut*, in a gentle
tone of voice; a vote, a ballot; ~ *yang
terbanyak*, a majority of votes; *kelebihan* ~, id., *pungutan ~ rakyat*,
plebiscite; *ber*~, aloud; to make audible,
to 'open one's mouth'; *dengan sebulat*
~, unanimous; *~kan*, to utter, give utterance to, to express; *membaca ber*~, to
read aloud; *besarkan* ~, to raise the

voice; (*alat*) *pengeras* ~, a loud-speaker;
merendahkan ~, to lower the voice.

suarang [KN], *persuarangan*, N.S. the
common property acquired by man and
wife.

suari [KN], *bantal* ~, an ornamental pillow
used in marriage ceremonies.

suasa [KN], gold alloyed with copper.

suasana [KN], surrounding circumstances,
'atmosphere', 'complexion'; ~ *siasah*,
the political atmosphere; ~ *riuh-heboh*,
a noisy scene.

suat [KS], whimsical, capricious.

suatu [KS], one; *se*~, each, every; the essential meaning of ~ is rather 'a' than
'one' as a numeral; ~ *hari*, one day; ~ is
often used in the sense of 'a sort of'
(something), 'very like', 'what might be
called a'; *saya nampak ~ lembaga*, I
saw a sort of shape; *se*~, something,
something or other.

subahat [KN], Ar. an accomplice.

subam [KS], dull (of metallic lustre).

subang [KN], a large ear-stud (in some
places this stud is worn by maidens
only and is discarded on marriage).

subhana [KN], Ar. praised be; *Allah --hu*.
God to Whom be praised; ~ *wa-taala*
(s.w.t.), God, Ever to be Praised, Most
High.

subud, see *susila*.

subur [KS], quick-growing, healthy (of
plants), fertile; *tanah ini* ~, this land is
fertile.

suci [KS], Skr. pure, clean; holy; *Tanah
Suci*, the Holy Places of Islam; ~ *hati*, a
heart free from malice or deceit; *Maha-
*~, the All-pure; God; *~kan*, (polite) to
circumcise; also, to sterilize; *~-hama*,
sterile, germ-free.

suda [KN], sharp-pointed bamboo splinters (used as caltrops).

sudah [KKtr], Pers. done, finished; marks
the perfect tense; *setelah* ~, when it
was finished; *~kan*, to complete; to
finish; to 'finish off' (a job); *penyudah*,
fulfilling, realisation, culmination; *yang
~ ~*, let bygones be bygones; *ke~an*, the
end; finally; the result; *kalau peraduan*

berke~an; dengan kalah-menang, if there is a definite result to the contest; often contracted in speech and in light writing to *dah.*

sudi [KK], 1. pleased, ready; *jikalau ~,* if you like; *~kan,* to like ; to care for; to approve of; *~lah,* pray, be pleased to; *~- tak ~,* willy-nilly; *ke~an,* benevolence, readiness, willingness; 2. Kel., Treng. to try, test.

sudip [KN], large flat rice-ladle; a spatula.

sudu [KN], a ladle; a spoon; the bill of a duck; *~ itik,* a duck's bill; *siput ~,* a shell (*Haliotis* sp.); *tulang ~ hati,* the xiphoid process; *menyudu,* to nuzzle with the beak (as a duck looking for food).

sudut [KN], a corner, a nook, an angle; viewpoint; *anda harus melihat keadaan ini dari ~ lain,* you have to see the situation from a different angle.

suf [KN], Ar. a cloth-fabric, camelot.

Sufi [KN], Ar. *ilmu ~,* Sufiism, mysticism.

sugar [KK], *menyugar,* to pass the fingers through the hair.

sugi [KN], *ber~* [KK], to rub the point of a stick against anything; putting out, e.g., a torch by rubbing off the burning portion; cleaning the teeth in the old-fashioned Malay way. 2. = *sogeh* 2.

suguh [KK], *menyuguh,* to serve food to a guest.

sugul [KS], Ar. mournful, depressed.

sugun [KK], 1. forcing down with violence; seizing, the hair or throat and so forcing down an adversary. 2. dishevelled (of hair).

suhu [KN], Ind. temperature.

Suhun [KN], *~an,* a Javanese royal title; also *Susuhunan* and *Susunan.*

suih [KN], Ch. misfortune; bad luck; bring bad luck; *zaman ~,* bad times.

suji [KN], 1. embroidery; fancy needlework. 2. Hind. (Pen.) a coarse wheat-meal, semolina.

sujud [KK], Ar. prostrating in prayer; *~ sahwi,* the prostration of forgetfulness (performed just before the *salam* which ends the prayer to cover any inadvertent omission in the prayer).

suka [KK], Skr. liking, pleasure, enjoyment, *~ hati, ~ cita,* joyful, delighted; *~ raya,* uproarious delight; *~ hati tuan,* as you please; *~i,* to take pleasure in; to like; *~kan,* id.; *ke~an,* pleasure, enjoyment; Kel. to laugh; *~~ramai,* popular; *~rela,* voluntary; *pekerja ~~rela Amerika syarikat,* the United States Peace Corps; *~relawan,* a volunteer; *~duka,* joys and sorrows; *ber~~~an,* to have fun, enjoy oneself.

sukan [KN], sport; sports; *ahli ~,* a sportsman, athlete.

sukar [KS], difficult, arduous; *~ dicari,* hard to find; *~ beroleh dia,* id.; *masa ke~an,* difficult times; *~ dipercaya,* beyond one's wildest expectations.

sukat [KK], 1. *menyukat,* to measure area or capacity; mensuration; *~an,* measurement; a measure; (fig.) grading; *penyukat,* something used for measuring; *~an pelajaran,* syllabus; *satu ~(ab),* a measured dose; *timbangan dan ~an,* weights and measures; *menyukat panas,* to gauge the temperature; *ber~,* measured out; so, doled out, rationed. 2. provided that, supposing that, if, when; *~ air menjadi batu,* if (or when) water turns into stone, i.e., never.

suki [KS], excessive, abundant (of food).

sukma [KN], soul.

Surkrat [KN], Ar. Socrates.

suku [KN], 1. etym. a limb; quarter; a section; a tribe or division of the people; *~ jam,* a quarter of an hour; *rial dan ~,* dollars and quarter-dollars; *~~sakat,* family, clan; *~~bangsa,* tribe, clan; *tiga ~,* (sl.) 'cracked', 'potty'. 2. Pah., Kel. separate, different; *~ fasal,* a different affair.

sukum [KN], Ked. a muzzle to prevent buffalo-calves from suckling.

sukun [KN], the bread fruit (*Artocarpus incisa*).

sula [KN], Skr. a pointed stick; an impaling-post; *~kan, menyula,* to impale; to roast on a spit; *ter~,* impaled; *teri~,* a trident; *~* is sometimes used for a fixed blade on which coconuts are husked.

sulah [KS], bare, hairless, *lada* ~, white pepper.

sulai [KK], *ter*~, projecting (as branch of tree).

Sulaiman [KN], *Nabi* ~, King Solomon; famed for magical powers and for control of *jins* and such supernatural beings; also as Lord of the animal kingdom.

sulalat [KN], Ar. extraction, descent, origin; *Sulalat u.s.-Salatun*, the ancestry of kings — a Malay traditional history.

sulam [KN], 1. raised embroidery; *ber*~, embroidered; *barang ~an*, embroidered articles. 2. to replace a tree or an attap with a new one; interplanting; *getah ber*~ *nanas*, rubber interplanted with pineapples; *ber*~, interspersed, e.g., as comedy in a drama.

sulang [KK], 1. joining in a drink; inviting another person to drink with you; *minum ber*~-~*an*, exchanging drinks time after time. 2. sooty deposit.

Sulawesi [KN], Celebes.

sulbi [KN], Ar. *tulang* ~, the coccyx.

suidi [KN], Ar. Adam's apple (in the throat).

sule [KS], Hind. (Pen.) rheumatic pains; in a very weak state.

suli [KN], a grandson or great-grandson; a descendant.

suling [KN], 1. a generic name for flageolets; fifes and pipes; sometimes, a whistle. 2. Ind. *menyuling*, to distil, as perfumes; to refine, as oil; *penyuling*, distiller; *penyulingan*, distillation.

sulit [KS], obscure, out of the way, little known, secluded; private, secret, confidential; complicated; *ke*~*an*, a difficulty, difficult problem; *menyulitkan*, to hamper, cause difficulties to.

sultan [KN], Ar. sultan; *Sultan Al Muasam*, the august sultan, i.e., the Sultan of Turkey; ~ was formerly a personal title taken by any ruling prince; its use now implies that the ruler is independent; *ke*~*an*, sultanate, territory ruled by a ~, monarchy; ~*ah*, consort of a sultan.

suluh [KN], a torch; a spy; a scout; *penyuluh*, a scout or spy; *terang seperti ber*~ *bulan matahari*, as clear as if lighted by both moon and sun, i.e., clearly proved; *menyuluh* [KK], to light with a torch; *ber*~, so lit.

suluk [KN], Ar. a form of mysticism; *amalan* ~, the practice of this mysticism (which sometimes takes the form of a sort of spiritualist seance).

sulung [KS], senior, eldest, first in age; *anak* ~, eldest son; often abbreviated to *Long*; *gigi* ~, milk teeth; ~ *tahun*, beginning of the year; *buah* ~, first fruits; *nobel* ~, a first novel.

sulur [KS], rising upwards; ~ *tiang*, top mast; also, a shoot (e.g., of a bush); esp. a creeping shoot; a runner; *penyulur*, id.; *menyulur*, to creep; *suluran*, plants which climb by twisting round a support.

Sumatera [KN], *Pulau* ~, Sumatra; possibly from *Kampung Semudera*, the 'village on the Ocean', a seat of government of the rulers of the old State of Pasai; see *semudera*.

sumbang [KK], 1. improper, revolting, incestuous; unseemly, improper; ~ *di mata*, an eyesore; *anak* ~, a child of incest; ~ *bagi pandangan*, a disgusting sight; 2. Ind. to contribute; ~*an*, a contribution; ~*sih*, contribution, assistance, aid; *menyumbang*, to make a contribution.

sumbar [KK], Jav. *ber*~, reproaching, reviling.

sumbat [KN], ~*kan*, *menyumbat* [KK], to cork up, stop an orifice, to plug; to put a stopper into anything; to stuff in; *menyumbat- nyumbatkan ke dalam*, to keep stuffing in (as food into mouth); *ter*~, plugged up; *penyumbat*, a stopper; *menyumbat mulut*, to gag.

sumber [KN], source, origin; *ber*~, originate from, rest upon; *ber*~*kan*, have as a source.

sumbi [KK], replacing an injured part; putting new planks into a boat; patching; to 'stop' a tooth; ~ *mas*, a gold stopping or crown; *ber~ dengan permata*, studded with gems — cf. **pasak**.

sumbing [KS], notched, dented, jagged; *gelak ~*, a sickly laugh; *bibir ~*, hare-lip; *ke~an*, a cleft, notch, (fig.) a flaw, fault, e.g., in style.

sumbu [KN], 1. a fuse; a slow match, wick; *~ pelita*, the wick of a lamp; *kena ~*, (coarse) to be made a fool of, to be led up the garden path. 2. *sumbu badak*, the horn of a rhinoceros.

sumbul [KK], 1. *menyumbul*, to pour out, as grain from a cut bag or as a crowd from a building; sometimes used for 'projecting'. 2. a small basket with lid.

sumpah [KK], oath; *~an*, vow, promise; *ber~*, to take an oath; *ber~ taat-setia*, to take an oath of allegiance; *memberi ~*, to administer the oath; *angkat ~*, to take the oath; *melanggar ~*, to break an oath; to swear falsely; *makan ~*, id.; *~i*, to lay a curse on; *menyumpah*, swearing, reviling, cursing; *~-~*, a name given to the Malayan 'chameleons' *(Calotes versicolor* and *C. cristatellus)*.

sumpil, Jav. = *sumbat*.

sumpit [KN], *~an*, a blowpipe; *~kan*, to kill (anything) with the blowpipe; *menyumpit*, to use the blowpipe; *~-~*, (1) the well-known shooting fish *(Toxotes jaculator)*; (2) a small *mengkuang*, rice bag.

sumsum [KN], Ind. marrow, pith.

sumur [KN], Ind. a well, source; *~ digali air terbit*, (prov.) to get more than one's expectation.

sunat [KN], circumcision; *tukang ~*, a circumciser; *~kan*, to circumcise; to enjoin as commendable.

Sunda [KN], *orang ~*, a Sundanese.

sundai [KN], N.S. sloping, slanting.

sundal [KN], a harlot, a prostitute, lewd; whore; *per~an*, prostitution; *~ malam*, the tuberose; often called gardenia.

Sundari [KN], the Fair (a woman's name).

sundang [KN], a Bugis short sword with cockatoo hilt, sometimes with wavy blade.

sundut [KN], Ar. a generation; *dari ~ ber~*, for many generations; also *sunut*.

sungai [KN], a river; a flowing stream of some size; *anak ~*, rivulet; *pergi ke ~*, (polite) to obey a call of nature; *surat ~*, Joh. an old form of land-title, the holder of which held the basin of a river — cf. **kangka**; *~ mati*, a backwater.

sungga [KN], Jav. a spur, a goad; a caltrop.

sungging [KN], picturing flowers or ornamental paterns in paint (such as gold paint), etc.

sungguh [KS], genuine, true, real; *~ hati*, earnestness; sincerity; *~pun*, although; *~-~*, really, genuinely; *se~nya*, in all truth; in all reality; *~-~i*, to strive vigorously or strenuously; *ke~an*, sincerity, wholeheartedness, earnestness.

sungkah [KK], *menyungkah*, to gobble (food).

sungkai [KN], 1. a tree *(Peronema canescens*-order *Verbenaceoe)*. 2. *Hantu Sangkai*, an evil spirit that molests hunters.

sungkal [KK], to turn up (as a ploughshare turns up the earth); *~ bajak*, a ploughshare.

sungkap [KK], pulled loose; *kuku ter~*, a finger-nail or toe-nail torn from the quick.

sungkawa [KN], *bela~*, condolence.

sungkit [KN], 1. *kain ~*, silk cloth shot with gold or silver. 2. to prise up.

sungkup [KN], covering, as under a hollow bowl or vessel.

sungkur [KK], rooting up, scooping up, shovelling up; a net of triangular shape pushed through mud and water so as to catch shrimps; *~ sangkar*, sprawling; *Sang Sungkur*, Mr Rotter, i.e., the pig; *jatuh ter~*, to fall sprawling, flat on the face; *menyungkurkan diri*, to throw oneself down on one's face.

sunglap [KN], jugglery; *main ~*, to juggle; to engage in double- dealing; *main ~ politik*, to play political tricks.

sungu [KN], Jav. horn.

sungut [KN], 1. grumbling; *ber~*, to

murmur; to mutter. 2. antennae, feeler, tentacle.

sunjam [KK], head downwards; *ter~*, hung up by the heels.

sunti [KN], lumps on roots of certain plants, esp. ginger; *anak dara ~*, a young girl whose breasts are just developing.

suntih [KK], chipping off.

suntik [KK], *menyuntik*, Ind. to inject; to vaccinate; *~kan*, injection, inoculation, vaccination.

sunting [KK], to wear stuck behind the ear (as flowers are occasionally worn); *~kan*, to wear in the hair; to 'crop the flower in season'; to decorate; to introduce, insert (articles in paper); *anak dara ~*, a girl who has just attained marriagable age; *penyunting berita*, news-editor.

suntuk [KKtr], overlong; too late, very late; *sehari ~*, all day long; *waktu ~*, time is up; *orang tua ~*, an old man who apes young ways; *kesuntukan waktu*, shortness of time; *masa ~*, time is short; *~ malam*, late at night; *fikiran ~*, shortsighted view.

sunyi [KS], Skr. lonely, solitary, desolately quiet, deserted; *ke~an*, silence, quiteness, stillness; *ber~ diri*, to live apart (as does a hermit); *~ sepi*, dead quiet; *~ senyap*, lonely and deserted, very quiet.

supaya [KPhbg], in order that.

sura [KN], 1. Skr. hero; man of men. 2. Ar. *bulan Sura*, a name given to the month *Muharram*.

surah [KN], 1. Ar. a subdivision or chapter of the Koran; *~ yasin*, the chapter chanted to a dying person. 2. = *syarah*.

surai [KN], 1. the combing or dressing of the hair; the hair itself (when speaking of a prince or princess). 2. *ber~* [KK], to break up, disperse (as people at a meeting); *menyuraikan*, to cause to disperse, to break up (a meeting). 3. *roti ~*, a sort of pancake.

suralaya [KN], Skr. the abode of the gods; the Hindu Olympus.

suram [KS], dark, gloomy, clouded (of the brightness of the sun or of the countenance); *~kan lampu*, to dim, turn down, a lamp.

surat [KN], Ar. a writing of any sort; a letter; *~an*, a document; handwriting; *isi ~*, the contents of a letter or document; *muka ~*, the written page; *~ kiriman*, a letter, an epistle; *~ pelekat*, a poster; *~ putus*, Ked. a grant (title for land); *~ tandatangan*, a signed acknowledgement; (us.) an I.O.U.; *~ wakil*, a power of attorney; *~ wasiat*, a will; *~ terbang*, an anonymous or pseudonymous letter; *~ melayang*, id.; *~ asmara*, love-letter; *~ beranak*, birth-certificate; *~ cucuk*, vaccination certificate; *~ khabar*, a newspaper; *~ edaran*, a circular; *~ akuan*, recommendation, as for a post; in some localities, a document evidencing title to land; *~ rantai bahagia*, 'chain of happiness letter'; *per~khabaran*, the Press; *~kan*, to cause to be written; *ter~*, written; inscribed; sometimes 'written' in the sense of being predestined; *orang yang percaya bahawa mujur malang sudah tetap ter~*, those who believe that good and bad fortune are definitely written; *menyurat*, to write; *per~an*, literature; the art of letter-writing; *~ menyurat*, to correspond, exchange letters; *batu ber~*, an inscribed stone.

Surati [KN], from Surat (in India).

surau [KN], prayer house.

suri [KN], Skr. a queen; royal; = *permai~*; *rama aji ibu ~*, royal father and queenly mother; the parents of a prince; *~ rumahtangga*, queen of the household; poet. for one's bride, wife.

suria [KN], (poet.) the sun; *Sang Suria*, Mr Sun.

suriakanta [KN], Ind. magnifying glass; lens.

surih [KN], *~~*, Pk. descent, lineage.

surmah [KN], Pers. a collyrium made of antimony.

suruh [KK], *menyuruh*, ordering; given instructions; *~an*, an order, a command; *~~an*, messengers; *~kan*, to order; to instruct; *pe~jaya,* a commissioner; *Pe~jaya Tanah,* Commissioner of Lands; *Pe~jaya Tinggi,* High Commissioner; *Pe~jaya Pengangkutan Jalanraya,* Commissioner for Road Transport; *Pe~-Sumpah,* Commissioner for Oaths; *pe~,* a messenger, orderly; *~anjaya,* a commission; *~anjaya Diraja,* a Royal Commission.

surut [KS], 1. ebbing (of the tide); *air ~,* the ebb-tide; *air sudah jauh ~,* the tide has ebbed a long way; to go down (as a swelling); *ter~,* taken aback, disconcerted. 2. = *sorot.*

susah [KS], difficult; uneasy; *~ hati,* sad; *~kan* to vex; *ke~an,* trouble, affliction; *menyusah-payahkan,* to harass, cause trouble to; *~-payah,* difficulties, troubles; *menyusahkan,* to vex, to cause difficulty; *jangan ber~-payah,* don't go to a lot of trouble; *jangan ~-~kan,* don't worry yourself about.

susila [KS], Ind. morals, morality; *ke~an,* moral behaviour; ethical; *amalan demikian tidaklah ~,* such practices are not ethical; *~ budi darma,* (the Movement), for Morality, Wisdom and Righteousness, generally referred to as *Subud,* a mystical movement originating in Indonesia; held by some to be contrary to the teaching of Islam; the leader is Sumohadiwidjojo (Pak Suhuh) of Jakarta.

susu [KN], the breast; milk; *air ~,* milk; *~i,* to suckle; *menyusukan,* id.; *menyusu,* to be suckled; *~ bundar,* hemispherical breasts; *~ kopek* or *~ lanjut,* pendulous breasts; *~ rimau,* the sclerotium or resting-place of a fungus; *dapur ~,* the outer portion of the breast; *hujung ~,* the nipple generally; the extremity; *puting ~,* the nipple proper; *tampuk ~,* the nipple and dark circle round it; *buah ~,* Jamaica honeysuckle *(Passiflora laurifolia); ~ getah,* latex; *~ tepung,* powdered milk; *~ tin,* tinned milk; *~ hidup,* fresh milk; *~ pekat,* condensed milk; *~ dibalas dengan tuba,* (prov.) to get small thanks for one's pains.

susuh [KN], a small projection; the (natural) spur of a fighting-cock.

susuk [KK], 1. *menyusuk,* to found (a city). 2. manner, bearing, mien; *~ jijak,* id.; *~ badan,* build (of body), figure. 3. a loop; a button-hole; *~ intan, ~ mas,* a diamond or small gold plate let into the flesh by old-fashioned women as a semi-magical beautifier. 4. = *cucuk.*

susul [KK], 1. following up; *menyusul,* to follow (in order), to succeed, esp. as events or as following in a procession; rarely, to pursue; *gerakan menyusul,* pursuit (by troops). 2. Ked. stuff, hard to work (as wood); hard to comb (as hair).

susun [KN], lying rows one above the other, double (of flowers); *ber~~,* in layers; nesting into one another, as vessels; *~(an),* such a nest; *~an ayat,* syntax; *menyusun,* to arrange in layers (e.g., as plates); to sort out; to compile; to stack; *menyusun teriti,* to frame a treaty; *ter~,* neatly arranged; even, as teeth; *penyusun,* arranger, compiler, organiser; *penyusunan,* arrangement, compilation, structure.

susup [KK], to slip under (as in getting under a fence); *menyusupkan,* to place under; to insert under; *menyusup,* to slip under and in; (met.) to infiltrate; to crouch low in order to get under something or to hide; *penyusupan,* conveying in secret, smuggling; *lari ~-sasap,* running in headlong flight (as through all obstacles).

susur [KN], *~an,* outskirts, outer borders; *~an pantai,* outer edge of beach; *~an kota,* outer walls of fort; *~an tangga,* banister; *menyusur,* to skirt; to hug (the shore); to edge past; *kapal penyusur,* a coasting vessel; *menyusur-galur,* to trace back to origin, thoroughly go into.

susut [KS], shrinking; diminishing in size; thinning down; *~ tubuh,* to lose flesh, slim; *menyusut,* decrease, depreciate, lessen.

sut [KN], Ked. rear, hindmost, fag-end; *~nya,* in the end.

sutera [KN], Skr. silk; *kain* ~, a silk sarong, *payung* ~, a silk umbrella; *ulat* ~, silkworm.

sutli [KN], Hind. (Pen.) coarse thread for canvas.

Syaaban [KN], Ar. the eighth month in the Muslim calendar; popularly known as *bulan ruah (arwah)*, i.e., the month in which departed spirits should be prayed for.

syair [KN], Ar. poem; *ahli* ~, a poet; *penyair*, id.

syafaat [KN], Ar. intercession; *memberi*, ~, to give the Blessing.

Syafei [KN], Ar. the founder of the Shafeite school *(mazab)* of Islamic law to which Malays belong.

syah [KN], Pers. King, sovereign; a royal title; ~ *johan*, ruler of the world; ~ *mardan*, king of men; ~ *bandar*, habour master; ~ *alam*, Lord of the World, honorific used as an address to kings; ~ *alam di rimba*, Jungle Lord of the World, a playful epithet given to the mousedeer in folklore stories (in this connection ~ is sometimes corrupted to *salam* or replaced by *syaikh*).

syahada [KS], noble, fine, handsome.

syahadan [KKtr], furthermore — a common exordium to a paragraph, moreover.

syahadat [KN], Ar. attestation; the confession of faith; the creed.

syahbandar [KN], see *syah*.

syahid [KN], Ar. *mati* ~, dying a martyr, killed in a holy war.

syahmat [KN], check-mate.

syahuat [KN], Ar. voluptuous sensation, orgasm; *menambahkan* ~, to intensify sensation (of aphrodisiacs).

syahur, = *sahur*.

syaikh [KN], Ar. a title given to Arabs who are not descendants of the Prophet; *turun* ~, to go into a mediumistic trance; sometimes, to be beside oneself with rage; ~ *Haji*, a class of Shaikhs who by custom instruct and advise would-be pilgrims to Mecca, pilgrimage agent; *syaikh alam di rimba*, see *syah*.

syair [KN], poem, *ber*~, compose a poem.

Syaitan [KN], Ar. an evil spirit; a devil; Satan; also *Setan*.

syak [KK], Ar. doubt, suspicion; ~ *hati*, suspicious; *tidak* ~ *lagi*, undoubtedly, certainly; ~ *wasangka*, prejudice, suspicion, distrust.

syakar [KN], Pers. sugar.

syaksyih [KN], Ar. personality, individual person; *tidak menyentuh* ~, no personal allusion intended.

Syam [KN], *negeri* ~, Syria.

syamsu [KN], Ar. the sun; *ketika* ~, when the (astrological influence of the) sun is in the ascendant.

syara [KN], Ar. *hukum* ~, Muslim law.

syarah [KN], Ar. a lecture, address; *ber*~ [KK], to lecture.

syarat [KN], Ar. article or clause in a contract, a condition; *mencukupi* ~, to fulfil conditions; *hilang* ~, to fail to meet conditions.

syariat [KN], Ar. ordinance of God; liturgy and ritual of Islam.

Syarif [KN], Ar. noble; a title of descendants of the Prophet through Husain.

Syarifah [KN], Ar. noble; a title given to women descended from the Prophet; also *Saripah* and (coll.) *Cik Pah*.

syarikat [KN], Ar. the joint earnings of husband and wife; a partnership; a mercantile firm, company; ~ *penerbangan*, an airline; also *serikat*; a society, union; ~ *berkerja-sama*, a cooperative society; *Amerika* ~, the U.S.A.; *Bangsa-bangsa* ~ *(bersatu)*, the United Nations; *kedai* ~, co-operative shop; ~ *permodalan*, finance company; investment company.

syatar [KN], Ar. a line (on paper).

Syawal [KN], Ar. the tenth month in the Muslim calendar.

syirik [KN], Ar. the heresy of attributing partners to God, contrary to the doctrine of His unity.

Syed [KN], *Said*.

syok [Ks], Ar. pleasant; entrancing; ~ *pada*, to be keen on, attracted by, desire (a woman).

syor [KN], Ar. (lit, distilled honey), advice,

counsel; proposal, recommendation — cf. **mesyuarat**.

syubahat [KN], Ar. an accomplice; *ber~*, to act as an accomplice; to collaborate (with the enemy).

syuhada, [KN], witness.

syukur [KN], Ar. thanks; *beribu ~*, thousands of thanks; *mengucap ~*, to give thanks; *ber~*, to be thankful; *~lah!*, thank God!; *ke~an*, thankfulness, gratitude.

syurga [KN], Skr. heaven; also *sorga*; *~ dunia*, heaven.

T

taajal [KKtr], haste, hasty, hastily.

taakul [KK], reason out (a matter etc.).

taala [KS], Ar. most high; *Allah* ~, God Most High.

taassub [KS], Ar. dogmatic, opinionated, bigoted; ~ *pada agama,* fanatically religious.

taat [KS], Ar. obedient, submissive; *men~i,* obey, abide, observe; *ke~an,* obedience, loyalty, fidelity; ~ *setia,* loyal; *yang* ~, yours obediently; *yang* ~ *di bawah perintah,* your obedient servant.

taayat [KK], Ar. *duduk* ~, sitting back after prostration in prayer.

tabah [KS], 1. a hand's breadth. 2. *ber~,* to be bold, persevere; *menabahkan,* make bold or stout-hearted; Ind. calm, cool, resolute; *ke~an,* resoluteness, perseverance, spirit.

tabak [KN], Ar. a box, a casket; a present of food taken by a departing guest.

tabal [KN], Ar. a kettledrum used at the installation of a ruler; *~kan* [KN], to install; *ber~,* to ascend the throne; to be crowned (of a ruler); *per~an,* ascending or ascension to the throne.

taban [KN], *getah* ~, gutta-percha; *pokok* ~, the gutta-percha tree *(Dichopsis gutta).*

tabaraka, Ar. may (he) be blessed.

tabia [KN], Hind. from Ar. (Pen.) a small tambourine.

tabiat [KN], Ar. character, nature; ~ *semula jadi,* innate characteristics, natural disposition; *ber~ pemalas,* naturally lazy; *rosak* ~, depraved; *sudah ber~,* to be altered in character (for the worse), esp. of a person who is 'failing as death approaches', to 'go downhill'; *buang* ~, id. see *alam.*

tabib [KN], Ar. a physician practising Arabic medicine.

tabii, see *alam.*

tabik [KN], excuse, greeting (as from an inferior); *memberi* ~, to greet, to courteously salute or recognise; *minta* ~, to excuse oneself; to apologise in advance for any unintentional breach of etiquette; *membalas* ~ *kehormatan,* to take the salute, e.g., at a march-past.

tabir [KN], hangings; drapery; *ber~,* curtained; *menabiri,* decorated with drapes or curtain; ~ *besi,* the iron curtain.

tabrak [KN], Ind. a bump, a crash; *menabrak* [KK], to bump into, collide with.

tabuh [KN], a striker for a drum or keys; a long cylindrical drum; *~kan,* to beat this drum; *~~an,* all sorts of percussion instruments.

tabun [KK], *menabun,* to rise straight up, as smoke; *~an asap,* a column of smoke.

tabung [KN], a cylindrical vessel of bamboo for papers, water, money; a quiver; *penabung,* saver, depositor; ~ *wang,* a money-box; (fig.) a fund, a nest-egg; ~ *mogok,* strike fund; ~ *pena,* the barrel of a fountain pen; ~ *derma darah,* donors' blood-banks; ~ *bunga,* a shrub *(Ixora pendula);* balik *menabung,* Pk. to return empty-handed, failed.

tabur [KK], 1. the scattering of seed or flowers; dispersing; *~kan* or *menabur-kan,* to sow; *ber~an,* scattered about; *penabur,* person who scatters something; shot (for cartridges).

tabut [KN], Ar. the ark of the convenant; (Pen.) a Hindu processional emblem; also the caper ark carried in procession on the 10th *Muharram,* when the deaths of Hassan and Husain are commemorated.

tadah [KK], intercepting or catching a falling object; ~kan tangan, to stretch out the hands with the palms upwards (as in Muslim prayer); beralih ~, to change one's attitude, alter views; berpaling ~, id.; kecik tapak tangan, nyiru di~kan, my hands being small, I hold out a winnowing-tray; i.e., over-whelmed with gratitude for incredible generosity; menadahkan botol, to put a bottle under (a tap) so as to receive water, to catch running water in a bottle.

tadbir [KK], Ar. government; men~kan, to govern, administer; to command (troops); pen~, in charge, in command; per~an, the Administration; pen~an, administration, pen~an amanah, a mandate.

tadi [KKtr], just a moment ago; immediately past; baharu ~, a moment ago; malam ~, last night; yang tersebut di atas ~, aforesaid.

tadung [KK], 1. Pen. tertadung, stumbling against, e.g., a creeper. 2. ber~, settling or forming on the sides, as scum.

tafahus [KN], investigation; menafahuskan, to investigate.

tafakur [KN], Ar. reflect; plunged in meditation; ber~, to meditate silently; tunduk ber~ selama dua minit, to observe a two-minute silence.

tafsir [KN], Ar. ~an, detailed description (opposed to ijmal); from the Koran; elucidation; interpretation of meaning, definition; penafsiran, id.

tafta [KN], Ar. twisted silk, taffeta.

tagak [KK], putting off, procrastination; ter~~, hestitating dawdling; menagak, ignore, defy, stop.

tagan [KN], the stakes in a sweep; the 'pool'.

tagar [KN], a peal of thunder.

tagi = tagih.

tagih [KK], menagih, to importune, clamour for, to dun for (a debt); ke~, craving (from constant indulgence) for, e.g., tobacco, opium or alcohol.

tah [Partikel], a suffix expressing interrogation or doubt; = entah, ini~ gamba-

rannya?, is this his portrait?

tahajud [KN] sembahyang ~, night prayer.

tahan [KS], 1. holding out against, sustaining; stopping; menahani, to restrain or resist; to bear up against; to stand (anything); to detain; to restrain; to last; to stop, e.g., a vehicle, a passerby; ber~, to hold out, to endure; orang ~an, a detainee; per~an, defence; Menteri Per~an, Minister of Defence: memper~kan, to defend; to maintain; menahan nafsu, to control the passions; tidak ter~, irresistible, unbearable intolerable; ke~an, power of endurance; ~ muda, to retain a youthful appearance; ~ habuk, dust-proof; ~ air, water-proof; ~ api, fire-proof; ~ karat, rust-proof; ~ gegar, shock-proof; ~ golek, hard to upset, of a boat; ~ uji, to stand up to a test; ~ lambung gelombang hidup, to stand up to the tossing of the waves of life. 2. setting (traps); ~ lukah, to set a fish-trap.

tahana [KN], greatness, majesty; ber~, to sit in majesty; to be present (of a prince).

tahang [KN], a large wooden tub.

tahar [KK], to keep on a course in spite of unfavourable winds.

tahi [KN], filth, mucus, dirt, ordure, feculence, lees, grounds; ~ angin, light fleecy clouds; words of little account, windy talk; ~ air, scum on water; ~ besi, rust; ~ candu, opium dross; ~ gergaji, sawdust; ~ harus, drift- wood; ~ ketam, shavings; ~ lalat, a freckle, a mole; ~ mata, mucus from the eye; ~ minyak, refuse in making oil; oil-residue, (fig.) scum; ~ panas, prickly heat; ~ penyakit, valetudinarian; ~ telinga, wax in the ear; ular ~ kerbau, a snake (Coluber radiatus); ~ arak, sot; ~ candu, opium addict; ~ bong, Kel. bookies at bull-fights; membuat kerja hangat-hangat ~ ayam, to work as hotly as fowls' droppings, i.e., start enthusiastically and then cool off, a 'flash in the pan' (because fowls' droppings quickly cool); *bunga ~ ayam*, lantana; marigold; *anjing makan ~, adakah patut kita makan ~ juga*, if a dog eats excrement, should we do the same?, i.e., don't meet dirty tricks with dirty tricks; also *taik*.

tahil [KN], a tael; 1 oz.

tahir [KS], pure, unspotted.

tahlil [KN], Ar. religious chanting; continually repeating the name of God.

tahmld [KN], praise to God over and over again.

tahniah [KN], Ar. congratulations, felicitation; *mengucap ~*, to offer congratulations; *~ dirinya*, his personal congratulations.

tahu [KK], 1. to know; *beri ~*, to inform; *dengan se ~ saya*, with my knowledge; as far as I know; *dengan tak se~—*, without the knowledge of—; *sepanjang pengetahuan saya*, to the best of my knowledge; *ke~an*, knowledge, sense, capacity for understanding; *ke~i* or *menge~i*, to know; *tak ke~an*, beyond belief; confused, bewildering *penge~an*, knowledge, learning; *berpenge~an*, knowledgeable; *penge~an am*, general knowledge, *buat tak ke~an*, to 'muck about', act irresponsibly; *tak ber~an*, wildly, recklessly; *tidak berke~an rupa*, unrecognisable (e.g., as a mutilated corpse); *~ menahu*, to have knowledge of, be cognizant of; *pemberi ~*, a notification; *orang yang berpenge~an*, well-informed person. 2. Ch. a sort of flat yellow cake of bean curd.

tahu [KN], *burung ~*, Kel. the Malayan koel (a cuckoo which lays in crows' nests); also a sort of barbet which has a note like that of the koel.

tahun [KN], year; *~ baru*, the new year; *ber~~*, for years, chronic; *ber~*, to plant one's annual crop of rice; *~an*, annual (event); *hari ulang-~*, anniversary; *~ Masihi*, A.D.; *pokok ~*, a perennial tree; *menahun*, perennial; chronic; *~ lompat*, leap-year; *~ kebisatan*, id.; *~*

hijrah, the Muslim year; cf. **sanat**; *~ lima-puluhan*, the fifties.

tahyat [KN], Ar. formal greetings.

taiku [KN], Ch. (Borneo) leprosy.

taikung [KN], Ch. the captain of a junk.

Taiwan [KN], Formasa.

taj [KN], Ar. crown, diadem.

taja [KK], to start, set up, establish; *menaja*, to promote (e.g., a competition); *penaja*, a promoter, a sponsor; *~an*, sponsorship.

tajak [KN], a sort of scythe — for cutting grass, weeds, etc., in rice-fields.

tajam [KS], sharp; *akalnya ~*, he was sharp mentally; *~ mulut*, caustic; *~kan*, *memper~kan*, to sharpen; *~ bertimbal*, sharpened at both ends; *ke~an*, sharpness, acuteness.

tajau [KN], a large earthenware jar.

taji [KN], the artificial spur of a fighting-cock; *membulang ~*, to fasten on the spurs; *ber~*, wearing metallic spurs.

tajin [KK], *~kan*, to soak, e.g., cloth with rubber to make it waterproof.

tajuk [KN], 1. an aigrette, a tuft, a sheath (with flowers in it) worn in the hair; *~ mahkota*, the aigrette or apex of a crown. 2. the knee-pieces in a house. 3. caption, headline; title; *~ rencana*, leading article.

tajur [KS], running out into the sea; *penajur*, a row of fishing-stakes to drive fish into a trap.

tajwid [KN], Ar. a grammatical accuracy; writing (Arabic) correctly; correct pronunciation and intonation (while reading the Koran).

tak = *tidak*, not.

takah [KN], Ked. the slow loris.

takak [KN], *kain ber~*, a sarong made up of two pieces.

takal [KN], Eng. a pulley, a block.

takar [KN], 1. an earthenware vessel with a narrow neck; esp. for ginger; used for 'dice-box'. 2. *burung ~*, the barbet; also *takau; se~*, of the same amount.

takat [Informal], as far as; up to a point reached, as on a journey; *~ pinggang*, up to the waist; *~ lutut*, up to the knee;

~ *air pasang,* high-water mark; *se~ ini,* so far, up to now.

takbir [KN], Ar. 1. the saying 'God is great'; *~ulihram,* the first ~ in the liturgical prayers; *mengangkat ~,* to raise the cry, 'God is great'; *laungkan ~,* id. 2. interpretation or elucidation, esp. *~ mimpi,* the interpretation of dreams; *men~kan mimpi,* to interpret dreams.

takbur [KS], proud, conceited, arrogant.

takdir [KN], Ar. will; the decree of Providence; that which is ordained by God; *sudah ~ Allah,* it was predestined; *ke~an,* predestination.

takhta [KN], Pers. a throne.

takhyul [KN], Ar. imagination, foresight; imaginary; sometimes, intoxication; *orang yang mempercayai ~,* imaginative people, superstitious people; *pemikiran yang ~,* superstition; *faham ~,* id.; also *tahyul.*

taki [KK], *menaki,* to debate, to dispute, to argue.

takik [KN], a cleft; *menakik* [KK], to cut slightly, to tap (a rubber tree).

taklid [KN], Ar. complete submission; a staunch believer of what others say; *secara ber~,* with blind obedience; without due consideration.

taklimat [KN], briefing.

takluk [KK], subdued, dependant, a colony, dependency; *pejabat jajahan ~,* colonial office; *menakluki,* to bring into subjection.

takrim [KN], Ar. honour, respect.

taksir [KN], 1. Ar. negligence, carelessness. 2. (Dutch) *menaksir,* estimte, valuation, assessment.

takuk [KN], a notch; a sort of step created by cutting out a piece from the outer portion of a tree-trunk; ~ *takak,* notched, jagged; *kepala penakuk,* the cleft at the top of a screw; *bendera ~,* a swallow-tailed flag.

takung [KK], *ber~,* stagnating, fermenting; *menakung air,* to be under water, covered with 'flood' water; *ter~,* stagnant; static; *~an,* a pond; a reservoir; *~an ikan,* a fish-pond; an aquarium.

takup [KN], a small tuberous jungle-plant.

takut [KS], fearful; *~i,* to fear; *~kan,* to be afraid of; *ke~an,* panic, fright; *penakut,* a coward, timorous; ~ *kesitsit,* helpless with fear; *menakutkan,* to frighten.

takwa [KN], Ar. 1 piety, devotion to religion. 2. = *tekua.*

takwim [KN], Ar. calendar; almanac.

takziah [KN], Ar. condolence; *mengucap ~,* to express condolences.

takzim [KS], respect, reverence.

takzir [KN], punishment.

tal [KN], 1. the Palmyra palm; also *lontar.* 2. *buah ~,* Kel. colour of cattle, black with brown or grey shoulders.

tala [KN], Skr. 1. harmonious response; *ber~~,* taking up a strain in turn; *se~,* attuned; *penala,* a tuning-fork; *menalakan,* to tune (a musical instrument). 2. Hind. a padlock.

talai [KS], negligent; = *lalaim.*

talak [KN], Ar. divorce; *tiga ~,* the full divorce; the triple divorce; *gugurkan ~,* to pronounce a divorce (by the husband); *menjatuhkan ~,* id.; *menebus ~,* to obtain a divorce by payment (of the wife); *gila ~,* divorce-mad, a description of a man who divorces his wife in a fit of temper and annuls the divorce immediately afterwards.

talam [KN], a metal tray; ~ *dua muka,* double-faced, treacherous.

talan [KN], a tree (*Saraca* sp.); also *gapis.*

talang [KN], 1. a kind of horse-mackerel (*Chorinemus* sp.). 2. *bujang ~,* a bachelor or childless widower; a man 'without encumbrance'.

talar [KK], permit, let, allow; = *biar.*

tali [KN], 1. cord, rope, anything of a cord-like appearance; ~ *air,* a runnel; ~ *air pembuang,* an outlet drain; *Jabatan ~ Air dan Parit,* the Drainage and Irrigation Department; ~ *harus,* the thin line of drift-wood marking the flow of a current; ~ *kulit,* a strap; ~ *pinggang,* a girdle, a waistband, belt; ~ *pusat,* the umbilical cord; ~ *temali,* cordage, rigging; ~ *kanjang,* a specious rogue, charlatan; ~ *keranjang*, id.; ~ *barut*, tool, cats-paw; *se~ ayam*, a bit of string just long enough to tether a fowl, i.e. a very short piece; *janganlah membelek tepi kain orang, pada hal kain sendiri se~ ayam*, don't fix your gaze on the edge of someone's else's sarong; in fact, your own is only as long as a fowl-tether, i.e., look at the mote in your own eye; let not the pot call the kettle black; (as to his use of *tepi kain*, see **tepi**); *ber~-arus*, in a continuous stream; ~ *pendarat*, a hawser; ~ *tambat*, painter of boat or leash of an animal; *per~an*, bonds, ties; *pe~an darah*, the ties of blood relationship; *memper~kan*, to include; to be based on. 2. a money value — 121/2 cents, Sp.

talibun [KN], an ode.

talikom [KN], Eng. telecommunications; ~ *antara-bangsa*, international telecommunications.

talkin [KN], Ar. a prayer or formula recited at a burial; *membaca* ~, to recite this formula, to conduct a funeral.

talu [KK], *ber~-~*, continuous, uninterrupted, in unbroken succession.

talun [KK], echoing back.

tamak [KS], Ar. covetous; greed.

tamam [KS], Ar. ended, e.g., of a prayer.

taman [KN], a garden; a pleasure-ground; ~ *hiburan*, an amusement park; ~ *kanak-kanak*, kindergarten; ~ *indera*, id.

temasya = *termasa*.

tamat [KKtr], Ar. ended; terminated; *penamat*, final; used to mean the 'passing' of an examination, 'completing' a course.

tamadun [KN], Ar. civilisation; also *sa-madun* and ~*dun; ber~*, civilised, cultured.

tambah [KN], increase by repetition or by continuation; *nasi* ~, a second helping of rice; ~*an pula*, again, further- more; *menambahkan*, to increase; *penambahan*, an addition, an appendix; ~ *penambahan kata*, (gram.) an affix; *menambah kata*, to continue, say further,

as in the course of a speech; ~*an masa*, extra time (in a match).

tambak [KN], 1. banking; filling, levelling up; a dam, embankment; *jalan* ~, a causeway, a road raised above the level of the surrounding fields. 2. *ikan* ~, *bawal* ~, a fish (*Stromateus niger*).

tamban [KN], a generic name given to a number of sardine-like fish of the herring tribe.

tambang [KN], 1. ferrying for money; a ferryboat; the fare paid for passage on a boat; ~*an*, a regular trip; *perahu penambang*, a ferryboat. 2. to put medicine over-night at a tomb or sacred place to improve its efficacy. 3. Ind. a mine; ~ *minyak*, an oil-well.

tambar [KN], a kind of medicine which helps to prevent malaria, etc.

tambat [KK], fasten up; ~*i, menambatkan*, to tie up; *ter~*, tethered (of an animal), moored (of a boat); ~*an*, mooring-place; landing-stage; *menambat hati*, to win the affection of.

tambi [KN], Tam. a messenger, a peon, an orderly.

tambul [KN], 1. refreshments (esp. drinks), dessert. 2. *ber~*, to act; *penambul*, an actor; a juggler; an acrobat.

tambun [KS], plump, stout, fat; *menambunkan*, to fatten up; *ber~-~*, in piles, in heaps, accumulated.

tambung [KS], insolent, rude, unmannerly; *menambungi*, to treat a person insolently.

tambur [KN], 1. Hind. a drum of European type, *tukan* ~, drummer. 2. silt or mud suspended in water.

tambus = *timbus*.

taming [KN], Jav. a small buckler used by heroes of romance.

tampa [KK], *menampa*, to form an opinion; to conjecture, suspect; *salah* ~, misconception.

tampah [KN], winnowing tray.

tampak [KK], being visible; *itu perubahan yang tidak begitu nampak*, it was a subtle change; ~*nya serupa mas*, it looks like gold.

tampal [KK], plastering, posting up; ~*kan*, to stick on; to paste on; to patch; *ber*~, patched.

tampan [KS], 1. handsome, smart, having 'presence'; looking well; suitable, befitting, *tiada se*~, it does not seem right or look well; ~-~ or *te*~, a shoulder napkin worn by attendants at a Malay court; *ber*~ *dengan* ..., on a par with, commensurate with. 2. stopping the progress of a moving body (as a boy stops a football with the side of his foot).

tampang [KN], 1. flat; *penampang*, the flat side of anything; a face, e.g., of a bevel or a pyramid; *penampang muka*, profile; facial expression. 2. a tin token or medium of exchange, formerly used on the East Coast: 16 cents went to the dollar. 3. cutting and tying up (as the umbilical cord is severed); plant cuttings for grafting or planting out. 4. a tree *(Artocarpus Gomeziana)*; ~ *burung (Ficus vasculosa)*; ~ *manis (Artocarpus Lakoocha)*, id.

tampar [KK], slapping; to slap; ~*i*, to slap; ~*an*, the giving of a slap; smack, blow; ~*an nyamuk*, the area between the shoulder-blades, where only a quick slap can dislodge a mosquito.

tampas [KS], 1. lopping off (small prominences). 2. = *tempias*.

tampi [KK], *menampi*, winowing by tossing up and down on a sieve; *penampi*, winnow; *menampi dada*, heaving of the breasts; *to' ke*~, an owl *(Ketupa javanensis); darah sebagai di*~, disturbed, alarmed, excited.

tampik [KK], fault-finding, censure; *menampik*, to spurn, to reject; *penampikan*, refusal, rejection.

tampil [KK], to come forward, to come out in front; (fig.) to 'crop up', as a subject in conversation; *dia menampilkan cerita yang amat menarik*, he came up with the most interesting story.

tampin [KN], a small plaited *mengkuang* bag for sago.

tampuk [KN], the point of junction of stalk and fruit; the little bit of stalk us. left on plucked fruit; the central point of converging lines; a boss in ornament; holder into which, e.g., an electric light bulb is fitted; ~ *susu*, the teat and the dark circle round it; *ikan* ~-~, a fish *(Gerres oblongus);* ~ is used (fig.) for nerve-centre, pivot; ~ *kerajaan*, the 'reins of Government'; *memegang* ~ *kerajaan*, to be in power.

tampul [KN], a wild mangosteen.

tampung [KK], 1. patching; piebald; *badak* ~, a tapir. 2. to catch a falling object (as a cricket-ball is caught); *tahan* ~, id.; *menampung*, to receive into a place, to find room for, supply a place for; ~*an*, a receptacle; ~ *sampah*, a rubbish bin; *penampungan*, accommodation, quarters; *sekeolah menampung seratus orang murid*, a school providing accommodation for a hundred pupils; *menampung tangan ke langit*, to hold up the hands to heaven in prayer (the hands being spread to receive blessings, cf. **tadah**).

tamsil [KN], Ar. example, metaphor, analogy; parable, simile.

tamu [KN], guest — cf. **jamu**; ~ *agung*, guest of honour; *te*~, guests; *ber*~, visit.

tan [KN], 1. Hind. ~ *kuda*, a stable. 2. ~, see *intan*. 3. ~ *Sri*, a title of honour in the bestowal of the *Yang dipertuan Agung;* carried by holders of the Order (see **darjah**) *Panglima Mangku Negara*.

tanah [KN], earth, ground, land; a country; ~ *air*, homeland; ~ *liat*, clay; ~ *tenggala*, arable land; ~ *bolong*, bitumen, asphalt; *tupai* ~, treeshrew *(Tupaia* sp.); *ular* ~, certain snakes *(Typhlops* sp.); ~ *raya*, ~ *besar*, mainland; *minyak* ~, kerosene; ~ *air* is often used to mean 'native country'; ~ *gambut*, peaty soil; ~ *merah*, red earth, esp. laterite; ~ *hidup*, occupied land; ~ *mati*, abandoned land; ~ *makin meninggi*, rising land; ~ *campuran*, compost; ~

campuran yang sudah berayak halus, finely sifted compost; *sistem pemilikan ~,* system of land tenure; ~ is also used for 'ground', i.e., the plain surface of material on which the pattern is superimposed.

tanak [KK], *ber~,* to cook (rice) by steaming away the water in which it is placed; *sepe~ nasi,* the time it takes for rice to boil — a primitive measure of time (about 20 minutes).

tanam [KK], to plant, to bury in the earth; ~ *~an,* planted crops, plants; *menanam,* to plant; *menanam wang,* (fig.) to invest money; *menanam fahaman,* to inculcate views, indoctrinate; *menanam cacar,* to vaccinate; *menanam ketumbuhan,* id.

tanau [KN], N.S. a sp. of parroquet, = *pialang.*

tanda [KN], 1. sign, token, mark, emblem; *ber~,* marked labelled, stamped; ~ *bacaan,* the vowel points; ~ *tangan,* a signature; ~ *mata,* a keepsake, personal souvenir; ~ *perniagaan,* a trademark; ~ *melintas jalan,* a marked road-crossing; *tangani,* to sign; *~i, menanda,* to put a mark on; (fig.) to be betrothed to; *per~,* a sign, indication; ~ *hidup,* a keepsake; ~ *tanya,* a question mark; ~ *penyambung,* a hyphen; ~ *kurang,* a minus sign; ~ *tambah,* a plus sign; ~ *kali,* a multiplication sign; ~ *kurung,* brackets; ~ *seruan,* an interjection; ~ *bahagi,* division sign; ~ *baca,* punctuation mark; ~ *waktu,* time-signal (esp. on radio); *ikan ~~,* a fish *(Lutianus sillaoo).* 2. *per~,* an excutioner; see **tandal** 1.

tandak [KN], 1. dancing; *ber~,* to dance (generally of old-fashioned step-dances). 2. = *tandup.*

tandan [KN], the stem of fruit that grows in bunches; a cluster, a bunch of coconuts; the main bunch made up of layers (*sikat*) of bananas.

tandang [KN], 1. wandering; travelling; *orang ~ desa,* a vagrant; *ber~,* to visit a person's house for a chit-chat; *ber~*

tidur, to sleep anywhere; *ber~ bilik orang,* to visit a peron's room; *rumah ber~ duduk,* a house to stay in.

tandas [KN], 1. a privy (polite). 2. *menandaskan* [KK], Ind. completely finished, done for; stripped clean, bare. 3. = *tandus.*

tandil [KN], Tam. the head of a gang of coolies; a petty officer — subordinate to the *serang* on a ship.

tanding [KS], a division, a comparison; a lot; *se~,* equal in size, equal, on a par; *tidak ada ~nya,* matchless, incomparable; *per~an,* a competition; *ber~,* to take part in a competition, to enter; *memper~an,* to enter, e.g. a horse; *se~ dengan,* comparable with, worthy to be classed with.

tandu [KN], a hammock-litter; stretcher, palanquin; *menandu,* to carry in a palanquin.

tanduk [KN], horn (of two-horned animals); *~~,* a creper *(Strophanthus dichotomus); ber~,* horned; *menanduk,* to butt; (fig.) to head the ball at football; *capang, cakang, capah,* widespread (horns); *kerutuk, kupit,* of narrow spread; *ragum,* Ked. id.; *sodok,* projecting forward; *terkelepek,* drooping; *macam ~ diberkas,* like horns fastened together, simile for ill-assorted partners or imperfect co-operation; *menantikan kucing ber~,* to wait for cats to grow horns, i.e. futile hope; *macam ~ dengan gading,* like horns and tusks, i.e. affinities; *(seperti) telur di hujung ~,* (like) an egg on the tip of a horn, i.e., in a precarious situation.

tandun [KN], *zaman ~,* the immemorial past.

tandup [KN], Kel. a dam; also *tandak* and *tandap.*

tandur [KN], 1. Jav. to plant. 2. holding up by means of a string; *tali ~,* a string for pulling up chicks.

tandus [KS], waste, barren, of land; fallow; (fig.) baffled, dried up, of hope, enthusiasm; *ke~an,* wilderness, desolation; sometimes, (fig.) failure of enterprise; emptiness or vanity of way of life; also *tandas*.

tang, an abbreviation for *tentang*; ~ *mana?*, where?, at what spot?; ~ *tunggul itu*, by that stump.

tangan [KN], hand; forearm and hand; handle; sleeve; ~ *baju*, sleeve; ~ *kemudi*, the handle of a rudder; *ibu* ~, thumb; *sapu* ~, handkerchief; *tanda*~, signature; *tapak* ~, palm; *di* ~ *saya*, in my possession; *panjang* ~, thievish; *dalam* ~, easy job; 'in the bag'; *penangan*, might, power; ~ *kasar*, clumsy; *pantas* ~, deft; *belakang* ~, the back of the hand; *tumit* ~, the heel of the hand; ~ *bertuah*, a lucky hand, as of a gardener having 'green fingers'; ~*kan*, to punish with the hand, buffet; ~*i*, id.; *jangan campur* ~, hands off, stay out of this; *pindah* ~, to change hands.

tangas [KN], fumigation; *ber*~ [KK], to steam; heating; ~ *hidung*, steaming the nostrils (as in snuffling steam for a cold); *penangasan*, nasal inhalation; vapour.

tangga [KN], ladder, staircase; *anak* ~, a step; a rung of a ladder; *rumah*~, a home-stead; *ber*~~, at fifth or sixth hand; *rumah*~, family; Pk. often used to mean 'my husband'; *te*~, neighbours; ~ *gaji*, wage-scale; ~ *sulung*, the top rung of a ladder; ~ *bongsu*, the bottom rung; ~ *nada*, musical scale.

tanggah [KN], *penanggah* or *penanggahan*, a kitchen in a palace.

tanggal [KK], 1. loosened; spontaneous severance or fall; to get detached, fall off, 'come off', as a fitting; ~*kan*, to remove, to take off, e.g., clothes; *menanggalkan*, id.; *penanggalan*, an evil spirit; a flying head and viscera. 2. [KN], Ind. date (time).

tanggam [KN], 1. a groove at the end of a beam; *ter*~, mortised together; driven firmly in. 2. to keep awake, to control (the freedom of a wife, husband).

tanggang [KK], *menanggang*, propping up, buttressing; = *sagang*.

tanggap [KS], ~*an*, [KN], concept, perception; *menanggapi*, to react to, to answer, to reply to, opinion, view.

tanggar [KK], 'putting through' work; *menanggar*, managing to get things done.

tangguh [KN], putting off, postponement; *ber*~, to postpone, delay; *penangguhan majlis*, adjournment of meeting; *ucapan penangguhan*, speech on the adjournment.

tangguk [KN], a landing-basket or lift-net used by fishermen; *menceduk ayer dalam* ~, to draw water in a landing-net, mere waste of time.

tanggul [KN], bobbing (of a boat's bows) — cf. **anggul**.

tanggung [KK], bearing up under; standing security for; ~*kan*, to support a burden; *ter*~, to be borne, supportable, sustained; ~ *belanja*, to make oneself responsible for expenses, esp. as a Chinese mining advancer; *ber*~*jawab*, responsible, liable; ~ *jawab bersama*, collective responsibility; ~*an berhad*, limited liability; *menanggung*, to be responsible for, support (a person); *makan* ~, free food supplied; 'all found'.

tangis [KN], weeping; ~*i*, to weep, to shed tears; *menangis*, id.; ~*kan*, to mourn for anyone; *pemenangis*, a mourner; *tulang rimau menangis*, the manubrium.

tangkai [KN], stalk, haulm, stem; ~ *hati*, the aorta; (fig.) a term of endearment, 'my heart'; ~ is also used of a handle, esp. a protruding handle, e.g., of a pan; ~ *pena*, pen holder.

tangkal [KN], a talisman, charm; ~ *sawan kanak-kanak*, a talisman against convulsions; ~ *polong*, jocular sl. for necktie.

tangkap [KK], capture, gripping, clasping, catch, seize, apprehend; ~*an*, toils, captivity, arrest; *(ikan)* ~*an*, the catch (of fish); *menangkap*, to seize, capture; to arrest; (fig.) to catch sight of; to deduce; to 'catch on' (to an idea); *menangkap basah*, to catch red-handed, in the act; *ter~*, captured.

tangkas [KS], nimble, swift, rapid, agile; *ke~an*, agility, rapidity, quickness.

tangki [KN], Hind. water-tank.

tangkil [KK], 1. sticking one tenuous object (e.g. paper) on another. 2. to dodge (a strike).

tangkis [KK], *menangkis*, to guard, to parry; *~an*, to intercept (a blow); to ward off; *bunyi senjata gemerencang ber~an denagan senjata lain*, the clash of weapons on weapons; *menangkis* is sometimes used (fig.) for retort, verbal riposte; *meriam penangkis*, anti-aircraft guns. 2. *bulu ~*, badminton.

tangkul [KN], a name given to groundnets, or nets and screens which catch fish by being pulled up with a winch; *menangkul*, to catch fish with a *~*; *pukat ~*, a wide ground- net (the sides of which are raised up when fish are over the net, thus preventing their escape).

tangkup [KN], capturing anything under a hollow, e.g. a fly under a cupped hand; *ber~*, closing over, folding over, as an arched wave; *menangkup muka dengan tangan*, to bury the face int he hands; *ber~-rapat*, in close formation; coalesced; *ter~*, up-turned, as a box.

tanglung [KN], 1. Ch. a Chinese latern. 2. Pk. a red millipede

tangsi [KN], 1. ch. a strong gut used in fishing lines. 2. barracks; the canteen.

tantang [KK], *menantang*, to defy; *~an*, challenge.

tani [KN], Ind. agriculture; *kaum ~*, peasants, farmers; *petani, pak ~*, id.; *per~an*, agriculture; *pejabat per~an*, Department of Agriculture.

tanjak [KN], projecting, sticking up; a pointed headress; *ber~ kaki*, standing on tip-toe.

tanju [KN], a bracket-lamp.

tanjul [KN], a sort of fishing-rod with a noose instead of a hook at the end; to hook in, tie in, as thread when mending a net; *~ hidung*, (fig.) to try to get a hold over someone, to 'get one's

hooks into'.

tanjung [KN], a cape, a promontory, a headland, the end of a straight stretch of road; George Town, Penang, is generally known to Malays as 'Tanjong', because the town grew up on a promontory *(Tanjung Penaga)*.

tanpa [KKtr], Ind. without.

tanya [KK], *ber~*, to ask a question; *ber~kan*, to inquire about; *per~an*, a query, inquiry; question; *borang per~an*, questionnaire; *ter~-~ sendiri*, to ask oneself.

tap [KK], *pe~*, to dab on, as medicine.

tapa [KN], Skr. asceticism; austerities undergone by hermits; *berbuat ~*, to practise these austerities; *ber~*, id.; *per~*, austere, ascetic; hermit; *ber~*, (fig.) to hibernate; to lie dormant; *orang per~an*, a hermit; *ahli per~*, id. 2. see **tapah**.

tapah [KN], *ikan ~*, a giant catfish *(Wallago tweediei)*, the largest Malaysian fresh-water fish; also *tapa*.

tapai [KN], 1. a preparation of steamed *pulut* rice fermented with yeast; *arak ~*, a spirit made from this preparation. 2. Treng. a rabbit.

tapak [KN], the palm (of the hand); the sole (of the foot or a shoe); sometimes, hoof or paw; *se~*, a step; *bekas ~ gajah*, an elephant's foot-prints; *~ itik*, a herb *(Floscopa scandens)*; *~ kaki*, the sole of the foot; *~ Sulaiman*, the seal of Solomon; the pentaclo; the five-pointed star-fish; *main ~ empat*, (N.S.) a fox and geese game; *~ rumah*, the site of a house; *~ jalan*, the line of a proposed road; *~ hidup*, livelihood; *~ catur*, a square on a chess-board; *~ bertolak*, stepping-off place, staring place; *berbentuk ~ kuda*, shaped like a horseshoe, as, e.g., a table; *ber~*, to have a foothold; *ber~ di-*, sited at; *memecah ~ empat*, (sl.) to give someone a hiding (from a movement in the fencing dance, *silat)*; *menapak*, to stride out; to track; *se~ demi se~*, step by step.

tapak-tokul [KN], efforts, pioneer work,

struggles.

tapal [KN], Ind. frontier, boundary; ~ *batas*, id.

tapih [KN], Jav. long sarong, unsewn and worn as a skirt by Javanese women; *ber~*, to wear a sarong as a skirt, i.e., from the waist downwards, not from the breast downwards *(berkemban)*.

tapis [KK], 1. *~kan*, to filter, pass a liquid through cloth; *se~*, a generation; *~an*, any kind of filter; *~an minyak*, an oil-refinery; so, (fig.) *~an berita*, news-censorship; *lembaga ~an filem*, film-censorship board. 2. the Ceylon iron-wood *(Messua ferra)*.

taptibau [KN], *burung ~*, the great-eared nightjar.

tapuk [KN], a scab, a scar, pockmark, the remains of the pistil in a fruit — cf. **tampuk**.

tara [KN], equal (of altitude); even; parity; *se~*, on a level with; *tiada ~nya*, peerless; *menara bukit*, the ridge of a range of hills.

taraf [KN], status; standard; *se~*, equal status; *~ hidup*, standard of living; *menye~kan*, to place on a par.

tarah [KK], 1. *menarah*, to rough-hew. 2. *ber~*, has been levelled.

taram [KS], 1. gloomy, overcast (of sky). 2. Pah. salt-lick. 2. bear a grudge.

tarang [KN], *pe~an*, a hen's nesting-place.

tarbil [KN], a pellet-bow; also a catapult.

tari [KN], dancing (by swaying the arms and body); *menari*, to dance; *membuang !*, to dance a wild dance, 'shake a leg'; *~an gelek perut*, the belly dance; *penari*, dancer.

tarik [KK], *menarik* or *menarikkan*, to draw to or after oneself; to pull; to drag; to draw in (a long breath) or prolong (a note in singing); *~-~*, *te~*, accordion; *menarik hati*, to attract attention, interest; *~ balik*, to withdraw (as a charge); *~ diri*, to withdraw, as from a contest, to stand down; *~an bumi*, the force of gravity; *daya (kuasa) penarik*, power to attract, charm; *~*

(naik), *to* hoist (a flag); *penarik*, portage; place where a boat can be hauled overland.

tarikat [KN], Ar. the path to truth (of mystics); now used sometimes for (political) doctrine.

tarikh [KN], Ar. date; era; period of time; *pada ~ itu*, at that time; *ber~*, dated.

taring [KN], long canine tooth projecting outwards, as of a boar or an ogre; = *siung*; *misai ber~*, a turned-up moustache.

taris, [KK], fastening, tying up, = *ikat*.

taru [KK], *ber~*, to sound (of the *nafiri* or of the royal trumpet).

taruh [KN], depositing; receiving or placing in a safe place; staking; betting; *ber~*, to stake; *menaruh*, to retain or preserve; to keep; to harbour; *pe~kan*, to entrust or confide; *menaruh hati pada*, to have a liking for; *menaruh mata pada*, to have one's eye on, covet; *menaruh kasihan*, to feel pity; *menaruh dendam*, to harbour a grudge; *memper~kan nyawa*, to risk one's life (put it at stake); *pe~an*, a deposit; a bet.

taruk [KN], the long shoot of a tree or plant; not often used of a newly sprouted shoot on a branch *(tunas)*; *ber~*, sprout.

taruka [KK], Ind. to level to found (a town).

tarum [KN], the indigo plant *(Indigofera tinctoria)*; as an adjective, ~ means 'dark-coloured'; so applied to certain animals and fishes.

tarung [KN], (onom.) a deep booming sound; Ind. *ber~*, [KK] to fight; *per~an*, fight, struggle; *memper~kan jiwa*, to risk one's life (in a struggle); *batu penarung*, a stumbling-block.

tas [KN], 1. a tree *(Kurrimia panniculata)*, the wood of which is believed to frighten away tigers. 2. Ind. a handbag.

tasak [KK], *menasak*, to stop bleeding; *ubat ~*, a styptic.

tasauf [KN], Ar. Islamic mysticism.

tasbih [KN], Ar. a rosary; *buah ~,* prayerbeads; *mengucap ~,* count one's beads, *mengira-ngira ~,* id.; *membilang ~,* id.; *bunga ~,* the canna; *bunga pisang ~,* id.

tasik [KN], a lake, a mere (Jav.); the sea; *~ pauh janggi,* the great ocean; *~-~,* a plant *(Adenosma capitatum).*

taslim [KN], *~kan,* to convey safely (a letter) in epistolary language.

tasydid [KN], Ar. the diacritical mark signifying that the letter over which it is placed is doubled.

tasyrikh [KN], Ar. *ilmu ~,* the science of anatomy.

tata [KN], Ind. order, arrangement, rules; dominant standards of behaviour, etc.; *~ susila,* rules of morality; *~ usaha,* administration; *~ rakyat,* civic duties; *~ bahasa,* grammar; *~ cara,* etiquette; *~ tertib,* rules of behaviour, discipline; *~ negara,* politics.

tatah [KK], inlaying, embedding, sticking into; *ber~kan ratna mutu manikam,* studded with gems.

tatal [KN], a shaving.

tatang [KK], carrying on the upturned palm of the hand, or any similar surface; carrying with extreme care; cherishing; *sebagai menatang minyak yang penuh,* as if carrying a vessel of oil on the palm of the hand, i.e. with meticulous care.

tatap [KK], close visual examination (such as a watchmaker gives to the works of a watch); *menatap,* to examine; to watch, to keep a look-out; *~an,* inspection, scrutiny, something that is looked upon.

tatih [KK], *ber~,* to toddle along (of infants); to walk with uncertain steps; *ber~-~ membaca,* to stumble through a reading.

tating [KK], take up with both hands.

tatkala [KN], Skr. the time when, at the time when; *pada ~ itu,* at that time; *~ ia lagi muda,* while he was still a child.

taubat [KS], Ar. repentant.

taucang [KN], Ch. a Chinese queue; a pigtail.

taufan [KN], a great storm, a typhoon.

taufik [KN], Ar. divine aid.

tauge [KN], Ch. bean sprouts.

tauhid [KN], Ar. the doctrine of the unity of God; single-minded, devoted to duty; *dengan ~ hatinya,* determinedly, unhestitatingly.

tauke [KN], Ch. a 'towkay', an employer of labour; owner of a large business, shop etc. also *tokeh.*

taul [KK], securing an oar by attaching it with cord to the gunwale; the thole strap.

tauladan = *tuladan.*

taulan [KN], Tam. friend, comrade.

tauliah [KN], a letter of authority, 'commission'; a charter, e.g., of an accountant; *surat ~,* credentials, e.g., of an ambassador; *ber~,* commissioned; certificate, duly authorised, in a post or profession.

taun [KN], Ar. a murrain, an epidemic, esp. cholera.

taung [KN], dust-storm.

taup [KK], *ber~,* to close up, cohere, coalesce; *biduk lalu, kiambang ber~,* the boat passes and the duckweed closes up behind it, i.e., a quarrel does not long separate people who are really intimate; *~kan,* to (cause to) fit closely together.

Taurit [KN], Ar. the Pentateuch; the books of Moses.

taut [KN], 1. a night-line with a rod. 2. to draw tightly together, fasten closely; *ber~,* at full stretch; *memper~kan,* stick together again; *hati ber~,* eager, agog; *tempat ~an,* place where (e.g., parasitic insects cling); a variant of *taup.*

tawa [KK], *ter~,* laughing; *ter~ ~,* to laugh continuously; *ter~ mengejek,* to laugh derisively; *ter~ kecil,* to giggle; *menggigil ter~,* to shake with laughter; *~ terbahak-bahak,* to guffaw; *~ sendirian,* to laugh inwardly, have a quiet laugh; also *ketawa.*

tawaduk [KS], humble, respect, obedient.

tawaf [KK], Ar. making a circuit of the

Kaabah during the Haj pilgrimage.

tawak [KN], ~-~, a small gong or sounding-board used to summon people to a meeting.

tawakkal [KN], Ar. surrender to God's will; trust in God; *ber~*, to trust in God.

tawan [KN], *~an*, a captive; *menawan hati*, to win over, convert to friendship; *~an sebagai tebusan*, a hostage; *~an perang*, a prisoner of war.

tawar [KS], 1. tasteless, without flavour or distinctive characteristic; harmless, ineffective, of drug; frustrated, of a spell; *menawarkan hati*, to discourage; *air ~*, fresh water (as distinct from salt); *~ hati*, disinclined, disillusioned; *lauk yang ~*, tasteless food; *tepung ~*, rice-flour and water used in ceremonies to frustrate evil; *~i* or *menawari*, to meet a spell with a counter-charm; to frustrate; *penawar*, an antidote; a protective talisman; *~-ibir*, absolutely tasteless. 2. bargaining; offering; *~ menawar*, haggling over a price; *~an*, an offer; *dasar ~-menawar secara kolektif*, policy of collective bargaining; *menawarkan diri*, to offer oneself (as for a task).

tawarikh [KN], Ar. annals; history.

tawaruk [KN], sitting posture (forbidden during prayer).

tawas [KN], alum.

taya [KN], *mentua ~*, elderly relatives by marriage other than the parents-in-law.

tayammum [KN], Ar. ablution with sand for lack of water.

tayang [KK], to raise fist or weapon; to brandish; to display; to show, as a film; *~an perdana*, the premiere of a film; *~an pertama*, the 'first house'; *menayang tangan*, to hold up the palm of the hand, as when checking someone.

tayar [KN], tyre.

tebah [KK], beating a flat surface, e.g. the breasts or a carpet; *menebah dada*, to beat the breast.

tebak [KK], a heavy cutting or chopping blow; *se ~*, a piece (of wood) lopped off from a log.

teater [KN], theatre.

tebal [KS], thick (of cloth, paper, planking, etc.); *muka ~*, brazen-faced; *~ hati*, hard-hearted; *muka ~*, poker-faced; *menebal muka*, to conceal one's feelings, esp. not show one's discomfiture; *~* is often used now for 'thick' of jungle or fog.

teban [KN], stakes in gambling, money deposited.

tebang [KK], *menebang*, to fell heavy timber; *burung ~ mentua*, the helmeted hornbill.

tebar [KK], sowing, or spreading by a sweeping round-arm motion; *~ jala*, to throw a casting-net; *menebar*, to scatter; to send round, issue (as invitation cards); *menebar jala rambang*, to cast a wide net, i.e., make inquiries far and wide or, sometimes, make indiscriminate arrests; *ber~*, spread out before one, as a view.

tebas [KK], to fell small scrub, clear undergrowth — cf. **tebang**; *penebas*, Kel. a fighting bull which strikes downwards with its horns — cf. **tikam**; *menebas-menebang*, to clear away all growths, big and small.

tebat [KK], damming, esp. of damming a stream to catch fish or to create a fish-pond; barring; barricading; closing to traffic; a dammed fish pond.

tebeng [KN] Treng. persisting, worrying.

tebeng [KK], 1. spread out; expanded, as a sarung or piece of embriodery is spread out to show the pater; *menebeng*, to show oneself off, as a woman. 2. a screen. 3. eat, sleep etc., in someone else's home without payment.

teberau [KN], a name given to several large grasses (esp. *Sacharum arundinaceum, S. Ridleyi* and *Thysanoloena acarifera)*; they are kinds of wild sugarcane; *musang ~*, a kind of civet-cat.

tebiat = *tabiat*.

tebing [KN], the bank of a river or canal.

tebu [KN] sugar-cane; *ular katang ~,* banded karait *(Bungarus fasciatus); tahu membezakan ~ dengan teberau,* able to distinguish between sugar-cane and teberau grass, i.e., not easily misled; not born yesterday; *se katam ~,* a (cut) section of sugar-cane; *ada ~ di bibir mulut,* he has sugar-cane on his lips, i.e. he has the blarney; *~ masuk mulut gajah,* irretrievably lost.

tebuan [KN], a hornet; *~ tandang,* Treng, a carbuncle, large boil.

tebuk [KS] *menebuk,* to bore; gnaw, thrust; making a cylindrical hole in anything; sinking a shaft or well; *nyiur sudah di~ tupai,* the coconut has been bored by a squirrel; vulgar way of saying, she's no virgin; *bertebak-~,* riddled, pierced in many places.

tebuk [KK], a heavy thrust.

tebus [KK], *menebus,* to redeem from mortgage or pawn; to purchase a slave from someone else; *wang ~an,* ransom money; *~ malu,* expiate a shame; *hamba ~an,* a bought (debt) slave; *orang ~an, a hotingo;* in early days an indentured (Javanese) labourer, whose employer had paid up the money due on his passage in exchange for his services.

tedeng [KN], Ind. sheltering, covering; screen from sun; *~ mata,* blinkers; eye-shades.

teduh [KS], still, after storm and rain; sheltered; *ber~,* to take shelter; *tempat ~,* shelter, a place sheltered from the elements.

tedung [KN], *ular ~,* a generic name given to hooded snakes and to some snakes resembling them; *ular ~ senduk,* the cobra *(Naia tripudians); ular ~ selar* or *ular ~ abu,* the hamadryad *(N. bungarus); ular ~ matahari,* a small brilliantly-coloured snake *(Doliophis bivirgatus); ular ~ liar,* a snake *(Zamenis korros).*

tega [KS], indifferent, showing no sympathy.

tegah [KN], *~kan* or *menegahkan,* to pro-hibit, hinder.

tegak [KS], stiffly erect, bolt upright; *sudut ~ lurus,* a right angle; *menegakkan benang basah,* trying to make wet cotton stand up, a hopeless waste of time; also *cegak.*

tegal [KN], cause; reason, *~ apa,* why?, = *kerana apa?*

tegang [KS], taut, outstretched, at its full span; *ke~an,* tension, strained relations; *ber~,* eager, agog; *ber~ meris,* stubborn and vociferous (in argument); *ber~ urat leher,* id.; *memper~kan,* tense up.

tegap [KS], sturdy; *badan ~,* id.; *menegapkan,* strengthen.

tegar [KS], stiff, unyielding, obstinate, inflexible; *~ hati,* stiff-necked.

tegas [KS], emphasize; definite; *~nya,* in short; *menegaskan,* to stress; *dengan ~,* firmly; *bersifat ~,* firm in manner; *dengan ~,* categorically.

teguh [KS], firm; fast; stable; tight (of a knot); rigidly adhered to (of a promise); *di-ikatnya ~ ~,* he tied it very tightly; *~ hati,* determined, staunch.

teguk [KK], gulping; a mouthful; *se~,* a mouthful; as much as one can gulp down; *menyeguk air,* to drink in gulps; *minum sekali ~,* to drink in one gulp; often abbreviated to *gok.*

tegun [KK], *ter~,* immobile, stiff, speechless, frozen into immobility by fear or expectancy.

tegur [KK], *menegur,* to address, greet; to accost, salutation; to criticise; *~ sapa,* courtesy; friendly greetings; *~i,* to address; *tak ber~,* not on speaking terms; *orang ke~an,* a person accosted (by an evil spirit), i.e., not very well, down in the dumps; *tak sanggup menghadapi ~an,* cannot stand criticism.

teh [KN], 1. Ch. tea; *daun ~,* tea (in leaf form); *air ~,* tea (prepared for drinking); *keladak ~,* used tea-leaves; *~ kosong,* tea without milk. 2. = *Putih* as a proper name.

teja [KN], Skr. glowing red clouds.

teji [KN], (= swift) Pers. *kuda* ~, a Pegasus; a winged steed; better *tezi*.

teka [KK], Skr. *meneka,* to guess; ~*-teki,* riddles; conundrums; ~*an,* guess-work; ~ *silang-kata,* crossword puzzle; ~ *kata,* word-puzzle; *peraduan* ~ *bola sepak,* football pools; *penekaan,* solution.

tekad = *itikad* [KN], will, purpose, believing firmly.

tekak [KN], 1. palate; *anak* ~, the uvula; *umpan* ~, an appetizer; *penyakit* ~, swollen tonsils. 2. *ber*~, to argue stubbornly. 3. = *teka.*

tekan [KK], to press, e.g., to obtain a squeeze or impression of an inscription or mould; ~*an,* pressure, e.g., political; ~*an nada,* stress, emphasis; *menekan,* to press, subject to steady push; ~*-menekan,* to apply pressure, esp. of petty persecution; to put down, suppress; cf. **tekap.**

tekang [KN], 1. a thwart; a cross-beam to resist pressure at its extremities and not to support a weight resting on it. 2. slag.

tekap [KK], resting the flat of the hand on anything, e.g., closing a child's mouth in jest to prevent him speaking; blotting with a pad; ~*kan,* to imprint, impress (mark); cf. **tekan.**

tekat [KN], embroidery; *ber*~ *mas,* embroidered in gold; *menekat,* embroidering.

tekebur [KS], Ar. proud, arrogant; esp, of lack of due respect to dignitaries; *jangan* ~, guard your tongue; be careful how you express yourself (as to a dignitary or in a holy place); *ber*~, boastful; to boast.

tekis [KK], 1. ~*kan,* to explain. 2. too close to the edge.

tekoan [KN], Ch. a tea-pot; also *tekor.*

teks [KN], texts, original words of an author, short passage taken from a religious book as a topic of discussion.

teksi [KN], taxi.

tekua [KN], *baju* ~, a long sleeveless jacket worn by women.

tekuh [KN], head of a warehouse; Ked.

period; = *masa;* ~ *mana?,* when?

tekuk [KK], *ber*~ *lutut,* to bend one's knees.

tekukur [KN], the turtle-dove; *padang* ~, a plain abandoned to doves, a desolate place; *burung sewah* ~, the Indian koel *(Eudynamis honorata); ular sawa* ~, a snake *(Coluber melanurus); macam* ~, *tahu mengangguk sahaja,* like a turtle-dove, nods his head at everything, i.e., no ideas of his own, a yesman.

tekun {KS}, assiduous, attentive; *ber*~ *mengaji,* to study attentively or assiduously.

tekup [KS], covering with the hand; catching by so covering.

tekur [KK], 1. *menekur,* to lower or bow the head; *menekurkan kepala,* to bow the head. 2. insufficient of cash.

tela [KN], a passage in a Malay house connecting the kitchen with the main building.

tela [KN], the pan of a firearm.

telaah [KN], Ind. *menelaah* [KK], to study, to scrutinize carefully.

telabai [KN], prov. saying, adage.

teladas [KN], a shallow rapid.

telaga [KN], Skr. a well, or a pool serving as a well (rather than a bricked well, which is generally *perigi);* ~ often covers the area fenced off for ablutions generally, including the well.

telagah [KK], *ber*~, to have an argument, dispute.

telah [KKtr], 1. did, was — a word giving a preterite meaning to the passage in which it occurs; ~ *dilihat itu,* when that was seen; *se*~, after. 2. *menelah,* to predict; ~*an,* a prediction.

telak [KN], Ked. a money-box of bamboo.

telampung [KN], drift-wood, a float.

telan [KK], *menelan,* to swallow; accept something unpleasant; *per*~, a draught.

telang [KN], long patches (as a pattern); *buluh* ~, a bamboo *(Gigantochloa* sp.).

telangkai [KN], a marriage-broker.

telanjang [KKtr], naked, stripped; ~ *bulat,* stark naked; ~ *bogel,* id.; *ber*~, nude;

bare; *menelanjangi,* expose.

telap [KN], 1. penetrating, working in, percolating; permeate, porus, absorbent. 2. a receptacle, = *bekas.* 3. mottled, blotched.

telapak [KN], site, position; (fig.) a demesne; a variant of *tapak.*

telapakan [KN], *duli ~,* a royal title; *tanah ~,* N.S. land held for and from chiefs by feudal tenure.

telatah [KN], manners, behaviour, ways; idiosyncracies, 'little ways'.

telatai [KN], N.S. 1. chicks, rattan blinds. 2. the lid of a rice-tun.

telatak [KN], Pah. a small raft.

telaten [KS], careful and patient (in doing a work); conscientious, painstaking, unremitting.

telau [KN], patchy (of colouring or of light); dappled, brightness with darkness; *ber~--~,* patchy, light and dark, as when the sun shines through leaves; *ber~ bagai panas di belukar,* patchy like sunlight (shining through) bushes; (met.) for uneven justice.

teledek [KN], dancing girl.

tele [KK], *ber~--~,* to chatter, to talk rubbish; *~du* [KN], an otter.

teledur [KS], idler, lazy, sleepy-head, inattentive, indifferent, a sluggard — cf. **tidur.**

telefon [KN], telephone; *menelefon* [KK], speak by telephone.

telekan [KK], *ber~,* to rest one's head on one's arms.

tekelu [KK], *ber~,* to lean on one's elbows.

telekung [KN], a praying-veil — used by Muslim women.

telempap [KN], *se~,* a hand's breadth.

telanan [KN], a cleaning-frame — used by a copper-smith.

teleng [KS], *ter~,* cocked on one side (of the head); heeling, tilt; *menelengkan,* a lie on one's back.

telengkoh [KN], part of a fortification that is distinguished from the rest (a military fort).

telepa [KN], = *celepa,* a small tobacco box.

telepuk [KN], printing in gilt on cloth; geometric pattern generally; marquetry.

telerang [KN], quartz; *mas ~,* reef gold, in contrast to alluvial gold *(mas urai)* and nuggets *(mas bertongkol).*

telinga [KN], the ear; the handle of a vessel; *~ bedil,* the pan of a gun; *~ kera,* a plant *(Henslowia Lobbiana); anak ~,* the tympanum; *cuping ~,* the lobe of the ear; *daun ~,* the outer frame of the ear; *lubang ~,* the orifice of the ear; *gendang ~,* ear-drum; *pelipatan ~,* the rim of the ear; *ber~ nipis,* 'thin-eared', i.e., touchy, quick to take offence; *~ lintah,* sharp-eared; *lembut ~,* easily talked round, easily cozened; *tebal ~,* 'thick-eared', won't listen; *menerusi lubang ~nya terus-menerus,* it goes in one ear and out the other; *membesar-besarkan ~,* to strain the ears; *ikan korek ~ buaya,* a fish *(Gastrotoceus baiculeatus).*

telingkah [KN], ways, behaviour, conduct; an idiosyncrasy, a foible, a trait differing from that of most people; *ber~* [KK], to differ; to fail 'to keep in step', unorthodox; to be inconsistent in one's actions; cf. **tingkah.**

telipuk [KN], a small, white, star-like waterlily.

teliti [KS], Ind, care, attention; *meneliti,* to examine carefully; *ke~an,* accuracy.

telor [KS], to mispronounce, esp. as a foreigner, accent.

teluk [KN], a bay, a bight, a curve, a bend; *~ rantau,* bends and reaches (in a river); territories generally; *telok belanga,* Malay dress without collar; *~i* (as in *bunga teluki*) pink carnation.

telungkup [KK], *menelungkup,* upside down; *menelungkupkan,* place something upside down.

telunjuk [KN], the index finger; *di bawah kuit ~,* under the twitch of an index finger, i.e. at the beck and call of, subservient to.

telur [KN], egg; fish-roe; *~ asin,* preserved

eggs; ~ *buaya,* a crocodile's egg; ~ *ter-ubuk,* the roe of the *terubuk* fish *(Clupae kanagurta);* ~ *dadar,* omelette; *menelurkan,* to bring forth, be responsible for, produce; *ber~,* lay egg.

telut [KK], 1. *ber~,* to kneel; *ter~,* to slip to one's knees, to be forced to one's knees, as in the course of a fight. 2. = *lut.*

telutak [KN], tip of leaf, petal, fruit.

tema [KN], Ind. theme (of a story).

temabur [KK], besprinkled, scattered, numerous; *bintang ~,* a constellation - cf. **tabur.**

teman [KN], 1. friend, colleague, companion; *~i,* to attend on; ~ *hidup,* life companion, mate. 2. Pk. I, me — a term of affectionate conversation.

temandang [KN], garb, get-up, general appearance.

temaram [KS], *terang ~,* dusky, gloomy, doubtful light.

temarang [KN], = *temaram.*

Temasik [KN], an old name for Singapore island.

temasya [KN], Pers, a show, a spectacular festivity; the sights of a place; also *ter-masa.*

tembadau [KN], a name given in Borneo to the small wild ox *(Box sondaicus,* and also in some dialects to *Bos min-dorensis).*

tembaga [KN], Skr. copper, bronze, brass; ~ *kuning,* brass; ~ *merah,* copper; ~ *putih,* nickel; ~ *suasa,* an alloy of gold and copper.

tembak [KK], shooting, firing shots; *men-embak,* to fire shots; penembak, marksman; *melepaskan ~an,* to open fire; *menembak jatuh,* to shoot down; *menembak mati,* to shoot dead; *terk-ena ~,* hit with a bullet etc.; *ber~-~an,* exchange shots; ~ *sasaran,* target-practice; ~ *sekali gus,* to fire a volley; ~ *serentak,* to fire a salvo; ~ *hormat,* to fire a salute; ~ *tabik kehormatan,* id.; *pasukan penembak,* firing-squad.

tembakau [KN], Hind. tobacco; ~ *Jawa,* locally grown tobacco; ~ *Belati,* to-bacco imported from Europe; ~ *kero-sok,* dried tobacco leaves.

tembakul [KN], i*kan ~,* the mud-fish; also *belodok.*

tembam [KS], plump; soft and prominent (as cheeks).

tembam = *tembam.*

tembang [KN], 1. songs, sung by dancing-girls. 2. fish.

tembarung [KN], a protruding attic.

tembatu [KN], preternaturally hard (of fruit).

tembelah [KN], a quiver for darts; *tabung ~,* id.

tembelang [KS], rotten (of eggs, when the chicken is not yet formed, = *kemeruk);* met. for rotten-ness of character; *nampak ~ nya,* he showed 'the cloven hoof', showed his 'true colours'; *buka ~,* to 'show up' a person, make clear his true character; cf. **kemungkus.**

tembelian [KN], a type of fresh water fish.

tembeliung = *puting beliung.*

tembelok [KN], an edible barnacle which eats into wood, a ship-worm.

tembera [KN], i*kan ~,* a carp *(Labeobar-bus tambra).*

temberam [KN], a river fish trap.

temberang [KN], 1. a stay (connecting the mast and a spar). 2. wild bragging, big talk; *tunjuk ~, membuat ~,* to talk big, brag; *kaki ~,* a 'blow-hard', braggart; ~ *lapuk,* a lot of damned rot; *~kan,* to bluff a person, deceive by putting on an act; *jual ~,* lying; *tukang ~,* boaster.

temberih [KN], a jew-fish *(Sciaena* sp.).

temberek = *tembikar.*

tembereng [KN], a bit; a section; splinter of porcelain, broken segment; a curved or sharp edge; ~ *tajam,* a sector.

tembesu [KN], a tree *(Fagroea fragrans);* also *tembusu.*

tembi [KN], an outward elbow-thrust.

tembikai [KN], a water-melon *(Citrullus edulis).*

tembikar [KN], china-ware, pottery; glazed earthenware; shards; broken pottery used by children in playing games such as *tuju lubang*.

tembil [KN], a stye in the eye.

tembilang [KN], long-shafted spade; = *pencebak, perejang*.

tembok [KN], 1. an embankment; a masonry wall; *kaki ~,* the foundations of a wall; *~ Berlin,* the Berlin Wall. 2. *menembok,* to cool a liquid by stirring it or by pouring it from one vessel to another. 3. to perform magical incantations (to injure).

tembokor = *bokor*.

tembolok [KN], the crop of a bird; used contemptously for 'belly', when speaking of a greedy, slefish person; *dia ingat ~ dia sendiri sahaja,* he thinks only of his own belly.

tembosa [KN], *kuih ~,* a kind of puff or patty.

tembuk [KK], *menembuk,* perforated, rent, torn; rotten or hollow (of the teeth); eaten through; to pierce, make an opening; holed, as a boat; *ber~ penuh dengan ukiran,* covered with incised carvings.

tembuku [KN], knob, a hard projection; inner ledges or lumps cut under gunwale of dug-outs — cf. **buku.**

tembung [KN], a long cudgel or quarterstaff; *ber~* [KK], to meet, knock up against; to clash head-on or (fig.) of the clash of ideas or meeting of glances.

tembuni [KN], the caul; *~ kecil,* the placenta; also *temuni* and *uri temuni*.

tembus [KK], broken through, perforated, holed; *~an,* a breach (as in a dam); a tunnel; Ind. a carbon copy; *menembusi,* go through.

temenggang [KN], *burung ~,* the white-winged jay.

Temenggung [KN], a Malay dignitary of high rank.

temenung [KS], 1. pensive. 2. a sea fish.

temiang [KN], 1. *akar ~,* a liana *(Lettsomia peguensis).* 2. *buluh ~,* a slender sp. of bamboo, from which the aborigines make their blow-pipes.

temikai = *tembikai*.

temin [KN], an iron ferrule connecting the spear-head with its shaft; mounting metal band; a ferrule at the base of a keris-sheath; ring of a baby's 'teat'.

Temir [KN], *orang ~,* an aboriginal tribe in Northern Malaya.

temoleh [KN], a carp *(Barbus tor)*.

temolok = *tembolok.*

tempa [KK], hammering, beating; working metal with the hammer — cf. **tempawan;** *menempa wang,* to mint money; *besi ~an,* wrought iron; *menempa sejarah,* do something new.

tempah [KK], to engage in advance; retaining services; *penempah bidan,* the fee paid in advance to a midwife; to 'order' (to be made); *menempah belanga,* to order pots (at a kiln); *menempah teket,* to book a ticket; *~an,* ordered, made to order.

tempala [KN], the hop or spring of a fighting chevrotin.

tempang [KS], 1. lame; limping, halt; *pangku-pangku ~,* limping slightly. 2. a fish-trap like a miniature *kelong,* set in streams.

tempap [KK], 1. to bring down the flat of the hand forcibly on any surface. 2. a hand's breadth.

tempat [KN], place, locality; *~ mengaji,* a school; *~an,* local; *akhbar ~,* local papers; *sudah ber~,* has found an abode, is not a mere wanderer; *ber~ di,* stationed at; *menempatkan,* to house, to place, to find a place for; *kawasan penempatan,* a settlement, esp, of refugees; *~ kediaman,* dwelling place; *~ kelahiran,* birth place; *~ tumpah darah,* native country; *~ jin bertandang,* uninhabited place; *sudah pada ~nya,* suitable, proper.

tempaus [KN], *ikan ~,* a whale; also *paus.*

tempawan [KN], beaten, wrought (of metals); *mas ~,* hammered gold — the pale yellow colour of which is a simile for an admired complexion.

tempayak [KN], the larvae or grubs of wasps, bees, etc.

tempayan [KN], an earthenware jar for

storing water; *mulut* ~, a babbler, can't keep a secret.

tempe [KN], Ind. a soya-bean cake.

tempel [KK], *menempelkan,* stick something to; *menempel,* stick on.

tempelak [KN], to twit a person with a blunder or mistake; *kena* ~, to get a rebuff, humiliate.

tempeleng [KN], a box on the ears, slap.

temperas [KK], scattered about by leakage; *ber~an* [KN], spilt all about a place.

temperas [KN], a red sand-flea.

tempiar [KK], *ber~* or *ber~an,* fleeing in all directions; scattering.

tempias [KN], beating in (of rain); *kena* ~, (fig.) to suffer consequences of something indirectly.

tempik [KN], to cheer; the war cries of an advancing army; *ber~* [KK], to shout, cry aloud; to bell, of a deer; to trumpet, of an elephant; *ber~ sorak,* to shout and cheer.

tempinah [KN], the water balsam *(Hydrocera triflora).*

tempinis [KN], a well-known hardwood tree *(Sloetia sideroxylon);* iron-wood, calebrated for its durability.

tempo [KN], tempo, speed at which music is played.

tempoh [KN], Port. time (esp. in the sense of further time for payment; extension of time); ~ *hari,* recently, 'the other day; *minta* ~, ask for time.

temponek [KN], the monkey-jack *(Artocarpus rigida).*

temporok = *porok.*

tempoyak [KN], a preserve made of salted durain.

tempoyok [KN], black ants.

tempua [KN], *burung* ~, the weaver-bird; *ikan* ~, a fish *(Barbus apogon).*

tempuh [KK], a violent onslaught; charging; *menempuh,* to assault, to storm; to enter on (as a newly-made road); to use (as a route); to meet, encounter, as dangers; to undergo, as a test.

tempuling [KN], a barbed fish-spear.

tempunai [KN], a monkey-bread tree *(Artocarpus rigida).*

tempur [KK], *ber~,* colliding, clashing, to come to blows, to fight; *per~an,* collision, fight, battle; *per~an darah,* bloodshed.

tempurung [KN], a piece of coconut-shell; ~ *kepala,* a skull; the body of a mandoline-like musical instrument; ~ *lutut,* the knee-pan; *sisik* ~, the loggerhead turtle *(Thalassochelys caretta);* ~ *naik ke gansa,* the bit of coconut-shell aspires to be bell-metal, a symbol of incongruity; *seperti katak bawah* ~, (prov.) narrow (ideas), narrow-mindedness.

temu [KK], 1. coming together at the same spot; an interview, meeting; *ber~,* to meet; *sampai ber~ lagi,* till we meet again; *per~an,* meeting; the act or place of meeting; one's affinity; *memper~kan,* to fix up; *ber~ belakang,* back-to-back; *per~an empat mata,* a tete-a-tete; *ber~ muka,* face to face; ~*ramah,* interview; ~ *tanya,* ~ *selidik,* interrogation; ~*duga,* interview, interview for questioning; audition; ~ *uji,* id.; *penemuan,* a discovery, esp. scientific. 2. a generic name given to a number of wild gingers *(Scitamineoe);* ~ *kunci,* a small cultivated ginger *(Koempferia pandulata);* ~ *kunyit,* turmeric *(Curcuma longa);* ~ *lawak,* a white turmeric, the zedoary *(Curcuma zedoaria).*

temucut = *cemucup.*

temukus = *kemungkus.*

temukut = *lemukut.*

temut [KK], throbbing, of the fontanelle.

tenaga [KN], strength, power, energy; ~ *kuda,* horse-power.

tenang [KS], calm, smooth, still (of water); also by extension, of mind, behaviour; *menenangkan,* to calm down; *ke~an,* rest, calm, quiet.

tenar [KS], an uproar; a row, esp. of a noise likely to be heard by others; *jangan buat* ~, don't let the neighbours hear; *ke~an,* popularity; *calon itu beru-*

saha mencari ke~an, the candidate is seeking popularity.

tenat [KS], Ind. grave, serious (of condition); tired out, exhausted, fatigued.

tenda [KN], Port. awning; hood of rikisha.

tendang [KK], kicking out; *bertumbuk ber~,* with cuffs and kicks; *~an pertama,* kick-off (football); *~an sudut,* corner.

tendas menendas [KK], to cut off, to sever, esp. to decapitate.

teng [KN], ch. a Chinese lantern.

tengadah [KK], looking upwards; to look up.

tengah [KN], midst, middle; the half, the centre; in the middle of (in point of time); whilst; *~hari,* midday; *~ naik,* halfgrown; *~ mengajar,* while he was teaching; *se~,* a half; a fair quantity; some; *se~ pada se~nya,* a number of them, some of them; *~ jalan,* on the way; *sama ~,* right in the middle; *per~an bulan,* the middle of the month; *menge~kan,* to bring forward, as a proposal; *orang ~,* a middleman; an arbitrator; *jalan ~,* a compromise; *kaum per~an,* the middle classes; *abad per~an,* middle ages; *se~ rasmi,* semi official; *penengah,* situated in the middle.

tengar [KN], a tree of the mangrove type — the bark of which is used for tanning *(Ceriops candolleana).*

tenggala [KN], Skr. a plough; *tanah ~,* arable land; *padi ~,* seed-padi; *menenggala,* to plough; *alur ~,* a furrow.

tenggalung [KN], a civet-cat *(Viverra tangalunga); pagar ~,* the railing round the stern-gallery of a Malay ship.

tenggan [KN], rolls of fat on the limbs or body.

tenggang [KK], 1. sharing; *~-menenggang,* sharing alike. 2. [KN] a period, a limited time, e.g. the length of a king's reign.

tenggara [KN], south-east; the S.W. monsoon; *timur menenggara,* E.S.E.; *selatan menenggara,* S.S.E.; *~ mandi,* a strong S.E. wind; *angin ~,* south east

wind; *musim ~,* monsoon season (April to October).

tenggat [KN], limit, extreme point; *dari ~ ini ke ~ itu,* from this extremity to that.

tenggek [KK], 1. squatting, perching, like a bird or ape; *ber~,* to squat; *ber~ di belakang,* used (sl.) for coming late into an enterprise; *~kan,* to put something quite high up; *berjalan ~,* to walk with bent knees. 2. wearing the headdress at a rakish slant.

tenggelam [KK], to sink, to be submerged, to disappear from the surface; *matahari ~,* sunset; *suratannya timbul ~,* the written characters on it were partly visible, partly effaced; *~kan,* to submerge; *penenggelaman,* sinking; *~-timbul,* bobbing up and down, appearing and disappearing.

tenggelung, Ked. = *penanggalan* — cf. **tanggal.**

tengger = *tenggek.*

tenggik [KK], tossing rice up and down when winnowing.

tenggiling [KN], a sort of ant-eater or armadillo *(Manis javanica); atap batu sisik ~,* tiled roofing.

tenggiri [KN], the Spanish mackerel.

tenggorok [KN], Ind. throat, palate; *pangkal ~,* the largynx.

tenggulung [KN], millipede which rolls up into a ball when touched; also *senggulung.* 2. *musang ~,* a civet.

tengik [KS], rancid (of oil); oily-looking (of water), unpleasant smell or taste.

tengka [KDpn], Pah. between, = *antara; menengka,* to stand between; (fig.) to negotiate.

tengkalak [KN], a long narrow fish-trap with inturning spikes at the broader end, or else *(~ onak),* made of sticks with inturning thorns.

tengkalang [KN], small granary on posts.

tengkalik [KKtr] & [KS], topsy-turvy, higggledly-pigggledy (as the contents of a ransacked room).

tengkaluk [KN], unripe but edible (of fruit).

tengkang [KN], the space between the

eyes.

tengkar [KK], *ber~,* to quarrel, to dispute; to have a squabble; *ber~an,* quarrelling, arguing; *~i,* to stir up a quarrel; *per~an,* an altercation, also *tengkarah.*

tengkarang [KN], a corner, recess, space; *api ~,* a fire in a hearth.

tengkarap [KS], ruined, destroyed.

tengkawang [KN], a (Borneo) tree *(Diplocnemia sebifera);* see **kawang.**

tengkel [KN], round droppings of goats, pill.

tengkelang = *kelang.*

tengkerong [KN], a fish *(Sebastes stolizkoe)* — also known as *kerong-kerong.*

tengkes [KS], unequal in size to its fellows; insufficeintly developed; deformed, of overlapping toes.

tengking [KN], snarling; *menengking* [KK], to speak angrily.

tengkolak [KN], Ind. a broker, middleman.

tengkolok [KN], a head-wrapper, a kerchief used as a head-dress.

tengkorak [KN], a skull, the cranium; *ringgit ~,* the 2 1/2 guilder piece.

Tengku [KN], a royal title which more or less = *Raja;* the practice as to the persons entitled to it varies in different States; probably not a variant of *tuanku;* see **tuanku** and **engku;** *Tengku Mokkota,* heir to the throne.

tengkuh [KN], Ch. opium-dross prepared for re-smoking.

tengkujuh [KN], season of heavy rain; wet monsoon.

tengkuk [KN], the nape of the neck, the neck generally; *bulu ~,* mane.

tengkuluk [KN], head-cloth.

tengkurap [KK], Ind. lying prone.

tengkuyung [KN[, 1. a kind of cowrie. 2. sago-bark.

tengok [KK], looking at, peering at; tǫ see.

tengung-tenging [KS], Pk. mooning, absent-minded.

tenjak [KK], Pah. to walk with toe or heel lifted, as a person with sore feet.

tentang [KDpn], opposite; facing; at, touching, regarding; *~an,* opposition; *ber~an dengan,* opposite to; *ber~ mata,* face-to-face; *menentang,* to face (as a man faces an opponent); to oppose; *kuasa penentangan,* right of veto; in its adverbial use often abbreviated to *tang,* cf. **batal;** *penentang,* one who opposes; *se~,* right in front of.

tentawan [KN], *akai ~,* a water-producing vine *(Conocephalus suaveolens).*

tentera [KN], skr. troops; army; *~laut,* naval forces; *~ darat,* land forces; *~ udara,* air forces; *~ berkuda,* cavalry; *~payung terjun,* parachute troops; *~ biasa,* regular troops; *~ lasak,* trained troops; *~ daerah,* territorial troops; *~ wataniah,* id. *anggota ~,* member of the armed forces; *ke~an,* army.

tenteram [KS], quiet, calm, peaceful; *ke~an umum,* the public peace; *men~kan,* clam, quieten.

tentu [KS], certain, definite; indubitable, positive; *khabar yang ~,* reliable news; *ter~,* fixed, definintely; to fix; to settle up (a dispute); *tidak menentu,* not sure, indefinite; *ber~an,* securely based, stable, as a government; *ke~an,* commands, rules, esp. of god; *penentuan nasib sendiri,* self-determination; *kepala buntut tidak ~,* unorganised, planless.

tenuk [KN], a tapir *(Tapirus malaynus);* *badak ~,* id. — cf. **badak tampung, badak murai.**

tenun [KN], the art or process of weaving; *~an,* method or style of weaving; *salah ~an,* a fault in the fabric; *ber~,* to weave; *te~,* the praying-mantis; *siti ~,* id.

tenung [KK], to gaze fixedly; *~kan,* to discover (e.g., a lost object) by divination; *penenung,* a fortune-teller.

tenusu [KN], dairy; *lembu ~,* dairy cattle; *ladang ~,* dairy farm.

tenyeh [KK], *menenyehkan,* to press and pinch; to rub and press, as in erasing or in putting out a cigarette; *~~ puntung rokok di bibir meja,* rubbing out the cigarette-butt on the edge of the table; cf. **tonyok**.

teologi [KN], theology.

teorem [KN], theorem.

teori [KN[, theory.

tepak [KN], (onom.) a light slap, pat or blow with the flat of the hand.

tepak [KN], a rectangular (Palembang-made) box containing sirih-chewing requisites; *menerima ~,* to receive a proposal of marriage (for one's daughter); *menolak ~,* to reject such a proposal; *menterbalikkan ~ sirih,* to turn over such a box (as a sign of repudiation of the bride); cf. **pinang**.

tepala [KN], *ikan ~,* a small pond-fish; a sp. of fighting fish.

tepam [KK], laying the palm of the hand on anything or passing the palm of the hand over anything (as a man in the dark trying to make out the character of some object).

tepas [KS], 1. brimful, full up. 2. *empat ~ dunia,* the four quarters of the earth; = *empat penjuru alam.* 3. material composed of interwoven laths, etc., for making walls, etc.

tepat [KS], exactly; hitting the spot exactly; *~ pada waktunya,* punctual to the minute; *menepati pada,* directed to, affecting; *barat ~,* due west; *matahari ~,* exactly noon; *penuh !,* just exactly full; *ber~,* to carry out in its exactness, e.g., *ber~ janji,* to carry out one's promise; *memandang ~-~,* to gaze fixedly; *~kan,* to place exactly; to set (the hands of a watch); *menepati,* to fulfil; to reach the standard of; *se~--~nya,* with complete exactness.

tepeh [KN], an edible salt-water shell-fish (unidentified).

tepek [KK], to affix by plastering.

teper [KK], = ceper.

tepi [KN], edge, border, margin, brink; *menepi,* to step to the edge; to edge off; to step aside; *ke~kan,* to shelve (as a proposal); to oust; to leave out (as a player from a team); to set aside, over rule (an order, etc.); *~ kain* (the edge of one's sarung) is used to convey the idea of the limitations of a person; also his private personal affairs; *menjaja-jajakan hal ~ kain orang,* to hawk round malicious gossip; *jagalah ~ kain sendiri,* i.e., look who's talking, or mind your own business; *orang luar ~,* an outsider, a person having no part in a matter; *~an,* the shallows by the edge of a river; also a river bath-house cum lavatory; *perempuan ~ jalan,* a 'street-walker'; see **sedar** and **tali**.

tepi [KN], a knuckle-duster.

tepis [KK], knocking aside, warding off; *~kan,* to strike or push aside; *~-menepis,* to fence.

tepok [KS], crippled, e.g. with no legs.

tepu [KS], full to the brim, full (of sails).

tepuk [KK], clapping, slapping; patting; *menepuk dada,* to beat the breast; *~ lalat,* the flap which Malays use for catching grasshoppers; *~ tangan,* to clap the hands; *~-sorak,* to applaud loudly (shouting and clapping); *~-sorak yang bergemuruh,* thunderous applause; *ber~ tangan sebelah, tak akan berbunyi,* if you clap with one hand only, no sound will result, i.e., all two-sided affairs need reciprocity, e.g. it takes two to make a quarrel, or you cannot hope to succeed alone; *menepuk pelanduk,* to call a mousedeer by patting the ground (in imitation of a stamping challenge).

tepung [KN], flour, meal, powdery substance; *~ beras,* rice flour; *~ gandum,* wheaten flour; *~ sari,* pollen; *~ tawar,* a powder used for cooling the skin; it is mixed with the leaves of the *setawar* plant and is sometimes sprinkled as a bar to bad luck; *~ sabun, ~ pencuci,* soap flakes; detergents.

tepus [KN], gingerwort; generic for many wild Zingiberaceæ.

tera [KN], the royal seal, stamp or impression; *belum ber~,* it is still unsealed; *me~i,* to stamp documents or coins in the mint; *juru~,* an engineer; *juru~ kerja kanan,* senior executive engineer; *ter~,* reproduced (of a picture); printed; stamped, of a coin.

terada, Ind. = *tiada*.

terajang [KK], trampling under foot; to stamp down on anything; *tendang* ~, kicking and stamping (as a horse); *sepak-*~, id.; (fig.) to kick up a great row, make a great disturbance.

teraju [KN], Pers. scales; a balance; the loose string joining the extremities of a kite; tent strings; a keyman, party boss, person in a position to pull strings; the 'reins of government', key position; *memegang* ~, to be in control; *~kan*, id.

terak [KN], 1. a fowl's laying-place. 2. tin refuse after smelting. 3. *penuh* ~, absolutely full; chock-full; *elok* ~, perfectly beautiful.

teral [KK], to insist, verbal pressure or importunity.

teraling [KN], *kayu* ~, a wood used in house-building *(Tarrietia simplicifolia)*.

teran [KK], to strain (in easing oneself); the impulse in labour.

teranas [KN], good anchorage; firm seabottom.

terang [KS], clear, bright; obvious, evident; ~ *hati*, clear-sighted; ~ *berderang*, bright and clear, brightly lit up; ~ *cuaca*, clear daylight; *di tengah-tengah* ~, quite openly; in broad daylight; *terus* ~, frankly; *ke~an*, elucidation, clearing up, explanation, proof; formal statement; *ke~an bersumpah*, statement on oath; *~kan*, to clear (land); to explain; *~-temarang*, very bright; *penerangan*, information; publicity; *pegawai penerangan*, Publicity Officer.

terangkik [KN], a bamboo receptacle for palm-juice.

terap [KN], 1. a tree *(Artocarpus Kunstleri)*, the bark of which is used by Sakais as cloth; *kulit* ~, the bark so used; *getah* ~, bird-lime made from the sap of this tree. 2. *keris te~an = keris terapang*. 3. *~kan*, to cut out (dough) into shapes; *penerap*, the cutter so used.

terapang [KN], a metal covering for the keris-sheath.

teras [KN], hard wood in a tree; *ber*~, having a solid core; ~ is also used (fig.) for good sifted grain as opposed to broken grain *(melukut)* and chaff *(sekam)*; *ditinting, ditampi* ~, winnowing out the good grain; (fig.) investigating the character and antecedents of a person, e.g., a prospective bridegroom; so ~ is used for a vital point, essence; main stay; ~ *terunjam gubal melayang*, the hard core stands fast when the soft wood blows away, i.e. true loyalty cannot be shaken; *ber~kan*, based on, founded on.

terasi [KN], a preparation of fish and prawns (better known as *belacan*).

terasul [KN], Ar. letter-writing; *ilmu* ~, knowledge of epistolary forms; *kitab* ~, a treatise on letter-writing.

teratai [KN], a kind of water-lily.

teratak [KN], a lean-to; a humble hut; a depreciatory way of describing one's own dwelling; *meneratak*, to build a hut.

teratu [KN], Port. torture; *tempat* ~, a torture-chamber.

terau [KK], *menerau*, to spin thread.

terawang, see **awang** 2.

terawih [KN], Ar. evening prayer (7.30 pm) in the month of Ramadan.

terbang [KK], flying, to fly; *belum* ~ *lalat*, before the flies are astir, i.e. the very early morning; ~ *arwah* or ~ *semangat*, 'the flight of the spirit of life'; lost (of consciousness); *ber~an*, flying in flocks; *binatang kecil yang ber~an*, small flying creatures; *penerbangan*, a flight, a journey by air; aviation; ~ *dengan teratur*, to fly in formation; *~-~ jatuh*, to flutter along, as young bird learning to fly.

terbit [KK], issuing out of; to arise, to emerge; *matahari* ~, the rising sun; ~ *rimba*, issuing from the forest; *yang* ~ *daripada hati yang jernih*, proceeding from a pure heart; *penerbit*, a publisher; *penerbitan*, publication.

terbul [KN], a fresh-water carp.

terbus [KN], Ar. tarboosh, a fez.

terbut [KN], a heavy wooden bolt used in ship-building.

terenang [KN], a large squat water-vessel of earthenware or metal.

terendak [KN], a conical sun hat; ~ *Cina,* the Chinese pattern of sun-hat (which is not a perfect cone but slopes inwards); sometimes used or shade of a lamp; *siput* ~, a shell *(Phorus solaris).*

terengkas, see *tulis.*

terentang [KN], a large forest-tree *(Campnosperma auriculata);* its timber is sued in match-making.

teri [KBil], Skr. three, triple (in certain expressions only, e.g., ~-*buana,* the three worlds; ~*sula,* a trident).

teriak [KN], a cry, a scream; *ber*~ [KK], to cry out; *meneriaki,* call out loudly.

terigu [KN], Port. flour.

terik, N.S. = *tarik.*

terima [KK], *menerima,* to receive, to obtain; ~ *kasih,* the acknowledgement of the receipt of kindness; thank you; thanks; ~ *kasih daun keladi,* rhyming sl. for *kalau boleh hendak lagi,* if possible, I want some more, i.e., gratitude which is a lively sense of favours to come; *salah* ~, misunderstand; ~ *nasib,* leave everything to fate, submissive (to God); *penerimaan,* acceptance, reception; *dapat di*~, acceptable; *menerima apa adanya,* to accept things as they are.

teripang [KN], a sea-worm prized by Chinese as a delicacy *(Holothuria edulis); ikan* ~, a fish *(Saurus indicus).*

terisula, Skr. a trident; see *teri* and *sula.*

teritik [KK], *ber*~, dripping, dropping continually in small drops — cf. **titik.**

teritip [KN], a small sea-slug (which eats into piles and ships' bottoms); a small barnacle.

terjak [KK], kicking out (as a horse).

terjemah [KK], Ar. translation; interpretation; *men*~*kan,* to translate; *pen*~, a translator; *pasukan pèn*~*an foto tentera,* Army Photographic Interpretation Unit.

terjun [KK], to leap or jump down; *air* ~, a waterfall; ~ *dari atas kuda,* to leap off a horse; ~*kan,* to let drop; *bidan (dukun)* ~, (met.) midwife (not engaged before).

terka [KK], Skr. guess-work; *menerka,* to guess; to conjecture, estimate by conjecture; cf. **teka;** *penerkaan,* guess, suspicion, supposition.

terkam [KK], leaping or springing forward; *seperti singa hendak menerkam,* like a lion about to spring.

terkap [KK], catching under a concave surface.

terkul [KN], *senapang* ~, a rifle; muzzle, loading gun.

terkup [KN], (onom.) the dull clash of flat non-metallic substances; the butting of rams; *ber*~, clashing head-on, as rams, or (fig.) of disputants; *menerkuptan,* to make (animals) fight, to set at each other.

terlalu [KKtr], too, very, excessively; *ke*~*an,* excessive, extreme.

terlampau [KKtr], extreme, excessive, too much.

terlantar, see *lantar.*

termasa, = *temasya.*

terminologi [KN], terminology.

termometer [KN], thermometer.

termos [KN], thermos.

ternah [KS], unprecedented, unusual, extra-ordinary; *si*~, a dressed-up idiot — a term of abuse.

ternak [KN], breed; *orang* ~, aborigines; *ber*~, to breed (livestock); *ber*~ *ayam,* to breed poultry; *ber*~ *ayam secara intensif,* to keep poultry on the intensive system; *pen*~, breeder.

ternang [KN], a squat big-bellied water-jar.

terobos [KK], Ind. *menerobos,* to burst through, thrust through.

teroka [KK], *meneroka,* to open up new village etc.

teromba [KN], N.S. a song of origin (Minangkabau).

terompah [KN], wooden clogs.

terompet [KN], Eng. trumpet; *siput* ~, a

shell *(Triton variegatus)*.

terongko [KN], Port, a prison; a cell.

teropong [KN], a tube; a tubular or telescopic instrument; a telescope, a speculum; ~ *api*, a bellows; ~ *tuma*, a microscope.

teowong [KN], tunnel.

terpa [KK], *menerpa*, to dart forward; *salah* ~, (fig.) to make a big mistake, 'put one's foot in it'.

terpal [KN], Hind. (from Eng.) a tarpaulin; a driving-apron; *muka* ~, brazen-faced.

tertawa [KK], to laugh; see *tawa;* ~ *kecil*, to giggle; ~ *besar*, to laugh loudly; *men~kan*, to laugh at; *di~kan*, to meet with laughter.

tertib [KS], Ar. 1. order, rank, precedence; decorous behaviour, deference to superiors; deferential; *tata* ~, discipline; ~ *sembahyang*, the order of prayer, ritual; *ke~an*, order, 'law and order'. 2. becoming modesty, i.e., of people who do not presume.

terubin [KN], a fish-trap with a falling door; also *tubin*.

terubuk [KN], *ikan* ~, the hilsa *(Alosa* sp.) of which the Malays recognise two varieties: ~ *padi* and ~ *korin; telur* ~, the roe of this fish used as a sort of caviare.

terubul [KN], a tree *(Ixora grandifolia).*

terubung [KN], a granary; a padi-barn.

teruk [KS], severe (of illness or of a beating).

teruka, = *seroka*.

terum [KN], a word of command to elephants to make them kneel.

terumbu [KN], a reef or rock visible at low tide but covered at high water.

teruna [KN], Skr. an unmarried youth; *muda* ~, a stripling; *ayam* ~, a cockerel.

terung [KN], a vegetable; the brinjal or aubergine; ~ *pipit*, a very small green brinjal *(Solanum torvum* and *S. verbascifolium)*, esteemed as a delicacy; ~ *masam*, the tomato.

terumtum [KN], a sea-shore tree *(Aegiceras mujus).*

terup [KN], Ar. *daun* ~, playing cards; *main* ~, to play cards.

terus [KKtr}, right through; straight; in a direct line through or across; at once, without delay; ~*an*, a canal or cutting joining two reaches of river; ~ *mata*, second sight; *menerusi*, through, via; *cakap* ~*-terang*, to speak frankly; *meneruskan*, to carry on with, push forward (a plan); *menerusi*, go through; ~*kan!*, get on with it!; ~*menerus*, openly, defintely; *ber~an*, unceasingly; *berjalan* ~, to go straight on; *se~nya*, then onwards.

terusi [KN], Tam. vitriol, sulphuric acid.

terwelu [KN], rabbit.

tesmak [KN], spectacles, glasses.

tetak [KK], hacking, notching; ~*kan*, to strike (anything) with a cutting weapon; *menetakkan*, id.; *menetak*, to give a cutting blow.

tetal [KS], close (of the pattern of a cloth); without wide interstices; of close texture; compressed; *kuih* ~, a cake made of *pulut* rice with coconut-milk, sugar and egg; compressed in a mould.

tetampan [KN], an embroidered kerchief of silk worn ceremonially on the shoulder by court attendants.

tetamu [KN[, guests; *rumah* ~, guest house; = *tamu-tamu*, see *tamu; ruang tamu*, sitting room.

tetangga [KN], neighbour.

tetap [KKtr], 1. fixed (of tenure or residence); definitely decided; *setelah* ~ *bicara itu*, when that matter was settled; *menetapkan*, to fix, determine; *per~*, fixed, determined, assured; *menetap*, to settle down, establish oneself, take up permanent residence; *setiausaha* ~, Permanent Secretary; *ke~an*, conclusive decision, resolution, resolve, order. 2. blotting up; sucking up moisture; ~ *hati*, steadfast; ~ *iman*, steadfast in faith; ~ *harga*, price is fixed.

tetapi [KPhbg], Skr. but; used in writing instead of *tapi*.

tetas [KK], *menetas*, to be hatched (of eggs); ~*kan*, to pick (as fastenings), slit open, cracked.

teteguk [KN], a small owl — perhaps a dialectic name for the pungguk *(Glaucidium brodii).*

tetak [KN], the nipple of the breast; *memberi ~,* to suckle; *~ bengek,* trifles, items of no importance, small things, trivial matters.

tetel [KN], inferior meat (sinews, soft cartilage, etc.) consumed by the poor.

tetes [KN], drop, droplet; *menetes* [KK], to drip.

tetua [KN], blotchy freckles, larger than *tahi lalat.*

tewas [KS[, failure; being worsted; *~ perangnya,* the battle was going against him; *di~kan,* beaten by; *menewaskan,* defeat; *ke~an,* suffer, defeat.

teyan [KN], Ch. *ber~,* to club together and subscribe a fund.

tezi [KN], Pers. *kuda ~,* a Pegasus, a winged horse, swift (of steeds).

thabit [KKr], fixed, confirmed, proved.

thani [KBil], the second.

tiada, is not there, there is not; used in writing for *tidak ada; ~lah ia di sini,* he is not here; *kerana ke~an,* owing to the absence of; *dengan ~,* without; *di~kan,* deny, discontinue, abolish.

tiak [KN], a type of bird that eats padi.

tian [KN], Ind. the uterus of a pregnant woman.

tiang [KN], a pillar, a post, a mast, a vertical support; *~ agung,* the mainmast; *~ topang,* the foremast; *~ bendera,* a flag-staff; *~ seri,* the central pillar in a Malay house; *separuh ~,* half-mast; *bendera dinaikkan separuh ~,* the flag was flown at half-mast; *setengah ~,* 'up the pole', 'balmy', esp. of men who are woman-mad; *~ negara,* source of a nation's strength.

tiap [KS[, *~-~,* each, every; *se ~,* id.; *pada ~-~ hari,* everyday; *~-~ mereka itu,* every one of them; *se~ kali,* at a time.

tiarap [KK], *ter~,* lying on one's face (of a man); bottom upwards (of a boat); *~kan,* to turn (anything) face downwards; to invert; *meniarap,* to assume such a position.

tib [KN], Ar. book of charms, a treatise on medicine or magic or astrology.

tiba [KK], to arrive; 'putting in' at a port (of a ship); 'landing' (of a blow); *~-~,* suddenly, unexpectedly; then it happened that; *se~nya,* as soon as he arrived; *getah diangkat, kuaran ~,* the bitterns arrived at the very spot just after the bird-lime had been taken up, i.e., rotten bad luck, or 'just missed the bus', or be more patient another time.

tidak [KKtr], no, not; *~kan,* to deny the existence of; *ke~an,* non-existence; *se~-~nya,* at any rate, in any case, at least; *pada ~ baik ada,* something is better than nothing, i.e. it'll have to do; *kalau ~,* unless; *~ boleh ~,* without fail; *~ lain dan ~ bukan,* none other than.

tidur [KK], to go to bed; to sleep; *~ lelap,* deep sleep; *~kan,* to put to sleep, e.g., an infant; *~ lelap,* fast asleep, deep slumber; *menyanyi menidurkan budak,* to sing a child to sleep; *ter~,* fallen asleep, deep in sleep; *ke~an,* over-slept; *~-~ ayam,* to sleep fitfully, doze, fail to get a good sleep; *~ meniduri,* to put to sleep or to sleep with (a woman).

tiga [KBil], three; *ber~,* in a party of three; *ke~,* all three; *yang ke~,* third.

tika [KN], a reel of thread.

tikai [KN], Ind. a disagreement; *ber~,* to disagree; to quarrel; involved in a dispute; *per~an,* a dispute; controversy; *diper~kan,* in dispute; *memper~kan,* to dispute.

tikal [KN], a 'tical'.

tikam [KK], *menikam,* stabbing, spearing, piercing (of thorns); *ber~-~an,* stabbing at one another; *ter~,* stab accidentally; *mati kena ~,* death from a stab or from a spear-thrust; *~kan,* to drive (a pointed weapon) into anything; *penikam,* Kel. a fighting bull which strikes upwards with its horns; *mari ~!,* (fig.) place your stakes!, have a go!; *penikam,* (fig.) a bettor, one who bets; *ber~ lidah,* to have a fierce argument; *judi ~ ekor,* a sort of lottery, based on selecting the correct digit; *permainan ~-~*, games such as are found at fairs, at which prizes may be won by skill at throwing, etc.

tikar [KN], a mat; *bentangkan ~,* to spread a mat; *ber~kan,* to use (anything) as a mat; to sleep on; *~ mas,* (fig.) for a wealthy marriage; *ganti ~,* change the mat, (fig.) to marry one's deceased wife's sister; *~ tantal,* bedding, *~ bantal,* mat and pillow; *~ bangkar,* thick coarse mat; *~ sembahyang,* praying mat.

tikas [KN], the line of sea-weed and driftwood on a beach, showing the extreme point reached by the tide.

tikus [KN], a generic name for rats and mice; *~ ambang bulan,* Raffles Gymnura; *~ buluh,* a name for the bamboo-rat *(Rhizomys sumatrensis),* better *dekan; ~ mondok,* the common brown rat; *~ rumah,* the common house-mouse *(Mus musculus); ~ tanah,* the field-mouse *(Mus decumanus); ~ turi,* the musk-shrew *(Corcidur amurina* and *C. coerulea); angin ~,* uncertain winds; *gigi ~,* small regular teeth; *lubang ~,* the cavity in which the body is laid in a Malay grave; *kerana marahkan ~ rumah terbakar,* house burnt down to spite rats, i.e., don't 'throw out the baby with bathwater', be discreet in your reforms; *seperti ~ basah,* like a wet rat, i.e. crestfallen, humiliated; *seperti ~ baiki labu,* like a rat repairing a gourd, of a job botched by a hopelessly unsuitable person.

tilam [KN], a mattress; *~an,* id.; *kain ~,* bedsheet, bedspread.

tilan [KN], the spiny eel.

tilik [KK], to look long and fixedly at anything; carefully examining; *tempat ~,* a cynosure of all eyes; *tukang ~,* a man gifted with second-sight; a fortune-teller; *ahli ~ nasib,* id.; *~-menilik,* scrutinizing each other.

tim [KN], Ch. stewing; *pe~an,* a stew-pan; *nasi ~,* steamed rice.

timah [KN], tin; lead; zinc; *~ putih,* tinned iron; *~ hitam,* lead; *~ sari,* zinc; *bijih ~,* alluvial tin; *~ jongkong,* block tin; *memasak ~, menuang ~,* to smelt tin; *~ salut,* tin-foil; *ikan ~-~,* a fish *(Lutianus lineolatus?); pokok ~-~,* a small tree *(Ilex cymosa); dahulu ~ sekarang besi,* (prov.) to lose prestige (respect).

timang [KN], balancing; to balance in the hand, to poise, as a spear; to toss up and down (as an adult playing with a very young child); to dandle; *~-~an,* a pet name or nursery name; *nama ~an,* pet name; *menimang-nimang,* to cuddle; *dia menimang-nimang bayinya,* she's cuddling her baby.

timba [KN], a small bucket; a dipper; *~ ruang,* well in a boat; *menimba,* to bale.

timbal [KS], *ber~an,* in equipoise; matching; *~an,* an assessor (juryman); an assistant; a deputy; *se~ dengan,* equal to, on a parity with; *~-balik,* reciprocity, mutual toleration; reciprocal; balanced; *se~,* in equilibrium; symmetrical (of, e.g., two parts); *ber~an,* id.; *tajam ber~,* sharpened at both ends.

timbang [Ks], estimating the weight of anything; considering the pros and cons of a question; *batu ~an,* measure of weight; *~kan,* to weight; *penimbang,* the weighter; *~ semula,* to reconsider; *~ rasa,* considerate, to be sympathetic, to sympathize; *dengan tidak ber~-~,* without due consideration; *hilang per~an badan,* to lose one's balance; *(ada) per~an yang baik,* well-balanced; *per~an,* consideration; *diper~kan,* under consideration.

timbau [KK], adding to piece so as to lenghten anything; *papan ~,* upper strake of a boat.

timbuk [KK], *menimbuk,* to strike downwards with the flat of the fist.

timbul [KK], appearing on the surface, floating, emerging from below; appearing, coming into view, esp. from below; in relief, standing out, as veins; to crop up, as a subject; *gambar*

~, a bas-relief; a statue; ~ *tenggelam*, appearing and disappearing —as the letters of a half-erased inscription; *bulan* ~, the new moon; *penimbul,* that which causes a thing to come to the surface — used esp. of a charm of invulnerability *(kebal penimbul* or *penimbul raksa),* (based on the belief that quick-silver absorbed into the system will rush to any spot struck by a weapon and so prevent the weapon penetrating beneath the skin); *menimbulkan,* to bring to the surface, so, (fig.) to cause to appear, bring out, cause; to exhibit clearly; *menimbulkan kebimbangan,* to arouse anxiety; *menimbulkan syak wasangka,* to arouse suspicion.

timbun [KN], a heap; *~i, ~kan,* or *menimbunkan* to heap up anything; *ber~-~,* in heaps; piled one on top of the other.

timbus [KK], filling up or blocking a cavity; *~i,* to fill up (a grave), to cover over, bury; *ter~,* buried, as in a landslide.

timpa [KK], falling down on; striking in its fall; *di~ batu,* struck down by falling stones; ~ *rasa,* to bear the brunt of anything; ~ *perasaan,* id.; *di~ daulat,* struck down by the power of dead kings; *menimpa,* to strike in one's fall; to fall upon; *sudah jatuh, di~ tangga,* to fall and have the ladder fall on top of you, i.e. misfortune follows misfortune.

timpal [KS], Ind. *se~,* in proportion, suitable, fitting.

timpang [KS], lame; *kaki kirinya* ~, he's lame in the left leg.

timpas [KN], low-water; exhausted (spring, well), dried up; ~ *pernama,* very low tide.

timpuh [KK], *ber~,* to sit with the legs turned to the right and bent back towards the body, while the left arm rests on the ground, as Malay women sit.

timpus [KS], disproportionately narrow; lacking in beam (of a boat).

timu [KN], by right (de jure); correct, of action; *~~,* id.

timun [KN], generic for cucumbers; also ~ *batik,* the squash melon; ~, Kel. a watermelon; ~ *Cina,* Kel. cucumber; *Awang* ~, nickname for armless and legless cripples; ~ *dendang,* a passionflower *(Passiflora foetida);* ~ *hutan,* ~ *Belanda,* the grenadilla *(Passiflora quadrangulis);* also *men~; anak-anak* ~, adopted girl (with a view to subsequent marriage).

timur [KN], east; ~ *laut,* N.E.; ~ *padang,* E.S.E.; ~ *tenggara,* ~ *menenggara,* id.; *bintang* ~, morning star; *ke~an,* oriental.

tin [KN], tin; *buah* ~, tinned fruit; *susu* ~, tinned milk.

tindak [KK], Ind. *ber~,* to act, take action; *~kan,* action, effort; *~-tanduk,* various activites; *~-balas,* reaction.

tindan [KK], lying loosely one on the other (of a pile of books or similar objects); *se* ~, a disorderly heap.

tindas [KK], to press hard on, to oppress, to crush; to squash, as an insect; *menindas,* tc repress; to oppress; *dia ketua pejabat yang menindas pekerja-pekerjanya,* he's the type of boss that exploits his workers; *ter~,* oppressed; *penindasan,* harshness, oppression; persecution; *penindas,* a tyrant.

tindih [KK], lying one over the other; *yang rebah di~,* the fallen is pressed under (still further); the unfortunate are oppressed; *ber~,* lying one over the other (as bodies on a battlefield); overlapping; sometimes used of animals copulating; *menindih,* to pin down, as debris pins down a person under it; *penindih kertas,* a paper- weight.

tindik *menindik* [KK], pricking through a thin surface; to pierce the ear.

tingau [KN], a sort of needle-cum-comb instrument used in making or repairing nets.

tinggal [KKtr], remaining over or behind; to stay, to be left; abiding in a place; to live, to dwell; ~ *nadi,* with life alone left, ruined; ~ *arwah,* have died; ~ *tu-lang,* very thin; ~ *nama,* leaving the good or bad name behind; *~i,* to leave behind; to abandon; *~kan* or *meninggalkan,* id.; *ke~an,* abandonment; left out, not included, left behind; *peninggalan,* absence; heritage; *harta peninggalan,* property left behind; *se-peninggalan,* in the absence of (so-and-so); every since; *tertinggal,* left behind, abandoned; *meninggal,* to pass away, die; ~ *lagi,* furthermore; *tidak ke~an,* not overlooked; *ke~an zaman,* old-fashioned, out-of-date; *ke~an masa,* id.; *ke~an keretapi,* missed the train.

tinggi [KS], high, lofty; ~ *hati,* proud; ~ *diri,* arrogant, snobbish; *dia daripada golongan ~,* he has class; *tempat ~,* altitude; *tingkat ~,* high level; *~-rendah,* uneven (of surface); undulating; (fig.) inequalities; *meninggi,* to rise high, as sun or voice; *meninggi langit,* sky-high; *kian meninggi,* rising, as ground; *meninggikan,* to raise, e.g., the head of a recumbent person or the voice; to elevate standard, quality; *majlis ter~,* Supreme Council.

tinggir [KK], *ber~,* to perch; cf. **tenggek.**

tinggung [KK], *ber~,* to sit on one's heels, squat like a toad or dog on its hind legs.

tingkah [KN], 1. ways, behaviour, manners; ~ *laku,* id.; sometimes, odd behaviour, manners; foibles; mannerisms; *ber~,* capricious. 2. Ind. *meningkah,* to answer, retort; (drumming) in time or in harmony.

tingkal [KN], Hind. (from (Skr.) borax, solder.

tingkap [KN], a window; ~ *kipas,* louvered window, ~ *magun,* ventilator.

tingkat [KN], a deck, a flooring, a storey — taken as a measure of height or size; *kapal tiga ~,* a three-decker; *ber~~,* in storeys; in stages; in tiers, multi-storied; *meningkat,* to rise to, to reach (a stage in development); to rise in scale, to progress; to esalate; *meningkat*

menjadi peperangan besar, to escalate into a big war; *~an,* ranking; classification; grading; *~an gaji,* wage-scale.

tingkil [KN], a bunch, a cluster (of fruit).

tingkis [KS], sad, sorrowful.

tingting [KN], 1. to hop on one foot. 2. to ring coins (to test them).

tinjau [KK], *meninjau,* to observe, look at, crane neck to see; to reconnoitre; (fig.) to consider, examine (merits of); *meninjau-ninjau,* to go sight-seeing; to survey in a group; *ter~~,* craning the neck to see; playing Peeping Tom; ~ *belukar,* beautiful sight from a distance (scrubby near-by); *~an* is sometimes used for 'a review' of a book; *peninjauan,* investigation, inquiry, survey; *pasukan peninjau,* recce unit in the Army.

tinju [KN], a fist; boxing; *ber~,* to box; *ahli ~,* a boxer; *ahli adu ~,* id.

tinta [KN], Port. ink.

tinting [KK], to winnow with a swaying motion; to investigate, sift (reports); to ring a coin (to test it).

tiong [KN], hill mynah.

tipis [KS], thin, delicate, exiguous; remote; *kemungkinan berjaya ~ sekali,* the chances for success are very remote; *menipis,* to wax thin; (fig.) to become slight, as hopes; *menipiskan,* to dilute, esp. with water; to thin out; cf. **nipis.**

tipu [KN], deception; ruse, trick; *bohong dan ~,* lies and misrepresentations; *menipu,* to deceive; *penipu,* a cheat; *~-daya,* fraud; *ter~,* swindled, deceived.

tir [KN], the rook or castle in chess.

tirah [KK], *ter~,* to take a cure; *pe~an,* sanatorium, health resort.

tirai [KN], Tam. a curtain; ~ *kelambu,* mosquito-curtains.

tiram [KN], an oyster; *burung ~,* the osprey.

tiri [KN], 'step' — in expressions like step-child *(anak ~),* step-father *(bapa ~)* and step-mother *(mak ~); menganak~kan,* treated as a stepson, mistreated.

tiris [KS], oozing through, dripping; leak

(roof, boat, etc.); *atapnya ~,* the roof is leaking.

tiru [KK], *meniru,* to copy, to imitate; *~an,* an imitation.

tiruk [KN], a long unbarbed fish-spear; *burung !,* the snipe *(Callinago stenura* and *G. coelestis); burung te~,* id.; *nyamok ~,* the anopheles mosquito; *miniruk,* to spear fish — cf. **tirus.**

tirus [KS], thin and tapering to a point; *padi menirus,* the ear of rice in its earliest stage — cf. **tiruk.**

titah [KN], the utterance of a prince; *~ Sultan,* the Sultan says; *ber~,* to speak (of a prince).

titi [KN], a bridge consisting of a fallen trunk, plank, branch, or a made bridge over a stream; *meniti,* to pass over such a footway; *~an,* anything that will serve as a bridge at a pinch; *ber~,* to make one's way along (e.g., a branch).

titik [KN], 1. a drop; (fig.) a point; an item; a full-stop; a dot; *~ dua,* colon; *~ api,* the focus (of a lens); *~ pertemuan,* crucial point of a dispute; sometimes, the common ground in a dispute; *~ hitam,* black spot (weak point, difficulty); *~ tolak,* inception, starting-point; *garisan ber~,* dotted line; *menintik, ber~,* to drip; *se~,* a drop; *menitik-beratkan,* to lay great stress on, treat as important. 2. a heavy racking blow (as in administering torture); *mas di~,* hammered gold; *biar ~ jangan tumpah,* (prov.) half a loaf is better than no bread.

titir [KN], a swift rapping movement; to beat certain drums and gongs; *di~ canang pemanggil,* the summoning gong was beaten.

titis [KN], slow dropping; the dropping of sticky liquids — cf. **titik;** *ke~an darah yang akhir,* the last drop of blood; *~an pena* (fig.), composition.

tiub [KN], tube.

tiung [KN], 1. the mynah *(Aracula intermedia* and *Gracula javanensis); ~ batu* or *~ belacan,* the Eastern broad-billed roller *(Eurystomus orientalis); ~ karat,* a large sp. of mynah with a blue 'flash'

on its wings. 2. *~ Hua,* Ch. China.

tiup [KK], blowing; the action of a current of air upon anything; *alat ~an,* wind instruments; *buntal di~,* a blown-out *buntal* fish; *ber~,* to blow (of the breeze); *~an,* gust; *saya berasa ada ~an angin,* I felt a gust of wind.

toakau [KN], Ch. a twakow; a type of barge, us. driven by sail or motor.

tobak menobak [KK], square-cut; trimmed square (of the nails).

tobat [KS], Ar. repentant; giving up (an evil practice); *ber~,* to repent one's ways; *~kan,* to absolve from sin; *~ nasohah,* complete repentance; *~!,* an exclamation denoting strong negation; never! never!; also *taubat.*

toboh [KN], in groups; *ber~-~,* in clusters.

tocang [KN], plaits; *ber~, menocangkan,* to wear the hair in plait.

todak [KN], a saw-fish; also used for a swordfish.

togel = *dogel,* [KS], tailless; *menogelkan,* made tailless.

togok [KN], limbless; with stumps for limbs; *berlayar ~,* to sail with only a storm-sail set; *si ~,* the long-nosed clown in a Javanese *wayang.*

toha [KN], Ch. a mourning-band; so, an armband generally.

tohok [KN], a sort of harpoon with a rope attached; *menohok,* to stab downwards, as with a harpoon.

tohor [KS], shallow, owing to drying-up of water; *kapur ~,* white-wash; *ber~,* 'stranded' (very hungry or despairing).

tojang [KN], a temporary prop or support; *penojang kaki,* a foot-rest.

tok [KN], 1. *~ duit,* money-box. 2. a contraction for *datuk,* q.v.; *~-~,* knocking sound.

tokak [KN], 1. an ulcer on the shin. 2. biting (in fighting and not for eating). 3. *~-takik,* unevenly cut, patchy (as hair or a hedge).

tokek [KN], split areca-nut.

tokek [KN], (onom.) the gecko.

token [KN], Ch. a counter, a small disc used in gaming.

toko [KN], Ch. a warehouse or store; ~ *buku,* book shop; *ber~,* has a shop.

tokoh [KN], character, quality, type — of goods; (fig.) an important person, a leader; *ber~,* of good appearance; of high quality.

tokok [KN], a small increase; to throw something in over and above; *~-tambahnya,* increases; (fig.) exaggerations.

tokong [KN], 1. a treeless rock; a barren island; ~ *pulau,* (lit.) rocks and isles, an archipelago. 2. Ch. a Chinese temple, or sacred image. 3. bobbed (of hair).

tolak [KK], repelling; keeping off; rejecting; to subtract; ~ *bara,* ballast; ~ *bala,* a propitiatory offering against misfortune; *~an,* to push away; *menolakkan,* id.; *cabang penolak,* a ploughshare; *ber~,* to start out, commence a journey (probably because in the old days practically all journeys had to be by boat); *ber~,* to push off; *ber~ pinggang,* arms akimbo; *ber~ ansur,* to compromise, to give-and-take; *~-tarik,* opposing one another, pulling in opposite directions, as influences, ideas; ~ *tepi,* to put aside; to ignore; 'to say nothing of', even if — is not taken into account; ~ *sebelah,* apart from, not including.

toleh [KK], *menoleh,* a side-look; *menoleh ke belakang,* to look back; *menolehkan muka,* to turn (his, her) head; *per~an hari,* the turning point in the sun's course (when it seems to descend precipitately).

toleran [KS], tolerant; *~si,* tolerance.

tolok [KN], matching; a peer or equal; *tidak ber~,* matchless; *tiada ~-bandingnya,* id.

tolol [KS], thick-headed, stupid; *orang ~,* blockhead, esp. of a man so acts without thinking; a variant of *tolo; ke~an,* stupidity.

tolong [KK], aid, assistance; favour, mercy, help; *~an,* assistance; *menolong,* to help; *penolong,* an assistant; *~!,* help me, so, in effect, please!

tom [KN], (Dutch) the bridle; *tail ~,* the reins.

toman [KN], *ikan ~,* a murrel *(Channa micropeltes).*

tombak [KN], a spear, a pike, a halberd; ~ *benderang,* spears with horsehair attached to them (as emblems of rank); ~ *kerajaan,* State spear; ~ *rambu,* a spear with a fringe or tassel under the spear-point; ~ *sayang,* a gaff for close-hauling a sail; ~ *sagang,* a sheerlegs, a crane; *ber~-~an,* to fight each other with lances.

tombol [KN], a knob, e.g., on a door; *ikan* ~ *mas,* a fish *(Thymnus thunnina).*

tombong [KN], 1. a lump, a knob; ~ *nyiur,* the seed-bud of a coconut. 2. arrogant; = *sombong.*

tomong [KN], a short squat gun, a sort of howitzer.

tompok [KN], a patch, as of ground, colour or clouds; a small heap; *bert~-~,* mottled; in small heaps; *kucing ~,* a tabby cat.

toncit [KN], a tuft of hair, small queue; '*Benggali ~',* cry of rude boys to Sikhs.

tong [KN], (Dutch) a tun, tub, barrel; ~ *sampah,* dust-bin; ~ *kosong berbunyi nyaring,* (prov.) empty vessels make the most sound.

tonggak [KN], 1. a snag. 2. a straight upright shoot coming from the roots, e.g., of the bamboo or mangrove tree; ~ *batu,* an upright boulder; a pillar, a megalith or menhir; ~ *hidup saya,* the prop, mainstay, of my life. 3. to empty out.

tonggang [KK], to invert, e.g., a bottle; a variant of *tonggeng.*

tonggek [KS], jutting out (of the posterior); *men~-~kan punggung',* to stick out the behind.

tonggeng [KK], lift the posterior (as in leap-frog); to invert a vessel to drain it; ~ *buyung,* aslant.

tonggok [KK], *ber~,* heap; *se~,* a heap; a pile; *ter~,* standing out as (an eminence); *Pak ~,* derisive nickname for anyone who sits lumpishly, contributing nothing to the discussion.

tonggong [KK], heaping up — cf. **tonggok**.

Tongkah [KN], 1. ~ (or *Pukit*), the capital of the Thai western States; also called in Malay *Hujung Salang* (Junk Ceylon, as anglicised); *relau* ~, a common type of smelting-furnace. 2. *papan* ~, a plank used to make one's way over mud-flats; 3. *menongkah air*, to travel against the current. 4. to lengthen a garment by sewing on a piece at the top.

tongkan [KN], a movable trap door of a Malay house.

tongkang [KN], a barge, a lighter, a very large open boat.

tongkat [KN], a vertical prop, a crutch, a walking stick; propping up from below; ~ *ketiak*, a crutch; *menongkat*, to sustain, to prop up; *~-enam-sembilan*, Kel. a short truncheon or cosh; *tinggi menongkat langit*, tall enough to prop the sky, abnormally tall, 'veritable Atlas'; ~ *waren*, a constable's truncheon; *ber~an*, supported by, depending on.

tongkeng [KN], 1. the rump; *tulang* ~, the coccyx; *di~*, behind. 2. *bunga* ~, the Tonkin creeper *(Pergutaria minor)*.

tongkol [KN], a knob; a roundish lump, or cob, or clod, or hank (of thread); *mas* ~, nugget gold; *ikan* ~, a tunny.

tongong [KS], slow of wit.

Tongsan [KN], Ch. China.

tongtong [KN], a hollow log or a large bamboo hung up as a sort of gong, struck to summon people to work or prayer or as an alarm; also ~ and *ke~*.

tonil [KN], Ind. the stage; a play.

tonjol [KN], a bulge, a protuberance; *ber~*, to bulge; *menonjol keluar*, to bulge out, e.g., as eyes; *menonjolkan muka*, to poke one's head out; *menonjolkan*, to bring forward, thrust into attention; *menonjol-nonjolkan diri*, to push oneself forward, to brag.

tonton [KK], Ind. *menonton*, to look at, watch (a spectacle); cf. **nonton** and **tuntun**. 2. *memper~kan*, show, éxhibit; *~an*, something that is seen or watched.

tonyok [KK], rubbing, scrubbing; rooting (as a pig); *si~*, is sometimes used jocularly for 'pig'; Mr Rooter.

top [KN], 1. a vessel with very bluff bows; *layar* ~, a lug-sail with a long yard. 2. ~- ~ = *tiba-tiba*, see *tiba*.

topang [KN], a forked support, a forked or angular prop; *layar* ~, a fore-sail; ~ *basikal*, the stand of a bicycle; *ber~ dengan tangan*, supporting oneself on one arm, as when rising from a recumbent position; *ber~ dagu*, chin in hand.

topekong [KN], Ch. a Chinese joss.

topeng [KN], masked Javanese dancers; a mask.

topes [KN], a precipitously sloping bank.

topi [KN], Hind. a sun-hat, a hat generally.

topong [KN], a small bag for holding *belacan*.

torak [KN], 1. *anak* ~, the spool (in weaving); *batang* ~, the spool rod. 2. *ubi* ~, a kind of potato. 3. a small cuttle-fish. 4. a rolling pin; *menorak*, to roll out (dough); *papan penorak*, board for such rolling, pastry board; *bulat* ~, cylindrical.

Toran [KN], Pers. Tartary, Turkestan.

torang [KN], the knot at the corner of a mesh.

toreh [KK], = *turis; penoreh*, a rubber-tapper.

torek [KN], a running at the ears; a buzzing in the ears, presaging deafness.

totok [Ks], full-blooded; = *jati; dia anak desa* ~, he's a pure country boy.

toya [KS], physical weakness.

toyah [KN], a long pole used as a thrusting-pole in fighting.

tradisi [KN], tradition, customs; *ber~*, with a tradition; *masyarakat tradisional*, traditional society.

trafik [KN], traffic; *polis trafik*, traffic police.

tragedi [KN], tragedy.

traktor [KN], tractor.

trampil [KS], skillful; *ke~lan*, skill.

triwarsa [KN], three years.

triwulan [KN], quarterly.

tua [KS]. old, matured, aged, senior; deep (of colouring); sometimes, fully formed and ready to pick, though not necessarily ripe, as bananas; *orang ~ suntuk,* old man trying to be young; *orang ~,* an old man; the head of a family; a village elder; *orang ~ saya,* 'my old man'; *ke~,* a headman; person in charge; *pak ~,* an uncle older than one's father; *merah ~,* deep red, dark red; *Yang Diper~,* president (as of a club); *penge~,* senior in charge; president; *menge~i,* to head; *dia menge~i delegasi itu,* he headed the delegation; *Ke~ Turus Tentera Bersenjata,* Chief of Staff of the Armed Forces; *Ke~ Negara,* Head of State.

tuah [KN], luck; lucky chance; *ber~,* lucky, luck-bringing; *~ ada, untung tak ada,* he has luck but doesn't profit by it; strictly speaking, *~* is the share of good luck which each man is fated to have, his destiny; *tak tertikam ~ oleh berani,* destined good luck cannot be destroyed by valour.

tuai [KN], a peculiar cutter used for reaping padi (a few stalks only being cut at a time); *menuai,* [KK], to cut padi with this; *penuaian,* harvesting.

tuak [KN], fermented spirit made from palmjuice, toddy.

tual [KK], sever, cut into lengths.

tuala, Port. a napkin; a towel; *~ mandi,* a bath-towel.

tualang [KN], *pokok ~,* a large jungle tree, remarkable for its grey-green foliage and stately appearance; it is said to be particularly favoured as a home for bees; hence, *ber~,* to 'swarm' (of bees); to range, to wander; *pe~,* wanderer, so, unprincipled person, opportunist, e.g. *pe~ politik,* political opportunist; mere adventurer, knave; *pe~an,* knavery; *teksi pe~,* 'pirate' taxi.

tuam [KK], to apply a hot dry poultice to a diseased part, to mould (as soft clay for pots); *~ sejuk,* cold compress; *~* is sometimes used (fig.) for 'give it to someone hot and strong'.

tuan [KN], Mr. a mode of address to men of some position; used by lovers of both sexes to one another; an owner; *~ kedai,* shopkeeper; *~ rumah,* householder; sometimes, host; *~ punya,* your; an owner; *ber~kan,* to take service under; to acknowledge (someone) as a master; *dewan per~an,* House of Lords; *ke~an,* ascendancy, dominating position (in the State); *~ku,* a title used in addressing a reigning price; in Perak used in addressing the *Raja Muda* and *Raja Bendahara; yang diper~,* the supreme lord; *yam~,* id.; *Yang Diper~ Agung,* the Paramount Ruler of Malaysia; *Yang Diper~ Negara,* the Head of State (in Singapore).

tuang [KK], to pour out, empty out a liquid; to cast (metal); *menuangkan,* id.; *~~,* a bamboo blown into noisily by way of signal; also *te~,* a siren; *te~ udara,* microphone; radio; *besi ~an,* castiron; *wang ~an,* metal money, coins; *~* is used locally (sl.) for 'bolt', run off.

tuap [KN], a splint of rattans.

tuar [KN], a riverine fish-trap made of inturning thorns.

tuas [KN], 1. a lever; to apply leverage in torture. 2. to skedaddle. 3. Pen. a form of fishing in which branches of foliage are anchored so as to attract fish by the food and shelter they provide (the fishing is done by hook and line — cf. **unjam**).

tuat [KN], 1. a mark indicating a good fishing ground. 2. *ke~,* a wart.

tuba [KN], a plant *(Derris elliptica),* with a root the sap of which has stupefying properties and is used in fishing; *menuba,* to fish in this way; *~ tikus,* arsenic.

tubagus [KN], a title of nobility.

tuban [KN], *~~,* the discharge preceding delivery; the liquor amnii.

tubi [KK], to devote, give oneself up heart and soul to anything; *ber~~,* persistently.

tubin [KN], 1. a fish-trap with a falling

door; also *terubin*. 2. the fourth day
hence.

tubing [KK], to droop slightly.

tubir [KN], a steep river-bank or shelf
under water; *ber~*, shelving away; *~
mata*, eye-socket.

tubruk [KN], to spring on, leap on;
ber~an, to have a collision.

tubuh [KN], the body in the anatomical
sense; the bodily frame; the seat of
physical sensation; *panas rasa ~ku*, I
feel warm; *bekas ~*, a garment that has
actually been worn; *berse ~*, having
carnal intercourse; *batang ~*, trunk of
the body; *~ kapal*, the hull of a ship;
nama ~, personal name (as opposed to
title); *tengah ~ lalu*, past middle age;
ber~, to flesh up, fill out; *~ kerajaan*,
constitution; *per~an*, organisation;
~kan, to set up, establish; *Per~an
Kebangsaan Melayu Bersatu*, United
Malay National Organisation, commonly called *Pekembar (Umno)*; *undang-undang ~*, rules of the constitution; *per~an kesihatan sedunia*, World
Health Organisation; *~* is sometimes
used to mean a person, 'a body'.

tubuk [KN], a wooden lance for spearing
teripang.

tuding [KK], 1. aslant; at an angle; a 'pulling' stroke in contradistinction to a
straight drive. 2. Ind. *menuding
kepada*, to point at; cf. **tuduh**.

tuduh [KK], accusation (esp. slanderous);
blame; *menuduh*, to accuse; *~* basically carries the idea of 'point the finger at' and so can be used in the sense
of, guess which, pick the right one;
~an, allegation; *~an itu tidak beralasan*,
the allegation was groundless.

tudung [KN], a veil; a hollow cover; covering up; *~ saji*, a large dish-cover; *siput
~*, a shell *(Trochus pyramis)*; *~an*, a
veil; *~i* or *~kan*, to enshroud; *ber~
lingkup*, closely veiled.

tugal [KN], a pointed stick used for making holes in the ground in which rice-
seed is dropped; *padi ~*, rice so
planted; *~an*, Kel., Treng. unirrigated

rice-fields (opposed to *cedungan*).

tugar, = *tugal*.

tugas [KN], Ind. task, duty, function; *~kan*,
to assign duties; *ber~*, on duty; *masa
ber~*, in working hours; *pe~*, official;
person who is given the duty of.

tugu [KN], monument, pillar, esp. memorial stone; *~ peringatan perang*, war
memorial.

Tuhan [KN], God; *ke~an*, divinity, belief in
God.

tuhfat [KN], Ar. *~ul-ajnas*, 'a gift of miscellanies' — a term used in polite letter-writing to describe the letter and
the gifts which theoretically accompany it.

tuhmah, [KN], slander, suspicion.

tui [KN] 1. a tree *(Ixonanthes icosandra)*.
2. Ch. the pool (gaming).

tuil [KN], a lever for tilting up a heavy
mass; to carry a burden over the shoulder on a stick with another stick over
the other shoulder to support it; to
lever up; *alas penuil*, fulcrum for leverage.

tujah [KK], to thrust, poke.

tujang [KN], prop, support, aid; shank;
ber~, (sl.) to 'bolt', run off; a variant of
tunjang.

tuju [KN], pointing at; making for; *se~*, in
harmony, agree; *~i*, to aim at, to make
for; *menuju*, to point towards; to injure
by turning evil spirits upon; *~ lubang*, a
game played with marbles or like
objects; *penuju*, lines of stakes for di-
verting fish, etc., into a trap; *~an*, aim,
objective, idea.

tujuh [KBil], seven.

tukal [KN], 1. a measure for thread; = 16
skeins; a hank; *se~*, united, mutually
assisting. 2. a dent or mark left on the
skin, the skin not being broken.

tukang [KN], a craftsman, a skilled
workman; *~ besi*, a blacksmith; *~ cap*, a
printer; *~ cukur*, a barber; *~ kasut*, a
shoemaker; *~ kayu*, a carpenter; *~ mas*,
a goldsmith; *~ tilik*, a fortune-teller; *~
gigi*, a (wayside) dentist (otherwise
doktor gigi); *~ roti*, baker; *~ lelong*, auc-

tioneer; ~ *silap mata,* conjuror; ~ *jahit,* tailor; ~ *kebun,* gardener; ~ *sukat,* surveyor; ~ *ukur,* id.; ~ *paip,* plumber; ~ *air,* water-carrier, scullion; ~ *letrik,* electrician; ~ *cat,* house-painter; ~ *batu,* mason; ~ *rumah,* id.; ~ *pelan,* draughtsman; ~ *ubat,* druggist; ~ *wang,* cashier; ~ *gambar,* photographer; ~*an,* piece of handi-work, artifact; instruments of craft; *per~an,* handicraft, craftsmanship, 'a trade'; *sekolah per~an,* a trade school; *burung* ~, a name sometimes given (owing to its note) to the night-jar and sometimes to the coppersmith bird; ~ is also used figuratively; e.g., ~ *hasut,* an agitator; ~ *ekor,* one who 'follows the crowd', has no initiative or ideas of his own; ~ *sah,* a 'rubber-stamp', a per-son in nominal authority.

tukar [KK], to change, substituting one thing for another; *ber~,* to exchange; ~ *menukar,* to barter; *secara per~an ba-han,* on a system of bartering raw materials; *ber~ tangan,* to change hands (as on a sale); *menukar-balikkan,* to transpose.

tukas [KK], *menukas,* N.S. to accuse of immorality; to accuse without evi-dence.

tukil [KN], a bamboo vessel for carrying liquid, = *tabung.*

tukik [KK], *menukik,* to plunge or fly downwards.

tukul [KN], 1. a small hammer; *menukul,* to hammer, strike with a hammer. 2. a log.

tukun [KN], a sunken rock — cf. **tokong.**

tul [KN], Eng. a thole-pin.

tuladan [KN], an example (to follow); also *tauladan;* cf. **simpadan.**

tulah [KN], Ar. calamity consequent on sacrilege or extreme presumption; *ke~an,* the curse resulting from such conduct; ~ *papa,* the curse of poverty generally.

tulang [KN], a bone; ~ *buku lali,* ~ *Alah 'mak,* (coll.) ankel; ~ *kucing,* funny-bone; ~ *belakang,* the dorsal vertebrae; ~ *belikat,* the shoulder-blade; ~ *dayung,* id.; ~ *caping,* the xiphoid process; ~ *kering,* the tibia; ~ *betis,* fibula; ~ *rusuk,* the ribs; ~ *selangka,* the collar-bone; ~ *sulbi* or ~ *tongkeng,* the coccyx; ~ *rawan,* the sternum, breast-bone; also used for cartilage; ~ *muda,* cartilage; *bertindih* ~, the 'closest' method of stiching thatch; *bertemu* ~, the next closest; — cf. **karang;** *berat-~,* lazy; *ringan-~,* energetic; *lidah tak ber~,* unreliable, empty talker; *kuasa* ~ *empat kerat,* the power of the four bones (of hands and feet), i.e. the bare hands (of an anarmed person); *angin sejuk sampai ke~ hitam,* a cold wind penetrating to the marrow of the bones; *penyakit dalam* ~, arthritis; *penyakit sendi,* id.

tular [KK], Ind. infectious, contagious; *penyakit menular,* infectious disease; ~*an,* infection.

tulat [KN], the third day after this, the day after the day after tomorrow.

tulen [KS], genuine; pure, unalloyed.

tuli [KS], 1. deaf; *menulikan,* to deafen. 2. ~*~,* a loop of rattan or metal wire tied on the stem of a keris-sheath, now as an ornament only.

tulis [KK], painting, figuring; *juru~,* a scribe, a clerk; ~*an,* writing; *menulis,* to write; *penulis,* writer; *ter~,* written; ~*an ringkas,* shorthand, us. *teringkas; gori-san teringkas,* symbols used in short-hand.

tulus [KS], sincere; earnest; ~ *ikhlas,* hon-est and sincere; *ke~an hati,* honesty.

tuma [KN], a small insect, a sort of louse; used as a synonym for the infinitely tiny.

tumang [KN], a wooden tent-peg, a teth-ering peg; an arrangement of three sticks for cooking.

tumbang [KK], to fall heavily; toppling down (as a large tree); *menum-bangkan,* to overthrow; ~ *harapan,* lost hope.

tumbas [KS] to the bitter end, to the last drop — a strong expression of completion.

tumbuh [KK], sprouting up, springing up (of any growth); to grow (of plants); ~ ~an, plants generally; ke~an, an eruptive disease; small-pox; ber~, to sprout up (of plants).

tumbuk [KK], to strike a pounding blow; ~ lada, a small dagger; ~ rusuk, (fig.) to bribe; ~ rusuk biar senak, if you give a man a punch in the ribs, see that he is winded, i.e., if you give a bribe, make sure that it is enough; ke~an, a company, troop; an army division; penumbuk, a fist; a punch; penumbuk besi, an iron knuckle-duster.

tumis [KK], to cook in oil and seasoning.

tumit [KN], heel (of the foot); ~ tiang, the trunk of a mast.

tumpah [KK], spilling; shed; ~ ruah, poured out; tempat ~ darah, birthplace; ~kan, to pour out; to empty out; per~an darah, spilling of blood in war, battle.

tumpang [KK], menumpang, to lodge; to take shelter with; to take advantage, e.g. of a lift in a car, of another's learning, etc.; penumpang, a passenger; saya hendak menumpang tahu, will you be so kind as to tell me; please, I just want to know; menumpang menanak, to have the privilege of someone else's fire for cooking; menumpang bercakap, to join in a conversation; saya nak ~ bertanya, I venture to ask; menumpang hidup pada, to depend on for livelihood.

tumpar [KK], Pk. dead.

tumpas [KK], crashed badly; destroyed; exterminated; failed disastrously, as an enterprise; menumpaskan, crush, destroy; ke~an, defeat.

tumpat [KS], filled up (of a hollow); solid; menumpat, to stop up an orifice; menumpatkan, pack tightly; ter~, full to the brim; ~-mampat, crammed.

tumpu [KN], having a footing on; resting on; melompat berse~, to jump from a take-off place; ber~, to have a footing somewhere; to have a place to 'take

off' from; tidak menumpu laut, have no footing on the sea; ber~ dengan..., adjacent to, marching with; ~an mata, cynosure of all eyes; tempat ~an, base, centre of operations; ~an harapan, centre of one's hopes; ~an kemarahan, target for anger, for abuse; ~an ejekan, target for ridicule, butt; ~an perhatian, focus of attention; tempat ~an ramai, popular resort; menumpukan fikiran pada, to concentrate attention or thoughts on; menumpukan perhatian pada, to concentrate attention on; menumpukan kesalahan pada, to fix the blame on; tempat ber~kan kaki, take-off place; ~an kaki, id.; ber~ dahulu baharulah melompat, i.e., look before you leap; menumpukan mata dan telinga kepada, to give one's whole attention to; menumpukan harapan kepada, to base one's hopes on, rely on.

tumpul [KS], blunt; pisau ~, blunt knife; fikirannya ~, (idiom) he is dull; ke~an, bluntness, dullness; menumpulkan, to blunt.

tumputinggi [KN], vertex.

tumpur [KS], loss by leakage; frittering away; destroyed; ruined; menumpurkan, to destroy, to ruin.

tumu [KN], a sea-shore tree (Diymocarpus crinitus).

tumus [KS], ter~!, falling on the face; sprawling.

Tun [KN], an old Malay title, revived as a title for the holders of the Orders S.M.N. and S.S.M., see darjah.

tuna [KS], 1. Skr. a wound; ter~, wounded = luka. 2. a kind of eel.

tunai [KN], ready (of money); cash down; wang ~, ready money; menunaikan, to realise (one's hopes); to carry out (policy); to implement (a promise); menunaikan fardhu Haji, to perform the duty of going on pilgrimage to Mecca.

tunak [KN], attachment, devotion (as of a retainer); steady, direct, of gaze.

tunakarya [KK], unemployed, ke~an

[KN], unemployment.

tunam [KN], the match applied to a cannon.

tunang [KN], fiance, troth, betrothal; *peluru ~*, a bullet pledged (by sorcery) to take effect; *ber~*, to be engaged to be married; *per~an*, engagement.

tunas [KN], a young shoot sprouting from a branch; *membuang ~*, to prune a tree of shoots; *~ harapan*, ray of hope.

tunasila [KN], *tunasusila*, immorality, prostitution, immoral.

tunda [KK], 1. towing; *sampan ~*, a dinghy; *pancing ~*, to troll for fish; *tali ~*, a tow-line; *kapal ~*, a tug. 2. to succeed, follow up, as a drink after a meal; to be delayed, fail to make progress.

tunduk [KK], stooping, bowing, lowering the head; (fig.) to give way, submit; *~ menyembah*, to bow in salutation; *~ tengadah*, to look down and then up (as a man trying to compose a letter); *menundukkan kepala*, to bow the head; *dia menundukkan lawannya*, he had defeated his rival; *ilmu penunduk*, a magic art for procuring the submission of a person.

tundun [KN], the mons Veneris.

tundung [KK], banish from a house, a country.

tungau [KN], a black sand-flea.

tunggak [KK], 1. stump of a felled tree. 2. Ind. arrears; *menunggak*, (to be) in arrears.

tunggal [KBil], sole, single, one; *anak ~*, an only child; *babi ~*, a solitary boar; *Sang Yang ~*, the one God; in grammar *~* is used to mean singular.

tunggang [KK], 1. astride; riding; *menunggang kuda*, to ride. 2. upside down; *~ langgang*, (run) helter, skelter; head over heels; disordered, haphazard; *~ balik*, upside down; *~ tunggit*, bowing very deep as in prayer; bobbing up and down; *~kan*, to invert, as a glass; cf. **tonggeng**. 3. determined, decided; *hatinya ~ nak pergi*, he was determined to go.

tunggu [KK], *~i*, to watch over; *menunggu*, to wait for; *ber~*, to be on the watch; *di~ kedatangannya*, waiting for his arrival; *penunggu*, a watchman; penunggu pintu, a porter; *hantu penunggu*, a tutelary spirit; *dipilih menunggu*, to draw a bye in a competition.

tunggul [KN], 1. the stump of a tree; butt; *~-~* or *te~*, the upstanding stump of a rainbow (believed to be portentous); *~* is used (fig.) to mean a mere stump, a 'stick'; *diam menunggul*, to remain stupidly silent. 2. a flag-staff; a standard. 3. *penunggul*, a propitiatory offering given as an indemnity or a guarantee (e.g., a hostage) to a victor. 4. *penunggul*, a heavy lump of wood to which an animal is tethered to prevent him running away; probably from 1.

tungkap [KK], tongue-tied, dumbfounded, silent through nervousness; opening the mouth and saying nothing; *~-haup*, 'finished off', 'done for'.

tungku [KN], an arrangement of stones constituting a primitive stove; *batu ~*, the stones so used; a hot stone used as a poultice; *~ kera*, a white-ants' nest; *~ lekar*, cooking stove and stand, i.e., cooking apparatus generally; used in Trengganu as a polite equivalent for 'wife'.

tungkul [KK], *menungkul*, surrender, bow.

tungkum [KK], *menungkum*, lie prone, invert.

tungkus [KS], deeply embedded in anything; *~-lumus*, deeply involved (in some effort); actively working; immersed in (some task, etc.).

tunjal [KK], a thrust downwards to give impetus to an upward motion.

tunjang [KK], a prop; the shank, of a leg; the tap-root, of a tree; *berjalan menunjang*, to trudge along, go on 'Shanks's mare'; *~an*, a support; also used for subsidy, allowance, given as aid; *mengayun ~*, to 'swing the shanks', trudge along; *ber~kan*, based on; relying on.

tunjuk [KK], ~*kan* or *menunjukkan,* to point out; to show; to display; ~ *perasaan,* to 'demonstrate', display organised expression of opinion; *menunjukkan mata,* to put in an appearance (as at a function); *menunjukkan pendirian,* to take a stand; *per~an,* a show, an exhibition; *per~, pe~,* guidance, indication, directions; a clue; a 'tip'; ~-*ajar,* to instruct by demonstration, to demonstrate how to do something; *memberi* ~-*ajar,* to give a demonstration; to teach, to advice; *menunjuk-nunjuk,* to 'show off'; cf. **telunjuk.**

tunjung [KN], the white water-lily.

tunku [KN], a variant of *tengku.*

tuntun [KK], 1. to lead, conducting, guiding — by means of some connecting link as a man leading a horse with a rope. 2. *menuntun,* to flock in crowds (to any performance); to visit (a spectacle); to 'see a show'; to view; *penonton,* visitor (as to a show), spectator; ~*an,* a spectacle, something worth looking at; *per~kan,* to display, exhibit to view; also *nonton* and *tonton.*

tuntung [KN], 1. a large river-turtle *(Callagur picta).* 2. a pointed tip.

tuntut [KK], *menuntut,* to claim; following after, intently seeking; ~ *ilmu,* to pursue knowledge, esp. religious for higher education; ~*an malu,* claim for damages for defamation; *penuntut,* student, candidate; *menuntut balas (bela),* to take revenge.

tunu [KK], 1. to burn up, consuming by fire. 2. to rub one thing against another; *ter~,* burnt up; *penunu,* person who burns.

tupai [KN], a generic name for squirrels; ~ *biji nangka,* the tupaia *(Tupaia ferruginea);* ~ *galang perahu,* Raffles' squirrel *(Sciurus rafflesi);* ~ *jinjang* = ~ *nandung;* ~ *kampung,* a squirrel *(Sciurus notalus);* ~ *nandung,* a squirrel *(Sciurus bicolor);* ~ *tanah,* a tree-shrew; ~ *kerawak,* a large hand-some parti-coloured squirrel; ~-~, cleats, as for a bar on a door; in Malay folk-lore the squirrel is regarded as having an exceptionally full sex-life, as is the rabbit in England; see *cula* and *tebuk; se pandai-pandai* ~ *melompat, ada kalanya jatuh ke tanah,* however smart the squirrel, sometimes, he falls to the ground, smartness fails at times or, in some contexts, pride goes before a fall; ~-~, cleats.

turap [KN], Ar. covering, plastering, lining; *ber~,* covered, plastered; *menurap jalan,* to surface a road with tar or other substance; *tepas ber~,* lath and plaster work.

turas, [KN] filtration; *menuras* [KK], straining through cloth.

turi [KN], Skr. *tikus* ~, a name given to the musk-shrews, = *tikus kesturi.* 2. *pohon* ~, a small tree bearing edible leaves.

turis [KK], scratch (a line or mark), to tap rubber; also *toreh.*

Turki [KN], Turkish.

turun [KK], coming down; dismount; to fall, of rain; to 'get up', of a storm or wind; ~*an* or *ke~an,* descent, origin; *ke~an Arab,* of Arab descent; ~ ~*an,* by descent; *adat* ~ *temurun,* long established custom; *menurun,* to decline, worsen, as business; a declivity; *umur dia dah menurun,* he's past the prime of life, 'going downhill'; *munurunkan,* to lower; *menurunkan harga,* to lower prices; *menurunkan harga diri,* stoop; *saya tidak menyangka dia akan menurukan harga diri demikian rendah,* I didn't think he'd stoop so low; *menurunkan tandatangan,* to affix one's signature; *dengan suara menurun,* in a lowered voice; *pe~kan,* to subjoin, place below (as a note); ~ *takhta,* to abdicate; *ke~an raja,* dynasty; *raja* ~- *Temurun,* hereditary ruler; *habis ke~annya,* died out, extinct; ~-*naik,* to fluctuate.

turus [KN], erect; the uprights of a fish-trap; ~ *negeri,* a pillar of the state; ~ is used (fig.) for the staff of a commander.

turut [KK], following in succession after; following advice or instruction; ~an, an example; menurutkan, to take anything as an example to follow; menurut bekas kaki, to track; pak ~, one who follows the crowd, a yes-man; ~ hati, doing as one pleases, following one's inclinations; ~ kalah, to give way, give in; ~ serta dalam, to take part in (e.g., a function); ~ tertawa, to join in the laugher; ber~-~, successively, one afer the other; tiga tahun ber~-~, three successive years; ~ is used for 'following suit' at cards; saya yang menurut perintah, your obedient servant; menurut jadual, on schedule; menurut rencana, according to plan; menururt urutan, in order; menurut perhitungan, by one's calculation; menurut-nurut, to follow or obey slavishly; tidak mahu menurut-nurut, 'won't be led'.

tus [KK], evaporated, dried up; ~kan, to draw off (water, as in cooking).

tusuk [KN], thin and sharp instrument used for picking and piercing needles; menusuk [KK], pierce, prick, stab something; menusuk-nusuk, to infuri-ate a person.

tut [KK], to graft (by creating new roots on a half-severed branch).

tutuh [KK], menutuh, to lop off the branches from the trunk after or before felling a tree; ~ lari, 'skedaddle'; ber~, Pk. to come to blows.

tutuk [KK], 1. to break or crush rattans into a sort of fibrous pulp; (fig.) to guzzle. 2. a tree (Hibiscus macrophyllus).

tutul [Ks], Jav. spotted; macan ~, leopard; = harimau bintang.

tutup [KK], closing up; shutting; covering; a lid or cover; setahun ~, a full year; ~ bumi, a weed (Elephantopus scaber); ~kan, to close, to shut up; menutupkan, id.; sidang ter~, a sitting (of Council) in camera; perbicaraan secara ter~, court hearing in camera; menutupi kesalahan, to cover up for; bagi penutupnya, finally, to wind up; ber~-rapat, tightly closed.

tutur [KN], utterance; ber~, to speak; ~an, speech, enunciation; delivery; ~-kata, id.; bahasa per~an, the spoken language; ber~, talk, converse.

U

uak [KN], *meng~*, to low; to bellow (of buffaloes).

uap [KK], *meng~*, yawn.

uar [KN], *~-~*, public proclamation; *~-~kan*, to proclaim, publish.

uba [KN], a sago-vat.

ubah [KK], change, alteration; *meng~kan*, to alter (a thing); *ber~*, to be altered; *meng~*, to transplant young rice; *tak ~ macam*, exactly like; *ber~-~*, changing from time to time; *tak dapat di~*, immutable; *~elok*, to renovate (house); *~suai*, to modify.

uban [KN], grey (of the hair); *ber~*, to be grey or grizzled; to age; *ciak ~* or *pipit ~*, the white-headed munia (*Amadina maja*).

ubang [KK], to cut a curved groove in a log so as to fit it to another; to cut notches or chips in a tree or log.

ubar [KK], *ber~*, to become loose; to open out; *ber~ hati*, to speak from the heart; *meng~*, to open out, unroll, uncoil.

ubat [KN], a drug, a medicine, a chemical, a magic simple, a philtre; 'medicine' in the sense of magic; *~ cacing*, a remedy for intestinal worms; *~ bedil*, gunpowder; *~ guna*, a philtre; *~ hati*, a solace, a comfort in distress; *~ cungkil*, vaccine; *~ tepung*, medicine in powder form; *~ cair*, medicine in liquid form; *~ pengasih*, love-philtre; *~ biji*, pills; *~ gosok*, liniment; *~ letupan*, explosives; *~ tidur*, sleeping-draught; *~ (tidur) berlebihan*, an over-dose (of sleeping-draught); *~ tawar jampi*, healing spells; *tukang ~*, a druggist; *meng~kan*, to apply medicine to; to treat; *meng~i*, id.; *peng~*, a remedy; *ber~*, to receive treatment; *tidak ter~*, incurable.

ubi [KN], a generic name for yams and tuberous roots; *~ kentang*, the common potato (*Solanum tuberosum*); *~ kayu*, tapioca; *~ keledek*, sweet potato; *~ halia*, artichoke; *~ keladi*, yam; *meng~-~kan*, to 'work on' a stubborn person so as to soften him; *~ nasi*, *~ jinjang*, the common yam (*Discorea alata*); *~ pasir* (*Discorea pentaphylla*); *diam ~*, to be silent but still mentally active; *ikan ~*, a murrel (*Channa lucius*).

ubin [KN], *batu ~*, a floor-tile; also hard granitic stone for road-metal.

ubun [KN], *~-~*, the crown of the head, the fontanel.

ubur [KN], *~-~*, a large jelly-fish; *payung ~-~*, a fringed umbrella.

ucap [KK], *meng~*, to utter; prayers (give thanks to God); to make a speech; *meng~ syukur*, to give thanks; *meng~ tasbih*, to tell one's beads; *peng~an*, *~an*, speech; elocution, oral delivery, enunciation; *meng~* by itself is used to mean 'to ejaculate', a prayer or invocation; *~an perpisahan*, farewell speech.

uda [KN], = *muda;* it is used as a familiar name for fourth or fifth son.

udam [KS], dulled; faded (of colouring); dimmed (of brilliancy).

udang [KN], a generic name for prawns and shrimps; *~ galah*, the crayfish; *~ bari-bari*, a small prawn appearing seasonally in shoals off the East coast and used for making *belacan; ~ geragau*, a very small shrimp; *~ lobok*, the prawn; *~ sungai*, the freshwater prawn; *raja ~*, a name given to kingfishers in the south and to large sand-pipers in the north of the Peninsula; *mata ~*, pop-eyed; *~ kering*, dried shrimp; *ada ~ di sebalik batu*, there's a prawn behind the stone, i.e., look out; there's more in this than meets the eye; in Malay the prawn often typifies stupidity; *seperti ~, tahi di kepala*, to be heavy in debt;

otak ~, stupid; ~ *tak sedarkan diri bongkok,* the prawn doesn't realise that it is humped, met. for complacence; *banyak ~ banyak garam,* rhyming slang for *banyak orang banyak ragam,* temperaments vary; also *hudang.*

udani [KN], a title.

udap [KN], ~-~*an,* ingredients of all sorts that go to make up a salad.

udara [KN], Skr. the atmosphere; the heavens; *tempat hampa ~,* a vacuum; *keadaan ~,* the state of the weather; *pertukaran (tukar) ~,* ventilation; *lubang ~,* ventilator; *corong ~,* ventilation shaft, as on a ship; *pesawat ~,* aeroplane; *angkatan ~,* air force; *peng~an,* aeration.

udarakasa [KN], atmosphere.

udi [KS], ill-luck.

udik [KN], upstream.

udut [KK], *meng~,* to smoke cigarette; *peng~,* a smoker.

ufti [KN], Skr. tribute; also *upeti.*

ufuk [KN], Ar. the horizon.

ugahari [KS], Skr. fair, even, equal, parity; *teman yang ~,* a friend on an equal social footing; a modest friend.

ugama [KN], Skr. creed, religion, also *igama* and *agama; beragama,* with a religion, religious.

ugut [KK], *meng~,* to menace, frighten; to intimidate, to threaten; ~-~ *beruk,* threats of the pig-tailed monkey (which chatters furiously), i.e., mere bluff.

uik [KK], *meng~,* to quack; sound of vomitting.

uit [KK], to move slightly.

uja [KK], *meng~,* give encouragement, support, hope, arouse anger, infuriate.

ujang [KN], name used to address a son, boy.

ujar [KN], Skr. utterance, speech, saying; ~-*nya,* he (or they) said.

uji [KK], to test, applying a touchstone to anything; *batu ~,* a touchstone; ~*an,* a test; *berlari meng~ masa,* to do a timed run; ~*an akal,* intelligence test; *tabung ~,* test tube; *peng~,* tester.

ukik [KN], a game played with coins.

ukir [KK], to engrave; incise patterns; carve; ~*an,* carving; ~ *kencana,* carvings on gold; *peng~,* carver, engraver.

ukup [KN], perfuming (cloth, etc.) with incense; *peng~* or *per~an,* the frame over which the cloth is laid and under which incense is burnt.

ukur [KN], linear measurement; *meng~,* to measure; *tukang ~,* a surveyor; ~*an,* measurement, size, as of a shoe; ~*an saku,* pocket size; ~*an hawa,* climatic temperature; *tak ber~,* unlimited, issued without stint, as rations; *ber~an,* of a measurement (length) of.

ulam [KN], leaves, herbs, fruits, etc. that is eaten raw with rice.

ulama [KN], Ar. learned men generally; one learned in the Scriptures; the plural of *alim.*

ulang [KKtr], repetition of action; ~ *tahun,* anniversary; ~*kan,* to repeat; *ber~,* repeatedly; ~-*aling,* backwards and forwards; *hari ~ tahun,* anniversary; *mahkanah ~ bicara,* Appeal Court; *pelawanan ~an,* return match; ~ *kaji,* review, reconsideration; *kursus ~ kaji,* refresher course; ~ *periksa,* to revise, re-examine; ~*an cetak,* a reprint.

ulap [KN], ~-~, broth made of coconut-milk and yam *(Colocasia antiquorum).*

ular [KN], a generic name for snakes, e.g., ~ *sawa,* a python; ~ *sawa cindai,* reticulated python; ~ *tedung senduk,* a cobra; ~ *danu,* Ked. a rainbow; ~ *naga,* a dragon; ~ *kapak,* the pitvipre; ~ *tedung selar,* the hamadryad; ~ *selimpat,* the sea-snake; ~ *bakau,* the large spotted viper; ~ *katang tebu,* the banded kriat; ~ *lidi,* the painted bronze-back snake; ~ *sawa tikus,* the common rat-snake; ~ *cintamani gajah,* the Penang temple-viper; ~ *pucuk,* the green whip-snake; ~-~, a pennon, a streamer; ~ *jangan disangka keli,* don't mistake a snake for a catfish, i.e., appearances may be misleading and dangerous.

ulas [KN], a covering, wrapper, ~*an,* id.; *se ~ durian,* a durian pip with the flesh on it; ~*an,* analysis, review; commentary, comments; ~*an selari,* running commentary; ~*kan,* to analyse, review, comment; *peng*~, a commentator; *meng*~, to cover envelope; to comment.

ulat [KN], a generic name for a number of worms, a maggot; ~ *bulan,* millipede; ~ *bulu,* a hairy caterpillar; ~ *sutera,* the silkworm; *kaki kena* ~ *air,* 'Singapore foot'; *macam* ~, crowded with people; *ber*~, with maggots.

uli [KK], knead, squeezing down, pressing or ramming down.

ulit [KK], ~*kan,* to sing (a person) to sleep; *meng*~*kan,* id.; *meng*~, to croon; to sing a lullaby; *peng*~, a lullaby.

ulung [KN], Ind. principal, leading, experienced (statesmen), smart and crafty (criminals).

uman [KK], ~-~, long-winded; a bore; *meng*~, to drag on a story monotonously.

umang [KN], ~-~, a hermit-crab.

umat [KN], Ar. people, mankind; follower of a certain religion.

umbai [KN], *ter*~, dangling, hanging down loosely.

umbang [KN], ~ *tali,* a sling.

umbang [KN], 1. colossal; *naga* ~, a great sea-dragon. 2. *meng*~, to make a trip, voyage (of a ship). 3. *meng*~, to lie moored between two cables; *meng*~*ambing,* to rock gently to-and-fro, to float lazily, (met.) to dilly and dally; swaying this way and that; sometimes, wave-tossed; (fig.) in an uncertain position; ~-*ambingkan,* to shake to impair stability.

umbara [KK], = *kembara.*

umbi [KN], the roots of a tree or a tooth; *akar* ~, id; 'to the very roots'.

umbuk [KN], N.S. *meng*~, to coax, wheedle.

umbut [KN], 1. the soft heart of the upper portion of a palm; the palm-cabbage. 2. *ikan* ~-~, a freshwater fish, *Cyprinid* genus *(Barynotus microlepis).* 3. *meng*~, to 'get to the heart of things' (in an investigation); *meng*~ *nyawa,* to slay.

umpama [KN], Skr. example, instance,

similar case; *se* ~, for instance; ~*an,* a proverb; ~*kan,* to liken to, to compare.

umpan [KN], bait; food to attract fish or animals; ~ *tekak,* an appetiser; *meng*~, *meng*~*i,* catch an animal, fish by using a bait; *kail sebentuk,* ~ *seekor,* you have only one hook and one (worm) as bait, i.e., husband your resources; ~ *peluru,* cannon-fodder.

umpat [KN], disparaging, evil-speaking, slandering; cursing; ~*i,* to revile; *meng*~, to be abusive; to slander.

umpil [KK], *meng*~, to lever up; to paddle (a canoe) by resting the paddle on the gunwale and levering outwards; *peng*~, a lever.

umpuk [KN], heap, pile; *ber*~, in heaps, *se*~ *batu,* a pile of stones.

umum [KS], 1. Ar. obscure, involved, complicated, difficult. 2. general, common, public; *pada* ~*nya,* generally; *perintah* ~, General Orders; *belum diketahui* ~, not yet generally known; *secara* ~, generalised (as criticism) not definte (place); *rapat* ~, a public meeting; *meng*~*kan,* to announce; *peng*~*an,* public announcement, proclamation, communique.

umur [KN], Ar. life; age (length of life); *lebih* ~, older, esp. over-age; *setengah* ~, middle-aged (but generally used to describe clothes, etc., which are part-worn); *separuh* ~, middle-aged (rather of people); *lalu separuh* ~, past middle age; *ber*~ *lebih,* older, 'of a certain age'; *panjang* ~, tenacious of life; *se*~ *hidup,* all one's life; *se*~*ku,* as long as I live; *kalau ada* ~ *saya,* if I live so long, if I am 'spared'.

unai [KS], soft, moist and odorous — as perfumed oil.

unam [KN], an edible shell-fish (*Murex* sp.).

uncang [KN], 1. ~-*uncit,* by driblets, by fits and starts; *menbayar* ~-*uncit,* to pay bit-by-bit. 2. a cloth slipknot for money; a pouch.

uncat [KK], lifting and lowering, moving a thing up and down as a bait before fish;

~-~, id.

undak [KK], *meng~*, not to make headway (of a ship); *laut peng~*, a choppy sea against which it is difficult to make headway; *~-andik*, vacillating.

undan [KN], 1. *burung ~*, the pelican *(Pelecanus philippensis)*. 2. *ber~*, to be protracted; to drag; to dawdle. 3. *ber~*, Pk. to look truculent.

undang [KN], 1. *~-~*, laws, statutes, ordinances, codified enactments; *~*, the title of the chiefs of Sungai Ujong, Rembau, Jelebu, Johol; *~-~ antara bangsa*, International Law; *majlis ~an*, Legislative Council; *per~an*, legislation; *~-~ tentera*, military law. 2. Ind. *meng~*, to invite; *~an*, an invitation.

undi [KK], lot; a die; *buang ~*, to cast lots; to cast a vote; *buah ~*, die, dice; *~an*, a lottery; an election, voting; *ber~an*, to take part in an election; *meng~*, to vote; draw lots, ballot; *peng~*, voters; *~an yang terbanyak*, a majority of votes; *bercabut ~*, to draw lots (with sticks of unequal length); *~ pemutus*, casting vote; *~ sulit*, secret ballot; *meluluskan satu ~ tidak percaya terhadap*, to pass a vote of no confidence in; *memancing ~*, to canvas for votes; *kertas ~*, a ballot paper.

undil [KN], a money-box; a money-bag.

unduk [KN], 1. *~-~*, the sea-horse *(Hippocampus* sp.). 2. *~-andal*, in swift succession.

undur [KN], 1. *meng~*, retreat, lose ground, to give way; *meng~kan diri*, to withdraw, to make good one's retreat; *meng~kan waktu*, to put back the time fixed for an event; *meng~kan*, to cause to retreat, repulse. 2. *~-~*, a sp. of insect — the ant-lion.

ungap [KK], *meng~*, to gasp for breadth.

ungar [KN], an edible salt-water fish; a snapper *(Lutlanus argentimaculatus)*.

unggas [KN], a bird; *~ dewata*, the bird of paradise; *~ angkasa*, birds that fly high up in the sky.

unggat [KS], 1. stiffly, erect. 2. *~-unggit*, to wobble about, as a table with legs of unequal length.

unggis [KK], *meng~*, to gnaw, to nibble; (fig.) to scrape open, to scrabble open (a hole); also *hunggis*.

unggul [Ks], Ind. superior, of highest standard; *ke~an*, superiority.

unggit = *ungkit*.

unggun [KN], a pile of rubbish for burning; a banked fire, a bonfire; a fire lit as a 'smudge' for insects; *men~*, to bank a fire; to make a 'smudge'.

ungkai [KK], *meng~*, untie, loosen, undone.

ungka [KN], a gibbon *(Hylobates lar* or *H. agilis)*.

ungkal [KS], obstinate; *dia ~ mendengar nasihat orang lain*, he turns a deaf ear to other people's advice.

ungkap [KK], 1. *ter~-~*, gasping with open mouth. 2. Ind. *meng~*, to express an idea; *~an*, a phrase, an expression.

ungkil [KK], *meng~*, to lever up — cf. **umpil**; *tidak dapat di~ dengan besi hangat*, inseparable.

ungkit [KK], bringing up again; raking up old stories; *ter~-~*, jogging up and down; see-saw motion; *meng~*, *jangan meng~ perkara lama*, don't bring up old issues.

Ungku = *Engku*.

ungkur [KK], *ber~-~an*, retreating in different directions; dispersing.

ungsi [KK], Ind. *meng~*, to flee; to migrate; *peng~*, migrants; refugees.

ungu [KN], purple; deep reddish-brown; rich dark colouring; *~ manis*, royal purple.

unifom [KN], uniform.

unik [KS], unique.

unit [KN], unit, thing or group that is complete in itself.

unjam [KK], *meng~*, 1. to thrust anything vigorously into the ground; *ter~*, firmly embedded, firmly fixed. 2. Kel., Treng., Pah. an arrangement of branches and leaves anchored with stones on a fishing-ground to afford shelter to fish; *buang ~*, to place this arrangement in position — cf. **tuas**.

unjap [KN], Ked. = *injap.*

unjuk [KK], offering (anything); putting (a thing) forward; *~kan* or *men~kan,* to hold out.

unjun [KK], lifting and lowering a bait in order to attract fish to it.

unjur [KK], to stretch out forwards; *bel~,* to stretch out one's legs (when sitting); *belum duduk, sudah bel~,* stretching out the legs before sitting down, i.e., hasty and ill-considered action; *meng~kan diri,* to stretch oneself out, as on a bed.

unsur [KN], Ind. basic material, element; *ber~kan agama,* having a religious element; characterised.

unta [KN], Hind. camel; *burung ~,* an ostrich.

untai [KS], hanging loosely, dangling; *ter~ ~,* hanging in strings; *~an kata,* a phrase.

untal [KS], 1. *~antil,* swaying loosely. 2. *se ~,* an armful; as of sticks, straw.

untang [K], pendulous, swaying, *~-anting,* id.

until [KN], *se~,* a small ball or pill; a small quantity; *ber~-~,* bit-by-bit; *meng~,* to work (e.g., clay) into pellets.

unting [KN], a bunch of rice plants for transplanting; a small skein of thread; a unit of measurement for thread.

untuk [KDpn], 1. share, allotted portion, for; *per~an,* fixed provision, government 'vote', allocation. 2. in order that...; with a view to...; for the purpose of...; for the benefit of....

untung [KN], gain, advantage; fortune; profit; destiny; *mendapat ~,* to derive profit; *bawa ~,* to put up with what comes, submit to fate; *mengadu ~,* try one's luck; *~ sagu,* second-best luck (sago being less desirable than rice); *~ batu tenggelam, ~ sabut timbul,* stone is fated to sink, coconut-husk to float (some are born unlucky, some are born lucky); *~ sekarung, rugi seguni,* a bag full of profit and a sackful of loss; an illusory profit, a Pyrrhic victory; *sistem cari ~,* the system of the profit incentive.

untut [KN], elephantiasis.

upacara [KN], ceremony; *~ perlantikan,* inaugural ceremony.

upah [KN], payment for service rendered; fee, wage, bribe; *~kan,* to engage a person's services; *meng~kan,* id.

upak [KK], 1. *meng~,* to stir up a smouldering heap of ashes; *meng~ api,* to revive a fire (by poking or stoking). 2. *~ apik,* inconsequent (of talk); mischievous or inconsistent talk.

upam [KK], *meng~,* to burnish, polish, give lustre to stones and metals.

upar [KK], Ind. *meng~,* to roll (e.g., dough) between the hands so as to make a ball; *meng~-ng~,* to rub gently.

upas [KN], Jav. poison generally; the poison of the *~* tree *(Antiaris toxicaria)* in particular; blood poison, esp. for darts.

upaya [KN], Skr. means, resources; effort, plan; *tak ada ~* or *tak ada daya ~,* destitute of all means; helpless; moneyless; *ber~,* try hard; *ke~an,* ability to do something.

upih [KN], the tough flower-sheaths of certain palms; *timba ~,* a bucket or dipper made of these sheaths. 2. *burung ~,* the Southern painted stork.

upik [KN], *si ~,* Miss So-and-so (of a girl whose name one does not wish to mention).

ura [KN], discussions, talks; proposal, suggestion, request; *ber~-~,* to talk over anything; to discuss the pros and cons.

urai [KS], loose, dishevelled, inadhesive; *mas ~,* gold dust; *~kan,* to undo, to unloosen, to explain; to analyse; *meng~,* to open out, to become loose, to unfold; *ter~,* undone, dishevelled (of hair).

urap [KN], *~an,* cosmetics; *ber~-~an,* to adorn oneself with cosmetics.

urat [KN], 1. nerve, sinew, fibre, vein, muscle; *~ belikat,* the dorsal muscles; *~ tanah,* a snake *(Typhlops* sp.); *salah ~,* a strained sinew; *~ sarap,* nerve-fibre; *~ nadi,* artery; *~* is used as a numeral co-efficient for bracelets, hairs, threads, etc. 2. Ar. *gila ~,* lascivious; *meng~,* to womanise; ~ here is connected with *a~*, q.v.

uri [KN], the afterbirth; *sangkut ~,* failure of the afterbirth to come away, adherent placenta; *~an,* a brazier's mould after use.

urung [KK], 1. crowding; *di~ semut,* covered with ants; *meng~,* swarming everywhere, as ants, flies. 2. *meng~,* to fail to make progress; *meng~kan,* to check, to cause to miscarry, to put off. 3. *mas ~,* iron pyrites.

urup [KN], *kedai ~~~,* a money-changers' shop; *meng~ wang,* to change money.

urus [KK], 1. rubbing, scrubbing, stroking — more refined than the word *gosok.* 2. *meng~kan,* to attend to, arrange, superintend, put right; *~an,* affairs, dealings; *ber~an,* engaged in, have (business etc.) dealings with; *peng~,* manager, superintendent; *tidak ter~,* neglected, untidy; *~an rumahtangga,* domestic management; *ber~,* establish contact in order to settle something.

urut [KK], to rub with the hands, massage, shampoo; *janggut di~,* a forked beard.

usah [KK], *tak ~,* needless; it is unnecessary; never mind; don't; *~kan,* so far from; = *jangankan.*

usaha [KN], Skr. diligence, industry; efforts, steps; *ber~,* industrious; *meng~kan diri,* to exert onese; *per~an tanah,* agriculture; *menumpukan ~ (dalam),* to bend one's energies (on); *melakukan ~,* to take steps; *menjalankan ~,* id.; *~wan,* industrialist, entrepreneur.

usai [KK], *~kan,* to set in order, arrange, as hair, or dress or affairs.

usam [KS], dull, tarnished (of metal).

usang [KS], shrivelled up internally (of grains of padi, etc.); *rumah ~,* an abandoned house (of which only the outer shell remains); arid, barren (of land); obsolete (of a word or a system); drawn, haggard (of face); rotted (of wood); worn, shabby (of clothes).

usap [KK], *meng~,* to apply a thin coating, e.g., of paint; to mop up; to rub gently, to stroke; *meng~~~,* to stroke and ca-

ress.

Usdik [KN], Ind. short for *undang-undang* 1945, *socialism ala Indonesia demokrasi terpimpin dan keperibadian,* i.e., the law of the Constitution 1945, Indonesian socialism, guided democracy and Indonesian personality.

usia [KN], skr. length of life, life; *sepanjang ~,* all one's life; *~ lebih tinggi,* older; *lagu lanjutkan ~ Baginda King,* the tune, 'God Save the King'.

usik [KK], *meng~,* to tease, chaff, worry with impertinent questions; to interfere with, molest; esp. of making improper advances to a woman; *ber~,* disturbed, teased; *~an,* teasing, *peng~,* teaser.

usir [KK], *meng~,* to pursue; to expel, to evict; *mereka meng~ seekor anjing liar,* they chase away a wild dog; *peng~an,* eviction.

uskup [KN], bishop; *ke~an,* bishopric; *~ agung,* archbishop.

usrah [KN], Ar. family, stock, esp. of a royal house.

usta [KN], Hind., Pen. a barber.

ustaz [KN], master, lord, religious teacher.

ustazah [KN], woman religious teacher.

usul [KN], 1. Ar. beginnings, origins — the plural of *asal; asal ~,* the antecedents or early history of anything; *~galur,* lineage, antecedents. 2. manner; *~ jijak,* bearing; *~ sifat,* ways; *~ menjunjukkan asal,* manners display descent. 3. request, proposal; *meng~kan,* to propose, 'move'; *~ perubahan,* proposed amendment; *kemukakan ~ tak yakin terhadap,* to bring forward a motion of no confidence in; *kemukakan ~ tak percaya terhadap,* id. 4. Kel. to question, make inquiries; *~ periksa,* thorough inquiries.

usung [KK], *ber~,* carried in a litter slung from a pole; *~an,* a litter; *meng~,* to carry on the shoulders or on a litter, etc.; *mereka meng~ jenazah,* they carried a corpse; *~an mayat,* bier.

usus [KN], Ind. intestine, gut, alimentary canal; *~ besar,* the large intestine; *~ buntu,* the appendix.

Uswah Hasanah, Ar. the good Exemplar, i.e. the Prophet and His ways.

utama [KS], 1. Skr. excellence, eminence; excellent, eminent; principal; *hasil ~,* principal (main) product; *gandum adalah hasil ~,* wheat is a staple product; *yang ter~,* the most eminent; *tuan yang ter~,* His Excellency; *meng~kan,* to exalt; to treat as of prime importance; *ke~an,* special position, special privilege. 2. Skr. the breath (of life); *~ jiwa,* id. (a term of endearment); *air ~ jiwa,* the water of life.

utara [KN], 1. Skr. the north; *~ tepat,* due north; *~ barat laut,* N.N.W.; *~ timur laut,* N.N.E.; *angin ~,* a northerly wind; *musim ~,* the N.E. monsoon. 2. *meng~kan,* to declare, to expound; *meng~kan ceramah,* to deliver a talk or lecture.

Utarik [KN], Ar. the planet Mercury.

utas [KN], 1. a coil, a skein; *se~ manik-manik,* a string of beads or corals; *ber~ permata,* with a string of precious stones. 2. a craftsman; *~an,* craftsmanship.

utau [KN], Ch. the secret sign between masons or members of secret societies; password.

utih [KN], name used to address the fourth child in the family.

utopia [KN], system of administration that is perfect (impossible to achieve).

utuh [KS], Ind. sound, firm; undamaged; *ke~an,* solid state, stable condition.

utus [KK], *meng~,* send on an embassy; *~an,* an envoy, a mission; *menteri ~an,* ambassador; *per~an,* communication, the 'mesage' contained in a story, etc.; *per~an rasmi,* official communication; *meng~ surat,* to correspond.

uyung [KS], shaking, swaying.

uzur [KN], Ar. sick, unfit; *meng~kan,* to plead incapacity, to make excuses in order to avoid doing something; *ke~an,* debility; *ke~an jauh,* the disability of distance (being a valid excuse for not attending Friday prayer).

W

wa [P], Ar. and.

waad [KN], Ar. bond, contract, = *janji; ber~*, to conclude a treaty.

wabak [KN], Ar. plague, pestilence, epidemic; ~ *taun*, cholera epidemic.

wabakdu [P], and after that....

wad [KN], ward.

wadi [KN], dry riverbed in the desert.

wadah [KN], tray, plate.

wadar [KN], warder, jailer.

wadas [KN], stony ground.

wadat [KN], state of living unmarried.

wadun [KN], Jav. a woman.

wafat [KK], Ar. to die.

wah [Kseru], exclamation, expressing surprise, admiration.

wahai [Kseru], exclamation, expressing sadness, inviting attention.

waham [KN], Ar. conjecture, suspicion.

wahi [KN], Ar. a vision, a divine revelation; also *wahyu, mewahyui,* to inspire.

wahid [KBil], Ar. sole, single.

wa-imma...wa-imma, Ar. either...or.

waja, Ind. = *baja* 1.

wajah [KN], Ar. countenance, visage; often used in a caption to a photograph with the meaning of 'the depicted countenance of', so that in such contexts it practically comes to mean 'photograph, picture'.

wajar [KS], right, fitting; *se~nya*, rightly, properly; *perkara itu dianggap sesuatu yang ~,* it's considered to be s. th. natural; *tidak ~,* abnormal.

wajib [KK], Ar. obligatory, required by religion; cf. **perlu**; so, necessary, imperative, right; *ke~an,* duty; *menunaikan ke~an,* to carry out one's duty; *di~kan,* compulsory (as education); *pihak yang ber~,* the responsible authorities.

wajik [KN], a sweetmeat made from glutinous rice with sugar and coconut cream; *potongan ~,* lozenge-shaped

(from the usual shape of the sweetmeat), cut diagonally.

wak [KN], 1. ~-~, the gibbon, = *ungka.* 2. *burung ~-~* = *ruak-ruak* 2. 3. uncle, 'daddy'; gaffer; grand-dad; granny (all as informal modes of address).

wakaf [KN], Ar. devoted to religious purposes; *tanah ~,* land bequeathed for religious use (such as to build mosque); in Kelantan ~ is used more particularly of public shelters built by charitable people; *ber~,* to donate land property etc. for religious purposes.

wakil [KN], Ar. agent, attorney, representative; *me~i,* to represent; *me~kan,* to appoint as deputy or agent, to depute; ~ *rakyat,* people's representative (member of parliament); *dewan per~an,* House of Representatives; *per~an,* a deputation.

waktu [KN], Ar. time, occasion, opportunity; *lima ~ sembahyang,* the five times of daily prayer: *subuh* (dawn), *zuhur* (mid-day), *asar* (afternoon), *maghrib* (evening), *isya* (nightfall); *tidak menurut ~,* not keeping to fixed time; unpunctual; at irregular times; *sepanjang ~,* continually; *se~-~,* on occasions.

wal'afiat [KS], hale and hearty, in excellent spirit.

walad [KN], son of, child of.

walakin [P], Ar. and yet; but; still.

walang [KS], Jav. sad, sorrowful, melancholy.

walau [KPhbg], Ar. although; ~ *bagaimana pun,* somehow or other; ~ *apa jadipun,* whatever happens, under all circumstances, 'at all costs'.

walhal [KKtr], Ar. in fact, actually.

walhasil [KS], in the end.

wali [KN], 1. Ar. a viceregent; a guardian of an unmarried woman; a deputy; ~

Allah, a saint; ~ *ikrab,* guardian by virtue of nearest blood-relationship, as opposed to ~ *hakim,* guardian appointed by Court; ~ *kota,* Ind. mayor. 2. *pisau* ~, a small lancet-like knife. 3. a shoulder-cloth worn by Court pages.

walimah [KN], a feast.

walimana [KN], Skr. a harpy; a legendary man-bird, still sometimes figuring in decorations.

walimatulurus [KN], a marriage feast.

Wallah, Ar. God! — an exclamation of astonishment.

wallahu, Ar. ~ *alam,* God is all-knowing; God knoweth best.

wam = *ruam.*

Wan [KN], a title given to descendants of great chiefs not of royal rank; locally a polite affix to the names of respected persons.

wang [KN], money, cash; ~ *tunai,* ready money; ~ *runcit,* petty cash; ~ *pertaruhan,* reserve fund; deposit; ~ *leburan,* metal money; coins; ~ *kertas,* notes; ~ *bunga,* interest, ~ *belanja,* money for everyday use; *ke~an,* finance; *kedudukan ke~an,* financial position; ~ *pendahuluan,* a deposit; ~ *muka,* a down-payment; (*wang* orignally meant a small coin now obsolete).

wangi [KS], fragant, perfumed; *air* ~, scent, perfume; ~-~*an,* perfumes; *me~kan,* cause to be fragrant, sweet smelling.

wangkang [KN], Old Jav. — (cf. **Fiji wangka**) a Chinese ocean-going junk.

wangsa [KN], race.

wanita [KN], Ind. female; a woman (more polite than *perempuan); ke~an,* womanhood.

wanta [KN], Skr. nature; pomegranate.

wap [KN], vapour, steam; *ber~,* steamy.

warak [KS], Ar. pious.

warangan [KN], 1. arsenic. 2. = *berangan.*

waras [KS], Ind. cure, convalescence, good health; healthy, sane, sensible; *berfikirian* ~, sane, sensible.

warga [KN], Skr. family, people; ~-*negara,* citizen; *menjadi* ~-*negara,* to be naturalised; ~ *dunia,* stateless person;

ke~negaraan, citizenship.

warip [KK], Jav. alive; ~ *waras,* alive and well.

waris [KN], Ar. heir; inheritor or potential inheritor; used in a wider sense than the English 'heir' it means anyone eligible to inherit under any circumstances; ~ *negeri,* be heir to; *pe~an,* a relic (of a past age); ~ *takhta,* heir to the throne.

warkat [KN], Ar. a writing; a letter; also *warkah.*

warna [KN], Skr. colour; shade of colour; *ber~-warni,* in diverse colours (esp. of films); *berubah* ~, to blush, to flush up.

warta [KN], Skr. news, tidings; ~ *nya,* the report was; ~ *berita,* the news of the day; ~*wan,* a journalist; ~*wan-wanita,* a female journalist; *ke~-wanan,* journalism; ~ *kerajaan,* Government Gazette.

Waruna [KN], Skr. the god of the ocean, Varuna.

warung [KN], Jav. a booth or stall.

was, Treng. = *waswas.*

wasangka [KN], concern, suspicion; *syak* ~, id.; *menaruh* ~, to suspect.

wasi [KN], Ar. an executor of a will.

waslat [KN], Ar. a will; *me~kan,* to bequeath; leave by will.

wasilkan [KK], Ar. to convey (a letter) — epistolary language.

wasir = *bawasir.*

wasitah [KN], medium, go-between.

waspada [KS], Ind. clear; clear understanding; *ber~,* alert, on the qui-vive, cautious, be on guard; *ke~an,* cautiousness.

waswas [KS], Ar. care; worried, anxious, doubt, suspicious.

wat [KN], Thai. a watt; a Buddhist temple.

watak [KN], Ar. character; used esp. for a character; ~ *utama,* id.; *membawakan* ~, to represent a character, take the part of; *per~an,* characterization.

watan [KN], Ar. birth-place; often used to mean 'native land'.

watania [KS], that is related to the fatherland; Ar. the adjective of *watan;* also

~*h; tentera* ~*h,* Territorial Forces.

watas = *batas.*

wati [KN], Skr. 1. the firmament; the universe. 2. that which denotes a lady, woman.

wau [KN], a kite flown by boys.

wawancara [KN], interview.

wawas [KN], ~*an,* insight.

wayang [KN], 1. an old-time theatrical performance whether by living actors (*wawung*) or a shadow or marionette show (~ *kulit*); ~ *gelap,* ~ *gambar,* a cinema; ~ *kulit sahaja,* just a shadow show, i.e., (fig.) 'a bit of theatre, not to be taken seriously; ~ *golek,* puppet show. 2. *ikan* ~, a fish *(Zanchis cornutus); panggung* ~, theatre; *anak* ~, stage actor, actress.

wazih [KS], Ar. clear, distinct.

wazir [KN], Ar. a vizier, a minister.

wenang [KN], Ind, power, authority; *kekuasaan yang se*~-~, absolute power; tyranny; *ke*~*an,* authority to do something.

wet [KK], to heave upwards as in prising open a box or when turning a boat with a side-ways heave of a paddle; also *uit.*

wetan [KN], Jav. the east.

wibawa [KN], Ind. *ke*~*an,* conscientious care, sense of responsibility; prestige, authority; *ber*~, have the authority to give orders.

widuri [KN], a tree.

wijaya [KN], Skr. and Jav. victorious; *bunga* ~ *mala,* a legendary flower which brought all it touched to life.

wijil [KN], Jav. a gallery in an audience-hall.

wijung [KN], Jav, the large squirrel *(Sciurus bicolor),* = *tupai nandung.*

wilada [KN], *mandi* ~, a ceremonial bathing for a woman after confinement.

wilahar [KN], a pool, a mire; also *lahar.*

wilayah [KN], Ind, province, territory.

win [KN], Eng. a winch, crane.

windu [KN], Ind, a cycle of eight years.

wira [KN], Skr. a man, a hero; *per*~, heroic.

wirid [KN], Ar. extra, personal prayers said after the ritual prayers *(sembahyang); baca* ~, to say such prayers; also *wirit.*

wirun [KN], Ind. a pleat.

wizurai [KN], Port. viceroy.

wong [KN], (Sundanese) a man; = *orang; wayang* ~, an old-time play with living actors (in Java).

wujud [KN], Ar. a being; to come into being, to be created, to exist; ~*kan,* to bring into being, to create; also *ujud; ke*~*an,* existence.

wuzu [KN], Ar. ritual ablutions required before prayer; *mengambil* ~, to perform such ablutions; also *wudu.*

Y

ya [KKtr], yes; that is so; ~ *tidak pun*, whether it is so or not; *seia sekata*, unanimity; ~ *tak* ~, yes indeed, that may well be; *kalau* ~ *pun bukan*, anyhow, at any rate; *meng~kan*, to assent.

Yahudi [KN], a Jew, Jewish.

Yahya [KN], Ar. John; *injil* ~, the gospel according to St. John.

Yajuj [KN], Ar. the giant Gog.

yakin [KS], Ar. certain, positive, confident, definite; convinced, firmly believing; *ke~an*, faith, confidence; *me~kan*, to convince; *me~i*, to believe firmly, certain.

yakni, Ar. that is to say; i.e.

yakut [KN], Ar. a jacinth.

Yaman [KN], Ar. *negeri* ~, the Yemen.

yam tuan [KN], sovereign; = *yang dipertuan;* see *tuan.*

yang [KN], 1. divinity, godhead; *sembah~*, worship; *ke~an*, the abode of the old divinities; paradise; fairy-land; *sang~*, holy god — a title given to the major divinities only; *~~*, god of gods: a similar title. 2. an expression having the force of a relative bringing the word or clause following it into relation with that which precedes, e.g., *masa baik*, a fortunate time, a lucky moment. 3. a title of little distinction; an abbreviation of *dayang.*

yarkan [KN], Ar. jaundice.

yasin [KN], Ar. a chapter of the Koran supposed to be read to the dying.

yatim [KS], Ar. orphaned, desolate, fatherless; *anak* ~, a fatherless child; ~ *piatu*, orphan.

yaum [KN], Ar. day; *~ul-kiamat,* the day of judgment.

yayasan [KN], Ind, edifice; foundation.

yengki [KN], Eng, Yankee; term applied to the costume and behaviour of certain young men — jeans and cowboy get up; *budak-budak* ~, young men of this type.

yu [KN], a generic name for sharks, dogfishes and rays resembling sharks; ~ *bengkung*, the hammer-headed shark; ~ *gila (Chyloscillium indicum)*; ~ *laras (Mustelus manazao)*; ~ *rimau (Galeocerdo rayneri)*; ~ *sambaran*, the ground shark; ~ *bodoh*, the basking shark; ~ *gergaji*, the saw-fish.

yuda [KN], Ind. war.

Yunan [KN], Ionia, Greece.

Yup [KN], a designation, = *Kulup.*

yuran [KN], subscription (as to a club); fees, contribution.

Yusuf [KN], Ar. Joseph; *nabi* ~, the biblical Joseph; a Malay proper name; also *Jusuh.*

Z

zabad [KN], Ar. civet — cf. jebat.

Zabaniah [KN], Ar. chief of the fiends of hell.

zabib [KN], Ar. raisins, dried fruit.

Zabur [KN], Ar. kitab ~, the psalms of David.

zadah [KN], Pers. sprung from son of; haram ~, ill-begotten, illegitimate; halal- ~, legitimate.

zahid [KN], Ar. a hermit, an ascetic.

zahir [KS], 1. = lahir; 2. Ar. clear, manifest; born; also (coll.) lahir; ~kan, to express; ~-batin, both openly and secretly.

zaif [KS], Ar. weak, feeble.

zakar [KN], Ar. the male organ of generation.

zakat [KN], Ar. a tithe paid by Muslims; beri ~ and ber~, to pay the tithe.

zakiah [KS], Ar. pure, honest, upright (of the heart), (fuad), in epistolary language.

zalim [KS], Ar. tyrannical, oppressive, cruelly unjust; also dzalim.

zaman [KN], Ar. long period of time, age; ~ puntung berasap, long, long ago (when fires were always kept in); ~ silam, dark ages; but more often used in the Indonesian sense of 'past ages'; dimakan dek ~, showing the corrosive effects of time (of an old building); menurut ~, to keep up with the times; ketinggalan ~, out of date; se~, of the same period, contemporary; sampai akhir ~, till the end of time.

zamrud [KN], Ar. emerald.

Zamzam [KN], Ar. the Zemzem well at Mecca.

Zanggi [KN], 1. Pers. Zanzibari; African; pauh ~, the tree believed to grow at the 'heart of the seas'; buah pauh ~, the double coconut. 2. Pers. warlike.

zanji [KK], Ar. ber~, to chant the praises of the Prophet.

zapin [KN], Kel. an Arabian dance.

zat [KN], Ar. essence, true nature; trace elements; organic nutritional elements, esp. vitamins; that in which a thing's special potency lies; ~ makanan, nutritious elements in food, esp. vitamins; ~ darah merah, red blood corpuscles.

ziarah [K], 1. Ar. a pilgrimage to a tomb or shrine; also, pay a visit (to a sick person, a friend); men~i, to go on a pilgrimage. 2. ~ cina, a Chinese cemetery; also ziarah.

zina [KN], Ar. illicit intercourse; ber~, to commit fornication or adultery; melakukan ~, id.; also zinah.

zindik [KN], Ar. a heretic, atheist.

zirafah [KN], Pers. a fabulous monster, giraffe.

zirah [KN], Pers. baju ~, a coat of mail.

zu [KS], Ar. possessed of; endowed with; ~lkarnain, the possessor of two horns; also dzu.

Zuhal [KN], Ar. the planet Saturn.

Zuhrah [KN], the planet Venus; also bintang kejora.

zulfakar [KN], At. name of a famous sword presented by the Prophet to his son-in-law, Ali; sometimes used as a proper name, but as a name it is generally written Dulfakar.

Zulhijjah [KN], Ar. the pilgrimage month, often called bulan Haji, the twelfth month of the Muslim calendar.

Zulikha [KN], Ar. the traditional name of Potiphar's wife.

Zulkaedah [KN], Ar. the month of the Truce (in which Arab feuds cease); the eleventh month of the Muslim calendar.

zuriat [KN], Ar. descendants, seed, offspring.

Introduction : English-Malay Section

This section of the dictionary aims at supplying in a compact form an English-Malay vocabulary suited to the needs of English-speaking students who wish to get a good start in Malay. It is intended to be used in conjunction with the Malay-English section of the dictionary, with which it is interlinked. So it is important that users of it should make a practice of looking up in the Malay-English section each Malay word entered herein. Sometimes they will get no further information, but in very many instances they will find other shades of meaning and cognate expressions and, indeed, alternative meanings or, at any rate, find out whether the word is a local word or not.

Space is also saved by the interlinking method. Thus 'science' is translated herein as *ilmu*. Look up *ilmu* in the Malay-English section and over 50 sciences and quasi-sciences will be found. Look up "smile" and it is *senyum*. In the Malay-English section 15 cognate expressions appear, from "broad smile" to "attempt at a smile"

So this section is considerably smaller in bulk than the Malay-English section. Not that the difference in size is caused merely by the interlinking system. I have not attempted to enter here all the Malay words entered in the other section nor do I think it is desirable to do so, especially in the case of words relating to flora, fauna and customs, which are explained rather than translated therein.

Treat this section carefully. A dictionary in which the user's language comes first may easily mislead; so much may depend on the context (though the link with the Malay-English section offsets this difficulty to a considerable extent).

Also remember that if you do not find a required word herein, it may well be that the choice of the word to be used in Malay depends on the context; the Malay 'approach' often differs widely from the English.

A difficulty which can be overcome only by practice is that of selecting out of several virtual synonyms the right word to use in speech. To a very small extent I have avoided misleading the student on this point by placing the more colloquial word, if any, first in an entry.

I have been deliberately sparing of information about pronouns and conjunctions. Their use (and avoidance) must be learned in the practical school of speech and reading.

A student nowadays will want to be informed of new terms and adaptations meeting modern ideas. Thus to give a small selection of such terms contained herein, he will want to know the Malay used for e.g. short and long term planning (I have underlined the relevant entry herein); vote of no confidence: multi-racial State; break off diplomatic relations; social welfare; profit incentive; free enterprise; atomic fall-out; agreement in principle; moral support; lie in state; a majority of votes; non-aligned and many other 'modernistic' terms.

Such terms may fairly be described as artificial coinage, as indeed they were originally in English. But the student may be surprised at the number of everyday-life expressions which are paralleled in ordinary 'homely' Malay. To take a few examples: castles in the air, first come first served; tied to mother's apron-strings; don't bite off more than you can chew; keeping up with the Joneses; borrowing from Peter to pay Paul; Utopia; cheaper in the long run. There is nothing forced about the Malay translations of these expressions. They are mentioned here largely as illustrating the fact that in translating one must translate the idea, not necessarily the words. So, a mushroom of smoke from an explosion is described in Malay as an umbrella; both similes are equally apt: words different, idea the same. So it will be seen that in Malay short-lived <u>enthusiasm</u> is aptly described by reference to fowls' droppings, and a changeable person, compared in English to a <u>weathercock</u>, is in Malay compared to a species of snail.

But it must always be borne in mind that not every English idiom is paralleled precisely in Malay and an attempt to find parallels in every instance is likely to result in driving a number of square pegs screaming into round holes.

I remark that even 'artificial coinages' are often simple and ingenious. How would a non-Malay have translated <u>suicide-squad</u>? And the idea behind the translation of <u>block of flats</u> is genuinely and delightfully 'Malay'.

Students are at first confused by the Malay system of affixation. They must learn the prefixes and suffixes (which are a vital element of Malay, and used by Malays in both speech and writing). But, as a concession to beginners, wherever a prefixed word occurs I have given the unprefixed form in brackets after it, unless the unprefixed form occurs elsewhere in the entry. If only a suffix is affixed, the student should be able to find the root-word without difficulty.

For the convenience of students I have included a brief statement on numerals and the calendar and a note on numeral coefficients.

A.E.C.

Index of Abbreviations

The list below is supplementary to that contained in the Malay-English section of the dictionary on page vi. It replaces the abbreviations for parts of speech in Malay.

adj.	adjective		*pp.*	past participle
adv.	adverb		*prep.*	preposition
conj.	conjunction		*pron.*	pronoun
fig.	figurative		*v.aux.*	auxiliary verb
int.	interjection		*v.intr.*	intransitive verb
lit.	literally		*v.tr.*	transitive verb
n.	noun			

A * placed after a Malay word indicates that there is a special reason for looking it up in the Malay-English section of the dictionary (though, as mentioned in the introduction, users of the dictionary should make a practice of so looking up Malay words anyway).

An Anglicism is shown between inverted commas.

N.B. — The part of speech to which the first (English) word in each entry belongs is noted against it. No parts of speech are, as a rule, noted against subsequent words contained in the entry. It is thought that, in practice, the arrangement of subsequent words is such that no confusion will be caused by this system. Especially it must be borne in mind that in many cases it is impossible to allocate a Malay word definitely to any one part of speech.

A

A-1, adj. (sl.) nombor satu.

A.A. guns, n. meriam penangkis (tangkis).

A.D., n. tahun Masihi (T.M.).

aback, adv. taken ~, tercengang (cengang), tergamam (gaman), tergemap (gemap).

abacus, n. sempoa, dekak-dekak.

abandon, v. tr. leave behind, meninggalkan (tinggal); to ~ an enterprise, cease one's efforts, melepas (lepas) tangan; see pack; ~ed, tertinggal; not looked after, terbiar (biar) begitu sahaja; esp. as task dropped when half-done, terbangai (bangai), terbengkalai (bengkalai); fig. gone to the bad, sudah rosak tabiat, sudah berjahat (jahat); fail to help, (sl.) paling punggung.

abase, v. tr. degrade, menghinakan (hina); to ~ oneself, merendahkan (rendah) diri.

abash, v. malu; rupa tikus basah (looking like wet rats); **abashed,** adj.

abate, v. intr. lessen, berkurangan (kurang); (as storm or disease), reda; (as rain), teduh sikit.

abattis, n. barrier of felled trees, reba, ranggas.

abattoir, n. tempat membantai (bantai) lembu dan sebagainya; pajak potong.

abbreviation, n. singkatan; see **contract.**

abdicate, v. tr. turun takhta.

abdomen, n. perut. (bahagian bawa).

abduct, v. tr. bawa lari, colek.

abeam, di rusuk.

Abel, n. the Biblical character, Habil.

aberration, n. luar ke biasaan (biasa); menyimpang (simpang).

abet, v. tr. assist or incite offender, menghasut (hasut), menjadi (jadi) subahat.

abhor, v. tr. benci(kan); feeling ~rence, merasa ngeri, getik.

abide, v. menerima (terima); bersetuju (setuju), mematuhi.

abjure, v. tr. swear abstience from, mengharamkan (haram); ~d, pantang; see **abstain.**

able, adj. competent, cergas, cekap; ability, kebolehan (boleh); ~-bodied, badan tegap.

ablutions, n. generally, mandi-manda; ritual cleansing of the lower orifices of the body, istinja; required before prayer, wuduk; to perform such ~, mengambil (ambil) wuduk; after coition, mandi junub; after defilement (e.g., by touching a pig), sertu; see **bath, clean, cleanse, wash.**

abnormal, adj. luarbiasa, ganjil.

abolish, v. tr. do away with, as a custom, hapuskan, menyinkirkan (singkir), menbasmikan (basmi).

abominable, adj. dasyat, sumbang.

aboriginal, adj. asli, bumiputera, pribumi; see **Jakun, Sakai, Semang, Temir** in the Malay-English section.

aborted, p.p. frustrated, bantut, gagal; abortion of child, keguguran (gugur); to cause an abortion, menggungurkan (gugur) anak.

about, adv. all around, sekeliling, sekitar; approximately, lebih kurang, kira-kira; ~ to (just going to), tengah hendak; see **concerning.**

above, adv. on top, (di) atas; ~-board (openly, without secrecy), dengan terang-terang (fig.); in the air-space of, di angkasa.

abraded, p.p. (kulit) terlucut (lucut); (kulit) terkelupas (kelupas).

abreast, adv. in a line, berbaris, sebaris (baris).

abridge, v. tr. shorten (e.g., a book), ringkaskan.

abroad, adv. di luar negeri, di negeri

orang.

abrogate, v. tr. cancel (as law), batalkan, mansuhkan.

abrupt, adj. in manner, bersifat (sifat) kasar; ~ly (of hasty action), secara mendadak (dadak), terburu-buru, tergesa-gesa; 'just like that' (without more), begitu sahaja.

abscess, n. bernanah.

abscond, v. int. melarikan (lari) diri; 'make oneself scarce', mengilangkan (hilang) diri.

absence, n. during the ~ of, sepeninggalan (tinggal); absent, not present, tak ada, tiada; as from a meeting, tidak hadir; absent-minded, nyanyuk, mamun, pelupa; see **absorb.**

absolute, adj. unrestricted, tidak terbatas (batas); (as of agent's authority), mutlak; ~ly, wholly, sama sekali.

absorb, v. tr. to suck up moisture, menyerap (serap), menjerap (jerap); ~ed in thought, berfikir jauh; duduk temenung; as in some task, ralip, leka; ~ed (as liquid), mesra.

abstain, v. intr. as from certain foods, memantangkan (pantang); to keep oneself apart from, menjauhkan diri daripada; to ~ from voting, berkecuali (cuali).

abstract, adj. tidak berupa; tidak nyata; tidak terang; not concrete.

abstracted, adj. 'in a brown study', duduk teringa-inga, duduk termenung (menung).

abstruse, adj. profound, dalam; hard to understand, sukar difahami.

absurd, adj. incredible, mustahil; rubbish, majhar; nor worthy of consideration, tidak menasabah bukan-bukan; nonsense, karut.

abundant, adj. as crops, menjadi-jadi; abundance, mewah; abound, bersepah-sepah; galore, belanar; see **rife.**

abuse, v. tr. to revile, maki, bermaki-hamun; 'snarl at', menengking (tengking); insult, menhina (hina), menista (nista); 'tell off', mengata-ngata (kata); see **filth.**

abut, v. intr. to border on, bertumpu (tumpu) dengan, seperenggan dengan; ~ment of wall, sangga tembuk.

abyss, n. keleburan.

accede, v. tr. consent (to proposal), bersetuju, sudi; ~ to (as a party), menjadi ahli; when changing parties, lompat masuk.

accelerate, v. to increase one's speed, berlari (lari) bertambah (tambah) laju, mempercepatkan; a car, memecut (pecut) kereta; quicker!, cepat!

accent, n. peculiar mode of pronunciation, pelat; as foreign ~, telor; intonation; tekanan suara, rentak suara, runtunan suara; nasal ~, sengau.

accept, v. tr. as a task, sanggup; see **receive;** ~ as true (and act on), pakai.

access, n. jalan masuk; ~ible (as an official), mudah didekati.

accident, n. kemalangan (malang); serious ~, nahas.

acclaim, n. menerima (terima); mengakui (aku).

acclimatized, v. and adj. thoroughly habituated to new surroundings, sebati; see **accustomed.**

accommodate, v. tr. supply a place for, be able to hold (as a building), menampung (tampung), menempatkan (tempat).

accompany, v. tr. buat kawan, mengikut (ikut); menemani (teman); escort, mengiring; musical accompaniment, iringan muzik.

accomplice, n. subahat.

accomplish, v. tr. a plan, laksanakan; ~ed, talented, berbakat (bakat).

accordance, n. in ~ with, menurut (turut).

accordion, n. tarik-tarik, 'kodian'.

accost, v. tr. tegur; stop (someone) in order to address, mengadang (adang).

account, n. narration, cerita; statement, keterangan (terang).

account, n. kira-kira, hisab; accountant, akauntan.

accountable, adj. having to account for, kena jawab; bertanggung-jawab.

accumulate, v. tr. to gather together (as

wealth), mengimpun (himpun), kumpul; *heaped up (as sand),* bertimbun-timbun; *see* **collect.**

accurate, *adj. correct,* betul; *exact,* tepat.

accursed, *adj.* kutuk, bedebah, celaka, laknat; ~ *be*—!, kutuklah—!

accuse, *v. tr. charge,* menuduh (tuduh); *blame,* salahkan.

accustomed, *adj.* biasa; *to accustom oneself to,* menyesuaikan (suai) diri pada.

ache, *n.* sakit; *tooth-~,* sakit gigi.

achieve, *v. to accomplish,* mencapai (capai).

acid, *adj. to the taste,* masam, asam; *acrid,* kelat; *(chemical) corrosive ~,* terusi; *vitriol,* air api; *acetic ~,* cuka getah; *nitric ~,* asam sendawa; *sulphuric ~,* asam belerang; *tannic ~,* asam samak.

acknowledge, *v. tr.* mengaku (aku); *(as a duty),* sanggup.

acorn, *n.* buah pokok oak.

acquaintance, *n. person known slightly,* kenalan.

acquiesce, *v. intr. not objected,* sudi.

acquire, *v. tr. come to have,* mendapat (dapat), mencapai (capai).

acquit, *v. tr.* memutuskan (putus) tak salah; *discharge,* lepaskan; *acquittal,* hukum lepas.

acrobat, *n.* penambul (tambul).

across, *prep.* seberang; *as, lying ~,* melintang (lintang); *spanning,* merentangi (rentang), menyeberang *run ~,* lari menlintas (lintas).

acrostic, *n. word puzzle,* teka-kata.

act, *n. deed,* perbuatan (buat); *of a play,* babak, penggal; *take action,* bertindak (tindak); *to ~ a play,* berlakon (lakon), bermain (main) wayang, bermain sandiwara; *to take a part in a play,* mengambil (ambil) peranan; *acting (as deputy),* pemangku (pangku); ~ *on (news),* pakai; *to 'put on an ~' (behave affectedly, try to make an impression),* membuat (buat) kelakuan, mandai-mandai (pandai), mengada-ngada (ada); ~ *of God, natural calamity,* bencana alam.

action, *n. see* **act;** *court ~,* bicara; *to take ~ in court,* mendakwa (dakwa).

active, *adj.* cergas; hidup *(as in live wire).*

activities, *n. efforts, steps,* tindakan, usaha, kegiatan (giat); *active,* ringan tulang, lincah; *(diligent),* rajin; *(mentally),* cergas; *(of a volcano)* hidup; *still functioning, as an organisation,* 'aktif'.

actor, *n.* pelaku (laku) wayang, pelakon (lakon); *actress, id.*

actual, *adj. real,* yang sebenar; *actually in truth,* sebenarnya; *as it happened,* pada halnya.

acute, *adj. shrewd,* tajam akal.

Adam, *n.* Nabi Adam; *Adam's seed,* bani Adam; *Adam's apple (in throat),* buah lekum (halkum).

adapt, *v. tr. to modify something,* padankan, sadorkan (sadar); ~ *oneself to,* menyesuaikan (suai) diri dengan.

add, *v. tr. increase,* menambahkan (tambah); ~ *up,* jumlahkan; *put in a bit more,* tokok.

addicted, *adj.* ~ *to, as opium,* ketagih (tagih) candu, tahi candu; *as to drink or gambling,* kaki minum, kaki judi.

addled, *adj.* tembelang, kemungkus.

address, *n. as of letter,* alamat; *to ~, speak to,* tegur; *deliver a speech,* memberi (beri) ucapan, berpidato (pidato).

adept, *n. proficient,* mahir, pakar, ahli; *scientist,* ahli 'sains'.

adequate, *adj.* cukup, padan; *fully ~,* patut padan; *(of means) enough to live on,* cukup makan.

adhere, *v.* patuh, menurut (turut) apa yang ditetapkan.

adjacent, *adj. lying near,* berdekatan (dekat; bersebelahan (sebelah).

adjourn, *v. intr. as a court, or meeting,* ditangguh (tangguh); *(a case),* gantung bicara.

adjust, *v. tr. make small corrections to, e.g., dress,* membetulkan, mematut-matutkan (patut); *as a watch, see* **set;** *adjustment of accounts,* penyelarasan (laras) kira-kira.

adjutant, *n.* ~ *stork,* burung botak, burung dahu; *in the army,* pembantu (pegawai).

administer, v. tr. to manage, perintah, uruskan (urus), mengelola (kelola); a government, mentadbirkan (tadir); letters of administration (of the state of a deceased person), surat kuasa; ~ an oath, memberi (beri) sumpah; rules of administration, tata usaha.

admiral, n. laksamana.

admire, v. tr. to praise, memuji (puji); to wonder at, mengagumkan (kagum); ~rs, 'fans', peminat (minat); hero-worship, menjulang-julang; memuja (puja).

admit, v. tr. acknowledge, mengaku (aku); allow inside, bawa masuk, benarkan masuk.

adolescent, remaja, pemuda (muda); of a girl, pemudi, anak dara sunti; see **teenager.**

adopt, v. tr. take over, as a plan, ambil alih; choose (e.g., a plan), menurut (turut); act on, pakai; ~ed child, anak angkat; ~ive father, bapa angkat

adore, v. tr. worship, memuja (puja), menyembah (sembah); (fig.) as a girl, memuja; ~d one, pujaan hati.

adorn, v. tr. menghiaskan (hias); ~ oneself (as a woman), bersolek (solek).

adrift, adj. berhanyut (hanyut), terapung-apung.

adult, adj. cukup umur, dewasa; an ~ who behaves childishly, fails to 'be his age', ibu keladi.

adulterate, v. tr. mix with base ingredients, bercampur (campur) dengan (lain benda) dengan tujuan hendak menipu (tipu).

adultery, n. zina; to commit ~, melakukan (laku) zina, berkendak (kendak).

adumbrate, v. tr. to indicate faintly, to fore-shadow, membayangkan (bayang).

advance, v. intr. to come or go forward, esp. as troops, mara (ke depan); step, come out in front, tampil; progress (as in studies or economy), maju; ~ a proposal, kemukakan (muka); (esp. as a scheme), majukan; an ~ (as on a con-

tract), pendahuluan (dahulu), (as for expenses), belanja; to make (improper) ~s to a woman, mengusik (usik); to ~ a clock or time of event, cepatkan.

advantage, n. favourable circumstance, kelebihan (lebih).

adventure, n. a happening, kejadian (jadi); occurrence, peristiwa; to 'go a-roving', merantau; rover, perantau; to 'try one's luck' (seek one's fortune), mengadu (adu) untung; mere ~r, knave, petualang (tualang).

adverse, adj. opposed, menentang (tentang); of wind, sakal.

advertisement, n. iklan; to advertise goods, mengiklankan barang; to advertise oneself (show off in order to attract notice), menonjolkan (tonjol) diri, kemukakan (muka) diri.

advice, n. nasihat, syor; guidance, panduan; precept, anjuran; advise, memberi (beri) nasihat; urge to, ajak; warn, ajar; coax, memujuk (pujuk).

advocate, n. (in court) peguam, membantu dalam soal-soal guaman (guam).

adze, n. beliung, rimbas.

Aeolian harp, n. (a sort of musical instrument made by some of the aboriginal tribesmen; a very large bamboo has stops cut in it resembling those of an organ and the bamboo is then fastened near the top of a high tree where the wind causes it to emit plaintive notes), buluh perindu (rindu).

aerated waters, n. minuman meruap (ruap).

aeroplane, n. kapal terbang.

afar, adv. from ~, dari jauh.

affable, adj. peramah (ramah), manis mulut.

affair, n. perkara; (circumstances), hal; in human relationship, hubungan sulit.

affect, v. tr. produce effect on, memberi kesan; see **connect;** adversely ~, mengganggu (ganggu); ~s one's health, mengganggu kesihatan (sihat).

affected, adj. to be ~, pose, berlagak (lagak), bergaya-gaya; (esp. with ~

mannerisms), berkelitah (kelitah); *make a pretence of action,* mengadangada (ada); ~ *adversely,* terjejas (jejas).

affection, *n.* kasih sayang; ~*ate,* penyayang; pengasih (kasih).

affidavit, *n.* surat sumpah, surat ikrar.

affiliated, *p.p.* bergabung (gabung); berkerabat (kerabat).

affinity, *n. esp. as suitable match,* jodoh pertemuan (temu), serasi.

affirm, *v. intr. state,* mengaku (aku), menyatakan (nyata).

affix, *v. tr. place, as stamp,* bubuh; *fix on,* kenakan; *stick up, as poster,* pelekat (lekat); *stick on,* lekatkan; *in grammar,* inbuhan (inbuh); penambahan (tambah).

affluent, *adj. in wealth,* makmur, kaya, kaya-raya.

afford, *v. tr. be able to spare (money),* tahan belanja; *have sufficient means,* mampu (nak).

Afghan, *n.* orang Kabuli (dari Afghanistan).

afraid, *adj.* takut, kagit; *shaky with fear,* kenaling; *'having the wind up',* kecut perut; *see* **fear.**

afresh, *adv. once more,* semula.

after, *prep.* ~ *that,* lepas itu; *behind,* di belakang; ~ *that time at which,* sesudah, selepas, setelah.

afterbirth, *n.* uri.

aftermath, *n. of crops, ceding,* buah di bujunq.

afternoon, *n.* lepas lohor, sudah beralih (alih) hari; *late* ~, petang, (waktu) matahari condong.

afterwards, *adv.* kemudian, lepas itu.

again, *adv.* lagi; *yet* ~, pula; *all over* ~, semula; ~ *and* ~, berkali-kali; *once more,* sekali lagi.

against, *prep.* lawan; *as in 'leaning* ~', pada; ~ *the current,* menongkah (tongkah) air; ~ *the wind,* menyongsang (songsang) angin.

agate, *n.* batu akik.

age, *n. length of life,* umur, usia; *epoch,* zaman; *of-*~ *(grown up),* cukup umur,

dewasa; *over-*~ *(as for an examination),* lebih umur; ~*d, old,* tua; ~*d (five years),* berumur (lima tahun); ~*less (unaffected by old* ~*),* tidak makan tua; *or by passage of* ~*s,* tak lapuk dik zaman; *'shows his* ~', umur dia dah menurun (turun); *past prime (esp. of a woman),* kering sabut.

agenda, *n.* acara, 'agenda'.

agent, *n.* wakil; *trusted servant,* orang harapan; *secret* ~ *(political),* perisik (risik) rahsia; *see* **power.**

aggravate, *v. tr. make worse,* memberatkan (berat), memburukkan lagi.

aggression, *n.* pencerobohan (cerobo); *non-*~ *pact,* perjanjian (janji) tidak serang-menyerang; *aggressive,* garang.

aggrandize, *v. tr.make larger,* memperbesarkan (besar).

aggrieve, *n. to pain,* menyakitkan (sakit); melukakan (luka).

aghast, *adj.* tertegun; terpogun; *see* **startle.**

agile, *adj.* pantas, tangkas; pantas-ligas.

agitate, *v. tr. a liquid,* kacaukan; *disturb, throw into confusion,* kacaukan; ~, *in an uproar, as a community,* heboh, gempar; *of a person,* risau, gugup; *agitator, person who stirs up trouble,* tukang asut, batu api.

agnostic, *n.* antara percaya dan tidak akan wujudnya tuhan.

ago, *adv.*—sudah;—dahulu; *two years* ~, dua tahun dahulu.

agree, *v. intr. be pleased,* suka; *acquiesce,* sudi; *concur,* bersetuju (tuju); *come to an* ~*ment,* berpakat (pakat), berjanji (janji); *can't* ~ *(can't get on together),* tak berlaga (laga) angin; ~*ment,* perjanjian, ~*ment, esp. as in settlement of dispute,* kata sepakat; ~*ment in principle,* persetujuan pada asasnya; *undertake to do (task),* sanggup.

agriculture, *n.* pertanian (tani); *viewed as an in* ~, perusahaan (usaha) tanah; *engage in* ~, bercucuk (cucuk) tanam; *Department of* ~, jabatan (jabat) pertanian.

aground, *adj.* terkandas (kandas), tersakat

(sakat); *see* **strand.**

ague, *n.* demam gigil.

ahead, *adv.* depan, di muka; *go ~,* jalan dahulu; *get ~ (prosper),* naik daun; *make progress at school or in the world,* maju; *get ~ in a race,* maju ke depan; *~ of expected time,* lebih dahulu; *surpass fellows,* jadi lebih (pada).

aid, *n.* bantuan; *foreign ~,* bantuan asing; *first ~,* pertolongan (tolong) cemas; *see* **help and revive.**

aide-de-camp, *n.* juruiring, 'adikong'.

aigrette, *n.* tajuk.

ailing, *adj.* sakit.

aim, *v. intr.* tenang, petar; *direct, as a missile,* mengarahkan (arah); menghalakan (hala), mengacu (acu), *poise and ~, e.g., a spear,* membega (bega); *a purpose,* tujuan; *esp. as political,* haluan.

air, *n.* udara, angin; *climate,* hawa; *to ~ (as clothes),* anginkan; *the ~ in a tyre,* angin; *~-tight,* kedap udara; *the upper ~,* angkasa; *Air Force,* angkatan udara; *~-mail,* 'mel' udara; *airship (lighter than ~),* kapaludara, 'belun'; *~-raid,* serangan udara; *~-field,* padang kapal terbang; lapangan udara, *id.; ~-port, ~-base,* pangkalan udara; *to ~ in the sun,* jemurkan; *to take the ~ (go for a walk, drive, holiday trip, etc.),* makan angin; *~-conditioning (cooling system),* penghawa (hawa) dingin, alat-penyejuk (sejuk); *~ in the sense of mien, bearing,* gaya; *with an ~,* dengan bergaya; *give oneself airs,* mengada-ngada (ada); *have a change of ~,* beralih (alih) angin.

ajar, *adj.* renggang sikit; terkuak (kuak) (sikit).

akimbo, *adj. with arms ~,* bercekak (cekak) pinggang.

akin, *adj.* ada hubungan (kekeluargaan).

alas! *int.* aduh! aduhai!

albino, *adj. lacking colouring pigment in hair and skin,* balar; *an ~,* orang sabun.

albumen, *n.* bahagian putih telur.

alcove, *n. recess,* cerok.

alert, *adj.* berjaga-jaga, berwaspada (waspada), amaran.

Alexandria, *n.* Iskandriah.

algae, lumut (laut).

alias, *n. name,* samaran; *pen-name,* nama pena.

alien, *n. foreigner,* orang dagang, orang asing.

alight, *adj. as flame,* bernyala (nyala), hidup, *to ~, descend, as from car,* turun; *see* **perch.**

align, *v. tr. form up in lines,* membanjarkan (banjar); *esp. of troops,* membariskan (baris); *to ~ oneself with,* berpihak (pihak) kepada, menyebelahi (belah); *non-aligned,* berkecuali (cuali); *badly aligned, as houses,* congkahmangkeh.

alike, *adj.* serupa; *exactly ~,* tak ubah (macam); *closely resembling,* seakanakan; *fitting the same category,* sebabat; *the spit'n image,* saling tak tumpah.

alimony, *n. maintenance after divorce,* nafkah.

alive, *adj.* hidup, bernyawa (nyawa).

all, *adj.* semua, segala, sekalian; *with exception,—*belaka; *~ over the place,* merata-rata; *entirely,* habis; *~ day,* sepanjang hari; *~ right!,* baiklah!; *~ kinds of,* serbaneka.

allegiance, *n. citizen owing ~,* rakyat; *to swear ~,* bersumpah (sumpah) taat setia; membaca (baca) ikrar taat setia.

allegory, *n.* cerita ibarat.

alleviate, *v. tr.* meringankan (ringan).

alley, *n.* lorong kecil.

alliance, *n.* perikatan (ikat).

allocate, *v.* menetapkan (tetap) bahagian.

allot, *v. tr. distribute,* bahagi (bahagi); *assign duties,* tugaskan; *as financial shares,* menguntukkan (untuk), aguhkan.

allow, *v. tr.* beri, kasi; *permit on request,* bernarkan; *let be,* biar; *~ance,* 'elaun'; *as for expenses,* belanja; *entertainment ~ance,* belanja hiburan, elaun hiburan; elaun sara hidup, *cost of living ~ance;* elaun gantian tetap, *commuted ~ance; to make ~ance for the current,* mengambil (ambil) basi harus.

alloy, *n. mixture,* campuran; *of gold,* emas muda.

allude to, *v. tr. mention,* menyebut (sebut) (hal); *touch on,* menyentuh (sentuh), menyinggung (singgung); *recall (memory of),* kenangkan hal.

alluring, *adj. in appearance, of a girl,* genit, penarik (tarik).

ally, *n.* bersatu dalam perdamaian (damai).

almanac, *n.* takwim.

almightly, *adj.* mahakuasa; akhar.

almond, *n.* buah badam; *~-eyed,* mata sepet.

almost, *adv.* dekat, hampir; *(of escaping accidents),* nyaris.

alms, *n.* sedekah; *religious rate for relief of poverty, etc.,* zakat, fitrah; *see* **charity.**

alone, *adj. (of a person),* seorang; *all ~,* seorang diri, sendirian; *without ties,* sebatang kara; *sole, single,* tunggal; *~ with (one other person),* berduaan (dua) dengan.

along, *prep. through the length of,* sepanjang; *~side,* berganding, berkepil (kepil); *running ~side, as road with river,* selari dengan.

aloof, *n. to remain ~ (from),* menjauhkan (jauh) diri (dari), menyingkirkan (singkir) diri (dari); *as a neutral,* berkecuali, *taking no part,* tidak campur tangan, duduk memandang (pandang) sahaja; *see* **neutral.**

aloud, *adj.* dengan suara kuat; *to read ~,* membaca dengan suara nyaring.

alphabet, *n.* abjad.

already, *adv. have ~—,* sudah; *~ in being or in place,* sedia.

also, *adv.* juga, jua.

alter, *v. tr.* mengubahkan (ubah); *v. intr.* berubah; *alteration, as new system,* peralihan (alih).

alternately, *adv.* berganti-ganti; *on alternate days,* lat sehari; *alternating,* selang-seli; silih-berganti; *alternating current,* arus bolak-balik, arus ulang-alik.

alternative, *n. another way,* lain jalan.

although, *conj.* sungguhpun, walaupun, meskipun, mentang-mentang.

altogether, *adv. wholly,* sama sekali; *completely,* habis; *in all details,* serba; *~ white,* serba putih.

altitude, *n.* tingginya.

alum, *n.* tawas.

always, *adv.* selalu; *every time,* tiap-tiap kali; *inevitably occurring,* ada-ada sahaja; *what one must expect,* memang; *it's ~ like that,* memang begitu; *at any time, at any time whatever,* bila-bila masa sahaja.

amalgamate, *v. tr. unite (societies, etc.),* menggabungkan (gabung), mencantumkan (cantum), menyatukan (satu).

amazed, *adj.* hairan, tercengang (cengang), kagum; *amazing ('like nothing on earth'),* bukan buatan, ajaib, menakjubkan (takjub).

ambassador, *n.* duta; *~ at large,* duta rencam; *Minister sent on a speacial mission,* menteri utusan.

amber, *n.* gaharap.

ambergris, *n.* ambar.

ambiguous, *adj. of uncertain meaning,* samar-samar.

ambitious, *adj.* bercita-cita tinggi, hemat tinggi.

amble, *v. tr. trot,* berlari (lari) anak.

ambulance, *n.* ambulan, kereta sakit.

ambush, *n. to lie in ~,* mengendap (endap); *to be ~ed,* kena endap, serang endap.

amen, *int.* amin.

amend, *v. tr. correct,* betulkan; *(as a law),* pindakan; *proposed ~ment,* usul pindaan; *~s,* ganti rugi.

amenities, *n. facilities,* kemudahan (mudah).

America, *n. the United States,* Amerika Syarikat.

amethyst, *n.* batu kecubung.

amidships, *n.* pinggang (kapal).

amiss, *adj. out of order,* salah; *to take amiss,* salah anggap.

ammonia, *n.* sadir, garam amonia.

ammunition, *n.* ubat (senapang), peluru, bahan letupan.

amnesia, *n.* hilang ingatan.

amnesty, *n.* pengampunan (ampun) beramai-ramai.

among(st), *prep. surrounded by,* di tengah-tengah; *between,* antara; *among themselves,* sesama (sama-sama) sendiri.

amoral, *adj.* biadab, kurang sopan, tiada adal.

amount, *n. total of,* banyaknya, jumlahnya; *to the ~ of—,* sebanyak—.

amphibious, *adj.* boleh hidup di darat dan dalam air.

amputate, *v. tr. cut off (limb),* kerat; *having lost a limb,* kudung.

amuck, *v. intr. to run ~,* mengamuk (amuk).

amulet, *n. talisman,* tangkal, azimat.

amused, *adj.* geli hati; *amusing,* lucu, jenaka; *to amuse oneself,* main-main, berhibur-hibur, berfoya-foya; *amusement park,* taman hiburan.

anaemia, *n.* kurang darah; *anaemic in appearnce,* pucat (masai).

anaesthetic, *n.* ubat bius; *insensitive, esp. part of body after injection,* pelali, lasa; *see* **opiate.**

analogy, *n.* kias; *draw an ~,* mengambil (ambil) kias; *analogous to,* seperti, seakan-akan, tamsil ibarat.

analyse, *v. tr.* mengurai (urai), memisahkan (pisah); *analysis,* analisa.

anatomy, *n. science of bodily structure,* ilmu tasyrikh, ilmu urai tubuh.

ancestors, nenek moyang; *a male ancestor,* moyang; *ancestral land,* tanah pesaka; *ancestry,* keturunan (turun).

anchor, *n.* sauh; *long-fluked ~,* jangkar; *fluke,* kuku; *to ~,* berlabuh (labuh); *to cast ~,* campak sauh; *weigh ~,* bongkar sauh; *~age,* labuhan.

ancient, *adj.* lama, lanjut umurnya, kuno; *~ days,* zaman purbakala, zaman puntung berasap (asap), zaman Tok Adam.

and, *conj.* dan.

anemone, *n. sea-~,* rembong.

aneurism, *n.* busung darah.

anew, *adv.* semula.

angel, *n.* malaikat, malak; *the ~ who is the custodian of Death, Izrael; the two angels who examine the dead,* Nakir and Munkar.

angle, *n. space between two meeting lines or (fig.) point of view,* sudut, segi; *at right ~s to,* lurus tegak pada; *to ~, fish with line,* mengail (kail), memancing (pancing).

anglicism, *n. use of English idiom or wording,* bahasa keinggerisan (Inggeris).

angry, *adj.* marah; *wrath,* murka; *to get ~,* meradang (radang); *as resentful,* sakit hati, in a temper, menyebal (sebal).

angular, *adj. having ~ projections, not smooth,* bersanding (sanding).

animal, *n.* binatang, haiwan; *wild ~s generally,* margastua.

aniseed, *n.* adas manis.

ankle, mata kaki; *anklet,* gelang kaki; *~-joint,* buku lali.

annals, *n.* sejarah, tawarikh.

annex, *v. tr. take possession of (territory),* menakluki (takluk); *'grab', 'gobble up',* membolot (bolot), *to join or add,* menyambung (sambung).

annihilate, *v. tr.* menghapuskan (hapus), membasmikan (basmi).

anniversary, *n.* hari ulang tahun.

announce, *v. tr. proclaim publicly,* mengumumkan (umum); *publish news, etc., esp. on radio,* siarkan; *radio ~r,* juruhebah; *part-time radio ~r,* juruhebah sambilan.

annoy, *v. tr. mock,* giat; *tease,* usik; *continually tease, plague,* sakat-sakat; *make ~ing noise,* bising; *~ed,* jauh hati.

annual, *adj.* tahunan.

annul, *v. tr.* batalkan, mansuhkan.

anoint, *v. tr. apply (ointment, oil, etc.),* bubuh; rubon, menyapukan (sapu); *by dripping liquid on,* cucurkan (air pada), renjiskan (air pada).

anomalous, *adj.* gangil, luar biasa.

anonymous, *adj.* tak bernama (nama); *~ letter,* surat terbang, surat layang.

another, *adj.* lagi satu; *a different one,* lain.

answer, *n.* jawaban; *to reply to question,*

jawab, memberi (beri) jawab; *to reply to letter,* membalas surat; *to reply to a hail,* menyahut (sahut); *~able,* bertanggungjawab (tanggung).

ant, *n.* semut; *flying ~,* kelekatu; *tailor-~,* kerengga; *large black biting ~,* kongkiak; *white ~s,* anai-anai; *~-hill,* busut, pongsu; *~-lion,* undur-undur.

antarctic, *n.* kutub selatan.

ant-eater, *n. pangolin,* tenggiling.

antennae, *n. of insects,* sesungut, ketek.

anthem, *n. national ~,* lagu kebangsaan (bangsa); *to sing the national ~,* menyanyikan (nyanyi) lagu kebangsaan, *the Malaysian national ,* Negaraku.

anthropology, *n.* ilmu kaji manusia.

anti-, *prefix, opposed to in sympathies, esp. racial,* membenci (benci); *esp. as in policy,* menentang (tentang), melawan (lawan); *as aiming at counteracting or doing away with, e.g., disease, vice,* pencegah (cegah); *see* **A.A. guns.**

anticipate, *v. tr. hope,* harap; *expect,* menduga (duga), jangkakan.

antidote, *n.* (ubat) penawar (tawar).

antiquated, *p p. out of date,* ketinggalan zaman, *(sl.)* lapuk, kuno, usang.

antiquity, *n.* zaman purba.

antler, *n.* tanduk (rasa); *tine of ~,* rangga.

anus, *n.* jubur, dubur.

anvil, *n.* landasan.

anxiety, *n apprehension,* khuatir; *nervous state,* kecemasan (cemas); *to feel ~,* menaruh (taruh) kuatir.

anxious, *adj.* bimbang, gelisah, cemas; *worried,* risau.

anyhow, *adv.* bagaimanapun; biar bagaimanapun; *(at any rate),* setidak-tidaknya; *(not less),* sekurang-kurangnya.

apart, *adj. separated,* berasingan (asing), terpencil (pencil), suku; *(three feet) ~,* jaraknya (tiga kaki); *~ from,* selain dari.

apartheid, *n.* dasar membeda-bedakan (beda) kulit, dasar menyingkirkan (singkir) kaum.

apathetic, *adj. lacking spirit,* kurang semangat; *showing no interest,* diam

menunggul (tunggul), buat acuh tak acuh.

aperient, *n.* (ubat) julap, pencahar (cahar).

aperture, *n. as in a wall or as a loophole,* lumpang; *see* **hole.**

apex, *n.* kemuncak, puncak.

aphorism, *n.* pepatah.

aphrodisiac, *n.* ubat menambahkan (tambah) syahwat; ubat nafsu berahi.

apologise, *v. tr.* minta maaf.

apoplexy, *n.* sawan terjun; *to have an apoplectic fit,* kena sawan terjun, kena lintasan (hantu).

apostate, *n. from Islam,* murtad.

apostle, *n.* rasul (Allah).

appalling, *adj.* ngeri, dahsyat.

apparatus, *n.* alat, perkakas, pesawat, radas.

apparently, *adv.* rupa-rupa, nampaknya.

apparition, *n.* penjelmaan (jelma); *ghost,* hantu.

appeal, *n. earnest request, esp. to authorities,* rayuan; *to ~ to a higher Court,* masuk 'apil'; *~ Court,* mahkamah ulang bicara, mahkamah rayuan; *public ~, as for funds,* seruan.

appear, *v. tr. present oneself,* hadir; *come into sight,* tampak, nampak, muncul; *esp. on surface,* timbul; *as a ghost,* menjelma.

appearance, *n.* rupa, roman; *bearing,* gaya; *to put in an ~ (as at a function),* menunjukkan (tunjuk) muka; *to keep up ~s; (i) avoid the possibility of scandal,* memeliharakan (pelihara) cakap; *(ii) avoid loss of dignity,* menjaga (jaga) maruah; *(iii) do something merely for ~s' sake,* melepaskan (lepas) batuk di tangga; *see* **eye, humbug, hypocrisy.**

appease, *v. tr. calm by coaxing,* membujuk (bujuk); *as by policy,* mententeramkan (tenteram), *esp. of appeasing an angry person,* menyejukkan (sejuk) hati; *see* **pacify.**

appendix, *n. to book,* penambahan (tambah), lampiran; *vermiform ~,* usus buntu; *appendicitis,* radang usus buntu; to append, subjoin, peturunkan (turun).

appertaining to, adj. relating to, berkenaan (kena) dengan.

appetite, n. craving for food, selera, nafsu makan; appetizer, umpan tekak; appetizing, rousing the ~, yang menggecarkan (gecar) selera, yang membuka (buka) selera; having no ~, nafsu makan bertambah (tambah) kurang; to indulge one's ~, menjamu (jamu) selera.

applause, n. tepuk sorak; thunderous ~, tepuk sorak yang gemuruh, soraksorai.

appliance, n. alat, perkakas; to apply, put on spot, bubuh; wipe on, sapu; ask for, minta; bring into contact with, kenakan; apply brake; kenakan 'berek'; apply oneself to studies, bertekun (tekun)

applicant, n. as for a job, (orang) yang meminta (minta); application, permintaan; permohonan (mohon).

appoint, n. to an office, melantik (lantik).

appointment, n. jawatan, jabatan, perlantikan.

apportion, v. tr. divide into shares, membahagi (bahagi), mangagihkan (agih), faraidkan.

appraise, v. tr. estimate worth of, nilaikan (nilai), taksirkan (taksir).

appreciate, v. tr. esteem, menghargai; realise existence of, insaf (akan), sedar (akan).

approach, v. tr. draw near, sampai dekat; berdekat dengan, berhampiran (hampir) ke; mendekati; mendatangi; get close to, rapat; ~ (as a person as for advice), mendapatkan (dapat); ~able (open to reason), boleh kira, boleh berunding (runding).

appropriate, adj. fitting, patut, padan, bersesuaian (sesuai), berpatutan; see **opportune.**

approve, v. tr. as a request, benarkan, kabulkan; as in order, sahkan; formal approval, izin.

approximate, adj. agak-agak, hampir

tepat (for measurement).

apron, n. as worn by child, bedung.

apt, adj. appropriate, as a quotation or an answer, kena; quick on the job, cekap.

April, n. bulan April.

aptitude, n. as in skills, ketrampilan (trampil), kecenderungan (cenderung) yang semula jadi.

aquarium, n. tangki ikan.

aqueduct, n. saluran air.

Arabia, n. negeri Arab; Arab Saudi, Saudi Arabia

arable, adj. ~ land (suitable for ploughing), tanah tenggala.

arbitrary, adj. of power, sewenangwenang, memenang.

arbitrator, n. orang tengah; to arbitrate, jadi orang tengah.

arbour, n. punjung.

arcade, n. as in narrow passage, lorong tempat jualan (toko).

arch, ~way, n. curved structure, pintu gerbang; gapura; see vaulted; ~ed, curved, melengkung (lengkung); to ~ the neck, as a horse or a heron, menggelekkan (gelek) leher.

archaic, adj. no longer in use, tak dipakai lagi, usang; kolot, ketinggalan (tinggal) zaman.

archipelago, n. gugusan pulau, nusantara, kepulauan (pulau).

architect, n. ahli ilmu binaan, jurubina, akitek.

arctic, n. kutub utara.

area, n. extent, luasnya; as of jurisdiction, kawasan.

areca-nut, n. buah pinang; ~ pounder, gobek; ~ scissors, kelati, kacip.

arena, n. gelanggang; for bull-fights, bong.

argue, v. intr. bicker, bertengkar (tengkar); discuss, berbicara (bicara); debate, berunding (runding), berdebat (debat); have a dispute, berbantah (bantah); have a fierce argument, bertikam (tikam) lidah; argument (reason advanced for or against), hujah; ground adduced, alasan.

arid, adj. kering; of soil, kersang, gersang;

esp. as waste land, tandus.

arise, *v. intr. come into notice, as a problem,* timbul; *get up,* bangun.

aristrocrats, *n.* kaum ningrat, bangsawan.

Aristotle, *n.* Aristu.

arithmetic, *n.* ilmu kira-kira, ilmu hisab, ilmu hitung, *do mental ~,* congak.

ark, *n.* tabut, bahtera; *Noah's ~,* bahtera Nabi Noh.

arm, *n.* lengan; *~pit,* ketiak; *~ful,* sepemeluk (peluk); *~-in-~,* berganding (ganding) tangan; *with open arms,* dengan tangan terbuka (buka); *~-rest (of chair),* pengalas tangan.

armada, *n.* angkatan laut.

armistice, *n.* perdamaian (damai) sementara, gencatan senjata.

amlet, *n. band worn round the arm,* toha; *(of metal),* gelang kana.

armour, *n.* baju besi, baju zirah; *~ed vehicle,* kereta perisai.

armoury, *n.* gudang senjata, pusat senjata.

arms, *n.* senjata alatan perang; *heraldic ~,* lambang; *the Armed Forces,* Angkatan Bersenjata.

army, *n.* angkatan darat, tentera darat, bala tentera; *territorial ~,* tentera wataniah.

aroma, *n. as in smell,* bauan wangi; *in feeling,* keadaan mengasyikan (asyik).

around, *adv. and prep,* sekeliling.

arouse, *v. tr. as emotions,* menimbulkan (timbul), mendatangkan (datang).

arrange, *v. tr. promote, as a plan,* menganjurkan (anjur); *put in order,* mengaturkan (atur); *'get up',* kira, iktiarkan; *~ in layers,* menyusun (susun); *make an ~ment with (come to an understanding with),* berpakat (pakat) dengan; *put together, as flowers,* mengarang karang); *~ hair,* berdandan (dandan); *see* **promote.**

arrangement, *n.* peraturan; *the thing as arranged,* aturan; *~s (preparation in readiness),* persediaan (sedia).

array, *n. of battle,* ikatan perang, *draw up in ~,* membariskan (baris).

arrears, *n. debt,* hutang; *money still unpaid,* hutang yang tersangkut (sangkut).

arrest, *v. tr.* tangkap, rigap.

arrive, *v. tr. come datang; reach destination,* sampai; *reach spot aimed at,* tiba; *on arrival (as soon as (he) ~d),* apabila sampai sahaja (dia); sebaik sahaja (dia) datang.

arrogant, *adj.* sombong, angkuh, hidung tinggi, *esp. in behaviour to superiors,* takbur, *uppish,* ranggi; *warning against arrogance,* padi makin berisi (isi) makin tunduk, *the fuller rice-ear, the lower it bows its head.*

arrow, *n.* anak panah.

arrowroot, *n.* berohi.

arsenal, *n.* gudang senjata.

arsenic, *n.* warangan.

art, *n. fine ~,* seni; *human skills,* ketrampilan (trampil).

artery, *n.* pembuluh (buluh) darah.

arthritis, *n.* penyakit (sakit) (dalam) tulang, penyakit sendi.

artichoke, *n.* ubi halia.

article, *n. thing,* benda, barang; *clause,* bab, fasal; *as in newspaper,* rencana, makalah; *leading ~,* tajuk rencana, *~ of faith,* rukun; *~ made, artifact,* bekas tangan, tukangan.

articulated, *adj. having joints,* bersendi (sendi); *to articulate, speak,* bertutur (tutur) dengan jelas.

artificial, *adj. not natural,* buatan, rekaan; *imitiation,* tiruan; *false,* palsu; *~ leg* kaki sambung, kaki buatan; *~ teeth,* gigi palsu; *~ insemination,* memasukkan (masuk) mani seseorang ke dalam rahim seseorang isteri kerana inginkan anak.

artillery, *n. branch of the Army,* pasukan meriam.

artisan, *n. skilled handicraftsman,* tukang yang berkemahiran (mahir).

artist, *n.* ahli seni; seniman, *painter,* jurulukis.

as, *adv. and conj. ~ such ~,* seperti; *in the function of,* sebagai; *~ far ~,* setakat; *~ far ~ I know,* yang saya tahu; *so long ~,* selama, selagi; ~ if, seolah-olah.

asafoetida, n. inggu.

ascend, v. intr. mount, naik; as hill, mendaki (daki); climb, memanjat (panjat); as a river, mudik

ascertain, v. tr. dapat tahu, menentukan (tentu).

ash, n. abu, abuk; ~-tray, bekas abu.

ashamed, adj. malu; to feel small; to feel oneself as big as an ant; merasa (rasa) diri sendiri sebesar semut.

aside, adv. di sebelah; to stand ~ (take no part), menyingkirkan (singkir) diri; duduk di tengah; put ~, menepikan (tepi).

ask, v. tr. question, tanya; for, minta; after, as an invalid, tanya hal; ~ to (request to act), ajak; interrogate, menyoal (soal), soal siasat, respectfully inquire, tumpang bertanya.

askance, adv. look ~ at, memendang (pandang) serong pada, menganggap (anggap) sepi.

askew, adj. our of true, inclining to one side, mereng, senget; twisted, awry, erut.

aslant, adj. not in straight line, serong, tuding; not completely vertical, condong.

asleep, p.p. tertidur (tidur), fast ~, lena; see **sleep.**

aspect, n. in appearance, perwajahan (wajah); bidang.

asphyxiated, p.p. lemas.

aspire, v. intr. concentrate one's hopes (on), mencita (kan); aspirations, citacita, hasrat.

assail, v. menyerang (serang).

assault, v. tr. strike, pukul; make an attack on (fortress, etc.), melanggar (langgar), menyerang (serang), menyerbu; ~ craft, perahu serbu.

assay, v. tr. test (metal, etc), menguji (uji).

assemble, v. intr. berhimpun (himpun), berkumpul (kumpul); call together, menghimpunkan; put together (as machine), pasang.

assembly, n, as crowd in street, kumpulan orang, perhimpunan (himpun)

orang; for a purpose, as for deliberations, majlis; right of ~, hak berkumpul; see **council and sit.**

assent, v. intr. express agreement, bersetuju (setuju), mengiakan (ia).

assert, v. tr. maintain, mengaku (aku), menyatakan (nyata); declare, menegaskan (tegas); ~ oneself (as in face of oppression), angkat muka; to be self-~ive, push oneself, suka menonjolkan (tonjol) diri; see **claim.**

assess, v. tr. fix amount of value, taksirkan, nilaikan.

assessor, n. in a trial, pengapit (apit); penilai.

assets, n. harta benda, modal.

assiduous, adj. in studies or duties, rajin, tekun.

assign, v. as a share, memberi (beri); to a job or duty, tugas; ~ment, tugasan.

assimilate, v. tr. menyamakan (sama); united, berpadu (padu); ~d to environment and associations, sebati, sesuai.

assist, v. tr. menolong (tolong), membantu (bantu); 'good offices', as in helping to settle a dispute, jasa baik; so to ~, memberi (beri) jasa baik; ~ant, penolong; of certain functionaries, muda; Menteri muda, (the ~tant Minister).

associate, v. intr. ~ with, bercampur dengan; berdamping (damping) dengan; an association, persatuan (satu) gabungan (gabung).

assume, v. tr. to take it to be that, I ~, pada pendapat (dapat), saya.

assurance, n. to give an ~, memberi (beri) jaminan, memberi pengakuan (aku).

assuredly, adv. tentu, nescaya.

astern, adv. di belakang, di buritan, go ~, 'gustan'.

asthma, n. sesak dada, sesak nafas, sakit lelah, semput.

astonish, p.p. terperanjat (peranjat); terpegun (pegun), to go 'right up in the air' with ~ment (and annoyance), melambung (lambung); see **amazed.**

astray, adj. tersesat (sesat); to lead ~, esp by deceit, mengelirukan (keliru), see deviate.

astride, adj. tunggang; straddling, terkangkang (kangkang),tercelapak (celapak).

astringent, adj. in taste, kelat.

astrology, n. ilmu bintang; astrologer, ahli nujum.

astronaut, n. angkasawan.

astronomy, n. ilmu falak; astronomer, ahli falak.

astute, cerdik, panjang akal.

asylum, n. mental ~, rumah sakit orang gila; rumah sakit otak; political ~, perlindungan (lindung) undang-undang, perlindungan politik, suaka politik.

at, prep. place, di (and now, sometimes, time); time, pada (sometimes place); ~ first, mula-mula; ~ last, akhirnya.

atheist, n. one who denies the existance of God, orang yang menidakkan (tidak) adanya Tuhan; orang kufur, see **heathen;** disbeliever in Divine Providence, kufur nikmat.

athlete, n. ahli sukan, olahragawan; athletics, sukan, panca lumba, olahraga.

athwart, adj. as, jammed across, sengkang; lying ~, melintang (lintang).

atmosphere, n. surrounding the earth, udara; (fig.) mental ~, suasana.

atom, n. ultimate particle of matter, zarah 'atom'; bomb, 'bom atom'; ~ic power, kuasa atom.

atone, v. intr. expiate (sin), menebus (tebus).

atrocious, adj. sangat kejam; atrocity, kekejaman.

atrophied, p.p. of limbs, lesut.

attach, v. tr. tie, ikat; as in joining things together, hubung; one thing onto another, as when assembling a pipe, sambung; seize by court order, 'sil'; girl to whom one is ~ed, gadis pautan hati.

attache, n. pembantu (bantu) dalam kedutaan (duta), jinjangan kedutaan.

attack, v. tr. as troops, menyerang (serang, terkam, langgar, verbally, membidas (bidas), mencela (cela), menyelar (selar); counter-~, serang balas.

attain, v. tr. reach, gain, mencapai (capai),

find one's way to, mendapatkan (dapat).

attempt, v. tr. in doing, to try, mencuba (cuba), ikhtiar.

attend, v. intr. be present, ada; esp. at meeting, hadir; to listen carefully, perhati (hati) baik-baik; ~ants, pengiring (iring); to ~ mosque, berjemaah (jemaah); ~ to (e.g. grievance, demands), melayani (layan); well-~ed, of a function, ramai; poorly ~ed, lengang; rapt attention, khusyuk.

attest, v. tr. a document, menandatangi (tanda tangan) jadi saksi.

attire, v. to dress, memakai (pakai).

attitude, n. bodily posture or behaviour, sikap; mental ~, corak fikiran; way of thinking, stand-point, pendirian (diri).

attitudInise, v. intr. posture, show affectation, berlagak-lagak; esp. of woman seeking to attract men, melaram (laram).

attorney, n. power of ~, surat kuasa.

attract, v. tr. (attention, interest or as a magnet), menarik (tarik); allure, memikat (pikat) hati; ~ive, of a girl, manis, genit,; magnetic ~ion, tarikan besi berani.

attribute, n. characteristic quality, sifat.

attrition, n. wearing down by friction, haus.

auction, n. lelong; to sell by ~, jual lelong; to buy at ~, tangkap lelong; ~eer, tukang lelong.

audible, adj. dapat didengar; barely ~, sayup, balam-balam.

audience, n. viewers, penonton (tonton), para pendengar (dengar); to have an ~ (with a Ruler), menghadap; ~ Chamber, balairong.

audit, v. tr. memeriksa (periksa) kira-kira.

audition, n. personal test-interview, temuduga, temu-uji.

auger, n. gerodi, penggerik (gerik), bor.

august, adj. worthy of veneration, azim.

August, n. bulan Ogos.

Aunt, n. emak saudara, emak su; '~ty' acik.

aura, n. of noxious person or object, imbasan.

auriferous, *adj.* mengandungi (kandung) emas.

auspicious, *adj. luck-bringing, of a date or moment,* sempurna; ~ *moment,* saat yang sempurna; *see* **lucky, propitious.**

austerity, *n. practice of* ~, riazah; *to practise* ~, as a hermit, berbuat (buat) tapa.

authentic, *adj.* sah; sahih; asli.

author, *n.* pengarang (karang), pereka (reka).

authority, *n. power,* kuasa; *'authorities consulted' (by an author),* buku-buku sebagai paduan; *the authorities, esp. governmental,* pihak yang berkuasa (kuasa); *responsible authorities,* pihak yang bertanggung (tanggung) jawab, pihak yang berwewenang (wewenang).

autobiography, *n.* riwayat hidup sendiri.

autocracy, *n.* 'otokrasi', kekuasaan (kuasa) diri, bergerak (gerak) sendiri, automatis.

autograph, *n.* tanda tangan sendiri.

autonomous, *adj.* berkerajaan (raja) sendiri.

autopsy, *n.* pemeriksaan (periksa), pembedahan (bedah) mayat.

autumn, musim buah.

auxillaries, *n. (troops),* pasukan pembantu (bantu).

available, *adj. ready to hand,* sedia.

avarice, *n.* tamak, loba.

avenge, *v. tr. a defeat,* menebus (tebus) kekalahan (kalah); *an insult,* hapuskan arang di muka; *see* **vengeance.**

average, *n. to strike an* ~, *on the* ~, pukul rata; ~ *price,* harga rata; *of ordinary standard,* sederhana.

averse, *adj. disinclined,* segan.

avert, *v. tr. ward off ,* mencegah (cegah), menjauhkan (jauh); *esp. as misfortunes,* menolak (tolak); *'one's face,* paling (muka).

avid, *adj. eager for,* ingin.

avoid, *v. tr.* menjauhkan (jauh) diri daripada, ~ *danger–or (shirk) work,* mengelakkan (elak); *see* **dodge.**

await, *v. tr.* tunggu, menantikan (nanti), mengharapkan (harap).

awake, *v. intr. not asleep, cease to sleep,* sedar, jaga; ~ *with a start,* terkejut dan terjaga.

awaken, *v. tr.* gerakkan daripada tidur, kejutkan.

award, *n.* hadiah, anugerah.

aware, *adj.* sedar, insaf (akan); *I am well* ~, saya bukan tak tahu.

awash, *adj. level with the waves, of a rock,* (batu) berendam (rendam).

away, *adv. off with you!* pergilah! nyah! berambus! (ambus), *see* **down;** *to go* ~ *(move to another place),* berpindah (pindah).

awe, *n. stand in* ~ *of,* disegani.

awful, *n. terrible,* dahsyat; ~*ly (sl. very),* bukan main.

awhile, *adv. for a time,* sementara, buat sementara.

awkward, *adj. clumsy,* kekuk; *with hands,* kasar tangan; *with feet,* kaki bangku; *of behaviour or speech,* canggung.

awl, penggerek.

awning, *n.* kajang, tenda; *see* **canopy.**

axe, *n.* kapak.

axis, *n.* paksi; pasak; *the Axis Power,* kuasa-kuasa pasak.

axle, *n.* aci, gandar roda; ~-*pin,* cabi.

B

B.C., *adv.* sebelum Masihi.

babble, *v. intr. talk incoherently or excessively,* meleter (leter); ~*r, loose-tongued,* bocor mulut.

baby, *n.* kanak-kanak (kecil), bayi; *new-born* ~, anak yang baru lahir.

bachelor, *n.* bujang; *young* ~, (anak) teruna.

bacillus, *n.* kuman, hama.

back, *n. hinder part,* belakang; *dorsal muscles,* tulang belikat; ~ *to front,* balik bokong; *come or go* ~, balik, kelek; ~ *of chair,* sandaran; *take* ~, *receive* ~, ambil balik; *lying on* ~, telentang (lentang); ~ *to* ~, bertemu (temu) belakang; *turn* ~ *on,* membelakangkan; *go* ~*wards and forwards,* berulang-alik (ulang); *walk* ~*wards,* (berjalan) jalan punggung ke hadap; ~*water (reverse oars),* lais, surung dayung; *a* ~*water (still water of stream),* sungai mati; ~ *(reverse, esp of car)* 'gustan'; *to support,* menyokong (sokong); *try to win,* menangkan; *take side of,* berpihak (pihak) pada; *prefer, as probable winner, net (on),* bertaruh (taruh)suit (sebelah); pilih; *behind one's* ~, balik belakang.

backbite, *v. tr.* membuat (buat) fitnah atas, mengumpat (umpat).

backbone, *n.* tulang belakang.

backcountry, *n.* ulu, daerah pendalaman (dalam), darat.

backfire, *v. intr. as a car,* tembak asap.

background, *n.* ~ *part of scene,* latar belakang.

backward, *adj. behind-hand in progress,* mundur, ke belakang.

bad, *adj. wicked,* jahat; putrid, busuk; *not* ~*!* jadi juga!

badge, *n.* lencana.

baffled, *adj.* terkecewa (kecewa), gagal.

bag, *n. suit-case,* "beg"; *kit-*~, buntil; *rattan* ~, kudai; *matting* ~, karung; *woman's hand-*~, tas; *make-shift* ~ *formed by tying together ends of some material,* punjut.

baggage, *n.* bebarang, barang-barang.

baggy, *adj. as trousers, etc., which have lost their crease,* sudah patah sait, sudah patah kanji.

bail, *n. security for appearance,* jaminan; ~*or,* orang jamin.

bail, *v. tr. to* ~ *out (water),* menimba; *a* ~*or (tin),* timba; *to* ~ *(enter into a* ~ *bond),* mengikat (ikat) jamin; *from plane,* terjun.

bait, *n.* umpan; *to* ~ *(worry with jeers or molest in small ways),* sakat-sakat, cucuk-cucuk.

bake, *v. tr.* membakar (bakar), memanggang (panggang); ~*r,* tukang roti.

balance, *n. pair of scales,* neraca; *steel yard,* dacing; ~*-sheet,* neraca kira-kira; *see* **weigh;** *equilibrium,* keseimbangan; *well-*~*d,* berimbang; *be in equilibrium,* bertimbang (timbang) betul, bertimbalan (timpal); ~ *of power,* imbangan kuasa, *to lose one's* ~, hilang pertimbangan badan; *to reel and fall,* huyung-hayang langsung rebah.

balcony, *n.* langkan; *projecting porch,* anjung.

bald, *adj.* botak; *as with shaven head,* gondol.

bale, *n.* bandela; *see* **bundle;** ~ *out, see* **bail.**

balk, baulk, *n. of timber,* balak; *to* ~, thwart, halangkan, kecewakan.

ball, *n.* bola; ~*-bearings,* kacang-kacang; *anggur roda; small round mass,* kepal; *roughly circular lump, as of mud,* segumpal.

ballast, *n.* tolak bara.

balloon, *n.* belon.

ballot, *n.* undi; *see* **vote.**

ballyhoo, *n. to make a* ~ *about, boost,*

gembar-gemburkan.

bamboo, *n.* buluh, aur, bambu; *edible --shoots,* rebung; *~-rat,* dekan, babi tanah; *flattened ~ used for cheap walls,* pelupuh (lupuh).

ban, *v. tr. as unlawful,* haramkan; *~ned area,* kawasan larangan; *to ~ entry,* menyekat (sekat).

banana, *n. tree,* pokok pisang; *a comb of ~s,* sesikat pisang; *main bunch,* setandan pisang.

band, *n. of colour,* jalor; *of music,* 'ben', pancaragam; *~-stand,* pondok pancaragam; *as for the arm,* toha; *for carrying burden on back,* ambin; *sound of musical ~,* gedak gedik, cepak pong; *as of robbers,* gerombolan; *tight ~, esp of rubber,* ketang.

bandage, *v. tr.* membarut (barut), membalut (balut); *something bound round, to strengthen,* simpai; *a ~,* kain balut.

bandit, *n. robber,* penyamun (samun) perompak (rompak); *terrorist,* pengganas (ganas); penjahat (jahat).

bandolier, *n.* sandang kartus.

bandy, *v. tr. ~ about, keep talking of (as a person's name),* membawa-bawa; *~ words,* bertengkar (tengkar) (dengan).

bandy-legged, *adj. (or bow-legged),* pengkar.

bang, *v. tr. ~ the door,* hempaskan pintu; *~ on the table,* menghentak (hentak) meja; *~! pong!*

bane, *n.* bencana.

bangle, *n.* gelang; gelang tangan; gelang kaki.

banish, *v. tr.* buang negeri; *see* **restrain.**

banister, *n.* susuran tangga; langkan tangga.

bank, *n. sloping margin of river,* tebing; *the left ~ of a river going upstream,* seberang kiri; *the right ~ going upstream,* seberang kanan; *on both ~s,* seberang-menyeberang; *see* **shelf;** *sand~, shoal, earth~,* batas; *to ~ up, make a ~,* menambak (tambak); *for custody of money,* ~; *donors' blood-~,* tabung derma darah; *to ~ (a fire),* runggun.

bankrupt, *adj.* bankrap, muflis; *to go ~,* jatuh bankrap.

banner, *n.* panji-panji, sepanduk; *on two poles,* pemidang; *stretched across (road),* kain rentang.

banquet, *n.* majlis makan.

banter, *v. intr. jest lightly,* bersenda gurau (senda); seloroh.

baptism, *n.* baptis, pembaptisan.

banyan, *n. lage sp. of fig-tree,* pokok jejawi (jawi-jawi).

bar, *n. as of door,* kayu sengkang; *of river,* alangan (di kuala sungai); *iron ~,* batang besi; *as of window,* jerjak, ruji; *as lattice-work,* kisi-kisi; *see* **exclude.**

barb, *n.* ruit, duri pandan; *~ed wire,* dawai berduri.

barbarian, *n.* orang liar; orang yang tidak bertamadun.

barber, *n.* tukang cukur, tukang gunting (rambut).

bare, *adj. smooth,* licin; *stripped, as of leaves,* loncos, gondol, bolos; *devoid of covering,* bogel; *'topless' dresses,* pakaian dedah dada; *see* **naked;** *with the ~ hands (without weapons),* dengan kuasa tulang empat kerat.

bare-faced, *adj. shameless, impudent,* tak silu-silu, muka tebal; *see* **shame.**

bare-footed, *adj.* tak berkasut (kasut); *(sl.),* berkaki (kaki) ayam.

bare-headed, *adj.* tak bertopi (topi); *(sl.),* berdogol (dogol); bergondol (gondol).

bargain, *v. intr. chaffer,* tawar-menawar; *collective ~ing,* dasar tawar-menawar secara 'kolektik'.

barge, *n. lighter,* tongkang; *another type, usually driven by sail or motor,* toakau; *to ~ through (an obstacle),* merempuh (rempuh), merapah (rapah); *~ in, melanda (landa) masuk.

bark, *n. of tree,* kulit kayu; *outer part of palm trunk,* ruyung; *to ~, of a dog,* menyalak (salak).

barn, *n. covered structure for storage of graip,* jelapang; rengkiang; *(small),* kepuk.

barnacle, *n. (various sp.),* berangas, teritip, kapang, tembeluk.

barracks, *n.* 'berek', tangsi, kaman.

barracuda, *n.* ikan alu-alu.

barrel, *n.* of gun, laras; wooden vessel, tong, pipa, tahang, legir; of fountain pen, tabung (pena).

barren, adj. incapable of producing children, mandul; arid, of land, tandus, dangkal, kersang, gersang; (fig.) of a useless way of life, gersang; (esp. as worked-out), usang; of a tree, not developed properly, tak subur; having attained a good size, but fruitless, besar gabuk.

barricade, v. tr. rebat, tebat; esp. as road-blocks; rintangan (jalan).

barter, v. tr. to exchange goods, etc., for something other than money, (berniaga dengan cara) tukar-menukar.

base, adj ignoble, hina; of action, keji.

base, n. of tree, perdu; of operations, pakaian, tempat tumpuan; as pedestal, lapik, alas; -d on (as a policy), berdasarkan (dasar); ~less, tak beralas (alas), tak berasas (asas); ~d on (having as an essential element), berteraskan (teras); to ~ one's hopes on, menumpukan (tumpu) harapan pada.

bashful, adj. shy, pemalu (malu); showing ~ness, tersipu-sipu.

basin, n. mangkuk, jeluk; metal ~, batil.

basis, n. basic substance of, dasar; forming ~, basic, pokok, asasi.

bask, v. intr. berjemur (jemur).

basket, n. raga, bakul; back ~, knapsack, ambung; rubbish-~, pongkis, saki; waste-paper ~, raga (bakul) sampah; plaited ornamental ~, rombong; hamper, keranjang.

bastard, n. illegitimate child, anak haram, born out of wedlock, anak di luar nikah; (abusive); anak haram, haram-zadah; of uncertain father, anak gampang.

baste, v. tr. renjis minyak.

bat, n. (flying), kelawar.

batch, n. number of objects collected together, kumpulan; part of a larger total of objects, bahagian.

bath, v. intr. mandi; bathroom, bilik mandi; ~-tub, tong mandi; ~-water jar, tempayan; bathing-cloth or dress, kain basahan; Chinese bathing clout, cokin.

bathe, v. intr. (in sea), mandi (laut).

batter, v. tr. dash violently against, membanting (banting), membantai (bantai).

battle, v. intr. berperang (perang); struggle, berjuang (juang); clash, bertempur (tempur); ~-field, medan peperangan.

baulk, v. tr. prevent, menghalang (halang), mencegah (cegah); interfere with so as to tend to thwart (movement, action), mengganggu (ganggu).

bawdy, adj. as a story, lucah.

bay, n. sea in opening of land, teluk; space, as in car-park, ruang; to ~, of hounds, menyalak (salak); sound of baying, keng, keng, keng.

bayonet. n. 'benet' sangkur.

bazaar, n. pasar, lorong tempat gerai-gerai jualan.

be, v. intr. exist occur, ada.

beach, n. pantai; ~ed, drawn up on shore, tersadai (sadai); see **aground, strand.**

beacon, n. for signalling, suar; survey ~, bairup.

beads, n. manik, manik-manik, esp of coral ~; merjan; rosary, tasbih.

beak, n. of bird, paruh; of fish, jolong.

beam, n. of timber, kasau, rasuk; of light, sinaran.

beamy, adj. broad, as boat, buntak, daup.

bean, n. kacang; soya ~, kacang kedelai; ~ sprouts, tauge; beancurd, tahu; soya-~ cakes, tempe; ~-pole, junjung.**bear,** n. beruang; bear-cat, benturung.

bear, v. tr. see **carry;** endure, tahan, menanggung (tanggung), menderita (derita); ~ a child, beranak (anak); (more formal), bersalin (salin); ~ fruit, berbuah (buah); ~ oneself, comport oneself, membawa (bawa) diri; ~ yourself as you should, baik-baik membawa diri; ~ a grudge, menaruh (taruh) dendam; ~ with, put up with, as a tiresome person, bersabar (sabar).

beard, n. janggut; a full ~, bauk.

bearing, n. mode of carrying oneself, gait, carriage, gaya, pembawaan (bawa).

beast, *n. animal,* binatang, haiwan; *see* **animal;** *proverbial '~ of burden',* kerbau; *he makes me just a ~ of burden,* menjadikam (jadi) hamba (sahaya).

beat, *v. tr. strike,* pukul; *drub,* balun; *with end of stick, as drum,* palu; *~ up (ingredients with spoon),* lecek, enjut; *~ in, as rain,* tempias; *thrash, with cane,* belasah; *of the heart,* berdebar (debar); *heart-~,* detik jantung; *~ing fast, of heart,* girap-gemirap; *~en down, as a crop by storm,* ranap; *as grass by weight,* terlendat (lendat); *~ metal,* menempa (tempa), menitik (titik); *see* **flat;** *~ the breast,* mendebik-debik dada, menebah-nebah (tebah) dada; *'~ it' (sl.), rush madly away,* buka langkah seribu *(sl.); see* **hit** and **away.**

beautiful, *adj.* cantik, molek; *esp. as a sight,* indah; *beauty-parlour,* kedai solek; *beautician,* pesolek; *beautify (decorate e.g. a town),* perindahkan (indah).

becalmed, *adj.* (kapal) kematian (mati) angin.

because, *conj.* sebab, fasal, oleh sebab; *~ of,* kerana, lantaran.

beche-de-mer, *n. sea-slug,* teripang.

beckon, *v. intr.* gamit.

bed, *n. sleeping-place,* tempat tidur; *~stead,* katil; *charpoy,* manja; *platform-~,* pentas, pangking; *pallet,* ranjang; *raised ~ for planting,* batas; *seed-~,* semaian; *~ of river,* perut sungai; *as bottom surface of sea, river,* dasar laut (sungai); *bedding,* tikar bantal; *~-ridden,* duduk terlentang (lentang) sahaja; *'make' a ~,* kemaskan tempat tidur; *'go out of ~ the wrong side' (grumpy),* cuka dimakan pagi ini; *(but makan cuka may also mean, get a 'telling off', be rebuked); 'uneasy ~-fellows',* seperti durian seambung dengan timun, *(like a durian in the same basket as a cucumber); a ~ of cockles, oysters, etc.,* benih (kerang, tiram); *~room,* bilik tidur; *bridal ~,* pelamin (lamin).

Bedouin, *n.* orang Badui.

bee, *n. honey ~,* lebah; *bees-wax,* lilin lebah; *carpenter-~,* kumbang; *midget ~,* kelulut; *mason-~,* angkut-angkut; *~-eater,* burung beberek (berek-berek).

beef, daging lembu; *steak,* bifstik.

beetle, *n.* kumbang; *esp. the coconut-~,* kekabur (kabur-kabur); *dung ~,* gulingtahi.

before, *adv.* dahulu; *beforehand,* terlebih dahulu; awal-awal; *conj.* sebelum.

beg, *v. tr. ask for,* minta; *beseech for,* mohon; *ask for alms,* minta sedekah; *beggar,* pengemis (kemis) (Ind.), peminta sedekah.

beget, *v. tr.* memperanakan (anak).

begin, *v. intr. commence,* bermula (mula); *take first step in,* mulai, melagang (lagang); *~ning, inception,* permulaan; *starting point,* pangkalan; *(as of period),* awal; *origin,* asal.

beguile, *v. tr. persuade by wheedling,* kecek-kecek; *~d by promises,* terjual (jual) dek janji; *by smooth talk,* termakan (makan) kata-kata orang.

begrudge, *v. tr.* sakit hati terhadap; iri hati kepada.

behalf, *n. on ~ of,* atas nama, *esp. in signatures,* bagi pihak.

behave, *v. intr. conduct oneself,* membawa (bawa) diri; *behaviour, conduct,* kelakuan (laku); *natural course of action,* resam, resmi; *odd behaviour, mannerisms, 'antics',* gelegat, telatah; *~ as, act like,* berlagak (lagak) sebagai; berkelakuan.

behaviour, *n.* perangai, tingkahlaku, tabiat.

behead, *v. tr.* pancung kepala, penggal kepala, penggal leher.

behind, *prep.* di belakang, di sebalik, di balik; *the posterior,* punggung.

belch, *v. intr.* bersendawa.

believe, *v. tr.* percaya; *be convinced,* yakin; *adhere to (as creed),* menganuti (anut); *~r, adherent,* penganut, *staunch ~r,* beriman (iman); *see* **convinced.**

belittle, *v. intr. disparage,* mempermudahkan (mudah), mencuaikan (cuai), memperkecilkan (kecil).

bell, *n.* loceng, genta; *cattle-~,* kertuk,

418

keroncong; *to ring a* ~, pukul loceng; *(by swinging)*, goyang loceng; *to* ~, *of a deer,* bertempik (tempik).

bellow, *v. intr. as a bull,* menguak (uak); *as in pain,* meraung (raung).

bellows, *n.* hembusan, alat untuk meniup api.

belly, *n.* perut; *(contemptuously),* tembolok; *~ing out, of sails,* kepuh, *swag-bellied,* perut gendut, perut buncit; *the 'bag' of the* ~, kelungsong perut.

belonging, *v. intr. be the property of,* hak; *this belongs to me,* ini hak saya; - punya; *this is mine,* ini saya punya; *~s, luggage,* barang-barang, *property,* hartabenda.

belt, *n.* tali pinggang; *girdle,* bengkung; *cross-~,* sandang; *stuck in one's ~ (as a knife),* tersisip (sisip) di pinggang.

bench, *n. a long seat,* ambin; *in a court,* kerusi hakim, *back ~er,* barisan belakang.

bend, *v. intr. as tree in wing,* melentur (lentur); *as laden branches,* meluyut (luyut); *as when riding a bicycle,* membongkok; *~ head,* tunduk; *as a river,* melengkuk (lengkuk), melengkung (lengkung); *~ this way and that, esp. up and down (as a plank),* meleding-leding; *~ a bow,* melenturkan (lentur) panah; *bent,* bengkok; *stooping,* bongkok.

beneath, *adv.* bawah.

benefaction, *n.* jasa, derma.

benefit, *n.* untung; *esp. as aid,* manfaat; *material benefits generally, not necessarily money,* faedah.

benighted, *adj. overtaken by night,* kemalaman (malam); *involved in intellectual and moral darkness,* jahil.

benumbed, *adj.* kebas, lali.

bequeath, *v. tr.* mewasiatkan (wasiat).

beri-beri, *n.* penyakit lembik, penyakit biri-biri.

berserk, *v. tr. to go* ~, mengamuk (amuk).

berth, *n. place to anchor,* tempat berlabuh (labuh).

beside, *prep.* di sisi, sebelah, di rusuk; *by*

the edge of, di tepi; *to be ~ oneself (with rage),* mengamuk (amuk).

besides, *adv.* lagi pun; *in addition to,* selain daripada; di samping.

besiege, *v. tr.* mengepung (kepung).

besmear, *v. tr.* melumur (lumur) dengan memalit (palit); conteng.

bespattered, *p.p. as with mud,* berselekeh (selekeh), terperecik (recik).

besprinkle, *v. tr.* merenjis (renjis), simbahkan.

best, *adj. most good,* yang baik sekali, yang terbaik; *to the ~ of (his) ability,* dengan seboleh-bolehnya, dengan sedaya-upaya.

bestir oneself, *v. reflex,* mengorak (orak) langkah.

bet, *v. intr.* bertaruh (taruh) (duit); *(on),* sebelah; *place one's stake,* tikam.

betel-nut, *n. see areca-nut; ~-leaf,* sirih; *betel-box,* tepak; *salver carrying requisites for ~-chewing,* cerana; *dried ~-nut,* pinang kotai.

betray, *n. for money,* menjual (jual); *'do the dirty on',* buat khianat atas; *to be ~ed (let down by one's friends),* sokongan membawa (bawa) rebah; *see* **collaborate, desert, traitor.**

bethrothed, *p.p.* bertunang (tunang).

better, *adj. more good,* lagi baik; *to become* ~, bertambah (tambah) baik; *improve, make progress,* maju; *feeling* ~, merasa (rasa) lega; *(you) had* ~, lebih baik; *one's '~s',* orang atasan.

between, *prop. and adv.* (di) antara; *in the space* ~, di celah; *~ ourselves (privately),* sesama (sama-sama) kita.

beware, *v. intr.* jaga, (jaga) baik-baik; *keep a watchful eye on,* awasi.

bewildered, *p.p.* terkeliru (keliru), terpegun (pegun); *'mazed',* bingung; *uncertain how to act,* serba-salah fikiran; *confused,* terpinga-pinga.

bewitched, *p.p. under a spell,* terkena (kena) sihir, terkena pukau (terpukau), terkena restu, terkena pesona.

beyond, *adv. and prep.* balik sana, sebelah sana; *esp. of river or sea,* seberang.

bezoar, *n.* buntat; *(magical),* guliga, mestika.

bhang, *n. Indian hemp,* ganja.

biased, *adj.* berat sebelah; *bias, inclination towards,* kecendurangan (cenderungan); *prejudice,* prasangka.

Bible, *n. see* **Scriptures.**

bicker, *v. intr.* bertengkar (tengkar).

bid, *v. intr. at auction,* tawar; *~ to do something,* suruh.

bier, *n.* jenazah, kereta mayat; *simple plank ~,* papan long.

big, *adj.* besar.

bigamy, *n. to commit, to have two husbands (wives) contrary to law,* menduakan (dua) laki (isteri).

bigoted, *adj.* taasub (pada agama), keras beragama.

bilge, *n. of ship,* ruang (kapal); *~-water,* air ruang.

bilingual, *adj. n.* boleh bertutur (tutur) dalam dua bahasa, dwibahasa.

bilk, *v. intr, dishonestly avoid payment of fare,* ponteng, menipu (tipu).

bill, *n. account,* kira; *of bird,* paruh; *proposed statute,* rang undang-undang, bakal undang-undang.

bin, *n. for rice,* belubur, baluh; *see* **barn;** *rubbish-~,* tong sampah.

bind, *v. tr. tie,* ikat; *~ up, as a wound,* balut; *as a book,* menjilid (jilid); *as a cricket bat,* kerbat; *pinion the legs,* rempong; *~ with bonds or as a cracked staff,* simpaikan, bingkaikan, bandut.

biography, *n.* riwayat hidup.

bird, *n.* burung, unggas; *birds of a feather flock together,* enggang sama enggang, pipit sama pipit, *(hornbills with hornbills, sparrows with sparrows).*

birth, *n. ~day,* hari jadi, hari lahir, hari ulang tahun; *(of royalty),* hari keputeraan (putera); *practice of ~-control,* amalan mencegah (cegah) beranak (anak); *woman in child-~,* perempuan nifas; *~day celebrations of a prince,* perayaan (raya) hari puja umur; *to sing ~day greetings,* menyanyikan (nyanyi) lagu selamat ulang tahun; *~-mark,* cacat bawaan; *~place,* tempat tumpah

darah; *~ certificate,* surat beranak (anak); *~day of the Prophet,* Maalud; *see* **bear, born, contraceptive, planning.**

bisect, *v. tr.* kerat dua, bagi dua.

bishop, *n. in chess,* gajah.

bit, *n. piece,* keping; *tiny piece,* secebis; *for horse,* lagam, kang; *~-by-~,* beruntil, berdikit-dikit; *to champ the ~,* mengulum (kulum) lagam.

bite, *v. tr.* gigit; *as an insect,* ketip; *as a dog,* kokak; *as a snake,* pagut, patuk; *as brakes,* makan; *as a fish taking bait,* senjah, makan, cagut; *~ the lips,* mengetap (ketap) bibir; *tear with teeth,* pepak; *once bitten, twice shy,* sekali tersengat, selalu teringat, *(once stung, always remembered).*

bitch, *n.* anjing betina; *v. to complain,* mengadu (adu), menyalahkan (salah).

bitter, *adj.* pahit; *acrid,* kelat; *sour,* masam, asam; *esp as fighting,* sengit; *plant proverbial for ~ness,* putarwali, seruntun.

bittern, *n. (various sp.),* burung pucung, burung gelam, burung kuaran; *tiger-~,* burung kuak.

bitumen, *n.* tanah bolong, bahan aspal atau tar.

black, *adj. dark,* hitam; *definitely ~,* hitam legam; *shiny ~,* hitam berkilat (kilat).

blackboard, *n.* papan tulis, papan hitam.

blackhead, *n.* bintik jerawat.

black magic, *n.* ilmu sihir.

blackmail, *n. to extort money by threats,* memaksa (paksa) wang (dengan mengugut), minta wang secara paksa.

black-market, *n.* pasar gelap.

black out, *n. a period of darkness,* sewaktu tanpa cahaya, gelap gelita; *loss of consciouness,* hilang ingatan (ingat), lupa..

blacksmith, *n.* tukang besi.

bladder, *n. gall-~,* hempedu; *urinary ~,* pundi-pundi kencing.

blade, *n. leaf,* daun; *of oar,* daun dayung; *of knife,* mata pisau.

blame, *v. tr.* salahkan, mencela (cela); *~-worthy,* bersalah; *to fix the ~ on,* menumpukan (tumpu) kesalahan (salah) kepada.

blank, *adj. (not written on or empty),* kosong; *of cartridge,* kosong, hampa.

blanket, *n.* selimut, kambeli.

blarney, *n.* tebu di bibir mulut, *(honey on the lips): see* **beguile** *and* **wheedle.**

blaspheme, *v. intr. talk or impiously,* menghina (hina) Tuhan, *blasphemy, n.*

blast, *n. rush of wind,* hembusan angin; *of heat,* bahang; *as of an explosion,* habil; *to* ~ *(esp rock with explosives),* letupkan (batu dengan bahan peledak); *see* **blow.**

blather, *v. intr.* merepek; *(description of a ~skite),* seperti kuda kencing ke depan, *(like a horse urinating forward; see* **chatter.**

blaze, *v. intr.* bernyala (nyala); *of flame shooting upwards,* marak; *with fierce heat,* membahang (bahang); *to* ~*s with* —*! pergi mampus dengan* —*!*

bleach, *v. tr.* memutihkan (putih); *~ing materials,* ubat peluntur (luntur).

bleak, *adj. of weather, cold and cheerless,* tidak cerah; tidak memberi harapan.

bleary, *adj. of eyes,* rejeh, mata bilis.

bleat, *v. intr.* mengembek (embek), membebek (bebek).

bleed, *v. intr. emit blood,* berdarah; *v. tr.* ~ *surgically,* petik darah.

blemish, *n.* cacat.

blend, *v. tr. mix,* mencampur (campur), mencampur-aduk; ~ *so as to become one,* sebati.

blessing, *n. bestowed of Divine favour,* berkat; *as special favour in time of need,* rahmat; *timely help,* mengantuk (antuk) disurungkan bantal, *(having a pillow passed to one when sleepy); to bless, give a* ~, *as a priest),* memberi (beri) syafaat; *God's blessings, delights,* nikmat; *utter a* ~, mengucap (ucap) doa selamat, *the Blessed,* yang berbahagia (bahagia); *esp as opposed to the Damned,* (yang celaka).

blind, *adj.* buta; *night-~,* rabun ayam; *to ~fold,* tutup mata (dengan kain); *to obey ~ly (without question);* menurut

(turut) perintah begitu sahaja; *believe ~ly,* percaya melulu (lulu); ~ *alley,* jalan buntu; ~ *in one eye,* buta sebelah; *play* ~ *man's buff,* main Cina buta; main tangkap ibu; *short-sighted,* buta larangan; rabun; *the near-~ leads the* ~, sirabun memimpin (pimpin) si buta.

blink, *v. intr.* pejam celek; *as a light,* terang gelap, *blinking hard,* terkebil-kebil; *esp as in bright light,* mata berpinar (pinar).

blistered, *p.p.* melecup (lecup), melecur (lecur), melecet (lecet), melepuh (lepuh).

blitz, *n.* serangan (serang), mengejut (dari udara).

block, *n. as for chopping,* landasan; ~*ed as a hole,* tersebu (sebu), tersumbat (sumbat); *as a drain,* terkambus (kambus); *to shut off,* tutup; ~ *up, as a watercourse,* mengempang (empang); *as a hole with clay,* tumpat; *see* **barricade, blockade.**

blockade, *v. tr. an entrance, traffic entering,* menyekat (sekat).

blond(e), *adj. of skin,* kulit putih; *esp. of a girl, 'honey-coloured',* putih kuning.

blood, *n.* darah; ~*-stained,* berlumur (lumur) darah; ~*-sucker (fig.),* lintah darat; *high ~-pressure,* penyakit (sakit) darah tinggi; ~ *transfusion,* perpindahan (pindah)darah; ~ *donor,* penderma (derma) darah; *'it runs in the ~',* baka dia sahaja begitu; ~*-bank,* tabung darah; *fainting at the sight of* ~, mabuk darah; *having a feeling of a rush of* ~ *to the heart,* terserap darah (serap); tersimbur (simbur) darah, darah meruap (ruap); *feeling the* ~ *run cold,* merasa (rasa) kering darah; *to 'wade through* ~' *'have a* ~ *bath',* mengarung (arung) darah; ~*-money,* diat; *red* ~ *corpuscles,* zat darah merah, biji darah merah.

bloom, *v. intr.* berkembang (kembang); *bear flowers,* berbunga (bunga).

blossom, *n.* bunga, kuntum; *of a palm,* mayang.

blot, *n. black spot,* titik hitam; ~*ted,*

smudged, terpalit (palit).

blotched, adj. with different colours, bertompok-tompok.

blotting-paper, n. kertas lap, kertas kembang.

blouse, n. blaus, pakaian atas wanita.

blow, v. intr. as wind, bertiup (tiup), berpuput (puput); puff, snort, mendengus (dengus); ~ hard, mengembus (embus); ~ nose, buang ingus, mengembuskan (embus) hidung; ~ away (of wind), some light object, melayangkan (layang), terbangkan; ~ a whistle, tiup siti; ~ (an egg), buang isi (telur); ~ down (as a tree), tertumbang (tumbang) buat dek angin; ~n off course, terbabas (babas); ~ up (by explosion), letupkan; ~ up with dynamite, membongkar (bongkar) dengan spidul; he blew his brains out, dia tembak diri, terpancur (pancur) otaknya, puffing and ~ing, termengah-mengah, cungap-cangip; ~pipe, sumpitan; see **blast.**

blue, adj. biru, light ~, biru muda; dark ~, biru tua; sky ~, biru langit; bluish, kebiru-biruan; ~ (powder for washing), nila.

bluff, v. intr. buat gempar sahaja, hentak sahaja; 'talk big', membuat temberang; membohong (bohong), menipu (tipu); empty threats, gertak sambal; bedil buluh; ugut-ugut beruk.

blunder, n. kesilapan (silap) yang bodoh.

blunderbuss, n. pemuras.

blunt, adj. tumpul; esp of point, dumpu; ~ side of blade, paparan (pisau).

blurred, adj. indistinct, kabur, samar-samar; balam-balam.

blurt out, v. tr. expressed by the word 'shot out', kata sudah terlanjur (lanjur).

blush, v. intr. berubah (ubah) muka (menjadi (jadi) merah); berubah warna muka.

board, n. plank, papan; to ~ (ship), naik kapal; on ~, atas kapal; a ~ (Commission), lembaga; commission, suruhanjaya; curry-~, sengkalan; pastry-~, papan penorak (torak).

boast, v. intr. cakap besar, melepas (lepas) cakap; ~ful, suka bercakap besar.

boat, n. (generally), sampan, perahu; ~-hook, 'bodok'; see **canoe, junk, ship, dinghy.**

bobbed, p.p. of hair, (rambut) tukung.

bob-up-and-down, v. tr. (as a cork), tenggelam-timbul; esp. as a boat, angguk-angguk; as the long locks of a runner, terjembak-jembak; always bobbing up (sl.), esp. of a person whom one meets unexpectedly from time to time, hilang-hilang timbul; to bob up, as from behind a wall, melonjak (lonjak).

bodkin, n. jarum cucuk; esp for mending nets, cuban.

body, as opposed to soul, jasad; anatomical, badan, tubuh; ~guard, retinue, asykar sebagai pengawal (kawal) diri; personal ~guard, pengawal peribadi; dead ~ (human), mayat; carcase, bangkai; bodily (as opposed to 'spiritual', rohani), jasmani.

bogey, n. ~-man, momok; to make a ~ of, momok-momokan.

bogus, pseudo, pura-pura, see **false, imitate.**

boil, n. bisul.

boil, v. intr. to come to the ~, mendidih (didih); ~ up, bubble, menggelegak (gelegak); to bring water to the ~, masak sampai mendidih; to ~ (e.g. an egg), rebus; to ~ rice, menanak (tanak) nasi; ~ing point, had mendidih; ~ over, melembak (lembak).

bolster, n. bantal guling, bantal panjang; 'Dutch wife', bantal peluk.

bolt, n. selak, kancing; wooden cross-~, kayu sengkang; metal pin, pasak; ~ of a rifle, pesawat senapang, '~' senapang; to ~ (sl. run away), cabut lari.

bomb, n. 'bom' atom ~, 'bom' jarah, 'bom' atom; time ~, 'bom' jangka; ~-blast, gegaran 'bom'; to drop a ~, menggugurkan (gugur) 'bom', menjatuhkan (jatuh) 'bom'; ~ disposable squad, pasukan pembersih (bersih) 'bom'.

bond, *n. as, security* ~, 'bon' jamin; ~*s, fetters,* belenggu, rantai (kaki), sengkela; *(fig.)* ~*s of custom,* bingkai adat; *as of affection of relationship,* pertalian (tali); *to enter into a* ~, mengikat (ikat) jamin; *to be 'bound over',* kena 'bon' jamin.

bone, *n.* tulang; *bony, having prominent* ~*s; esp. in face,* tulang menyendul, menjendul (jendul); *(fig.) to be a* ~ *of contention between,* perkara yang dipertikaikan.

bonfire, *n.* unggunan api.

bonus, *n. in payment,* gaji tambahan (tambah), bonos.

book, *n.* 'buku', 'buk'; *esp. as a religious* ~, kitab; *to* ~ *(a ticket),* menempah (tempah) tikit; ~*-shelf,* rak-rak buku.

bookcase, *n.* almari 'buku'.

boom, *n. across river-mouth,* batangan; *of sail,* pokoki (kaki) layar; *to - out, as a big clock,* berdentum (dentum); *as guns,* degum-degam bunyinya; *see* **trumpet.**

boost, *v. tr. to make a great fuss about,* hebuhkan, gembar-gemburkan; ~ *prices,* menaikkan harga; ~ *(scheme, goods), in a noisy,* tub-thumping *way,* dentam-dentamkan; *see* **push.**

boot, *n.* kasut 'but'; ~*-laces,* tali kasut; ~*-trees,* kayu sengkang kasut; ~ *of a car,* buntut (kereta).

booth, *n.* warung, pondok.

booty, *n.* barang rampasan.

borax, *n.* tingkal.

border, *n. edge,* tepi; *to a garment,* sibar-sibar; *see* **boundary, frontier.**

bore, *v. tr.* tebuk, kerbuk; *as for water,* gali lubang; *bored (as by long story),* bosan, jemu.

born, *p.p. to be* ~, beranak (anak), lahir; *locally* ~ *(of foreign race),* peranakan; *(if Chinese),* baba; ~ *by breech presentation,* beranak menyongsang (songsang), ~ *by Caesarean operation,* beranak dengan jalan pembedahan (bedah); *still-*~, mati dalam kandungan; anak kebebangan (bebang).

borrow, *v. tr.* pinjam.

bosom, *n.* dada.

boss, *n.* majikan, ketua pekerja.

botch, *n. v. tr. and intr. see* **mess.**

botany, *n.* ilmu tumbuh-tumbuhan.

both, *adj. and adv.* dua-dua; *the two of them,* kedua-duanya; ~ *- and,* baik - baik; *not only - but,* - lagi - lagi; ~ *large and strong,* besar lagi kuat lagi; *on* ~ *sides (esp. of a river or road),* seberang-menyberang; ~, *of a pair,* dua belah; ~ *hands,* dua belah tangan.

bother, *v. tr. annoy,* mengacau (kacau), mengusik (usik); *pester, molest,* mengganggu (ganggu); ~*!,* kacaulah!

bottle, *n.* 'botol', balang; *gourd-*~, labu air.

bottom, *n. as of box,* bawah; *as of hill,* kaki; *buttocks,* punggung; *see* **bed;** ~*less (as lake),* tak terduga (duga) dalamnya; *the* ~ *one (under a pile),* yang terkebawah (bawah).

bougainvillea, *n.* pokok bunga kertas.

bough, *n.* dahan.

boulder, *n. large detached stone,* batu besar; *upright* ~ *or megalith,* tonggak batu, tonggak hidup.

bounce, *v. intr.* mengambul (ambul), memantul (pantul), menganjal (anjal).

bound, *v. tr. see* **jump;** ~*less,* tak terbatas (batas).

boundary, *n.* sempadan, perenggan, mentara; *esp.* ~ *marked by a bank,* batas.

bounty, *n. as of a Ruler,* limpah kurnia.

bouquet, *n.* karangan, jambangan bunga.

boutique, *n.* kedai pakaian berfesyen.

bow, *n.* panah; ~*-legged (or knockkneed),* pengkar; *to walk* ~*-legged,* berjalan (jalan) tenggek.

bow, *n. of boat,* haluan.

bow, *v. intr.* menunduk (tunduk) kepala (memberi hormat); ~*ed (stooping),* bongkok; ~ *the head in prayer,* merukok (rukok); *slightly* ~*ed,* bongkok udang, terkedek; ~*ed, but still tough,* bongkok sabut; *to the head, esp. in grief,* menekur (tekur) kepala.

bowels, *n.* isi perut; *see* **defecate.**

bowl, *n.* mangkuk; *of metal,* batil; ~ *for flowers,* pasu.

box, *n.* peti; *carton,* kotak; *money-~,* tabung duit, tok duit; *~-number,* peti surat; ~ *fish,* ikan buntal; *to* ~, bertinju (tinju); ~ *ears,* tempelang; *see* **case.**

boy, *n.* budak (jantan); ~ *scout,* budak pengakap (kakap); *young Tamil,* tambi.

Boyan, *n.* pulau Bawean.

boycott, *v. tr.* pulaukan, 'memboikot'.

brace, *v. tr. to* ~ *oneself (as to meet danger),* beranikan diri; ~ *up!,* gagahlah!

bracelet, *n.* gelang (tangan).

bracken, *n.* resam, daun resam.

brackets, *n. enclosing words, etc.,* tanda kurung.

brackish, *adj.* payau.

brag, *v. tr. see* **boast,** *empty ~gart, expressed by* masuk bakul angkat sendiri, *(one who talks as if he could get into a basket and lift it by himself).*

braille, *n. system of printing for the blind,* huruf timbul bagi orang buta.

brain, *n. (physical, but sometimes, centre of thought),* otak; *intelligence,* akal.

bran, *n. rice-polishings, 'sharps',* dedak, *imported,* busi.

branch, *n. limb spreading from tree,* cabang, dahan; *minor* ~, carang; *of road or river,* cabang, cabang sungai, *of road,* simpang; ~ *of an association,* bahagian; *minor, cawangan; small local* ~, ranting; *as of education,* jurusan.

brand, *n. mark,* cap, jenama; *to* ~, cap, selar; *half-burned log,* puntung; *(fig.)* ~, *stigmatise as,* mencapkan sebagai, menyelarkan sebagai.

brandish, *v. tr.* tayangkan; melunjakkan (lunjak); *(threateningly),* mengacu-acukan (acu); *wave about,* melelakan (lela), melambaikan (lambai).

brash, *adj. lacking refined manners,* tak berbahasa (bahasa), kurang ajar; *cheeky,* megah.

brass, *n.* tembaga (kuning).

brassiere, *n.* kutang, coli, kain pengampu (ampu) susu.

brave, *adj.* berani; *of great prowess,* gagah; *dauntless,* teguh semangat;

never giving up, berani candang.

bravo!, *int.* bagus.

brawl, *v. intr.* bergaduh (gaduh).

brawn, *n. muscular part of the body,* tubuh; otot.

bray, *v. intr.* bertempek (tempek).

brazen, *adj. shameless,* tak tahu malu, tidak silu-silu, muka tebal, muka papan, muka terpal.

brazier, *n. anglo,* keran; *esp. for heating or for incense,* perapian (api).

breach, *n. to commit a* ~ *of etiquette,* langgar bahasa; *of law,* langgar undang-ungang; *of promise,* mungkir; ~ *of trust,* pecah amanah; *a* ~, *as in dam,* tembusan.

bread, *n.* roti; *a loaf or hunk of* ~, seketul roti; *cupatti,* rot perata; *~-fruit,* sukun.

breadth, *n.* lebarnya; *of an orifice,* bukanya.

break, *v. tr.* ~ *into pieces,* pecahkan; *fracture, patahkan: sever,* putuskan; ~ *a promise,* mungkir (janji); ~ *off (a projection),* kepak; ~ *open as a box,* kopak; ~ *in (as thieves),* pecah masuk; ~ *against, as waves,* menghempas (hempas), membanting (banting); ~ *back (as game),* patah balik; ~ *journey at,* singgah di; ~ *in,* train *(as animals),* latihkan, perjinakkan (jinak); *elephants with brutal methods,* renap; ~ *through (obstacle),* merempuh (rempuh); ~ *off (as flower-head),* getis, runtas; *to* ~ *off relations, 'part-brass-rags',* berputus (putus) arang; *broken-hearted,* hancurhati, remuk-hati; *~-up, as a police a meeting,* menyuraikan (surai), mencemperakan (cempera); ~ *wind,* kentut; *'~' (change course) of a ball,* terpesong (pesong); *broken but not broken off,* sekah.

breakfast, *n.* makan pagi, sarapan.

breast, *n. chest,* dada; ~ *of a woman,* mam, susu, buah dada; *dress, showing* ~ *(topless),* pakaian bogel dada.

breastwork, *n.* benteng.

breath, *n.* nafas; *short of* ~ *(esp. on account of asthma),* sesak nafas, termengah-mengah; *windpipe,* saluran pernafasan; *breathing space*, tempoh melepas (lepas) ngap; *draw in ~, as before muscular effort*, mendengu (dengu); *out of ~*, putus nafas; *with bated ~*, dengan nafas yang tertahan-tahan; *to give a ~er*, memberi (beri) bernafas; *the hot ~ of fire*, hawa api.

breathe, *v. intr. inhale*, menarik (tarik) nafas; *exhale*, membuang (buang) nafas; *hold breath*, tahan nafas; *to ~ again (fig.)*, berbalik (balik) semangat; *~ fire*, menghembuskan (hembus) api.

breed, *v. intr. produce offspring*, mem-biak (biak); *to raise (poultry, etc.)*, pe-lihara, menternak (ternak), mem-biakkan (biak); *race*, bangsa, *ill-bred*, kurang bangsa; *well-bred, of good family*, bangsawan, anak orang baik-baik; *stock*, baka; *thoroughbred*, jati, belum bercampur (campur) baka; *of mixed ~*, kacuk-baka

brewery, *n.* kilang masak 'bir'.

bribe, *n.* (wang) suap, rasuah, (wang) sogokan; *to give a ~*, memberi (beri) suap, tumbuk rusuk biar senak, *if you give a ~, make sure that it is enough (lit. if you give a man a punch in the ribs, make sure that it winds him).*

brick, n. batu bata, batu bipang.

bride, bridegroom, *n.* pengantin; *bridal dais*, mempelai.

bridge, *n. anything serving as a ~*, gertak; *esp. ~ with hand-rail*, jambatan; *pontoon--*, gertak lampung; *suspension ~*, gertak gantung; *anything that can be used as a ~ at a pinch*, titian; *~-head (as a base for operations)*, pangkalan; *drawbridge*, jambatan angkat.

bridle, *n.* tali ras.

brief, *adj. as a writing*, ringkas; *of life*, singkat; *in ~*, pendeknya, pendek kata.

brigade, *n. in the army*, briged.

bright, *adj. shiny*, kilat; *gleaming*, gilang-gemilang; *~ and flashy, of clothes*, gamat; *of colours*, cerah; *~ly lit up, as by moon or lamps*, terang benderang; *shining ~*, terserlah (serlah); *~en up, look cheerful*, berseri (seri) muka.

brilliant, *adj.* cemerlang, gemerlap; *a ~*

(diamond cut in two flat faces), 'ber-lian'.

brim, *n. edge, brink of water*, tepi air, gigi air; *of hat*, birai; *~-full*, penuh menjun-jung (junjung), penuh merombong (rombong); *~ming over*, penuh, mera-bung (rabung).

brindled, *adj. of a dog*, nibung.

brine, *n.* air asin; air laut.

bring, *v. tr.* bawa; *~ in*, bawa masuk; *~ out*, bawa keluar; *~ up*, pelihara, bela, mendidik (didik); *~ forward, as a proposal*, kemukakan (muka), memajukan (maju); *~ up (a subject)*, menimbulkan (timbul); *~ up again as (an old matter)*, ungkit, mengulangi (ulang) semula; *keep ~ing up*, membangkit-bangkitkan (bangkit); *I can't ~ myself to...*, saya tak sampai hati nak...; *cause to come, as clouds ~ rain*, mendatangkan (datang); *retort to someone who persists in ~ing up a stale subject*, rumah sudah, pahat berbunyi (bunyi), *(the house is finished, but the chisel is still heard).*

brinjal, *n.* terung.

brink, *n. of water*, pergigian (gigi) air, pinggiran (pinggir); *see* **edge.**

bristling, *adj. spiky*, menceracak (ceracak); *esp. as a chevaux-de-frise*, jangkuh-mangkuh, *as spears, guns*, carried by a host, bercerancang (cerancang); *as young plants just sprouting up*, merebu; *a bristle*, bulu (kasar), bulu remang; *see* **quill.**

brittle, *adj.* rapuh, mudah pecah

broad, *adj. (as opposed to narrow)*, lebar; *extensive*, luas; *as of chest*, bidang; *beamy*, buntak, dempak; *~-minded*, berfikiran (fikir) luas.

broadbill, *n.* burung hujan, jajang.

broadcast, *n.* siaran radio, *to make a ~*, membuat siaran di radio, *radio station*, stesyen pancaran radio.

broadside (on to), *adj.* melintang (lintang) (dengan); *~ guns*, meriam pem-inggang (pinggang kapal).

broke, *p.p. (sl.)*, papa, licin, muflis; *(vulg.)*, tercalat (calat).

broker, *n. marriage--*, telangkai; *to act as*

a ~ *(in seeking out opportunities),* pukul lubang.

bronze, *adj.* perunggu, gangsa.

brooch, *n.* kerusang, kerongsang.

brood, *v. intr. as over wrongs,* makan hati; *meditate,* termenung (menung); *on eggs,* mengeram (ram); *recall to mind,* mengenangkan (kenang).

broom, *n.* penyapu (sapu), 'berus'; *hard* ~, penyapu lidi.

broth, *n. liquid food,* hirupan; *rice-gruel,* bubur.

brothel, *n.* rumah pelacuran (lacur), rumah jahat; *Chinese* ~, rumah loki; *the 'madam' of a* ~, ibu ayam.

brother, *n. elder* ~, abang, kakak; *younger,* adik; *full* ~, abang (adik) seibu (seemak) sebapa; ~*-in-law,* ipar; ~*s (or* ~*s and sisters),* adik-beradik; ~*hood, band of* ~*s,* persaudaraan (saudara).

browbeat, *v. intr.* menggertak (gertak).

brown, *adj.* hitam manis, perang; *chocolate-coloured,* 'coklat'; *pale* ~, hitam pudar; *very dark* ~, hitam tua.

brows, *n.* dahi.

bruised, *adj.* lebam; ~ *with effusion of blood,* pecah ke darah; *as fruit, having a soft spot,* bertobek (tobek).

brunt, *v. intr. bear the* ~, *be the chief sufferer,* timpa rasa; *do most of the work,* memikul (pikul) berat.

brush, *n.* 'berus', *feather-*~, bulu-ayam; *to* ~, sapu 'berus'; *hair-*~, 'berus' rambut; *tooth-*~, 'berus' gigi; *paint-*~, 'berus' lukisan; ~ *off or away,* kibaskan.

brusquely, *adv.* dengan kasar.

brutal, *adj.* kejam; ~ *act,* angkara.

bubble, *n.* buih, gelembung; *to* ~, as boiling water, menggelegak (gelegak); *to* ~ *up, as a spring,* membuak (buak), membobok (bobok).

bucket, *n.* baldi.

buckle, *n.* pending, kancing, *to* ~ *(bend under pressure),* kerut.

bud, *n.* kudu; *flower-*~, kuntum; *budded, see* **graft.**

budge, *v. intr. shift position slightly,* berganjak (ganjak); *fig. of yielding, giving away,* berganjak, beralah (alah); *he*

won't ~ *an inch,* dia tak berganjak setapak pun.

budget, *n. of Government,* belanjawan, anggaran belanja.

buffalo, *n.* kerbau; *wild* ~, seladang.

bug, *n.* ulat; *bed-*~, pijat.

bugbear, *n. special object of dread,* momok.

bugle, *n.* sejenis tiupan.

build, *n. physique,* perawakan (awak), susuk badan; raga.

bulb, *n. of a plant,* bebawang (bawang-bawang), ubi.

bulbul, *n.* burung merbah; *yellow-crowned* ~, burung barau-barau; *red-whiskered* ~, merbah jambul.

bulge, *n.* tonjol; ~ *out,* tersembul (sembul), membonjol (bonjol).

bulk, *n. the majority,* kebanyakan (banyak).

bull, *n.* lembu jantan; *buffalo* ~, kerbau jantan; ~*'s eye,* mata sasaran.

bull-dozer, *n.* kereta penyodok (sodok) tanah; jentolak.

bullet, *n.* peluru.

bulletin, *n. short official statement,* kenyataan (nyata) rasmi; *medical* ~, kenyataan perubatan (ubat).

bullock, *n.* lembu (kasi).

bulwark, *n.* benteng.

bump, *n.* benggul; *small swelling,* bincul; ~*y of road,* tinggi-rendah, lekak-lekuk; *to '*~ *into', knock up against unexpectedly,* terjeremba (dengan); *noise of a cart* ~*ing along,* gedak-gedak; ~ *(something) against (something),* hempaskan, senggukkan; ~ *up against, encounter unexpectedly,* tersua (sua) dengan; *see* **collide.**

bunch, *n. of flowers,* seikat; *of keys,* sejambak.

bundle, *n.* bungkus (an); *of sticks or other disconnected objects,* se berkas.

buoy, *n.* bairup; *see* **float.**

buoyant, *adj. able to float,* dapat timbul, dapat terapung (apung); *of spirits,* (ber)gembira.

burden, *n.* beban, pikulan.

burgle, *v. tr.* pecah masuk; *anti-burglar*

device, alat pencegah (cegah) pencuri.

burly, *adj.* badan tegap, jagur.

burn, *v. tr.* bakar; *consume by fire,* tunu; *~ed up,* hangus; *~ to the ground,* bakar runtuh; *~t, scorched by being left too long on the fire, of food,* hangit; *to ~ one's fingers (suffer from injudicious action, esp. meddling),* kedapatan (dapat) budi; *a ~ed child dreads the fire,* sekali tersengat, selalu teringat, *(once stung, always remembered).*

burnish, *v. tr. rub, esp. metal to give it a gloss,* upam, menyepuh (sepuh), gilap.

burrow, *n.* lubang; *to ~,* mengeruk (keruk) lubang; *see* **dig.**

bursar, *n. in an institution, a person who has charge of money;* pengumpul (kumpul) wang (yuran); *~y,* biasiswa.

burst, *v. intr. Into pieces,* pecah; *~ on explosion,* pecah meletup (letup); *as shell,* meletup; *a ~ of fire,* letusan; *to ~ through (a barrier),* merempuh (rempuh); *as water through a leak,* membobos (bobos).

bury, *v. tr.* tanam; *a corpse,* kebumikan (bumi); *entomb,* kuburkan, makamkan; *entombed (lit. or fig.), as a letter under a pile of papers,* berkubur; *~ face in (pillow),* sembam muka ke (bantal); *buried, as by a landslide,* terkambus (kambus), tertimbus (timbus), *see* **funeral;** *to ~ by thrusting down into water or mud,* membenamkan (benam).

bush, *n.* pokok kecil, anak pokok; *scrub,* semak.

business, *n. to be engaged in ~,* berniaga; *in buying and selling (some commodity),* berjual-beli (jual); *~-man,* saudagar; *~ circles,* kalangan peniaga (niaga); *~ expert,* ahli perniagaan; *mind your own ~,* ini bukan hal awak; *rather in the sense of 'look to your own faults',* jaga tepi kain sendiri.

bustle, *v. intr. bustling about, excitedly busy,* sibang—sibuk; *hurrying here and there,* cucas-cucas ke sana ke mari; *bustling along, as a crowd of shoppers,* berbondong-bondong; *never still,* macam lipas kudung, *(like a cockroach which has lost a limb).*

busy, *adj. having a lot of work,* kerja banyak; *too ~ to do something,* tak senang; *short-handed,* tak menang tangan; *'rushed',* tengah sibuk; *harassed,* lorat.

but, *conj.* tapi, tetapi.

butler, *n.* pembantu (bantu) rumah lelaki; jongos; khadam.

butcher, *v. tr. to cut up a carcass,* bantai.

butt, *v. tr. strike with horns,* menanduk (tanduk), senggut.

butter, *n.* mentega; *tinned ~,* mentega 'tin'; *fresh ~,* mentega segar, baru.

butterfly, *n.* rama-rama, *see* **moth;** kupu-kupu.

buttocks, *n.* punggung.

button, *n.* butang, kancing; *~hole,* lubang butang, susuk butang,

buttress, *n. as of wall,* sangga, tiang penyokong (sokong); *like projections at the base of certain trees,* banir; akar tunjang; *(fig. support),* menyokong.

buxom, *adj. well fleshed, esp. of a woman,* muntil.

buy, *v. tr.* beli.

buzz, *v. intr.* berdengung (dengung); *of the continuous ~ing of small insects which seems to fill the jungle,* terngiang-ngiang; *having a ~ing in the ears, e.g. after a blow,* merasa (rasa) terngiang-ngiang di telinga; *(fig.) of head as a result of continuous chatter,* bingit kepala; *a ~ of talk,* desiran orang; *of a bee round a flower (dengung is rather of a swarm),* bersering (sering); *'~ off!' (rude),* nyahlah! hincit!; *~ing (of ears),* bengang.

by, *prep. (agent),* dik, oleh; *near to,* dekat; *hard ~,* tang, tentang; *~ means of (e.g., vehicle),* dengan.

by-pass, *a ~ road,* jalan simpangan.

by-product, hasil pecahan, hasil sampingan.

bye, *n. to draw a ~ in a competition,* dipilih menunggu (tunggu).

bye-bye, *v. intr. (to children) go to sleep,* bum! *goodbye,* selamat tinggal.

C

cabbage, *n.* kobis; *palm-~,* umbut.

cabin, *n.* bilik (di dalam kapal), kamar (di dalam kapal), 'gebeng'.

Cabinet, *n. of Ministers,* jemaah menteri, Kabinet.

cable, *n. (hawser),* pendarat (darat); *(wire)* dawai; *(chain)* rantai; *telegram,* kawat.

cackle, *v. intr. (as hen),* berkiok (kiok); *(with laughter),* menggelekek, mengekek (kekek), mengilai (ilai).

cadence, *n.* irama.

cadet, *n. person under instruction, esp. military,* pelatih (latih).

cadge, *v. tr.* mengemis

cafe, *n.* kedai kopi, kedai makan.

cage, *n. as for birds,* sangkar; *generally,* kurungan; *large ~, esp. as used for prisons,* penjara.

Cain, *n. the Biblical character,* Kabil.

Cairo, *n.* Kahirah.

cajole, *v. tr. persuade or soothe by flattery,* membujuk (bujuk).

cake, *n. generally,* kuih; *~s of all sorts,* kuih-muih; *Malay ~s (various types, commonly),* penganan, juadah; *Western-type ~,* 'kek'; *to ~ (form into mass),* berbeku (beku); *selling like hot ~s,* laris seperti goreng pisang panas; *he wants to eat his ~ and have it,* tepung pun dia mahu, kuih pun dia mahu, *(he wants both the flour and the ~).*

calabash, *n.* labu.

calamity, *n.* mala petaka, nahas, bala, bencana.

calculate, *v. intr. reckon, esp. with figures,* menghitung (hitung), mengira (kira), buat anggaran; *calculator,* pengira (kira), mesin pengira.

calendar, *n.* 'kalendar', takwim.

calf, *n.* anak lembu; *of leg,* betis.

calico, *n.* belacu.

calibre, *n. of a tube or a gun,* garis pusat corong; saiz peluru; *of someone,* nilai seseorang, kaliber.

Caliph, *n.* Khalifah.

call, *v. tr. summon,* panggil; *give name to,* panggil; *shout, hail,* laung, kelur; *~ to get up,* bangunkan, panggil; *~ to prayer,* berazan (azan), berbang (bang); *~ to (appeal to),* menyeru; *exclaim,* berseru (seru); *~ in (as a port),* singgah; *pay a visit,* melawat (lawat); *'drop in',* mampir; *visit Ruler,* menghadap (hadap); *a deer-~,* pipit rusa; *pigeon-~,* buluh dekut; *~-up (for service),* kerahan umum; *to be ~ed-up,* menerima (terima) kerahan.

caligraphy, *n.* seni lukis atau seni tulis khat.

calliper, *n.* jangka.

callosity, *n. hard skin,* berulang.

callous, *n.* kejam, tak ada hati.

callow, *adj. young and raw,* mentah, belum tahu hal, belum banyak makan garam, hijau lagi.

calm, *adj.* tenang, tenteram; *unruffled,* tabah; *keep ~!,* sabar!, bertenanglah!; *(don't get worked up!),* jangan melatah (latah); *to keep ~,* bersabar (sabar), bertenang (tenang) diri; *becalmed,* (sudah) kematian (mati) angin.

calorie, *n.* sukatan haba.

caltrop, *n. pointed stakes left as trap for enemy,* ranjau, suda.

calyx, *n.* sari bunga, perdu kelopak bunga.

cambered, *adj. of a road,* berimbalan (imbal).

Cambodia, *n.* negeri Kemboja, Kampuchia.

camel, *n.* unta.

camera, *n.* kamera; *a sitting (of Council) in ~,* sidang tertutup (tutup).

camouflage, *n.* samaran.

camp, *n.* perkhemahan, khemah, kem;

hut-ments, pondok.

campaign, *n.* gerakan, kempen; *to launch a* ~, melancarkan (lancar).

camphor, *n.* kapur barus.

can, *v.* aux be able to, boleh; *know how to,* pandai, tahu; *manage to,* dapat, *cannot,* tak boleh; *of physical effort,* tak lalu, tak larat.

canal, *n.* terusan; *joining two rivers,* sungai gali, sungai korek; *artificial runnel,* tali air; *artificial channel,* bandar air.

cancel, *v. tr.* batalkan; ~*led,* mansukh; *strike out,* potong.

candid, *adj. of speech,* terus-terang.

candidate, *n. for position,* calon.

candle, *n.* dian, lilin; ~-*stick,* kaki dian.

cane, *n.* rotan; *to get the* ~, kena rotan; *to* ~, *swish,* sebat, bedal; *sugar-*~, tebu.

canna, *n.* bunga pisang tasbih.

cannon, *n.* meriam; *fire a* ~, pasang meriam; ~-*fodder,* umpan peluru.

canoe, *n.* kolek; *dug-out* ~, sagur, jalur, serempu.

canon-law, *n. of Islam,* hukum syarak; *of Christianity,* hukum gereja.

canopy, *n.* sengkuap, langit-langit (lelangit); *temporary thatched covering esp. over a boat,* tersendeng (sendeng).

cantankerous, *adj.* bengkeng.

canvas, *n.* kain layar, kembes.

canvass, *v. tr.* ~ *for votes,* mencari undi; *'chase up' votes,* memancing (pancing) undi.

canyon, *n. gorge,* gaung, jurang.

cap, *n.* kopiah, songkok; *skull-*~, ketayap.

capable, *adj.* cekap, berupaya.

capacity, *n. cubic content,* muatan; ~ *for a job,* kelayakan (layak), kesanggupan (sanggup); *in the* ~ *of,* sebagai.

cape, *n. headland,* tanjung.

caper, *v. intr.* prance, jig, gelinjang, menari-nari (tari).

capital, *n. of State,* ibu kota; *wealth for business,* modal; *esp. as opposed to interest,* pokok; ~*ists,* kaum pemodal; ~ *letters,* huruf besar.

capitulate, *v. tr.* menyerah (serah) (diri).

capon, *n.* ayam kasi.

capricious, *adj.* ada angin, ada banyak kerenah, macam kelembuai, ada banyak kelitah; *to act* ~*ly,* bertingkah (tingkah).

capsized, *p.p.* telangkup (langkup), terbalik (balik).

capstan, *n.* putaran sauh.

captain, *n.* 'kapitan; *of a Malay or Arab junk,* nakhoda; *of a Chinese junk,* taikung, *of a fishing boat,* juragan.

caption, *n.* tajuk.

captivate, *v. tr.* menawan (tawan) hati, mengambil (ambil) hati.

car, *n.* kereta, *motor* ~ (kereta) 'motokar'; *armoured* ~, kereta perisai.

carat, *n, unit of weight for gold,* mutu, *but one* mutu = 2.4 ~*s.*

caravan, *n.* company travelling together, kapilah, kofilah.

caraway-seed, *n.* jintan, jemuju.

carbuncle, *n. a sort of large boil,* bisul besar, tebuan tandang, Inas.

carcass, *n.* bangkai.

cardamom, *n.* buah pelaga.

card-board, *n.* kertas papan.

cards, *n. playing* ~, daun terup; *hearts,* lekuk; *clubs,* kelawar; *spade,* 'sped'; *sekopong; diamonds,* 'dimon'; *a pack,* sepotong (daun terup), sekepala (daun terup), *a card for invitations,* kad jemputan (jemput); *identity* ~, kad pengenalan (kenal).

care, *v. intr.* don't ~, tak peduli; *ignore,* tak hirau; ~ *for, be fond of,* sayang; -*free,* herhati (hati) lapang, luleh-luleh; ~ *of (in addresses),* dengan alamat.

careen, *v. tr.* to turn (vessel) on to its side (in order to clean), sendengkan, merengkan.

career, *n.* means of livelihood, mata pencarian (cari); *jalan kehidupan (hidup);* *as holder of an office,* jawatan; kerjaya.

careful, *adj.* hemat, cermat; *be* ~*!,* jaga (baik-baik)!; *gingerly,* berhati-hati; ~*ly (thoroughly),* dengan saksama, dengan teliti.

careless, *adj.* cuai, lalai; ~*ly,* secara cuai; *carelessness,* alpa.

caress, *v. tr.* membelai (belai); *exchang-*

ing ~es, bercumbu-cumbuan.

cargo, n. muatan.

caricature, n. gambar sindiran.

carnal, adj. (as opposed to spiritual -, rohani), jasmani.

carnivorous, adj. of beast of prey, buas.

carp, v. intr. 'pick holes', cela-mencela, mencari-cari, kesalahan.

carpenter, n. tukang kayu.

carpet, n. hamparan, permaidani, hambal; 'red ~', permaidani merah; to spread (a ~), bentangkan.

carriage, n. wheeled vehicle, kereta; bearing, gaya.

carrion, n. daging busuk; carcase of animals, bangkai.

carry, v. tr. convey, bawa; ~ on the shoulder, pikul; by the tips of the fingers, jinjing; as a bag, bimbit; under the arm, kelek, kepit; as in a sack or in the womb, mengandung (kandung); pick-a-back, mengokok (kokok); remove, transport, angkat; something heavy, angkut; in mouth, as a dog, gunggung; in fist or in claws, genggam; on head, junjung; on back, as in knapsack, esp. as travellers, hawkers; galas; across both arms like a bale of firewood, cempung; on shoulder, as gun, memanggul (panggul); in scarf on back, mengambin (ambin); on carrying stick, mengandar (kandar); on a stretcher, mengusung (usung); wrapped in belt-cloth, mengendung (kendung); ~ out, as a plan, menjalankan (jalan), melaksanakan (laksana), melakukan (laku); ~ away, make off with, bawa lari; esp. as swag, menggondol (gondol); ~ off, grab, membolot (bolot); ~ in, bawa masuk; ~ out, bawa keluar; carrier on bicycle, lanting.

cart, n. kereta; bullock-~, kereta lembu; waggon, pedati.

cartilage, n. tulang muda.

cartoon, n. caricature, gambar sindiran, 'kartun'; design, sketch for a painting, (rajah) bakal gambar.

cartridge, n. ubat senapang, kartus, peterum.

carve, v. tr. incise pattern, mengukir (ukir); slice up, menghiris (hiris), meracik (racik); quarter, bantai.

cascade, n. air terjun.

case, n. instance, kali, embak; in ~, kalau-kalau; Court ~, bicara, kes guam; civil ~, bicara mal; criminal ~, bicara jenayah, bicara 'polis'; box, etc.; suit-~, 'beg'; receptacle, generally, bekas; packing-~, pak; small-~, tas; casket, cembul.

cash, n. ready money (~ down), wang tunai.

cashew nut, n. buah janggus, buah jambu golok, buah gajus.

cask, n. tong, legir.

casket, n. cembul, cepu.

cassock, n. jubah.

cassowary, n. burung kesuari.

cast, v. tr. as dice, lots, buang; as net, tebar, buang, campak; skin, meluruh (luruh); see **vote;** ~ anchor, berlabuh (labuh); metal, menuang (tuang); ~ away, discard, campak, buang; down violently, hempaskan; to ~ oneself into, esp. fig., menceburkan (cebur) diri ke dalam; see **throw;** ~ iron, besi tuangan; having a ~ in the eye, juling bahasa.

castaway, n. see **strand.**

caste, n. kasta; ~-mark on forehead, pilis.

casting-net, n. jala.

castle, n. kota; stronghold, benteng; in chess, tir, rukh; '~s in the air', angan-angan Mat Janin.

castor, n. small wheel, kerek.

castor-oil, n. minyak jarak.

castrate, v. tr. kasikan, kembirikan.

casually, adv. not earnestly or attentively, secara sambil lewa, acuh tak acuh.

casualities, n. as in war, kecederaan (cedera).

casuarina, n. pokok ru.

cat, n. kucing; wild ~, kucing hutan; when the cat's away, the mice will play, bila kucing tidak bergigi (gigi), tikus berani melompat (lompat) tinggi, (when the ~ has lost its teeth, the rats dare to leap *high.*

catalogue, *n.* daftar barang-barang, senarai barang-barang.

catalyse, *n.* cerakin.

catamaran, *n.* perahu katir, kolek katir.

catapult, *n.* 'lastik', tarbil.

cataract, *n.* air terjun; *opacity of lens of eye,* buta bular; *the film in* ~, selaput mata.

catch, *v. tr. generally, in trap or as police,* tangkap, rigap; ~ *in the act,* tangkap basah; *as in war,* menawan (tawan); *an illness,* kena; *grip, hold, as a bolt,* makan; *snap up,* cakup; ~ *hold of,* pegang; *to* ~, *take hold, of a flame,* lekat, hinggap; *to* ~ *falling water by putting (a bottle) under it,* menadahkan (tadah) (botol); *the* ~ *(of fish),* (ikan) tangkapan; *as of a device,* persilapnya; *see* **caught.**

catechise, *v. tr.* bersoal (soal)-jawab.

category, *n. sorts,* jenis; *types of people,* golongan, babat; *esp. of the eight classes of persons eligible to receive a share of tithe,* sinf.

catepillar, *n.* ulat, bulu.

cater, *v. to provide and serve food,* pembekal (bekal) makan dan minum.

catfish, *n. (commonest spp.); freshwater, small,* ikan keli; *large,* ikan tapa; *marine,* ikan sembilang.

catgut, *n.* tangsi.

cat's eye, *n. precious stone,* baiduri.

cattle, *n. oxen and buffaloes,* lembu kerbau; *wild ox,* sapi, banteng; *wild buffalo,* seladang.

catty, *n. weight* of 1 1/3 *lb.,* kati.

caught, *p.p. as by thorns,* tersangkut (sangkut); *as rubbish on a snag,* terlembat (lembat); *as by foot,* tersembat (sembat); *as in mud,* terbenam (benam): *see* **catch.**

caul, *n.* tembuni.

cauldron, *n.* kawah, kancah.

caulk, *v. tr. stop up seam with pitch, etc.,* pakal; *pitch for* ~*ing,* gegala (gala-gala), minyak ladan.

cause, *n.* sebab; *basic* ~, pokok pangkal; *origin,* punca, asal; *to* ~, *bring about,*

membawa (bawa), menyebabkan (sebab); *give rise to,* menimbulkan (timbul); *result in,* mengakibatkan (akibat); *bring, as clouds bring rain,* mendatangkan (datang).

causeway, *n.* jalan tambak.

caustic, *n.* ~ *liquid,* air api; *see* **acid;** *of tongue,* kata yang pedas, tajam.

caution, *n. warning,* amaran; *care,* teliti; *to* ~, memberi amaran; *cautiously,* berhati-hati.

cavalry, *n.* tentera berkuda (kuda).

cave, *n.* gua (batu); ~ *in, collapse, as wall,* roboh.

cavil, *v. intr. to make pretty criticisms,* mencela-cela.

cavity, *n. hollow within solid body,* rongga; *see* **hole.**

cease, *v. intr. generally,* berhenti (henti); *esp. of rain,* sidang, scriat, teduh; ~ *to be, die out, as a custom,* luput; *a* ~*-fire,* gencatan senjata, berhenti tembak-menembak.

ceaseless, *adj. incessant,* tak putus-putus, bertalu-talu; bertubi-tubi.

cede, *v. tr. transfer territory,* menyerahkan (serah), memindahkan (pindah).

ceiling, *n.* pagu, 'siling', langit; *to 'hit the* ~' *in wrath or astonishment,* melambung (lambung).

Celebes, *n.* Sulawesi.

celebrate, *v. tr. (as event),* merayakan (raya); meraikan (rai); *celebration,* perayaan.

celebrated, *adj.* ternama (nama), terkenal (kenal); *see* **famous.**

celibate, *n. resolved not to marry,* berpantang (pantang)nikah; *live a bachelor life,* hidup membujang (bujang).

cell, *n. room,* bilik (kecil); *body-*~, buli-buli.

cellular, *adj. not solid, of material,* mabung; *see* **porous.**

cement, *n.* simen; *fig. to* ~ *the bonds of friendship, esp. political,* mengeratkan (erat) pertalian (tali) persahabatan.

cemetery, *n.* perkuburan (kubur);

Chinese ~, jirat Cina.
censer, *n.* perasapan (asap).
censorship, *n.* tapisan (berita); *film* ~ *Board,* lembaga penapis filem.
censure, *v. tr.* mencela (cela).
census, *n.* banci, cacah jiwa.
cent, *n.* 'sen', duit.
centipede, *n.* lipan, halipan.
centralise, *v. tr.* memusatkan (pusat).
centre, *n.* tengah-tengah; *central point,* pusat; ~ *of attention,* tumpuan mata, tumpuan perhatian (hati).
century, *n.* kurun, abad.
cereal, *n. processed edible grain (*strictly *of pounded young rice),* emping.
ceremony, *n.* upacara; *ceremonial custom,* istiadat; *correct ritual,* tertib; *see* **magic;** *master of ceremonies at Court,* datuk istiadat; *generally,* juru acara.
certain(ly), *adj. adv.* tentu, nescaya, pasti; ~ *not,* sekali-kali tidak.
certificate, *n.* surat (keterangan) (terang); *birth-*~, surat beranak (anak); *vaccination* ~, surat *cucuk;* ~ *attesting a fact,* surat akuan; *as,* ijazah, sijil.
cesspool, *n.* limbah, acar.
Ceylon, *n.* Seri Langka.
chafed, *p.p. scraped by friction,* kena geseran, kena haus.
chaff *n. separated grain husks,* sekam; *see* **husk;** *to* ~, *banter,* menggiat (giat), bergurau (gurau).
chain, *n. series of loops of metal or distance of 22 yards,* rantai; *fetters,* belenggu; *neck*~, kalung; ~*-shot,* peluru bolang-baling (baling); ~ *of mountains,* banjaran gunung, deretan gunung.
chair, *n.* kerusi; *easy-*~, kerusi malas; *rocking* ~, kerusi ungkang-ungkit; ~*man,* pengerusi; *to play musical* ~*s,* lumba merebut (rebut) kerusi; *to* ~ *(carry in triumph),* menjulang (julang).
chalice, *n.* piala (gereja).
chalk, *n.* kapur.
challenge, *v. tr. to urge to action,* ajak; *esp. as to a contest,* mencabar (cabar); ~ *cup,* piala cabaran.
chamber, *n. as for meetings,* dewan;

large room or open space in cave, ruangan.
Chamberlain, *n.* Dautk Istiadat.
chameleon, *n.* sesumpah (sumpah).
champion, *n. as in-*sport, johan, juara, jaguh; *as in a struggle,* pembela (bela), pejuang (juang).
chance, *n. opportunity,* peluang; *hoped for prospect,* 'can'; *by* ~, *just by* ~, kebetulan (betul) pula; *to take a* ~ *(try one's luck),* mengadu untung (adu), buang nasib; *see* **destiny, fortune, luck.**
Chancellor of the Exchequer, *n.* Menteri Kewangan (wang).
change, *v. tr. to ex*~, menukar (tukar); ~ *clothes,* bersalin (salin (pakaian); *alter,* mengubah (ubah); ~ *position of,* mengalih (alih); *to be altered,* berubah; ~ *one's shape by magic,* menjelma (jelma) menjadi—; ~ *one's mind,* berubah fikiran; ~, *balance due,* baki, duit yang lebih; *small* ~, duit kecil, duit pecah; *small silver,* 'seling'; *to* ~ *money,* menukar wang, mengurup (urup) wang; *to* ~ *hands* (of *property),* berpindah (pindah) tangan; ~ *the subject,* mengalih pokok perbualan (bual); ~ *sides, join another political party,* melompat (lompat) masuk —; ~ *one's views,* beralih tadah; *veer,* ~ *direction, of wind,* berkisar (kisar); ~ *course,* beluk; *changeable,* berubah-ubah *(in temper),* macam kelembuai; *as winds, times,* pancaroba; *a* ~ *(transformation),* as of policy,* peralihan.
channel, *n. as in river,* alur; *artificial and (*fig.),* saluran; *runnel,* tali air; *navigable course at sea,* arungan; *of radio or television,* saluran (radio, televisyen).
chant, *v. intr. as prayers,* membaca (baca); ~ *religious verses,* berzikir (zikir); ~ *the praises of the Prophet,* berzanji; *intone esp. a tale,* mengidung (kidung); *Arabic chants,* kasidah.
chaos, *n. extreme confusion,* kacau -bilau, purak-peranda, kelam -kabut, lintang-pukang; *state of* ~, keadaan (ada) kacau-bilau, *etc.*

chapel, n. private place of worship, not a mosque of general assembly, surau, bandarsah.

chaperon, n. pengiring (iring).

chapter, n.. bab; of the Koran, surah.

character, n. set of writing symbols, huruf; mental ~, moral nature, tabiat, perangai; reputation, nama; ~ in a novel or play, watak, pelaku (laku); natural ~ (not the result of environment or training), tabiat semula jadi; good and bad points in ~ of person, jahat baiknya.

characteristics, n. distinguishing traits, sifat; to characterise, sifatkan sebagai—.

charcoal, n. arang kayu.

charge, n. care or custody of, jagaan; price demanded for doing work, upah; accusation, tuduhan, exhortation (to duty, etc.), amanat; to attack at a run, menerkam (terkam), meluru (luru), menyerbu (serbu).

charity, n. money given to institutions for helping those in need, derma; charitable works, derma bakti, amalan, khairat; to give, esp. land, for charitable purposes, wakafkan; see **alms, works.**

charm, n. attractive quality, budi, budi bahasa; words acting as a ~, petua, mantera; book of ~s, etc., buku tib; to recite (a ~), membaca (baca); see **talisman;** ~ing (of a girl), genit, manis; ing to talk to, peramah (ramah) mulut.

charred, p.p. scorched and blackened by fire, rentung.

chart, n. carta peta laut; weather ~, peta angin.

charter, n. plagam; to ~ (vehicle or vessel) for agreed sum, sewa; written grant of rights to, e.g. an accountant, tauliah.

chary, adj. berhati-hati.

chase, v.tr. hambat; pursue, mengejar (kejar); hunt, memburu (buru); ~ away, halau.

chasm, n. gaung, jurang; see **abyss.**

chaste, adj. not irregular in behaviour (of a woman), sopan santun.

chat, v.intr. berbual (bual), berborak (borak), berceloteh (celoteh).

chatter, v.intr. talk incessantly and trivially, mereta-reta; as birds, mengicak (kicak), mericau (ricau); ~box, tukang borak; engage in empty ~, bergibang-gibang; sound of ~, esp. of children, pok-pek pok-pek; ~ing, of teeth, terantuk-antuk, menggelatuk (gelatuk).

chauvinistic, adj. excessively patriotic, gila kebangsaan (bangsa), terlampau cintakan tanah air.

cheap, adj. murah; dirt-~, dapat terpijak (pijak); ~er in the long run (of expensive quality goods), alah beli, menang pakai, (worsted when you buy , you win when you use).

cheat, v. tr. tipu; by small tricks, e.g., by giving short weight, celok; 'steal a march' (get a dishonest advantage), potong 'trip' (sl.), to act crookedly, esp. by ~ing in games, elat; see **deceive, swindle.**

check, n. in chess, sah; ~ to the queen, mar; opened ~, aras; ~-mate, mat; to ~, cause to cease, as disease, mencegah (cegah); ~ed, in square pattern, corak tapak catur; ~ by comparing, as in proof-reading, semak; see **restrain.**

cheek, n. side of face, pipi; cheeky, megak; see **saucy.**

cheer, v. intr. sorak; shout and ~, as a crowd, bertimpik (tempik) sorak; to ~ (someone) up, menghiburkan (hibur) hati; to ~ up, perk up, oneself, angkat mata.

cheerful, adj. suka hati, periang (riang); of ~ countenance, muka berseri (seri).

cheese, n. keju.

chemicals, n. ubat-ubatan, bahan kimia.

chemist, n. research ~s, ahli kimia; druggist, tukang ubat.

cheque, n. written order to a bank, surat janjian (janji) bank, cek.

cherish, v. tr. look after, pelihara, mendidik, bela.

chess, n. catur.

chest, n. breast, dada; box, peti; large ~,

saharah.

chestnut, *n.* buah berangan.

chew, *v. tr.* mamah; *munch,* kunyah-kunyah, membaham (baham); ~ *the cud,* mamah-biak; *don't bite off more than you can* ~, tepuk perut, tanya selera, *(pat your stomach and ask how your appetite is.)*

chicken, *n. baby chick,* anak ayam.

chicken-pox, *n.* jeluntung, cacar air.

chicks, *n. sun-*blinds, bidai.

chief, *n. leader,* ketua (tua), penganjur (anjur), pemimpin (pimpin); *local headman,* penghulu; *principal in importance,* utama.

chiku, *n.* buah ciku, buah sawa, buah sawanila.

child, *n. infant,* kanak-kanak, bayi; *offspring,* anak; *of royalty,* putera, puteri; *to treat as a (mere)* ~, memperbudak-budakkan; *mere* ~, budak makan pisang; ~*ish, of behaviour,* keanak-anakan; *adult who behaves* ~*ishly,* ibu keladi; *still tied to mother's* apron-strings, duduk di bawah ketiak emak lagi.

childbed, *n. woman in* ~, perempuan nantikan (nanti) hari, melarikan anak.

childhood, *n.* masa kecil lagi; *from* ~, dari kecil lagi.

chilli, *n. long pepper,* cabai, cili.

chilly, *adj.* dingin.

chimney, *n.* ceropong, serombong.

chin, *n.* dagu; ~ *in hand,* bertopang (topang) dagu.

China, *n.* benua China, negeri China, Tongsang, Tionghoa, Tiongsan.

chinaware, *n.* barang tembikar, 'porselin'.

chink, *v. intr. to emit sound as of coins striking together,* berdencing (dencing), berdering (dering); *a crevice,* celah.

chintz, *n.* kain cita.

chips, *n. of wood,* bahan kayu, serpih-serpih; *as flying fragments,* perecik (recik); *chipped,* sompik, serpih; *having little bits knocked out,* rompis-rompis.

chirp, *v. intr. as a bird,* mengicak (kicak); *sound of* ~*ing,* cit, cit, cit; *as a cricket,* berdesing (desing).

chisel, *n.* pahat.

chock, *n. block, as for checking motion of wheel,* (kayu) sengkang; *wedge,* baji.

chock-full, *adj.* penuh sesak.

choice, *n. act of choosing,* pemilihan (pilih); *selected,* terpilih; *Hobson's* ~ *(have to take what there is),* kena ambil apa sahaja.

choke, *v. tr. see* **throttle;** ~*d, of a pipe, etc.,* tersumbat (sumbat), tersebu (sebu), tersebat (sebat); *esp. as of an airlock,* senak; ~*d, of a person,* tercekik (cekik); *(something) stuck in throat,* terlekat (lekat) di kerongkong.

cholera, *n.* penyakit (sakit) taun, penyakit muntah -muntah dan cirit-birit; ~ *epidemic,* waba penyakit taun.

choose, *v. tr.* pilih; *see* **fastidious.**

chop, *v. tr. hack at,* tetak; *mince,* cincang; *cut wood up,* belah kayu; ~ *down,* tebang; ~ *bushes,* tebas; ~*per (short jungle heavy* ~*per,* kelewang; ~ *off, as a branch,* cantas; ~*ped off,* putus kena tetak; ~*ping-block,* landasan.

chopsticks, *n.* sepit; penyepit makanan.

chorus, *n. refrain.* dendang.

Christ, *n.* Nabi Isa; *Christian,* Masihi; *esp. Roman Catholic,* Serani; *generally,* Christian.

Christian, *n.* orang-orang yang beragama Kristian.

Christmas, *n.* hari besar bagi orang-orang yang beragama Kristian, Krismas.

chronic, *adj. of invalid,* mengidap (idap) sakit; *lasting year in, year out,* menahun (tahun).

chronicle, *n. of events,* riwayat.

chrysalis, *n.* kepompong.

chrysanthemum, *n.* bunga kekwa.

chubby, *adj.* (muka) tembam.

chuckle, *v. tr.* menggelekek (gelekek).

chunk, *n. lump of clod,* gumpal.

chupatti, *n.* roti cepati.

church, *n.* gereja.

churn up, *v. tr.* ~ *up (water),* palung; *for*

children's play, papan gelungsur.

chute, *n. artificial channel for water,* palung; *for children's play,* papan gelungsur.

chivalvous, *adj. relating to chivalry;* perwira (wira).

chop, *v. of cutting,* menetas (tetas); memenggal (penggal); memotong (potong).

cicada, *n.* riang-riang; cengkerik.

cigar, *n.* cerutu; cerut.

cigarette, *n.* rokok; *the little handmade ~, wrapped in nipah leaf,* rokok daun; *~ case,* bekas rokok, lopak rokok; *~-end,* puntung (rokok).

cinders, *n.* bara api.

cinema, *n. (show),* wayang gambar; *(half),* panggung (wayang); *see* **picture.**

cinnamon, *n.* kulit kayu manis.

cipher, *n. figure O,* kosong, sifar; *system of secret writing,* tulisan rahsia.

circle, *n. round plane figure,* bulatan; *ring for sport;* gelanggang; *for bull-fight-*ing, bong; *to ~, as a plane,* berlegar; *~t,* lingkaran; *to ~, en~, the stratosphere,* melingkari angkasa lepas; *to sit in a ~,* duduk melengkung; *~s (persons having a common centre of interest),* golongan, kalangan; *semi ~,* keluk.

circular, *adj. round,* bulat; *globular,* bundar.

circular, *n. document sent round to a number of persons,* surat edaran (edar); surat pengedaran, 'sekelar'.

circulation, *n. (of paper),* siaran; *(of blood),* peredaran (edar) darah.

circumcision, *n.* sunat, khatan; *to be circumcised,* bersunat; *to circumcise,* sunatkan, *(sl.)* sucikan, cuci; *circumcisor,* tukang sunat, Tok Modin.

circumference, *n.* lilitan, lilit bulatan (bulat).

circumlocution, *n. talking round and round a subject,* cakap berbelit-belit.

circumstance, *n.* hal, peri hal, hal ehwal; *~s (state),* keadaan (ada).

circumvent, *v. tr. get the better of by artfulness,* memperdayakan (daya).

cistern, *n.* tangki.

citadel, *n.* kota.

cite, *v. tr. ~ as authority,* mensaksikan (saksi); *collect (opinions, rulings),* memetik (petik); *~ (summons to Court),* 'saman'.

citizen, *n. person owing allegiance,* rakyat, warga negara; *inhabitants,* isi (negeri); *~ship,* kerakayatan; *city,* kota (besar), kota raya; *sense of ~ship,* kesedaran (sedar) bernegara; *'civics',* tata negara.

citronella oil, *n.* minyak serai.

civet-cat, *n.* musang.

civil, *adj. of a case, not criminal,* (bicara) mal, (bicara) yang tidak berkenaan (kena) dengan polis; *~ war,* perang saudara; *~ servant,* pegawai awam.

civilian, *n.* orang 'preman', orang awam; *civvies (~ clothes),* pakaian 'preman'.

civilization, *n.* tamadun, peradaban (adab), mudun.

claim, *vtr. as of right,* menuntut (tuntut); *profess fact,* mendakwa; *dun (for a debt),* menagih (tagih).

clairvoyant, *n.* petung (tenung), tukang tilik, orang terus mata.

clam, *n.* (siput) kima.

clammy, *adj.* melengas (lengas).

clamour, *n. confused hubbub,* gempur, bunyi riuh rendah; *to emit ~,* geger; *to ~ for (make vociferous demand),* gaduh-gaduh minta; *make a great noise, of a crowd,* kegemparan (gempar).

clan, *n.* puak; *family group,* suku.

clang, clank, *v. intr. emit loud metallic sound,* berderang (derang), bergerancang (gerancang).

clap, *v. intr.* tepuk tangan; *~ hand to, esp. a painful place,* menekup (tekup); *~per of bell,* anak (genta); *~per worked by hand,* kelontang, kelenting.

clarify, *v. tr.* mejelaskan (jelas), menerangkan (terang).

clash, *v. intr. to meet in conflict,* bertimpur (timpur); *as meeting head-on,* berterkup (terkup), bertembung (tembung); *not fit in with,* bertentangan (tentang) dengan, tidak sesuai dengan; *sound of clashing,* bunyi gemerencang, berdencing (dencing).

clasp, *n. for fastening,* kancing; *(clip),* sepit; *to ~ (embrace),* memeluk (peluk); *grasp,* pegang; *as a climber ~ a tree,* kapuk; *~ hands (shake hands),* berjabat (jabat); *~ the hands,* berdakap (dakap) tangan.

clasp-knife, *n.* pisau lipat.

class, *n. (school),* darjah, 'kelas'; *of society,* lapisan bangsa, 'kelas', golongan (bangsa), kalangan (bangsa); *esp. of persons in an age*-group, lingkungan; *~mate,* kawan se 'kelas'; *'upper-~''* (*of society),* orang atasan; *'lower-~es',* orang bawahan; *'middle-~es',* kaum pertengahan (tengah); *~-struggle,* perjuangan antara kelas.

classify, *v.* membahagikan (bahagi); menentukan (tentu).

clause, *n.* fasal, ceraian, bab.

claw, *n.* kuku; *of crab, prawn,* sepit; *to ~,* mencakar; *scape by ~ing motion,* mengokot (kokot).

clay, *n.* tanah liat.

clean, *adn. free from dirt,* bersih; *to ~,* cuci, membersihkan; *wash,* basuh; *by rubbing and scrubbing,* mengincah (kincah); *~ oneself after defecating,* cebuk *; ~ the teeth,* menggosok (gosok) gigi; *'~ed out'* (sl.), licin; *(vulg.),* tercalat (calata).

cleanse, *v. tr. to ~ oneself ceremonially after ritual defilement,* samak; *such cleansing,* sertu; *see* **ablutions.**

clear, *adj.* terang; *~ and established,* sabit, sahih; *limpid,* jernih, hening; *obvious,* nyata; *~ and bright, as in moonlight,* terang benderang; *to see clearly, have an uninterrupted view,* nampak jelas; *~, of daylight,* cerah; *of skin,* cerah; *to ~ away (dishes),* angkat pinggan mangkuk, kemaskan pinggan mangkuk; *~ away, disappear, as mist,* hilang; *~ a way, by cutting,* merambah (rambah) jalan *; generally,* buka jalan; *to ~ jungle,* terangkan, bersihkan; *by felling trees and bushes,* menebang

(tebang) menebas (tebas); *~ the head, e.g., by going on a holiday,* melapang-lapangkan (lapang) fikiran; *~ one's name (from suspicion, etc.),* membersihkan (bersih) nama; *a clearing (in jungle),* cerang; *a ~ing for planting,* ladang; *overgrown ~ing,* repuh; *to ~ weeds (in rice-field) with tajak,* menajak, merempeh (rempeh); *to ~ throat,* berdahak (dahak), berdaham (daham), melepaskan (lepas) batuk; *~ and distinct (of view or sound),* lantang; *~-out, as nose,* mancung; *~-cut, of features,* muka bagai diraut; *~ as daylight, esp. of an offence,* terang seperti bersuluh (suluh) bulan matahari, *(as ~ as if lighted up by the sun and the moon).*

cleats, *n. (to receive a bar, etc.),* tupai-tupai.

cleave, *v. tr.* membelah (belah); *cleft, fissure,* celah; *crack,* retakan; *'cleavage' (between breasts),* lekuk dada, rengkahan dada.

clemency, *n.* bertimbang rasa; belas; lemah lembut.

clench, *v. tr. ~ the fist,* genggamkan tangan.

clerk, *n.* kerani.

clever, *adj.* cerdik, pintar; *(skilled),* pandai; *'try to be ~',* memandai-mandai.

cliff, *n.* gunung (curam).

climate, *n.* hawa, iklim; *see* **zone.**

climax, *n. culmination (of a movement or a story),* puncak; *reach a ~,* memuncak.

climb, *v. tr. ascend,* memanjat (panjat); *clamber up (hill),* mendaki (daki); *swarm up,* naik mendepang (depang); *'~ down', (give way),* beralah (alah), tunduk; *~ing-loop (for feet),* sengkelit; *the ~ing perch,* ikan pepuyu (puyu-puyu).

clinched, *adj. finally settled,* selesai, tetap; *clinch (come to grips),* bergomol (gomol).

cling, *v. tr. hold on to,* pegang; *as to side of wall,* melekap (lekap); *clinging tightly to,* berpaut pada.

clink, *v. intr.* berbunyi (bunyi) garing, berdencing (dencing).

clip, *n.* sepit; *to ~ (cut off ends),* pangkas; *clipped, as a moustache,* kompot, kontot.

clique, *n.* puak; *to form cliques,* berpuak-puak.

clitoris, *n.* kelintit.

cloak, *n.* baju layang, baju labuh; jubah; *see* **robe.**

clock, *n.* jam, arlogi; *alarm-~,* jam loceng; *o'clock,* pukul; *3 o'clock,* pukul tiga; *hands of a ~,* jarum jam; *set a ~,* tepatkan jam; *wind a ~,* kuncikan jam; *advance a ~,* cepatkan jam; *retard a ~,* perlambatkan (lambat) jam; *fast,* deras; *slow,* lambat; *stopped,* mati.

clod, *n.* sebingkah tanah, segumpal tanah.

clog, *n. wooden shoe,* terumpah; encumbrance, galangan, kongkongan.

close, *adv. near,* dekat; *~ friend,* kawan biasa, kawan karib; akrab; *~ly woven,* kedap, tetal.

close, *v. tr. shut,* tutup, katup; *hermetically,* pengap; *~ with a crash,* mengertap (kertap); *bang,* hempaskan; *~ up (draw nearer),* rapat; *~ up (fold, as a flower),* kuncup; *~d, 'bunged up', of eye,* bakup; *~d down, ceased to operate, of a business,* gulung tikar.

clot, *n.* sekepul, segumpal; *~ted, as blood,* bergumpal-gumpal; *coagulated,* beku; *viscous,* kental; *blood in great ~s,* berkopah-kopah.

cloth, *n.* kain; *a bolt of ~,* sekayu kain.

clothes, *n.* pakaian; *esp. of ordinary Malay dress,* kain baju; *frock (Western style),* 'gaun'; *working ~,* pakaian lasak; *~-line,* tali sampai, ampaian kain; *see* **dress.**

cloud, *n.* awan; *a mass of ~s,* gumpalan awan; *storm-~,* pokok ribut; *cirrus ~s,* mega-mega; *red sunset ~s,* teja; *~y (day),* (hari) redup; *overcast with dark ~s,* (hari) mendung; *~ed over, as a peak,* disaput awan; *rising in ~s, of smoke,* berkelun (kelun); *in thick ~s, of smoke,* berkepul (kepul), berjabu (jabu).

clove, *n.* buah cengkih.

clown, *n.* orang lawak, pelawak, orang kelakar; *buffoon,* badut.

club, *n. heavy stick,* tongkat, belantan; *see* **cosh;** *~-footed,* kaki cepoh; *~ suit at cards,* kelawar; *social ~,* kelab, persatuan (satu); *night-~,* 'kelab' malam.

clue, *n. guiding sign,* tanda, petunjuk (tunjuk).

clump, *n. as of bamboo,* rumpun, perdu; *small thicket,* gumpung; *~, ~, as sound of feet,* degam degum; *to give a ~ over the head,* memberi (beri) ketupat Bangka-hulu.

clumsy, *adj.* kekuk; *with hands,* kasar tangan; *with feet,* kaki bangku; *as of style,* canggung, janggal; *comment on someone who ruins what he is working on,* tikus membaiki (baik) labu, (the rat repairs the gourd).

cluster, *n.* serangkai, segemal; *dangling in ~s,* beruntai-runtai; *a ~ of coconuts or bananas,* setandan (nyiur, pisang); *of islands,* gugusan.

clutch, *v. tr. seize hold,* tangkap, cengkam; *~ at,* cekau; *see* **cling;** *a ~ of eggs,* telur sesarang.

cluttered, *p.p. lying about untidily,* berkaparan (kapar).

coach, *n. of a railway train,* gerabak; *of team,* juru latih.

coagulate, *v. tr. by adding acid,* bekukan.

coal, *n.* arang batu.

coalesce, *v. intr. unite,* bersatu (satu); *as particles,* bertaup (taup).

coalition, *n.* penyatuan (satu), percantuman (cantum); *~ government,* kerajaan (raja) campuran.

coarse, *adj.* kasar.

coast, *n.* pantai; *~-line, littoral,* pesisiran (sisir) pantai; *to hug the ~,* menyusur (susur) pantai; *coaster (ship),* kapal penyusur; *~-guard,* pengawal (kawal) pantai.

coat, *n. Malay loose jacket,* baju; *long ~, such as surgeon's gown,* jubah; *~ of arms,* lambang.

coat, *v. tr. apply a ~, esp. of paint or metal,* menyalut (salut), mengusap

(usap); ~ed with gold, bersalut emas.

coax, v. tr. pujuk, bujuk.

cobra, n. ular tedung (senduk); hamad-ryad, ular tedung selar.

cobweb, n. sarang labah-labah; jaring labah-labah; old abandoned ~s, sawang.

coccyx, n. bone at end of spinal column, tulang tongking, tulang sulbi.

cock, n. male fowl, ayam jantan; fighting ~, ayam sabung; to hold a ~-fight, menyabung (sabung) ayam; ~pit, gelanggang (ayam).

cockatoo, n. kakatua.

cockroach, n. lipas.

coconut, n. nyiur, kelapa; ~ husk (coir), sabut; copra, kelapa kering; ~ milk, air nyiur; ~ cream, santan; seed-bud of ~, tombong, kumbuh; coco-de-mer, pauh janggi.

cocoon, n. kepumpung, belencas.

coddle, v. tr. over-indulge, manjakan.

code, n. for messages, tulisan rahsia; of behaviour, see **decent.**

codicil, n. supplement to will, penamba-han (tambah) wasiat.

coeval, adj. of the same epoch, sezaman.

coffee, n. kopi, kahwa; ~ berries, buah kopi; ground ~, serbuk kopi.

coffin, n. keranda, larung, long; ~ of an eminent person, esp. royalty, jenazah; bearers of such ~, pengusung (usung) jenazah.

cog, n. gigi roda.

cognate, adj. descended from the same ancestor, seketurunan (turun), serum-pun.

cognisance, n. to take ~ of, make oneself aware of, mengambil (ambil) tahu.

cohabit, v. intr. live together as husband and wife, bersetubuh (tubuh), berse-keduduk (duduk), duduk suami isteri.

cohere, v. intr. to stick together, melekat (lekat); see **coalesce.**

coil, n. as of rope, lingkaran; as of hair, gelong; ~ing, as a river or snake, ber-belit-belit; to ~ round, melilit (lilit); ~ cup, as a rope, memuntal (puntal); a ~ for winding thread or for the passage of electricity, kumparan, puntalan.

coin, n. metal money, wang leburan; ~age, currency, mata wang; silver ~, wang perak; copper ~, wang tembaga; gold ~, wang emas; esp. those used for ornament, 'paun'; gold pieces of fabled treasure, dinar mas; to make (mint) ~s, menempa (tempa) wang; to ~ false money, membuat (buat) wang palsu; to '~ money', (sl.) make big profits, buat duit.

coincidence, n. just a ~, kebetulan (betul) sahaja; what a ~!, kebetulang pula!; coinciding with (agreeing with, of the same value), bersamaan (sama) dengan; coincidental in time, berte-patan (tepat) masanya dengan.

coir, n. coconut-fibre, sabut.

colander, n. fine sieve for kitchen use, kaluk.

cold, adj. sejuk; esp. as unpleasantly ~, dingin; a ~, selesema; to catch ~, kena selesema; having nose blocked up, hidung tersebu (sebu).

colic, n. senak perut, mulas perut; esp. that caused by shell-fish, cika.

collaborate, v. intr. mutually assist, tolong-menolong; esp. of assisting en-emy, bersubahat (subahat); see **col-league, co-operate, traitor.**

collapse, v. intr. fall while upright, rebah; as building, etc., roboh, runtuh, terjela-bak (jelabak).

collar, n. of coat, leher baju; for tie, 'kollar'.

collar-bone, n. tulang selangka.

collate, v. to examine, memerhati (per-hati) dan membandingkan (banding); to arrange, menyusun (susun).

collateral, n. property as a promise, cagaran (cagar).

colleague, n. rakan, rakan sejawat.

collect, v. tr. ~ here and there, mengutip (kutip); gather together, memungut (pungut); pick up here and there, forage for, meramu (ramu); see **accu-mulate, assemble.**

collection, n. ~ of people or of articles into one spot, kumpulan; of money or *prized objects,* kutipan; *esp. of odd-ments,* ramuan.

college, *n.* maktab.

collide, *v. intr.* terantuk (antuk) (dengan); *knock against,* langgar; ~ *with,* berlanggar dengan; *colliding with one another, as ships adrift,* rempuh-merempuh.

colloquial, *adj.* bahasa pasar (bazaar), bahasa basahan.

collusion, *n. to act in* ~, berpakat (pakat).

colon, *n. large intestine,* usus besar, saluran isi perut; *punctuation mark,* tanda titik dua.

colony, *n. dependency,* jajahan (takluk); *colonist (settler in new country),* penyeroka (seroka).

colour, *n.* warna; *of varied* ~*s,* bermacam-macam warna, aneka warna; ~*s* (of *regiment),* panji-panji; ~*ed* (not *black and white),* berwarna-warni; *to change* ~ *(esp. to blush),* berubah (ubah) warna muka; *to show* ~ *prejudice,* membezakan (beza) warna kulit.

column, *n. pillar,* tiang; *large pillar,* turus; *of newspaper,* ruangan, halaman; ~*ist,* penulis (tulis) pojok; *fifth* ~*ist,* musuh dalam kelambu.

coma, *n. in a* ~, (dalam keadaan (ada)) tak sedarkan diri.

comb, *n. of cock,* balung; *for hair,* sikat, sisir; *of honey,* sarang lebah; *of bananas,* sikat (pisang).

combat, *v. tr. fight to get rid of, esp, some evil,* memberantas (berantas), membanteras (banteras); ~ *falsehood with falsehood,* lagakan kepalsuan (palsu) dengan kepalsuan.

combine, *v. tr. unite, as organisations,* bergabung (gabung); *as weld together,* menggembling (gembling); ~*d,* 'telescoped', bergaung; *see* **alliance, join, unite.**

combustible, *adj. easily burned,* mudah terbakar (bakar).

come, *v. intr.* datang; ~ *here!,* kemari; ~ *in,* masuk; ~ *out,* keluar; *emerge.,* terbit; ~ *to surface,* timbul ~ *up,* mount, naik; ~ *down,* turun; ~ *up, of a plant,*

tumbuh; ~ *up, of a plant,* tumbuh; ~ *off, as a fitment,* tanggal; *peel off, flake off,* lekang; *time to* ~, masa yang akan datang, kemudian hari.

comedy, *n.* sandiwara, (filem) lawak jenaka; *comedian,* orang lawak, pelawak, lelucon.

comet, *n.* bintang berekor (ekor).

comfort, *v. tr.* menghiburkan (hibur); *a* ~, *solace in distress,* ubat hati; *baby's* ~*er,* 'titty', puting (isapan kanak-kanak).

comfortable, *adj. at ease,* berasa (rasa) senang; *esp. of circumstances,* lega; *feeling* ~, berasa nyaman, berasa lega; *as roomy clothes,* lapang, selesa.

command, *n.* hukum; *of God,* firman; *of a Ruler,* titah; *to be in* ~ *of,* memerintah (perintah); mentadbirkan (tadbir); ~*ing Officer,* pegawai Pemerintah; *General Officer* ~*ing,* Panglima Agung; ~*er in Chief,* panglima tertinggi (tinggi); *words of* ~, kata-kata perintah baris.

commemorate, *v. tr.* menjadikan (jadi) peringatan (ingat); *see* **celebrate.**

commence, *v. tr.* mulai.

commensurate, *adj. proportionate to,* seimbang dengan.

comment, *v. intr.* mengulas (ulas); ~*ator.* juru ulas; ~*ary, elucidatory notes forming part of book,* penafsiran (tafsir); *as in a review or on radio,* ulasan 'komentar'; *running* ~*ary,* ulasan selari.

commerce, *n.* perniagaaan (niaga); *commercial law,* undang-undang perniagaan; *Chamber of Commerce,* dewan perniagaan.

commission, *n. brokerage,* komisen; *'tea-money',* duit kopi; *Government Board,* badan, lembaga; *warrant of appointment,* tauliah; *Royal Commission, esp. for some investigation,* Suruhanjaya Diraja.

commissioner, *n.* Pesuruhjaya (suruh).

commit, *v. tr.* ~ *sin,* melakukan (laku) dosa.

committee, *n.* jawatankuasa, panitia.

commodious, *adj.* selesa, lapang luas.

commodity, *n.* barang dagangan.

common, *adj.* *constantly met with,* selalu berjumpa (jumpa); *the ~ people,* orang kebanyakan (banyak), rakyat jelata; *~ sense,* akal; *~place (happens every days),* perkara basahan, biasa; *no ~ man, outstanding,* bukan sebarang orang; *in ~ use, as word,* lazim; *to hand in abundance,* belanar; *~ knowledge,* masyhur; *the ~ weal (general good),* kebajikan (bajik) am; *usual,* biasa; *House of Commons,* dewan orang ramai, dewan rakyat, *'~'' (inferior, of goods),* 'koman'.

commotion, *n.* bunyi gempar, *in ~ (esp. of populace),* hebuh.

communicate, *v. tr. as news,* memberi tahu (beri), berkhabar (khabar); berhubung (hubung).

communication, *v. news,* khabar; *official ~,* perutusan (utus) rasmi; *~s (means of access, etc.),* perhubungan (hubung).

communique, *n.* pengumuman (umum), kenyataan (nyata).

communist, *n.* komunis, *communism,* faham komunis.

community, *n. group, racial or otherwise,* kaum; *esp. (racial or religious),* suku; *generally, of persons having a common interest,* golongan, masyarakat; *Community Centre,* balai rakyat.

compact, *adj. as closely grained,* padat, pukal; *as an organisation,* bersatu (satu) padu.

companion, *n.* kawan, teman, saing, rakan.

company, *n. commercial firm,* syarikt, perkongsian (kongsi); *limited ~,* syarikat berhad (had); *the ~, persons assembled, esp. at a party.,* majlis orang.

compare, *v. tr.* membandingkan (banding); *as in checking proofs,* menyemak (semak); *incomparable,* tidak ada bandingan, tidak bertolok (tolok).

compartment, *n. space partitioned off,* ruang, petak; *room partitioned off,* bilik bersekat (sekat).

compass, *n. for showing direction,* pedoman; *pair of compasses for describing circles,* jangka; *points of the ~,* mata angin.

compassion, *n.* kasihan; *to feel ~,* berasa (rasa) kasihan, berasa belas kasihan; *see* **mercy.**

compatible, *adj.* sesuai, seraksi, sejodoh.

compatriot, *n.* teman sebangsa; teman senegara.

compel, *v. tr.* paksa.

compensate, *v. tr. pay amount of loss or damages,* ganti kerugian (rugi), *compensation,* ganti rugi, belanja kerugian; *for defamation,* ganti rugi bagi saman molu, wang timbang malu; *workmen's compensation,* pampasan pekerja (kerja).

compere, *n.* juru acara.

compete, *v. intr.* bertanding (tanding); *strive to get ahead, vie,* berdahulu-dahuluan (dahulu); *~ for,* merebut (rebut); *participant in competition,* peserta (serta).

competent, *adj.* cekap; *reliably efficient,* handalan (handal).

competition, *n.* pertandingan (tanding), peraduan (adu); *beauty ~,* peraduan cantik; *rivalry, esp. in trade or armaments,* saingan.

compile, *v. tr. collect and arrange (facts, etc),* menyusun (susun); *see* **compose.**

complacent, *adj. blind to one's own faults, expressed by the saying, 'the prawn doesn't realise that it is humpbacked',* udang tak sedarkan dirinya bongkok.

complain, *v. intr. as to authority,* mengadu (adu) hal, merayu (rayu), mengeting (keting); *grumble,* bersungut (sungut); *enter ~t at police station,* membuat aduan di balai polis; *~ant (in Court),* aduan; *~t,* rayuan, aduan.

complete, *n.* lengkap, sempurna; *of period,* cukup, genap; *finished,* sudah; *to finish, as task,* perhabiskan,

menyudahkan, ~ly, wholly, sehabis-habis, sama sekali, semata-mata.
complexion, n. air muka; rupa paras.
complicated, adj. terkusut-kusut; sulit; rumit; berselirat (selirat).
compliment, n. pujian.
compose, v. tr. as a book, mengarang (karang); esp. as poetry, menggubah (gubah); ~r, pengarang, penggubah; ~d of (portions), terdiri (diri) dari.
composition, n. karangan, rencana.
compositor, n. setter of type, penyusun (susun) huruf, pengatur (atur) huruf.
compost, n. made-up mixture of soil, tanah campuran.
compound, n. composed of several elements, campuran; ~ed medicine, electuary, maajuan; chemical ~, sebatian.
comprehend, v. tr. faham, mengerti (erti); comprehensive, on a broad scale, secara luas; comprehensive school, sekolah anika jurusan; see include.
compress, v. tr. to squeeze between two surfaces, mengapit (apit); by constriction, as a python, mencerut (cerut); a ~, cold pad, penjaram (jaram), tuam sejuk; hot ~, tuam panas; ~ed, as by weight, padat; esp. as sunken loose earth, mampat.
comprise, v. tr. consist of (parts), mengandungi (kandung); ~d of, terdiri (diri) dari.
compromise, v. intr. bertolak (tolak) ansur, cari jalan tengah berlebih-kurang (lebih).
compulsory, adj. (dengan) paksa, termesti (mesti), diwajibkan.
compute, v. tr. mengitung.
comrade, n. rakan, teman; ~-in-arms, teman seperjuangan (juang); as political term, saudara.
concave, adj. cekung; lekuk.
conceal, v. tr. see hide.
concede, v. tr. admit a right or responsibility, sanggup; mengizinkan; menyetujui.
conceited, adj. sombong; bongkak.
conceive, v. tr. a child, mengadung

(kandung); see pregnant; an idea, mendapat (dapat) fikiran, menampa (tampa); couldn't ~ that, tak sangka sekali-kali.
concentrate, v. tr. give one's whole attention to, menumpukan (tumpu) mata dan telinga kepada, menumpukan perhatian (hati) kepada; ponder thoroughly, berfikir (fikir) masak-masak.
concentric, adj. having a common centre, sepusat.
concern, n. anxiety, bimbang; to feel ~, berasa (rasa) bimbang; no ~ of mine, bukan hal saya; as far as I am ~ed, buat diri saya, bagi pihak saya sendiri.
concerning, prep. with regard to, berkenaan (kena) dengan, tentang, fasal, dari hal.
concession, n. special right or privilege, hak yang khas, hak yang istimewa; make some ~, give way a little (in a dispute), beralah (alah) sikit.
conciliate, v. tr. win over by kindness, etc., menawan (tawan) hati, memujuk (pujuk); induce to a peaceful settlement, mendamaikan (damai).
concise, adj. ringkas; singkat.
conclude, v. tr. to draw a conclusion, mengambil (ambil) kesimpulan, in conclusion, pada penutupnya (tutup); you can draw your own conclusion, anda boleh membuat kesimpulan sendiri; see deduce.
concoct, v. tr. ~ erraudos, mengada-adakan (ada) (alasan); a plot, memasakkan (masak) pakatan.
concubine, adj. gundik.
concur, v. tr. bersetuju (tuju); see unanimous.
concurrent, adj. serentak, serempak.
concussion, n. sound of loud crash, dentuman; kerusakan (rusak) otak.
condemn, v. tr. in Court, hukumkan, menjatuh (jatuh) hukum (atas); blame, salahkan; ~ to death, menjatuhkan hukum mati atas.
condescend, v. intr. lower oneself, merendahkan (rendah) diri; show geniality

to inferiors, beramah-tamah (ramah) dengan orang bawahan.

condiments, *n. relish to be eaten with meal,* sambal.

condition, *n. stipulation,* syarat; *state,* keadaan (ada), hal.

condole, *v. intr.* mengucap (ucap) takziah, mengucap belasungkawa, menyatakan (nyata) belasungkawa.

condone, *v. tr. treat (offence) as nonexistent.* biarkan begitu sahaja.

conduce, *v. intr. tend to produce an effect,* membawa (bawa) kepada.

conduct, *n. behaviour,* kelakuan (laku), tingkah laku.

conduct, *v. tr. to lead, guide,* bawa, memandu (pandu); *esp. by hand,* memimpin (pimpin); ~ *a band,* memimpin pancaragam; *a case or business,* menjalankan (jalan); *esp. a business,* menguruskan (urus); *lightning ~or,* kawat kilat.

conduit, *n.* pancuran air, saluran air (yang besar), bandar air, gedung air), *yang* besar), bandar air, gedung air; *esp. of bamoo,* pembuluh (buluh).

cone, *n.* kerucut; *rising to a ~,* merunjung (runjung).

confectionary, *n. various cakes, etc.,* kuih-muih.

confederate, *n.* sahabat; *confederation,* persekutuan (kutu), gabungan.

confer, *v. tr. (as litle , favour)* mengurniai (kurnia), menganugerahi (anugerah); *to meet for discussion, as councillors,* bermesyuarat; *to sit in ~ence,* bersidang (sidang); *~ence,* persidangan; *round table ~ence,* persidangan meja bundar; see **argue.**

conference, *c.* persidangan (sidang).

confess, *v. tr.* mengaku (aku); *the (Muslim) ~ion of faith,* syahadat, kalimah alsyahadat.

confide, *v.* mengadu (adu) hal diri.

confident, *adj.* yakin.

confidential, *adj. not to be disclosed generally,* sulit, rahsia.

confine, *v. tr. shut up,* tutup; *keep in ~ment,* kurungkan; *keep in seclusion,*

pingit.

confirmed, *adj. as news,* sah; *definite,* tetap.

conflict, *n.* see **battle;** *~ing, inconsistent,* tidak sesuai (dengan), berselisih (selisih) (dengan).

confluence, *n. of rivers,* pertemuan (temu) (sungai).

conform, *v. intr. in ~ity with,* menurut (turut), seleras dengan, secocok dengan; *when in Rome, ~ to Roman ways,* masuk kandang kambing membebek (bebek), masuk kandang kerbau menguak (kuak), (when you enter a goat-pen, you should bleat; when you enter a buffalo pen, you should low).

confront, *v. tr. to face,* menentang (tentang), menghadap (hadap) muka; *'~ation' (the Indonesian formerly avowed policy towards Malaysia),* konfrantasi.

confused, *adj. in disorder,* kelam kaut, kacau bilau; *'regular shamber',* habis kucar kacir; *at sixes and sevens,* simpang perenang; *in indescribable confusion,* tak karuan.

congeal, membeku (beku).

congenial, *adj. of kindred spirit,* seraksi (dengan).

congenital, *adj. born with one (as disease, weakness),* bawaan baka (dia) memang begitu, sejak dilahirkan.

conger, *n. large marine eel,* malung.

congested, *adj. as population,* penuh sesak; *~ area,* kawasan sesak; *packed together,* berasak-asak.

congratulate, *v tr.* mengucap (ucap) tahniah kepada; *well done!,* bagus! syabas!

congregate, *v. intr.* berkumpul (kumpul), berhimpun (himpun), berkerumun (kerumun); *congregation,* jamah para makmum.

conjecture, *v. intr. form opinion on scanty* grounds, gamak, menampa (tampa); *see* **guess.**

conjurer, *n.* tukang silap mata.

connect, *v. tr join up,* hubungkan; *join on,* sambung; *~ion, as coupling,* penyambung; *see* **join;** *connected with,* berkaitan (kait) dengan, bersangkut (sangkut) paut dengan; berkenaan (kena) dengan; *closely connected,* bertali (tali) rapat.

connoisseur, *n. expert,* ahli, pakar.

conquer, *v. tr. bring country into subjection,* menakluki (takluk); *defeat,* mengalahkan (kalah); *overcome,* mengatasi (atas), kalahkan.

conscience, *n. faculty warning against wrong-doing,* (kata) hati, suara hati.

conscientious, *adj.* cermat; *reliable,* handalan; *thorough and impartial,* saksama.

conscious, *adj. aware (of),* sedar, sadar; *realise,* insaf akan.

conscription, *n. general call-up,* kerahan umum.

consecutive, *adj.* berturut-turut.

consent, *v. intr.* setuju; *esp. in the sense of ~ing unwillingly,* rela; *see* **agree.**

consequence, *n.* akibat; *in ~,* sebab itu.

consider, *v. tr. weigh over,* timbang; *think well,* berfikir (fikir); *regard as,* menganggap (anggap) sebagai; *~ate,* ada fikiran, ada timabng rasa; *see* **kind.**

considerable, *adj.* banyak; *no ordinary,* bukan sebarang, bukan alang kepalang.

consign, *v. tr. entrust for delivery,* kirim; *~ment of goods,* sambutan dagangan, pengiriman barang.

consist, *v. intr. ~ of,* terdiri (diri) dari.

consistent, *adj. ~ with,* sesuai dengan; tetap dengan; *acquire consistency,* 'jell', membeku (beku); *begin to firm up, as liquid or the flesh of a coconut,* meliat (liat).

consolation, *n.* hiburan; *~ prize,* hadiah sagu hati; *~ race,* lari timbang rasa.

console, *v. tr.* menghiburkan (hibur), menyejukkan hati (sejuk).

consolidate, *v. tr. strengthen,* memperkukuhkan (kukuh).

consortium, *n. business combination,* perkongsian (kongsi), konsortium.

conspicuous, *adj. attracting attention,*

yang menarik (tarik) perhatian (hati); *standing out boldly, as a tower,* tersergam (sergam); *to be ~, show oneself off, as in a new suit,* meledangkan diri (ledang).

conspire, *v. intr.* berpakat-pakat (dengan); *a conspiracy,* komplot, pakatan.

constant, *adj. faithful,* taat setia.

constellation, *n.* rangkaian bintang, susunan bintang, bintang temabur.

consternation, *n.* kegemparan (gempar) kerana ketakutan (takut).

constipation, *n.* sembelit.

constituency, *n.* kawasanundi (undi); *constituent (voter),* pengundi, pemilih (pilih); *constituents of a mixture,* ramuan.

constitute, *v. tr. establish (a body),* menubuhkan (tubuh).

constitution, *n. of State,* pertubuhan (tubuh), perlombagaan (lembaga); *law of the ~,* dasar negeri, undang-undang tubuh kerajaan (raja); *a ~al State,* negara berperlembagaan; *a ~al monarch,* raja berperlembagaan; *of body,* pembawaan (bawa) tubuh, resam tubuh.

constrict, *v. tr. encircle and squeeze, as a python,* mencerut (cerut).

construct, *v. tr.* membina (bina); *see* **build;** *~ive, criticism,* 'kritik' yang membina.

consul, *n.* 'konsul'; *Consul General,* 'konsul' agung.

consult, *v. tr. ask advice of,* minta nasihat; *deliberate,* berunding (runding); *to hold ~ations,* mengadakan (ada) rundingan.

consume, *v. tr. use up by eating or buy fire,* makan; *finish off,* perhabiskan (habis).

contact, *v. tr. come into ~ with (physically),* kena (pada), menyentuh (sentuh); *make ~ (in an electrical circuit),* jangkit kena; *make ~ with, approach (as for discussions),* mendapatkan (dapat); *to come into ~ with danger,* menempuh (tempuh) bahaya; *be in communication with,* berhubung

(hubung dengan).

contagious, *adj. of diseases,* menjangkit (jangkit), menular (tular).

contain, *v. tr. have within as contents,* berisi (kan), mengandungi (kandung); *as cargo,* bermuat (muat); *contents,* bekas; *contents of letter,* bunyi, isi.

contaminated, *adj. made dirty, as water,* kena kotoran, kena pencemaran (cemar); *containing harmful germs,* mengandungi (kandung) hama penyakit (sakit).

contemplate, *v. intr. to be sunk in thought,* termenung (menung), tafakur.

contemporary, *adj. of the same age,* sebaya; *of the same period,* sezaman.

contempt, *n.* penghinaan (hina); *to commit ~ of Court (by disobeying an order),* bantah hukum (mahkamah); *by an insult,* menghinakan mahkamah; *see* **despise.**

contend, *v. intr. see* **competition;** *~er (person aiming at a championship),* pencabar (cabar); *clash,* bertimpur (timpur); *make an assertion,* menyatakan (nyata), menegaskan (tegas).

contented, *adj. satisfied,* puas hati; *tranquilly happy,* lapang hati, senang hati; *to one's heart's content,* puas-puas, sampai puas.

contentious, *adj. prone to bicker,* suka bertengkar (tengkar); *noisily ~,* kerasterak.

contents, *n. generally,* isi; *of a ship,* muatan; *of a letter,* bunyi (surat), isi (surat).

contest, *n.* perlawanan (lawan); pertandingan (tanding); *see* **competition, contend.**

contest, *v. intr.* impugn, *truth of statement,* menafikan (nafi), menyangkal (sangkal); *~ or compete for (prize, seat in Parliament),* merebut (rebut); *esp. for a seat in Parliament,* bertanding (tanding).

contiguous, *adj.* seperenggan (dengan), bertumpu (tumpu) dengan.

continent, *n. land-mass,* benua.

contingent, *n. quota of troops,* pasukan; *contingency, possible event,* yang berlaku di luan dugaan.

continual, *adj. as in unbroken line or stream,* berjujuh (jujuh); *without a break,* tak putus-putus, tak berhentihenti; *through whole period,* sepanjang masa (itu); *~ly,* selalu, bertalu-talu.

continue, *v. tr. as journey or speech,* meneruskan (terus); *go on, as activities,* berlangsung (langsung), berjalan (jalan) terus; *to ~, proceed with (e.g., a speech or studies),* melanjutkan (lanjut); *to be ~d (of story),* bersambung (sambung); *as before,* masih, lagi; *~! (get on with it!),* teruskan!; *in continuation,* selanjutnya; *continuity,* kesinambungan (sinambung).

contorted, *adj. twisted out of true,* erut.

contour, *n. of hill,* lereng.

contraband, *n.* barang larangan, dagangan gelap.

contraceptive, *n. birth-control drug,* ubat penjarang (jarang) beranak (anak), ubat menyekat (sekat) beranak; *~ pill,* 'pil' mencegah (cegah) hamil.

contract, *n.* 'kontrak', perjanjian (janji); *make a ~,* berjanji, mengikat (ikat) 'kontrak'; *contractor,* pemborong (borong); *marriage ~,* akad nikah.

contract, *v. intr. as opposed to 'expand',* kempis; *expanding and contracting,* kembang kempis; *tighten,* bercerut (cerut).

contradict, *v. tr. deny statement,* menyangkal (sangkal), menafikan (nafi); *~ictory to,* bertentangan (tentang) dengan.

contrary, *adj. of wind,* sakal; *to, e.g., regulations,* bersalahan (salah) dengan; *to act ~ to,* melanggar (langgar); *on the ~,* sebaliknya; *opposed to, inconsistent with,* berlawanan (lawan) dengan.

contrast, *v. tr. compare,* membandingkan (banding); *in strong ~ to,* berlainan (lain) sangat dengan.

contravene, *v. tr.* melanggar (langgar).

contretemps, n. unexpected hitch, aral gendala.

contribute, v. tr. make a contribution, menyumbang (sumbang); a contribution, as to a club, yuran; as to a newspaper, langganan; see **donation.**

contrite, adj. menyesal (sesal) kesal.

contrive, v. intr. devise, find a way, cari jalan, cari akal; ikhtiar.

control, v. tr. mengendalikan (kendali), menguasai (kuasa); manage, mengelola (kelola), mengurus (urus); be in charge of, menyelenggara (selenggara); get under ~, terkawal; be in ~, of party of body), memegang (pegang) teraju; ~ passions, menahan (tahan) nafsu; ~ grief, menahan sedih; birth~ see **contraceptive;** ~s, restrictions, larangan, sekatan; price~~ kewalan harga.

controversy, n. perselisihan (selisih), pertikaian (tikai); tengkarah.

oontrovert, v. tr. dispute the truth of, membantah (bantah).

convalesce, v. tr. be in process of recovering strength after illness, menunggu (tunggu) baik daripada sakit.

convene, n tr. call together, mengumpulkan (kumpul), memanggil untuk mesyuarat.

convenient, adj. easy to use, senang memakai (pakai); useful, berguna (guna); conveniences (useful amenities), kemudahan (mudah).

conventions, n. accepted rules of behaviour, adat kebiasaan (iasa); the bonds of custom, bingkai adat; the ~, 'decencies' of behaviour, e.g., in controversy, sopan santun; conventional, usual, biasa.

converse, v. intr. berbual (bual); topic of conversation, pokok perbualan.

convert, v. tr. to another faith, mengubah (ubah) anutan; to be converted (to other views), beralih (alih) tadah; a ~ (to Islam), mualaf; (from Islam), murtad.

convex, adj. cembung.

convey, v. tr. take from one places to another, bawa; transfer propertly by deed, tukar nama; see **carry, remove, transport, transfer.**

convict, n. orang salah; pesalah (salah); ~ion, hukum salah; Indian transported ~ of former days, banduan; to ~, hukumkan salah.

convince, v. tr. bring to firm belief, menyakinkan; convinced, yakin, percaya bulat-bulat.

convoy, (war-ship), v. tr. escort, mengiring (iring), mengawal (kawal); ships so escorted, iring-iringan kapal.

convulsions, n. infantile disorder, sawan.

coo, v. intr. of doves, berperam (peram), berkukur (kukur).

cook, v. tr masak; rice, menanak (tanak); see **boil, fry, roast,** steak; a ~ (Chinese), kuki; (Malay), juru masak; palace chef, gerau; ~ing stove of stones, tungku.

cool, adj. not hot, sejuk; of behaviour, tenang; ~ed down to berable temperature, siau; keep ~!, sabar!; ~ing-system, see air.

coop, n. for fowls, reban, lau, kurungan; small basket-~, serkap; see **confine.**

co-operate, v intr. berkerjasama (kerja); mutually help, tolong-menolong, bantu-membantu, begotong-royong (gotong); in ricefields, menderau (derau); for a feast or special task, berantam (rantam); co-operative society, syarikat kerjasama.

cope, v. intr. contend on equal terms, boleh tahan; ~ with, get the better of, memperdayakan (daya); ~ with (difficulties), mengatasi (atas).

copper, n. tembaga (merah); ~s (~ coins), wang tembaga.

copra, n. kelapa kering; ~ drying rack, salaian.

copulate, v. tr. bersetubuh (tubuh); (coarse), ancuk; (of animals) ~aka (baka); 'cover', bertindih (ti'

copy, n. reproduction of salinan; fair ~, salinan '

nan bersih, *id.; duplicate,* salinan pertama; *imitation,* tiruan; *single-specimen of book, etc.,* naskhah; *to ~, make a ~,* menyalin (salin); *imitate,* meniru (tiru); *mere copyist,* tahu meniru sahaja; *copyright reserved,* hak pengarang (karang) terpelihara (pelihara), hak cipta terpelihara.

conquet, *v. intr. put on enticing airs (of a woman),* menjual (jual) lagak, melaram (laram).

coral, karang; *coraline growths,* bunga karang; *~ beads,* merjan.

cord, *n.* tali (kasar); *cordage, rigging,* tali temali.

cordial, *adj. heartily-friendly,* peramah (ramah).

cordon, *v. tr. ~ off place guards over access,* mengepung (kepung), menyekat (sekat) jalan ke.

core, *n. of boil,* punat; *of fruit,* empulur; *centre hard position of tree,* teras, *(also used (fig.) for the hard ~, mainstay, of a movement).*

coriander, *n.* ketumbar.

cork, *n. the substance,* libut, gabus; *stopper,* penyumbat (sumbat); *~-screw,* pembuka (buka) botol.

corn, *n. wheat,* gandum; *hard skin,* belulang.

corner, *n.* bucu; *in road,* selekuh; *in road or river,* liku; *sharp turn,* siku; *angle,* sudut, penjuru; *every nook and ~ of the country,* seluruh pelusuk negeri; *the four ~s of the earth,* empat penjuru alam; *to turn a ~,* beluk selekuh; *to ~ (cut off retreat),* mengepung (kepung); *~-boy (young ruffian),* kutu bandar; *to ~, buy up, whole stock,* memborong (borong); *see* **opportunity.**

coronation, *n.* kemahkotaan (mahkota).

corporation, *n. body of persons legally constituted,* perbandanan.

corporeal, *adj. as opposed to spiritual,* jasmani; *connected with the body,* mengenai (kena) tubuh.

corpse, *n.* mayat; *(honorific),* jenazah.

correct, *adj.* betul.

correspond, *v. intr. exchange letters,* mengutus (utus) surat, surat-menyurat; *corresponding to, parallel or analogous to,* bersesuaian (sesuai) dengan; *of the same value as,* bersamaan (sama) dengan.

corroborate, *v. tr. support statement or a speaker,* menyokong (sokong).

corrode, *v. intr. suffer corrosion,* makan diri, dimakan karat.

corrugated iron, *n.* atap 'zin'; *a corrugation, on hard substance, e.g., a horn,* gerat; *~ into wrinkles,* berkerut-kerut; *see* **crinkled, flute.**

corruption, *n. venality,* korupsi; *see* **bribe.**

corvee, *n. exaction of unpaid labour,* kerah.

cosh, *n. small cudgel used, esp. in Kelantan by bad characters,* tongkat enam sembilan; *in a form resembling a small axe,* kapak bungkus, kapak kecil; *to ~,* godam.

cosmetics, *n.* barang solekan (solek), urap-urapan; *see* **lip, powder, rouge.**

cost, *n.* harga; *~ of living,* belanja hidup; *~s, expenditure,* belanja, biaya; *~ly,* mahal; *at all ~s, whatever happens,* walau apa jadi pun.

cot, *n. for baby, swinging ~,* ayunan, buaian.

cote, *n. for animals,* kandang; *for pigeons,* peranja merpati.

cotton, *n. the material,* kapas; *thread,* benang; *tree- ~,* kapok; *~ cloth,* kain kapas; *'~-tree',* kekabu (kabu-kabu); *printed ~ cloth,* cita.

couch, *n. sofa, settee,* 'kaus'.

cough, *n.* batuk.

council, *n.* mesyuarat, majlis; *to sit in Council,* bersidang (sidang); *Council Hall,* dewan majlis undangan.

counsel, *n. to take ~ together,* muafakat, berpakat (pakat).

counsellor, *n.* penasihat, peguam.

count, *v. tr.* mengira (kira); *tot up,* hitung; *enumerate,* bilang; *~ing your chickens before they're hatched,* burung terbang di-pipiskan lada, *(grinding the spices while the bird is still on the* *wing*).

counter, *n. in shop,* meja; ~-attack, serang balas.

counterfeit, *adj.* palsu, lancung; *imitation,* tiruan.

counterfoil, *n. see* **butt.**

counterpane, *n.* gebah, seperai.

counterpart, *n. in partnership,* teman seperkongsian.

countless, *adj.* tidak terbilang (bilang), tidak terhitung (hitung).

country, *n. state,* negeri, negara; *esp. as inhabited settlement,* negeri; *~side,* desa; *~man, rustic,* orang kampung; *territory,* tanah air; *my ~!,* ibundaku!, negaraku!

coup d'etat, *n. seizure of power,* perebutan (rebut) kuasa.

couple, *n.* pair, sepasang; *esp. of bride and bridegroom,* sejoli; *married ~,* sekelamin, suami isteri.

couplet, *n. pair of verses,* bait.

coupling, *n. link, esp. between railway coaches,* (rantai) penyambung (sambung); *hooked ~,* penyangkuk (cangkuk).

courage, *n. see* **brave;** *pluck up ~,* beranikan diri.

course, *n. followed by river of range of hills,* larian; *race-~,* padang lumba kuda; *channel, alur; ~ of action or progress,* aliran; *~ of study,* kursus; *extension ~,* pelajaran (ajar) lanjutan; *~, direction,* arah; *to change ~,* mengalih (alih) arah, beluk; *driven off ~,* terbabas (babas), terbias (bias); *successive parts of meal,* hidangan; *refresher ~ of studies,* kursus ulang kaji; *of ~ (certainly),* tentu; *(why ask?),* apa lagi?; *(naturally, what else can you expect?),* memang.

court, *n. palace,* istana; *~ staff, generally,* orang dalam; *~ of law,* mahkamah, balai; *~ martial,* mahkamah tentera; *~yard,* halaman, *to ~ (seek in marriage),* meminang (pinang), melamar (lamar); *~ disaster, run needless risks,* mencari (cari) bahaya.

courtesy, *n.* budi, budi bahasa; *geniality,*

ramah tamah; *courteous,* beradab (adab), berbudi; *soft-spoken,* mulut manis; *demure,* sopan; *well-bought-up,* masuk ajar; *'by ~ of—',* dengan ihsan—.

cousin, *n.* pupu.

cove, *n. small bay,* teluk kecil.

cover, *v. tr. overlie,* tutup, bertindih (tindih); *all over, as clouds,* meliputi (liput); *as with dish,* tudungkan; *~ right over from on top, as by dome,* menyerkup (serkup); *~ oneself (wrap up),* berselubung (selubung); *~ up, (keep dark),* pengap; *to take ~,* berlindung (lindung) *~ (place to take cover),* tempat berlindung, *~ed with (ants),* dihurung (semut); *as by water or weeds,* acap dek (air, rumput); *encased in gold,* bersalut (salut) emas; *to ~, as a creeper a wall,* menyeliputi (seliput); *dish ~,* tudung saji; *~ of a book,* kulit buku; *~ed with a roof,* berbumbung (bumbung); *with an awning* berkajang (kajang).

coverlet, *n.* gebar, seperai.

covet, *v. tr.* ingin nak mendapat (dapat), *'have one's eye on',* menaruh (taruh) mata pada; *eye covetously,* menginding (inding), melangut (langut); *covetous,* tamak, loba.

cow, *n. female ox,* lembu betina; *~herd,* gembala lembu; *~-house,* kandang lembu.

cowardly, *adj.* penakut (takut), cabar hati, dayus, bacul.

cower, *v. intr. stoop right down,* membongkokkan (bongkok) diri; *~ing when moving along,* menyeronut (seronut), menyusup (susup).

cowrie, *n.* siput gerus.

coy, *adj. shy,* pemalu (malu); *displaying ~ness,* tersipu- sipu.

crab, *n.* ketam; *~ usually eaten,* ketam batu; *soft-shelled ~,* kepiting; *king~,* belangkas, *boring ~,* ketam jabut; *hermit ~,* umang-umang; *to ~, criticise unfairly,* disparage, mencela-cela.

crack, *n.* retak; *rift,* celah; *split,* belah.

crack, *v. intr. of some hard substance,*

meretak (retak); *of, e.g., rind of fruit,* merekah (rekah); *to ~ (emit sudden sharp noise),* berderap (derap) bunyinya.

crack, *v. tr. to ~, as a flea,* menindas (tindas).

cracker, *n. fire-*work, mercun, petas; *to let off ~s,* membakar (bakar) mercun, membuang (buang) mercun.

crackle, *v. intr. emit smallpopping noises, as under-water coral,* meletup (letup).

cradle, *n.* ayunan, buaian, endul.

craft, *n. skilled handicrat,* pertukangan; *~sman,* tukang.

crafty, *adj.* cerdik, panjang-akal.

crag, *n. steep sharp rock,* batu cancang.

cram, *v. tr. as in ~ming in,* mengasak (asak), menjejalkan (jegal).

cramp, *n.* simpul mengkarung, kejang urat; *~ed, as quarters,* picik, sempitl *see* **narrow.**

crane, *n. bird,* burung *pala; machine,* 'win', kren; *~-fly (daddy-long-legs),* gantih-gantih; *to ~, strech out neck to see,* meninjau (tinjau), memanjangkan (panjang) leher.

cranium, *n. brain-pan,* batu kepala, jemala; *skull,* tengkorak.

crash, *v. intr. as a plane,* jatuh terhempas (hempas); *~ in ruins,* roboh berderai (derai); *fall with a heavy ~, as a building,* roboh berdegum (degum); *— with a terrific ~,* hadamat bunyinya.

crate, *n.* keranjang, pak; *see* **box, case.**

crater, *n. of volcano,* kawah (gunung api), genahar (gunung api); *of extinct volcano,* lobuk (gunung api).

crave, *v. tr. have a strong desire for,* ingin akan; *as a pregnant woman,* mengidamkan (idam); *as drugs,* berasa (rasa) ketagih (tagih).

crawfish, *n.* udang galah.

crawl, *v. intr. esp. on hands and knees,* merangkak (rangkak); *on belly,* merayap (rayap), menjalar (jalar); *underneath, e.g., a fence,* menyusup (susup).

creak, *v. intr.* keriat-keriut, berkeruit, ber-

derak derak, berkiut (kiut).

cream, *n.* 'kerim', *top of the milk,* kepala susu; *ice-~,* 'ais kerim'; *finest portion of something, essence,* pati; *coconut ~ (expressed from the flesh),* santan; *~ of society,* buntat masyarakat; *~ coloured,* berwarna (warna) duku; *of skin,* putih-kuning.

creased, *adj. as a dress,* berkedut, (kedut), kumal; *a neat ~,* sait.

create, *v. tr.* menjadikan (jadi), menciptakan (cipta), mewujudkan (wujud); *the Creator,* tuhan yang menjadikan alam, Khalik ulkhalka; *~d things,* khalayak, makhluk.

creature, *n.* haiwan, makhluk.

creche, *n.* tajaka, taman jagaan (jaga) kanak-kanek.

credit, *n. reputation for action,* nama; *credentials (of high official, e.g., an ambassador),* tauliah; *see* **steal.**

credulous, *adj.* mudah di percaya; *to play on people's credulity,* memperdayakan orang; *see* **superstitious.**

creed, *n. faith in which one believes,* agama; *faith in Islam,* iman; *the ~ of Islam,* syahadat, *statement of the ~,* dua kalimah syahadat.

creek, *n.* teluk, suak, serukan.

creel, *n. angler's fishing-basket,* kantung, keruntung.

creep, *v. intr.* menjalar (jalar), merayap (rayap); *as a snake or a creeping plant,* menyelar (selar); *~ under, (from fear),* seram bulu tengkuk; *(from repugnanace),* berasa (rasa) ngilu; *a creeper (plant),* pokok menjalar; *liana,* akar.

cremate, *v. tr.* membakar (bakar) mayat.

crescent, *n. ~ moon,* bulan sabit.

crest, *n.* jambul; *~ of wave,* puncak gelombang; *heraldic ~,* lambang; *see* **peak.**

crestfallen, *adj. mortified, as by defeat,* kecewa; putus asa; *as 'with tail between legs' (fig.),* macam tikus basah.

crevice, *n.* celah.

crew, *n.* kelasi, anak perahu.

cricket, *n. insect,* kerdik, cengkerik.

crime, *n.* perbuatan (buat) jenayah,

kesalahan (salah) pada undang-undang.

cringe, *v. intr. bend obsequiously,* membongkokkan (bongkok) diri; *behave obsequiously to,* angkat-angkat.

crinkled, *adj. fuzzy, of hair,* pepuah; *by heat, as frying meat,* melecur (lecur); *in little folds, as hair, paper,* berketakketak.

cripple, *n. deformed or maimed person,* orang tepuk, orang cacat; *see* **lame, maimed.**

crisis, *n.* 'krisis', masa kecemasan (cemas); *esp. of illness,* kemulut, *delicate situation,* waktu *yang* genting; *to become critical, reach a difficult point of a problem,* meruncing (runcing).

crisp, *adj.* rangup; *esp. of cooked food,* garing; *not soggy, of rice,* kersai, serul, pulan.

criss-cross, *adj.* silang, simpang-sisu.

criterion, *n. principle to be followed in judging,* kayu ukur, kriteria..

critic, *n.* pengkritik; *~ism,* kritikan *~al, of a situation,* genting, meruncing (runcing).

criticise, *v. tr.* menegur (tegur) mengupas (kupas); *esp. adversely,* mengecam (kecam); *as 'pick holes in',* mencacat (cacat); *attack verbally, esp. in speech,* membidas (bidas).

croak, *v. intr. as a frog,* berkeruk (keruk); berdengking (dengking); *loud and deep, as bull-frogs,* menguak (kuak); *(sl.) to die,* mampus.

crockery, *n.* pinggan mangkuk.

crocodile, *n.* buaya.

crook, *n. stick with ~ed handle,* tongkat berkaluk (kaluk); *see* **cheat.**

crooked, *adj.* bengkok; *in character,* hati; *dishonest, esp. as faithless,* curang; *esp. bent at end, as hockey-stick,* cengkok; *lop-sided,* merebeh (rebeh).

croon, *v. intr. as to a child,* mengulit (ulit); *as a tune,* bersenandung (senanadung).

crop, *n. of bird,* tembolok; *to ~ (cut off ends),* memangkas (pangkas); *~ up, as*

a subject in conversation, timbul, tampil.

cross, *adj. out of temper,* merungsing (rungsing); *'got out of bed the wrong side',* sudah makan cuka pagi ini.

cross, *n. esp. as religious emblem,* salib; *Red Cross,* sengkang merah; palang merah; *mark as signature,* pangkah.

cross, *v. tr. esp. as river,* menyeberang (seberang); *traverse, as sea,* mengarung (arung); *dash ~,* melintas (lintas); *~ out,* potong; *lying ~,* melintang (lintang); *don't ~ him (humour him),* jangan melintas angin dia; *~ over (to another political party),* lompat (masuk—); *~ something that serves as a bridge,* meniti (titi); *with ~ed legs,* bersilang (silang) kaki.

cross-bar, *n. on buffalo's horns or on goal,* kayu palang; *of fence,* rembat; *as of door,* kayu sengkang.

crossing, *n. marked road--,* tanda melintas (lintas) jalan; *of wild animal in jungle,* lintasan; *of the sea,* harungan.

crossword puzzle, *n.* teka silang kata.

croton, *n.* pokok puding.

crouch, *v. intr. as for a spring,* menyeranggung (seranggung), mendekam (dekam); *as over a carcase or on nest,* mengeram (ram); *as in getting under an obstacle,* menyusup (susup); *bend low, as when riding a bicycle,* membongkok (bongkok); *~ huddled up, as a sick person,* merengkok (rengkok).

crow, *n.* burung gagak; *~-pheasant,* burung but-but; *to ~, as a cock,* berkokok (kokok); *as a baby,* mengagah (agah).

crowd, *n. assembly of people,* kumpulan orang; *small ~, knot of people,* gumpalan orang; *in ~s,* beramai-ramai; *in packed crowds,* berjejal-jejal, berasak-asak, penuh sesak; *see* **assembly.**

crown, *n.* mahkota; *Crown Prince,* putera mahkota; *~ of head,* batu kepala; *cap affixed by dentist,* sumbi.

crow's-nest, *n. look-out post,* tempat meninjau (tinjau).

crucify, *v. tr.* menyalibkan (salib); *to be*

crucified, kena salib; *a crucifix,* salib.

crude, *adj. untreated,* mentah; *in manners,* kasar.

cruise, *v. intr. sail here and there,* belayar (layar) untuk bersuka-suka, menjelajah (jelajah); *go touring,* melancong (lancong); *~r (warship),* kapal penjelajah.

crumble, *v. intr. to pieces,* relai; *crumbling,* as *loose soil,* gembur; *to ~, as a wall,* berpesai-pesai, berketai (ketai); *rotting away,* reput puih, bangsai; *crumbly, not sticky, of soil, of fine tilth,* leroi; *esp. of rice,* serul,

crumbs, *n. of food,* rimah.

crumpled, *adj.* terperonyok (ronyok); *esp. as clothes,* kumal; *having lost neat crease,* (sudah) patah sait, (sudah) patah kanji.

crunch, *v. tr.* membaham (baham), kunyah-kunyah; *~ noisily,* kerkah-mengerkah; *tear, at,* pepak; *sound of ~ing,* kerup-kerup.

crusade, *n. holy war,* perang suci; *on behalf of Islam,* perang sabil; *on behalf of Christianity,* perang salib.

crush, *v. tr.* menghancurkan (hancur); *~ to powder,* melumatkan (lumat), pirek; *~ed (smashed to pieces),* remuk, terkecai (kecai); *flattened out,* penyek; *~ed in, as a hat,* terpersuk (persuk) ke dalam.

crust, *n. hard outer part, as of bread,* kulit; *adhering to the side of pan in cooking,* kerak.

crutch, *n. walking instruments for cripple,* tongkat ketiak; *the perineum,* celah kangkang, kerampang.

crux, *n. difficult point,* kesulitan (sulit); *essential difficulty,* kesulitan yang utama; *see* **difficulty.**

cry, *v. intr. weep,* menangis (tangis); *see* **scream.**

cryptic, *adj. hard to understand,* rahsia.

cryptogram, *n.* tulisan rahsia.

crystal, *n.* hablur.

cubic, *adj. ~ foot,* kaki padu.

cubicle, *n.* bilik (bersekat) (sekat), petak.

cubit, *n. distance between elbow and fin-*

gertip, hasta; *(=two span* (jengkal)).

cuckoo, *n.* burung takhu; *~! (call of children playing hide-and-seek),* celut!; *~-shrike,* burung kuangkuit.

cucumber, *n.* mentimun, (timun).

cud, *n. chewing the ~,* kunyah-kunyah, mamah-biak.

cuddle, *v. intr. mutually embrace,* berdakap-dakapan; *~ up, as a child,* menyongkom (songkom).

cuddlesome, *adj. of a child, cute, exciting affection,* geram.

cudgel, *n.* belantan; *see* **cosh;** *fig. to ~ one's brains,* memeras otak.

cue, *n. sign for action,* isyarat; *for billiards,* tongkat 'biliad'.

cuisine, *n. in cooking,* cara masakan (masak).

cul-de-sac, *n. blind alley,* jalan sekerat (sahaja), jalan buntu, jalan mati.

culminate, *v. intr. reach final point of development,* meningkat (tingkat) ke; *reach peak,* memuncak (puncak).

culpable, *adj,* bersalah (salah).

culprit, *n. to a person,* persalah (salah).

cult, *n. a ritual or adoration looked on as superstitious by those who do not agree with it,* puja; *~ of personality,* pemujaan tokoh.

cultivate, *v. tr. raise a crop of,* menanam (tanam); bertani (tani); *see* **agriculture.**

culture, *n.* kebudayaan (budaya), peradaban (adab); *see* **civilisation.**

culvert, *n.* pelubung.

cumin, *n. ~ seed,* jintan putih.

cumulative, *adj. piled one on top of the other,* bertimbun-timbun.

cunning, *adj.* cerdik, licik.

cup, *n. tea-~,* cawan, mangkuk; *goblet, chalice,* piala; *challenge ~,* piala cabaran; *esp. league ~,* piala pusingan; *to form a ~ with the hands,* merangkup (rangkup) tangan; *to take up (water) with ~ped hands,* meraup (raup); *to ~ under the hand, e.g., a fly,* menangkup (tangkup), mencekup (cekup); *as injured spot, e.g., eye,* menekup (tekup).

cup, *v. tr.* to treat with a ~ping glass or horn, membekam (bekam).

cupboard, *n.* gerobok; *esp. for clothes,* almari.

cupola, *n.* kop, kubah.

cupid, *n.* the god of love; dewa kecintaan, dewi asmara.

curd, *n. of milk,* dadih; ~led, coagulated, beku; to ~le into clots, bergumpal (gumpal).

cure, *n.* remedy, ubat; efficacious ~, ubat mujarab; to ~ (treat), mengubati; heal, menyembuh (sembuh); preserve (leather), samak.

curfew, *n.* order enjoining time after which people may not be abroad, perintah berkurang (kurang); to impose a ~ order, mengenakan (kena) perintah berkurung.

curio, *n.* curious object such as is sought by collectors, benda yang ajaib, benda yang pelik.

curious, *adj.* strange, ganjil, pelik; see **inquisitive.**

curl, *v. intr.* mengeriting (keriting), mengerinting (kerinting); ~ed ('permed') hair, rambut kerinting; curly, keriting, kerinting, ikal; ~ing pin, sepit rambut; to ~ up (as a dog), mengerikut (kerikut); locks ~ed upwards 'flick-ups', roduk-rambut; to ~ up in heat, melenting (lenting).

curlew, *n.* burung kendi.

currant, *n.* kismis.

current, *adj. in circulation, esp. of money,* laku; currency, matawang.

current, *n. of water,* arus, aliran; of electricity, aliran 'elektrik', 'karan'; direct ~, 'karan' searah; alternating ~, 'karan' bolak-balik; to make way against the ~, monongkah air (tongkah); to make allowance for the ~, mengambil (ambil) basi harus.

curriculum, *n.* aliran pelajaran (ajar), rencana atau perancangan pelajaran, kursus.

curry, *n.* kari, gulai; to ~, gulaikan; ~-stuffs (spices), rempah-pawah; slab for pounding ~-stuffs, sengkalan; to ~ favour, cari muka; see **suck.**

curse, *v. tr.* swear and ~, sumpah seranah; to ~ someone, denounce with ~s, mengutuk (kutuk), sumpahi; see **accursed;** to use foul language, mencarut (carut); a ~, bane, suatu bencana.

cursory, *adj. without attention to details,* hastily, tergesa-gesa, sambil lewa; with a ~ glance, selayang pandang.

curt, *n. as a letter or speech,* ringkas; ~ly, dengan ringkasnya.

curtain, *n.* tirai, tabir, langsir; the Iron Curtain, tabir besi, tirai besi; Bamboo Curtain, tabir (tirai) buluh; 'chicks', bidai; mosquito ~, kelambu.

curtly, *adv.* dengan ringkas, dengan tegas; curt, of speech, singkat, tegas.

curved, *adj.* lengkung, melentik (lentik); a ~, kelok; of a kris, lok; well-~, of a girl, tubuh potongan gitar (sl.), (shaped like a guitar).

curvet, *v. intr. as a horse,* menari-nari (tari).

cushion, *n.* bantal; something to sit on, lapik punggung.

cuspidor, *n.* ketur.

custard-apple, *n.* buah nona.

custom, *n. established usage,* adat; to follow the ~, menurut (turut) adat; to violate a ~, melanggar (langgar) adat; see **accustomed** and **usual;** long-established ~, adat turun temurun; acquired habit, kebiasaan (biasa).

customer, *n.* pelanggan (langgan).

customs, *n.* Customs Department, jabatan (jabat) kastam; ~ duty, cukai, bea; excise duty, cukai dalam; ~ tariff, daftar cukai.

cut, *v. tr.* potong; sever, kerat; ~ off retreat, mengepung (kepung); ~ with scissors, menggunting (gunting); ~ off, as supplies by blockade, menyekat (sekat); take short ~, merentas (rentas), memintas (pintas); ~ in, as when driving, patah masuk; to ~, of clothes, gunting (pakaian); ~ into lengths, as timber, tual; esp. as sugar-cane, katamkan; ~ throat, or person, kerat leher; see **kill, behead;** ~ way through *(jungle)*, meredah (redah); merambah (rambah); *lop off,* pancung, cantas; ~ *down expenditure,* menjimatkan (jimat) perbelanjaan (belanja); ~ *open, as a box,* mengopek (kopek); *see* **split, whittle.**

cutlass, *n.* cenangkas.

cuttings, *n. newspaper-~,* guntingan surat khabar, potongan surat khabar; *a cutting (for planting),* anak keratan.

cuttlefish, *n.* sotong; *sepia of ~,* pangsi.

cycloid, *n. as in geometry,* lengkok; lengkungan.

cyclone, *n.* ribut taufan.

cylinder, *n.* 'selindar', kebuk; ~ *shaped object generally,* gelendung; *cylindrical in shape,* bulat torak, laras.

cynosure, *n.* ~ *of all eyes,* tumpuan mata.

cyst, *n.* risa; *if suppurating,* risa lendir.

D

D.V., *adv. Deo Volente, if God wills,* In-syaAllah

dab on, *v. tr. as medicine,* petap (tap).

dad, *n. father;* ayah; abah; bapa; bapak.

dagger, *n.* kris keris; *small types of ~s,* tumbuk lada, kerambit, badik.

daily, *adv.* tiap-tiap hari.

dainty, *adj. as a girl,* jelita, kecil molek.

dais, *n.* pentas, geta, peterana; *for throne,* singgahsana, teniat; *bridal d.,* pelamin.

dally, *v. intr. dawdle about,* berlengah-lengah.

dam, *n.* empang, tandup, panggung; *bund,* ban; *barrage,* empangan, bendung.

dam, *v. tr. check flow of water,* mengempang (empang), membendung (bendung); *esp. as a small stream for the purpose of catching fish,* tebat.

damaged, *p.p.* rosak; *see* **compensate.**

damascening, *n. on blade, esp. of* kris, pamur.

dame, *n. a woman,* perempuan muda; perawan, gadis.

damned, *adj.* celaka; *accursed, see* **accursed;** *I'm damned if I will-,* haram saya tak mahu-.

damp, *adj.* lembap.

damsel, *n.* gadis, perawan; *of Court,* dayang.

dance, *v. tr.* menari (tari); *Malay square ~,* ronggeng; *a ball,* pesta tari-menari; *to perform rhythmic dances, esp. solo,* berlagak (lagak) irama; *as midges,* berkelebang (kelebang); *see* **curvet, caper.**

dandle, *v. tr. as a baby,* timang.

dandruff, *n.* kelemumur.

dandy, *n.* orang pesolek (solek), orang peraga (raga), peragawan.

danger, *n.* bahaya, merbahaya; *to encounter ~s,* menempuh (tempuh) bahaya; *hidden ~s, esp. from an under-*ground movement, of an animal apt to attack, bahaya tersembunyi; *see* **fierce.**

dangle, *v. intr. as suspended,* bergayut (gayut); *esp as legs of sitting person,* berjuntai (juntai); *slackly, as broken limb,* terkulai (kulai); *in clusters, as fruits,* beruntai-untai; *as bunches,* terkontal-kantil (kontal).

dank, *adj. oozy, unwholesomely damp,* berlendir (lendir), melengas (lengas); *watery,* berair (air).

dappled, *adj. mottled,* bertompok-tompok; *in patches of colour or of light and shade,* bertelau-telau.

dare, *v. intr.* berani; *I daresay (it's quite likely),* harus juga.

dark, *adj. with little or no light,* gelap, kelam; *pitch-~,* gelap gulita; *of deep colour,* tua; *~ red,* merah tua; *as opposed to 'blond',* hitam, *~ and gloomy,* suram, *~, of clouds,* mendung; *to 'keep ~', see* **hush.**

darling, *adj. term of endearment: 'apple of my eye',* buah hati; *'light of my eyes' (esp. o a child),* cahaya mata; *sweetheart,* kekasih (kasih); *'sweetie',* manis; *'bunch of sweetness',* gula batu.

darn, *v. tr.* rajut, jerumat.

dart, *n. as for blow-pipe,* anak damak; *to ~ across,* melintas (lintas); *to ~ along,* melancar (lancar); *to ~ about, as a fish,* berkirap (kirap); *~ forward, as to attack,* menerpa (terpa).

dash, *v. tr. to rush swiftly,* berkejar (kejar), meluru (luru); *to ~ down, hurl violently,* hempaskan; *to 'cut a ~', esp. by lavish expenditure,* buat besar hentak.

data, *n. facts; information,* butir-butir; keterangan (terang).

date, *n. fruit,* buah kurma; *day of*

occurence, hari bulan, tarikh; *out of ~,* ketinggalan (tinggal) zaman, kolot; *up to ~,* menurut (turut) zaman; *up ~,* mengemas (kemas) kini.

datura, *n.* kecubung.

daughter, *n.* anak perempuan; *~-in-law,* menantu (perempuan); *step-~,* anak tiri (perempuan).

dawdle, *v. intr.* melengah-lengah; *esp. as 'potter about',* berleka-leka; *working half-heartedly,* berkerja (kerja) sambilewa.

dawn, *n.* (waktu) matahari naik (terbit), subuh; *grey of ~,* pagi-pagi buta, dinihari.

day, *n.* hari; *'the other ~',* hari itu, kelmarin, tempuh hari; *~ of Judgment,* hari kiamat; *~-book (showing daily sales),* buku pendapatan (dapat) harian; *~-break (in poetry),* fajar menyinsing (singsing); *all ~ long,* sepanjang hari; *for one whole ~,* sehari suntuk; *in a ~ or two,* esok lusa; *'one of these ~s',* esok-esok.

day-dream, *v. intr.* berkhayal-khayal, berangan-angan; *see castle; sunk in thought,* termenung (menung).

daylight, *n.* siang.

dazed, *adj.* berasa (rasa) pening; *as from a blow,* terlengar (lengar); *see dizzy.*

dazzled, *adj. temporarily blinded by brightness,* silau, seriau mata; *~ and blinking,* mata berpinar (pinar).

dead, *adj.* mati; *of a Ruler,* mangkat; *'croaked',* mampus, haup; *destined hour,* ajal; *death,* maut; *'no longer with us',* sudah pergi dahulu; *'more ~ than alive',* of a sick person, bernyawa (nyawa) ikan; *as dull and spiritless,* hidup segan, mati tak mahu; *~-heat (in race),* seri; *~ and buried',* mati berkalang (kalang) tanah; *~ened, of sound,* bengap; *drug to ~en pain,* ubat penghilang (hilang) rasa sakit; *see die.*

dead-line, *n.* waktu, jangkamasa sesuatu kerja diselesaikan.

dead-lock, *n. state of affairs in which no progress is possible,* kebuntuan (buntu).

deadly, *adj. of wound,* parah.

deaf, *adj.* pekak, tuli; *hard of hearing,* berat-telinga; *~en the ears,* membengangkan (bengang) telinga; *~ened (fig.), feeling muzzy in the head from noise or stream of conversation,* bingit kepala.

deal, *v. tr. to distribute, esp. cards,* bahagi; *~ in (goods),* berniaga (niaga); *be a seller of (goods),* berjual (jual); *~ with, negotiate with,* berkira (kira) dengan; *~ at, be accustomed to buy (goods) at,* biasa membeli (beli) (barang-barang) di-; *~ with, see to (an affair),* bicarakan, kerjakan; *'~ with', (sl.) in the sense of 'chastise', 'attend to',* kerjakan, beri bagian.

dear, *adj. expensive,* mahal; *object of affection,* kekasih (kasih); *my ~ (at opening of a letter to a friend),* yang diingati; *see darling.*

dearth, *n. scarcity,* kekurangan (kurang).

death, *n.* maut; *angel of ~,* malak al-maut; *near to ~, very feeble,* bernyawa (nyawa) rapuh, bernyawa ikan; *life and ~ struggle, battle to ~,* perjuangan (juang) hidup mati; *see dead, die.*

debar, *v. tr. to serve to exclude form course of action,* menjadi (jadi) sekatan, menjadi halangan; *to refuse admittance,* tidak dibenarkan masuk.

debark, *v. intr. naik ke darat, mendarat.*

debase, *v. tr. to lower standard of (esp. money),* merendahkan (rendah) mutu.

debate, *v. intr.* berdebat (debat); *see confer, argue.*

debauch, *v. tr to lead from the paths of virtue,* sesatkan; *ruin character of,* rosakkan; *~ed, given up to sensual indulgence,* jangak, biasa menurut hawa nafsu sahaja.

debilitate, *v. tr.* melemahkan (lemah).

debit, *n.* piutang, hutang piutang.

debouch, *v. tr. emerge into open,* terbit.

debris, *n. strewn fragments of fallen buildings,* runtuhan; *as broken or torn pieces,* reja; *as of a wrecked plane,* bangkai; *as of a meal,* sisa; *oddments left over,* kalat-kalat.

debt, *n.* hutang; *to get into* ~, lekat hutang orang; *debts receivable,* piutang; *always in* ~, *incurring a new* ~ *to settle an old one, 'borrowing from Peter to pay Paul',* tutup lubang, gali lubang, *(i.e., digging a hole to fill up another hole).*

decade, *n.* dasarwarsa; masa selama sepuluh tahun.

decadent, *adj.* mundur.

decanter, *n. long-necked bottle,* balang.

decay, *get rotten,* menjadi (jadi) reput; *decline in quality,* merosot (rosot), mundur; ~*ed, as a result of damp,* lapok; *esp. as timber,* bangsai; ~*ed tooth,* gigi kena makan dek ulat.

deceased, *adj. the late; of a ruler,* marhum; *of a Muslim generally,* Allahyarham, gemulah, arwah; *of a non-Muslim,* mendiang (diang); *generally,* simati.

deceit, *n.* helah, tipu helah; tipu daya.

deceitful, *adj.* curang, penipu (tipu).

deceive, *v. tr.* outwit, memperdayakan (daya); *play a trick,* membuat (buat) helah; *mislead,* mengelirukan (keliru); *bamboozle, 'two-time',* buat kayu tiga; ~*d, 'talked into' some action,* termakan (makan) kata orang, *'get caught out',* terkena (kena); *see* **cheat, swindle.**

decent, *adj. seemly,* berpatutan (patut), senonoh; *'the decencies', accepted code of behaviour in, e.g. controversy,* sopan santun.

decide, *v. tr.* memutuskan (putus); *make up mind,* menetapkan (tetap) fikiran; *decision,* keputusan; *as esp. in Court,* kerat; *'last word',* kata putus.

decimal, *adj.* perpuluhan (puluh).

decipher, *v. tr. succeed in reading,* dapat membaca (baca), memecahkan (pecah) rahsia.

deck, *n.* geladak, 'dek', ~*-house,* kajang magun; *as of a bus,* tingkat; *two-~er bus,* 'bas' dua tingkat.

declare, *v. intr. assert emphatically,* menyatakan (nyata); *declaration of war,* perisytiharan (isytihar) perang, pernataan perang.

decline, *v. intr. deteriorate, see* **decay;** *period of* ~, zaman pudar; *as a business or prosperity,* merosot (rosot), menurun (turun); *as an offer,* menolak (tolak).

declivity, *n.* menurun (turun).

decompose, *v. intr. crumble to pieces,* berketai (ketai); *see* **decay.**

decorate, *v.tr.* menghiaskan (hias), perindahkan (indah); *decorative pattern,* bunga.

decorum, *n. seemliness,* tertib, menurut (turut) adat; *decorous (of behaviour),* sopan santun; *see* **decent.**

decoy, *v. tr. (fig.) entice into a dangerous situation,* memikat (pikat); *bird used as a* ~, denak, burung pemikat (pikat).

decrease, *v. intr.* makin berkurang (kurang); *see* **diminish.**

decree, *n. order,* perintah; *of Ruler,* titah; *of God,* firman; *of a Court,* keputusan (putus), hukum, 'dikri'; *to issue a* ~, mengumumkan (umum) perintah.

decrepit, *adj. esp. of aged person,* renta.

decry, *v. tr. disparage,* mempermudahkan (mudah).

dedicate, *v. tr. devote to pious purposes,* menjadikan (jadi) wakaf.

deduce, *v. tr.* dapati, mengambil (ambil) kesimpulan (simpul); *deduction,* pendapat (dapat).

deduct, *v. tr.* memotong (potong), menolak (tolak).

deed, *n. action,* perbuatan (buat), tindakan; *great efforts,* tapak tokul; *good* ~, jasa; *legal document,* surat, cap.

deem, *v. tr. regard as* sifatkan sebagai; menganggap (anggap) sebagai.

deep, *adj. profound, as water or as studies,* dalam; *of colour,* tua; ~ *red,* merah tua; *of sleep,* lena, lelap, jendera, nyenyak; ~, *of voice,* garau; ~ *in thought,* duduk tafakur, duduk berfikir (fikir).

deer, *n.* sambhur, rusa; *barking* ~, kijang; *mouse-*~, pelanduk kancil; *larger species,* napuh; *Mr Mousedeer,* Sang Kancil; *in folk-lore,* Syah Alam di rimba, *(Jungle Lord of the World).*

defacto, *adj. adv. in actual fact,* sebenarnya, yang sebenar.

deface, *v. tr. damage the surface (of something),* merosakkan (rosak) permukaan (muka) (sesuatu benda); *of a coin,* merosakkan sekah (matawang).

defame, *v. tr.* mencemarkan (cemar)nama.

defeat, *v. tr.* mengalahkan (kalah); ~ed, kalah, alah, tewas; ~ist, bersifat (sifat) mengalah (alah); *see* **eat.**

defecate, *v. intr.* berak, buang air besar; *to have a good motion,* berak lawas; *to ~ hurriedly (in sudden diarrhoea),* memburan (buran), terberak.

defect, *n. blemish,* cacat, keburukan (buruk); *weak point,* kekurangan (kurang); *defective,* ada cacatnya, pincang.

defend, *v. tr. watch over, guard,* jaga diri, *to ~ someone, esp. in Court,* membela; *as one's country,* mempertahankan (tahan); *means of self-defence,* pelindung (lindung).

defendant, *n. in suit,* yang kena adu.

defer, *v. tr. postpone,* menangguhkan (tangguh).

deferential, *adj.* sopan santun; *deference,* tertib; *to show ~ to,* menghormati (hormat), segani.

deficient, *adj.* kurang; *deficiencies, weak points, esp. in a scheme,* retak belah.

defile, *v. tr. to pollute,* mencemarkan (cemar), nodai, (noda).

define, *v. tr. state precisely,* menentukan (tentu), menjelaskan (jelas); *definite answer,* kata putus; *having a definite result (not a draw),* berkesudahan (sudah) dengan kalah menang; *specific,* tepat; *definition, interpretation of precise meaning,* tafsiran, takrif.

deflate, *v. tr. let air out,* buang angin; ~ed, kempis, kurang angin, memek.

deflected, *p.p. from course,* terpesong (pesong), terbias (bias); *see* **deviate.**

deflowered, *p.p. no longer a virgin,* hilang dara; *'ruined',* rosak; *(sl.) 'the coconut has been bored by a squirrel',* nyiur sudah ditebuk tupai.

deformity, *n. disfigurement,* cacat rupa.

deft, *adj.* cekap-tangan, ringan tangan.

defy, *v. tr. oppose,* menentang (tentang); *utter defiance,* memengkis (mengkis); *defiant,* tak mahu tunduk; *determined not to yield,* pantang beralah (alah).

degenerate, *v. intr. to loose one's herditary good qualities,* membuang (buang) baka; *decline in quality,* merosot (rosot); *as decadent,* mundur.

degrade, *v. tr. reduce in rank,* menurunkan (turun) pangkat; *see* **disgrace, insult.**

degree, *n. unit of measurement,* darjah; *diploma,* ijazah; *persons having University ~s,* orang berkelulusan (lulus) 'universiti', *by ~s, gradually,* beransur-ansur.

deify, *v. tr. treat as a god,* memperdewakan (dewa).

deign, *v. intr. condescend to (do), be so good as to,* sudi; *see* **demean.**

deject, *v. tr.* membatutkan (bantut) hati; ~ed, kurang semangat, terbengok (bengok), berhati (hati) mutu; murung; *esp. as ~ed and miserable in appearance,* moyok.

delay, *v. intr. be tardy,* lambat; *dilly-dally,* melengah-lengah; *keep putting off,* bertangguh-tangguh.

delegate, *n. a representative,* wakil, utusan; *to commit authority to,* mewakilkan (wakil), memberi (beri) kuasa kepada.

delete, *v. tr. strike out,* potong.

deliberate, *v. intr. see* **confer, debate, discuss;** ~ly, on purpose, sengaja.

delicacy, *n.* makanan yang lazat-lazat.

delicate, *adj. weak,* lemah (badan-nya); *fine,* halus rumit; *(fig.) of situation, problem,* rumit, runcing.

delicious, *v. tr.* sedap, lazat, enak.

delight, *v. tr. to fill with pleasure,* menyukakan (suka) hati, menggiurkan (giur).

delimit, *v. tr. fix boundaries,* menentukan (tentu) perenggan.

delinquent, *n. frequent offender,* penjahat (jahat).

delirious, *adj.* mengigau (igau); *to rave in delirium,* meracau (racau).

deliver, *v. tr. as letters,* sampaikan; *hand over,* serahkan; *set free,* bebaskan; *from restraint,* lepaskan; *~y, manner of ~ing a speech,* tuturan.

delude, *v. tr.* mengelirukan (keliru).

deluge, *n. big flood,* bah besar, banjir; *(fig.) of rain,* hujan bagai dicurah-curah.

delusion, *n.* khalyalan.

delve, *v. in research work,* kajian (kaji) mendalam (dalam).

demand, *v. tr. to request as of right,* menunutut (tuntut); *in ~, of goods,* laku; *in great ~,* larap, laris.

demean, *v. tr. ~ oneself (to), condescend to,* merendahkan (rendah) diri (untuk); *(very formally, in Court language, of a Raja 'deigning to proceed'),* bercemar (cemar) kaki; *act in an undignified manner,* hilang maruah; *deliberately ~ oneself for gain,* menjual (jual) maruah; *see* **deign.**

demeanor, *n. expression,* air muka; *behaviour,* kelakuan (laku).

demigod, *n.* dewa, dewata; *demigoddess,* dewi.

demobilise, *v. tr.* membubarkan (bubar) (tentera).

democracy, *n.* 'demokrasi', kuasa ramai; *'guided ~',* demokrasi terpimpin (pimpin).

demolish, *v. tr.* merobohkan (roboh), meruntuhkan (runtuh).

demon, *n.* syaitan, hantu.

demonstrate, *v. tr. prove,* menerangkan (terang), membuktikan (bukti); *display,* menunjukan (tunjuk), memperlihatkan (lihat); *display organised expression of opinion, esp. political,* tunjuk perasaan (rasa); *giving instruction by demonstration,* memberi (beri) tunjuk ajar.

demoralised, *adj.* lemah semangat.

demote, *v. to lower in rank,* turun pangkat, kedudukan (duduk).

demur, *v. intr. protest,* membantah (bantah).

demure, *adj.* sopan santun.

den, *n.* kandang binatang buas seperti singa.

dengue, *n. ~ ferver,* demam ketulangan (tulang).

denigrate, *v. tr. criticize so as to show the worst side,* mencela-cela sahaja.

denounce, *v. tr.* mengutuk (kutuk) mengganyah (ganyah).

dense, *adj. as leaves,* lebat; *as foilage,* rimbun; *as a thicket,* semak sangat; *as fog, jungle,* tebal.

dented, *adj.* kemik; *covered with dents,* kemuk-kemik.

dentist, *n.* 'doktor' gigi.

deny, *v. tr. not admit,* tidak mengaku (aku); *definitely ~,* menidakkan (tidak); *repudiate (suggestion),* menafikan (nafi), menyankal (sangkal); *undeniable,* tak dapat dinafikan.

deodorant, *n.* wangian (wangi) wangi-wangian.

depart, *v. intr. go away,* berlepas (lepas); *esp. of prince,* berangkat (ankat); *proceed,* berjalan (jalan); *proceed on journey,* beridar (idar); *~ 'bag and baggage',* angkat bungkus, berdondong (bondong); *'buzz off',* angkat kaki; *(rude),* angkat puggung; *'beat it!',* ambus! nyah! *~ure, leaving,* pemergian (pergi); *see* **go, start, leave, walk.**

department, *n. of government* pejabat (jabat), jabatan; *of a business,* bahagian.

depend, *v. intr. ~ on,* bergantung pada; *that which all depends on (as regards result),* hujung pangkalnya; *~ for a living on,* bergantung (gantung) hidup pada; *it ~s on, rest with,* terpulang (pulang) kepada.

dependants, *n.* anak buah.

dependency, *n.* negeri takluk, jajahan.

depict, *v. tr.* menggambarkan (gambar); menunjukkan (tunjuk).

deplore, *v. tr. feel regret at,* sesalkan.

deploy, *v. intr. spread out, esp. as troops,* berjarak (jarak); *to form (troops) into line,* membariskan (baris).

deport, *v. tr.* buang negeri.

deportment, *n. manner, bearing,* sikap, gaya; *behaviour,* kelakuan (laku).

depose, *v. tr. remove, esp. a ruler,* pecatkan, makzulkan.

deposit, *v. tr. esp. in bank,* pertaruhkan (taruh), menyimpan (simpan); *part payment,* wang pendahuluan, *see* **earnest.**

deposition, *n. statement in evidence,* keterangan (terang).

deprave, *v. tr.* merosakkan (rosak) tabiat; *~d,* sehabis-habis jahat, rosak tabiat.

depreciate, *v. tr. to belittle,* mempermudahkan (mudah), mencuaikan (cuai); *to sink in value or esteem,* merosot (rosot); *depreciation, lessening in book value,* pengurangan (kurang) nilai.

depressed, *adj. on low spirits,* hati buntu, gundah gulana; *lost heart,* tawar hati; *the '~ classes' (very poor),* kaum melarat; *depression, business depression,* kemelesetan (meleset); *indentation,* lekuk; *~, as damp soil by a weight,* lembang; *depression (considerable area whose surface is lower than its surroundings),* lembahan.

deprive, *v. tr. take away, rights, etc.* melucutkan (lucut).

depth, *n.* dalamnya.

depute, *v. tr. see* **delegate;** *deputy, substitute for an official,* timbalan, naib, pemangku (pangku); *deputation,* perwakilan (wakil); *spokesman,* jurucakap.

derailed, *p.p. of a train,* terkeluar (keluar) dari landasan, terlepas (lepas) dari landasan.

derange, *v. state of mental (mind) disorder,* hilang akal, hilang fikiran; tidak waras; gila.

derelict, *adj. abandoned,* tertinggal (tinggal); *abandoned and neglected,* usang, terbiar (biar) begitu sahaja; *of a vessel, drifting aimlessly,* berhanyut (hanyut); *(fig.) of penniless stranger,* terlantar (lantar).

deride, *v. tr.* mengejek; *cries of derision,* suara ejekan; *derisive cheers,* sorak seranah.

derived, *p.p. ~ from,* asalnya daripada, asal-usulnya daripada.

derris, *n.* akar tuba.

descend, *v. intr.* turun; *as river,* menghilir (hilir); *descendants,* anak cucu; *(seed),* zuriat, cucu cicit; *(remote),* piat-piut; *descent, lineage, origin,* keturunan; *Ruler by descent,* raja berasal (asal).

describe, *v. tr. make clear,* menerangkan (terang), menjelaskan (jelas); *an event,* menceritakan (cerita) hal, *~ as, characterize as,* mensifatkan (sifat) sebagai; *description (appearance),* rupa; *indescribable,* tidak terperi (peri).

desecrate, *v. tr. befoul,* menodai (noda), mencemarkan (cemar); *with filth,* menajiskan (najis); *as by high-handed trespass,* menceroboh (ceroboh) masuk.

desert, *n. a tract of sand,* padang pasir; *uninhabited wilds,* hutan belantera; *as waste land,* padang tekukur, tanah tandus; *'~ed' (poorly attended, as a place of public resort),* lenggang; *having no one to look after it,* tak berpenghuni (huni).

desert, *v. tr. as a soldier, to abscond,* melarikan (lari) diri (dari tentera); *~ to the enemy,* belut; *to abandon,* meninggalkan (tinggal) (begitu sahaja).

deserve, *v. tr.* patut menerima (terima), patut mendapat; *to ~ well of (bring benefits to),* berbuat (buat) jasa kepada.

dessicated, *p.p. drained of moisture,* kering kontang.

design, *n. scheme,* ikhtiar, rancangan; *aim,* tujuan; *intention,* maksud; *geometrical ~,* rajah; rekabentuk.

design, *v. intr. intend to,* berhajat (hajat) nak, bermaksud (maksud); *dressdesigner,* pereka (reka) 'fesyen', pencipta (cipta) 'fesyen'.

desire, *v. tr. to want,* hendak, ingin, berkehendak (hendak); *esp. of a pregnant woman,* mengidamkan (idam); *~ to,* bermaksud nak; *set one's heart on,* membubuh hati pada; *see* **love;** *desires, as ambitions,* cita-cita, *to ~ (a woman),* memberahikan (berahi).

desist, *v. intr. cease from some action,* berhenti (henti); *as call to cease temporarily,* nanti dahulu.

desk, *n.* meja tulis.

desolate, *adj. lonely,* sunyi, sepi.

despatch, *v. tr. send to destination,* mengirim (kirim); *esp. of troops,* menghantar (hantar).

desperate, *adj.* tak ada harapan lagi, putus harapan, putsu asa; *at wit's end,* kehabisan (habis) akal, mati akal.

despicable, *v. tr. consider ~,* benci; *treat as ~,* menghinakan (hina); *look down on,* memandang (pandang) rendah pada; *look with contempt on,* memandang keji pada; *look lightly on,* mengabaikan (abai), menganggap (anggap) sepi pada.

despondent, *adj.* tawar hati, putus asa.

despotic, *adj. to act as despot,* bermaharaja (maharaja) lela; *see* **arbitrary, autocracy.**

destiny, *n. fate (kismet),* nasib; *the Will of God,* takdir Allah; *destined hour (of death),* ajal; *submit to ~, take what comes,* bawa nasib, bawa untung; *no man can command his ~,* tuah dan malang manusia tidak berbau (bau), *(human good luck and bad luck have no smell (so that no steps to anticipate them can be taken), bad luck cannot be pushed away, good luck cannot be drawn towards one,* malang tak dapat ditolak, mujur tak dapat diraih.

destitute, *adj. pauper,* papa; *'the poor and the needy',* orang fakir; fakir miskin.

destroy, *v. tr.* membinasakan (binasa), membasmikan (basmi), memusnahkan (musnah); *esp. as 'do away with' (e.g. bad customs),* membanteras (banteras), memberantas (berantas); *wipe out,* hapuskan; *utterly by fire (or fig.)* meleburkan (lebur); *~ed by fire,* habis terbakar (bakar), hangus.

destroyed, *p.p.* binasa, punah; *reduced*

to dust. jadi abu angin.

desultory, *adj. nor regulated,* tidak teratur (atur); *occasional, as a job,* sambilan.

detach, *v. tr. untie,* buka; *separate,* mengasingkan (asing); *get ~ed, as a fitment,* tanggal; *~ment (of troops),* pasukan.

details, *n.* butir-butir, buah-butir, perincikan (inci); *ins-and-outs, finer points, minutiae,* seluk-beluk; *in detail,* dengan panjang lebar, perincian; *to detail (assign persons for duties),* tugaskan.

detain, *v. tr.* menahan (tahan); *detainee,* orang tahanan.

detect, *v. tr. descry,* nampak; *find out,* dapat tahu; *~ a secret,* bongkar rahsia; *~ing device (for mines, etc.),* alat pencari (cari), alat pengesan (kesan).

detective, *n.* mata-mata gelap.

deter, *v. tr. limit action,* membataskan (batas); *check,* menahan (tahan); *frighten,* menakutkan (takut); *~red (by having learnt a lesson),* serek.

deteriorate, *v. intr. be reduced in quality,* mengurang (kurang); *esp. as economic position,* merosot (rosot); *as state of affairs,* menjadi (jadi) bertambah (tambah) buruk; *go to the bad,* berjalan (jalan); *be past its best e.g., as a fruit-tree,* melawas (lawas); *see* **decay.**

determined, *adj.* berhasrat (nak), berazam (nak), bertekad (nak); *fixed determination,* nekat; *of determined nature,* teguh-hati; *unyielding in determination to,* berkeras nak; *determinedly,* mati-mati; *self-determination,* penentuan (tentu) nasib sendiri; *strong-minded, won't be led,* tidak menurut-nurut (turut).

detest, *v. tr.* benci, getik (akan).

detonate, *v.* memulakan (mula) atau menyebabkan (sebab) letupan.

dethrone, *v. tr.* turunkan dari takhta.

detour, *n. to make a ~,* memintas (pintas).

detrain, *v. intr.* turun dari kereta api.

detritus, *n. rock debris,* runtuhan batu-batu.

devaluate

devaluate, v. tr. *lower nominal value of currency,* menurunkan (turun) nilai wang.

develop, v. intr. *come to a more advanced state,* berkembang (kembang), bertambah (tambah) maju; *to ~ a film,* cuci (filem); *~ment, as of a country,* pembangunan; *esp. as of education,* perkembangan.

deviate, v. intr. *enter new way,* menyimpang (simpang); *from course, esp. as ship,* terbabas (babas); *deviating widely, esp. as from policy,* terpelencung (lencung); *see **deflected**.*

device, n. *trick,* suatu akal; *mechanical catch,* persilap (nya); *appliance,* alat, pesawat; *emblem, e.g., on shield or coin,* lambang.

devil, n. *of hell,* syaitan, setan, *evil spirit,* hantu, iblis; *to the ~ with,* pesetan kepada.

devise, v. tr. *a plan,* mencari (cari) ikhtiar, mencari akal.

devolve, v. intr. *be thrown back on someone (as task or right to property),* pulang kepada.

devote, v. tr. *~ one's energies to,* menumpukan (tumpu) usaha kepada; *~d to (spending one's time in doing, etc.),* leka; *esp. as to a child or a loved one,* tersangkut pada; *devotion to God or good works,* kebaktian (bakti); *always performing religious duties,* beramal (amal) ibadat.

devout, adj. *in religion,* beriman (iman); *in practice of good works,* berbakti (bakti), beramal (amal).

dew, n. embun.

dewlap, n. gelambir.**dexterous,** adj. pantas tangan; *see **deft**.*

diabetes, n. penyakit (sakit) kencing manis.

diagnose, v. tr. menganal (kenal) penyakit (sakit).

diagonal, adj. lintang bujur.

diagram, n. *drawing showing geometrical figures, etc.,* rajah; gambarajah.

dial, n. *face of clock,* permukaan (muka) jam; *sun-~,* jam bayang matahari; *~ a*

number, memutar (putar) nombor telefon.

dialect, n. *local variety of language,* bahasa daerah, loghat.

dialogue, n. *conversation between two people,* soal jawab; *esp. written ~ in a play, etc.,* dialog.

diameter, n. perepang (repang), garis tengah-tengah; garisan pusat.

diamond, n. intan; *brilliant,* 'berlian'; *suit of cards,* 'dimon'; *~ pattern,* belah ketupat, potongan wajik; *~ in the rough,* intan mentah; *a rough (unpolished) ~ (lit. and fig.),* intan tak bersepuh (sepuh); *~ dust (tiny ~s set close together),* intan podi.

diaphanous, adj. *esp. of clothers,* jarang.

diarrhoea, n. cirit, cirit-birit; cahar.

diary, n. buku harian.

dibble, v. tr. *sow or plant in littel holes,* tugal.

dice, n. dadu, buah dadu; *throw ~,* buang dadu; *~-box,* takar (dadu).

dictation, n. rencana.

dictionary, n. kamus.

didactic, adj. *of a person,* bersifat (sifat) mengajar (ajar); *of a writing,* mengandungi (kandung) pengajaran (ajar).

die, v. intr. mati; *pass away,* meninggal (tinggal); *called to God,* sampai hukum; *(semi-sl.),* kalu, hilang; *go to Eternity,* pulang ke alam baka; *~ away, of wind,* mati; *~ away gradually, of sound,* makin lama makin sayup; *~ out, fall into disuse, as a custom,* luput; *~ out, as a species,* habis keturunannya (turun); *dying,* sudah nak mati; *at death's door,* tinggal nadi sahaja, bernyawa (nyawa) ikan, menantikan (nanti) hari; *may you be cursed by God and ~ standing up! (i.e., may you ~ with your boots on!),* dikutuk Allah mati terdiri (diri); *see **dead, death**.*

diet, n. *one's usual food,* makanan; *on a ~ (refraining from certain foods),* makan berpantang (pantang).

different, adj. lain, berlainan (dengan); *difference, point of difference,* kebedaan (beda); *to ~iate,* membedakan;

difference of opinion, perselisihan (selisih); to differ, not be 'in step', not harmonize, bertelingkah (telingkah); see **discriminate.**

difficult, adj. payah; troublesome, susah; arduous, sukar; ~y (~ point), galangan, kesukaan, aral, gendala; the snag is-, yang tersangkut (sangkut) inilah; '~ (hard to deal with), mua.

diffused, adj. as news, tersibar (sibar); see **pervade.**

dig, v. tr. gali; esp. as ~ through, korek, korok; ~ out, as with pin, colek, cungkil; ~ up, as a plant, korekkan; turn over the surface or excavate mencebak (cebak); ~ with mattock, mencangkul, menyangkul (cangkul); to make sly digs at, harass in petty manner, mencucuk-cucuk; a sly ~, bit of sarcasm, sindiran; see **exhume.**

digestion, n. penghazaman (hazam).

dignitary, n. claim to respect, maruah; dignified in manner or gait, bergaya (gaya); preserving one's dignity, bermaruah; undignified, of behaviour, hilang maruah.

digress, v. intr. (from subject of e.g., speech), menyimpang (simpang) dari pokok (pidato), merembat-rembat (kepada).

dilapidated, adj. buruk, robak-rabik, kopak-kapik, robek.

dilate, v. intr. expand, berkembang (kembang); as inflated, kembung.

dilatory, adj. lambat.

dilemma, n. difficult position, kesulitan (sulit); expressed by the aphorism, '(go) right and your mother dies., (go) left and your father dies', kanan mati emak, kiri mati bapa.

diligent, adj. rajin; esp. as in studies, bertekun (tekun).

dilute, v. tr. menipiskan (tipis); campur.

dim, adj. kabur, suram; ~-sighted, mata kabut; faint and flickering, of a light, malap; dimly visible, balam-balam; ~med, of eyes by tears, balam-balam; to ~ (a light), samarkan, redupkan; suramkan.

dimensions, n. ukuran; size, besarnya.

diminish, v. intr. susut; as contents of container, meluak (luak); get progressively less, beransur (ansur) kurang.

dimple, n. sarang pipit, lesung pipit.

din, n. riuh rendah.

dinner, n. makan malam.

dinghy, n. jongkong.

dip, v. tr. as pen in ink, cicah; dye, celup; ~per, timba; of coconut-shell, gaying; to ~ a flag, menjunamkan (junam) bendera.

diptheria, n. penyakit (sakit) kerongkong.

diploma, n. sijil, diploma.

direct, adj. straight on, terus; make a ~ hit, kena pasang; ~, as tax, secara langsung; as a hit or a question, pepat; to instruct to (do), suruh; to ~ (a business, project), mengarahkan (arah); directive, arahan.

direction, n. quarter, jurusan; in the ~ of, hala ke, arah ke; hard by, sebelah; ~s (for action), aturan; (for taking medicine), pelisa; to change ~, berpaling (paling) arah; see turn.

director, n. pengarah (arah); directive, arahan, 'direktif'.

dirt, n. kotoran; on the body, daki; filth, esp. excrement, najis; dirty, kotor, cemar; esp. of clothes or skin, comot; esp. as face, cemuas; '~y' money, duit lendir.

dis, prefix, when a word carrying this prefix means the direct opposite of the unprefixed word, the Malay word corresponding to the unprefixed word can generally be used preceded by tidak: to believe, percaya; to ~-believe, tidak percaya.

disabled, adj. ~ person, orang cacat; to disable, put out of action, melumpuhkan (lumpuh); physical disability, cacat badan; injured, put out of action, as in a fight, patah (sl.).

disagree, v. intr. tidak bersetuju; ~ment perselisihan (selisih); as, not get on with, tidak berlaga (laga) angin dengan.

disappear, v. intr. lenyap, lesap, ghaib;

461

be lost to sight or perception, hilang; missing *(not in its normal place),* sudah tak ada; *make oneself scarce,* menghilangkan (hilang) diri.

disappointed, *adj. foiled in aspirations,* kecewa; *dissatisfied,* tidak puas hati, hampa hati; *distressed,* susah hati; *suffer a great disappointment,* kena kempunan.

disapprove, *v.* tidak bersetuju; membangkang (bangkang).

disarm, *v. tr.* melucutkan (lucut) senjata; *lay down arms,* meletakkan (letak) senjata.

disaster, *n.* nahas, malapetaka, bencana; *see* **accident, plague.**

disavow, *v. tr. deny as action or promise,* menyankal (sangkal), tidak sanggup.

disband, *v. tr. as troops,* membubarkan (bubar).

discard, *v. tr. throw away,* buang campak; *as weed out,* singkirkan, ketepikan (tepi).

discern, *v.* dapat melihat, (lihat); memahami (faham).

discharge, *v. tr. unload (cargo),* punggah; *an employee,* buang kerja, pecat; *duty esp. religious duty,* menunaikan (tunai); *a gun,* melepaskan (lepas) tembakan.

disciple, *n. pupil,* murid; *follower,* pengikut (ikut), *esp. religious follower,* penganut (anut).

discipline, *n.* 'disiplin', tatatertib.

disclose, *v. tr. (secret),* buka (rahsia), bongkar (rahsia).

discomfited, *adj.* kecewa.

disconcerted, *adj.* tergamam (gamam).

disconnect, *v. tr. break connection of something with something,* putuskan.

discontented, *adj.* tidak puas hati; *peevishly ~,* merungsing (rungsing).

discordant, *adj. as sounds,* janggal; *as opinions,* berselisih (selisih); *not fitting in,* tidak bersuai (suai), bertelingkah (telingkah).

discount, *n.* wang potongan.

discourage, *v. tr. reduce confidence,* membantutkan (bantut) hati, mena-

warkan (tawar) hati; *see* **depressed.**

discourteous, *adj.* biadab; *rough,* kasar.

discover, *v. tr. find,* jumpa; *find out,* mendapat (dapat) tahu; *~y, esp. scientific,* penemuan (temu), pendapat (dapat); *~ secret,* buka rahsia, bongkar rahsia.

discreet, *adj. careful and practical,* berakal (akal), bijak; *cara bijaksama.*

discrepance, *n.* pertentangan (tentang).

discretion, *n.* akal; *left to (your) ~,* ikut timbangan (tuan), terpulang (pulang) kepada timbangan (tuan).

discriminate, *v. tr. by showing partiality,* memilih (pilih) bulu; *particularly by favouring relatives,* memilih kasih; *by showing colour prejudice,* memilih kulit, membedakan (beda) warna kulit; *by showing racial prejudice,* memilih bangsa; *~ against, show bias against,* menganak-tirikan (tiri); *~ in favour of,* menganak-emaskan (anak), melebihkan (lebih), mengagung-agungkan.

discus, *n.* cakera; *used in sports,* piring lemparan; *throw the ~,* baling piring lemparan.

discuss, *v. tr. talk over,* berkira (kira), berbicara (bicara), berbincang (bincang), berunding (runding); *~ions,* ura-ura, rundingan, diskasi.

disease, *n.* penyakit (sakit).

disembark, *v. intr.* naik ke darat, turun ke darat, mendarat.

disembowel. *v. tr.* buang isi perut.

disfigured, *adj. marred in appearance,* bercacat (cacat).

disfranchise, *v. tr. deprive of right to vote,* menghapuskan (hapus) hak memilih (pilih).

disgrace, *v. tr.* memberi (beri) aib; *~d,* kena malu, hilang maruah; *~ful affair,* perkara keji; *a mark of ~ (as opposed to an honour),* suatu aib, suatu kehinaan (hina); *see* **insult.**

disguise, *n.* samaran; *to ~ oneself (as),* menyamar diri (sebagai).

disgusted, *adj.* berasa (rasa) cicek, berasa lan; *fill with disgust, make feel* 'positively sick', meloyakan (loya) tekak; disgusting! nasty!, esp. as a word of warning to children, jijik!

dish, n. vessel, pinggan; ~-cloth, kain lap; a particular ~ (food), hidangan; ~ of dressed food, sajian; to ~ up, hidangkan.

disharmony, n. pertelingkahan (telingkah) tiada persetujuaan.

disheartened, adj. lemah-semangat, tawar hati.

dishevelled, adj. of hair, kusut-masai; of hair, floating loose, teruarai (urai), menggerbang (gerbang); of clothing, serbah-serbih.

disintegrate, v. intr. separate into component parts, terkecai (kecai), menjadi (jadi) abu angin; fall to bits, relai.

dislocated, adj. cerai sendi.

disloyal, adj. derhaka, tidak setia; esp. of a spouse, curang.

dismal, adj. of appearance, muram.

dismantle, v. tr. take to pieces, as a machine, rombak, rongkal; see **demolish.**

dismayed, adj. surprised and alarmed, hilang semangat; see **startle.**

dismiss, v. tr. from job, buang kerja; more formal, pecatkan; a court case, buang bicara; to be ~ed, kena buang kerja.

dismount, v. intr. turun.

disobey, v. tr. bantah (hukum).

disorders, n. esp. civil disturbances, pergolakan (golak), kucar-kacir; riots, huru-hara; chaotic conditions, porak peranda, kekacauan, (kacau); disorderly, to behave in a disorderly manner, meliar (liar), buat kacau.

disorganised, adj. at 'sixties and sevens', simpang-perenang, colak-colang.

disown, v. tr. refuse to admit ownership or responsibility, tidak mengakui.

disparage, v. tr. speak or think lightly or slightly of, buat mudah, mempermudahkan, merendah-rendahkan, mencela.

dispel, v. tr. clear away (as anxiety), menghilangkan (hilang); (seperti kecemasan) (cemas).

dispense, v. tr. from a duty, membebaskan.

disperse, v. intr. go various ways, as a crowd, bersurai (surai); to part and ~, as clouds, berkuak (kuak); ~d, placed here and there, berselerak (selerak).

displace, v. tr. place in wrong place, salah letak; ~d person, orang pelarian (lari).

display, v. tr. see **show;** show ostentatiously, as banners, paparkan; to ~, of bird showing its plumage when seeking a mate, mengigal (igal).

disposition, n. innate character, perangai, tabiat, orangnya; Ahmad has a generous ~, Ahmad itu pemurah (murah) orangnya.

dispute, n. difference of opinion, perselisihan (selisih); feud, sengketa; territory in ~, tanah sengketa; see **argue, bicker, quarrel.**

disregard, v. tr. not take into account, tidak menimbang (timbang) hal -, tidak mengacuhkan (acuh), mengabaikan (abai), tidak kira; overlook, as a fault, biarkan begitu sahaja.

disrepair, n. in state of, dalam keadaan (ada) robak-rabek, buruk.

disrepute, n. busuk nama.

disrespectful, adj. cheeky, megak; not showing due deference, kurang sopan, kurang hormat.

dissect, v. tr. cut open, esp. in order to examine, membelah (belah), bedah.

disseminate, v. tr. pamphlets, news, views, menyibarkan (sibar), menyiarkan (siar).

dissent, v. intr. tidak bersetuju; dissension, perselisihan (selisih), pertikaian (tikai).

dissipate, v. tr. squander, membuang tak tentu, memboroskan (boros); waste, membazir.

dissipated, adj. following a frivolous or dissolute way of life, leceh, jalang.

dissolve, v. intr. hancur, melarut (larut); a society or Parliament, bubarkan.

distance, n. interval of space, jauhnya; between two objects, jaraknya; distant, jauh; *of relationship,* renggang.

distil, *v. tr. as perfume,* sulingkan; *water,* kukuskan.

distinct, *adj. easily discernible,* terang, lantang; *different,* berlainan (lain), berasingan (asing).

distinction, *n. point of difference,* perbedaan (beda); *mark of honour,* tanda kehormatan (hormat), tanda kemulian (mulia); *marks in examination earning* ~, markah kepujian (puji); cemerlang.

distinguished, *adj. of renown,* ternama (nama), mulia, masyhur.

distorted, *p.p. see* **twist.**

distribute, *v. tr.* membahagi (bahagi), *property of intestate under Islamic law,* faraizkan; *the distribution of e.g., various species of animals, i.e., places where they are to be found,* penyibaran (sibar); *see* **disseminate.**

district, *n.* daerah, jajahan; *District Officer,* pegawai daerah, ketua (tua) daerah.

disturb, *v. tr. break calm, etc.,* mengacau (kacau); *violently or noisily,* mengganggu (ganggu); *~ed from sleep,* terjaga (jaga) tidur; *see* **disorders.**

disunite, *v. tr. break up concord, as of a party,* memecah (pecah)-belahkan; *'set by the ears',* mengadu-dombakan (adu).

ditch, *n.* parit; *see* **gutter.**

dive, *v. intr. plunge below water,* menyelam (selam); *plunge down head-first, as a plane or from a springboard,* menerjun (terjun), menjunam (junam); *~r,* juru selam; *to ~ for pearls,* menyelam mutiara.

diverge, *v. tr.* menyimpang (simpang), ikut lain jalan.

diverse, *adj.* bermacam; banyak macam.

divert, *v. tr. alter channel, as of stream,* membelukkan (beluk); *~ed, as a missile,* terpesong (pesong); *prevent passage by dam,* empangkan; *~ (traffic),* menyimpangkan (simpang), melencongkan (lencong); *as funds to wrong use,* ketepikan.

divide, *v. tr. split into two parts,* belah dua, kerat dua; *as arithmetically,* bahagi; *~ land into portions,* pecah-pecahkan; *see* **disunite.**

dividend, *n. on capital,* pembahagian (bahagi), seru.

divine, *adj. of or from God,* keTuhanan (Tuhan); *a (minor) divinity,* dewa.

divine, *v. tr. to tell (future, etc.) by magic or inspiration,* meramalkan (ramal), menilik (tilik); *to discover by divination,* tenungkan (tenung); *the art of divination,* ilmu firasat.

division, *n. of troops,* ketumbukan (tumbuk), *esp. of rice-field,* petak.

divorce, *n. under Islamic law,* penceraian; *full ~,* talak tiga; *to ~ (wife),* menceraikan (cerai), menjatuhkan (jatuh) talak tiga; *~ by judicial decree,* fasakh; *on wife's application,* khula.

divulge, *v. to make public,* mengumumkan (umum); pecahkan rahsia.

dizzy, *adj. as from drink or drugs,* mabuk; *with sleep,* terpisat-pisat; *as from a blow,* terlengar (lengar); *slightly ~, 'groggy', esp. from drink or drug,* pening lalat; *see* **giddy.**

do, *v. tr.* buat, bikin; *suffice,* jadi; *done! (in striking a bargain),* sah!; *'~' (disable, etc.),* kerjakan, buat; *that will ~! (suffice),* jadilah!; *that will ~! (stop it!),* sudahlah!

docile, *adj.* patuh.

dock, *n.* 'dok', limbungan; *floating ~,* 'dok' lampung; *~yard,* limbungan kapal.

doctor, *n. of Western medicine,* 'doktor'; *Malay herbalist,* dukun, bomoh; *Chinese herbalist,* sengse; *for branches of medicine, see under* **ilmu.**

document, *n. esp. a letter,* surat; *a writing,* suratan, tulisan.

dodge, *v. intr.* elak; *~ aside,* berkelit (kelit); *~ behind a tree,* berkelit balik pokok; *~ this way and that,* berkelit-kelit, mengelak-ngelakkan (elak) diri.

dog, *n.* anjing, *cur,* koyok; *wild ~,* serigala; *~ged by bad luck,* dirundung malang; *let sleeping ~s lie,* sarang tebuan jangan dijolok, *(don't poke a hornet's nest)*.

doiley, *n.* kain pelapik (lapik) pinggan.

doll, *n.* anak-anak, anak patung, gambar, patung, boneka.

dollar, *n.* ringgit.

dolphin, *n.* ikan lomba-lomba; *to sport in the sea, of a ~,* main gelumbang.

domain, *n sphere, or scope of,* e.g., *science,* kalangan, bidang; *area as of jurisdiction,* kawasan.

dome, *n.* kecubung, kop, kubah.

domestic, *adj. pertaining to the household,* yang berkenaan (kena) dengan rumahtangga; *of animals, kept by man,* - kampung; *~cat,* kucing kampung; *~ science,* urusan rumah tangga; *to ~ates, reduce (animal) to dependence on man,* menjinakkan (jinak); *see* **jinak.**

donation, *n. to charity,* derma; *allowance given for support,* wang bantuan, tunjangan; *to donate,* mendermakan, menghadiahkan (hadiah).

donkey, *n.* kaldai.

don't, *v. aux,* jangan; *no need to,* tak usah; *~ trouble to,* tak payah.

doom, *n. fated day of death,* ajal; *Doomsday,* hari kiamat.

door, *n.* pintu; *~ knob,* tombol pintu; *uprights of a ~,* jenang pintu; *threshold,* ambang (pintu); *body of ~,* daun pintu; *lintel,* bendul pintu, palang pintu.

dormant, *v. intr. to lie,* bertapa (tapa).

dose, *n. a measure of medicine,* satu sukatan (ubat); *over-~,* ubat berlebihan (lebih).

dot, *n.* titik, noktah; *~ted line,* garisan bertitik; *dotted about, situated here and there,* berselerak (selarak).

dotard, *n.* orang tua nyanyuk, orang tua agut-agut; *useless old ~,* tua bangka.

double, *adj. folded in two,* berlipat (lipat) dua; *of a flower,* berlapis (lapis) dua, berkelopak (kelupak) dua; *~ the size,* dua kali lebih besar; *~-barreled gun,* senapang laras dua; *to ~, make ~,* gandakan; *~-faced,* talam dua muka, bermuka dua; *~s (contest),* bergu (gu).

doubt, *n. uncertainty, suspicion,* syak, kesangsian (sangsi); *~less,* tidak syak lagi; *~ful, of events,* tidak tentu; *feeling ~ful (as to proper course of action),* bercabang (cabang) hati; *anxious,* bimbang.

dough, *n.* adunan, tepung.

dove, *n. ground-~,* burung merbok; *turtle-~,* burung tekukur; *brown spotted ~,* burung balam; *(fig.), pair of turtle-~s (young lovers),* sepasang merpati.

dovetailed, *p.p.* tertanggam (tanggam), berbajang (bajang).

dowdy, *adj. lacking smartness, of clothes,* lusuh.

down, *adv. to lower plane,* ke bawah; *go ~,* turun; *~ with! (do away with!),* singkirkan!, punah!, hapuskan!, hancurkan!, basmikan!

down, *n. fine soft hair,* bulu kapas.

dowry, *n.* mas kahwin, mahar.

doze, *v. tr. sleep for a short time,* terlayang (layang) sekejap, lena pelanduk; *esp. of having a fitful sleep,* tidur-tidur ayam.

draft, *n. of document,* rang; *a ~ law,* gubahan undang-undang, rang undang-undang; *rough ~,* rangka.

drag, *v. tr.* heret, hela; *~ trailing after one,* runtun, seret; *to ~, of anchor,* melarut (larut); *~ging on slowly, as time,* larat; *~ging on and on, as a speech or a dispute,* meleret-leret, melarut-larut.

dragon, *n.* naga; *~-fly,* sesibur (sibursibur), belalang patung; *'~'s blood', (a resin),* jernang.

drain, *n. ditch,* parit; *by street or house,* longkang; *Drainage & Irrigation Department,* pejabat (jabat) tali air dan parit; *irrigation runnel,* tali air; *outlet ~,* tali pembuang (buang); *to ~ off water in cooking,* tuskan.

drama, *n. stage play,* lakunan, sandiwara, 'drama'.

drastic, *adj. as measures,* keras.

draught, *n. current of air,* angin, hembusan udara (bayu); udara; *~ of a ship (depth of water it draws),* makannya dalam air.

draughts, n. the game, dam; ~-board, papan dam; the pieces, buah dam.

draw, v. tr.·as a cart, tarik, hela; as a sword, cabut, hunus; apart, as curtains, singkap, selakkan; a picture, melukis (lukis); ~ towards one, as with stick or foot, kuis, raih; ~ up in line, banjarkan, bariskan; ~ tight, as a knot, menjerut (jerut); a ~er (as of a table), laci; ~ers (undergarment), celana dalam; ~n (of a contest), seri; ~ and haggard, of face, lesu, usang, ~n and pallid, pucat lesi; of cheeks, kempung; ~n and sunken, cengkung-mengkung.

dread, n. takut, menakutkan, membenci (benci).

dream, v. intr. bermimpi (mimpi); have a nightmare, mengigau (igau); visions of the future, angan-angan; see **castle, daydream.**

dredge, n. kapal pengorek (korek), kapal lombong.

dregs, n. sediment, keladak, kerodak; '~ of society', sampah masyrakat.

drench, v. kuyup; basah kuyup.

dress, n. pakaian; woman's frock (Western style), 'gaun'; to ~, put on clothes, berpakai; 'doll oneself up', pasang badan; ~ing-table, meja solek; to ~, 'furnish' the surface of cordage, leather, samak.

dribble, v. intr. as a baby, melejeh (lejeh); to ~ in football (take ball on oneself), bawa (bola); with clever footwork, mengelecek (gelecek) (bola); ~ away, as money wasted or embezzled, cicir.

drift, v. intr. berhanyut (hanyut), mengapung (apung), mengatung (atung); fig. of a person, who never settles down, merempat (rempat) (ke sana sini); a '~er', waster, orang hanyut; drifted (piled up, esp. by the wind), bertimbun-timbun; ~-wood, on beach, kayu godar; on water, kayu apung.

drill, v. intr. berbaris (baris) berkawad (kawad); do physical ~, bersenam (senam); to ~ a hole, menggerek (gerek); a ~, jara, bor, penggerek, to ~, as a dentist, culek.

drink, v. intr. minum; strong ~, minuman keras; to lap, sip, menghirup (hirup); to 'have a nip', 'wet one's whistle', membasah (basah) tekak.

drip, v. intr. menitik (titik), meniris (tiris); sound of ~ping, detap-detap.

drive, v. tr. as a car, bawa; be at the wheel, pegang stering; ~r, derebar; in formal language, pemandu (pandu) kereta; ~ away, ~ off, halau; ~ out, nyahkan, usir; ~n firmly in, tertanggam (tanggam), terunjam (unjam); see **stick.**

drone, v. intr. emit a sound as of passing bee or bullet, berdengung (dengung); ~ a song, esp. a chorus, berdendang (dendang); esp. as intoning a tale, mengigung (kidung); see **buzz.**

drongo, n. burung cawi.

droop, v. intr. as head of plant, tunduk; esp. as laden branches, meluyut (luyut); of wilted flower, layu; curl over and ~, as tendrils of a weeping tree or as dogs' ears, melempai (lempai); ~ing, of head, from weariness, longlai.

drop, n. se titik; to ~ (fall, of a small object, as from pocket), titik, cicir; to (let) ~ from above, as a bomb, jatuhkan, gugurkan; ~ off, as an attachment, tanggal; see **fall;** ~ in, stop on the way, singgah; pay a casual visit, mampir; ~pings, dung of animals, etc. tahi; to drop (dismiss, e.g., member of a committee or a team), ke tepikan, singkirkan; to ~ in ~s, as tears, berlinang (linang).

dropsy, n. busung (air).

dross, n. worthless residue, kalat-kalat; left after processing, hampas; scum formed in smelting, sanga; opium ~, tengkuh, tahi candu.

drought, n. musim kemarau.

drowse, v. in slumber, melelapkan (lelap) mata; letih; memabuk (mabuk).

drown, v. intr. mati lemas (dalam air); to ~ (someone) as by thrusting into water or mud, membenamkan (benam); also (fig.) to ~ a voice, as does, e.g., a storm.

drug, n. ubat; dadah; madat; ~s generally,

ubat-ubatan; *herbal ~s,* akar periuk; *narcotic ~s,* kena pukau, kena sekut, kena kecubung, kena madat, kena ganja; *see* **addicted.**

drum, *n.* gendang; *esp. mosque ~,* gendang raya, beduk; *esp. military ~,* tambur; *~s and fifes,* tambur dan suling; *to beat (a ~),* memalu (palu).

drunk, *adj.* mabuk (arak); *'booze-hound',* tahi arak, kaki minum.

dry, *adj.* kering; *~ and stiff, of hair, arid, of land,* kersang; *~ season,* musim kemarau; *to hang up to ~ (clothes),* menyidai (sidai), menyedal (sedal); *see* **air;** *to ~, as fish or copra over a fire,* salaikan; *to rub ~,* mengesat (kesat).

dual, *adj. in couples, combined,* berangkap (rangkap); bertarung, (tarung).

duck, *n.* itek; *~-weed,* kiambang; *like water off a ~'s back,* seperti air di daun keladi, *like water on an aroid leaf (which proverbially lets water run off easily); to ~ the head,* tunduk.

due, *adj. fallen ~, of a debt,* sudah cukup tempoh; *exactly, of points of the compass,* tepat; *~ west,* barat tepat; *in ~ course (at the proper time),* pada waktu yang patut; *sooner or later,* lambat laun.

duet, *n.* nyanyian (nyanyi) oleh dua orang penyanyi.

dugong. *sea cow,* duyung.

dug-out, *n. canoe,* sagur, jalur serempu.

dull, *adj. of colour,* sebam, seput; *of a day,* redup; *of light,* suram; *of sound of a coin, not ringing properly,* bengap; *see* **stupid.**

dump, bisu; *struck ~,* terkelu (kelu); *as by a magic spell,* kena pembongkam (bongkam).

dumbfounded, *adj.* tercengang (cengang)./

dumpy, *adj. short and thick or fat,* buntak.

dun, *v. tr. importune for payment,* menagih (tagih) hutang; menuntut (tuntut) hutang bertubi-tubi.

dune, *n. sand ~,* busung pasir, tanah beris.

dupe, *n. cheated,* tertipu (tidup); terpedaya.

dung, *n.* tahi, najis.

duplicate, *n. copy of document,* salinan; *see* **copy.**

durable, *adj. long-wearing,* tahan lama; *hard-wearing,* tahan lasak.

dusk, *n.* (waktu) senjakala; (waktu) samar muka.

dust, debu, abuk, abu; *'to bite the ~',* membaham (baham) tanah; *to ~ (flick with cloth),* kerpas; *~-bin,* tong sampah; *to 'throw ~ in the eyes',* mengabu mata.

Dutch, *adj.* Belanda; *'~ treat',* belanja Korinci.*

duty, *n. job,* kerja; *pious duties,* ibadat; *imposed by religion or as a social ~,* kewajiban (wajib); *enjoined as a ~ by religion,* perlu, fardu; *assigned ~,* tugas; *customs ~,* cukai ('kastam'); *dutiable,* kena cukai; *import ~,* cukai masuk; *export ~,* cukai keluar; *~-free,* bebas dari cukai.

dwarf, *n.* orang kerdil, orang katik.

dwindle, *v. intr.* susut, bertambah (tambah) kurang.

dye, *n.* air celup.

dynamite, *n.* spidul, dinomit.

dynasty, *n.* keturunan (turun) (raja).

dysentry, *n.* buang air darah, cirit darah.

dyspepsia, *n.* salah hazam, sakit perut.

E

each, *adj.* tiap-tiap; ~ *separate,* masing-masing.

eager, *adj.* ~ *to,* ingin nak, gemar nak; *excited and* ~, girang.

eagle, *n.* *white-bellied sea-*~, lang siput; *as symbol,* rajawali.

eaglet, *n.* anak burung nasar.

ear, *n.* telinga; *within* ~-*shot,* sepelaung (laung), kelur dengar; ~-*ring,* subang; *dangling* ~-*rings,* anting-anting; *small* ~*rings,* orlit; *stud* ~*rings,* kerabu; ~*s of padi,* bulir padi, gemal padi; *'in one* ~ *and out the other',* menerusi lubang telinga (nya) terus menerus.

earl, *n.* gelaran bangsawan.

early, *adv. quickly,* cepat; *before time,* awal; *before others,* lebih dahulu; ~ *in the morning,* pagi-pagi; *it is too* ~ *(the time has not yet arrived),* belum cukup (jam, bulan); *a day* ~, sehari terdahulu.

earmark, *v. tr. assign (fund) to a specific purpose,* cadangkan, menguntukkan (untuk).

earn, *v. tr. get,* mendapat (dapat), menerima (terima); ~ *wages,* makan gaji; ~*ings,* pendapatan.

earnest money, *n. money paid to confirm contract,* cengkeram; *deposited with tender,* wang cagaran.

earnestly, *adv. seriously, determinedly,* sungguh-sungguh, bermati-mati; *with all sincerity,* bersungguh-sungguh.

earnings, *n. pl.* pendapatan, nafkah.

earth, *n. physical,* bumi; *the world we live in,* dunia; *soil,* tanah.

earthly, *adj.* jasmani, kebendaan, keduniaan.

earthenware, *n.* barang tembikar.

earthquake, *n.* gempa bumi, gerak bumi; ~ *shock,* gerak gempa, gegaran gempa.

ease, *n.* kelapangan, kesenangan; *ill at* ~, gelisah, malu. *v. tr.,* menenangkan,

memudahkan.

easel, *n.* sandaran papan tulis (papan lukis).

east, *n.* timur.

easy, *adj. not difficult,* mudah; *free from difficulty or pain,* senang; *in* ~ *circumstances,* lega; *easily,* dengan senangnya; *'in the bag',* dalam tangan; *without an effort,* berdarat (darat) sahaja; ~ *chair,* kerusi malas; *take it* ~!, sabarlah!; *an* ~ *mark (* ~ *to deceive),* lembut-telinga, (lembut-telinga, tentu orang pulaslah, *if you have soft ears, people will twist them, i.e., take advantage of you.)*

eat, *v. tr.* makan; *(courtly),* santap; *(rude) gobble up,* muntah kedarahkan; *guzzle,* gasak, balun, baham; ~ *(solid) food without rice,* meratah (ratah); *devour (jocular),* mengganyang (ganyang); *completely defeat,* makan dengan tahi sekali *(sl.) see* **mince.**

eaves, *n.* cucuran atap.

eavesdrop, *v. intr.* mendengar percakapan orang lain secara rahsia.

ebb, *v. intr.* surut.

ebony, *n.* kayu arang.

ebullient, *adj.* (perasaan) yang tidak tertahan-tahan.

eccentric, *adj. odd, whimsical,* (i) gila bahasa, anih, ganjil; (ii) bulatan-bulatan yang tidak mempunyai pusat yang sama.

ecclesiastic, *n.* alim ulama, pendeta, paderi.

echo, *n.* bahana; *to re-*~, bergema (gema).

eclipse, *n.* gerhana, matahari (bulan) sakit.

economy, *n. state of resources,* perekonomian (ekonomi); *economist,* ahli ilmu ekonomi; *economical (saving),* jimat-cermat; *planned* ~, ekonomi teratur (atur); *economic pressure, 'sanctions',* penekanan (tekan) ekonomi, hukum iktisad; *to economise,* menjimatkan (jimat) wang.

ecstasy, *n.* keghairahan.

eczema, *n.* kudis.

eddy, *n. small whirlpool,* olak air; *esp. in stream,* puaran air; *wind,* pusaran angin.

edge, *n.* tepi; *of knife,* mata; *to ~ forwards or backwards, move along a little,* beranjak (anjak); *edging up, as a shy child,* terkesut-kesut; *to ~ along, of a coaster,* menyusur (susur) (pantai); *having one's teeth 'on ~',* berasa (rasa) ngilu, berasa geli geliman.

edible, *adj.* dapat dimakan; *not forbidden food under Islamic law,* halal.

edit, *v. tr. prepare for publication,* menyusun (susun); *compose,* mengarang (karang); *~ion,* cetakan; *~orial,* lidah pengarang, tajuk rencana; *news-~or,* penyunting (sunting) berita, pengarang berita kumpulan.

educate, *v. tr.* memberi pelajaran (ajar), mendidik (didik); *mengasuh train,* melatihkan (latih); *well ~d,* (orang) terpelajar; *Department of Education,* jabatan (jabat) pelajaran; *pursue higher education,* menuntut (tuntut) ilmu; *educationist,* pakar pendidik.

eel, *n.* ikan belut; *spiny ~,* ikan tilan; *marine ~, conger,* malung.

efface, *v. tr. wipe out,* menghapuskan (hapus).

effect, *n. result produced,* akibat, hasil; *to take ~, prevail, come into use,* berlaku (laku); *take ~, as 'hit the spot', as, e.g., a smart repartee,* kena; *come into ~, as law,* berjalan (jalan) kuat kuasa; *owing to the ~ of (wind),* buat dek angin; *to the ~ that, implying that,* maksudnya; *in ~,* pada hakikatnya.

effective, *adj. producing results,* berhasil (hasil) berkesan (kesan); *of medicine, tried and trusty,* mujarab; *sure to act,* mustajab.

effervesce, *v. intr.* meruap (ruap), membuih.

efficacious, *adj.* berkesan, mujarab.

efficient, *adj.* cergas, cekap; *reliable,* handalan.

effiminate, *adj.* kewanitaan.

effigy, *n.* gambar; *rough shape, figure,* lembaga, patung.

effluent, *n.* anak sungai yang mengalir dari sungai yang besar, tasik.

efforts, *n. strenuous activities,* usaha, tapak tukul; *to make an effort, exert oneself,* gagah; *making great ~,* terkial-kial, berusaha bersungguh-sungguh.

egg, *n.* telur; *to lay an ~,* bertelur; *shell of ~,* kulit telur; *broken ~-shell,* kelumpang telur; *boiled ~,* telur rebus; *fried ~,* telur goreng; *to ~ on (incite),* menghasut (hasut); *so as to make mischief,* mengacum (acum).

egret, *n.* burung bangau, burung kutur.

Egypt, *n.* negeri Mesir.

either, *adj. one of the other,* salah satu; *~—or—,* atau—atau—.

ejaculate, *v. intr. exclaim suddenly, esp. as in invocation,* mengucap (ucap); *see* **exclaim.**

eject, *v. tr. expel,* buang, halau.

elaborate, *adj. & v. tr.* menerangkan dengan panjang lebar.

elapse, *v. tr.* berlalu (lalu); *be lost and gone,* luput.

elastic, *n. piece of ~,* 'lastik'; *springly, as rope,* dapat menganjal (anjal) kenyal; *~ity,* *n.* sifat boleh kembali menjadi bentuk yang asal.

elated, *adj.* besar-hati, bangga.

elbow, *n.* siku; *to nudge with the ~,* singgung; *(roughly),* sinjuh.

elder, *adj.* lebih tua; *~s (as respected older people),* orang tua-tua.

eldest, *adj.* tertua (tua); *~ child,* anak sulung.

elect, *v. tr.* memilih (pilih); *act of ~ion, choice,* pemilihan; *general ~ion,* pilihan raya; *by-~ion,* pilihan raya kechil; *State ~ions,* pilihan raya negeri; *to hold an election,* mengadakan (ada) pilihan raya; *right to free ~ions,* hak pemilihan yang bebas; *see* **vote.**

electricity, *n.* api elektrik, kuasa elektrik, tenaga elektrik.

electuary, *n. compound medicine,* makjun.

elegant, *adj. smart,* segak, tampan, lawah.

element, *n.* anasir, unsur; *in chemistry,* zat; *undesirable ~s (politically),* anasir yang tidak diingini; *subversive ~s,* anasir subversif; *'snakes in grass',* jari lipan.

elephant, *n.* gajah; ~ *keeper, mahout,* gembala gajah; *ankus,* kosa; *howdah,* kop, rengka; *saddle,* rengka; *rutting, of* ~, meta, turun minyak.

elephantiasis, *n.* untut.

elevate, *v. tr. raise higher, as head of recumbent person or fig. as rank, status, material prosperity,* meninggikan (tinggi).

elf, *n. mischievous imp,* jembalang; *invisible elves of the jungle,* orang bunian, lembuyan, siluman.

eligible, *adj. qualified to be chosen,* layak.

eliminate, *v. tr. remove, get rid of,* menghilangkan (hilang); *'weed out', push aside,* menyingkirkan (singkir), ketepikan (tepi); *do away with, wipe out,* menghapusskan (hapus), membasmikan (basmi).

elite, *n. the 'top people',* orang atasan, lapisan atas, golongan orang yang terpelajar (terbaik dalam masyarakat).

elliptical, *adj. of oval shape,* bujur telur, bulat bujur.

elocution, *n.* tuturan, cara mengucap.

elongate, *v. tr.* panjangkan.

elope, *v. tr. make a runaway marriage,* kawin lari.

eloquent, *adj.* fasih; *having a ready flow of words,* pitah.

elsewhere, *adv.* di tempat lain.

elucidate, *v. tr.* menerangkan (terang), menjelaskan (jelas).

elusive, *adj. shunning observation,* suka menjauhkan (jauh) diri.

emaciate, *v. tr. make lean, waste,* menguruskan (badan).

emanate, *v. tr.* ~ *from, have its origin in,* berasal (asal) dari.

emancipate, *v. tr. set free,* bebaskan; *~d, no longer kept secluded, of girls,* lepas pingitan.

embankment, *n.* batas; *esp. as for road,* tembuk; *bund,* ban; *causeway,* jalan tambak.

embalm, *v. tr. preserve,* mengawetkan, (mayat).

embargo, *n. order forbidding entry of (goods),* sekatan (barang-barang).

embarrassed, *adj. feeling ~,* merasa (rasa) malu; *to feel ~ and reluctant,* merasa segan; *looking shy and sheepish, esp. of a girl,* tersipu-sipu.

embassy, *n.* kedutaan (duta).

embedded, *adj. firmly fixed,* terunjam (unjam); *as in mud,* terbenam (benam).

ember, *n.* bara api.

embezzle, *v. tr.* melesapkan (lesap) wang, menggelapkan (gelap) wang.

emblem, *n. symbol,* lambang.

embrace, *v. tr.* memeluk (peluk), mendakap (dakap); *put arm round,* kapuk; *(fig.) include, comprise,* merangkum (rangkum).

embrocation, *n.* minyak urat.

embroidery, *n.* tekat; *embroidered cloth,* kain bertekat, kain bersulam, barang sulaman; *to insert ornamentation,* menyulam (sulam), menekat (tekat).

embroil, *v. tr. draw into a quarrel,* membabit (babit); *excite two parties against one another,* mengadu-dumbakan (adu), lagakan.

embryo, *n.* punat, lembaga, lembaga di peringkat awal kelahiran sesuatu seperti manusia, binatang dsb.

emend, *v. tr. remove errors,* meminda (pinda); *put right,* membetulkan (betul).

emerald, *n.* zamrud.

emerge, *v. intr. come into view from confined space,* terbit; *as appearing on surface,* timbul, munchul; *'~nt nation',* negara muncul, negara yang sedang membangun.

emergency, *n. sudden juncture requiring prompt action,* saat yang genting; *public ~,* masa kecemasan (cemas), darurat; *to proclaim a state of e~,* menyatakan (nyata) keadaan (ada) darurat.

emery, *n.* ~ *stone,* batu las.

emigrate, *v. intr.* berpindah (pindah) (ke negeri lain), merantau (rantau).

eminent, *adj.* *of recognised superiority,* utama, unggul.

emissary, *n. envoy,* utusan.

emit, *v. tr. give out, put forth, cause to go out,* mengeluarkan (keluar); *shoot out (as water, rays),* pancarkan; *spray out,* menyembur (sembur); *if the real meaning is to be the source from which something comes, the effect may be attained by the use of the prefix* ber-: *~ting smoke,* berasap; *~ting flame,* berapi; *or* asal *(origin) may be used: originating from,* berasal dari; *see* **exude.**

emolument, *n. (usually in pl.) profit from employment, salary,* gaji, pendapatan.

emotion, *n. ~s generally,* hawa nafsu; *feeling deep ~,* terharu (haru); *~al (unsteady in ~s),* kepala angin; *heart, a seat of ~s,* hati; *see* **feel.**

emotive, *adj.* membangkitkan perasaan jiwa yang kuat.

emphasis, *n. significance on words,* tekanan suara; *to emphasise (treat as serious),* mengambil (ambil) berat; *to lay stress on, munitik beratkan (titik).*

employ, *v. tr.* memakai (pakai) (sebagai orang gaji); ~er, tuan, tauke, majikan.

empower, *v. tr. give power to,* memberi (beri) kuasa kepada; *enable,* membolehkan (boleh).

empty, *adj.* kosong; *void of expected contents,* hampa, sambang; *abnormally unfrequented, as a market street, etc.,* lengang; *to ~ out,* curahkan; *~ out contents,* buang isi; *emptiness,* kehampaan, kekosongan.

emulate, *v. intr. copy,* meniru (tiru); *emulating one another,* berdahulu-dahuluan (dahulu).

enact, *v. tr. make a law,* membuat (buat) undang-undang, meluluskan (lulus) undang-undang.

encamp, *v. tr.* berkhemah (khemah); *see*

camp.

encase, *v. tr. put into case, surround as with case,* memasukkan ke dalam sarung, sampul, bekas dll.

encircle, *v. tr. to form a circle around,* melengkungi (lengkung), melingkari (lingkar); *see* **surround.**

enclose, *v. tr. as in letter,* sertakan; *fence off,* memagarkan (pagar); *enclosure generally,* kurungan; *esp. as for animals,* kandang.

encounter, *v. tr. as enemy or as dangers,* menempuh (tempuh); *'knock up against', come face to face with,* tersua (sua) dengan, terjeremba (jeremba) dengan.

encourage, *v. tr.* buat galak; *stimulate,* buat perangsang (rangsang); *raise morale,* menghidupkan (hidup) semangat; *incite,* mengasut (asut); *'~' (allow to take liberties),* beri muka; *urge to further action,* memberi (beri) dorongan (kepada).

encroach, *v. int. intrude on others' right,* menyalahi, melanggar hak.

encumbrance, *n.* halangan, kongkongan.

encyclopaedia, *n.* kamus, ensiklopedia.

end, *n. extreme point,* hujung; *of period,* akhir; *latter part of period,* penghujung; *~ of a piece of string, etc.,* punca; *~ of an event,* kesudahan (sudah); *tamat; 'at a loose ~' (having nothing to do),* duduk bergoyang-goyang kaki; *in the ~,* lama-lama, akhirnya; *in the long run,* lama-kelamaan; *that's the ~ (no more to be said or done),* habis perkara, habis bicara; *ended (terminated),* selesai, berakhir.

endeavour, *v. try (to do), strive, n. attempt, effort,* usaha, ikhtiar.

endemic, *adj. of a disease, regularly found in a locality,* (penyakit) yang selalu terdapat di daerah yang tertentu.

endless, *adj.* tidak berkesudahan (sudah); *the ~ past,* azal; *the ~ future,* akhirat.

endure, *v. tr. put up with,* tahan; *undergo,* menanggung (tanggung); *suffer,* menderita (derita); *tolerate patiently,* sabarkan; *put up with it, 'lump it'*, ber-ela-rela.

enemy, *n.* musuh; *personal enemy*, seteru.

energetic, *adj.* rajin, ringan-tulang.

enervate, *v. tr.* melemahkan (lemah) badan.

enfeeble, *v. tr.* melemahkan.

enforce, *v. tr. as a law*, menjalankan (jalan), menguatkuasakan.

engage, *v. tr. take on person for work*, memberi (beri) kerja; *for a task*, mengupah (upah); *~d to marry*, bertunang (tunang).

engine, *n.* 'injin', jentera; *~er*, jurutera; *locomotive*, kepala keretapi.

English, *adj.* Inggeris; *England*, negeri England; *~ language*, (bahasa) Inggeris.

engrave, *v. tr.* mengukir (ukir).

engrossed, *adj. absorbed in something*, ralip, asyik; *~ in a book*, ralip membaca (baca) buku.

engulf, *v. tr. swallow up*, menelan.

enhance, *v. tr. increase*, menambahkan (tambah); *heighten (e.g., standard)*, mempertinggikan (tinggi).

enigma, *n. riddle, puzzling person or thing*, sesuatu yang membingungkan.

enjoin, *v. tr. lay down (practice, line of conduct) as fitting*, mengharuskan (harus).

enjoy, *v. tr. like*, menikmati, suka; *~ oneself*, bersukaria; *'have a good time'*, buat 'joli', berseronok-seronok, bere-nak-enak, berpoya-poya; *~able*, seronok.

enlarge, *v. tr. make bigger*, memperbesarkan (besar); *make extensive, as territory*, meluaskan (luas); *increase space or scope of*, perlapangkan (lapang), meluaskan (luas).

enlighten, *v. tr. instruct, inform, shed light on*, memberi penjelasan atau keterangan.

enlist, *v. tr. enter in list or roll*, mendaftarkan (daftar); *to be engaged for military service*, menjadi (jadi) asykar, masuk tentera, masuk berkhidmat (khidmat).

enliven, *v. tr. as a ceremony with music*, menyerikan (seri), memeriahkan (meriah).

enmity, *n. hatred, hostility*, bermusuhan, kebencian.

enormity, *n. great wickedness or crime*, kekejaman, kezaliman, kesalahan yang besar.

enough, *adj.* cukup; *~ to live on*, cukup makan; *~ to go on with*, cukup pakai; *adequate*, berpada-pada; *~! (stop it)*, sudahlah!; *(that will do, suffice)*, jadilah; *see* **suffice**.

enraged, *adj.* meradang (radang); *'get steamed up'*, naik 'marah'.

enslave, *v. tr.* memperhambakan (hamba).

entangled, *p.p.* terkusut-kusut, terbojot (bojot); *caught up, as in thorns*, tersangkut (sangkut); *in a noose*, terjerat (jerat).

enter, *v. tr. come or go in*, masuk; *~ (e.g. name in book)*, masuk(kan); *~ a competition*, bertanding (tanding); *entrant*, peserta (serta); *entrance fee*, bayaran masuk.

enterprise, *n. bold undertaking*, kegiatan yang memerlukan semangat dan usaha yang bersungguh-sungguh.

entertain, *v. tr. as host*, menjamu (jamu); *esp. as officially or on a large scale*, merayakan (raya); *as with music, etc.*, menghiburkan (hibur).

enthrone, *v. tr. as ruler*, menabalkan (tabal).

enthusiasm, *n.* keghairahan, gembira; *football enthusiast*, kaki bola; *see* **addicted, fan**; *to display an ~ which quickly cools*, membuat kerja hangat-hangat tahi ayam, *(to do a job as hotly as fowls' droppings (which quickly cool)*.

entice, *v. tr. persuade with allurements*, membujuk (bujuk), memikat (pikat).

entire, *adj. all*, semua; *the ~ world*, seluruh dunia.

entitled, *adj. having a right (to)*, berhak (hak) (nak).

entrain, *v. intr.* naik kereta api.

entrance, *n.* jalan masuk.

entranced, *p.p. lit and fig.* terpesona pesona.

entreat, *v. tr. ask earnestly,* memohon (mohon), merayu (rayu).

entrench, *v. tr. surround or fortify with trench,* di kelilingi oleh kubu pertahanan; yang diperkukuhkan.

enumerate, *v. tr. count one by one,* menghitung (hitung) satu persatu.

enunciation, *n. of speech,* tuturan, pertuturan (tutur).

envelope, *n. of letter,* sarung surat; *generally,* sampul.

environment, *n.* alam sekitaran, alam keliling.

environs, *n.* daerah sekitar (bandar).

envisage, *v. tr. conjure up a picture of, imagine,* menggambarkan (gambar) (dalam hati).

envoy, *n.* utusan; *ambassador,* duta.

envy, *n. malicious jealousy,* dengki, iri; *envious,* irihati, berasa (rasa) dengki, menaruh (taruh) dengki.

epidemic, *n.* wabak.

epilepsy, *n.* sawan babi, gila babi.

episode, *n. happening,* kejadian (jadi), peristiwa (istiwa); *in a play,* adigan.

equal, *adj.* sama; *of ~ size,* sama besar; *of ~ status,* setaraf; *of ~ rank,* sepangkat; *equality, as of pay,* persamaan; *to ~,* menyamai; *~ to (not inferior to),* tak kalah dengan; *to treat (e.g., different communities) as equals,* menyama-ratakan (sama).

equanimity, *n. composure, calm,* ketenangan.

equator, *n.* khatulistiwa.

equilibrium, *n. see* **balance**.

equipment, *n.* kelengkapan (lengkap).

era, *n.* zaman.

eradicate, *v. tr.* membantun (bantun); *pull up roots and all,* mencabut (cabut) dengan akar sekali; *(fig.) get rid of completely,* membasmikan.

erase, *v. tr.* menghapuskan (hapus); *scratch out,* mengikis (kikis); *rub out,* padam.

erect, *adj.* tegak; *to ~,* mendirikan (diri);

~ion (structure generally), bangunan; *esp. temporary,* peranja; *~ of ears,* tercacak (cacak).

erode, *v. tr. rub away, eat away, gradually,* mengikis (kisis), makan, mengeruk (keruk).

errand, *n. short journey on which person is sent with message, goods etc.,* perjalanan pendek untuk membuat sesuatu.

erratic, *adj. of actions, conforming to no apparent principle,* tak ketahuan (tahu); *of course,* tak tentu arah.

error, *n. blemish in behaviour,* khilaf; *mistake,* kesilapan (silap).

erupt, *v. intr. of volcano,* meletup (letup), meruap (ruap).

escalate, *v. intr. rise step by step, esp. to a dangerous state of affairs,* meningkat (tingkat) menjadi-jadi.

escapade, *n. irresponsible piece of conduct,* suatu kenakalan (nakal).

escape, *v. intr.* lari; *get away,* lepas lari; *get clear away,* melarikan diri; *'make oneself scarce',* bawa diri; *~ with one's life,* melepaskan (lepas) nyawa; *have a narrow ~, expressed by use* of nyaris tak *(almost);* nyaris tak kena tembak, *(narrowly ~d being shot); in the South* nyaris *alone is used in this sense.*

escort, *v. tr. attend,* ikut; *see off,* hantar; *as formal guard,* mengawal (kawal), mengiring (iring).

esoteric, *adj. secret, e.g. mystical,* batin.

especially, *adv.* istimewa.

espionage, *n. spying or using spy,* amalan mengintip.

esprit de corps, *n.* taat setia yang mengukuhkan dan menyatu-padukan anggota-anggota satu kumpulan.

essay, *n.* rencana.

essence, *n.* sari, zat; *esp. as extract,* pati.

essential, *adj. of prime importance,* terutama (utama), penting sekali.

establish, *v. tr. set up (partly, system, business, etc.),* menubuhkan (tubuh), menciptakan (cipta); *~ oneself, settle in,* menetapkan (tetap); *household,* rumah tangga; *to keep up two ~ments* *(presumably with a wife or concubine in each),* simpan dua periuk, *(keep two cooking pots); Establishment Office,* pejabat (jabat) perjawatan (jawat).

estate, *n. plantation,* kebun, ladang; *see* **plantation;** *of deceased person,* harta simati, harta gemulah.

esteem, *v. tr. think highly,* menghargai, menghormati, menyanjungi.

estimate, *n.* anggaran; *guess,* agak; *to ~,* membuat (buat) anggaran.

estuary, *n. tidal mouth of river,* kuala, muara.

etcetera, etc., dan lain-lain (dll); *'and what have you',* apalah; *and so on (more of the same kind),* dan sebagainya.

eternal, *adj.* kekal, abadi; *~ly,* sampai selama-lama, sampai akhir zaman; *imperishable, as heaven,* baka; *the World of Eternity,* alam baka.

ethics, *n. moral principles,* akhlak, kesusilaan (susila); *(rules of ~),* tata susila.

etiquette, *n.* adat, adat-istiadat; *to commit a breach of ~,* langgar adat; *rather a breach of good manners,* langgar bahasa.

eulogy, *n.* (ucapan, shaer) sebagai pujian.

eunuch, *n.* orang kasim, lelaki yang sudah dimusnahkan kejantanannya.

Eurasian, *adj.* orang Serani.

Europe, *n.* Eropah.

evacuate, *v. tr. withdraw from (fort),* mengundur dari (kota); *~ people,* memindahkan (pindah) orang; *~ (troops),* mengundurkan (undur); *see* **defecate.**

evade, *v. tr. dodge,* mengelakkan (elak); *as a tax,* melarikan (lari); *evasive, as in answering,* berdolak-dalik (dolak).

evaluate, *v. tr. find or state amount or value of,* menentukan nilai sesuatu.

evanesce, *v. intr. fade away gradually, as dew,* meresap (resap).

evaporate, *v. intr.* sejat, tus.

Eve, *n. wife of Adam,* Siti Hawa.

even, *adj. of surface,* rata; *of numbers,* genap; *'~' (in betting) on a fighting bull in Kelantan,* sali ganda; *~ly balanced,*

on an ~ keel, bertimbang (timbang) betul.

even, *conj.* pun *(enclitic); ~ so,* biar pun begitu.

evening, *n.* petang.

event, *n. happening,* kejadian (jadi); *occurrence,* peristiwa (istiwa); *in the ~ of—,* jikalau sekiranya; *~ually, sooner or later,* lambat-bangatnya.

eventuality, *adv. in the end,* perkara yang akan muncul, yang kemudian akan jadi.

ever, *adv.* pernah, *(esp. as negative: I have never been to Singapore,* saya tak pernah pergi Singapura); *for ~,* sampai selama-lama.

every, *adj.* tiap-tiap; *~ single,* masing-masing; *~ day,* tiap-tiap hari, (se) hari-hari; *~ other day,* lat sehari; *an ~-day affair,* perkara basahan; *~day clothes,* pakaian lasak; *~where, all over the (country, world),* merata-rata (negeri, dunia); *anywhere at all,* di mana-mana pun.

evict, *v. tr.* membuang (dari rumah), menghalau (halau) (dari rumah).

evidence, *n.* keterangan (terang), bukti.

evil, *adj.* jahat, durjana; *sin,* dosa.

evince, *v. tr. show, indicate,* memperlihatkan, melahirkan, membuktikan, menunjukkan.

ex-, *prefix, former,* bekas; *the former Minister,* bekas menteri; *esp. as having finished course, service (of scholar, soldier),* lepasan.

exacerbate, *v. tr. aggravate, irritate,* mengganggu, menyakitkan hati seseorang, menjadikan lebih teruk, (mengenai penyakit, kesakitan, dll).

exact, *adj. precise,* tepat; *strictly correct,* betul-betul.

exaggerate, *v. tr.* melebih-lebihkan (lebih), memperbesar-besarkan (besar).

exalt, *v. tr. raise high in ranks, etc.,* mengutamakan (utama).

examine, *v. tr.* periksa; *~ (a problem) minutely,* meneliti (teliti), halusi; *(visually),* membedek (bedek), membelek

(belek); *scrutinize, e.g., accounts,* menyelidik (sellidik); *examination papers,* kertas soalan; *viva voce examination,* soalan (ujian) jawabmulut, temu uji.

example, *n. to follow,* tuladan; *to avoid,* sempadan; *for ~,* misalnya; *such as,* seperti; *don't follow the bad ~ of others,* kalau anjing makan tahi, adakah patut kita makan tahi juga? *(if dogs eat dung, that does not justify us in doing so); illustrative ~,* misalan.

excavate, *v. tr.* menggali (gali), mencebak (cebak); *excavations (diggings),* penggalian.

exceed, *v. tr.* melampaui (lampau), mengatasi (atas); *~ingly,* terlampau; *to ~ one's powers,* melebihi (lebih) kuasa.

excellent, *adj. of great merit,* utama; sangat baik, cemerlang; *His Excellency,* Tuan yang terutama, *~! (well done!),* bagus!; *(of a person),* bergeliga (geliga), *(of outstanding excellence, a 'jewel').*

except, *prep. not including,* tidak termasuk (masuk); *leaving aside,* kecuali (cuali); *without ~ion,—*belaka.

exceptional, *adj.* luar biasa; *no ordinary—,* bukan sebarang—.

excerpt, *n. as from a book,* kutipan, petikan.

excess, *n. amount by which a thing exceeds,* yang lebih; *~ively,* terlampau; *~ive,* berlebih-lebihan.

exchange, *v. tr.* bertukar (tukar); *rate of ~,* harga tukaran wang; *~ in reciprocity, interchange,* berbalas-balas; *exchanging smiles,* berbalas-balas senyum; *~ blows/words,* berkelahi.

excise, *n.* cukai; *to ~ (cut out from document),* potong.

excite, *v. tr. ~ to love,* memberahikan (berahi); *rouse,* menggalakkan (galak); *stir up to attack (of a fighting cock or bull),* mengoja (oja); *~d, elated,* besarhati; *with anger,* naik panas; *wildly ~d, as populace,* gempar, heboh; *'worked up',* naik geram; *don't get ~d!* sabar!; *full of eagerness, zest,* gerang; *to get*

'worked up', throw a temper, naik angin, *(not, 'get the wind up'); exciting, as a film,* meriah.

exclaim, *v. intr.* berseru (seru); *see* **ejaculate.**

exclude, *v. tr. shut out from privilege, etc.,* mengasingkan (asing), menyingkirkan (singkir); *excluding, exclusive of,* tidak termasuk (masuk).

excrement, *n.* tahi, najis.

excrete, *v. tr. separate and expel, (waste matter) from the system,* membuang, mengeluarkan.

excruciating, *adj. extremely painful,* (kesakitan) yang amat sangat.

excursion, *n. to go on an ~, a pleasure trip,* pergi makan angin, melancung (lancung).

excuse, *n. reason,* sebab; *grounds alleged in ~,* alasan; *incapacity alleged in ~,* keuzuran (uzur); *mere ~,* suatu elah.

excuse, *v. tr.* maafkan; *~ me!,* minta maaf; *as modest greeting,* tabik!

execute, *v. tr. carry out (as plan),* melakukan (laku), menjalankan *as capital punishment,* membunuh (bunuh) mengikut (ikut) hukuman; *executioner,* pertanda.

exempt, *adj. as from tax,* bebas; *~ed,* dikecualikan (cuali); *see* **immune.**

exercise, *n. to take ~,* cari penat, membuang (buang) kejang; *esp. of physical or mental ~,* riadah.

exertions, *n. to put forth great ~,* terkial-kial; *with all one's might,* sedaya upaya.

exhale, *v. intr.* membuang (buang) nafas.

exhausted, *adj. tired out,* letih lesu, penat; *used up,* putus, habis.

exhibit, *v. tr. show,* tunjuk; *as for sale,* mendedahkan (dedah); *display,* memperlihatkan (lihat); *see* **expose;** *an ~, show,* pertunjukan, pameran.

exhilarate, *v. tr. cheer, enliven, gladden,* menggembirakan, menyenangkan.

exhume, *v. tr.* membongkar (mayat).

exile, *v. tr.* buang negeri; *hound out of a place,* tondong; *an ~, deportee,* orang buangan; *expatriate,* perantau (rantau).

exist, *v. tr.* ada, wujud.

exodus, *n. departure esp. in considerable number,* hal meninggalkan beramai-ramai.

exorcise, *v. tr. expel evil spirits or influences,* mengusir (hantu) menghalaukan setan dari tubuh manusia; *esp. after killing a deer,* buang bahadi.

expand, *v. intr. dilate, increase in bulk or area,* berkembang (kembang); *to ~ (extend), e.g.* one's estate, meluaskan (luas); *expanding and contracting (as, e.g., a jelly-fish),* kembang-kempis; *~ed metal,* besi silang.

expect, *v. tr. wait expectantly for,* menanti-nantikan; *hope,* harap; *believe,* percaya; *calculate, anticipate,* menduga (duga), menjangka (jangka); *regard as probable,* sangka; *~ant of death or of a baby,* menantikan (nanti) hari; *beyond ~ation,* di luar dugaan, *also expressed by the saying,* pucuk dicita, ulam mendatang (datang), *(I hoped for a shoot and vegetables arrived).*

expeditionary force, *n.* pengiriman tentera, pemergian ke sesuatu tempat untuk menyiasat.

expel, *v. tr.* buang, halau, nyahkan.

expense, *n.* belanja; *expenditure (as opposed to income),* perbelanjaan; *expensive,* mahal.

experiment, *n.* percubaan (cuba); *test,* ujian.

expert, *adj.* pandai, cekap; *~ in, esp. science, quasi-science and art,* ahli; *esp. in the sense of 'learned in',* pakar; *esp. in handicraft,* tukang; *esp. in work other than handicraft,* juru.

expiate, *v. tr. make amends for (sin),* menebus (tebus) (dosa).

expired, *p.p. as truce, licence,* tamat tempoh; *of period,* times, luput; *see* **dead**.

explain, *v. tr.* menerangkan (terang), menjelaskan (jelas), menegaskan (tegas); *~ meaning of,* ertikan; *ah, that ~s it, fits the facts,* patutlah.

explicit, *adj. expressly stated,* terang, dengan tegas.

explode, *v. intr.* meletup (letup), mencetus (cetus); *thud of explosion,* dentum, meletus, mengeluarkan perasaan marah.

explore, *v. intr. journey about distant countries,* menjelajah (jelejah) di negeri yang jauh-jauh; *~r (traveller),* menyelidiki, memeriksa, pengembara (kembara); *(traveller far afield),* perantau (rantau).

export, *v. tr. take (commodities) out of the country,* bawa (dagangan) keluar negeri, eksport; *~ duty,* cukai eksport.

expose, *v. tr. as for sale,* mendedahkan (dedah); *open,* membuka (buka); *as a secret,* mengupas (kupas); *(waiting about) ~d to the elements,* bersapai (sapai), berjenggi (jenggi), berpanas (panas) berembun (embun); *open to the sky, as an unroofed boat,* terdedah; *to ~ the person,* menampakkan (nampak) aurat, membuka (buka) aurat; menelanjangi, membeberkan (kesalahan orang); *to lift the sarung so as to ~ the person,* selakkan kain.

expound, *v. tr.* menerangkan (terang), menghuraikan.

expression, *n. of face,* air muka; *combination of words,* istilah, rangkaian (kata); *~less, of face,* muka tebal, muka bersahaja (sahaja).

expropriate, *v. tr. nationalise,* menjadikan (jadi) milik negara; *confiscate,* merampas (rampas).

expunge, *v. tr. erase, strike out,* menghapuskan, memadam.

extant, *adj. still existing (as, e.g., a document),* yang masih wujud.

extend, *v. tr. enlarge area (as of estate),* meluaskan (luas); *prolong,* melanjutkan (lanjut); *stretch out (hand),* hulur (tangan); *to stretch, reach out (as a mountain range),* merentang (rentang); *~ed (in open order),* berjarak (jarak); *extension (as to a building),* tambahan.

extenuating circumstances, *n.* sebab-

sebab atau keadaan yang meringankan (ringan) kesalahan (salah).

exterminate, *v. tr.* memusnahkan (musnah).

external, *adj.* sebelah luar; *outside the country,* di luar negeri, lahir.

extinct, *adj.* habis mati, tumpas; *died out,* habis keturunannya (turun); punah.

extinguish, *v. tr.* membasmikan (basmi); mencabut dengan akar-akar; *see* **destroy.**

extol, *v. tr. praise to the skies,* puji melambung (lambung), mengagungkan (agung).

extort, *v. tr.* ~ *money,* memaksa wang.

extricate, *v. tr. get (person, thing, oneself (from confinement, difficulty),* melepaskan, memerdekakan, menguraikan (benang).

exuberant, *adj. in high spirits, effusive,* mewah, segar, limpah, bersemangat.

exude, *v. intr. trickle out,* meleleh (leleh), berlinang (linang); *exuding moisture,* berair (air); *to be ~d in drips,* berdenih (denih); *see* **emit.**

exultant, *adj.* kembang-hati; *to shout in exultation,* bersorak (sorak), kegembiraan.

eye, *n.* mata; ~*brows,* bulu mata; ~-*socket,* lekuk mata, tubir mata; ~*wash (humbug),* pengabuk (abuk) mata; ~*sore (disgusting sight),* sumbang bagi pandangan; *black* ~ *(bunged up),* mata bakup; *have one's* ~ *on, covet,* menaruh (taruh) mata pada; *to make* ~*s, ogle,* main mata; *to* ~ *longingly,* menginding (inding), melangut (langut); ~*sight,* penglihatan.

F

fable, *n.* cerita ibarat, cerita-cerita dongeng.

fabric, *n. woven material,* kain tenunan, rangka.

fabricate, *v. tr. invent, (fact)* mereka-reka, membuat-buat, memalsukan; *fabrication, n.* pemalsuan, rekaan.

fabulous, *adj. marvellous,* seperti cerita ajaib.

facade, *n. face of building,* hadapan (rumah), muka (rumah).

face, *n.* muka, wajah; *to pull a long ~,* menarik (tarik) muka dua-belas; *(grimace),* cebik; *'lose ~',* hilang milang maruah; *facing towards—,* menghadap (hadap) ke-; *~ to ~,* bertentang (tentang) muka; *~ upwards,* telentang (lentang); *~ downwards,* tertiarap (tiarap); *to ~, encounter, as dangers,* menempuh (tempuh); *oppose,* menentang (tentang); *~d with, as danger,* tersua (sua) dengan; *~, meet confidently, not shy to meet,* berdepan (depan) dengan; *poker~d,* muka tebal; *sour~d,* muka masam; *pleasant~d,* muka manis; *~ lifting,* menegangkan kulit muka supaya kelihatan lebih muda.

facilitate, *v. tr. render move easy,* memudahkan (mudah); *facilities (amenities),* kemudahan.

fact, *n. affair,* hal, perkara; *plain (statement of) ~,* kenyataan (nyata); *a plain ~,* satu hakikat; *in ~,* pada halnya, pada hakikatnya; *in actual truth,* sebenarnya.

faction, *n.* pihak, puak, golongan yang tidak puas hati.

factitious, *adj. artificial, not genuine,* tiruan, dibuat-buat, tidak asli.

factor, *n. element in a result,* faktor; *reason,* sebab; *component part, see* **element**.

factory, *n.* kilang, pabrik.

fade, *v. intr.* turun (warna); *lose colour (esp. as metal),* luntur; *as flower,* layu, malap; *esp. as washed out,* kepudaran.

faeces, *n. see* **excrement**.

fail, *v. intr. as plan,* tak jadi; *not succeed,* tak berjaya (jaya), gagal, tak sampai-sampai; *in examination,* tidak lulus; *fall short, not come up to standard (of progress),* mundur; *(sl.) 'didn't stick' (of a plan),* tak lekat; *(do it) without ~,—* jangan tidak.

failing, *n. natural fault,* keburukan (buruk), kelemahan, kekurangan, cacat; *to be '~' (to 'go downhill', of the weakening of faculties of a person nearing death),* bertabiat (tabiat).

faint, *v. intr. lose consciousness,* pengsan, menyelap (selap); *unconscious,* tak sedarkan diri; *feel ~,* naik pitam; *feeling ~ at the sight of blood,* mabuk darah; *~, of sound or sight,* sayup, redam, *~-hearted, adj.* pengecut.

fair, *adj. just,* adil, saksama; *right and proper,* patut, memuaskan; *of complexion,* putih; *a ~ (market),* pasar.

fairy, *n.* pari, hantu pari; *'~' beings generally,* orang halus, (orang halus are invisible beings who can take human shape and human size); *nymph,* bidadari; *~land,* negeri kayangan.

faith, *n. belief in religious doctrine or divine truth,* kepercayaan.

faithful, *adj.* setia; *true,* benar; *yours ~ly,* yang benar; *see* **loyal**.

faithless, *adj.* derhaka, tak setia; *tidak jujur; deceitful,* curang.

fall, *v. intr. ~ down,* rebah; *esp. as from an elevated position,* jatuh; *of heavy, bulky object, as building, rock,* runtuh; *as leaves, ripe fruit,* luruh; *esp., prematurely,* gugur; *of rain,* turun; *crash, as plane,* jatuh terhempas (hempas); ~ *with a thud,* berdentum (dentum); ~ *to pieces,* bercetai-cetai; ~ *on,* timpa; ~ *into (a hole),* terperosok (perosok); ~ *on face,* tersembam (sembam); *of water in a river, flood, etc.,* surut; *of level in contents in a container,* luak; ~ *behind (fail to keep up),* lepas ke belakang; *flop down and cover, as a tent,* menghempap (hempap); *'bite the dust',* membaham (baham) tanah; ~*en to pieces, as after a smash,* pecah lerai; *see* **crumble**; ~*ing ground (sloping downwards),* menurun (turun); *water*~, air terjun, air melata (lata).

fallacious, *adj. containing fallacy, misleading,* palsu, bohong, gambaran yang tidak betul.

fallow, *adj. temporarily uncultivated,* (tanah) rang.

false, *adj. as story,* bohong, dusta; *as teeth or coin,* palsu, lancung; *to play* ~, *esp. of husband or wife,* berlaku (laku) curang.

falter, *v. intr.* ~ *in spirit,* semangat sudah melampau (lampau); *hesitating,* teragak-agak; *in speech,* gagap; *with faltering voice, as under stress of emotion,* dengan surara terputus-putus.

fame, *n. condition of being widely known or much talk about,* ternama, keharuman, kemasyhuran.

familiar, *adj. of friend,* rapat, karib; *over-*~, *disrespectful,* bebas sangat; *on* ~ *terms with, esp. a superior,* manja dengan; ~ *spirit, (demon attending sorcerer),* guru; ~ *imp,* polong, pelesit; *see* **intimate**.

family, *n.* keluarga, 'famili'; *of a man,* anak-bini; ~ *group,* suku; *dependants,* anak-buah; *genus, stock,* baka, rumpun; *'*~*-man',* orang beranak-bini, orang berumah-tangga (rumah); *Royal* ~, keluarge di raja, kerabat diraja; ~ *planning,* rancangan beranak, berancangan keluarga; *man (woman) of good* ~, anak orang baik.

famine, *n.* kebuluran (bulur).

famous, *adj.* masyhur; *celebrated,* terkenal (kenal); *notable (person),* (orang) kenamaan (nama); *world-*~, masyhur di seluruh dunia.

fan, *n.* kipas; *a '*~*' (enthusiastic supporter, e.g., of a team),* peminat (minat).

fanatical, *adj.* taksub (pada agama).

fancy, *n. vague impression,* perasaan (rasa); *imagination,* angan-angan, khayalan; *anomalous,* ganjil; ~ *dress,* pakaian ganjil; *fancier (of cocks, doves, etc.),* peminat (minat).

fantasy, *n. fanciful story,* cerita khayalan, 'fantasi'.

far, *adj.* jauh; ~ *(bigger),* berganda-ganda lebih (besar); ~*ther,* lagi; *gone too* ~, *exceeded reasonable bounds,* sudah melampau (lampau), terlanjur (lanjur); *by the best,* yang sebaik-baiknya; *so* ~ *(up to now or up to here),* setakat ini; ~*-sighted,* berfikiran (fikir) luas; ~ *from it! (not like that at all),* tujuh bukit tujuh lurah jauhnya *(seven hills and seven valleys away).*

farce, *n.* cerita lawak jenaka.

fare, *n. cost of passenger's conveyance,* tambang; *food provided, diet,* makanan.

farewell, *int. & n. goodbye,* selamat tinggal.

farm, *n.* ladang.

fascinate, *v. tr.* memikat, (pikat) hati, menambat (tambat) hati.

fashion, *n. manner,* cara; *in dress,* fesyen.

fast, *adj. swift,* deras, laju; *esp. as a runner,* tangkas; *of colour, not fading,* tidak luntur; *firmly fixed,* tepap, kejat, teguh, kukuh.

fast, *n. religious,* puasa; *the fasting month,* Ramadan, bulan puasa.

fasten, *v. tr.* ikat; *tether, moor,* tambat; *pinion,* mengilas (kilas).

fastidious, *adj. hard to satisfy,* sangat pemilih (pilih), cerewet.

fat, *adj.* gemuk; *Fatty,* si gedempal; *plump,* tambun; *well-fleshed,* muntil; *pot belly,* perut buncit; *swag belly,* perut gendut; ~*-head,* bodoh.

fatal, *adj. of wound,* parah, yang membawa maut, celaka.

fate, n. see **destiny.**

father, n. bapa, pa'; *daddy,* abah; *more formal,* ayah; *sire,* ayahanda; *'my old man',* orang tua saya; *~-in-law,* pak mentua; *step-~,* pak tiri; *elder 'in-laws', generally,* mentua taya; *~-land,* tanah air, ibu pertiwi.

fathom, n. *measure of six feet,* depa; *to ~ (sound),* menduga (duga); *to cast the lead,* membuang (buang) perum; *~less,* tak terduga.

fault, n. *flaw,* cacat, rekah, celah; *at ~,* salah; *to find ~,* cari salah; *the best of us has ~s,* gading mana yang tak retak? *(what ivory has no cracks?); ~less,* sempurna, tanpa kesalahan.

fauna, n. *animals of a region,* haiwan.

favour, see **discriminate, suck.**

favourite, adj. *best loved,* yang disayang sekali; *in bull-fighting,* ganda; *non-~, e.g., hobby,* kegemarannya (gemar); *to 'play ~s',* memilih (pilih) kasih.

fawn, n. baby sambhur, anak rusa; *~-coloured,* langsat; *~ on, as for favours,* angkat-angkat; *see* **suck.**

fear, v. tr. takutkan, kembimbangan, kecemasan; *trembling with ~,* berketar-ketar (kerana takutan); *~less,* berani, gagah; *~some,* yang menggentarkan; *see* **afraid.**

feasible, adj. *that can be done,* dapat dikerjakan, dapat dijalankan.

feast, n. *sumptuous meal,* kenduri; *~ in honour of the dead,* bewah; *'~ for the eyes',* jamuan mata; *jocular exclamation on seeing a well-spread table, what a ~!,* bukan memapan (papan), menarah (tarah), *(lit., not sawing into planks, rough-hewing, but rhyming slang for* bukan makan muntah kedarah, *not food a guzzle).*

feat, n. *notable act, esp. of valour,* kegagahan, perbuatan (pahlawan); *adj.* cekap, tangkas, cepat.

feather, n. bulu (burung); *long tail-~, esp. of cock,* lawi; *~less,* tak berbulu, bogel; *a ~ in his cap (reason for pride),* suatu kemegahan (megah).

feature, n. *part(s) of the face,* air muka;

prominent article in newspaper, rencana yang terpenting dalam suratkhabar.

feckless, adj. *flightly,* kepala angin.

federated, adj. bersekutu (kutu); *federation,* persekutuan.

fee, n. upah; *to a local herbalist,* pengkeras; *retaining ~ of a midwife,* penempah (tempah) bidan; *school ~s,* yuran sekolah.

feeble, adj. lemah; *to walk feebly,* berjalan (jalan) longlai.

feed, v. tr. memberi (beri) makan; *be responsible for food of,* tanggung makan; *fed-up,* jemu, bosan.

feel, v. tr. merasa (rasa); *explore by touch,* meraba (raba), menjamah (jamah); *to put out ~ers (with a view to negotiations),* merisik-risik; *~ing,* perasaan; *to hide one's ~ings,* menebal (tebal) muka; *see* **antennae.**

feint, v. intr. acah; *make as if to,* buat-buat nak; *see* **pretend.**

felicitation, n. ucapan selamat.

fell, v. tr. *a tree,* menebang (tebang).

female, adj. perempuan; *of animals,* betina.

fence, n. pagar; *wire ~,* pagar dawai; *to ~ (as with swords),* bersilat (silat).

fend, v. intr. *~ for oneself,* mencari (cari) kehidupan (hidup) sendiri; *v. ward off, keep off,* mengelak, menangkis, menolak.

fender, n. *ship's ~,* daperas, pagar dawai yang mengelilingi tempat membara api.

fermented, adj. berperam (peram); *with yeast,* beragi (ragi); *~ rice-spirit,* tapai.

ferocious, adj. *fierce, cruel,* kejam, ganas.

fern, n. pokok paku-pakis; *bracken,* resam.

ferry, n. 'feri', perahu penambang (tambang); *v. tr.* menyeberangkan.

fertile, n. subur, see **manure.**

fervent, adj. *hot, ardent, intense,* panas, hangat, ghairah, bersungguh-sungguh.

fester, v. intr. meliau (liau), naik kelurut,

bernanah.

festival, *n.* hari raya, hari besar, pesta; *popular occasion,* temasya, suatu keramaian (ramai); *celebration,* hari perayaan; *festivity,* kegembiraan berpesta.

fetch, *v. tr.* bawa.

fetters, *n.* belenggu, sengkela, rantai; *wooden block impeding movement,* kongkongan; *used also (fig.) for '~' in the sense of handicaps.*

feud, *n.* sengketa, permusuhan.

fever, *n.* demam; *feverish,* dedar.

few, *n.* sikit, sedikit; *as a minute fraction,* segelintir; *quite a ~,* beberapa juga.

fez, *n.* tarbus.

fibre, *n.* serabut, serat; *esp. of coconut,* sabut; *esp. from sugar-palm,* ijuk.

fickle, *adj. not loyal,* tidak setia; *changeable,* berubah-ubah, hati-hati hari; *'weathercock',* macam kelembuai; *~ness,* sifat selalu bertukar fikiran.

fictional, *adj. of a story,* dongeng; *lying,* dusta, bohong.

fidget, *v. intr.* menggelisah (gelisah); *~y,* lesah; *unable to keep hands to oneself, always fiddling,* membuat (buat) lasak tangan; *must touch,* gatal tangan; *can't keep still,* seperti cacing kepanasan (panas), *('like a worm caught out in the sun'); always on the move ('like a maimed cockroach'),* macam lipas kudung.

fie, *int.* cis!, ceh!

fief, *n. territory held,* (tanah) pegangan, tanah yang disewa daripada tuan besar di zaman feudal.

field, *n.* padang, lapangan; *~ of battle,* medan perang; *(fig.) sphere of action, etc.,* bidang, lapangan, jurusan; *meadow,* lembahan; *see rice.*

fiend, *n.* iblis, syaitan, orang zalim.

fierce, *adj.* garang, bengis; *apt to attack man or his stock,* ganas; *as beast of prey,* buas.

fife, *n.* suling.

fig, *n.* buah ara; *one cannot gather figs of thistles,* tanam lalang, tak akan tumbuh padi, *(if you plant lalang grass,*

rice won't come up).

fight, *v. intr.* melawan (lawan); *of animals,* berlaga (laga); *in war,* berperang (perang), bertempur; *cock-~ing,* sabung ayam; *have a fist ~,* lawan bertumbuk (tumbuk), berkelahi; *~ to the death,* berjuang (juang) bermatimatian; *see* **combat.**

figurative, *adj.* sebagai ibarat, kiasan.

figure, *n. number,* angka; *rudimentary ~, shape, depicted ~,* lembaga; *bodily measurements,* ukuran badan; *shape, esp. of a woman,* potongan tubuh, potongan badan, raut tubuh (badan); *a shapely ~ (curved in the right places),* tubuh potongan 'gitar'; gosh! *what a marvellous ~ she has!,* perempuan berbadan kur semangat, *(vulg. sl., i.e., a woman whose ~ makes you say, gosh! my soul!);* v. menggambarkan, mengkhayalkan; *~ out,* menghitung.

figure-head, *n. of ship,* gambar di haluan kapal; *of boat,* angkun; *mere symbol, as Head of State,* lambang (sahaja); rubber-stamp, tukang cap, tukang sah.

filch, *v. tr. steal, pilfer,* mencuri.

file, *n. tool,* kikir; *of papers,* 'fail'; *filings,* tahi kikir, serbuk kikir; *a ~ of people,* sebaris, sebanjar, sederet (orang); *in single ~,* berekor-ekor, berbuntutbuntut; *fail,* tempat menyimpan surat dll. yang telah disusun.

fill, *v. tr.* mengisi (isi); *~ in, as hole,* kambus, timbus; *~ a tooth,* pasak, sumbi; *~ up,* mengisi sampai penuh; *~, bank up, as a swamp before building,* menambak (tambak); *to ~ out, of a sail,* berkembang (kembang), mengepuh (kepuh); *drink (eat) one's ~,* minum (makan) hingga kenyang.

fillet, *n. for the hair, snood,* cekak rambut, daging rusuk.

film, *n.* 'filem'; *see* **cinema, picture;** *a thin membrane,* selaput, selupat.

filter, *n.* tapisan air, saringan air, penuras; *~ in, as moisture,* meresap (resap) masuk.

filth, *n.* najis, kotoran; *use ~y language,* mencarut (carut), menceceh-ceceh.

fin, *n,* sirip; *foral* ~, ridip.

final, *adj.* *at the end,* terakhir; *~ly,* akhirnya.

finance, *n.* *management of money,* kewangan (wang); *financier,* saudagar wang; *to* ~, *pay for, as a scheme,* membiayai (biaya).

find, *tr.* jumpa; ~ *out,* dapat tahu; *~ing, conclusion,* kesimpulan (simpul); *decision,* keputusan (putus).

fine, *n.* denda; *to cut from wages,* potong; *capital,* elok; *delicate,* halus; *in* ~ *particles, as sand,* gebu; *of clothes,* indah; *minced or ground* ~, lumat-lumat.

finger, *n.* jari; *~-prints (as identification),* cap jari; *(as casual mark),* bekas jari; *to* ~ *(feel with ~s),* meraba (raba), menggamak-gamakkan; *between* ~ *and thumb,* menggentel-gentel; *see* **fidget;** *'green ~s',* tangan bertuah (tuah); *little* ~, jari kelingking; *fourth* ~, jari manis; *~-tip,* hujung jari.

finical, finicking, finicky, *adj.* *excessively fastidious or fussy,* cerewet.

finish, *v.* *tr.* perhabiskan (habis), menyudahkan (sudah); *terminated,* selesai; *it's all up!,* selesai!; ~ *a course of study,* menamatkan (tamat); *a good '~er',* seperti cencaru makan petang, *(like the horse-mackerel, eating in the evening); ~ing stroke,* pukulan terakhir untuk membunuh seseorang; *to put the ~ing touch,* melakukan pekerjaan yang terakhir supaya lengkap atau sempurna.

finite, *adj.* terbatas (batas).

fire, *n.* api; *fiery blast,* bahang api; *to catch* ~, lekat api; hinggap api; *~-engine,* bomba api; *on* ~, bernyala (nyala); *set* ~ *to,* membakar; *~-wood,* kayu api; *to* ~ *off (a cannon or ~works),* pasang; *to* ~ *(a gun),* tembak, bedil; *~-works,* bunga api; *Chinese '-crackers,* mercun, petas; *~-arms,* senjata api; *firefly,* kelip-kelip; *smudge-~ (to repel insect),* unggunan api; *'~-brand' (trouble-maker),* batu api; *a* ~ *e.g., a burning building,* kebakaran (bakar); *a* ~ *for warming,* api diangan; *see*

brazier, stove; *~-escape,* tangga kecemasan; ~ *extinguisher,* alat pemadam api; *~-hose,* saluran air yang diperbuat dari getah khas untuk memadam api; *there's no smoke without* ~, tak ada angin, tak akan pokok bergoyang (goyang), *(if there was no wind, the trees would not shake); out of the frying-pan into the* ~, lepas dari mulut harimau, masuk ke mulut buaya, *(escaped from the mouth of a tiger into the mouth of a crocodile); to play with* ~, bermain (main) api.

firm, *adj.* *stable,* teguh, utuh; *hard to shake,* kukuh; *sturdy,* tegap; *firmly in place,* teguh; *not crumbling, as rock, not flabby as flesh,* pejal; *firmed up, as dug earth,* mampat; *as flesh or coconut or fruit,* meliat (liat).

firm, *n.* *business* ~, syarikat, perkongsian (kongsi); *Chinese* ~ *name,* cap.

firmament, *n.* *the sky with its stars and clouds,* langit, cakrawala.

first, *adj.* yang pertama; *at* ~, mula-mula; *previously (before all),* dahulu; *at* ~ *glance (prima facie),* sepintas lalu; *~-born,* anak sulung; *by extension,* sulung *is also used for e.g.,* ~ *novel—* 'nobel' sulung; ~ *aid,* pertolongan cemas; ~ *time,* kali yang pertama; *this is the* ~ *time I—,* baharu sekali ini saya,—; ~ *come* ~ *served,* yang dahulu didahulukan.

first-fruits, *n.* *first products of season,* bungar.

fish, *n.* ikan; *to* ~ *(angle),* mengail (kail) memancing (pancing); *with unweighted line, as for cuttle~,* mengambul (ambul); *~ing-line,* tali kail; *fishing-rod,* joran; *~-fry, baby* ~, anak marak; *minute ~-fry and sea-organisms,* plankton, bunga air; *to* ~ *in troubled waters (profit by misfortunes of others),* menangguk (tangguk) di air keruh.

fisherman, *n.* penangkap (tangkap) ikan, pengail, nelayan, fishy, bau hanyir (ikan), sesuatu yang tidak boleh dipercayai.

fissure, n. celah, retakan.

fist, n. genggam; 'bunch of fives', buku lima; to clench the ~, genggamkan tangan.

fit, n. sudden passing attack of epilepsy, etc., sawan; healthy, strong, sihat, segar; for sudden seizure, etc., see **convulsions, epilepsy.**

fit, v. tr. ~ on, as a gadget, kenakan; ~ up, set up, pasang; ~ out; as an expedition, melengkapan (lengkap); well-~ting, of a suit, pandan; to work by 'fits and starts', (showing an enthusiasm which quickly cools), membuat (buat) kerja hangat-hangat tahi ayam; ~ness, kesihatan kesegaran.

fitful, adj. of wind, see **gusty.**

fittings, n. alat, perkakas; small fitting, gadget, gerendek; **adj.** becoming proper, kena, padan, sesuai.

fix, v. tr. as a fitting, kenakan; 'fix' ('settle hash'), kerjakan, ~ed, of data or price, tetap, tentu; ~ed price, harga mati; ~ eyes on, menumpukan (tumpu) mata pada; in a ~ (in difficulties), terselit (selit), dalam keadaan kesukaran, berketial (ketial); harassed, lorat, sesak.

fizzle, v. intr. hiss or splutter feebly, berdesis keluar; ~ out, come to lame conclusion, berakhir dengan kegagalan.

flabbergasted, adj. terperanjat (peranjat), tercengang-cengang.

flabby, adj. lembik; as breasts, kelemping.

flaccid, adj. flabby, hanging loosely, lembik, lemah, lembut.

flag, n. bendera; pennon, panji-panji; to hoist a ~, pasang bendera; to fly (or wave) a ~, kibarkan bendera; ~-staff, tiang bendera; the Indonesian flag, Sang Merah Putih; to raise a ~, naikkan bendera; to lower a ~, turunkan bendera; half-mast, separuh tiang.

flagrant, adj. of a offence, glaring, obvious, (kesalahan) (salah) yang menjolok (jolok) mata; see **clear.**

flair, n. talent, berbakat, kepandaian.

flake, n. a ~, secebis; tiny bit, kepingan; to ~ off (as plaster), lekang.

flamboyant, adj. over-decorated, terhias (hias) sangat; **see flashy,** (orang) yang suka menunjuk-nunjuk.

flame, n. api; tongue of ~, lidah api, liukan api; flaming, bernyala (nyala); ~ high, flare up, marak; ~ with anger, naik panas; ~-thrower, alat penyembur (sembur) api; to burst into ~, ~ high, menyala (nyala).

flamingo, n. burung bangau.

flank, n. rusuk, sisi.

flap, v. intr. as a flag, berkibar-kibar, berkirap (kirap); ~ wings, berkepak-kepak, mengibas-ngibaskan (kibas) kepak, id.; ~ up and down, as long hair of a person running, terjembak-jembak; a ~, e.g., bit of page turned down, kelepek; 'flapper' (young girl barely nubile), anak dara sunti.

flare, v. intr. ~ up, of fire, marak, berkobar (kobar); rise high, menjulang (julang); (fig.) of enthusiasm, etc., berkobar; see **flame.**

flash, n. cahaya, sinaran api; to ~ a torch, suluh; ~-light, lampu suluh, lampu picit; to ~, of lightning, sabung-menyabung, berkilau-kilau, memancar (pancar); briefly (of summer lightning), mengenyit (kenyit).

flashy, adj. as clothes, gamat; over-bright, of colour, garang.

flask, n. 'botol'; small ~, buli-buli.

flat, n. rata, datar, hampar; ~tened, squashed ~, penyek; as building by bomb, ranap; as shallow basin, leper; not rounded, pipih; not edged, pepat; ~, low-lying land, tanah pamah; of a tyre, 'pancit'; ~-bottomed (boat), lepap; to ~ten out (iron) by hammering, leperkan; bamboo by hammering, melupuh (lupuh); ~ (having lost effervescence), mati; a ~ failure, gagal sama sekali; a ~ (apartment), '~'; block of ~s, rumah pangsa; ~ and round, as a coin, bulat leper, bulat pipih; without projections, papak; ~-roofed house, rumah papak; the ~ of a sword, kaparan pedang; ~-*iron,* alat seterika.

flatter, *v. tr.* puji-puji, lomis-lomis, gula-gulakan; *see* **suck.**

flatulent, *adj.* segah-perut; *see* **wind.**

flaunt, *v. tr. to ~ oneself (esp. in a new dress),* meledangkan diri, peraga (raga).

flavour, *n.* rasa; ~*less,* tawar ibir, tawar ambar; ~*ing (adding spicy taste),* per-encah (rencah), ramuan perasa (rasa), asam garam.

flaw, *n.* cacat; *as weakness (in metal or figuratively),* retak-belah.

flaxen, *adj.* kuning pucat.

flay, *v. tr. remove skin,* lapah, buang kulit; menyiat, *(fig.) attack verbally,* mem-bidas (bidas).

flea, *n.* kutu anjing; *sand-~,* temperas, tungau.

fledged, *adj. (of birds) with fully grown wing feathers,* mendapat bulu; *able to fly,* dapat terbang.

fledgeling, *n. young bird just fledged,* anak burung yang baru pandai ter-bang, orang yang belum berpengala-man.

flee, *v. intr. see* **escape, run.**

flesh, *n.* daging; *esp. as opposed to skin and bones,* isi; *to put on ~,* bertubuh (tubuh); 'in the ~' (in person), hidup-hidup, se benar-benar; *to lose ~,* susut-tubuh; *own ~ and blood,* sedarah sed-aging.

flexible, *adj.* lemah-liat, lembut melentur (lentur), (sikap) longgar.

flick, *v. tr. as ash off cigarette,* menjentik (jentik); *a catch,* petik.

flicker, *v. tr. as a dying lamp,* malap; *shine intermittently, as the lamp of a lighthouse,* terang gelap, terang gelap; mengerlip (kerlip).

flight, *n. a journey by air,* penerbangan (terbang); *see* **air.**

flighty, *adj. irresponsible,* kepala angin.

flimsy, *adj. as building,* gegai; *as paper,* tipis dan ringan.

flinch, *v. intr. make a slight involuntary movement,* tersentak (sentak).

flipper, *n.* sirip, lebar; kaki perenang yang

dibuat dari getah.

flirt, *v. intr. make eyes,* bermain (main) mata; berpoya-poya; *verbally,* bergu-rau (gurau); *exchange endearments,* bercumbu-cumbu; *flirtatious (fond of 'giving the eye'),* panjang-mata; *hav-ing a roving eye, esp. of a man,* mata keranjang, mata rambang.

flit, *v. to move lightly and quickly,* pergi dari satu tempat ke tempat yang lain dengan cepat.

float, *v. intr. esp. to the surface,* timbul, ~*ing along,* terapung (apung); *a ~, as of a net,* pelampung (lampung); *see* **drift.**

flock, *n. as of birds,* sekawan, sekumpulan; *to ~ together,* berk-erumun (kerumun).

flood, *n.* air bah, banjir; yang mencurah-curah; 'young' (preliminary) ~, lik; ~-water, air sebak; ~-gate, pintu air.

flog, *v. to beat severely with a rod of whip as a punishment,* membelasah.

floor, *n.* lantai; ~-*tiles,* batu ubin; *storey,* tingkat.

flop, *v. intr. fall with a ~,* jatuh berdebap (debap), jatuh berjelepak (jelepak), re-bah, gagal.

flotilla, *n.* sekumpulan kapal perang yang kecil.

flotsam, *n.* kaparan; *drift-wood,* kayu apung.

flounce out, *v. intr. leave abruptly and impatiently,* merenyah (renyah) keluar, merenjas (renjas) keluar; keluar atau bergerak dengan marah; *see* **depart, walk.**

flounder, *v. intr. as a stranded fish,* menggelupur (gelupur), melibas-libas; ~ *about, esp. in mud or water,* menggeludar (geludar).

flour, *n.* tepung; *sago ~,* tepung sagu; *ref-use sago ~,* serampin; *rice ~,* tepung beras.

flourish, *v. intr. prosper,* maju, bertam-bah (tambah) makmur; *to ~, as a weapon,* tayangkan, *esp. of threatening by* ~*ing,* mengacu-ngacukan; ~, *grow luxuriantly as a tree,* merambak (rambak); *as plants,* *esp. weeds,* meriap (riap).

flout, *v. to disobey openly and scornfully,* menentang.

flow, *v. intr.* mengalir (alir); *trickle,* meleleh (leleh); *~ing, a robe,* labuh; *of loose hair,* lepas labuh.

flower, *n.* bunga; *~-pot or vase,* pasu bunga; *posy,* karangan bunga; *to ~,* berbunga; *bed or stand of ~s,* jambangan bunga; *~ing plant,* pokok bunga.

fluctuate, *v. intr. as prices,* turun-naik.

fluent, *adj. of speech,* lancar, fasih, berabuk (abuk), pitah.

fluid, *adj.* cair.

fluke, *n.* tersaruk (saruk); *of anchor,* kuku (sauh), untung, nasib baik.

flume, *n. wooden water-channel,* palung.

flush, *v. intr. to get hot in the face,* berubah (ubah) warna muka; *~ with (one a level with),* separas dengan.

flustered, *adj.* tergamam (gamam), serba salah firkiran, membingungkan.

flute, *n.* suling; *~d, striated,* bergelugur (gelugur).

flutter, *v. intr. as a flag,* melambai-lambai, berkibar-kibar, berkirap (kirap); *as a dying fowl,* menggelupurkan (gelupur) sayap; *~ down, as leaves,* melayang (layang) jatuh; *~ along, of a young bird,* terbang-terbang jatuh.

flux, *n. a state of continual change,* sentiasa berubah-ubah.

fly, *n.* lalat; *blow-~, blue-bottle,* langau; *gad~,* pikat; *banana-~,* bari-bari; *sand-~,* agas, rengit; *cwatter,* tepok-lalat; *~ing fish,* ikan belalang; *~ing fox,* keluang; *~catcher,* murai gila, cencala; *~-over,* jejatas; *~-wheel,* roda besar untuk memutar mesin.

fly, *v. intr.* terbang; soar, melayang (layang); *~ a flag,* kibarkan bendera; *~ a kite,* main wau, main layang-layang; *~ into a passion (rage),* menjadi marah sekali.

foam, *n.* buih.

focus, *n. of lens,* 'fokas', titik api; *~ of attention,* tumpuan perhatian (hati).

foe, *n. enemy, opponent,* musuh, seteru.

foetus, *n. earliest embryo,* alkah; janin;

see **embryo.**

fog, *n. see* **mist;** *~ged, of a film,* kabur.

foible, *n. weak point, fault,* sifat kelemahan seseorang.

foiled, *p. p.* kecewa, gagal, bantut; *to foil (a scheme),* membantutkan.

fold, *v. tr.* melipat (lipat); *to ~ the arms,* peluk tubuh; *~ over, as a corner of page,* kelebet; *to hang in ~s, of skin,* menggelambir (gelambir); *to ~, as an umbrella,* kuncupkan; *a ~,* lipatan, lapisan; *~ for animals,* kandang.

foliage, *n.* daun-daunan.

follow, *v. tr. accompany);* ikut; *~ behind,* ikut dari belakang; *go after,* turut; *succeed, ~ in point of time or as in a procession,* menyusul (susul); *pursue,* mengejar (kejar); *~er,* pengikut; *personal adherents,* anak-buah; *to ~ a creed,* menganut (anut); *~ immediately behind (a person),* membuntut (buntut),

folly, *n. foolishness,* kebodohan.

foment, *v. tr. as a boil with hot cloth,* demah, tuam; *as disturbances,* menimbulkan (timbul) (kucar-kacir); *see* **poultice.**

fond, *n. to be ~ of,* sayang; *see* **addicted, like, love.**

fontanel, *n.* ubun-ubun.

food, *n. a meal,* makan; *diet,* makanan; *main part of meal other than rice,* lauk; *a snack,* alas perut; *dressed ~,* sajian; *to have a meal, generally,* makan nasi; *see* **provisions.**

fool, *n. typical ~ of fiction,* Pak-Pandir, Pak Kaduk; *to play the ~,* main gila; *see* **stupid;** *to make a ~ of oneself,* membodohkan (bodoh) diri; *v. play the ~, trifle, cheat,* memperdayakan, menipu.

foot, *n.* kaki.

football, *n.* bola sepak; *to play ~,* main bola sepak; *~ pools,* peraduan (adu) teka bola sepak.

foothold, *n. to get a ~, establish oneself on a spot,* bertapak (tapak); tempat berpijak; *~, place to take off from, as in jumping,* tempat bertumpu (tumpu).

footprint, *n.* kesan kaki, bekas tapak;

footsteps, bunyi jejak kaki.

foppish, *adj.* pesolek (solek), anggun, kacak.

for, *prep.* ~ *the benefit of,* bagi, untuk; ~ *the sake of,* kerana, demi kepentingan.

forage, *n. food for horses,* makanan kuda *and* lembu.

forbid, *v. tr.* larang, tegah; ~*den by religion,* haram; *by custom or medical advice,* pantang; ~*den area,* kawasan larangan; *God* ~*!,* dijauhkan Allah!, siah peralih!, haram!; ~*ding of aspect,* penggerun (gerun).

force, *n. strength, power,* kuasa, tenaga, kuderat; *might,* penangan (tangan); *by* ~, dengan keras; *coercion,* paksa; ~*d labour,* kerah; *to use criminal* ~ *to,* menggunakan (guna) kekerasan (keras) jenayah kepada; ~*s (troops),* tentera; *a* ~ *(body of troops),* pasukan; *the Forces,* Angkatan bersenjata (senjata); *to be in* ~, *as a law,* berlaku (laku) berjalan (jalan) kuat kuasa; *a* ~, *of wind,* sekencang; *a storm of a* ~ *of 120 miles per hour struck Hong Kong,* ribut taufan sekencang 120 batu sejam memukul (pukul) Hong Kong; *to* ~, *compel,* paksa; ~ *open, as a box,* kopek, gajai; ~ *away through,* merempuh (rempuh), melanda (landa); ~*d labourer,* buruh paksa; ~*ful,* hebat, kuat.

forceps, *n.* angkup-angkup.

ford, *n.* tempat mengarung (arung), tempat merandai (randai).

forecast, *n.* ramalan; *to* ~, meramalkan.

forefathers, *n.* nenek moyang.

forehead, *n.* dahi.

foreigner, *adj.* orang dagang, orang asing; *as outsider,* orang luaran; ~ *parts,* negeri orang, rantau orang; *(viewed as the temporary abode of expatriates),* perantauan; *foreign affairs,* hal ehwal luar.

foreman, *n.* mandur; *esp. of Tamils,* tandil; *esp. of Chinese,* kepala; *person in charge, generally,* ketua (tua).

foresee, *v. to be aware of or realise beforehand,* membayangkan sesuatu yang mendatang, mengetahui lebih dahulu.

foreshadow, *v. tr.* membayangkan (bayang).

foresight, *n.* kebolehan mengetahui kehendak-kehendak masa hadapan.

foreskin, *n. prepuce,* kulup, kulit luar pada bahagian penghujung kemaluan kaum lelaki.

forest, *n. see* **jungle**; ~ *officer,* pegawai hutan.

foretell, *v. tr. see* **forecast**.

forethought, *n. careful thought and planning for the future,* fikiran dahulu, kebijak-sanaan.

foreword, *n.* kata pengantar (hantar), pendahuluan (dahulu).

forever, *adv.* sampai selama-lamanya.

forfeited, *p. p. as a pledge,* luncur, lelap; *reverted to—,* pulang kepada—; *see* **confiscate**.

forged, *adj. of a document or currency,* palsu.

forget, *v. tr.* lupa(kan); *don't* ~, jangan lupa, jangan tak ingat.

forgive, *v. tr.* maafkan, ampunkan; *as a debt,* halalkan.

fork, *n. table* ~, garpu; *of a tree or river,* cabang, cawang; *turning on road,* simpang; *of bicycle,* sepit udang; *forked fish-spear,* serampang; ~ *of lower limbs,* celah kangkang, pukang.

form, *n. aspect,* rupa; *shape,* bentuk; *to take the* ~ *of (mode of manifestation),* merupakan; *in due* ~, dengan sepertinya; *to* ~, *as a party,* menubuhkan (tubuh); *by combining (*~*s a company or Cabinet),* menyusunkan (susun).

formal, *adj. customary,* beradat (adat); *according to official custom,* rasmi.

former, *adj.* yang dahulu; *ex-,* bekas; *in* ~ *times,* zaman dahulu.

Formosa, *n.* Taiwan.

formula, *n.* petua, rumusan; *magical,* mantera.

formulate, *v. to express clearly and exactly,* menyatakan.

fornication, *n.* zina, mukah.

forsake, *v. tr.* meninggalkan (tinggal).

fort, *n.* kota; *Fort Canning,* Bukit Larangan.

forth, *adv. out, onwards, forwards,* selanjutnya, ke luar; *from this day* ~, sejak hari itu.

fortify, *v. tr. strengthen,* kukuhkan; *make fortifications,* membuat (buat) kota (benteng, kubu).

fortnight, *n.* dua minggu.

fortuitous, *adj.* kebetulan (betul) sahaja.

fortune, *n. see* **fate, luck;** *to seek one's* ~, mengadu (adu) untung; *fortunate,* bernasib baik; ~-*teller,* tukang tilik, pentenung (tenung); *'ups and downs of life', see* **up.**

forward, *adv. to the front,* ke depan; *go* ~, *advance,* mara; *come out in front, step* ~, tampil; *over-familiar,* bebas sangat; *lacking modesty, of a woman,* bisi; *see* **advance.**

foster, *v. tr. grudge,* menaruh (taruh) (dengki, dendam); ~-*child,* anak angkat; -*mother (wet-nurse),* ibu susu.

foul, *adj. stinking,* busuk; *a* ~ *(as stroke in game agains the rules),* tak aci.

found, *v. tr.* asaskan; *to lay a* ~*ation stone,* meletakkan (letak) batu asas; *well* ~*ed,* cukup berasas; ~*ations of a building,* asas, alas; *see* **form.**

foundling, *n.* anak buangan, anak pungutan.

foundry, *n.* bengkel, kilang peleburan.

fountain, *n. as spring,* mata air, pancaran ayer; *artifical* ~, basut; ~ *pen,* pena tabung; *as source,* punca.

fowl, *n.* ayam; ~-*house, reban,* lau ayam; *jungle* ~, ayam hutan.

fraction, *n. (mathematics),* pecahan; *a* ~ *(minute number),* segolintir.

fracture, *n. breaking or breakage, especially of a bone,* (tulang) yang patah.

fragile, *adj.* mudah pecah; *brittle,* rapuh, raka, repas.

fragments, *n.* pecahan (barang-barang); *flying* ~ *(e.g., of a bomb),* perecik (recik); *splinters, chips,* serpihan, serpih-serpih; *a little bit,* butiran.

fragrant, *adj.* wangi, harum.

frail, *adj. not strong,* lemah; ~*y, n. weak-*

ness, kelemahan.

frame, *n. as of spectacles,* bingkai; *as of picture,* lengkungan; ~*work,* rangka; *for stretching cloth for embroidery or hides for drying,* pemidang; *to* ~ *(as a treaty),* menyusun (susun), membentuk (bentuk); *to* ~ *in outline, as a plan,* merangkakan.

francise, *n.* hak mengundi (undi), hak memilih.

frangipanni, *n.* bunga cempaka, bunga kemboja, bunga kubur.

frank, *adj. sincere,* jujur; *of a speech,* terus terang; ~*ly (concealing nothing),* dengan tidak berselindung (selindung).

frantic, *adj. having lost self-restraint,* hilang akal; *to rage* ~*ally,* mengamuk (amuk).

fraternize, *v. intr. behave in friendly manner,* beramah-tamah (ramah).

fraud, *n.* tipu-daya.

frayed, *adj.* haus sikit, compang-camping, cobak cabik, sobik-sobik.

freckles, *n.* tahi lalat; *large blotchy* ~, tetua; bintik-bintik yang terdapat pada kulit, terutamanya pada kulit muka.

free, *adj.* bebas; *set* ~, *escaped,* lepas; *independent,* merdeka; ~ *and easy,* bebas, leluasa, badar; ~ *speech,* kebebasan bercakap (cakap); ~*dom of the Press,* kebebasan persurat-khabaran (surat); ~*dom of worship,* kebebasan beragama (agama); *right of* ~ *assembly,* hak berkumpul (kumpul); ~ *elections,* pemilihan (pilih) bebas; *i.e., private, enterprise,* usaha secara perseorangan (orang); ~ *association (esp. between sexes),* pergaulan (gaul) bebas; *see* **emancipated;** *working freely, as a wheel or as a plan,* (jalan) lancar; *to* ~ *from (by stopping),* mencegah (cegah); *to* ~ *from hunger,* mencegah kelaparan (lapar); *to get something* ~, dapat percuma; *freely (without let or hindrance),* dengan leluasa, dengan lepas bebas; *see* **independent.**

freeze, *v. intr. to become ice,* membeku

(beku), menjadi (jadi) 'ais'; *freezing point*, titik beku; *(fig.) to keep absolutely still*, mematikan (mati) diri.

freight, *n.* muatan.

French, *adj.* Perancis.

frequent, *adj. see* **often;** *to go often or habitually to*, berulang-ulang ke.

fresh, *adj. of water*, tawar; *esp. of milk, not tinned or dried*, hidup; *of fish, not dried*, basah; ~ *caught*, baharu tangkap.

fret, *v. intr.* merana (rana), makan hati; ~ *and fume*, marah sekali.

fretwork, *n.* kerawang.

friable, *adj. easily crumbled*, mudah renyuk, mudah rusak.

friction, *n.* haus, pergeselan (gesel); *(fig.)*, persinggitan (singgit), pergeseran.

friend, *n.* kawan, teman, saing, sahabat; *one's circle of* ~*s*, sahabat handai; *see* **acquaintance, intimate;** *to establish* ~*ly relations (esp. politically)*, menghubungkan (hubung) silatul rahim; *goodwill, esp. between peoples*, muhibbah; *to tighten the bonds of* ~*ship*, mengeratkan (erat) pertalian (tali) muhibbah; ~*ly, affable*, peramah (ramah) (orangnya); *to be on* ~*ly terms with*, beramah dengan, berbaik (baik) dengan; *in a* ~*ly atmosphere*, dalam suasana ramah mesra; ~*ly match*, peraduan (adu) secara persahabatan (sahabat).

frighten, *v. tr.* menakutkan (takut).

frill, *n.* rupul, rambu-rambu, jerumbai (ucapan penulisan) yang berbunga.

fringe, *n. border of loose threads or tassels,* rambu-rambu, jerumbai; *of a bride*, andam; *of hair on forehead or neck*, gigi rambut, anak rambut; *see* **edge.**

fritter, *v. to waste little by little, esp. on trivial things,* membazir, membuang masa.

frivolous, *adj. lacking a serious purpose*, tidak bersungguh-sungguh, tidak mustahak.

frizzy, n. of hair, pepuah, kejur.

frog, *n.* katak, kodok; *tadpole*, anak berudu.

from, *prep.* dari, daripada.

frolic, *v. to play about in a lively cheerful manner*, bergurau senda.

frond, *n.* pelepah.

front, *n. forepart*, muka; *in* ~, di muka depan, di hadapan; *the* ~ *(battlefild)*, medan peperangan (perang); ~ *line*, garis peperangan; ~ *yard*, halaman; ~ *door*, pintu depan; ~*age*, bahagian hadapan sesuatu kawasan atau bangunan.

frontier, *n.* perenggan, sempadan, tapal; ~ *area*, daerah perbatasan (batas); *natural* ~, perenggan semula jadi.

froth, *n.* buih, busa, berbual kosong.

frown, *v. intr. knit brows*, berkerut (kerut) dahi; ~*ing*, masam-muka.

frozen, *v.* beku.

frugal, *adj.* jimat-cermat.

fruit, *n.* buah; *embryo* ~ *as it appears when the blossom has dropped*, putik; *(fig.)* ~*s (as of labours)*, hasil; *first-*~*s*, bungaran, buah dara, buah sulung; *by their* ~*s you may know them*, sebab buah dikenal (kenal) pohonnya.

fruitless, *adj.* tak berhasil (hasil), sia-sia.

frustrated, *p. p. as a plan*, gagal, bantut; *to frustrate*, mensia-siakan; menghalangi; *having a feeling of frustration*, berhati buntu, berasa (rasa) hampa hati, terkecewa (kecewa).

fry, *v. tr.* goreng; *in oil with seasoning*, tumis; *fish* ~ *(baby fish)*, anak ikan.

fuddle, *v. make stupid esp. with alcoholic drink*, minum minuman keras sampai memabukkan.

fugitive, *n. hunted man*, orang buruan.

fulcrum, *n.* tempat tumpuan, titik sandaran, sanggatuas.

fulfil, *v. tr. as a plan*, melaksanakan (laksana), menunaikan (tunai).

full, *adj.* penuh; *chock-*~, penuh sesak; *as sails*, kepuh, tepu; ~ *of (containing)*, berisi (isi); *to hit* ~ *(in the right place)*, kena pasang; *(if not* ~ kena sipi); *brimful*, mumbung; ~, *of the mouth*, kemumbu; ~*-time job*, pekerjaan (kerja) sepenuh masa; *half-~ of water,* berair (air) separuh.

full-grown, *adj.* sudah besar, cukup umur, dewasa.

fulsome, *adj. excessive, disgusting by excess,* (pujian) yang melampau atau berlebihan.

fumes, *n.* wap asap; *to fumigate,* merabun (rabun), asapkan.

fun, *n. to have ~,* buat 'joli', main-main; keseronokan, kegembiraan, keriangan; *see* **enjoy;** *~ny, as a story,* lucu; *see* **joke;** *~-fair,* pasar ria; *to make ~ of,* mengolok-olokkan (olok).

function, *n. duty,* tugas; *role,* peranan; *see* **ceremony.**

fund, *n.* tabung, dana; *a provision set aside,* persediaan (sedia), cadangan.

fundamental, *adj. of the first importance,* terutama (utama), terpenting (penting); *see* **basis.**

funeral, *n. to conduct a ~,* membaca (baca) talkin; *a ~,* kerja kebumikan mayat; *see* **bury.**

fungus, *n.* kulat, cendawan; *poisonous ~,* cendawan mabuk; *fungoid disease on plants,* lapuk, jamur.

funnel, *n.* corong, serombong.

fur, *n.* bulu, *a ~,* kulit berbulu.

furious, *adj. raging, very angry, violent,* sangat, geram.

furnace, *n.* genahar, relau.

furniture, *n.* perkakas rumah, perabutan; *furnished,* lengkap (dengan perkakas).

furrow, *n. slight hollow,* suak; *in skin,* kerut; *made by plough,* alu (tenggala).

further, *adv.* lagi; *furthermore,* tinggal lagi, lagi pun.

fury, *n. to be in a ~,* merampus (rampus); keberangan, kemarahan yang amat sangat; *to 'blow one's top',* mengamuk (amuk).

fuse, *n.* sumbu; *slow match,* colok; *fusible wire in electrical circuit,* fius.

fuss, *v. intr. ~ round,* berkalut (kalut); *make a great ~ about,* hebuh-hebuhkan; kerewelan, kecerewetan yang tidak menentu; *agitate, esp. about a small matter,* gaduh-gaduh; *see* **bustle.**

fussy, *adj. (in the habit of) making a fuss,* cerewet.

futile, *adj. useless, worthless, frivolous,* sia-sia, tak berguna.

future, *n. the ~,* hari kemudian; *another time,* lain kali; *times to come,* masa yang akan datang, masa depan; *one of these days,* esok-esok; *see* **prospective**

G

gab, n. (informal) chatter, bercakap-cakap, berbual; he has the gift of the ~, dia pandai bercakap berdolak-dalik.

gadabout, n. person who goes here and there idly, kaki rambu.

gadget, n. a small mechanical device or tool, perkakas.

gag, v. tr. menyumbat (sumbat) mulut.

gain, n. laba; see profit.

gainsay, v. to deny or contradict, menyangkal, menidakkan.

gait, n. jalannya, gaya berjalan.

galaxy, n. bintang termabur; for Milky Way, see milk.

gale, n. angin ribut.

gall, n. bile, hempedu; ~-bladder, pundi-pundi hempedu, kandung hempedu; ~-stone, batu dalam kandung hempedu; tiny ~-stones, batu-batuan; to suffer from ~-stones, sakit kencing batu.

gallery, n. hall for display of picture, etc., balai.

gallop, v. intr. berlari (lari) dengan kencang.

galore, adj. (sl.) in numbers, belanar, mewah (berlebihan).

gambling, n. judi; gambler, tahi judi; licensed ~-house, rumah perjudian.

game, n. a ~ permainan (main); Olympic Games, sukan Olympik; Game Warden, pengawal (kawal) margasetua.

gang, n. esp. of bad characters, gerombolan, kumpulan orang jahat.

goal, n. see prison.

gap, n. celah, lumpang; broken by gaps, as a fence or teeth, rongak, rompang.

gape, v. intr. open-mouthed, nganga; as an entrance, terlopong (lopong), terlangah (langah).

garage, n. shed for car, 'garaj', bangsal kereta; repair shop, bengkel membaiki kereta, dll.

garbage, n. see rubbish.

garble, v. tr. twist (facts, sstatement) so as to pervert, memutar-balikkan (putar).

garden, n. kebun bunga; esp. as public ~, taman; open space attached to house, halaman; ~er, tukang kebun.

gardenia, n. bunga, cempaka tanjung.

garland, n. kalung bunga, karangan bunga.

garlic, n. bawang putih.

garotte, v. tr. strangle, kujut; see throttle.

garrulous, adj. bocor-mulut, lidah panjang, suka bercakap, peleter.

gashed, adj. rabak, luka yang dalam.

gasp, v. intr. cungap-cangip, berngap-ngap, sesak nafas.

gastronomer, n. orang yang suka makanan enak.

gate, n. pintu.

gather, v. tr. collect, mengutip (kutip); ~ (objects) together, memungut (pungut); assemble, berhimpun (himpun), berkumpul (kumpul), berkerumun (kerumun); see fester.

gauche, adj. socially awkward, kaku; canggung; esp. with strangers, perak.

gauge, n. of capacity, alat penyukat (sukat); of depth, alat pengukur.

gaunt, adj. lean and haggard, kurus dan cengkung.

gauze, n. khasah, kain kasa.

gay, adj. happy, riang; lively, as a tune, rancak; bright, gaudy, as clothes, gamat.

gaze, v. tr. intently, memandang dengan tetap; see look.

geese, n. (pl.) goose, angsa.

gelatine, n. agar-agar.

gelding, n. kuda kasi, kuda kembiri.

gem, n. permata, manikam; dust of ~s (tiny ~s set close together), podi; see bezoar.

genealogy, *n.* silsilah.

general, *n.* 'jeneral', panglima perang; *not restricted or particular,* umum; *not ~ly known,* belum diketahui (tahu) umum; *in ~,* umumnya, amnya.

generally, *adv. by common practice,* lazim; *see* **accustomed, usually;** *in general (as opposed to, in particular),* amnya.

generation, *n. persons born in the same period,* generasi, angkatan, sundut.

generous, *adj.* murah-hati, pemurah, tangan(nya) terbuka (buka); *charitable,* dermawan.

genial, *adj.* peramah (ramah).

genius, *n. any great natural ability,* orang yang berbakat istimewa.

gentle, *adj.* lemah-lembut; *esp. of speech,* manis; *gently! (carefully),* baik-baik!; *(slowly),* perlahan-perlahan!

gentleman, *n. of good birth,* anak orang baik; *courteous and considerate,* berbudi (budi); *gentlemen!,* tuan tuan sekalian!

genuine, *adj. true,* benar; *pure, as a race,* jati; *not imitation,* asli; *unalloyed,* tulin.

genus, *n. group of animals, etc., with certain common characteristics,* rumpun, golongan.

geometry, *n.* ilmu ukur, ilmu bangun, geometri.

germ, *n.* kuman, hama.

germinate, *v. intr.* cambah, berbenih.

gesticulate, *v. intr.* kuit-gamit, pergerakan tangan dan lengan atau kepala sebagai isyarat bercakap atau sambil bercakap.

get, *v. tr. obtain,* dapat, beroleh (oleh); *take,* ambik, ambil; *incur,* kena; *~ arrested,* kena tangkap; *~ up, as from bed,* bangun, bangun tidur, bangkit; *~ out of the way!,* lalu!

ghastly, *adj. to look at,* ngeri, mengerikan sumbang bagi pandangan; *~ pale,* (pucat) tetak tak berdarah (darah), pucat lesi.

ghost, *n.* hantu; *spirit of the dead,* arwah; *~ly,* berhantu.

giant, *n. of legend,* raksasa.

gibberish, *n. incoherent talk,* percakapan (cakap) kelalut; *to talk ~,* meraban (raban), meracau (racau).

gibbon, *n. black,* siamang; *brownish,* ungka, wak-wak.

gibe, *v. to jeer,* memperli, mengejek.

giddy, *adj.* pening-kepala; *from rush of blood to the head,* naik pitam; *from vertigo,* gayat; *having a swimming in the head,* mata berpinar-pinar; *~-brained,* tidak berfikir terlebih dahulu.

gift, *n.* pemberian, hadiah, bakat.

gigantic, *adj.* besar-raksasa; *abnormally tall,* tinggi menongkat (tongkat) langit.

giggle, *v. intr.* menggelekek (gelekek), tertawa (tawa) kecil; *sound of giggling,* kekek, kekek.

gild, *v. tr.* celup mas, menyadur (sadur) mas; *~ing, gold paint,* air mas.

gills, *n. of fish,* isang; *of cock,* gelambir.

gimmick, *n. a trick, device, or mannerism used for attracting notice or publicity,* cara istimewa memperolehi publisiti.

ginger, *n.* halia; *wild ~,* lengkuas; *Chinese ~-jar,* takar, situn.

gingerly, *adv. with attentive care,* berhati-hati.

girder, *n.* gelegar.

giraffe, *n.* zirafah.

girdle, *n.* bengkung, gendit.

girl, *n. female child,* kanak-kanak perempuan; *young unmarried ~,* budak perempuan, anak dara; *damsel, gadis; esp. Chinese ~,* nona.

girth, *n. see* **circumference;** *of horse,* tali perut.

gist, *n. substance (of talk, etc.),* kesimpulan (simpul), intisari.

give, *v. tr.* beri; *~ up (an attempt),* melepaskan (lepas) tangan; *~ and take (of mutual concessions, compromise),* bertolak-ansur (tolak); kompromi; *to ~ way (yield),* beralah (alah), tunduk; *budge,* berganjak (ganjak); *as a tree in the wind,* melentur (lentur); *under pressure or weight (fig.),* beri; *sag,* melendut (lendut); *at seams,* retas, bertas; *~ in, esp. in face of threatening* *power,* berela-rela.

gizzard, *n.* hempedal, pedal.

glad, *adj.* suka-hati, sedap-hati; *elated,* besar-hati; *joyful,* riang, bergembira (gembira).

gladden, *v. to make glad,* menggembirakan, menggirangkan.

glance, *v. intr.* kelih; ~ *sideways,* kerling; ~ *at,* menjengah (jengah); *cast a ~ at,* membuang (buang) pandangan pada; *esp. coyly,* melirikkan (lirik) mata pada; *at first ~,* sepintas lalu; *to hit a glancing blow (not fully),* kena sipi.

gland, *n.* kelenjar.

glare, *v. intr. look fierce,* memandang (pandang) dengan mata terjegil (jegil) (dengan mata terbeliak (beliak)); ~ *with rolling eyes, so as to alarm,* mencerlangkan (cerlang) mata pada; *ferocious ~,* mata menyinga (singa); *glaring, of fire or red colour,* sahang; *of bright colours or of lights,* garang, memancarkan cahaya yang menyilaukan.

glass, *n. the substance,* kaca, 'gelas'; *drinking ~,* 'gelas'; *mirror,* cermin; *powdered ~,* serbuk kaca; *see* **spectacles,** telescope.

glaze, *n.* sepuh.

gleaming, *adj.* gilang, gemilang, cemerlang.

glean, *v. tr.* ~ *aftermath of rice-fields,* merajau (rajau); *pick up here and there,* meramu (ramu); mengutip (kutip) di sana sini.

glen, *n.* ceruk gunung, lembahan.

glib, *adj. fast talking,* fasih, petah.

glimmer, *n. a faint gleam,* berkelip-kelip.

glimpse, *n.* selayang pandang, sekelibat.

glitter, *v. intr.* berkilau (kilau), gilang.

gloat, *v. intr. to feast the eyes, pleasurably, greedily or malignantly,* menjamu (jamu) mata; *smirking slyly,* tersenyum (senyum), sumbing; *don't ~ over the misfortunes of others,* pelepah di atas jatuh, pelepah di bawah jangan gelak, *(lit. when a frond from above falls, let not the lower fronds laugh).*

globe, *n. of the world,* bulat dunia, peta

bumi berbentuk bola.

gloomy, *adj. not bright,* muram, suram; *as dejected,* murung.

glorify, *v. to praise highly,* membanggakan, memuliakan.

glorious, *adj. splendid,* agung, luhur.

glory, *n.* nama yang megah; glorious, mulia; *splendid, as a victory,* cemerlang; *an age of ~,* zaman kemegahan (megah); *God's Glory,* kekayaan (kaya) Allah Taala.

glossary, *n.* daftar kata-kata yang sulit; ~ *of phrases,* daftar istilah.

glossy, *adj. as hair,* licau, licin-licau; *esp. with oil,* lecuk; *shiny,* berkilat (kilat), menggilap.

glove, *n.* sarung tangan.

glow, *v. intr. as heated metal,* memijar (pijar); *of radiant face,* berseri (seri); ~*ing bright, of a light,* terserlah (serlah); *the ~ of a fire,* bahang; *the sunset ~ (and the spirit personifying it),* mambang.

glower, *v. to stare angrily,* memandang dengan perasaan sangat marah.

glue, *n.* perekat; ~*d (fig.) to seat (of a 'chair-borne' person),* terpaku (paku) di kerusi.

glut, *n.* bekalan yang berlebihan.

gluttonous, *adj.* pelahap (lahap), gelojoh.

gnarled, *adj. rough and knobby,* gerutu, monggol.

gnash, *v. tr.* ~ *the teeth,* mengetap, menggertakkan gigi.

gnaw, *v. tr.* menggigit sedikit-sedikit, mengunggis; *noisily, as rats,* menggerit-gerit.

gnome, *n.* jembalang.

go, *v. intr.* pergi; *proceed,* berjalan (jalan); ~ *out,* keluar; *as a fire,* mati; ~ *in,* masuk; '~', *of an engine,* jalan; ~ *up,* naik; ~ *down,* turun; *(fig.) as a flood or a swelling,* surut; ~ *off (explode),* meletup (letup); *in one ~, (as, at the first attempt),* sekali harung; *see* **depart;** *who goes there?,* siapa itu?

goad, *n.* kayu yang tajam hujungnya untuk menghalau (memacu) lembu; *(fig.)*

~ *of the senses,* godaan nafsu.

goat, *n.* kambing; *~herd,* gembala kambing; *wild ~,* kambing gerun.

gobble, *v. tr. see* **eat;** *eat with loud smacking noises,* makan terkecap-kecap, makan dengan gelojoh dan bising.

goblin, *n.* bota, hantu jahat dan buruk rupanya.

God, *n.* Allah; *the Lord ~,* Tuhan; *the Most High,* Allah Taala; *the Creator,* Tuhan yang menjadikan alam; *the One Above,* Tuhan Yang Esa; *in the hands of ~,* berserah (serah) kepada Allah; *~ knows the truth,* wallahu alam; *by ~!* Wallah; *~ not recognised by Islam,* dewa, dewata; *~dess,* dewi; *~ly,* beriman (iman).

goddess, *n.* dewi.

godsend, *n. timely bit of luck,* suatu rahmat; *see* **blessing.**

goggle-eyed, *adj.* mata udang, mata terbeliak (beliak), mata yang tersembul.

goitre, *n.* beguk, gondok.

gold, *n.* mas, emas; *~-plated,* besadur (sadur) mas; *~smith,* tukang mas; *hammered ~,* mas dititik; *'fool's ~'* (iron pyrites), mas urung; *(woman) ~-digger,* (perempuan) mata duitan.

gong, *n.* gong; *small ~,* tawak-tawak, bendir; *esp. to accompany proclamations,* canang.

gonorrhea, *n. a venereal disease,* penyakit kencing nanah, penyakit perempuan, gonorea.

good, *adj.* baik; **fine,** elok; **splendid!,** bagus!; *~ at (doing. etc.),* pandai; *~s,* barang-barang, dangangan; *'~',* as a king in cards when the ace has been played, hukum; *he's a ~ chap,* baik orangnya; *good, esp. as virtue, opposed to sin,* pahala; *do ~ works,* beramal (amal), berjasa (jasa), berbakti (bakti).

goodbye, *int. as from host,* selamat jalan; *as from guest,* selamat tinggal; *au revoir,* ketemu (temu) lagi; *bon voyage,* selamat belayar (layar), selamat sampai.

goodwill, *n. see* **friend.**

goose, *n.* angsa; *'~-flesh',* seramkulit, tegak bulu roma kerana sejuk atau ketakutan.

gore, *v. tr. pierce with horn,* sempuh; menusuk (dengan tanduk); *a ~, gusset,* pesak.

gospels, *n. see* **scriptures.**

gossip, *v. intr.* berbual (bual), bergebang-gebang, berborak (borak), berlabun-labun; *to hawk round (esp. malicious) ~ about people's private affairs,* menjaga-jagakan (jaga) hal tepi kain orang, orang yang suka mengumpat.

gouge, *n.* pahat kuku; *to ~ out,* cungkil.

gourd, *n.* labu.

government, *n.* kerajaan (raja); *esp. republican,* pemerintah (perintah); *administration,* pentadbiran (tadbir); *the Administration,* pertadbiran; *puppet ~,* kerajaan (raja) patung, kerajaan boneka; *~ in exile,* kerajaan buangan.

grab, *v. tr. snatch,* rebut; *appropriate,* bolot; *by a quick movement,* cakup, menyambar (sambar); *reach out and ~ at,* cekau; *see* **snatch.**

grace, *n. of God,* rahmat, tempoh; *a week's ~ to settle the bill,* tempoh seminqqu lagi untuk melunaskan pembayaran.

graceful, *adj. in movement, as a girl,* lemah lembut, lemah gemalai, julita.

graceless, *adj. shameless,* tak tahu malu.

gracious, *adj. kindly in manner,* peramah (ramah); *be ~ly pleased to —,* sudilah — .

grade, *n. (school),* darjah; *(rank),* pangkat; *as of quality,* peringkat, mutu; *grading,* tingkatan.

gradually, *adv.* beransur-ansur; *bit-by-bit,* beruncit-uncit, berdikit-dikit.

graduate, orang berkelulusan (lusus) 'universiti', siswazah; *M.A.,* sarjana; *B.A.,* sarjana muda.

graft, *v. tr.* kawinkan (pokok), senyawakan (pokok), tut; *to bud-~,* mencantum (cantum); *official corruption, see* **corruption.**

grain, *n. a ~ of any sort,* biji; *for seed,*

benih; *various kinds of* ~, biji-bijian; *the* ~ *of wood,* corek, lorek, belak; *see* **vein;** *go (be) against against the* ~ *(idiom)* bertentangan atau berlawanan dengan kemahuan.

gramophone, *n.* peti nyanyi.

grammar, *n.* nahu, tata-bahasa.

grand, *adj. imposing, as a building,* hebat.

grandchild, *n.* cucu; *great* ~, cicit; *grandfather,* datuk, tok; *(familiar),* wak; *grandad,* tok aki; *grandmother,* nenek; *(familiar),* opah; *great grand-parent,* moyang; *teaching your grandmother to suck eggs,* orang tua diajar makan pisang, *(lit. teaching an old man how to eat a banana).*

granite, *n.* batu besi.

grant, *n. Government title to land,* 'geran'; ~ *in aid,* wang bantuan; *compassionate* ~, wang sagu hati; *to concede a request,* membenarkan (benar), mengizinkan (izin); memenuhi (permintaan) mengabulkan memperkenankan meluluskan; *bestow,* kurniai, anugerahi; *to* ~ *as a prayer,* kabulkan, makbulkan; *to take for* ~*ed, of confidence regarding a future event, can be expressed by the use of* tak boleh tidak *(cannot be), as I take it for* ~*ed that Jusoh will win,* saya yakin tentu Jusuh menang — tak boleh tidak; *of accepting gifts without showing gratitude: by the use of* begitu sahaja *(just like that), as, he showed no gratitude to me at all — he accepted it just like that,* dia tidak mengenang (kenang) budi saya sedikit pun — dia menerima (terima) begitu sahaja; ~*ed that (even through, admitting that),* biar pun.

granular, *adj.* berbutir-butir.

grapes, *n.* buah anggur.

grapnel, *n.* jangkar, candat, sejenis sauh yang mempunyai lebih dpd. dua cangkuk.

grapple, *v. intr. come to grips,* bergumul (gumul); ~ *with,* cangking, bergelut, cuba menyelesaikan sesuatu (masalah) dll.

grasp, *v. tr.* pegang; ~ *tightly,* pegang kuat-kuat; ~*ing,* tamak.

grass, *n.* rumput; *thrust-*~, rumput jolok-jolok, lalang laut; *a coarse* ~ *which gives its name to* ~ *slippers,* sambau; *creeping swamp-*~, rumput kumpai; ~ *window,* perempuan yang ditinggalkan buat sementara oleh urusan perniagaan dll.

grasshopper, *n.* belalang.

grate, *v. tr. scrape,* rasp, memarut (parut), mengikis (kikis); ~*r,* kukuran; *grating (bars),* kisi-kisi; *grating noise,* kerak, kerak.

grateful, *adj. to be* ~, mengenang (kenang) budi; *to be under an obligation to,* berhutang (hutang) budi; *to show gratitude by action,* balas budi.

gratifying, *v. tr. please, delight, satisfying,* memberikan kepuasan atau keseronokan.

gratis, *adv. without charge,* percuma.

gratitude, *n. being thankful,* perasaan berterima kasih atau kesyukuran.

gratuitous, *adj. uncalled for, as insult,* tak berfasal-fasal; ~ *insult,* penghinaan yang tidak pada tempatnya.

gratuity, *n.* hadiah, bayaran sagu hati; *tip,* duit kopi.

grave, *adj. of illness,* teruk, tenat; *of wound,* parah; *of situation,* genting; *of face,* muram, tidak berseri (seri), *of* ~*st importance that...*penting sekali bahawa...

grave, *n.* kubur; *tomb,* makam; ~*stone,* nisan; *the* ~ *(to which all come),* liang lahad; *to carry to one's* ~ *(as a memory or a scar),* bawa mati; *esp. non-Muslim* ~, jirat.

gravel, *n.* batu kerikil; *small stones in bladder; see* **gall.**

gravity, *n. force of* ~, tarikan bumi.

gravy, *n.* kuah.

graze, *v. tr.* makan rumput; ~*d (very slightly abraded),* jejas.

grease, *n.* lemak, minyak pekat, carbi; *greasy,* licin, berminyak; *a greasy road,* jalan yang licin.

great, *adj.* besar; *The Great Wall of China,* Tembok Besar Negeri China; *a ~ painter,* pulukis terkenal; *take ~ care,* sangat berhati-hati; *a ~ occasion,* peristiwa penting; *in compounds,* maha; agung; *Alexander the Great,* Iskandar Zulkarnain, (Iskandar yang Agung).

grebe, *n.* itik air.

Greece, *n.* Yunan.

greed, *n. esp. for money,* tamak loba; *~y for food,* gelojoh, pelahap (lahap); *having a mind only for his own belly (esp. of a dishonest official),* condong ke perut; *~ily,* dengan rakus.

green, *adj.* hijau; *jungle-~,* hijau daun; *dark ~,* hijau tua; *light ~,* hijau muda; *bright light ~,* hijau pucuk pisang; *greenish,* kehijau-hijauan. *Some shades of colour which in English are called blue are called ~ by Malays.*

greet, *v. tr.* memberi (beri) salam, menegur (tegur); *address courteously,* memberi tabik, menyapa (sapa); *see* **welcome.**

gregarious, *adj.* hidup berkawan (kawan), hidup bermasyarakat.

grenade, *n.* bom lempar, bom tangan.

grey, *adj.* kelabu; *of hair,* uban; *charcoal-~,* warna abuk robok.

grief, *n.* dukacita, sedih, kepiluan yang amat sangat.

grievance, *n. having a ~,* kecil hati muysykil; *dissatisfied,* tidak puas hati; *see* **complain.**

grimace, *n. and v. intr. see* **face.**

grill, *n.* besi bersilang yang dipasang pada tingkap dll.

grin, *v tr.* terjeringing (jeringing), menyeringai (seringai), tersengih (sengih).

grind, *v. tr. esp. as curry-stuffs,* pipis, giling; *as in sharpening,* asah, kilir; *esp. as grain,* mengisarkan; *grindstone,* batu asah; *(revolving),* batu kisar; *~ the teeth,* mengerat (kerat) gigi, mengertak (kertak) gigi.

grip, *v. tr.* mencengkam (cengkam), pegang kuat-kuat; *as brakes,* makan.

gripes, *n.* senak-perut, (yang mulas-mulas rasanya).

grist, *n. corn for grinding,* biji-bijian (spt. padi, gandum dan lain-lain) yang hendak ditumbuk.

gristle, *n.* tulang muda.

groan, *v. tr.* mengerang (erang), merintih (rintih), mengeluk (keluh).

groin, *n.* pangkal paha, lipat paha.

groom, *n.* gembala kuda, sais, pengantin lelaki, *v.* melatih seseorang untuk sesuatu jawatan.

groove, *n.* lurah, aluran; *on a gramophone record,* pusaran; *routine, rut,* cara hidup yang menjadi kebiasaan.

grope, *v. tr.* gagau-gagau.

gross, *adj. coarse,* kasar; *ill-bred,* kurang ajar; *(fig.) of profits or takings,* kasar.

ground, *n. surface of earth,* tanah, bumi; *bottom of sea or river,* dasar; *underlying part, esp. of cloth on which pattern is worked, prevailing colour,* tanah.

groundnuts, *n.* kacang tanah.

grounds, *n. alleged, motives,* alasan; *sediment,* keladak; *enclosed land attached to house,* halaman rumah; *groundless, as rumours,* tak berasas (asas); *without reason,* tak ada sebab-sebab yang munasabah.

ground-swell, *n.* alun.

group, *n.* sekelumpuk; *in ~s,* berkobok-kobok; *a party, small body,* rombongan; *in small ~s,* berkusu-kusu; *to be photographed in a ~,* bergambar (gambar) ramai; *a ~ of islands,* gugusan pulau; *a number of persons classed together as regards age, views, etc.,* lingkungan; *age-~ of thirty and under,* lingkungan tiga puluh tahun ke bawah; *esp. literary groups,* angkatan.

grouse, *v. int. and n. grumble,* mengomel, bersungut, omelan.

grovel, *v. int. throw oneself down,* merebahkan diri di hadapan orang yang ditakuti seolah-olah meminta belas kasihan; *fall at feet of,* menyembah (sembah) kaki; sujud, *see* **cringe.**

grow, *v. intr. as a plant,* tumbuh; *~ up,* menjadi (jadi) besar; *increase, increasingly,* bertambah (tambah); *~ apace, as* *weeds,* meriap (riap).

growl, *v. intr.* mengaum (aum), menggerung (gerung); *emit low rumbling ~,* menderam (deram).

grudge, *n.* dengki, dengam; *to harbour (a ~),* menaruh (taruh) (dengki, dendam), iri hati.

gruel, *n.* bubur.

gruff, *adj. of voice,* garau, bengis atau kasar (kelakuan).

grumble, *v. intr.* bersungut; *see* **nag.**

grumpy, *adj.* perengus (rengus), merungsing (rungsing).

grunt, *v. intr.* menggerut (gerut), mengorok (korok); mengeluarkan bunyi spt. bunyi mendengkur yang kuat; *make throaty noises as some birds and fishes,* berdengut (dengut); *a ~er (fish),* ikan gerut-gerut.

guano, *n. manure formed by excrement of bats or sea-birds,* baja tahi kelawar, baja tahi lurung laut.

guarantee, *n.* jaminan; *to ~ (as a debt),* menjamin; *make oneself responsible for (an expense),* menanggung (tanggung).

guard, *v. tr.* mengawal (kawal); *watch over,* jaga menunggu (tunggu); *off ~,* tak berhati-hati; *to ~ against,* berhati-hati terhadap; *~ of honour,* barisan kehormatan (hormat); *royal ~s,* pengiring (iring) raja; *personal bodyguard of troops,* asykar sebagai pengawal (kawal); *Home Guard,* pengawal kampung.

guardian, *n. under Islamic law,* wali; *~ angel,* malaikat pelindung.

guava, *n. (sp.)* buah jambu, buah jambu bul.

guess, *v. intr.* agak, menerka (terka); *as, hazard an opinion,* gamak; *make a wild ~, make a 'shot in the dark',* buang serkap jarang.

guest, *n. at a party,* orang jemputan, tetamu (tamu), dif; *~ of honour,* dif kehormat, tetamu agung, tetamu terhormat.

guide, *v. tr. show the way,* menunjuk (tunjuk) jalan atau arak; *to ~,* memandu (pandu), memimpin (jadi) ikutan;

something to direct the eye, pedoman; *guiding principle or aim,* pedoman, panduan; *spiritual ~ (also used of familiar spirit),* guru; *girl ~,* pandu wanita; pandu puteri; *right guidance in religion,* hidayat; *see* **example.**

guilty, *adj.* salah; *plead ~,* mengaku (aku) salah.

guinea-fowl, *n.* ayam mutiara, ayam peru.

guinea-pig, *n.* tikus belanda, marmot, *(idiom)* orang dan lain-lain yang dijadikan percubaan sains; korban percubaan.

guitar, *n.* 'gitar'; *to play the ~,* petik 'gitar'.

gulf, *n. as indentation on coast,* teluk; *chasm,* gaung, jurang; *inlet,* serokan; *(fig.) ~ dividing communities, etc.,* jurang.

gullet, *n.* kerongkong.

gullible, *adj. easily deceived,* mudah percaya; mudah diperdayai, mudah dibohongi; *easily cheated,* mudah tertipu (tipu), lembut-telinga.

gulp, *v. tr. ~ down,* teguk; *~ it down!,* teguk sekali!; *a ~,* seteguk; *see* **swallow.**

gum, *n.* perekat, getah; *to ~,* merekat (rekat), pelekat (lekat); *the ~s,* gusi.

gun, *n. shot-~, rifle,* senapang, bedil; *pistol,* 'pistol'; *cannon,* meriam; *'stick to one's ~s' (refuse to give way),* pantang beralah (alah); *spring-gun,* belantik (lantik).

gunpowder, *n.* ubat senapang.

gunwale, *n.* bordu, rubing, bibir dinding perahu.

gurgle, *v. intr. as water in a pot,* menggelegak (gelegak); *as a spring,* membobok (bobok).

gush, *v. intr. spout out,* memancut (pancut), memancar (pancar); *as contents of a cut sack,* terburai (burai), menyumbul (sumbul).

gusset, *n.* pesak.

gusty, *adj. blowing intermittently,* terjal; *a gust,* puputan angin.

gut, *n. intestinal canal,* usus; *intestines,* isi perut; *as for fishing-line,* tangsi, keberanian, ketekunan.

gutta-percha, *n. wild rubber,* getah perca, getah taban, getah jelutung.

gutter, *n. esp. by road,* longkang; *esp. on house,* saluran; ~-*snipe,* kutu bandar.

guttural, *adj. of speech,* garau, garuk.

gymnastics, *n. see* **physical.**

gynaecology, *n.* ilmu penyakit (sakit) kandungan, ilmu sakit puan.

gypsies, *n. nomads,* kaum melara (lara).

gyrate, *v. move in circle or spiral, revolve,* bergerak mengelilingi sesuatu bulatan dll, berputar.

gyrate, *v. intr.* berputar (putar).

H

habit, *n.* kebiasaan; tabiat; *custom,* adat; ~*ual,* telah menjadi biasa, lazim; *having the (opium)* ~, ketagih (tagih) (candu).

hack, *v. tr. as with axe,* menetak (tetak); memotong (potong); mengerat (kerat).

hackles, *n. on neck of cock,* bulu leher ayam jantan.

heckneyed, *adj. see* **stale.**

haft, *n. of knife,* hulu.

haggard, *adj. sunken and pallid, of face,* letih; lesu.

haggle, *v. intr.* tawar-menawar.

hail, *n.* hujan ais; hujan batu; *to* ~ *(greet),* memberi (beri) salam; *call to,* laung (kan); *loud-*~*er,* alat pembesar (besar) suara.

hair, *n. of human head,* rambut; *of body and of animals,* bulu; '~*-do',* sanggul; ~ *in a mess,* gumpalan rambut; *'bun',* siput; ~*-style,* dandanan rambut; ~*-pin,* cucuk sanggul; ~*-clip,* sepit rambut, *bobbed* ~, rambut tokong; *'permed'* ~, rambut keriting, *see* **curly;** *to have* ~*-cut,* bergunting (gunting) rambut; ~*-dresser,* tukang gunting; pendandan rambut; ~*y,* ramus; ~ *stylist,* juru dandan; ~ *dressing saloon,* kedai mendandan rambut; ~*-dryer,* alat pengering (kering) rambut; ~*-net,* jala rambut; ~*-raising,* menakutkan (takut); menggerunkan (gerun).

hairless, *adj.* tak berambut (rambut); *see* **bald.**

half, *n. and adj.* setengah, separuh; *precisely* ~, seperdua (dua); *to cut in* ~, kerat dua; ~*-mast,* separuh tiang; ~*-way (on a journey),* separuh jalan; ~*-baked,* setengah (tengah) masak, tiga suku; ~*-blood,* kacuk-baka; ~*-full,* berisi (isi) separuh; ~*-grown,* tengah naik; ~*-hearted, of action,* acuh tak acuh, sambil lewa; *a* ~ *(of a game divided into two equal periods),* separuh masa, babak; ~ *a loaf is better than no bread,* tak ada rotan akar pun berguna (guna).

hall, *n. public room,* balai, dewan; *large chamber for business or social occasions,* dewan besar.

hallucination, *n.* khayalan, maya.

halo, *n.* lingkaran cahaya.

halt, *v. intr.* berhenti (henti); ~*ing, not fluent, of reading,* membaca (baca) bertatih-tatih; *of speech broken, esp. by emotion,* (dengan) suara terputus-putus.

halve, *v. to divide, to share equally between two,* membahagi dua.

ham, *n.* daging peha babi yang digaram dan diasapi.

hamadryad, *n.* ular tedung selar.

hammer, *n.* martal, tukul; *of a gun,* burung senapang; *to* ~ *(work metal with* ~*),* menempa (tempa), menitik (titik).

hammock, *n.* buaian, ayunan.

hamper, *n.* keranjang; bakul yang berisi bahan makanan, hadiah dsb.; *to* ~ *(cause difficulty),* menyulitkan (sulit), menghalang (halang).

hand, *n.* tangan; ~ *of clock,* jarum (jam); ~*kerchief,* sapu tangan; ~*cuffs,* gari; ~*ful,* segenggam; *double* ~*ful,* serangkum; *double handful,* seraup; ~*in-*~, berpegang (pegang) tangan; ~*icrafts,* pertukangan (tukang); ~*iwork,* bekas tangan; *to* ~ *round,* mengedarkan (edar); *hold out,* unjukkan; *pass (as a dish),* sorongkan; ~*-hold,* pegangan; *having a 'good* ~' *for some work, as having 'green fingers' for planting,* bertangan (tangan) sejuk; ~*s up!,* angkat tangan!; *on the other* ~ *(of contrasted facts),* sebaliknya; *with bare* ~*s (weaponless),* dengan kuasa tulang empat kerat; ~*grenade,* bom lempar; ~*out,* pemberian derma, surat sibaran.

handicap, n. circumstance placing a person at a disadvantage, kongkongan, halangan; as in a (foot-) race, kuyu; weight on a horse, pikulan, bawaan; ~ped person (physically), orang cacat.

handle, n. esp. of a knife, hulu; as of a vessel, telinga; as of a tool, tangan; long ~, as of a pan, tangkai; ~-bars of bicycle, tangan 'basikal'; as of a paddle or hoe, batang.

handsome, adj. cantik, bagus rupanya, rupawan; of a man, orang gagah, kacak tampan; see **pretty.**

handwriting, n. tulisan tangan, khat; mere scrawl, seperti cakar ayam.

handy, adj. clever with hands, cekap (tangan).

hang, v. intr. gantung; ~ing out, of tongue, terjulur (julur), terjelir (jelir); ~ down, as hair or branches, melampai (lampai); to ~ up (as on a peg), sangkutkan; sentenced to be ~ed, kena hukum gantung; see **dangle.**

hank, n. coil of yarn, etc., setukal.

hankypanky, n. trickery, kongkalikong; to indulge in ~, main kongkalikong.

Hansard, n. laporan rasmi mengenai kegiatan-kegiatan di Parlimen.

haphazard, adv. without selection of direction, tak tentu arah; of violent action, buta tuli; of wild, ill-considered action, tak ketahuan (tahu), serampangan.

happen, v. intr. jadi; esp. of continuing event, berlaku (laku); as it so ~ed, kebetulan (betul) pula; and then it suddenly ~ed that, tiba-tiba.

happy, adj. senang-hati, (ber)gembira; having a feeling of euphoria, berasa (rasa) nyaman; see **glad, please;** ~-go-lucky, adj. taking events cheerfully as they happen, sentiasa suka hati, sesenang-senang.

harakiri, n. suicide involving disembowelment, formerly practised by Japanese officers when in disgrace, membunuh diri.

harass, v. tr. continually worry, menggoda (goda), merundung

(rundung); cause a lot of trouble to, menyusah-payahkan (susah); victimize in petty ways, tekan-menekan.

harbour, n. shelter for ships, river-mouth, kuala; ~-town, bandar; anchorage, perlabuhan (labuh); natural ~, perlabuhan semula jadi; artificial ~, perlabuhan buatan; ~master, syahbandar; to ~ (resentment, pity, anxiety, etc.), menaruh (taruh) (dengki, belas, bimbang).

hard, adj. keras; ~ of hearing, berat telinga; ~ labour (in prison), kerja berat; ~ work, kerja keras; to work ~, bekerja kuat; ~-up, dalam kepicikan (picik); ~ times, masa kesukaran (sukar); ~ when it should be soft, as badly cooked potatoes, ganyut; ~en, menjadi keras; ~ly, hanya sedikit; hampir-hampir tidak; ~y, kuat teguh.

hardship, n. kesusahan (susah); life of ~, hidup melarat, hidup sengsara.

hard-wearing, n. tahan lasak.

hare-lip, n. bibir sumbing.

harmful, adj. of an animal, jahat; yang mencederakan, bisa; causing sickness, mendatangkan (datang) penyakit (sakit); he was not harmed in any way, dia tidak kena apa-apa; the raja did nothing to him, did not harm him, raja tidak pengapakan (apa); harmless, jinak, tanpa salahnya; see **damaged, hurt, injured, wound.**

harmonious, adj. compatible, seraksi (dengan), selaras sesuai (dengan); agreeing, bersetuju; vocal harmony, paduan suara.

harpoon, n. tempuling.

harrow, n. sisir.

harsh, adj. unfeeling, kasar, keras; of voice, garau.

harvest, n. time to cut (rice), musim menuai (tuai), musim mengetam (ketam); produce, hasil.

hastily, adv. bergopoh-gapah; esp. of rash haste, terburu-buru; make haste!, cepatlah; hasty, of speech or action, lancang.

hat, n. topi; conical sun-~, terendak; take

one's ~ off to, menyatakan hormat kepada.

hatch, v. intr. come out of egg, menetas (tetas); see **sit.**

hate, v. tr. benci(kan), getek.

haul, v. tr. menarik (tarik); tangkapan, penghasilan; ~ after one, menghela (hela); ~ in (a line), karau; ~ up (an anchor), bongkar; haulage, pengangkutan;; heavy transport, pengangkutan (angkut).

haunch, n. pangkal paha.

haunted, adj. berhantu (hantu); by a tutelary spirit, berpuaka (puaka); of a person, di rasuk hantu.

have, v. tr. ada (pada — , di tangan —).

hawk, n. burung lang; v. tr. to peddle, berjaja (jaja), meraih (raih); v. intr. to clear one's throat of phlegm noisily, berkahak-kahak, berjeluak (jeluak); sound of such ~ing, gerehak, gerehak.

hawker, n. penjaja.

hawser, n. tali pendarat (darat), tali tebal, kebel.

hay, n. rumput kering, ~wire, bingung, keliru, kusut.

haze, n. embun asap; see **mist, vapour.**

he, pron. dia, ia; the person mentioned above, beliau; the '~' in children's games, ibu.

head, n. kepala; crown of ~, batu kepala; ~-waters of river, hulu; ~man (of parish), penghulu, penggawa; generally ketua (tua); ~cloth, tengkolok, setangan (sapu-tangan); to 'lose one's ~', hilang akal; ~ache, sakit kepala; ~-over-heels, tunggang-langgang; won by a ~ (in horse-racing), menang jarak kepala; won by a short ~, menang jarak domol; ~land, tanjung; ~-quarters, ibu pejabat (jabat); (military), markas besar; ~strong, degil; obstinate, keras kepala; ~line, tajuk; ~scarf (for Malay women), kain lepas, selendang; (if covering both shoulders), kelubung; Head of State, ketua negara, yang di pertuan (tuan) negara; to ~ a ball, at football, menanduk (tanduk); ~master, pengetua sekolah; ~way, pembangunan.

head-hunt, v. intr. mengkajau (kajau); head-hunter, pemburu kepala manusia.

healthy, adj. sihat; of a plant, subur.

heap, n. longgok; to ~ together, menimbunkan (timbun); 'heaps' (galore), belanar; heaped (of a full measure), penuh menjunjung (junjung), mumbung.

hear, v. tr. dengar; get news, dapat khabar; court hearing, perbicaraan (bicara).

hearsay, n. rumour, khabar angin; only according to what people say, mengikut (ikut) kata orang sahaja.

hearse, n. jenazah, kereta mayat.

heart, n. (anatomical), jantung; seat of the emotions, hati; haven't got the ~ to —, tak sampai hati nak —; in (my) innermost ~, dalam hati kecik (saya); learn by ~, hafal; hearts suit at cards, lekuk; ~-wood of a tree, teras; ~less, kejam; ~ily, dengan ikhlas, dengan jujur, dengan berselera; having 'no bowels', tidak berhati perut; ~beat, degupan jantung; ~break, yang menyayat hati; ~ disease, penyakit jantung; ~ failure, kegagalan perjalanan jantung; ~felt, ikhlas.

heat, n. panas, hangat; to ~ up, jerangkan; perhangatkan; on ~ (of an animal), biang; see **randy.**

heathen, n. kafir; as a term of abuse, keparat; see **scriptures.**

heave, v. tr. exert strength, paut; menghela, menarik (nafas); ~ up, as by pressing on a lever, wet; rise and fall, of breast, meriak-riak, turun naik.

heaven, n. syurga; ~ on earth, syurga dunia; ~ly, yang sangat menyenangkan.

heavy, adj. berat; as rain, moustache, foliage, lebat; as stodgy cake, bentat; ~ and stolid, of face, daup.

heckle, v. mengemukakan banyak soalan yang sukar dalam mesyuarat umum.

hector, v. intr. bluster, bully, sergah, jerkah.

hedge, n. pagar (hidup).

heel, n. tumit; ~ over, senget, mereng.

height, *n.* tingginya.

heirs, *n. potential ~ under Islamic law through relationship,* waris; *heirloom,* pesaka; *Heir Apparent,* Raja Muda, Tengku Mahkota.

hell, *n.* neraka, jahanam; *the hottest ~,* neraka jahim; *the pains of ~,* seksa neraka; *to ~ with,* persetan (setan) pada.

helm, *n.* kemudi; *~sman,* juru mudi; *to take the ~,* pegang kemudi; *tiller,* bam kemudi.

help, *v. tr.* tolong; *aid, back up,* bantu; *shout for ~,* jerit minta tolong; *there's no ~ for it,* apa boleh buat?; *~less,* tak terdaya; *~less and bewildered,* seperti orang buta kehilangan (hilang) tongkat, *(like a blind man who has lost his stick); timely ~ to a friend in need,* mengantuk (antuk) disorongkan bantal, *(having a pillow passed to one when sleepy); material ~ (as opposed to moral support),* bantuan kebendaan (benda); *see* **support.**

helter-skelter, *adv. in disorderly haste,* hempas-pulas; bertempiaran; *through all obstacles,* susup-sasap.

hem, *n.* kelim, kelipat; *to ~ in (block escape routes),* mengepung (kepung).

hemp, *n. 'Indian ~',* bhang, ganja *material for ropes,* rami; *~en rope,* tali rami, tali Manila, tali belati.

hen, *n.* ibu ayam.

henceforword, *adv.* dari sekarang, seterusnya.

henna, *n.* inai.

herald, *n.* bentara; *~ic devices,* lambang.

herbivorous, *n.* yang makan tumbuh-tumbuhan sahaja.

herbs, *n.* daun-daunan; *medicinal ~,* akar periuk; *herbage,* rumput; *herbalist, see* **doctor.**

herd, *n.* sekawan, sekumpulan; *~sman,* gembala.

here, *adv.* (di) sini; *come ~!,* marilah!; *~! (take it),* nah!; *~ and there,* di sana sini; *~abouts,* dekat di sini, tidak jauh; *~after,* kemudian, pada masa yang akan datang; *~by,* dengan ini; *~tofore,*

dahulu; hereupon, selepas itu; *~with,* bersama dengan ini.

hereditary, *adj.* turun-temurun; *~ property,* pesaka; *inherited traits,* baka.

heresy, *n. false doctrine,* bidaah, agama sesat; *a heretic,* orang bidaah; *forbidden by religion,* haram; back-slider, rosak iman.

heritage, *n.* warisan.

hermaphrodite, *n.* orang papak, banci, pondan, kedi.

hermit, *n.* orang pertapaan (tapa), zahid; *to live a ~'s life,* bersunyi (sunyi) diri; *~-crab,* umang-umang.

hernia, *n.* burut.

hero, *n.* ceteria, kasteria; *great warrior,* pahlawan, perwira; *~ine,* serikandi; *to ~-worship,* menjulang-julang; *praise to the skies,* memuji (puji), melambung (lambung).

heron, *n.* burung seriap; *night-~,* burung pucung, burung gelam.

hesitating, *adj. undecided,* pecahbelah hati, teragak-agak, bercabang (cabang) hati, ragu-ragu; *un~ly,* tak ragu-ragu.

heterodox, *adj.* menyimpang dari kepercayaan rasmi.

heterogenous, *adj. made up of people or things that are unlike each other,* berbeda jenis.

hew, *v. tr. chip at,* tetak; *~ down,* menebang (tebang); *rough-~,* menarah (tarah); *rough-~n,* sembulu.

hibernate, *v. intr.* bertapa (tapa), tidur di musim dingin.

hibiscus, *n.* bunga raya.

hiccough, *v intr.* tersedak (sedak).

hide, *v. intr.* bersembunyi (sembunyi); *slip out of sight,* menyorok (sorok); *to conceal, as a treasure,* pendam, sembunyikan; *'make oneself scarce',* menghilangkan (hilang) diri; *play ~-and-seek,* main menyorok; *'keep dark',* menggelapkan (gelap), penyapkan; *a ~ (for a hunter),* up a tree, ran; *on the ground,* bumbun; *thick skin,* belulang.

hidebound, *adj.* berfikiran sempit.

hideous, *adj. very ugly,* hodoh.

higgledy-piggledy, *adv. in utter confu-*

sion, lintang-pukang, simpang-pere-nang; sarabara, bercampur-aduk, tidak tersusun, tidak teratur.

high, adj. tinggi; ~-minded, berhati (hati) mulia; sky-~, tinggi melangit (langit); ~lands, daerah pergunungan (gunung); to treat in a ~handed manner, memperkudakan (kuda).

Highness, His, n. Duli yang maha mulia; Your ~, tuanku.

hilarious, adj. riang gembira, meriah.

hill, n. bukit, guar, gun, banggul; ~ock, anak bukit, ~y, berbukit-bukau; foot~s, pekakian (kaki) gunung.

hilt, n. hulu.

hinder, v. tr. menghalangkan; hindrance, halangan, galangan, gendala.

hinge, n. engsil.

hint, n. analogy, kias, isyarat; conveyed by irony, sindiran; meaning intending to be conveyed, purport, maksud; meaning underlying words, makna batin; can take a ~, tahu mengenal (kenal) kilat di air, (can recognise lightning (from its reflection) in the water.

hinterland, n. upriver, hulu; ~ area, daerah pendalaman (dalam).

hip, n. pinggang, temenggak; to place hands on the ~, akimbo, bercekak (cekak) pinggang.

hire, v. tr. (things), menyewa (sewa); (a person), mengupah (upah); ~car, kereta sewa; to charter, sewa; ~-purchase, belian dengan bayaran beransur-ansur.

hiss, v. intr. as a hot iron in water, berdesar (desar), berdesir.

history, n. tawarikh, sejarah; ~ of (story of), hikayat; historian, ahli sejarah.

hit, v. tr. pukul; pound, tumbuk; as a mark, kena; 'slosh', hempuk; ~ and run, as guerrilas, pukul cabut; see **beat.**

hitch, v. menyentak, merenggut, sangkut, tersangkut.

hitch-hike, n. pengembaraan dengan menumpang kenderaan secara per-cuma.

hither, adv. ke sini, ke mari; ~ and thither, ke sana ke mari.

hoard, v. tr. save up, simpan; stow away unused, pendap.

hoarse, adj. (suara) garuk (suara) serak, (suara) parau.

hoax, n. olok-olok (sahaja), mengakali seseorang secara bergurau.

hobble, v. intr. ~ along, jalan berdengkut-dengkut, jalan tertempang-tempang.

hobby, n. favourite occupation, not one's main business, suatu kegemaran (gemar); regular practice, amalan.

hocus-pocus, n. trickery, percakapan atau perbuatan yang bertujuan untuk menyimpangkan perhatian seseorang dari sesuatu.

hoe, n. for rice-fields, tajak.

hoist, v. tr. as a flag, pasang, naikkan, tarik naik; fly, mengibarkan (kibar); as with a crane, angkat.

hold, v. tr. grasp, pegang; ~ out (offer), unjuk; ~ out (as hand), hulurkan; to persist in resistance, bertahan (tahan); to ~, conduct, cause to take place, e.g., a party, discussions, a function, an election, a meeting, a festival, mengadakan (ada); ~ fast to (political principles), berpegang (pegang) pada (pendirian (diri) politik); ~ a championship title or high position, menyandang (sandang); ~ out hands palm-upwards in prayer or as a begger, menadah (tadah) tangan; held up, as a plan or journey, tergendala (gendala); ~er into which, e.g., an electric-light bulb, is fitted, tampuk; ~ of ship, ruang kapal, perut kapal; ~-back, rasa ragu, rintangan; ~fast, pegangan kuat; ~-up, perompakan, perampasan; ~er, pemegang, pemilik; ~ing, tanah milik, kawasan kepunyawaan.

hole, n. lubang; small aperture, liang; small cavity, rongga; crevice, celah; large cavity, darang; pitted with ~s, berpesuk-pesuk; ~d, perforated, tembuk, tembus; full of ~s through which light shines, as roof, bintang-bintangan; to bore a ~, tebuk.

holiday, n. cuti, hari kelepasan (lepas); public ~, hari kelepasan umum (hari cuti awam); *school* ~ *(at end of term),* cuti penggal; ~ *resort,* tempat perangi-nan (angin).

Holland, *n.* negeri Belanda.

hollow, *adj.* geronggang, berongga (rongga); *a* ~, *cavity,* rongga; *small* ~, lekuk; ~ *space, e.g., under house,* kolong; ~*ed out,* berlurah (lurah).

holy, *adj.* suci, kudus; ~ *water,* air tolak bala; *a* ~ *man,* aulia; *Holy Land, esp. Mecca,* tanah suci.

homage, *n.* takzim, sembah; *to pay* ~, menyembah, menjunjung (junjung) duli; *to pay (fig.) tribute to (for merit),* memberi (beri) hormat kepada.

home, *n. house,* rumah; *household,* rumah-tangga; *native land,* tanah air; ~*sick,* merindukan (rindu) rumahtangga; *a Home (charitable insti-tution),* rumah amal, darul ihsan; *old persons' Home,* rumah kebajikan (bajik) orang tua; *East West,* ~'s *best,* hujan mas perak, negeri orang, hujan keris lembing, negeri kita (baik juga negeri kita), *(it rains gold and silver abroad and daggers and spears at* ~, *yet* ~ *is best);* ~-*made,* buatan sendiri; ~-*work,* kerja rumah; *make yourself at* ~, buat macam rumah sendiri; ~*stead,* rumah desa; ~*ly,* sederhana, biasa, menyebabkan sseseorang teringat atau terkenang kampung halaman; Home Secretary, menteri hal ahwal dalam; *Home Guard,* pengawal (kawal) kampung.

homosexuality, *n.* cinta sejenis, per-hubungan (hubang) jenis sesama jenis; *see* **sodomy.**

hone, *n.* batu canai, batu asah.

honest, *adj. sincere,* benar; *of integrity,* jujur; *trustworthy,* (orang) harapan, sadik-amanah; *see* **trust.**

honey, *n.* manisan lebah, madu; ~-*comb,* lilin lebah; *like bees round a* ~-*pot,* sep-erti kucing dengan panggang, *(like a cat and the roast),* seperti kumbang menyeri (seri) bunga, *(like a bee busy about a flower).*

honeymoon, *n. to go on a* ~, berbulan

(bulan) madu.

honorary, *adj.* yang kehormat (hormat).

honour, *n. mark of distinction,* tanda ke-hormatan (hormat), suatu kemulian (mulia); ~*able (in character),* jujur, ikhlas; *the Honourable,* yang berhor-mat.

hood, *n. of a car,* bumbung (kereta); *esp. of* rikisya, tenda; tudung kepala.

hoodwink, *v. to deceive,* menipu.

hoof, *n.* kuku; *to show the cloven* ~ *(dis-close one's blemish),* tunjuk tembe-lang; tapak kaki binatang seperti kuda.

hook, *n. fish-*~, mata kail; *unbarbed many-pointed* ~ *(used particularly for catching cuttle-fish),* candat; *a* ~*ed ar-ticle generally,* cangkuk, gancu; ~ *to hang something on,* penyangkut (sangkut); *to* ~ *down (esp. fruit),* kait; *by* ~ *or by crook,* berhutang (hutang) bergolok (golok), *(by borrowing or by using a knife).*

hoop, *n. as for barell,* simpai; *child's* ~, kereta; ~-*ing-cough,* batuk rejan.

hop, *v. intr.* terloncat-loncat; *as a flea,* jintat; *as, 'lolloping along',* terkidat-kidat, jalan mengenjak-ngenjak (enjak); ~*ping* 'along, *as a kangaroo,* terkinja-kinja.

hope, *v. intr.* harap; ~*s,* aspirations, cita-cita; ~*less,* putus harapan, putus asa; *at wits' end,* kehabisan (habis) akal; *centre of* ~*s,* base of ~*s,* tumpuan harapan; *I* ~ *that — (would that),* minta-minta, moga-moga, *all* ~*s exceeded,* pucuk dicita, hulam mendatang (datang); *(I* ~*d for a (mere) shoot and got a vegetable).*

horizon, *n.* kaki langit; ufuk; *just lying on the* ~, *of rising sun or moon,* mengam-bang (ambang).

horizontal, *adj.* melintang (lintang).

horn, *n.* tanduk; *of rhinoceros,* sumbu; *of dragon,* cula; ~*less,* dogol; *tine of a* ~, rangga handuk; ~ *of a car,* 'hon'.

hornbill, *n. (many spp.) small black* ~, burung langling, burung kelengkeng; *rhinoceros* ~, burung enggang.

hornet, *n.* tebuan; ~*s' nest,* sarang

tebuan.

horoscope, *n.* ramalan bintang.

horrifying, *adj.* dahsyat; *horrified,* berasa (rasa) ngeri.

horse, *n.* kuda; *pack-~,* kuda beban; *~-back,* menunggang kuda; *~-laugh,* ketawa bising; *~-sense,* akal sihat; *race-~,* kuda lumba; *gelding,* kuda kasi; *~-power,* kekuatan (kuat) kuda.

horticulture, *n.* ilmu penanaman bunga, buah-buahan dan sayur-sayuran.

hose, *n.* bomba, getah penyalur air.

hospitable, *adj.* suka menjamu (jamu) orang, murah hati.

hospital, *n.* rumah sakit, hospital; *~ ward,* 'wad', ruangan rumah sakit.

host, *n. master of the house,* tuan rumah; *person giving the entertainment,* orang yang menjamu (jamu).

hostage, *n.* orang tawanan sebagai tebusan.

hostel, *n.* rumah tumpangan; *esp. for students,* asrama.

hostility, *n. between States,* permusuhan (musuh); *between individuals,* perseteruan (seteru); *on mutually hostile terms,* saling bermusuh-musuhan; *see* **battle, enemy, fued, war.**

hot, *adj. esp. of sun-heat,* panas; *esp. as warm and stuffy,* hangat; *as of curry,* pedas; *as ginger,* pedar; *sultry,* panas terik, panas cing; *see* **heat;** *~-news,* berita yang terakhir diterima; *~ stuff,* orang yang tegar, mahir dan penuh perasaan; *~head,* orang degil, *~-tempered,* lekas marah.

hour, *n.* jam; *hourly,* tiap-tiap jam.

house, *n.* rumah; *the ~hold inmates,* isi rumah; *~hold,* rumah-tangga; *see* **establishment;** *~wife,* suri rumahtangga, *~-keeping money,* duit pasar, belanja pasar; *to ~,* find accommodation for, menempatkan (tempat); *~ of assembly,* dewan; *the 'first ~' at the cinema,* tayangan pertama.

hover, *v. tr.* menduyung-duyung; berlegar-legar di udara (burung); (orang) yang menunggu-nunggu; *~craft,* kapal yang dapat berjalan di air dan daratan;

as a fish hanging with waving fins in the current, berleduk-ledak; *appear to remain motionless, as fish in water, bird in air, and esp. moon on horizon,* mengambang (ambang).

how?, *adv.* macam mana?, mana?, bagaimana?; *~ do you do?,* apa khabar?; *~ much?,* berapa (harga)?

however, *adv. (despite what may be said),* biar bagaimanapun; *see* **nevertheless.**

howl, *v. intr.* melolong (lolong).

hubbub, *n. noisy disturbance,* ingar-bangar, bising; *esp. of quarrelling,* herukperuk.

huddle, *v. intr. ~ together,* berhimpit-himpit; *(sitting, lying) ~d up,* berlepoh-lepah (lepoh); *(lying);* (berbaring) (baring), terjelepoh (jelepoh), merengkok (rengkok); *as a sick person,* terkokol-kokol (kokol); *to ~ oneself up in a small space, as when hiding,* berkemas (kemas) diri.

hug, *v. tr.* memeluk (peluk), mendakap (dakap); *to ~ the shore,* menyusur (susur) pantai.

hull, *n. of ship,* badan (kapal).

hum, *v. intr. as a bullet or bees,* berdengung (dengung); *as a swarm of bees, as insects in the jungle, as a wire in the wind,* ternggiang-ngiang (ngiang); *sing with closed lips,* bersenandung (senandung), berdahamkan (daham) nyanyi.

human, *adj. see* **man;** *~ity (benevolence, justice, etc.),* kemanusian (manusia).

humble, *adj.* rendah-hati.

humbug, *n.* auta, dusta, bohong; *a ~,* orang yang suka menipu; *blatant rot,* temberang lapuk; *a piece of ~ (something done for show);* wayang kulit sahaja, *(just a puppet-show); see* **appearances, eye, hypocrisy.**

humiliate, *v. tr. see* **insult;** *a humiliation,* suatu kehinaan (hina); merendahkan; *to feel ~d,* merasa (rasa) diri sebesar semut, *(to feel oneself the size of an ant).*

hummock, *n. low rounded ridge, esp. between stretches of rice-fields,* matang, permatang, gong; *see* **hill;** anak bukit.

humorous, *adj.* jenaka, lucu.

humour, *v. tr.* *indulge whim,* ikut angin; *see* **cross.**

hump, *n.* *as of bullock,* engguk, ponok, bonggol; *--backed,* bongkok.

hunched, *adj.* *(sitting)* ~ *up,* (duduk) terpungguk (pungguk), (duduk) terbenguk (benguk).

hungry, *adj.* *lapar; ravenous,* kemaruk; *having stomach pinched in,* kempis perut.

hunt, *v. tr.* berburu (buru).

hurl, *v. tr.* baling; ~ *down,* campak.

hurly-burly, *n.* keriuhan.

hurricane, *n.* ribut taufan.

hurry, *n. and v. tr. and intr. in a ~,* terkocoh-kocoh; *see* **hastily.**

hurt, *adj.* *pained,* sakit; *wounded,* luka; *injured,* cedera; *in feelings,* tersinggung (singgung) perasaan (rasa); *to ~ feelings, 'upset' someone,* menggeludak (geludak) perasaan (rasa); *touch 'on the raw', on a sensitive spot,* betul-betul kena pada batang hidung (nya), *(hit (him) right on the nose).*

husband, *n.* laki; *more formal,* suami.

hush!, *interjection,* diam!, sengap! cus!; *don't make a noise,* jangan ingar; *-- money,* wang tutup mulut; *to ~ up (as a scandal),* penyapkan; *see* **hide.**

husk, *n.* *of grain,* antah, sekam; *of coconut,* sabut; *-ed coconut,* nyiur gubal; *to ~,* kupaskan.

husky, *adj.* *of voice,* garau.

hustle, *v. intr.* *of people struggling in a crowd,* bergelut-gelut.

hut, *n.* pondok, teratak; *temporary shelter,* dangau; *primitive shack, esp. of bamboo,* gobok; *lean-to,* pondok pisang sesikat.

hybrid, *adj.* kacuk baka.

hydrant, *n.* pancaran air.

hydrocele, *n.* sakit pasang-pasang.

hydrophobia, *n.* penyakit (sakit) anjing gila.

hygiene, *n.* kebersihan (bersih).

hymen, *n.* selaput dara.

hyoid bone, *n.* tulang amris.

hypnotize, *v.* menjadikan seseorang seakan-akan tertidur serta di dalam penguasaannya.

hypochondriac, *n.* tahi penyakit (sakit); *an imaginary illness,* penyakit khayal.

hypocrisy, *n.* *pretence,* pura-pura; *dissembling, as with false smiles,* bermuka-muka; *double-dealing,* lidah biawak; *see* **humbug, pretend;** *hypocrite,* munafik.

hysterical, *adj.* *to get ~,* melatah (latah), menyelap (selap).

I

I, *pron.* saya, aku.

ice, *n.* air batu, 'ais'; *refrigerator,* peti 'ais'; ~-*cream,* 'ais krim'; ~*berg,* bongkah 'ais', gunung 'ais'.

idea, *n. (theory),* buah fikiran; *(plan),* suatu akal; *see* **think.**

ideals, *n.* yang indah, unggul, yang dianggap sempurna; *hopes and aims,* cita-cita; *having lofty* ~, bercita-cita mulia.

identical, *adj.* serupa, sama juga.

identify, *v. tr.* camkan, mengenalpasti.

identity card, *n.* 'kad' pengenalan (kenal).

ideology, *n.* 'ideoloji', fahaman yang digunakan untuk dasar pemerintah.

idiom, *n.* jalan bahasa.

idiosyncrasy, *n.* telingkah.

idle, *adj. see* **lazy, loose, unemployed;** *vain, purposeless, of talk,* omong kosong, keretaan (reta).

idol, *n. image as object of worship,* berhala; *to worship* ~*s,* memuja (puja) berhala; '~ *of the people',* pujaan ramai; ~*ised one (sweetheart),* pujaan hati; *see* **image.**

if, *conj.* kalau, jikalau, jika, sekiranya, andainya.

ignorant, *adj.* jahil.

ignore, *v. tr. pretend not to recognise,* buat-buat tak kenal; tidak memperdulikan; *take no notice of or action about,* tidak ambil tahu, biarkan sahaja; *disdainfully* ~, mengabaikan (abai); *put aside, refuse to consider,* tolak tepi.

iguana, *n.* biawak, bewak.

ill, *adj. out of health,* sakit, uzur; ~*ness (disease),* penyakit; *(state of being* ~*),* kesakitan; *fall* ~, jatuh sakit.

ill-bred, *adj.* salah didik, kurang sopan, bangsa-kurang; *badly brought-up,* kurang ajar; *ill-favoured,* hodoh, buruk rupa; *ill-mannered,* biadab; *ill-natured,* peradang, pemarah; *ill-fated,* malang.

illegal, *adj.* salah pada undang-undang; *esp. as contrary to religious law,* haram; ~*ly,* secara haram; *surreptiously* ~, gelap.

illegible, *adj.* sukar untuk dibaca (baca); *mere scrawl,* cakar ayam.

illegitimate, *adj. of child,* haram, dilahirkan di luar nikah; *see* **bastard.**

illimitable, *adj.* tak berbatas (batas), tak berhad (had).

illiterate, *adj.* buta huruf; *completelly* ~, buta kayu; *to stamp out illiteracy,* membasmikan (basmi) buta huruf.

illuminated, *p. p. brightly lit up, artifically or by the moon,* terang benderang.

illusion, *n.* khayalan, angan-angan sahaja.

illustrated, *p. p. as a book,* bergambar (gambar).

image, *n.* patung; *in Chinese temple,* tok pekung; patung, arca; *reflection,* bayang; imej.

imagination, *n.* angan-angan, khayalan, imaginasi; *see* **picture;** *impression,* perasaan (rasa); *imagine (conceive),* sangka; *I imagine (i.e., I suppose),* gamak sahaya.

imbalance, *n. lack of balance,* tidak seimbang.

imitate, *v. tr.* meniru (tiru); *to follow as an example,* turutkan, mengikut jejak; *be a mere imitator,* ikut-ikut sahaja; *mimic,* ajuk.

immaculate, *adj. spotlessly clean,* bersih, tidak cacat, murni.

immature, *adj.* muda (lagi); *raw, callow,* mentah; *callow,* belum tahu hal.

immediately, *adv. straightaway,* selalu, dengan tiada bertangguh; *without more ado,* serta-merta; *while opportunity offers,* dan-dan; *see* **promptly.**

immemorial, *adj.* sejak zaman berzaman.

immense, adj. exceedingly great, tersangat besar, hebat.

immerse, v. tr. membenamkan (benam), merendamkan (rendam); deeply '~d' (involved) in some task, tungkuslumus.

immigrant, n. orang pindahan dari luar negeri.

immodest, adj. unseemly, tak senonoh; of a woman, bisi; generally, tak tahu malu, tak silu-silu.

immortal, adj. kekal, abadi; to ~ize, esp. in fame, mengabadikan; see **eternal.**

immune, adj. invulnerable, kebal; from a disease, balu; not susceptible to, tak alah pada; as from a tax, bebas; to immunise (as by injections), kebalkan.

immutable, adj. tak dapat berubah (ubah).

imp, n. jembalang, polong, pelesit.

impact, n. collision, pukulan, bentrokan, perlanggaran; kesan.

impair, v. to damage, to cause weakening of, merosakkan, melemahkan.

impale, v. tr. sulakan; spitted, terpacak (pacak).

impartial, adj. tidak berat sebelah; just, adil, saksama; see **equal.**

impasse, n. deadlock, kebuntuan (buntu)

impatient, adj. (by nature), tak tahu sabar; (losing patience), tak boleh sabar lagi.

impediment, adj. kongkongan, halangan; see **difficult.**

impel, v. tr. drive to action, mendorong (dorong); cause to move forward, menjalankan (jalan); launch, melancarkan (lancar).

impenetrable, adj. cannot be pierced, tak dapat ditembus, peluru tak lut, kebal.

imperialism, n. faham penjajahan (jajah).

impersonate, v. tr. disguise oneself as, menyamar (samar) diri sebagai; make oneself look like, merupakan (rupa) diri sebagai; act as if one were, berlagak (lagak) sebagai; take the role of, melakukan (laku) peranan; assume (by magic) the shape of, menjelma (jelma) menjadi (jadi).

impertinent, adj. biadab; uppish, sombong, kurang ajar.

impervious, adj. not able to be penetrated, tidak dapat diresapi.

impish, adj. nakal.

implacable, adj. not to be appeased, tak dapat didamaikan; pitiless, tidak menaruh (taruh) kasihan.

implant, v. tr. fix firmly in, cacak; a plant or ideas, menanam (tanam).

implement, n. alat, perkakas, pesawat; to ~ (put into effect), menjalankan (jalan), melakukan (laku).

implicate, v. tr. membabitkan (babit), melibatkan (libat); implication (significance), maksud.

implicit, adj. implied though not made explicit, terkandung, termasuk juga.

import, v. tr. bawa masuk negeri, mengimport; ~s, dagangan masuk.

important, adj. as requiring action, mustahak, penting; not ~ (not likely to lead to any serious consequences), tidak menjadi (jadi) hal, bukan apa; that's no skin off my nose, perkara itu tidak menjadikan kudis, (that matter doesn't give me the itch); person or transaction, besar; Very ~ Person, pembesar; principal, main, utama; see **personality.**

importunate, adj. making persistent requests, yang mendesak berkali-kali.

impose, v. tr. as a tax, mengenakan (kena).

imposing, adj. to the eye, hebat, yang mengagumkan.

impossible, adj. tak boleh jadi, mustahil!, mana boleh?

impotent, adj. helpless, tak terdaya (daya); sexually, mati pucuk.

imprecation, n. see **curse.**

impression, n. notion, perasaan (rasa); mark, bekas, kesan; left on mind, kesan; to impress (leave a memory of), memberi (beri) kesan; arouse admiration, mengagumkan (kagum).

impressive, adj. to the eye, as a building, hebat (pada pandangan).

improbable, adj. tak akan (jadi), tak

mungkin.

impromptu, *adj.* dengan tidak bersiap (siap) dahulu.

improper, *adj. unseemly,* tak senonoh; *obscene,* lucah.

improve, *v. intr. as sick person,* beransur (ansur) baik; *as a student,* beransur pandai, maju; *as relieved from pain or poverty,* lega; *attain higher standard,* meningkat (tingkat) ke atas; *to ~, make better, as conditions of life,* mengelokkan (elok), membaikkan (baik); *to get better generally,* bertambah (tambah) baik.

impudent, *adj. cheeky,* megak, nakal; *shameless,* tak silu-silu.

impugn, *v. to express doubts about the truth or honesty of,* mengesyaki, menyatakan kekhuatiran.

impulsive, *adj.* ikut gerak hati sahaja.

impunity, *n. exemption from punishment,* bebas dari hukuman atau cedera.

in, *prefix when denoting 'not', can often be expressed by placing* tidak, *or in the case of a verb,* tak dapat, *before the positive word: ~delible,* tak dapat dihapuskan; *also by the use of* tidak *with the prefix* ter-: *~curable,* tak terubat (ubat).

in, *prep. (space)* di; *~side or within the space of,* (di)dalam; *~ certain contexts,* pada.

inappropriate, *adj.* tidak sesuai (dengan), tidak kena (pada masa).

inaugurate, *v. tr. initiate the public usse of (building, etc.),* merasmikan (rasmi).

inauspicious, *adj. ill-omened, of time for action,* nahas, malang, celaka.

incalculable, *adj.* tidak terhitung (hitung).

incantation, *n.* mantera, petua; *to utter ~s,* menjampi (jampi), membaca (baca) petua.

incapable, *adj. not up to the job,* tidak cekap; *not qualified,* tidak layak.

incarnation, *n. an embodiment in human form,* penjelmaan (jelma); *in animal form,* jadi-jadian.

incendiary, *adj. malicious setting on fire of property; (of bomb, etc.) intended to cause fires,* pembakaran, penghasutan.

incense, *n.* kemenyan, setanggi, dupa.

incentive, *n. impelling to line of action,* umpan (fig.); *to serve as an ~, stimulate,* buat perangsang (rangsang); *the 'profit ~',* 'sistem' cari untung.

incessant, *adj.* tak putus-putus, berjujuh (jujuh).

incest, *n.* sumbang; *to commit ~,* melakukan (laku) sumbang (dengan).

inch, *n.* 'inci'; *give an ~ and he wants an ell,* beri betis, hendakkan paha, *(give the calf and he wants the thigh).*

incident, *n.* kejadian (jadi), peristiwa (istiwa).

incise, *v. tr. as a pattern,* mengukir, (ukir); *lightly as a rubber tree,* menuris (turis), menoreh (toreh); *make a very small incision,* petik; *surgically,* membelah (belah); *surgical incision,* pembelahan; *on a rubber tree,* caruk; *~d,* terukir; *esp. as opposed to 'in relief',* tenggelam.

incite, *v. tr.* hasut; *~ to rage,* mengapi-apikan (api).

incivility, *n.* kelakuan (laku) biadab.

inclined, *adj. sloping, leaning over,* condong; *~ to,* condong hati nak, cenderung hati nak; *to ~ to the right or left when walking,* berjalan (jalan) serung.

include, *v. tr.* mengandungi (kandung), masuk(kan); *to comprise, cover,* meliputi (liput); *'embrace',* merangkum (rangkum); *including,* termasuk; *not excluding,* tidak ketinggalan (tinggal).

incognito, *adj. to be ~,* memakai (pakai) nama samaran.

incoherent, *adj. not coherent, inconsequential,* tiada hujung pangkal, tidak bersambung.

income, *n.* pendapatan (dapat); *~ tax,* cukai pendapatan.

incomparable, *adj.* tak terlawan, tiada taranya, tak berbanding (banding).

incompatible, *adj. not affinities,* tidak seraksi; *esp. of proposed bride and* *bridegroom*, bukan pertemuan (temu); *inconsistent with*, bertentangan (tentang) dengan, tidak sesuai dengan, berlawanan (lawan) dengan; *inconsistencies (differences, as between two stories)*, perbedaan.

incomprehensible, *adj.* tidak dapat dimengerti; *can't make head or tail of it (of a document)*, tidak dapat difahami.

inconceivable, *adj.* tak terupa (rupa) dek akal, tidak dapat dibayangkan, digambarkan.

incongruous, *adj. not in harmony or agreement*, canggung, tidak selaras, tak seimbang, *incongruity, n.*

inconsiderate, *adj.* tidak berfikir (fikir), tidak timbang rasa; *see* **selfish.**

inconsistent, *adj. see* **incompatible.**

inconspicuous, *adj.* tidak nyata, tidak menarik perhatian.

incontrovertible, *adj. cannot be denied,* tidak dapat dinafikan.

increase, *v. intr.* bertambah (tambah); *increasingly* — , bertambah — ; *rise in scale, stage by stage,* meningkat (tingkat); *~ number of,* memperbanyakkan (banyak).

incredible, *adj.* mustahil; *preposterous,* tak masuk akal, mana bulih?; *it can't be,* masakan!; *when pigs fly* —, kalau kucing bertanduk (tanduk) baharu —, *(when cats get horns, then (and not till then) —).*

increment, *n.* tambahan (gaji).

incubate, *v. tr. sit on eggs,* mengeram (ram).

inculcate, *v. tr. as doctrine,* menanam (tanam) ke dalam hati; *teach persistently,* mengajarkan (ajar) bertubi-tubi.

incur, *v. intr. as loss, punishment, wound,* kena, tertimpa, mendatangkan.

incurable, *adj.* tak terubat (ubat).

indebted, *adj.* berhutang (hutang); *heavily in debt,* banyak terhutang wang; *~ for kindness,* terhutang budi; *~ for benefits,* berhutang jasa.

indecent, *adj.* lucah, tidak senonoh, biadab.

indecorous, *adj.* tidak senonoh,

melanggar sopan santun.

indeed, *conj.* sesungguhnya.

indemnify, *v. tr. guarantee against loss,* menjamin; *enter into an ~ bond,* mengikat (ikat) jamin; *compensate,* mengganti (ganti) kerugian (rugi).

independent, *adj. as a State,* merdeka; *as an individual, e.g., a politician,* bebas; *as not controlled by Government, of an institution,* bersendiri (sendiri); berdikari; *of ~ means,* jaga harta sendiri; *see* **autonomous.**

indescribable, *adj.* tidak terperi (peri); *as of a hopeless state of confusion,* tak ketahuan (tahu), tidak dapat digambarkan.

indict, *v. tr. prosecute,* mendakwa (dakwa); *charge,* menuduh (tuduh), menuntut.

indifferent, *adj. taking no interest,* bersikap (sikap) acuh tak acuh.

indignant, *adj. moved by anger or scorn,* berang (marah) terutamanya kerana ketidakadilan atau tuduhan yang tidak patut.

indigenous, *adj. native,* asli.

indigestion, *n.* makan tidak hazam; *flatulence,* segah-perut; *stomach-ache,* sakit-perut.

indigo, *n.* tarum, nila.

indirect, *adj. as taxation,* secara tidak langsung; *to suffer consequences ~ly (like a person getting wet indoors),* kena tempias.

indiscreet, *adj. loose-tongued,* bocor mulut; *dangerous babbler,* cabulmulut, tak bijaksana.

indiscriminately, *adv. without aim, without thought,* buta tuli; *without selection,* tak pilih-pilih; *of eating,* ambil makan; *'everything goes' (of an unscrupulous or greedy person),* bujur lalu, lintang lalu, *(lengthways it gets through and crossways it gets through).*

indispensable, *adj.* perlu, sangat mustahak, tidak boleh diketepikan.

indisposed, *adj. ill, sick,* sakit.

indistinct, *adj. faintly visible or audible,*

sayup, redam; *visible, as through a haze,* balam-balam; *vague, not clear,* samar-samar.

individual, *adj. an ~,* seorang; *~ism,* perseorangan; *see* **personality.**

indoctrinate, *v. tr. instil (political or religious) doctrine, esp. by gradual and crafty methods,* menanam (tanam) (fahaman, 'ideoloji') ke dalam hati.

inducement, *n. through the ~ of, through the persuasion of,* dengan pujukan —; *through the incitement of,* dengan asutan —.

indulge, *v. tr. freely gratify a person, 'spoil',* memanjakan (manja); *give undue licence to,* beri muka; *~ oneself,* memuaskan (nafsu, dll).

industries, *n. manufactures, etc.,* perusahaan (usaha).

industrious, *adj. rajin,* berusaha (usaha); *esp. in studies,* bertekun (tekun); tabah.

ineffable, *adj.* tidak dapat dibayangkan, tidak terperi, tak terkatakan.

inept, *adj.* tidak layak; tidak pada tempatnya; janggal.

inevitable, *adj.* tak dapat dielakkan (elak), atau dihindarkan; *it must be that,* tak dapat tidak; *the ~ hour (of death),* ajal.

inexact, *adj.* kurang tepat/saksama.

inexperienced, *adj. 'raw',* mentah; *'green',* hijau lagi; *unsophisticated,* belum tahu hal; *see* **experience.**

infant, *n. legal,* belum cukup umur, belum baligh, belum dewasa; *see* **baby, child.**

infantry, *n.* tentera berjalan (jalan) kaki.

infect, *v. tr.* menjangkit (jangkit) kepada; hinggap kepada; *~ious,* berjangkit, menular (tular); *~ion,* kuman, jangkitan.

infer, *v. tr.* dapati, mengambil (ambil) kesimpulan (simpul).

inferior, *adj.* kurang baik; *one's '~s',* orang bawahan; *~ to —,* tak boleh lawan —, tidak sebanding dengan —; *esp. in depreciation of one's own effort,* yang tidak sepertinya.

infertile, *adj. as an egg, seed,* sambang.

infest, *v. tr. as vermin, pirates, swarming*

unresisted, bermaharajalela (lela), berleluasa (leluasa), didapati dengan banyaknya; *a river ~ed with crocodiles,* sungai yang banyak buaya.

infidel, *n. pervert from Islam,* murtad; *back-slider,* rosak-iman; *see.* **heathen.**

infidelity, *adj. see* **false, traitor.**

infiltrate, *v. intr. as skirmishers or as subversive elements,* menyeluk (seluk), menyusup (susup), menyeludup (seludup); *as fluid,* mesra.

inflamed, *p.p. as feelings or as a wound,* radang; *swollen,* bengkak; *inflammation of the lungs,* radang paru-paru.

inflammable, *adj. easily burned,* mudah terbakar (bakar).

inflate, *v. tr. pump up, as a tyre,* mengisi tayar dengan udara; *~ prices, raise artifically,* tarik harga; *~ the chest,* membusungkan (busung) dada, melembungkan (lembung) dada.

inflexible, *adj. unyielding,* tegar hati, keras.

influence, *n.* pengaruh (aruh); *to get ~ over a person ('lead by the nose'),* tanjul hidung, cucuk hidung.

inform, *v. tr.* berkhabar (khabar), beri tahu, maklumkan, bilang; *'~ation received',* suatu rahsia; *police ~er,* hantu polis; *~ation, news,* khabar; *esp. in the nature of an official statement,* penerangan (terang), maklumat; *well ~ed,* berpengetahuan; *Minister of Information,* Menteri Penerangan (terang).

informally, *adv. not officially,* secara tidak resmi.

infringe, *v. tr. as rules,* melanggar (langgar) (peraturan, dll).

ingratiate, *v. tr. ~ oneself, seek favour,* cari muka; membuat sesuatu supaya disayangi.

ingredients, *n.* ramuan, perawis.

inhabit, *v. tr.* duduk di, tinggal di, diam di; *esp. as be domiciled in,* bermastautin (mastautin) di-; *~s,* isi negeri, penduduk, penghuni (huni).

inhale, *v. tr. draw in breath,* tarik nafas; *breathe in, suck in,* hisap; *snuffle up,* hidu; *as for a cold,* tangas hidung.

inharmonious, *adj. not fitting in,* tidak sesuai (dengan); *as music or language,* canggung, janggal.

inherit, *v. tr.* menerima (terima) sebagai pesaka; mewarisi (waris).

inimitable, *adj.* tak dapat ditiru, tak ada bandingnya.

initials, *n.* huruf pangkal.

initiate, *v. tr. take the lead in,* menganjurkan (anjur); *initiative,* 'initiatif'; *to take the initiative, be a pioneer,* merintis (rintis) jalan; *he lacks intiaitive,* kurang ikhtiar; daya utama; dia menantikan (nanti) ikan timbul, *(he waits for the fish to come to the surface); just 'follows the crowd',* jadi pak turut, jadi tukang ekor; *the 'lead', the main impulse behind a movement,* daya utama; *afraid to take the initiative,* takut mengikut (ikut) jalan tak berentas (rentas), *(afraid to follow a way, the trace for which has not been cut).*

inject, *v. tr. by syringe,* cucuk, menginjik ('injik'), menyuntik (suntik); *give an intravenous ~ion,* cucuk urat; *give an intra-muscular ~ion,* cucuk kelasa; *to give an anti- (cholera) ~ion,* cucuk pencegah (taun).

injured, *p.p.* luka, cedera.

injustice, *n.* aniaya, ketidakadilan.

ink, *n.* dakwat, tinta; *~-pot,* bekas dakwat.

inland, *adj. away from the sea,* sebelah hulu, sebelah darat, pedalaman.

innate, *adj. see* **natural.**

innocent, *adj.* tak calah; *of sin,* tak berdosa (dosa).

innovation, *n.* pembaharuan (baharu).

innuendo, *n.* sindiran.

innumerable, *adj.* tak terhitung (hitung).

inoculate, *v. tr.* menanam (tanam) benih penyakit (sakit); *see* **inject, vaccinate.**

inquest, *n.* penyiasatan (siasat) kematian (mati).

inquire, *v. tr. ask,* tanya; meminta keterangan; *'nose around',* menjolok-jolok; *make discreet inquiries,* merisik (risik), menyelidiki; *thorough inquiries,* usul periksa; *preliminiary inquiry (in*

Court), pemeriksaan awal; *see* **investigate.**

inquisitive, *adj.* suka sangat mengambil tahu hal orang, ingin tahu; *see* **spy.**

ins-and-outs, *n. subtleties, niceties, finer points, 'ropes',* seluk-beluk.

insatiable, *adj.* tak puas-puas, tak boleh kenyang.

insect, *n.* binatang yang merayap (rayap), serangga.

insensible, *adj.* tak sedarkan diri, tidak peka, tidak dapat merasakan; *see* **anaesthetic, faint.**

inseparable, *adj. cannot be parted,* tak dapat diceraikan, atau dipisahkan; seperti keroncor* dengan belangkas, *(like a pair of king-crabs).*

insert, *v. tr.* masuk(kan); *as knife into belt,* menyisip (sisip); *esp. between two surfaces,* selitkan; *as an article in a newspaper,* suntingkan.

inside, *prep. and adv.* (di)dalam; *~out,* balik-bokong; *an ~ (at football),* apit; *'~ job',* pencuri (curi) dalam selimut, *(a thief in the blanket).*

insignia, *n. badge,* lencana; *symbol or arms,* lambang; *regalia,* alat kerajaan (raja), alat pawai; *~ of rank,* tanda pangkat; *of an order,* pingat.

insincere, *adj.* tidak jujur, tidak sungguh; *~ invitation,* ajak* ayam; *see* **humbug.**

insipid, *adj.* tawar hambar.

insist, *v. intr. on doing something,* berkeras (keras) nak.

insolent, *adj.* sombong, angkuh; *esp. in showing lack of respect to dignitaries,* takbur.

inspect, *v. tr.* periksa; *look closely at,* bedek, belek; *oversee,* menyelia (selia).

inspiration, *n.* ilham.

instal, *v. tr. in office,* melantik (lantik); *as Ruler,* tabalkan; *put in position,* menempatkan (tempat); *as machinery,* pasang; *equip with,* melengkapkan (lengkap) dengan; *military ~lations (buildings),* bangun-bangunan tentera.

instalment, *n.* ansuran; *pay by ~s,* bayar berangsur-angsur; *particularly of ~ of repayment to a money-lender,* gusti.

511

instance, *n. occasion of an occurrence,* kali; *for ~,* misalnya.

instant, *n. an ~,* saat, sekejap; *~ly,* pada saat itu juga; *before you could say Jack Robinson,* tak dan baca bismillah, *(before you could say, in God's Name); see* **once.**

instead, *prep.* ganti; selain daripada.

instigate, *v. tr. urge to,* ajak; *incite,* hasut.

instinct, *n. innate propensity,* naluri.

institute, *v. tr.* mendirikan (diri), menubuhkan (tubuh); institut.

instruct, *v. tr. teach,* mengajar (ajar); *train,* melatih (latih); *~ions to be followed: command,* hukum; *precept,* petua; *for guidance,* panduan; *for taking medicine,* pelisa.

insubordinate, *adj.* bantah, derhaka, melawan.

insult, *v. tr. humiliate publicly,* menghinakan (hina), menjatuhkan maruah, sapu arang di muka; *an ~,* penghinaan (hina); *to swallow an ~,* menelan (telan) penghinaan.

insurance, *n.* 'insuran'; *(fig.) security against event,* jaminan; *life ~,* insuran nyawa.

insurrection, *n.* pemberontakan (berontak), penderhakaan (derhaka).

intact, *adj.* sempurna.

integrate, *v. tr. combine into a whole,* menyatukan (satu); *integration, harmonious union,* berpaduan (padu); *racial integration,* 'integrasi'.

integrity, *n.* kejujuran (jujur).

intellect, *n.* akal; *~ual; wise,* bijak; *learned,* terpelajar (ajar); *an ~ual,* cendekiawan; *the ~uals,* kaum cerdik cendekia.

intelligence, *n.* akal; *~ test,* ujian menduga (duga) akal; *~ quotient (I.Q.),* darjah kecerdasan (cerdas), angka kecerdasan; *'~' (secret sources of information, etc.),* sumber perisikan (risik); *Central ~ Agency,* pusat perisik America; *see* **officer.**

intelligent, *n.* berakal (akal), cerdas; *the 'intelligensia',* orang cerdik-pandai.

intend, *v. intr. going to,* hendak; *(more definite),* berhajat (hajat); *intention (purpose),* hajat; *(aim),* tujuan; *(fixed purpose),* niat, hasrat.

intensify, *v. tr. as efforts,* memperhebatkan (hebat); mempergiatkan; *to keep (fowls) on the intensive system,* menternak (ternak) (ayam) secara intensif.

intentionally, *adv.* sengaja.

interdependent, *adj.* saling bergantung (gantung).

interest, *n. on money,* bunga (wang), faedah; *as usury,* riba; *~s (rights, concerns),* kepentingan (penting); *~ed in,* minat, perhatian; *connected with (e.g., an enterprise),* berhubung (hubung) dengan.

interesting, *adj. attractive, entertaining,* yang menarik (tarik) hati, seronok; *to take an interest in (usually in negative),* ambil pusing.

interfere, *v. intr.* campur, masuk tangan; *~ with, molest,* usik; *act obstructively,* ganggu; *meddle with,* kotak-katikkan, *'tread on people's toes',* memijak (pijak) benang* arang orang; *poke nose in private affairs,* menjaga-jaga tepi* kain orang.

interior, *adj. inside,* dalam; *hinterland,* darat, hulu, daerah pendalaman.

interlaced, *adj. as links of of a chain,* jerait; *as fingers,* berkait (kait).

interlinked, *adj. as links in a chain,* berjeraitan (jerait), jerepet; *joined at the ends,* bersambung (sambung); *hooked on to one another or (fig.) connected with,* berkait (kait).

interlude, *n. short entertainment, e.g., betweeen acts of play,* selangan, selingan.

intermediary, *n. go-between,* orang tengah, (orang) perantara (antara).

interminable, *adj.* tak putus-putus; *esp. as a speech,* meleret-leret.

intermittent, *adj.* berselang-selang.

intern, *v. tr.* mengurung (kurung); *~ee,* orang tahanan.

internal, *adj. as, home affairs,* dalam negeri; *purely ~ question,* soal rumahtangga sahaja.

international, adj. antara bangsa; ~ law, undang-undang antara bangsa.

interplant, v. tr. menyulam (sulam).

interpret, v. tr. menterjemahkan (terjemah), mentafsirkan —; ~er, juru bahasa; ~ation of dreams, takbir mimpi; explain abstruse words, etc., esp. in a religious book, mentafsirkan (tafsir).

interrogate, v. tr. menyoal (soal), periksa; interrogation, temu tanya, penyoalan.

interrupt, v. tr. by words, masuk mulut; interpose a remark, menyampuk (sampuk), mencelah (celah); noisy ~ions (as to a speech), kata-kata mengganggu (ganggu); to ~ communications, mengganggu perhubungan (hubung).

interspersed, adj. scattered about here and there, berselerak (selerak); alternating with, bersulam (sulam), selangseli.

interval, n. selang; recess, masa rihat.

intervene, v. intr. campur tangan.

interview, v. tr. meet, berjumpa (jumpa), bertemu (temu), 'interbiu'; be received in audience, menghadap (hadap); test ~ for a job, etc., temuduga, wawancara.

intestine. n. qut, usus.

intimate, adj. of friend, karib, rapat, bermesra-mesra, kenal-biasa; to associate ~ly with, berjinak-jinak dengan.

intimidated, p.p. put off action through fear, tergerapak (gerapak); mengancam, mengugut.

intolerable, adj. tidak tertahan (tahan), tidak terderita (derita).

intolerant, adj. see **bigoted**; ~ of, have no patience with, tak sabarkan; lacking sympathy, tidak bertimbang (timbang) rasa.

intonation, n. runtunan suara.

intoxicant, n. intoxicating liquor, minuman keras; see **drunk**.

intricate, adj. berjalin-jalin, rumit, sulit; intricacies (of a problem or a building), selok-belok.

intrigue, v. intr. pakat-pakat, rancangan rahsia; work for some end, cari jalan;

work tortuously, pintas-memintas; engage in dirty politics, main 'politik' kotor; engage in subtle ~s, menjalankan (jalan) jarum-jarum.

introduce, v. tr. make person known to another, memperkenalkan (kenal); bring forward as a Bill or motion, memajukan (maju), kemukakan (muka); introduction (to book), pendahuluan (dahulu), kata pengantar (antar).

intrude, v. intr. barge in, merempuh (rempuh) masuk; trespass violently, menceroboh (ceroboh) masuk.

intuition, n. gerak hati; intuitive perception, mata hati, mengikut gerak hati.

invade, v. tr. masuk; attack, melanggar (langgar), menyerang (serang).

invalid, adj. not valid, tidak sah; as against the rules, tak aci.

invalid, n. person suffering from illness, orang mengidap (idap) sakit; see **valetudinarian**.

invaluable, adj. tak ternilai (nilai).

invent, v. tr. mereka (reka), mencipta; ~or, perekacipta.

invert, v. tr. as bottle, tonggengkan.

invest, v. tr. money, menanam (tanam) modal; be ~ed with, as high office, menyandang (sandang).

investigate, v. tr. periksa; esp. as police, siasat; make full examination, menyelidik; get to the heart of things, mengumbut (umbut).

inveterate, adj. rooted, as a habit, berakar-urat (akar), sudah menjadi (jadi) amalan.

invigilate, v. tr. mengawasi, mengawal, memerhati.

invincible, adj. tak terlawan (lawan), tak dapat dikalahkan.

invisible, adj. not in sight, tak nampak; not obviously visible (as owing to darkness), tak ketara; through magic art, halimun.

invite, v. tr. mengajak (ajak); to a party, menjemput (jemput), mengundang (undang); as welcome in, mempersilakan (sila); ~ formally or as in inviting *applications for a post,* pelawa; *written invitation,* surat jemputan, 'kad' jemputan.

involve, *v. tr. as a third party in a quarrel,* membabitkan *(babit);* ~*d (in affair, plot, etc.),* terlibat (libat), bersangkutan (sangkut); *not simple,* berserabutan (serabut); *see* **complicated, immersed.**

invulnerable, *adj.* kebal.

inward, *adj. mental, spiritual,* batin; *as opposed to material,* rohani.

irascible, *adj.* pemarah (marah); lekas meradang.

irksome, *adj. tiresome,* yang membosankan, yang mengganggu.

iron, *n.* besi; ~ *pyrites,* mas urung; *corrugated* ~ *(sheets),* atap 'zin'; *smoothing* ~, seterika; *strike while the* ~*'s hot,* jangan sejuk gulai di tungku, *(don't let the curry get cold on the stove).*

irony, *n.* sindiran.

irregular, *adv. not duly arranged,* tidak teratur (atur); *not allowed under rules,* tidak sah; *halting, of gait,* pincang-pincut; *as teeth, spikes,* berceranggah-ceranggah.

irrelevant, *adj. separate matter,* lain kira; *not connected with,* tidak berkenaan (kena) dengan.

irreligious, *adj. having no religion,* tidak beragama (agama); *back-slider,* rosak iman; *see* **heathen, heresy, pervert.**

irresponsible, *adj. see* **flighty**; *(acting) irresponsibly (hastily and thoughtlessly),* terburu-buru, tidak berfikir (fikir) dahulu, tak bertanggungjawab; *'mucking about' recklessly,* membuat (buat) tak ke tahuan (tahu); ~ *talker,* lidah tak bertulang (tulang).

irrigate, *v. tr.* mengairkan (air), menjiruskan (jirus); *irrigation runnel,* tali air, pengairan.

irritate, *v. tr. annoy,* menjengkelkan, menyakitkan hati; *make an irritating noise,* bising; *irritable,* lekas marah, bengkeng; *see* **nag.**

isinglas, *n. fish-gelatine,* lupa-lupa, belida.

island, *n.* pulau.

isolated, *p.p.* terpencil (pencil), terasing (asing); *in solitude,* keseorangan (orang).

issue, *v. intr. flow out (as a river),* mengalir (alir) keluar; *emerge,* terbit; *to* ~, *as a book or newspaper,* terbitkan, keluarkan; *an* ~ *(as of a newspaper),* keluaran (luar).

isthmus, *n.* segenting tanah.

it, *pron.* ia; *that thing,* benda itu.

itchy, *adj.* gatal, miang; *the* ~ , kudis.

item, *n.* perkara, acara, hal.

ivory, *n.* gading, danta.

J

jab, *v. tr. poke,* cucuk, jolok; *n.* cucukan, tikaman.

jacinth, *n.* batu yakut.

jack, *n. i. at cards,* pekak.

jacket, *n.* baju; *particularly Western style* ~, 'kot'.

jackfruit, *n. (sp.),* nangka, cempedak.

jagged, *adj. notched, as blade,* sumbing; *with gaps, as teeth,* rompang, rongak; *as partly broken surface with projections,* congkah.

jail, *n. see* **prison.**

jamb, *n. side-post of door,* jenang pintu.

jammed, *adj. between two surfaces,* tersepit (sepit), terselit (selit); *as in an aperture,* terserat (serat); *as a wheel against a post,* tersagat (sagat); *athwart an opening,* tersengkang (sengkang); *as part of a machine,* sudah 'jem'; *as crowded street,* penuh-sesak; *esp. as cars in a traffic-block,* berjejal-jeljal; *as key in lock,* terlekat (lekat).

January, *n.* bulan Januari.

Japan, *n.* negeri Jepun; *Japanese,* orang Jepun.

jar, *n. for bathroom,* tempayan; *small, for storing water,* guri; *small, esp. for ginger,* takar.

jarring, *adj. discordant, as misused word,* canggung; *to eyes or ears,* janggal.

jasmine, *n.* bunga melur, bunga melati.

jaundice, *n.* penyakit (sakit) kuning.

javelin, *n.* campak buang, pendahan, lembing (buang-buangan).

jaw-bone, *n.* tulang rahang.

jealous, *adj.* cemburu; *envious,* iri hati; *see* **envy.**

jeans, *n.* celana 'paip', jean.

jeer, *v. intr.* mengejek, mencemuhkan.

jelly, *n.* agar-agar, lengkong; *a thin Chinese* ~, cincau.

jelly-fish, *n.* ubur-ubur; *'water-flea',* am-pai-ampai; *large, stinging* ~, geronggong.

jemmy, *n. hooked iron used by burglars,* cangkuk tingkap.

jeopardy, *n. in* ~, dalam bahaya.

jeopardize, *v. tr.* membahayakan.

jerk, *v. tr.* sentak; *esp. of short sharp* ~, enjut; *to* ~, *flick, as a marble,* jintik.

Jerusalem, *n.* Baitul-mukadis.

jest, *v. intr.* bergurau (gurau), berseloroh (seloroh).

Jesus, *n.* Nabi Isa, al-Masih.

jetty, *n.* 'jetti', pangkalan, bagan.

Jew, *n.* orang Yahudi; *the children of Israel,* bani Israel.

jewellery, *n. generally,* barang mas, barang kemas; *gems,* permata; *jeweller,* tukang mas, jauhari.

jingle, *v. intr. as coins, etc.* berdencing (dencing), bergemerecang (gemerecang).

Job, *n. see* **work.**

jockey, *n.* 'joki', *to* ~ *up prices, force up artificially,* tarik harga, *v. tr. & i.* mem bohongi, mengakali, menipu.

jocose, *adj.* jenaka, lucu.

jinnee, *n. spirit able to appear in many forms,* jin, jin iblis.

jog, *v. intr. up and down, as on a rough road,* terunggit-unggit; *as when conforming to the gait of a horse,* mengikut (ikut) mengenjak (enjak) kuda.

John Bull, *n. (sl.),* Mat Salleh.

join, *v. tr. as a society,* masuk, jadi ahli; *to connect on,* sambung; *connect up,* hubung; *to* ~ *together in parallel strips,* menjalinkan (jalin); *to* ~ *(in doing),* turut (serta) —, ikut (serta) —; *to* '~ *up',* masuk tentera; *bring together, as severed portions,* cantumkan; ~*ted,* bersendi (sendi); *see* **connect.**

jointly, *adv.* bersama-sama.

joints, *n. as of body,* sendi; *nodes of*

bamboo, buku; *space between nodes,* ruas.

joists, *n.* jeriau, kayu palang.

joke, *n. intr.* kelakar, senda gurau; *practical* ~, lelucon yang dimaksudkan supaya seseorang menjadi bahan tertawa orang; *chaff, spoof,* menggiat (giat), memperolok-olokkan; *to jest,* berseloroh (seloroh), bergurau (gurau), berjenaka (jenaka); *play pranks, 'clown it',* berkelekar (kelekar); *only a* ~!, main-main sahaja!; *jokingly,* secara bergurau; *no* ~! *(serious matter, surprising),* bukan main!

jollification, *n. to have a* ~, bersuka-sukaan (suka), bersuka-ria, buat 'joli'.

jolt, *v. intr.* ~*ing up and down,* terungkit-ungkit, bergerak dengan terenjut-enjut.

joss, *n. Chinese sacred image,* tok pekong; ~*-sticks,* setanggi, kemenyan, gaharu Cina, colok.

jostling, *v. intr. as in a crowd,* bergelut-gelut, sondol-menyondol, berpusu-pusu.

journal, *n. daily record as diary,* buku harian, jurnal.

journalist, *n.* wartawan, pemberita (berita).

journey, *n.* perjalanan (jalan); *by sea,* pelayaran (layar); *by air,* penerbangan (terbang); *esp of a far* ~, pengembaraan (kembara).

joy, *n.* gembira, kemeriahan (meriah), keriangan (riang), kesukaan (suka); ~*s and sorrows,* suka duka.

jubilant, *adj.* sangat girang, bersorak-sorai, *jubilation, n., sorak-sorai.*

jubilee, *n. 50th anniversary,* hari ulang tahun yang kelima-puluh.

judge, *n.* hakim, *under Islamic law,* Kathi; *judgment (decision),* keputusan (putus); *Day of Judgment,* hari kiamat, yaum'l kiamat, hari pembalasan (balas), hari pengadilan (adil); *sit in judgment on, esp, in the sense of criticise adversely,* menghakimkan.

judicious, *adj.* bijaksana.

juggle, *v. intr.* main sunglap, *v. tr.* men-

ipu.

juice, *n. generally,* air; *esp. of palms, taken for making sugar, toddy, etc.,* nira; *sap,* getah; *expressed* ~, air perahan.

July, *n.* bulan Julai.

jumbled, *adj.* campur-baur; ~ *sale, n.* penjualan barang-barang lama (di gereja atau sekolah).

jump, *v. intr.* lompat; ~ *down,* terjun; ~ *up and down, as in excitement,* melonjak-lonjak; *see* **spring.**

junction, *n. of ways,* persimpangan (simpang); *joining point of woodwork, etc.,* perapatan (rapat); *place where roads cross,* simpang; *fork,* cabang; *esp. of rivers,* pertemuan (temu); sungai; *at this juncture,* dalam keadaan seperti sekarang ini.

June, *n.* bulan Jun.

jungle, *n.* hutan; *virgin* ~, rimba; *untrodden* ~, hutan banat; *secondary* ~, berlukar, rok; *when large and old,* belukar, tua; *scrub,* semak.

junior, *adj. in age,* lebih muda; *in seniority,* kiri; *in rank,* berpangkat (pangkat) lebih rendah.

junk, *n.* 1. *sailing vessel; Chinese,* wangkang, jong; *Malay,* perahu. 2. barang lama.

jurisdiction, *n. authority,* kuasa; *area of* ~, kawasan.

jurisprudence, *n.* ilmu hukum.

just, *adj.* adil.

justify, *v. tr. show that action was right,* menghalalkan (halal), membenarkan, membela, mempertahankan.

just like that, *adv. e.g., without obvious reason, without effort, without protest, without acknowledgement,* (dengan) begitu sahaja.

just now, *adv.* tadi; *recently,* baharu lagi; *a moment age,* baru saat ini.

jut out, *v. intr. as a promontory,* menganjur (anjur); *see* **project.**

juveniles, *n.* pemuda (muda) pemudi (mudi); budak-budak; *see* **teenagers.**

juxtapose, *v. tr.* meletakkan damping berdampingan, berjajar.

K

keel, *n.* lunas.

keen, *adj. see* **sharp;** *zealous,* giat; *determined on policy,* keras; *see* **fan.**

keep, *v. tr.* simpan; *as livestock,* bela, pelihara; ~ *out (drive away),* halau; ~ *off (repel),* tolak; *to* ~ *(continue undecayed),* tahan; *to* ~ *a promise,* pegang janji, menepati (tepat) janji; ~ *up with,* jalan sama cepat dengan; sejajar dengan; *to* ~ *up with the Joneses (the neighbours),* tak mahu mengalah (alah) dengan jiran.

keeper, *n.* pengawas (awas); penjaga (jaga); pemegang (pegang).

keepsake, *n.* tanda mata; cenderamata; kenang-kenangan; *something that has been worn,* bekas tubuh.

kettle, *n.* cerek, kendi.

key, *n.* anak kunci, kunci; *bunch of* ~*s,* se jambak kunci; ~*hole,* lubang kunci; ~*s of a piano,* mata 'piano'; *winding* ~, kunci, pemutar (putar); *to hold the* ~ *(fig.) (to a situation),* memegang (pegang) teraju.

kick, *v. tr.* tendang; *esp with the side of the foot,* sepak; ~*ing and stamping, as a restive horse,* tendang terajang.

kid, *n. young goat,* anak kambing.

kidnap, *v. tr.* membawa (bawa) lari, menculik (culik).

kidney, *n.* buah pinggang, ginjal.

kill, *v. tr. slay,* bunuh; *by cutting throat for food,* sembelih, potong; *cause death of,* mematikan (mati); *take life of,* ambil nyawa; *by squashing, as an insect,* tindas; ~ *time,* menghilangkan (hilang) masa; *'do for', 'do in',* pendekkan riwayat, hapuskan riwayat *(sl.).*

kiln, *n. furnace for baking bricks, etc.,* relau, genahar.

kin, *n. family,* keluarga; *of some descent,* seketurunan (turun); *kith and* ~, sanak saudara; *next of* ~, saudara kadim.

kind, *adj. benevolent, friendly,* pemurah (murah), baik hati, berbudi (budi); ~ *action,* jasa, budi baik, *treat* ~*ly,* berbuat (buat) budi pada, berbuat jasa pada; *be* ~ *to (help),* tolong.

kind, *n. sort,* bangsa, jenis; *type,* macam, corak; *species,* jenis.

King, *n. H.M. the Paramount Sultan of Malaysia,* Yang Dipertuan Agung; *H.M. the* ~ *of Great Britain,* Baginda 'King',; *generally,* malak; *constitutional monarch,* raja perlembagaan (lembaga).

kingfisher, *n.* burung pekaka, raja udang; *small variety,* binti-binti.

kinked, *adj. as wire,* terkehel; berbelit-belit, *v. tr.* berpintal, membelit. *kinky, as hair,* genjur.

kiss, *v. tr.* cium, *lip to lip, Western style,* mengucup (kecup).

kit, *n. personal equipment,* alat perlengakapan (lengkap); *outfit of tools,* alat-alat.

kitchen, *n. dapur; stove,* tungku; *oven,* dapur.

kite, *n. bird,* lang merah, lang ayam; *toy,* wau, layang-layang.

kitten, *n.* anak kucing.

kitty, *n. the pool in gaming,* tui.

knapsack, *n.* ambung, kantung yang di isi berbagai-bagai keperluan dan digalas di belakang.

knave, *n. in cards,* pekak; *unprincipled person,* petualang (tualang).

knead, *v. tr.* menguli (uli), meramas (ramas), mengadun (adun).

knee, *n.* lutut; ~*-deep,* takat lutut; *to kneel,* bertelut (telut), berlutut.

knick-knacks, *n. small oddments,* barang tetek-bengek, keropas-kerapis.

knife, *n.* pisau; *see* **chop.**

knight, *n. at chess,* kuda.

knit, *v. tr.* merajut (rajut), mengait (kait).

knob, *n.* tombol, cembul.

knock, *v. tr. as on door,* katuk, ketuk; *against,* langgar; *come into contact with,* terkena (kena) pada; *'~ up against', come across casually,* terjeremba (jeremba); *bump into here and there',* merodong (rodong); *~-out competition,* pertandingan (tanding) secara kalah mati (secara pukul mati); *~-kneed,* pengkar ke dalam.

knot, *n.* simpul; *in wood,* mata kayu; *node,* buku; *~ty point,* kesulitan (sulit);
~ted up, as roots, terpiuh (piuh).

know, *v. tr.* tahu; *get to ~,* dapat tahu; *~ a person,* kenal; *~ by sight,* biasa tengok; *~ well,* kenal biasa; *~ledge,* pengatahuan; *~ledge, esp. of arts and sciences,* ilmu; *y'~,* maklumlah; *God knows best,* wallhau alam; *common ~ledge,* pendapat ramai, masyhur.

knuckle, *n.* buku jari; *'bunch of fives',* buku lima; *~duster,* tepi, penumbuk (tumbuk) besi.

kohl, *n. eye-black,* celak.

L

laboratory, n. makmal.

labour, n. (political), buruh; Labour Party, Parti Buruh; hard ~ (in prison), kerja berat; ~ pains, kesakitan semasa hendak melahirkan anak; ~ Exchange, pusat mencari (cari) pekerjaan (kerja), pejabat (jabat) pendaftar (buruh); laborious, adj. rajin, bersungguh-sungguh; laboriously with prolonged physical effort, terkial-kial.

lace, n. renda; ~-edging, biku; shoe-~, tali kasut; gold ~, kida-kida mas.

ladder, n. tangga; rungs of ~, anak tangga; ~ made by lashing pieces of wood to a tree-trunk, sigai.

lade, v. tr. cargo, memuat (muat); heavily ~n, sarat.

ladle, n. senduk; to ~ out, cedok; made of a half-coconut shell pierced for a rough handle, gayung; esp. for cleansing after defecation, cebok.

lady, n. Malay, Cik, puan wanita; European 'mem'; Chinese, nyonya.

lake, n. tasik, danau.

lame, adj. limping, capik, kaki ringkat; lamed, tempang, kecok, pincang; see **hobble**; 'dot-and-carry-one', tiga 'sellndar'.

lament, v. intr. mourn loudly, meratap (ratap); able, of event causing grief, sedih.

lamp, n. lampu, pelita; street ~, lampu tepi jalan; table ~, lampu catuk; electric ~, pelita 'letrik'; pressure ~, lampu 'pam'.

lancet, n. pisau wali; to lance, belah.

land, n. tanah; dry ~, darat; main~, benua, tanah raya; ~ing-stage, pangkalan; ~-slide, tanah runtuh, tanah longsor; ~scape, pemandangan alam; arable ~, tanah tenggala; for rice-~s, see **rice**; to ~, naik ke darat, turun ke darat; esp. of troops, mendarat; set foot on ~, melangkahkan (langkah) kaki ke darat;

forced ~ing, pendaratan terpaksa (paksa); to ~ a blow, mengenakan tumbukan; system of ~-tenure, 'sistem' pemilikan (milik) tanah.

landlord, n. of house, tuan rumah; of land, tuan tanah.

lane, n. lorong; trace cut through jungle, rentis.

language, n. bahasa; ~ normally used by a person, bahasa pengantar (hantar); mother tongue, bahasa ibu; lingua franca, bahasa perantaraan (antara).

languish, v. intr. in sickness, merana (rana); (fig.) in jail, merengkok (rengkok).

lanky, adj. tinggi melonjong (lonjong), tinggi merunjau (runjau).

lantern, n. 'latin', kandil; Chinese ~, tanglung.

lap, n. riba, pangkuan; to ~ up, mengirup (irup), mencerup; sound of loud ~ping noises, cepak, cepak; take on ~, memangku, meriba.

lard, n. lemak babi.

large, adj. besar; of great extent, luas; on a ~ scale, secara besar-besaran.

largesse, n. coins scattered to the people, hambur-hambur, wang hamburan.

larvae, n. wrigglers, esp. of mosquitoes, jintik-jintik, omah-omah; of wasps, tempayak.

larynx, n. pembuluh (buluh) nafas.

last, v. intr. tahan; at ~, lama-lama, akhirnya; ~ year, tahun lalu; ~ (in time), yang akhir sekali; in space, yang di belakang sekali, yang sut sekali; esp. in race, dapat nombor curut, yang terkemudian (kemudian).

late, adj. lewat; too ~, terlewat; dawdling, lambat; ~ at night, jauh malam, larut malam; ~ in the evening, larut petang; too ~, terlewat (lewat), terlambat (lambat); esp. when a fixed time for, *e.g., entering for an examination, has lapsed,* (sudah) lepas masa; *the ~st (newest),* yang terbaru (baru) sekali; *no use crying over spilt milk,* apa boleh buat? nasi sudah menjadi (jadi) bubur, *(what can one do? the rice has got wet and turned to gruel); the ~, see* **deceased.**

lately, *adv.* akhir-akhir ini, baru-baru ini; *of late,* baru-baru ini, tempoh hari.

laterite, *n.* batu merah.

latex, *n.* susu (getah).

lath, *n.* beroti; *used for fastening thatch,* bengkawan; *in plastering,* tepas.

lathe, *n.* bindu; mesin bubut; *to turn in a ~,* melarik (larik).

lather, *n.* buih; *to form ~,* berbuih; *sweat,* peluh.

latitude, *n. line of ~,* garisan lintang.

latrine, *n. see* **lavatory.**

lattice-work, *n.* kisi-kisi; *lattice-shaped openings,* mata punai.

laugh, *v. intr.* gelak tertawa (tawa); *cackle with ~ter,* mengilai (ilai); *bellowing with ~ter,* terbahak-bahak; *~ feebly,* tertawa ambar; *sickly ~,* gelak sumbing; *to guffaw,* tertawa berdekah-dekah; *helpless with ~ter (lit. until the stomach aches),* tertawa sampai sakit perut; *to ~ inwardly, have a quiet ~,* tertawa sendirian; *he shook with ~ter,* (dia tertawa-tawa) sampai bergentar badannya, sampai bergoncang (goncang) bahunya; *see* **giggle;** *to be a ~ing-stock,* menjadi (jadi) ejek-ejekan orang.

launch, *v. tr.* melancarkan (lancar).

laundryman, *n.* 'dobi', benara.

lava, *n.* lahar.

lavatory, *n.* bilik air, jamban; *(polite),* tandas; *(polite) esp. public ~,* tandas awam; *water-closet,* jamban tarik; *see* **defecate, urine.**

lavish, *n.* pemurah (murah); *over-~,* pemboros (boros); *without stint, as supply of rations,* tak berukur (ukur); *to ~ (money),* menghamburkan, membuang-buang (wang).

law, *n.* undang-undang, hukum; *to break*

a ~, melanggar (langgar) undang-undang; *canon ~ (of Islam),* hukum syarak, hukum fikah; *international ~,* undang-undang antarabangsa; *~ful,* sah menurut (turut) undang-undang, halal mengikut hukum syarak; *~-abiding,* rukun; *living in a ~-abiding and peaceful way,* hidup dengan rukun dan damai.

lawn, *n.* halaman; *wide grassy expanse,* padang rumput.

lawyer, *n.* peguam (guam).

laxative, *n.* ubat melawaskan (lawas) buang air besar; *see* **aperient.**

lay, *v. tr. an egg,* bertelur (telur); *~ down arms,* meletakkan (letak) senjata, melucutkan (lucut) senjata.

layout, *n.* rencana umum, susunan.

layer, *n.* stratum, lapisan, petala.

lazy, *adj.* pemalas (malas), berat tulang; *'~-bones',* panjang-belikat; *mere drone,* tahu makan tidur sahaja.

lead, *n. the metal,* timah hitam; *the '~' on a fishing-line,* batu ladung; *sounding ~,* perum.

lead, *v. intr. go ahead,* jalan dahulu, bawa jalan; *~ by the hand,* pimpin; *as an animal,* heret; *see* **head, guide;** *~er, esp. political,* pemimpin (pimpin), penganjur (anjur); *esp. of a movement,* pelopor (lopor); *to ~ to, conduce to,* membawa kepada.

leaf, *n.* daun; *frond,* pelepah; *~y,* rendang, rimbun.

leaky, *adj.* bocor; *to leak (ooze through),* meniris (tiris); *the secret has leaked out,* rahsia sudah bocor; *a leakage,* bocoran.

lean, *adj.* kurus, rincing.

lean, *v. intr. ~ against,* bersandar (sandar) pada; *~ing over (out of perpendicular),* condong; *to ~, v. tr.,* sandarkan (pada); *to ~ athwart (as gun against a log),* langgung pada; *~ on someone's arm for support,* bertumpang (tumpang) sandar dilengan; *see* **support.**

leap, *v. intr. see* **jump;** *~-frog,* lompat katak.

learn, *v. tr. study,* belajar (ajar); *get to*

know, dapat tahu, dapat khabar; ~ *by heart,* hafal; *having '~ed one's lesson',* serik.

learned, *adj.* terpelajar (ajar), berilmu (ilmu), berpengetahuan (tahu), alim, arif; *esp. as great scholar,* pendita; *see* **expert.**

lease, *v. tr. to someone,* sewakan; *from some-one,* menyewa; *mining sub-~,* haptung; ~ *of Government monopoly or of orchard,* pajak; *a new ~ of life,* penghidupan baru.

leash, *n.* tali (tambat); *hold in ~,* mengekang, mengendalikan, menguasai.

least, *adj. smallest,* yang kecil sekali; *at ~,* sekurang-kurang; *(at any rate),* setidak-tidaknya.

leather, *n.* kulit (lembu).

leave, *n. of absence,* cuti; *permission,* izin; *to take one's ~ (depart),* minta diri; *to 'excuse oneself',* minta maaf; *to depart,* lepas; ~ *behind,* meninggalkan (tinggal); ~ *alone (left be),* biar(kan); ~ *go,* lepas(kan); *I'll ~ it to you,* terpulang (pulang) kepada timbangan tuan; *leavings (as of a meal)* sisa.

lecherous, *adj.* jalang; *see* **nymphomania, woman.**

lecture, *n.* syarah, kuliah.

ledge, *n. projecting rock,* batu menganjur (anjur); *a ~ window,* birai jendela.

lee, *n. side away from the wind,* bawah angin; *the ~ of the land,* abal-abal daratan; *go to ~ward,* mengekor (ekor) angin.

leech, *n.* pacat; *horse-~,* lintah; *(fig.) extortionate person,* lintah darat.

left, *adj. ~ (side),* kiri; *on the ~,* sebelah kiri; *~-handed,* kidal; ~ *behind,* tertinggal (tinggal); ~ *far behind,* juah ketinggalan, (sudah) lepas ke belakang; *see* **abandon.**

leg, *n.* kaki; *one-~ged,* berkaki tunggal; *two-~ged,* biped, berkaki dua; *four-~ged,* quadruped, berkaki empat; *to stand on one ~,* berdiri (diri) itik.

legacy, *n.* pemberian (beri) amanat; *devolving by reason of relationship,* pesaka, warisan.

legal, *adj. valid,* sah, halal, menurut (turut) undang-undang.

legend, *n.* cerita purba kala (yang dongeng), legenda, dongeng.

legitimate, *adj. esp. of child,* halal; *see* **legal,** sah menurut undang-undang.

leisure, *n.* senang, kelapangan (lapang), tidak terburu-buru.

lemon, *n.* limau puting; *~-grass,* serai.

lend, *v. tr.* pinjamkan, beri pinjam.

length, *n.* panjangnya; *at ~,* lama-lama; *~wise,* bujur; *to write ~y letter,* memanjangkan (panjang) kalam; *to ~en life,* melanjutkan (lanjut) umur.

lenient, *adj. of a person,* lemah lembut; *of a sentence,* ringan.

leopard, *n.* harimau akar; *the ~ cannot change his spots (character persists),* rupa boleh diubah, tabiat dibawa mati, *(appearance can be altered, but character remains to the grave).*

leper, *n.* orang sakit kusta; *(fig.) disgusting and contemptible person,* anak sumbang, anjing buruk-kepala; ~ *hospital,* rumah sakit kusta; ~ *settlement,* kawasan penempatan (tempat) orang-orang kusta.

less, *adj.* kurang; ~ *than (a specific number),* tak sampai —; *to become ~,* berkurang; *~en in size,* susut.

lesson, *n.* pelajaran (ajar); *piece for learning by heart,* hafalan; *to repeat such a ~,* mengucap (ucap), hafalan; *having 'learned a ~' (warned),* serek; *to get a sharp ~, esp. of a person who has tried to play a trick,* kedapatan (dapat) budi; *teaching, serving to instruct,* pengajaran.

lest, *conj.* takut —, supaya jangan —, supaya tidak.

let, *v. tr. ~ be,* biar; ~ *go,* lepaskan; *(nautical),* 'leggo'; ~ *us —,* baik kita —; *to be '~ down' (of failure of friends to help in time of need), expressed by the aphorism 'the support brings about the fall',* sokongan membawa (bawa) rebah; *see* **lease.**

lethal, *adj. of wound,* parah; *of weapon,* yang boleh menyebabkan (sebab) kematian (mati).

lethargic, *adj.* lemah, lesu; *'doesn't want to die and won't live',* hidup segan, mati tak mahu.

letter, *n. missive,* surat (kiriman), warkat; *~ of the alphabet,* huruf; *covering ~* , surat lampiran, surat yang disertakan; *~ box,* peti surat; *~ case,* bekas untuk mengisi surat.

lettuce, *n.* selada.

leukaemia, *n.* sakit barah darah.

level, *adj.* 1. rata, datar; *on a ~ with (in a horizontal plane),* separas dengan; *sea-~,* aras laut; *trimmed to a ~, as a hedge,* repang; *~-headed,* penyabar (sabar), sempurna akal; *standard of importance or merit,* peringkat; *to ~,* peratakan; *by filling,* menambak (tambak); *to ~ to the ground,* peratakan hingga paras tanah. 2. *~-headed,* sifat bijaksana.

lever, *n.* pengumpil (umpil), tuil; *to ~ up,* tuas, wet.

liable, *adj. as legally bound to,* bertanggung (tanggung) jawab nak; *~ to incur,* harus kena —.

liana, *n.* akar kayu, pokok menjalar (jalar).

libel, *v. tr.* membuat (buat) fitnah atas (dengan surat).

liberate, *v. tr. as from slavery,* bebaskan; *as from prison,* lepaskan.

liberty, *n. see* **free**.

library, *n. public,* balai pustaka, perpustakaan, kutub-khanah; *private,* tempat menyimpan (simpan) 'buku'.

lichen, *n.* lumut.

lick, *v. tr.* jilat; *'salt-~' (mineral spring to which wild animals resort),* sira, jenalek, jenut, bendang air hangat.

lid, *n.* tutup; *dish-cover,* tudung saji.

lie, *n.* bohong, dusta; *to tell lies,* cakap bohong; *Father of Lies,* Dajal; bunkum! karut!

lie, *v. intr. ~ down,* baring; *cast oneself down,* rebahkan diri; *~ face downwards,* meniarap (tiarap); *on the back,* terlentang (lentang); *on the side,* memering (mering).

lieutenant, *n. in Army,* leftenan; *second ~,* leftenan muda; *deputy,* pemangku (pangku), naib, wakil.

life, *n.* nyawa, jiwa; *period of ~,* umur, hayat, usia; *the ~ to come,* akhirat; *all (my) ~,* seumur hidup (saya); *tenacious of ~,* panjang umur; *lifesize,* sebesar dirinya; *way of ~,* cara hidup; *manner or state of a life,* kehidupan; *see* **biography;** *a matter of ~ and death,* perkara hidup mati, soal hidup mati; *long ~ and happiness to —,* selamat berbahagia (bahagia) —; *~-belt,* pelampung, kelampung (lampung).

lift, *v. tr.* angkat; *with an effort, 'hock',* angkut; *get a ~ (in a vehicle),* menumpang (tumpang) (kereta orang); *keep ~ing and lowering, as a bait before fish,* uncat-uncat.

light, *adj. not heavy,* ringan; *as timber,* lempung; *not in darkness,* cerah; *~ed up, esp. by moon or lamps,* terang benderang; *artificial ~,* cahaya terang buatan; *~ as of sun,* cahaya; *moon~,* terang bulan; *flame,* api; *to ~, set fire to,* pasang, lekat api, cucuh api; *show a ~ as with torch,* suluh; *a~, kindled,* hidup; *~ up, show sudden cheerfulness, of face,* berserilah (seri) (muka); *to ~en, e.g., a ship,* anggalkan; *~-fingered,* pandai mencuri; *~-hearted,* senang hati, riang hati; *~-heeled,* pantas.

lighter, *n. barge,* tongkang.

lighthouse, *n.* rumah api.

lightly, *adv. to treat ~ (as unimportant),* mengabaikan (abai), tidak mengambil berat; *deem too easy, not worth bothering about,* mencuaikan (cuai), permudahkan (mudah).

lightning, *n.* kilat; *summer ~,* kenyit; *~-bolt,* lintar; *struck by ~,* kena lintar, kena sambaran kilat; *~-conductor,* dawai penangkap (tangkap) kilat; *see* **flash**.

like, *prep.* seperti, sebagai, serupa dengan, bak; *see* **alike**.

like, *v. tr.* suka, gemar; *have a fancy for,* berkenan (kenan), minat.

likely, *adj.* harus, mungkin; *not ~,* tak

mungkin; *not bloody ~!* tak mungkin sekali!.

limb, *n. of body,* anggota; *of tree,* dahan, cabang, pokok.

lime, *n. caustic substance,* kapur; *quicklime,* kapur mentah; *to ~-wash,* sapu kapur; *bird-~,* getah burung, getah terap; *to catch, esp. with bird-~,* memikat (pikat) (dengan getah terap), menggetah; *the fruit,* limau asam, limau kapas.

limit, *n.* had; *speed-~,* had laju; *see* **boundary;** *~ed,* berhad, terbatas (batas); *~ed liability,* tanggungan berhad; *of intelligence,* singkat; *~ation, that which is lacking,* kekurangan (kurang); *flaw,* cacat; *to know one's ~ation,* kadarkan diri, tahu batasan.

limp, *adj. not stiff,* lembik, lembut; *see* **lame.**

limpid, *adj.* jernih, hening.

line, *n.* baris; *traced,* garisan; *on paper,* satar; *fishing-~,* tali kail; *~s (barracks),* 'berek', kaman; *~s on palm of hand,* retak tangan; *(standing) in a ~,* berbaris; *in ~ with the road,* mengiring (iring) jalan; *clothes-~,* penyidai (sidai) kain, tali sampaian; *body controlling conveyances (e.g., shipping or air),* syarikat (misalan, perkapalan (kapal) atau penerbangan (terbang); *~r (vessel on regular run),* kapal calu; *~ of unbaited hooks, 'spiller',* rawai; *front ~ esp. of war,* barisan depan, garisan peperangan (perang); *~s on face,* kerutan muka; *see* **row.**

linen, *n.* kain rami.

linger, *v. intr.* melengah-lengah, sambil-lewa.

linguist, *n.* ahli bahasa, pendita bahasa.

liniment, *n.* minyak urat, ubat gosok.

lining, *n. inner material,* alas, lapis; *~ of stomach, peritoneum,* selaput perut.

link, *n. of chain,* mata rantai; *as of friendship,* pertalian (tali); *~ed (connected),* berkait (kait), jerepet; *as basic ideas,* secucuk; *as businesses with common owners,* bergabung (gabung).

lintel, *n.* ambang pintu.

lion, *n.* singa.

lip, *n.* bibir; *~-stick,* gincu bibir; *hare-~,* bibir sumbing.

liquefy, *v. intr.* menjadi (jadi) cair.

liquid, *adj.* cair; *sloppy,* bonyor; *~ nourishment, such as broth,* irupan.

liquidate, *v. tr. debts,* menjelaskan (jelas); *fully ~d, of indebtedness,* langsai; *to ~, as an association, club,* bubarkan; *get rid of, remove, as opponents,* singkirkan; *destroy, wipe out,* meleburkan (lebur).

liquor amnii, *n. the discharge preceding birth,* tuban-tuban.

lissom, *adj. lithe, slender,* lampai, gemalai.

list, *n.* daftar, senarai, *see* **heel.**

listen, *v. tr.* dengar; *strain ears,* pasang telinga; *~ to, heed,* dengarkan; dengarkan kata enggang, makan buah belolok, *(if you ~ to a hornbill, you'll eat (inedible) belolok fruit; rhyming slang for,* dengarkan kata orang, terjun ke dalam lubuk, *if you ~ to talk, you'll fall into a deep pool).*

listless, *adj.* lalai, tak bermaya (maya).

literature, *n.* sastera; *literary man,* ahli sastera, pujangga.

litter, *n. for carrying a person,* tandu; *stretcher,* usungan; *~ed about,* tersepah-sepah; *as lying in a heap,* tersepuk (sepuk); *strewn about,* berkaparan (kapar).

little, *adj.* kecil; *a ~,* sikit, sedikit; *~ by ~,* berdikit-dikit; *slight, as hope,* tipis.

live, *v. intr. ~ at,* duduk di-, tinggal di-, diam di-, *if I ~ so long, if I am 'spared',* kalau ada umur saya; *long ~ —!,* hidup —!; *short-~d,* singkat-umur; *long-~d, hard to kill,* panjang-umur; *to ~ (support life),* hidup.

lively, *adj. esp. as music, dancing,* rancak.

liver, *n.* hati.

livestock, *n.* binatang ternak, hidup-hidupan.

livid, *adj. ~-blue, as a bruise,* biru lebam.

living, *adj. see* **alive;** *livelihood,* kehidupan (hidup); *(fig.)* periuk nasi; *sustenance,* nafkah; *calling,* mata pencarian (cari); *cost of* ~, sara hidup; *enough to live on,* cukup makan, *to live on a woman's earnings,* makan hasil perempuan; *on immoral earnings,* makan hasil perempuan jahat; *on immoral earnings or other 'dirty' money,* makan duit lendir; ~ *from hand to mouth,* (seperti ayam), kais pagi, makan pagi, kais petang, makan petang, *(like fowls, scratch in the morning and eat in the morning, sractch in the evening and eat in the evening); food and clothing (as an item in wages),* makan pakai.

lizard, *n.* cicak; *garden* ~, bengkarung; *monitor* ~, iguana, biawak, bewak; *large gecko,* tokek; *flying* ~, cicak kubin.

load, *n. cargo,* muatan; *burden,* beban, pikulan; *see* **lade;** *to* ~ *(a gun),* mengisi (senapang), isi kartus.

loaf, *v. intr.* duduk berlalai-lalai, duduk goyang kaki sahaja, bergelandang (gelandang); *for* ~ *of bread, see* **bread.**

loathe, *v. tr.* benci, getik, cicik.

local, *adj. belonging to a certain place,* tempatan; *peculiar to one place,* setempat; ~ *dialect,* bahasa daerah; *~ly born,* peranakan (anak).

lock, *n.* kunci; *padlock,* mangga kunci; ~ *of hair,* segombak rambut.

lockjaw, *n.* mulut terkunci (kunci), kaku-mulut.

locust, *n.* belalang kunyit.

lodge, *v. intr. with host,* menumpang (tumpang) di rumah —; *lodgings,* bilik sewaan.

loft, *n. space under roof,* pagu, loteng.

lofty, *adj.* tinggi; *(towering skywards),* serenjang; *exalted,* mulia, terhormat (hormat).

log, *n. unhewn piece of timber,* batang kayu; balk (baulk); balak; *apparatus for measuring ship's speed,* ikan-ikan.

loggerheads at, *adv. on unfriendly terms,* berseterumeru (seteru), saling bermusuh-musuhan (musuh), bertelagah (telagah); *to set at loggerheads,* lagakan, mengadu-dombakan (adu).

logical, *adj.* makkul, mengikut (ikut) 'logik', mengikut akal.

loins, *n.* pinggang; *~-cloth,* cawat; *Chinese bathing-clout,* cokin.

loiter, *v. intr.* berjalan (jalan) lambat-lambat, berlengah-lengah, merayau.

loll, *v. intr.* duduk bersandar (sandar), duduk, baring, bermalas-malas.

lonely, *adj.* sunyi, sepi, tanpa teman; *out of the way, as a dwelling,* jauh dari loceng.

long, *adj. in space,* panjang; *in time,* lama; *extended,* lanjut; ~ *relative to length,* bujur; ~ *without bulk as a tree or a Rugby football,* lonjong; *~-lived,* panjang-umur; *~-drawn out (case, speech),* meleret-leret; *~-winded,* sangat lanjut hingga membosankan; *to* ~ *for,* ingin; *(with nostalgia),* merindukan (rindu); *as a pregnant woman,* mengidamkan (idam); *as* ~ *as, whilst,* selagi; *see* **old, once.**

longitude, *n.* garisan bujur; *longitudinal,* mengikut (ikut) panjangnya.

look, *v. tr. and intr.* ~ *at, see,* tengok; ~ *carefully, as at a small object,* bedek, belek; ~ *long and earnestly,* renung, amat-amati; ~ *back,* ~ *around,* menoleh (toleh) (ke belakang); ~ *up (raise head),* tengadah; gaze, pandang; ~ *out!* jaga!; ~ *sideways (esp. when 'giving the eye'),* menjeling (jeling), mengerling (kerling); *see* **peep, peer, scrutinise, watch;** ~*! (esp. in advertisements),* awas; *to* ~ *longingly, as a hungry child,* menginding (inding), melangut (langut); ~ *up,* mendongak (dongak), mencongak (congak); ~ *before you leap, see* **chew;** ~ *back on, see* **recall.**

look-out, *n. observation post,* tempat-meninjau (tinjau).

loom, *n. hand-~,* kek; *weaving-apparatus generally,* perkakas tenun.

loom, *v. intr.* ~ *large, as the rising moon,* nampak terbambang (bambang); *appear indistinctly,* berbalam (balam); *I saw the* ~ *of the land,* saya nampak daratan berbalam-balam.

loop, *n.* sepit udang; *as a coil of rope,*

gelong; ~ *of a noose,* mata jerat.

loose, *adj.* longgar; *slack,* kendur; *as soil,* gembur; *having a ~ surface,* cerul; *as a tooth, ogeh,* onyak-anyik; *~ned, of hair,* terurai (urai), menggerbang (gerbang), sanggul terlepas (lepas); *not firmly fixed,* goyah; *~-tongued,* bocor-mulut, *un~d, as a shoelace,* terongkal (rongkal); *'at a ~ end',* idle, duduk goyang kaki sahaja; *~ly tied, as a sarong,* londeh; *see* **undo.**

loot, *n.* barang rampasan.

lop, *v. tr.* cut off, kerat, memangkas; ~, trim branches, before or after felling, menutuh (tutuh).

lopsided, *adj.* berat sebelah; *unbalanced, esp. in flight,* rebeh; *swaying and awry, as a vehicle,* incang-incut; *set unevenly,* tak seimbang.

loris, *n.* see sloth.

lose, *v. tr.* kehilangan (hilang); *suffer monetary loss,* rugi; *lost;* hilang; *astray,* sesat; *to ~ one's head,* hilang akal; *misplaced,* salah letak; *lost and bewildered,* seperti anak ayam kehilangan ibu, *(like a chick which has lost its mother).*

lot, *n. portion,* bahagian; *to draw ~s,* bercabut (cabut) undi, membuang (buang) undi; *the ~ fell in,* undi terkena (kena) pada.

lotion, *n.* ubat jelum; *hair ~,* minyak rambut.

loud, *adj.* kuat, keras; *high-pitched,* nyaring; ~ *and clear,* lantang; *~speaker,* alat pembesar (besar) suara, (alat) pengeras (keras) suara.

lounge, *v. intr.* duduk bersenang-senang; *see loll;* tempat berehat-rehat.

louse, *n.* tuma, kutu; *'lousy',* busuk.

love, *v. tr.* kasih; *(less strong),* sayang; *in ~ with,* asyik pada; *deeply in ~,* gila berahi; *madly in ~ (with),* 'crazy' *(about),* tergila-gila (pada); *'stuck on',* tersangkut (sangkut) pada; ~ *for the unattainable,* gila bayang; *infatuated (with wild and dangerous desire),* mabuk kepayang; *unrequited ~,* cinta yang tidak berbalas (balas); *romantic*

~, cinta; *passionate ~,* cinta berahi, asmara; *~-philtre,* ubat guna, ubat pengasih (kasih); *(aphrodisiac),* ubat menambahkan (tambah) syahuat; *to fall in ~,* jatuh cinta (pada); *to make ~,* berasmara; *exchanging endearments,* bercumbu-cumbuan; *~-lies-bleeding,* bunga balung ayam; *cupboard-~,* seperti bangau kasihkan kerbau, *(as the egret ~s the buffalo; the egret constantly attends buffaloes to pick up insects, etc., disturbed by them).*

love-bird, burung serindit.

low, *adj.* height and of voice, rendah; *~-lands,* tanah lembah; ~ *and obscene,* lucah.

low, *v. intr.* as cattle, menguak (uak), melenguh (lenguh).

lower, *v. tr.* pay out, as rope, hulurkan; *(something) by means of a rope,* labuhkan; *generally,* turunkan; ~ *away!, (nautical),* aris!; ~ *head, as a bull,* menyondol (sondol); ~ *voice,* merendahkan (rendah) suara; ~ *light, see* **turn.**

loyal, *adj.* setia, taat setia; *to do ~ service,* berbuat (buat) bakti; *take oath of ~ty,* bersumpah (sumpah) taat setia; *~ists (persons siding with Government),* pengikut (ikut) pemerintah.

lozenge-shaped, *adj.* belah ketupat, kelarai, potongan wajik.

lubricate, *v.* melicinkan dengan minyak.

luck, *n.* good or bad, nasib; *good ~,* untung, bertuah, mujur; *bad ~,* malang; *stroke of ~,* rezeki; *'windfall', durian* runtuh; *~y (bringing good ~),* bertuah (tuah); *esp. as a ~y rod or weapon,* dekar; *un~y (bringing bad ~),* sial; ~ *brought by an object or name,* sempena; *to try one's ~,* mengadu (adu) untung; *trust to ~,* bawa nasib; *dogged by ill-~,* dirundung malang; *see* **destiny.**

lucrative, *adj.* beruntung (untung) banyak; *yielding large revenue,* yang mendatangkan (datang) hasil banyak.

ludicrous, *adj.* absurd, laughable, yang menggelikan hati.

luggage, *n.* berbarang (barang-barang).

lukewarm, *adj.* pesam, suam.

lullaby, *n.* pengandui (andui), dondang; *to sing to sleep,* menyanyi (nyanyi) menidurkan (tidur) (budak), mengulit (ulit).

lumbago, sakit pinggang.

lump, *n. as of sugar,* ketul; ~ *sugar,* gula batu; ~ *on body,* benggul; *(cyst),* risa; *a* ~ *generally (e.g. of mud),* segumpal; *large chunk,* bungkah; *to pay in a* ~ *sum,* bayar pukal.

lunatic, *n.* orang gila; *see* **asylum, mad.**

lunch, *n.* makan tengah hari.

lungs, *n.* paru-paru; ~-*fish (mudfish),* ikan belodok, ikan tembakul.

lurch, *n. left in* ~, *abandoned in a crisis,* terbangai (bangai) begitu sahaja, tertinggal (tinggal) begitu sahaja, memulaukan seseorang semasa dia memerlukan bantuan.

lure, *n.* umpan.

lurk, *v. intr.* mengendap-endap.

lust, *n.* nafsu; ~*ful,* gasang.

luxuriant, *adj. of plants,* subur; *having thick foliage,* rendang; *growing apace, as weeds,* meriap (riap).

luxury, *n.* kemewahan; ~ *articles,* barang mewah; *a life of* ~, hidup mewah.

M

macabre, *adj. gruesome,* yang mengerikan (ngeri), menggerunkan.

Macassar, *n.* Pulau Mengkasar.

mace, *n. spice,* buah pala; *staff,* cokmar.

machine, *n.* 'mesin', jentera, pesawat; ~*ry generally,* alat jentera.

mackerel, *n. (many sp.) Spanish* ~, ikan tenggiri; *horse-*~, ikan cencaru.

mad, *adj.* gila; *eccentric,* gila bahasa, sasar, gong; *not quite right in the head,* tidak sempurna akal, otak mereng; *'half-baked',* tengah masak; *'a screw loose',* tiga suku; *'not quite right',* fikiran tidak siuman, mamai; *'balmy',* setengah tiang.

magazine, *n. periodical,* majalah; *for arms,* gudang senjata.

maggot, *n.* ulat; *fly-blown,* berula, berenga (renga).

magic, *n. to make* ~, jampi, main puteri; *black* ~, ilmu jahat; ~*al (as a sword),* ɔokti; ~*al power,* hikmat; ~*al bullet,* peluru petunang (tunang); *see* **sorcery.**

magnet, *n.* besi berani.

magnificence, *n.* keindahan, kemuliaan.

magnify, *v. tr.* membesarkan (besar); ~*ing glass,* kaca pembesar, teropong tuma.

maid, *n. virgin,* anak dara; ~*-of-honour,* dayang; *attendant,* pelayan (layan), pembantu rumah.

mail, *n. letters,* 'mel'; *air-*~, `mel' udara; *sea-*~, `mel' laut; ~*-train,* kereta (api) `mel'.

maim, *v. tr. to cripple, disable,* mencacatkan (cacat); *see* **mutilated.**

main, *adj. chief, principle,* utama; *(in certain expressions),* agung, ibu; ~*-mast,* tiang agung; ~ *or central pillar of a house,* tiang seri; *e.g., question or aim,* pokok.

mainland, *n.* benua, tanah raya.

mainstay, *n. chief support (esp. of a per-* son), tonggak (hidup); *esp. of a party,* teras.

maintain, *v. tr. nurture,* pelihara; *assert,* mengaku (aku), menyatakan (nyata); *look after, attend to,* selenggara; *see* **living, support.**

Majesty, *n. His* ~, Duli yang maha mulia seri paduka.

majority, *n. the* ~, *'most people',* kebanyakan (banyak) orang; *a* ~ *(of votes),* undian yang terbanyak, suara yang terbanyak.

make, *v. tr.* buat; ~ *up (of a woman),* berdandan (dandan), bersolek (solek) muka, bermekap ('mekap'); *to* ~ *up a quarrel,* berdamai (damai); *a* ~*-weight,* basi; ~*-belief,* rekaan, sesuatu yang tidak wujud; ~*r,* pencipta, pembuat.

malaria, *n.* demam kura.

Malay, *adj.* Melayu; Malaya, Tanah Melayu; *the* ~ *language,* Bahasa Melayu; *to speak* ~, bercakap Melayu.

male, *adj. of humans,* lelaki, laki-laki, *of animals,* jantan.

malicious, *adj.* dengki, hasad; *malice,* dengki, dendam; *to bear malice,* menaruh (taruh) dengki, menaruh dendam.

malignant, *adj. desirous of harming,* busuk-hati.

malinger, *v. intr. pretend to be ill,* pura-pura sakit.

malkoha, *n.* burung cenuk, burung sanuk, burung kerak nasi.

malnutrition, *n.* kekurangan makanan berzat.

mammal, *n.* binatang yang menyusukan (susu) anaknya.

man, *n. person,* orang; *male,* orang jantan, laki-laki; ~*kind,* manusia, insan; ~*ly,* mempunyai sifat-sifat lelaki.

manage, *v. tr. see* **control;** ~ *to (succeed in),* dapat; ~*r,* pengurus (urus), penguasa (kuasa); *'can ~' (cope with diffi-culties),* boleh terurus.

mandate, *n. commission of authority to act, etc.,* amanah.

mandolin, *n.* kecapi.

mane, *n.* bulu tengkuk.

manganese, *n.* batu kawi.

mange, *n.* kurap.

mango, *n. (various sp.)* buah mangga; *horse-~,* buah macang; *wild ~,* buah pauh; *large Indian ~,* buah mempelam.

mangrove, *n.* pokok bakau.

mangosteen, *n.* buah manggis, buah masta.

manifest, *adj. obvious,* nyata; *ship's ~,* penyata muatan kapal.

manifesto, *n.* pengumuman (umum), pernyataan (nyata), *'~'.*

manifold, *adj. of many kinds,* bermacam-macam; *very numerous,* berganda-ganda.

manner, *n. way of behaviour,* tingkah, laku gaya; *expression,* muka; *~s and customs,* adat kebiasaan (biasa), adat resam, adat dan perangai; *see* **courtesy.**

mannerism, *n. habitual trick of behaviour,* kebiasaan tingkah-laku atau ta-tasusila seseorang; *esp. of affectation,* lagak.

manoeuvres, *n. to engage in ~ (of troops),* berlatih (latih), pergerakan tentera; tipu muslihat.

mantis, *n. the praying ~,* tetenun, siti tenun, cengkadak.

manufactory, *n.* kilang, pabrik.

manure, *n.* baja, pupuk, serasah; *liquid ~,* baja air; *artificial ~,* baja buatan; *horse (cattle) ~,* tahi kuda (lembu); *well-rotten ~,* baja yang sudah lama terperam (peram); *see* **guano.**

manuscript, *n. writing,* naskhah tulisan tangan; *text of document,* naskhah.

many, *adj.* banyak; *numerous, of people,* ramai; *galore,* belanar; *not a few,* bukan sikit-sikit; *a considerable number,* sebilangan besar.

map, *n.* peta.

marble, *n.* batu pualam, batu marmar; *~s*

(played with by children), buah guli.

March, *n.* bulan Mac.

march, *v. intr. walk together in military manner,* berjalan (jalan) berbaris (baris).

margarine, *n.* mentega buatan.

margin, *n.* tepi; *side,* sisi; *of a document,* rusuk (surat).

mark, *n. sign,* tanda; *trace,* bekas parut; *school ~s,* markah; *identification ~,* ciri, tanda kenalpasti; *to ~ exam. papers,* memeriksa kertas-kertas jawaban.

market, *n.* pasar; *Sunday ~,* pasar Ahad; *Common Market,* Pasar Bersama (sama); *~s (outlets for trade),* pasaran.

marriage, *n. ceremony of ~,* majlis perkahwinan; *to take place (of ~),* berlangsung (langsung); *~ contract,* akad nikah; *to perform a ~,* menjalankan (jalan) akad nikah, menikahkan; *mixed ~,* kawin campuran; *~ ties,* pertalian (tali) kawin; *~able,* yang layak berkahwin; *see* **marry.**

marrow, *n. gourd,* labu; *of bones,* otak tulang; tulang sumsum; *(cold wind) penetrating to the ~ of the bones,* (angin sejuk) sampai ke tulang hitam.

marry, *v. intr.* kawin, nikah; *the marriage formula,* khutbah nikah; *to pronounce this formula,* membaca (baca) khutbah nikah; *married (of a man),* beristeri (isteri), berbini (bini); *(of a woman),* bersuami (suami), berlaki (laki); *to have a household of one's own (of a married man),* berumah (rumah) tangga.

Mars, *n. the planet,* bintang, Marikh.

marsh, *n.* paya.

martyr, *n.* (mati) syahid; *victim,* korban.

marvellous, *adj.* ajaib, menghairankan.

mascara, *n. eye-black,* celak.

mascot, *n. talisman,* tangkal, azimat.

mash, *v. tr.* lenyek; *beat into pulp,* lecek.

mask, *n.* topeng.

mason, *n.* tukang rumah; *~-bee,* angkut-angkut; *Masonic Lodge,* rumah kumpulan Freemason.

mass, *n. dense aggregate of objects,* gumpalan; *of people,* kumpulan; *small ~ or clump,* kelompok; *~ meeting,* rapat raksasa; *'the ~es'*, rakyat jelata, rakyat murba; *en masse,* beramai (rami); *to ~ (esp. troops),* menghimpunkan (himpun), mengkumpulkan (kumpul).

massage, *v. tr. with fingers and thumb,* picit; *by rubbing,* urut; *masseur,* juru urut, pelulut.

mast, *n.* tiang (kapal).

master, *n. employer,* tuan; *(if Chinese),* tauke; majikan, *schoolmaster,* guru; *(familiarly),* Cik-gu; *~piece,* pekerajaan kesenian yang amat indah.

masturbate, *v. intr.* merancap (rancap), melancap (lancap), melocok (locok).

mat, *n.* tikar; *prayer-~,* masalla; *of colour, not lustrous,* muram.

match, *n. contest,* peraduan (adu), pertandingan (tanding); *football ~,* perlawanan bola; *a ~ (whether as equal or as a soul-mate),* jodoh; *~less,* tidak dapat dibandingkan, tidak bertolok (tolok); *a perfect ~, 'made for one another',* seperti pinang dibelah dua, *to ~ against one another,* mengadu (adu); *well-matched (in a contest),* bertemu (temu) buku* dengan ruas.

matches, *n.* 'macis', goris api, korek api, gocek api; *matchbox,* kotak ('macis'); *wax vestas,* 'macis' bersepuh (sepuh) lilin.

mate, *n. associate,* kawan, teman, rakan; *room-~,* kawan sebilik; *life-~,* teman hidup; *play-~,* budak sepermainan (main); *check-~,* mat.

materialism, *n. exclusive attention to material things,* kebendaan (benda); *material as opposed to spiritual,* jasmani.

materials, *n. for manufacture,* perkakas, bahan; *raw ~,* bahan mentah; *to materialise (assume human form) or (fig.) of hopes,* menjelma (jelma).

matter, *adj. of hair,* kusut-masai.

matter, *n. see* **affair, pus;** *physical substance that which occupies space,* jirim; *it doesn't ~,* tak apa, tidak apa; *(it's of no consequence),* bukan apa; *(nothing will come of it, no one will bother about it),* tak akan jadi perkara;

'let be', biarlah.

mattock, *n.* cangkul; *shaft of ~,* batang, blade, mata.

mattress, *n.* tilam; *thin quilt ~,* lembik.

mature, *adj. (as ripe),* masak, matang; *mentally ~d,* fikiran yang dewasa, *of age,* cukup umur, dewasa; *years of discretion,* akal baligh.

mausoleum, *n.* makam.

mauve, *adj.* ungu manis.

maxim, *n.* bidalan, pepatah.

maximum, *n. in number,* yang terbanyak (banyak) sekali.

May, *n.* bulan Mei.

mayor, *n.* dutuk bandar.

mean, *adj. stingy,* kedekut, lokek, kelorek; *'tight-wad',* pidal; *as ~ as cats' meat,* kedekut tangkai jering; *~ to, see* **intend;** *~ing,* erti erti-kata, makna; *what the speaker is 'getting at',* maksud; *no ~ (no ordinary) —,* bukan sebarang —.

meander, *v. intr. as a river,* berliku-liku, bengkang-bengkok, berkelok-kelok.

means, *n. resources,* daya upaya; *as ~ to pay,* mampu; *by any ~,* dengan apa sahaja.

meanwhile, *adv.* buat sementara, sementara (itu) (ini).

measles, *n.* demam campak.

measure, *v. intr.* mengukur (ukur); *to ~ capacity,* menyukat (sukat); *~s of capacity, generally,* cupak gantang; *~s and weights,* sukatan dan timbangan; *a ~d stride,* langkah (nya) sebagai di atur; *~less,* tak terukur.

meat, *n.* daging; *as opposed to bones and skin,* isi.

Mecca, *n.* Makkah, Mekah; *the direction in which ~ lies,* kiblah.

mechanic, *n.* mekanik ('mesin', 'motorkar' and sebagainya); **mechanism,** *~al parts, 'works',* pesawat; *~al appliance,* pesawat berjentera (jentera), perkakas mekanik.

medal, *n.* bintang, pingat.

meddle, *v. intr. in affairs,* campur tangan; *interfere, obstruct,* mengganggu (ganggu); *with things,* membuat (buat) lasak tangan, kosek, kotek-katekkan, *mischievous busy-body*, penyeleweng (seleweng).

mediate, *v. intr. act as go-between*, jadi perantara (antara).

medicine, *n.* ubat; *art of ~*, ilmu kedoktoran (doktor), ilmu perubatan.

Medina, *n.* Madinah.

mediocre, *adj. moderate*, sedang, sederhana, tidak berapa baik, bermutu rendah; **mediocrity,** kesederhanaan, orang yang sederhana.

meditate, *v. intr.* tafakur, termenung (menung).

medium, *adj. not extreme, see* **mediocre;** *of ~ build*, badan gempal; *to go into a ~istic trance*, turun syaikh.

meek, *adj. not apt to resist*, bersifat (sifat) mengalah (alah).

meet, *v. tr.* berjumpa (jumpa); *as by appointment*, bertemu (temu) (dengan); *encounter (as dangers)*, menempuh (tempuh), tersua (sua) dengan; *be presented to*, bersalam (salam) dengan; *'knock up against'*, terserempak (serempak) dengan, terjeremba (jeremba) dengan; *~ face-to-face*, bertentang (tentang) dengan, bertemu (temu) muka; *~ing*, rapat, perjumpaan, mesyuarat; *as of Council*, persidangan (sidang); *General ~ing*, mesyuarat (persidangan) agung; *Extraordinary ~ing*, mesyuarat (persidangan) tergempar (gempar); *mammoth ~ing*, *mass ~ing*, rapat raksasa.

megalith, *n.* batu hidup.

megaphone, *n.* alat pembesar (besar) suara.

melancholy, *adj.* murung, sayu hati.

mellow, *adj. of voice*, lunak.

melon, *n.* temikai, semangka; *squash ~*, timun betik; *dried ~ seeds*, kuaci.

melt, *v. intr.* hancur; *liquefy*, menjadi (jadi) cair; *molten*, lebur; *melting point of metals*, titik lebur; *to ~ away, disappear, as guerillas*, meresapkan (resap) diri.

member, *n. of Council or Club*, ahli, anggota.

membrane, *n.* selaput.

memento, *n.* kenang-kenangan; *personal ~*, tanda mata.

memoirs, *n.* kenang-kenangan.

memorial, *n. stone ~*, batu peringatan (ingat); *esp. ~ pillar*, tugu peringatan; *war ~*, tugu peringatan perang.

memorise, *v. intr.* hafaz; *memory*, ingatan.

mend, *v. tr.* membaiki (baik); *put right*, perbaik; *~ a net*, bubul.

menstruate, *v. intr.* datang bulan, membawa (bawa) adat, datang kotor, datang darah; *the menstrual flow*, haid.

mention, *v. tr.* sebut; *allude to*, menyinggung (singgung).

menu, *n.* daftar makanan.

mercenary, *n. ~ troops*, asykar upahan, askar upahan; *always looking out for money*, mata duitan; *esp. of an official*, condong ke perut.

merchant, *n.* saudagar, pedagang, *merchandise*, danganan.

mercury, *n.* raksa.

mercy, *n. of God*, rahmat; *God the Merciful and Compassionate*, Allah itu pengampun lagi penyayang (sayang); *forgiveness*, ampun, maaf; *to show ~*, ampunkan; *~!*, ampun; *(less formally)*, tolong!; *to ask for one's life*, minta nyawa.

merely, *adv.* sahaja.

merge, *v. intr. be absorbed into a greater whole*, bercantun (cantum).

meridian, *n. sun's position at noon*, matahari rembang.

merit, *n. ~orious act*, jasa, bakti, amalan; *virtuous actions, esp. as opposed to sin*, pahala.

merry, *adj.* riang (hati); *to make ~*, beriang gembira.

mesh, *n.* mata (jaring, sirat); *close-~ed*, tetal, kedap; *wide-~ed*, jarang.

mess, *v. intr. to ~ together, esp. of labourers*, makan nasi kawah*, makan berkongsi (kongsi); *to make a ~ of (a job), bungle it*, ropak-rapikkan, mengacau-bilaukan (kacau), menggagalkan (gagal); *topsyturvy*, bongkar-bangkir; *'bound to make a ~ of it'*, tikus membaiki labu, *(the rat repairs the gourd)*.

message, *n. letter*, surat; *news*, khabar; *direction*, pesanan; *formal communication*, perutus; *'~'* *conveyed in a story, etc.*, perutusan, pengajaran (ajar).

metal, *n.* benda galian, logam.

metamorphosis, *n.* penjelmaan (jelma); *to change shape*, menjelma menjadi (jadi) —, berubah (ubah) rupa (bentuk).

metaphor, *n.* ibarat.

meteor, *n.* tahi bintang; *~ite*, batu halilintar; *Meteorological Department*, jabatan kajicuaca.

meter, *n. apparatus registering amount (e.g., of water, current), passing through*, alat pengukur (ukur), meter.

method, *n.* cara, jalan, kaedah; *regular procedure*, peraturan (atur).

meticulous, *adj. precise about details*, berhati-hati, teliti; sangat cermat.

metre, *n.* irama sajak.

mew, *v. intr.* mengiau (iau).

mica, *n.* abrak,

microbe, *n.* hama, kuman.

microphone, *n.* alat pembesar (besar) suara, corong radio; mikrofon.

microscope, *n.* teropong tuma, kaca pembesar (besar).

middle, *adj.* tengah; *midday*, tengah hari; *midnight*, tengah maiam; *central point*, pusat; *~ part of a period*, pertengahan; *~-aged*, setengah umur, separuh umur; *past ~ age*, tengah tubuh lalu; *'not so young as she was'*, kering-sabut.

middleman, *n.* orang tengah, (orang) perantara (antara).

midwife, *n.* bidan.

migrate, *v. intr.* berhijrah, berpindah (pindah) (ke negeri lain); *esp. as refugees*, mengungsi (ungsi); *wander abroad*, merantau (rantau).

migrant, *n.* binatang atau orang yang berpindah-pindah.

mild, *adj. of tone or policy*, lunak; *in temperament*, lemah-lembut; *of aspect or voice*, manis; *moderate*, sederhana.

mildew, *n.* lapuk, lumut; *spots of ~ on cloth*, tahi lalat.

mile, *n.* batu.

military, *adj.* yang berkenaan (kena) dengan tentera; *the ~ (the troops)*, (bala) tentera, perajurit (jurit); *~ law*, undang-undang tentera.

milk, *n.* susu*; *(~) in the coconut*, air nyiur; *~ expressed from the flesh of the coconut*, santan; *to ~*, perah susu; *Milky Way*, bintang bima-sakti, bintang temabur; *no use cyring over spilt ~*, apa boleh buat? nasi sudah menjadi (jadi) bubur, *(what can one do? the rice has (got wet and) turned to porridge.*

mill, *n.* kilang; *~-stone*, batu kisaran; *'~-stone round neck'*, kongkongan.

milled, *adj. ~ edge*, tepi yang berigi-rigi; *the milling*, penggerigian (gerigi).

millet, *n.* jelai.

million, *n.* juta; *~aire*, jutawan.

millipede, *n.* tanglung, senggulung; *luminous ~*, kelemayar.

mimic, *v. tr.* ajuk, tiru.

minaret, *n.* menara.

mince, *v. tr.* cincang, hiris halus-halus; *~-meat*, daging lumat campuran.

mind, *n. seat of emotions and thought*, hati; *perceiving faculty*, akal; *to make up one's ~*, tetapkan fikiran, memutuskan, menentukan tujuan; *can't make up ~*, berbelah hati, bercabang (cabang) hati; *the ~'s eye*, mata hati; *~ you — (bear this in ~)*, jangan tak ingat —.

Mindanoa, *n.* Magindanau.

mine, *n. excavation from which minerals are extracted, esp. surface ~*, galian, kalian; *dug deep*, lombong; *mining dredge*, kapal lombong, kapal pengorek (korek); *Mines Department*, jabatan galian; *military and naval ~*, ranjau, periuk api; *~-sweeper*, kapal penyapu (sapu) periuk api, kapal penyapu ranjau.

minerals, *n.* hasil galian, barang galian, logam.

minimum, *n. in number of amount*, yang terkurang sekali; *as a ~, at least*, sekurang-kurang.

minister, n. menteri; *Cabinet of Ministers,* Jemaah menteri; ~ *without portfolio,* menteri (negara) tidak berjabatan (jabat).

minor, adj. *the lesser,* yang kecil; *under age,* belum cukup umur, belum dewasa, belum sampai akal (baligh); *~ities (racial),* golongan (yang) kecil.

mint, v. tr. menempa (tempa); *~-impression, on a coin,* sekah.

minus, prep. *less, with the deduction of,* kurang, tolak.

minute, adj. *delicately small,* rumit, halus; *to investigate ~ly,* halusi.

minute, n. *(time),* 'minit'; *~s of meeting,* butir-butir mesyuarat.

minutiae, n. *trival points,* tetek-bengek; *subtleties, intricacies,* selok-belok.

miraculous power, n. mujizat; *(of a sorcerer),* ilmu, keajaiban.

mirage, n. pembayangan (bayang) udara, fatamorgana, sangkaan.

mirror, n. cermin (muka); *to look in a ~,* memandang (pandang) ke cermin.

mis-, prefix meaning *'amiss', 'wrongly': can often be expressed by placing* salah *before a positive word:* ~*understand,* salah faham; *~conception,* salah tampa.

misappropriate, v. mengambil dan menyalah-gunakan.

miscarry, v. intr. *of a child,* gugur; *of a plan,* tak berjaya (jaya), gagal; *fail to 'stick',* tak lekat.

miscellaneous, adj. *of various sorts,* bermacam-macam, rampai-rampai, berbagai ragam.

mischief, n. *deliberate,* khianat; *mischievous, as a child,* nakal; *can't leave ₍things alone,* gatal tangan; *deliberately harrying,* sakatan; *to make ~, incite to make trouble,* mengacum (acum); *~-maker, 'fire-brand',* batu api.

misconduct, n. *bad behaviour,* berkelakuan tidak senonoh.

misfire, v. intr. *of a gun,* tak meletup (letup).

misfortune, n. nasib buruk, malang, ben-

cana, geruh; *one ~ following another,* jatuh ditimpa tangga, *(to fall and have the ladder fall on top of you); ~ never comes singly,* malang tidak datang tunggal; *see* **luck.**

mislay, v. tr. salah letak, hingga payah didapati; *see* **miss.**

mislead, v. tr. mengelirukan (keliru), mempersesatkan (sesat); *not easily misled,* tahu membedakan (beda) tebu dengan teberau, *(call tell sugar-cane from teberau grass, which looks something like sugar-cane).*

misprint, n. tersilap (silap) cetak, salah cetakan.

miss, v. tr. *fail to hit thing aimed at,* tak kena; *as absent person,* merindukan (rindu); *~ing (disappeared),* hilang; *'haven't seen hide nor hair of him for two years',* sudah dua tahun tak nampak batang hidung dia, *(haven't seen the bridge of his nose for two years); ~ footing, see* **slip;** *(not in usual place),* sudah tak ada; *I've ~ed the train,* keretapi sudah lepas; *left behind by the train,* ketinggalan (tinggal) keretapi.

missile, n. *as from rocket,* peluru; *guided ~,* peluru berpandu (pandu).

mission, n. *persons sent as envoys,* utusan; *goodwill ~,* utusan muhibbah.

missionary, n. pengembang (kembang) agama; *Christian ~,* paderi; *esp. of Islam,* mubaligh.

mist, n. kabut, kabus.

mistake, n. silap; *blunder,* khilaf; *to 'put one's foot in it',* salah terpa; *the best of us may make a ~,* gajah pun kadang-kadang terdorong (dorong) juga, *(even the elephant stumbles sometimes).*

mistletoe, n. dedalu.

mistrust, v. tr. menaruh (taruh) syak kepada, tidak mempercayai.

misunderstand, v. tr. *fail to comprehend,* tidak mengerti (erti); *take in wrong sense,* salah faham.

misuse, v. tr. menyalah (salah)-gunakan.

mite, n. *parasite,* hama, tungau.

mitigate, n. *reduce severity of,* meringankan (ringan).

mix, v. tr. campur; *blend,* bancuh; *indissolubly blended,* sebati; *of ~ed breed,* kacuk-baka.

mob, n. *a crowd,* kumpulan orang; *to ~, crowd upon,* mengerubung (kerubung), mengerumun (kerumun), mengerubut (kerubut); *to get ~bed,* kena keroyok.

mobile, adj. *shifting position readily,* dapat bergerak (gerak).

mobilise, v. tr. mengerahkan (kerah); *issue mobilisation order,* mengumumkan (umum) kerahan tentera, mengumumkan 'mobilasi'; *demobilise,* membubarkan (bubar) tentera.

mock, v. tr. mengejek (ejek); *chaff,* menggiat (giat); *sham, imitation (as battle),* olok-olok.

mode, n. *way in which thing is done,* cara; *in music and (fig.) in temperament,* ragam.

model, n. contoh, acuan; *clothes-~,* peragawati (raga).

moderate, adj. *not extreme, tolerant,* sederhana; *to become less violent, as a storm,* reda.

modern, adj. 'modan', kini; *up to date,* menurut (turut) zaman.

modest, adj. *in demeanour,* santun; *not stuck up,* tidak sombong; *not excessive,* sederhana; *the truly great are ~,* padi makin berisi (isi) makin tunduk, *(the fuller the rice-ear, the lower it bows its head).*

modify, v. tr. *make minor changes in,* meminda (pinda).

moist, adj. lembap.

mole, n. *on skin,* tahi lalat.

molest, v. tr. *subject to international annoyance,* mengganggu; *worry,* mengusik (usik).

mollify, v. tr. *calm down,* menyejukkan (sejuk) hati.

Moluccas, n. *the ~,* Pulau Maluku.

moment, n. saat, ketika.

momentum, n. *carried on by its own ~, as a suddenly braked car,* terlajak (lajak).

Monday, n. Hari Isnin.

money, n. duit, wang, pitis; *~-box,* tabung duit; *slang words for ~,* 'lolly', 'the wherewithal', fulus, pasak seribu; *silver ~,* wang perak; *gold coinage,* wang mas; *copper ~,* wang tembaga; *notes,* 'not', wang kertas; *I can't make ~!,* aku bukan tukang cap* duit.

money-lender, n. *Indian ~,* Cetti; *financier,* saudagar wang; *'blood-sucker',* lintah darat.

mongoose, n. cerpelai.

mongrel, adj. *of mixed bred,* kacukbaka.

monk, n. rahib.

monkey, n. *(many sp.),* common *mustard-coloured ~,* kera, monyet; *black leaf-~,* lotong; *pig-tailed ~,* beruk.

monogamy, n. (adat) kawin satu.

monopoly, n. *by licence, esp. from Government,* pajak.

monotheism, n. kepercayaan (percaya) keesaan (esa) Tuhan.

monsoon, n. *the wet season,* musim hujan; *N.E. ~,* musim utara, musim tengkujuh, musim gelora; *S.E. ~,* tenggara.

month, n. bulan; *every ~,* tiap-tiap bulan; *~ly,* bulanan.

monument, n. batu peringatan (ingat), tugu peringatan.

moon, n. bulan; *~ seen in daylight (and so pallid),* bulan kesiangan (siang); *Mr. Moon,* Sang Rembulan *(poet),* *~beam,* pancaran sinaran bulan.

moor, v. tr. tambat; *~ing-post,* sembuang, tambatan.

moorhen, n. burung ruak-ruak; *purple ~,* burung pangling.

mop-up, v. tr. lap; *to mop face, eyes* mengesat (kesat); *~ (fig.), destroy last remnants (of enemy, etc.),* hapuskan saki-baki; *round up,* berkas; *make a clean sweep of,* menyapu (sapu) bersih.

mope, v. tr. duduk murung sahaja, merana (rana).

moral, n. *lesson to be remembered as a result of an incident,* ingatan; *deducible in, e.g., story,* pengajaran (ajar); *'message',* perutusan (utus).

morale, n. semangat, perjuangan,

keyakinan.

morals, *n. see* **ethics.**

more, *pron. and adv. further,* lagi; *plus,* lebih; *the ~ — the ~,* makin — semakin; *the older he gets the wickeder he gets,* makin tua, semakin jahat; *~ or less,* lebih kurang.

moreover, *adv.* lagipun, dan lagi, tambahan pula.

moribund, *adj.* menantikan (nanti) hari, nazak, bernyawa (nyawa) ikan.

morning, *n.* pagi; *daybreak,* dinihari; *see* **dawn;** *the ~ glory flower,* bunga kembang pagi.

Morocco, *n.* negeri Maghribi.

morose, *adj.* perengus (rengus).

mortal, *adj. of the world, not eternal,* fana; *~s,* insan, manusia; *likely to cause death, as a wound,* yang harus menyebabkan (sebab) mati.

mortar, *n. mixture for holding together bricks, etc.,* 'simen', perekat batu; *for pounding,* lesung; *short-cannon,* meriam katak, *~ board,* papan lepa.

mortgage, *v. tr.* gadai; *pledge as security,* sandar, cagar.

mosque, *n.* masjid, *leader of a ~,* Imam; *preacher,* khatib; *muezzin (who calls to prayer),* bilal, tukang bang; *caretaker,* siak; *~ elders,* lebai; *see* **chapel.**

mosquito, *n.* nyamuk; *~-net,* kelambu.

moss, *n.* lumut.

most, *adj.* terbanyak, yang banyak sekali.

moth, *n.* kupu-kupu, rama-rama; *clothes- '~',* gegat.

mother, *n.* emak; *(informal or of animals),* ibu, induk; *(formal),* ibunda, bunda; *~-in-law,* emak mentua; *step-~,* emak tiri; *~ tongue,* bahasa ibunda; *'tied to ~'s apron-strings',* duduk di bawah ketiak emak, *(staying under ~'s armpit).*

motherland, *n.* Ibu Pertiwi, tanahair.

mother-of-pearl, *n.* gewang.

motion, *n. proposal put to meeting,* usul, syor.

motive, *n. what impels to action,* maksud; *aim,* tujuan; *reason,* sebab.

motley, *adj. of many colours,* pancawarna.

mottle, *adj.* bertompok-tompok; *as timber,* barik, berbelak-belak.

motto, *n.* cogan kata, semboyan.

mould, *n. matrix,* acuan; *fungoid growth,* lapuk, jamur.

moult, *v. intr.* meluruh (luruh) bulu.

mound, *n. natural,* anak bukit; *artificial,* timbunan tanah; *pile,* longgok; *small ~,* monggok.

mountain, *n.* gunung; *~ range,* banjaran gunung.

mourn, *v. intr. lament,* meratap (ratap); *weep,* menangis (tangis); *~ing-band,* kabung, toha.

mouse, *n. see* **rat.**

mousedeer, *n. see* **deer.**

moustache, *n.* misai; *wearing a ~,* bermisai; *clipped ~* misai kompot; *heavy ~,* misai tebal; *stiff ~, esp. waxed,* misai denting; *~ with fiercely upturned ends,* misai taring; *~ esp. if drooping,* misai lebat; *thick up-twisted ~,* misai lebat menjungkit (jungkit) ke atas; *bristling ~,* misai kucing.

mouth, *n.* mulut; *of river,* kuala; *~-organ,* bangsi; *~ful, of food,* sesuap; *of drink,* seteguk; *to ~ (work ~ nervously to and fro),* komak-kamik; *word of ~,* cakap mulut; *by word of ~,* dengan lisan.

move, *v intr. ~ house,* berpindah (pindah); *be ~d or transported,* beralih (alih); *shift slightly,* berganjak (ganjak); *stir,* bergerak (gerak), menguit (kuit); *~ on!,* lalu!; *much ~d (by emotion),* terharu; *to ~ (something),* mengalih; *re~,* angkat; *~ments,* gerak geri; *~ment, esp. political,* gerakan; *to ~ to tenderness,* memberi (beri) rawan.

Mr., Mrs., Miss, *vocative to Malays,* Encik; *(informal),* Cik.

much, *adj.* banyak.

mucous membrane, *n.* selaput lendir.

mucus, *n.* lendir; *from nose,* ingus.

mud, *n. slush,* selut; *thick ~,* lumpur; *~dy, as road,* lecah; *~died, as clothing,* berlumur (lumur) selut; *crust of ~ on surface,* lanyau.

muddled, *adj.* porak-peranda, kacau bilau, kelam-kabut; *all in a tangle,* bers-erabutan (serabut); *unorganised, planless,* kepala buntut tidak tentu, *(uncertain which is the head and which the backside);* muddle-headed, bingung; *see* **mess.**

mudfish, *n.* ikan belodok, ikan tembakul.

mudguard, *n.* sayap kereta, 'madgad'.

muezzin, *n. the mosque official who calls to prayer,* bilal.

muffled, *adj. of sound,* bengap; ~ *up, as against the cold,* berselubung (selubung).

mufti, *n. plain clothes, 'civvies',* pakaian 'preman'.

mug, *n.* mangkuk; *metal* ~, *tankard,* cebok.

mule, *n.* baghal.

multifarious, *adj.* bermacam-macam.

multi-lingualism, *n.* dasar berbilang (bilang) bahasa.

multiply, *v. tr. (arith),* pukul, darab; *cause to increase manyfold,* melipat-gandakan (lipat); *to increase manifold, as population,* berkembang-biak (kembang); ~ *by two,* dua kali ganda; *see* **rife.**

multi-racial, *adj.* berbilang (bilang) bangsa, pelbagai bangsa; ~ *society,* masyarakat berbilang (pelbagai) bangsa.

mumble, *v. intr.* berngangut-ngangut, berkulat-kulat, bercakap dengan tidak jelas.

mumps, *n.* sakit benguk, sakit degum.

munch, *v. tr.* mamah, kunyah-kunyah, *sound of ~ing,* kerup-kerup.

municipality, *n.* majlis bandaran.

munitions, *n.* alat-alat peperangan (perang).

murder, *v. tr.* membunuh (bunuh) (dengan sengaja).

muscle, *n.* urat.

museum, *n.* sekolah gambar, 'muzium'.

mushroom, *n.* kulat, cendawan; *to spring up like ~s,* merecup (recup) bak cendawan; *to ~ (rise in a ~-shaped cloud),* naik berpayung (payung), membumbung (bumbung) berpayung; *(rise in umbrella-shape).*

music, *n.* 'musik'; *musical instruments,* alat 'musik'; *esp. of a band,* bunyi-bunyian.

musk, *n.* kesturi.

Muslim, *adj.* orang Islam; *to become a* ~, masuk Islam; *a convert to Islam,* mualaf.

muslin, *n.* khasah.

mussel, *n.* kupang; *fresh-water* ~, kijing.

must, *v. aux.* mesti, hendaklah, tak dapat tidak; *I* ~ *(have to) go to Ipoh,* saya kena pergi Ipoh; *I* ~ *(am compelled to) go to Ipoh,* saya terpaksa (paksa) pergi Ipoh; *to be* ~, *of an elephant,* turun minyak.

muster, *v. tr. as troops,* kumpulkan.

musty, *adj. stale,* basi; *sour,* masam.

mutilated, *p.p. deprived of a limb,* kudung, rompong, kontot, kompong.

mutiny, *v. intr.* berontak (rontak), pendurhakaan.

mutter, *v. intr.* merungut (rungut), mengomel.

mutton, *n. flesh of goat or sheep,* daging kambing; *specifically of sheep,* daging bebiri (biri-biri), ~ *head,* orang bodoh.

mutual, *adj.* saling, sefahaman; *see* **cooperate.**

muzzle, *n. of gun,* mulut; *snout,* muncung.

muzzy, *adj. feeling* ~ *in the head, as after a blow,* kepala terasa (rasa) bengal; *as a result of noise,* bingit; *see* **dizzy.**

mynah, *n. buffalo-~,* burung gembala kerbau; *(various sp.),* tiung.

myrtle, *n.* pokok kemunting.

mysterious, *adj. as supernatural,* ajaib, penuh rahsia; *a secret,* rahsia; *difficult problem,* kesulitan (sulit).

mysticism, *n.* tasauf; *the Mystic Path,* tarikat; *a form of* ~ *said to involve calling up spirits,* suluk; *a modern Movement,* Subud (susila*, budhi, dharma).

N

nag, *v. tr.* berleterkan; ~*ging (continually irritating, as e.g., a thorn under the skin),* terasa-rasa.

nail, *n. as of finger,* kuku; *spike,* paku; ~*varnish,* cat kuku.

naked, *adj.* telanjang; *esp. as with a suggestion of indecency,* berpukas (pukas); *to conceal one's* ~*ness,* menutup (tutup) aurat; ~, *unsheathed, of a blade,* terhunus.

name, *n.* nama, *nick~,* nama panggilan, jolokan; *pet-~,* timang-timangan; *pen-~,* nama pena; *pseudonym,* nama samaran.

namely, *adv. that is to say,* iaitu.

nap, *v. intr. to have a* ~, tidur untuk sekejap-masa.

nape, *n. of neck,* tengkuk.

napkin, *n.* sapu tangan, 'nipkin'; *nappy,* cawat kanak-kanak, kain lampin; *see* **swaddling-cloth.**

narrate, *v. tr.* cerita (kan), meriwayatkan.

narrow, *adj.* sempit; *as straitened,* picik; *of a gap,* genting; *'the* ~*s',* pergentingan; ~*-minded,* berfikiran (fikir) picik atau sempit, berakal (akal) singkat; *barely room to swing a cat,* selebar sekangkang kera, *(as broad as a monkey's straddle).*

nasal, *adj. concerned with the nose,* berkenaan (kena) dengan hidung; *of speech,* sengau.

nasty, *adj. of taste,* maung; *as warning to a child,* ~*! don't touch!,* jijik!

nation, *n. race,* bangsa; *State,* negara; ~*ality,* rupa-bangsa; ~*al anthem,* lagu kebangsaan; ~*al language,* bahasa kebangsaan, bahasa 'nasional'; *citizen,* anak negeri, warga negara; *see* **citizen, race;** *to* ~*ise,* menjadikan (jadi) milik negara.

native, *n. indigenous,* penduduk (duduk) asli, bumi-putera.

natural, *adj. not artificial or adulterated,* asli; ~ *trait,* sifat; *innate or provided by nature,* semula jadi; ~ *talent,* bakat semula jadi; *has become second nature to him,* sudah menjadi (jadi) darah daging pada dia; ~ *resources,* hasil bumi.

naturalised, *p.p. to become* ~, menjadi (jadi) warga negara.

naturalist, *n.* ahli ilmu isi bumi, ahli ilmu haiwan.

naturally, *adv. of course! (what else did you expect?),* apa lagi?; *(bound to be so),* sememangnya (memang), sewajarnya (wajar), menurut alam; ~ *curly (of hair),* keriting asli.

nature, *disposition,* tabiat, perangai; *sum of characteristics,* pembawaan (bawa); *the world of* ~, alam semula jadi.

nausea, *n. to feel* ~, mendugal (dugal), meloya (loya) tekak.

navel, *n.* pusat.

navigation, *n. the art of* ~, ilmu pelayaran (layer).

navy, *n.* angkatan laut.

near, *prep.* dekat; *see* **almost.**

neat, *adj. esp. as in dress,* cermat, rapi; *of clothes still well-pressed,* tak patah sait, tak patah kanji; *neatly arranged (as in layers or piles),* bersusun (susun) rapi.

necessary, *adj.* perlu, penting; *necessarily,* se mestinya.

neck, *n.* leher; *esp. back of* ~, tengkuk; ~*tie,* 'nek-tai', dasi; *(sl.),* tangkal polong, tali leher; *having a stiff* ~, leher berkiat (kiat); *stiff for no obvious reason,* salah-bantal.

necklace, *n.* tali leher, kalung.

needle, *n.* jarum; bodkin, cuban.

needs, *n.* keperluan (perlu), kepentingan (penting).

neglect, *v. tr.* biarkan, mengabaikan

(abai); ~ed, tak terjaga (jaga); *negligence,* alpa, cuai; ~*ful, slack,* lalai; *to ~ a partly finished job,* bengkalaikan.

negotiate, *v. intr.* berkira (kira) (dengan), berunding (runding) dengan; *see* **agree, arrange, discuss.**

Negro, *n.* Habsyi.

neigh, *v. intr.* meringkik (ringkik).

neighbour, *n.* tetangga (tangga-tangga), jiran; *the ~hood,* daerah berhampiran (hampir), daerah sekitar; *a dangerous ~,* seperti durian dengan mentimun, menggolek rosak, kena golek binasa, *(like a durian and a cucumber, if you roll on it, you are hurt, if it rolls on you, you are done for).*

nephew, niece, *n.* anak saudara, anak penakan, anak kemanakan.

nepotism, *n.* dasar pilih kasih; *see* **discriminate.**

nerve, *n.* ~*-fibre,* urat sarap; *to ~ oneself,* memberanikan (berani) diri.

nervous, *adj.* cuak, gelisah, *agitated,* gugup; *in a dither,* darah gemuruh.

nest, *n.* sarang; *of boar,* jerumbun; *to ~,* bersarang; *to ~ inside one another, as baskets, pots,* bersusun (susun); *he fouls his own ~,* dia memberakkan periuk nasi dia sendiri, *(he defecates Into hls own rlce-pot). N.B.* periuk nasi is often used *(fig.)* for *'household, establishment';* *he feathers his own ~,* dia mengisi (isi) tembolok dia sendiri, *(he fills his own belly).*

net, *n.* barrier *(and generally),* jaring; casting-~, jala; *seine-~,* pukat; *landing-~,* tangguk; *~, of profit,* bersih; ~*-ball,* bola jaring; ~*-work (radio),* rangkaian (radio); *design in ~-work, as lace,* selirat, sirat.

nettle, *n. poisonous tree-~,* jelatang.

neutral, *adj. to be ~,* duduk di tengah, tak bercampur (campur) tangan, berkecuali (cuali).

never, *adv.* ~ *yet,* tak pernah; ~ *(in the future),* sampai bila pun tak akan; ~*! (strong negation),* haram!; *Never-~ Land,* negeri antah*-berantah.

nevertheless, *adv.* dalam itu pun, itu

pun, biar pun begitu.

new, *adj.* baru.

New Guinea, *n.* Irian.

news, *n.* khabar, warta, berita; *to break (become generally known), of ~,* pecah; ~*-conference,* persidangan (sidang) akhbar; ~*-agency,* syarikat berita, kantur berita; ~ *summary,* ringkasan berita; ~*-reel,* berita bergambar; ~*-stand,* tempat menjual surat khabar.

newspaper, *n.* suratkhabar, akhbar; *daily ~,* harian.

next, *adj. in fixed time sequence,* depan, di muka (ini); ~ *day,* esok harinya; ~ *time (another time),* lain kali; ~ *to,* di sisi, se belah; *see* **side.**

nib, *n.* mata kalam.

nibble, *v. tr.* unggis-unggis; *esp. as a fish,* pagut.

nice, *adj. pleasing to the senses,* sedap, enak, lazat; *see* **ins-and-outs.**

niche, *n.* ceruk; ~ *in side of grave in which body is placed,* liang lahad.

nick, *n.* takik, takuk, kelar.

night, *n.* malam; *to spend the ~,* bermalam, menginap (inap).

nightjar, *n.* burung segan, burung tukang.

nimble, *adj.* pantas.

nip, *v. tr. pinch,* cubit; ~*ped between two surfaces,* tersepit (sepit); *to ~, as an ant,* ketip.

nipple, *n.* puting tetek.

nit, *n. egg of louse, etc,* telur kutu.

nitrates, *n.* nitrat; garam yang diperolehi dari tindakan asid nitrik ke atas sebarang alkali.

no, not, *particle,* tidak; *is ~,* bukan; ~ *yet,* belum (lagi); *see* **damned, likely;** ~ *one,* tidak seorang pun; ~ *at all!,* sekalikali tidak.

Noah, *n.* nabi Noh; *Noah's ark,* bahtera nabi Noh.

nobility, *n. the class of noblemen,* kaum bangsawan, kaum ningrat; *of ~ character,* berhati (hati) mulia.

nocturnal, *adj. in the night,* pada malam hari.

nod, v. intr. esp. as in assent, angguk; ~ding as from weakness, teragut-agut; a Nodder (person who assents to everything), (macam burung tekukur) tahu mengangguk-angguk sahaja; tukang ekor; ~ding from weariness or sleepiness, tersengguk-sengguk; see **yes.**

node, n. as in bamboo, buku.

noise, n. any sound, bunyi; din, clamour, bunyi hingar-bangar; hubbub, riuh-rendah; esp. of quarrelling, herok-perok, becang-becok; noisy scene (as at a meeting), suasana riuh-heboh; to make an annoying ~, bising; don't make such a ~, jangan hingar-hingar.

nomads, n. kaum melara (lara), kaum pengembara (kembara).

nominally, adv. atas nama sahaja.

nominate, v. tr. esp. as a candidate, menamakan (nama), **meletakkan** (letak) nama, mencalonkan.

non-aligned, adj. berkecuali (cuali).

non-fertile, adj. as an egg, sambang.

nonsense, n. karut; as a preposterous story, bukan-bukan, tak diterima dek akal; to talk ~, merapik (rapik); see **rave.**

nook, n. ceruk.

noon, n. tengah hari, lohor.

noose, n. jerat, racik; to draw tight a ~, jerut; rattan ~, as for deer, siding.

normal, adj. biasa, lazim; ~ly, biasanya, lazimnya; on ~ days, sehari sehari (hari); 'average', sederhana.

north, n. utara; N.E., timur; N.W., barat laut; ~ Pole, kutub utara.

nose, n. hidung; of animal, muncung, domol; beak of fish, jolong; hooked ~, hidung bongkok; snub ~, hidung kemek; high (well-cut) ~, hidung mancung; to '~ round' (make discreet inquiries), menjolok-jolok, (menyolok-yolok), mencari (cari) rahsia, merisik-risik; as pigs in rubbish, menyondong-nyondongkan (sondong) muncung pada; to cut off one's ~ to spite one's face, kerana marahkan tikus rumah terbakar (bakar), (burning the house to get rid of the rats).

nostalgia, n. rindukan kampung halaman, rindukan sesuatu yang telah dialami.

notable, adj. of an event, istimewa; ~ person, orang kenamaan (name).

notch, n. takuk, takik; ~ed, jagged, as knife-blade, sumbing; serrated, beringgit-ringgit, berenggil-enggil; much ~ed, tokak-takik.

note, n. brief record, catatan; in music, nada; to ~ (take congnisance), faham; ~-book, buku catatan; esp. one used as school exercise-book, buku rampaian; foot-~, catatan di bawah.

notice, n. intimation, pemberi (beri) tahu; esp. as legal ~, 'notis'; to ~, perhati (hati), petia; esp., nampak; realise, sedar (akan); ~-board, e.g., for road-signs, papan tanda; for legal ~s, etc., (papan) tempat menampal (tampal) 'notis'.

notify, v. tr. memberi (beri) tahu (kepada), melaporkan (lapor) (kepada).

notorious, adj. masyhur.

nought, n. ciper, kosong, sifir.

nourish, v. tr. sustain with food, pelihara, mendidek didik; ~ing (of food), yang menyegarkan (segar) badan.

novel, adv. new, baru; ~ty, pembaruan; fictitious prose tale, cerita dongeng, 'nobel'.

November, n. bulan November.

now, adv. sekarang (ini), ~adays, masa ini; in the present era, zaman ini.

nozzle, n. muncung.

nucleus, n. central part, pusat, punat.

nudge, v. tr. sigung, menyiku (siku).

nugget, n. bongkah emas, tongkol emas.

nuisance, n. to be a ~, mengacau (kacau).

null, adj. not valid, tidak sah; to ~ify, batalkan.

numb, adj. having 'pins and needles', kebas; deprived of sensation, sebar, lali; ~skull, orang dungu.

number, n. in series, 'nombor', bilangan; numeral, angka; cardinal ~, angka pokok, ordinal ~, angka berturut-turut.

numerous, adj. a large number, sebilangan besar; a lot, banyak —; see **galore,**

many.

nurse, *n. children's* ~, *Chinese,* amah; *Malay or Indian,* ayah; *Javanese,* Babu; *to* ~ *(look after) a child,* mengasuh (asuh); *to* ~ *a patient,* merawat; *hospital* ~, 'missi', jururawat; *wet* ~, ibu susu.

nursery, *n. for plants,* semaian; *for babies,* bilik kanak-kanak.

nut, *n.* buah keras.

nutrient, *n.* zat makanan.

nutmeg, *n.* buah pala.

nuzzle, *v. tr. as animal at teat,* menyondol (sondol), menyondongkan (sondong) muncung pada; *as a duck,* menyudu (sudu).

nymphomaniac, *n. having exaggerated sexual desire for women,* gila ekor, gila urat; *of woman,* biang keladi, gatal keladi, (ada) banyak minyak.

O

oakum, *n.* majum.

oar, *n.* dayung.

oath, *n.* sumpah; *to take the* ~ *of allegiance,* membaca (baca) ikrar taat setia, bersumpah (sumpah) taat setia.

obey, *v. tr.* menurut (turut) perintah; *esp. as, be subservient to,* patuhi; ~ *command of Ruler,* menjunjung (junjung); *obedient,* taat, patuh; *yours obediently,* yang taat (dibawah perintah).

object, *v. intr. as protest,* membantah (bantah); *to have ~ions about (doing),* berkeberatan (berat); ~*able,* tidak digemari, tidak disukai.

objective, *n. esp. military,* matlamat; *see* **aim.**

obligation, *n. to be under an* ~ *to,* berhutang (hutang) budi.

obligatory, *adj.* perlu, termesti (mesti).

oblique, *adj.* serong.

obliterate, *v. tr. wipe out,* menghapuskan (hapus); *destroy,* membasmikan (basmi).

oblong, *adj.* empat persegi (segi) memanjang (panjang).

obscene, *adj.* kotor, lucah.

obscure, *adj. as dark,* kelam; *of document,* umum; *esp. as little known,* sulit.

obsequious, *adj.* suka merendahkan (rendah) diri, suka membongkokkan (bongkok) diri, berleher (leher) lembut; *(to behave like a hen),* membawa (bawa) perangai ayam betina.

observe, *v. tr. keep under observation,* mengawasi (awas); ~*! (esp. as heading to advertisements),* awas!; *to act in conformity with,* menurut (turut); *an* ~*r, esp. at a conference,* pemerhati (hati).

obsolete, *adj.* usang, ketinggalan (tinggal) zaman, menjadi lapuk.

obstacle, *n.* halangan, aral; ~*-race, see* **race.**

obstetris, *n.* ilmu kebidanan (bidan).

obstinate, *adj.* degil, keras kepala, keras hati.

obstruct, *v. tr. way,* tutup; *as by blockade,* sekat; *by barricade,* rebat, rentang; *act ~ively,* mengganggu (ganggu).

obtain, *v. tr.* mendapat (dapat), beroleh (oleh); *attain to,* mencapai (capai).

obtuse, *adj. not pointed,* tak berhujung (hujung), tumpul, dempak, dumpu; *slow of perception,* dungu.

obviate, *v. tr. clear away, get rid of (danger, etc.)* menyingkirkan (singkir).

obvious, *adj.* nyata, terang; *to 'leap to the eye',* menjolok (jolok) mata; *clearly visible,* ketara.

occasion, *n. time of occurrence,* waktu; *instance,* kali, embak; *occasionally (now and then),* sekali-sekali.

occult, *adj.* ghaib, tersembunyi, rahsia.

occupy, *v. tr. reside in,* duduk di-; *as land,* perintah; *military* **occupation,** pendudukan tentera.

occur, *v. intr. happen,* jadi; *take place,* berlaku (laku); *it has just ~red to me,* baru saya teringat (ingat); *it simply never ~red to me that ——,* saya tak sangka sekali-kali ——; *continually ~ring,* menjadi-jadi; *as an idea,* terlintas (lintas) di hati; *of e.g. a species of animal, be met with, be found in,* terdapat (dapat) di-.

occurrence, *n.* kejadian (jadi), peristiwa (istiwa); *see* **occasion, event.**

ocean, *n.* lautan.

o'clock, *n.* jam; *two* ~, (jam) pukul dua, jam dua.

October, *n.* bulan Oktober.

octopus, *n.* (ikan), sotong, kerita.

odd, *adj. queer,* pelik, anih; *anomalous, not even, of numbers,* ganjil; *extra,* lebih; ~ *jobs,* pekerjaan tidak tetap, *as* side-line job, kerja sambilan; '~ fish' (queer customer), satu macam; to have an ~ (undescribable) feeling, berasa (rasa) agak berlainan; the ~s (in betting at bull-fights), ganda; in the sense of additional, lebih; a hundred dollars ~, seratus ringgit lebih.

oddments, n. odds and ends, keropas-kerapis, tetek-bengek, perca (kain dsb.).

odious, adj. hateful, mendatangkan benci.

off, adv. be ~!, nyah! hincit!; to come ~ (be detached), tanggal; from, dari; he jumped ~ the bridge, dia terjun dari jambatan.

offence, n. misdemeanour, kesalahan (salah); to give ~ to, hurt feelings of, menyinggung (singgung) perasaan (rasa); offended, jauh-hati.

offer, v. tr. in bargaining, tawar; hold out, unjuk; as to royalty or in a temple, sembahkan.

off-hand, adv. on the spur of the moment, without previous thought as in giving an answer, serta-merta, dengan tidak berfikir (fikir) dahulu; ~ed, to behave ~ly to (showing lack of courtesy or care), buat acuh tak acuh, buat endah tak-endah (terhadap (hadap)).

office, n. public appointment, jawatan, jabatan; place, pejabat; head ~, ibu pejabat; ~-boy, see **orderly**; 'good ~s', see **assist**.

officer, n. pegawai; military ~, pegawai tentera; civil ~, pegawai awam; staff ~, pegawai turus, pegawai 'staf'; duty ~, pegawai menjaga (jaga); intelligence officers, pegawai perisik (risik), pihak pengintip (intip) rahsia; commanding ~, pegawai pemerintah (perintah); liaison officer, pegawai perantara (antara); seconded ~, pegawai pinjaman; supply ~, pegawai perbekalan (bekal).

official, rasmi; ~ly, secara rasmi; an ~, pegawai kerajaan (raja); Government staff, kakitangan kerajaan.

offspring, n. anak; descendant, keturunan (turun).

often, adj. acap kali, kerap kali, selalu; again and again, berkali-kali.

ogle, v. intr. bermain (main) mata, memerhatikan seseorang dengan penuh bernafsu, apt to ~, panjang-mata.

ogre, n. gergasi.

oil, n. minyak; ~-palm, kelapa sawit; to ~ (surface), sapu minyak; as with ~-can, bubuh minyak; ~-well, telaga minyak; gingelly ~, minyak bijan, minyak lenga; coconut ~, minyak nyiur, minyak kelapa.

ointment, n. minyak, 'salap'.

old, adj. tua; of things, lama; the ~ days, zaman dahulu; the ancient days, (zaman) purba kala; 'not so young as she was', kering-sabut; stricken in years, dimakan umur; past best, as a fruit-tree, melawas (lawas); ~-fashioned, kolot, ketinggalan (tinggal) zaman, ~-fashioned ideas, fahaman kolot; see **age**.

olive, n. kana, zetun.

omen, n. padah, alamat; a good ~ for prosperity, alamat kebajikan (bajik).

omit, v. tr. not insert, leave, tinggalkan; leave out (as from team), ketepikan (tepi).

on, prep. a spot, di; (a day), pada; (top), di atas.

once, adv. sekali (sahaja); one day, pada suatu hari, formerly, dahulu; ~ upon a time, sekali persetua; at ~, (without more ado), serta-merta; at 'one go', sekali arung; ~ upon a time, no one knows when, zaman entah-berentah.

one, pron. se, satu, suatu, ~ of several, ~ or the other, salah satu; ~ by ~, satu persatu; ~ after the other, lepas se (orang) se (orang); the ~ Above, Tuhan Yang Esa.

onion, n. bawang.

only, adj. sahaja, hanya; sole, tunggal; not more than, baru; he is ~ two years old, umur dia baru dua tahun.

ooze, v. intr. ~ in, 'work in' mesra.

opal, n. baiduri.

open, adj. terbuka (buka); uncovered, as a

boat, terdedah (dedah); *~-mouthed,* ternganga (nganga); *~ed, as a fissure,* terenggang (renggang); *~-handed (generous),* dengan tangan terbuka; *~ly (without concealment 'in broad daylight'),* dengan terang-terang, berdepan-depan; *without attempt at concealment,* tak berselindung (selindung); *in ~ order (with spaces between),* berjarak (jarak); *~ to the public,* terbuka kapada (orang) ramai; *with an ~ mind,* dengan fikiran yang terbuka; *to speak ~ly (not privately),* bercakap (cakap) secara terbuka; *an ~ space,* tempat lapang.

operate, *v. tr. ~ on (of doctor),* membelah (belah); *operating theatre,* bilik pembedahan; *operation,* pembedahan; *police or military ~,* gerakan; *to put (a law, rules) into ~,* menjalankan (jalan) kuat kuasa.

opiate, *n. sleeping draught,* ubat tidur; *as used by thieves,* pukau, sekot; *painkilling drug,* ubat pelali (lali); *see* **anaesthetic.**

opinion, *n. view,* fikiran, *considered ~,* timbangan, hemat; **conclusion,** pendapatan (dapat); *impression,* perasaan (rasa).

opium, *n.* candu, madat; *to smoke ~,* makan candu, mengisap (isap) candu; *~-dross,* tengkuh, tahi candu; *see* **addict.**

opponent, *n.* lawan; *enemy,* musuh.

opportunely, *adv. just at the right time,* tepat pada waktunya; *to arrive ~ (esp. as, just in time for a meal),* langkah kanan.

opportunity, *n.* peluang: lowong, kesempatan; *a chance,* 'can'; *have time to,* sempat; *business ~,* lubang; *to seize the ~,* merebut (rebut) peluang; *an opportunist to be (having no defined plan),* serkup sahaja; *seize your ~ while you may,* jangan sejuk gulai di tungku, *(don't let the curry get cold on the stove); to seize an ~ to 'work a squeeze', esp., by cornering a product,* menahan (tahan) jerat* dipergentin-

gan (genting), *(to set a noose in a narrow place).*

oppose, *v. tr. resist,* melawan (lawan), menentang (tentang); *~d to (as in meaning),* sebalik dengan; *opposite (in front of),* depan; *(facing),* bertentang dengan, di muka; *the Opposition,* puak pembangkang (bangkang); *~r of a motion,* pembahas (bahas).

oppress, *v. tr.* menindas (tindas), memeras (peras); *~ion,* aniaya, penindasan; *~ive,* zalim; *of heat,* terik.

optician, *n.* pakar kaca mata, pakar cermin mata.

opus, *n. written work,* buah kalam, karya.

or, *conj.* atau.

orally, *adj. by speech,* dengan cakap mulut, dengan lisan.

orange, *n.* limau manis; *in colour,* (kuning) jingga.

orang-outang, *n.* mawas, mayas.

orator, *n. fluent speech-maker,* pandai berpidato; juru pidato; *see* **speech, spout.**

orbit, *n.* peredaran (edar).

orchard, *n.* dusun.

orchid, *n.* bunga 'okkid', bunga anggerik, sakat.

order, *n. direction,* perintah; *of Ruler,* titah; *Order of Chivalry,* darjah; *correct, of ritual,* tertib; *tranquillity,* sentosa; *arrangement,* peraturan (atur), *in ~ that,* supaya, agar; *in an ~ly manner,* secara teratur (atur); *~ly behaviour,* kerukunan (rukun), ketertiban (tertib); *out of ~ (of a mechanism),* rosak; *'won't go',* tak jalan; *General Order,* perintah umum; *see* **regular.**

order, *v. tr. direct,* suruh; *command,* beri hukum; *as Ruler,* titah; *as Government,* perintah; *to ~ goods,* pesan; *~ goods to be made or book (as tickets),* menempah (tempah); *made to ~,* tempahan.

orderly, *n. office ~,* 'ardali', 'peon', budak pejabat (jabat); *~ room,* bilik hukuman.

ordinary, *adj. habitual,* biasa; *such as commonly occurs,* lazim; *of normal type,* kebanyakan (banyak); *unimportant, trivial,* sebarangan.

ore, *n. esp. tin-~,* bijih; *~-bearing stratum,* karang.

organ, *n. of the body,* bahagian tubuh, perkakas tubuh.

organise, *v. tr. arrange,* mengatur (atur); *'get up', as a function,* kira; *systematise,* menyusun (susun), memperkemaskan (kemas); *set up,* menubuhkan (tubuh).

origin, *n.* asal; *ultimate cause,* pokok pangkal; *ultimate ~s,* usul asal.

original, *adj.* yang asli; *not an imitation,* bukan tiruan.

ornament, *n. decorative work,* perhiasan (hias); *an ~,* barang hiasan.

orphan, *n.* anak yatim; *without any kin,* anak piatu; *~age,* rumah anak yatim, daru'l ihsan; *child ~ed of its mother,* kanak-kanak kematian (mati) ibu.

ostracise, *v. tr.* pulaukan.

ostrich, *n.* burung unta, burung kasuari.

other, *adj.* lain; *an~,* lagi satu; *every ~ day,* lat sehari; *one or the ~,* salah satu.

otter, *n.* memerang, berang-berang.

ought, *v. aux.* patut.

out, *adv. not at home,* tak ada; *of a light,* mati, padam; *~ of, having finished,* putus, keputusan; *~ of spending money,* putus belanja; *~ of petrol,* keputusan benzin.

outdistance, *v. tr.* melancar (lancar) ke hadapan meninggalkan jauh di belakang.

outfit, *n.* kelengkapan (lengkap).

outflank, *v. tr.* mengepung (kepung).

out-house, *n.* rumah tambahan.

outing, *n. to go on an ~,* (pergi) makan angin.

outlaw, *n.* orang buruan.

outline, *n.* garisan lingkaran; *rough outlines (as of a plan),* garis-garis kasar, rangka corat-coret.

outrage, *n.* pencabulan (cabul), angkara.

outrank, *v. tr.* berpangkat (pangkat) lebih daripada.

outright, *adv. without reservations,* langsung, tak berlapik (lapik).

outside, *adv.* di luar; *~r (as stranger),* orang luaran.

outskirts, *n. (of town),* daerah sekitar bandar, perenggan bandar, susuran bandar, pinggiran bandar.

outstanding, *adj. pre-eminent,* utama; *of debts, not yet paid,* yang tersangkut (sangkut).

outstrip, *v. tr.* meninggalkan (tinggal) jauh di belakang, mendahului (dahulu).

outwit, *v. tr.* memperdayakan (daya), mengakalkan (akal).

outworks, *n. of fort,* susur(an) kota.

oval, *adj.* bujur telur, bulat bujur.

oven, *n.* dapur; *primitive stone or clay ~,* tungku.

over, *prep. more than,* lebih daripada; *see* **odd, overhead.**

overcast, *adj. (of sky),* (hari) redup, mendung; *as moon,* muram.

overcome, *v. tr. as difficulties,* mengatasi (atas).

over-dose, *n.* ubat berlebihan (lebih).

overflow, *v. intr.* melimpah (limpah), melembak (lembak); *~ banks,* melewati (lewat) tebing.

overgrown, *adj. (with weeds, etc.),* habis naik semak, semak-samun, acap dek (rumput, semak, lalang).

overhang, *v. tr. as rocks, as hair on brow,* menyerukup (serukup).

overhead, *adv.* di atas kepala; *pass overhead, as a bird,* (terbang) dari atas; *in the sky, as a plane,* di angkasa; *~ expenses (expenses of adminstration of a business),* belanja tetap.

overlap, *v. tr. partly cover,* bertindih (tindih); *closely, esp. as tiles,* bersirip (sirip).

overloaded, *adj.* sarat sangat.

overrate, *v. tr. praise excessively,* memuji (puji) sangat; *esteem too highly,* memuliakan (mulia) sangat; *treat as over-important,* mengambil (ambil) berat sangat.

overseer, *n. of labour,* mandur; *generally,* ketua; *see* **foreman.**

overshoot, *v. intr. go beyond mark,* telajak, (lajak).

overtake, *v. tr.* dapat kejar, memotong,

mendahului.
overthrow, *v. tr.* menumbangkan (tumbang); menggulingkan (guling).
overtures, *n. to make ~,* merisik-risik.
overturned, *adj. as a cup,* telangkup (langkup); *see* **upset.**
overwork, *v. tr.* menjadikan (jadi) kerbau, memperkudakan (kuda); *~ oneself,* bekerja (kerja) terlampau berat.

owe, *v. tr.* berhutang (hutang); *owing to (because of).*
owl, *n. (many sp.),* Scops *~,* burung jampuk; *orchard ~,* burung hantu; *hawk ~,* burung pungguk.
own, *v. tr. esp. as land,* memilik (milik).
ox, *n.* lembu (kasi); *see* **cattle.**
oyster, *n.* tiram.

P

pace, *n.* langkah; *to keep ~ with,* berjalan (jalan) sama cepat dengan; *(not left behind),* tidak ketinggalan (tinggal).

Pacific, *n.* lautan teduh.

pacify, *v. tr. appease, make peaceful,* mengamankan (aman); *esp. as two persons quarrelling,* mendamaikan (damai); *as angry person,* menyejukkan (sejuk) hati.

pack, *v. tr. as baggage,* berkemas (kemas), simpan barang-barang (dalam 'beg'); *make into a bundle,* bungkuskan; *'~ up' (abandon an enterprise),* gulung tikar; *~ed tight,* padat; *~ing, as shavings,* penyendal (sendal); *~ing case,* pak; *a ~ of cards,* sepotong daun terup; *~ed, crammed, as crowds, traffic,* berjejal-jejal; *~ in or down, as loose earth,* asak; *see* **congested.**

pact, *n.* perjanjian (janji), pakatan, perikatan (ikat).

pad, padding, *n. protective lining, etc.,* alas, lapisan; *~ded chair,* kerusi bertilam (tilam).

paddle, *n.* pengayuh (kayuh); *double-bladed ~,* kelibat.

padlock, *n.* mangga (kunci).

pagan, *adj.* musyrik, orang yang tidak menganuti sebarang agama terbesar.

page, *n. of book,* muka, halaman; *Court ~s,* budak kundang.

pail, *n.* baldi; *dipper,* timba.

pain, *n.* sakit; *twinge,* sengal; *exclamation of ~,* aduh!; *~-killing drug,* ubat penghilang (hilang) rasa sakit; *see* **opiate.**

paint, *n.* cat; *to ~,* sapu chat; *~ing,* gambar, lukisan cat; *the art of ~ing,* seni lukis.

painter, *n.* pelukis (lukis); *house-~,* tukang cat; *~ (rope to tie up boat),* tali tambat.

pair, *n. a set of two,* sepasang; *esp. as lovers,* sejoli; *as well-fitted to one an-* other, sejodoh, segu; *married couple,* sekelamin; *the other member of a ~,* gu.

palace, *n.* astana; *hall of audience,* balai.

palate, *n.* tekak.

pale, *adj.* pucat; *deathly ~,* toreh tak berdarah (darah).

pall, *n. cloth spread over dead,* kapan.

palm, *n. of hand,* tapak tangan.

pamper, *v. tr. over-indulge,* manjakan; *encourage to be cheeky,* beri muka.

pamphlet, *n.* risalah.

pan, *n. for cooking,* kuali; *large,* gerenseng; *wooden ~ used when washing for tin,* dulang; *to ~ for ore,* mendulang bijih, melanda (landa) bijih; *out of the frying-~ into the fire,* terlepas (lepas) daripada mulut buaya, termasuk (masuk) ka mulut harimau, *(escaped from the mouth of a crocodile into the mouth of the tiger).*

panic, *v. intr. be seized with sudden fright,* naik ketakutan (takut); *lose head,* hilang akal; *flee in disorder,* lari lintang-pukang; *agitated, 'in a flap',* gugup.

pant, *v. intr.* termengah-mengah, cungap-cungap.

panther, *n.* harimau kumbang.

papaya, *n.* buah betik.

paper, *n.* kertas; *writing papers,* kertas tulis; *bloting ~,* kertas lap; *toilet ~,* kertas jamban; *tissue ~,* (kertas) jeluang; *~-weight,* batu penindih (tindih) kertas; *worthless ~ (as forged money or as a miser's hoard),* kertas belacan.

par, *n. equality,* persamaan (sama); *on a ~ with,* bersamaan dengan; *of the same status,* setaraf (dengan).

parable, *n.* cerita ibarat.

parachute, *n.* payung terjun.

parade, *n. of troops,* perbarisan (baris); *passing out ~,* perbarisan tamat latihan; *to '~'* *(strut about, perambulate),* menunjuk-mujuk.

Paradise, *n.* firdaus; *the Garden of Delights,* jannat al'main; *bird of ~,* burung cenderawasih.

paraffin, *n.* minyak tanah.

paragraph, *n.* fasal, perenggan.

parallel, *adj.* sejajar (dengan).

paralysis, *n.* penyakit (sakit) lumpuh.

paramount, *adj. as supreme among Rulers,* agung; *generally,* terutama (utama).

paramour, *n.* kendak.

parapet, *n.* benteng.

parasite, *n. insect or (fig.),* kutu; *to be a ~ on (draw nutriment or living from),* menumpang (tumpang) hidup pada; *parasitic plants generally,* sakat-sakat; *see* **mistletoe.**

parcel, *n.* bungkus(an); *paper ~,* bungkus(an) kertas.

parch, *v. tr. dry by exposure to heat,* layur, salai.

pardon, *n. as after apology,* maaf; *as remission of sentence,* ampun.

pare, *v. tr. as fruit,* kupas; *esp. as stick,* raut.

parents, *n.* ibu bapa; *(more formal),* ayah bonda.

pariah, *n. social outcast in India,* pariah; *the Untouchables,* kaum yang tidak boleh disentuh.

parish, *n.* mukim; *parochial (having narrow views),* bernegeri-negerian (negeri); *~ioners,* anak buah; *see* **congregate.**

park, *n.* taman, kebun bunga; *car-~,* tempat meletak (letak) kereta, tempat simpan kereta; *to ~ a car,* meletak (letak) kereta (di-).

parliament, *n.* 'parlimen', dewan perwakilan (wakil), dewan rakyat.

parrot, *n.* burung bayan, burung nuri; *little Malay parrotquet,* burong pialang, burong puling; *~-fish,* ikan jumpung; *a red and green wrasse,* ikan bayan.

parry, *v. tr. ward off,* tangkis; *knock aside,* tepis.

part, *n.* bahagian; *~ cut off,* sekerat; *in these ~s,* sebelah sini, di daerah ini; *~-time job,* kerja sambilan; *a ~, e.g., of an examination, a play or a course,* penggal; *a (mechanical) ~ of a machine,* alat; *for my ~ —,* buat saya; *see* **role.**

part, *v. tr.* sibak; *as persons in one's way, as sun a mist, as curtains,* menguakkan (kuak); *~ed in the middle of hair,* terbelah (belah) di tengah, tersibak di tengah; *to become broken up and separate, as clouds,* berkuak (kuak); *to take ~ in, join in,* ikut, turut, ikut serta *(followed by a verb);* take *~ in canecutting,* ikut memotong (potong) tebu; *see* **participate, separate.**

participate, *v. intr.* ambil bahagian; *participants (as in a contest),* peserta (serta).

particle, *n. minute portion of matter,* jarah; *tiny piece,* sebutir, secebis, segelintir.

particular, *n. in ~,* istimewa, khasnya; *a detail, a piece of information,* butiran.

partition, *n. as in house,* dinding; *separating off,* sekatan; *splitting off, as territory,* pecahan; *room partioned off,* bilik bersekat.

partnership, *n.* perkongsian (kongsi), perniagaan (niaga); *partner,* rakan; *esp. in games,* pasangan, regu.

patridge, *n. black ~,* burung bertam; *longed-billed ~,* burung selanting.

party, *n. as to dispute,* pihak; *political,* 'parti'; *organised body,* pertubuhan (tubuh), badan; *tea-~,* jamuan teh; *feast,* kenduri; *a ~ (as of travellers),* rombongan, gerombolan; *(large) dinner-~,* majlis makan malam; *(large) social gathering,* ihtifal; *to give a ~,* mengadakan (ada) jamuan.

parvenu, *n. newly rich,* orang kaya baru; *upstart,* bongkok baru betul, si buta baru celik.

pass, *n. between hills,* genting bukit, bukit berapit (apit).

pass, *v. intr. ~ along,* lalu; *by,* lalu dekat; *~ by, as a person or periods of time,* berlalu; *slip away, as events or as a memory,* luput; *a ~ of football,* 'pas', bola hantaran; *through, as a crowd,* melulus (lulus); *to-and-fro,* lalu lalang, mundar-mandir; *through, by way of,* melalui; *by overtaking,* potong; *as cars going in opposite directions,* berselisih (selisih); *to ~ a dish,* sorong; *~ round,* idarkan; *an examination,* lulus, tamat; *when ~ing (on one's way),* sama lalu; *please ~ the —,* cuba kirikan —; *~ers-by,* orang lalu lalang.

passenger, *n.* penumpang (tumpang).

passion, *n.* to be in a, meradang (radang); *the ~s,* hawa nafsu; *~ate love,* cinta berahi; *~ fruit,* buah asyik.

password, *n.* utau, kata mengenal (kenal).

past, *adj. of time,* yang sudah, lalu, dahulu; *pass two o'clock,* pukul dua lebih.

paste, *n.* perekat; *to ~ on,* tepek, tampalkan.

pat, *v. tr.* tepuk.

patch, *n. and v. tr.* tampal, tampung; *a ~, as of colours,* setompok; *~y, as a partly obscured sunlight,* bertelau (telau).

path, *n.* lorong; *cut through jungle,* rentis; *bridle-~,* jalan enam kaki; *trail beaten by wild animals,* denai; *way through, opening that can be used as a ~,* lorongan; *by-~, unfrequented way,* jalan sulit; *private ~ (to which entry is forbidden),* jalan larangan.

pathetic, *adj.* yang menimbulkan (timbul) kasihan, yang menimbulkan perasaan (rasa) rawan, yang menginsafkan (insaf).

patient, *adj.* penyabar (sabar), pesakit.

patina, *n. surface gloss,* sepuh.

patrol, *n.* peronda (ronda).

patron, *n.* penaung (naung).

pattern, *n. as design on cloth,* corak; *decorative ~,* bunga; *colour scheme,* ragi; *see* **example.**

pauper, *n.* orang papa.

pause, *v. intr. halt for a moment,* beranggar (anggar),, berhenti sejenak.

pavement, *n. side-walk,* kaki lima; *paving stone,* batu ubin; *to 'pave the way' (lead up to, make possible),* merintis (rintis) jalan.

paw, *n.* kaki depan, tangan.

pawn, *v. tr.* gadai; *~-ticket,* surat gadai; *a ~ in chess,* bidak.

pay, *n. wages,* gaji; *fee,* upah.

pay, *v. tr.* bayar; *~ in full,* bayar jelas; *~ back,* bayar balik; *~ out (as rope),* hulurkan; *~ for it' (suffer for it),* timpa rasa; *to ~, show a profit of a business,* beruntung (untung); *down ~ment,* wang muka; *see* **advance, earnest money.**

peace, *n.* aman; *tranquillty,* sentosa, tenteram; *~ be with you!,* salam alaikum!; *may he rest in ~!,* kalu inna!; *to make ~,* berdamai; *sue for ~,* minta damai; *~ful co-existence,* hidup bersama-sama secara damai; *to make one's ~ with,* rejoin, a wife or a party, rojok pada; *member of (American) ~ Corps,* sukarelawan (Amerika Syarikat); *if you want ~, prepare for war,* berkubu (kubu) sebelum alah, *(make a stockade before you are defeated).*

peacock, *n.* burung merak.

peak, *n. of mountain,* puncak, kemuncak, mercu; *of hat,* birai.

pea-nuts, *n.* kacang tanah; *(when fried),* kacang goreng.

pearl, *n.* mutiara; *mother-of-~,* gewang; trochus, loklok; *to dive for ~s,* menyelam (selam) mutiara.

peas, *n.* kacang 'pis'.

peasant, *n.* orang kampung, petani (tani).

peaty, *adj. of soil,* gambut.

pebbles, *n.* batu kerikil.

peck, *v. tr.* patuk, pagut; *~ to pieces,* pagut putus-putus.

peculiar, *adj.* ganjil, pelik.

pedal, *n.* pengayuh (kayuh).

peddle, *v. tr.* berjaja (jaja), meraih (raih).

pedestal, *n.* alas, lapik.

pedigree, *n.* silasilah.

peel, *n.* kulit; *to ~,* kupas, buang kulit; *to ~ off, flake off,* lekang, mengelupas (kelupas).

peep, v. intr. intai; to play Peeping Tom, mengendap.

peer, v. intr, gaze intently, intai, intip; down-wards, canguk; **peer,** n. person's equal in rank or merit, duke, earl, orang bangsawam di negeri Inggeris.

peevish, adj. perengus (rengus), merungsing (rungsing), bengkeng.

peg, n. pating; as for tethering cattle, tumang; clothes' ~, penyangkut (sangkut) kain; to ~ together, pasak.

pelican, n. burung undan.

pell-mell, adv. 'at sixes and sevens', simpang-perenang; in disorder, hempaspulas.

pelt, v. tr. baling, lempar, merejam (rejam) batu ke atas; ~ing (or rain), (hujan) tak boleh celik mata.

pelvis, n. pinggul.

pen, n. kalam, pena; fountain-~, pena tabung; ~-holder, batang pena; a ~ for cattle, kandang.

Penang, n. Pulau Pinang; Georgetown, Tanjung; ~ Hill, Bukit Bendera.

pending, adj. still undecided, belum putus.

penetrate, v. tr. as a bullet, memasuki, menembus; as oil into bearings, mesra.

peninsular, n. semenanjung.

penis, n. pucuk, butuh, batang pelir; (sl.) pesawat, zakar; of a squirrel, cula; esp. of a child, kotek.

penitent, adj. bertaubat (taubat); remorseful, menyesal (sesal); having 'learnt lesson', serik.

pennon, n. panji-panji; streamer, ular-ular.

pension, n. 'pencen'; to go on ~, berpencen, bersara (sara); to place on the ~able establishment, masukkan dalam lingkungan bersara.

pensive, adj. termenung (menung).

people, n. orang; the public, orang ramai; the common ~, orang kebanyakan (banyak); subjects, rakyat; population, isi negeri; see **mass.**

pepper, n. lada.

perambulator, n. kereta bayi.

perceive, v. tr. with the eye, nampak; discover, conclude, dapati; apprehend, faham.

per cent, adj. peratus (ratus); payment on a ~age basic, upah mengikut (ikut) kiraan peratus.

perch, v. intr. hinggap, bertenggek (tenggek); habitual ~ing place, anggaran (burung); the climbing ~, ikan pepuyu (puyu-puyu).

perchance, adv. if ~ —, nyampang-nyampang kalau —, jikalau sekiranya.

percolate, v. intr. menapis (tapis), menelap (telap); see **absorb.**

peremptory, adj. ~ command, hukum paksa, tak boleh diingkari atau dibantah.

perfect, adj. intact, sempurna; without flaw, tak bercacat (cacat).

perforate, v. tr. tebuk; ~d, tembus; holed, tembuk; see **penetrate.**

perform, v. tr. carry into effect, as a plan, melaksanakan (laksana), menjalankan (jalan); as a ceremony, melangsungkan (langsung); ~ a play, melakukan (laku).

perfume, n. minyak wangi, air wangi, haruman; various ~s, bau-bauan.

perfunctory, adj. not thorough, tidak bersungguh-sungguh, sambilewa; done just for appearances' sake, muka sahaja!; see **appearance, humbug.**

pergola, n. punjung.

perhaps, adv. barangkali, andainya; 'could be', boleh jadi.

perimeter, n. garis keliling.

period, n. masa; epoch, zaman; women's '~', see **menstruate;** ~ic, ada masa, ada kala; ~ical (magazine), majallah; ~ical, berkala (kala); ~ical rises in wages, tambahan gaji berkala; ~ical issue, as of a magazine, penerbitan (terbit) berkala; ~! (sl.), that's that, no more to be said, habis perkara, habis bicara.

perishable, adj. will not withstand rough treatment, mudah rosak.

peritonitis, n. penyakit (sakit) radang selaput perut.

perjury, n. to *commit* ~, sumpah palsu (bohong).

permanent, adj. *meant to last,* tetap; *eternal,* kekal, abadi, baka; *for ~ wave, see* **curl, hair.**

permeate, v. intr. *see* **absorb, percolate.**

permission, n. kebenaran (benar); *(more formal),* izin; *a (written) permit,* surat kebenaran.

perpendicular, adj. tegak.

perpetual, adj. abadi, kekal.

perplexed, adj. terkeliru (keliru); *'mazed',* bingung.

persecute, v. tr. *treat cruelly,* menyiksakan (siksa); *persistently harry,* mengejar-ngejar (kejar), tekan-menekan.

persevere, v. intr. bertahan (tahan); *perseveringly (persistently),* bertubi-tubi, bermati-mati.

Persia, n. negeri Farsi, Iran.

persimmon, n. buah pisang kaki.

persistently, adv. berperi-peri, tidak lepas-lepas; dengan gigih, dengan tekun; *see* **persevere.**

person, n. *individual human being,* orang; *self,* sendiri, diri; *in ~ (in the flesh),* hadir sendiri.

personage, n. *prominent person, 'personality'* pembesar (besar), tokoh.

personality, n. *distinctive character,* peribadi, sahsiah; *a ~, prominent personage,* tokoh, pembesar (besar); *character, as the attributes of a person,* keperibadian; *his ~ is good, 'he's a good chap',* baik orangnya; *cult of ~,* pemujaan (puja) tokoh.

personnel, n. *staff,* kakitangan.

persuade, v. tr. memujuk (pujuk); *win over,* menawan (tawan) hati.

pertaining to, adv. berkenaan (kena) dengan.

pervade, v. intr. *be diffused, as scent,* semerbak.

pervert, v. tr. *lead astray,* mengelirukan (keliru), menyesatkan (sesat); *see* **garble,** *a ~ (from Islam),* murtad.

pest, n. *agricultural pests generally,* bina-tang atau serangga perosak; *chief ~ of rice,* pianggang, kesip, cenangau.

pester, v. tr. *worry,* mengusik (usik); *interfere with,* mengganggu (ganggu), menggoda (goda), merunut (runut).

pestilence, n. hawar, sampar; *epidemic,* waba.

pestle, n. alu, antan.

pet, n. *~ animal,* binatang kesayangan (sayang); *to keep as a ~,* simpan buat main; *my ~! (to animal),* didik!

petal, n. kelopak bunga.

petition, n. surat rayuan.

petrify, v. intr. membatu, menjadi batu.

petty, adj. runcit; *trifling,* remeh; *triffles,* tetek-bengek.

petulant, adj. lekas marah, bengkeng; *see* **play.**

pew, n. bangku gereja.

phase, n. *as of events,* peringkat; *~d (by calculated degrees),* bertingkat-tingkat.

pheasant, n. burung kuang, burung kuau.

phial, n. buli-buli, *'botol'* kecil, pelis.

philanthropist, n. orang dermawan.

philosophy, n. falsafah; *philosopher,* failasuf, ahli falsafah.

phlegm, n. *generally,* lendir; *in nose,* ingus.

phosphorescence, n. pendar, kolomoyar.

photograph, v. tr. mengambil gambar; n. gambar foto.

phrase, n. rangkai kata; ungkapan.

physical, adj. berkenaan (kena) dengan badan; *~ training, gymnastics,* pelajaran (ajar) gerak badan; *to do ~ training,* bersenam (senam).

physique, n. *bodily structure,* susuk badan, bangun tubuh.

pick, v. tr. *as a flower,* petik; *~ off, as a flower,* getis, gentas, runtas; *~ pockets,* menyeluk (seluk) kocek; *~ a quarrel,* cari gaduh; *'~ on' (fault-find),* cari salah; *~ up (collect here and there),* mengutip (kutip); *as between finger and thumb,* cekuh; *select,* memilih (pilih); *as teeth,* cungkil; *~ed (specially selected),* terpilih; *~ holes, see* **cavil;** *~*

at, as a sore, kutil; ~ *to pieces,* mencetai (cetai); ~ *fibrous staff, as oakum,* jonjot; *grasp and* ~ *up, as a child or in wrestling,* merangkul (rangkul); ~ *up, take in the hand,* mencapai (capai).

pick-a-back, *n. to carry* ~, mengokok (kokok).

picket, *v. tr. to* ~, *guard,* mengawal (kawal); *of strikers,* berpiket (piket).

pickles, *n.* acar; *locally pickled anchovies, etc.,* budu; *fruit, etc., pickled in salt,* jeruk; *to pickle, generally,* pendap.

picnic, *v. intr.* berkelah (kelah).

picture, *n.* gambar; *diagram,* rajah; *moving* ~*s,* gambar bergerak (gerak); *to* ~ *to oneself,* gambarkan dalam hati, bayangkan; *see* **cinema.**

piebald, *adj. in stripes,* kuda belang; *parti-coloured,* tampung.

piece, *n.* sekeping; ~ *cut off,* sekerat, sepotong; *as in chess, etc.,* buah; ~*work,* pawah.

piecemeal, *adv. bit by bit,* berdikit-dikit.

pier, *n.* dermaga, pangkalan, tembok laut.

pierce, *v. tr. as with a spear,* menikam (tikam); *ears for ear-rings,* tindik; *go right through,* lantas; ~*d right through,* tembus; *see* **penetrate.**

piety, *n.* kesalehan, kesucian.

pig, *n.* babi; *euphemism,* kerbau Cina, kerbau pendek; *wild* ~, babi hutan; ~*headed, impervious to advice,* tak ternasihat (nasihat); *to buy a* ~ *in a poke,* membeli kerbau di padang, *(to buy a buffalo in the field, i.e. without having a good look at it).*

pigeon, *n. domestic,* merpati; *green,* punai; *wood-*~, pergam; *pied imperial* ~, burung rawa; *carrier-*~, merpati 'pos'.

pigtail, *n.* tocang.

pile, *n. piece of timber, driven into the ground,* pancang, tiang; *heap,* longgok, timbunan; *in piles,* bertimbun-timbun; *to* ~ *up, 'build up', of water under pressure,* membuak (buak).

piles, *n. haemorrhoids,* bawasir, wasir.

pilgrimage, *n.* ziarah; *pilgrims to Mecca,* jemaah Haji; *to go on* ~ *to Mecca,* naik Haji, pergi ziarah ke Mekah; *to fulfil the duty of going on* ~, menunaikan (tunai) fardu haji.

pillar, *n.* tiang; *large* ~, turus; *memorial* ~, tugu peringatan (ingat); ~ *of State,* turus negeri.

pillion, *n. to sit* ~, membonceng (bonceng) (di belakang).

pillow, *n.* bantal; ~*-case,* sarung bantal.

pilot, *n. of aircraft,* pemandu (pandu) juruterbang; *of ship,* malim; *helmsman,* juru mudi.

pimp, *n.* barua.

pimple, *n.* bintat, jerawat; *numerous small pimples,* bintik-bintik.

pin, *n.* peniti; *drawing-*~, paku payung; *hair-*~, cucuk sanggul; *metal* ~ *for pegging or rivetting,* pasak; ~*ned down, e.g., by a fallen tree,* tertindih (tindih); '~*s and needles' (tingling),* kebas, semut-semut; *to* ~*-prick (annoy in petty manner, harass),* mencucuk-cucuk; *safety-*~, peniti baju, 'pin' penyemat (semat); *to* ~ *together,* sematkan.

pincers, *n. nippers,* sepit, cunam; *large,* kakatua.

pinch, *v. tr.* cubit, picit; ~*ed between two surfaces,* tersepit (sepit); *to '*~*' (pilfer),* sauk; ~ *off, as a bud,* getis; *a* ~ *(as of salt),* sejemput.

pincushion, *n.* bantal jarum.

pine, *v. intr.* merana (rana); ~ *for love or for regret for a person,* bercintakan (cinta); *from nostalgia or longing,* merindukan (rindu).

pineapple, *n.* buah nanas; ~*-factory,* kilang mengetin ('tin') nanas.

pinion, *v. tr. to tie so as to prevent escape, as by tying the legs of a fowl,* merempung (rempung), menambatkan (tambat); ~ *(arms),* mengilas (kilas), mengikat lengan.

pink, *adj.* merah muda; *deep* ~, merah jambu; *bright* ~, kesumba.

pinnacle, *n.* mercu.

pioneer, *n.* perintis (rintis); *esp. in a struggle,* pelopor.

pious, *adj.* beriman (iman), berbakti

(bakti), wara.

pip, n. biji (buah); *on a card,* mata daun terup.

pipe, n. *for carrying water,* 'paip', pembuluh (buluh); *for smoking,* 'paip'; (sl.), dapur; *musical instrument,* suling, seruling; *voice-~,* saluran suara.

piquant, adj. *as, spicy in taste,* pedas.

pirate, n. perompak (rompak), lanun.

pirouette, v. intr. *spin round as in dancing,* memusing-musingkan (pusing) badan.

piston, n. 'piston', omboh.

pit, n. *hole,* lubang; *large, of mine,* lombong; *abyss,* keleburan; *to ~ (match) against another,* mengadudombakan, melagakan; *~ted with holes,* berdarang-darang, berpesukpesuk; *with pock-marks,* mopeng; *~fall (for game),* serling, pelubang (lubang).

pit-a-pat, adv. *to go ~, of the heart,* berdebar-debar.

pitch, n. *for caulking,* gegala (gala-gala); *bitumen,* tanah bolong.

pitch, v. intr. *of a ship,* teranggul-anggul, berangguk-angguk; *to ~ (a tent),* hamparkan, dirikan.

pitcher, n. buyung, 'jak'; *~-plant,* periuk kera.

pith, n. empulor; *esp. of a sago-palm,* sagu.

pity, n. kasihan; *regret,* sayang; *to feel ~,* menaruh (taruh) belas kasihan; *what a ~!,* sayanglah!; *(stronger),* kesianlah!

pivot, n. *(fig.) basis from which action emanates,* pokok pangkal; *axis,* pasak.

placard, n. pelekat.

place, n. tempat; *to take ~,* berlaku (laku); *esp. as a ceremony,* berlangsung (langsung); *to ~ (in position),* bubuh.

plagiarise, v. tr. *steal from the works of others,* mencedok (cedok) kerangan orang, meniru-niru (tiru) sahaja; memplagiat; *plagiarism,* hasil, cedok.

plague, n. sampar, hawar; *(fig.) affliction,* bencana; *esp. as a term of abuse,* musibat.

plain, adj. *clear,* terang; *level tract,* tanah rata, dataran; *open ~,* padang; *simple,*

sederhana; *~ clothes, see* **mufti;** *having no pattern,* yang tidak bercorak (corak).

plaintiff, n. aduan, yang mendakwa (dakwa).

plaintive, adj. *arousing a sad feeling,* sayu; *arousing a feeling of nostalgia;* perindu (rindu).

plait, v. tr. anyam; *~ a net,* menyirat (sirat) jaring.

plan, n. peta; *way of doing,* jalan, ikhtiar; *proposal,* cadangan, syor; *to propose, suggest, (a ~),* mencadang; *'bright idea',* suatu akal; *worked out programme,* rancangan.

plane, n. *smoothing tool,* ketam.

planet, n. bintang beredar.

plankton, n. *minute floating sea-organisms,* bunga laut, bunga air.

plant, n. pokok; *herbage,* rumput; *vegetation generally,* tumbuh-tumbuhan; *to ~,* menanam (tanam); *~ out (seedlings),* meredah (redah), meredih (redih).

plantain, n. *fruit,* buah pisang; *the weed,* rumput taik babi.

plantation, n. kebun, ladang; *rubber-~,* kebun getah; *coconut-~,* kebun nyiur; *oil-palm-~,* kebun kelapa sawit; *coffee-~,* kebun kopi; *experimental ~,* kebun percubaan (cuba).

plaque, n. papan peringatan (ingat).

plaster, v. tr. sapu kapor; *~ on,* tepek; *sticking-~,* koyo.

plate, n. pinggan; *to ~, overlay with metal,* sadurkan; *electro-~d articles,* barang celup 'karan'; *gold-~d,* barang tersadur mas; *silver-~d,* barang tersadur perak.

plateau, n. dataran (di atas gunung).

platform, n. pentas; *dais,* gerai, teniat; *wedding dais,* pelamin (lamin); *~ bed,* pangking, geta; *esp. for drying fish and for the ~ of a railway station or a jetty,* pelantar; *(fig.) political ~, political standpoint,* pendirian (diri).

platitudinous, adj. *trite, hackneyed,* lusuh, usang.

play, v. intr. bermain; *~ football,* main

bolasepak; ~ *the piano,* petik 'piano'; ~ *the violin,* gesek biola; *to '~ the fool',* main gila; *to '~ up' (show tempera- ment),* meragam (ragam), mengolah (olah); *'try to be clever',* memandai- mandai (pandai); *behave petulantly,* membuat (buat) perangai, *(fig.) of en- gines, etc., '~ing up', giving trouble,* meragam; *thinking of nothing but ~,* leka bermain sahaja; *~-boy,* kaki 'joli'; *to '~ old Harry' (do as one pleases),* bermaharaja-raja)-lela, berleluasa (leluasa); *~mate,* budak sepermainan; *a ~ (dramatic piece),* wayang, sandiwara; *~-ground, esp. one at- tached to, e.g., a school,* halaman tem- pat bermain.

playing-field, *n.* padang bola.

plead, *v. intr. make earnest appeal,* merayu (rayu) hal; *to ~ for, esp. in Court,* membela.

pleasant, *adj. of expression,* (muka) manis.

please, *int.* cuba; *(more pleadingly),* tolong; *be ~d to, agree to,* sudi; *as host,* sila; *as you ~,* ikut suka (tuan); *to ~, give pleasure to,* menyukakan, (suka) hati, memujuk (pujuk) hati; *if God ~s,* insya' Allah; *~d,* suka-hati; *a pleasure, a delight,* suatu kegemaran (gemar); *doing as one ~s, following one's whims,* turut hati sahaja; *see under* **play.**

pleat, *n.* wiron, lipatan.

plebiscite, *n.* pungutan suara rakyat.

pledge, *n. a deposit as security,* cagaran, gadaian, jaminan; pertaruhan (taruh) sebagai jaminan; *solemn promise,* ikrar.

Pleiades, *n.* bintang ketika.

plenary, *n.* kuasa yang tak terbatas, pertemuan yang dihadiri oleh semua orang yang berhak menghadirinya.

plenipotentiary, *n.* wakil mutlak.

plentiful, *adj. many,* banyak; *mewah, ga- lore,* belanar; *abundant,* melimpah; *esp. as crops,* menjadi-jadi; *of money, wealth,* makmur.

pliable, *adj. as a bough,* lentur; *easily led,*

mudah terpengaruh; *easily talked round,* lembut-telinga.

pliers, *n.* angkup-angkup.

Plimsoll-mark, *n.* garisan tanda air.

plinth, *n.* pelapik (lapik), alas.

plod, *v. intr. ~ along,* mengayun (ayun) tunjang.

plop, *adv. sound,* debap; *to fall with a ~,* jatuh berdebap.

plot, *n. of land,* sekeping (tanah), sejoreng (tanah); *to ~,* berpakat-pakat; *a ~,* komplot; *the ~ of a story,* rencana, 'thema'; *area in rice-field bounded by* batas, petak.

plough, *n.* tenggala, bajak; *~share,* nayam.

plover, *n. (many sp.),* grey ~, burung cunglit; *golden ~,* burung keruit; lap- wing, burung duit-duit.

pluck, *v. tr. feathers,* cabut bulu; *a flower, see* **pick;** *~ up courage,* memberan- ikan (berani) diri.

plug, *n. for a hole,* penyumbat (sumbat); *~-hole,* cerat; *for a boat,* mata kakap; *of betel-leaf,* sepiak, sesogeh; *to ~ a crack by pushing, e.g., a rag into it,* pema- lam.

plumb, *n. plummet,* perum, batu duga, batu ladung.

plump, *adj.* tambun, tembam, montok.

plunder, *v. tr.* merampas (rampas); *to go ~ing,* menjarah (jarah).

plunge, *v. intr. throw oneself in impetu- ously,* menceburkan (cebur) diri, berkecimpung (kecimpung); *jump down,* menyelam, terjun; *as a restive horse,* lompat-hambur, terkerjang-ker- jang.

plus, *n. to be added on,* lebih.

pneumonia, *n.* demam rabu kembang, radang paru-paru.

poach, *v. intr. hunt illegally,* berburu (buru) secara haram; *shoot without a license,* menembak (tembak) tak ber- lesen ('lesen'); *hunt in a reserved for- est,* berburu di hutan larangan.

pocket, *n.* kocik, saku; *~-size,* ukuran saku; *~-money,* wang kocek, wang jajan; *~-knife,* pisau lipat; *(spending-*

money), belanja.

pock-marked, *adj.* mopeng.

pod, *n.* kulit, cemuk.

poem, *n.* syair, sajak; *quatrain,* pantun.

point, *n.* tip, hujung; *as of horns (tine),* rangga; *dot,* titik, noktah; ~*s (score),* mata; *won on* ~*s,* menang atas kiraan mata; *come to the* ~, pendekkan kata; *finer* ~*s (as of language or scheme),* selok-belok; *as of argument,* buku; *to* ~ *(a gun) at,* acukan (senapang) pada; ~ *out, show,* tunjuk; *to* ~ *with the chin,* memoncongkan (moncong) mulut kearah; ~ *at,* menuding (tuding) ke; ~*ed,* runcing.

poise, *v. tr.* balance in the hand, as a spear, timang, memperseimbangkan.

poison, *n.* stomach ~, racun; *blood* ~, bisa, dari ~, ipuh, upas; ~ *of the tree-nettle,* jelatang; *compounded slow* ~, santau; *trees with* ~*ous sap, which are dangerous to climb,* pokok rangas; *food-*~*ing,* sakit tersalah (salah) makan; keracunan makanan; *death from* ~, kematian (mati) termakan racun; *one man's meat is another man's* ~, pejatian (jati) awak kepantangan (pantang) orang, *(your tibits are forbidden food for others).*

poke, *v. tr.* cucuk; *from below, as fruit,* jolok; *esp. of stabbing from below,* radak; *to* ~ *one's head out,* menjengukkan (jenguk) kepala; ~ *around, as with a stick in water,* runjang.

pole, *n.* galah; *to* ~ *(a boat);* bergalah; *support for climbing plant,* junjung; *geographical* ~, kutub.

police, *n.* the ~, 'polis'; *a policeman,* mata-mata; ~-*station,* rumah pasung, balai polis; '~', mata-mata khas; ~-*informer,* hantu 'polis'.

policy, *n.* 'polisi', dasar; *course of action adopted,* muslihat; *standpoint,* pendirian (diri).

polish, *v. tr.* gosok; *'shine up',* gilap, upam; *as gems,* canai; ~*ed by lathe,* dilarik.

polite, *adj. see* **courtesy.**

politics, *n.* 'politik', siasah, tata negara;

politician, ahli 'politik'; *not politically minded,* buta 'politik'.

poll, *n. see* **vote;** ~-*tax,* cukai kepala.

pollen, *n.* sari bunga, benih bunga; *to pollinate (as does a bee),* mengenakan (kena) sari bunga, memasukkan (masuk) sari bunga.

pollute, *v. tr.* mencemarkan (cemar), nodai.

polygamy, *n.* practice of ~, permaduan (madu).

polyglot, *adj.* ahli berbilang (bilang) bahasa.

polytheism, *n.* kepercayaan (percaya) berbilang (bilang) bahasa.

pomegranate, *n.* buah delima.

pomp, *n.* with great ~, dengan segala kebesaran (besar).

pompous, *adj.* to be ~, membesarkan (besar) diri; *snooty,* hidung tinggi.

pond, *n.* kolam; *old mining hole filled with water,* lombong; *fish-*~, takungan ikan; *mud-hole,* londang.

ponder, *v. intr.* merenungkan (renung), tafakur; *think hard,* berfikir (fikir) dalam-dalam.

pool, *n.* in river, lubuk; *in gaming,* tui; *for ablutions at mosque,* kolah.

poor, *adj.* miskin; *destitute,* papa; *'cleaned out',* licin; *(course),* tercalat (calat); *in straitened circumstances,* dalam kepicikan (picik); *'the* ~ *and the needy'* (two of the eight categories of people entitled to receive tithe, see **category,** orang fakir miskin; *the 'under-privileged',* kaum melarat; *living from hand to mouth,* (macam ayam), kais pagi, makan pagi, kais petang, makan petang, *(like fowls), scratch in the morning and eat in the morning; sractch in the evening and eat in the evening);* having only the clothes one stands up in, sehelai sepinggang, *(one sarung) for one waist).*

populace, *n.* isi negeri; *the public,* orang ramai; *the 'masses',* rakyat jelata; *the common people,* orang kebanyakan (banyak); *(total) population,* bilangan penduduk (duduk).

popular, *adj. celebrated,* ternama (nama); *well-like,* sukai-ramai; *see* **idol.**

populous, *adj. thickly populated,* ramai penduduknya; *densely populated area,* daerah padat, kawasan sesak.

porcelain, *n.* 'porselin', tembikar.

porch, *n.* anjung; ~-*room,* serambi.

porcupine, *n.* landak.

pore, *n.* liang roma; ~ *over, (studiously read),* bertekun (tekun) membaca (baca).

pork, *n.* daging babi.

porous, *adj.* berliang-liang; *as absorbent,* telap; *as cellular; not solid,* mabung.

porpoise, *n. see* **dolphin.**

port, *n. left of ship looking forward,* kiri; ~-*hole,* lobang pot; *free* ~, pelabuhan (labuh) bebas; *see* **harbour.**

portable, *adj.* dapat diangkat; ~ *radio,* radio bimbit.

portentous, *adj. ominous,* berpadah (padah), luar biasa, menakjubkan.

portion, *n.* habuan, bahagian; *see* **share.**

portray, *v. tr. depict,* menggambarkan (gambar); *portrait;* gambar (wajah).

pose, *v. intr. behave in an artificial manner,* berlagak (lagak); ~ *as (pretend to be),* berlagak sebagai; *claim to be* mengaku (aku) diri menjadi (jadi).

position, *n. place,* tempat, kedudukan (duduk); *site,* letaknya; *state of affairs,* hal, keadaan (ada).

positive, *adj. definite,* tertentu (tentu), pasti, tegas.

possess, *v. tr. have title to, esp. land,* memilik (milik); ~*ions,* harta benda; *in my ~ion (in my hands),* di tangan saya; '~*ed',* (sudah) kenaikan (naik) hantu, (sudah) diserap hantu, (sudah) dirasuk hantu; *to* ~ *(as a spirit),* menjelma (jelma) ke dalam diri —, *(to become incarnate in the personality of —).*

possible, *adj.* boleh jadi, mungkin; *as soon as* ~, secepat mungkin; *as far as* ~, dengan seboleh-bolehnya, sedapat-dapat-nya.

post, *n. appointment,* jawatan, jabatan; *occupation,* kerja; *place of duty (of a*

soldier), tempat mengawal (kawal); *to be* ~*ed (transferred),* berpindah (pindah); *to* ~ *(a letter),* mengirim surat; ~-*box,* tong surat; *box for letters to be collected at the Post Office,* peti surat; ~-*free,* bersih belanja 'pos'; *to* ~ *(place, esp. sentry) in position,* tempatkan; ~*mark,* cap 'pos'; ~*script,* tambahan surat; *see* **pillar, stake.**

poster, *n.* pelekat, sepanduk.

posterity, *n.* keturunan (turun); *grandchildren and great grandchildren,* cucu cicit; *future ages,* zaman yang akan datang.

post-mortem, *n.* pemeriksaan (periksa) mayat.

postpone, *v. tr.* tangguh; *to ask for* ~*ment (as for time),* minta tempoh; *put back time fixed for event,* mengundurkan (undur) waktu.

pot, *n. cooking* ~, periuk; *of earthenware,* belanga; *flower-*~, pasu bunga; ~*s-and-pans,* periok belanga; ~*tery,* tempat orang membuat (buat) periuk belanga; *(to a guest), take* ~-*luck!,* makanlah ada-ada sahaja!; ~*sherd,* tembikar; *glazed* ~, *as for ginger,* situn; *the* ~ *calls the kettle black,* keladi* kata kemahang gatal.

potato, *n.* ubi (kentang); *sweet* ~, keledek, setela.

pot-purri, *n.* bunga rampai.

potter, *v. intr. dawdle on job,* terkosel-kesel.

pouch, *n.* pundi-pundi, kandi-kandi, saku; *esp. for fisherman,* kantung.

poultice, *v. tr.* pupik, tuam.

poultry, *n.* ayam itik.

pounce, *v. intr.* menyambar (sambar), menukik.

pound, *v. tr.* tumbuk; *crush small,* pirik; *esp. spices,* pipiskin; ~*er for betel,* gobek.

pour, *v. tr.* ~ *out,* tuang, ~ *away,* curahkan; *to* ~ *out, as grain from a cut sack or people from a building,* menyumbul (sumbul); ~, *as water through a breach in a dam,* membobos (bobos); *as smoke from a fire,* naik berkepul-kepul;

of rain, mencurah-curah; *see* **gush.**

pout, *v. intr.* membuat (buat) mimik muka, mencemik, melebarkan bibir ke hadapan.

powder, *n.* serbuk; *gun-~,* ubat senapang; *face-~,* bedak, pupur; *~y, as fine sand,* gebu.

power, *n.* kuasa, tenga; *might, esp. of God,* kudrat; *active property, as of a magnet,* daya; *~ of attorney,* surat kuasa; *might, as striking ~,* penangan (tangan); *as ability to perform,* kadar; *to the best of my ~,* sekadar; *to hold political ~,* memegang (pegang) tampuk kerajaan (raja).

practice, *n. exercise to improve skill,* latihan; *to put (rules) into ~,* mengamalkan (amal) (petua); *practically speaking (virtually),* boleh dikatakan; *to practise one's religion,* beramal ibadat; *in ~ (as opposed to theory),* pada amalannya.

praise, *v. tr.* puji, sanjung.

prance, *v. intr.* gelinjang, menari-nari (tari), melompat-lompat kesukaan.

prank, *n. escapade,* suatu kenakalan (nakal); *to play ~s,* berjenaka (jenaka).

prawn, *n.* udang; *~-paste,* belacan; *(sl.),* mentega laut.

pray, *v. intr. ritually, sembahyang, for something,* hajat, berdoa (doa); *to say an extra ~er for some special purpose; to raise hands in ~er,* tadah tangan; *to ~ at immense length (sl.),* berdoa sampai dua kepuk* banyaknya; *the call to ~er,* bang, azan; *the five times of Islamic daily ~er,* lima waktu; *to ~ esp. at a shrine for a special purpose, accompanied by a vow,* berkaul (kaul); *to call to ~er,* suarakan bang.

preach, *v. intr.* membaca (baca) khutbah.

preamble, *n.* pendahuluan (dahulu).

precarious, *adj. insecure, dependent,* tidak tetap; *'like a bamboo on a riverbank' (apt to falling in),* seperti aur di tebing; *in a threatening situation,* seperti telur di hujung tanduk *('like an egg on the point of a horn'),* retak menanti (nanti), belah *('the crack awaits (is sure*

to be followed by) the split').

precautions, *n. to take ~,* berjaga-jaga; *take your ~ in good time,* berpayung (payung) sebelum hujan, *(get an umbrella before it starts to rain.*

precepts, *n.* petua; *esp. of traditional sayings of the Prophet,* hadis; *injunction, charge,* amanat.

precinct, *n. ground pertaining to a building,* kawasan, lingkungan sekeliling, halaman.

precious, *adj.* berharga (harga), bernilai (nilai), mahal; *of metal or gems,* mulia.

precise, *adj.* jitu, tepat, saksama, teliti.

precipice, *n.* batu curam.

precipitate, *adj. of action, over-hasty,* gopoh-gapah, terburu-buru; *to ~ (hasten), e.g., a crisis,* mencetuskan (cetus).

precis, *n. abstract,* pati; *summary,* ringkasan.

precise, *adj. exact,* tepat.

predacious, *adj. of animals, subsisting by capture of prey,* buas.

predecessor, *n. previous (holder of position),* yang memegang (pegang) jawatan dahulu; *see* **ex-.**

predestination, *n. the Will of God,* takdir Allah; *'written',* tersurat (surat).

predict, *v. tr.* meramalkan (ramal); *foreshadow,* membayangkan (bayang).

predominate, *adj. foremost in importance,* terutama (utama); *v.* mengatasi, menguasai, melebihi.

preen, *v. intr. of a bird,* menyelisik (selisik) bulu, menghiasi diri.

preface, *n.* pendahuluan (dahulu), kata pengantar (hantar).

prefer, *v. tr.* lagi suka; *give special position or attention to,* mengutamakan (utama), mengagung-agungkan; *~able, adj.* lebih baik dpd, lebih disukai dpd.

pregnant, *adj.* bunting; *(more polite),* hamil; *(sl.),* berbadan (badan) dua; *to 'carry',* mengandung (kandung); *in early stage of pregnancy,* bunting kecil; *in last stage, heavy with child,* bunting sarat; *'expectant',* menantikan (nanti) hari.

prejudice, *n.* prasangka; *to ~, impair the prospects of, e.g., a conference,* mengece-wakan (kecewa); *prejudicial, adj.* mempengaruhi, merugikan; *see* **discriminate unfair.**

preliminary, *adj. what comes first,* yang terdahulu (dahulu); *by way of ~,* sebagai pendahuluan, *~ inquiry (in Court),* pemeriksaan (periksa) awal.

premature, *adj.* sebelum waktunya; *~ birth,* beranak (anak) kurang bulan.

premier, *adj. foremost,* yang terutama (utama), yang penting; *the Premier,* Perdana Menteri.

premier, *n. first showing of a film,* tayangan perdana.

premonition, *n.* alamat (akan terjadi sesuatu), firasat.

preoccupied, *adj. as 'in a brown study',* ralit, asyik, khusuk.

prepare, *v. tr. see* **ready;** *preparations (articles made, steps taken, by way of preparation),* persediaan (sedia); *be ~d to (undertake to),* sanggup hendak; *not afraid to,* berani; *~d to swear to it,* berani sumpah.

prepay, *v. tr. in advance,* membayar lebih dahulu.

preposterous, *adj. utterly absurd,* mustahil, karut sahaja, tak diterima dek akal.

prepuce, *n.* kulup.

prerogative, *n. special power, esp. of a sovereign,* hak istimewa.

presage, *n. sign of something to come,* alamat, tanda.

presence, *n.* adanya; hadapan; *in the ~ of his friends,* di hadapan sahabat-sahabatnya; *~ of mind,* akal budi, dingin kepalanya.

present, *adj. to be ~,* ada; *(more formal),* hadir, *a ~, gift,* hadiah; *small gift brought by caller,* buah tangan; *gift or grant,* pemberian (beri); *to ~ (as prizes at a show,* sampaikan; *to a Ruler,* persembahkan (sembah); *as a play or film,* persembahkan, menghidangkan (hidang); *as a singer a song,* memperdengarkan (dengar); *the ~ation, as of prizes or of a story,* penyampaian; *to*

make a voluntary conveyance of property, hebah; *a gift inter vivos,* pemberian hidup, hebah; *at ~,* sekarang.

preserve, *v. tr. keep safe,* pelihara, melindungi; *see* **pickles.**

preside, *v. tr. be head of,* jadi ketua (tua); menage, mengelola (kelola); *be chairman,* jadi pengerusi (kerusi).

president, *n.* 'presiden', ketua negara; *of a Club,* yang di pertua (tua).

press, *v. tr. e.g. as a bell, taken; as a catch,* petik; *exert ~ure on,* mendesak (desak); *between two surfaces,* mengapit (apit); *with the tips of the fingers,* picit; *~ down with weight,* henyak; *a ~ (as for printing),* apitan; *the Press,* persurat (surat)-khabaran; *freedom of the Press,* kebebasan persurat-kabaran.

prestige, *n.* pengaruh (aruh), gengsi; *reputation,* nama.

presume, *v. tr. and intr. see* **assume.**

presumptuous, *adj. esp. as not showing due respect,* takbur, *see* **arrogant, pompous.**

pretend, *v. intr.* buat-buat; *piece of pretence,* pura-pura; *'put on', e.g., esp. appearance, of emotion,* sengajakan, mengada-ngadakan (ada); *see* **appearance.**

pretext, *n.* alasan; *to find a ~ (to harm someone),* cari helah.

pretty, *n.* cantik, molek; *daintily ~,* comel; *dainty morsel, 'nice little bit of stuff',* sirih kuning; *rosy-cheeked,* jambu; *see* **beautiful.**

prevail, *v. intr.* menang; *get the upper hand,* naik tangan; *see* **win.**

prevaricate, *v. intr.* berdalih (dalih), berdolak (dolak)-dalik, cakap berbelit-belit (belit).

prevent, *v. tr. forbid,* larang, tegah; *restrain,* tahan; *not allow,* tak beri; *avert, as disease,* menyekat, (sekat), mencegah (cegah).

previous, *adj.* yang dahulu.

prey, *n.* mangsa; *victim,* korban; *beast of ~,* binatang buas.

price, *n.* harga; *cost ~,* harga pokok; *~less,* tak ternilai; *~-control,* kawalan harga;

jockey up ~s, tarik harga; *fetch a good
~*, mendapat harga yang berpatutan.

prick, *v. tr.* cucuk, tusuk; *so as to pierce,*
tikam; ~ *up ears (lit.),* (binatang) men-
jongkitkan (jongkit) telinga; *(fig.),* pasang telinga; *to have ~ing pains,* terasa
(rasa) berduri-duri; *~ly,* berduri (duri);
~ly heat, ruam.

pride, *n. proper ~,* maruah; *prideful,*
megah; kesombongan (sombong); *to
be proud of,* membanggakan
(bangga), *see* **arrogant, pompous.**

priest, *n. (generally),* guru agama; *Buddhist or Hindu,* sami; *Christian,* paderi;
(lay) leader of a mosque, Imam; *esp. of
old-time religions,* pendita.

primary, *adj. initial,* yang pertama; dasar,
permulaan; *concerned with rudiments,
as a school,* rendah; *forming basis,*
pokok.

primitive, *adj. belonging to ancient
times,* purbakala; *out-of-date,* ketinggalan (tinggal) zaman; *roughly
made,* buatan kasar.

prince, *n. son of a raja,* putera, anak raja;
Crown Prince, Raja Muda, Tengku
Mahkota; *'put not your trust in ~s',* tiga
perkara jangan dipercaya, pertama
laut, kedua api, ketiga, raja.

princess, *n.* puteri.

principal, *adj. most important,* utama,
terpenting (penting); ~ *actress,* seri
panggung; *head of an institution,*
kepala, ketua (tua); *of a school,* guru
besar; pengetua; *the ~ (sum),* pokok;
see **capital.**

principle, *n. basic rule of conduct,* rukun,
'prinsip'; *the Five Principles of the Indonesian Republic,* pancasila; *basis,*
dasar; *basic ~s of doctrine,* lunas-lu-
nas, asas-asas; *agreement in ~,*
persetujuan (tuju) pada asasnya.

print, *v. tr.* cetak, cap; *~er,* tukang cap; *~ed
reproduced, as a photograph in a
newspaper,* tertera (tera); *mark left on
surface,* bekas; *see* **finger.**

priority, *n. to give ~ to,* mengutamakan
(utama).

prise, *v. tr.* ~ *out,* cungkil; ~ *up,* ungkit,

tuil.

prison, *n.* 'jel', penjara, gok; *~er (convict),*
orang salah, banduan; *~er of war,*
orang tawanan perang.

private, *adj. (confidential, secret),* sulit;
(not open to all), larangan; *(secluded),*
sunyi dan tersendiri *(of property),* not
Government, hak orang; *(not controlled by Government),* bersendiri
(sendiri); ~ *enterprise,* usaha secara
perseorangan (orang); ~ *parts,* kemaluan (malu), aurat; *a ~ letter,* surat peribadi.

privilege, *n.* hak istimewa; *(as exemption),* kebebasan; *(as special concession),* perlantikan (lantik), pelonggaran
(longgar).

privy, *n. see* **lavatory.**

prize, *n.* hadiah; *a ~ scholarship,* biasiswa
hadiah.

pro-, *prefix, favouring, sliding with,*
memihak (pihak) kepada; *~s and cons
(of a plan),* baik buruknya; ~ *tem.,* buat
sementara.

probable, *adj.* harus, mungkin.

probe, *v. tr.* menduga (duga); *surgical ~,*
jarum.

problem, *n.* soal, tanda-tanya; *as puzzle,*
teka-teki; *esp. political or economic,*
masaalah.

proceed, *v. intr. go on one's way,* berjalan (jalan); terus, maju terus; *procedure,* peraturan (atur); *Court ~ings,*
perbicaraan (bicara).

process, *n. method,* jalan cara, pencer-
naan, cara menghasilkan; *to ~ (in
manufacture),* memproseskan (proses)
see **treatment.**

procession, *n.* perarakan (arak); *esp. as a
rally,* pawai.

proclaim, *v. tr.* mengumumkan (umum),
isytiharkan; *make widely known,* siarkan, menguar-uarkan; *'~ from the
house-tops',* see **trumpet.**

prodigal, *adj. over-lavish,* boros; suka
menghamburkan wang; *see* **waste.**

produce, *n. products,* hasil; *waste products,* hampas; *natural products,* hasil
bumi; *to ~ (bring out),* bawa keluar;

memperlihatkan bukti kenyataan; *bring forward to the public,* kemukakan (muka); *as a play,* mengarahkan (arah).

profess, *v. tr. represent,* mengaku (aku); ~ *oneself to be,* mengaku diri jadi —; ~ *a creed,* menganuti (anut); ~*ion, source of livelihood,* mata pencarian (cari); *post,* jawatan; ~*or,* mahaguru.

profile, *n.* tampang muka.

profit, *n.* untung, faedah; *gains,* laba; *on a* ~*-sharing basis,* secara pawah; ~ *and loss,* laba rugi; *the* ~ *incentive,* 'sistem' cari untung.

profound, *adj. deep (as the sea or (fig.) doctrine),* dalam; *a* ~ *interest,* minat yang mendalam; ~ *books,* buku-buku yang dalam isinya.

profuse, *adj.* amat banyak, melimpahlimpah.

programme, *n. details of intended proceedings,* acara; *planned* ~, rancangan; *printed,* 'program', sekelar.

progress, *v. intr. get on, improve,* maju; *now in* ~, sedang berlangsung; *progressive (as policy)* 'progresif'.

prohibit, *v. tr.* larang, tegah.

project, *n. see* **plan.**

project, *v. intr. as a promontory,* menganjur (anjur); *as branches,* terkulai (kulai); *sticking out from a surface,* tercagul (cagul); *side-ways over a boundary, as branches,* terjulai (julai); *upwards, as crag,* menjolok (jolok); *see* **protrude.**

projectile, *n.* peluru.

proletariat, *n.* rakyat jelata.

prolific, *adj. of offspring,* biak, peridi; *a* ~ *author,* pengarang yang banyak hasilnya.

prolong, *v. tr.* melanjutkan (lanjut).

prominent, *adj. distinguished,* utama, besar; *as slightly protuberant,* tersembul (sembul), tersempal (sempal); *as teeth,* jongang; *as bones,* menjendul (jendul); *to give prominence to (as a specially important question),* mengutamakan (utama); *(treat as serious),* mengambil (ambil) berat.

promiscuous, *adj. mixed without distinction,* campur baur; *not fastidious,* tak memilih.

promise, *v. tr.* berjanji (janji); *accept responsibility for (a task), undertake to,* sanggup; *to make a firm* ~, berjanji teguh-teguh.

promontory, *n.* tanjung.

promoted, *p.p. to be* ~, naik pangkat; *to be demoted,* turun pangkat; *promoter, as of a plan,* penganjur (anjur); *esp. of a theatrical enterprise,* penaja (taja).

promptly, *adv. at once,* lekas; *quickly,* cepat.

promulgate, *v. tr.* mengumumkan (umum), memberitahukan.

prone, *adj. lying face downwards,* tertiarap (tiarap); ~ *to,* cenderung pada; ~ *to error,* cenderung berbuat salah.

pronounce, *v. tr.* menyebut (sebut), mengucap (ucap); *mis-*~, salah sebut; ~ *with a peculiar accent,* pelat; *esp. with a foreign accent,* telor.

proof, *n. evidence,* keterangan (terang), bukti; *water-*~, tahan air; *a waterproof (coat),* baju hujan; *bullet-*~, peluru tak lut; *fire-*~, tahan api; *dust-*~ tahan habuk; *rust-*~, tahan karat; *shock-*~, tahan gegar; *bomb-*~, tahan 'bom'; *splinter-*~, tahan serpihan 'bom'; ~*-sheet,* cetakan pertama.

prop, *n.* galang, sangga, sokong, tiang; ~*s for keeping boat on beach upright,* jeremang; *see* **support.**

propaganda, *n. propagation of a doctrine, etc.,* dakyah, 'propaganda'.

propagate, *v. tr. disseminate doctrine, etc.,* menyiarkan (siar), menyibarkan (sibar); *to multiply, breed freely,* berkembang (kembang) biak.

propel, *v. tr. give forward motion to,* menggerakkan (gerak) ke depan, mendorong, menyorong maju; *as, hurl,* membalingkan (baling); *as a projectile,* melontarkan (lontar), melancarkan (lancar); *push along,* sorong; ~ *with a flick, as a marble,* jintikkan; *propeller,* kipas.

proper, *adj. suitable,* patut; *conforming to*

etiquette, dengan sepertinya.

property, *n.* harta benda; *esp. of land,* milik; *fief,* pegangan; *special attribute, as of medicine,* khasiat.

prophesy, *v. tr.* meramalkan (ramal), menelah (telah).

prophet, *n.* nabi; the Prophet, Nabi Muhammad (sallalahu alaihi wassalam); *He who must be obeyed,* Junjungan; *the Good Exemplar,* Uswah Hasanah; *one who predicts the future,* tukang ramal; *see* **astrology.**

prophylactic, *n.* ubat penawar (tawar), ubat pencegah (cegah) penyakit (sakit).

propitiate, *v. tr. appease,* menyejukkan (sejuk) hati.

propitious, *adj.* ~ *moment,* saat yang baik; *a ~ influence, as carried by a name or an object,* sempena; *see* **auspicious.**

proportion, *n. in ~ to,* sekadar, seimbang dengan; *~ate,* setimbang, seimbang; *in ~ (pro rata),* seukor (itu).

propose, *v. tr.* mencadangkan (cadang); menganjurkan, (anjur), mengemukakan (muka); *(esp. in Council),* mengusulkan (usul); *~ marriage to,* meminang (pinang), melamar (lamar); *to receive a marriage proposal for one's daughter,* menerima (terima) cerana (tepak); *to reject such a proposal,* menolak (tolak) cerana (tepak); *to ~ as a candidate (for election),* calunkan.

proprietor, *n.* tuan, yang empunya, tuan punya.

prorogue, *v. tr. close sitting (of Council),* menangguhkan, mengundurkan, tidak meneruskan sidang.

prose, *n.* 'prosa'.

prosecute, *v. tr.* mendakwa (dakwa), ambil 'saman', menuntut; **prosecutor,** *n.* pendakwa; *Public Prosecutor,* Pendakwa Raya.

prospect, *v. intr. esp. for tin,* mencari (cari) (bijih), *n.* kemungkinan, pengharapan.

prospective, *adj. (as opposed to ex-),*

bakal.

prosper, *v. intr.* maju; *~ous (of a country),* makmur; *as a business or a person,* mewah.

prostitute, *n.* perempuan jahat; *'fly-by-night',* kupu-kupu malam; *streetwalker,* perempuan tepi jalan; *esp. as a term of abuse,* sundal; *to live on the proceeds of prostitution,* makan hasil perempuan jahat; *prostitution,* persundalan, pelacuran (lacur).

prostrated, *adj. as by grief or shock,* terbang semangat, terbang arwah; *lying on face,* tertiarap (tiarap); *to prostrate oneself,* rebahkan diri; *in prayer,* bersujud (sujud).

protect, *v. tr.* jaga, melindungi (lindung); *watch over,* mengawal (kawal), menunggu (tunggu), memelihara, *Protectorate,* negeri naungan; *~ion money,* wang perlindungan (lindung).

protest, *v. intr.* membantah (bantah), memprotes ('protes'); *written ~,* surat bantahan; *complain,* mengadu (adu) hal; *a ~ (as, complaint to Government),* rayuan.

protrude, *v. tr. put out (as tongue),* menjelirkan lidah; *stuck out (as long object from a bundle),* terjenguk (jenguk), tercuping (cuping), tercuking (cuking); *just projecting (as baby's teeth),* mentat, recup.

protuberance, *n.* bonggol, boncol, tonjol.

protuberant, *adj.* tersembul; *esp. as stomach,* buncit, gendut; *of eyes,* mata udang, mata belalang; *of buttocks,* tonggek; *see* **project, prominent.**

proud, *adj. of high spirit,* tinggi-hati; *~ly, of gait,* dengan bergaya (gaya); *see* **arrogant glory, pompous, pride.**

proverb, *n.* perumpamaan (umpama), pepatah.

provide, *v. tr. make available,* mengadakan (ada); *give,* memberi (beri); *bring,* membawa (bawa); *~ for family,* menyarai keluarga.

provided, *that, conj.* asal, asalkan.

province, *n.* daerah, wilayah; *provincial-*

ism, faham kedaerahan.

provision, *n. as financial,* cadangan wang, peruntukan (untuk) wang; *generally,* persediaan (sedia); *~s (foodstuffs, etc.),* barang makanan; *esp. as for journey,* bekal; *as for an army,* pelabur (labur).

provisional, *adj.* sementara.

provoke, *v. tr. give rise to (esp. emotions),* menimbulkan (timbul); *make mischief,* mengacum (acum); *rouse to anger,* memarahkan (marah).

prow, *n.* haluan, kapal.

prowl, *v. intr.* merayau (rayau), bersiar (siar) berkeliaran (mencari mangsa).

proximity, *n.* berhampiran (hampir).

proxy, *n.* wakil, orang yang ganti.

prudent, *adj.* bijak.

pry, *v. intr.* mengintai (intai), menintip (intip); *make secret enquiries,* merisik (risik); *Paul Pry,* tukang mengintai (intai).

psalms, *n. (of David),* (kitab) zabur.

pseudonym, *n.* nama samaran.

psychiatrist, *n.* 'doktor' jiwa.

puberty, *n.* akil baligh.

public, *adj.* umum; *the ~,* orang ramai; *in ~,* tengah orang ramai; *~ opinion,* pendapatan (dapat) orang ramai, pendapatan umum; *open to the ~,* terbuka (buka) kepada ramai; *Public Works Department,* jabatan kerja raya; *in ~ (in the sense of openly, not in secret),* berdepan-depan; *~ interests,* kepentingan (penting) umum, *not in the ~ interest,* tidak sesuai dengan kepentingan umum.

publicity, *n. to seek ~,* menonjolkan (tonjol) diri, mencari (cari) publisiti; *to 'publicise',* mengumumkan (umum) merata-rata, heboh-hebohkan; *Publicity Department,* pejabat (jabat) penerangan (terang); *to get a lot of ~ (get talked about),* jadi sebutan, jadi buah mulut orang; *(get stared at),* jual muka.

publish, *v. tr. as book,* menerbitkan (terbit); *as news,* siarkan, mengumumkan (umum).

puckered, *adj. as a scar,* berkedut

(kedut), jerejut.

pudding, *n.* kuih.

puddle, *n.* lopak, paloh; *puddly land,* tanah lopak, tempat air bertakung (takung).

puff, *v. intr. exhale sharply, as when blowing out a light,* hembus; *to blow,* tiup; *a ~ of wind,* puputan angin; *~ing, as short-winded,* bongek; *~ed out, as by air,* menggelembung (gelembung); *see* **swell;** *~er-fish,* ikan buntal; *to ~ oneself out, as a ~er-fish,* melembung (lembung); *see* **blow, pant.**

pull, *v. tr.* tarik; *drag,* hela; *~ up or out,* cabut; *~ down (as structure),* robohkan, rombak; *tug,* rentak; *~ in jerks (used of the jerky ~ of an engine running badly),* rentap; *~ at, as the breast or an ice-cream,* nyonyot; *~ up, as sarong,* selakkan; *~ tight (slip-knot),* jerut.

pullet, *n.* ayam dara, ayam* panggang-perenggi.

pully, *n.* 'takal', kapi.

pulpit, *n.* mimbar.

pulpy, *adj. as fruit (i.e., not a hard fruit),* lunak; *as rice,* bonyor; *as soft under pressure,* lembik; *to pulp (beat into pulp with a spoon, etc.)* lecek.

pulsate, *v. intr.* berdenyut (denyut), menggembut (gembut); *the arterial pulse,* nadi.

pulverise, *v. tr. crush very small,* melumatkan (lumat); *~d,* hancur luluh, remuk redam; *become dust before the wind,* menjadi (jadi) habuk angin.

pumelo, *n.* limau besar.

pumice-stone, *n.* batu timbul.

pump, *n.* 'pam'; *to ~ up, esp. a tyre,* 'pam' angin; *a ~ for throwing water to extinguish fires,* bomba; *monitor for throwing a jet of water, esp. in a mine,* (jentera) pemancut (pancut) air; *suction ~,* 'pam' penyedut (sedut) air.

pumpkin, *n.* labu.

punch, *v. tr. with fist,* tumbuk, gocoh; *as a stamp,* cap.

punctual, *adj. at the right time,* tepat pada waktunya, menurut (turut) waktu betul; *be ~!*, jangan lewat!.

punctured, *adj. of a tyre,* 'pancit'; *it's a slow puncture,* angin meresip (resip) sahaja keluar; *to pierce a thin object, as ears for ear-rings,* tindek; *holed, as the 'skin' of a boat, etc.,* tembuk.

punish, *v. tr. formally order ~ment,* hukumkan; *esp. with whip,* mendera (dera); *'give what-for' (sl.),* beri bahagian; *see* **fine, prison.**

puny, *adj. thin and under-sized,* kurus ceding.

pupil, *n. at school,* anak murid, pelajar (ajar); *of eye,* anak mata.

puppet, *n.* patung, boneka; *~-show,* wayang kulit.

puppy, *n.* anak anjing.

pure, *adj. free from dirt,* bersih; *as heart,* murni, suci.

purgative, *n.* julap, pencahar (cahar).

purgatory, *n.* alam berzakh.

purge, *v. tr.* membersihkan (bersih); *(fig.) to get someone out of the way, liquidate,* menyingkirkan (singkir).

purple, *adj.* ungu manis.

purpose, *n.* hajat, maksud; *on ~,* sengaja; *common ~, as of conspirators,* maksud bersama (sama).

purr, *v. intr.* mendengkur (dengkur).

purse, *n. pundi-pundi; pouch,* kantung, saku; *woman's bag-~,* tas.

pursue, *v. tr. run after,* hambat; *go in pursuit,* mengejar (kejar); *esp. as in a game,* memburu (buru); *follow up,* turut.

pus, *n.* nanah.

push, *v. tr. ~ along,* sorong; *~ away,* tolak; *~ and shove, as people in a crowd,* bergelut-gelut; *~-cart,* kereta sorong; *'~ off' (from the bank when starting a journey by water),* bertolak (tolak), *(so often used (fig.) for 'starting out'); to '~ one-self' (of a self-assertive person),* menonjolkan (tonjol) diri; *'play up' to superiors with a view to profit,* cari muka; *to ~ one's wares, increase sales, see* **jockey;** *~ed in,* stove in, terpersuk (persuk).

put, *v. tr. ~ down,* letak; *~ away,* simpan; *~ away to keep,* taruh; *~ away carelessly, shove aside,* peruk; *~ in its place,* bubuh; *~ on (as dress),* pakai; *~ off, postpone,* tanggoh; *~ aside, earmark,* cadangkan; *~ together, tidy up,* kemaskan; *'~ the shot',* baling peluru; *melontar* (lontar) besi; *'~ off one's stroke', disconcerted,* tergamam (gamam); *~ out (fire),* padam; *~ up with,* tahan, sabarkan; *~ back (clock),* undurkan; *~ forward,* cepatkan.

putative, *adj. a ~ father,* Pak Sanggup.

putrid, *adj.* busuk; *~ and stinking,* busuk, melantung (lantung).

putty, *n.* 'simen', dempul.

puzzle, *n.* teka-teki.

pylon, *n.* menara.

python, *n.* ular sawa.

Q

qua, *conj. in the capacity of, as,* sebagai.

quack, *v. intr.* membebek (bebek), menguik (uik).

quadruped, *n.* binatang berkaki (kaki) empat.

quail, *n.* puyuh; *button-~,* pikau.

qualified, *adj. for a job,* layak; *by examination,* berkelulusan (lulus); *by virtue of certificate or registration,* bertauliah (tauliah).

quality, *n.* mutu, tokoh; *~ goods,* barangan yang bermutu; *precious or not 'everyday',* barang yang berharga; *~ of mind,* sifat.

quandary, *n. see* **dilemma;** *in a ~, uncertain what to do,* dalam keadaan serba salah.

quarrel, *v. intr.* berkelahi (kelahi); *brawl,* bergaduh (gaduh); *bicker,* bertengkar (tengkar); *dispute noisily,* berbalah (balah); *disagree,* berselisih (selisih); *~some,* lekas marah, kaki gaduh; *to pick a ~,* cari fasal, cari gaduh; *sound of noisy ~,* herok-perok, becang-becok; *~some,* kaki gadoh; *esp. as recalcitrant,* babil; *see* **loggerheads;** *it takes two to make a ~,* bertepuk (tepuk*) tangan sebelah tak akan berbunyi (bunyi).

quarry, *n. for stone,* tempat pecah batu; *prey,* mangsa; *the game hunted,* perburuan (buru).

quarter, *n.* sesuku, seperempat (empat); *to ask for ~,* minta nyawa.

quarters, *n. lodging-place,* tempat tumpang; *to find ~ for,* menempatkan (tempat); *see* **barracks, lodge.**

quartz, *n.* telerang.

quash, *v. tr. as a Court sentence,* batal-kan.

quantrain, *n.* pantun.

quaver, *v. intr. to emit ~ing notes when singing,* mengerenek (renek); *of the voice of a person deeply moved,* menggigil (gigil).

quay, *n.* bagan, pangkalan.

queen, *n.* raja permaisuri; *Queen of England,* baginda 'kuin'; *in cards,* nyonya; *in chess,* menteri; *~ regnant,* raja perempuan; *~ consort,* raja permaisuri; *(fig.),* ratu; *beauty ~,* ratu cantik.

queer, *adj.* ganjil, pelik; *see* **odd.**

quench, *v. tr. fire,* memadamkan (padam) api; *thirst,* melepaskan (lepas) dahaga; *see* **slake.**

question, *v. tr.* tanya; *examine, periksa, a ~,* soal; *~naire,* borang pertanyaan.

queue, *n. to ~ up,* beratur utk menunggu gilirah; *see* **pigtail.**

quibble, *v. intr.* berdolak (dolak)-dalik.

quick, *adj.* cepat, tangkas bangat; *~-witted,* tajam-akal, ringan-kepala; *to ~en one's pace,* cepatkan langkah.

quicksilver, *n.* raksa.

quid, *n. of betel or tobacco,* sepiak, sesogeh.

quiet, *adj. still,* sepi; *of business,* lengang; *retiring,* pendiam (diam); *not restive, as a horse,* mandum; *to keep ~,* senyap, berdiam diri.

quill, *n.* bulu; *~-feathers,* lawi; *~s of porcupine,* duri landak.

quiver, *n.* tabung (anak damak, anak panah); *to ~,* mengetar (ketar), bergentar (gentar).

quotation, *n.* kutipan (dari buku).

R

Rabbi, *n.* pendita Yahudi.

rabbit, *n.* arnab, tapai; *(among foreigners),* kucing Belanda; *hutch,* kandang arnab.

rabies, *n.* penyakit (sakit) anjing gila.

race, *n.* group having common ancestors, bangsa; *racial stock, descent,* rupabangsa; *racial,* berkenaan (kena) dengan bangsa; *racialism,* perkauman (kaum).

race, *n.* contest of speed, perlumbaan; *horse-~,* lumba kuda; *obstacle ~,* lari berhalangan (halang); *walking ~,* lumba berjalan (jalan); *long-distance ~,* lari jarak jauh; *short-distance ~,* lari jarak dekat; *cross-country ~,* lari merentas (rentas) desa; *relay ~,* lari berganti-ganti; *arms ~,* persaingan (saing) senjata.

rack, *n.* para; *esp. in kitchen,* rak; *esp. for drying fish,* salaian, pelantar; *for drying hides or for printing negatives,* pemidang; *to ~ one's brains,* memerah (pera) otak.

radiant, *adj.* berseri (seri), bercahaya, bersinar-sinar.

radio, *n.* 'radio'; *announcer,* juruhebah, ponyiar (siar); *see* **broadcast;** *national '~',* 'radio' bercorak (corak) kebangsaan (bangsa); *commercial ~,* 'radio' bercorak perniagaan (niaga); *~ network,* rangkaian radio

radish, *n.* lobak.

raft, *n.* rakit.

rafter, *n.* main ~, kasau; *minor rafters,* jeriau.

rag, *n.* a ~, seperca kain; *~ged,* koyak-rabak, compang- camping; *to hold a ~ (of freshmen at college),* mengadakan (ada) plonco*.

rage, *v. intr. as a fire,* bercabul (cabul); *to be in a ~,* meradang (radang), naik berang; *see* **angry.**

raid, *n. a sudden attack,* serangan; *air ~,* serangan udara; *so to attack,* menyerang, menyerbu (serbu); *~ of police,* geledah, serbuan; *to go on a plundering expedition,* menjarah (jarah).

rail, *n.* 'rel'; *~way train,* keretapi; *passenger train,* keretapi penumpang, *goods train,* keretapi muatan; *~way station,* 'stesyen' keretapi; *platform,* pelantar keretapi; *the line (esp. the sleepers),* landasan keretapi; *to travel by ~,* naik keretapi; *coach,* gerabak; *compartment,* petak keretapi; *truck,* gerobok; *see* **mail.**

rain, *n.* hujan; *period of heavy ~,* (musim) tengkujuh; *pouring with ~,* hujan mencurah-curah; *~ in sunshine,* hujan panas; *~coat,* baju hujan; *~ing 'cats and dogs';* hujan tak boleh celek mata.

rainbow, *n.* pelangi, ular danau, lanum.

raise, *v. tr.* lift up, angkat; *lift to higher position,* tinggikan; *make stand up,* mendirikan (diri); *to an upright position,* menegakkan (tegak); *increase, as taxes or wages,* menambahkan (tambah), menaikkan (naik); *~ voice,* menguatkan (kuat) suara; *~ disorders,* menimbulkan (timbul) kucar-kucir; *~ anchor,* bongkar sauh; *(his) voice was raised,* suara(nya) makin meninggi; *see* **breed, rise.**

raisin, *n.* kismis.

rake, *n. for use in garden, etc.,* pencakar (cakar), penggaruk.

rally, *v. tr.* muster troops again, kumpulkan kembali; *~ (troops) by voice,* mengalak (alak); *a ~ (gathering for some common purpose),* pawai.

ram, *n.* kambing (biri-biri) jantan; *to ~ (in charge),* melanda (landa), merempuh (rempuh); *(fig.),* menanduk (tanduk); *~ down,* lantak; *~ in,* asak.

563

ramble, *v. intr. walk without definite route,* berjalan (jalan) tak tentu arah, merayau (rayau), bersiar (siar); *grow here and there (of climbing plants),* menjalar (jalar), merayap (rayap); *rambling (of a story),* tak tentu hujung pangkal; *of speech, in delirium,* kelalut, tak tentu; *as oration or writing,* berjelajela; *not keeping to the point,* bersimpang- siur (simpang); *to rave,* meracau (racau).

ramification, *n.* keadaan bercabang-cabang, percabangan.

rampage, *v. intr. behave violently, storm, esp. as in angry boss (fig.),* mengamuk (amuk); *as predatory animals or bandits,* mengganas (ganas).

rampant, *adj. unchecked, as crimes,* menjadi-jadi; *inevitably occurring,* ada-ada sahaja.

rampart, *n.* benteng, kota, kubu; pertahanan.

ramrod, *n.* pelantak (lantak), antar-antar.

ramshackle, *adj. of a building,* sangat tua dan hampir roboh.

rancid, *adj.* masam, tengik; *stale,* basi.

rancour, *n.* dengki, kebencian; *rancorous, adj.* pendendam, menaruh (taruh) dendam.

random, *n. at ~, haphazard, to strike out at ~,* pukul buta tuli; *shoot 'into the brown' (without picking out a bird),* tembak merambang (rambang); *select at ~,* buang serkap jarang; *having no definite objective,* tak tentu arah, sembarangan.

randy, *adj. of a man,* gila urat, ketagih (tagih) (perempuan); *of a woman,* gatal keladi, miang, ketagih (jantan); *see* **nymphomaniac.**

range, *n. distance,* jauhnya; *the ~ of a weapon,* sepenjulat (julat) (peluru, meriam); *rifle-~,* padang tembak, padang sasaran; *the mound behind the targets,* benteng sasaran; *a ~ of mountains,* sebanjaran gunung.

rank, *n. row,* baris; *grade,* pangkat; *smelling ~ly,* berbau (bau) hapak; *growing ~ly, as weeds,* meriap (riap).

rankle, *v. intr. cause recurrent pain as an old wound or a thorn or (fig.) a mental injury,* terasa-rasa; luka hilang, parut adakah-hilang? menjadi kenangan pahit, *(the wound has gone, but has the scar gone ? (it still ~s)).*

ransack, *v. tr.* selongkar; menggeledah.

ransom, *v. tr.* menebus; *~ money,* wang tebusan.

rant, *v. intr. utter loud boastful talk,* cakap berdegar-degar; *rave,* meracau (racau).

rape, *v. tr.* merogol (rogol); *outrage,* berbuat (buat) cabul pada; *seizing, taking, by force;* menculik dengan paksaan.

rapid, *adj.* laju; cepat, deras, pesat; *rapids,* jeram; *less steep,* cegar.

rapt, *adj. unconscious of reality,* lupakan daratan, asyik; *as in a 'brown study',* duduk ralip sahaja.

rare, *adj.* jarang jumpa; *hard to come by,* payah; *~ly,* jarang-jarang; *see* **odd.**

rash, *n. spots on skin,* bintik-bintik; *esp. as prickly heat,* ruam; *skin-eruption,* kayap; *~ly,* terburu-buru; lancang; *to court disaster,* mencari (cari) bala.

rasp, *n.* kukuran; *to ~,* kukur, memarut (parut).

rat, *n.* tikus.

ratchet, *n.* gerigi; *the stop on a ~,* sangga (gerigi).

rate, *v. estimate value or worth of,* menilai, (nilai) menaksir (taksir).

rates, *n.* cukai rumah.

rather, *adj. somewhat,* sikit, sedikit, agak, kira-kira.

ratify, *v. tr. as a treaty,* mengesahkan (sah).

ration, *n. fixed daily allowance of food,* catuan, rangsum; *v. tr.* mencatu; merangsum.

rattan, *n.* rotan.

rattle, *v. tr. & i. ~ about,* bergerodak (gerodak), bergerancang (gerancang); mengucapkan (ucap) dengan cepat; *~ (to be shaken),* orok-orok; kelentong; *sound of rattling,* gemerencing.

ravage, *v. tr. destroy,* memusnahkan (musnah) (harta orang), membinasakan (binasa).

rave, *v. intr.* meracau (racau); *ravings,* igau-igauan.

ravine, *n.* gaung, jurang.

raw, *adj.* uncooked, mentah; *(fig.) inexperienced,* mentah lagi, hijau, belum banyak makan garam; *that touched him on the ~ (hit him on a sensitive point),* betul-betul kena pada batang hidungnya, *(hit him right on the bridge of his nose).*

ray, *n.* sinaran; *to emit rays,* bersinar; *a sp. of fish,* ikan pari.

razor, *n.* pisau pencukur (cukur).

re-, *prefix, back to former state, often expressed by* balik; *to ~capture,* menawan (tawan) semula; *all over again, yet once more,* semula; *to ~-elect,* memilih (pilih) semula.

reach, *v. tr. arrive (at),* sampai; *by stretching,* mencapai (capai), cekau; *attain point aimed at,* mendapatkan (dapat); *~ing down to (as hair to shoulders),* jejak ke; *~ for,* cekau; *as high as one can ~,* tinggi se jengkau; *out of ~,* tak tercapai (capai); *as of a blow 'landing',* tiba; *a ~ (of a river),* rantau.

reactionary, *adj. not progressive (of policy),* kolot; penentang (tentang) kemajuan.

read, *v. tr.* membaca (baca); *~ aloud,* membaca dengan suara nyaring; lantang; *~ right through,* membaca terus menerus, *~ silently,* membaca senyap, membaca dalam hati; *unreadable,* tak berbaca; *see* **handwriting.**

ready, *adj.* siap, mustaid; *all ~,* siap sedia; *to make (something) ~, prepare,* siapkan; *get ~ to,* bersiap untuk; *~ to, about to,* bersedia; *~ cash (cash down),* wang tunai; *cash in hand, expense money,* belanja; *out of ~ cash,* putus belanja; *~-made,* tersedia, siap dibeli, *be ~! stand prepared!,* besedialah!; *to be ~ to, agree to,* sanggup, bersetuju (setuju).

real, *adj. genuine,* betul, benar; *as purebred,* jati; *really,* sungguh.

realise, *v. tr. apprehend clearly,* sedar

(kan), insaf akan, tahu benar-benar; *take in meaning,* faham; *to be ~d, as hopes,* berhasil (hasil); *see* **succeed;** *you must ~ that,* jangan tak tahu—, kamu hendaklah sedar bahawa....

reap, *v. tr.* mengetam (ketam), menuai (tuai); *with a sickle,* menyabit (sabit), mencerut (cerut).

rear, *v. tr. livestock,* berternak (ternak); *bring up,* pelihara, bela, mendidik (didik); *in the ~, behind,* sebelah belakang; *to ~ (stand up on hind legs),* berdiri tegak.

reason, *n.* sebab; *faculty of ~,* akal; *~able, as a proposal,* menasabah; *of a person, ready to listen,* boleh berundung (runding), sedia mendengar; *as a price,* berpatutan (patut); *be ~able! (think of the consequences),* ingat dahulu!; *acceptable to a thinking person,* dapat diterima dek akal; *for some ~ or other,* entah mengapa sebabnya; *grounds, ~s alleged,* alasan.

rebate, *n.* potongan.

rebel, *v. intr.* berontak (rontak), menderhaka (derhaka).

rebound, *v. intr.* mengambul (ambul) menganjal (anjal), melantun.

rebuke, *v. tr. an argument or opinion,* menyangkal (sangkal)

recall, *v. tr. summon back,* panggil kembali (balik); *call to mind,* teringat (ingat); mengenang kembali; *remind oneself or others of, 'dwell on',* kenangkan hal.

recede, *v. intr. as water,* surut; *business recession,* kemelesetan (meleset).

receive, *v. tr.* terima; *as a guest,* sambut; *a (social) reception,* sambutan; *reception room (for guests),* ruang tamu; *of a Ruler,* balairong, balai menghadap (hadap); *reception committee,* panitia sambutan; *see* **welcome;** *receipt,* 'resit'.

recent, *adj.* baru; *~ly,* baru-baru ini, tempoh hari.

receptacle, *n. (generally),* bekas.

receptionist, *n.* penyambut (sambut) tetamu (tamu).

recess, *n. vacation,* rehat; *as small hollow,* ceruk, celah.

recipe, *n.* petua, ramu-ramuan, resipi.

reciprocate, *v. tr.* berbalas-balasan (balas); tukar-menukar.

recite, *v. tr.* membaca (baca), mengucapkan (ucap).

reckon, *v. tr. compute numbers,* hitung.

reclaim, *v. tr. take back,* ambil kembali (balik); menuntut supaya dikembalikan; *waste land,* memugar (pugar), tanah tambak.

recline, *v. intr.* berbaring (baring); *lean back,* bersandar (sandar).

recognise, *v. tr.* mengecam (cam); *know,* kenal, ~ *the existence of (as a new Government),* iktiraf, mengakui (aku).

recoil, *v. intr. as a gun,* tendang.

recollect, *v. tr. see* **recall.**

recommendation, *n. letter of* ~ *(esp. of an applicant),* surat (pujian); *to recommend (a person),* 'rekomenkan'; ~ *(of a course of action), advice,* nasihat, syor.

recompense, *v. tr. reward for a good deed,* membalas (balas) jasa; *pay a reward,* membaya (bayar) hadiah; memberi ganjaran (ganjar).

reconcile, *v. tr.* mendamaikan (damai); *to be ~d to, make peace with (a separated wife or (fig.) a political party),* merujuk (rujuk) kepada; ~*d, friends again,* berbaik (baik) semula; ~ *oneself (to misfortune), see* **resign.**

recondite, *adj. abstruse,* umum, dalam; sukar dimengerti, sulit, kabur.

reconnoitre, *v. intr.* meninjau (tinjau), mengintip (intip); *recce unit,* pasukan peninjau.

reconsider, *v. tr.* timbang semula.

reconstruct, *v. tr. institutions,* menyusun (susun) semula; membangunkan (bangun) semula.

record, *n.* ~ *of facts, etc.,* 'rekod'; *State ~s,* 'rekod' kerajaan (raja); *gramophone ~,* piring peti nyanyi; *long-playing ~,* piring aneka lagu; *limit hitherto attained, best performance,* 'rekod'; *to set up a ~,* membuat (buat) 'rekod'; mencipta (cipta) 'rekod'; *to equal a ~,* menyamai

(sama) 'rekod'; *to beat a ~,* mengatasi (atas) 'rekod'; *to ~, note,* menulis (tulis), mencatat (catat); *by inscribing indelibly,* merakam (rakam); *tape-~er,* alat perakam (rakam); *tape-~er,* alat perakam suara; ~*s (documents),* catatan; *a ~ing, e.g., of a song,* rakaman.

recover, *v. tr. get back,* ambil balik; dapatkan semula; *be healed,* sembuh; *from illness,* sudah baik, segar balik, siuman; *'perk up',* angkat mata; *recovery,* pemulihan (pulih); kewarasan; kesembuhan.

recriminations, *n. to indulge in* ~, tuduh-menuduh; menyalahkan.

recruit, *n.* askar baru, 'rekrut'.

rectify, *v. tr. put right,* memperbaiki kesalahan.

recuperate, *v. intr.* memulihkan (pulih) badan; beransur sembuh sesudah sakit; *mentally,* melapangkan (lapang) fikiran.

recurrent, *adj.* berulang-ulang; *see* **rife.**

red, *adj.* merah; ~*dish,* kemerah-merahan; *the Red Cross,* Palang Merah.

redeem, *v. tr.* menebus (tebus).

redress, *v. tr. make up for wrongs, etc., expressed as, e.g., lighten suffering,* meringankan (ringan) penderitaan (derita); *or, do away with afflictions,* menghilangkan (hilang) bencana, *also;* membutulkan (betul), memperbaiki (baik) sesuatu kesalahan.

reduce, *v. tr. make less,* mengurangkan (kurang); ~ *price,* menurunkan (turun) harga, memotong (potong) harga.

redundant, *adj.* berlebih-lebih, terlalu banyak; melimpah.

reed, *n. see* **sedge.**

reef, *n. coral* ~, batu karang; *hidden rock,* tukun; *rock just awash,* batu berendam (rendam); *of ore,* telerang; *in a sail,* setinggi; *to ~ sails,* mengandakkan layar (andak).

reel, *n. fishing-~,* kili-kili; *as for cotton or generally,* gelendong; *to ~ (stagger),* huyung-hayang.

refer, *v. tr.* ~ *to,* menyebut (sebut) hal

(nama); *hand over (decision) to*, pulangkan pada, merujukkan (rujuk) pada; *~ence number*, angka rujuk.

referendum, *n.* pungutan suara rakyat.

refined, *adj. as speech,* halus; *mannerly,* beradab (adab); berbudi bahasa; *to refine, as oil,* menapis (tapis), menyaringkan (saring); *oil-refinery,* kilang penyaringan minyak, kilang penapisan minyak; *~, of material generally,* murni; bersih, jernih.

reflection, *n. as in a mirror,* bayang; *to throw back (light),* pantulan cahaya; *to reflect, ponder,* berfikir (fikir).

reflex, *n. ~es, ~ action,* gerakbalas.

reform, *v. tr. put an end to abuses,* pembaruan; menghapuskan (hapus) unsur-unsur yang buruk; *reconstitute,* memperkemaskan (kemas); *turn over a new leaf,* bertukar (tukar) daun; *repent,* bertaubat (taubat); *to improve (e.g. conditions of people's lives),* membaikkan (baik); *reshape,* membentuk (bentuk) semula; *~ character (rehabilitate by teaching),* memulihkan (pulih) akhlak (tabiat), mendidik (didik) semula.

reformatory, *n.* sekolah budak-budak nakal.

refractory, *adj. esp. as a child,* babil, nakal; 'won't be told', tak makan ajar; *as a horse,* candi; *generally,* begar; *see* **stubborn.**

refresh, *v. tr. feeling ~ed,* berasa (rasa) lega, berasa nyaman; *to ~ (reinvigorate), (as does a breeze, a holiday),* menyegarkan (segar) badan; *light ~ments,* hidangan ringan; *a snack,* alas perut; *a 'wet',* pembasah (basah) kerongkong.

refuge, *n.* perlindungan (lindung); *~e,* orang pelarian (lari), orang buruan.

refund, *v. tr.* bayar balik; dikembalikan (kembali).

refurbish, *v. tr. to make clean or bright again;* mencuci bersih atau mengilatkan semula.

refuse, *n. what is left after processing,* hampas; *see* **rubbish.**

refute, *v. tr. to prove that (a statement or opinion or person) is wrong,* membuktikan kesalahan.

regalia, *n.* alat kerajaan (raja).

regent, *n.* pemangku (pangku) raja.

regime, *n. system of government,* 'rejim', sistem pememerintahan (perintah).

register, *n.* daftar; *to ~,* mendaftarkan, *[v. tr. & i.]* mencatat.

regret, *v. intr. to feel ~,* menyesal (sesal).

regular, *adj. at ~ times,* bertentu (tentu) waktunya; *in a ~ (orderly) manner,* secara teratur (atur), dengan sepertinya; *systematic,* cukup teratur; *~ troops,* tentera biasa; *~ly (daily),* tiap-tiap hari; *without a break,* tidak berselang-selang, tidak putus-putus.

regulations, *n.* undang-undang; peraturan.

regurgitate, *v. tr. to bring (swallowed food) up again to the mouth,* memuntahi.

rehabilitate, *v. tr.* memulihkan (pulih).

rehearse, *v. intr. practise before appearance,* berlatih (latih).

reign, *v. tr.* bersemayam (semayam) di atas takhta kerajaan (raja).

rein, *n.* tali ras; *(fig.) to hold the ~s of government,* memegang (pegang) tampuk kerajaan (raja).

reinforcements, *n.* bala bantuan; perihal menguatkan (kuat), memperkukuhkan (kukuh).

reinstate, *v. tr. re-establish in former position,* meletakkan (letak) balik.

reiterate, *v. tr. repeat again and again,* menyebutkan (sebut) berulang-ulang.

reject, *v. intr.* menolak (tolak); *~ emphatically, 'scout',* menolak mentah-mentah, menolak bulat-bulat.

rejoice, *v. intr.* bersuka (suka)-ria.

relapse, *n. to have a ~,* bentan.

relate, *v. tr.* ceritakan hal.

relation, *n. in ~ to, in connection with,* berhubung dengan; *~s (feelings between persons),* perhubungan; *friendly ~s,* silatulrahim; *to establish friendly ~s (between),* memperatkan (erat) hubungan (antara); *break off diplomatic ~s,* memutuskan (putus) hubungan 'diplomatik'; *resume diplomatic ~s,* membuka (buka), memulihkan (pulih) semula hubungan 'diplomatik'; *Public Relations Officer (Information Officer),* pegawai perangan (terang); *see* **relative.**

relative, *n.* kinsman, saudara; *distant ~,* saudara renggang, saudara bau bacang; *(my) own flesh and blood,* darah daging (saya); *~s within the prohibited degrees of marriage,* muhrim: *if not within these degrees,* ajnabi, halal-nikah.

relaxed, *adj. not taut,* kendur; *relax!,* beristirahat!; *to relax, as reglations,* melonggarkan (longgar), melembutkan (lembut); *to relax (ease one's mind, be less tense),* melegakan (lega) fikiran, melapang-lapangkan fikiran.

relay, *n. in relays,* berganti-ganti.

release, *v. tr.* lepas(kan); membebaskan (bebas).

relent, *v. intr. feel pity,* menaruh (taruh) kasihan.

relevant, *adj.* berhubung (dengan), kenamengena (dengan).

reliable, *adj. worthy of confidence,* kepercayaan (percaya); *trusty, re-doubtable,* handalan; *trustworthy,* amanah; *as, efficacious, of medicine,* mujarab; *certain to act,* mustajab; *something to rely on, 'rock to cling to',* tempat pautan.

relic, *n. (of a past age or event),* warisan (zaman dahulu).

relief, *n. in ~, of a craving,* timbul.

relieved, *adj. as after illness,* berasa (rasa) lega; *as after shock,* pulang semangat; *as from worry,* lapang hati; *feel ~, feel better, 'buck up',* angkat mata; *to relieve oneself, see* **defecate, urine.**

religion, *n.* agama; *religious (pious),* beriman; *staunchly religious,* taat pada agama, kuat beragama; *irreligious (backslider),* rosak iman; *to perform one's religious duties,* beribadat (ibadat); *one's faith, that which one professes,* anutan; *see* **scriptures.**

reluctant, *adj.* segan, enggan.

rely, *v. intr.* harap (pada), bergantung (gantung) pada; *see* **reliable.**

remain, *v. intr.* tinggal; *~der,* baki; *~s, as leavings after meal,* sisa; *useless remnants,* kalat-kalat; *torn shreds,* reja-reja; *as residue after processing,* hampas; *~s of a demolished building,* runtuhan bangunan; *as wreckage, e.g., of a plane,* bangkai.

remarkable, *adj. worth noticing,* menarik perhatian; **exceptional,** luar biasa.

remedy, *n.* ubat, penawar (tawar).

remember, *v. tr.* teringat; *bear in mind,* simpan di hati; *as far as I ~,* yang saya ingat, sepanjang ingatan saya; *see* **recall.**

remind, *v. tr.* ingatkan, beri peringatan.

reminiscences, *n.* kenang-kenangan.

remit, *v. tr. send (money),* kirimkan; *as debt,* maafkan, halalkan; *as punishment, by authority,* ampunkan.

remnants, *n. last ~,* saki-baki; *what is left over, the excess,* yang lebihnya; *see* **remain.**

remorse, *n.* sesal, kesal; *it's better to be ~ful before the act; what's the good of ~ after it?,* sesal dahulu pendapatan (dapat); sesal kemudian tiada gunanya?

remote, *adj.* jauh, terpencil (pencil); *lonely,* sunyi; tersendiri; *far from the beaten track,* jauh dari loceng.

remove, *v. tr. carry away,* angkat; *strip off, as cloth,* papas; *see* **move.**

renegade, *n.* penderhaka (derhaka), pembelut (belut); *from Islam,* murtad.

renounce, *v. tr. abandon,* meninggalkan (tinggal); *surrender,* menyerahkan (serah); *cease to associate with,* menjauhkan diri dari; *~ one's throne,* turun takhta.

rent, *n.* sewa; *Government '~' on land,* hasil; *see* **lease.**

reorganise, *v. tr.* memperkemaskan (kemas), mengatur (atur) semula.

repair, *v. tr.* membaiki (baik); *put right,* memperbaiki (baik).

reparation, *n.* ganti-rugi.

repay, *v. tr.* bayar balik; menebus (tebus);

~ *an obligation,* balas budi; *see* **revenge, vengeance.**
repeal, *v. tr. a law,* batalkan, mansuhkan.
repeat, *v. tr.* mengulang (ulang), (kata) sekali lagi; *as a lesson learned by heart,* mengucapkan (ucap); ~*edly,* berulang-ulang.
repel, *v. tr. as attack,* menolak (tolak); *drive away,* halau; *keep off,* menjauhkan (jauh); *see* **prevent, repulse.**
repent, *v. tr.* bertaubat (taubat); '*turn over a new leaf',* mulakan hidup baru; berubah sikap; *see* **remorse.**
repercussion, *n. reactions to event,* gerak-balas, kesan-balas, gema; *see* **reactions.**
replace, *v. tr. put back in former place,* simpan balik; *put in a subsitute,* ganti baru.
reply, *v. tr.* jawab; *as in* ~*ing to a shout,* menyahut (sahut); *to a letter,* balas surat.
report, n. narration, cerita; *esp. as official,* penyata (nyata), laporan; *esp. to police,* 'repot'; *school* ~, penyata kemajuan (maju) pelajaran (ajar); *to* ~ *oneself,* melaporkan diri; ~ *of a gun,* bunyi senapang; ~*er,* wartawan.
representative, n. agent, wakil; *attorney,* kuasa; *elected* ~, calon; *mission,* utusan; *to represent oneself to be*—, mengaku (aku) diri jadi—; *see* **pose;** *proportionate representation,* perwakilan (wakil) porimbangan (imbang).
repress, *v. tr.* menindas (tindas).
reprimand, *v. tr.* memberi (beri) amaran; *criticise,* menegur (tegur); *to 'give a roasting',* gulaikan; *to 'get it hot',* makan cuka; *'get a rocket',* kena sembur.
reprint, *v. tr.* mencetak lagi; *a* ~, ulangan cetak.
reprisals, *n. to make* ~, membalas (balas).
reproduce, *v. tr.* ~ *species,* membiakkan (biak) jenis.
republic, *n.* 'republik', jamhoriah.
repudiate, *v. tr. reject,* menolak (tolak); *disavow, as a debt,* menyangkal

(sangkal), tak mengaku (aku); *as a promise,* mungkir; *refuse to accept responsibility for,* tak sanggup terima tanggungjawab.
repulse, *v. tr. cause to give ground,* mengundurkan (undur); penolakan.
repulsive, *adj. (to look at),* sumbang bagi pandangan; *(1) find it* ~ *to look at,* benci memandangnya, meluat perangainya; *to have a feeling of repulsion,* berasa (rasa) lan, meluak (luak).
reputable, *adj. of good repute,* ternama, bernama baik; *repute,* nama.
request, *v. tr.* minta; *beseech,* mohon; *a* ~, permintaan; *esp. to the authorities,* rayuan; *by public* ~, atas permintaan (minta) ramai.
require, *v. tr.* hendakkan, memerlukan (perlu), membutuhkan (butuh); *express a desire for,* minta; *requisites, articles needed for a task,* peralatan (alat), keperluan.
requisite, *adj. necessary to success,* diperlukan.
requite, *v. tr.* membalas (balas).
rescind, *v. tr. an order,* batalkan; *a promise,* tarik balik (keputusan).
rescue, *v. tr.* menyelamatkan (selamat).
research, *n. critical investigation,* penyiasatan (siasat), penyelidikan (selidik); *to study,* mengkaji (kaji); *Rubber Research Institute,* badan pengkaji getah.
resentful, *adj.* sakit-hati, sebal-hati, terkilan (kilan); *to brood* ~*ly,* makan hati; *preserve a* ~ *silence,* diam lepu; *to 'take to heart',* ambil (di) hati.
reserve, *v. tr. set aside,* cadangkan; *Government reserved land,* 'reseb', Melayu, kawasankhas Melayu; *land* ~*s for religious or charitable purposes,* tanah wakaf; *stockpile,* persediaan (sedia); ~ *troops,* tentera simpanan.
reserved, *adj. not apt to talk much,* pendiam, ~ *but mentally active,* diam ubi, *(because the silent and hidden potato is busy underground).*
reservoir, *n.* danau buatan, kolam air.
reside, *v. intr. see* **live;** *esp. as domiciled,*

bermastautin (mastautin) di-; *residential land,* tanah perumahan (rumah).

resign, *v. tr.* meletakkan (letak) jawatan; *to tender ~ation,* minta berhenti; meletakkan (letak) jawatan; *stop work,* berhenti (henti) kerja; *~ oneself (accept the inevitable),* merelakan (rela) diri.

resin, *n.* damar.

resist, *v. tr.* melawan (lawan), menentang (tentang).

resolute, *adj.* teguh-hati, tabah.

resolution, *n. of meeting,* keputusan (putus); ketetapan pendapat yang telah diambil dalam suatu mesyuarat; *to make a ~ to,* berniat (niat) hendak.

resort, *n. place frequented by the public,* tempat tumpuan orang ramai; *for animal ~, see* **lick.**

resound, *v. intr. fill place with sound,* bergema (gema); *see* **echo.**

resources, *n.* daya upaya; sumber; *resourceful,* panjang-akal; *means of support whether obtained from produce or from manufacture,* penghasilan (hasil).

respect, *v. tr.* menghormati (hormat); *show deference to,* segani, memuliakan (mulia); *self-~,* maruah, harga diri; *~ful,* sopan, tertib; *~able (decent and well- behaved),* sopan santun; *~ful,* penghormat.

respective, *adj.* masing-masing.

respiration, *n.* pernafasan (nafas).

responsible, *adj. to be ~ for expenses,* bertanggungjawab (tanggung); *as surety,* jamin; *to be answerable,* dipertanggung-jawabkan; *to take the responsibility,* mengambil tanggungjawab; *the ~ parties,* pihak yang bertanggung-jawab; *true originator of event,* pokok pangkal; *to 'carry the can', bear the brunt,* timpa rasa.

rest, *v. intr.* hilang penat; rihat; *to take a ~, 'stand easy',* bersenang (senang) diri; melepaskan (lepas) lelah; *have a restful time,* melegakan (lega) badan; *see* **relax;** *R.I.P.,* kalu inna; *it rests with— (to decide),* terserah (serah) kepada—; *see* **leave.**

restaurant, *n.* kedai makan, restoran.

restive, *adj. as a horse,* candi; kuda yang enggan mara ke hadapan.

restless, *adj.* resah; *see* **bustle, fidget;** *of eyes, never steady,* liar; *looking this way and that nervously,* terbelingas (lingas).

restore, *v. tr. put back,* mengembalikan (kembali) memulihkan, menghidupkan semula; *give back,* beri balik; *re-establish (health, peace, etc.),* memulihkan (pulih); *also* memperbaharui.

restrain, *v. tr.* menahan (tahan); *restriction by Government control,* kawalan; *subject to legal limits, e.g., as sale of rubber,* berdasarkan pada kawalan undang-undang; *~ yourself!,* sabar!; *you should ~ your emotions (or lusts),* jangan mengikut (ikut) hawa nafsu; *to ~ one's feelings,* menahan perasaan (rasa); *see* **feelings.**

restricted, *p.p. kept within bounds,* bersekat (sekat); terbatas; *person whose area of residence is ~ by Government order,* orang buangan tempatan; *to impose restrictions,* mengenakan (kena) sekatan; *~ area,* kawasan larangan; *see* **control.**

result, *n. end,* hasil, kesudahan (sudah); *consequence,* akibat; *decision, issue,* keputusan (putus); *to ~ (happen),* jadi; *see* **definite.**

resurrection, *n.* kehidupan (hidup) kembali; *to resurrect,* menghidupkan (hidup) kembali (balik); *see* **revive.**

resuscitate, *v. tr. & i. to bring or come back from unconsciousness,* memulihkan pernafasan.

retail, *n.* runcit.

retaliate, *v. tr.* membalas (balas).

retch, *v. intr.* belilah (lilah), menjeluak; bunyi seakan-akan hendak muntah.

retinue, *n.* pengiring (iring).

retire, *v. intr. cease work,* berhenti (henti) kerja; *~ on pension,* berpencen, bersara (sara); *retiring (not sociable),* suka membawa (bawa) diri, tak suka menengahkan (tengah) diri; *see* **retreat.**

retract, *v. tr. as a statement,* membatalkan (batal) tarik balik; *as claws,* menyorokkan (sorok).

retreat, *v. intr. go back, beat a ~,* mengundur (undur); *make good one's ~,* mengundurkan diri.

retrench, *v. tr. cut down expenditure,* menghematkan (hemat) perbelanjaan (belanja); mengurangi (kurang).

retrograde, *adj. reversing progress,* mundur; *~ step,* langkah mundur.

return, *v. intr.* balik, kelik; kembali; *go off home,* pulang; *to send back (as goods),* kirim balik; *~ ticket,* 'tikit' pergi-balik; *~ match,* pelawanan (lawan) ulangan; *~ing good for evil,* jahat dibalas baik.

reveal, *v. tr. a secret,* membuka (buka) rahsia; *'let cat out of bag',* membongkar (bongkar), mendedahkan (dedah) rahsia; *divine revelation,* wahi.

revenge, *n.* bela; *to seek ~,* tuntut bela; *take ~,* membalas dendam; *~ a defeat,* menebus (tebus) kekalahan (kalah); *blood money,* diat; *see* **requite.**

revenue, *n. esp. of State,* hasil, perolehan (oleh); *income,* pendapatan (dapat).

reverberation, *n.* bahana; berkumandang (kumandang) menggema (gema); *to reverberate,* berbahana, bergaung (gaung), bergema (gema).

revere, *v. tr.* memuliakan (mulia), menghormati (hormat).

reverse, *v. tr. a car,* 'gustan'; mengundurkan; *turn backwards, as a revolving part,* akaskan; *~ a decision,* batalkan; *as, against the grain, song sang.*

revert, *v. tr. of property,* pulang (kepada).

revet, *v. tr. strengthen sides of drain, etc.,* mengukuhkan (kukuh), menupang (tupang).

review, *n. of troops,* pemeriksaan (periksa) barisan; perbarisan pentadbiran (tadbir); *of a book,* ulasan, kecaman, sorotan.

revile, *v. tr. & i.* mencerca, mencaci maki, menghinakan.

revise, *v. tr.* memeriksa (periksa) lagi; *as studies,* ulang-kaji; *amend,* meminda (pinda); *re-examine,* ulang periksa, mengkaji semula.

revive, *v. tr. bring back to life, vigour or consciousness,* menghidupkan (hidup) balik; *by artificial respiration,* memulihkan (pulih) nafas.

revoke, *v. tr. cancel,* batalkan.

revolt, *v. intr. see* **rebel.**

revolve, *v. intr. orbit,* beredar (edar); *go round,* berpusing (pusing); *rotate on axis,* berputar (putar) pada paksi; *as round a central point,* berkisar (kisar); *revolution (political),* pemberontakan (berontak).

reward, *n.* hadiah; ganjaran.

rheumatism, *n.* pirai; penyakit sengal-sengal.

rhinoceros, *n.* badak (hempit).

rhyme, *n.* sajak.

rhythm, *n.* irama.

rib, *n.* tulang rusuk; *of leaf,* lidi; *of boat,* kong.

ribbon, *n.* pita.

rice, *n. growing,* padi; *husked,* beras; *cooked,* nasi; *parboiled,* beras rebus; *glutinous,* pulut; *broken ~,* beras háncur, melukut; *~-paper,* jeluang; *~field, wet,* bendang, sawah, tanah cedungan; *dry,* tanah tugalan; *hill padi,* padi huma, padi bukit; *hill ~field,* ladang; *aftermath,* padi ceding; *early padi, padi rengan; Rangoon ~,* beras Pegu.

rich, *adj.* kaya, hartawan; *of food or of voice,* lemak; *of soil,* gemuk; *to en~ oneself,* mengayakan (kaya) diri.

rickets, *n.* penyakit (sakit) lembik, penyakit riket.

ricochet, *n. intr.* melantun (lantun), memantul (pantul).

rid, *v. tr. get ~ of, as throw away,* buang; *cause to cease (as, e.g., pain),* menghilangkan (hilang); *'root out',* membasmikan (basmi), hapuskan, singkirkan; *make a clean sweep of,* menyapu (sapu) bersih.

riddle, *n.* teka-teki; *~d (e.g., with bullets),* bersarang-sarang, tembus-menembus melubangi dengan peluru.

ride, *v. tr. (horse, bicycle),* tunggang, naik.

ridge, *n.* cangkat; *flattened top of hill,*

penara (tara); *hummock between rice-fields,* matang, gong; *low bank, esp. between rice-plots,* batas; *roof-~,* rabung; *between furrows,* awat.

ridicule, *v. tr.* mengejek (ejek); *(taunt),* menggiat (giat).

rife, *adj. continually occuring, as crimes, etc.,* menjadi-jadi; meluas (luas) *'always with us',* ada ada sahaja.

rift, *n. crack,* retak; *split,* belah; *fissure,* celah.

rigging, *n.* tali temali.

right, *adj. (hand),* kanan; *fitting,* patut; *correct,* betul; *fair claim,* hak; adil; *~ of assembly,* hak berkumpul (kumpul); berhimpun (himpun); *conjugal ~s,* nafkah batin; *serves (him) ~,* patutlah!; (sl.), padan dengan muka dia; *let him suffer!,* biar dia rasa.

righteousness, *n.* dharma; keadilan, hal patut.

rigid, *adj.* keras, kaku; *as in death,* keras jegang.

rigmarole, *n.* cakap angin, cerita yang tak ada hujung pangkalnya; tak bertalian.

rikisha, *n.* beca, lanca; *trishaw,* beca roda tiga.

rim, *n. edge,* tepi; *raised ~,* bingkai; *as of plate,* sembir; *as of pot,* bibir; *see* **brim.**

rind, *n.* kulit.

ring, *n. for finger,* cincin; *a keepsake ~, esp. an engagement ~,* cincin tanda; *circular appliance,* gelang, gelung; *for cattle-fights,* bong; *arena, generally,* gelanggang; *nose-~s for cattle,* kelikir, kili-kili; *~s of a tree,* belak yang bulat; *to ~ bell,* pukul loceng; *to ~ (a coin to test it),* penting, tinting; *emit a ~ing noise, as a telephone,* berdering (dering).

ringworm, *n.* kurap.

rinse, *v. tr. wash in clear water,* bilas, kincar.

riot, *n.* huru-hara, musuh, rusuhan.

rip, *v. tr. sharply,* carik.

ripe, *n.* masak; *fully formed, but not yet soft,* mengkal; *dead-~ (and hard),* kemirau; *to put away (esp. bananas), to ~n,* peram.

ripple, *n.* riak; *esp. as 'cat's paws' at sea,* keracak.

rise, *v. tr. esp, as sun or moon,* naik, terbit; meninggi; *from bed,* bangun; *stand up,* bangkit berdiri (diri); *spring up to feet* bingkas berdiri; *just lying on the horizon (of sun or moon),* mengambang (ambang); *~, of price,* naik meningkat (tingkat); *~ from (have origin from),* berasal (asal) dari; *~ high (e.g., of prices, hopes, smoke),* menjulang (julang); *~ to a peak, climax,* memuncak (puncak); *voice rising to an angry pitch,* suara mengalun (alun) kasar; *~ to a level with clouds,* mengaras (aras) awan; *~ (swell with yeast), of dough,* kembang, melumbung (lembung), memual (mual); *rising ground,* tanah makin meninggi (tinggi); *a ~ in wages,* tambahan gaji; *to give ~ to, cause, see* **cause.**

risk, *n. danger,* bahaya; risiko; *to ~ one's life,* mempertaruhkan (taruh) jiwa, menyabungkan (sabung) jiwa; *esp. of a soldier,* gadai nyawa; *'chuck ones life away',* buang nyawa; *run needless ~,* cari bahaya.

ritual, *n.* upacara; *to perform a ~,* melakukan (laku) upacara.

rival, *n.* lawan, saingan, tandingan; *unrivalled,* tak terlawan, tak boleh lawan; *in ~ry (trying to outdo one another),* berdahulu-dahuluan; *a ~ (second) wife,* madu.

river, *n.* sungai; *bed of ~,* dasar sungai; *~side,* tepi sungai; *see* **stream.**

road, *n. way,* jalan; *banked ~,* tembok; *corduroy ~,* jalan raya, jalan batang; *~ sign,* papan tanda jalan; *tarmac ~,* jalan bertar ('tar').

roar, *v. intr.* meraung (raung); *emit growling ~, esp, as a tiger,* mengaum (aum); *as a storm,* menderu (deru).

roast, *v. tr.* panggang, bakar; *in ashes,* bembam.

rob, *v. tr.* menyamun (samun), merompak (rompak).

robe, *n. esp. as long Arab ~,* jubah; *woman's long ~,* kebaya.

robin, *n. magpie-~,* murai.

rock, *n.* batu (besar) *bed-~,* batu hampar; *to ~ (oscillate), as a boat,* oleng-oleng; *as a cradle,* berayun (ayun); *as tree in the wind,* bergoyang (goyang); *~ to-and-fro,* lenggok-lenggang; *see* **wobble.**

rod, *n. fishing-~,* joran; *generally,* batang; *cane,* rotan.

role, *n. part played,* peranan; *to sustain a ~,* mendukung (dukung) peranan, memainkan (main) peranan.

roll, *v. tr. as with a ~er,* giling; *~ up,* gulung; *~ up (sleeves),* singsing (lengan baju); *~ over (run over),* gelek; *~ along (as stone down slope),* golek; *between palms of hands,* kusal, gisal; *~ out (as flour),* giling; *move with ~ing gait,* melenggang (lenggang); *see* **rock;** *as swaying from side to side,* liangliuk; *of boat,* berenggut-enggut, angguk-angguk; *to ~ oneself up into a ball, as a hedgehog and some insects,* bergulung; *~ up between finger and thumb, as a pill,* menggentel (gentel); *~, e.g., dough between the palms of the hands so as to make a ball,* mengupar (upar) *~ing-pin,* torak, batu giling; *to ~ out, as dough,* menorak; *~ the eyes,* bolak-balikkan mata; *~ (sound with vibration, as thunder),* bergemuruh (gemuruh); *~ing over and over,* tergolek-golek; *a ~ (list),* dafter; *~ of fat,* tenggan; *a ~ of cloth,* segulung kain; *a ~er (as for the road),* penggiling; *long wave,* alun; *roller to assist the pulling along of, e.g., a boat,* galang.

romance, *n.* cerita percintaan, peristiwa (urusan) percintaan.

romanised, *adj. ~ script,* huruf rumi.

Rome, *n.* Rum; *Roman,* Rumawi; *when in ~, do as the Romans do,* masuk kandang kerbau, menguak (kuak), *(when you enter a buffalopen, low).*

roof, *n.* bumbung; *thatched ~,* atap rumah.

room, *n.* bilik; kamar; *large semi-public ~, chamber,* ruang(an), *reception-~,* ruang tamu; *see* **cubicle.**

roomy, *adj. spacious,* selesa; *as clothes or car,* lapang-luas.

root, *n.* akar; *tap-~,* tunjang; *other main ~,* umbi; *branching ~, as of mangrove,* jangkar; *the ~ (fig.), as of trouble,* pokok pangkal; *to ~, as a pig,* tonyok, menyungkur (sungkur), menyondongkan (sondong) mencung kepada; *~ of a word,* umbi; *'~ed to the spot' (as amazed or startled),* tertegun (tegun).

rope, *n.* tali (kasar); *(fig.) the ~s, finer points connected with a job,* selok-belok.

rosary, *n.* tasbih.

rostrum, *n. platform,* pentas; pulpit, mimbar.

rot, *v. intr.* menjadi (jadi) busuk; *crumble to pieces,* reput puih, reput relai; *~ away, esp. of wood,* bangsai; *see* **decay;** *~!,* karut!; *a lot of damned ~ (esp. of a 'tall' story),* temberang lapuk.

rotate, *v. intr. see* **revolve;** *in rotation (by turn),* bergilir-gilir, berganti-ganti; *as in rotation of crops,* bertukar-tukar.

rouge, *n.* gincu, bedak pemerah (merah) pipi.

rough, *adj.* kasar; *to the touch,* kasap, gerapu; *see gnarled; of the sea,* kocak, berombak (ombak) *besar; of a gem unpolished,* mentah, tidak bersepuh (sepuh); *the ~ and the smooth (of life),* baik buruknya; *~ly (adv.),* kira-kira, lebih kurang, secara kasarnya.

round, *adj.* bulat; *~ed,* bundar; *of number,* genap; *a~,* sekeliling; *all ~ (the town),* merata-rata (bandar); *to go on ~s,* melakukan lawatan biasa untuk memeriksa sesuatu; *in a patrol,* meronda (ronda); *to ~ up (as criminals),* berkas; *a ~ (in boxing),* pusingan.

routine, *n. regular duties,* kerja biasa, 'rutin'.

row, *n. commotion, noisy dispute, see* **quarrel, riot;** *sounds of quarrel, esp. of family quarrel,* hiruk-pikuk; *uproar,* riuh-rendah; *esp. as of brawl,* hingar-bangar; *esp. of heated argument,* becang-becok; *frightful commotion (sl.),* kiamat dunia.

row, *v. intr.* berdayung (dayung); *a ~, esp. of troops,* baris; *esp. of trees,* nirai; *as a line, of teeth, persons, chairs, etc.,* deret.

rowdy, *n.* samseng, orang yang suka bertengkar.

rowlock, *n.* 'taul'.

royal, *adj,* diraja; *~ty,* bayaran dari syarikat lombong dll kepada tuan punya tanah, royalti.

rub, *v. tr.* gosok; *as in striking a match,* gesek; *roughly, so as to cause friction,* haus; *as in scrubbing,* gonyoh; *in scouring,* kincah; *as in cleaning the teeth,* sugi; *as in massage,* urut; *~ out,* hapus, padam; *gently between palms of hands,* mengusal (kusal); *~ with gentle friction, as when applying rouge,* menggesel (gesel); *or in touching something when passing; as when stubbing out a cigarette,* tenyeh; *~ hands together,* menggenyeh-genyeh tangan; *~ eyes,* menggenyeh mata; *~bed sore,* haus-haus; *rubber eraser,* getah pemadam; *rubber stamp (lit.),* cap getah; *(fig.) mere figure-head, see* **roll.**

rub-a-dub, *n.* bunyi gendang.

rubber, *n.* getah.

rubbish, *n.* sampah; *~-bin,* tong sampah; *~!,* karut!; *hole for dumping ~,* acar; *dirty garbage,* kotoran.

rubble, *n.* pecahan batu.

ruby, *n.* batu delima.

rucked, *adj. ~ up,* berkedut (kedut).

rucksack, *n.* ransel, *same as* kantung yang dipikul di belakang.

rudder, *n.* kemudi.

rude, *adj. rough,* kasar; *unmannerly,* kurang ajar, biadab, tak tahu adat; *disrespectful,* kurang sopan; *see* **offhand;** *behave ~ly (make a 'rough house'),* menceroboh (ceroboh).

rudiment, *n.* dasar permulaan; organ yang tak sempurna.

ruffian, *n.* samseng, kacang hantu.

rug, *n.* selimut, ambal.

ruined, *adj. destroyed,* binasa; *(financially),* jatuh 'bengkerap'; *~ in charac-*

ter *(esp. as a girl),* rosak; *ruins of buildings,* runtuhan bangunan; *~, of a country or an enterprise,* terlingkup (lingkup); *falling into ruin, of a building,* robak-rabik.

rule, *v. tr.* perintah; *administer,* mentadbirkan (tadbir); *Ruler,* raja, pemerintah; *school ~r,* kayu 'rul', penggaris (garis), pembaris (baris); *~s of life,* rukun; *~s of politeness,* adab; *dominant standards, accepted method of regulating,* tata, tatabahasa; *grammar, esp. on a point of religion,* fatwa; *customary ~s, esp. of tribal law,* pantang-larang; *~s of conduct,* petua; *laid down by authority,* undang-undang.

rumble, *v. intr.* berderam-deram; *as thunder,* bergemuruh (gemuruh); *faintly, far away,* mendayu-dayu; *as empty stomach,* berkeroncong (keroncong).

rummage, *v. intr. search,* menyelongkar (selongkar).

rump, *n.* punggung binatang.

run, *v. intr.* berlari (lari); *'hare off',* cabut lari; *~ down (disparage),* mencela (cela); *~ over (as with car),* gelek; *~ out of (ready money),* putus (belanja); *~ off with,* bawa lari; *~ (as paint),* turun berdenih (denih); *~ for one's life,* bawa nyawa; *~ wild, live an undisciplined life,* meliar-liar; *~ away (of a horse),* lari meliar; *~-wild (having reverted to wild state), of an animal,* jalang; *to ~ a film,* putarkan; *~ner-up (in championship),* naib (johan); *~ners (on a pole),* katang-katang; *~ner (creeping stem),* sulur; *~ning (consecutive),* berturut-turut.

runt, *n. particularly small offspring,* anak keladi.

rupture, *n.* hernia, burut, putus (perhubungan).

ruse, *n.* muslihat, tipu.

rush, *n. see* **sedge.**

rush, *v. intr.* berkejar (kejar); *~ at,* terkam; *as in chase,* hambat; *~ frantically over all obstacles,* lari susup-sasap.

russet, *adj.* kuning kemerah-merahan (merah).

rustic, *adj. countryman,* orang kampung,

orang hulu, orang desa; ~ *dress,* pakaian orang desa.

rustle, *v. intr. as leaves in wind,* berdesar (desar), berperas-peras.

rusty, berkarat (karat).

rut, *n. wheel-marks,* bekas roda; ~*ting, of elephant,* menta; *of deer,* biang.

ruthless, *adj. cruel,* kejam, zalim; *having no 'bowels',* tidak berhati (hati) perut.

S

sabbath, *n.* hari istirahat, (hari Sabtu bagi orang Yahudi dan hari Ahad bagi orang Kristian).

sabotage, *n.* khianat; *saboteur,* pengkhianat.

sack, *n.* guni; *small ~,* guntil; *of plaited material,* karung; *to ~ (sl.), dismiss,* buang kerja; diberhentikan (henti) kerja.

sacred, *adj.* suci; *hallowed by associations,* keramat.

sacrifice, *n.* korban.

sacrilege, *v. tr. to common ~,* menghinakan (hina) tempat yang suci, mencemarkan (cemar) tempat yang suci.

sad, *adj. of a person,* susah-hati, sayu-hati, sedih-hati; *of news,* sedih.

saddle, *n.* zin, pelana; *pack-~, of elephant,* rengka; alas pelana.

safe, *adj.* selamat; *iron box,* peti besi; *~ty first!,* biar lambat asal selamat!; langkah keselematan; utamakan keselamatan; *to ~guard,* melindungkan (lindung); *a ~-guard (e.g., a special clause in a constitution or lit.),* pelindung, kawalan; *a place of safety, refuge,* perlindungan, suaka.

sag, *v. intr.* melendut (lendut), melentur (lentur).

sago, *n.* sagu; *refuse ~ flour,* serampin; *the ~-palm,* pokok rembia.

sail, *n.* layar; *sailing ~,* kapal layar; *sailor,* kelasi (kapal), pelaut (laut).

saint, *n.* wali Allah.

sake, *n. for the ~ of,* kerana.

salary, *n.* gaji.

saliva, *n.* air liur.

sallow, *adj.* putih bahasa; wan, *of a dark person,* perang-perus.

salt, *n.* garam; *~y,* masin; *~ed,* masin, asin; *preserved in ~,* jeruk; *brackish,* payau; *to ~ away (lit. and fig.),* pendap; *to pickle in ~,* menggarami.

saltpetre, *n.* sendawa, mesiu.

salubrious, *adj.* yang menyegarkan.

salute, *v. tr.* memberi (beri) salam kepada, memberi tabik kepada; *(more formal),* memberi hormat kepada; *to fire a ~,* menembak (tembak) tabik hormat; *to take the ~ (as at a march past),* membalas (balas) tabik kehormatan.

salvo, *n. to fire a ~,* menembak (tembak) sekali gus.

same, *adj.* sama; *just like,* serupa; *on a parity with,* bersamaan dengan; *the ~ day,* hari itu juga, sama sehari; *'six of one and half a dozen of the other',* dua kali lima sepuluh juga, *(twice five still makes ten); so (sl.),* awak dua kali lima dengan dia, *(your're just as bad as he is).*

sample, *n.* contoh.

sanctimonious, *adj.* munafik, pura-pura alim.

sanction, *n.* izin; *economic 'sanctions' (penalties),* hukum iktisad, penekanan (tekan) ekonomi.

sand, *n.* pasir; *~-fly (sp.),* agas, temperas, rengit, kekapur (kapur-kapur); *~-paper,* mempelas; *~-bag,* karung pasir, bantal pasir; *~y (in colour),* (warna) langsat; *~-piper,* burung kedidi; *~bank,* beting; *quicksand,* pasir apung, pasir jerlus, *see* **shoal.**

sandal, *n.* capal.

sandalwood, *n.* kayu cendana.

sane, *adj.* sempurna-akal.

sanitation, *n. hygiene,* kebersihan (bersih); *sanitary science,* ilmu kesihatan (sihat).

sap, *n.* getah; *sapwood,* gubal.

sapphire, *n.* batu nilam.

sarcasm, *n.* sindiran; *sarcastic,* tajam mulut.

sari, *n.* pakaian perempuan India.

sarong, n. kain sarung, kain; *short ~ worn with trousers,* samping.

sash, n. *(worn over shoulder),* selendang, kain lepas; *esp. as ~ of insignia,* sandang.

satchel, n. kandi-kandi, kantung.

sated, p.p. kenyang, puas, jemu.

satellite, n. *follower,* pengikut, ikut-ikutan; *~ State,* negara patung; negara satelit; *see* **sputnik.**

satiate, v. tr. memuaskan sepenuhnya; mengenyangkan.

satin, n. seti, antelas.

satire, n. sindiran.

satisfactory, adj. cukup baik, memberi (beri) puas-hati; *will do,* jadilah.

satisfied, adj. puas-hati.

saturated, adj. *through steeping,* jerap, lecap; *waterlogged,* keairan (air); *see* **wet.**

Saturday, n. hari Sabtu

sauce, n. 'sos'; *soya-bean ~,* kicap; *saucepan,* kuali.

saucer, n. piring.

saucy, adj. *as a child,* manja; *saucily provocative, of a girl,* naik lemak; *see* **cheek, rude.**

savage, adj. *fierce,* bengis, garang; *~s (primitive people),* orang liar; *see* **fierce.**

save, v. tr. *help in danger,* tolong; *secure safety of,* selamatkan; *lay by,* simpan; *Post Office Savings Bank,* 'Bank' simpanan pejabat (jabat) 'Pos'; *a good ~r, economical, pandai berhemat (hemat);* *to ~ (money, time),* menjimatkan (jimat); *to sing God ~ the King (Queen),* menyanyikan (nyanyi) lagu Allah lanjutkan usia baginda 'King' ('Kuin'); *see* **safe.**

saviour, n. penyelamat.

saw, n. gergaji; *~-mill,* kilang papan; *~-fish,* ikan todak, yu gergaji; *~-dust,* habuk gergaji, serbuk gergaji.

say, v. intr. kata; *as a ruler,* titah; *as a prophet or high dignitary,* sabda; *a ~ing,* pepatah; *Sayings of the Prophet,* hadis.

scab, n. *on sore,* kuping, keruping;

sejenis penyakit kulit yang terdapat terutamanya pada kambing biri-biri.

scabbard, n. sarung (keris, pedang).

scaffold, n. *temporary platform,* peranja, aram-aram, panggar, perancah.

scald, v. tr. *as fowl, to remove feathers,* celur; *to get ~ed,* lecur.

scales, n. *as of fish,* sisik; *steelyard for weighing,* neraca, dacing; *marks showing the various weights,* mata dacing; *tongue showing marks,* lidah dacing; *rod,* batang dacing; *series of degrees,* tangga; *wage-scale,* tangga gaji; *to fake the ~,* makan dacing; *on a large scale,* secara besar-besaran; *on a small scale,* secara kecil-kecil.

scalp, n. kulit kepala.

scamp, n. *good-for-nothing,* kacang hantu.

scamped, p.p. *of work, not carefully done,* terserempak (serempak), sergut.

scamper, v. intr. *to trot along not at full speed,* berlari (lari) anak.

scan, v. tr. *turn eyes successively to each part of (face),* memandang (pandang) menyeluruhi (seluruh) (muka), melihat sepintas lalu.

scandal, n. *disgraceful incident,* perkara keji, khabar honar; *to talk ~,* menjual (jual) nama orang; *the 'talk of the town',* buah mulut; *~-monger,* seseorang yang melakukan fitnah; *to go round telling tales,* bawa mulut; *~ (scandalous behaviour) 'willout',* bangkai gajah dapatkah ditudung dengan nyiru? *(can the carcase of an elephant be covered with a tray?); see* **appearance, slander.**

scanty, adj. *not thick, sparse,* jarang; *exiguous,* tipis.

scar, n. parut; *see* **wale.**

scarce, adj. jarang jumpa, payah (dapat); *in short supply,* berkurang (kurang).

scarecrow, n. *contrivance for scaring birds, figure looking like a man,* orang-orang; *acting by noise,* selayut, baling-baling.

scarf, n. *to support child carried on back,* ambin; *loose cloth round neck,* sebai;

577

tudung.

scarlet, *adj. the colour of the hibiscus flower,* merah menyala (nyala).

scatter, *v. tr. as seed,* tabur, hambur; *~ed about,* bertaburan; *dotted here and there,* berselerak; *esp. of an army,* pecah-belah, cerai-berai; *~ed, as a crowd by rain or by police,* bercempera (cempera); *to run ~ing right and left,* lari lintang bujur, lari bertempiaran (tempiar); *to ~, disseminate here and there,* serakkan; *to be smashed and ~ed about in bits,* tersepai (sepai); *see* **litter.**

scavenge, *v. tr. remove refuse,* mengangkat (angkat) sampah; *pick up what one can here and there,* meramu (ramu); *~r n.* binatang yang makan bangkai binatang lain.

scene, *n. part of act in a play,* babak; *incident in play,* adegan; *a sight,* pemandangan (pandang); *noisy ~,* suasana riuh-heboh; *to make a ~ (minor disturbance),* buat kelaku (laku); *~ry (of the theatre),* hiasan pentas, 'dekor', 'dekorasi'; 'flats', papan 'dekor'; *behind the ~s (not publicly),* di belakang layar; **scenario,** *n.* rencana lakon sandiwara (atau filem).

scent, *n. as of game,* bau, *perfume,* air wangi; *see* **smell, frangrant, perfume.**

sceptical, *adj. disinclined to believe,* tak berapa percaya; *not easily talked over,* tak mudah termakan (makan) kata orang.

schedule, *n.* jadual.

scheme, *n.* rancangan, ikhtiar, gagasan, skim.

scholarship, *n. grant to student,* biasiswa.

school, *n.* sekolah; *kindergarten,* taman kanak-kanak; (tajaka); *~ (group) of religious thought,* mazhab.

science, *n.* ilmu; *knowledge,* pengetahuan (tahu); *scientist,* ahli 'sains'; *domestic ~,* kesenian (seni) rumahtangga.

scissors, *n.* gunting; *for betel-nut,* kacip,

kelati.

scoff, *v. intr.* mengejek (ejek); mencemek; memperli.

scold, *v. intr. rebuke sharply,* marahkan; *revile,* cerca, hamun; *'go for', 'tell off',* mengata-nyatakan (kata).

scoop, *v. tr. as with a ladle,* cedok; *as when bailing,* menimba (timba); *as with hands,* kaup; *shovelling up,* menyodok (sodok).

scope, *n. area of action,* bidang.

scorch, *v. tr.* melayur (layur); *smell of ~ing, esp. of cooked food,* hangit; *to singe,* siut; *~ed,* terselar, tercelur (celur); *to '~ the earth',* melebur (lebur) bumi.

score, *n. a ~,* dua puluh, sekodi; *~d off (unexpectedly worsted),* kanjal; *~ off, in argument,* menang cakap; *total of marks, etc., obtained,* jumlah mata (markah).

scorpion, *n.* kala jengking.

scour, *v. tr. rub clean,* mengincah (kincah); *as a swift stream,* mengikis (kikis), mengorek (korek); menggosok; mencari sesuatu dengan segera.

scout, *v. tr.* mengakap (kakap), mengintip, mengintai; *see* **reconnoitre;** *boy ~,* budak pengakap; *Chief ~,* pengakap agung; *Cubs,* anak serigala.

scrabble, *v. tr. scratch at, as fowls,* kais-kais; *as when drawing something towards one, e.g., with a stick,* kuis; *~ open (to make a hole),* unggis-unggis.

scramble, *v. intr. make one's way by clambering, crawling, etc.* merapah; *~ up,* meragang; mendaki.

scrap, *n. small detached piece,* seperca, secebis; *see* **remain;** *~ iron,* besi buruk.

scrape, *v. tr.* kikir; *lightly, as when playing the violin,* gesek; *~ clean, as when removing the scales of fish,* siang; *as in grating,* purat; *as wheel against post,* tersanggit (sanggit) pada, tergeser (geser) pada; *with iron instrument,* kokot.

scratch, *n.* calar; *covered with ~es,* golok-galar; *to ~ as an itchy place,* garu; *as* *fowls,* kais, cakar; *withdraw name,* potong nama.

scrawl, *n. untidy writing (sl.),* cakar ayam.

scream, *v. intr.* menjerit (jerit), berteriak (teriak), memekik (pekik).

screech, *v. intr. in excitement or anger,* melenting *(lenting); as a cat,* melalak (lalak); *(as brakes),* mencicit (cicit); *see* **scream.**

screen, *n.* tebeng; *against sun,* dinding hari; *as curtain,* tabir, tirai, layar; *lattice-work,* kisi-kisi; the *'silver ~',* layar perak; *to ~ off, as hide the view of,* mendinding (dinding), mengadang (adang); *to ~, investigate antecedents of,* menyaringkan (saring).

script, *n. of play,* senikata.

scriptures, *n.* kitab (suci); *people possessing ~ recognised by Islam, i.e., Muslims (Kuran), Jews* (Taurat *the Old Testament* and kitab Zabur, *the Psalms) and Christians,* (Injil, *the gospels); others are 'pagan'* (musyrik) *or 'heathen'* (kafir); *those 'possessing ~' are* ahli al'kitab, *people of the Book* or ahli al'ahad, *people of the Covenant.*

scrotum, *n.* kandung buah pelir.

scrub, *v. tr. rub hand,* gonyoh, sental; *small jungle,* **semak,** belukar rok.

scruple, *n.* keberatan (berat).

scrupulous, *adj. painstakingly careful and thorough,* berhati-hati.

scuffle, *v. intr. to struggle confusedly with pushing about,* bergelut-gelut.

scullery, *n.* tempat mengincah (kincah).

sculpture, *v. tr.* mengukir (ukir), memahat (pahat); **sculptor,** ahli pahat.

scum, *n. impurities that rise to the surface of liquid,* buih, ruban; *on tide-rip,* kekat; *in smelting,* sanga; *~ of society,* sampah masyarakat.

scruf, *n.* kelemumur.

scuttle, *v. intr. dash hurriedly, esp. as in and out of obstacles,* menyelinap (selinap), lari susup-sasap; *to ~ (deliberately sink) (a ship),* sengaja menenggelamkan (tenggelam).

scythe, *n.* pedang (rumput); *for weeds in rice-fields,* tajak.

sea, *n.* laut; *the ocean,* lautan, bahar; *~-weed (sp.),* setu, rengkam (karang), agar-agar, jepang, akar bahar; *~-sick,* mabuk laut, mabuk ombak; *~-anemone,* rembung; *~-horse,* unduk-unduk, kuda-kuda laut; *seamanship,* ilmu pelayaran, keahlian belayar.

seal, *n. of wax,* cap; *royal ~,* tera; *~ing wax,* lak; *~ing wax palm,* pokok linau; *marine mammal,* gajah mina, anjin laut; *to ~ off a road,* menyekat (sekat) jalan.

seam, *n.* jahitan, kelim.

seance, *n. to hold a ~ to call up spirits,* berhantu (hantu); *to effect a special purpose, such as curing the sick,* main puteri, minduk; *see* **shaman.**

search, *v. tr. a person,* periksa; *look for,* cari; *rummage,* selongkar; *see* **investigate.**

season, *n.* musin; *'in ~' (on heat, of animals),* biang; *~able (apt to the occasion),* tepat pada saat dan waktunya; *to ~ (lay up a natural product until fit for use),* peram.

seat, *n.* tempat duduk; *as in Council,* kerusi; *see* **bench, chair, stool.**

secede, *v. intr.* memisahkan (pisah) diri (daripada), menarikkan (tarik) diri (daripada), mengundurkan diri.

seclude, *adj. of place,* sunyi; *kept in seclusion, as an unmarried girl,* pingitan.

second, *n. of time,* saat, detik; *~er, supporter (as of a proposal),* pembantu (bantu), penyokong (sokong); *the ~ (next after the first),* yang kedua (dua); *to come ~ (in a race),* dapat 'nombor' dua; *~ sight (enabling the possessor to see the future or distant objects),* terus mata; *~ helping of rice,* nasi tambah; *~ in a duel,* pengapit (apit); *~-hand,* sudah dipakai, 'sekenhen'.

secret, *n.* rahsia; *confidential, not to be divulged,* sulit; *~y, stealthily,* curi-curi, bersulit-sulit; *top ~, of a document,* sangat rahsia; *~ Service,* perkhidmatan rahsia; *~ agent (political),* perisik (risik) rahsia; *~ society,* kongsi gelap; *~ code,* tulisan rahsia.

secretary, *n.* setiausaha; *private ~,* setiausaha sulit; *personal ~,* setiausaha peribadi; *honorary ~,* setiausaha yang kehormat (hormat); *Permanent ~,* setiausaha tetap.

sect, *n.* mazhab.

section, *n.* bahagian kecil daripada bahagian yang lebih besar; *of a writing,* fasal, ceraian; *as a small party,* seksi; *of community,* suku, puak, golongan; *of fruit,* ulas; *of bamboo,* ruas; *used as pipe,* kancung; *~ of fruit, e.g., esp. a durian, containing the edible part,* pangsa.

sector, *n. division,* bahagian; *as of jurisdiction,* kawansan.

secure, *v. tr.* melindungi, menyelamatkan, *~ the doors and windows;* mengunci jendela dan pintu.

security, *n. peacefulness,* keamanan (aman) keselamatan (selamat); *~ Council of the United Nations,* Majlis Keselamatan Bangsa-bangsa Bersatu (satu); *~ forces,* pasukan keselamatan; *~ (for debt, etc.),* jamin.

sedate, *adj.* sopan santun.

sedge, *n. (sp.),* menderung kercut, sendayan, mensiang.

sediment, *n. see* **dregs.**

sedition, *n.* asutan derhaka.

seduce, *v. tr. lead astray,* menyesatkan (sesat), memikat (pikat); *outrage,* berbuat (buat) cabul kepada; *take virginity,* merosakkan (rosak) anak dara; *seduced (girl),* sudah hilang dara; *(sl.),* nyiur sudah ditebuk tupai, *(the coconut has been bored by a squirrel); 'wolves' who are a danger to maidens,* musang, lelaki hidung belang.

see, *v. tr.* tengok, lihat; *esp.,* nampak; *interview,* berjumpa, 'interbiu'; *~ off,* hantar; *understand,* faham; *~ to (deal with),* kira, bicarakan; *see* **look.**

seed, *n.* biji, *for sowing,* benih; *Adam's ~ (human kind),* bani Adam; *descendants,* zuriat; *~-bed,* semaian; *~ling,* anak pokok.

seek, *v. tr. see* **search;** *~ out (as for advice),* mendapatkan (dapat).

seemingly, *adv. apparently,* rupa-rupa, rupanya.

seep, *v. intr. ooze out or in,* meniris (tiris), meresap (resap), meresip (resip).

see-saw, *v. intr. ~-sawing, unsteady, of planks forming a flooring,* jongkit-jongkitan; *to play ~-saw,* main enjut-enjut, main ungkang-ungkit.

seethe, *v. intr. as water,* menggelegak (gelegak), mendidih; *as ants,* mengurung (urung), berenyut (renyut).

segment, *n. part cut off,* sekerat; *natural ~ of fruit,* ulas; *cavity containing such a ~,* pangsa.

segregate, *v. tr.* mengasingkan (asing); *see* **confine, restrict.**

seize, *v. tr.* pegang; *catch,* tangkap; *as in struggle,* merebut (rebut); *grab, make off with,* membolot (bolot); *~ and grapple with,* cangking.

seldom, *adv.* jarang.

select, *v. tr.* memilih (pilih).

self, *n. individuality,* diri; *I my~,* saya sendiri; *~-sufficiency, esp. in food supplies,* kecukupan (cukup) sendiri; *~-supporting,* bergantung (gantung) kapada dirinya sendiri; *~-control,* penguasaan (kuasa) diri; *~-centred,* mementingkan diri sendiri; *right of ~-determination,* hak penentuan (tentu) nasib sendiri; *do it your~ kit,* alat-alat bertukang (tukang) sendiri; *~-assertive, pushing,* bersifat (sifat) naik daun.

selfish, *adj.* hakap, ingat hal dia sendiri sahaja, mementingkan (cari) periuk nasi (dia) sendiri, ingat tembolok (dia) sendiri; *see* **avarice.**

sell, *v. tr.* menjual (jual); *cheap sale,* jualan murah; *clearance sale,* jualan sapu; *sold out,* habis dijual; *a Sale, esp. for charity,* majlis jual beli, beramal; *to market, ~ in trading centres,* memasarkan (pasar); *see* **demand.**

semen, *n.* mani, air mani.

semi-official, *adj.* secara setengah rasmi.

semolina, *n.* suji.

senate, *n.* dewan negara.

send, *v. tr.* hantar; *by the hand of a per-*

son, kirim; ~ off (player from field), buang padang.

senile, adj. a ~ person, orang tua nyanyuk, orang tua agut-agut; as useless old dotard, orang tua bangka.

senior, adj. in rank, kanan (pada); in age, lebih tua (pada).

sensational, adj. as news, yang menggemparkan (gempar), yang mengharukan (haru); agitated as a result of such news, heboh; a sensation (exciting occurrence), suatu kegemparan.

sense, n. feeling perasaan (rasa); good ~, akal; the five ~s, pancaindera.

sensible, adj. having good sense, berakal (akal), berfikiran (fikir) waras; to be ~ of (realise existence of), sedarkan.

sensitive, adj. easily moved to emotion, mudah terharu (haru); peka; liable to moods, lekas naik angin; as an instrument, rumit; ~ plant, keman, rumput simalu.

sentence, n. in grammar, ayat, kalimat; of Court, hukuman.

separate, adj. asing, suku; to ~, as fighters, lerai; part company, bersurai (surai); dissolve intimacy, berparak (parak), berputus (putus) arang; having a gap between, renggang; disassociate oneself from, mengasingkan diri dari.

September, n. bulan September.

septic, adj. meliau (liau); to go ~, naik kelurut; exuding pus, menanah (nanah).

sequel, n. of story, sambungan; result, akibat.

series, n. siri; serial story, cerita bersambungan (sambung).

serious, adj. of wound, parah; of illness, teruk, tenat; to take ~ly, seem important, mengambil berat; ~ matter (causing trouble), perkara panjang; ~, not in jest, 'serius'.

sermon, n. khutbuh; to preach a ~, membaca khutbah.

serrated, adj. beringgit-ringgit; as jagged, gerigis.

servant, n. employee on wages generally, orang gaji.

serve, v. intr. in the Forces, berkhidmat (khidmat); the public services, perkhidmatan; dish up, sajikan; wait on, melayan (layan); look after, nurse (sick person), merawat (rawat); ~ well, do much for, membuat (buat) jasa kepada; to ~ as (perform function of), buat; this stick can ~ as a weapon, kayu ini boleh buat senjata; religious service, ibadat; ~ right, see **right.**

session, n. persidangan (sidang).

set, v. tr. a trap, tahan; ~ up (a contrivance), pasang; ~ aside (as a fund), cadangkan; ~ aside (disregard, not given a place to), ketepikan (tepi); ~ down, letak; ~ heart on, bubuh hati pada; to ~ (from fruit), of blossom, berputek (putek); solidly, as jelly, berbeku (beku); ~ with (diamonds), bertatah (tatah) (intan); to ~ (of sun), masuk, jatuh; ~ the teeth, mengetapkan (ketap) gigi; ~ a watch, tepatkan jam; ~ a sail, buka layar; a ~ (a number of things belonging together), selengkap, satu 'set'; a ~, e.g., social, of people, golongan.

settee, n. 'kaus'.

settle, v. tr. as a quarrel or a debt, selesaikan; ~ in full, jelaskan; settled, wound up (of an account), langsai; to take up abode, duduk, bertempat (tempat); bermastautin; (as colonist), menyeroka (seroka); penempatan, to ~ (as loose earth), mampat; (as sediment), mendak; to '~ his hash' (make an end of him), kerjakan dia; to ~ (subside a little in yielding earth, of a building), terendap-endap; ~ down permanently (in new abode), menetap (tetap); to ~, e.g., refugees, menempatkan (tempat); see **perch.**

settlement, n. inhabited area, negeri; see **settle;** a peaceful ~ (of a dispute), penyelesaian (selesai) secara damai.

severe, adj. as sentence, keras; see **serious.**

sew, v. tr. jahit; sewing machine, 'mesin'

jahit; *tack up*, jelujur; *~ing-basket*, bakul jahitan.

sewer, *n. pipe for carrying off refuse*, 'paip' mengalirkan (alir) kotoran.

sex, *n.* jenis kelamin; *to have special relations with*, mengadakan (ada) perhubungan jenis dengan; *book of information about ~*, buku pengetahuan (tahu) 'sex'; *see* **adultery, cohabit, copulate, fornication.**

shabby, *adj. of clothes*, buruk, lusuh, *~, of an ungenerous person, esp. of one who seeks to reclaim a gift*, buruk siku.

shackle, *n. v. tr.* belenggu.

shade, *n.* naung (an); *shady (of a tree)*, rendang; *a shady place*, tempat tedoh; *lamp-~*, tudung lampu; *see* **shelter.**

shadow, *n.* bayang; *~-show*, wayang kulit.

shaft, *n. as of spear*, batang; *of cart*, bam.

shaggy, *adj. of hair*, kusut-masai, panjang-kusut.

shake, *v. tr.* goncang; *as in loosening*, mengogah (ogah); *~ hands*, berjabat (jabat) tangan, berjabat salam; *shaky (not firmly in place)*, onyak-anyik, bergoncang; *not firmly implanted*, kolak-kalek; *shaky in construction*, gegai; *(as a weak hand)*, terketar-ketar; *to ~ the head*, geleng kepala; *~ out (as a wet cloth)*, kiraikan, kebaskan; *to ~ oneself (as a wet dog)*, mengirai-ngiraikan (kirai) badan; *to ~ the fist*, melonjakkan (lonjak) tangan; *to ~ up (a bottle)*, mengocak (kocak); *to ~ up (fig.), (cause consternation to)*, menggemparkan (gempar); *to ~ to and fro as when shaking down fruit*, hinggut; *when loosening a stake*, oleng-alengkan; *see* **tremble, sway;** *to ~ to and fro, as a disturbed branch*, berembih (rembih); *shaking with emotion, e.g., anger, laughter*, badan (nya) menggigil (gigil).

shallow, *adj. of water*, cetek, cangkat dangkal; *esp. as partly dried up*, tohor; *as a flat dish*, leper.

sham, *n. see* **pretend;** *imitation*, tiruan; *false*, palsu; *'mock'*, olok-olok.

shaman, *n. person in charge of a seance to conjure up spirits*, poyang, tok minduk.

shame, *n.* malu; *to feel ~*, berasa (rasa) malu; *to put to ~*, memberi (beri) malu, memberi aib; *better death than ~*, biar putih tulang, jangan putih mata; *~less*, tak tahu malu, tak silu-silu; *brazen-faced*, muka papan; *see* **insult.**

shank, *n. stem*, tangkai, gagang; *of leg*, betis, tunjang; *tibia*, tulang kering; *to 'shake one's ~s' (trudge along)*, mengayun (ayun) tunjang; *of a tool*, puting; *spindle-shanked*, berkaki (kaki) bangau.

shape, *n. form*, bentuk; *appearance*, rupa; *a '~' (figure dimly seen or imagined)*, suatu lembaga; *figure*, susuk badan.

shapely, *adj. of a girl, graceful*, berbentuk elok, jelita; *(sl.), curved in the right places*, potongan 'gitar'; *nicely rounded*, gemuk gempal.

share, *n.* bahagian, habuan; *as in a partnership*, hun; *in a company*, syer, saham; *plough-~*, nayam; *to ~ a room*, berkongsi (kongsi) bilik; *~-holder*, pemegang saham.

shark, *n.* ikan yu, jerung.

sharp, *adj.* tajam; *~-pointed*, runcing, landat; *to ~en (a blade)*, asah, kilir, gabus; *to a point*, rancung; *exactly, punctually*, tepat, betul-betul; *five o'clock ~*, pukul lima tepat; *~ed at both ends*, tajam bertimbal (timbal); *~, of criticism*, pedas; *hunger ~s (lit, polishes up) the wits*, perut kosong penggilap (gilap) otak.

shave, *v. tr.* mencukur; *to have a ~*, bercukur; *(sl.), cuci muka; shaving-brush*, 'berus' cukur; *the ritual shaving of a child's head*, akikat; *shavings*, tatal (kayu).

she, *pron.* dia.

sheaf, *n.* seikat; *of long objects such as sticks*, seberkas.

sheath, *n. generally*, sarung; *calyx of flower*, kelopak; *flower-~ of certain palms*, upih.

shed, *n.* bangsal; pondok, *see* **hut;** *to ~*

(as leaves, feathers), meluruh (luruh); *(tears)*, menangis (tangis); *(blood)*, menyimbahkan (simbah) darah.

sheep, *n.* (kambing) bebiri (biri-biri), domba; *shepherd,* gembala kambing; *'wolf in ~'s clothing'*, musang berbulu (bulu) ayam, *(civet-cats in fowls' plumage)*.

sheet, *n.* *for bed,* cadar; *thick ~,* selimut; *a ~ of paper,* selembar kertas, sehelai kertas; *winding-~, shroud,* kapan; *of a sail,* tali kelat; *of rubber,* sekeping getah.

shelf, *n.* *plank,* papan para, para-para; *~ of rock projecting from rock-face,* batu menganjur (anjur), batu membonjol (bonjol); *to lay ~, as a proposal,* ketepikan; *to shelve away, of ground,* melandai (landai).

shell, *n.* *as of egg, nut or mollusc,* kulit; *military,* periuk api; *coconut-~,* tempurung (nyiur); *half coconut-~ used as a measure,* cupak; *~-fish (generally),* siput, kerang-kerangan; *the broken egg-~ from which a chick has emerged,* kelompang (telur); *to ~ (remove ~),* mengupas (kupas), buang kulit.

shelter, *n.* *~ed place,* perlindungan (lindung), tempat berlindung, tempat teduh; *to take ~,* berlindung; *esp. from sun,* bernaung (naung), berteduh; *as a natural ~ from wind,* abal-abal; *temporary ~ in rice-fields,* dangau; *sun-sail, dinding hari: air-raid ~,* 'shelter', perlindungan (lindung); *bus ~,* pondok perhentian (henti) 'bus'.

shelve, *v. tr.* *lay aside, as a plan,* ketepikan (tepi); *shelving away, as a shallow,* melandai (landai).

sherbet, *n.* 'serbat'.

shield, *n.* perisai; *oblong ~,* jebang; *(fig.)*, pelindung (lindung).

shift, *v. tr.* *veer, of wind,* berkisar (kisar); *move slightly,* anjak; *(working) in shifts,* berganti-ganti; *see* **move.**

shilly-shally, *v. intr.* berdolak-dalik (dolak); ragu-ragu.

shimmering, *adj.* *appearing to diffuse tremulous light,* berbelau-belau; *as a confused number of lights (such as those of a distant town or of a tree lighted up by fireflies)*, berkelip-kelip, gemerlapan; *as the surface of the sea when shadows chase one another over it,* berkelipan.

shin, *n.* tulang kering; *see* **shank.**

shine, *v. intr.* bersinar (sinar); *shiny,* kilat; *shining, as a happy face,* berseri (seri); *as eyes,* bercahaya (cahaya); *as well-oiled hair,* lecok; *shining out brightly,* terserlah (serlah).

shingles, *n.* ruam saraf; rusuk atap, batu kerikil.

ship, *n.* kapal; *see* **steamer.**

shirk, *v.tr.* *slack on job,* curi tulang, curi masa; *apt to ~,* culas; *~ (a task),* mengelakkan (elak), diri dari (kewajipan, tugas ds.)

shirt, *n.* kemeja, baju.

shiver, *v. intr.* menggeletar (ketar) menggigil (gigil); *to have the cold shivers,* berasa (rasa) seram sejuk.

shoal, *n.* *shallow place in sea,* gosong; *sand-bank,* beting; *bar at river-mouth,* alangan; *of fish,* sekawan (ikan), sekumpulan (ikan); *to swim in ~s,* melewar (lewar).

shocked, *p.p.* *startled,* terkejut (kejut), terperanjat (peranjat); *shocking,* dahsyat, ngeri; *to be affected with horror or amazement,* menggemparkan (gempar); *to get an electric shock,* terkena karan; *shock troops,* askar penggempur (gempur).

shoddy, *adj.* buruk, rendah mutunya.

shoe, *n.* kasut, sepatu; *a pair of ~s,* sepasang kasut ; *high-heeled ~s,* kasut tumit tinggi; *pointed ~s,* kasut runcing ke hujung; *horse-~,* ladam, sepatu kuda; *to ~ a horse,* pukul ladam, pasakkan sepatu kuda; *see* **slipper.**

shoot, *v. tr.* menembak (tembak), membedil (bedil); *a shot,* satu das; *top ~ of plant,* pucuk; *side ~,* tunas, taruk; *small shot,* penabur (tabur), kacang-kacang; *to ~ forward, as in a race,* melancar (lancar) kehadapan; *to ~ in the (leg)*, menembak kena (kaki); *to ~ up, as a flame,* menjulang (julang); *as a flying object or as a bird,* melambung (tinggi); *to ~ ahead,* meluru (luru) ke depan; *~ing-range,* padang tembak.

shop, *n.* kedai; *big store,* toko; *~keeper,* tuan kedai, pekedai; *if Chinese,* tauke kedai; *to do one's ~ping,* pergi ke kedai, pergi membeli-belah (beli), berbelanja.

shore, *n.* pantai, tepi laut; *to hug the ~,* menyusur (susur) pantai.

short, *n. not tall,* pendek, rendah; *not long,* pendek, pandak, singkat; *abbreviated,* ringkas; *of time,* suntuk; *in ~,* pendeknya; *~age,* kekurangan (kurang), kesempitan (sempit; *~-sighted (lit.), blind; (met.),* berakal (akal) pendek, berfikiran (fikir) suntuk; *~-lived,* singkat umur; *'Shorty',* si Cembul; *~s,* seluar pendek, seluar kotong; *a ~ cut,* cara memperoleh atau mengerjakan (kerja); *~ of what is needed (as a piece of string or a sum of money),* cupul.

shorthand, *n.* teringkas (tulisan ringkas); *~-hand typist,* jurutringkas.

shortly, *adv.* tak lama lagi; *~ before —,* sejurus sebelum —; *~ afterwards,* sejurus kemudian, selang tak berapa lama.

shot, *n. a ~ (one time of firing),* satu das; *sound of a ~,* bunyi senapang; *sound of three ~s,* bunyi senapang tiga kali; *a ~gun,* senapang patah; *a '~ on the dark',* see **guess.**

shoulder, *n.* bahu; pundak, *~-to-~,* berganding (ganding) bahu, bahu-membahu; *~-blade,* belikat; *~ of meat,* lemusir; *the area between the ~-blades,* tamparan nyamuk; *~-strap,* lidah bahu; *to carry on the ~,* memikul (pikul); *across the ~, as a gun,* memanggul (panggul); *over the ~ as a bag or an Order,* menyandang (sandang).

shout, *v. intr.* keriau; *esp. as cheer,* sorak; *as hail,* laung; *~ excitedly, as a crowd at a match,* berteriak, memekik-mekik (pekik); sorak-sorai (sorak).

show, *v. tr.* tunjuk; *display,* memperlihatkan (lihat); memamerkan (pamer), *esp. as expose for sale,* mendedah (dedah); *as a film,* tayangkan; *~ off,* peraga (raga); *esp. as a woman trying to attract a man,* melaram (laram); see **exhibit, pose;** *to ~ oneself off (as in a new dress),* meledangkan (ledang) diri; *to ~ off something (to advantage),* megahkan; *to '~ up' (disclose true character),* buka tembelang; *~ off, display (e.g., valour),* menunjuk-nunjuk (tunjuk).

shreds, *n.* reja-reja, cebis-cebis.

shrill, *adj.* nyaring, langsi.

shrine, *n. grave-~,* makam; *place having revered associations,* keramat.

shrink, *v. intr. or shrivel,* kecut; *as a sack,* kempis; *get less,* susut; *get tight,* bercerut (cerut); *to ~ from, have scruples about (doing),* berkeberatan (berat) hendak, tak sampai hati hendak; see **diminish.**

shrivel, *v. intr.* kecut; *curl up, as leaf,* mengerutkan, kerepot; *~led face,* muka yang berkerut; *in heat,* melenting (lenting), melecur (lecur).

shroud, *n. winding-sheet,* kain kapan; *~ed with mist,* terlindung (lindung) dek kabut, di saput kabut.

shrug, *v. tr. ~ shoulders,* mengangkat (angkat) bahu.

shudder, *v. intr.* menggigil (gigil), menggeletar (geletar).

shuffle, *v. tr. cards,* mengocok (kartu), rombakan; penyusunan semula (kabinet).

shun, *v. tr.* menjauhkan (jauh) diri dari, mengelakkan (elak).

shut, *v. tr.* tutup, katup; *~ tight,* tutup rapat; *~ eyes,* pejam mata; *an umbrella,* kuncupkan; *~ up!,* senyap!, diam!; see **confine.**

shuttle, *v.t. & i.* bergerak ulang-alik.

shy, *adj. bashful,* pemalu (malu); *showing coyness,* tersipu-sipu; *reluctant,* segan; *as game,* cega, culas; *ring-~ (of a fighting bull),* pemeleng (meleng); *water-~,* putera garam; *work-~, (as* afraid of the sun), putera lilin; *as a nervous stranger,* seperti rusa masuk kampung, *(like a deer entering a village).*

sick, *adj.* sakit, uzur; *to fall ~,* jatuh sakit; *sea-~,* mabuk laut, mabuk ombak; *see* **vomit.**

sickle, *n.* sabit, cerut; *small ~,* keri.

sickly, *adj. of taste,* maung; *of a person,* badan lemah, sakit-sakit, berpenyakitan; *see* **chronic, hypochondriac.**

side, *n.* rusuk, sisi; *as in dispute,* pihak; *~s, flanks, of a hill,* lereng (an) bukit; *on this ~,* sebelah sini; *on the right (left) hand ~,* sebelah kanan (kiri); *lying on the ~,* memereng; *along~ the —,* berganding (ganding) - berkepil (kepil) pada; *~ with (in a dispute),* masuk sebelah, menyebelahi, berpihak kepada; *sitting ~-by-~,* duduk bertindih (tindih) lutut, bergandingan; *to 'mark a bit on the ~' (get a bit of profit for oneself, licitly or otherwise while doing a job),* expressed as 'drinking while diving', sambil menyelam (selam) minum air; *~line job,* kerja sambilan; *see* **support.**

side-track, *v. tr. put off dealing with (problem, person),* ketepikan (tepi).

slege, *n.* kepungan (kepung); *to lay ~ to a city,* mengepung sebuah kota.

sieve, *n.* ayakan; *to sift,* mengayak, meninting (tinting); *(fig.) sift facts,* mengayak (saring), meninting.

sigh, *v. intr.* mengeluh (keluh); *~ for, see* **yearn.**

sight, *n. power or ~,* pelihat (lihat); *spectacle observed,* pemandangan (pandang); *to go ~-seeing,* melancung (lancung), meninjau-ninjau (tinjau); *out of ~, not visible,* tak ketara; *lost to ~,* lenyap; *out of ~, out of mind,* hilang, di mata, hilang di hati; *at first ~,* sepintas lalu; *I can't stand the ~ of,* saya benci tengok; *'~ for sore eyes',* rezeki mata; *see* **feast.**

sign, *n. indicating something,* tanda, alamat, petunjuk (tunjuk); *mark,* bekas; *shop ~,* papan tanda kedai; *road ~-*

post, papan tanda jalan; *to ~ (a document),* bubuh tanda tangan, menandatangani; *to mark a ~ (esp. by gesture),* memberi (beri) isyarat; *mark, indication,* ciri; *to make the ~ of the Cross,* buat isyarat pangkah (di dada).

signal, *n.* isyarat; *(by sound),* semboyan.

signify, *v. tr. to mean,* bererti (erti); menandakan.

silent, *adj. not speaking,* diam; *keeping quiet,* senyap; *to hold one's peace,* berdiam diri; *to 'stay mum',* membongkam (bongkam); *to be, or pretend to be tongue-tied,* membatu (batu); *to be mute,* membisu (bisu); *to be 'as ~ as the grave',* membisu mayat; *tight-lipped,* berbunyi (bunyi) batu, berbunyilah dia, *(he will not open his mouth until stones do so); to meditate in silence,* bertafakur (tafakur); *to keep a two minutes silence,* (tunduk) bertafakur selama 'minit'.

silhouette, *n.* bayangan.

silk, *n.* sutera.

sill, *n.* ambang (pintu); *window-~,* ambang tingkap.

silt, *n. sand,* pasir; *mud,* lodak, selut; *banked up ~,* tanah enap; *~ed up,* terkambus (kambus); *(as a pipe),* sebu; *see* **tailings.**

silver, *n.* perak; *small ~ (coins),* 'seling'; *~-fish (insect),* gegat.

simile, *n.* ibarat, perbandingan (banding).

similar, *adj.* sama, serupa, semacam.

simple, *adj. easy,* mudah; *artless,* bodoh; **unsophisticated,** belum tahu hal; *not elaborate,* sederhana, bersahaja (sahaja); *insular, inexperienced,* seperti katak di bawah tempurung, *(like a frog under a coconut-shell); not that ~,* not born yesterday, tahu membedakan (beda) tebu dengan teberau.

simultaneous, *adj.* serentak, serempak; *at that very moment,* pada saat itu juga; *as in 'getting it done in one', 'not making two bites of a cherry',* sekali lalu, sekali arung; *all together (as a volley),* sekali gus.

sin, *n.* dosa, hal yang dianggap tidak baik;

forbidden by specific religious law, haram; *to commit* ~, membuat (buat) dosa, melakukan (laku) dosa; *mortal* ~, dosa yang tidak dapat diampunkan.

since, *conj.* *ever* ~, semenjak, dari semenjak, dari semenjak, sejak.

sincere, *adj.* jujur, ikhlas, tulus hati; ~*ly*, dengan sungguh-hati; *yours* ~*ly*, yang benar.

sinecure, *n.* *to have a* ~, makan gaji buta.

sing, *v. intr.* menyanyi (nyanyi); *chant*, membaca (baca); ~ *to sleep*, mengulitkan (ulit); *crowd-~ing*, nyanyian beramai-ramai; *the art of* ~*ing*, seni suara.

Singapore, *n.* Singapura; *old name*, Temasik.

singe, *v. tr.* siut, menghanguskan; menghitamkan permukaan kain.

single, *adj.* *sole*, tunggal; *unmarried*, bujang; *in* ~ *file*, berekor-ekor, berbuntut-buntut.

sink, *v. intr.* tenggelam; *founder*, karam; *sunken, as cheeks*, cengkung, caung; *as in mud (also of sun and of a blade in object struck)*, terbenam (benam); *of sun*, jatuh, masuk; ~ *in, as grave or post*, menderut (derut); *as a spoon into jam*, terserelum (serelum); *sunken, of eyes*, terpersuk (persuk) ke dalam, *esp. of cheeks*, cengkung; *of soil*, terendapendap.

sip, *v. tr.* menghirup (hirup), menyedut (sedut).

siren, *n.* *sound instrument*, tetuang (tuang), semboyan; *of ship*, peluit; *to sound, as a* ~, berbunyi (bunyi).

sister, *n.* *younger*, adik (perempuan); *elder*, kakak; ~*-in-law*, ipar (perempuan).

sit, *v. intr.* duduk; *tailor-fashion*, bersila (sila); *as a hen*, mengeram (eram); *of a Council*, bersidang (sidang); *squat on heels*, bertinggung (tinggung), menjongkok (jongkok); *as Malay women, with legs turned to the side*, bertimpuh (timpuh); ~*tight, refuse to move, as a trespasser*, bercokol (cokol); *to* ~ *with crossed legs*, duduk bersilang (silang)

kaki, duduk bersila (sila) panggung; ~ *up, as in bed*, bangun duduk; ~ *propped up*, duduk bersandar (sandar); ~ *down heavily, 'plump' oneself down*, menghenyakkan (henyak) badan (ke kerusi); *for an examination*, mengambil peperiksaan.

site, *n.* tapak (rumah); ~*d at*, terletak (letak) di.

situation, *n.* *of building*, letaknya; *state of affairs*, keadaan (ada); *circumstances*, suasana.

size, *n.* besarnya; *area*, luasnya; *measure*, ukuran, 'sais'.

skien, *n.* *bundle (of yarn)*, unting.

skeleton, *n.* rangka; *'mere* ~*'*, tinggal tulang sahaja.

sketch, *n.* *drawing*, lukisan; *rough outlines*, garisan kasar.

skewer, *n.* cungkit daging; tusuk daging.

skid, *v. intr.* *slide, of wheels on slippery surface*, terlancut (lancut), terlajak (lajak), melongsor (longsor) tergelincir (gelincir).

skilful, *adj.* *proficient*, pandai, cekap, mahir.

skim, *v. intr.* ~ *along the surface, as a swallow*, melayap (layap).

skimp, *v. tr.* *supply scantily and grudgingly*, menjimatkan (jimat), menghematkan (hemat); ~*y, of an allotment of food (sl.)*, hanya segenggam kera, *(only as much as a monkey could hold in one hand)*, hilang celah gigi pun tidak, *(not enough to fill the gap between one's teeth)*; *'what there is of it'*, *'such as there is'*, seada-adanya.

skin, *n.* kulit; *dry hide or callus*, belulang; *to* ~, buang kulit; *flay*, lapah; ~*ny*, kurus.

skip, *v. tr.* *omit when reading*, melangkah (langkah), melangkau (langkau); *v. intr. as capering, frisking*, gelinjang, terloncat-loncat, melompat-lompat anak.

skull, *n.* tengkorak; *the occipital bone*, godok kepala.

sky, *n.* langit; *atmosphere*, udara; ~*scraper*, bangunan pencakar (cakar) langit.

slab, *n.*kepingan batu; papan dll.

slack, *adj. as rope,* kendur; *listless,* lalai; *of trade, business,* lengang.

slag, *n.* tekang, terak; *embers,* bara.

slake, *v. tr.* ~ *thirst,* minum puas puas, memuaskan dahaga.

slam, *v. tr. shut or throw down with a bang,* menghempaskan (hempas).

slander, fitnah, pesona; *to* ~, buat fitnah atas; besmear name, cemarkan nama.

slanting, *adj. not vertical,* condong; *not parallel,* serong; *narrow, of eyes,* sepet.

slap, *v. tr.* tampar, lempang, sepak; *box ears,* tempeleng.

slapdash, *adj.* terburu-buru.

slash, *v. tr.* cencang; hack, tetak.

slat, *n.* bilah.

slate, *n. (school),* batu tulis, papan batu.

slaughter, *v. tr. for food,* sembelih, potong; *see* **abattoir.**

slave, *n.* abdi, hamba; *to* ~ *(work hard),* membanting (hanting) tulang; *fettered (fig.), (not free to act),* terkongkong (kongkong); ~ry, 'sistem' perhambaan.

sledge, *n.* bentung.

sleek, *adj. as animal's coat,* licau; *esp. of hair,* licin.

sleep, *v. intr.* tidur; *deep in* ~, *overslept,* ketiduran; *fast a*~, lena, lelap, nyenyak, jendera; **sleepy,** mengantuk (kantuk); *to dose,* telayan (layan) sekejap; *'catnap',* lena pelanduk; *'hog it',* membuta (buta); *get to* ~, lelapkan mata; *put to* ~, menidurkan; *sleeping draught,* ubat penidur; *'*~ *out', as a vagabond,* bertandang (tandang) tidur; *railway* ~*er,* (kayu) landasan.

sleeve, *n.* lengan baju.

slender, *adj. esp. of body, ramping,* langsing; *straight and* ~, *as a tree,* lonjong; *of neck,* jinjang; ~ *in the middle, as a waist,* genting; lissom, lampai; *see* **slight, thin.**

slice, *n.* sepotong, sehiris seracik; *to* ~ *up,* hiris, meracik; ~ *off,* sayat.

slide, *v. intr.* melongsor (longsor), gelongsor; *see* **chute.**

slight, *v. tr. disdain,* menghinakan (hina);

show indifference to, capak; *treat as inferior,* menganak-tirikan (anak); *of hopes, tips; of body,* rincing.

slim, *adj. see* **thin;** ~*ming drugs,* ubat menguruskan (kurus) badan.

slime, *n. mucus,* lendir; *mud,* selut.

sling, *n.* ali-ali; kain pengampu (ampu) lengan, endul lengan; *slung on back, as a rifle,* tersandang (sandang) pada bahu.

slink, *v. intr.* ~ *about,* menginak (kinak); ~ *out abashed,* keluar macam tikus basah, *(go out like wet rats);* menyelinap.

slip, *v. intr.* (kaki) tergelincir (gelincir); *miss footing,* tersalah (salah) langkah; ~ *off or down (of an attachment),* lucut; *as a bracelet,* lurut; *a* ~ *in anticipation,* sangkaan meleset (leset); ~*pery,* licin; *it just* ~*ped out (as an indiscreet remark),* kata sudah terlanjur (lanjur); *to* ~ *in,* ~ *along,* ~*ping down (as a badly fastened sarong),* rembah-rembeh londeh, terlengser (lengser); *to* ~ *something into or under something,* menyusupkan (susup); *as a knife into a belt,* menyisipkan (sisip); *to* ~ *through (e.g., a thicket),* soronot, melulus (lulus), menyelinap (selinap); *halfcrouching,* menjelonok (jolanak); *to* ~ *down, as loose sand on the side of a pit,* terebis (rebis); ~ *of the tongue,* kata terdorong (dorong), kata terluncur (luncur); *there's many a* ~ *twixt cup and lip,* nasi tersenduk (senduk) tidak termakan (makan), *(the rice is spooned up, but not eaten).*

slipper, *n.* (kasut) 'selipar'; mules, kasut seret; *grass-slippers,* kasut sambau.

slipshod, *adj. slovenly, of work,* serampangan, leceh; *of dress, see* **slovenly.**

slipway, *n.* limbungan, galangan (perahu).

slit, *n.* belah; *to* ~, membelah; *rip up,* hiris; ~-*eyed,* mata sepet.

slogan, *n.* cogan kata.

sloping, *adj. as a declivity,* landai; *out of the perpendicular,* condong; *leaning at an angle,* sendeng; *a slope (gentle hill),* menurun (turun); *slopes of hill,* lereng bukit; *to slope arms,* sendeng senjata; *see* **heel.**

sloth, *n.* the slow loris, kongkang, kera duku.

slouch, *v. intr.* ~ *along,* berjalan (jalan) berdembai-dembai; *sit ~ed up,* duduk berlepah-lepuh (lepah); *with stomach sticking out,* duduk terserdih (serdih); *see* **loll.**

slough, *n.* of snake, selumur; *deep swamp,* redang; *to change skin,* bersalin (salin) kulit.

slovenly, *adj.* of dress, serbah-serbih; *of work,* serempak, serampangan.

slow, *adj.* lambat; *~ly,* perlahan-perlahan; *~-witted,* berat-kepala; *a 'go-~' (of workers),* kerja lambat-lambat, *~coach,* pelengah.

sluggard, *n.* orang yang pemalas.

sluggish, *adj.* pemalas (malas); *in movement,* berat-kaki; *lacking energy, 'wet',* lembam, lembab.

sluice-gate, *n.* pintu air, kunci air; *sluice-channel* (flume), palung; *drain carrying off surplus water,* parit buang).

slump, *v. intr.* of business, meleset, merosot (rosot).

sly, adj. cerdik, pintar.

smack, *v.tr. see* **slap;** *to ~ the lips,* terkecap-kecap; *to ~ of, be suggestive of ,* berbau (bau) -, bercorak (corak) -.

small, *adj.* kecil; *minute,* halus.

smallpox, *n.* ketumbuhan (tumbuh), cacar; *pock-marked,* mopeng.

smart, *adj.* in dress, lawa, tampan, kacak; *as a cut,* pedih; *clever,* cerdik; *to ~en one-self up,* bersolek (solek), bercantik-cantik; *make small adjustments to appearence,* mematut-matutkan. (patut) diri.

smashed. *adj.* terkecai (kecai), tersepai (sepai); *see* **break.**

smattering, n. of a subject, serba sedikit.

smear, *v. tr.* conteng, palit, lumurkan; *be~ed, esp. of mouth,* sememeh; *esp. as with mud,* berlumur.

smell, *n.* bau; *to ~ (perceive by ~),* cium; *sniff* at, hidu; *bad ~ (~y),* bau busuk; *~ing horribly, esp. as of stale urine,* hancing; *stinking,* hapak, hanyir; *sweet ~,* bau wangi; *~ing of -,* berbau -; *get the ~ of,* dapat bau -.

smelt, *v. tr.* melebur (lebur), masak.

smile, *v. intr.* tersenyum (senyum); *show amusement,* gelak; *see* **grin.**

smirk, *v.* tersengih.

smoke, *n.* asap; *smoky,* berasap; *to rise in spirals (of ~),* berkelun (kelun); *in clouds,* berkepul (kepul); *to ~,* isap, makan ('paip', 'sigaret', cerutu), merokok (rokok); *no smoking!,* dilarang merokok!; *rubber ~house,* rumah salai getah; *plume of ~,* tabunan asap.

smooth, *adj.* licin; *as path,* rata; *as of voice, mellow,* lunak; *or of liquid, not lumpy,* lunak; *working ~ly, as a plan,* jalan dengan lancar; *not angular,* tak bersanding (sanding); *to ~, esp. hair, by stroking,* mengusap-usapkan; *to ~ off, as with sandpaper,* melampas (lampas); *or a plane,* memaras (paras); *a '~ customer' (sl.),* pisau cukur.

smothered, *adj.* lemas; *(fig.) by weeds, etc.,* acap.

smoulder, *v. intr. still smoking,* berasap (asap) lagi; *still containing hot embers,* berbara (bara) lagi.

smudge, *n.* smear, palit; *as fire to repel insects,* unggunan; *~d, as a letter,* tercalit (calit)

smuggle, *v. tr.* bawa masuk (keluar) barang larangan, menyeludup (seludup); *~d (the subject of clandestine import or export),* gelap.

snack, n. *slight hurried meal,* alas perut, lapik perut, jalan; *to eat ~s, eat between meals,* makan sambil-sambil; kudapan.

snag, *n. sticking in stream,* tonggak canggung; *see* **difficulty.**

snail, *n. amphibious ~,* kelembuai.

snake, *n.* ular, *~-charmer,* tukang sihir ular.

snap, *v. intr. speak with sudden irritation,* membentak (bentak); *'fly out at',* sergah; *~ped off,* putus; *~ up (grab),* cakup.

snare, *n. a trap for catching birds or animals, usually with a noose,* jebak, jerat, perangkap.

snarl, *v. intr. growl,* mengaum (aum); *(fig.) speak ill-temperedly,* menengking (tengking); *~ing, showing the teeth, as a nervous dog,* terkerenyang-kerenyang.

snatch, *v. tr.* merebut (rebut); *tear away,* renggut; *(fig.) ~ a moment (legitimately or otherwise) to do something,* curi masa; *~ roughly at,* merentap (rentap).

sneak, *v. intr. & (i) carry tales,* bawa mulut, mengendap, menyelinap.

sneer, *v. intr. make a wry face,* mencemik (cemik), mencebik (cebik); mencemuh (cemuh), *make ~ing remark,* mengejek (ejek), menyindir (sindir); *a ~ing smile,* senyum sumbing.

sneeze, *v. intr.* membersin (bersin).

sniff, *v. tr. ~ up,* hidu, sedut.

snigger, *v. intr. see giggle, laugh.*

snipe, *n.* burung berkik; *in North,* burung tiruk; *painted ~,* burung meragi.

snobbish, *adj. looking down on alleged inferiors,* tinggi-hidung, sombong.

snoop, *v. intr.* meninjau (tinjau), mengintip; *~er,* tukang mengintai (intai).

snore, *v. intr.* mendengkur (dengkur), mengeruh (keruh).

snort, *v. intr.* mendengus (dengus), mengembus-embuskan nafas.

snout, *n. of animal,* muncung, domol; *of fish,* jongor, jolong.

snow, *n.* salji.

so, *adv. like that,* begitu; *and ~ -,* jadi -; *Mr. ~-and-~,* si anu, si anu, si polan; *Master ~-and-~,* si Buyung; *Miss ~-and-~,* si Upik; *~~, not really good, but not very bad,* begitu hal sahaja.

soak, *v. tr.* rendam; *steep,* memyeduh (seduh); *~ in (as wate, as oil into bearings, as advice),* mesra; *~ up,* menyerap (serap); *~ed to the skin,* basah lencun, basah kuyup; *~~away,* cesspool, limbah, acar.

soap, *n.* sabun; *a cake of ~,* sebuku sabun;

~~suds, air sabun; *froth,* buih.

soar, *v. intr.* melayang (layang); *~ right up into the sky,* terbang mengawan (awan); *shoot upwards,* melambung (lambung); *(fig.) of prices,* meningkat (tingkat) tinggi.

sob, *v. intr.* tersedu-sedu, teresak-esak.

sober, *adj. ~ed up,* siuman.

sobriquet, *n. a nickname,* nama samaran.

society, *n. the community,* masyarakat; *an association,* kesatuan (satu), kongsi; *secret ~,* kongsi gelap; *social welfare,* kebajikan (bajik) masyarakat; *sociable,* beramah-tamah (ramah).

sociology, *n.* ilmu masyarakat.

socket, *n. hollow for something to fit in,* sendi lubang; *eye-~,* lekuk mata.

socks, *n.* sarung kaki, 'stokin'.

sodden, *adj. of food,* lecuh, bonyor.

sodomy, *n.* semburit; *to commit ~,* main semburit, main berjantan (jantan); *see* **homosexuality.**

sofa, *n.* kaus.

soft, *adj. lembut; yeilding to pressure, as a cushion,* lembik, empuk; *of timber,* lempung; *~ened, as by cooking,* empuk; *through over-cooking,* lodoh, *(also used of over-ripe fruit); of ground,* becak, lecak, lembut; *~-hearted,* berhati (hati) lembut, baik hati; *of fruit,* lunak.

soggy, *adj. of food, esp. rice,* bonyor, benyal; *of soil,* becak, lecak.

soil, *n. (i) the loose upper layer of earth,* tanah, *(2) v. tr. to make or become dirty,* mengotori.

solder, *v. tr.* patri (kan).

soldier, *n.* askar, 'sojar', soldadu.

sole, *n. fish,* ikan lidah; *of foot,* tapak kaki; *one and only,* tunggal, **solely,** *adv.* cuma, hanya, semata-mata.

solecism, *n.* kesalahan dalam menggunakan satu-satu bahasa.

solid, *adj. not hollow,* tumpat; *compact, not cellular or porous,* pukal; *as, united or welded together,* berpadu (padu); *firm, not flabby,* pekal; *political ~arity (mutual loyalty),* setia-kawan.

soliloquise, *v. intr.* bercakap (cakap)

seorang diri, bercakap sendirian.

solitary, *adj. not gregarious,* tunggal; *all alone,* seorang diri; *as without family ties,* sebatang karah; ~ *confinement,* kurungan berasing (asing); *separated, apart,* terasing; *a 'lone wolf',* kera sumbang.

Solomon, *n.* Nabi Sulaiman.

soluble, *adj.* dapat larut, dapat menjadi (jadi) cair.

solution, *n. chemical,* larutan; *of a puzzle,* penekaan (teka); *to solve (a difficulty or problem),* dapat menyelesaikan (selesai), memecahkan (pecah); *see* **settle.**

solvent, *n. chemical ~,* pelebur (lebur).

some, *adj. a small quantity,* sikit, sedikit; *~one (unnamed),* orang; ~ *people (out of a number),* setengah orang, beberapa orang; *~what (to ~ degree),* sikit, agak; *~one or other (out of a number),* salah seorang, *~how or other,* entah macam mana; *(gone) ~where or other,* entah ke mana; *~thing or other (I don't know what),* entah apa; *~ething or other,* sesuatu; *~times,* kadang-kadang, ada kalanya; ~ *time or other,* tak sekali sekali; *see* **soon.**

somersault, *v. intr. to turn a ~,* bertunggang-langgang (tunggang), jungkir balik.

son, *n.* anak jantan, anak laki-laki; *~-in-law,* menantu; *step-~,* anak tiri.

song, *n.* lagu, nyanyian; *the art of ~,* seri suara.

soon, *adv.* lama lagi; *~er or later,* lambat-laun; *as ~ as,* sebaik sahaja, seelok sahaja; *in the sense of provided only ~,* asal; *the ~er the better,* makin cepat semakin baik.

soot, *n.* jelaga.

soothe, *v. tr. pacify,* mengamankan (aman); *allay anger of,* menyejukkan (sejuk) hati, melembutkan (lembut) hati; *as console,* menghiburkan (hibur), meredakan (reda).

soothsayer, *n.* tukang ramal; tukang telek.

sophisticated *adj. complicated, elaborate,* canggih.

sorcerer, *n.* ahli sihir.

sore, *adj. feel ~,* berasa (rasa) sakit; tingling, perit; *see* **abraded, smart, ulcer, wound.**

sorry, *adj. troubled,* susah-hati; *sad,* sayu, sedih hati; *remorseful,* sesal; *sorrow,* duka cita; *I'm ~! (as an apology),* minta maaf!; *what's the good of saying '~' now?,* sesal dahulu pendapatan (dapat), sesal kemudian apa gunanya?, *(i.e., remorse before-hand is beneficial, but what's the use of subsequent remorse?).*

sort, *n. kind,* macam; *race,* bangsa; *species,* jenis; *to ~ (set apart),* asingkan; ~ *out (as letters),* memilih-milih (pilih), asing-asingkan, lain-lainkan; *separate into piles or lots,* menyusun (susun); *of all sorts,* bermacam-macam.

soul, *n. of dead person,* arwah; *as opposed to body,* sukma, jiwa; *spirit,* semangat, roh; *units of population,* jiwa.

sound, *n.* bunyi; *~ing-lead,* perum; *see* **fathom;** *(fig.), make cautious inquiries,* merisik-risik, *~-proof,* tidak memasukkan bunyi.

sour, *adj.* masam; *see* **bitter.**

source, *n. of a stream,* mata (air), sumber; *of information,* punca, sumbir; *origin,* asal; *basic origin,* pokok pangkal.

soursop, *n. durian Benggal,* durian Belanda.

south, *n.* selatan; *S.E.,* tenggara; *S.W.,* barat daya; *South Pole,* kutub selatan; *S.S.W.,* selatan daya; *S.S.E.,* selatan menenggara (tenggara).

souvenir, *n.* kenang-kenangan; *personal ~,* tanda mata, cenderamata.

sovereignty, *n.* daulat.

sow, *v. tr.* menabur (tabur) (benih); ~ *the seeds of (fig.), do what will result in (e.g., disturbances, etc.),* semaikan, membibitkan (bibit).

space, *n. a place for something,* tempat, ruang; ~ *between,* jaraknya; ~ *underneath, as ~ under a bungalow,* kolong; *part left blank on printed form, 'box',* kotak; *double spacing (in typing),* ('taip') langkah sebaris; *outer ~,* angkas lepas; *spacious,* luas, selesa.

spade, *n.* penggali (gali); mattock, cangkul.

Spain, n. negeri Spanyol.

span, *v. tr. see across; a ~ (space between thumb and forefinger),* sejengkal.

spangles, *n.* kida-kida, kelip-kelip.

spare, *adj. extra,* lebih; *~-part,* barang-barang gantian; *~ tyre,* tayar tambahan (simpanan); *~ time,* masa lapang, waktu terluang (luang).

spark, *n.* bunga api; *to ~le,* gilang.

sparrow, *n. birds of ~ type generally,* burung pipit; *tree-~ (locally),* burung gereja, burung raja; *Java ~,* burung jelatik; *white-headed '~',* pipit uban.

spatter, *v. tr. be~ed (as with mud),* berselekeh, kena recik; *~ed about, as blood, brains,* bersemburan (sembur).

spatula, *n.* sudip.

speak, *v. intr.* cakap; *as of a person able to ~,* bertutur (tutur); *~ out (frankly),* cakap terus terang *(as opposed to circumlocution -* cakap berbelit-berlit); see **chat, chatter, say; spokeman,** juru cakap; *not on speaking terms,* tak bertegur (tegur).

spear, *n.* lembing, tombak; *fish-~,* serampang; *harpoon,* tempuling; *wooden or bamboo ~,* seligi.

special, *adj.* khas; *out of the ordinary, strange,* ganjil; *of extra quality, as a film,* istimewa (sl.); *Special Branch,* polis rahsia; *~ feature,* suatu keistimewaan (istimewa).

specific, *adj. definitely formulated,* tertentu (tentu); khusus.

speck, *n. small spot,* titik; *soft ~ in fruit,* tobek; *~led,* berintik-rintik; *of a hen,* borek.

spectacle, *n. a ~,* temasya, pemandangan (pandang).

spectacles, *n.* cermin mata; *contact ~,* cermin lekat; *~-frame,* bingkai (cermin mata).

spectacular, *adj.* istimewa, menarik perhatian.

spectator, *n.* penonton (tonton).

speculate, *v.i.* mengagak-agak, mengadu untung.

speech, *n. oration,* ucapan, pidato.

speed, *n.* lajunya, derasnya; *esp. of wind,* kencangnya; *~-limit,* had laju; *correct ~ (for camera),* kecepatan (cepat) yang betul.

spell, *v. intr.* mengeja; *a ~ in incantations,* restu, pesona, petua; *to utter (a ~),* membaca (baca); *~bound, as by an orator,* terpesona.

spend, *v. tr. (money),* belanjakan (wang); *(time),* menghabiskan (masa); *~ing money,* belanja; *~thrift,* pemboros.

spew, *v. intr. & tr.* muntah.

sphere, *n. see* **field.**

spices, *n.* rempah-rempah, bumbu.

spick-and-span, *adj.* cermat dan bersih.

spider, *n.* labah-labah; *large ~, believed venomous,* pesan-pesan; *hunting ~,* harimau lalat.

spike, *n.* paku (panjang); *stuck in ground as an obstacle to enemy, etc.,* ranjau; suda.

spilt, *p.p.* tumpah; *scattered,* tersimbah (simbah).

spin, *v. tr. make thread,* memintal (pintal), menggantih; *make cloth,* tenun; *revolves, as a top,* berputar (putar); *whirling,* ligat.

spinach, *n.* bayam; *a sort of convolvulus used as ~,* kangkung.

spine, *n. backbone,* tulang belakang; *prickle,* duri.

spirit, *n. alcohol, arak, as opposed to body,* semangat; *tutelary ~,* hantu penunggu (tunggu), puaka; *~ual,* rohani; *~s of the dead,* arwah.

spirited, *adj. as a horse,* ranggi; *see* **morale.**

spiritualism, *n.* ilmu ghaib.

spit, *v. tr. to stick (meat) on ~,* pacak, cucuk; *to eject saliva,* berludah (ludah); *to ~toon,* ketur.

spite, *n.* dengki, *spiteful,* iri hati.

splash, *v. intr. ~ about, as bathers,* berketimpung (ketimpung); *to get ~ed,* kena recik, kena sembur; *~ed up, as water or mud by a wheel,* terpercik

(percik); *sound of splashing,* cerup; *as of person hurrying through wet ground,* celum-celam; *to plunge in with a big splash,* berkecimpung (kecimpung); *(fig.) to make a big ~ (by lavish and ostentatious spending),* buat besar hentak.

spleen, *n.* kura.

splendid, *adj.* cemerlang; *~! (well done!),* bagus!; *that's a bit of luck,* mujurlah!

splice, *v. tr.* sambat, cantum.

splinter, *n.* selumbar; *flying fragments,* perecek (recek), serpih.

splints, *n. as for broken bone,* kayu penganduh (anduh).

split, *v. tr. and intr.* belah; *~ in two,* belah dua; *to ~ up, as a party,* berpecah-belah (belah); *as an over-ripe melon,* merekah (rekah); *(as at seams),* betas.

spoilt, *p.p. (sl.),* jahanam; *as a child,* manja; *to ~ (over-indulge),* manjakan, muakan.

spoke, *n. of wheel,* jari-jari.

sponge, *n.* bunga karang; *~ cake,* buah ulu.

spontaneous, *adj. automatic, not forced,* dengan sendirinya; spontan.

spoof, *n.* olok-olok (sahaja), menipu, memperdaya.

spool, *n.* gelendong; *~ on to which spun thread is wound,* rahat.

spoon, *n.* sudu; *tea-~,* camca; *large ~,* senduk; *to ~-feed, as a child,* suapkan.

sports, *n. see* **athlete.**

spot, *n. mark,* titik; *a black ~,* titik hitam; *as of rash,* bintik; *~ted,* belang cicak; *with numerous small ~s,* berbintik-bintik, *on the ~,* pada ketika, itu; *~less,* bersih.

spout, *v. intr. as water,* memancur (pancur); *to ~, as an orator,* mencurut (curut); *as a whale,* memangus (pangus); *water-~,* puting beliung; *the ~ of a kettle,* muncung; *open ~ (as that affixed to a rubber-tree),* saluran; *as of a hole,* pancur.

sprained, *p.p. of a muscle,* salah urat; *esp. by making a false step,* terpelecuk (pelecuk).

sprawling, *adj. falling,* terpelanting (pelanting); *lying,* sungkur-sangkar; *esp. of corpses,* tergelimpang (gelimpang), terjerumus (jerumus), terbongkang; *esp. of falling flat on one's face,* jatuh tersungkur;· *fall spread-eagled,* jatuh terjangkang (jangkang).

spray, *n. from waves,* buih, recikan air; *to break in ~,* pecah bersembur; *leafy shoot,* carang, *to ~, as with hose,* menyembur (sembur), menyiram (siram); *esp. of a strong jet,* memancut (pancut); *a ~, sprig, of leaves or flowers,* cangkis.

spread, *v. intr. as fire or disease,* melarat (larat), merebak (rebak); *to ~, esp. as sails,* membabarkan (babar); *as a mat,* bentangkan, hamparkan; *as butter,* sapu; *as wings,* kembangkan; *as a skin-disease,* meroyak (royak); *as a creeping forest-fire, vapour,* menjalar (jalar); *in all directions, as weeds, creepers and (fig.) trade,* merambak (rambak); *as news,* pecah (merata-rata); *see* **disseminate, open, scatter;** *~ out (interspaced),* jarak; *~ing, of a tree,* rimbun, rendang.

sprig, *n. see* **spray.**

spring, *n. of water,* mata ayer; *hot ~,* air hangat, bendang air hangat; *to ~ (leap),* lompat; *~ up (as from a sitting position),* bingkas bangun; *as a plant,* bertumbuh (tumbuh); *~ up from the ground, as mushrooms,* merecup (recup); *see* **sprout;** *~, esp. in attack, as a tiger,* menghambur (hambur); *~ at (as prey),* terkam; *~ back (as a bent bamboo),* bidas; *sprung, of a trap,* bingkas; *~-gun,* belantik (lantik); *(European) season of ~,* musim bunga; *a ~, as of a watch,* 'sepering', pegas; *mineral ~,* mata air logam; *springy, as a mattress,* berenjut-enjut.

sprinkle, *v. tr.* siram, merenjis, simbahkan; *esp. as dashing drops of water over,* renjiskan, *(used esp. of the bathing of a tame bird with water from the mouth); esp. with a light stream as* *in baptism,* cucurkan.

sprocket, *n.* gigi jentera.

sprout, *n.* tunas; *to ~ (of a branch),* bertunas; *put out a ~ (of a seed),* cambah; *~ up (from the ground),* bertumbuh (tumbuh); *just appear above ground,* mentat, merecup (recup).

spruce, *adj. see* **smart, spick and span.**

sprue, *n.* penyakit (sakit) seriawan.

spur, *n. of cock; natural,* susuk, jalu; *artificial,* taji; *to bind on the artificial ~s,* membulang (bulang) taji; *to ~ (urge on a horse),* pacu.

spurt, *v. intr. see* **gush, spout;** *quicken pace,* cepatkan langkah, memancut, menyembur.

sputnik, *n.* bulan rekaan, bulan buatan.

spy, *n.* suluh, 'sepai'; *to ~,* mengintip (intip); *a 'nosey' or inquisitional person,* tukang mengintai (intai).

squad, *n.* pasukan.

squall, *n. sudden short storm,* angin badai; *to ~, of children,* menangis (tangis) terciar-ciar.

squander, *v. tr.* menghabis-habiskan; membazir (wang, masa dll) *see* **waste.**

square, *adj.* empat segi; *a ~ (as on chessboard),* tapak; *~d, checked, pattern,* corak tapak catur; *a ~ (open space enclosed by buildings),* lapangan.

squash, *v. tr. as an insect,* tindas; *~ed flat,* penyek.

squat, *v. tr. see* **sit;** *short, and fat,* gemuk ketut, pendek gemuk; *tubby,* buntak; *to ~ (occupy land without legal security),* menduduki secara haram; mencangkung.

squeak, *v. intr.* berdecit (decit).

squeal, *v. Intr.* menjerit (jerit).

squeamish, *adj.* lekas loya, lekas mual.

squeeze, *v. intr. as in milking,* perah; *constrict,* cerut; *with fingers,* picit; *between two surfaces,* apit; *as dough with hands,* ramas; *(fig.) ~, extort money,* memeras (peras) wang; *to ~ oneself (through),* meluluskan (lulus) diri; *for working a '~',* see **opportunity.**

squinting, *adj.* mata juling.

squirrel, *n.* tupai; *flying '~',* kubung; *ground ~,* kuas.

squirt, *v. intr. ~ out,* memancit (pancit), memancut keluar, menyembur.

stab, *v. tr.* tikam, *esp. as ~bing upwards (through floor),* radak; *downwards,* rujah; *to have stabbing pains,* mencucuk-cucuk sakit (nya).

stable, *n. for cattle generally,* kandang; *esp. for horse,* tan (kuda), 'setal' (kuda); *firm,* kukuh, tetap, teguh; *firmly based, as a Government,* berketentuan (tentu); *to stabilise,* mengukuhkan; *stability of the State,* keutuhan (utuh) negara.

stack, *n. a pile,* timbunan; *to ~, arrange in lots of piles,* menyusun, (susun).

stadium, *n.* 'stadium'.

staff, *n. of flag,* tiang; *as support,* tongkat; *assistants,* kakitangan; *of army,* 'staf', turus; *Chief of Staff,* ketua, turus agung.

stage, *n. platform,* pentas; *as of development,* peringkat, tingkat; *to ~ (put on the ~, of a play),* mementaskan.

stagger, *v. intr.* huyung-hayang, melilau (lilau); *see* **totter.**

stagnant, *adj.* berladung (ladung), tertakung (takung); *having ceased to flow,* mati.

staid, *adj. of quiet demeanour,* sopan.

stain, *n.* kotoran, noda; *~less (pure),* suci, murni; *of steel,* tahan karat.

stair, *n.* tangga; *up~s,* atas loteng, tingkat atas.

stake, *n.* pancang; *support,* turus; *line of ~s leading fish into a trap,* penajur (tajur), penuju (tuju); *to place a ~ (bet),* bertaruh (taruh) duit; *place your ~s! (try your luck!),* mari tikam!

stale, *adj.* basi; lapuk, *interesting, as news joke, story,* basi, lusuh.

stalk, *n.* tangkai, gagang; *to ~ (walk with long strides),* melangkah (langkah) guntai; *to follow furtively,* menurut (turut) terendap-endap, mengekor (ekor) diam-diam.

stall, *n. for selling,* gerai, meja, warung;

see **stable.**

stalwart, *adj.* tinggi gagah.

stammer, *v. intr.* gagap; *speaking jerkily,* cakap terbabak-babak, cakap merangkak-rangkak; *with broken utterance, esp. as weeping,* cakap dengan suara terputus-putus.

stamp, *v. tr.* hentak kaki; *a (postage) ~,* 'stem'; *to ~ (impress with die),* cap; *to ~ on,* pijak; *~ down,* latam; *~ out, as bad practices,* membasmikan (basmi).

stampede, *v. intr. rush away wildly,* berkeliaran (liar) lari hempas pulas, *rushing here and there, as frightened hens,* berbebar (bebar), berlari kacau bilau.

stand, *v. intr.* berdiri (diri); *a ~ (base),* pelapik (lapik), alas; *bicycle-~ (fixed to bicycle),* topang 'basikal'; *~ for cars, etc.,* tempat perhentian kereta; *~-point (as policy),* pendirian; *angle, point of view,* segi, sudut; *forked ~, as for a telescope or a light swivel-gun,* cagak; *'~ out', as veins or as a sculpture in relief,* timbul; *~ back~ (get out of the way),* lalu!, ke tepi!; *~ (as a candidate),* bertanding (tanding) (sebagai calun), mencalunkan diri; *~ on end (of hair, from fright),* seram (bulu tengkuk); *to '~' (cost),* tanggung (belanja); *~ by (promise, condition, policy),* berpegang (pegang) pada, bersetia (setia) pada; *support,* menyokong (sokong); *can't ~ (endure),* tak boleh tahan; *can't ~ (intensely dislike),* bencikan; *~ up to a test,* tahan uji.

standard, *n. school class,* darjah; ukuran *emblem,* cogan; *ensign,* panji-panji; *level of quality,* mutu, tingkat; *~ of living,* cara kehidupan (hidup), taraf hidup, darjah hidup; *of authoritatively verified ~ (as weight of measure),* piawai; *the ~ gantang,* gantang piawai.

standardize, *v. tr.* menetapkan bentuk yang dijadikan ukuran.

star, *n.* bintang; *constellation,* susunan bintang; *a person's astrological ~,* raksi; *~ of a play (female),* seri panggung; *film-~,* bintang 'filem'; *~-*

fish, ripang.

starch, *n.* kanji; *well-~ed,* keras berkanji.

stare, *v. intr.* mengintai (intai); *glare,* menjegel (jegel); *staring eyes (as from fear),* mata buntang.

starling, *n.* burung cemperling, burung perling.

start, *v. intr. on way,* permulaan, bermula, berjalan (jalan); *set out,* bertolak (tolak); *sail away,* berlayar (layar); *of an engine,* 'stat'; *get going, factory, business, machinery,* menghidupkan (hidup); *make sudden involuntary motion,* tersentak (sentak); *give a violent ~, as in pain,* melantun (lantun); *~ing point,* pangkal jalan; *'stepping-off place',* tapak bertolak (tolak); *see* **begin.**

startle, *v. tr. with an abrupt or threatening movement,* sergah, jerkah; *~d,* terkejut (kejut), terperanjat (peranjat); *'struck all of a heap',* tertegun (tegun).

starvation, *n.* kebuluran (bulur); *to die of ~,* mati kebuluran, mati lapar; *to starve (keep short of food),* laparkan.

state, *n. civil community,* negara, negeri; *existing position,* hal; *condition,* keadaan (ada); *~sman,* negerawan; *~smanship, science of administration,* tata negara; *~ of affairs,* kedudukan (duduk) hal; *to lie in ~,* meletakkan jenaah dengan penuh istiadat di khalayak ramai sebelum dikebumikan.

stately, *adj. as a building,* hebat; *of movements, manner,* bergaya (gaya).

statement, *n.* kenyataan (nyata), keterangan (terang).

static, *adj. as opposed to flowing of water,* bertakung (takung).

station, *n. post,* tempat; *railway ~,* 'stesyen'; *police ~,* balai, rumah pasung; *~ platform,* pelantar ('stesyen'); *~ at,* bertempat (tempat) di.

stationary, *adj. not moving,* tidak bergerak (gerak).

stationery, *n.* alat tulisan, peralatulis (peralatan tulis).

statistics, *n.* statistik, perangkaan.

statue, *n.* gambar timbul; *~tte,* patung.

status, *n. rank,* pangkat; *standing,* taraf.

staunch, *adj.* teguh-hati; *see* **loyal;** *to ~ (check flow of blood),* menahan (tahan), menasak (tasak).

stave, staved in, *adj. (as box, hat),* terpersuk (persuk) ke dalam.

stay, *v. intr. remain,* tinggal; *as with host,* tumpang; *a ~ (connecting mast and spar),* temberang.

steadfast, *adj. firm in position,* tetap; *as firmly embedded,* kejat; *mantap solid and stable,* kukuh; *steady! (hold fast!),* tahan!

steal, *v. tr.* mencuri (curi); *'pinch',* sauk, celok; *(sl.) '~ a march' (sneak an unfair advantage),* potong 'trip'; *~ the credit (for what someone else has done),* cedok jasa orang; *also expressed by the aphorism, the cow gave the milk, but the wild ox got the credit,* lembu punya susu, sapi punya nama.

stealth, *n.* berbuat sesuatu dengan diam-diam.

steam, *n.* wap; *to ~ (cock with ~),* kukus; *if rice,* menanak (tanak); *to 'get all steamed up' (with anger and excitement),* naik 'stim'.

steamer, *n.* kapal api, kapal wap; *~ on regular run,* kapal calu; *tramp ~,* kapal liar.

steam-roller, *n.* penggiling (giling).

steel, *n.* besi waja; *to ~ oneself (in face of danger),* memberanikan (berani) diri.

steep, *adj.* curam; *to ~ (infuse in water),* menyeduh (seduh).

steersman, *n.* juru mudi.

stem, *n. of tree,* batang; *of flower,* tangkai, gagang; *to ~ (make head against) current,* menongkah (tongkah) harus; *against wind,* menyongsong (songsong) angin.

stenographer, *n.* jurutringkas.

step, *n. pace,* langkah; *a ~ on stairs,* anak tangga; *~-father,* bapa tiri; *~-mother,* emak tiri; *~-child,* anak tiri; *to keep in ~,* mengikut (ikut) rentak kaki; *out of ~,* tersesat (sesat) langkah; *not keeping in ~ (fig.) (following courses not approved by associates),* bertelingkah

(telingkah); to take ~s, act, mengambil (ambil) langkah; *a ~ in promotion,* tangga; *~ping-stone,* batu loncatan; *~ping-off place, see* **start.**

sterile, *adj. germ-free,* suci-hama; mandul, tidak subur *see* **barren.**

stern, *adj. of vessel,* buritan,; *harsh,* keras; *of forbidding aspect,* penggerun (gerun), garang.

stertorous, *adj.* mendengkur.

stick, *n.* kayu; *walking-~,* tongkat; *carrying-~,* kayu kandar; *to ~ (as gum),* lekat; *to ~ up (as a poster),* pelekat, tampalkan; *to ~ on, paste on,* tepek; *to ~ fast (as in mud),* terbenam (benam); *(as in thorns),* tersangkut (sangkut); *to ~ in (as a stake),* cacak; *~y,* likat; *~ insect,* belalang ranting; *stuck-up (conceited),* tinggi-hidung; *'~-in-the-mud',* Pak Tonggok; *~ing-out (of ears),* jabing; *~ing up,* terjolok (jolok); *as a stake,* tercacak; *as ends of moustache,* menjungkit (jungkit) ke atas; *to ~ one's neck out (rashly place oneself in a vulnerable position),* mengalangkan (alang*) leher suruh sembelih, *(stretch out one's neck and tell them to cut one's throat); see* **project.**

stiff, *adj. of muscles,* kejang, lenguh lumpuh; *of joints,* berkiat (kiat); *hard to bend,* kaku; *cold, unemotional, not relaxed (fig.),* kaku; *as hair,* kejur; *esp. as moustache,* berdenting (denting); *of wind,* kencang; *as in death,* keras jegang; *~ as in death, esp. in imprecations,* mati kojol; *as paper or cloth,* sering.

still, *adv. as before,* lagi, masih; *nevertheless,* juga.

still, *adj. as water,* tenang; *keep ~,* jangan bergerak (gerak), jangan menguit (kuit); *~-born,* mati dalam kandugan; *~ waters run deep (a silent man may be a deep thinker),* diam ubi*; *(~ waters may contain dangers),* air tenang jangan disangka tidak ada buaya *(because water is ~, it does not follow that there are no crocodiles).*

sting, *v. tr.* sengat, ketip; *a ~, e.g., of a*

wasp, sengat; ~ *(spine), of certain fish,* sonak, duri.

stingy, *adj.* kedekut, kelorek, kekel, medit.

stint, *v. tr. supply in niggardly way,* menghematkan (hemat), menjimatkan (jimat).

stipulate, *v. tr. & intr. to demand or insist upon as part of an agreement,* menentukan, menetapkan syarat.

stipulation, *n.* syarat janji.

stir, *v. tr.* kacau; *esp. as boiling rice,* karih; ~ *up ingredients so as to mix or to ~ up water, as bathers,* godak; *see* **chum up;** ~ *up (as trouble),* menimbulkan (timbul) kucar-kacir.

stirrup, *n.* rakap.

stitch, *v. tr. see* **sew;** *a ~ in time saves nine,* berpayung (payung) sebelum hujan, *(get an umbrella before it starts to rain).*

stock, *n. family group,* rumpun; *racial group,* rupa-bangsa; *genus,* baka; *descent,* keturunan (turun); *of gun,* buntut; ~-*in-trade,* barang-barang (yang sedia).

stockade, *n.* kubu, benteng.

stodgy, *adj. as a cake,* bentat, payah dicerna.

stomach, *n.* perut.

stone, *n.* batu; *to ~,* merejam (rejam).

stooge, *n. see* **traitor.**

stool, *n.* bangku; *to fall between two ~s,* tersepit (sepit) di tengah, *(pinched in between).*

stoop, *v. intr.* tunduk, membongkok (bongkok).

stop, *v intr.* berhenti (henti); *of rain,* teduh, seriat sidang; *restrain,* larang; *detail,* tahan; ~ *up, plug,* sumbat; ~ *passage, as by blockade,* sekat; *to ~ a tooth,* pasak, sumbi; ~ *up (a hole),* tumpat; ~ *at (on the way), see* **touch;** ~ *(e.g., a passing vehicle or person),* tahan; *a full ~ (gram.),* titik; ~-*page, esp. in anus or uterus,* bebang; ~*per,* penyumbat.

store, *n. household ~,* 'stor'; *warehouse,* gudang; *see* **shop;** *to ~,* simpan; ~ *away, 'salt away',* pendap.

storey, *n. adjutant ~,* burung botak, burung dahu; *the Southern painted ~,* burung upih.

storm, *n.* ribut; *to ~ (a position),* menggempur (gempur); *see* **cloud, typhoon.**

story, *n.* cerita; *narrative, romance,* kisah, hikayat; *esp. as formal statement of facts,* riwayat; *serial ~,* cerita bersambung (sambung); *travelling ~-teller,* selampit; *see* **statement.**

stove, *n. for warming,* perapian (api); *dapur, for '~ in', see* **stave.**

stow, *v. tr. pack away,* menyimpan dengan penuh perhatian; *put away casually,* peruk.

stowaway, *v. intr. get a free passage by hiding in ship,* curi-curi naik kapal.

straddle, *v. intr.* terkangkang (kangkang), tercelepak (celepak).

straggle, *v. intr. to move in loose irregular order,* berderai-derai, berduyunduyun, bercerai-berai (cerai); *lagging,* berlambat-lambat (di belakang); *astray,* tersesat (sesat).

straight, *adj.* lurus; ~ *on,* terus; *vertical,* tegak; *to keep a ~ course,* mendudu (dudu); *direct of gaze,* tepat; *to ~en out (become ~) under pressure (as a hook taken by a heavy fish),* terleka (leka); *to ~en out (a difficulty or a tangled skein),* selesaikan; *(a bent bar),* luruskan, ~*forward.*

strain, *v. tr.* tapiskan, saringkan; *to ~, as in easing oneself,* teran; *esp. as in child-birth,* rejan; ~ *the ears,* besar-besarkan telinga; ~*ed (as twisted joint),* tergeliat (geliat); *see* **sprained;** ~, *breed,* baka; ~*er, filter,* tapisan; *small ~er,* kaluk.

strait, *n. narrow water passage,* selat, terusan.

strand, *n. shore,* pantai; *of rope,* lembar; ~*ed, as castaway,* terdampar (dampar); *as cut off from help,* tersekat (sekat); *as hopelessly astray,* tersesat (sesat); *as penniless stranger,* terlantar (lantar); *(fish) left ~ed by receding water,* (ikan) kekeringan (kering) air; *see* **aground.**

strange, *adj. unusual, surprising,* ganjil luar biasa, anih.

stranger, *n. foreigner,* orang dagang, orang asing; *outsider,* orang luaran; *(of a bewildered ~),* seperti rusa masuk kampung, *(like a dear entering a village).*

strangle, *v. tr. see* **throttle;** mencekik leher.

strap, *n.* tali kulit, mengikat.

strategem, *n.* daya, muslihat, suatu akal.

stratum, *n.* lapisan bumi.

straw, *n.* jerami, roman.

stray, *v. intr. as from herd,* lepas; *a~,* sesat; *run wild (of a domestic animal),* jalang; *off-course, of a projectile,* kesasaran (sasar), menyimpang.

streaked, *adj.* coreng; *esp. of an animal,* koreng.

stream, *n.* anak sungai; *current,* harus; *artificial runnel,* tali air; *up~,* ulu; *to go up~,* mudik; *down~,* hilir; *to go down~,* menghilir; *on the down~ side (of an object),* sebelah olak; *to ~ along (of crowds),* berduyun-duyun; *in a continous ~,* bertali-arus (tali).

streamer, *n. (long ribbon),* ular-ular.

street, *n.* jalan (raya); *broad ~ (esp. as business-centre),* lebuh.

strength, *n.* tenaga; *see* **power.** **strong;** *to ~en (as fortifications),* kukuhkan, menguatkan.

stress, *v. tr. to lay ~ on, treat as important,* menitik-beratkan (titik), menekankan; *emphasis (by tone of voice),* tekanan suara; *time of ~,* masa kecemasan (cemas), masa kesukaran (sukar).

stretch, *v. tr. pull taut,* tarik regang; *~ oneself,* buang kejang; *'~ one's legs' (take a little exercise),* buang kebas; *~ out one's legs (when in a sitting position),* belunjur (lunjur); *to ~ in specified direction, as a mountainrange,* merintang (rintang); *to ~ oneself out, as on a bed,* mengunjurkan (unjur) diri, mengaparkan (kapar) badan; *for ~ neck', see* **crane;** *~ outwards (hands or as skin on a drum),*

mengedangkan (kedang); *lying ~ed our, as a corpse,* terbujur 'bujur'; *a ~ of rice fields,* sebidang (sawah); *~ing far, as view,* terpampang (pampang); *to ~ out, as hand,* hulurkan; *~er,* usungan, tandu; *to carry on a ~er,* mengusung.

stretcher, *n.* tandu, usungan.

strew, *v. tr.* hamburkan, taburkan.

strict, *adj. requiring implicit obedience,* keras; *careful, as watch,* teliti, rapi; *as agreement,* teguh; *strictly speaking (in actual fact),* sebenarnya.

stride, *n.* langkah; *to ~ out,* cepatkan langkah, mengayun (ayun) tunjang; *to walk with long ~s,* melangkah guntai; *with measured ~,* langkahnya sebagai teratur (atur).

strike, *v. tr.* pukul; *see* **beat;** *~ a light,* lekat api, petik, panciskan, 'macis'; *to go on ~,* mogok*; *general ~,* hartal; *to ~ loudly, of a clock,* berdentang (dentang); *'struck all of a heap' (with excitement, astonishment or anger),* tertegun (tegun), terserap (serap) darah; *~ the eye, attract attention,* menjolok (jolok) mata.

string, *n.* tali; *a ~ of fish,* secucuk ikan; *a ~ of beads,* seutas manik.

strip, *n. a ~, esp. of land,* sejoreng; *eps. of cloth,* selerang; *to ~ off, remove,* memapas (papas); *~ped, denuded,* licin, bolos, melucutkan (lucut) menanggalkan (tanggal).

stripe, *n.* jalur; *~ denoting rank,* markah (tanda pangkat); *Mr. Stripes (the tiger),* Tok Belang.

strive, *v. intr. esp. politically,* berjuang (juang); *~ for,* merebut (rebut).

stroke, *v. tr. to rub gently,* gosok, urut; *esp. caressingly,* mengusap (usap); *to have a ~ (as of apoplexy),* kena lintasan (hantu); *apoplexy,* sawan bangkai, sawan terjun.

strong, *adj.* kuat; *of wind,* kencang; *of drink,* keras; *firm,* kukuh; *as coffee,* pekat; *a (military) '~-point',* benteng, *~hold,* tembok yang kukuh.

strop, *n.* pegilap (gilap), pegabus (gabus); *hone,* batu asah.

struggle, v. intr. as to escape, meronta-ronta; as jostling crowds, bergelut-gelut; for possession of, merebut (rebut); esp. politically, berjuang (juang); struggling along, terkial-kial; wildly, as a drowning man, terkapai-kapai; thrashing about, as in water, menggelodar (gelodar); helplessly, as flies in web, berpuli-puli; a ~, for power, pergelutan, perjuangan.

strut, v. intr. walk proudly; berjalan (jalan) dengan bergaya (gaya) atau cara yang sombong.

stub, n. of cigarette, etc., puntung; of counterfoil, tunggul; to ~ one's toe against, tersaruk (saruk) pada, terseradung (seradung) pada; ~ ^ut (lighted end), sugikan, tenyeh.

stubble, n. of rice, etc. jerami.

stubborn, adj. degil, keras-kepala; obdurate, keras-hati.

stud, n. collar-~, butang dasi; ~ded with (e.g., diamonds), bersumbi (sumbi), bertatah (tatah) (intan).

studious, adj. involving study, rajin, tekun.

study, v. intr. to be at school, mengaji (kaji), bersekolah (sekolah); to ~ (a specific subject), mengkaji (kaji); to pursue knowledge, menuntut (tuntut) ilmu; student, penuntut, pelajar (ajar), maha-siswa, (anak) murid; to ~ attentively, bertekun (tekun) mengaji.

stuff, v. tr. pack in tightly, mengasak (asak); to fill, mengisi (isi); ~fed tight, padat; ~fing, as for a fowl, inti; ~ed up, as nose by a cold, tersebu (sebu); to ~ into (e.g., shavings into a hole), menyumbat (sumbat) — ke dalam —.

stuffy, adj. over-warm, hangat; atmosphere of crowded room, udara bersesak-sesak.

stumble, v. intr. terdorong (dorong); bertemu secara kebetulan, trip up by catching one's foot on something, tersaruk (saruk) pada, terserandung (serandung) pada; by putting one's foot in a hole, terperlus (perlus), terperosok (perosok), to ~ along, berjalan (jalan)

jatuh bangkit; esp. as a baby, bertatih-tatih (tatih); ~ through a reading, berta-tih-tatih membaca (baca); stumbling-block (difficulty in the way), halangan; see **trrip.**

stump, n. tunggul; as of cigarette, puntung.

stunted, adj. ketut, bangkut; set back in growth, tergencat (gencat); undersized of men and animals, kerdil; esp. of fowls, katik.

stupefied, adj. with drink, drugs, mabuk; (fig.) by noise, bingit (kepala).

stupid, adj. dungu; simple, bodoh; dull, bebal; 'mazed', bingung; unsophisticated, belum tahu hal; 'wet', lembam; simpleton, tolol; 'bone from the neck up', seperti udang*, tahi di kepala, (like a prawn, dung in the head); crassly ~, jahil; 'bloody fool', buta perut.

sturdy, adj. passively strong, tegap, kukuh; sturdily built, tegap-badan.

stutter, v. intr. & tr. berkata (bercakap) dengan gagap.

stye, n. kandang babi.

sty, n. in the eye, ketumbit, bintil.

style, n. way, method, type, cara; fashion, fesyen; smartness, 'setail, gaya.

subdue, v. tr. forcibly, memperkosakan (kosa), menguasai (kuasa); menindas (tindas) menundukkan see **suppress.**

subject, n. matter, perkara; person owing allegiance, rakyat; academic ~, mata pelajaran (ajar); branch of study, jurusan; ~ of conversation, pokok per-bualan (bual); ~ to (tax), kena (cukai); ~ of a story, bahan cerita.

submarine, n. kapal selam; under the sea, di bawah laut; on the sea-floor, di dasar laut.

submit, v. intr. give in, tunduk; offer no resistance, beralah (alah), berserah (serah); admit defeat, mengaku (aku) kalah.

subscription, n. as to Club, yuran; to newspaper, langganan; as contribution, sumbangan.

subservient, adj. ~ to, di bawah kuit

telunjuk*; *to make* ~, tanjul* hidung;
see **obsequious.**

subside, *v. tr. as water or a swelling,*
surut; *as storm,* reda; *settle, as dug
in, of earth,* mampat, berderut (derut); *cave
in, of earth,* runtuh; *sink slightly, esp.
as a heavy building,* terendap-endap.

subsidy, *n.* wang bantuan.

substitute, *n.* ganti, *substitution n.*
penggantian, tukar ganti.

subtle, *adj. ingeniously minute,* rumit;
halus; *cunning,* kebijaksanaan.

subtract, *v. tr. away,* tolak; *deduct,*
potong.

suburbs, *n.* daerah di sekitar bandar,
pinggiran bandar.

subvert, *v. tr. overthrow (esp. the
Government),* mengguling(kan),
menumbangkan (tumbang); *subversive,* 'subersif'; *subversive activities,*
kegiatan (giat) 'subersif'.

succeed, *v. intr. take the place of,* ganti;
to win, menang; *go well,* jadi; *esp. as
an enterprise,* berjaya (jaya); *in succession (succeeding one another),* berganti-ganti; *in turn,* bergilir-gilir; *one
after the other,* berturut-turut, lepas se
(orang) se (orang).

succint, *adj. brief but clear,* tegas,
cingkat, jelas, pendek.

suck, *v. tr. as sweet in mouth,* kulum; ~ *at,
as a bit of ice,* kebam; ~ *in,* isap; *draw
up by suction, as vacuum-cleaner,*
sedut; *(fig.)* ~ *up, curry favour,* cari
muka, mengampu (ampu) (bodek);
~*ing-fish,* ikan gemi.

suckle, *v. tr.* menyusukan (susu).

suddenly, *adv.* tiba-tiba, sekonyong-
konyong.

sue, *v. tr.* mendakwa (dakwa); ~ *for peace,*
minta damai.

suet, *n.* minyak sapi.

suffer, *v. tr. undergo,* kena; *endure,*
tahan, menderita (derita); *put up with,*
menanggung (tanggung); *from an
illness,* mengidap (idap) penyakit
(sakit) —; ~ *for it (pay the penalty),*
timpa rasa; ~*ing,* sengsara, penderitaan (derita).

sufficient, *adj.* cukup, padan; *reasonably
~,* lumayan.

suffocated, *p.p.* lemas.

sugar, *n.* gula, syakar; ~-*cane,* tebu; ~-
palm, pokok kabung, pokok nau.

suggest, *v. tr. put forward, as a plan,*
menganjurkan (anjur), kemukakan
(muka); *recommend,* cadangkan,
sarankan.

suicide, *n. to commit ~,* bunuh diri; *(fig.)
of running foolish risks,* tahan jerat,
sorong kepala, *(set a noose and thrust
your head into it),* buang nyawa,
menjerat leher sendiri; ~-*squad,*
pasukan berani mati.

suit, *n. a ~ of clothes,* selengkap pakaian.

suitable, *adj. qualified,* layak; *proper,*
patut, berpatutan; *compatible,* sesuai,
sejodoh; *harmonising,* secocok, ~ *to,
fitted for,* padan dengan; *adapted to,
as tools,* serasuk dengan.

suitcase, *n.* 'beg'; *see* **bag.**

sulky, *adj.* merajuk (rajuk); ~-*looking,* bermuka (muka) masam; *see* **surly.**

sully, *v. tr.* mencemarkan (cemar), menodai (noda), mengotorkan (kotor).

sulphur, *n.* berlerang.

sum, *n. total,* jumlah; *to ~ up,* meringkas-
kan (ringkas); *in short,* pendeknya; *a ~
of money,* sejumlah wang.

summary, *n.* ringkasan.

summer-house, *n.* balai peranginan.

summit, *n.* mercu, puncak, kemuncak; ~
Conference, persidangan (sidang)
kemuncak.

summon, *v. tr. send for, tell to come,*
panggil; *by a hail,* laungkan; *take out
Court ~s,* mengambil (ambil) 'saman'.

sump, *n.* limbah, acar.

sun, *n. matahari; (poet),* Sang Suria; ~-
rise, matahari naik, matahari terbit; ~-
set, matahari masuk, matahari jatuh,
matahari terbenam (benam); *nearing
~-set,* matahari condong; ~-*shine,*
panas (matahari); ~-*shade (parasol),*
payung; *screen against the ~,* dinding
hari; ~-*dial,* jam bayang matahari; *to ~
oneself,* berjemur; ~-*beam,* sinar
matahari; ~'s *rays,* cahaya matahari;

~*ny day,* hari panas; ~*burnt,* kena makan* dek hari; ada hujan ada panas, *sometimes it's* ~*ny, sometimes rainy, rhyming equivalent for* ada hari boleh balas, *one day we will be able to repay (esp. repay a wrong, i.e., have revenge); in the (heat of the)* ~, tengah-tengah panas; ~*-bird, spider-hunter,* burung jerejik.

Sunday, *n.* hari Minggu; hari Ahad.

supercilious, *adj.* hidung tinggi, angkuh, bongkak, sombong.

superficial, *adj. as thought, knowledge,* dangkal, cetek; *as would, affecting the skin only,* kena kulit sahaja; hanya di bahagian luar sahaja.

superintend, *v.tr.* menyelia (selia), mengawasi (awas), mengelola (kelola).

superior, *adj. better,* lebih baik daripada; *one's superiors,* orang atasan.

supernatural, *adj. occult,* ghaib; *magical,* sakti; ~*ly created animal,* jadi-jadian.

superstition, *n. fantastic belief,* khayalan, kepercayaan karut, faham tahyul; *playing on people's* ~, mempergunakan (guna) kepercayaan karut seseorang.

supervise, *v. tr. see* **superintend.**

supple, *adj.* lemah liat; *of a person,* lembut-pinggang, mudah bengkok atau lentur.

supplement, *n.* tambahan; *as makeweight,* basi.

supply, *v. tr. bring,* membawa (bawa); *supplies,* perbekalan (bekal); *esp. of an army,* pelabur (labur); *stocks,* persediaan (sedia).

support, *n. pillar,* turus, tiang; *post,* pancang; *prop,* tongkat; *forked or angular prop,* topang; *for climbing plant,* junjung; *for back,* sandaran; *for keeping beached boat upright,* jeremang; *moral* ~, sokongan batin; *mainstay of (my) life,* tonggak hidup (saya); *to* ~, *generally and esp. by buttressing,* sokong; *to back up, assist,* membantu (bantu); *by propping from below,* menongkat; *to stand up for, help to win,* menangkan; menangkan; *to* ~

from below, as a sling for a broken arm, mengampu (ampu); *to bring up (as child),* pelihara; *financial* ~, wang bantuan, wang tunjangan; *to walk with* ~, be helped along, berpapah (papah); *be responsible for, e.g., a family,* tanggung belanja; ~ *oneself,* menanggung diri; *serve as a foundation for,* mengalas (alas); *prop from below,* menopang (topang); ~*ers, 'fans',* peminat (minat); *of a political party,* penyokong.

suppose, *v. intr. & tr. see* **think;** *I* ~, gamak saya; *supposing* —, kalau misalan —, mengandaikan (andai).

suppress, *v. tr. as opposition,* menindas (tindas); *as disturbances,* menekan (tekan); *as news,* penyapkan (sapan); *hide, as feelings,* pendam; ~ *signs of discomfiture, etc., on one's face,* menebal (tebal) muka; *wipe out,* menghapuskan (hapus), membasmikan (basmi).

suppurate, *v. intr.* menanah (nanah).

supreme, *adj. in rank,* agung, tertinggi (tinggi); *Supreme Head of the Armed Forces,* panglima tertinggi tentera bersenjata (senjata).

sure, *adj.* tentu; *convinced,* yakin; *there can be no doubt that* —, tidak syak lagi —, ~*ty,* orang jamin, jaminan.

surf, *n.* pecahan ombak, hempasan ombak; ~*-bathing,* main gelombang.

surface, *n.* muka; *whole superficial area,* permukaan; *to come to the* ~, timbul; *to* ~ *a road with tar, etc.,* menurap (turap).

surfeit, *n. much of something,* hal terlampau kenyang.

surge, *v. intr. rise in wave-like motion,* meluap (luap); ~ *up, heave up, as sea,* mengambung (ambung); *see* **pour.**

surly, *adj.* perengus (rengus), merungsing (rungsing), marah-marah.

surmise, *v. intr.* gamak, menjangka (jangka), menerka.

surmount, *v. tr. as difficulties,* mengatasi (atas).

surname, *n.* nama keluarga.

surpass, *v. tr.* mengatasi (atas), melampaui (lampau).

surplus, n. yang lebih; see **remain.**

surprised, adj. hairan; surprising, ajaib, pelik; taken by ~, sergap; ~ attack, serangan secara mengejut (kejut).

surrender, v. intr. serah diri; mengaku kalah, hand over, serahkan, no ~!, pantang menyerah!

surreptitious, adj. done secretly or stealthily, dengan diam-diam; secara mencuri-curi.

surround, v. tr. mengepung (kepung); ~ings, sekeliling, sekitar.

surveillance, n. pengawasan (awas).

survey, v. tr. land, mengukur (ukur), menyukat (sukat); inspect, memeriksa (periksa), menyelidik (selidik); meninjau (tinjau).

survive, v. intr. escape (a disaster), terlepas; be still alive, ada lagi, hidup lagi; terus hidup; if I ~ (if I live so long), kalau ada umur saya; survivors (of a disaster), yang hidup, orang yang terselamat; survival, hal terselamat.

suspend, v. tr. from duty, gantung jawatan; see **hang.**

suspense, n. state of anxious uncertainty, kegelisahan (gelisah), keragu-raguan; atmosphere of tension, suasana ketegangan (tegang), to wait expectantly, duduk ternanti-nanti.

suspicious, adj. feeling ~, syak-hati, curiga; to harbour suspicion, menaruh (taruh) syak; to arouse suspicion, menimbulkan (timbul) syak.

suzerainty, n. kedaulatan (daulat).

svelte, adj. lissom, but well-fleshed, muntil; esp. of a young girl, ramping sedang naik.

swaddling-cloth, n. for infant, lampin, barut.

swag, n. barang rampasan, barang curian (curi).

swagger, v. intr. walk with ~ing gait, melenggang (lenggang), jalan terhegeh-hegeh; 'cutting a dash', esp. by lavish expenditure, buat besar hentak; see **boast, show.**

swallow, v. tr. telan; ~ whole, telan bulat;

take food by ~ing without chewing as a python, makan melulur (lulur); the bird, burung layang-layang; cave-~ (which makes edible nests), ibu gua, induk gua.

swamp, n. paya; deep ~, redang; ~ed (flooded with water, of a boat), keairan (air); see **puddle.**

swanky, adj. ranggi; moving along swankily, dengan bergaya, penuh gaya; see **swagger.**

swarm, n. as of bees, sekawan (lebah), se kumpulan (lebah); to ~, run about in great numbers (as insects), menghurung (hurung), mengerumit-mengeramat (kerumit), mengerotong (kerotong); ~ everywhere, all over the place, as children, ants, berbelar (belar); ~ up (a tree), naik mendepang (depang).

sway, v. intr. as a tree in the wind, bergoyang (goyang); swing rock, berayun (ayun); berbuai (buai); as branches in wind, liang-liuk, slah-layah; this way and that, as in wind, berlenggan-lenggan; esp. as if about to fall, terlayah (layah); under the ~ (government) of, di bawah perintah; see **shake.**

swear, v. intr. bersumpah; take an oath, angkat sumpah; cursing and ~ing, sumpah serapah.

sweat, n. peluh; esp. as '~ of the brow', keringat; bathed in ~, mandi peluh; kerja kuat, exude surface moisture (of wall, etc.), melengas (lengas).

sweep, v. tr. menyapu (sapu); make a clean ~, menyapu bersih.

sweet, adj. manis; melodious, merdu; ~-smelling, harum, wangi; ~s, manisan, halwa; loaf-sugar or sugar-candy, gula batu; ~heart, kekasih (kasih), buah hati; ~ie! (to a girl), manis!

swell, v. intr. as rice when boiled, muai; as leavened bread or as a box-fish, melembung (lembung); see **dilate;** ground-~ at sea, alun, swollen, bengkak; distended, buncit; puffy, sembap; (esp. from dropsy or beri-

beri), basal; *as a stream,* sebak; *to ~ out the chest,* membusungkan (busung) dada.

swerve, *v. intr. deviate from course,* membelok (belok) dengan tiba-tiba, terpelencong (lencong), terpesong (pesong); *esp. as driven from course,* terbias (bias), terbabas (babas); *turning aside,* terbenok (benok), terbelok (belok).

swift, *adj.* laju, tangkas; *see* **swallow.**

swim, *v. intr.* berenang (renang); *to ~ breast-stroke,* berenang katak; *on the back,* berenang belakang; *to do the 'crawl',* berenang merayap; *~ming expert,* ahli berenang; *~ming pool,* kolam renang; *with '~ming eyes,* berair (air) mata; *'~ming' head, see* **giddy.**

swing, *n. as for children,* ayunan; *to ~ from direct course (of a ship),* merewang (rewang); *to and fro, as a moved ship,* mengumbang-ambing (umbang); *this way and that, as a pendulum,* berayun-ayun; *see* **sway.**

swirl, *n. of water,* olak air, riak; *to ~, as a skirt,* mengimbau (imbau).

switch, *v. tr. whip with ~,* rempit, senawat, sebat; *~ on (current),* pasang, buka; *~ off,* padam, matikan; *a ~,* 'suis; to press a ~, petek 'suis'.

swoop, *v. intr.* menyambar (sambar),

menukik (tukik).

sword, *n.* pedang.

swordfish, *n.* ikan todak.

sycophant, *n.* kaki ampu, tali barut; *see* **suck, traitor.**

syllabus, *n.* sukatan pelajaran (ajar).

symbol, *n.* alamat, lambang, 'simbol'; *to ~ise,* melambangkan; *~s in shorthand,* garisan tringkas.

symmetrical, *adj. equally balanced,* setimpal.

sympathy, *n.* insaf, 'simpati'; *to feel ~,* timbang rasa; *to express ~ (esp. as agreement with views),* menyatakan (nyata) 'simpati', menyuarakan (suara) 'simpati' (bagi); *see* **condole.**

symptoms, *n.* gejala, gejala penyakit (sakit), tanda-tanda penyakit.

synchronise, *v. tr. make items (of occasions) correspond,* menyamakan (sama) waktu; *~d (fixed at the same time),* serentak.

synonym, *n. word having same meaning,* kata seerti.

synopsis, *n.* ikhtisar, ringkasan.

syntax, *n.* susunan ayat, jalinan bahasa.

synthetic, *adj.* buatan, tiruan.

Syria, *n.* negeri Syam.

syringe, *n. (for inoculation),* jarum cucuk.

system, *n. co-ordinated plan of working,* 'sistem'; *see* **method, regular.**

T

table, *n.* meja; *~-cloth,* kain meja, alas meja; *to lay the ~,* mengatur (atur) meja; *to clear the ~ (remove dishes, etc.),* angkat pinggan-mangkuk.

taboo, *adj. forbidden, esp. by custom,* pantang, pemali (mali); larangan keras; tabu.

tacit, *adj. saying nothing, silent,* berdiam, dengan tidak diucapkan.

tack, *v. intr. turn aside sharply (of a ship),* belok; *~ to and fro,* berpal-pal.

tackle, *n. ropes, etc.,* tali temali; *appliances,* alat

tact, *n.* kebijaksanaan akal; *~ess,* tak ada akal; *thoughtless,* tidak berfikir dahulu; *delicate and careful, of speech or methods,* halus.

tail, *n.* ekor; *~ings (sand-tailings),* pasir hampas, pasir-pasir buangan lombong; *see* **silt;** *to put ~ between legs (of a dog),* mencawatkan (cawat) ekor; *~ light,* lampu belakang; *'~s', of a coin when tossed,* bunga, *(as opposed to 'heads',* kepala).

tailor, *n.* tukang jahit; *~-bird,* burung cakcak.

take, *v. tr.* ambil; *convey,* bawa; *~ off,* buka, tanggalkan; *~ (capture) a piece (e.g., at chess),* pukul; *~ (capture) a town or prisoners (in war),* menawan (tawan); *~ over (a plan or a business),* ambil alih; *to ~ place (of a function),* berlangsung (langsung), berlaku (laku); *place to ~ off (for a jump or fig.),* tempat tumpuan; *there! ~ it! (in handing something),* nah!

tale, *n. see* **statement, story;** *~-bearer,* kaki bawa mulut.

talent, *n.* bakat; *natural ~,* bakat semula jadi.

talisman, *n.* tangkal, azimat.

talk, *v. intr. utter words,* bertutur (tutur); *converse,* berbual (bual); *gossip,* ber-

gebang-gebang; *blather,* berleter, *~ over,* berura-ura; *to get '~ed about',* jadi sebutan; *the '~ of the town',* buah mulut; *~ative,* lidah panjang, bibir nipis; *clever ~er,* pitah mulut; *~ative, esp. as a child,* petis; *a ~, esp. on the radio,* ceramah; *wild irresponsible ~,* keretaan (reta); *to hold ~s (negotiate),* mengadakan (ada) rundingan; *big ~er, lazy worker,* ringan mulut, berat punggung, *(light mouth, heavy stern); see* **speak.**

tall, *adj.* tinggi; *abnormally ~,* tinggi menongkat (tongkat) langit.

tamarind, *n.* pokok asam Jawa.

tambourine, *n.* rebana.

tame, *adj.* jinak; tidak liar atau ganas.

tamer, *n.* penjinak (binatang).

tan, *v. tr. by steeping,* samak.

tangled, *adj.* terkusut (kusut), terbojot (bojot), berserabutan (serabut).

tank, *n. for water,* tangki, takungan; *esp. for ablutions at mosque,* kolah; *military,* kereta kebal; *~er,* kapal minyak.

tantrum, *n. to be in a ~,* naik angin.

tap, *n.* pili (ayer), pemutar (putar) 'paip' ayer; *to ~ (a rubber tree),* menuris (turis), menoreh (toreh); *runnel on ~ped rubber tree,* caruk; *its spout,* saluran; *to ~ (a person) lightly with fingers (as when drawing his attention),* cuit; *to emit a ~ping sound (as a typewriter),* berdetik-detik; *to put a bottle under (a ~) so as to catch the water,* menadahkan (tadah) 'botol'; *(on a door),* katuk; *~-root,* tunjang.

tape, *n. narrow,* tali; *broad,* pita; *'red ~',* 'birokrasi'; *measuring-~,* tali ukur; *to record on ~,* pitakan; *to run such a ~,* putarkan pita; *see* **record.**

tapering, *adj.* tirus ke hujung; *to a point,* runcing.

tapioca, *n.* ubi kayu.

tapir, *n.* badak tampung; kipan; tenuk.

tar, *n.* minyak 'tar'.

target, *n.* sasaran; *(fig.)* ~ *for anger,* tumpuan kemarahan (marah); *(fig.) objective,* matlamat.

tariff, *n. of Customs,* daftar cukai.

tarnished, *adj. of metal,* usam, kusam, sebam.

tarpaulin, *n.* kain terpal.

tassel, *n.* jumbai, rumbai, gunjai; rambu.

taste, *n.* rasa; *to* ~, merasa, cecap; *to 'savour',* mengecapkan (kecap); *tasty,* sedap, perisa; ~*less,* tawar; *in bad* ~ *(offends the aesthetic faculty),* tidak manis.

tattered, *adj.* cubik-cabik, koyak-rabak; compang-camping.

tattoo, *v. tr. mark patterns on skin,* mencacah.

tatty, *adj.* selekeh; comot.

taunt, *v. tr.* menggiat (giat), mengejek (ejek); menghina (hina); mencela (cela); *make nasty digs,* mencucuk-cucuk.

taut, *adj. as rope,* tegang, regang; *esp. as a full sail,* mencing, kepuh.

tax, *n.* cukai; *to impose a* ~, mengenakan (kena) cukai.

tea, *n.* teh; ~-*pot,* teko (cerek), tekuan; ~-*party,* jamuan teh; ~-*spoon,* camca; ~-*cup,* cawan.

teach, *v. tr.* mengajar (ajar); ~*er,* guru; *(familialy),* Cikgu; *esp. as tutor,* pengajar (ajar); *training,* latihan; *group* ~*er,* Guru Kumpulan; *visiting* ~*er,* Guru Pelawat (lawat).

teak, *n.* kayu jati.

teal, *n.* burung belibis.

team, *n.* pasukan.

tear, *n. from eyes,* air mata; *eyes glistening with* ~*s,* mata berkaca-kaca; ~-*gas,* 'gas' pemedih (edih) mata.

tear, *v. tr. pull apart,* koyak; *tattered,* koyak-rabak; ~ *down (as a poster),* soyak; *rip,* carik; ~ *up,* koyak buang; ~ *out (as a nest),* renggut; *torn off (as a nail),* tersungkap (sungkap); ~ *at, pull at roughly,* meragas (ragas); ~ *the*

heart (of grief), menyayatkan (sayat) hati; *torn through (of an edge),* rabit; *having a bit torn out,* terkobak (kobak); *gaping* ~, cabak.

tease, *v. tr.* usik; *chaff,* giat, memperlikan (perli); *worry,* sakat.

teat, *n.* mata susu, puting.

tedious, *adj.* (yang) membosankan (bosan), memuakkan (muak).

telecommunications, *n.* telekomunikasi.

telegram, *n. to send a* ~, mengirim telegram, mengutus kawat; *wireless* ~, telegram, tak berdawai (dawai).

telephone, *n. to* ~, telefon; menelefon; ~*box,* kandang telefon; *the instrument,* gagang telefon, tangkai telefon, *mouthpiece,* mulut gagang telefon.

telescope, *n.* teropong.

tell, *v. tr. relate,* berkhabar (khabar), beri tahu, bilang; *narrate,* cerita(kan); *direct to,* suruh; ~ *tale (n)* pengadu. pengumpat.

temerity, *n.* keberanian yang berlebih-lebihan.

temper, *n. in a bad* ~, berhati (hati) sebal, sudah naik berang; *see* **angry;** ~*ed, of metal,* berbaja (baja).

temperament, *n. to show* ~, *'play up',* meragam (ragam), mengolah (olah); ~*al,* ada angin, macam kelembuai, *to 'throw a* ~', *get 'worked up',* naik angin; ~*s vary,* banyak banyak udang, banyak garam, *(many prawns, much salt; rhyming equivalent for* banyak orang, banyak garam, *many men many forms of mood).*

temperate, *adj. of climate,* sederhana.

temperature, *n.* darjah panas, suhu; *(of air),* ukuran hawa; *to 'have a* ~', naik demam.

temple, *n.* tokong; *esp. Hindu,* kuil.

temples, *n. the* ~ *of the forehead,* pelipis (lipis).

temporary, *adj.* sementara; *as opposed to eternal,* fana.

temptation, *n. urge of the senses,* godaan nafsu.

tenant, *n.* orang yang menyewa (sewa)

(rumah).

tender, *adj. as meat,* empuk, lembut; *a ~ (for a contract),* pemborongan (borong), tender; *v. tr. & intr.* menawarkan.

tendon, *n.* urat; *~ Achillis,* urat keting.

tendril, *n. of plant,* padung, sulur.

tense, *adj.* tegang.

tent, *n.* khemah.

tentacle, *n.* sungut, ampai-ampai, jari-jari.

tenure, *n.* hak milik, masa jabatan *(of office)* kedudukan tetap *(as professor).*

tepid, *adj.* pesam, suam; *as cooled to a bearable temperature,* siau.

term, *n. school ~,* penggal; *~s (as of contract),* syarat; *on good ~s with,* baik dengan; *long ~ plan,* rancangan jangka panjang; *short ~ plan,* rancangan jangka pendek; *not on speaking ~s,* tak bertegur (tegur).

tern, *n.* burung camar.

terrible, *adj.* dahsyat.

territory, *n. of a State,* tanah air; *particularly area of sovereignty,* daerah, tentera wataniah.

terrorist, *n.* pengganas (ganas).

test, *n.* ujian; *to ~,* menguji, menjalankan (jalan) ujian; *to try out,* mencuba (cuba); *intelligence ~,* dugaan akal.

testicles, *n.* buah pelir, bodek.

testimonial, *n.* surat (pujian); surat akuan.

tetanus, *n. lock-jaw,* kejang-mulut, kaku-mulut; *kancing mulut (gigi).*

tête-à-tête, *adv. face to face,* bertemu (temu) muka.

tether, *v. tr.* menambat (tambat).

text, *n. original document,* nasykah; *sentence in book,* ayat; *traditional relig ious ~s,* hadis.

text-book, *n.* buku pelajaran (ajar), buku 'teks'.

textiles, *n.* kain-kain, barang tenunan.

texture, *n. of cloth,* jaringan, tenunan, susunan kain.

than, *prep.* pada, daripada.

thanks, *n. to express ~,* mengucap (ucap) terima kasih; *esp. to God,* mengucap

syukur; *to be thankful,* mengenang (kenang) budi; *thank God!,* al-hamdulilah! syukurlah~; *~ to —,* dengan berkat —; *with the help of —,* dengan pertolongan (tolong) —.

that, *adj.* itu; *~ is, i.e.,* iaitu.

thatch, *n.* atap.

thaw, *v. intr. warm into liquid state,* menjadi (jadi) cair, hancur.

theathre, *n.* panggung (wayang); *the performance,* wayang.

theme, *n. subject matter of a story,* perkara, bahan tema; *popular ~ of conversation,* buah mulut.

then, *adv. at that time,* la itu; *in that period,* masa itu; *after that,* lepas itu; *~ only,* baharulah.

thence, *adv.* sana, kerana itu; kemudian, *~ forth,* sejak itu.

theory, *n. the sphere of speculative thought,* teori.

there, *adv.* (di) situ; *over ~,* sebelah sana; *yonder,* nun; *~! (take it!),* nah!

therefore, *conj.* sebab itu, oleh sebab itu.

they, *pron.* dia orang, dema, depa, dia, mereka itu.

thick, *adj. as plank,* tebal; *as rain, moustache, leaves,* lebat; *as cordage,* kasar; *of liquids,* pekat, kental; *of undergrowth,* semak sangat; *dense, as fog, jungle,* tebal; *luxuriant, as shady tree,* rendang; *of smoke,* berkepul (kepul), membukat (bukat); *of mist,* pekat.

thicket, *n.* gompong, semak, rimbun.

thief, *n.* penouri (ouri).

thigh, *n.* paha.

thimble, *n.* sarung jari.

thin, *adj. of body,* kurus; *'skin and bone',* kurus koring; *'bag of bones',* tulangnya berjerangkang (jerangkang); *slight scrawny,* rincing, macam cicak disalai, *(like a dried-up lizard);* *of objects,* nipis, tipis; *as cordage,* halus; *of liquids,* cair; *as hair, foliage,* jarang; *to lose flesh,* susut tubuh; *to ~ out,* tipiskan; *~-skinned (quick to take offence),* bertelinga (telinga) nipis.

thing, *n.* benda, barang.

thingumjig, *n. something whose name slips one's memory,* anu itu.

think, *v. intr. be of opinion,* fikir; *have an idea,* ingat; *cogitate,* berfikir; *weigh up points,* timbang; *have an impression,* rasa; *form an idea,* sangka; *I ~ (my impression is that),* rasa saya; *(my general impression is that),* perasaan saya; *(in my opinion),* pada fikiran saya; *(in my humble opinion),* pada fikiran saya yang bodoh ini; *(in my considered opinion),* pada timbangan saya, pada hemat saya; *(I am convinced that),* saya yakinlah; *(it has just occurred to me that),* baharu saya teringat; *(I have an inkling that),* sangka saya; *(I suspect that),* saya syak; *(I have it in my mind that),* gamak saya; *(I guess that),* agak saya; *deep in thought,* termenung (menung), melengung (lengung).

thirsty, *adj. thirst,* haus, dahaga.

this, *adj.* ini; *~ one,* yang ini.

thorn, *n.* duri, onak, selumbar; *'a ~ in the flesh' (a continual source of irritation or worry),* terasa-rasa bagai duri dalam daging.

thorough, *adj. as an investigation,* saksama; *to enquire ~ly,* halusi; *to study (a subject ~ly,* mengkaji (kaji) secara mendalam (dalam); *~bred (racially pure),* jati, belum bercampur (campur) baka; *genuine,* sungguh; *if you do something, do it ~ly,* mandi biar basah; *(when you bath, get wet); to the full,* jenuh; *to think out ~ly,* fikir masak-masak.

thrash, *v. tr. see* **beat.**

thread, *n.* benang; *to ~ (beads),* mencucuk (cucuk) (manik).

threaten, *v. tr.* mengugut (ugut), mengancam (ancam); *~ed (as under test, in danger),* terduga (duga); *make ~ing gesture,* gertak, jerkah; *see* **bluff.**

thresh, *v. tr. separate grain from stalk by beating,* membanting (banting); *by treading,* mengirik (irik).

threshold, *n.* ambang (pintu).

thrift, *n.* hemat; *~y,* jimat-cermat; *~less,* boros.

thrilled, *adj.* riang-hati; *thrilling, filling with delight,* menggiurkan (giur); *cause the heart to beat fast,* mendebarkan (debar) hati.

thriving, *adj. of plants,* subur; *of a country,* makmur, maju.

throat, *n.* kerongkong; *viewed as neck,* leher; *uvula* anak tekak.

throb, *v. intr. esp. as heart,* berdebar (debar); *esp. as a boil,* nyut-nyut, berdenyut (denyut).

throes, *n. desperate or agonizing struggle,* perasaan sakit pedih;

throne, *n.* takhta; *dais on which ~ stands,* singgahsana.

throng, *v. intr.* berkerumun (kerumun); *in ~s,* berjelai-jelai.

throttle, *v. tr. compress throat, strangle,* mencekik (cekik) leher; *garotte (with cord),* kujut.

through, *adv. straight ~,* terus; *melalui penetrating right ~,* lantas; *as by the help of,* dengan pertolongan (tolong) —; *no ~ road, see* **cul-de-sac;** *~out, (adv. & prep.)* seluruhnya.

throw, *v. tr.* melontar (lontar), lempar, baling; *hurl,* campak, pekong; *chuck,* tauk; *~ away,* buang; *~ down or off, as a horse,* menghumbankan (humban); *to 'floor',* menggulingkan (guling); *to ~ oneself down,* rebahkan diri, *to ~ a game, deliberately lose it,* cicirkan permainan.

thrust, *v. intr. stab,* tikam; *menusuh (tusuk) poke,* cucuk, jolok; *~ upwards,* radak; *~ into the ground,* unjam, cacak; *spit,* pacak; *to ~, e.g., a spear, into,* merodokkan (rodok) —ke.

thud, *v. intr. as heavy guns or a heavy falling object,* berdentum (dentum).

thumb, *n.* ibu jari (tangan), jempul; *under the ~ of (under the control of),* di bawah kuit telunjuk; *rule of ~,* peraturan yang berdasarkan pengalaman.

thump, *n. sound of a ~,* degum bunyinya.

thunder, *n.* guruh, guntur; *rolling ~,* guruh gemuruh; *reverberating ~,* guruh berdegar-degar; *~-bolt,* halilintar, petir;

'~-struck', tertegun (tegun).
Thursday, n. hari Khamis.
thus, adv. begitu, demikian, begini.
thwart, v. tr. foil purpose, melintangi (lintang); merintangi, ~ a whim, melintas (lintas) angin; ~ed, gagal.
tiara, n. gendik.
tick, n. insect, cengkenit; to ~, as a clock, berdetik (detik).
ticklish, adj. geli, geletek; ~, requiring great care, of a job, renyah; a tickling in the throat, perit kerongkong.
tide, n. flood-tide, air pasang (naik); high ~, air pasang penuh; execeptionally high ~, air naik merabung (rabung); ebb ~, air surut; dead low water, air timpas; to turn, (air) berbalas (balas); tidal, berpasang-surut; ~-rip (line of scum, etc.), kekat, tali harus; high-water mark, takat air pasang, bakat; line of driftwood marking high water-mark, tikas air pasang.
tidy, adj. kemas; esp. as of clothing, cermat; to ~ oneself up, mematut-matutkan (patut) diri.
tie, v. tr. see **fasten;** a ~ (in a game), seri; neck~, tali leher 'nektie', dasi; (sl.), tangkal polong; ties (as of friends), pertalian (tali).
tiffin, n. makan tengah hari; ~carrier, siak mangkuk tingkat; ~basket, rantang.
tiger, n. harimau, rimau; Mr. Stripes, Tok Belang; man-eating ~, rimau pemakan (makan) orang; prone to attack man or stock, rimau ganas.
tight, adj. ketat, erat; hold ~!, pegang kuat-kuat; shut ~, tutup rapat; of a knot, teguh; 'as ~ as a drum' (of stomach from overeating), macam rebana disedak; ~ so as to squeeze, cerutan; as a band, ketang.
title, n. roof-~, atap, genting; floor-~, batu ubin.
till, prep. & conj. hingga, sampai. v. tr. mengusahakan (mengerjakan) membajak tanah.
tilted, p.p. terjonkit (jongkit); ~ on one side, tersendeng (sendeng), mering; to tilt one's head up, congak; to tilt as to

invert (esp. a bottle), tonggeng; see **heel, tip.**
timber, n. balak; ~-trees, kayu balak; various sorts of ~, kayu-kayan; see **tree.**
time, n. period, masa; era, zaman; occasion, waktu; instance, kali, embak; respite, tempoh; what's the ~?, jam pukul berapa?, at what ~?, pukul berapa?, keep ~ with music, menurut (turut) irama; as by tapping the foot, gencok; timely, tepat pada waktunya; ~-table, jadual waktu; it's ~ (as for an appointment), sudah cukup jam; haven't ~ (too busy), tak senang; ~ in which something can be done, sempat; in ~ to cut throat (of a wounded bird, thus rendering it permissible for food), (halal), sempat sembelih; in ~ (not late), tidak lewat, tepat pada waktunya; it can't (or couldn't) be done in the ~, tak sempat; spare ~, masa kelapangan, (lapang); to find ~, snatch a moment for something, curi masa; a favourable juncture, peluang (luang); to make ~ (find ~ somehow), meluangkan (luang) waktu, melapangkan (lapang) waktu; to while away the ~, bagi perintang (rintang) waktu; full ~ work, pekerjaan (kerja) sepenuh masa; part-~ work, pekerjaan sambilan; to do a timed run, lari menguji (uji) masa; not keeping ~, so as to present a spectacle of confusion (e.g., oars not going in together, body of troops marching anyhow), colak-caling; see **step;** ~-worn, dimakan zaman.
timid, adj. pengecut (kecut), bacul, segan, takut-takut
tin, n. the metal, timah; ~-ore, bijih; ore-bearing stratum, karang; block ~, timah jongkong; a ~ (container), 'tin'; to preserve in a ~, mengetin.
tinder, n. rabuk.
tingle, v. intr. berasa (rasa) perit.
tinkle, v. intr. melenting (lenting), berdering (dering), berbunyi (bunyi) tingting.
tinsel, n. perada, mas kerajang.
tiny, adj. terkecil (kecil); esp. of a baby,

kenit; *dwarfish,* kerdil, kerdil, ketut; *see* **minute** *(adj.).*

tip, *n. point,* hujung; *gift,* duit kopi; *pointed ~,* tuntung; *to ~ up on side,* sendengkan; *lenghtways,* jongkitkan; *see* **tilted.**

tipsy, *adj.* mabuk.

tiptoe, *n. on the ~,* berjingkit-jingkit, terginjat-ginjat, bertinjit (tinjit), bertanjak (tanjak) kaki; *running gingerly on ~,* lari bertinjit-tinjit.

tirade, *n.* hamburan atau ucapan marah-marah yang panjang lebar.

tired, *adj.* letih; *~ out,* penat; *(limbs) having lost power,* (anggota) patah layak; *~ out,* tak terlarat (larat); *'dog-~',* melenguh; *see* **sated.**

tiresome, *adj. as a job or a person,* cerewet, renyah.

tissue, *n. bodily ~,* jaringan tubuh; *muscular ~, as opposed to veins,* kelasa; *~ paper,* (kertas) jeluang.

tit for tat, *n. return stroke,* tepuk balas tampar; bagaimana tindakan, begitulah balasannya.

titivate, *v. intr. smarten oneself up,* bersolek (solek); *see* **toilet.**

title, *n. of rank,* gelaran; *of book,* nama, mauzuk, judul, tajuk, gelar; *land ~,* 'geran' tanah; *right,* hak.

titter, *v. intr. & n. giggle,* tertawa berdekah-dekah.

tittle-tattle, *n. malicious gossip,* mengumpat.

to, *prep.* ke, kepada; *~ and fro,* berulang-alik (ulang), mundar-mandir; *~ rock, shake, oscillate (object) ~ and fro, e.g., an object in water, so as ~ cleanse it,* oleng-alingkan; *see* **shake.**

toad, *n.* katak puru.

toast, *n.* roti panggang, 'tos'; minum untuk menghormati seseorang.

tobacco, *n.* tembakau.

today, *adv.* hari ini.

toboggan, *n.* sejenis kereta peluncur yang dipakai dilereng gunung bersalji.

toddle, *v. intr. as a child,* bertatih-tatih; *stumble along,* berjalan (jalan) jatuh-bangkit.

toddy, *n. palm-wine,* tuak.

toe, *n.* jari kaki, *big ~,* ibu jari kaki.

together, *adv.* bersama-sama; berkumpul, *all ~ (at the same moment),* sekali gus; *one escorting the other, in convoy,* beriringan (iring).

toilet, *n. to make one's ~ (of a woman),* berhias (hias), bersolek (solek), berdendan (dendan); *~ requisites,* alat pesolek; *~ paper,* kertas jamban.

token, *n.* tanda, alamat.

tolerable, tolerant, *adj.* sederhana.

tolerate, *v.tr. put up with, leave unmolested,* membiarkan (biar), menahan (tahan) mengizinkan.

tomato, *n.* terung masam, 'tomato'.

tomb, *n. see* **grave.**

tome, *n.* buku yang besar dan berat.

tomorrow, *adv.* besok, esok; *the day after ~,* lusa.

tone, *n. of voice,* nada; *esp. of rising voice,* alunan suara.

tongs, *n.* penyepit, sepit.

tongue, *n.* lidah, lisan; *~ of flame,* lidah api, liukan api; *guard your ~,* jaga mulut; *esp. before dignitaries,* jangan tekebur; *a word spoken cannot be recalled,* telajak (lajak) perahu boleh balik, terlajak cakap tak boleh balik, (*a boat which has gone too far can return; a word which has gone too far cannot);* *for 'slip of ~' see* **slip;** *put out ~,* hulurkan lidah; *with ~ continually shooting in and out, of a snake,* lidahnya terjelir-jelir.

tonight, *n.* malam ini; *the coming night,* malam karang.

tonsils, *n.* biji rengkong; *swollen ~,* penyakit (sakit) tekak.

too, *adv. also,* — juga, — jugak, — jua; *in an excessive degree,* sangat, terlampau (lampau), terlalu (lalu).

tool, *n.* pesawat, perkakas; *appliance,* alat; *~-bag,* karung perkakas; *to use (a person) as a ~ (i.e., for one's own purposes),* memperalatkan, *'~ (cat's paw),* tali barut.

tooth, *n.* gigi*; *large canine ~,* siung; *molar,* geraham; *wisdom ~,* geraham bongsu; *to set the teeth,* mengetapkan (ketap) gigi; *~-pick,* cungkil gigi; *~-brush,* berus gigi; *~ache,* sakit gigi; *~less,* tak bergigi, tinggal gusi sahaja.

top, *n. toy,* gasing; *to play with ~,* main gasing, *(topside),* atas; *summit,* kemuncak; *~-heavy,* berat di atas; *to '~ up' (add a little),* tokok sikit.

topaz, *n.* manikam kuning.

topic, *n. general ~ of conversation,* buah mulut, pokok perbualan (bual); *subject-matter discussed,* perkara.

topple, *v. intr. fall from vertical to horizontal position,* tumbang.

topsy-turvy, *adv.* bongkar-bangkir, golek-galik, tunggang-langgang, lintang-pukang.

torch, *n. resinous,* damar, jamung, andang; *electric ~,* lampu picuit, lampu suluh; *blow-~,* (alat) penyembur (sembur) api; *Olympic ~,* obor Olympik.

torment, *v. tr. torture,* menyiksa (siksa), mendera (dera); menyakiti; *worry,* menganggu (ganggu), menggoda (goda), mengusik (usik).

tornado, *n.* angin puting beliung.

tortoise, *n. (sp.)* kekura (kura-kura), baning, juku-juku; *'~-shell',* kulit karah, sisik karah; *see* **turtle.**

tortuous, *adj.* bongkang, bengkok; berkelok-kelok, berbelit-belit.

torture, *n.* azab; *see* **torment.**

toss, *v. tr. throw high,* lambungkan; *dandle,* timang; *coin, before game,* nenting duit, lontar duit, *~ing, as ship at sea,* toleng-oleng, anggik-anggik; *wave-~ed,* dilambung ombak; *~ed aside (as a garment),* tersepuk (sepuk).

total, *n.* jumlah; *totally, wholly,* habis, sama sekali.

totem, *n.* benda, (binatang, tumbuhan) yang dianggap suci dan berkaitan dengan keluarga.

totter, *v. intr.* huyung-hayang, melilau (lilau); *~ along (as a wounded man),* melelong-lelong.

touch, *v. tr. contact, esp. with hand,* sentuh; *esp. as in feeling something,* tepam, meraba (raba); *put hand on,*

pegang; menjamah (jamah); *come into contact with,* terkena (kena) pada; *handle,* jamah; *~ (at a port),* singgah di-; *~ on, mention,* menyebut (sebut), menyinggung (singgung); *touching, moving the feelings,* yang mengharukan (haru); *sadden,* yang menyedihkan (sedih); *~ down, of a plane, descend,* turun; *actually make contact with the ground,* mencecah (cecah) (tanah); *drooping down and touching — (esp. of hair),* jejak ke —; *get in ~ with (approach for advice, discussions, etc.),* mendapatkan (dapat); *~ing (with regard to),* tentang, berkenaan dengan; *~-stone,* batu uji.

touchy, *adj. easily angered,* lekas marah; *quick to take offence,* bertelinga (telinga) nipis.

tough, *adj. as meat,* liat; *a ~ (rowdy),* samseng.

tour, *v. intr. travel about,* menjelajah (jelajah); *go on a sight-seeing ~,* melancung (lancung); *~ round casually,* bersiar-siar; *go on a study ~ to —,* melawat (lawat) — sambil belajar (ajar); *a ~, trip,* darmawisata; *~nament,* pertandingan, sayembara.

tout, *n.* penjual yang mendesak.

tow, *v. tr. pull after one,* menghela (hela); *as a vessel,* menunda (tunda), menyeret.

towards, *prep.* hala ka-, arah ke; *in relation to,* terhadap (hadap).

towel, *n.* tuala; *face-~,* tuala tangan; *bath-~,* tuala mandi; *sanitary ~,* kain penyerap (serap) kotoran; *(but sometimes cawat is used).*

tower, *n.* menara; *~ing high,* tersergam (sergam), terseranjang (seranjang); menjulang tinggi.

town, *n.* bandar, pekan; *as opposed to country,* negeri; *Town Hall,* dewan bandaran; *~-limits,* lingkungan bandar; *~-planning,* rancangan bandar.

toy, *n.* barang mainan; *to ~, with (finger lightly),* gamak-gamakkan, meraba-raba.

trace, *n. mark left behind,* bekas; *sign,*

tanda; *cut through jungle*, rentis; *marked out for new road*, tapak (jalan); *for fishing-line*, perambut.

track, *n. series of traces showing where something has passed, of wild beasts*, denai, selarung; *path*, lorong; *~s*, *footmarks*, kesan, bekas kaki, jejak; *to ~*, menurut (turut) kesan.

tract, *n. of land*, daerah.

tractable, *adj.* bersifat menurut, penurut, taat.

trade, *v. intr.* berniaga, berdagang (dagang), berjual-beli (jual); *~-mark*, tanda perniagaan, cap dagangan; *President of the Board of Trade*, penguasa (kuasa) lembaga perniagaan (niaga); *free ~*, perdagangan bebas.

tradition, *n. long-established custom*, adat kebiasaan (biasa); *~al religious sayings*, hadis; *tale handed down*, cerita purba kala, cerita warisan.

traffic, *n. coming and going, esp. on road*, lalulintas; *to ~, engage in commerce*, berdagang (dagang); lampu isyarat.

tragedy, *n.* sandiwara sedih; kecelakaan.

tragic, *adj. distressing*, sedih.

trail, *v. tr. draw along behind*, seret; *follow, ikut dari belakang; trailing behind, as a loose appendage*, terjela-jela; *as a crowd, in a long straggling line*, berderai-derai; *the ~ of a comet*, ekor; *to ~ (follow closely)*, mengekor; *as 'weeping' branches*, melampai (lampai).

train, *n. see* **rail;** *to ~ (undergo training)*, berlatih; *trainer (of athletes)*, juru latih; *of fighting animals*, juara; *~ing other than athletic*, pendidikan (didik).

trait, *n. item in character*, sifat, ciri, perangai.

traitor, *n.* perderhaka (derhaka); *'tool', collaborator, 'stooge'*, tali barut; *saboteur*, pengkhianat (khianat); *'tool'*, alat; *to turn ~*, membelut (belut); *see* **column.**

trajectory, *n. of a bullet*, perjalanan (jalan) (peluru); *to rise in ~*, membumbung (bumbung).

tramp, *v. intr. to ~ along*, berjalan dengan langkag yang berat, mengayun (ayun) kaki; *see* **vagrant;** *sound of ~ing*, derap derap; melanyak, memijak.

trample, *v. tr.* pijak; *of the trampling of soil by buffaloes before rice cultivation, or of trampling in general, esp. in anger*, lanyak.

trance, *n. to go into a ~, as a medium*, turun syaikh; *keadaan khayal as immersed in speculation*, lupakan daratan; *as oblivious of surroundings*, lupakan diri.

tranquil, *adj. as life*, tenteram, sentosa, sejahtera; *~ity, n.* ketenangan, kesentosaan.

transact, *v. tr. carry through (business)*, menjalankan (jalan); *~ion*, perjanjian perdagangan.

transcend, *v. tr. pass beyond the range of*, mengatasi (atas), melebihi (lebih), melampaui.

transfer, *v. tr. property*, tukar nama; *change residence*, berpindah (pindah); *change place of work*, tukar tempat kerja, *voluntary conveyance of property*, hebah.

transfixed, *adj. pierced right through*, terpacak (pacak), tembus; *(fig.) rooted to the spot, e.g., by astonishment*, tertegun (tegun); *see* **impale, spit.**

transformation, *n.* perubahan rupa, penjelmaan.

transfuse, *v. tr. see* **blood.**

transgress, *v. tr. esp. a law*, melanggar (langgar), melampaui.

transition, *n.* peralihan, perubahan dari satu keadaan kepada yang lain.

transitory, *adj. of the world*, (alam) fana, (alam) maya.

translate, *v. tr.* menyalin (salin) kepada bahasa —, menjadikan (jadi) bahasa —, menterjemahkan (terjemah).

transliterate, *v. tr.* memindahkan (pindah) huruf ke huruf —.

translucent, *adj.* hening, jernih, lut-cahaya.

transmit, *v. tr. pass on, as news*, menyiarkan (siar); *esp. by radio*, memancarkan (pancar); ~ter, alat peman-car 'radio'.

transparent, adj. jernih, hening; of diaphanous clothing, jarang; obvious, nyata.

transplant, v. tr. memindahkan (pindah); of rice-seedlings, mengubah (ubah).

transpire, v. intr. berpeluh, berlaku.

transport, v. tr. convey on a large scale, mengangkut (angkut); a ship conveying troops, kapal pengangkut tentera; to ~ to new houses or overseas, memindahkan (pindah).

transpose, v. tr. menukar-balikkan (tukar).

trap, n. perangkap; noose, jerat, racik; break-back ~, apit-apit; large marine fish-~s, kelong, jermal, types of river fish-~s, bubu, belat; to set (a ~), tahan; to set up (an elaborate ~), pasang; spring-~, sembat; small cage-~ for birds, jebak; net for birds, lapun; see **noose.**

trapdoor, n. pintu geladak.

travel, v. intr. make a journey, see **journey, tour;** go wandering abroad, merantau (rantau); ~ler' palm, pokok payung; ~ler, pengembara (kembara).

traverse, v. tr. cross, esp. as sea, mengharung (harung); melintang make way through esp. jungle, meredas (redas).

travesty, n. misrepresentation grotesquely incorrect, olok-olok sahaja.

trawler, n. kapal menghela (hela) pukat.

tray, n. metal, talam; wooden, dulang; basket-work, sayak; salver for betelnut, etc., cerana; large elaborate salver, kerikal; small metal ~ (e.g., card-~), ceper; winnowing ~, badang, nyiru.

treachery, n. see **betray, column, traitor,** tidak jujur atau tidak setia, khianat.

tread, v. tr. put foot on, pijak; set foot on (land on), melangkahkan (langkah) kaki ke-menjejak; see **trample.**

treason, n. derhaka; pengkhianatan.

treasure, n. hoard of precious articles, kumpulan mata benda yang bernilai (nilai); ~-trove, harta karun*, harta terpendam (pendam), ~r, orang yang

menjaga perihal kewangan; bendahari.

treasury, n. khazanah, perbendaharaan.

treatment, n. behaviour (to), kelakuan (laku) (terhadap) (hadap), layanan; treat well (be kind to), buat baik dengan; treat badly (be unkind to), buat tak baik dengan, buat tak patut dengan; to treat (a sick person), mengubatkan (ubat), merawat (rawat); to treat (adopt a certain method of dealing with a subject, of a writer), mengolahkan (olah); to treat, subject material to process under heat, masak; to stand treat, menanggung (tanggung) belanja; a 'Dutch treat' (each person paying his own share), belanja Korinci*; an entertainment, jamuan; a favourite enjoyment, suata kegemaran (gemar); great bit of luck, rezeki.

treaty, n. 'teriti', perjanjian (janji); to frame a ~, menyusun (susun) 'teriti'

treble, adj. tiga ganda, lipat tiga.

tree, n. pokok, pohon; shoe-~, (kayu) sengkang kasut; family ~ (genealogical), susur galur (keturunan) keluarga, asal usul.

trellis, n. kisi-kisi.

tremble, v. intr. mengetar (ketar), menggigil (gigil), menggementar (gementar), kerana takut.

tremendous, adj. hebat, sangat besar, dahsyat.

trench, n. ditch, parit; entrenchment, kubu.

trend, n. as of opinion, aliran, arah aliran (fikiran)

trepidation, n. kegemparan, ketakutan.

trespass, v. intr. enter violently, menceroboh (ceroboh) masuk, melanggar (langgar).

trestle, n. kuda-kuda.

trial, n. in Court, bicara, guam; experiment, percubaan (cuba); test, ujian; to have a ~ of strength (with), mengadu (adu) kekuatan (kuat) terhadap (hadap).

triangle, n. segi tiga.

tribe, n. puak, suku.

tribute, *n. payment made in sign of dependence,* ufti; *the golden flower formerly sent to Siam as a sort of ~ by the Northern Malayan States,* bunga* mas; *tributary river,* anak sungai.

trick, *n. stratagem, musihat,* suatu akal; *deceit,* tipu daya; *secret of a mechanical device,* persilapnya; *to ~ (get the better of by a ~,* memperdayakan; *to act ~ily in politics,* main sunglap politik; *see* **cheat.**

trickle, *v. intr.* meleleh (leheh); *drip,* menitik (titik); *in drops, as tears,* berlinang (linang); *as tears or as paint,* berdenih (denih).

tricolour, *n. ~ flag,* bendera corak tiga, bendera berbelang (belang) tiga.

tricycle, *n.* 'basikal' beroda (roda) tiga.

trifling, *adj. as 'no harm done',* bukan apa; *perkara kecil, hal yang tidak penting, of no importance,* remeh; *not amounting to much,* tidak seberapa; *to trifle with (fool with a pretence of, e.g., affection),* memperolokkan (olok).

trigger, *n.* picu, pemetik senapang; *to press (the ~),* memetik (petik).

trim, *v. tr. clip ends,* pangkas; *not baggy, of clothing,* ringkas, rapi; *see* **level, lop.**

trinity, *n. a whole consisting of three parts,* tiga serangkai; *a religious ~,* tiga senyawa, tritunggal.

trio, *n. as of performers,* tiga sekawan, tiga serangkai.

trip, *v. tr. ~ up,* bentih kaki; *see* **stumble;** *to go on a (holiday) ~,* pergi makan angin, melancung (lancung).

tripartite, *adj.* terdiri daripada tiga bahagian.

triple, *adj.* tiga kali lipat; *~ts,* anak kembar tiga.

tripod, *n.* penopang, kamera dll, bangku yang berkaki tiga.

trishaw, *n.* beca (k) roda tiga.

trite, *adj. see* **stale;** *adj.* (fikiran, pendapat perasaan) basi; biasa.

trivial, *adj. commonplace,* perkara basahan; *of no account,* gampang; *(of an event or action),* won't lead to *trouble,* tak akan jadi perkara.

troll, *v. intr. to ~ for fish,* memangcing (pancing) tunda.

troops, *n.* tentera, bala tentera, askar; *in ~ (as monkeys),* (secara) berpuak-puak; *to troop the colour,* mengarak (arak) panji.

trophy, *n. kept as a memento of success,* piala kemenangan (menang).

tropic, *n. ~ of Cancer,* Garisan Sartan; *of Capricon,* Garisan Jadi; *the tropics,* negeri-negeri panas, kawasan hawa panas; *see* **zone.**

trot, *v. intr.* berlari (lari) anak.

trouble, *n. affliction,* kesusahan; *causing such ~,* susah; *don't ~ to,* tak payah; *don't go to a lot of ~,* jangan bersusah payah; *to try to get someone into ~,* cari het; *'make ~', seek a quarrel,* cari fasal; *in ~ (in difficulties),* lorat; *esp. as, pressed by debt,* sesak, dalam kepicikan (picik); *to 'ask for ~' (by some illconsidered action),* buat geruh-gerah; *~-maker,* tukang hasut; *to make ~ (out of some incident, 'make something of it'),* buat fasal.

trough, *n.* palung; *between waves,* lembah gelombang.

trousers, *n.* seluar; *European style,* 'pantalun'; *Indian style,* celana; *jeans,* celana 'paip', jean; *of a woman 'wearing the ~',* kemudi di haluan, *(the helm is in the bows).*

truant, *n. to play ~ from school,* lari dari sekolah, tak menghadiri kelas.

truce, *n.* gencatan senjata.

truck, *n. railway ~,* gerobok.

truckle, *v. intr.* tunduk, merendahkan diri.

trudge, *v. intr. ~ along,* berjalan kaki dengan susah payah, mengayun (ayun) betis.

true, *adj.* benar, sungguh; *yours truly,* yang benar; *truth,* kebenaran; *actual fact,* hakikat; *~, in the sense of racially pure,* jati.

trumpet, *n.* 'terompet'; *a Malay royal ~,* nafiri; *the Last Trump,* sangkakala; *to blow a ~,* meniup (tiup) 'terompet'; *to ~ (of an elephant),* bertempik (tempik), menggeru (geru), berdering (dering); *(fig.) to proclaim loudly, boost,* genbar-gemburkan, heboh-hebohkan; *'blowing one's own ~',* seperti burung cenuk menyebut (sebut) diri, *(like the malkoha repeating its own name).*

truncheon, *n.* tongkat, tongkat waran, martil; belantan kecil.

trunk, *n. of tree,* batang; *base of ~,* perdu; *of elephant,* belalai; *standing dead tree-~,* punggur; *soft ~as of a banana-tree,* rias; *~ call,* (telefon) panggilan jauh.

trust, *v. tr.* kepercayaan, keyakinan, harap pada; *breach of ~ (esp. criminal),* pecah harapan; *~-worthy,* (orang) amanah; *to fail in one's ~,* pecah amanah; *~ed servant, confidential agent,* orang harapan; *~ee,* pemegang (pegang) amanah; *see* **believe.**

truth, *n.* kebenaran, kenyataan, kesungguhan.

try, *v. tr.* cuba berikhtiar, berusaha, *'have a ~',* take a chance, buang nasib; *have a ~! (place your stakes!),* mari tikam!; *~ on (clothes),* mengacukan; *see* **test, trial.**

tub, *n. wooden ~,* tong, tahana; *see* **cask, jar.**

tube, *n.* 'tiub'; *bamboo ~,* pembuluh (buluh); *see* **pipe.**

tuberculosis, *n.* batuk kering, penyakit paru-paru.

tuberose, *n.* bunga sundal malam.

Tuesday, *n.* hari Selasa.

tuft, *n. as of grass or hair,* gombak; *top-knot,* toncit; *long lock or crest,* jambul; *flower-~,* jambak.

tug, *v. tr. pull sharply,* rentak; *~-of-war,* tarik tali; *now comes the ~ of war! (a close contest),* bertemulah (temu) buku dengan ruas, *(the node meets the inter-node); heave,* paut; *as a fish,* enjut; *a ~,* kapal tunda; *see* **pull.**

tuition, *n.* bimbingan, (bimbing) pengajaran (ajar).

tumble, *v. intr & tr.* jatuh tunggang-langgang, jatuh berguling.

tumour, *n.* barah; bengkak, tumbuh.

tumult, *n. in a ~,* heboh, gempar; keributan *see* **row.**

tune, *n.* lagu, nada; *measure, beat,* irama, *to ~ (adjust notes of instrument),* menyamakan (sama) suara, menalakan (tala); *tuning fork,* penala; *out of ~,* 'jangling', janggal.

tunnel, *n. artificial passage through rocks, etc.,* tembusan, terowong; *esp. of railway,* gua keretapi.

tunny, *n.* ikan tongkol, ikan aya.

turban, *n.* serban.

turbid, *adj, of water,* keruh, bukat; *esp. as troubled,* gelodar.

turkey, *n.* ayam peru; *(chiefly among foreigners),* ayam Belanda.

tumeric, *n.* kunyit.

turn, *v. intr. around,* pusing; *~ up (arrive),* datang; *~ up (light),* bersarkan (api); *~ on (as light),* pasang; *~ off,* padam, matikan; *~ on (as water),* buka; *~ off,* tutup; *~ down (light),* perkecilkan (kecil) api, redupkan api; *~ up sound,* kuatkan suara; *~ down sound,* rendahkan suara; *~ over (as a page),* singkap; *~ over, riffle through (pages, papers),* membalik-balikkan (balik); *invert (as a glass),* tonggingkan; *~ over on (its) side,* sendengkan; *~ with a lathe,* melarik (larik); *~ down (request),* tolak; *~ a corner,* membelok (belok) selekoh; *~ head nervously this way and that,* terbelingas (lingas); *~ over, generally,* terbalikkan; *esp. as in righting a boat,* telentangkan (lentang); *~ up (as sleeves),* singsing, sisil; *~ over earth, as by ploughing,* sungkal; *as by rooting (of a pig),* sungkur; *(esp. by digging),* bongkar; *to ~ (a handle),* putarkan; *to change direction,* belok; *to ~ right round,* pusing belakang; *to do a good ~ to,* berbuat (buat) jasa pada; *to '~', begin to '~' sour (esp. as milk),* melawas (lawas); *to ~ over in bed,* berkalih (kalih) tidur; *to ~ into (become),* menjadi (jadi); *(assuming new shape by magic),* menjelma (jelma) menjadi; *up~ed (as box),* tertangkup (tangkup); *taking ~s,* bergilir-gilir, bertukar-ganti (tukar); *diverge,* simpang; *to ~ the head,* paling (kepala); *a ~ing in the road,* simpang; *one's ~,* giliran; *see* **revolve, rotate, upset, upside-down.**

turnip, *n.* lobak.

turquoise, *n.* batu pirus; (batu permata yang hijau kebiru-biruan).

turtle, *n. green ~,* penyu; *leathery ~,* kambau, agal; *~ providing 'tortoise-shell',* karah; *large river ~,* tuntung; *small,* jelebau; *sea ~s, generally,* ibu telur.

tusk, *n. of elephant,* gading; *of boar,* taring; *~-like canine teeth,* siung.

twang, *v. intr. as a bow-string,* berdeting (deting).

tweezers, *n.* angkup-angkup, penyepit (sepit).

twice, *adv. on two occasions,* dua kali, dua embak; *~ three makes six,* dua kali tiga jadi enam; *~ as big,* dua kali lebih besar.

twiddle, *v. tr. this way and that, as a knob,* liang-liukkan, putar-putarkan; *to '~ one's thumbs',* duduk goyang kaki sahaja, *(just sit and swing one's legs).*

twig, *n. ranting; sprig,* carang.

twilight, *n.* waktu senja kala, waktu samar muka.

twinge, *n. of pain,* sengal.

twinkle, *v. intr.* mengerlip (kerlip); *descriptive,* lip lap, lip lap.

twins, *n.* anak kembar.

twirl, *v. tr. as a moustache,* memutarkan (putar); *to spin round quickly, as a top,* ligat.

twist, *v. tr. as in opening a bottle or extracting a screw,* putarkan, liang-liuk; *as yarn,* pilin, pintal; *~ed, as joint,* tergeliat (geliat); *kinked,* terkehel (kehel); *awry,* erut; *to ~ up, as in making rope,* memintal (pintal); *~ and turn, as a restless sleeper,* menggeliat-geliat; *~ed out of true, esp. as a joint,* terpelekoh (pelekoh); *~ing and turning, as a path,* biang-biut; *~ing facts, see* **garble.**

twitch, *v. tr. give a short sharp tug,* enjut; *as tail,* menggenyitkan (genyit); *pull or jerk slightly,* menguitkan (kuit).

twitter, *v. intr.* mengicak (kicak), menggericau (gericau).

type, *n. specimen,* contoh; *having certain attributes,* corak, ragam; *of the same ~,* sebabat; *a '~' (nasty fellow) (sl.),* satu macam; *~writer,* 'mesin' 'taip'; **typist,** juru 'taip'; *see* **shorthand.**

typhoid, *n.* sejenis pentakit usus yang mudah berjangkit.

typhoon, *n.* 'taufan'.

tyrannical, *adj. oppressive,* zalim; *absolute power,* kekuasaan (kuasa), yang sewenang-wenang.

tyre, *n. band round wheel,* kerek; *rubber ~,* 'tayar'; *solid ~,* 'tayar' getah padu.

U

ubiquitous, *adj. occurring everywhere,* terdapat (dapat) di mana-mana pun; *always present, can't get away from it,* ada-ada sahaja; *world-wide,* serata dunia.

udder, *n.* tetek.

ugly, *adj,* hodoh.

ulcer, *n.* barah; *small superficial ~,* benta; *large ~,* cabuk.

ultimatum, *n.* kata-dua.

ultra vires, *adj.* luar kuasa; *to act ~,* melebihi (lebih) kuasa.

umbilical, *adj. ~ cord,* tali pusat.

umbrage, *n.* rasa tersinggung, rasa kecil hati.

umbrella, *n.* payung.

umpire, *n.* orang yang dilantik untuk mengadili pertandingan bolasepak dll; pengadil.

un-, *prefix in the sense of 'not': can often be expressed by placing tidak before the positive form of an adjective: ~becoming (esp. as dress),* tidak senonoh.

unaccountably, *adv. somehow or other,* entah macam mana; *'without rhyme or reason',* tak berfasal-fasal; *tidak dapat di pertanggung-jawabkan.*

unaffected by, *adj. see* **proof.**

unanimous, *adj.* (ahli) semua bersetuju; *~ly,* dengan sebulat suara; *unanimity,* seia sekata.

unbridled, *adj. as anger,* tidak tersekat-sekat.

unceasingly, *adv.* tak putus-putus.

uncertain, *adj. not settled,* tak tentu; *varying, fickle, as times, fate,* pancaroba; *see* **change, fickle.**

uncle, *n.* paman, pakcik; *as polite address to a stranger,* wak.

unclean, *adj. dirty, see* **dirt;** *ceremonially impure, esp. as food,* haram; *detestable, esp. as food,* makruh.

uncoil, *v. tr.* mengorak (orak).

uncomfortable, *adj.* berasa (rasa) tak senang; *as from heat or other cause, 'hot and bothered',* berasa rimas; *feeling ~ (restless, not relaxed),* berasa gelisah.

unconditional, *adj.* tak bersyarat (syarat).

unconscious, *adj. having swooned,* pengsan tidak sedarkan diri; *prostrated by shock,* terbang arwah; *as heedless, esp. of danger,* loleh-loleh; *not realizing, tak sedar (akan); as 'dreaming',* lupakan daratan.

unconstitutional, *adj.* tidak sah di sisi perlembagaan.

uncouth, *adv. see* **rude;** *'rough diamond',* intan yang tidak bersepuh (sepuh).

undecided, *adj.* hesitant, bercabang (cabang) hati, ragu-ragu; *awaiting a decision,* belum putus lagi.

under, *prep.* di bawah.

underdogs, *n. poor and uninfluential people,* orang bawahan; *see* **underprivileged.**

underdone, *adj. not fully cooked,* kurang masak.

undergo, *v. tr.* menanggung (tanggung), menderita (derita); *incur, kena; meet danger or test,* menempuh (tempuh); *be subjected to, punishment, training,* menjalani (jalan).

undergraduate, *n.* mahasiswa (yang belum berijazah).

underground, *adv.* di bawah tanah; *to work '~', esp. of insidious subversion,* menggungting (gunting) kain dalam lipatan; *see* **column, intrigue, subvert.**

undergrowth, *n.* semak.

underhand, *adj. in a secretive manner,* secara gelap, curi-curi.

underling, *n.* orang bawahan; *staff, esp.*

subordinate staff, kaki tangan.

undermine, *v. tr.* menggali (gali) di-bawah; melemahkan dasarnya. *see* **underground.**

under-nourished, *adj.* tidak mendapat makanan yang berzat.

under-privileged, *adj. not in a prosperous state,* ~ *communities,* kaum mela-rat.

underrate, *v. tr. look upon as unimportant or (as a task) too easy,* buat mudah, mencuaikan (cuai).

under-signed, *adj.* yang bertanda (tanda) tangan di bawah ini.

understand, *v. tr.* mengerti (erti), faham.

undertake, *v. tr. as a duty,* sanggup; ~ *to -* , mengaku (aku) nak - .

undertone, *n. lowered voice,* suara rendah.

undertow, *n. backwash of waves under the surface,* arus songsang.

underwear, *n.* pakaian dalam.

undignified, *adj. (of behaviour),* hilang marwah.

undisciplined, *adj. of troops, not trained,* tidak terlatih (latih); *won't listen to instructions,* tak makan ajar; *refractory, begar.*

undo, *v. tr. as knot,* rongkal; *as hair,* uraikan; *unfasten,* buka.

undoubtedly, *adv.* tentu, nescaya, tidak syak lagi.

undress, *v. tr.* buka pakian, tanggalkan pakaian.

undue, *adj.* tak patut, tidak wajar, tidak pada tempatnya.

undulating, *adj, of land,* tinggi-rendah; *as broken country,* berbukti-bukau (bukit); *as drawn lines,* berombak (ombak).

undutiful, *adj.* derhaka.

uneasy, *adj.* tak sedah hati, khuatir.

unemployed, *adj. having no job,* tak bekerja (kerja); *out of work,* menganggur (anggur).

uneven, *adj, odd, of numbers,* ganjil; *as surface,* tidak rata; *full of little holes or puddles, of road,* lekok-lekok; *as sewing or as crinkled paper,* keretut; *as*

badly cut hair or hedge, tokak-takik, capuk-capuk; *see* **undulating.**

unexpected, *adj.* tak disangka; *the* ~ *always happens,* mujur tidak berbunyi (bunyi), malang tidak berbau (bau), *(i.e., good luck makes no noise, bad luck has no smell).*

unfair, *adj. not right,* tidak patut; *not impartial,* berat sebelah; *gross injustice,* aniaya; *to act unfairly,* elat; *see* **cheat, discriminate.**

unfaithful, *adj. esp. as spouse,* curang.

unforgettable, *adj. (engraved on the heart),* tergoris (goris) di hati; tidak dapat dilupai.

unfortunate, *adj. see* **luck;** ~*ly* -, sayangnya -

ungrateful, *adj.* tidak mengenang (kenang) budi; *often expressed by the aphorism the bean forgets its pod,* kacang melupakan (lupa) kulit.

uniform, *n.* ~ *dress,* 'unifom', pakaian seragam; *conforming to the same standard,* seragam; *similar,* serupa; *of* ~ *size,* sama besar; ~*ity, consistency,* kesa-ragaman.

unify, *v. tr.* menyatukan (satu), gabungkan; *so as to have one being,* senyawakan; *see* **blend, united.**

unilaterally, *adv. acting on one's own,* secara bersendiri (sendiri).

unimportant, *adj.* alang kepalang; tidak penting

union, *n. of workers,* kesatuan (satu) buruh; *of States,* kesatuan; *(merger),* percantuman (cantum), serikat, syarikat.

unique, *adj. only one of its kind,* tunggal; *unequalled,* tak berbanding, (banding).

united, *adj.* bersatu (satu); *in concord, esp. politically,* bersatu-padu; *all pulling together,* serentak; *cohering, as particles,* bertaup (taup); *unitary State,* negara kesatuan; *United Nations,* Bangsa-bangsa Bersatu; *United States,* Amerika Syarikat; *United Arab Republic,* Republic Arab Bersatu; *doctrine of the unity of God,* tauhid; *to unite, combine, as parties,* bergabung

(gabung); ~ *we stand, divided we fall,*
bersatu teguh, bercerai (cerai) runtuh.

universal, *adj. all over the world,* merata-
rata dunia, di seluruh dunia; *applicable
to all cases,* meliputi (liput), umum;
~ly, adv. secara menyeluruh.

universe, *n.* alam semesta.

unlawful, *adj.* melawan (lawan) undang-
undang, tidak sah pada undang-
undang; *esp. as breach of religious
law,* haram.

unless, *conj.* kalau tidak, kecuali.

unlimited, *adj.* tak berhad (had), tak ber-
sukat (sukat).

unload, *v. tr. as cargo,* punggah; *a gun,*
buang (cabut) kartus.

unlock, *v. tr.* buka (kunci).

unlucky, *adj. esp. as a day not right for an
enterprise,* nahas; *see* **luck.**

unmanly, *adj.* bukan lelaki, dayus.

unmarried, *adj. (bachelor or widow(er)),*
bujang; *without encumbrances,*
bujang talang.

unobtainable, *adj. not on sale,* tak terbeli
(beli).

unpack, *v. tr.* ~ *contents,* bongkar; *see*
unload.

unpick, *v. tr. as a rope,* tetas.

unpropitious, *adj. as day for action,*
nahas; *see* **unlucky.**

unprovoked, *adj. as an attack,* tak berfasal-fasal.

unqualified, *adj. without conditions,* tak
bersyarat (syarat); *complete, as support,* credence, sepenuh-penuh, bulat-
bulat, melulu (lulu); *not fit for post,* tak
layak; *not having passed the necessary
examination,* tak berkelulusan (lulus);
not certificated, tak bertauliah
(tauliah); *not an expert in the science
of-,* bukan ahli ilmu.

unravel, *v. tr.* mengorak (orak), mengurai
(urai).

unrecognisable, *adj. as a mutilated
corpse,* tak berketahuan (tahu) rupa.

unreliable, *adj.* tak berkepercayaan (percaya), tak boleh harap; *mere plausible
talker,* lidah tak bertulang (tulang);
empty braggart, golok kayu, cakap

besar.

unrest, *n. esp. political,* kegelisahan
(gelisah); *see* **disorders.**

unripe, *adj.* belum masak, *still hard,* kirau;
fully formed, but not ripened, mengkal.

unseated, *p.p. of an elected member,* terlucut (lucut) dari kerusinya; *from a
horse,* terjatuh (jatuh), tercampak
(campak).

unsightly, *adj.* buruk, menyakitkan mata.

unsophisticated, *adj. artless, not used to
worldly ways,* belum tahu hal; *simple,*
bodoh; *'raw',* mentah; *'green',* hijau;
lacking worldly experience, belum
banyak makan garam; *not mature,* belum lepas laku.

unspeakable, *adj.* tak terkata-kata lagi,
jangan sebut!, *see* **indescribable.**

unsporting, *adj. see* **cheat, unfair;** *to
play rough,* main kasar; *can't take a
beating,* terkena pada batang masam
muka, *(i.e., cheering when he gets into
a fish, scowling when he gets into a
log).*

unsteady, *adj. moving unevenly, jerky,*
terincut-incut; *see-sawing up and
down, as a plank when trodden on,*
jongkang-jongkit; *not firmly fixed,* tidak tetap; *shaky in construction,* gegai;
as a post, goyah; *walking or talking
unsteadily (from weakness),* meraban
(raban).

untidy, *adj. esp. of dress,* serbah-serbih;
of hair, terurai (urai), kusut-masai, rupa
nenek Semang; *as a room,* semak
sungguh (sl.); *littered with things,*
bersepahan (sepah).

until, *conj.* sampai, sehingga.

untreated, *adj. of materials,* mentah.

unwell, *adj.* tak sedap badan; *see* **sick.**

unwilling, *adj.* segan, enggan.

unwind, *v. tr.* mengorak (orak).

unworthy, *adj. as for post, honours,* tidak
layak; *deemed ~ of notice (as a petition, etc.),* disifatkan seperti kentut
semut.

unyielding, *adj. persisting in course,*
berkeras (keras) sahaja.

up, *adv.* atas; *see* **ascend;** *life has its ups*

and downs, air ada pasang surutnya; the ~s and downs of life's destiny, tenggelam timbulnya nasib hidup, peredaran (edar) dunia.

up-country, n. sebelah ulu, sebelah darat, daerah pendalaman (dalam).

uphill, adv. to go up a hill, naik bukit; a way going ~, gun, jalan mendaki (daki).

uphold, v. tr. menyokong (sokong), mendukung (dukung).

upkeep, v. tr. look after, jaga; cherish carefully, bela; maintain, selenggara; cost of ~ is excessive, mahal tali dari kerbau, (the buffalo's rope costs more than the buffalo).

upper, adj. sebelah atas.

uppish, adj. bersifat (sifat) naik daun, sombong, angkuh; see **cheek.**

upright, adj. vertical, tegak; in character, jujur.

uproar, n. hingar-bangar, gegak gempita, riuh-rendah; esp. at a 'stormy' meeting, keributan (ribut), riuh-heboh; see **commotion.**

uproot, v. tr. pull up, cabut; tear out roots and all, membantunkan (bantun).

upset, p.p. terbalik (balik), telangkup (langkup); mentally, risau; hard to ~, of a boat, tahan golek.

upside-down, adj. bottom-up, see **upset;** head-over-heels, tunggang-langgang; head downwards, kepala ke bawah; inverted, sungsang.

upstairs, n. atas loteng.

upstart, adj. expressed as, a newly straightened humpback, bongkok baharu betul; and a blind man who has newly got his sight, si buta baharu celik; presumptuous ~, kaduk naik junjung, (the (worthless) kaduk vine climbs the pole meant for the betel vine); noveau riche, orang kaya baharu; ungrateful ~, see **ungrateful.**

upstream, adv. sebelah ulu; to travel ~,

mudik.

urban, adj. berkenaan dgn. kota (bandar).

urbane, adj. berbudi bahasa, sopan-santun.

urge, v. tr. move to action, ajak; press, mendesak (desak), mendorong (dorong), mengesa (gesa); the ~ of the senses, godaan nafsu; urgently, dengan segera.

urine, n. air kencing; to urinate, mengencing, buang air kecil; diuretic, medicine to promote urination, ubat melawaskan (lawas) kencing.

usage, n. customary practice, adat kebiasaan (biasa); manner of using, pemakaian (pakai).

use, v. tr. pakai; make ~ of, put to ~, menggunakan (guna); ~ful, berguna; ~ as a tool to forward one's own purposes, memperalatkan (alat); ~less, tak jadi benda, sia-sia sahaja; past service, tak terpakai; (1) used to ~, dahulu (saya) ~.

usual, n. biasa, lazim; as ~, seperti biasa; ~ly, biasanya, selalunya, pada umumnya; on normal days, sehari hari.

usurp, v. tr. seize (power), merebut (rebut) kuasa; merampas (kuasa, takhta).

usury, n. excessive interest, riba; see **interest;** usurer, lintah darat, (land horse-leech).

uterus, n. rahim; of a pregnant woman, tian.

utilise, v. tr. menggunakan (guna).

Utopia, n. imaginary country, negeri antah-berantah.

utter, v. tr. mengucap (ucap), suarakan; enunciation, tuturan; adj. sama sekali, sesungguhnya.

utterly, adv. completely, sehabis-habis, langsung

uttermost, adj. paling, utmost.

uvula, n. anak lidah, anak tekak.

V

vacant, adj. kosong, lowong; *vacancy,* tempat kosong.

vacate, v. tr. cease from occupying, meninggalkan (tinggal).

vacation, n. waktu tidak bekerja, cuti, liburan.

vaccinate, v. tr. tanam cacar, cucuk; *vaccine,* ibu cacar, benih cacar, ubat cucuk; *vaccination certificate,* surat cucuk.

vacillate, v. intr. show indecision, raguragu, bimbang; *'blow hot and cold',* sorong sentak.

vacuum, n. tempat kosong tidak berudara (udara), tempat hampa udara; ~ *brake,* 'brek' angin; ~-*cleaner,* pembersih hampagas.

vagabond, n. see **vagrant.**

vagary, n. canda, luarbiasa, anih (tentang tingkah laku dan sebagainya).

vagina, n. saluran peranakan (anak).

vagrant, n. orang bangsat; *traveller here and there,* pengembara (kembara); *to live the life of a* ~, hidup merempat (rempat) ke sana ke mari, bertandang (tandang) desa; *a 'drifter',* orang hanyut; *see* **nomads.**

vague, adj. not clear, samar-samar, umum.

vain, adj. haughty, sombong; *fond of posing,* suka berlagak (lagak); *in* ~, sia-sia, cuma-cuma; *tired out for nothing,* buat penat sahaja.

valediction, n. selamat tinggal, minta diri, kata-kata ucap selamat (perpisahan).

valetudinarian, n. person compelled or disposed to live the life of an invalid, tahi penyakit (sakit).

valid, adj. sah; *as coin,* laku.

valley, n. lembah, lurah; ~ *floor,* lembahan.

value, n. harga, nilai; *valuable,* berharga, bernilai; *expensive,* mahal; *to* ~ *(appraise),* nilaikan, taksirkan.

vampire, n. evil spirit, pontianak, langsuir, penanggalan.

vandal, n. one who commits brutish mischief, pengkhianat (khianat); orang yang suka merosakkan hasil-hasil seni, keindahan alam dsd.

vanished, p.p. not to be seen in usual place, sudah tak ada; *lost and gone,* hilang; *disappeared,* lenyap; *as by magic,* ghaib; *as a past era,* luput.

vapour, n. wap; *to have a* ~ *bath,* bertangas (tangas), mandi wap.

varicocele, n. huluran.

variety, n. a class of things; *varieties in sound, colouring, amusements, etc.,* ragam; *various,* bermacam-macam serba neka; ~ *show,* pertunjukan (tunjuk) anika ragam.

varnish, n. sampang, minyak 'bernis'; *glaze,* sepuh.

vase, n. pasu (bunga).

vaulted, adj. of roof, kubah; *the vault of heaven,* cakerawala.

veer, v. intr. of wind, berkisar (kisar); berubah hala (haluan).

vegetable, n. sayur; *vegetation,* tumbuh-tumbuhan; ~s *side-dishes,* ulam; *vegetarian,* orang yang berpantang (pantang) makan daging.

vegetate, v. intr. to live like a plant without seeing the world and without ideas, duduk seperti katak di bawah tempurung, *(to live, like a frog under a coconut-shell).*

veil, n. tudung muka, kelubung; *closely* ~*ed,* bertudung lingkup; *to* ~, hang down, as hair, so as to cover, melingkupi; ~*ed treats,* ugutan, berselindung (selindung); *won by women pilgrims,* bergok; *women's praying*-~, telekung.

vein, *n.* urat (darah); *jugular ~,* urat leher; *artery,* pembuluh (buluh) darah; *~ of leaf,* lidi; *~ed, of wood,* berlorik-lorik, barik, corik.

velocity, *n.* lajunya.

velvet, *n.* beledu; *'on ~', 'sitting pretty' (free grub and no work),* makan tanggung, berak cangkung *(coarse).*

venerate, *v. tr.* memuliakan (mulia), menghormati (hormat), segani.

venereal, *adj. ~ disease,* sakit perempuan, sakit kelamin; *gonorrhea,* sakit kencing nanah; *syphilis,* 'siflis'.

veneer, *n. gloss,* sepuh.

vengeance, *n.* bela; *to take ~,* menuntut (tuntut) bela, membalas (balas) dendam; *see* **avenge, revenge.**

venomous, *adj.* beracun, berbisa, menaruh dendam.

vent, *n. small orifice,* liang (udara); *to ~ one's spite,* melepaskan (lepas) dendam.

veranda, *n.* beranda, serambi.

verge, *n. border strip,* pinggiran.

vermicelli, *n.* laksa, mihun; *cylinder for making ~,* kebuk.

vermin, *n. agricultural pests generally,* mara; *of the body,* kutu.

versatile, *adj. quick to deal with contigencies,* pantas akal; yang cergas dan pintar dalam berbagai perkara.

verse, *n. of poem,* rangkap (syair).

versus, *prep. against,* lawan.

vertebrae, *n.* ruas tulang belakang.

vertebrate, *n.* binatang bertulang belakang, haiwan verteberit.

vertical, *adj.* tegak lurus.

vertigo, *n.* gayat; hal pening kepada, pusing kepala, pitam.

very, *adv.* sangat, terlalu; *'uncommonly',* bukan main; *not ~,* tak berapa.

vest, *n.* baju dalam; memberi hak kepada.

veterinary surgeon, *n.* 'doktor' binatang, 'doktor' haiwan.

veto, *n. right of ~,* hak undi membatal (batal), kuasa penentangan (tentang).

vex, *v. tr. continually annoy,* menyakat (sakat) mengganggu; *pester,* merundung (rundung).

via, *prep. by way of,* melalui (lalu).

vibrate, *v. intr.* bergentar (gentar), menggeletar (geletar).

vice, *n. immorality,* maksiat; *anti-~ squad,* pasukan pencegah maksiat; *the appliance,* ragum.

vice-versa, *adv.* (dan) akasnya, (dan) sebaliknya.

vicious, *adj. of animals, generally,* jahat, buruk, ganas; *of a large animal,* barak; *esp. of a horse,* candi; *~ spiral,* kenaikan sesuatu akibat kenaikan yang berterusan bagi benda lain.

vicissitudes, *n. the ~ of life,* peredaran (edar) dunia; *like grass in the middle of the road, now up, now down,* engkapengkip bagai rumput di tengah jalan; *see* **up.**

victim, *n.* korban, mangsa.

victory, *n.* kemenangan (menang), kejayaan (jaya); *fruits of ~,* hasil kemenangan; *a Pyrrhic ~ (~ that is as bad as a defeat),* untung sekarung, rugi seguni, *(winning a bagful and losing a sackful),* menang sabung, kampung tergadai (gadai), *(winning a cock-fight but pawning your home (to do it)).*

victuals, *n. food-stuffs,* barang makan; *supplies, esp. for a journey,* bekalan; *esp. for an army,* pelabur (labur).

vie, *v. intr. to strive in rivalry,* berdahulu-dahuluan (dahulu), bersaing (saing), merebut (rebut).

view, *n. expanse presented to the eye,* pemandangan (pandang), awas; *considered opinion,* timbangan, hemat; *conclusion,* pendapatan (dapat); *point of ~,* segi, sudut.

vigilant, *adj. see* **alert.**

vilify, *v. tr.* mencemarkan (cemar) nama, mencaci (caci).

village, *n.* kampung; *New Villages (under the Emergency Regulations),* kampung pemindahan (pindah); *~ belle,* seri kampung.

villainous, *adj.* durjana.

vindicate, *v. tr. remove a stigma from the reputation of,* menghapuskan (hapus) arang dari nama; *show truth of,* membuktikan (bukti) kebenaran (benar); *establish merit of (e.g., policy)*, mengisahkan (sah); *see* **justify.**

vindictive, *adj.* menaruh dendam, pendendam.

vinegar, *n.* cuka.

violate, *v. tr. rights,* mencabul (cabul); *see* **breach, rape.**

violence, *n.* kekerasan (keras), pencerobohan (ceroboh); aniaya, angkara.

violin, *n.* biola; *to play the* ~, gesek biola.

viper, *n.* ular kapak.

virgin, *n. (female),* anak dara; *(male),* anak teruna; *Virgin Mary,* Siti Meriam; ~*ity,* dara, bikir; *(fig),* pati santan; *see* **hymen.**

viscous, *adj.* kental.

visible, *adj. as having come into sight,* nampak, tampak; *perceptible to the eye,* ketara; *visibility,* batas pemandangan (pandang).

vision, *n. object seen in imagination,* khayalan; *a revelation through a* ~ *or dream,* wahi; *apparition,* penjelmaan (jelma); ~*s of the future,* angan-angan, visi; *for power of* ~, *sight, see* **sight.**

visit, *v. tr.* melawat (lawat), mengunjung (kunjung), *'drop in',* mampir; ~ *a shrine or a sick person,* menziarah (ziarah); *have an audience with,* menghadap (hadap), ~*ing card,* 'kad' nama, *a short* ~, lawatan sengkat.

visualize, *v. tr.* angan-angankan, menggambarkan (gambar) dalam hati.

vitamin, *n.* 'vitamin', zat 'vitamin'.

vivid, *adj. of colour,* gamat, cerah, jelas, terang, bersemangat.

vocabulary, *n.* kitab tughat; daftar kata, kosa kata, perbendaharaan kata.

vociferous, *adj. loud and insistent in speech,* riuh-mulut, riuh-rendah.

voice, *n.* suara; ~-*pipe (e.g., on a ship),* saluran suara; *see* **enunciation, volatile,** *adj. evaporating rapidly,* mudah menghawa (hawa), mudah menguap (uap); *see* **evaporate.**

volcano, *n.* gunung berapi; *active* ~, gunung berapi hidup; *extinct* ~, gunung api mati; *see* **crater, erupt.**

volley, *n. to fire a* ~, menembak (tembak) sekali gus.

voluntarily, *adv. acting on one's own,* dengan bersendiri (sendiri).

volunteer, *v. intr. to offer oneself,* menawarkan (tawar) diri; ~*s (troops),* tentera sukarela.

vomit, *v. intr.* muntah; *see* **nausea.**

vote, *n.* suara; *ballot,* undi; *ballot-box,* peti undi; *voting-station,* tempat mengundi; *constituency,* kawasan mengundi; ~*r,* pengundi; *right to* ~, hak memilih (pilih); *casting* ~, undi pemutus (putus); *to propose a* ~ *of no confidence in* -, memajukan (maju) usul tidak percaya kepada -; *out-*~*d,* kalah suara , kalah undi; *to* ~ *for,* mengundi menyokong (sokong); *to* ~ *against,* mengundi menentang (tentang); *a* ~ *of money, financial provision,* peruntukan (untuk).

vow. *v. intr.* berniat (niat); bernazar (nazar); *pledge oneself,* berikrar (ikrar); *fulfil a* ~, membayar (bayar) niat, membayar kaul.

vouchsafe, *v. tr.* sudi memberikan (sst) atau berbuat (sst); ~ *a reply,* sudi menjawab.

voyage, *n.* pelayaran (layer).

vulgar, *adj. coarse,* kesar; *mannerless,* biadab.

vulture, *n.* burung reng; (burung nasar).

vying, *v. intr.* merebut, bersaingan.

W

wad, *n.* nal; *stopper,* penyumbat (sumbat), sendal.

waddle, *v. intr.* berjalan (jalan) berlenggang-lenggang, jalan teregehegeh, berjalan terkedek-kedek.

wade, *v. intr.* merandai (randi); *ford,* mengharung.

wag, *v. tr. as a dog its tail,* mengotek-ngotekkan (kotek) (ekor); *very vigorously,* mengibas-ngibaskan (kibas) (ekor); *the ~tail,* burung kedidi bukit.

wages, *n.* gaji; *for task,* upah.

waggle, *v. tr. to ~ to and fro, e.g., when cleaning something in the water,* oleng-alingkan; bergoyang, menggoyangkan.

waif, *n. having no home,* orang hanyut; *see* **vagrant, wander.**

wail, *v. intr.* meratap (rata); menangisi.

waist, *n.* pinggang; *~ of ship,* peminggang kapal.

wait, *v. intr. as desist,* nanti; *~ for,* tunggu; *~ for expectantly,* menantikan (nanti); *'count the days'* duduk bilang hari; *~ing-room,* bilik menunggu; *~ a moment!,* nanti dahulu!; *~ on (as at table),* melayan (layan).

waive, *v. tr. remit a debt,* halalkan.

wake, *n. of a ship,* aluran (kapal); *eddies caused by passage,* olak yang disebabkan oleh lintasan kapal; *in the ~ of,* berikutan dengan, sesudah, setelah; *see* **awake.**

wale, *n. weals, on skin,* balur-balur, bilai, bilur; *cane-marks,* bekas rotan.

walk, *v. intr.* berjalan (jalan) kaki; *'pound along',* berjalan dengan langkah yang berat; *'~ out' (as from a meeting),* angkat kaki; *go for a ~ (take the air),* makan angin; *stroll about,* bersiar (siar); *get a ~-over (in a contest or an election),* menang dengan tak payah bertanding (tanding).

wall, *n. solid,* tembok; *more filmsy, esp. as inner ~,* dinding; *~-eyed,* mata bular.

wallet, *n.* saku, uncang, kantung; dompet.

wallow, *v. intr.* berkubang (kubang).

walrus, *n.* gajah mina; *same as* anjing laut.

wander, *v. intr.* berjalan (jalan) tak tentu arah, merayau (rayau), mengembara (kembara); *esp. as nomads,* melara (lara); *go '~ing,* merantau (rantau); *~ here and there, having no fixed abode,* bertandang (tandang), merempat (rempat); *to ~ mentally, as in a fever,* lupakan diri, tak sedarkan diri; *~ in speech, talk incoherently,* meraban (raban); *see* **delirious.**

wane, *v. intr. get less,* berkurang (kurang); *susut esp. as moon,* susut; *as power,* mundur.

want, *v. tr.* mahu; hendak, memerlukan (perlu); *don't ~,* tak mahu, tak sir; *need,* hendak; *long for,* ingin; *see* **crave, require.**

wanton, *adj.* nakal, galak, suka bermain-main.

wantonly, *adv.* dengan sewenang-wenang, dengan sembarangan.

war, *n.* perang; *cold ~,* perang dingin; *holy ~,* perang sabil; *declaration of ~,* perisytiharan perang (isytihar); *~ of nerves,* perang urat saraf; *~ of words,* perang mulut; *cold ~,* perang dingin; *civil ~,* perang saudara; *~like, bellicose,* bersemangat (semangat) perang; *the art of ~,* keahlian (ahli) perang; *~-ship,* kapal* perang.

warden, *n. of hostel,* pengawal (kawal) asrama.

ward off, *v. tr. a blow,* menepis, menangkis.

wardrobe, *n. cupboard,* almari, gerobok.

warehouse, *n.* gudang, gedung.

warm, *adj. moderately hot,* siau; *to ~ up (food, water),* jerangkan, perhangatkan (hangat); *see* **hot, tepid;** *a ~ welcome,* sambutan yang hangat.

warn, *v. tr. by advice,* ajar; *by admonition,* beri amaran; *by prohibition,* larang; *bid beware,* suruh jaga; *~ing! (as heading to a notice or a bit of moralising),* ingat!, hubaya-hubaya!; *take heed!, observè!,* awas!; *look out!,* jaga!

warp, *v. intr.* meleding (leding); *the ~ (in weaving),* loseng, keadaan bengkok, melengkung.

warrior, *n.* parajurit, jurit; *~-chief,* panglima.

wart, *adj.* ketuit.

wary, *adj. acting with caution,* berhati-hati; *apprehensive of danger, of game,* cega; *on the qui vive,* berwaspada (waspada); *looking nervously this way and that,* terbelingas (lingas).

wash, *v. tr.* (basuh); *clean,* cuci, bersihkan; *~-up (dishes),* cuci pinggan mangkuk; *~ the hands,* basuh tangan; *to ~ for tin-ore,* melampan (lampan); *~ed up (on the beach),* terdampar (dampar) (di pantai); *~able (of clothes),* tahan cuci; *~er-man,* 'dobi', benara; *~ed out, see* **fade;** *sea-~ed rock,* batu mandi ombak; *to ~ away, carry in current,* mengalirkan (alir), menghanyutkan (hanyut); *see* **erode;** *to be ~ed away,* berhanyut, dibawa harus; *to ~ one's hands of an enterprise, drop out,* melepaskan (lepas) tangan; *for ~ of a chip, see* **wako.**

wasp, *n.* penyengat (sengat); *hornet,* tebuan; *blue ground-~,* aning-aning.

waste, *v. tr. expend to no purpose (money),* membazir; *~ (money), on frivolities,* 'jolikan'; *~ one's life,* mensia-siakan diri; *(time),* buang masa, hilang masa; *mere ~ of time,* sia-sia sahaja; *~ful (as a spend-thrift),* boros; *to ~ away (in sickness),* merana (rana); *~r (having no roots),* orang hanyut; *~ products (left after processing),* hampas; *~ land, see* **desert;** *see* **dissipate, vain.**

watch, *v. tr. look after,* jaga, berwaspada; *as a spectator,* tengok, menonton (tuntun); *keep ~,* tunggu; *~ over, as a sentry,* mengawal (kawal); mengawasi; *~man,* (orang) jaga; *a ~,* jam; *wristwatch,* jam tangan; *see* **alert.**

water, *n.* air, *~y, sloppy,* bonyor, benyai; *to ~ (of eyes),* berair; *to ~ (plants),* jirus air, siram air; *by springling or splashing,* menyimbah (simbah); *~-lily,* bunga teratai; *~ lotus,* bunga telipuk; *~-rail,* burung sintar; *~-cock,* ayam-ayam; *~-hen,* ruak-ruak; *~-spout,* puting-beliung; *~-proof,* tahan air; *a ~proof,* baju hujan; *~wings,* pelampung (lampung) berenang (renang); *~-supply,* bekalan air; *~-level,* paras air; *~line,* garisan air; *~-hyacinth,* keladi bunting; *~-wheel,* kincir; *~-gate, sluice-gate,* pintu air; *~ of life,* air utama jiwa; *holy ~,* air tolak bala; *to ~ (of the mouth),* menggecar (gecar); *see* **dribble, saliva;** *~s pertaining to a country,* perairan.

wattle, *n. wicker hurdle,* sasak.

wave, *n.* ombak, gelombang; *roller,* alun; *radio ~,* gelombang 'radio'; *wavy (of hair),* ikal manis; *naturally wavy,* ikal asli; *to ~, brandish,* lambaikan; *to ~ hand,* lambaikan tangan; *see* **brandish;** *to ~ slowly to and fro, as a fan,* melewa-lewakan; *to ~ (as a flag),* kibarkan; *to ~, as a field of grain in the wing,* meliuk-liuk; *crest of a ~,* puncak golombang; *trough of ~,* lombah gelombang; *see* **curl.**

waver, *v. intr. be undecided,* ragu-ragu, tergak-agak.

wax, *n.* lilin; *sealing-~,* lak, malau; *~ in the ears,* tahi telinga; *~ vestas,* 'macis' bersepuh (sepuh) lilin; *to ~ (bigger),* bertambah (tambah) (besar); *sealing-~ palm,* pokok linau.

way, *n.* jalan; *to ask the ~,* tanya jalan; *this ~ (direction),* ikut jalan ini; *this ~ (like this),* begini; *on the ~,* tengah jalan; *half-~,* separuh jalan; *~s and means,* daya upaya; *out of the ~!,* lalu!; *make*

~!, tepi sedikit; *open the* ~, beri jalan; *give* ~ *(yield),* tunduk, mengalah (alah); *a* ~ *through (though not a regular path),* lorongan; *to make* ~ *through (e.g. a crowd),* melulus (lulus); *for plan, scheme; for ~s, see* **behaviour;** *on the* ~ *(while passing),* sambil lalu; *that's his* ~ *(he's always like that),* dia memang begitu.

we, *pron. you and I,* kita; *excluding the person spoken to,* kami, saya, saya orang.

weak, *adj.* lemah, daif; ~ *spot (as in character or plan),* cacat, keburukan (buruk) *a* ~ *solution,* larut cair ; *see* **puny.**

weal, *n. see* **wale.**

wealthy, *adj.* kaya, hartawan; *the* ~, orang kaya-raya.

weaned, *adj.* cerai susu.

weapon, *n.* senjata.

wear, *v. tr.* pakai; *hard-~ing,* tahan lasak; ~ *in hair or behind ear,* suntingkan; *as an Order or bandolier across chest,* menyandang (sandang); ~ *off, gradually cease,* hilang; *see* **worn.**

wearisome, *adj. to be* ~, menjemukan (jemu), membosankan (bosan), melelahkan (lelah).

weather, *n.* keadaan (ada) udara, cuaca; *~-beaten,* makan dek hari; ~ *forecast,* ramalan cuaca; ~ *bureau,* pangkalan menyukat (sukat) cuaca; *~-cock (revolving pointer showing direction of wind),* baling-baling; *(fig.) changeable person,* macam kelembuai; *see* **cloud, rain, season, storm.**

weave, *v. tr.* tenun; ~*r,* tukang tenun; ~*r-bird,* burung tempu, ciak raya.

web, *n. of spider,* sarang (labah-labah); *to weave such a* ~, merakut (rakut); ~-*footed,* berkaki (kaki) itik.

wedding, *n.* perkawinan (kawin); *formal* ~ *feast,* walimat al'arus; ~ *reception,* majilis sambutan kawin; *see* **marriage, marry.**

wedge, *n.* baji; ~*d in,* terselit (selit); *to put something to serve as a* ~ *(e.g., to keep a door open),* menyendalkan (sendal); *peg serving to* ~, pasak; *a chock,* kayu

(batu) sengkang; *'the thin end of the* ~', lulus benang, lulus kelindan, *(if the thread goes through, the cord will go through).*

wedlock, *n.* keadaan menjadi suami isteri.

Wednesday, *n.* hari Rabu.

weeds, *v. tr.* merumput (rumput), menyuci (cuci) rumput; ~ *of all sorts,* rumput-rampai.

week, *n.* minggu, sejumaat, sepekan.

weep, *v. intr.* menangis (tangis); *a weeping tree (with thick drooping branches),* pokok rendang melempai (lempai).

weevil, *v. tr.* bubuk; *fruit-~,* kelarah.

weigh, *v. tr. find weight of or consider,* timbang; *weight,* beratnya; ~*ing machine,* 'mesin' timbang; *see* **scales;** *to put on weight (get fat),* tubuh bertambah subur (sl); *to lose weight,* susut tubuh; *'chuck weight about' (be pompous),* membesarkan (besar) diri; *a weight (on a horse),* bawaan, pukulan; *(on a line),* ladung kail; *(on scales),* batu dacing; *to sell by (catty) weight,* berjual (jual) timbang (kati); *weight-lifter,* pengangkat (angkat) berat; *weights and measures,* timbangan dan sukatan.

welcome, *v. tr.* menyambut (sambut); *formally,* mengalu-ngalukan (alu); ~*!* persilakan! sila, selamat datang!; *a warm* ~, sambutan hangat.

weld, *v. tr.* ~ *together,* memadukan (padu); *(fig.)* menggembleng (gembleng), menyatu-padukan (satu).

welfare, *n.* kebajikan (bajik); *social* ~, kebajikan masyrakat.

well, *n.* telaga, perigi; *fit,* sihat, segar; ~ *done!,* bagus!; *very* ~, baiklah!; ~ *of a ship,* ruang kapal; *central space in a house,* ruang rumah.

well-born, *adj.* anak orang baik, bangsawan.

well-informed, *adj.* berpengetahuan (tahu).

well-timed, *adj.* tepat pada waktunya.

welter, *v. intr.* ~ *in blood,* mandi darah;

see **wallow.**

west, *n.* barat.

wet, *adj.* basah; ~ *through,* basah lencun basah kuyup; ~ *nurse,* ibu susu; *bedraggled,* basah lokos; ~ *season,* musim hujan, musim gelora; *period of heavy rain,* musim tengkujuh.

whale, *n.* ikan paus.

wharf, *n.* pangkalan, bagan, dermaga.

what? *pron.* apa?; *whatever,* apa-apa; *what's his name (can't remember),* see **so.**

wheat, *n.* gandum.

wheedle, *v. tr.* coax, bujuk; *'butter-up',* lomis-lomis; *'talk round',* kecek-kecek; *'work-on',* mengubi-ubikan.

wheel, *n.* roda; *esp. of a machine,* jentera; *water-~,* kincir; *small ~, castor,* kerek; *steering-~ (of car),* stering; *to take the ~,* pegang stering; *helm,* kemudi; *to ~ (gyrate),* berlegar (legar); *change direction,* belok; *to ~ (a horse or vehicle),* membelokkan.

when? *adv.* bila?; *at the time ~,* waktu, apabila; *during the time ~,* (pada) masa; *at the (past) time ~,* tatkala.

where? *adv.* (di) mana?; *at what point?,* tang mana?

whet, *v. tr.* mengasah (asah), mengilir (kilir); ~ *the appetite,* buat umpan tetak, membuka (buka) selera, menarik (tarik) selera; ~*stone, n.* batu asah, batu canai.

whether, *conj.* adakah; apakah.

whey, *n.* air dadih.

which? *pron.* (yang) mana?; *that ~,* yang.

whiff, *n.* bau yang dibawa angin, sehembus nafas, seputut bayu.

while, *conj.* sementara, selagi, sambil; *during the time that,* semasa; *to ~ away the time,* menghabiskan (habis) masa, merintangkan (rintang) masa.

whimper, *v. intr.* merengek (rengek).

whine, *v. intr. as a child,* merengek (rengek), mendusi (dusi), mendongeng (dongeng).

whip, *n.* sauku, cabuk, cemeti; *to ~ (strike with swishing motion),* membedal (bedal), rempit, senawat; *with a cane,* merotan (rotan); *to ~ up with a jerk, as the arm of a trap or a flexible branch springing back into position,* membidas (bidas).

whirl, *v. intr. rotate,* berputar (putar), berpusing (pusing); ~*ing as a top,* ligat; ~*pool,* putaran air; ~*wind,* angin puting beliung, godaan angin, pusaran angin; *'in a ~' (frantically busy),* bersibuk, sibang-sibuk.

whisk, *n. fly-~,* tepuk-lalat; *lime-~,* podi. *v. tr. & intr.* bergerak cepat; membuat dengan cepat.

whiskers, *n.* jambang; *of cat, cat-fish, prawns, etc.,* sungut-sungut.

whisper, *v. intr.* bisik; ~*s, esp. of discontent,* desas-desus; *convert ~s,* risik-risik.

whistle, *v. intr.* bersiul (siul); *a ~,* siti; *to blow a ~,* tiup siti; *a ship's ~,* peluit.

white, *adj.* putih; *of hair,* uban.

whitebait, *n.* ikan bilis.

whiting, *n. whitewash,* kapur, *to whitewash,* sapu kapur; *a ~,* ikan bebulus (bulus-bulus).

whitlow, *n.* jari naik kelurut.

whittle, *v. tr.* meraut (raut).

whizz, *v. intr. as a bullet,* berdenung (dengung), berdesing (desing), berciung (ciung).

who? *pron.* siapa?; *(he) ~,* yang.

whole, *adj. all,* semuanya; *the ~ world,* seluruh dunia; *to swallow ~,* telan bulat; *see* **swallow;** *on the ~ (taking everything into consideration),* kalau hitung panjang, kalau ditimbang seluruhnya, pada keseluruhannya, secara keseluruhan; ~*-heartedly,* dengan sebulat hati; *wholly,* sama sekali.

wholesale, *adv.* borong; *of selling rice whole-sale (i.e., by the sack),* jual guni.

whorl, *n. one turn of a spiral; esp. of hair,* pusaran; *of markings on the hand,* siput.

why? *adv.* apa fasal? apa sebab? mengapa? buat apa? ~ *not? (what's against it?)* apa salahnya?

wick, *n.* sumbu.

wicked, *adj.* jahat, durjana.

wide, adj. lebar; *extensive,* luas; *broad of chest,* bidang; *~-spread, as horns,* capang, cakang; *width,* lebarnya; *width of orifice,* bukanya; *~-open, of an entrance,* terlopong (lopong); *~, of stride,* guntai.

widow, n. *by divorce,* janda; *by death,* balu.

widower, n. laki-laki kematian (mati) isteri, duda.

wield, v. tr. *power, weapon,* menegang (pegang); mempunyai dan menggunakan kuasa.

wife, n. bini; *more formal,* isteri; *fellow-~,* madu; *informally,* perempuan, orang rumah, orang dapur; *mate, life-companion,* teman hidup; *'queen of the household',* suri rumah.

wig, n. cemara; *added tresses, switch,* inti sanggul.

wild, adj. liar; *not domesticated, -* hutan; *~ cat,* kucing hutan; *run-~,* jalang; *~ly, recklessly,* buta tuli, tak ketahuan (tahu); *careless of direction,* tak tentu arah, terburu-buru.

wilfully, adv. (dengan) sengaja; *wilful (won't listen),* degil, babil, tak makan ajar.

will, v. aux. *of future action,* nanti; *going to,* nak, hendak; *want to,* mahu, mau; *willy-nilly,* mahu-tak-mahu; *~ of God,* takdir, iradat; *testament,* wasiat; *bequest,* umanat.

will-o'-the-wisp, n. jerambang; *(unseen) spirit leading travellers astray,* hantu wewer.

win, v. tr. *be victorious,* menang; *get the upper hand,* naik tangan; *succeed,* berjaya (jaya); *~ over (convert to friendship),* menawan (tawan) hati; *obtain, as a prize,* dapat, dapat merebut (rebut), memenangi (menang); *obtain, attain to,* mencapai (capai); *carry off, esp. as 'sweep the board',* membolot (bolot), menggondol (gondol); *to ~, 'touch', of a lottery ticket,* kena.

wince, v. intr. *start suddenly owing to pain,* tersentak (sentak); menggigil kerana takut.

wind, n. angin; *~less,* angin sudah mati, kematian angin; *see* **force;** *~ward,* atas angin; *leeward,* bawah angin; *to go to ~ward,* menyongsong (songsong) angin; *to go to leeward,* mengekor (ekor) angin; *periodical ~s,* angin berkala (kala); *trade ~s (constant ~s),* angin tetap; *see* **gust, shift, blow;** *'~-bag' (empty talker',* karung kosong; *to break ~,* kentut; *~fall (great and unexpected good fortune),* durian runtuh; *~ed (incapacitated by blow in ~),* sesaknafas; *~-pipe,* pembuluh (buluh) nafas; *'~ of change',* ribut perubahan (ubah).

wind, v. tr. *as a clock,* kuncikan; *esp. as in hoisting,* putarkan; *to ~ up a debate,* menggulung (gulung) debat; *~-up, (settle an affair, etc.),* selesaikan, menentukan (tentu); *~ing, as a river,* berbelit-belit, berliku-liku; bengkangbengkok.

window, n. tinkap; *French ~,* jendela; *shutter pushed out from below,* ebek.

wine, n. minuman keras (yang dibuat dr air anggur), wain.

wing, v. intr. sayap, kepak.

wink, v. intr. terkelip (kelip) mata, mengenyitkan (kenyit) mata.

winnow, v. tr. 1. menampi (tampi); *esp. by moving tray this way and that,* meninting (tinting), mengentek (entek). 2. memisahkan antara yang baik benar, berguna dll. daripada yang tidak.

wipe, v. tr. *on or off,* sapu; *~ dry,* kesat; *~ out, expunge,* hapuskan.

wire, n. dawai, kawat; *~less telegraphy,* telegraf tak berdawai; *barbed ~,* kawat berduri (duri); *~-netting,* kawat beranyam (anyam); *~-cutters,* gunting kawat; *wiry, of hair,* kasar, kasap; *to pull ~s (be in effective control),* memegang (pegang) teraju.

wise, n. bijak, arif.

wish, v. intr. mahu; *desire,* ingin (nak), bermaksud (maksud) (nak); *~ for, want,* hendak(kan); *'make a ~',* mencita; *see* **want.**

wistful, adj. *feeling sad,* berasa (rasa)

sayu-hati, murung; see **yearn.**

wit, n. akal, budi, kecerdasan otak, fikiran.

with, prep. dengan.

withdraw, v. tr. pull out, cabut; retract, as an accusation, tarik balik; as claws, menyorokkan (sorok); ~ (oneself), as from an association, tarik diri, pengunduran; as into a hole, menyorokkan diri; see **retreat.**

wither, v. intr. menjadi (jadi) layu; ~ed, as a limb, lesut; see **shrivel.**

within, adv. and prep. (di)dalam; ~ (a specified time), dalam (tempuh); before a specified time is up, tak dan; ~ a day (before a day is out), tak dan sehari.

withhold, v. tr. (-held) menahan, tidak memberikan, melawan.

without, adv. and prep. outside, di luar; as opposed to 'with', (kalau) tak ada, tak berdengan tiada, tanpa.

witness, n. saksi; to give evidence, naik saksi; ~-box, kandang saksi; to ~ (a document), menyain (sain) menjadi (jadi) saksi; to ~ (a spectacle), tengok, menonton (tonton), menyaksikan.

witty, adj. pandai bergurau (gurau), pelucu (lucu), pelawak (lawak) orangnya, pandai berkelakar, penuh jenaka; to pit one's wits (against), beradu (adu) akal (tirngau), at wits' end, kehabisan (habis) akal.

wizard, n. see **sorcerer.**

wobble, v. intr. bergoyang-goyang, berlenggang-lenggang; as a wounded bird in flight, mereben; wobbly, as a loose tooth, ogeh, onyak-anyik, goyak; not fitting in properly, longgar; as a table with uneven legs, unggatunggit; wobbling from side to side, as a loose wheel, merewang-rewang; see **rock.**

woes, n. hai-hui; woe!, alas!, aduh!; duka, kesedihan, kesengsaraan.

wolf, n. serigala (fig.) bold bad man, musang; see **sheep;** lone ~ (unsociable), kera sumbang; easy prey for 'wolves' (of an unprotected girl), rezeki musang.

wolfram, n. kaci.

woman, n. perempuan; more formal, wanita; ~-kind, kaum perempuan, keturunan (turun) Hawa; Chinese lady, nyonya; to ~ise, mengurat; womaniser, gila urat; keen and indiscriminate ~iser, belukang darat; 'dirty old man', tua lengkuas, makin tua semakin buas, (old as wild ginger is old, the older the hotter).

womb, n. rahim.

wonderful, adj. ajaib; no wonder! (just what one expected), patutlah!; see **admire, surprised.**

woo, v. tr. memikat hati perempuan, membujuk rayu.

wood, n. timber, kayu; see **jungle;** woodpecker, burung belatuk.

woof, n. weft, pakan.

wool, n. benang bulu.

word, n. perkataan (kata); two or three ~s, dua tiga patah; the ~s of a song, senikata.

work, n. occupation, kerja; to ~, bekerja; part-time ~, kerja sambilan; full-time ~, kerja sepenuh masa; piece-~, pawah; odd jobs, kerja panjang pendek; to 'do the donkey ~' (carry the chief burden), memikul (pikul) berat; '~ the fingers to the bone', banting tulang; to do good ~s, beramal (amal) (ibadat); a written ~ (typist), buah kalam, karya, (u ~, of a plan, jadi, berjaya (jaya); artistic ~, hasil seni; to '~ on' a person (to soften or persuade him), mengubi-ubikan (ubi); to 'get ~ed up' (be in an agitated state), naik angin; see **factory, mechanic.**

world, n. the earth, bumi, alam semesta, jagat; this ~ below, dunia, jagat; this ~ and the next, dunia akhirat; ~-wide, serata dunia, sedunia, seluruh dunia.

worm, n. cacing; round ~, cacing gelang; thread ~, cacing kerawit; hook-~, cacing halus, (also) cacing kerawit; tape-~, cacing pipih, cacing panjang; a 'wandering' intestinal ~ (ascaris?), cacing biar-biar; marine caddis-~, pumpun; ~-eaten, dimakan bubuk; of fruit, dimakan kelarah; marine wood-~, tembelok; *silk-~*, ulat sutera.

worn, *adj. shabby,* buruk, lusuh, usang; *~ by friction,* haus; *~ out (as clothes),* tak terpakai (pakai) lagi; *see* **tired.**

worry, *v. tr.* mengganggu (ganggu), menggoda (goda); **worried,** risau, khuatir; *as in a fluster,* menggelisah (gelisah); *don't ~ yourself about,* jangan susah-susahkan.

worse, *adj. not so good,* kurang baik; *more wicked,* lebih jahat; *to ~n (as state of affairs),* bertambah (tambah) buruk.

worship, *v. intr. see* **pray;** pemujaan, (puja) penyembahan (sembah); *perform religious duties,* beramal (amal)ibadat; *~ idols,* memuja (puja) berhala.

worth, *n.* nilai; *price,* harga (yang patut); *~less,* tak berguna (guna), tidak berharga; *see* **use.**

would-be, *adj. prefixed to a noun and expressing an aspiration to,* bakal; *~ Minister,* bakal menteri.

wound, *n.* cedera, luka; *~ed,* kena terluka; *slight ~,* luka ringan; *serious ~,* luka parah.

wrangle, *v. intr.* berkelahi, berbabil (babil), berbalah (balah), bertengkar (tengkar); berbantah.

wrap, *v. tr. a parcel,* bungkuskan; *as bandage,* balut; *as swathe in ~ping,* barut; *~ oneslf up, as on a cold day,* berselubung (selubung); *~ cloth, etc.,* round, membulang (bulang); *~per, generally,* sampul, pembalut (balut), pemalut (palut).

wreath, *n.* karangan bunga; *esp. for neck,* kalung bunga; *to garland with flowers,* mengikatkan (ikat) kalung bunga pada leher.

wrecked, *p.p. of a vessel,* pecah; kero-

sakan, sunk, karam; *run ashore,* terkandas; *see* **strand;** *wreckage (smashed body of ship or plane),* bangkai (kapal, kapal terbang); *pieces of wreckage,* pecahan (kapal), kaparan.

wrench, *v. tr. twist violently,* 1. merengkuh (rengkuh); renggutan, rentapan; 2. kesedikan kerana berpisah; *see* **twist.**

wrestle, *v. intr. come to grips,* bergomol (gomol); *(in contest),* bergelut, bergusti *v. tr.* merebut, merampas.

wretch, *n.* orang malang, orang bedebah, celaka.

wriggle, *v. intr. ~ along, as a snake,* menggeliang-geliut, *as an insect,* merayap (rayap); *squirm,* menggeletek (geletek); *writing and wriggling,* geliang-geliat; *to struggle and ~, as a stranded fish,* menggelupur (gelupur); *~ jerkily, as larvae in water,* menjintik-jintik; *wriggling along jerkily, as leeches,* terkelibat-kelibat; *to ~, esp. from discomfort,* menggerenyut-gerenyut.

wring, *v. tr.* memulas (pulas); *~ out (moisture),* perahkan; *~ the hands, as in pain,* mengibas-ngibaskan (kibas) tangan.

wrinkled, *adj.* berkedut (kedut), berkerut (kerut).

wrist, *n.* pergelangan (gelang) tangan.

write, *v. tr.* menulis (tulis), menyurat (surat); *calligraphy,* senitulis; *see* **handwriting.**

writhe, *v. intr. e.g., as a wounded person,* menggelupur (gelupur); menggeliat, mengerang (kerana kesakitan).

wrong, *adj. incorrect,* tidak betul; *morally ~,* tidak patut; *culpable,* salah; *made a mistake,* tersilap (silap); *got the ~ idea,* tersalah sangka, salah tampa; *see* **sin.**

X

xenophobia, *n.* perasaan (rasa) benci terhadap orang asing.

Xmas, *n.* hari Krismas, hari Natal.

X-ray, *n.* sejenis sinar elektromagnetik; *an*
~ *examination,* pemeriksaan (periksa)
dng menggunakan (guna) alat ~.

xylophone, *n.* gambang; zilofon.

Y

yard, *n.* ela; *of house,* halaman; *of mast,* peruan, andang-andang; *~-stick (fig.) basis of calculation or judgement,* pedoman.

yarn, *n. thread,* benang.

yacht, *n.* kapal layar untuk perlumbaan.

yawn, *v. intr.* menguap (kuap).

yaws *n.* puru.

year, *n.* tahun; *esp. of the Muslim era,* sanat; *Happy New Year!,* selamat tahun baru!

yearn for, *v. tr.* merindukan (rindu); *esp. as pregnant woman,* mengidamkan (idam); *symbolic of yearning for the unattainable; the owl yearns for the moon,* pungguk merindukan bulan.

yeast, *n.* ragi, tapai.

yell, *v. intr. & tr.* berteriak, menjerit, memekik.

yellow, *adj.* kuning; *~-brown,* warna duku; *sandy,* langsat.

yelp, *v. intr.* mendengking (dengking), salak.

Yemen, *n.* negeri Yaman.

yes, *particle,* ya; *'a ~-man who is over-conventional,* tukang ekor.

yesterday, *adv.* semalam, kelmarin; *the day before ~,* kelmarin dahulu; *not born ~,* bukan budak-budak makan pisang. *(not a banana-eating child).*

yet, *adv. still,* lagi, masih; *not ~,* belum lagi.

yield, *n. produce or return (as fruit or profit),* hasil; *to ~ (give way),* menyerah (serah), mengaku (aku) kalah.

yoga, *n.* ilmu yogi.

yoke, *n. single ~,* kok; *double ~,* igu, gu.

yolk, *n.* kuning-telur; *double-~ed egg,* telur dua sebandung.

yonder, *adv.* nun; *over there,* sebelah sana.

you, *pron.* tuan, encik, mika, awak, anda.

young, *adj. immature,* muda; *offspring,* anak; *~ bird,* anak burung; *adolescent,* belia; *'~ people', (~ster),* pemuda pemudi; *~est,* yang termuda; *the ~est child,* anak bongsu; *mere kid,* umur baharu setahun jagung; *see* **callow, teenagers.**

youth, *n. time of ~,* masa muda lagi; *a ~,* orang muda; *to retain one's ~ful appearance,* tahan muda; *World Youth Congress,* perhimpunan (himpun) belia sedunia.

yule, *n. yuletide,* Hari Krismas (Natal).

Z

zealous, *adj.* bersemangat (semangat), giat, rajin.

zebra, *n.* kuda belang.

zenith, *n. meridian,* rembang; bahagian langit yang tepat di atas kepala; *(fig.) highest point (e.g., of power),* puncak.

zero, *n.* O, kosong, sifir.

zest, *n.* semangat, kemahuan, seronok.

zinc, *n.* timah sari; *~-sheets (for roofing, etc.),* atap 'zin'.

zigzag, *adj.* bengkang-bengkok, berlikuliku; *to proceed in ~s,* berjalan (jalan) simpang-siur.

zip, *n. ~-fastener,* kancing tarik, 'zip'.

zodiac, *n. signs of the ~,* bintang duabelas, rasi.

zone, *n. area, as of jurisdiction,* kawasan; *as division of the earth,* daerah bahagian bumi; *torrid ~,* daerah (berhawa) panas (hawa); *frigid ~,* daerah (berhawa) dingin; *temperate ~,* daerah (berhawa) sederhana.

zoo, *n.* kebun binatang; *~logist,* ahli ilmu haiwan.

zoom, *v. intr. soar steeply upwards,* melambung (lambung) tinggi.

HIPPOCRENE MASTER SERIES

This teach-yourself language series, now available in six languages, is perfect for the serious traveler, student or businessman. Imaginative, practical exercises in grammar are accompanied by cassette tapes for conversation practice. Available as a book/cassette package.

MASTERING FRENCH

0746	ISBN 0-87052-055-5	$11.95 BOOK
1003	ISBN 0-87052-060-1	$12.95 2 CASETTES
1085	ISBN 0-87052-136-5	$24.90 PACKAGE

MASTERING GERMAN

0754	ISBN 0-87052-056-3	$11.95 BOOK
1006	ISBN 0-87052-061-X	$12.95 2 CASSETTES
1087	ISBN 0-87052-137-3	$24.90 PACKAGE

MASTERING ITALIAN

0758	ISBN 0-87052-057-1	$11.95 BOOK
1007	ISBN 0-87052-066-0	$12.95 2 CASSETTES
1088	ISBN 0-87052-138-1	$24.90 PACKAGE

MASTERING SPANISH

0759	ISBN 0-87052-059-8	$11.95 BOOK
1008	ISBN 0-87052-067-9	$12.95 2 CASSETTES
1097	ISBN 0-87052-139-X	$24.90 PACKAGE

MASTERING ARABIC

0501	ISBN 0-87052-922-6	$14.95 BOOK
0931	ISBN 0-87052-984-6	$12.95 2 CASSETTES
1101	ISBN 0-87052-140-3	$27.90 PACKAGE

MASTERING JAPANESE

0748	ISBN 0-87052-923-4	$14.95 BOOK
0932	ISBN 0-87052-938-8	$12.95 2 CASSETTES
1102	ISBN 0-87052-141-1	$27.90 PACKAGE

Ask for these and other Hippocrene titles at your local booksellers!